1992

EDUCATIONAL PSYCHOLOGY AND INSTRUCTIONAL DECISIONS

The Dorsey Series in Psychology

Consulting Editor **Wendell E. Jeffrey** University of California, Los Angeles

Nelson F. DuBois
George F. Alverson
Richard K. Staley

all of the
State University of New York
at Oneonta

EDUCATIONAL PSYCHOLOGY AND INSTRUCTIONAL DECISIONS

1979

The Dorsey Press Homewood, Illinois 60430
Irwin-Dorsey Limited Georgetown, Ontario L7G 4B3

ISBN 0-256-02056-6
Library of Congress Catalog Card No. 78–70013

Printed in the United States of America

1 2 3 4 5 6 7 8 9 0 K 6 5 4 3 2 1 0 9

Preface

The purpose of this text is to introduce prospective teachers or anyone interested in any aspect of instruction to that body of knowledge, called educational psychology, in a manner that is useful in different instructional contexts. Further, we have attempted to present a systematic interpretation of educational psychology as a discipline worthy of pursuit for its own sake.

Writing this text, we were guided by the three apparent commonalities of almost all introductory texts in educational psychology. First, the subject matter of our field must be presented thoroughly. Second, the book must emphasize application. Finally, the book should be eclectic enough so that instructors of different theoretical orientations can use it. In this respect, our book is no different than other introductory educational psychology texts; it is *thorough, practical,* and *eclectic.*

We believe, however, that an introductory text in educational psychology should go well beyond these qualities. In our opinion, strict adherence to the traditional topical approach to areas of study in educational psychology at times makes it very difficult for potential teachers to see the utility of much of what educational psychology has to offer in a real instructional context and thus to make more enlightened instructional decisions.

Further, strict adherence to the traditional topical approach in educational psychology can leave the potential teacher with a fragmented conceptualization of what our field has to offer and how the information can best be used for instructional decision making. The traditional topical approach tends to leave out or minimize a great deal of psychological or related information necessary for competent instructional decision making because it does not happen to fit nicely within the traditional topical framework. Finally, the traditional topical approach is deceptively thorough—thorough in *reproducing* our field as it now exists, but not thorough in analyzing what is needed to make enlightened instructional decisions. In other words, we are suggesting that the traditional topical approach to our field may be less than structurally adequate to facilitate transfer of training in instructional contexts.

Recently many educational psychologists have begun to recognize some of the apparent deficiencies with the traditional topical approach to educational psychology. Englander (1976) puts it well. According to Englander, our discipline should:

1. cut the umbilical cord to traditional psychology
2. focus on the *acts of teaching* and learning as it *takes place in a classroom context*

3. focus on the *nature of the individual in relationahip to the objectives* of the program
4. make an attempt to *integrate* the various segments of teacher education.

In addition, Hunt and Sullivan (1974) submit that educational psychologists ought to study those types of decisions teachers have to make, and then organize their studies and books around those decisions rather than around pure psychological topics. Further, Shavelson (1976) suggests that potential teachers should be asked to examine their beliefs and philosophy of education, and then to integrate those beliefs with their teaching skills.

In agreement with these authors, we have attempted to organize many parts of our book utilizing their suggestions in a manner that is somewhat unique to our field. Essentially, we have conceptualized teaching to consist of five fairly distinct roles that require competent decision making. Regardless of the level of teaching, the subject matter to be taught, or the philosophy of the teacher, the teacher must perform reasonably well in the following five roles: (1) program developer, (2) program implementer, (3) a socializing agent, (4) a link between the classroom and community, and (5) a developing professional. These roles are based on the various tasks that confront teachers.

As stated previously, given these roles, we have found it necessary to abandon as a unit some of the traditional topics in our field because those topics span a variety of instructional roles and decisions. In other words, rather than attempt to *reproduce* the educational psychology literature as it has been traditionally presented, we have tried to *reconceptualize* our field to retain the content of educational psychology that is thought to be important to educational psychologists, while at the same time reorganizing and adding topics that should aid a teacher to make more competent instructional decisions. In essence, we have not tried to ask the question: What has the field of educational psychology produced? but rather ask the question: If I were in a classroom teacher's role how could I apply the content of educational psychology?

In the process of writing this text, we have attempted to nudge our field a little toward the shift we see coming in educational psychology, to organize our field around *instructional questions* rather than *psychological* topics. Recognizing that our profession has been concerned with the psychological topical approach, however, we have maintained some of the traditional topics for the sake of continuity and for ease of dealing with our field as it has been traditionally presented. We felt that a blend of both approaches was the most useful strategy at this time in our history as a discipline.

To start the book, we address many of the broad beliefs and issues that face teachers in their various roles, followed by some basic information germane to understanding some of the later chapters in the book. From these broad considerations, we then discuss the teacher's role as a program developer. Returning to some of the earlier topics in the book while emphasizing the application of educational psychology, the next section of the book focuses on the teacher's role as program implementer. The remainder of the book addresses topics concerning the teacher's role as a socializing agent, as well as the teacher's role as a link between the classroom and the community, and the role of a teacher as a professional. In the latter section of the book, some topics that various instructors would look for in a traditional educational psychology text are included. Certainly these topics could be easily covered earlier in the course.

By using a spiraling approach to the topics in the text, we feel we have been better able to include those topics crucial to instructional decision making in much more depth than is found in traditional texts. Further, this strategy was used to enhance transfer from topic to topic. In this context, we make no apology for repeating some material in different ways in several chapters.

Finally, we strongly urge the reader to consider the topics in this book in the context of the total educational institution, and to make decisions in a thorough and systematic manner. In our opinion, too often the textbooks in our field have been neither thorough nor systematic in addressing the types of decisions facing teachers. Further, many of the texts do not ask their readers to apply the psychological findings of our field to make well-thought out instructional decisions. This book constantly prods the reader to make tentative instructional decisions based on careful planning.

Because of the orientation of this text, at the conclusion of reading this book the student should be better able to:

1. Plan systematically for instructional events.
2. Identify how the concepts and principles discussed in this book can be used to implement an instructional event.
3. Identify many of the current problems facing our field and offer some plausible strategies for dealing with these problems.

ACKNOWLEDGMENTS

A book always has many people who work behind the scenes supporting an author's work. We have many people to thank. The reviewers of our text, Merlin C. Wittrock, University of California at Los Angeles; Raymond W. Kulhavy, Arizona State University and Jerry Davidson, Consulting Editor at Dorsey Press, have been very helpful and supportive of our efforts. Our thanks are also extended specifically to our colleagues who have reviewed or helped us on individual chapters: Harry Bergstein, Oneonta State; Tim Boggs, Oneonta State; Dennis Hocevar, University of Southern California; Jean London of the library staff at Oneonta State and Robert Seidenstadt, Oneonta State.

Special thanks also go to the whole library staff at Oneonta who have been tremendously helpful in finding references on our behalf.

Many students have also helped to make this book a reality. Specific thanks go to Oneonta State students Ken Kiewra and Sue Leonard for reading early editions of the manuscript as well as to hundreds of other students from Oneonta State and Hartwick College who had to read various typewritten versions of the manuscript and made helpful suggestions to us.

Our gratitude is also extended to all those people who worked on the photographs for the book. Photographers Richard Alverson and Fred Ricard did an outstanding job for us. Additional thanks go to John McNamara, Howard Lynch, and Howard Dunbar from the Sidney, New York Public Schools; Paul Lambert and Barry Gould from the Cooperstown, New York Public Schools, and Mr. Judd and Mr. McGuire from the Albany Public Schools as well as all the classroom teachers for allowing us to take pictures in their respective schools. In addition, we would like to thank

Jerry Reese, Registrar of the New York State Historical Association, for permission to search and use historical photos from the Smith-Telfer collection.

We wish to thank the teachers of the Sidney Elementary Schools for helping to shape the applied nature of the text by calling our attention to many difficult problems and making many critical comments about the utility of some theoretically "sound" recommendations.

Our final thanks are extended to Ellen Brown, our fabulous secretary, who typed almost the entire manuscript for us, and to Maria Zamelis and Lenore Foster for typing small sections of the book, as well as to our families who tolerated us for what seemed to be an interminable project.

March 1979

Nelson F. DuBois
George F. Alverson
Richard K. Staley

Contents

Chapter 1

The profession of teaching and educational psychology

THIS BOOK is about how to become an effective instructional decision maker and an effective teacher. As such, the information is organized and presented in a manner to help you prepare for any instructional decision-making situation or any teaching role in which you may eventually find yourself. Of a very practical nature, yet with a strong theoretical basis, this book blends the theoretical with the practical.

After reading this book, you should be able to analyze thoroughly any instructionally related situation within the total context of the schools and generate a *reasonable-realistic solution to the problem*. We hope your solution will be clear and insightful, and will not take the form of a "that's the way it was done to me" justification. Your solution should be based on a blend of what educational psychology has to say about the solution as well as the reality of the total instructional situation within which the problem is encountered.

From our perspective, the purpose of writing this educational psychology book is to provide you with some useful insights about the instructional decision-making process as it is related to the society at large, the nature of our schools and classrooms, the nature of the students passing through our schools, and the various roles of the teacher in this process. In order to make wise instructional decisions, the teacher needs to consider all these factors at various times in the decision-making process.

FACTORS INFLUENCING DECISION MAKING IN THE SCHOOLS

Society

In essence, the schools are a product of the wishes of the society. Society dictates which general outcomes should be achieved in the schools as well as which ones should *not* be achieved. To be sure that the proper outcomes are achieved, society is responsible for providing the resources to the schools, as well as monitoring the outcomes of the schools, usually in a very haphazard unsystematic way. Whenever there appears to be an imbalance in this process, you can be sure that the local citizenry will speak out. Our point in discussing such a broad amorphous variable as society is to emphasize that educational administrators and teachers alike *must* carefully consider the wishes of the society. If the general school program, the teacher's behavior, or the student outcomes are not consonant with the wishes of society, the school and/or the teacher will be in great difficulty. Careful planning is needed in this area. In this book, you will learn how to convert fuzzy and disorganized goals into clear and organized objectives. You will also learn how to systematically evaluate specific students as well as different aspects of a total school program. Throughout the book you will be encouraged to give these topics serious consideration. All too often the educational establishment has tried to promote poorly conceived outcomes and has failed to systematically evaluate its programs (witness the "back-to-basics" trend of the schools).

The schools

To understand the purposes of this book, it is important for you to consider briefly several functions of the schools as institutions. Influenced by many interrelated political, economic, and social variables, the schools have been asked to carry out two complementary purposes: *to educate and instruct the young.* The popular distinction between *education* and *instruction* is useful for our discussion, although later we argue that it is impossible to separate the two functions in any precise meaningful way.

Somewhat broader in scope, *education* refers to the process whereby the schools, and even society, develop the students' general capabilities to solve unknown, previously unencountered problems in the future, which benefits either the individual or society. We say a person is "educated" when he/she is a knowledgeable, competent problem solver. From a narrower perspective, *instruction* is the deliberate arrangement of the student's environment to produce a specific *known* outcome in a specified situation.

In our opinion, any *instructional* strategy used by a teacher must be consonant with the *broad educational goals* of the school as well as with *specific instructional objectives.* Too often, instructional strategies are used by teachers with little or no consideration of how they might help a student to achieve the broader goals of the schools; hence the student comes to perceive school as fragmented, piecemeal, and largely purposeless. In addition, too often the specific objectives of the curriculum have not been clearly specified, with the result that students learn a great deal of trivia.

At various times you will have to resolve some discrepancies between what the field of educational psychology suggests might be the best instructional solution to a particular problem and a contrary opinion offered by either the society at large or the school administration. Likewise, the reality of the school structure will force you to modify some of the principles you will learn in this book. Throughout this text we attempt to constantly discuss the research findings of our field in relation to the realities of the schools and classroom. Such topics as designing and evaluating school programs and designing optimum classroom environments are thoroughly discussed. You will learn how to identify and choose important objectives, and how to arrange the instructional environment accordingly.

The teachers

Given the specific role of bringing about the desires of the society at large within the constraints of a school system, the public school teacher is required to implement the goals of our society in an acceptable manner. For example, having read some research suggesting that giving grades to a student who is very interested in a topic may interfere with the student's intrinsic motivation (Deci, 1975), the teacher still has to assign letter grades. Attempting to present material at the student's level of comprehension, the teacher might get accused of "watering down" the curriculum. Such compromises have to be made by teachers all the time. Many of these "Catch 22" decisions occur and, as unfortunate as it might be, solutions must be to the satisfaction of those in authority.

Not only do teachers have to resolve those types of conflicts, but teachers also have to resolve conflicts between their professional lives and their personal lives. For example, throughout this book you will read that frequent relevant practice and appropriate feedback are very important instructional practices that need to be implemented. While the ideal instructional strategy may warrant such an approach, what should the teacher do who is assigned from 125 to 150 students a day? Certainly, the reality of the classroom situation must be considered. Either the teacher gets outside help in providing the necessary feedback (volunteer parents, teacher aides, or other students), or the teacher modifies the assignments by providing either fewer or shorter assignments. Faced with these unpleasant decisions, teachers have to work within the system as best they can to help the students achieve a desirable level of competence, while at the same time attempting to improve those aspects of the system that can be improved.

To be a good teacher requires skills in analyzing programs, designing programs, preparing programs, implementing goals, and evaluating outcomes. Further, good teachers have certain personal qualities that help them in interpersonal skills with students. All these points are thoroughly discussed throughout this book.

The students

Students are what the schools are all about. Having students with widely differing academic skill levels and diverse interests in the same classroom, the teacher must attempt to match the student characteristics with the instructional program (Figure 1–1). Essentially it is the teacher's task to bring about competent, independent learners and problem solvers who are self-motivated and are generally capable of performing in group situations.

FIGURE 1–1
Although students may look alike, their needs vary considerably

To be able to match different students with different instructional techniques and strategies requires that a teacher be competent in observational and evaluation strategies; that is, the teacher should be able to assess a student's general level of entering behavior (those general characteristics that will influence what a student learns) as well as very specific characteristics of a student with respect to specific objectives. The skills needed for individualization and for assessing a student's response patterns are thoroughly discussed throughout the book.

Summary of the teacher's role

In one sense, this book is about you, about the type of classroom you will want to be in as a teacher, about the types of student-teacher interactions you will have with your students, and about your teaching goals. Although teachers generally work within complex school systems or simlar institutions where a significant number of decisions are predetermined, any teaching role of necessity still requires a great deal of individual decision making. For example, let us assume you are already a teacher. It really is not important to consider the grade level, the nature of your students, or the nature of the subject you are assigned to teach. What is really important is how you think you will *behave* as a teacher. On what basis will you decide upon the objectives for your classroom? How will you develop an understanding of your students so that you can provide appropriate learning environments?

How will you evaluate the progress of your students, your effectiveness as a teacher, and the total effectiveness of your program? How will you sequence the events in your classroom? How much freedom will you allow the students? To what extent will your classroom be teacher-centered or student-centered, and for what reasons? What types of routines will you establish? What types of general methods will you use? Any teaching role requires that these questions be answered honestly, realistically, and skillfully. Although this book can provide you with some useful suggestions for most of these questions, your ultimate decisions will be a unique blending of *what you know* and *how you feel* about each of them. The constraints of the school system will also have to be considered in your deliberations.

All we ask of you is that you develop a well-thought-out rationale for your teaching behavior. *Do not* adhere to one viewpoint which limits your decision-making capabilities. *Do* develop a clear set of goals from which your instructional decisions can be based; then integrate your decisions around your goals.

THE RELATIONSHIP OF EDUCATIONAL PSYCHOLOGY TO INSTRUCTIONAL DECISION MAKING

Educational psychology is a loose confederation of other psychological disciplines—a theoretical discipline that attempts to understand what happens in the schools and why it happens there. It is also a discipline that attempts to give teachers some useful information about the best "bets" of teaching—how to facilitate learning in a variety of contexts.

The domain of educational psychology

As an applied branch of psychology, educational psychology specifically studies those variables that allow for better *prediction, control,* and *understanding of behavior* within or related to an instructional context. Focusing on instructional-related questions, educational psychologists have traditionally studied such broad topics as:

1. Child development issues related to school behavior, adjustment, and motivation.
2. The characteristics of learners and the nature of individual differences.
3. Strategies for planning and implementing instructional events.
4. Strategies for designing tests and measuring behavior.

The origins and orientation of educational psychology

Having as a cornerstone the belief that teaching can be partially analyzed from a scientific perspective, our field has its roots in the scientific method and scientific inquiry. Stemming from the early work of Johann Friedrich Herbart (1776–1841) and Edward L. Thorndike (1874–1949), the belief has persisted that teaching is partially a scientific endeavor. Herbart, for example, believed that teaching should be viewed as a systematic sequential strategy for implementing objectives. According to Herbart, all teaching strategies should consist of the formal sequence: preparation, presentation, association, generalization, and application. Many current instructional psychologists have analyzed instructional tasks from essentially the same framework. The belief that instructional events can be analyzed in terms of sequences and hierarchies is very much a part of current thinking; therefore Herbart's insistence that instructional strategies should be analyzed systematically and scientifically is his legacy to our field.

Thorndike was also an early contributor to our field (Figure 1–2). From a careful analysis of the theories of transfer held in the early 1900s, Thorndike demonstrated that studying subjects such as mathematics or Latin is not really useful in increasing one's intellect. His ideas have had a great impact on current theories of the transfer of training and thus, some would propose, Thorndike should be considered the originator of modern educational psychology. Regardless of who eventually is considered the originator, the common characteristic of Herbart's and Thorndike's work is their insistence on the use of the scientific method for analyzing instructional questions.

We hope you do the same as a teacher. *Do not ignore your intuitive hunches!* And do not ignore the data on teaching. All we ask of you is to question your decisions and *verify the decisions after they are implemented.*

Current concerns and trends in educational psychology

Borrowing from the general discipline of psychology, the discipline of educational psychology in the past has not asked some of the necessary and complex instructional questions. As Gage (1964) points out, psychologists have traditionally studied theories of learning and development. Focusing on how a person learns and/or develops is not the same as asking how a teacher can influence a person to learn. These are different questions and need different research strategies. The answers about how a person learns leaves the practitioner with very little information about how to structure an instructional event or the general classroom environment to facilitate learning. Recently these points have been recognized, with the result that increasingly sophisticated, systematic studies are being conducted on various aspects of the instructional process over which educators have some control.

Courtesy of Teachers College, Columbia University

FIGURE 1–2
Edward L. Thorndike (1874–1949) made significant contributions on the transfer of training research

For example, Jerome Bruner (1966), the well-known cognitive psychologist, proposed that we need theories of instruction that address the following questions:

1. With this student's predisposition to learn in the following manner, what should be my instructional strategy?
2. How should I best structure the body of knowledge I want my students to learn so that they will learn the material most efficiently?
3. How can I best sequence this material to facilitate the student's learning?
4. How should I best implement rewards, punishment, and feedback to facilitate reaching my goals?

Asking even more specific and systematically developed questions, Glaser (1976a) suggests that we need instructional theories that answer the following questions:

1. How should an instructional designer, or classroom teacher, go about analyzing a complex task? Specifically, how can an instructional decision maker identify the competencies of a student that are needed for the student to complete a complex task at a high level of proficiency?
2. What factors should an instructional decision maker consider in analyzing a student's state (entering behavior) with reference to an assigned task? Which characteristics of a student should be assessed?
3. When providing the student with a task to complete, what environmental conditions should be established to foster learning and the acquisition of competence in the student? According to Glaser, theories need to be developed that provide the teacher with strategies for producing competent problem-solving students.
4. How might a student's competencies best be assessed? Not only should we be concerned with assessing a student's competency, but we also must ask what

type of effects different instructional strategies might have on students in related areas of competency.

Notice the specificity of Glaser's suggestions. While Bruner's and Glaser's points must be thoroughly researched, we should not fall into the trap of being unable to see the forest through the trees. Olson (1976b), for example, suggests that while a particular instructional strategy might be excellent for facilitating a specific objective or series of objectives, what might be the long-term cumulative effects of specific instructional strategies on a student's general competence or attitude?

Focusing on specific instructional strategies or programs designed to bring about a set of specific objectives, this short-sighted research strategy will not provide us with information about the long-term effects of specific strategies on the broader cognitive and attitudinal goals of education. Achieving specific objectives at the expense of broader goals is certainly an undesirable outcome of instruction.

In addition, Olson (1976b) says that we need theories of instruction that:

1. Specify the nature of human knowledge—particularly how the knowledge is acquired by humans and is represented in the mind.
2. Identify under what conditions we might want a student to just "muddle" through a task because we cannot specify the prerequisite skills very well.
3. Relate the acquisition of knowledge and skills to human performance on terminal tasks.

As can be seen from the previous examples, educational psychologists are beginning to ask instructional-type questions based on decisions that teachers have to make in the classroom.

Focus of study: Different approaches

As you should be able to determine by now, those factors that contribute to learning in a classroom context are highly complex. Essentially, psychologists of three broad orientations have studied behavior in complex classroom settings, and we will argue strongly in this book that all three orientations are needed to effectively arrive at valid instructional decisons.

The behavioral approach. Probably one of the more basic historical issues in psychology stems from the 200-year-old Locke-Leibnitz controversy. Believing that a baby's mind is akin to a sheet of "white paper void of all ideas," Locke posited in his treatise "Some Thoughts Concerning Education" that it is from a baby's *experience* that the baby acquires knowledge of the environment. Emphasizing environmental strategies for increasing a student's performance, present-day behaviorists such as B. F. Skinner have essentially adopted the basic Lockean position. Since behavior is thought to be the result of experience, it is very important to identify clearly which specific experiences bring about which behavioral outcomes in individual children. More precise than other psychologists, the behaviorists have generally emphasized the study of small units of behavior. Further, because of their orientation, behaviorists have not emphasized the study of internal thought processes or internal motivational/attitudinal variables which supposedly could contribute to complex classroom behavior. While we believe this viewpoint to be very limiting in a classroom context, much progress has been made in psychology because of the precise nature of identifying environmental variables that contribute to and modify both cognitive and attitudinal behavioral patterns. To ignore some of the findings and techniques of the behaviorists would be tragic.

The cognitive approach. As contrasted with the behaviorists, the cognitive or information-processing psychologists are on the Leibnitz side of the Locke-Leibnitz controversy. The Leibnitzian viewpoint, while not denying the influence of the environment, suggests that innate ideas and various internal thought processes are important mechanisms from which knowledge may be acquired. Essentially, modern-day cognitive psychologists study complex behaviors by identifying the underlying processes, such as perception and memories, thought to facilitate overt behavior. From an instructional decision-making perspective, cognitive psychologists have been asking questions about how to increase students' memory abilities as well as how to increase students' overall competency with problem solving. In other words, in order to understand complex human behavior, one has to understand the underlying mechanisms that produce that behavior. It is very clear that our field is moving in this direction. Chapters 4 and 5 address these issues in depth.

The motivational/attitudinal approach. Believing that basic attitudes and motivation are even more important outcomes of instruction than any cognitive content of a course, some educational psychologists have spent their time studying the origins of attitudes and motivation. Certainly one of the prime goals of education is to produce students who have positive attitudes toward school-related subjects and who desire to learn solely for the value of learning. Students are not just "cerebral." They have feelings and attitudes, and these feelings and attitudes may either increase learning or interfere with learning, depending upon the internal state of the student (Figure 1–3). Without some type of motivation, students are unwilling to approach their schoolwork. In fact, teachers often complain that the unmotivated student is the most serious problem facing our schools!

It is our point of view that the competent teacher needs to understand some of the precise behaviorist principles to analyze specific environmental events, needs to under-

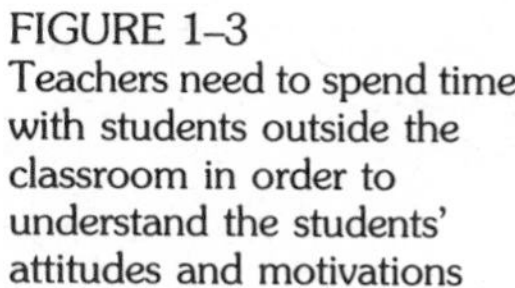
FIGURE 1–3
Teachers need to spend time with students outside the classroom in order to understand the students' attitudes and motivations

stand many of the cognitive principles to plan for instruction, and needs to understand the principles of motivation in order to increase the student's desire to learn. As we pointed out before, the complete teacher should be able to analyze, design, prepare, implement, and evaluate instructional programs. Knowledge of various behavioral, cognitive, and motivational principles is the foundation for those decisions.

ORGANIZATION OF THIS BOOK

In order to help you arrive at some provisional instructional decisions, the organization of this book is designed to simulate the sequential decision-making process you will likely undergo as you plan for instructional events. Starting with some broad questions about the purposes and foundations of education, each chapter progessively begins to focus on the real instructional decisions you will ultimately have to make.

To give you an idea of the scope of this text, some of the following questions are representative of the topics addressed in depth in this book:

1. With so many objectives to teach in one year, I cannot ever seem to plan for the objectives, let alone teach them. What are some strategies that should be used to increase my planning proficiency?
2. Some of my students never seem to finish their work, and they do not seem to care about school. What should be done with them?
3. Yesterday's class was a disaster. The students were frequently getting into trouble. Nothing seemed to go right. What could have gone wrong and how could the class have been organized more effectively?
4. I know some of the students do not understand their work, but I do not know how to analyze their specific problems.
5. All I hear about in education classes is individualization. If they would just show how individualization can be accomplished, I would be happy. With so many different students with different interests and skills in a classroom, I do not see how it is possible to individualize.
6. I really wish I could get my students to be creative problem solvers but nothing seems to work. In fact, half the time the students do not seem to know the basic facts.
7. I do not understand it. Some teachers appear to conduct classrooms in which very little fooling around occurs, and yet other teachers seem to be in charge of a circus. What gives?
8. Teaching would be great except for evaluation. How can I evaluate my students in an effective non-time-consuming manner?
9. Great—I am going to be a teacher and nobody ever taught me how to use the library. Until the other day, I thought ERIC was the name of the librarian!

To help you answer these questions, this book is divided into major sections that deal with different professional roles and decisions common to all teachers. Teachers have to (1) plan and develop programs; (2) implement programs, including evaluating their effectiveness; (3) act as a link between the school and community; (4) teach socialization skills; and (5) make other professional decisions of considerable importance. The chapters in this book are organized around these general themes.

HOW TO USE THIS BOOK

Each chapter is introduced by a general overview of the topic, followed by three to five objectives. Inserted in each chapter at various locations are some boxed questions pertaining to what you read. At the end of each chapter is a summary of the chapter, answers to the boxed questions, a self-quiz covering the total chapter, and answers to the self-quiz. We urge you to make use of these aids.

The general overview and objectives are designed to help you organize your thoughts as you read the chapter. As you go through the chapter you may want to attempt to answer the objectives. The boxed questions are designed to have you recall some important material you have just read. If you cannot answer these questions as you read them, perhaps you should reread that section of the chapter. At the end of the chapter you will find a chapter quiz. You should *not* take this quiz until you have studied the chapter thoroughly. Its purpose is to determine whether you are ready to take a test on this chapter. If you do poorly on the unit quiz (score below 80), chances are you did not study the chapter very effectively. Incidentally, if you are a poor student, we would suggest that you read Chapters 10 and 16 at the start of the course. A lot of the material in those two chapters deals with useful hints on how to be an effective student.

ONE FINAL COMMENT

Most texts do not suggest that the reader develop a workable instructional model, synthesize diverse concepts and principles, and justify preliminary decisions and resolutions of problems. This text asks that you become alive and think for yourself. We do not want you to *reproduce* the field of educational psychology; we want you to *produce* justifiable preliminary solutions to complex decisions and problems related to teaching based on your beliefs and knowledge of psychology. Our contention is that teaching is purposive behavior that is intended to promote *learning* and positive *attitudes* in students. Regardless of your psychological and philosophical beliefs, you must be able to transform your beliefs into a personalized integrated teaching model from which you will operate as a teacher. We feel that it is important for you to develop a well-conceptualized model of teaching because your general belief cannot help but be reflected in your classroom behavior. To know what you stand for and why you stand for it is thus the first step in becoming a competent instructor.

In order that you synthesize your instructional strategies into a unique, well-organized plan, you are asked to build upon your decisions in the early part of the book and use these decisions in the latter section. For example, your behavior as a teacher is based ultimately on your concepts about the nature of students, your philosophy of education, your objectives for an instructional event, and the general method(s) you choose. Rarely is a potential teacher given the opportunity to think about how instructional strategies are derived, and how strategies might be integrated. Decision making is highly complex, and many of the variables influencing decisions are subjective (such as a philosophy, your propensity to respond to people in a particular manner, and your beliefs about the nature of people). It would appear to be important to have potential or practicing teachers identify those variables that apparently influence their decisions. Perhaps a more enlightened professional would result—one who has done a lot of searching while attempting to develop a well-thought-out rationale for his/her role as a teacher.

SECTION I

FOUNDATIONS FOR EDUCATIONAL AND INSTRUCTIONAL DECISIONS

Undoubtedly in your student role you have observed teachers with varying degrees of competency. We predict that your *best* teachers, although varying considerably in their styles, gave the appearance of knowing what they wanted, possessed the skills and determination to reach their goals, and were strongly committed to the teaching profession.

Section I of this book is designed to help you develop and clarify your professional goals and to provide you with some general information about educational psychology so that you might have a strong foundation from which to derive your teaching style.

In Chapter 2, "The goals of education: Philosophical perspectives," four major philosophical schools of thought are presented. Chapter 3, "The characteristics of humans: Psychological perspectives," discusses viewpoints concerning the underlying psychological characteristics of people. Chapters 4 and 5 on the processes of learning provide a thorough overview of contemporary models of learning from which teaching decisions are based. Finally, Chapter 6, "The process of decision-making: Systems perspective," develops a framework for viewing the educational process as movement toward long-range goals.

Taken together, these chapters cover the basic issues that must be answered by anyone grappling with the questions of *what* and *how* to teach.

Chapter 2

The goals of education: Philosophical perspectives

> **If education seems to deteriorate, if it seems to become more and more chaotic and meaningless, it is primarily because we have not settled on satisfactory arrangements of society, and because we have both vague and diverse opinions about the kind of society we want. Education cannot be discussed in a void, our questions raise other questions, social, economic, financial, political. . . . To know what we want in education, we must know what we want in general, *we must derive our theory of education from our philosophy of life.***
>
> ***T. S. Eliot, 1950***

SINCE THERE APPEARS to be a very close relationship between a teacher's general philosophical position and the teacher's behavioral patterns, and since many of the educational and instructional decisions teachers have to make are decided on the basis of philosophical questions, we thought it appropriate to address these questions early in the book. Being competent with various psychological and instructional skills without having first questioned the underlying purposes of education makes a teacher a technician rather than an educator—sort of analogous to a beautifully designed car without an engine.

Schools, by their very institutional nature, have broad goals. These goals are the basis upon which programs are developed and classrooms are organized. They are derived from a society's explicit and implicit philosophical positions. Educational philosophies are the origins as well as the guiding framework from which our educational and instructional decisions are derived and monitored. To be aware of the differing philosophical questions and viewpoints is one of the first steps to becoming an educator rather than a technician.

As this chapter unfolds you will begin to see that the beliefs you have about psychology are closely related to your general philosophical beliefs about education and life in general. It is for these reasons that a chapter on the philosophy of education precedes our discussion of the implications of educational psychology for teachers.

This chapter is designed to have you identify some of your broad beliefs about the purposes of education. At the end of this chapter, you should be able to generate some *provisional* answers to some complex questions concerning your beliefs about the purposes of education, the nature of the curriculum, and some roles you intend to play as a teacher. Related to your beliefs about education are your beliefs about the nature of people. At the end of Chapter 3 you ought to be able to identify more clearly how your beliefs about education and about the psychological nature of people are interrelated. Being able to identify your preferences should aid you in your decision-making role as a teacher. Everyone has biases and preferences. Becoming and remaining aware of your biases and preferences should be important factors as you plan for your classroom objectives and interact with students.

Notice that we emphasize the provisional nature of your answers. We hope you will continue to question your purposes and methodologies as an educator throughout your professional career, and as you experience various successes and failures in teaching you will be able to change your ideas accordingly. We believe the more you think about these issues in the early stages of your professional development, the better able you will be to develop successful systematic instructional strategies commensurate with your beliefs about education. It is relatively easy to know what you are against; it is a little harder to *specify your goals* so that others can understand your viewpoints and so that your goals can help guide your behavior as a teacher.

The chapter is divided into two sections. In the first section, an attempt is made to identify several issues related to the overall goals of education and to discuss what is meant by the term *education.* The second section of the chapter discusses the four general educational philosophies of perennialism, essentialism, progressivism, and reconstructionism. Each philosophy is studied in terms of the basic assumptions of the philosophical position, the nature of the learner, the activities of the learner in a school setting, the roles of a teacher, and the content of the curriculum. At the conclusion of this chapter you should be able to:

1. Derive a functional definition of "to educate."
2. Explain why any human-made environment is necessarily a function of human values.
3. Compare the philosophies of perennialism, essentialism, progressivism, and reconstructionism on the following points:
   a. The basic assumptions of each philosophical position.
   b. The nature of the learner.
   c. The activities the learner should be doing in the classroom, and the outcomes of instruction.
   d. The roles of the teachers.
   e. The content of the curriculum.
4. Express your own views on the issues presented in the third objective.

THE PHILOSOPHICAL ISSUES OF MOST CONCERN TO EDUCATORS

The last ten years have not been easy ones for educators in the United States. Besieged by attacks from liberals, moderates, conservatives, radicals, and independents alike, the educational establishment has found itself in a defensive posture. In times of relative affluence, peace, honesty in government, stability of values, and racial harmony, members of a society generally agree upon the purposes of education, but when a society begins to have doubts about its own purposes, that society of necessity begins to ask some penetrating questions.

Eventually those questions focus on the purpose of education. For example, which of the following should the educational establishment emphasize?

1. The truths thought to transcend all cultures (the classics).
2. The transmission of the current cultural values, including the skills necessary to function within the culture.
3. The adjustment of the student to the culture by providing the student with a variety of choices.
4. The skills and attitudes necessary to change the culture for the better.
5. Some combination of the above.

Although questions such as these have been raised for many years, there is no unanimity of opinion on which of these points should be emphasized. Educators cannot afford, however, to continue to mimic the ostrich; these questions must be addressed satisfactorily. Because of our increasing emphasis on accountability, poorly founded answers will not be tolerated by society at large. As Hutchins (1972) so aptly states, "A large, conspicuous, elaborate, expensive institution on which the hopes of a nation have been pinned cannot hope to escape attack in a period of national distress unless it can show that it has intelligent purposes and it is achieving them." Coleman (1972), for example, suggests that often the students have outgrown the schools because the schools are not really helping the students to become more productive and contributing members of the family, community, and country. Can we effectively counter Coleman's criticism?

To arrive at a reasoned position about the purposes of education takes a lot of thought and effort. One of our contentions is that all too often educators and teachers have not carefully considered the purposes of education. Possessing the technical skills to implement programs with psychological precision, educators and teachers all too often have not considered the *whys* of the curriculum. The end product of this short-sighted thinking, in our opinion, has resulted in carelessly developed, fragmented instructional programs that lack substance and are "trendy" in their orientations. Lacking clear, well-thought-out purposes, our schools have been confronted with apathetic, confused, and alienated students. These students sense a mismatch between their education and the world of work, family, and community, and many are unwilling to put forth any significant effort toward their schoolwork. Our lack of purpose has resulted in numerous critics who rightfully point out some of the problems of our current system without adequately addressing the questions of the schools' outcomes and without suggesting realistic instructional programs to reach the desired outcomes within the financial and social constraints of our schools.

Representative of some of the outcome-type questions that have been posed recently are letters written by concerned teachers in a 1976 edition of the National Education Association's *Today's Education:*

> I agree . . . that standards are slipping.
>
> Enrollments in elective physical science courses throughout the country are declining. In my high school, the student body has increased from 3,000 in 1968 to 5,000 in 1975, while enrollment in elective physical science courses has dropped more than 50 percent. Enrollment in advanced placement physical science has dropped to zero.
>
> . . . the declining enrollment in elective high school physical science is a national trend. . . .
>
> . . . in the past decade the youth movement has featured a "revulsion against all things technological" and . . . the problem centers on the priorities of our young people, not the quality of instructional programs.
>
> I believe students should be "forced" into taking courses matched to their abilities. [From a high school chemistry teacher] (Stappler, 1976)

Or consider this letter from a frustrated teacher:

> As a teacher of eleventh and twelfth grade English, I find the controversy over the problem of "slipping" standards to be my greatest source of frustration because of the equally controversial issue of teacher accountability.
>
> Why did these kids get to the twelfth grade without learning to read and write?
>
> If I hear one more person tell me that I must not be motivating my students, I'll scream my head off. It is time that parents and students themselves take some of the responsibility for motivation. I refuse to entertain my students into learning; it is too time-consuming, too difficult; and completely frustrating because it doesn't work.
>
> . . . I don't intend to give up yet on myself or my students, but with the arbitrary and contradictory guidelines and dictates that I receive from "higher up," my resolves cannot and will not last forever. [From a 27-year-old high school teacher] (Wright, 1976)

These letters represent real problems experienced by concerned teachers. We believe that letters such as these are symptomatic of many of the problems facing our schools. Stated bluntly, our educational establishment is somewhat confused. Caught between several major social trends, our educational establishment often appears to be at cross purposes, unable to determine priorities and to act upon them. For example, one major problem concerns giving students a great deal of freedom to determine their own direction while insuring that they possess the basic skills to function as an informed adult in our complex society. If the students opt not to acquire the skills, what is our response? If the students do not possess the knowledge and attitudes necessary to determine their own direction, what is our response? If the students don't care, what is our response?

Regardless of the philosophical and psychological orientations of educators and teachers, most of the important educational questions can be reduced to the pragmatic questions: What should be the *outcomes* of our educational system? and What appear to be the viable *processes* to reach our outcomes? The outcome question is steeped in philosophy, whereas the process question has its basis in educational psychology.

To make this point clearer, consider the recent work by Scandura (1977a) on problem solving. According to Scandura, the overall goal of our curriculum efforts should be to produce students who are capable of solving categories of problems that cut across content areas. When seen from this perspective, it is the task of curriculum experts to identify those higher-order rules that are applicable to a variety of problem-solving tasks. Rather than including in our curriculum many unimportant objectives that appear to have little bearing on problem solving, we must be more selective with what we want students to do with their time. To repeat, it should be the task of the curriculum constructor to identify the finite set of rules needed to solve important problems. Obviously the philosophies help us to decide which set of problems should be addressed.

From a decision-making base, however, it should be apparent to the reader that the "outcomes" questions of the philosophers and the "process" questions of educational psychologists are closely related and cannot be neatly untangled. This relationship becomes very apparent when we carefully consider the various definitions of the verb *to educate.*

According to *Webster's Third International Dictionary, to educate* is derived from the verb *educare*—to rear, bring up, to lead. Four definitions are provided in Webster's dictionary:

a. To develop by fostering to varying degrees the growth or expansion of knowledge, wisdom, desirable qualities of mind or character, physical health, or competence. . . .
b. To train by formal instruction and supervised practice. . . .
c. To provide with information. . . .
d. To bring about an improvement in, or a refinement of. . . .

Several underlying themes are implicit in these definitions. Initially, you should be aware that regardless of which definition you prefer, a *change in behavior is implicit.* Secondly, if you read these definitions carefully, each implies that *value judgments* must be made. What should be trained? Who is to say what is wisdom? What is a desirable quality of the mind? What information should be provided? What improvement should occur? Finally, it should be noted that a *teacher* or outside agent plays a major role in the educative process (Figure 2–1); the verbs *develop, train, provide,* and *to bring about* all strongly suggest that someone other than the student is partially

FIGURE 2–1
The teacher plays a major role in the educative process

responsible for the educative process. This does not imply, of course, that a student cannot take a great deal of the initiative in learning, just that an outside agent or teacher plays a significant role in the process. Notice how the philosophical and psychological questions are both incorporated in the definition. Both the outcome question and the process question are implied. Let us briefly consider the relationship between these questions.

SUBJECTIVITY IN TEACHER PERSPECTIVES

Rarely do teachers conceptualize well-developed, consistent, formal philosophical systems from which teaching strategies evolve. Rather, most teachers appear to be relatively pragmatic about teaching. This does not mean, however, that teachers do not possess *very strong* opinions about the purposes of schools, the nature of students, and how classrooms should be run. You should be aware that your beliefs about schools and students are probably fairly consistent. You should also be aware that your beliefs are subjective and somewhat unique to your own way of thinking. And you should be aware that your beliefs are closely related to what you decide to read about education, what you think is important in educational psychology, and what you will remember and use from this textbook as a teacher. Finally, irrespective of certain constraints placed upon teachers from society at large and the school system in particular, the teacher's behavior in the classroom necessarily is a reflection of the teacher's beliefs. The point we wish to make is that we cannot escape from our subjectivity, nor can we hide from it. Acting as a filter, buffer, and distorter, our subjectivity is closely related to the types of classrooms we conduct.

As an example in the psychological realm, teachers with a cognitivist persuasion tend to read different books and journals than do teachers with a behaviorist persuasion.

Teachers oriented toward a humanist viewpoint not only tend to read different books and journals than do behaviorists or cognitivists, but they also tend to emphasize different types of goals and objectives in the classroom. This does not mean, however, that any of these viewpoints is necessarily instructionally incompatible with other viewpoints or that any of the viewpoints are necessarily wrong. It does mean, however, that often a person possessing a strong viewpoint is likely not to be knowledgeable about alternative viewpoints. The tragedy of this superficial narrowness is that none of the viewpoints has covered all of the philosophical and psychological "truths." *Each of the varying viewpoints identified in this book appears to have some validity for aiding a teacher to become a better educational and instructional decision maker.* For example, many of those teachers espousing a progressivist philosophical orientation (to be mentioned soon) appear to be very much opposed to the psychological behaviorist orientation, and yet, upon careful analysis, there is nothing necessarily incompatible between those two viewpoints. You should be aware that complex decision making, by its very nature, is somewhat subjective. There is often no compelling logic behind many of the philosophical and psychological decisions we make as teachers—often a "psycho-logic" prevails.

Before you read any further in this chapter, we thought it would interest you to complete the accompanying brief questionnaire. This questionnaire is designed to assess your beliefs about various philosophical issues related to educational and instructional decision making.

QUESTIONNAIRE ON PHILOSOPHICAL BELIEFS ABOUT EDUCATION

Instructions: Read each statement and circle the number that best represents your view.

1. I believe the main focus of education should be the study of those basic "truths" and creative works that transcend every age and culture in order that students may best adapt to the human condition.

Strongly disagree	*Moderately disagree*	*Slightly disagree*	*Neutral*	*Slightly agree*	*Moderately agree*	*Strongly agree*
1	2	3	4	5	6	7

2. I believe the main focus of education should be the study of our culture and our times in order that the student may readily adapt to our culture.

Strongly disagree	*Moderately disagree*	*Slightly disagree*	*Neutral*	*Slightly agree*	*Moderately agree*	*Strongly agree*
1	2	3	4	5	6	7

3. I believe the main focus of education should be centered around providing students with many enriching experiences rather than exposing them to a fixed curriculum in order that they may pursue their own interests.

Strongly disagree	*Moderately disagree*	*Slightly disagree*	*Neutral*	*Slightly agree*	*Moderately agree*	*Strongly agree*
1	2	3	4	5	6	7

4. I believe the main focus of education should be to study our culture and other cultures in order that the student may want to change those situations in our culture that need changing.

Strongly disagree	*Moderately disagree*	*Slightly disagree*	*Neutral*	*Slightly agree*	*Moderately agree*	*Strongly agree*
1	2	3	4	5	6	7

5. Upon graduation from public school, our students should possess the mental discipline to be capable and desirous of pursing the "best" humanity has to offer.

Strongly disagree	*Moderately disagree*	*Slightly disagree*	*Neutral*	*Slightly agree*	*Moderately agree*	*Strongly agree*
1	2	3	4	5	6	7

6. Upon graduation from public school, our students should possess the skills and attitudes necessary to adjust to our society.

Strongly disagree	*Moderately disagree*	*Slightly disagree*	*Neutral*	*Slightly agree*	*Moderately agree*	*Strongly agree*
1	2	3	4	5	6	7

7. Upon graduation from public school, our students should have developed a well-adjusted, individual lifestyle.

Strongly disagree	*Moderately disagree*	*Slightly disagree*	*Neutral*	*Slightly agree*	*Moderately agree*	*Strongly agree*
1	2	3	4	5	6	7

8. Upon graduation from public school, our students should want to be able to identify and solve problems of social significance.

Strongly disagree	*Moderately disagree*	*Slightly disagree*	*Neutral*	*Slightly agree*	*Moderately agree*	*Strongly agree*
1	2	3	4	5	6	7

9. The curriculum should prepare the student for the future by emphasizing the three R's in elementary school. At the secondary level, the college-bound student should receive a general education with an emphasis on the classics, grammar, math, and science. The non-college-bound student should continue to receive a broad education, but the emphasis should shift to skill training.

Strongly disagree	*Moderately disagree*	*Slightly disagree*	*Neutral*	*Slightly agree*	*Moderately agree*	*Strongly agree*
1	2	3	4	5	6	7

10. The curriculum should prepare the student for the future by emphasizing the three R's in elementary school. At the secondary level, the curriculum should be a "miniature of the world" in order to prepare the student to live in our democratic culture.

Strongly disagree	*Moderately disagree*	*Slightly disagree*	*Neutral*	*Slightly agree*	*Moderately agree*	*Strongly agree*
1	2	3	4	5	6	7

11. The curriculum should focus on a variety of social experiences, projects, problems, and similar activities. The basic skills, such as the three R's, are to be learned through student-initiated activities.

Strongly disagree	*Moderately disagree*	*Slightly disagree*	*Neutral*	*Slightly agree*	*Moderately agree*	*Strongly agree*
1	2	3	4	5	6	7

12. The early school years should focus on a variety of group experiences and activities. The basic skills, such as the three R's, are to be learned through student-initiated activities. The last several years of high school should focus on the economic, political, scientific, artistic, educational, and social problems of our culture.

Strongly disagree	*Moderately disagree*	*Slightly disagree*	*Neutral*	*Slightly agree*	*Moderately agree*	*Strongly agree*
1	2	3	4	5	6	7

Being aware of your own biases, preferences, and "psycho-logic" concerning educational and instructional issues might help you to become more open to alternative or complementary viewpoints, and thus become a more enlightened decision maker. Furthermore, you might develop a clearer insight into your purposes as a teacher.

Later in the chapter we will provide you with a scoring key to evaluate your responses to the various questions. Before turning to the scoring key we recommend that you read the chapter first. By doing so, your evaluation of your responses should be more meaningful to you. It would also be interesting to see if you change your mind after reading the rest of the chapter.

AN INESCAPABLE FUNCTION OF THE SCHOOLS: TO TRANSMIT VALUES

Have you ever questioned, or even wondered, why our educational system is as it is today? Why do we provide the opportunity for formal schooling for students between the ages of 5 and 18? What are the general purposes of our schools? Who should our schools educate? What should the students be able to do upon graduation from our schools? What should we do with students who refuse to conform to the basic rules of the school? To what extent should our schools take on the responsibilities of teaching values? Which values should be taught? Who should teach the values? Who should decide which values to teach? To what extent should our schools be relevant? The list of questions appears endless. This chapter attempts to address some of these *value*-laden issues.

At a broad level, the schools necessarily have to transmit the general values of our society. At a narrower level, it is our contention that the types of goals, objectives, assignments, specific teaching strategies, and choices the teacher makes available to students, whether the teacher is aware of it or not, are closely related to the teacher's general philosophy and value system. Further, within the constraints placed upon the teacher, the daily routines of the classroom and the general methods used by the teacher are also a reflection of the teacher's philosophical orientation and values.

In fact, it is our contention that teachers, because of their prescribed roles, are constant purveyors of values. A teacher's role automatically dictates this *inescapable* function. To teach is to value! To facilitate and guide learning is to value. To choose to respond or not to respond is an expression of a value.

Every classroom is filled with values. If a teacher assigns a lesson, the teacher does so because the lesson is deemed worthy. If a teacher lets the students make a great number of choices, the teacher does so because the choices are considered worthy. It is impossible for humans to design environments that are valueless because every human interaction is based on values. And whether consciously designed or not, a classroom purposefully imparts many values. Snyder (1971) makes this point by suggesting that the classroom contains a "hidden curriculum" component. The hidden curriculum consists of all those stimuli in the classroom, including the teacher's responses, that elicit or shape a student's response and that are not formally a part of the explicit curriculum (Figure 2–2). A set of encyclopedias, a teacher's smile, the seating arrangement, the routines of the class, and the general activities of the class are some examples of the hidden curriculum. And we should point out here that the hidden curriculum can have a very positive or negative outcome depending upon how it is structured.

FIGURE 2–2
Classrooms impart many values that are not part of the formal curriculum

We mention the hidden curriculum because you should be aware that it is as much a reflection of the goals and values of the class as is the formal curriculum and specified objectives, and it can have a very definitive impact upon students. We also mention the hidden curriculum concept because of an issue that is raised from time to time concerning the school's role with reference to imposing values upon students. Some educators have taken the position that the school environment should be basically value-free and that it is generally wrong to impose values upon students. Educators of this persuasion usually feel that learning should be an organic experience; it should grow from within the child and be spontaneous. The learner knows best. All the teacher should do is to facilitate this process. Carl Rogers (1967), for example, suggests that the only learning that significantly influences behavior is self-discovered learning, and, therefore, the outcomes of *teaching* are either unimportant or fruitless. A. S. Neill (1960), the founder of Summerhill, a radical school in England noted for its permissiveness, stated that his school had "to renounce all discipline, all direction, all suggestion, all moral training, and all religious instruction."

In his book, Neill goes on to say that "all any child needs is the three R's—the rest should be tools and clay and sports, theater, paint, and freedom." This statement makes it very clear that Neill also attempted to foster certain values in his school. His statement also makes it very clear that he favored some activities and outcomes over others. All of those previous stimuli or instructional practices that Neill chose to have in his school environment are based on his educational philosophy. Choice itself is a value. His school could have just as easily had scientific laboratories, machinery, shops, and programmed instructional materials. The types of books, materials, and activities made available to students in any school are based necessarily on the staff's values! The absence of certain stimuli also implies a great deal about values.

Obviously Neill had an expectation, or at least a strong desire, that students at Summerhill would choose to do something *worthwhile* with the tools, clay, sports, theater, or paint, or else these objects and activities would not have been a part of the environment.

What is the point of all this, anyway? We are suggesting that *any* school has a certain structure that implies discipline, direction, suggestion, and moral training. These qualities are an inescapable function of a school environment. The issue is to decide which aspects of the environment are to be emphasized and for what general outcomes. Schools are not purposeless institutions; they have a purpose and direction and they impart these values to their students (refer back to the hidden curriculum concept), no matter how subtly. Our contention is that *all* teachers interact with their students to bring about certain *behavioral* changes; the nature of these interactions is to a large extent a function of the teacher's values.

In our opinion the issue of whether or not a school should transmit or teach values is false. The nature of any type of teaching, even the type referred to by Rogers, is such that values are taught by adults to students, even if the teaching is not intentional. The real issue is: What values should be taught? A secondary issue necessarily follows: How can these values best be taught? It would appear that teachers ought to work hard to clearly identify their purposes and then to translate those purposes into a plan of action. Without this clarity of purpose we may discover to our dismay, if we have not already discovered it, that our schools are inadvertently conveying values and outcomes that we neither believe in nor wish to convey to our students.

Believing that our schools should have a sound philosophical basis from which our goals and the resulting classroom environments may be derived, we discuss in this chapter the four most influential educational philosophies that have had an impact on our schools. In agreement with the poet T. S. Eliot, we must derive our theory of education from our philosophy of life. Too often the important issues of education—the issues upon which the major institutional and instructional decisions have been made—have been given only a surface consideration.

1. State why Webster's definitions of *to educate* imply a change in behavior.
2. As stated in the first part of this chapter, it is impossible for humans to construct value-free environments. Any choice implies a value. Given the following list of objects or instructional practices found in a typical classroom or school, identify at least one possible value associated with each, and then explain what type of outcome a teacher might want to see occur with the object or instructional practice.
    a. A pile of art paper.
    b. An assignment of ten math problems.
    c. Seats arranged in groups of four.
    d. A class discussion on a controversial topic.
    e. A choice of three different long-term projects.

THE FOUR PHILOSOPHIES

Let us see how educational philosophy might help us address the question of values. Philosophy is basically the study of the questions: What is real? What is true? and What is good? To help you consider these questions in an educational and instructional context, we discuss the philosophies of perennialism, essentialism, progressivism, and reconstructionism (Brameld, 1971; Morris, 1962). These four viewpoints are the cornerstones from which most of the major educational and instructional decisions are currently derived. As a generalization, most of the important philosophical questions concerning education and instruction can be reduced to the broad issues raised by these philosophies.

You should be aware, however, that these general philosophical systems are not necessarily mutually independent of one another in all issues. We present these four viewpoints as separate philosophies only because of their historical significance. On many issues it is difficult to identify which position is represented. While reading the remainder of this chapter, you should view each of these philosophical positions as a semi-integrated approach to the questions concerning reality, truth, and goodness.

To assume that any one of these philosophical positions has covered "the truth" on an issue would be premature. To feel that you have to choose one of the four philosophies as a basis for your professional behavior is also premature. The purpose of this chapter is to get you to think about these issues—to be aware that a well-thought-out foundation is needed upon which to base your future decisions. To do less than that is unfair to the students you will have.

Perennialism

According to the perennialists, education should focus on the *essence of reality, truth, and value.* Believing that there are certain principles that transcend every age—principles that are timeless, spaceless, everlasting, and absolute—educators must identify these principles and *transmit* them to the young. From the perennialist perspective, the failure of our society and our educational system has been that neither of these institutions has discovered the essence of the ultimate questions. The philosophical mood of this orientation appears to be restorative, that is, to restore the culture to a previous condition (Brameld, 1971). Plato, Aristotle, and Thomas Aquinas, three of the greatest Western philosophers, have strongly influenced this movement.

1. What is the nature of the learner? From the perennialist perspective the learner is viewed as a *rational* being who possesses the ability to solve problems only after the mind is disciplined to think rationally. The methods of reasoning (deductions and inductions) are indispensable tools of perennialism, as is the scientific method.

Plato's concept of "ideas" appears to be particularly appropriate here. Humans should constantly search for the highest good, that which is universal and eternal. These ideas should be the criteria upon which daily decisions are made. In a clarification of Plato's basic pronouncement, Aristotle postulated a theory that the world is a single cosmic order of increasing perfection, a movement from impure matter to pure form where form and matter fuse at the apex of development. We should study the world from this perspective.

According to the perennialists, students should be viewed in the same manner; that is, it is possible for students to progress from mere potentiality (impurity of matter) toward a greater degree of actuality (purity of form), but only if the student is able to transcend material reality (Brameld, 1971). Most people fall far short of what they are capable of becoming. This position is very similar to the humanist and cognitivist point presented later in this book. In conclusion, an individual has the *capacity* to grow only if the mind is disciplined to think and has a purpose, thus transcending physical reality.

2. What should the learner be doing? A perennialist would advocate having the learner study the basic content of the intellect and spirit. Particular emphasis

FIGURE 2–3
Learning from books is an important part of perennialism

would be placed on mathematics, languages, logic, and the great books in order that the learner develop high levels of rationality, spirituality, and a competent intellect (Figure 2–3). The essence of reality, truth, and goodness should be pursued through reasoning and well-developed creative intuition. As a result, it is believed that a well-disciplined mind should be the end product of this type of education—a mind capable of identifying the essence of reality, truth, and value.

3. What should the teacher be doing? From the perennialist perspective, the teacher's role is one of *imparting* the appropriate knowledge and mental discipline to the student. The educational philosopher M. M. Adler (1942) notes that teaching is essentially one of two processes: either a teacher can operate upon a student to insure that the student acquires what is needed, or a teacher can cooperate with the student to help the student unfold an underlying potential that is thought to already exist. Essentially, these positions evolve from the Locke-Leibnitz controversy of the late 1600s. You will recall from Chapter 1 that Locke maintained that an infant's mind is analogous to a blank slate *(tabula rasa).* According to Locke experiences of the external world serve the function of filling up the slate. Leibnitz, on the other hand, posited that the mind of an infant is self-motivated and actively seeks out what it wants for its own good. Depending on your view about the nature of human development, within this philosophical orientation you could play a Lockean role, a Leibnitzian role, or a combination of both. Regardless, your position would be to insure that the learner acquires the appropriate *eternal* principles of life, partially by presenting those principles to the student and partially by having the student discover those principles as the student develops.

4. What should be the content of the curriculum? The perennialist views the purpose of education from a quasi-absolutist perspective; that is, since there exists a *universal* body of knowledge as well as certain processes that allow an individual to comprehend the essence of the universe (reality, truth, and goodness), it is the duty of the educational establishment to teach *that essence* and *those processes* that will allow an individual to understand the essence of the universe.

To understand this viewpoint a little more thoroughly, let us travel back in time to ancient Greece. According to Plato, humans possess three qualities: appetite, will, and reason. It is the purpose of education to enhance these qualities. For the truly competent, Plato believed that education should consist of the subjects found in Figure 2–4.

FIGURE 2–4
Plato's outline of education

Age	*Subjects or focus of life*
0–20	Two R's, music, gymnastics, military training
20–30	Mathematics, science
30–35	Philosophy
35–50	Practical experience in life

Notice in the figure how the curriculum flows toward philosophy, which is seen as the ultimate prerequisite for life's practical experiences. As an aside, it is interesting to note that our age requirements for representatives, senators, and the presidency as specified in the Constitution parallel Plato's model. At the time of the early Renaissance, the perennialist university curriculum generally consisted of the trivium (logic, rhetoric, and grammar) and the quadrivium (music, astronomy, geometry, and arithmetic).

Today, the perennialists take the position that education should prepare the student for the future. This belief is based on the premise that a child is still basically potential rather than actual. For the elementary-school-aged child, the three R's, in addition to history, geography, science, literature, and a foreign language, are considered the appropriate curriculum. At the secondary level, both a general education and skill training are stressed. For college-aged students, the emphasis is on mathematics, logic, rhetoric, and grammar, as well as the great books. This type of curriculum, according to the perennialists, should guarantee advanced reasoning skills and exposure to the perennial ideas of humankind. Perennialists are particularly distressed at colleges for the disorganized mish-mash of fragmented and overlapping courses offered. To prepare a student for the future, the student should be well grounded in the basics.

As an example of the perennialist orientation, consider the new core proposal developed by Harvard University for all Harvard undergraduates. Aware that the college-aged students of the 1970s lack a common, broad cultural knowledge, Harvard, (1978) has proposed that all graduates should "acquire a basic literacy in major forms of intellectual discourse." The Harvard proposal then defines the core areas as literature and the arts, history, social and philosophical analysis, science and mathematics, and foreign languages and culture. In addition, a basic competency in expository writing is required of all students. According to the Harvard report, the new proposal is founded on the question: "What are the characteristics of an educated person and how can curricular requirements help to foster these?" It is interesting to note that the new Harvard proposal is based on its definitions of what an educated person is generally capable of doing in each of these areas. Based on a carefully developed set of goals founded on the perennialist viewpoint, the Harvard undergraduate proposal is likely to have a very strong impact on higher education in the near future. Perennialism is becoming very much alive in higher educational circles.

Essentialism

The nucleus of the essentialist position is based on the premise that the *cultural patterns leading up to and including the present need to be preserved* and transmitted to students. This eclectic movement originated during the Renaissance and focuses on the orderly structure and content of a curriculum, guided discipline, and similar goals. As Morris (1962) observed, the essentialist position is located at the "trailing edge" of the present. With its orientation toward the assimilation of a body of knowledge (i.e., the cultural patterns leading up to the present), the essentialist viewpoint possesses a certain closeness to the perennialist position.

The main difference between the essentialist's views and the perennialist's views centers on the emphasis the curriculum should spend on attaining a worldwide perspective on the problems and common history of humankind compared to a more pragmatic concern for producing students who are capable of adjusting specifically to our culture. As a generalization, the philosophical mood of essentialism is transmissive (to transmit the culture) and conservative (Brameld, 1971) in its orientation.

Two basic goals permeate the essentialist philosophy:

a. To generate a set of beliefs in a student so that the student is able to adjust to a culture that is becoming increasingly scientific, industrial, and secular.
b. To insure that these beliefs endure.

According to the essentialists, education should not serve the function of cultural moderation (the progressivists) or transformation (the reconstructionists); rather the learner ought to be able to re-represent the current culture. To simplify their position, the essentialists emphasize reproductive learning (i.e., learning the cultural traditions) rather than productive problem solving; *adjustment* to the culture rather than significant change of the culture. This does not mean that the essentialists are opposed to significant change or productive problem solving; quite the contrary, they are in favor of both of these outcomes. Their main emphasis, however, is toward the reproductive end of the scale; one has to be able to reproduce the old before one can produce the new.

1. What is the nature of the learner? There is no well-defined viewpoint about the nature of the learner that necessarily results from an essentialist's educational beliefs. Basically the learner is seen as *adaptable.*

2. What should the learner be doing? The learner should be studying the subject matter content about his/her secular, scientific, and industrial culture in order to adjust to the same. At the conclusion of the student's education, the student should be able to reproduce accurately that which is real, true, and good about the culture (Brameld, 1971).

3. What should the teacher be doing? As an essentialist, the teacher must insure that the students obtain a sense of their own culture. The education should stress adequate *mastery* of the history and current status of the culture. To reach these goals the teacher's role is one of *conveying,* guiding, instructing, and *disciplining* students toward that end.

4. What should be the content of the curriculum? According to Brameld (1971), the essentialist's curriculum should be a miniature of the world—"a rich, sequential, and systematic curriculum based on an irreducible body of knowledge, skills, and attitudes common to a democratic culture." A series of subject fields is the basic curriculum. If a teacher leans toward philosophical idealism (the belief that ideas should be at the core of the curriculum), the curriculum should emphasize literature, intellectual history, philosophy, religion. If the teacher is closer to the realist's philosophical persuasion (the belief that curriculum should emphasize practical adaptation), math, science, and vocational preparation take on increasing importance.

We chose to group together the perennialist and essentialist movements because both of these viewpoints have the following common characteristics.

a. The emphasis is on mastering facts, information, and ideas in order to be a better thinker. Because of this cognitive emphasis, the learner is required to engage in a great deal of assimilative, reproductive-type learning. Further, language is the vehicle used most frequently to transmit the knowledge, hence there is a great emphasis on learning from books.
b. The teacher's role is generally oriented toward transmitting a body of knowledge or transmitting discipline to students.
c. The structure and content of the curriculum are relatively fixed; providing students with a lot of choice is not considered necessary.
d. Adjustment to the society (essentialist) and the conservation of the universal heritage of humankind (perennialist) are important goals.
e. Both of these movements are distressed by the lack of concern for insuring that a fixed body of knowledge is transmitted to students.

Progressivism

The progressivists start out with premises that on the surface are very different from the perennialist and essentialist viewpoints. Representative of the progressivist viewpoint is the suggestion that our activities and experiences in life are ultimately responsible for influencing our thought processes and philosophy of life, which lead us to our way of life. In other words, experiencing is more important in determining our thinking than thinking is in determining our living. This philosophical position has its origins in pragmatism and empiricism, a belief that people should *try out their ideas* before believing in them. According to the progressivists, it makes very little sense to think for the sake of thinking; rather one should think with a purpose in mind.

FIGURE 2–5
A variety of experiences are necessary to develop the whole child

It is interesting to note that the progressivists also owe their origins to the great Greek philosopher Plato, who coined the phrase "learning by doing." Instead of focusing their educational philosophy on a fixed content or structure, the progressivists stress the role of experience in the development of the learner. Experience is both spiritual and material, complex and simple, intellectual and emotional; therefore, proper experiences enhance the likehood that a "whole child" will develop (Brameld, 1971) (Figure 2–5). Comenius, the 17th-century Moravian bishop, was one of the first to suggest that instruction should fit the child, which, of course, is one of the basic tenets of individualized instruction. Rousseau, another romantic, progressivist advocate, submitted that schools ought to be child-centered rather than content- or teacher-centered. This philosophy focuses on the process of change; it places its faith on the individual's capacity to originate solutions to complex problems rather than on the universal "truths of the past or the relative truths" of an existing culture. It is for these reasons that this philosophy has been accused of being content-free or rootless.

According to the essentialist viewpoints, for example, the progressivist orientation toward problem solving and experience places the learner in the absurd situation of having to solve problems without the necessary knowledge or mental discipline to gain very much from the experience. We will have a great deal to say about this point throughout the book. Furthermore, the progressivists do not emphasize a fixed curriculum to the same extent as do the perennialists and essentialists. Essentialists argue that progressivists are likely to produce rootless, restless, undisciplined students.

1. What is the nature of the learner? The progressivists believe that learning evolves over time toward higher and higher levels of complexity; this evolution is natural and will ultimately result in intelligent behavior. The environment plays a critical role in this evolutionary process, not from a deterministic model as postulated by some behaviorists, but from an interactionist perspective as suggested by the cognitivists identified in Chapter 1. The learner is viewed as a *selector* of stimuli in the environment (the cognitivist position) rather than as a *reactor* to stimuli (the radical behaviorist position).

2. What should the learner be doing? Unfortunately, there is a great deal of confusion about this question. John Dewey, the foremost advocate of the progressivist viewpoint, would be very upset with many of the schools that currently call themselves progressive. One of Dewey's main goals was to create educational institutions in which learners could develop distinct "patterns of living" based upon experimentation. The scientific method is at the core of this philosophy, in which the student is required to control and systematically examine experience in cause-and-effect patterns.

This philosophy does not imply that children should be allowed to "do their own thing," as professed by some pseudo-progressivists and misinformed critics of this approach. While learning is believed to originate with the felt needs, curiosities, and interests of a learner and is, therefore, quasi-individualistic, the teacher should play a very active role in *expecting and demanding excellence!* The child should develop, in concert with other children, a disciplined mind; a mind in which profound questions are asked and pursued for long periods of time; a mind fused with emotionality in order that work and play become united; a mind that is not afraid to solve complex problems and thrives upon change. Basically, this philosophy centers on the *process* of thinking rather than on the *content* of thinking. Stated another way, the philosophy is process-oriented rather than content or product-oriented.

3. What should the teacher be doing? The teacher plays several extremely important roles as a progressivist:

a. The teacher should demand and expect excellence!
b. The teacher should play an active-aggressive role in interaction with learners, rather than a passive-laissez-faire role.
c. As with all other philosophical approaches, the teacher should clearly define the desired outcomes of instruction, particularly since this philosophical system places much faith in experimentation and the scientific method.
d. The teacher should be sure that appropriate experiences and environmental stimuli are available in order to facilitate the defined objectives.
e. To a large extent, the teacher should become a facilitator of research-type projects. Independent study projects at the college level and the British tutorial system are examples of this approach.
f. Based on the empiricist viewpoint, the teacher should be monitoring the classroom environment continually to determine whether the program is a success.

4. What should be the content of the curriculum? Since the progressivist is concerned mainly with process and change, the content of the progressivist curriculum is less fixed. Basically, the content is change itself, the important and sometimes controversial issues of life (Figure 2–6). In fact, the unsettled, non-agreed-upon issues are actively studied. Essentially, the subject matter centers around social experiences, problems, projects, and similar activities rather than around specified topics and activities. Ideally, the student is taught how to observe and manage change. Those skills necessary to manage change are taught to the student as the skills are needed and an interest in them is expressed.

Reconstructionism

Comparing reconstructionism to the other three philosophical viewpoints is difficult. First of all, reconstructionism shares with perennialism the concern for producing highly competent thinkers, shares with the essentialists the orientation toward the present culture as an object of study, and shares with the progressivists the orientation toward experimentalism. The purpose for producing highly competent individuals, however, is quite different here than in the other three philosophies. The perennialists, essentialists, and, to a lesser degree, the progressivists all have a vested interest in maintaining many elements of the status quo. The reconstructionists, on the other hand, are interested in initiating social change of considerable magnitude; they may be viewed as utopian in their thoughts. They share some of their views with Plato's *The Republic,* Augustine's *City of God,* More's *The City of the Sun,* Mumford's *Culture of Cities,* and other writers who may be characterized as utopian in vision.

FIGURE 2–6
Learning to cooperate in groups is a progressivist goal

The reconstructionist's main premise is that our culture has failed and as humans, we have the capability to make our culture what we want. The emphasis of this position is on defining important new cultural goals while developing the means to reach these goals. Rationality is the essence of this position. According to the reconstructionist, a thorough-going transformation is needed if Western society is to survive. Wars, racism, poverty, and unnecessary conflicts have plagued humans from our earliest origins. These phenomena are caused by humans, therefore these same phenomena may be eliminated by humans. Change cannot occur, however, unless the masses desire change; therefore the reconstructionist emphasizes the process of change within a group. Group consensus is thought to be a necessary component of the classroom process. If significant change is ever to occur in our society, the majority must agree upon certain economic, political, scientific, aesthetic, educational, humane, and world-order values, while keeping minority rights in mind. Change is a difficult process, and we ought to prepare our students for it.

Before we proceed, you ought to be aware that this viewpoint has actually had very little impact on curricular decisions. We have included this position in the book, not because of the influence of this viewpoint on curriculum decision making, but simply because there are an increasing number of critics who feel that our schools should be more concerned with the types of problems addressed by those activists advocating this position.

1. What is the nature of the learner? Many of the beliefs about the nature of learners are similar to the progressivist philosophy; the differences are subtle. Essentially, reconstructionists emphasize the social nature of learning as it relates to group responsibility, commitment, and arrival at a *group* consensus.

2. What should the learner be doing? The learner should solve problems of social significance and then act upon the solutions. According to the reconstructionists, students should not engage in problem solving just because it is a method used in thinking; the student should actually solve real social problems. In essence, this viewpoint asks the learner to search for the utopian way of life. Improvement of humankind through social commitment is the goal. Work is the source of all human value, and this work should be fulfilling, not degrading. The learner should be particularly competent in the scientific method, for according to the reconstructionist, science, when properly used, has the potential to become the salvation of the modern era.

3. What should the teacher be doing? The teacher is a facilitator and synthesizer of information and experiences whose duty is to help weave together the various themes of a relatively structured curriculum. Generally, the teacher's role in this viewpoint is quite closely related to that of the progressivist position, but they differ radically in terms of the goals desired of students. The progressivists are committed to cultural moderation; the reconstructionists are committed to significant change within the society.

4. What should be the content of the curriculum? In actuality, as stated previously, the reconstructionist viewpoint has not yet been implemented in its entirety, although some of the ideas have been incorporated into existing programs. It is interesting to note that although the reconstructionist philosophy may be incorporated into the total school curriculum, the emphasis has been placed on the last two years of high school and the two years of junior college. It is thought that the earlier schooling a child receives can be brought to fruition in this four-year span, and that the earlier schooling serves as a prerequisite for problem solving. An example of a possible reconstructionist program is summarized in Figure 2–7 (Brameld, 1971).

FIGURE 2–7
Course content: Reconstructionism

1st year (11th grade)	1. Motivation toward the program 2. Economic-political reconstruction (community—worldwide)
2d year (12th grade)	1. Challenging problems, methods, needs, goals—science 2. Challenging problems, methods, needs, goals—art
3d year (1st year college)	1. Where do we want to go in organization and practice of education? 2. Where do we want to go in organization and practice of relations to one another as human beings?
4th year (2d year college)	1. Techniques and strategies for attaining agreed-upon goals 2. Reconsideration of all major areas—a synthesis

3. Take a current issue such as the environment or the government's response to poverty, and state how a teacher would handle the topic from each of the four philosophical viewpoints mentioned in this chapter. Include in your discussion statements about:
   a. The type of outcome the teacher would like to achieve.
   b. The types of activities in which the students would be engaged.
   c. The specific role the teacher would likely take in dealing with the topic.

FIGURE 2–8
Summary of the perennialist, essentialist, progressivist, and reconstructionist philosophical-educational viewpoints

Philosophy	*Focus of the philosophy (orientation)*	*Nature of the learner*	*Content of the curriculum*	*Teacher's role*	*Expected outcome of the learner*	*Criticism of current educational practices*
Perennialism	To discover the absolute principles of reality, truth, and value; should transcend society; great deal of book learning	Capable of learning, rational, intellectual, receptive	Great books, logic, math, languages, classics, structure-oriented	To transmit knowledge; promote intellectual discipline; "purity"	Should be able to identify the "absolute principles" and behave accordingly; highly rational, well-disciplined	An eclectic mish-mash, purposeless, producing incompetent, illiterate relativists; a spiritual and intellectual bankruptcy exists
Essentialism	To discover principles of reality, truth, and value of our culture; identify our heritage; adjust to our scientific, secular, industrial culture	Receptive spectators of ideas of nature	Idealism: symbols and ideas (history, literature); realism (math, science), structure-oriented	To transmit knowledge; demonstrate	Should "re-present" the culture accurately	Perennialist—irrelevant; progressivist—too restless, disorderly, leaves education to serendipity, produces incompetence
Progressivism	To experience reality, experiment; grounded in pragmatism; learning is natural	An active problem solver; uses both intellect and feelings	Social sciences, many group experiences, projects, science, much choice, process-oriented	To facilitate, groups and guide projects	Competent problem solver; work and play should become one; a doer	Perennialist—not practical enough, not grounded in experience; essentialist—too authoritarian, doesn't produce motivated learners and doers
Reconstructionism	To realize our potential as humans; transform the world into the ideal; orient to the future (the possible)	Capable of rational problem solving	The basics; but use the basics to transform society; change imperative; goals to change society; process-oriented	Basically same as progressivists, but to insure proper change of society	Citizen who desires significant changes and is competent to carry out plans	Simply not relevant, reproduces the past, produces uncommitted citizens

SUMMARY

In the beginning of the chapter, we attempt to point out that our schools are vulnerable to criticism because a common purpose and a justifiable orientation of public education appear to be lacking. Often trendy in their thinking, educators must come to realize that a reasoned position concerning the basis for our schools is sorely needed.

To help you consider these issues, four of the most influential philosophies of education are discussed. See Figure 2–8 for a summary of these viewpoints.

How do you feel about these viewpoints? We should point out that although each of these philosophical viewpoints necessarily emphasizes different orientations, they are not logically incompatible. There is no reason at all why the best features of each viewpoint could not be integrated into a synthesized eclectic model. What would you think of an educational philosophy that emphasizes producing students who are able to: *identify* the "absolute principles" of all time and *behave* in accordance with those principles (perennialism), *represent* the current culture accurately (essentialism), *solve* complex problems competently with an attitude that work and play are one (progressivism), and *desire* significant change in those aspects of our society that need changing irrespective of one's vested interests (reconstructionism)?

Carefully identifying your goals is one of the first steps along the road to becoming a teacher. Recognizing that you have strong biases and that your biases will be closely related to what you read professionally and how you ultimately treat students in your classroom is another important consideration. To distinguish between those values that ought to be imparted to students and those that ought not to be imparted is difficult. Now score the questionnaire you took at the beginning of the chapter to see how you stand on some of these issues. How do you think your beliefs will be related to your behavior as a teacher?

ANSWER KEY TO PHILOSOPHICAL BELIEFS QUESTIONNAIRE

The questions have been grouped into four categories representative of the four philosophical positions presented in this chapter. Record your scores for each question and total your score.

	Total score
1. Perennialism—Represented by Questions 1, 5, and 9	_____
2. Essentialism—Represented by Questions 2, 6, and 10	_____
3. Progressivism—Represented by Questions 3, 7, and 11	_____
4. Reconstructionism—Represented by Questions 4, 8, and 12	_____

Caution: You should be aware that forced-choice questionnaires such as this may not represent your true beliefs. You may have felt that some of the statements are appropriate for some students, but not for others. Or you may have felt that some of the statements are appropriate for a specific age level but not for another age level. Or you may have felt that none of these statements accurately represents your viewpoint. Finally, you may have felt that a combination of these statements between the categories best represents your views.

Given the limitations, we shall attempt to interpret what your score may mean. A score from 18 to 21 in any category indicates a strong preference for that philosophical position. A score from 15 to 17 indicates a moderate preference. At the other extreme, a score from 1 to 3 indicates an extreme dislike for the category, while a score from 4 to 6 indicates a moderate dislike. Scores from 7 to 14 fall in the "no strong preference" category.

A high *perennialist* score indicates a strong preference for the classics and the "Renaissance" ideal. A high *essentialist* score indicates a strong preference for a pragmatic view of education. Education should produce people to perform competently in our society. A high *progressivist* score indicates a strong preference for individualism and social adjustment. A high *reconstructionist* score indicates a strong preference for those who believe we are capable of creating a better society. Educators should take an active role in changing the society and should be utopian in orientation. A low score for any of these categories represents the opposite viewpoint.

SELF-TEST

1. Generate a functional definition of *education.*
2. In a conversation with a high school teacher from Merchantsville, Mr. Dullard stated that teachers should promote *intellectual* discipline while attempting to insure that students develop an attitude that work and play can be integrated. Which combination of philosophical attitudes does this combination represent?
   a. Perennialism – essentialism.
   b. Perennialism – progressivism.
   c. Perennialism – reconstructionism.
   d. Essentialism – progressivism.
   e. Essentialism – reconstructionism.
   f. Progressivism – reconstructionsim.
3. The criticism: "While the ideals underlying your philosophical position are wonderful, your position is really not germane to today's concerns of the individual and society" might best be leveled *against* the ______________________.
   a. Perennialists.
   b. Essentialists.
   c. Progressivists.
   d. Reconstructionists.
4. The perennialist perceives the student as being rational and capable of solving problems only after the student has achieved:
   a. Sufficient personal experiences to relate to.
   b. A proper attitude about life.
   c. Sufficient discipline necessary to think rationally.
   d. A prescribed role dictated by the educational institution.
5. Consider this conversation: **A:** "I don't care what you think about education, the most important consideration for our students is to have them adjust to our society. They must live in our society, and therefore they must be adjusted to it." Also consider: **B:** "Many of the problems we've had in our society have been created by people who have not been well adjusted. Although the academic subjects should be taught, a great deal of consideration should be given to a person's personal adjustment. One of the goals of the school should be to instill positive attitudes toward work in general." These two philosophical positions differ on a couple of key points. What position does **A** represent, and what position does **B** represent? Choose the correct combination.
   a. Perennialist – essentialist.
   b. Perennialist – progressivist.
   c. Perennialist – reconstructionist.
   d. Essentialist – progressivist.
   e. Essentialist – reconstructionist.
   f. Progressivist – reconstructionist.
6. Which of the four philosophical positions represents a utopian analysis of society?
   a. Perennialism.
   b. Essentialism.
   c. Progressivism.
   d. Reconstructionism.
7. The criticism: "You really don't know what your objectives are" could probably best be leveled against the ______________________.
   a. Perennialists.
   b. Essentialists.
   c. Progressivists.
   d. Reconstructionists.
8. Which of the following two philosophical positions emphasizes group projects?
   a. Perennialist – essentialist.
   b. Perennialist – progressivist.
   c. Perennialist – reconstructionist.
   d. Essentialist – progressivist.
   e. Essentialist – reconstructionist.
   f. Progressivist – reconstructionist.
9. Who would say this to whom: "It is through experience that our children learn, not through philosophical ideas of men long gone."
   a. Progressivist to perennialist.
   b. Essentialist to reconstructionist.
   c. Progressivist to essentialist.
   d. Reconstructionist to essentialist.
10. With the divorce rate rising significantly, a practical course on "Marriage and the Family" should be an

integral part of every student's high school education in order that potential married couples might better adjust to their marriages. This position would *most* likely be espoused by the ______________.

a. Perennialists.
b. Essentialists.
c. Progressivists.
d. Reconstructionists.

ANSWER KEY TO BOXED QUESTIONS

1. All four of the verbs used by Webster (to *develop, train, provide,* or *bring about* improvement) imply that the learner is in a particular state and will change as the result of being exposed to education, i.e., from undeveloped to developed, untrained to trained.
2. *a.* A pile of art papers: *value*—artistic expression and skill; *outcome*—able to produce an acceptable art project.
   b. An assignment of ten math problems: *value*—competent, independent problem solver; *outcome*—able to solve specified math problems.
   c. Seats arranged in groups of four: *value*—cooperation; *outcome*—able to work together in a group and cooperate on assignments to do group assignments correctly.
   d. A class discussion on a controversial topic: *value*—good discusser, independence of thought; *outcome*—develop good discussion skills, able to arrive at solutions to controversial topics in a reasoned, logical, impassionate approach to problem solving.
   e. A choice of three different long-term projects: *value*—involvement, hard work, commitment; *outcome*—able to organize and execute a long-term project, will want to approach other tasks that involve commitment and a long-term involvement.
3. Consult Figure 2–8. If your answers to the three parts of the question emphasize the content in the appropriate categories of that figure, then you are on the right track. If not, perhaps a short rereading of the second part of the chapter would be in order.

ANSWER KEY TO SELF-TEST

1. Any definition that implies a change in the state of the learner with an external agent having some role in the matter is appropriate.
2. *b*
3. *a*
4. *c*
5. *d*
6. *d*
7. *c*
8. *f*
9. *a*
10. *b*

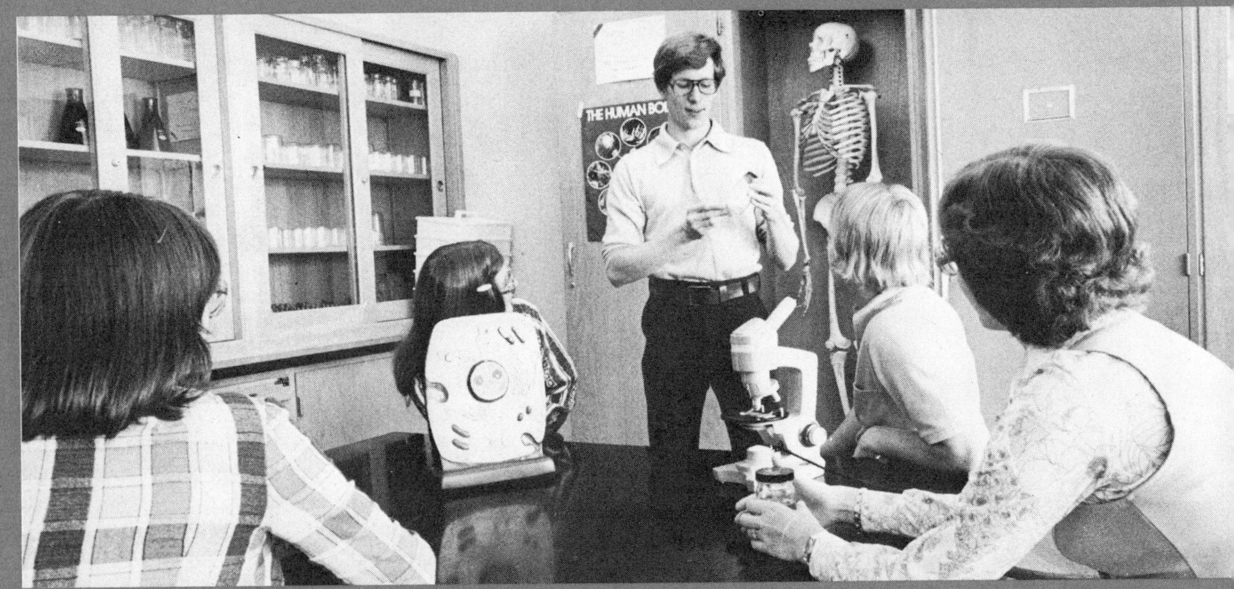

Chapter 3

The characteristics of humans: Psychological perspectives

AT THIS POINT IN YOUR LIFE you have already developed a personal set of beliefs about the basic motivations and other characteristics of humans. Those beliefs (you may not be able to verbalize them very well) are based on your lifelong set of experiences. In this chapter we do not attempt to change them. We do hope, however, to aid you in seeing those beliefs more clearly in the context of a school setting because they influence your interactions with other people. In your professional life you will interact with students, parents, and colleagues from a wide range of backgrounds. We believe a broad, well-integrated perspective will aid you in identifying their points of view and how they relate to or differ from your own. In this way you can be more effective in these interactions.

To develop your perspective, we first explore some limitations of humans as observers. Next we discuss the main perspectives from which psychologists have investigated the nature of people. Following this are several conclusions derived from personality and learning theory approaches and the impact we believe they have had on educational practice. The final two topics attempt an integration of the various points of view and the implications they have for teachers.

After studying the chapter you should be able to:

1. Define several major perspectives that psychologists have used to describe the general characteristics of humans and a variety of their conclusions.
2. Classify specific statements people may make as to their beliefs about human nature.

HUMANS AS OBSERVERS OF HUMANS

It has been said that "fish will be the last to discover water." The same may be true for human attempts to determine the nature of humans. If we fail, however, it will not be due to a lack of effort. Many people, over a long period of time, in many contexts, and from many perspectives have worked on the problem (Boring, 1950). It is more likely that failure will be due to the fact that individuals have a limited perspective, which affects their judgment.

To illustrate the point of a limited perspective, let us imagine the human population as a giant school of fish swimming past a coral reef. The general perspective of those fish at the head of the school may be that life is bountiful, interesting, and good and that the basic nature of fish is one of explorer. Others in the leading edge, depending on their experiences, may see life as fraught with dangers from lurking enemies and view their basic nature as trying to survive in a conflict with their environment. The conflict arises between their needs and hostile forces in the environment that threaten their safety and survival.

Those fish in the center of the school may also see life as a conflict, but for them the conflict is between members of the school over space, food, and rules of navigation. It is likely that these fish will view their basic nature as being a social organism, greatly influenced by interactions with other members of the species.

To those poor fish at the rear of the school, life may not appear as bountiful and beautiful. In fact, to them life may appear to be a miserable existence and their basic nature is to endure the sufferings of a meager life in a murky world.

Whereas some of the leading fish may think the primary issue to be considered should be the course to be taken, others, sighting sharks in the distance, may argue that defense should be the primary issue. Those fish close to the coral reef may argue that crowding should be the main issue, while those in the middle of the school would also want to include individual rights. Alas and alack for those fish at the rear of the school, the only thing clear may be that the main issue should be the prevention of water pollution.

In view of the considerable amount of knowledge that has been accumulated in the brief history of human beings, it would seem that we should be able to rise above ourselves and view the human species more objectively than the fish in our analogy. This is rather difficult to do apparently, because our perceptions are shaped in subtle ways, which we shall elaborate upon in later chapters. What we will do now is explore some of the different perspectives that have been developed by psychologists.

DIFFERING GENERAL PERSPECTIVES

There are many ways in which psychologists tend to differ in their viewpoints. We present two major dimensions on which they are divided. The first is based on the general nature of humankind and makes a distinction between the cognitivists and the behaviorists. The second dimension is based on the major content of theories that have been developed, namely, personality and learning.

Cognitivist versus behaviorist's viewpoint

The field of psychology is an outgrowth of philosophy, and there is a fairly smooth transition of thought from one to the other (Spearman, 1937). As pointed out in the preceding chapter, the controversy in the late 1600s between Leibnitz and Locke is essentially centered on whether the mind of an infant is self-motivated and active in the selection of what is experienced from the environment or whether it is a reactive, blank slate to be filled in through experiences provided by the environment. The two positions were carried into the field of psychology as the faculty and associationists' positions. As Hilgard (1962, p. 14) expressed it, faculty psychologists (Leibnitzian tradition) believe that "the mind had a few principal faculties such as thinking, feeling, and willing that accounted for its activities. Association psychologists (Lockean tradition), on the other hand, "denied inborn faculties of the mind; instead, they limited the mind's content to ideas coming by way of the senses, which then became associated through principles such as similarity, contrast, and contiguity."

These two basic approaches still persist and affect present-day approaches to psychological research and its application to the classroom. With the passage of time, the terminology has changed and the Leibnitzian tradition is currently best represented by the cognitivist position, and the Lockean by the behaviorist. Because in this text, and no doubt from other sources, you will be faced with suggestions from authorities of both persuasions, we believe it is well to have a clear understanding of how they differ.

William D. Hitt (1969) offered a concise description of the two points of view in his comments about a symposium during which several leading psychologists expressed their differing views. According to the cognitivists, the basic human nature is dynamic and each individual is unique (Figure 3–1). For the cognitivists, the uniqueness stems from the ability to perceive, remember, think, and control actions. Because these abilities operate from birth, each individual is a potential that develops out of a unique set of experiences. As the world is experienced and stored in memory and later used in thought processes, each individual develops a personal, or subjective, world. Because each has a subjective world, we will never be able to completely predict an individual's

FIGURE 3–1
Each individual is unique

future behavior, nor can it be considered rational or irrational. Instead, it is arational; it just *is*. For psychologists of this orientation, the similarity between individuals exists in the basic psychological processes used to experience the environment.

As we mentioned in the preceding chapter, this position is compatible with a portion of the perennialist philosophy. You will recall that perennialists view students as having the potential to become rational problem solvers, but this potential needs to be developed through a carefully paced curriculum designed to systematically expose them to the basic truths humankind has so far discovered. To some extent the progressivists also agree with this position in that they believe the ability to solve problems is developed by interacting with the environment. To them the actual topics of the curriculum are less important than sheer exposure to change and the problems associated with change. In this way the rudimentary faculties of "thinking, feeling, and willing" mentioned by Hilgard (1962, p. 14) are developed and refined. The solutions a person arrives at may differ from the solutions of others and may seem irrational from that person's perspective, but they may be perfectly logical to the problem solver.

In opposition, the behaviorists see humans as governed primarily by events in the environment and to a large extent, similar to each other. To them, the similarity is a result of a common general environment affecting all of us. Each individual is simply a sum of the experiences provided by the environment. Because the world is real, humans learn what reality is and, therefore, are objective. Since humans learn about an objective, real world, they can be considered as acting in a rational or irrational manner in terms of that real world and are therefore predictable. For psychologists of this orientation, the major differences found between individuals result from exposures to different environments.

The essentialist and reconstructionist views are basically in agreement with the behaviorist since both positions place more emphasis on the exact content of the curriculum and the development of specific skills in relation to the environment. To the extent that the perennialists would stress presenting basic factual information for the learner to assimilate, this philosophical position is also consistent with the behaviorist viewpoint. The difference between the perennialists on one hand and the essentialists and reconstructionists on the other hand is that the latter would emphasize the utility of increasing the store of knowledge for its own sake and for adjustment to society, whereas the perennialists would view it more in terms of something to be used in developing the thought processes. Hilgard (1962, p. 14) points out that the behaviorists believe the "principles such as similarity, contrast, and contiguity" in the environment are sufficient to explain the process of learning and presumably the content of instruction should help to develop the ability to detect similarities, differences, and sequences.

Neither the behaviorists nor the cognitivists totally reject the position of the other; the difference lies more in the amount of emphasis placed on internal processes and external variables in the study and description of human beings. Believing that psychologists of both orientations should listen to each other, since each position has a useful model appropriate for the study of different problems, we try to follow Hitt's suggestion and draw from both perspectives.

1. What are the major ways in which the behaviorists and cognitivists differ in their basic orientations toward the nature of humans?

Personality versus learning theorist's viewpoint

Snelbecker (1974) notes that the field of psychology has passed through a period of developing "schools" of psychology in which various groups defined what they thought should be the content and methodology of the emerging science of human behavior. From that point, the field began to develop comprehensive theories of human behavior. The problem has proved more complex than could be accomplished with this type of theorizing, and recently smaller theories relating to specific aspects of human behavior are being developed.

The comprehensive theories were of two major types: personality and learning theories. These theories developed at approximately the same time but they did so fairly independent of each other. Mancuso (1970) suggests this independence may have been fostered by a difference between the professional roles of psychologists. The learning theorists developed their ideas primarily within an academic, experimentally based context where fairly narrow lines of investigation could be pursued in a scientifically rigorous manner. The primary concern was with identifying factors and principles that influenced human behavior. Differing from this, the personality theorists developed their theories in an applied context where the primary concern was with the immediate problems of people. The demands of trying to solve these immediate problems required a more global view than could be based on available research evidence. The personality theorists were, therefore, more speculative and deductive in their approach to theory development than were the learning theorists. The learning theorists tended to frown on this speculation and were more conservative, systematic, and inductive as they formulated their theories from research data.

Personality theories have had a great impact on the fields of psychology and education. In addition, through the popular press and the media, they have influenced the thinking of the general public. Learning theories have had a somewhat less dramatic and more delayed impact on education, but presently they are the dominant influence on psychological and educational practice. In keeping with this general historical trend, we first present some notions about basic human nature derived from personality theories and later explore some of those stemming from learning theories. We will not attempt to present any theories in depth but rather abstract from them the basic nature of humans expressed in each.

> 2. As a teacher what sort of a balance should I try to maintain between empirical knowledge and intuition as I try to solve the problems related to classroom instruction?

PERSONALITY THEORY VIEWPOINT

Maddi (1976) has developed an analytic framework for comparing and contrasting many of the personality theories that have been developed. The analytic framework is based on Maddi's belief that all of the many theories he has analyzed can be explained as conforming to one of three basic models of humans. Each of the three models has two versions. This makes six subdivisions into which Maddi classifies theories, depending on the basic view of humans expressed by the theory. His basic analytic framework can be represented as follows:

Conflict model	*Fulfillment model*	*Consistency model*
Psycho-social	Actualization	Cognitive dissonance
Intrapsychic	Perfection	Activation

Later when we get to the learning theories we will expand on this by adding the behaviorist and cognitivist models, each of which also has two versions. There is certainly no scarcity of views of human nature. To help you keep them separate and organized we will gradually fill in the different models and versions. As we did in the preceding chapter we will present a summary chart at the end of this chapter for quick reference to the main ideas.

Conflict model

One of the three models Maddi uses to classify personality theories is the conflict model. Theories falling within this category view people as constantly caught in a conflict between two opposing forces. At best, life can be only a momentary compromise between the two continuously conflicting forces.

Psychosocial version. The psychosocial version views the conflict as occurring between an individual as one force and society as the opposing force. The basis of the conflict arises within individuals. People are seen as having certain biological needs, which, if not met, create a state of deprivation in the body. These states of deprivation are experienced as tension or pressure in the form of instinctual stimulation. This stimulation, or psychic energy, is constantly arising from within the individual and, it is believed, must be released in some way. In order to satisfy these instinctual drives, a human being acts in an utterly selfish manner. It is this selfish nature that places humans in conflict with other individuals, their selfish desires, and the rules established in the society (Figure 3–2).

As an opposing force to these selfish individual desires, societies attempt to provide for the well-being of their members by establishing rules that equalize the opportunity for all members of a society to meet their biological needs. By establishing these

FIGURE 3–2
Selfish desires sometimes conflict with social rules

rules, society sometimes blocks the immediate and complete fulfillment of the selfish desires of individuals, thereby creating conflicts which people have to deal with throughout life. Some needs, such as those for air, water, food, and elimination, are so universal and necessary for life that societies have established institutions that usually allow for the regular gratification of these needs as they arise. Western societies, however, have not provided institutionalized ways for all members of society to satisfy the sexual instinct. Sigmund Freud, whose theory is the best-known example of this version, placed great emphasis on this instinct because of the conflict it creates. Another common example of conflict is between a person's desires for some of the conveniences or luxuries and a society's institutionalized means of obtaining them.

Another major assumption of psychosocial conflict theories is that people are not consciously aware of their selfish desires and the continual conflict they create. We are unaware of the desires and conflict because of defense mechanisms we use, which act to shield our consciousness from the unconscious desires. Because people use defense mechanisms, it is impossible to understand an individual simply by observing behavior. The psychosocial theorists believe that in order to see behind the defense mechanisms, it is necessary to use indirect means to expose a person's innermost thoughts. In the past this belief has guided the development of many personality tests and fostered their use by psychologists of this orientation.

Freud's basic theory has been modified by others so that current theories place greater emphasis on rational thought processes than on just instinctual functioning. One theory, transactional analysis, has also transformed the terminology from id, ego, and superego to child, adult, and parent, but the basic view of a conflict between a person and society remains unchanged; society is localized in the parental role.

This position has had several effects on educational practice. One effect is evident in the view that children should be encouraged to express their inner feelings so they do not become "bottled up." The belief is that if this happens the child may express feelings in an explosive manner or resort to defense mechanisms to release the inner tension. A second effect is evident in how some educators view certain behaviors, especially those classified as aggressive, sexual, or socially withdrawn. The behaviors may be quite common among children, but if the behaviors are observed in a context where the educators believe them to be inappropriate, an inference is often made that the behavior is a sign of some type of psychological disturbance. It is not viewed as a normal reaction to a particular situation, but something extra is read into it. Once a person perceives the behavior from this perspective, there is generally a feeling of incompetence and a reluctance on the part of the teacher to deal with it directly. Instead it is referred to a psychologist or psychiatrist. This has resulted in the schools hiring a great many psychologists and psychiatrists and many referrals to mental health clinics. The belief is that only these professionals have the competence to diagnose and cope with the underlying cause and not just treat the behavior. The behavior is seen as merely a symptom of the underlying cause. Proponents of the psychosocial model contend that changing the outward behaviors does not affect the underlying cause, which will simply be expressed in different behaviors.

The research evidence has not demonstrated any significant effectiveness of the clinical techniques associated with this position. Contrary to this position, the research does indicate that modifying a single behavior may be effective in bringing about long-term changes in an individual without substitution of other behaviors. This seriously questions the notion of an underlying cause of the type proposed by these theorists.

The research evidence has not, however, changed the belief of many people in a deeply rooted psychological cause of behavior, and they hesitate to tamper with some problems. They also have a great deal of faith that psychological testing will reveal the true cause that they cannot see.

Another related effect on educational practice is based on the belief that the innate desires must be expressed in one form or another due to the buildup of psychic energy. The practice is to allow students to work off this energy in more desirable channels, thereby avoiding its outlet in less desirable ways. The most notable example is when students are allowed to go to the gym to work out their frustrations and aggressions. There is some evidence that this actually may be counterproductive (Bandura & Walters, 1963).

Due to the extensive impact this theory has had, you may find that your views are somewhat consistent with this position. You are quite likely to encounter other educators or parents who express this view of humans. It is also apt to make you or them resistant to certain suggestions about how to cope with a limited range of behaviors that are commonly categorized as socially deviant. Because of the emphasis on deviant behavior, the view does not appear to have much impact on the major curriculum areas and associated instructional techniques.

Intrapsychic version. Differing from the view that people are in conflict with external forces, the intrapsychic version of the conflict model emphasizes a conflict between internal forces. The conflict, according to some theorists, is between a desire to become separated, distinct, and independent from others as one force, and a desire to merge with others, both physically and in thought, as the opposing force (Figure 3–3). Expressed differently, the conflict is between a desire to become independent and the need for the security and companionship of others.

Maddi (1976) also includes under this version theorists who assume the conflict is between (1) the ego, (2) the personal unconscious, and (3) the collective unconscious. In this framework, the ego is a person's conscious level of functioning. The personal unconscious is made up of socially unacceptable memories, and the collective uncon-

FIGURE 3–3
Internal conflict between the desires for separation and merging

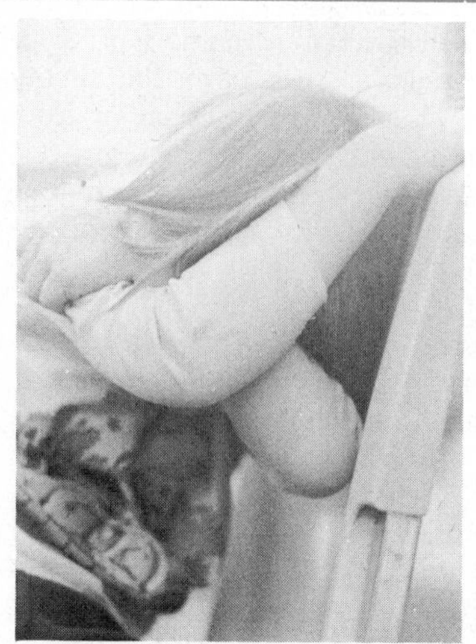

scious is a species memory that represents the accumulated experiences of humankind. The conflict between these forces threatens an individual's basic tendency to move toward selfhood, which is a balancing of all the conflicting forces in the personality.

While these theories have not had much impact on schools or the field of psychology, teachers often express the view that a child is "all torn up inside" due to some sort of perceived internal conflict. Schools are also concerned with the development of independence and the ability to develop friends. So, while the formal theories have not gained much popularity, some people apparently have informal theories that express the same viewpoint. Differences of opinion may exist between yourself and others about the amount of independence that should be expected and the effect that training children to be more independent will have on their emotional state.

To summarize thus far:

Conflict model

Psychosocial version—Humans are in constant conflict with their environment, and basic hidden drives will be expressed in some form.

Intrapsychic version—Humans are in a state of constant internal conflict between desires to become separated from and merge with others or between conscious and unconscious memories.

3. From personal experience, what are some statements you or others have made that reflect a belief in each of the versions of the conflict model? Also, what are some personal conflicts that are examples of each version of the model?

Fulfillment model

In both versions of the conflict model just discussed there is an assumption of two or more antagonistic forces that determine human nature. The fulfillment model differs by assuming only one major force. The force is internal and a person's basic tendency is toward a fuller expression of that force. In expressing this force, an individual may occasionally come in conflict with other forces in the environment, but the conflict is neither inevitable nor a dominant factor. "Indeed, when it occurs, it represents an unfortunate failure in living, rather than something unavoidable" (Maddi, 1976, p. 20). Maddi uses the terms *actualization* and *perfection* to refer to the two versions of the fulfillment model.

Actualization version. Theories conforming to the actualization version of the fulfillment model assume the single force to be some sort of a "genetic blueprint." The blueprint specifies the maximum limits of a person's capabilities, and the basic human nature is to express these capabilities to the fullest. The actualization version of the fulfillment model also stresses the expression of humanism. Currently the terms *humanists* and *third-force psychologists* are used to categorize these theories. The theories of Carl Rogers and Abraham Maslow, whose names you may already know, are examples of this position.

Rogers's view of people is that they are not basically selfish or in conflict with the world, but rather their primary tendency is to develop or actualize their innate potential to the fullest. This is accomplished by learning how to cope with the world and deal with conflict so as to maintain and enhance their lives in a manner that is compatible with one's personal growth as well as the needs of others. Conflicts are mainly encountered in dealing with other people and are viewed as counterproductive, because resolving the conflict takes time and energy away from fulfilling the goal of developing one's potential to the fullest.

At the biological level, this actualizing tendency is true for all forms of life, animal and vegetable. A unique, human form of the actualizing tendency is self-actualization or the tendency to grow and develop in a manner consistent with our self-concept or personal view of ourselves. The direction of development is toward an ideal concept of self. The self-concept is not genetically determined but is learned through social interactions. It develops out of a secondary need we have for positive regard. If we have received positive regard from others who are important to us or, expressed differently, if the attitudes of sympathetic others toward us have generally been positive, then we will develop a positive self-concept. Conversely, if the attitudes people have expressed toward us have been generally negative, then a negative self-concept develops. Presumably the regard others express toward us is based on their view of how well we have adjusted to our situation and potential level of capabilities. A positive self-concept is in essence, then, a belief in a high level of personal capability and esteem, which has developed because others have treated us as though we are highly capable, are of some importance, and have the potential to develop even further.

Another secondary need, that of positive self-regard, tends to keep the individual moving toward self-actualization. If we view ourselves as ideally having the potential to be even more capable but our behavior does not move us in a direction to express it, we will hold ourselves in low self-regard. If, on the other hand, we perceive ourselves as living up to our potential, then we will have a great deal of positive self-regard.

This approach has had considerable influence on schools, not only among many school psychologists but also among guidance counselors and classroom teachers. Those who follow this theoretical view emphasize, to a great extent, the importance of helping students to see and develop their inherent potentials. They believe it is important to interact with students in a positive, accepting manner, even if they do not always approve of some of the students' actions. The position does not recommend an absence of all constraints on behavior, but rather implies the manner in which we should express our views of a certain behavior, i.e., "I accept you as a person, although I disapprove of what you have just done."

More specifically this position emphasizes the need to help students develop a positive self-concept and to motivate them so they develop a high level of self-regard in fulfilling their potential. Possibly developing out of this position is the feeling some teachers have that "overachievers" may "break down" under the strain, since the concept implies a striving for a level beyond the innate capacity. The teacher who holds this view is also likely to believe that the student needs to learn to adjust to a "more realistic" set of goals.

Abraham Maslow's theory is the other major example of the actualization version of the fulfillment model. Maslow is basically in agreement with Rogers but does not emphasize the self-concept quite as much. Maslow suggests a hierarchy of needs that humans attempt to fulfill. The lower, or more primary, needs in the hierarchy are physiological needs, whereas the higher-level needs are psychological. The needs Maslow identified, in the ascending order in which they must be met, are the needs for physiological functions, safety and security, belongingness and affection, self-respect and self-esteem, and self-actualization. As we attempt to meet these needs, we encounter successes and failures, and out of these experiences we develop a self-concept. This views the self-concept more as a result of the process of trying to meet the hierarchy of needs, with less emphasis on it as a basic determinant of behavior as Rogers's position implies.

Maslow's position has had an impact on current educational practice somewhat similar to Rogers's, in that individual differences are considered important and should be encouraged to develop. The main emphasis is, however, to help the student progress through the hierarchy of needs, thereby fostering a positive self-concept. There is still an emphasis on positive, accepting interactions with the student, but these are more likely to occur as encouragement during attempts to meet the hierarchy of needs and as positive feedback to the student about accomplishments. In other words, a teacher who shares Maslow's view is likely to be positive and accepting but somewhat more directive than a teacher who shares Rogers's perception of human nature.

Perfection version. Whereas the actualization version refers to an unfolding of actual potential, the perfection version refers to a striving for an ideal regardless of potential (Figure 3–4). To accomplish the ideal or goal, a person must work hard rather than merely have an inherent potential unfold or develop, given an adequate environment.

A considerable number of very divergent theorists can be grouped within this position, including the loose conglomerate of theorists known as *existentialists.* No attempt is made here to present the differences between positions. As distinct theories, most are of little importance to educational practice beyond the common emphasis on striving to achieve new goals or levels of perfection.

An exception is the theory of Robert White (1959), which has focused a great deal of attention on the development of achievement motivation because of his emphasis

FIGURE 3–4
Perfection comes from striving for an ideal

on a basic human tendency to attempt to produce effects in the environment, which he calls *effectance motivation.* From experience gained through the attempts to affect the environment, individuals learn to be competent and develop a feeling of competence. It is out of this process that achievement motivation is developed, and many teachers rely on achievement motivation when they assign tasks to students. Teachers also assume a tendency on the part of students to want to learn about the world around them, which is similar to White's notion of effectance motivation. Teachers are prone, however, to assume that this natural tendency will generalize to all tasks, and they often ignore the need to foster achievement motivation through carefully matching tasks to a student's current level of achievement.

The existentialist position is also relevant to the school curriculum and expectations of students. As Maddi (1976, p. 125) expresses it, the existentialists emphasize "being genuine, honest, true, and making decisions and shouldering responsibility for them." Educators may not believe humans have a natural tendency in this direction, but they seem to believe it is their duty to mold humans in this way. Instruction aimed at moral development is consistent with this position but is probably not directly attributable to any particular theorist.

These two versions of the fulfillment Model can be summarized as follows:

Fulfillment model

Actualization version—A striving to attain some inherent level of potential.

Perfection version—A striving to attain ever higher levels of competence regardless of inherent potential.

4. From personal experience, what are some statements you have heard or made that reflect a belief in each of the versions of the fulfillment model? From the many people you have met in your life, which ones have seemed to be trying to attain some maximum level of inherent potential and which ones seemed to be constantly trying to achieve higher levels of perfection that they themselves have set?

Consistency model

The consistency model assumes that the basic tendency of humans is to maintain a certain consistency in terms of expectations or tension level. In this model there is more emphasis on the role of experience in a person's life and less on some inherent force or forces.

Cognitive dissonance version. The cognitive dissonance version of the consistency model views people as attempting to understand, predict, and control the world around them. Based on our experiences, we develop certain expectations about the sequence and likelihood of events occurring. If events, as they occur, match our expectations, all is well with us. If, however, events do not meet our expectations, then a certain amount of dissonance or discrepancy is set up between our thoughts and the information we are receiving (Figure 3–5). We react to this dissonance in various ways.

Not all theorists Maddi (1976) includes in this version are in agreement about how we react to dissonance. The various positions can be viewed as elaborations of a central theme. We have condensed the variety of opinions in the following presentation.

FIGURE 3–5
A discrepancy between expectations and information

One result of discrepancies between what we expect and the information we receive is a feeling of anxiety. This causes us to change our expectations so that they conform to the information we receive. At times, however, we may react by distorting the information to fit our expectations rather than the reverse, which is the more common reaction. Not all discrepancies necessarily lead to anxiety—only large discrepancies or, in other words, large amounts of cognitive dissonance. Small discrepancies actually result in pleasant feelings, which cause us to approach stimuli that have small amounts of novelty. A situation with a complete absence of discrepancies, where everything is completely predictable, would be boring due to the lack of novelty in stimuli. Too much novelty or discrepancy between expectations and actual events, on the other hand, would result in anxiety and a retreat from the situation.

While these theories have had some influence in the field of psychology, they have not had much direct impact on educational practice. One theorist, McClelland (McClelland, Atkinson, Clark, and Lowell, 1953), has had some influence, particularly in terms of developing achievement motivation, because he believes that learned motives develop out of our moving toward small amounts of discrepancy. Students introduced to small amounts of discrepant information, which they can master, develop a motive to achieve new levels of mastery. When provided with too much or not enough discrepancy, students do not have the opportunity to develop achievement motivation. McClelland's theory and subsequent research on achievement motivation have probably led to some of our present concern for pacing the presentation of tasks so that they are interesting and challenging for students but not overwhelming. In this way it has had an impact on motivational techniques that teachers use when presenting learning tasks. We try to avoid placing a child in a situation where there is too much novelty, which will lead to inattention or failure, or too much repetition of already acquired skills and hence no challenge to the student.

This position differs from the perfection version of the fulfillment model by emphasizing not a basic drive toward competence but rather the actual characteristics of the task. There is no assumption that the task has any intrinsic motivation beyond the amount of novelty it presents. It requires that a teacher match this quality of the task to the level of the students, thereby placing more responsibility on teachers for motivating students.

Activation version. The activation version contends that people attempt to maintain a consistent level of activation or tension. It is based on consistency in our accustomed level of excitement or alertness rather than consistency between our thoughts or expectations and the information we are exposed to. This version is based on research evidence indicating that the function of a part of the brain, know as the *reticular formation,* is associated with changes in our level of activity. The theory contends that from our daily experiences we learn to expect, or become adjusted to, a specific level and pattern of activity. Once we have developed this level of activation, our basic tendency is to try to maintain ourselves at that level.

There are three sources of stimulation that affect our activation level. One source is stimulation from the environment, which we receive through our receptor cells. A second is internal stimulation from receptor cells within the body. The third source of stimulation is the cortex or upper part of the brain and the stimulation is in the form of recollections and thinking. The total impact of these three sources of stimulation determines our level of activation at any one time. To maintain our customary level of activation, we learn certain behaviors; some behaviors to increase the impact of stimuli and some to decrease the impact. This position also assumes that we learn to anticipate the impact of stimuli and behave so as to insure that we are not exposed to large discrepancies between accustomed and actual levels of stimulation. If these avoidance efforts are not successful, we will be faced with a discrepancy that we will react to with escape behaviors aimed at reducing the discrepancy. The attempts may take the form of distorting reality to either increase or decrease the impact of the stimulation to which we are exposed.

Because we gradually become accustomed to particular types of stimulation, we need to continually expand our physical activities and become more subtle in our cognitive functioning. This insures that we will maintain a sufficiently high level of stimulation to match our preferred level of stimulation. In order to decrease stimulation, we learn to integrate various experiences into broad categories, thereby reducing the number of stimuli to which we need to react.

This version in itself has probably had very little impact on educational practice. This may not reflect so much the utility of the position as the times within which it was developed. As we have pointed out, there has been a shift in the field of psychology from general theories about the nature of people to smaller theories about particular aspects of human functioning. In this historical vein it is interesting to note that the earliest theories Maddi refers to are the conflict theories. In the 1950s, a great many theories conforming to the actualization and consistency models were developed somewhat simultaneously. The activation version, in the form we described, did not appear until the early 1960s. By then the inability of these broad theories to predict behavior in anything more than general terms was becoming apparent, and more attention was directed toward learning theory principles to understand human behavior. Before we turn to the learning theories, we summarized the consistency model as follows:

Consistency model

Cognitive dissonance version—People strive to maintain consistency between what has previously been learned and what is presently being experienced. Consistency is maintained by either distorting reality or modifying prior beliefs.

Activation version—People strive to maintain some acquired, optimal level of arousal by either approaching stimuli to avoid boredom or retreating from overly stimulating experiences containing too much novelty.

5. What are some statements you have heard or made that reflect a belief in each of the consistency model versions? What situations can you think of that have created cognitive dissonance for an individual, and what was their reaction to the dissonance? What situations have created an undesirable level of activation for an individual, and what was the person's means of achieving a more desirable level of activation?

LEARNING THEORY VIEWPOINT

As Maddi (1976) has pointed out, personality theorists have not concerned themselves with the topic of learning but simply assumed the existence of a learning process that accounts for differences between individual lifestyles. What we have presented thus far are theories about the aspects of human nature that help to explain the similarities between individuals, or as Maddi refers to it, the "core of personality" (p. 13). Distinct from the core for Maddi is the "periphery of personality," and theoretical statements about the periphery are intended to explain why people differ from one another.

Learning theorists also attempt to explain similarities and differences among people. For learning theorists, the core characteristics are not basic motivating tendencies but rather basic characteristics of how humans learn to act in specific, new ways. Periphery statements from learning theorists would involve descriptions of how the basic learning principles apply to an individual's life and result in a typical pattern of behavior. Learning theorists generally concern themselves not with why people learn but rather with how people learn. By doing this, learning theorists focus almost exclusively on the process, products, and environmental factors related to learning and ignore the aspects of humans on which personality theorists focus. As we mentioned earlier, they consider these issues too broad and vague for rigorous study and simply choose not to speculate about them, feeling it is unnecessary to do so.

Whereas most personality theorists have followed the tradition of Leibnitz, the earliest American learning theorists have their philosophical roots in the Lockean tradition and are classified as behaviorists. Slightly later in Europe, learning theorists of the Leibnitzian position developed. Currently, these cognitive-type theories are much more accepted in America and are being actively researched.

We have used the behavioral and cognitive headings as two basic models of human nature in addition to the three Maddi suggests. The focus of the models is, as we have indicated, much narrower and limited to the nature of people in relation to learning. Giving two versions of each model is an attempt on our part to organize the wide differences between theorists in each camp into a simplified description.

Behavioral model

As mentioned earlier, the basic position of the behaviorists inherited from Locke and the British associationists is that there is a real world out there and humans start out in life as a blank slate, which is gradually filled in through experience (Figure 3–6). Knowledge is gradually built up through a process of developing associations between stimuli in the environment and specific actions or behaviors. In the behaviorist view the major problem is to determine those stimuli in the world that foster the development of new behaviors. Two major positions have developed to explain how these associations are formed. To some behaviorists the results of behavior are the critical factor, while others argue that simply having two stimuli occur in close temporal proximity to each other is all that is necessary for associations to form. The terms *reinforcement* and *contiguity* are generally used to refer to the two positions or versions of the behaviorist model.

Reinforcement version. One of the most influential early American learning theorists was Edward L. Thorndike. He established a strong trend toward the reinforcement position and laboratory experimentation with animals. Results of his experiments with cats learning to escape from a box convinced Thorndike that learning is gradual and the result of trial and error. In Thorndike's view, those associations between stimuli and behaviors that were successful were "stamped in" and those that were unsuccessful were "stamped out." He did not find any evidence of thinking or reasoning on the part of the animals, although he did not deny its existence. What affected whether or not a behavior would be stamped in was whether it led to a satisfying state. If a particular behavior led to a "satisfier," it was stamped in; if the behavior led to an "annoyer," it was stamped out. In this way the bond between associations is strengthened by satisfiers and weakened by annoyers. The basic notions of Thorndike's theory have stood up well to subsequent research studies.

FIGURE 3–6
The blank slate is filled through experience

Thorndike's application of his theory to classroom procedures led him to emphasize drill rather than insight and understanding. He did, however, believe that students should be informed about the characteristics of a good performance so that inappropriate behaviors are not practiced. This would be necessary, presumably, so that a successful performance would be recognized and thereby lead to a satisfying state for the learner. Possibly because of Thorndike's emphasis on drill, many educators of today use the term *reinforcement* synonymously with *practice*. Psychologists use the term to refer to those events following a particular behavior that tend to increase the likelihood of it occurring in the future. The term *reinforcement* as used in the psychological literature is therefore more synonymous with *reward* than with *practice*.

Following in a vein similar to Thorndike's is B. F. Skinner. At the present time, Skinner's influence is having a strong impact on educational practice as well as on other areas of behavioral change and the field of psychology in general. In Chapter 4 we will outline several principles associated with reinforcement that have developed out of this tradition and are extremely useful for classroom teachers.

Contiguity version. At approximately the same time Thorndike was developing his theory, Ivan Pavlov, a physiologist, was conducting his famous experiments. He conditioned dogs to salivate at the sound of a bell as well as at the sight of meat powder. This led him to believe that animals and humans learn through forming associations. Pavlov differed from Thorndike in that he did not consider the effect of behavior to be the factors determining whether associations are formed and strengthened. According to Pavlov, the timing and repetition of stimuli are the important factors leading to the development of associations. Pavlov believed that organisms have innate reflexes to certain stimuli. Other stimuli, if presented close in time prior to the original stimulus, become associated and also lead to the occurrence of the reflexive behavior. In time, the original stimulus does not need to be present and only the newly associated stimulus is needed to bring about the reflexive behavior. In other words, it is not the effects of behavior but the more or less contiguous (closely spaced in time and/or space) presentation of stimuli that is important.

Pavlov's notion that contiguity is a major factor in relation to the basic nature of humans was adopted by Guthrie, who formulated the position in terms of a psychological theory rather than a physiological theory. Guthrie also developed the idea that associations actually develop all at once rather than through a slow buildup. The apparent slow buildup, according to Guthrie, is due to an increasing number of associations between the various stimuli in the situation and the resulting response. The more associations there are, the more likely that the stimulus will result in the response.

Guthrie's theory has been expanded by mathematical learning theorists, but probably of more relevance to schools is the position of Bandura and Walters (1963). They proposed that a large proportion of human learning, especially social learning, is the result of observation. They contend that observation of other individuals is all that is necessary for the learning of complex behaviors. To Bandura and Walters, reinforcement is not necessary for learning but is necessary for performance. In other words, reinforcement or the possibility of reinforcement will determine whether or not we demonstrate what we have learned, but learning itself occurs simply by having an individual observe another person modeling a particular behavior.

This has important implications for educational practice in that it places a great deal of importance on supplying children with desirable models of behavior to imitate. Simply telling children how to behave is not likely to be effective if we do not ourselves behave in a similar manner. We shall go into this position in much greater detail in the following chapter.

We have summarized the two versions of the behavioral model as follows:

Behavioral model

Reinforcement version—A person's basic ability to learn is controlled by the reinforcement received following performance of some behavior.

Contiguity version—A person's basic ability to learn is controlled by the occurrence of closely timed events or closely spaced stimuli and the observation of this closeness.

> 6. What are some statements or comments you have heard or made that indicate a belief in the behaviorist position? List some reinforcers that increase your likelihood of learning. Also list some stimuli that bring about a particular feeling or alert you to perform a certain action.

Cognitive model

The final model of human nature that we have included is that of the cognitivists. As we have already pointed out, the cognitivists, instead of viewing humans as being primarily stimulated by the environment, see people as being more active in acquiring knowledge. The cognitivists are more interested in the inherent and acquired capabilities of humans than in specific environmental effects on the individual. They do not question that the environment has an effect, but they are more inclined to stress the interactive effect between the environment and humans. Their description of the nature of humans is, however, primarily described in terms of (1) inner, innate processes or (2) acquired capabilities. We have subdivided the cognitivists therefore into the information-processing version and, for want of a better term, the structure of knowledge version.

Information-processing version. A group of European psychologists known as the "Gestaltists" were the earliest learning theorists associated with this position. Max Wertheimer was the founder of the movement; he worked primarily with perception and the ways in which we tend to superimpose organization upon what we see and hear. The Gestaltists believe that an entity is not merely the sum of its parts but is something over and above this. From his work Wertheimer proposed several laws of perceptual organization which he believed were a basic part of human nature and influence our perception of reality. As an example, look at Figure 3–7 and ask yourself what you see.

To answer the question, you are likely to "see" a pattern of diagonally slanted, alternating rows of dots and circles. To "see" rows slanting up to the left where the dots and circles alternate within the row is much more difficult.

FIGURE 3–7
Perceptual effects of proximity and similarity

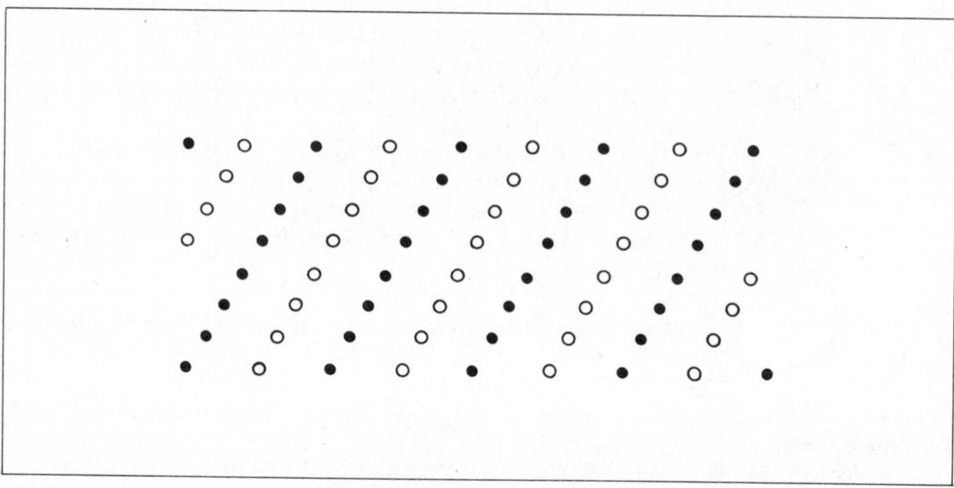

It was from phenomena such as these that the Gestaltists were led to conclude that learning is not merely the gradual buildup of associations but rather a matter of perceptual reorganization imposed upon stimuli so that they are seen in new patterns. This reorganization is an active process engaged in by humans, and when it is achieved it results in new insights.

From this start other perceptual processes have been postulated until now the information processors have very elaborate models that include a series of processes. We shall not attempt to present them here but do so in a later chapter. For now we merely wish to point out that cognitivists in this group have identified several separate processes that they believe are involved in human learning and performance. While these processes are distinct, they do interact with each other. In other words, one process may have a direct influence on the immediate functioning of another process. The processes include those associated not only with the intake of information from the outside world but also with the storage of information, retrieval of information from storage, and the process of organizing information into action. The information-processing version points out the complex series of interacting cognitive processes that may be set in motion by a single stimulus from the environment. What for the behaviorists is a simple, single stimulus becomes for the cognitivists a complex series of internal, interacting events, which may result in a specific behavior.

At least one effect of the information-processing version is evident in the schools. Many perceptual testing and training materials have been developed and used by schools. There are also many teachers and psychologists who use a perceptual explanation for a child's inability to learn. For example, a child's inability to read may be explained as due to some deficit in the child's visual or auditory perceptual processes. This does not mean that the child's visual or auditory receptors are defective but rather that at the next step in the process the stimuli are not perceived appropriately. Quite often perceptual or auditory training is initiated to develop the perceptual skills. Research evidence does not support this approach very well, and some recent findings suggest that the memory process rather than the perceptual process may have more to do with the child's learning difficulty (Vellutino, Steger, Moyer, Harding & Niles, 1977). We cover these issues in greater detail in the following chapters and present this example simply to give the flavor of this version.

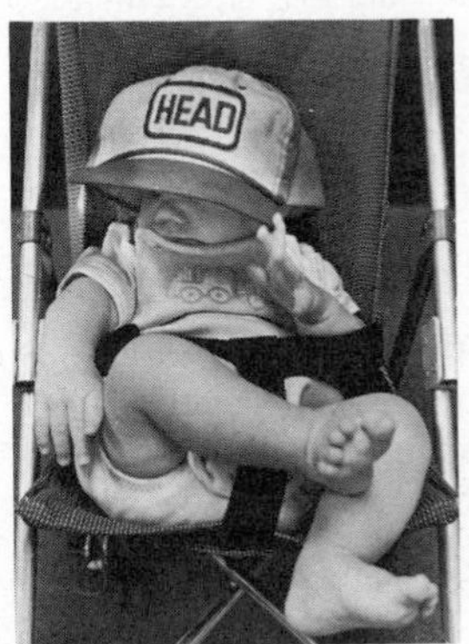

FIGURE 3–8
Within the head are cognitive processes and the products of learning

Structure of knowledge version. Theorists in this group are not so interested in the psychological processes involved in learning as they are in the products of learning (Figure 3–8). The products are usually described in terms of cognitive capabilities, which we describe in greater detail in Chapter 5. Due to a research need for objectivity, these cognitive capabilities may be expressed in the outward signs that are used to assume that the capability has been acquired. This often clouds the distinction between behaviorists and cognitivists. While cognitivists may use behavioral statements to describe the acquired capability, behaviorists often use a statement of a cognitive capability as a shorthand means of referring to a general class of responses. Strict behaviorists would not resort to the use of these cognitive capabilities but would confine themselves to statements that simply describe the relationship between stimuli and responses without reference to the internal capabilities of the learner. On the other hand, cognitivists interested primarily in the development and structure of knowledge will focus on the unit of knowledge developed and its relationship to prior knowledge and the acquisition of new knowledge.

Some theorists we would list as belonging in this group study very broad capabilities. Piaget is the most notable example of this orientation. A great deal has been written by and about Jean Piaget, a Swiss biologist/psychologist. Although his work has covered a long time span, it was not until the 1950s that he had much influence in America. His influence was initially upon the area of child development.

Piaget (1963) believes there are two *biological functions* that determine basic human nature: adaptation and organization. Adaptation to one's environment is Piaget's definition of intelligence. The second function, organization, is responsible for the interrelatedness of our actions.

In addition to the two biological functions, Piaget suggests two *intellectual functions* that are a basic part of human nature. These functions, assimilation and accommodation, are involved in adaptation, or intellectual development. Assimilation allows us to integrate our present experiences with our previously learned patterns of behavior. Accommodation is the process whereby we reorganize our learned patterns of behavior to correspond to an ever-changing environment. These two intellectual functions could place Piaget in the information-processing version. While the concepts are part of Piaget's theory, they are in very simplistic contrast to the information-processing outline of processes. Piaget's main emphasis is more on the development of intellectual stages. The biological and intellectual processes are simply used to describe the process of intellectual development, which, according to Piaget, starts from an innate reflex level and gradually progresses through several stages in a fixed sequence. The attainment of each stage allows an individual to function at a more sophisticated level than was possible at the preceding level.

Due to the complexity of Piaget's theory, we do not wish to expand on this brief description at this point. However, we do so in a later chapter because his theory has had, and is having, considerable influence on school practices. The theory is probably the most complete and up-to-date general explanation of children's intellectual development and functioning, and followers of Piaget are enthusiastic in their attempts to apply his ideas in the classroom. As Sullivan (1967) notes, Piaget's theory has some relevance for educational practice, but it is probably somewhat premature to adopt it as a prescription for the structure and sequencing of subjects to be covered in the school and the particular type of learning environment needed. Sullivan also believes that some of the enthusiasm is a self-serving tactic by proponents of the discovery approach, which is not too well substantiated by the theory. Our position is that, while Piaget's theory is a monumental effort in helping to understand human behavior, one has to be cautious in adopting recommended educational practices that are purportedly developed from a Piagetian base.

Jerome Bruner's view of humans is from the same general perspective as Piaget's, but the two differ in their views about the stages that define intellectual development. Bruner contends that the stages are related to intellectual development of specific topic areas and this position has led him to state, "Any subject can be taught effectively in some intellectually honest form to any child at any stage of development" (1960, p. 33).

According to Bruner, human intellectual development occurs in three stages or modes of representing the world. The first stage is called *enactive.* This involves learning through actual activity. As an example, if we were to teach a young child to get from one place to another, we would have to have the child physically move from the starting place to the goal. The second stage is the *iconic.* This stage allows us to deal with images rather than being dependent on actual objects and actions. At this stage we could indicate on a map the route the child should take, as long as the map has sufficient details to represent relevant landmarks to which the child will need to respond. At the third stage, called *symbolic,* humans are able to deal with words and symbols to represent reality. At this stage we would be able to direct the child from one point to the other with verbal directions or a much more abstract map and set of symbols.

Bruner has also investigated various types of conceptual strategies that humans use in solving problems. He believes that these strategies develop as a result of actively attempting to solve problems, and therefore he has been a strong advocate of *guided* discovery learning.

Opposed to Bruner's enthusiasm for the discovery approach to learning, David Ausubel contends that the utility of discovery learning is rather limited. He believes that humans develop general concepts and gradually refine and subdivide them with increased experience. For this reason, Ausubel recommends that we provide learners with what he calls "advance organizers." The advance organizers allow a child to organize experiences into a meaningful framework only if they are provided prior to the experience. Discovery learning only allows an individual to organize experiences after they have occurred.

Both Bruner and Ausubel (1960) have a great deal of influence on educational practice today and we refer to their work often in the following chapters.

The main point in these three structure of knowledge positions is that the development of knowledge is not totally dependent upon environmental factors but is also dependent upon the sequential development of certain cognitive capabilities. Ausubel describes the structure in terms of the general framework required. Piaget describes it in terms of very general types of cognitive capabilities. Bruner describes more limited capabilities in terms of acquiring a specific topic or solving a particular problem or class of problems.

Starting from a considerably different point, Gagné (1965) has also developed a statement about the development and structure of knowledge. His theory originally dealt with relatively small units of knowledge, but more recently (Gagné, 1972) he has expanded it to include broader capabilities of the type described by Bruner. The position describes in relatively fine detail the development of broad capabilities, and for this reason it appears to be a productive approach for use in the classroom since precise learning tasks can be identified. Probably the greatest utility associated with Gagné's position is the specification of the learning conditions associated with developing each of the cognitive capabilities. Starting from a behaviorist position, Gagné has in effect developed a cognitive theory describing the development and structure of knowledge, and this blending of the two positions enhances the utility of his work.

We summarize the two versions of the cognitive model in the following way:

Cognitive model

Information-processing version—People's basic nature to learn is controlled by the various cognitive processes acquired through inheritance and developed by interacting with the environment.

Structure of knowledge version—People's basic nature to learn is controlled by the content of previous experience and the cognitive structure imposed on that experience.

7. What are some statements or comments that you have heard or made that reflect a belief in the two cognitive versions of human functioning? What are some cognitive processes that you believe account for the learning process? What are some examples of prior knowledge that you believe are necessary for further learning to occur?

INTEGRATION OF VARIOUS VIEWPOINTS

FIGURE 3–9
Perspectives can vary

While there are differences between particular points of view, this does not mean that they are incompatible (Figure 3–9). As Hitt pointed out, it would be well for theorists of the two major positions to begin trying to integrate each other's views into their own efforts. Gagné, whether intentionally or not, has done this to some extent. In developing the content of this text, we have attempted to follow Hitt's suggestion by drawing on a variety of sources that we believe are compatible in terms of psycho-educational design of instruction.

The various philosophies covered in the preceding chapter lay the groundwork for the integration. As we pointed out, the four philosophies emphasize different goals. The perennialist philosophy emphasizes the acquisition of the basic principles that govern our world. This does not negate the essentialist philosophers' emphasis on learning the basic state of our world as it exists today. It seems worthwhile not only to understand the principles that govern our world, but also to have a firm understanding of its present state. The philosophies of the progressivists and the reconstructionists have more implications for how we should use our knowledge of the principles and state of our world. The progressivists contend that we should develop individuals who are problem solvers, and the reconstructionists suggest the direction our problem-solving efforts should take. In order to solve significant social problems, one must first have a basic understanding of the problem, the factors affecting it, and the problem-solving skills appropriate for the task. From this perspective we see the four philosophies as a well-rounded set of guides for determining educational goals rather than a four-sided argument about which philosophy to adopt.

To the same extent that philosophies differ, so also do psychological theories. Rather than differing on the same aspect of functioning, we believe that most psychological theories differ as to the aspect of human functioning they attempt to explain. As Maddi (1976) has pointed out, the personality and learning theorists have been dealing with different issues.

The personality theorists have attempted to explain the basic human tendencies that account for similarities between individuals. This encompasses the most basic motivations involved in human functioning. The three general themes Maddi has identified in personality theories also appear to be addressing different issues. It is not difficult to believe that at times individual human desires are in conflict with society's desires. If this were not so, we would have little need for laws to govern individual behavior. It is also not difficult to believe that humans have some inner conflict between wanting to become more independent and still desiring to congregate with other humans. The areas of child development and marital adjustment are prime examples of where these conflicts manifest themselves. This does not mean, however, that humans do not also attempt to develop their capabilities to higher levels of functioning as the fulfillment theories suggest. There is a great deal of evidence to suggest that human endeavor does tend to develop higher and more complex levels of functioning as the actualization theorists believe. It does not seem that one should have to choose between the actualization and the perfection theories. Instead, it appears possible that a portion of human motivation is in terms of an innate tendency to develop personal capabilities to their fullest, and at the same time we find some ideal model toward which we strive to fashion our own behavior. In other words, humans tend to practice and perfect newly acquired behaviors to a mastery level and they also tend to fashion behavior after some ideal model they have selected.

The conflict and actualization models emphasize the actions of humans as they relate to the environment around them. In the psychosocial version of the conflict model, the focus is on attaining certain objects to gratify our needs. The intrapsychic version of the conflict model emphasizes approach and avoidance tendencies toward other humans. Both versions of the actualization model emphasize learning to function in harmony with the environment in order to achieve higher levels of competence in coping with it. All these positions appear to be dealing with human endeavor as it relates to achieving a level of adjustment or compromise between a person and the environment, with the possibility that there also may be a motivating force moving us to higher levels of functioning in attaining this adjustment.

In contrast, the consistency models appear to be emphasizing a motivation to also attain a certain level of internal functioning. The cognitive dissonance theorists point up a need for humans to maintain consistency among their thoughts, actions, and perceptions of the world. This is very close to Piaget's notion of adaptation that comes about through the functions of assimilation and accommodation. When we are assimilating our experiences we find consistency between what is happening and what we expect. When we do not find this consistency, the discrepancy would lead to cognitive disequilibrium, which Piaget believes leads to accommodation or a revision in our cognitive structure. The activation version of the consistency model implies a discrepancy between levels of arousal rather than between thoughts. This may simply be a more refined version of consistency based on a larger portion of the functioning of the nervous system or the interaction between affective and cognitive learning. This seems to be accomplished in the activation version by taking into account the input value from both of these types of learning and the resulting effect on behavior.

The learning theorists fill a serious gap in the personality theories, since all theorists agree that human behavior is almost all a result of learning, even though some inherited tendencies may give it a general direction. Personality theories do not deal with the process whereby the behaviors are learned but instead deal with the implications of various learned lifestyles.

The dichotomy between the cognitivists and the behaviorists is also one on which an educator does not need to take a stand. The behaviorists have described in considerable detail the effects of various environmental stimuli and contingencies on learning. To this the cognitivists have added some insight into how the learner tends to process, distort, store, and pursue information. If one takes the position of the interactionist, then it is easy to accept both positions as having some degree of accuracy but neither position as offering a complete description of human nature as it relates to the classroom and formal education. Instead the two models and two versions of each seem necessary to describe the basic nature of humans as learners. This four-way description of humans as learners in conjunction with the six basic directions of human behavior provided by the personality theorists is not so much a statement about the chaotic state of affairs in the field of psychology but rather a statement about the many facets of human behavior, the ability to adapt to the environment, and the ability to actually change it to suit human needs.

As we did in the preceding chapter we have presented the various perspectives in the form of a table at the end of the chapter.

IMPLICATIONS FOR YOU AS A TEACHER

Perception of the school system

First of all, as we have already pointed out, the four philosophies help to establish the purpose of the educational system. Recognition of these varied but compatible goals of the school system should help you to analyze not only the formal aspects of the school curriculum but also its informal aspects. The informal aspects to a large extent involve the social training and work habits fostered by the school. These topics do not have the same formality as reading, mathematics, science, social studies, and other subject areas, but when you listen to educators and parents alike it is unmistakable that schools are intended to turn out socialized individuals ready to take an active part in the social and economic community.

The psychological views of humans should also be applied when viewing the school system, since the system is designed for humans (Figure 3–10). Such issues as how the system is compatible and incompatible with human tendencies to behave and learn should be raised constantly. Whereas the philosophies primarily address the goals of education, the psychological theories address the process of education. This distinction is not as clear-cut as we have indicated, but it may help you to clarify where schools are going and how they are trying to get there.

Perception of students

Since you will be on the front line of the interaction between schools and students, your ability to see clearly the distinctions we have been emphasizing about human nature should help you to look at your students from a broader perspective. By doing this you may be able to see their position more clearly and also be able to help them to see and accept the views of yourself and others. Your main focus as a teacher is to foster in your students certain changes in the level of their functioning.

FIGURE 3–10
The school system is designed for humans

The better you understand the nature of your students and the system within which you are working, the better prepared you will be to bring about those changes. For an auto mechanic to not know how a car operates would be absurd. For a teacher not to have a good solid understanding of the basic characteristics of humans and how they learn is just as absurd. Too often, however, the views expressed by teachers indicate a knowledge that is naive, superficial, or actually distorted by popular myths.

Perception of parents

One task of teachers is to interact with parents. Given the large number of children you will come in contact with, you are likely to be confronted with parents covering the full range of views presented. They are not likely to recognize that their views are limited and therefore biased. They may, because of limited perspective, hold very strongly to their opinions and have difficulty accepting differing views. Having a broad perspective can help you to identify their positions and how they may differ from yours. This insight and a large dose of diplomacy in how you approach the differences may help you through some otherwise difficult situations.

Perception of colleagues

What we have said about your views of parents is also applicable to your views of other members of the school staff. You may have a common title and task but this does not mean you will share a common viewpoint on many issues. Tenure laws were passed to preserve this diversity of opinion between educators. Besides adding a great deal of stability and freedom for teachers, it also provides a great deal of

FIGURE 3–11
Summary of five models and two versions of each model of general human nature

Conflict model	*Fulfillment model*	*Consistency model*	*Behavioral model*	*Cognitive model*
Psychosocial version—Humans are in constant conflict with their environment, and basic, hidden drives will be expressed in some form.	Actualization version—A striving to attain some inherent level of potential.	Cognitive dissonance version—People strive to maintain consistency between what has previously been learned and what is presently being experienced. Consistency is maintained by either distorting reality or modifying prior beliefs.	Reinforcement version—A person's basic ability to learn is controlled by the reinforcement received following performance of some behavior.	Information-processing version—People's basic nature to learn is controlled by the various cognitive processes acquired through inheritance and developed by interacting with the environment.
Intrapsychic version—Humans are in a state of constant internal conflict between desires to become separated from and to merge with others, or between conscious and unconscious memories.	Perfection version—A striving to attain ever higher levels of competence regardless of inherent potential.	Activation version—People strive to maintain some acquired, optimal level of arousal by either approaching stimuli to avoid boredom or retreating from overly stimulating experiences containing too much novelty.	Contiguity version—A person's basic ability to learn is controlled by the occurrence of closely timed events or closely spaced stimuli and the observation of the closeness.	Structure of knowledge version—People's basic nature to learn is controlled by the content of previous experience and the cognitive structure imposed on that experience.

diversity in the views to which students are exposed. This seems appropriate when one considers the diversity of views a person encounters following the school years. However, this diversity among colleagues may make decision making more difficult and create a certain level of friction. Again, by seeing your position and that of those you work with more clearly, you may be able to arrive at decisions that all can live with more quickly and amicably.

SUMMARY

The biased nature of human observers was noted. The expression of this bias in the cognitivist and behaviorist perspective was described, as well as the bias between personality and learning theorists. The basic nature of humans was then described in terms of the conflict, fulfillment, and consistency models derived from personality theories, and the behaviorist and cognitivist models derived from learning theories. Two versions of each model were presented, resulting in a ten-category perspective of human nature (Figure 3–11). How these views complement and add to each other was considered. As a final topic, this ten-category perspective and the four philosophies presented in the preceding chapter were applied to your relationship with the school system, your students, their parents, and your colleagues.

SELF-TEST

1. Select *all* of the following that are consistent with the cognitivist position.
   - *a.* Humans are primarily governed by events in the environment.
   - *b.* Basic human nature is dynamic and each individual is unique.
   - *c.* The mind has a few faculties such as thinking and feeling that account for its activities.
   - *d.* The mind's content is limited to those ideas coming from the senses.
   - *e.* A person's behavior cannot be judged as being rational or irrational.
2. Select *all* of the following that describe the personality theorists in relation to the learning theorists.
   - *a.* Work in a more applied context.
   - *b.* More systematic.
   - *c.* More conservative.
   - *d.* More concerned with the immediate problems of people.
   - *e.* More likely to theorize beyond established research data.
3. It is the author's view that a teacher would:
   - *a.* Select one of the models described and consistently work from that position.
   - *b.* Work from an integration of the various models.

   Below is a list of the various psychological views of the nature of humans. Following the list are several statements. For each statement, select the letter of the position that best matches it.

   - *a.* Conflict, psychosocial.
   - *b.* Conflict, intrapsychic.
   - *c.* Fulfillment, actualization.
   - *d.* Fulfillment, perfection.
   - *e.* Consistency, cognitive dissonance.
   - *f.* Consistency, activation.
   - *g.* Behavioral, reinforcement.
   - *h.* Behavioral, contiguity.
   - *i.* Cognitive, information processing.
   - *j.* Cognitive, structure of knowledge.
4. "I have just got to help Henry develop a better self-concept if he is ever going to live up to his potential."
5. "Golly gee is that Mary active! She is constantly on the go and if I don't give her something to do she will think up something on her own."
6. "Boy, Jane certainly sets some very high goals for herself. The way she works, she may just reach them."
7. "Poor Jim, he is so quiet today. Maybe he is all torn up inside because he wants to go on the Boy Scout hike but is afraid he will get homesick."
8. "Even though Richard is very quiet he seems to have a mean streak and I have the feeling that someday he may explode and hurt somebody. It is so hard to tell about these things."
9. "I wouldn't let George out of my room until he had corrected his paper. I didn't want him to leave with those crazy answers."
10. "I don't think Myron has the background for that course."

ANSWER KEY TO BOXED QUESTIONS

1. *Behaviorist orientation*
   - Reactive
   - Mind is a blank slate that is filled from experience
   - Sensory organs are the source of information input
   - Knowledge is developed through principles of association
   - Individuals are highly similar
   - Consistency in environment and human reaction to it make prediction of behavior possible
   - Rationality of human behavior can be judged on the basis of principles operating in a real and consistent world

   Cognitivist orientation
   - Self-motivated and dynamic
   - Active in selection of what is experienced in environment
   - Mind has a few principal faculties that are innate
   - Each individual is unique and develops a personal world
   - Uniqueness of individuals makes prediction of behavior impossible
   - Behavior of individuals can not be judged rational or irrational—it is what it is

2. This question has no exact answer. The balance will depend upon your knowledge of the empirical evidence and the contingencies operating in the decision-making situation. However, it does seem counterproductive to use procedures that ignore or are contrary to well-researched learning principles. This is often done through ignorance of the empirical knowledge. The well-informed individual is more likely to follow sound principles but may have to shift them to reach broader, more abstract goals than are obvious in the immediate content of instruction.

3. For the psychosocial version the comments should reflect a basically self-centered and unconscious nature to human behavior that is beyond the control of the individual and if blocked will simply appear in another form. The actions should be self-centered and ignore or violate the rights of others. The individual would not view the action as a violation of the rights of others but would be able to give a rationalization for the social acceptability of the bahavior.

   For the intrapsychic version the comments should reflect some inner turmoil a person is experiencing in regard to deciding whether to act independently or fall back on the security of the company or reassurances of others. The actions would to some extent be limited to less than completely independent action. The person may not view the restrictions on activities as being due to a need for the security of other individuals, but may rationalize the action as being determined by some socially acceptable responsibility or attachment to one or more individuals. The rationalization may also be a denial of the desirability of the goals the independent action would have brought about.

4. For the actualization version the comments should reflect a comparison between a person's capabilities and some inherent potential. In many cases the reference may be about a person who is seen as having a potential that is limited by some biological factor. Individuals this version may remind you of are likely to be unusual in that they are obviously limited in their potential or have some outstanding biological characteristic that allows for a considerably greater degree of development or opportunity.

   For the perfection version the comments should stress the setting of new goals without reference to any inherent potential and/or stress the systematic striving to attain some individually determined goal. The main characteristic of individuals you have been reminded of should be that they seem to be working toward some specific goal or trying to develop one or more skills to a high level of proficiency.

5. For the cognitive dissonance version the statements should express a discrepency between what was expected and what was happening, or that some individual was reacting in a manner inconsistent with the situation and reflected a distortion of reality or a change in beliefs. The situations should also exemplify a discrepency between what was expected and what occurred. The person's actions would have to indicate that he/she misperceived the actual situation and acted in accordance with expectations, or actions reflected a change in beliefs.

   For the activation version the statements would have to indicate that the person was in a situation that was too active, stimulating, or confusing to suit the person's desires, or the person found the situation too boring, repetitious, or inactive. The situations should be ones where demands are being made on the person's ability to cope with stressful situations, or there is a lack of any stress on the individuals involved and they react so as to reduce, remove, or avoid high levels of stress and try to increase or seek out additional environmental stimulation in low-stress situations.

6. For the reinforcement version the comments should emphasize the consequences of behavior, and most especially external events, as having an influence on the acquisition of specific response capabilities. Examples of reinforcers can include almost anything since different things act as reinforcers for different individuals. The essence of a reinforcer is, however, to increase the performance of behavior.

   For the contiguity version the comments should stress the relationship between the occurrence of a stimulus and a behavior that occurs almost as a reflexive act or feeling. Examples of stimuli may range from red lights to social situations, and the reactions can include almost all acts or emotional responses.

7. For the information-processing version the comments should refer to the use of, need for, or existence of some

internal process associated with learning, retention of a capability, or performance of a capability. The processes would involve what is generally described with terms such as *attending to, thinking, remembering,* or *putting their mind to it.* In later chapters we cover the information-processing approach in greater detail, and with that additional information you should be better able to recognize instances of cognitive processes people may be using or referring to.

For the structure of knowledge version the comments should reflect a belief that some prior level of knowledge or cognitive functioning is needed or missing in order for a later level of learning to occur. The examples can range from very specific bits of factual information to very broad and general cognitive strategies related to problem solving.

ANSWER KEY TO SELF-TEST

1. *b, c,* and *e*
2. *a, d, e*
3. *b*
4. *c*
5. *f*
6. *d*
7. *b*
8. a
9. *h*
10. *j*

Chapter 4

The process of learning: Behaviorist perspective

IN THE PRECEDING TWO CHAPTERS we have discussed the manner in which a teacher's conceptions of educational philosophy and human nature affect educational practices. Educational practices reflect not only a teacher's philosophies of education and human nature but also the teacher's view of the learning process. For example, a teacher who believes that learning is an active process and that the best way to get students actively involved in learning is through practice of the to-be-learned skills will most likely use an instructional method that requires or at least provides the opportunity for the student to practice the skill to be learned. Conversely the teacher who perceives learning as a passive process in which the student receives information from the environment is going to use methods that transmit information via some medium and do not require any active participation on the part of the student (i.e., practice of a skill).

The facilitation of learning is at the core of the educational process. In the course of their school careers, students acquire a tremendously diverse set of learned capabilities. To illustrate this point, consider the differences in the following tasks likely to be encountered by most students: learning to hit a softball, to spell a word, to use an art medium such as water colors, to classify different animals according to a taxonomy, or to conduct a science experiment designed to test a specific hypothesis.

In this chapter and in Chapter 5 we will explore how such diverse learned capabilities are both similar and unique. The underlying processes of learning will be examined from several different contemporary viewpoints. Our overriding concern is to lay a foundation of scientific knowledge about the learning process that will serve as a data base for the decision-making process in learning and teaching. In keeping with our model of teaching as a decision-making process, we remind you that a crucial and recurring decision-making situation facing a teacher relates to the attainment of desired learning outcomes in the classroom.

The objectives for this chapter are:

1. Define learning and describe conditions affecting the accuracy of a teacher's inference about learning.
2. Describe conditions influencing verbal learning from the behaviorist perspective.
3. Analyze an episode of learning into the components of the respondent conditioning paradigm.
4. Distinguish between types of consequential stimuli.
5. Identify examples of stimulus control in operant conditioning.
6. Describe the four major factors determining the learning and performance of modeled behaviors.

SOME TERMS AND DEFINITIONS FOR THE UNDERSTANDING OF LEARNING

Before we go further, we need to clarify the meaning of certain basic terms used to discuss learning. Given the central importance of learning to educational psychology, you will encounter these terms in numerous chapters as you read through this book. We shall look first at the definition of learning, then at the distinctions between learning and performance and between learning and remembering. Following this the components of a learning task will be defined and explained.

Definition of learning

The scientific study of learning has occupied educational and psychological researchers for well over 75 years. You would expect widespread agreement about such an extensively studied phenomenon; however, researchers are divided into different theoretical orientations or "schools." As Hilgard and Bower (1975) point out, the disputes among most learning theories are centered around facts and interpretations of these facts and not a definition of learning. So most, if not all, learning theorists will accept a common definition of learning, which Hilgard and Bower (p. 17) give as:

> Learning refers to the change in a subject's behavior to a given situation brought about by his repeated experiences in that situation, provided that the behavior change cannot be explained on the basis of native response tendencies, maturation, or temporary states of the subject (e.g., fatigue, drugs, etc.).

This definition restricts learning to behavioral change that can be accounted for on the basis of interaction with an environment (i.e., experience). If a behavioral change can be shown to be the result of some factor other than experience, then we do not consider it to be learning. As Hilgard and Bower point out in their definition, alternate explanations for behavioral changes are native response tendencies, maturation, and temporary states. An infant crying because an open diaper pin is sticking him is not an instance of learning; it is a native response tendency. The infant's crying is a reflexive action to the painful stimulus. A child crying because in the past crying has lead to contact with and comforting by the parents is an instance of learning. In this case a behavior change (an increase in crying) is attributable to experience (past occasions of parents comforting the child).

Voice change, the appearance of sexual characteristics, and increased physical strength are bodily transformations that are not a matter of learning but are rather parts of the process of maturation. The development of such structures and other maturational phenomena are activities taking place within the person and are determined largely by hereditary factors. To be sure, other variables such as nutrition and disease can have an influence on these maturational changes, but learning is not a significant factor.

Temporary behavioral changes produced by such factors as fatigue or the ingestion of drugs are excluded as instances of learning. After a strenuous game of handball you may be unable to thread a needle. Then following a brief period of rest your hand is sufficiently steady to allow you to thread the needle. Here, the behavior change disappears after a short period of time along with dissipation of fatigue.

Learning and performance

Learning is a process that occurs within a person, and as such is a private event that cannot be directly observed by another person. The result or product of learning is the capability to perform a certain behavior in a given situation. The performance of a behavior in a given situation is a publicly observable event. So we say that behavioral performance is an indicator of learning; it is not learning but a product or result of learning.

The occurrence of learning can be inferred only from the observation of a behavioral performance. For a teacher, the occurrence of learning is verified by performance of a behavior in a given stimulus situation in which the student previously could not perform that behavior (Figure 4–1). The first-grade teacher infers that Marybeth has learned the alphabet when she is observed to say all 26 letters of the alphabet in the correct order. The physics teachers infers that George has learned Ohm's law when he is observed to write the formula. The basketball coach infers that Michele

FIGURE 4–1
Learning is inferred from performance

has learned to dribble the ball when she is observed to bounce the ball with one hand as she runs down the court.

Learning and remembering

As we have just seen, learning is the acquisition of an internal state that makes possible a particular performance capability. This internal state is stored in our memory and the process of activating such a stored internal state is remembering. This implies that learning and remembering are directly related because what is available for remembering is determined by what is learned.

The distinction between learning and remembering means that most frequently on a test, a teacher is observing memory or retention of a learned performance rather than learning directly. Therefore the performance on the test reflects not only the influence of learning but also forgetting, because retention or remembering equals learning minus forgetting. This is important because it means that retention is influenced by factors other than those affecting learning. As we shall see in Chapter 5, retention is jointly determined by factors operating during learning, storage in memory, and activation from memory.

Components of a learning task

We shall now consider in more detail some of the technical terms we use to talk about learning and performance. The concepts of behavior and stimulus situation will be defined and their use explained.

Behavior. *Behavior* is defined simply as any act or movement on the part of the learner. Behaviors that are directly observable are referred to as *overt* behaviors. Many behaviors of interest to the teacher, though, are not directly observable because they take place "within the skin" of the learner; we refer to such behaviors as *covert* behaviors. The occurrence of a covert behavior can be inferred if and only if that covert behavior leads to an overt behavior or produces some other observable effect.

Consider the following example. Archie Medes, a math teacher, asked Dougie, "Bobbie had 12 apples and gave 6 to Ann, and then met Dick who gave him 4, of which he shared 2 with Mike. How many apples does Bobbie now have?" Dougie sits there for 10 to 30 seconds and then answers, "He ended up with eight apples!" In this instance Dougie saying eight apples is the overt behavior; obviously preceding this behavior and following Mr. Medes's question, Dougie engaged in thinking, which in this case was the arithmetic operations of adding and subtracting. We refer to the adding and subtracting that went on "in Dougie's head" as covert behaviors, and the evidence from which we inferred their occurrence was the overt verbal behavior of "He ended up with eight apples!"

Stimulus situation. The stimulus situation is defined as the environment of the person at any given time. Psychologists usually consider a person's environment to be composed of many stimuli or potential stimuli, and so we use the term *stimulus situation* to connote the complexity of the learner's environment. A further distinction is made by dividing a stimulus situation into two classes of stimuli: functional and nominal stimuli. The functional stimulus is the stimulus element or elements that must be present is a stimulus situation to cue or start the learned behavior. The nominal stimulus is the total array of stimuli or potential stimuli present in the learning situation.

Consider the stimulus situation in learning to distinguish yield-right-of-way signs from stop signs. The environment in which these traffic signs are encountered is exceedingly complex, yet the learner need only attend to one or two stimulus characteristics within the environment. These characteristics are the shape and color of the two traffic signs. So, the functional stimulus for putting on the brakes until the car comes to a complete stop is a red octagonal shape on the right side of the road. The stimulus situation or nominal stimulus contains many potential stimuli such as cracks in the pavement, people on the sidewalk, houses along the way, and cars passing in the other direction.

As we shall see in the design of instruction, an important job of the teacher is to analyze the stimulus situation of the given learning situation in order to identify the stimulus element that is to become the functional stimulus. Identifying the appropriate functional stimulus and insuring that the student actually attends to it are tasks of considerable importance in facilitating learning.

Conditions affecting the accuracy of a learning inference. Making inferences about whether or not a student has achieved a desired learning goal is one of the major daily decisions made by a classroom teacher. The reason it is such an important decision is that the business of school is to teach students knowledge and skills that will help when they leave school, therefore effort should be expended to insure the validity (accuracy) of any such decisions. Since the capabilities resulting from learning are to be beneficial at a future date, the teacher's inference about learning is also a prediction about the future performance of a student. Consequently it behooves a teacher to be aware of the conditions that affect the accuracy of inferences about learning.

Number of observations. The first condition to be considered and one of the more important factors influencing inferences is the number of observations on which our inference is based. Assume you have observed John spell *dictionary* correctly on five separate occasions and you have observed him spell *regulation* once. Now are you more willing to bet five dollars that he knows how to spell *dictionary* or that he knows how to spell *regulation?* Other factors being equal, the larger our sample of observations, the greater will be our confidence in our inference and our prediction of the student's future performance of the desired behavior.

Related to the number of observations is the concept of the degree of learning. Suppose that everyday for a week Mr. Jones, a sixth-grade teacher, gave a spelling test. On this spelling test everyday was the word *bicycle.* Mike spelled it correctly all five times, Sue three times, and Chuck once. Who learned to spell *bicycle* best? Most people would agree that Mike did best because he performed the desired behavior five out of five times and therefore he learned it to the greatest degree of the three students. It can be said then that degree of learning is another indicator of the validity of our learning inference. The rule here is that the greater the degree of learning exhibited by a student, the greater is the accuracy of our inference about the attainment of learning.

Stimulus conditions surrounding performance. The next point concerns the conditions surrounding the performance of the behavior, because improper conditions invalidate the performance as evidence of learning. Returning to Marybeth and the alphabet, suppose you as the teacher have decided that acceptable evidence of learning the alphabet is to be able to say in order all 26 letters. You decide to test your hypothesis that Marybeth has learned the alphabet, so in class you ask her to stand up and recite the alphabet. She gets up and says all the letters, but you notice that sitting in back of her Carolyn whispered letters on three separate occasions. Are you going to accept this performance as evidence of learning the alphabet? You probably would not, because Marybeth had been given help or hints as to the correct behavior. The conditions surrounding the performance of the behavior must not give away or clue the behavior, otherwise you would not know if the person could perform that behavior unaided. Consequently you could not accept this performance as evidence of learning. To put it another way, the stimulus conditions surrounding the performance should reflect as nearly as possible the real-world situation in which the student will be expected to perform after leaving school. Therefore there should be no stimulus clues or hints present that will not be present in real-world conditions.

Up until now in the chapter, we have tried to make the point that some of the most important decisions you will make daily as a teacher concern learning. These decisions will be based on observations of student behavior, and the accuracy of these observations will be affected by conditions that must be considered. We have attempted to describe these conditions and the language educational psychologists and teachers use to refer to them. Much of what has been presented in this section of the chapter will be presented again and in greater detail in other chapters. One of the reasons for presenting this discussion of the conditions surrounding the performance of behavior has to do with current practice in education. It is quite common to speak of the goals of education in terms of behavior change or performance capabilities to be acquired by students.

1. Which of the following statements are critical attributes of a definition of learning?
   a. Change in behavior.
   b. Internal state.
   c. Resulting from experience.
2. Describe the relationship between learning and performance; between learning and remembering.

LEARNING: THE BEHAVIORIST TRADITION

We mentioned in Chapter 3 that behaviorist models of learning developed out of the philosophical school of British associationism associated with John Locke. Models of the learning process based on the tenets of behaviorism can be further separated into contiguity and reinforcement theories. The contiguity model predicts that an association between a stimulus and a response will be formed or strengthened when the two occur together in close temporal or spatial relationship. With the reinforcement model, associations are developed and strengthened by the consequences of the response. In the remainder of this chapter we will examine the major learning principles derived from these two behaviorist positions.

CONTIGUITY THEORIES

Perhaps most closely related to the British associationism tradition are the behaviorist theories based on the contiguity principle. Associations by temporal and spatial contiguity were two of the four basic laws of association formulated by this school of philosophy. Two important traditions in contiguity theory will be examined: verbal learning and respondent conditioning.

Verbal learning

In 1885 Hermann Ebbinghaus originated the experimental study of verbal learning by publishing the results of his work on the topic. Ebbinghaus devised a basic unit for his study of verbal learning, the nonsense syllable or, as it is most frequently referred to today, the "trigram." His intention was to study the formation and retention of associations from the "very beginning" and in order to do this he needed to eliminate the effects of prior experience from the learning process. Ebbinghaus eliminated prior experience by constructing trigrams from all possible consonant-vowel-consonant combinations (CVC's) that were not words in the German language.

Ebbinghaus, who served as his own subject, would study a number of trigram lists until he could recite them in correct order twice without error. After learning the lists to this criterion, he would put them aside for a period of time and then relearn them to this same criterion. In this way his measure of retention was the savings in time required to relearn the lists compared with the time spent in the original learning. For example, to learn a set of eight lists may have taken 20 minutes, but to relearn these lists after a one-day rest may have required 14 minutes. That would be a savings score of six minutes. Ebbinghaus found that forgetting was most rapid immediately following learning and decreased as time progressed. Figure 4–2 depicts Ebbinghaus's famous curve of forgetting.

Verbal learning tasks. Most studies of verbal learning have used one of three basic types of learning tasks: paired-associate learning, serial learning, and free recall. Each of these tasks, while requiring the learning of associations among verbal material,

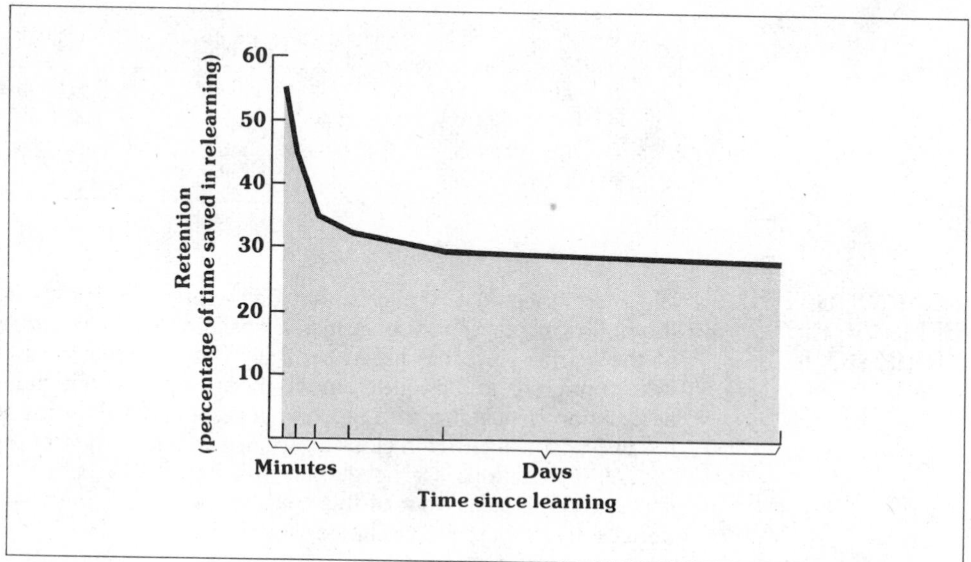

FIGURE 4–2
Curve of forgetting from research on nonsense syllables by Ebbinghaus

places different demands on the learner. Furthermore, each has a counterpart in classroom tasks faced by every school child.

One type of learning task is the paired-associate task. With this type, the learner is presented with a list of paired trigrams or words. For each pair, one trigram or word is designated the stimulus term and the other is the response term. The learner's task is to associate each response term with its appropriate stimulus term for the entire list, hence the name "paired-associate" learning.

Learning in a paired-associate task proceeds through two phases: the response learning phase and the associative phase (Underwood & Schulz, 1960). In the first phase, or response learning, the learner must become able to produce the trigram as a response. After having learned to produce a trigram as an integrated response, the learner must associate it with its respective stimulus term. If the response terms in a paired-associate task are either low in meaningfulness or difficult to pronounce, then the major requirement of the task would be the response learning phase. In a case where the response terms are high in meaningfulness or easy to pronounce, the major learning requirement would reside in the associative phase of learning.

Many tasks that we encounter in school fall into the category of paired-associate learning. The elementary school child learning arithmetic facts, such as $2 + 2 = 4$ or $6 \times 6 = 36$, or acquiring a sight vocabulary in reading is performing paired-associate tasks; as is the high school student memorizing vocabulary words for the next unit in French, or the chemistry student who must learn the symbols and atomic weights and numbers for all the elements in the periodic table. Many other learning tasks in school and in daily life fit into the paired-associate paradigm, which might explain why the paired-associate task is one of the most popular tasks for the study of verbal learning.

A second type of task used in the study of verbal learning is the serial learning task. This type requires the learner to reproduce in sequence a list of trigrams or words according to the order of their presentation. So this task requires the person to learn not only a set of trigrams or words but also their order of occurrence.

An interesting and common characteristic of serial learning is the serial position effect. Simply stated, the largest number of errors tend to occur in learning those terms at the middle of the list. Words at the beginning and end of the list are more readily learned than words in the middle of the list. This phenomenon is referred to as the "serial position effect." Data from a study demonstrating the serial position effect are illustrated in Figure 4–3.

FIGURE 4–3
Pattern of errors typifying the serial position effect

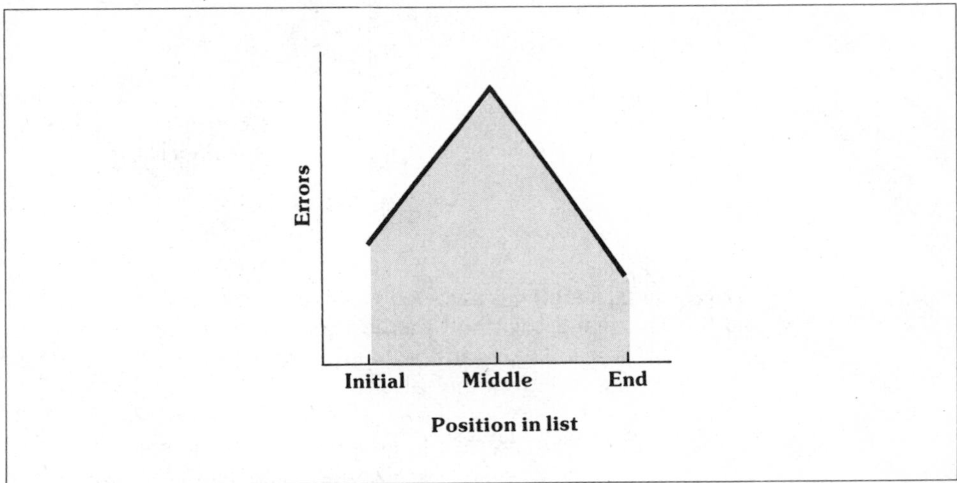

The serial position effect can be modified by making a word in the middle more distinctive or novel in comparison with the other words. This modification of the serial position effect is shown in Figure 4–4. Notice that the term in the middle of the list was learned much better than the surrounding words.

This modification of the effect is attributable to the novelty of the term in the middle of the list. For example, suppose the following list of words is to be learned in a serial learning study:

pink
black
yellow
beige
orange
five
silver
purple
white
gray

All of the words in the list are colors except *five*, so *five* is a novel term. A novel and distinctive term is learned and remembered better than less novel terms. This phenomenon is called the "von Restorff effect."

FIGURE 4-4
The von Restorff effect in serial learning

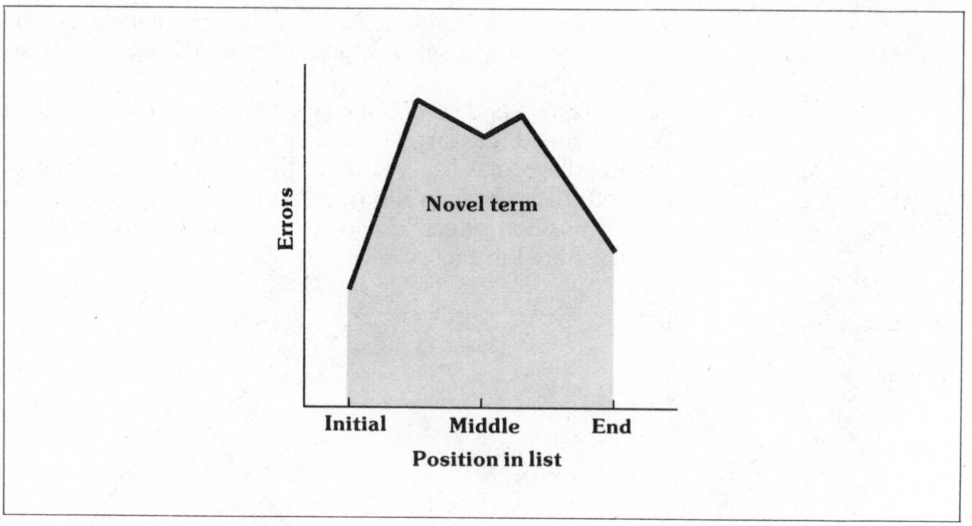

Serial learning is involved in any everyday task in which the order of recall is important. The first-grade child memorizing the alphabet or the numerals 1–19 is engaging in serial learning, as in the high school student who must learn to recite the geological epochs in chronological order.

A third learning task frequently used in the study of verbal learning is the free-recall task. This task is basically the same as serial learning with one big exception. In free recall, the learner does not have to recall the list in any particular order but is free to recall the terms in any order. The major task for the learner, then, is to recall as many of the terms as possible.

With a free-recall task we typically observe the phenomenon of clustering. This was first demonstrated in a study by Bousfield (1953). In this study, the learners were given a list of 60 words divided into four equally occurring conceptual categories: animals, proper names, professions, and vegetables. During the study trials, the words were presented in random order, but the learners had a tendency to organize the words in recall. That is, words belonging to a given conceptual category tended to be clustered together in recall.

Discussion of this organizational process in memory will be postponed until the next chapter because of its central importance to cognitive formulations of the learning process. Free recall is involved in classroom learning tasks whenever the student must learn a set of facts. Students who must learn four major events leading up to the Revolutionary War are demonstrating free recall; so are the students who must name ten counties in their home state or four or five important industrial products of their state.

Factors influencing the acquisition and retention of verbal learning. As we have seen, associations between verbal stimuli are basically formed by contiguity. However, other variables influence the formation and retention of such verbal associations. This is evidenced by the fact that some associations are acquired and retained better than others. Two basic factors affecting the acquisition and retention of verbal associations that have been investigated extensively within the contiguity framework are meaningfulness and practice.

Meaningfulness. Ebbinghaus originally developed nonsense syllables because he thought them devoid of any meaning since they never would have been associated with any prior experiences. Much subsequent research has proved Ebbinghaus's assumption to be false. Even nonsense syllables differ in terms of their meaningfulness, and this meaningfulness is a major determinant of their ease of learning.

Meaningfulness can be measured in numerous ways, but regardless of the way it is measured, it is related to the rate of learning. Glaze (1928) developed the first measure of meaningfulness in verbal learning. He presented individual trigrams to people and asked if each suggested an association to them—not what association or how many, just whether the trigram suggested an association. From this, he calculated the percentage of people answering yes for a given trigram as the association value of that trigram. Research has shown that even this rather simple measure of meaningfulness is a powerful predictor of the learnability of verbal material.

A different measure of the meaningfulness of a trigram is the frequency of its occurrence in the language of the learner. For example, Underwood and Schulz (1960) determined the frequency of every possible trigram in 15,000 words of print and found this frequency to predict ease of learning. Figure 4–5 illustrates typical learning curves for materials of varying meaningfulness.

Both measures of meaningfulness are good predictors of how quickly verbal material will be learned. Furthermore, meaningfulness is an excellent indication of how well

FIGURE 4–5
Learning of verbal material as a function of its meaningfulness (1 is least meaningful and 4 is most meaningful)

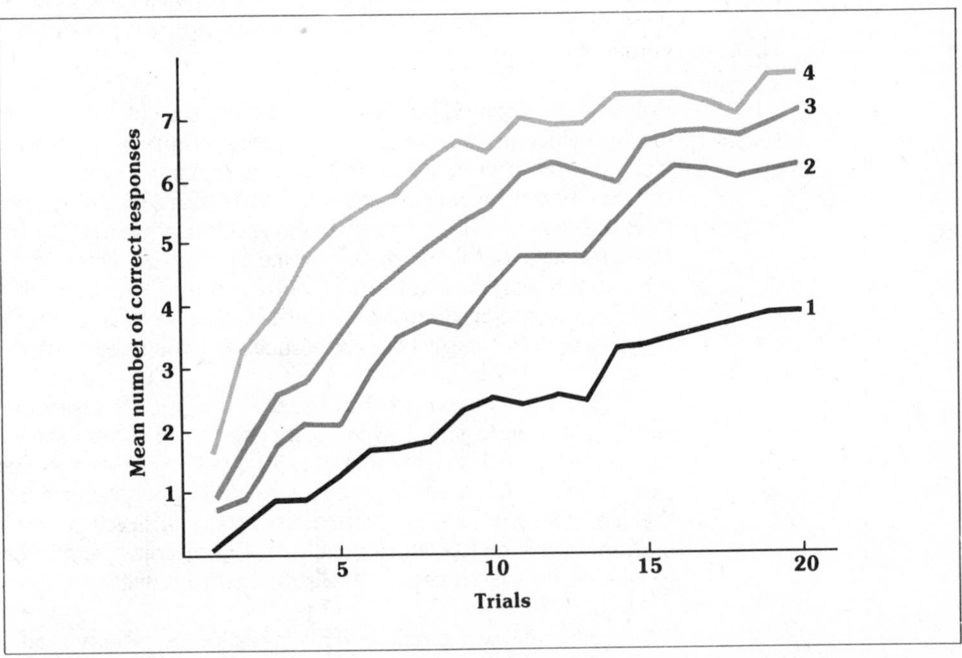

Source: Underwood and Schulz (1960).

verbal learning will be remembered. If we are willing to assume that the degree of meaningfulness increases as we go from nonsense syllables to substance, then we conclude that the rate of forgetting decreases as meaningfulness increases.

The research into the effects of meaningfulness on the acquisition and retention of verbal material should not be interpreted as a rationale for not teaching verbal material low in meaningfulness to the learner. For instance, technical terms and other specialized vocabulary, while initially not very meaningful to the novice, can be essential for greater mastery of a discipline as learning progresses. As we shall see later in this chapter, other factors such as practice can overcome the tendency to quickly forget low-meaningfulness material. For the teacher the implication is this: when the material to be learned by the students is likely to be low in meaningfulness, more care and time must be expended to insure that it is learned adequately.

Practice. A basic premise of the contiguity theory is the law of frequency. This states that the number of contiguous pairings of a stimulus and response influences the association established between them, such that as the frequency increases so does the strength of the association. Each pairing of a stimulus and response is referred to as a "practice trial." Researchers examining conditions that make practice more efficient have focused on three conditions: distributed versus massed practice; whole versus part learning, and overlearning.

Distributed versus massed practice. Much research has been conducted in an attempt to determine whether a practice period should consist of trials interspersed in some manner with rest intervals or a number of trials without any rest intervals provided. The former type is called *distributed practice* and the latter is *massed practice.* It had long been known that distributed practice facilitates the learning of a performance involving bodily movements, such as swinging a golf club (for further discussion of practice conditions in the learning of motor skills, see Chapter 11). Many psychologists were willing to generalize these findings with motor skills to performances involving verbal responses.

Subsequent research by Benton J. Underwood (1961) has shown the effects of distributed practice to be considerably more complex than the preceding generalization from motor to verbal learning held it to be. Underwood concluded that distributed practice had a facilitative effect in the response learning phase of a paired-associates task but not in the associative phase. Consequently, the most benefit to be derived from the use of distributed practice should be when the verbal material is low in meaningfulness to the learner. With verbal material high in meaningfulness to the learner, the major demand of the learning task is that of association of terms, and hence we would expect no differences between distributed and massed practice.

Furthermore, Underwood has observed that the effects of distributed practice on verbal learning are quite small when compared with other factors in the learning situation. Furthermore, the length of a rest interval necessary to demonstrate the distributed practice effect is so small that it is hard to imagine any learning situation outside of the laboratory, including such often-cited examples of massed practice as a student cramming the night before a quiz, not containing rest intervals of sufficient duration to qualify for classification as distributed practice.

Whole versus part practice. This question is whether all the verbal material to be learned should be practiced at once (the whole method) or divided into parts with each part practiced to mastery separately (the part method). Quite often a modification of the part method, called the "part-progressive method," is used to learn verbal material. With the part-progressive method, the material is divided into parts and as each part is mastered it is then combined with its preceding part.

Deese and Hulse (1967) state that the decision to use the part or whole method in practicing verbal material depends upon the kind of structural relationship among the verbal material. If the relationship among the verbal items suggests more or less coherent subunits to the learner, then the part method would be a more efficient practice method. If no such substructures exist, then the whole method is preferred.

Consider the following sets of facts:

Set A

The capital of South Carolina is Columbia.
The major industrial products of South Carolina are textiles.
The chief agricultural product of South Carolina is tobacco.
The climate of South Carolina is temperate.
The capital of Florida is Tallahassee.
The major industry of Florida is tourism.
The chief agricultural product of Florida is citrus fruit.
The climate of Florida is semitropical.

Set B

The major industrial products of South Carolina are textiles.
The major industry of Florida is tourism.
The major industrial products of Michigan are automotive products.
The major industrial product of Oklahoma is petroleum.
The major industry of Pennsylvania is steel.
The major industry of West Virginia is coal.
The major industrial products of Maine are shoes.
The major industry of Oregon is lumber.

Application of the part method would be most appropriate to Set A, and we would have two parts: a set of four facts about South Carolina and a set of four facts about Florida. Set B does not suggest division into parts; rather what must be learned with Set B is eight distinct associations of states and products.

To quote Deese and Hulse (1967, p. 304):

> . . . the part-whole problem resolves itself into the study of the internal arrangements of material to be learned. Whether or not it is sensible to split some task up into two or more parts depends upon whether or not the interrelations within the task are such that the splitting makes the task structurally simpler or more difficult.

Overlearning. Everyone is familiar with the old saying "practice makes perfect." This saying is true in two related ways: (1) the more common interpretation is that the more you practice a skill, the more expert your performance becomes; and (2) the more practice, the better the skill is retained in memory. In the laboratory this better retention as a result of continued practice was studied through a procedure labeled *overlearning.* A learner practices a set of verbal learning materials until a criterion of one errorless trial is reached, and any practice after that is considered overlearning.

For example, if it took 20 trials to reach the criterion of one errorless performance, then 50 percent overlearning would be 10 more trials, 100 percent would be 20 more trials, and so on.

Results of studies on overlearning reveal that continued practice after mastery facilitates retention. As the amount of overlearning increases so does the amount of verbal material retained by the learner. The implication of overlearning for the classroom is clear. The more important the information to be learned is, the more practice should be given to it and this practice should continue beyond mastery. Most typically material is not practiced to mastery by the average student, but according to this principle practice should actually go past mastery.

Respondent conditioning

The second form of contiguity theory is based on the work of the famous Russian physiologist and Nobel laureate, Ivan Petrovich Pavlov. His studies of the modification of salivation to food in dogs set the foundation for the future work in this area. Respondent conditioning, often referred to as "classical conditioning," describes learning in situations in which reflexive behaviors become associated with new stimuli.

The classic experiment in psychology that extended the principles of respondent conditioning to humans was performed in 1920 by the preeminent behaviorist John B. Watson and his associate Rosalie Raynor. In this study they demonstrated that a young child could acquire an emotional response through respondent conditioning. Observations of a one-year-old child named Albert had led to the conclusion that the only detectable fear he exhibited was one of unexpected loud noises. On several occasions Watson had struck an iron bar with a hammer while Albert's attention was diverted, and on these occasions Albert responded with a startled look and cried.

Albert's fear was a reflexive reaction to the stimulus of an unexpected loud noise. Within the respondent conditioning paradigm, a reflexive response is an *unconditioned response* (UCR), and the stimulus that elicits such a response is an *unconditioned stimulus* (UCS). This relationship between an unconditioned stimulus and an unconditioned response is referred to as a *reflex arc;* it can be expressed schematically as:

Unconditioned stimulus ⟶ Unconditioned response
(loud noise) (crying)

Reflexes, such as Albert's crying, come to be elicited by new stimuli through contiguity. In Watson and Raynor's study the presentation of a white rat was paired with the loud noise. After several pairings, the white rat was presented to Albert without the accompanying noise, whereupon Albert started crying and fell over to cover his face. This previously neutral stimulus of a white rat had come to elicit an emotional response in Albert by being paired closely in time with the unconditioned stimulus of a loud noise. Now the white rat is called a *conditioned stimulus* (CS) and the crying elicited by this CS is a *conditioned response* (CR). The entire process of respondent conditioning can be illustrated by the following four steps:

1. Unconditioned stimulus ⟶ Unconditioned response
   (loud noise) (crying)
2. Neutral stimulus
   (white rat)
   ↕
   Unconditioned stimulus ⟶ Unconditioned response
   (loud noise) (crying)

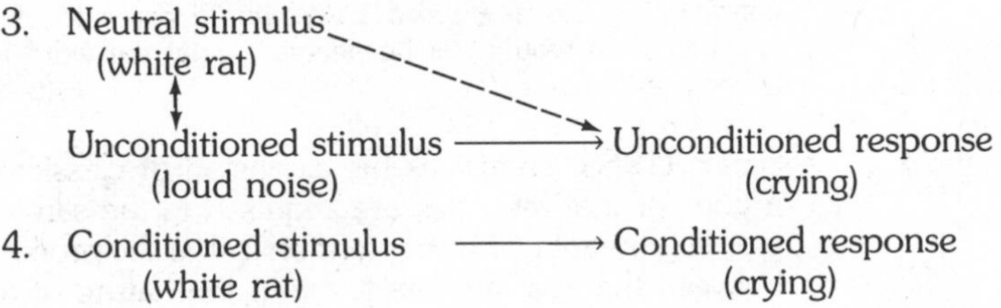

In the case of Albert, several contiguous pairings between the white rat and loud noise were sufficient to produce a strong fear response. This rapid establishment of a conditioned response was due mainly to its nature. Fear responses, because of their importance to the survival of the organism, are learned more quickly than other classes of responses. For these other classes the association between a conditioned stimulus and a conditioned response is strengthened gradually by repeated pairing of the conditioned stimulus and unconditioned stimulus. Thus we see that in respondent conditioning, as in verbal learning, the law of frequency is a basic principle.

Watson's contention that human emotions are modified through the conditioning process has received further support from subsequent researchers. Staats (1968) reported a series of studies that illustrate how attitudinal and other emotional responses can become associated with verbal stimuli within a respondent conditioning framework. In one of these studies, Staats, Staats, and Crawford (1962) used a simple conditioning procedure to demonstrate the manner in which the emotional meaning of words may be acquired. A list of 25 words was used as the verbal stimulus in this study. One word from the list was chosen as the conditioned stimulus, and the experimental group had this word paired with an unconditioned stimulus of either a loud noise or a mild electric shock nine times as the list was presented repeatedly in random order. A control group received the unconditioned stimulus nine times too, but never in close association with the word chosen as the unconditioned stimulus.

After the above experimental treatment, emotional response to the word chosen as a conditioned stimulus was measured in two ways. The resistance of the skin to passage of a minute electric current was used since it is a well-documented indicator of emotional change. The other measure used required the person to rate the emotional connotation of the words used in the study. Results showed a change in skin resistance upon presentation of the conditioned stimulus word for the experimental group but not for the control group. Additionally, the experimental group rated the conditioned stimulus word as having more unpleasant meaning than did the control group.

Staats (1968) further extends the respondent conditioning paradigm to explain how we learn much of our basic vocabulary. In order to account for the growth of vocabulary through respondent conditioning, Staats relies on the principle of higher-order conditioning. This principle states that an already established conditioned stimulus can function as an unconditioned stimulus in the development of a new conditioned stimulus. Staats (1968, pp. 24–25) describes the process in the following quote:

> Let us say, using another example, that a child has through first-order conditioning of the type already described acquired a meaning to the word BAD. That is, the child has received aversive stimulation in contiguity with the presentation of the word stimulus. Let us also say that the child later on reads a new word *evil;* a word that he has never seen before, thus, to him a nonsense syllable. He is then told by a parent or teacher that EVIL MEANS BAD and he repeats this to himself several times. These experiences would constitute conditioning trials in which the word BAD would serve as the ^{uc}S and the word EVIL as the ^{c}S. Through this

conditioning the new word EVIL would come to elicit the same meaning response as the word BAD. It would not be necessary that the word EVIL ever be paired with an unlearned aversive stimulus.

Staats (1968) continues his extension of classical conditioning to offer a convincing argument that attitudes are acquired in the same manner as emotional or evaluative wording meaning. His contention is that the process is the same, and that the difference between the two appears to be in the nature of the stimuli involved.

The preceding research has illustrated quite convincingly that human emotions can be acquired and modified through the process of respondent conditioning. A question of perhaps greater practical significance is: Can negative emotions be eliminated through the same process of respondent conditioning? One means by which this could be accomplished would be to continue presenting the conditioned stimulus for the emotional response while not allowing it to be paired again with the unconditioned stimulus. This procedure is called "extinction" and the result is a cessation of the conditioned response to the conditioned stimulus.

Mary Cover Jones, a graduate student of John B. Watson, was the first person to report the elimination of a fear through a conditioning procedure (Jones, 1924). Ironically, she removed a fear of animals in a three-year-old child named Peter by applying a technique involving extinction. Jones proceeded by introducing the feared animal, a rabbit, into the room with Peter while he was eating. The rabbit was kept at a sufficient distance so that it did not frighten Peter and was gradually moved closer. Thus, Peter was repeatedly exposed to the conditioned stimulus without it being paired with an unconditioned stimulus for fear. Furthermore, the conditioned stimulus of a rabbit was repeatedly paired with stimuli such as food and the attention of an adult. If these stimuli are associated with any emotional responses, they would be pleasant and hence incompatible with a fear response.

Further discussion of the role of respondent conditioning in the development of attitudes can be found in Chapter 11. The major implication for the classroom teacher is that the experiences students have as they come into contact with school activities help form their attitudes through a simple process of contiguous association. Consequently the student who encounters continual failure in a subject quickly develops a negative attitude, whereas the student experiencing success develops a positive attitude.

3. After being stung by a wasp on the back porch of his grandmother's house, George is afraid to go on the porch again. Analyze this response in the respondent conditioning paradigm (i.e., identify the UCS, UCR, CS, and CR).

REINFORCEMENT THEORIES

In contiguity theories the major variable influencing the establishment of an association between a particular stimulus and response is a close temporal or spatial relationship, whereas for reinforcement theories the major variable is the consequences of the response in that situation. Put another way, reinforcement theorists postulate that a given response will become more or less frequent in a particular situation depending upon its consequence. Edward L. Thorndike, an early behaviorist and educational psychologist, referred to this principle as the Law of Effect. To Thorndike the two important types of consequences were satisfying and annoying states of affairs, which he (1913, p. 2) defined in the following terms:

By a satisfying state of affairs is meant one which the animal does nothing to avoid, often doing things which maintain or renew it. By an annoying state of affairs is meant one which the animal does nothing to preserve, often doing things which put an end to it.

Thorndike later modified the Law of Effect to emphasize the satisfying state of affairs as having a greater exertion on associations than the annoying state of affairs. However, the Law of Effect in one form or another is the basis of all reinforcement theories of learning. B. F. Skinner's operant conditioning theory can be viewed in this way as a major refinement and extension of Thorndike's Law of Effect. We shall now examine operant conditioning as an example of reinforcement theories of learning. (In the past decade operant conditioning has probably had greater impact on educational practice than any other learning theory.)

Operant conditioning

Early behaviorists, such as John B. Watson, thought all behavior could be explained by the principles of respondent conditioning. The explanation was a simple matter of demonstrating how complex behaviors were built of simpler behaviors and established through conditioning.

Within a relatively short time it became apparent that the principles of respondent conditioning were insufficient to explain all behavior. The model of human beings based totally on respondent conditioning is that of reactor. We say that an unconditioned stimulus or a conditioned stimulus elicits or draws out a response; so the response is the reaction to the stimulus. In respondent conditioning action is initiated by the stimulus or environment and not by the person. Yet our own experiences and other evidence tells us this is not the case in most human behavior. Humans are said to engage in *purposive* behavior. We, rather than the environment, are the initiating agents in much of our behavior. After we have acted on our environment, the consequences of that action determine whether or not we will behave in a like manner in the future. In other words, much of our behavior acts on our environment rather than merely reacting to it, and herein lies the distinction between operant and respondent behavior.

Consider the following example of operant conditioning reported by Harris, Johnston, Kelley, and Wolf (1964), and while you read the description attempt to contrast this process with that of respondent conditioning. The study involved a three-year-old girl in a preschool situation who engaged in "excessive" crawling. Excessive crawling was defined as spending most of her time crawling or in a crouched position with her face hidden from view. Observations of the child showed her to spend more than 80 percent of her time engaged in this behavior. A decision was made to alter the consequence of crawling, so the teacher was instructed to ignore the child when she crawled and to pay attention to her when she was engaged in any behaviors that involved running, standing, or walking. According to the authors this procedure resulted in a close-to-normal pattern of on-feet behavior within a week.

To determine if the teacher's shift in attention was indeed responsible for this change in behavior, it was decided to once again make attention dependent upon the occurrence of crawling and other off-feet behaviors. By the second day of this reversal the child was again spending 80 percent of her time off her feet. The procedure of paying attention to only on-feet behaviors was reinstated for a final time. The child was again engaging in on-feet behaviors for 62 percent of her time at the preschool within four days.

The study by Harris and colleagues illustrates the conditioning of operant behaviors, so with this in mind let us examine the differences between operant and respondent conditioning. To begin the discussion, no mention was made of any antecedent stimuli in the study. There is no suggestion of a stimulus that elicits the crawling behavior. Yet in the Watson and Raynor study of respondent conditioning, the crying response was clearly elicited by an antecedent stimulus, the loud noise. As we see in our example of operant conditioning above, there is no unconditioned stimulus to elicit the behavior, and the stimulus that altered the crawling behavior came after, not before, the behavior. Operant behavior is modified or conditioned by its consequences. So if respondent behavior reacts to the environment, then operant behavior acts upon the environment. The name given to the two types of conditioning by B. F. Skinner convey this distinction: *respondent* to respond to the environment and *operant* to operate on the environment.

Types of consequential stimuli

The consequences of operant behaviors referred to as "stimuli" within the reinforcement framework are classified on the basis of two dimensions: the direction of the behavioral change and the stimulus change operation related to that behavioral change. The change in a behavior brought about by the consequence of that action can be either an increase or a decrease in the performance of the behavior. If a stimulus increases the rate of the behavior it follows, then it is a *reinforcer.* A stimulus that results in a decrease of the operant behavior it follows is a *punisher.*

FIGURE 4–6
Types of consequential stimuli

Direction of behavior change	*Stimulus operation*	
	Present stimulus	*Remove stimulus*
Increase in behavior	Positive reinforcer	Negative reinforcer
Decrease in behavior	Type 1 punisher	Type 2 punisher

Reinforcers and punishers are further subdivided on the basis of the stimulus change operation involved in the behavior change process. The consequences of operant behaviors are to change the environment of the person. This change can be either the presentation of some new stimuli or the removal of some current stimuli. The presentation of some stimuli following a behavior results in an increase in the performance of that behavior and these stimuli are classified as reinforcers, whereas the presentation of other stimuli decreases the behavior they follow and so are called punishers. The same is true for stimuli that either increase or decrease behaviors that remove the stimuli from the environment of the person. Figure 4–6 illustrates the four types of consequence that can be derived from our two-way analysis. We turn our attention now to each type of consequential stimuli developed in the two-way classification table.

Reinforcement. Reinforcement is the procedure by which an increase in the frequency of operant behavior is obtained. Reinforcers follow operant behavior and are said to be contingent on the behavior's occurrence; that is, the reinforcer occurs only after the behavior has occurred. If the behavior does not occur, then the reinforcer does not occur. Reinforcers are of two types: positive and negative. Both increase the behaviors they follow, but they do it through opposite stimulus change operations.

Positive reinforcers must be presented after a behavior in order to increase it, whereas negative reinforcers must be removed following a behavior to increase it.

Positive reinforcement. By far the most frequent type of reinforcement to be utilized by the classroom teacher is positive reinforcement. The following two examples illustrate the procedure of positive reinforcement in a classroom context.

Hart and Risley (1974) increased the use of adjective-noun combinations and compound sentences in the speech of disadvantaged children through the use of positive reinforcement. They rearranged the school environment so that the students had to ask for most of the play materials during their free-play periods. Access to the play materials was contingent upon the child's utterance of a noun, then an adjective-noun combination, and finally a compound sentence. For instance, suppose a child wanted to play with a toy car that was on the shelf. At first in order to obtain the car the child would have to simply say "car." When he consistently said "car," the teacher would require him to add an adjective to describe the car, and so the child would then have to say "blue car" to obtain the car. Finally in order to receive the car for play the child would have to speak a compound sentence such as, "I want the blue car so I can play with it." The results indicated that being allowed to play with toys was a positive reinforcer for the children and increased their use of adjective-noun combinations and compound sentences. Furthermore, Hart and Risley concluded that the increased use of adjective-noun combinations and compound sentences was not restricted to free-play period but occurred in other periods of the school day as well.

Lahey and Drabman (1974) taught second-graders a sight vocabulary through the use of a technique referred to as "token reinforcement." The study involved both the acquisition and retention of a sight vocabulary of 30 words selected from the commonly encountered reading words. The children in both the reinforcement and no-reinforcement groups were taught to read the words during three separate acquisition sessions at which they were given a list of ten different words each. Acquisition of the ten words was determined by counting the number of trials (a trial was a single presentation of all ten words) before a student could read all ten words once without an error. Retention of all 30 words was measured immediately after acquisition of the third list and then two days later. Children in the token reinforcement group were given a token for each word read correctly during the acquisition sessions but not after the retention test. The tokens could be exchanged for pennies later. The children in the no-reinforcement group were simply told whether or not they had read the word correctly on each trial.

The graphs in Figure 4–7 compare the performance of the reinforcement and no-reinforcement groups on both acquisition and retention of the sight words. We can see from the graphs that the reinforcement group learned to read the words quicker and remembered more of them longer.

The tokens fit our definition of positive reinforcers because: (1) they are presented after the desired behavior (reading a word) and are contingent upon the desired behavior, and (2) they increase the performance of that behavior (in this case acquisition and retention are the measures of performance). You might be thinking that the other group in this experiment also learned the sight vocabulary words, since at the beginning of the experiment they could not read any of the words either. So what was the reinforcer for the control group? The answer is that the control group also

FIGURE 4–7
Average number of sight words read correctly per 10-word list in the combined retention tests.

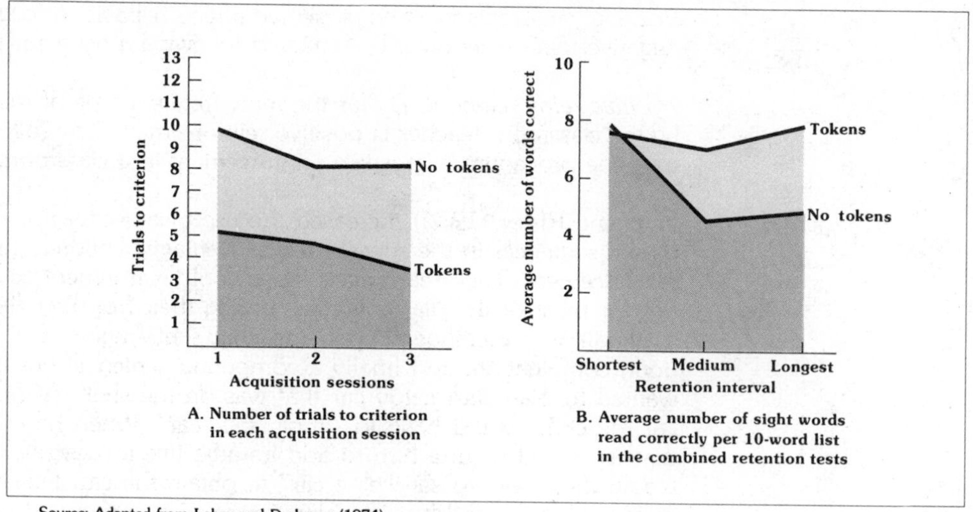

Source: Adapted from Lahey and Drabman (1974).

was reinforced but not with as strong a reinforcer as tokens. One reinforcer for the children in the control group was being told they were right when the word was read correctly. Being told one is right is a positive reinforcer closely related to attention, as illustrated in our previous examples of crawling and crying behaviors.

Negative reinforcement. Referring back to Figure 4–6, we see that negative reinforcers increase behavior rate just as do positive reinforcers; that positive reinforcers are stimuli that increase behaviors when they are presented, whereas the removal of negative reinforcers increases the behaviors that remove them. To illustrate negative reinforcement and to contrast it with positive reinforcement, we offer the following hypothetical example of classroom proceedings. Imagine yourself as an observer in Mr. Watson's sixth-grade class. You are focusing on the behavior of two students, Jim and George, and you keep a record of whether or not they turn in their math homework. For the first five days of your observation period, the teacher simply collects the homework and makes no evaluative comments one way or the other. The number of completed homework assignments for each student is shown in Figure 4–8. For the second five-day period, Mr. Watson told Jim that for every day he did not turn in his homework, he would have to stay one-half hour after school. Mr. Watson told George that for every completed homework assignment he would get five extra minutes of recess time. The rate of completed homework assignments for this second five-day period is also presented in Figure 4–8. After this second five-day period, Mr. Watson went back to collecting the homework assignments without any comment. The rate of completed homework assignments for this third period is also given in the figure.

Perusal of the records of both Jim and George show that the two different treatments had the same effect on the rate of doing homework. Both Jim and George increased their completion rate when Mr. Watson applied contingencies to this behavior. In Jim's case the increase in behavior can be attributed to negative reinforcement. Completion of the homework assignment removed the threat of detention. For George completion of the homework resulted in the presentation of extra recess time, hence positive reinforcement.

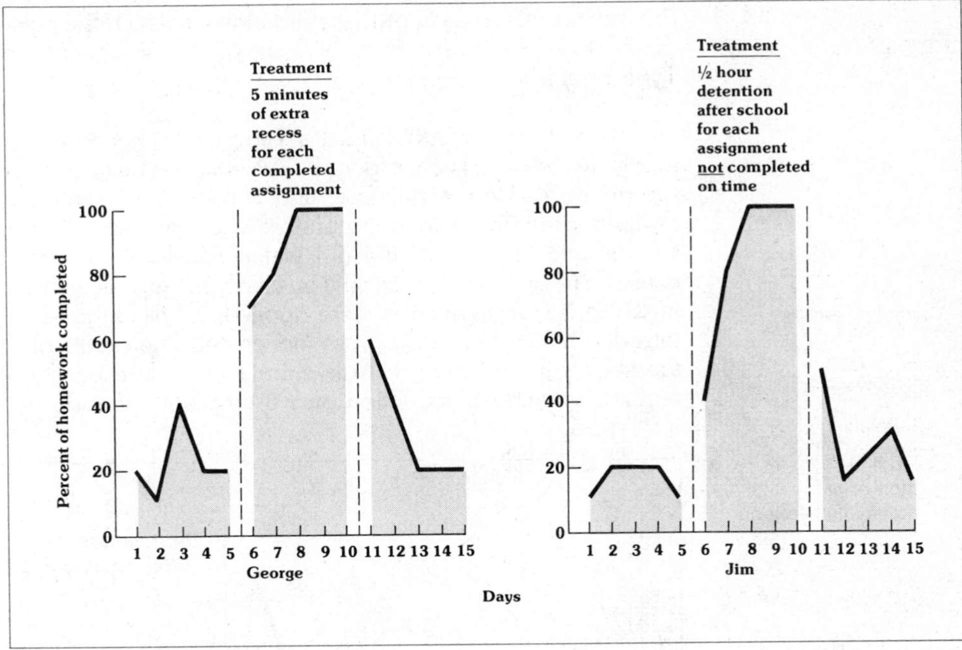

FIGURE 4–8
Hypothetical record of completed homework assignments

To summarize, this example demonstrated an increase in the rate of a behavior by the removal of a stimulus, negative reinforcement, and by the presentation of a stimulus, positive reinforcement. To be effective in increasing the performance of a behavior, both positive and negative reinforcers must be made contingent upon the occurrence of that response.

Basically, negative reinforcers are unpleasant or painful stimuli we try to escape or avoid, such as loud noises, extreme temperatures, boredom, or a dental drill. Behaviors that remove such a stimulus become strengthened and are therefore more likely to occur when we encounter that stimulus again in our environment. On the other hand, there are some stimuli that we try to approach; these are positive reinforcers such as a smile from a friend, a reward, or food. Behaviors that result in the presentation of such reinforcers tend to be repeated.

Punishment. In the preceding section we examined stimulus change operations that function to increase the performance of a behavior. Now we turn our attention to those stimulus change operations that decrease the behaviors with which they are associated. This class of stimulus change operations is referred to as "punishment." Just as there are two types of reinforcement, so there are two types of punishment. In the first type of punishment we find that the presentation of a stimulus results in a decrease in the behavior that produces it. The second type of punishment would be a decrease in performance resulting from the removal of a stimulus.

Type I punishment. Perhaps the most common type of punishment we encounter involves some Type I punishers. Our everyday experiences provide us with a wealth of examples—the careless person makes a mistake, the child who misbehaves receives a reprimand or even a spanking from her parent, the sunbather who falls asleep gets sunburned. In each of these situations in which the person is less likely to perform the behavior in the future as a result of its consequence, we have an example of a Type I punisher.

Greene and Hoats (1969) used a Type I punisher to reduce gross hyperactivity in a mildly retarded 18-year-old girl. This hyperactivity included excessive amounts of squirming, rocking, scratching, and continual adjustment of her hair and clothing. Furthermore, she reported discomfort when she had to sit for more than a few minutes. Greene and Hoats had the girl watch television in a room where her movements could be recorded automatically by electronic means. After a two-week baseline period in which no contingencies were applied, a brief interval of television distortion was introduced following each gross movement. The results of this punishment procedure are shown in Figure 4–9. This simple procedure quickly reduced the hyperactivity and maintained the reduction over a long time period.

FIGURE 4–9
Reduction of gross hyperactivity by television distortion

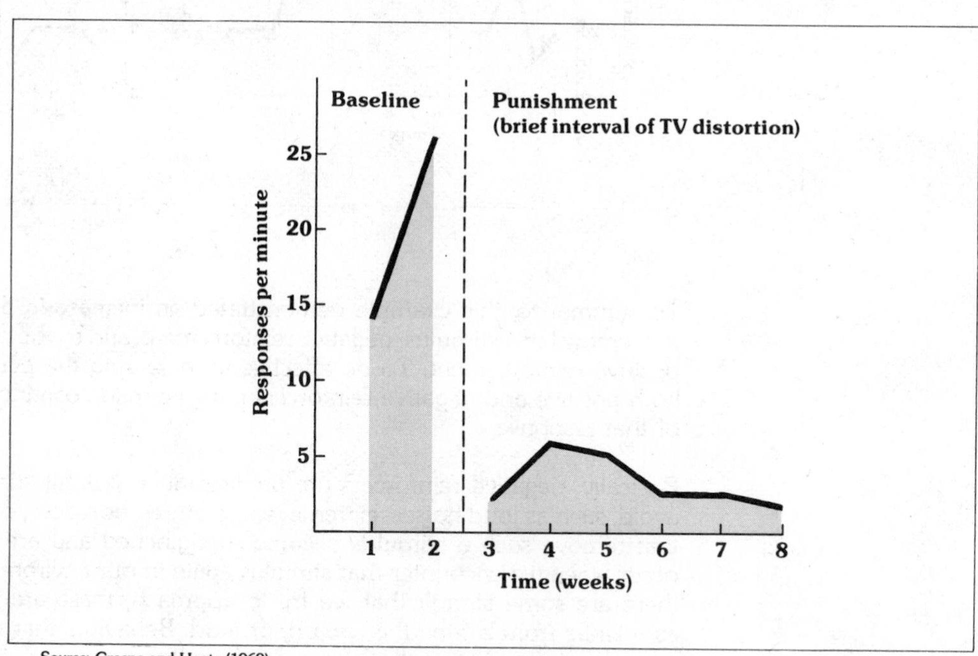

Source: Greene and Hoats (1969).

Type II punishment. The removal of a stimulus can cause a decrease in the performance of the behavior that produced that particular effect. This stimulus change operation is called Type II punishment and is illustrated quite well in a study by Knight and McKenzie (1974). In this study problem thumb-sucking was eliminated through the contingent withdrawal of bedtime reading. The parents of children in the study were instructed to stop reading when the children were thumb-sucking and not start again until the children removed their thumbs from their mouths. Independent observations of the children's thumb-sucking were taken. The study demonstrated that this simple punishment procedure was effective in reducing the thumb-sucking. In this case the stimulus change operation was the termination of oral reading, which may be interpreted as the removal of a stimulus contingent upon the performance of thumb-sucking. The effect was to reduce the likelihood that the child would suck her thumb and so it is the operation of Type II punishment.

Basic stimuli in operant consequences. Now that we have covered the range of reinforcers and punishers, it is probably apparent to you that while we have made four distinctions, we have been dealing with only two basic types of stimuli. That is to say, both positive reinforcement and Type II punishment involve the same stimulus in opposite change operations. The same relationship holds between negative reinforcement and Type I punishment.

Perhaps this relationship is best clarified by a specific illustration. In the study by Greene and Hoats cited earlier, we saw that distortion of a television picture dependent upon the occurrence of hyperactive behavior decreased such behavior. In this same study a different person could remove or avoid distortion of a television picture by completing a simple production-line task within a predetermined time period. In this situation, television distortion accelerated the work rate as measured by responses per minute, so we see that the stimulus has a different effect on performance depending upon the direction of the change operation in which it is involved. The same stimulus, television distortion, decreased responding when it was presented and increased responding when it was removed contingent upon performance.

While the preceding example demonstrates that the stimulus will function either as a negative reinforcer or as a Type I punisher depending upon the stimulus change operation, the same relationship could be shown between positive reinforcers and Type II punishers. This relationship points to the importance of considering both the stimulus change operation and the effect on future performance in classifying consequences of actions in operant conditioning. The environment acts in numerous ways to modify behaviors within the operant conditioning paradigm (Figure 4–10).

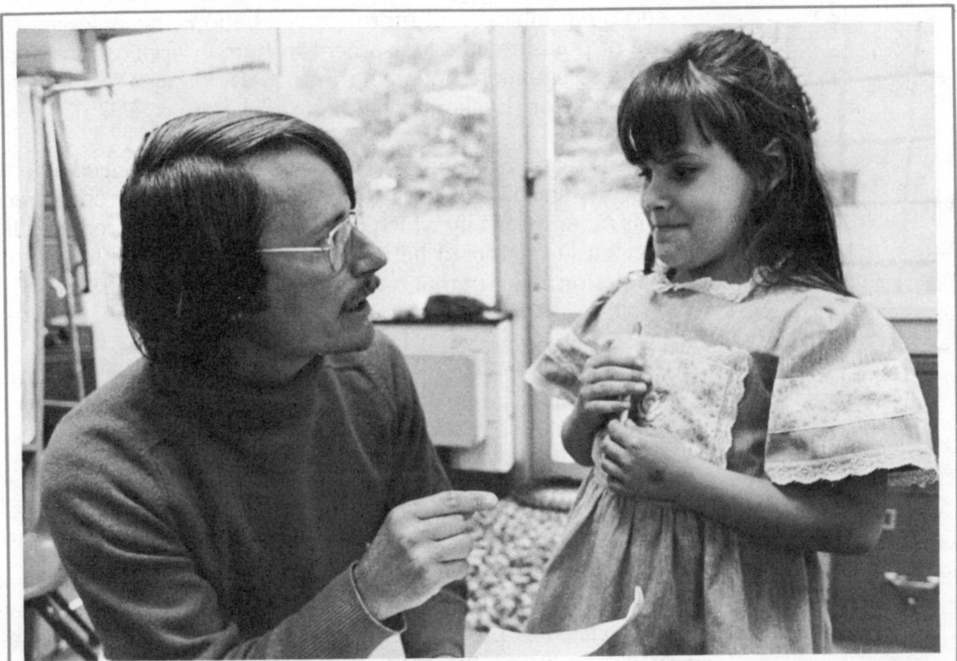

FIGURE 4–10
The consequences of behavior affect its future performance

Side effects of punishment. We have described punishment and reinforcement as having opposite effects. This is true in regard to their effects on the behaviors producing the reinforcement or punishment. However, punishment, particularly in applications to human problems, generates numerous undesirable side effects, which have led to the behaviorist aversion to the use of punishment.

Sulzer-Azaroff and Mayer (1977) list a number of possible disadvantages of the use of punishment in applied settings, three of which are withdrawal, aggression, and negative self-statements. One response to punishment is to withdraw or escape from the situation in which punishment occurs. A student who receives much punishment in school may escape by one of several means. The student may become a dropout and physically withdraw from the situation. Many students feeling greater pressure to remain in school may escape by some less overt method such as daydreaming or becoming sick.

Another reaction to punishment is aggression. The expression of aggression engendered by punishment can take many forms, ranging from verbal aggression such as sarcasm to acts of vandalism. Skinner (1968) has suggested that the high rate of vandalism directed toward school property can be attributed to the fact that the predominant method of controlling student behavior is punishment. Other research indicates that aggression is an unconditioned response to punishment. Furthermore, aggression as a response to punishment becomes more probable as the severity of punishment increases and the opportunity to escape decreases (Azrin & Holz, 1966).

Sulzer-Azaroff and Mayer assert that the use of punishment can influence the type of statements students make about themselves. A frequently punished student who often hears admonishments such as, "You're a bad boy!" may start making these statements about himself. After occurring in a number of situations, these negative statements become beliefs and part of the student's self-concept. For these reasons and other ethical and moral considerations, behaviorists recommend minimizing the use of punishment. Punishment in human applications should be restricted primarily to those situations involving immediate danger to the student or others affected by the behavior (Becker, Engelmann, & Thomas, 1975).

Extinction. Behaviors, as we have seen, are reduced when they lead to consequences called "punishment," but there is another type of consequence that reduces behaviors. This other means by which operant behaviors are reduced is called "extinction." When previously reinforced behaviors are no longer reinforced, the effect is a reduction in the performance of that behavior. The procedure by which the withholding of reinforcement decreases a behavior is extinction.

C. D. Williams (1959) demonstrated that temper tantrums in young children could be eliminated by an extinction procedure. A two-year-old child kept a parent or an aunt in his room at nap or bedtime by screaming and crying. The adult had to remain until the child went to sleep, which took up to two hours on occasions. According to Williams, the parents felt that the child enjoyed this control over them and that he resisted falling to sleep once in bed.

The child's parents were advised to put the child to bed in a relaxed and leisurely fashion, then to leave the room and shut the door. Figure 4–11 shows the effect of this extinction procedure on the child's behavior. On one occasion after extinction of the tantrums, the child screamed and the aunt reinforced the tantrum again by

FIGURE 4–11
Length of crying in two extinction series as a function of successive occasions of being put to bed

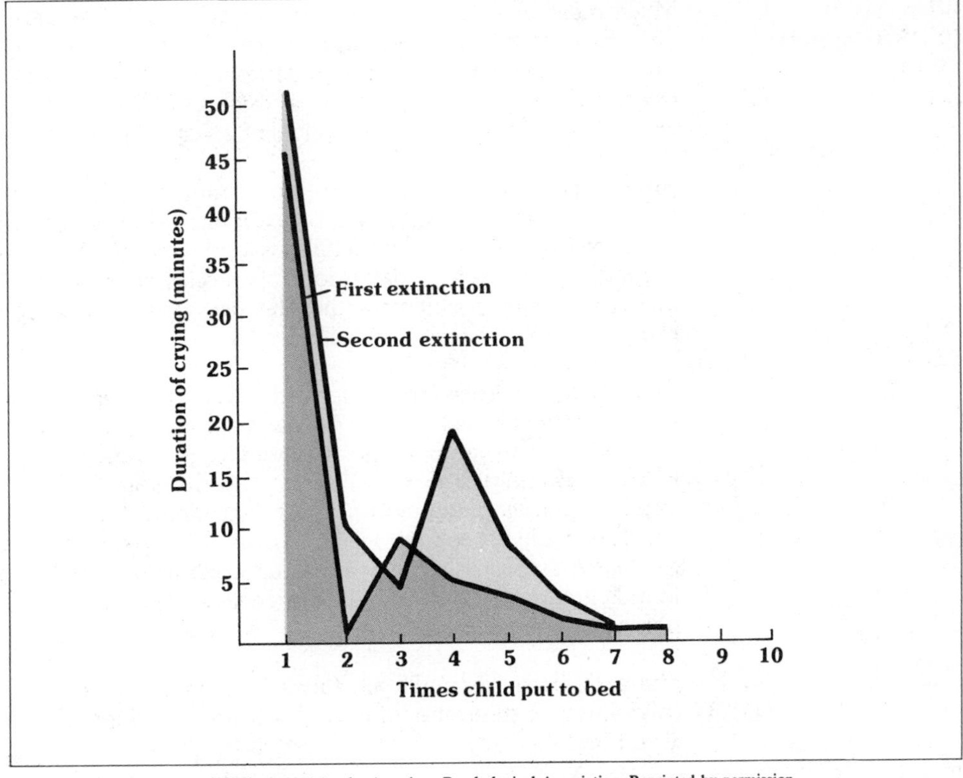

Source: C. D. Williams (1959).

staying with the child until he went to sleep. This single reinforcement reinstated the tantrums and made it necessary to perform the extinction procedure a second time.

Extinction should not be confused with Type II punishment. Both procedures reduce behaviors, but the stimulus change operations involved are different. Type II punishment occurs when the removal or withdrawal of a stimulus reduces a behavior; extinction of the procedure results when a stimulus is withheld and the result is a reduction in performance. The distinction is subtle but important. In the following section, patterns of reinforcement will be differentiated partially on the basis of the characteristic performances they generate when the person undergoes extinction of a learned response.

4. Determine the type of reinforcement or punishment operating in each situation below.
   a. Annabel rarely spoke above a whisper when called upon in class. To encourage her to speak up, her teacher had her stand and repeat her answer to the entire class. Annabel did not speak aloud again for days.
   b. On the Artic expedition, tinted goggles were worn to prevent snow-blindness.
   c. Lynn's parents told her that everytime they caught her sucking her thumb, she would lose 10 cents of that week's allowance. After instituting that rule, Lynn lost 20 cents in one week and then quit sucking her thumb.
   d. One night after supper Bill's father told a story to Bill, who listened very attentively. After that Bill's father regularly told Bill a bedtime story.
   e. Jane tried to teach her child to count by saying, "No, that's wrong" whenever the child made a mistake. The child never repeated those mistakes.

Effective use of reinforcement

Much research within the operant conditioning paradigm has been concerned with effective and efficient means to establish and maintain operant behaviors. Operant behaviors are established primarily through the method of successive approximations, often called "shaping." Behaviors, once established, are maintained at the desired level of performance by application of an appropriate schedule of reinforcement.

Shaping. To be effective, reinforcers must be contingent upon the occurrence of the desired performance; that is, a reinforcer is not delivered until the desired behavior is performed. However, in situations in which complex skills are being learned, the desired performance initially does not occur, so it cannot be reinforced in order to increase it. This problem of the first occurrence is solved by the use of a shaping procedure.

With a shaping procedure, closer and closer approximations to the desired performance are consecutively reinforced. An excellent example of a shaping procedure used in an academic program is the handwriting program developed by Barber (Brigham, Finfrock, Breunig & Bushell, 1972). This program teaches handwriting skills in three steps: tracing, copying, and independent handwriting. Each of these three steps can be viewed on a broad level as a closer approximation to the final skill, but also with each step smaller successive approximations to the printing of letters can be found. Figure 4–12 illustrates the sequence of successive steps within the tracing portion of the program.

The early frames actually are tubes containing dotted lines, and the learner draws a solid line over the dotted line staying within the tube. For example, below are frames 1 and 9.

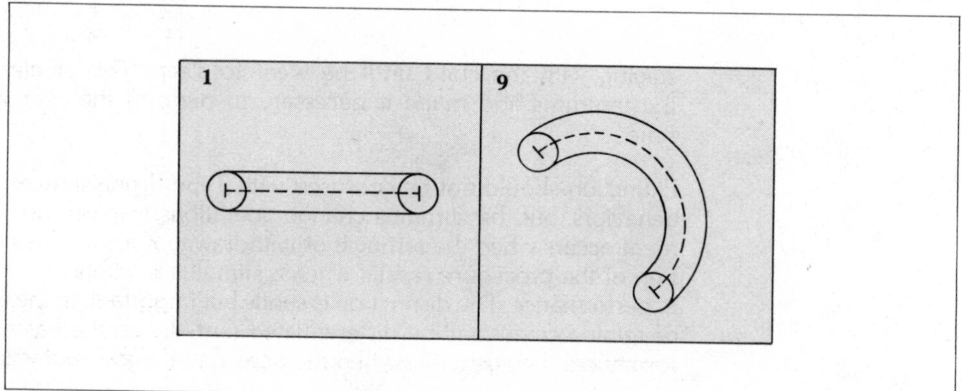

When the behavior to be learned has a low or no probability of happening, shaping is used to establish the desired performance through a progression of steps. This technique has proved very valuable in academic situations because many goals in the classroom require the establishment of complex skills that the student initially cannot perform. By using a shaping procedure, an instructor can teach the complex skills more effectively and efficiently than would otherwise be possible.

Schedule of reinforcement. Much learning research in the laboratory utilizes reinforcement on a continuous basis; that is, a reinforcer is given to the subject each

FIGURE 4–12
Sample figures from 24 of 32 steps in the handwriting program

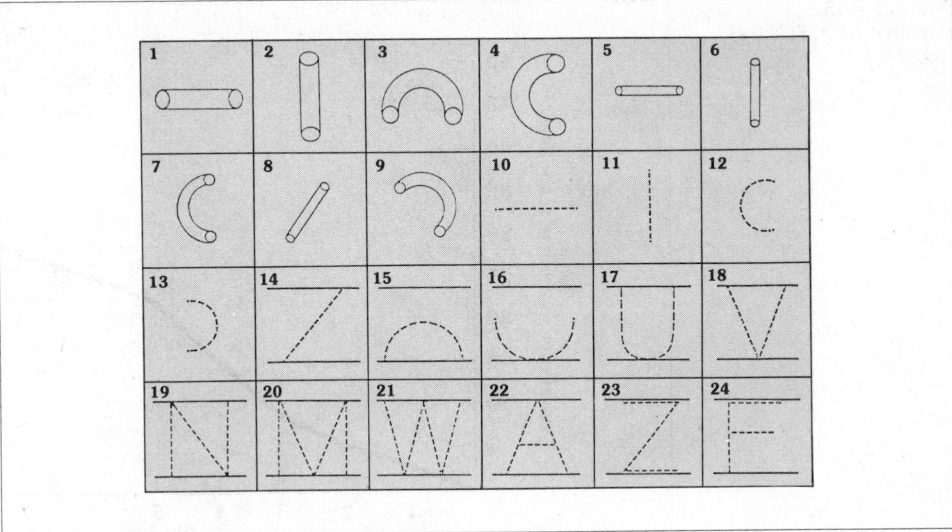

Source: Brigham, Finfrock, Breunig, and Bushell (1972).

time the behavior under study occurs. Yet in the real world outside the lab, this contingency seldom holds and reinforcements are administered on a more intermittent basis. These contingencies of reinforcement, whether continuous or intermittent, are referred to as "schedules of reinforcement."

We now turn to a consideration of the effects of reinforcement schedules on the performance of a behavior. First, we define the basic schedules. Previous mention has been made of the continuous schedule of reinforcement, where every occurrence of the behavior produces a reinforcer. This schedule produces the fastest increase in the frequency of a behavior. Continuous reinforcement is the best schedule to facilitate the learning of a new skill; however, as stated earlier, this schedule rarely is found operating in the world outside the psychologist's laboratory. More often than not, the schedule of reinforcement maintaining any behavior is some sort of intermittent schedule. These intermittent schedules can be categorized into two basic types: ratio and interval schedules. Ratio schedules are based on the number of responses emitted, and interval schedules are based on the passage of time. Ratio and interval schedules can be further subdivided into fixed and variable schedules. Fixed schedules are ones in which the ratio or interval required for reinforcement remains constant, whereas variable schedules have ratios or intervals that vary around some average value.

Each schedule of reinforcement produces a characteristic performance expressed as the *rate* of responding. These distinctive rates are best illustrated by a cumulative record such as the one shown in Figure 4–13. Notice that each point is not plotted from zero on the vertical axis as with noncumulative graphs, but rather moves cumulatively from the preceding *(X,Y)* coordinate. For example, at point A we see that four hours have elapsed and a total of 15 responses have occurred. Between points A and B, one hour expired and approximately six responses occurred.

Figure 4–14 illustrates the characteristic performance produced by each of the four basic intermittent schedules. The slope of the line reflects the rate of responding,

FIGURE 4–13
Hypothetical cumulative record

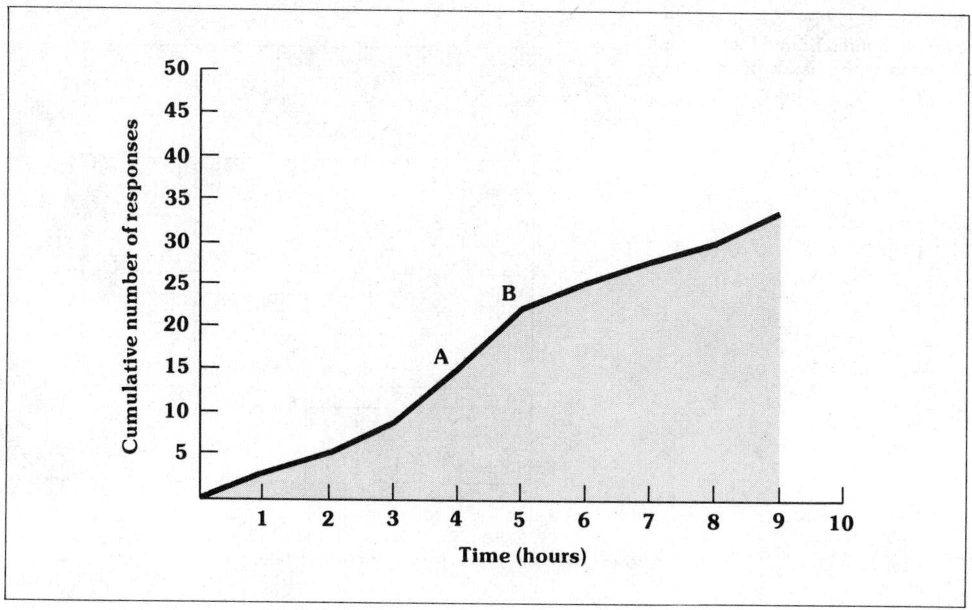

and the small graph in the lower right-hand corner indicates rates for various representative slopes. Additionally, the slash marks on each of the lines denote the occurrence of reinforcement.

Fixed ratio. On this schedule a reinforcement occurs every time the specified number of responses is performed. For example, a fixed ratio of 20 means that a reinforcer

FIGURE 4–14
Stylized records of responding under basic schedules of reinforcement

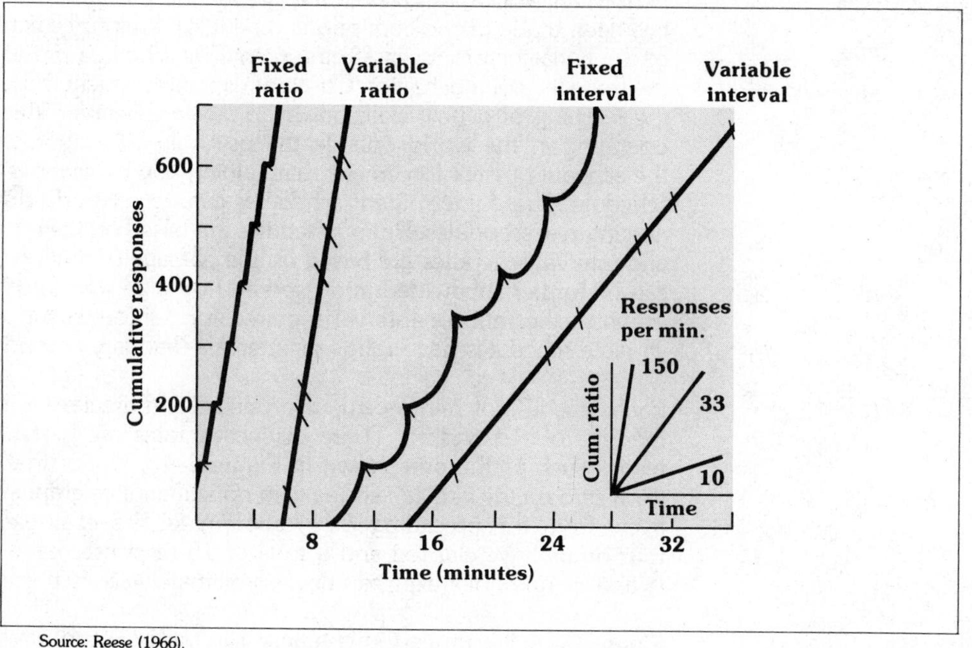

Source: Reese (1966).

will be delivered after 20 responses occur, then after the next 20, and so on. A fixed ratio of 75 would mean delivery of a reinforcer contingent upon the person performing the behavior 75 times, and after the occurrence of another 75, and so on, without the ratio varying.

Fixed-ratio schedules result in high steady rates of responding characterized by a pause in the responding immediately after the occurrence of a reinforcer. In other words, after the delivery of a reinforcer on a fixed-ratio schedule, the person stops responding. The length of this pause in responding on a fixed ratio schedule is a function of the magnitude of the ratio.

Variable ratio. With a variable-ratio schedule, the ratio varies around some average value. Suppose the schedule has a variable ratio of five, then one time a reinforcer is given after, say, three responses, then seven, then eight, then two. As you see, the number of responses necessary to produce a reinforcer varies around some average.

Of the four basic intermittent schedules, variable-ratio schedules produce the highest rate of responding. The rate on a variable ratio is a high sustained rate of responding without the pauses after reinforcement that are typical of the fixed-ratio schedule of reinforcement.

Fixed interval. In the beginning of this section, the interval schedule was described as being based on the passage of time. While this is true, it does not mean that reinforcement is delivered noncontingently after the elapse of a specified amount of time, rather the first response to occur after the time interval produces a reinforcer. An interval schedule is independent of the number of responses, since regardless of the number of responses emitted none will yield a reinforcer until the specified time interval has elapsed.

A fixed-interval schedule has an interval that does not vary, so that whatever the length of the interval, when it elapses the first response produces a reinforcer. Upon delivery, the same interval length starts anew, and when it elapses the first response to occur will result in a reinforcer. Fixed-interval schedules produce low overall response rates with pauses after reinforcement that give the cumulative record curve a characteristic scalloped effect.

Variable interval. A variable-interval schedule is an interval schedule in which the interval changes around some average value. The rate of responding produced by a variable interval is a low sustained rate without the pauses of the fixed-interval schedule.

In comparing these basic schedules, several regularities concerning response rates stand out. Each schedule produces a characteristic and distinctive rate of responding. Both ratio schedules produce a high rate of responding, while interval schedules result in lower response rates. Fixed schedules, ratio and interval, result in a distinct pause after reinforcement that is not present on variable schedules. Now we will move to a consideration of schedule effects on performance under conditions of extinction.

Schedules and extinction. The rate at which the performance of a response will decrease in extinction is a function of several variables—the number of prior reinforcers associated with the response and the schedule used to administer those reinforcers.

Here we will be concerned only with the effects of reinforcement schedules on responding in extinction. These effects can be summarized as:

1. Behaviors reinforced on a continuous schedule have the quickest decrease in response rate in extinction of the basic schedules.
2. The rate of responding in extinction following a ratio schedule tends to exhibit a burst of responding soon after extinction begins, with the intensity and frequency of these bursts decreasing as time into extinction increases.
3. Interval schedules tend to result in a slow, steady decline of responding in extinction.

Schedules and daily life. Schedules of reinforcement abound in our daily life or, as we referred to it earlier, the real world. Vending machines (most of them, anyhow!) pay off on a continuous schedule. The Las Vegas slot machine operates on a variable-ratio schedule, which explains why a slot machine "junkie" stands there and drops quarters into the slot at a rapid rate. Given the typical college course in which the instructor gives a midterm and final exam, you will find most students studying on a fixed-interval schedule. Studying immediately before the midterm or final has a very high probability of occurrence (most students recognizing this high probability refer to the phenomenon of cramming!), however, studying right after one of the exams has a very low probability (the typical post-reinforcement pause of a fixed interval). Another illustration of a fixed-interval schedule is found in the work habits of Congress (Weisberg & Waldrop, 1972). The enactment of legislation has its highest frequency just prior to adjournment. The rate of enactment is lowest

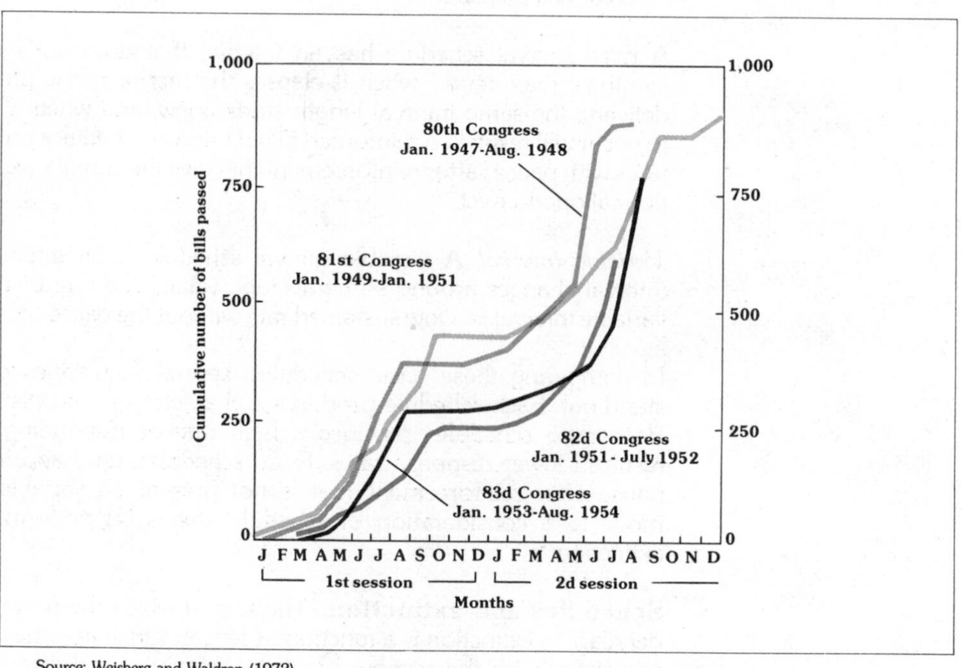

FIGURE 4–15
Cumulative number of bills passed during the legislative sessions of Congress from January 1947 to August 1954

Source: Weisberg and Waldrop (1972).

immediately following return from adjournment, thus producing the scallop effect of a fixed-interval schedule. This reinforcement schedule for Congress is shown in Figure 4–15.

In the classroom a teacher could utilize different reinforcement schedules to promote desired learning goals. To do this, the teacher must match the desired performance outcome to the appropriate schedule of reinforcement. If a shaping procedure is used to facilitate the acquisition of a new skill, then a continuous schedule is most effective. Those tasks necessitating rapid performance call for reinforcement on a ratio schedule. An interval schedule is best suited for tasks requiring persistence in the face of adversity, where reinforcers are scarce.

Stimulus control

In operant conditioning behaviors are increased or decreased according to the effects they have upon the environment of the person. So, we say that operant behaviors are under the control of their consequences; yet operant behaviors followed by a reinforcer, while becoming more frequent, are not performed on random occasions. Rather, operant behaviors tend to occur more frequently in certain stimulus situations. We say that they become associated with or are under the control of antecedent stimuli.

There is a difference in the nature of stimulus control in operant and respondent conditioning. According to operant theory, stimuli do not elicit operant behaviors as they do respondent behaviors. Instead, stimuli are said to set the occasion for operant behaviors. In those stimulus situations in which a behavior is followed by a reinforcer, the behavior becomes more probable in the presence of the stimulus, and thus it is said that the stimulus *sets the occasion* for the performance of the behavior.

Two opposite processes are said to comprise stimulus control: generalization and discrimination. Generalization occurs when different but similar stimuli come to control a common response. Discrimination occurs when similar but different stimuli come to control different responses.

Generalization. At the most basic level generalization occurs on the basis of similarity between stimuli, for example:

This is a wog.

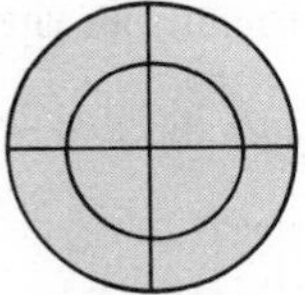

Which of these is a wog? A or B?

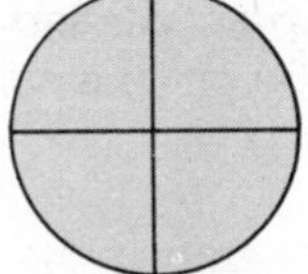

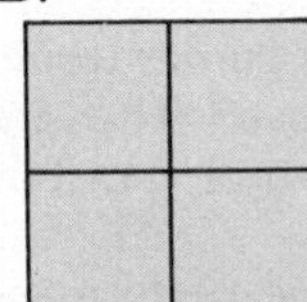

Most people would choose A because A looks most like the example of the wog. The advantage of generalization should be apparent. No two environment situations are ever identical, so if a behavior learned in one stimulus situation did not generalize to similar stimulus situations, then we will spend all of our time learning how to behave in all slightly different situations.

Generalization is strengthened or maintained through the use of reinforcement. The following diagram illustrates the basic model for teaching a generalization.

$$\left.\begin{matrix}S_1\\ S_2\\ S_n\end{matrix}\right] \cdot R_1 \longrightarrow S^R$$

Generalization has been described by Francis Mechner (1967, p. 85) as "the technical term for what is commonly called 'seeing similarities,' 'noticing common elements,' or 'disregarding differences.' " Getting into and driving a friend's car even though you have never been in it before is an example of generalization. So is the example of the young child who calls every dog "Bowser," the name of the family pet. With generalization, control of the behavior is shifted to stimulus situations differing from the original situation in which the behavior was reinforced.

Discrimination. If generalization is, as Mechner says, "seeing similarities," then discrimination is "seeing differences." We previously defined discrimination as responding differentially to two similar but different stimuli. The following diagram illustrates the basic model for teaching a discrimination:

$$\begin{matrix}S_1 \cdot R_1 \longrightarrow S^R\\ S_2 \cdot R_1 \not\longrightarrow S^R\end{matrix}$$

The following are some simple examples of discriminations:

1. Multiplying, instead of adding or subtracting, two numbers occurring with an ×.
2. Calling a friend's correct name upon seeing that friend.
3. Passing the bottle with white granules, instead of the one with black granules, when asked for the salt.
4. Stating the correct number, when shown any numeral between 0 and 9.

An effective means for teaching a difficult discrimination is the matching-to-sample technique. One such difficult discrimination for a young child is between the lowercase b and d. The basic matching-to-sample procedure would resemble the following:

Find the letter below that is just like the letter in the box on the left

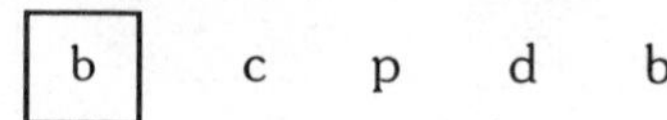

Of course, the learner would be given more practice, and finally the sample to match would be removed. Then the learner would be given a sample of letters and required to identify the b or d or both.

Chaining. The performance of complex operant behaviors involves a very subtle form of stimulus control involving discrimination. These complex behaviors can be analyzed in a chain of simpler responses in which each response produces the stimulus that controls the succeeding response.

Gilbert (1962) represents long division as the following response chain:

$S_1 \longrightarrow$	R_2	$S_2 \longrightarrow$	R_3	$S_3 \longrightarrow$	R_4
$d \div n$	Set up problem	$n\overline{)d}$	Estimate quotient and place it	$\begin{array}{r} q \\ n\overline{)d} \end{array}$	Find product and place it
$S_4 \longrightarrow$	R_5				
$\begin{array}{r} q \\ n\overline{)d} \\ \underline{p} \end{array}$	Subtract to get remainder				

Reprinted by permission of the author.

Notice that response 4, find product and place it, occurs only after the person has established the appropriate stimulus situation by performing response three, estimate quotient and place it. By analyzing a complex behavior into a chain of simpler responses, the student can be taught each simpler response individually and then the correct sequence in which to perform them.

SOCIAL LEARNING THEORY

Behavioristic theories of learning have had a difficult time explaining the human ability to rapidly master a complex behavioral performance. Operant analyses, perhaps the most successful, have tended to rely on chaining and shaping as the explanatory mechanisms for this phenomenon. Chaining, while it appears to describe fairly accurately the processes involved in the execution of a complex behavior, offers little explanation of how the performance was initially acquired. The burden in explaining the rapid acquisition of complex performances has fallen to the concept of shaping. As we saw earlier in this chapter, reinforcement in shaping is given for closer and closer approximations to the desired terminal behavior. This technique has been demonstrated to be effective in the acquisition of a wide variety of human behaviors from walking (O'Brien, Azrin & Bugle, 1972) to social behaviors like sharing (Cooke & Apolloni, 1976). The problem is that shaping, even though effective, is a slow process involving many trials and reinforcers, so it still does not account for the rapid acquisition of a complex behavior.

The ability to adequately handle the problem of rapid acquisition, as well as other issues in learning, has made social learning theory important in modern psychology. Observational learning, or how a person learns from observing the performance of another person, has been the central concept in social learning theory. Learning from observation is a very important concept in understanding how humans so quickly acquire complex performances without long periods of practice.

The leading exponent of social learning theory is Albert Bandura. A classic study by Bandura (1965) demonstrates quite well several of the basic principles of the theory. In this study children observed a filmed model engaging in a series of verbally and physically aggressive behaviors. The children were divided into three treatment groups differentiated on the basis of the effects of the observed model's aggression. One group of children saw a model who was severely punished for aggressive behavior. The second group observed a model receiving lavish praise and numerous delectable rewards for aggression. The other treatment group saw a film with no particular consequential stimuli following the display of aggressive behavior.

After viewing the film, all the children were tested to determine how much, if any, of the aggressive behavior they would imitate. The groups that saw the model reinforced or given no consequence performed significantly more aggressive behaviors than did the group that saw the model punished for aggressive behavior. Upon completion of this first test of imitative performance, the children in all three groups were then offered an incentive to imitate the aggressive behaviors they had previously observed. This addition of an incentive eliminated the differences in imitation of aggression among the three groups.

From this example we see a very important implication of observational learning—the consequences of a model's actions influence the performance of an imitative response, not the learning of such a response. In the Bandura study the children who saw the model punished were less likely than the other children to perform the punished acts. However, when they were offered an incentive to display the observed aggressive behaviors, they performed them as well as the other children. Apparently they had learned the behaviors but were not inclined to perform them.

Outcomes of observational learning

Liebert (1972) has described observational learning as resulting in two major classes of possible performance outcomes: imitation and counterimitation. Imitation occurs when the observer becomes more likely to perform the model's behavior or some other similar actions, whereas with counterimitation the observer is less likely to perform the modeled or similar behaviors. Liebert further subdivides both imitation and counterimitation into two more subclasses of performance.

Imitation consists of direct imitation and disinhibition. If an observer is more likely to copy the specific actions of a model after exposure to that model, then it is direct imitation; however, if there is an increase in the likelihood of imitating other actions in the same general class as the observed behavior, then it is disinhibition. Consider the young child who watches an older sibling take a handful of cookies and run out to play after their mother had informed them that they must wait until after supper for sweets. Now if the young child sneaks some cookies before supper too, it is direct imitation. But if the younger child is now more inclined to disobey this and other commands of the mother, it would be disinhibition. From this example we can conclude that disinhibition represents effects that go beyond those of direct imitation.

Counterimitation, as the name implies, occurs when the observer is less likely to perform the observed behavior of a model. Analogous to direct imitation, there is a direct counterimitation effect. There is also an inhibitory rather than a disinhibitory effect. Returning to our preceding illustration, imagine that the older sibling was caught with his hand in the cookie jar, was sent to his room to remain until supper, and was not allowed to have any cookies for dessert that night. What do you think would be the effects on the younger child in this case? Most probably the child would not be inclined to take any cookies, and if so this effect would be one of direct counterimitation. Furthermore if the effects went beyond this specific action and the child is now less likely to violate any of the mother's rules, it would be an inhibition effect.

Processes in [illegible]vational [illegible]g

Learning from observation is a complex process resulting in a varied set of outcomes depending on the context in which it occurs. Imitative effects do not occur in all social situations, and a sophisticated theory is necessary to explain such a complex

FIGURE 4–16
A social learning theory analysis of the processes in learning from observation

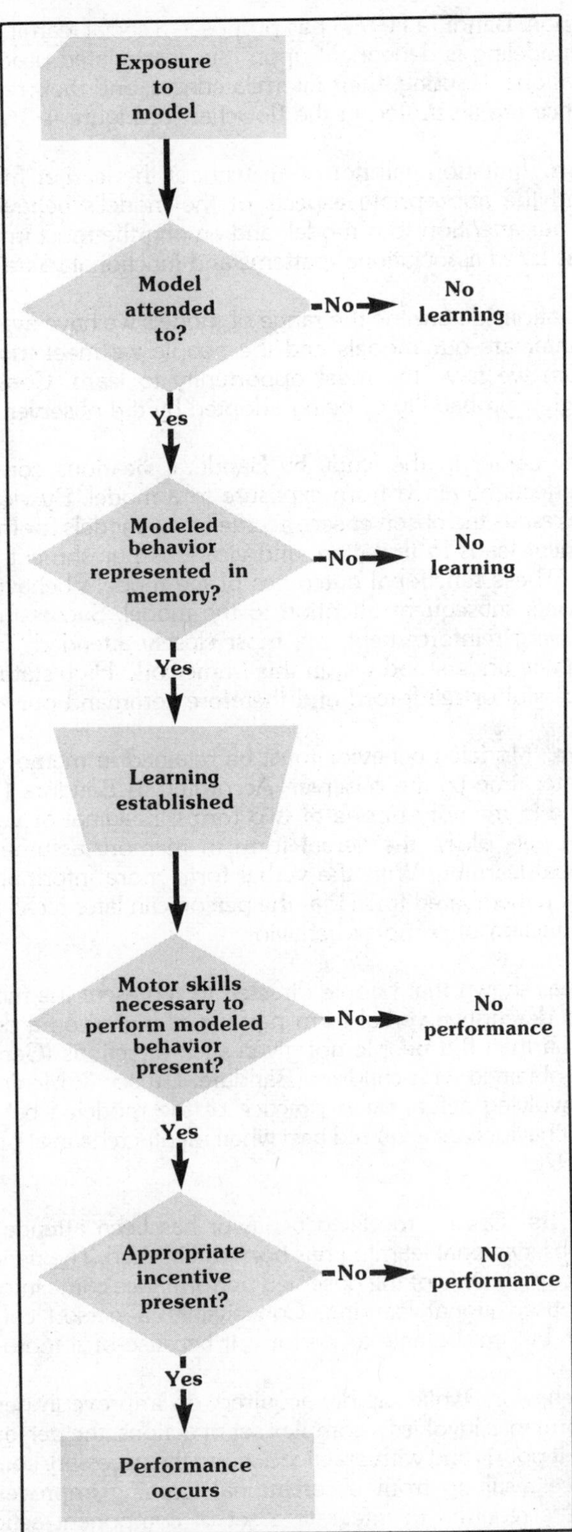

phenomenon. Bandura (1977) has proposed a social learning theory in which learning through modeling is dependent upon four interrelated processes. The four processes in observational learning, their interrelatedness, and their relationship to learning and performance are illustrated in the flowchart of Figure 4–16.

Attention. Imitation will not occur without the learner first having attended to the model and the appropriate aspects of the model's behavior. A number of factors influence our attention to a model, and among the most important of these Bandura (1973) has listed associational patterns and functional value of the modeled behavior.

Our associations determine the range of models we have available to us. Other people we encounter are our models and the people we meet most regularly are the ones from whom we have the most opportunity to learn. Consequently their behaviors have a higher probability of being adopted by the observer.

As we saw earlier in the study by Bandura, vicarious consequences determine the imitative effects obtained from exposure to a model. By vicarious consequences it is meant the results the observer sees accrue to the models for the performance. Vicarious reinforcement leads to imitation, and vicarious punishment leads to counterimitative outcomes. These functional outcomes of the model's behavior furthermore influence the observer's subsequent attention to the model. Successful models, the ones most often receiving reinforcement, are most closely attended. The appeal of high-status models can be understood within this framework. High-status models are more likely to be successful or reinforced and therefore command our attentiveness.

Retention. Modeled behavior must be retained in memory if it is to be performed at some later time by the observer. According to Bandura (1977), behavior patterns are retained in memory in one of two forms: imaginal or verbal terms. Especially as the person gets older, the verbal form in memory assumed greater importance in observational learning. With the verbal form more information can be remembered in an easily remembered form that the person can later recall and use as self-directions in the production of complex behavior.

Research has shown that people directed to represent the modeled behavior in either imagery or descriptive verbal form performed higher on a delayed test of behavioral reproduction than did people not given such directions (Gerst, 1971). Similar effects have been obtained with children (Bandura, Grusec & Menlove, 1966). Furthermore, research involving actual overt practice of the modeled behavior has demonstrated that such behaviors are acquired best when mental rehearsal precedes the overt practice (Jeffrey, 1976).

Motor skills. Once a modeled behavior has been attended to and represented in memory, observational learning has been established. The person's ability to reproduce the motor components of the observed performance come into play in the performance phase of observational learning. Conceivably, a person could learn a behavior by observation but not be able to perform it because of a motor deficiency.

Imitated behaviors, while rapidly acquired, do improve in performance with practice. If the performance involves a complex set of actions, the person may lack a component or perform it poorly and with practice acquire the necessary component. More probably, performance resulting from observational learning improves with practice because the person is required to integrate a set of component actions previously acquired in separate contexts. The person must now develop and learn the cues that will coordinate these particular components into an integrated sequence of actions.

Incentive. We have seen earlier that the vicarious or observed consequences of the modeled behavior have a large influence on the performance of the observer. Vicarious consequences lead to expectations on the part of the observer. Consequently, the observer is motivated to perform behaviors that lead to reinforcement for the model because the observer also expects to be reinforced for such actions. Vicarious punishment results in counterimitative effects because the observer expects direct punishment for these acts.

Bandura (1971) describes an important effect that vicarious reinforcement has on the incentive value of direct reinforcement. We develop an expectation about the level of reinforcement to be received for a given performance by observing what other people receive for performance of that action. In this manner the effectiveness of direct reinforcement in a diversity of situations is influenced. If the anticipated reinforcement falls below the person's expectation established through observation, performance is unlikely to occur.

FIGURE 4–17
Learning by imitation

Social learning theory has its origins in the behaviorist perspective on learning and this orientation is evident in its emphasis on reinforcement. Both learning and performance are influenced by reinforcement. We attend more closely to models who are reinforced for their actions, consequently we are more likely to learn from them. Through the process of observing a model we develop an expectation for the likelihood of reinforcement and the level of reinforcement (Figure 4–17). Incentive for performance occurs when the anticipated reinforcement in a particular situation meets or exceeds our expectation for that situation.

In important ways social learning theory has come to resemble modern cognitive conceptions of learning. The common element is the emphasis on the importance of representing the modeled behavior in memory. Retention and consequently later performance of a modeled action are facilitated when the observer is encouraged to mentally rehearse the action. In this regard social learning theory represents a bridge from behaviorist to cognitive theories of learning, and so it is with this theory that we end this chapter on the behaviorist perspective on learning. Chapter 5 will be an exposition of the cognitive perspective on learning. Attention will focus on the mental activities in learning and remembering that mediate between environmental stimulation and performance by the learner.

5. From a social learning theory perspective, should students be complimented by the teacher privately or in front of the class? Why?

SUMMARY

In this chapter we defined learning as an internal state of the person that makes possible specific performance capabilities. Factors to be considered by the teacher in making decisions about learning are the number of observations, level of performance, and conditions surrounding the performance. The behaviorist model of learning was presented and seen to involve two types of theories: contiguity and reinforcement theories. Contiguity theories postulate that an association between a stimulus and response is formed when the two occur in a close relationship of time or space. Reinforcement theories emphasize the consequences of a response in a given situation as the major determinant of an association. Finally, social learning theory was presented as a bridge between behaviorist and cognitivist constructions of the learning process. According to this view, learning by observation is facilitated when the observer attends to and mentally represents in some form the actions of the model.

SELF-TEST

1. Mr. Wolf, the drama teacher, noticed that four times during rehearsal of the first act Nelson had to look at his script. Mr. Wolf wisely concluded that Nelson needed more practice. What was amiss in the conditions surrounding Nelson's performance that led Mr. Wolf to infer that the desired learning had not occurred?
2. Which of the following is *not* an example of learning?
   a. Shivering when cold.
   b. Swinging a golf club.
   c. Preferring a book to television.
   d. Gardening.
3. A student is shown a square, a triangle, and a rectangle and he calls both the square and the rectangle "square." Apparently *four sides* was functioning as:
   a. A conditioned stimulus.
   b. A functional stimulus.
   c. A nominal stimulus.
   d. A prompt.
4. Which of the following is most probably the product of classical conditioning?
   a. Learning to make pottery.
   b. Enjoying classical music.

   c. Memorizing a poem.
   d. Printing one's name.

5. In which of the examples below would forgetting occur most rapidly?
   a. Student keeps reciting a poem even after she has said it twice without error.
   b. Student memorizes a passage out of *Time* magazine.
   c. Student memorizes a paragraph in a foreign language in which she is not conversant.
6. An infant will spend more time looking at a novel stimulus than a familiar stimulus. Apparently for infants a novel stimulus functions as:
   a. Positive reinforcement.
   b. Negative reinforcement.
   c. Type I punisher.
   d. Type II punisher.
7. Everytime Bob slurped his soup his mother made him leave the table. After five occurrences of this treatment, Bob quit slurping his soup. This is an example of:
   a. Positive reinforcement.
   b. Negative reinforcement.
   c. Type I punisher.
   d. Type II punisher.
8. Behaviorists advocate not using punishment in schools. State three reasons for this
9. A wine taster notices subtle flavors in a wine that most of us overlook. This illustrates:
   a. Discrimination.
   b. Generalization.
   c. Extinction.
   d. The nominal stimulus.
10. Ms. Lake, the high school principal, plans to hold a nonsmoking clinic at the school. She wants to obtain a guest speaker to relate personal experiences with smoking to the students. What would be the criterion for selecting such a speaker according to social learning theory?

ANSWER KEY TO BOXED QUESTIONS

1. Learning is an *internal state* of the person that makes possible the *performance of behavior* in a given situation *resulting from experience* in that situation. So all three are critical attributes of a definition of learning.
2. Learning makes possible performance, and learning is inferred from the observation of performance. Learning is the initial acquisition of an internal state, and remembering is the storage and activation of previously learned internal states.
3. Wasp sting ⟶ Fear
   UCS UCR
   ↕
   CS
   Back porch
   Back porch Fear
   CS ⟶ CR
4. *a.* Type I punishment
   b. Negative reinforcement
   c. Type II punishment
   d. Positive reinforcement
   e. Type I punishment
5. Students should be complimented in front of the class. Social learning theory views vicarious reinforcement as important in the learning and performance of imitative behavior.

ANSWER KEY TO SELF-TEST

1. Nelson needed the script as a cue for some of his lines. In the real situation in which Nelson is to perform, we do not want him to use such stimulus cues.
2. *a*
3. *b*
4. *b*
5. *c*
6. *a*
7. *d*
8. Behaviorists do not advocate punishment because it leads to withdrawal or escape, aggression, or negative self-statements.
9. *a*
10. Social learning theory would say to select a model with high status to the students. High-status models are more closely attended to and therefore the observer is more likely to learn from them.

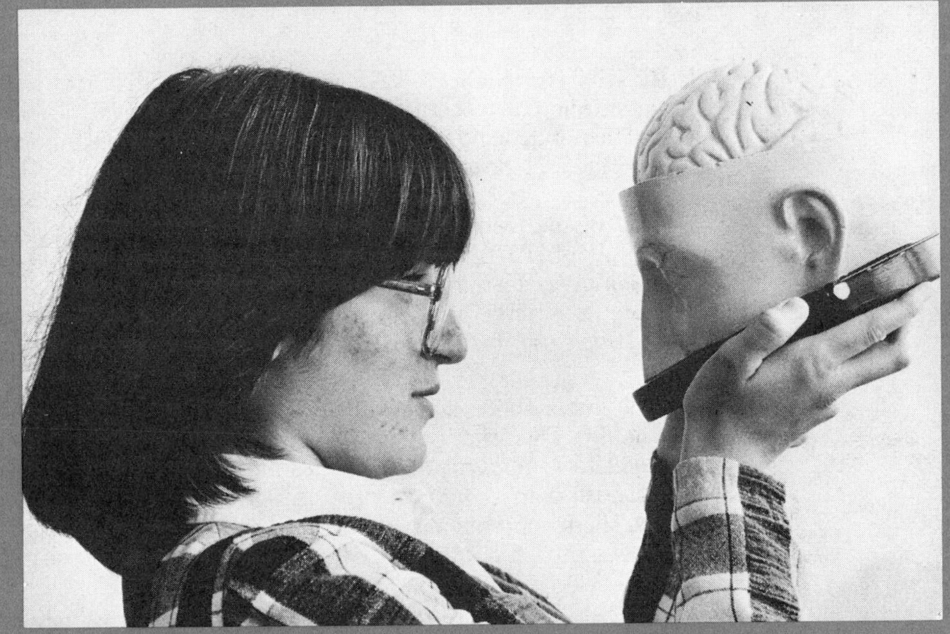

Chapter 5

The process of learning: Cognitivist perspective

COGNITIVE FORMULATIONS OF LEARNING stress the role of mental activities intervening between the environment and the person's action upon that environment. While not denying the importance of environmental influences upon the learner, cognitive theories do not give these influences the central role in explaining learning outcomes as do behaviorist theories. Instead cognitive explanations stress the critical role of the learner's activities in determining what is learned from any experience. Rothkopf (1970, p. 325) summarized the importance of a person's activities in determining the learning outcome of a situation very succinctly and humorously in his paraphrasing of an old adage: "You can lead a horse to water but the only water that gets into his stomach is what he drinks."

The first modern expression of a cognitive interpretation of learning was Gestalt psychology. This school of psychology was a reaction against the attempts of other psychologies to analyze mental activities into more basic elements. Gestalt psychologists believed that there was an organization or pattern to mental activity that went beyond the mere components, that to break these activities down into components and then to study each component separately destroyed the meaning that is the organization.

This view led to the famous Gestalt principle: the whole is more than the sum of its parts. Learning to a Gestalt psychologist was not the "stamping in" of an association between a stimulus and response by contiguity; rather, it was an organization of the various elements in a situation by the learner into a meaningful whole or pattern.

After reading this chapter you should be able to accomplish the following objectives.

1. Describe the structures and processes of the human information-processing system.
2. Specify the major causes of forgetting.
3. Identify the major qualitative changes in cognitive structures according to developmental theories of cognitive growth.
4. Describe the relationship between acquired knowledge and new learning.

AN OVERVIEW OF HUMAN INFORMATION PROCESSING

At present the cognitive perspective in psychology is experiencing very rapid growth covering the entire spectrum of human intellectual activities. At the core of most cognitive interpretations of learning and thinking is the memory system. The predominant model that has emerged from this research is the information-processing model. In this model of cognitive functioning the human information-processing system is viewed as analogous to the computer in many important ways.

The analogy between people and computers is not one of physical resemblance, but rather resemblance in operation. Both the computer and a person receive information from an environment, change this information into another form, store it for later use, retrieve the stored information at some later date, and use it in some manner. The value of the analogy between humans and computers as information processors has been stated by Hayes (1978, p. 135) as:

> . . . they provide an alternative to the black-box model which ignores internal processes. The fact that computers are complex and yet have objectively describable inner processes seems to have given us confidence that humans may have describable inner processes as well. We can use information processing models, then, to propose descriptions for the contents of the unopenable black-box.

The human information-processing system is composed of two components: structures and processes. Most cognitive theorists use the three memory structures first postulated by Atkinson and Shiffrin (1968): the sensory register, short-term store, and long-term store. These three structures are invariant features of the system and serve distinct functions in information processing. It should be noted that not all theorists accept this multistore model of memory, and many have offered different models [see Craik & Lockhart (1972) for an alternative memory model].

Processes are the operations at the disposal of the person for controlling the flow of information through the system. The processes determine the fate of information entering the human information-processing system and are largely under the voluntary control of the person, hence the importance of the person as an active agent in learning according to the cognitive perspective. Figure 5–1 is a simplified illustration of the human information-processing system, showing the structures and the processes relating the structures.

Let us briefly trace the path of an input through the human information-processing system. First, the informational input enters the sensory register and is held for a very brief time as a replica of the original environmental stimulus. Some of the information in the sensory register is selected by attention and transferred by pattern recognition to short-term store. Notice, as illustrated in Figure 5–1, that pattern recognition involves retrieving meaning about the incoming information from long-term store and sending this additional information to short-term store.

Once in short-term store, information is stored for a brief time and then is displaced by new incoming information unless rehearsal takes place. The input will be retained in short-term memory as long as rehearsal takes place. While in short-term store, information judged important by the individual will be encoded and sent to long-term store for permanent storage until it is needed at some future time.

In the following section the functions of each memory structure and the control processes in the acquisition and retention of new information will be examined. Since our definition of learning, stated in the preceding chapter, stressed the relative permanence of learning, the emphasis in our discussion will be upon short-term and long-

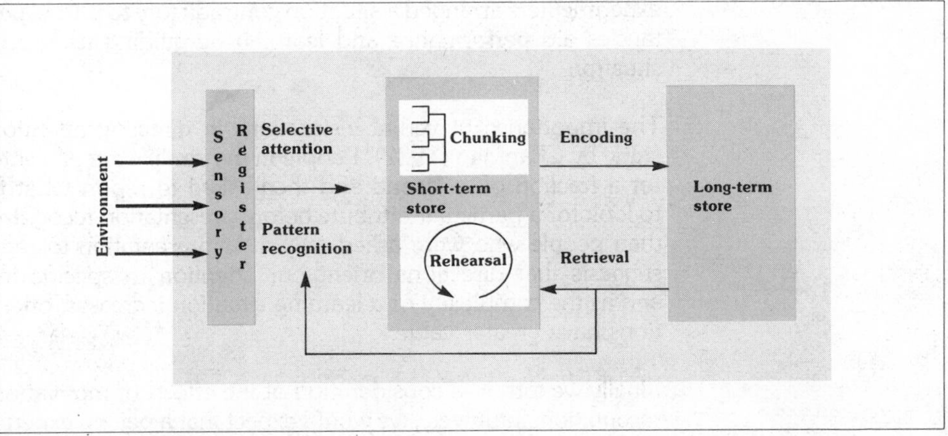

FIGURE 5–1
Information-processing model of human memory

term stores and the control processes for transferring information from the former into the latter. Additionally, the process of remembering or accessing information in long-term store for use in performing a skill will be examined.

Following the exposition of the human information-processing system in operation, attention will be given to theories that attempt to describe the way in which existing knowledge affects learning. Essentially these theories state that what is learned in any given situation is determined largely by what information the person already possesses in long-term store. We have named these theories *cognitive structure theories.*

SENSORY REGISTER AND INFORMATION TRANSFER TO SHORT-TERM MEMORY

The sensory register is the structure through which information about the world enters the information-processing system. Presumably, there is a corresponding register for each sense modality; however, research has focused primarily on the visual or iconic store and the auditory store. A series of ingenious experiments by Sperling (1960) determined the major attributes of the iconic store as: (1) unlimited capacity for information, (2) very rapid loss of information, and (3) no assigned meaning for information represented as raw sensations.

For information in the sensory register to be sent to short-term store, it must be selected and given meaning by the person. These processes are referred to as *attention* and *pattern recognition,* respectively. The information that will be attended to in a given situation and the meaning assigned to it are determined to a large extent by the person's expectancy in that situation. An expectancy is an awareness, belief, or anticipation that some event is very likely to occur in a given situation. Expectancies arise from three sources: (1) prior experiences or learning, (2) directions given to the person, and (3) motivation of the person.

A theme that will emerge throughout this book in various forms is that a person's current knowledge plays a critical role in determining what that person learns from any experience. Knowledge acquired through prior learning affects new learning in an important way by influencing the processes of attention and pattern recognition. For example, Bruner and Postman (1949) presented people with playing cards for a fraction of a second with the colors either reversed (black diamonds and red spades) or correct. The reversed cards were more difficult to recognize. Apparently people were attending to color because past experiences told them to expect red diamonds and black spades. Expectancy hindered performance in this case simply because the experimenters arranged a situation contradictory to past experience, but typically expectancies aid performance and learning by guiding us to important information in a situation.

The importance of verbal instructions in directing attention was demonstrated in a study by Chapman (1932). People in the study were presented with visual information for a fraction of a second and then asked to report what they saw. People directed to look for a particular attribute before presentation recognized it with greater accuracy than people who were asked only after presentation to report on that attribute. This suggests that directions orient our attention to specific information in a situation, and as the complexity of a learning situation increases, orienting stimuli such as directions have greater value.

Finally we turn to a consideration of the effects of motivation on attention and pattern recognition. Intuitively, we would expect that a person experiencing a particular motivational state would be more sensitive, or "tuned in," to goal objects associated with that motive. For example, when do you think you would be more likely to notice a McDonald's billboard? Immediately following your lunch or six hours after lunch? Research supports our intuition regarding motivation and attention (McClelland & Liberman, 1949; Wispé & Drambarean, 1953). In a state of motivational arousal we attend more closely to relevant information and select it for further processing.

1. Expectancies or learning sets can arise from which of the following sources?
   a. Prior experiences.
   b. Verbal directions.
   c. Motivation.
   d. All of the above.

SHORT-TERM MEMORY

Short-term memory is the immediate memory in our cognitive system and is characterized by three important attributes. Here, information resides while it is being used by a person, and this has led to the alternate name of *working memory*. Representation of the information in short-term memory is acoustical. Short-term memory is the bottleneck in the information-processing system because of its limited capacity. For information to be maintained in short-term memory it must be rehearsed periodically. Let us look at each of these characteristics of short-term or working memory more closely.

Conrad (1964) demonstrated that retention errors in short-term memory were due to acoustical similarities. He presented a series of letters visually and asked a person to recall all of them. Errors were based on acoustical features and not visual properties. For example, a person may mistakenly recall a T for a C, whereas an error based on visual features would be a response of G for C. Apparently, visual information is converted to auditory information for use in short-term store. As you read this page you are performing this process. Notice that you are transforming the print into sounds by saying the words to yourself.

Information in short-term store that goes unrehearsed is forgotten within a matter of seconds. Suppose you are calling someone whom you have never called before. Obviously you do not know the person's number, so you look it up in the telephone directory. Next you have to put the directory down in order to dial the number. You say the number once or twice in the interval between putting the directory down and dialing the number, and with this small amount of rehearsal you experience no trouble in retaining the number. But what would happen if immediately after you found the desired listing in the directory and had read it once, something prevented you from rehearsing the number again? How long do you think you would be able to remember the number with just this initial exposure? In an ingenious study, Peterson and Peterson (1959) duplicated this type of situation under controlled laboratory conditions. They were able to demonstrate that there is very little or no retention in short-term memory beyond an 18-second interval without rehearsal. In this study a person was shown a trigram briefly and then required to count backwards by threes from some specified number, thereby effectively blocking rehearsal. After a retention interval of 0–18 seconds, the person was asked to recall the trigram. Recall steadily decreased to less than 20 percent by 18 seconds.

Information could theoretically be retained indefinitely in short-term store by rehearsal. However, because of the limited capacity of short-term memory for information, this would essentially block all new learning by the person. This limited capacity of short-term memory is labeled the *memory span,* and it is measured by the number of items that can be immediately recalled in order after one presentation of a list of items. Most people can reliably recall seven items, but this can vary by two items in either direction depending upon the items used to measure recall. G. A. Miller (1956) has termed this the *magical number seven plus or minus two,* and he sees this as a fundamental characteristic of human information processing.

When the short-term memory span is filled, the only way for new information to enter is by replacing information already in the short-term store. The amount of information in short-term store can be stretched by a process of organization. Think of the memory span as having seven slots into which rehearsal places information. The information placed in a slot is called a "bit" and the actual amount of information in a bit can vary. Read the sequence of digits below:

8121659

The first time you read the digits you probably read them as eight–one–two–one–six–five–nine, or as seven discrete bits of information. But they could have been read as eighty one–twenty one–sixty five–nine, and with the latter reading we have only four bits of information containing the same information as the previous seven bits. This reorganization of information to increase the amount of information in short-term store is called "chunking."

Miller provides a demonstration of increasing memory span by chunking information in a study involving the learning of long chains of binary digits. By convention a binary digit is either 1 or 0, so in a chain of binary digits there are only four possible combinations of two digits: 00, 01, 10, or 11. Each of these combinations may be chunked into one digit, by 0 for 00, 1 for 01, 2 for 10, and 3 for 11. As illustrated in Table 5–1, this reorganization may be continued until chunks of six binary digits

TABLE 5–1
Ways of recoding sequences of binary digits

Binary digits (bits)		*1*	*0*	*1*	*0*	*0*	*0*	*1*	*0*	*0*	*1*	*1*	*1*	*0*	*0*	*1*	*1*	*1*	*0*
2:1	Chunks	10		10		00		10		01		11		00		11		10	
	Recoding	2		2		0		2		1		3		0		3		2	
3:1	Chunks	101			000			100			111			001			110		
	Recoding	5			0			4			7			1			6		
4:1	Chunks	1010				0010				0111				0011				10	
	Recoding	10				2				7				3					
5:1	Chunks	10100					01001					11001					110		
	Recoding	20					9					25							

represented by digits from 0 to 31 are derived. Figure 5–2 shows the size of the chain of binary digits recalled as a function of the chunk utilized by the learner. The principle, well taken from this study, is that the amount of information to be retained in short-term memory can be influenced greatly by the organization of this material undertaken by the learner. Again we see the importance of the learner's activities in determining the outcome of learning.

FIGURE 5–2
The span of immediate memory for binary digits is plotted as a function of the recoding procedure used. The predicted function is obtained by multiplying the span for octals by 2, 3, and 3.3 for recoding into base 4, base 8, and base 10, respectively

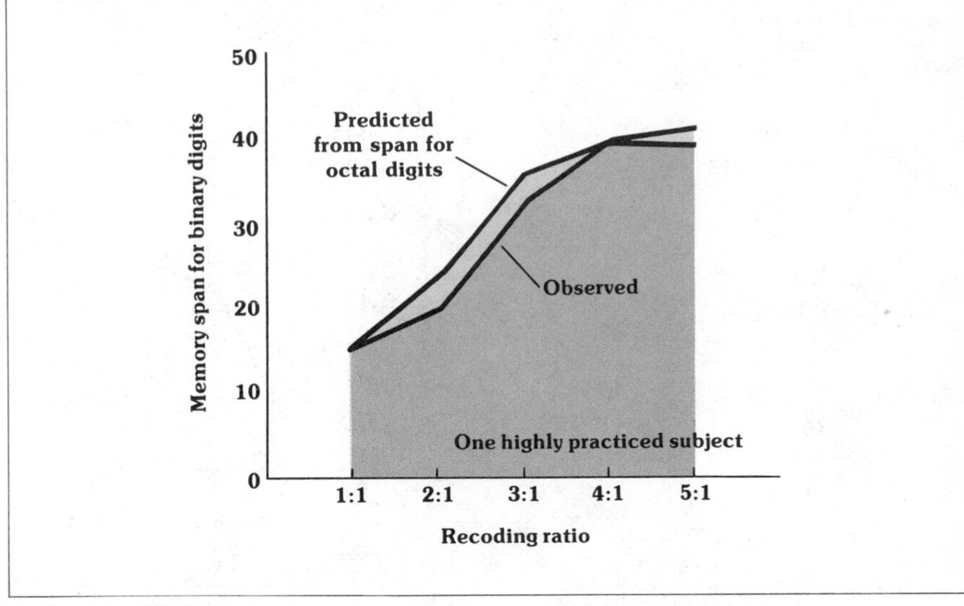

Source: G. A. Miller (1956).

2. Chunking in short-term memory has what effect?
   a. Eliminates old information.
   b. Puts new information into short-term memory.
   c. Reduces retroactive inhibition.
   d. Expands the capacity of short-term memory.

3. Which person below is probably trying to retrieve information in short-term memory?
   a. "Wait a minute it sounds like. . . ."
   b. "I think it means the same as. . . ."
   c. "Let's see, what was I doing that day?"
   d. None of the above.

THE TRANSFER OF INFORMATION TO LONG-TERM MEMORY

Both rehearsal and chunking are important processes in short-term memory because they determine which and how much information remains in the memory store. This is critical since information in the memory store is available for transfer to long-term memory. Now we wish to examine the processes that take information from short-term memory to long-term storage. Rehearsal and elaborative encoding are the processes responsible for this information transference. Elaborative encoding is the process by which a person makes to-be-learned information more meaningful by associating it with previous experiences of some sort. Again we shall see that these processes are activities under the control of the learner, so the learner determines to a large extent what information is transferred to long-term store.

Rehearsal

Rehearsal has a positive effect on the retention of information. A study by Rundus and Atkinson (1970) shows results typical of studies in this area; namely, that as rehearsal increases the amount of retention increases also. The learning task used by Rundus and Atkinson was a free-recall task. Persons in the study were required to rehearse the items in the list aloud, but other than that they could rehearse any item(s) in the list as much as they desired. Results of this procedure are shown in Figure 5–3.

FIGURE 5–3
Proportion of items correctly recalled as a function of rehearsal

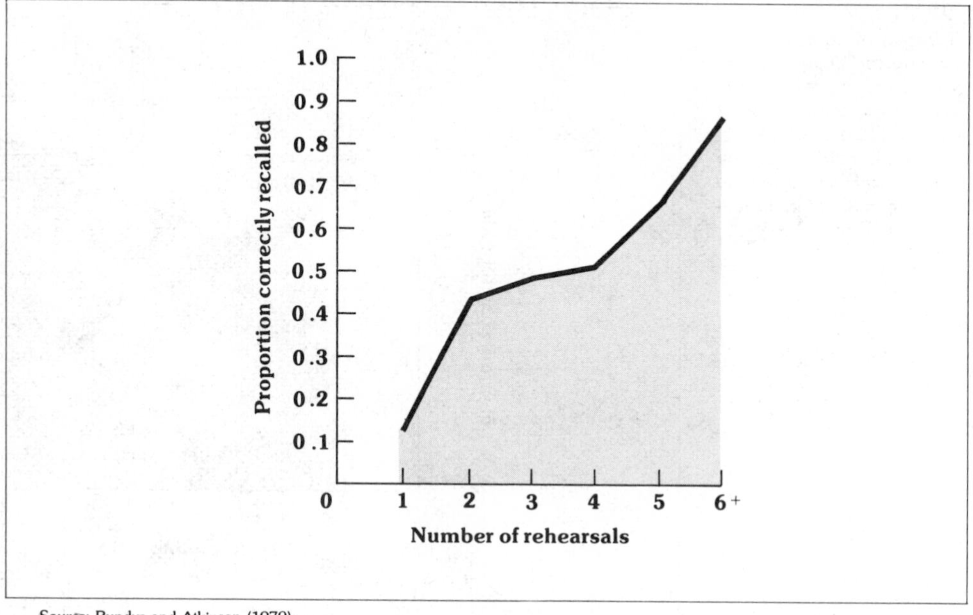

Source: Rundus and Atkinson (1970).

Craik and Lockhart (1972) contend that not all rehearsal facilitates transfer to long-term memory. Maintenance rehearsal, in which the person rotely repeats the information in acoustic form, keeps information in short-term storage but does not promote long-term retention. Research by Craik and Watkins (1973) supports this contention regarding maintenance rehearsal. However, it should not be concluded that rote rehearsal has no effect on long-term retention. A study by Woodward, Bjork, and Jongeward (1973) demonstrated that rote rehearsal influences long-term retention measured by recognition but not recall (Figure 5–4). According to Craik and Lockhart, elaborative rehearsal promotes transfer of information to long-term store. The major factor responsible for the effectiveness of this type of rehearsal is the elaborative encoding that occurs, and it is to this encoding that we turn in the next section.

Elaborative encoding

Elaborative encoding modifies the to-be-learned information in some manner that is more meaningful to the learner, and this modified or elaborated representation is what gets stored in long-term memory. Paivio (1971) has postulated a dual-coding theory of memory in which there are two systems or modes of memory representations or elaborative encoding strategies. The imagery system stores information in images that are direct analogues to objects and actions based on perceptual qualities (i.e., shape, tone, smell). The other system is verbal, and information is stored in this mode in an abstract linguistic form that is only arbitrarily related to objects or actions. While these two systems are independent, they are related in the sense that information can be simultaneously encoded in both modes. According to Paivio, when this dual encoding occurs, retention of information is enhanced beyond single encoding.

Imagery. Imagery has a long history in the philosophical inquiry into the mechanisms of the mind. Traditionally, imagery is the mental representation of an object that is not present, and it has been considered by many to be a basic element in the operation of the human mind. Research by Paivio, Smythe, and Yuille (1968) examined the

FIGURE 5–4
Rehearsal is an important process in learning and retention

separate effects of imagery and verbal encoding on learning. Three lists of paired associates were developed for the study from a pool of words with known imagery and verbal meaningfulness values. List I words were equated for verbal meaningfulness and allowed to vary in imagery value, List M words were equated for imagery and meaningfulness was allowed to vary, and both imagery and meaningfulness were allowed to covary in List IM.

As the results in Figure 5–5 show, words high in imagery were recalled better than words high in verbal meaningfulness, suggesting that different processes are involved in learning the two types of information. Also words high in both values were learned the best, which supports the superiority of dual encoding.

Bower (1972) reports a simple and interesting study on imagery as a learning strategy. The study involved a paired-associates task in which the terms were unrelated concrete nouns, such as DOG–BICYCLE. People in the experimental group were instructed to associate the two terms by imagining a mental picture in which the two objects interacted in some manner; they were given several illustrative examples. People in a control group, not directed to use an imagery strategy, were simply told to learn to give each response term when presented with the corresponding stimulus term. The two groups were compared on both immediate and delayed retention, and the perfor-

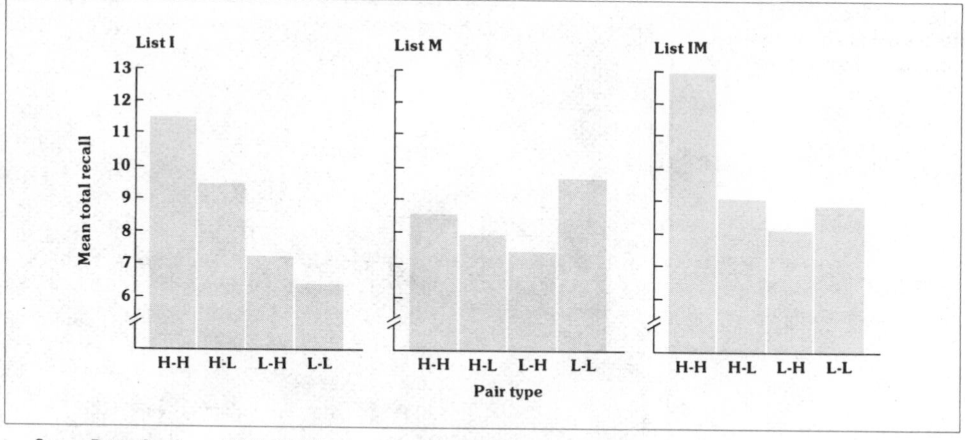

FIGURE 5–5
Mean total recall over four trials as a function of high (H) and low (L) values of the stimulus and response attributes of pairs in three paired-associates lists

Source: Paivio, Smythe, and Yuille (1968).

mances of both groups are depicted in Figure 5–6. The differences between the two groups are all the more exciting when one stops to think that there was no attempt to prevent people in the control group from using an imagery strategy. Furthermore, Bower states that interviews following the study turned up some people in the control group who reported using imagery or verbal encoding strategies.

Bower also found that imagery facilitated recall only when the learner utilized it to relate the stimulus and response terms. One group was given instructions to imagine the noun pair, such as DOG–BICYCLE, interacting with each other (i.e., imagine a dog riding a bicycle). The other group was instructed in Bower's words: "to imagine the two objects separated in their imaginal space, like two pictures on opposite walls of a room. One object-picture was not to be influenced in any way by the contents of the other object-picture" (1972, p. 80). The group receiving the interactive instruc-

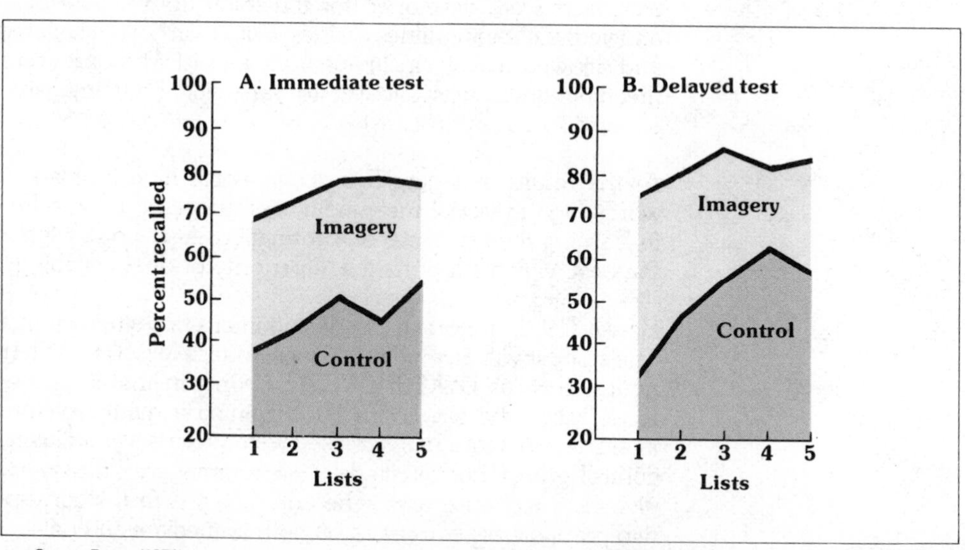

FIGURE 5–6
Immediate and delayed recall of five lists for imagery versus control subjects

Source: Bower (1972).

tions recalled 71 percent of the response terms, while the separation instructions group recalled only 46 percent of the response terms. This last figure is approximately the same as recall obtained from control groups given repetition instructions.

That the generation of mental imagery is an effective memory aid or mnemonic has been known since the ancient Greeks [see Adams (1976) for a description of these mnemonic devices]. One mnemonic device developed by the Greeks was the method of loci, in which an image of each item to be remembered is put in a particular location in some familiar place, say your living room. When you wish to recall the information, you first imagine yourself standing in your living room, then turn slowly to each place and locate each item stored there. Imagery such as the above works as an encoding strategy when the information is concrete in nature and has distinctive perceptual qualities that can be preserved in an image code. However, much verbal information is abstract in character and not amenable to storage as a concrete image. In this case encoding must take place in the verbal system.

Semantic encoding. Encoding, whether imagery or verbal, elaborates information into a form more meaningful to the learner. Suppose you were given a list of trigrams to memorize and one of these trigrams was VET. This could be encoded into a meaningful word like *veteran* and remembered in that form. Later upon recall it would be retrieved in the form *veteran* and decoded back into its original form VET. Rather than an image, the elaboration in this case is another verbal form that possesses meaning to you. This type of transformation is often referred to as a *natural language mediator.*

A study by Montague, Adams, and Kiess (1966) illustrates several important issues concerning natural language mediators. Persons participating in the study were presented with 96 paired associates of high or low association value for either a 15- or 30-second study interval on each paired associate. Each person was instructed to write down any natural language mediator that occurred during the study interval. On a recall test with 24-hour retention interval, stimulus terms were displayed consecutively to the learner, who was instructed to write the appropriate responses and any natural language mediators formed that could be remembered.

More encoding or mediators were formed under the longer study condition, and there were more mediators involved with high-association-value terms. The percentage of recall summarized across the study time and association value conditions was compared for three different categories of verbal terms. Paired associates learned by rote, those for which no mediators were formed during study, had a retention rate averaging 7 percent. Recall averaged 64 percent for those paired associates for which mediators were formed during study and that could be remembered at the time of recall. However, recall averaged only 2 percent for the paired associates from which mediators were formed during study but not remembered at the time of recall.

Two significant features of elaborative encoding emerge from this study. The formation of verbal mediators takes time and consequently is promoted by longer study periods. Next, in order to be effective, mediators must be remembered at recall time and then decoded for the required information. In this regard Prytulak (1971) found that the effectiveness of verbal mediators in retention decreases as the number of steps in the decoding process increases.

Another form of semantic encoding that is important in the learning and retention of verbal information is organization. Recall from Chapter 4 that Bousfield (1953) observed that people tend to cluster or organize information in their recall attempts. He gave them a list of 60 words comprised of 15 words each from four categories: professions, animals, proper names, and vegetables. During presentation the word order was random, but people tended to organize them by category in recall. This clustering represents the encoding of words from a category on the basis of shared meaning.

Further evidence for the effectiveness of organization in encoding information was obtained in a series of studies reported by Bower, Clark, Lesgold, and Winzenz (1969). They had college and high school students learn a list of related words organized by either a conceptual hierarchy or a random ordering. On retention tests, the conceptual hierarchy groups recalled two to three times the number of words as the random order groups. Students given the conceptual hierarchy had a meaningful framework into which they could encode the word list, and at recall they used this framework to generate the words. This function of an encoding strategy is called "retrieval" and in the next section we will describe this process more thoroughly.

4. Assuming all directions to be applicable, which of the following directions should best facilitate retention?
   a. Think of an animal it looks like.
   b. Think of a word that sound like it.
   c. Say it to yourself five times.
   d. Relate it to your previous experiences.
5. Thinking of the human memory as analogous to a library, which of the following would be the equivalent of a human encoding strategy?
   a. The check-out desk.
   b. The card catalog.
   c. The book classification system.
   d. The reference desk.

ACCESS TO KNOWLEDGE IN LONG-TERM MEMORY

Information that is rehearsed and encoded in working memory goes to long-term memory for storage until it is required by the learner. At some point in the future an occasion on which stored information is relevant to the person's performance may arise; when this occurs the desired information is accessed from long-term store and sent to short-term memory (the working memory). This process can and does break down, so that previously learned information sometimes cannot be recalled to the working memory. This failure to transfer information from storage in long-term memory to short-term memory is called "forgetting." Three major theories have been advanced to account for forgetting in long-term memory: decay theory, interference theory, and retrieval theory.

Decay theory of forgetting

The oldest theory of forgetting is decay or disuse theory. Essentially, the decay theory postulates that memory traces in the long-term memory weaken over time when the information is not used. Memory traces are physiological residuals of experiences left in the nervous system of the learner. Once the strength of a memory trace fades below a certain level, that memory trace is simply not available for activation by the learner. Decay theory is not today an important theory of forgetting, not necessarily because of its failure to explain forgetting but mainly due to its failure to lead to many testable hypotheses about the forgetting process.

Interference theory of forgetting

Interference theory has been the predominant theory of forgetting for the past decade. While the passage of time is the major determinant of forgetting in decay theory, it is what takes place during the passage of time that is of interest in the interference theory. Failure to recall information stems from the learning of other information, so that we may say that the learning of task X interferes with the recall of task Y. One of the first tests of the interference theory of forgetting was reported by Jenkins and Dallenbach (1924), who examined whether time (the independent variable in decay theory) or interference was the major cause of forgetting. Jenkins and Dallenbach had people memorize lists of nonsense syllables and tested them for recall of the lists at intervals up to eight hours after the original study of the syllables. One group slept after learning the lists, while another went about their normal waking activity. The recall of two typical people from the study is presented in Figure 5–7. Recall was lower overall after waking activity and declined further as time awake increased but did not decline with time sleeping. Consequently one is left to conclude that it is some aspect of the activities occurring over time that is responsible for forgetting and not the elapse of time per se.

FIGURE 5–7
Recall of learned syllables at various intervals after sleeping or remaining awake. Results are averages from two subjects

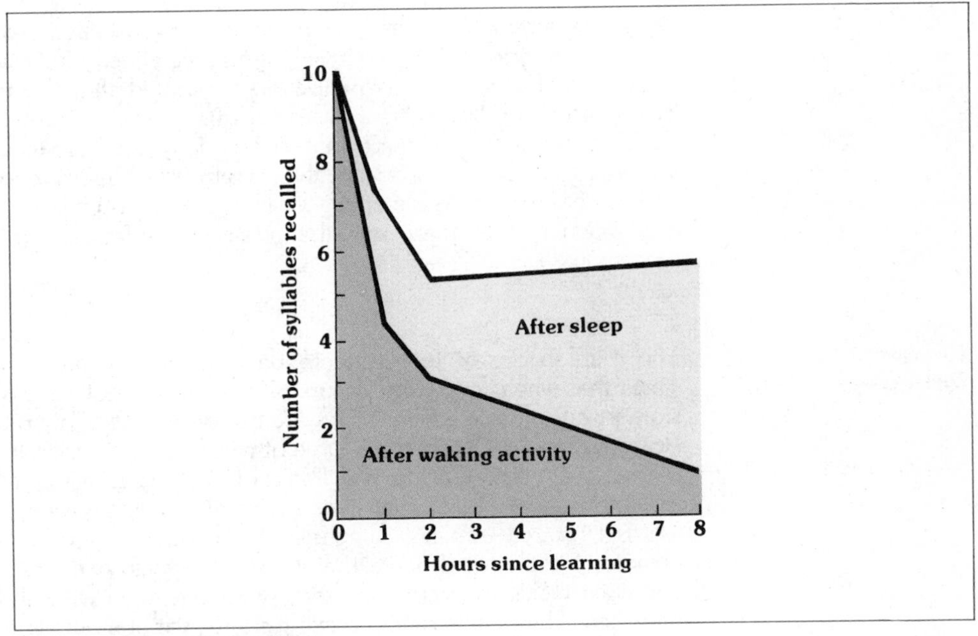

Source: Jenkins and Dallenbach (1924).

Interference effects are of two types depending on whether the interfering material was learned before or after the to-be-recalled material. These two types of interference can be simply and clearly illustrated by the experimental design used to study each. Retroactive interference occurs when new learning activity interferes with the recall of previously acquired information; the basic experimental design to study it is thus:

Experimental group	Learns Task A	Learns Task B	Recalls Task A
Control group	Learns Task A	Rest or other unrelated activity	Recalls Task A

Proactive interference occurs when previously acquired information interferes with the recall of newly acquired information:

Experimental group	Learns Task A	Learns Task B	Recalls Task B
Control group	Rest or other unrelated activity	Learns Task B	Recalls Task B

Research on interference effects has generally examined three major variables: similarity between the two tasks, practice, and the number of lists. As would be expected, the greater the similarity between the two lists, the more interference will be produced. The interference effect produced by the amount of practice depends upon whether it is practice on the task to be recalled or practice on the interfering task. Generally, the more a person practices on the recall list, the greater will be the amount of recall (conversely, interference will be less). Greater amounts of practice on the interfering task will produce higher interference effects.

Finally the amount of similar information previously acquired by the learner is related to the magnitude of the proactive interference effect (Underwood, 1957). In reviewing a number of studies, Underwood demonstrated that the number of lists a person learns before the recall of a given list affects the amount of recall of that list. This led Underwood to conclude that in our daily lives proactive interference is a more important source of interference than is retroactive interference. With proactive interference we have the possible effect of previous learning from a lifetime, which is conceivably much greater than, say, the possible interfering activities in a given 24-hour time span.

Retrieval theory of forgetting

The third theory of forgetting to be discussed is the retrieval theory. This theory states that when forgetting occurs information is not necessarily lost from long-term storage, but rather sufficient cues are not present to allow retrieval of the information. According to this theory the degree of recall depends upon the availability of appropriate retrieval cues. Tulving and Psotka (1971) used a free-recall task to demonstrate the importance of retrieval cues on recall. They presented people with lists of 24 words clustered into six categories, with the words grouped to make the clusters obvious. People involved in the study were given two types of recall tests: noncued and cued recall. In cued recall they were presented with all the category names they had seen. The results of the recall tests for various numbers of lists are presented in Figure 5–8. Cued recall showed minimum forgetting, whereas noncued recall showed a rapid decline in retention. The curve for noncued recall shows a strong retroactive interference effect, whereas the cued recall test does not show such an effect.

Retention is best when the context at the time of recall is consistent with the manner in which the learner encoded the information. The importance of encoding in determining effective retrieval cues was demonstrated in an experiment by Light and Carter-Sobell (1970) using a noun-recognition task. Semantic encoding was established by embedding the nouns to be learned in sentences involving specific adjectives. By changing the adjectives used, Light and Carter-Sobell could change the context in which a noun was presented at recognition, thus changing its meaning. For example, during the study period a person might see the noun, GRADE in the following context: The boy earned a GOOD GRADE on the test. On the recognition test the person would be shown a list of adjective-noun pairs and asked to identify the nouns previously seen. If the person was shown the adjective-noun pair GOOD GRADE, then acquisition and retrieval contexts were similar. A different semantic context could be established

FIGURE 5–8
Mean number of words recalled from a list of 24 words in three successive tests

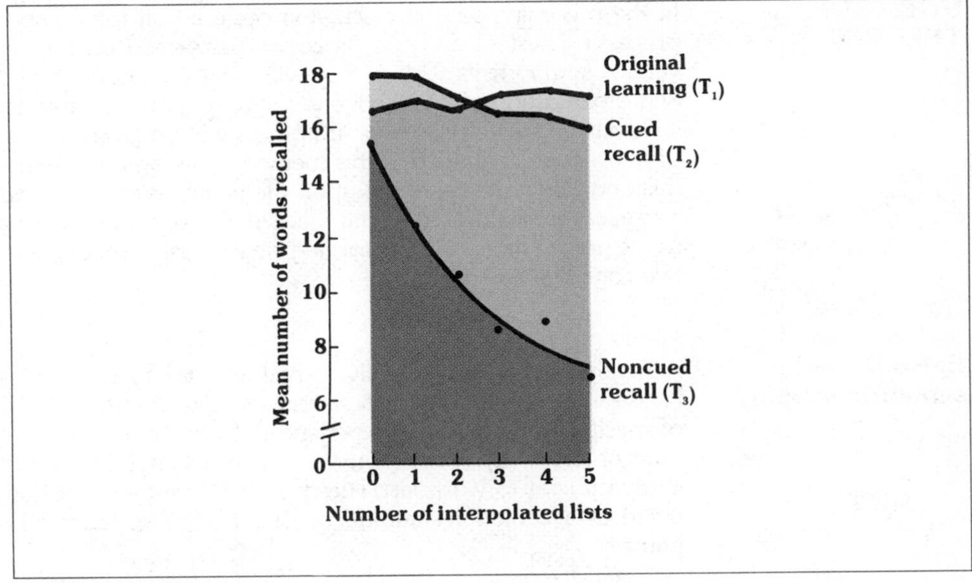

Source: Tulving (1974).

by presenting the adjective-noun pair STEEP GRADE. Correct recognition was highest when the semantic context was the same at retrieval as at acquisition. Further proof that the important context is semantic was found in the fact that the specific adjective could be changed and not affect recognition accuracy as long as the meaning of the noun was not changed. In our example this type of adjective substitution would be BAD GRADE for GOOD GRADE.

Retrieval theory relates elaborative encoding to the process of remembering. Earlier in this chapter we saw that the learner's encoding strategy is a major influence on the acquisition of information. Remembering from the information-processing perspective is a retrieval process related directly to the initial encoding of the to-be-remembered information. The form of encoding determines what will function as effective retrieval cues. If the context at the time of retrieval does not provide or lead to the appropriate cues, then recall of information will be poor. In Chapters 10 and 11 we will return to elaborative encoding strategies as an important consideration in the design of instruction.

We have surveyed the structures and processes by which we acquire and retain knowledge of the world. Our attention now will turn to a description of how this knowledge is represented and organized in long-term memory. Emphasis will be given to the role of this world knowledge in supporting cognitive functioning.

6. Which theory says that forgetting in long-term memory is really a problem of accessibility?
   a. Retrieval theory.
   b. Interference theory.
   c. Decay theory.
   d. Dual-coding theory.

7. According to Underwood, retroactive interference is a greater source of forgetting than is proactive interference. True or false?

STRUCTURAL THEORIES

In the preceding section discussion centered on the components of the information-processing system and the processes performed on incoming information by these various components. This section will focus on theories that describe the accumulation and organization of knowledge in memory and how such cognitive structures interact with our cognitive processes. Emphasis will be given to the important characteristics of knowledge contained in this memory store and the manner in which people utilize this knowledge in operating upon the world. We will consider these issues from two perspectives: a developmental view of the qualitative changes in thought structures as the person grows, and a learning view focusing on the essential attributes of cumulative cognitive structures.

Episodic and semantic memory

A major attribute of cognitive structures has been described by Tulving (1972) in his distinction between episodic and semantic memory. Episodic memory is the recall of specific events we have experienced. Events in this memory are related to a specific time or place. Episodic memory occurs when I remember that I wore my brown corduroy coat to work last Tuesday, that I saw a particular colleague the last time I dined at a certain restaurant, or that I left the paper I now need on my desk at home.

Information in semantic memory is not tied to a specific time or place, but rather is of a more general and abstract nature. Semantic memory is comprised of conceptual knowledge and is often referred to as our *world knowledge.* Instead of information concerning whether or not I wore a specific coat on a given date, semantic memory would contain information about what a coat is.

FIGURE 5–9
Example for illustrating semantic memory

The major function of semantic memory is to support cognitive processes and give meaning to our experiences. One simple illustration of this function is the way in which we interpret events in episodic memory by using our knowledge in semantic memory. To experience this function of semantic memory, look at the picture in Figure 5–9 and describe to yourself what you see. Information entered your episodic memory when you looked at the picture, and if you were asked to describe any pictures encountered while studying this chapter, you should be able to state: "I saw a picture of a man waterskiing while reading my ed. psych. text." Notice that upon seeing the picture you immediately interpreted it as that of a person waterskiing behind a powerboat. This interpretation occurred even though you had never seen that particular person and, more importantly, even though there is no boat visible in the picture.

The waterskiing example serves to illustrate two important points about semantic memory. First, you did not place only visual information in episodic memory but also categorized this particular instance as one of a man waterskiing. If you had not abstracted information about waterskiing from your past experiences, it would not have been possible for you to give the picture the interpretation that you did. More interesting than the simple categorization is the inference that the man is waterskiing behind a powerboat. From your general knowledge of waterskiing you knew that, even though not specifically shown, the man needs some vehicle to pull him, that the vehicle used on water is a boat, and that most probably the boat was a powerboat and not a sailboat. This ability, to construct inferences and conclusions from semantic memory that go beyond the given, points out its critical importance in our cognitive processes.

Schemata: Scaffolding of the mind. Sir Frederic C. Bartlett (1932) was one of the first modern psychologists to emphasize the role of world knowledge in learning and remembering. Through research involving memory for pictures and simple stories, Bartlett demonstrated that remembering is a constructive process. Information presented to a person undergoes change during the learning and remembering processes. These changes can both condense and elaborate the information to make it consonant with some aspect of our world knowledge. The component of world knowledge to which information is related during learning is called a "schema."

Bartlett referred to remembering as a constructive process because when we attempt to recall previously learned information we first retrieve the appropriate schema and then use it to construct the original information. The constructed information will tend to be consistent with the activated schema; therefore we may find inconsistent original information omitted and new consistent information added. According to Bartlett (1932, p. 213):

> Remembering is not the re-excitation of innumerable fixed, lifeless and fragmentary traces. It is an imaginative reconstruction, or construction, built out of the relation of our attitude towards a whole active mass of organised past reactions or experience, and to little outstanding detail which commonly appears in image or in language form. It is thus hardly ever really exact, even in the most rudimentary cases of rote recapitulation.

Anderson, Reynolds, Schallert, and Goetz (1977) have conducted research that demonstrates the importance of schemata in the comprehension of written discourse. Physical

FIGURE 5–10
Paragraph, test item, and recall protocols

Prison/wrestling passage

Rocky slowly got up from the mat, planning his escape. He hesitated a moment and thought. Things were not going well. What bothered him most was being held, especially since the charge against him had been weak. He considered his present situation. The lock that held him was strong but he thought he could break it. He knew, however, that his timing would have to be perfect. Rocky was aware that it was because of his early roughness that he had been penalized so severely—much too severely from his point of view. The situation was becoming frustrating; the pressure had been grinding on him for too long. He was being ridden unmercifully. Rocky was getting angry now. He felt he was ready to make his move. He knew that his success or failure would depend on what he did in the next few seconds.

Question

How had Rocky been punished for his aggressiveness?
a. He had been demoted to the B team.
b. His opponent had been given points.
c. He lost his privileges for the weekend.
d. He had been arrested and imprisoned.

Examples of theme-revealing disambiguations and intrusions

Prison theme
Rocky sat in his cell.
He was angry that he had been caught and arrested.
Wrestling theme
Rocky is wrestling.
Rocky was penalized early in the match for roughness or a dangerous hold.

Source: Anderson, Reynolds, Schallert, and Goetz (1977).

education and music education students read two short passages: a passage that could be given either a prison break or a wrestling interpretation, and another passage capable of being comprehended as an evening of card-playing or a rehearsal session of a woodwind ensemble. After reading the passages the students were given a free-recall test scored for theme-revealing statements and a multiple-choice test designed to determine which interpretation they had given each passage. The prison break/wrestling passage, a disambiguating test item, and examples of theme-revealing statements for the passage are reproduced in Figure 5–10.

A student's background did not influence the amount of information retained from the passages, but it did have a large effect upon the interpretation given each passage. Physical education students were more than twice as likely to give the prison break/wrestling passage a wrestling interpretation than were the music education students. Conversely the music education students were more than twice as likely to give the card/music passage a music theme than were the physical education students. These results are even more impressive when combined with the fact that the wrestling and music themes are the least likely interpretations of the typical person for the respective passages.

Schemata or knowledge structures comprising semantic memory are important determinants of cognitive functioning. What we *now* know strongly influences what we *can* know; therefore, it is important for education that you understand how schemata are acquired and interrelate with the learning and remembering processes. In the next section we will examine these issues from two perspectives: developmental theory and learning theory.

Developmental theories of cognitive growth

Developmental theories focus on the underlying factors that produce change in cognitive structures over the lifetime of a person. Most theories view these changes as a succession of stages through which a person passes in maturing. For our purposes a stage can be thought of as a constellation of schemata distinguishing one stage from another. All children in a given stage share a common general conception of the world and therefore act toward it in a similar manner. In this section of the chapter we will examine two influential theories of cognitive development: those of Jean Piaget and Jerome Bruner.

Jean Piaget's genetic epistemology: From reflex to reflection. Piaget's writings on the development of children's knowledge have extended over a period of 40 years. His work, while slow to gain acceptance among American psychologists for a myriad of reasons, has had a tremendous impact upon developmental psychology in the last decade or so. Piaget's description of the intellectual journey the child undertakes to adulthood has revolutionized our conception of the child as a thinker.

Cognitive growth is followed from the infant's reflexive actions on the world to the adult's sophisticated mental manipulation of the world, or reflection. Reflective thought is advantageous for adaptation to the world in a number of ways. A person can "try out" a course of actions mentally before actually performing it. In this way if the person decides a particular action is not likely to yield the desired results, the action may be reversed and another considered mentally. Given this reversibility of mental actions and the fact that an action may be performed much quicker mentally than physically, it may be concluded that reflective thought allows the person to consider a much larger set of possible routes to the desired goal than would be feasible if each had to be actually performed.

The qualitatively different thought patterns at each stage of development in Piaget's theory are reflected in the cognitive structures of the child. Cognitive structures are composed of representations and operations. A representation is a mental substitute for an external action or object in the person's environment. Piaget refers to such a representation as a *signifier* or *symbol.* A signifier can be very much like the object it represents such as a visual image, or it can bear only an arbitrary relation to the object it signifies such as a word. The development of representations frees the person from the present and allows consideration of the past or even the future. Operations are mental actions that can be performed upon representations. Classifying objects as belonging to the same class and dividing objects into two subclasses are both examples of operations that can act on representations.

From this general overview of Piaget's theory of cognitive development, we now move to a consideration of two further aspects: (1) the processes by which cognitive structures are acquired and elaborated, and (2) the major characteristics of cognitive structures defining each developmental stage.

Developmental processes. To Piaget, cognition is a type of biological adaptation to the environment. This adaptation involves two complementary processes: assimilation and accommodation. The process of assimilation occurs when the person incorporates an experience into an existing cognitive structure. Complementary to assimilation is the process of accommodation, whereby the person must change an existing cognitive structure to fit the new experience.

One of the authors of this book, an amateur naturalist, recently had an experience that illustrates the manner by which assimilation and accommodation function to bring about the growth of cognitive structures. One evening while going to his car in a parking lot adjacent to a pond on campus, he encountered two students busy prodding some unknown object in the grass with an umbrella. He overheard these students making such comments as "It's ugly! What is it? Does it bite? Is it poisonous?" Immediately upon seeing the object of the student's inquisitiveness, the author recognized it as a yellow-spotted salamander, a rare species for the geographic location concerned. In this case the author quite readily assimilated the novel animal into existing cognitive structure, but the college students were unsuccessfully trying to assimilate it into their existing structures. However, after the students were told that the animal was not a lizard or snake, but rather an amphibian called a yellow-spotted salamander, they were able to accommodate existing structures to this strange creature. From this encounter they evolved a new schema of animals indigenous to the geographic area to include a smooth-skin, lizard-like animal with yellow spots and living in and around fresh water.

This example demonstrates several further characteristics of adaptation by assimilation and accommodation. Any act of adaptation by the person toward the environment involves both assimilation and accommodation. The two students could not have acquired the new knowledge about salamanders in any meaningful way if they had not already possessed a schema to assimilate this information, so by reorganizing the schema to include this new information, accommodation occurred.

An experience too discrepant from existing schemata will not bring about adaptation or growth. Modification of a schema comes about when a new experience deviates only moderately from the person's current world knowledge. Experiences containing a small amount of new information lead to assimilation and accommodation, with the result being a slight modification of the cognitive structure involved. This process is repeated constantly, and over time qualitatively different cognitive structures emerge from those of the preceding stage.

Further explanation of cognitive growth and the factors influencing it can be found in Chapter 23, where Piaget's theory of cognitive growth will be considered as a view of human intelligence.

Developmental stages. Piaget's theory, as stated earlier, describes the evolution of human thought from reflexive action to reflection. This process of growth requires the building of cognitive structures or schemata consisting of internal representations and operations. This organized knowledge comes about from the person acting on an environment. Piaget (1970, p. 704) phrases it in the following manner:

> . . . Actually, in order to know objects, the subject must act upon them, and therefore transform them: he must displace, connect, combine, take apart, and reassemble them.
>
> From the most elementary sensorimotor actions (such as pushing and pulling) to the most sophisticated intellectual operations, which are interiorized actions, carried out mentally (e.g., joining together, putting in order, putting into one-to-one correspondence) knowledge is constantly linked with action or operations, that is, with *transformations*. . . .

In this section we will summarize the major qualities of the schemata marking each developmental stage of Piaget's theory.

Sensorimotor period (0–2 years[1]). In this period the child's knowledge of the world is represented in actions performed on the actual objects such as sucking, shaking, pulling, and looking. At first these actions are reflexes or random generalized movements, however, these are modified by experience and become coordinated with other actions and senses. Actions become means to ends; for example, the child moves an obstacle to a rattle and then grasps the rattle. Following this the child begins to repeat such successful actions and finally begins to explore for new means to a specific end.

Another important development in the sensorimotor period is construction of the object concept schema. Initially, it may be said of the infant that "out of sight, out of mind" is literally true. The infant will look at an object in the visual field but will not search for the object when it leaves the field. However, by the end of the sensorimotor period, the child will come to know that the permanent existence of an object and its movement in space are independent of its interactions with the child.

The first step in development of the object concept is visual search for an object that has left the child's field of vision; however, even eight-month-old children will not reach for an object that has disappeared from sight. At the next step in development of object permanence, the child will actively search for an object that has been removed, and finally the child adjusts the search to take account of movement of the object while out of view.

The culmination of the sensorimotor period occurs with the start of representational thought. Piaget (1954) describes the emergence of such thought from an observation of one of his three daughters, Lucienne. A gold watch chain has been placed in a matchbox and a small opening left in the box. Prior to this particular observation, Lucienne had learned to turn the box over and insert her finger to obtain the chain.

[1] Age spans are approximations and will vary as a function of individual and cultural differences.

FIGURE 5–11
Sensorimotor activities lay the foundation for later cognitive development

This time Piaget reduced the opening in the box so that Lucienne's ensuing attempt to retrieve the chain by the above strategy failed. After a pause, according to Piaget, Lucienne looked attentively at the opening. Next she opened and shut her mouth several times at first narrowly then wider and wider. Following this action, Lucienne pulled the box open with great certainty and obtained the desired chain.

In the above observation we see that Lucienne anticipated the solution to her problem and represented it motorically by opening and shutting her mouth before actually performing the necessary action. This capability to mentally manipulate the world through symbolic representation marks the transition to a higher stage of cognitive development (Figure 5–11).

Preoperational period (2–7 years). This period of cognitive development is often negatively conceptualized and is considered a transitional period. Because of the shortcomings of this period, the important advancement in thinking achieved by the preoperational child is overlooked. This major accomplishment is an increased capacity for symbolic representation by mental images primarily but also by language. Language and other symbols are an important form of representation because they allow the preoperational child to evoke past experiences.

Two major characteristics of the preoperational child contribute greatly to the negative view of this period: (1) egocentrism and (2) perceptual dominance of thought. Egocentrism is the inability to view the world from any perspective other than one's own. Piaget and Inhelder (1956) presented a three-dimensional model of three mountains to children and asked them to draw the mountains as they would be seen by a doll sitting across the table from the child. Regardless of the directions, preoperational children drew the scene from their own perspective, whereas older, concrete operations children drew it from the correct perspective. Apparently children at the preoperational stage are not capable of considering an event from a perspective other than the one they experience.

Thought processes during the preoperational period are perceptual-dominated; that is, they are influenced by the most salient physical features of a situation. This perceptual dominance of thought is quite readily evident in a situation involving conservation. Conservation, an important extension of the object concept, occurs whenever the child realizes that any attribute or quality retains its essential characteristics in spite of transformation of its physical appearance (Sigel & Cocking, 1977).

The prototypical Piagetian conservation task involves the conservation of quantity (Figure 5–12). In this demonstration the child watches while the experimenter pours liquid into two containers with equal dimensions. The experimenter adjusts the level of the liquid in the two containers until the child agrees that both contain an equal amount. Next the experimenter pours the liquid from one container into a taller, thinner container while the child watches, and again the child is asked to judge the equivalence of the liquids. This time the preoperational child responds that the taller container has more liquid. The reasons for this answer indicate that the preoperational child focused on the higher level of liquid in the thin container (or if the child said the thin container had less liquid, reason would indicate that the child had noticed how narrow its base was compared to the other container). The answers indicate that the child attended to a dominant perceptual characteristic of the situation and failed to realize that a change in one dimension (height) is compensated by a change in another dimension (width).

FIGURE 5–12
Typical reply of preoperational child to conservation of quantity problem

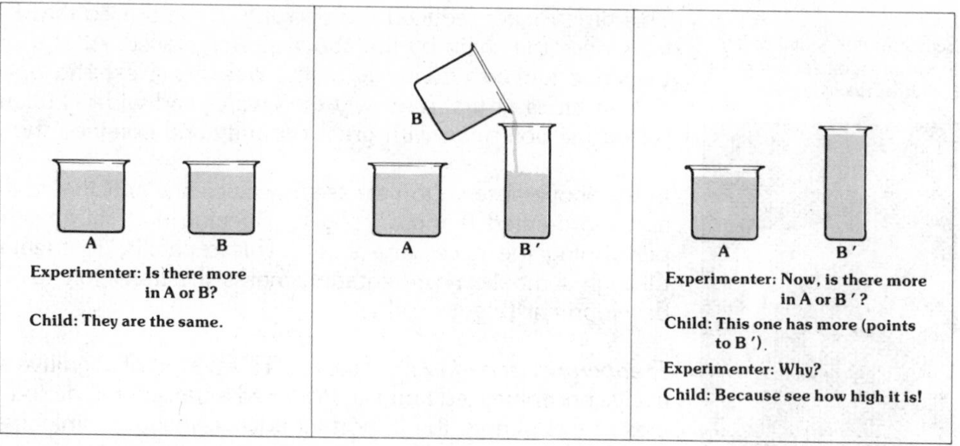

The perceptual dominance of thought is related to three other characteristics of thought that contribute to nonconservation in the preoperational period: centration, statism, and irreversibility (Ginsburg & Opper, 1969). Centration means the child thinks in terms of the separate features of a situation and does not integrate the features. As noted above on the conservation task, the child attends to either the height or the width of the new container but does not integrate this information and consequently does not realize that a change in one is compensated by a change in the other. Statism refers to the tendency to focus on static states and not operations. In the conservation task, the child views the columns of liquid and not the act of pouring. Additionally, thought in the preoperational period is characterized by irreversibility. The child does not yet understand that actions like pouring the liquid are reversible, that is, the liquid poured from container B into B′ can be poured back into B from B′.

The cognitive structures of the preoperational child, tied as they are to perceptual features of the environment, do not allow true operational thought. While the child in this period can engage in transductive reasoning (reasons from a particular to a particular), operational thought awaits the next period of growth.

Concrete operations period (7–11 years). Thought in the concrete operations period has transformed the preoperational child's centration to decentration, statism to dynamism, and irreversibility to reversibility. Decentration is the ability to focus on several dimensions and relate them. We would expect a concrete operational child who has achieved conservation to view the taller, thinner container and tell us, "This one is taller but the other one is wider." Having achieved dynamism, the child observes the liquid being transferred from one container to another, which makes it more likely that the reversibility of the act will be noticed. Understanding reversibility, the child will know that the liquid can be poured back into its original container. These qualities of thought help to free the person from immediate perceptual dominance and allow the emergence of operational thought.

In addition to the operation of conservation, class inclusion, seriation, and relational thought are important operations achieved in the concrete operations period. Class inclusion represents the ability to think about the whole and a part of it simultaneously. Suppose we present a child with 15 wooden beads, 10 painted red and 5 painted white. The child is asked, "Are there more red or wooden beads?" In order to answer correctly, the person must consider that the red beads are a subset of the set of wooden beads.

Another operation acquired by the concrete operations child is seriation. This refers to the ability to arrange in order a set of objects differing on some dimension. Seriation allows children to solve problems of one-to-one serial correspondence, a critical prerequisite for understanding numbers and basic arithmetic functions (Sigel & Cocking, 1977).

During the concrete operations period the ability to classify on the basis of the relationship between two dimensions is developed. For example a child is given three blocks of differing size; furthermore, two of the blocks are green and one is blue. The child is asked to point to the littlest green block and complies correctly.

The ability to carry out such mental operations is an important milestone in cognitive development. Rather than merely representing a static concrete world, the child is now operating on this world with reversible mental actions, a formidable intellectual tool. The next major development must await the formal operations period. The concrete operational child, while going beyond merely representing the concrete world to operating on it, is still restricted to it in mental operation. The class inclusion problem involving different colored beads would be insolvable if posed verbally. The concrete operational child must have the actual concrete objects present in order to support mental operations.

Formal operations period (11 years through adulthood). In this period the person moves from being able to consider what *is* to consider what *is possible.* Inhelder and Piaget (1958) demonstrate this ability to consider the hypothetical in a problem involving the determination of what influences the rate at which a pendulum swings. Four variables could be considered: weight of pendulum bob, length of string, height of release, and force exerted at release. Children in the formal operations period manipulate the variables so as to systematically check all possible explanations before arriving at a conclusion. However, concrete operational children tend to derive a conclusion prematurely (i.e., before checking all possibilities).

In this stage mature thought is reached when a person attains the ability to perform operations on symbols instead of on the actual objects. This represents the release of the thinker from the present because the person can manipulate objects that are not now present or that never have been! This characteristic makes possible not only more efficient adaptation but also creativity.

Jerome Bruner: Beyond the information given. Bruner's theory of cognitive development has been strongly influenced by the work of Piaget. Both theories conceive of cognitive development as qualitative transformations in the cognitive structure of the person. The span of both theories covers growth from the infant's immediate concrete world to the young adult's complex world of the possible.

The major differences between Bruner and Piaget relate to their explanations of the processes determining the growth of cognitive functioning. One such major difference concerns the degree of emphasis on culture as a force in cognitive growth. Bruner (1965, p. 1007) has stated:

> What is unique about man is that his growth as an individual depends upon the history of his species—not upon a history reflected in genes and chromosomes but, rather, reflected in a culture external to man's tissue and wider in scope than is embodied in any one man's competency. Perforce, then the growth of mind is always growth assisted from the outside. Since a culture, particularly an advanced one, transcends the bounds of individual competence, the limits for individual growth are by definition greater than what any single person has previously attained; the limits of growth depend on how a culture assists the individual to use such intellectual potential as he may possess. It seems highly unlikely—either empirically or canonically—that we have any realistic sense of the furthest reach of such assistance to growth.

The difference between Bruner and Piaget on the role of culture is one of degree. Piaget recognizes the role of the child's culture in promoting cognitive growth, but he has not made it a focal point of his work as Bruner has. However, the role of language in the development of thought does represent a theoretical difference between the two theories. Piaget views language growth as a result of increased cognitive growth, whereas Bruner views language growth as a strong influence on cognitive growth (Figure 5–13).

Modes of representation. Bruner does not describe the growth of knowledge as a succession of stages, instead he views it as the successive mastery of three systems of representation or encoding. Bruner (1973, p. 316) defines *representation* as "a set of rules in terms of which one conserves one's encounters with events." Each

FIGURE 5–13
Cognitive growth involves acquiring proficiency in symbolic representation

system is a medium by which knowledge is encoded and stored in semantic memory—these media are actions, images, and symbols. Bruner refers to each system, respectively, as enactive, iconic, and symbolic representation.

Enactive representation corresponds roughly to the sensorimotor period and, as in this period, an event is known in enactive representation by the actions performed on it by the knower. An infant who sees a rattle and then moves the arm as if shaking the rattle is demonstrating knowledge by enactive representation. A major limitation of enactive representation in cognition is that it is tied to the immediate.

Iconic representation is knowledge encoded in the medium of the image. Bruner (1964) uses the picture as a metaphor for the image. Like a picture, the image summarizes the event for which it stands by selective representation of features; however, there is a correspondence between an image and its referent such that an image of an event is recognizable from experiencing the event. This correspondence is lacking in the third system of representation—the symbolic mode. Words and other symbols have the important qualities of remoteness and arbitrariness. The word *umbrella* in no way can be said to resemble the object it represents. Yet look at the representations below and you should have no trouble in recognizing in one the image of an umbrella.

The properties of representational systems described above have important implications for their functioning as intellectual tools, a topic to be covered momentarily; but first a final word about mastery of the three modes as cognitive growth. Bruner defines growth as the successive mastery of the three representational modes, resulting in qualitatively different cognitive structures. However, unlike growth in stages there is not a loss of the ability to represent enactively as iconic representation is mastered, nor is a loss of iconic representation the result of mastery of symbolic thinking. The three systems coexist in a person and form different schemata supporting qualitatively different thought processes. The mature person brings to bear schemata from the appropriate mode for each given task.

Because of his emphasis on the role of language in thought, Bruner has studied most thoroughly the transition from iconic to symbolic representation and the differences in cognitive processing possible with these two representational systems. Several studies by Bruner and his associates will suffice to demonstrate the differences in abilities accompanying the transition from iconic to symbolic representation. Bruner and Kenney (1966) presented children between the ages of five and seven with a 3 × 3 matrix containing nine glasses varying in either diameter or height as shown in Figure 5–14 (except no glass or space was labeled as in the illustration). Each was shown the matrix, the glasses were scrambled, and then the child was asked to place the glasses back as before. After performance of this task, the glasses were scrambled once more, with glass A moved from space 1 to space 2. Again the child was asked to reconstruct the pattern, but this time with the stipulation to leave glass A in space 2. On the first task, called *reproduction,* there was no difference in correct performance as a function of age; however, on the second task, labeled *transposition,* most of the seven-year-old children but hardly any of the five-year-old children performed correctly.

FIGURE 5–14
Matrix with glasses differing in height and width

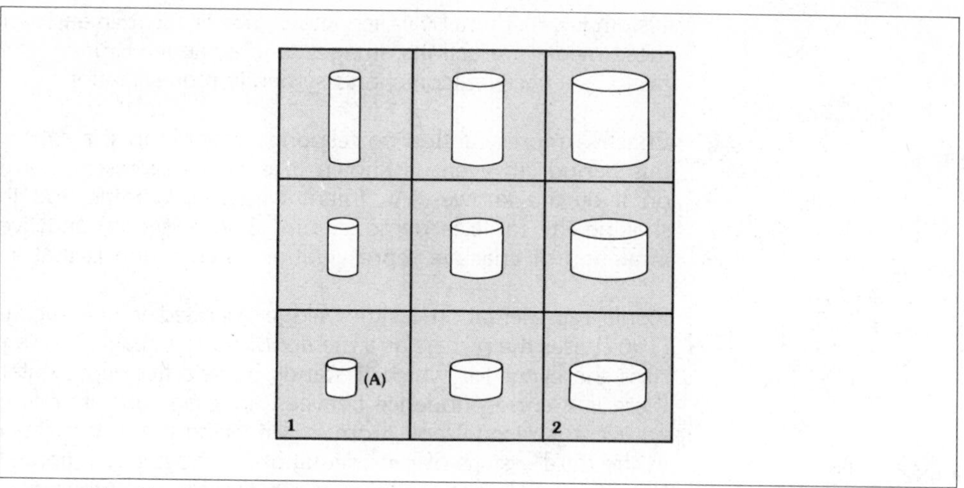

Source: Adapted from Bruner and Kenney (1966).

The reproduction task can be performed by copying from an image of the matrix in memory and so can be successfully performed by a person capable of iconic representation. Performance on the transposition task would be hindered by such a copying strategy, and indeed Bruner and Kenney (1966) report that the children who failed this task typically tried to return glass A to space 1. Children who were successful at the transposition task described the matrix in terms of height and width, like "It gets fatter going one way and taller going the other" (p. 165). Apparently, children capable of symbolic representation are freed from copying the static image of iconic representation and can reconstruct a number of alternate realities from the more abstract code contained in words.

The importance of this abstract quality or remoteness of language is demonstrated further in an experiment by Frank (1966). She tested children between the ages of four and seven in the classic conservation of quantity test depicted in Figure 5–12 to determine conservers and nonconservers. Next the conservation task was repeated, but this time a screen was placed in front of the containers as the liquid was poured from one to the other. With the screen still in place, the child was asked which now had more liquid in it. Conservation responses went from 0 to 50 percent among four-year-olds, from 20 to 90 percent among five-year-olds, and from 50 to 100 percent among six-year-olds.

The screen was removed and the children were asked which container had more. All the four-year-old children reversed their conservation responses, but all the older children maintained their conservation stances. They justified their answers with statements such as the following by a five-year-old, "It looks like more to drink, but it is only the same because it is the same water and it is poured from there to there." Figure 5–15 illustrates the results from Frank's study.

According to Bruner (1964, p. 7):

> It is plain that if a child is to succeed in the conservation task, he must have some internalized verbal formula that shields him from the overpowering appearance of the visual displays much

FIGURE 5–15
Percentage of children showing conservation of liquid volume before and during screening and upon unscreening of the displays

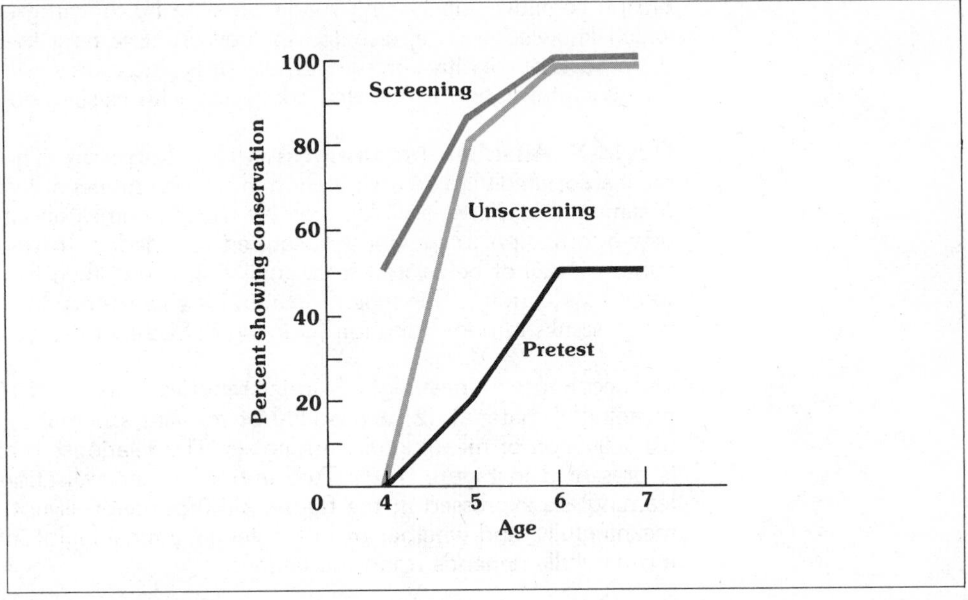

Source: Bruner (1964).

as in the Frank experiment. The explanations of the children who lacked conservation suggest how strongly they were oriented to the visual appearance of the displays they had to deal with.

The development of a symbolic representational system with its qualities of remoteness and arbitrariness allows the person to deal with a situation on the basis of qualities other than the perceptual. As opposed to a stage theory, Bruner does not postulate that a given mode of representation is eliminated and replaced by a succeeding mode, rather each mode is used in the pursuit of appropriate ends. The symbolic mode of representation is especially suited as an intellectual tool in the majority of cognitive tasks required in school experiences. This appropriateness is expressed in the following quote of Greenfield and Bruner (1969, pp. 647–48):

> The influence of [linguistic] encoding becomes stronger as cognitive conditions become more difficult, making an iconic approach to the problem increasingly ineffective and a symbolic approach more crucial. Such conditions are produced as the situation becomes less simultaneous and more a matter of memory and as the number of stimuli to be dealt with simultaneously approaches 7 ± 2, the limit of immediate perception and memory. . . . These generalizations about the conditions under which linguistic encoding will affect other cognitive operations must be further qualified. They hold only if a linguistic representation is available to the person in question and has been activated.

8. Both Piaget and Bruner would agree with which statements below?
   a. Growth proceeds from motor skills through perceptual skills to abstract thought.
   b. Language is a major factor in directing thought.
   c. Growth represents a qualitative change in cognitive structures.

Learning theories of cognitive growth

A major distinction between developmental and learning theories of cognitive growth is the focus of theoretical interest. Developmental accounts of cognitive growth center on the cognitive functioning made possible by the progressive changes in form by which knowledge is represented in memory. Learning theories focus on explaining the process of cognitive growth. Emphasis is placed on identifying conditions necessary for new information to become connected with existing cognitive structure.

David P. Ausubel: Meaningful verbal learning. The educational psychologist most associated with an assimilation-to-schema model of learning is David P. Ausubel. Meaningful learning, according to his theory, comes about when the learner relates new information to previously acquired knowledge. If the to-be-learned information is not or cannot be related to cognitive structure, then the resultant learning is said to be *rote* learning. This type of learning is characterized by a lack of comprehension, which results in poor retention (Dooling & Lachman, 1971; Dooling & Mullet, 1973).

The occurrence of meaningful learning requires three factors: (1) exposure to potentially meaningful material, (2) availability of relevant schemata in cognitive structure, and (3) activation of meaningful learning set. The relationship among these requirements is presented in Figure 5–16. Two important generalizations concerning meaningful learning are expressed in the figure: all information is not capable of being learned meaningfully, and whether or not potentially meaningful information will be learned meaningfully depends upon the learner.

Meaningfulness. In order for meaningful learning to occur, the information itself must have certain qualities. Such information has logical meaning according to Ausubel (1968), and the critical qualities it possesses are substantiveness and nonarbitrariness.

FIGURE 5–16
Schematic representation or requirements for logical meaningfulness, potential meaningfulness, and meaningful learning

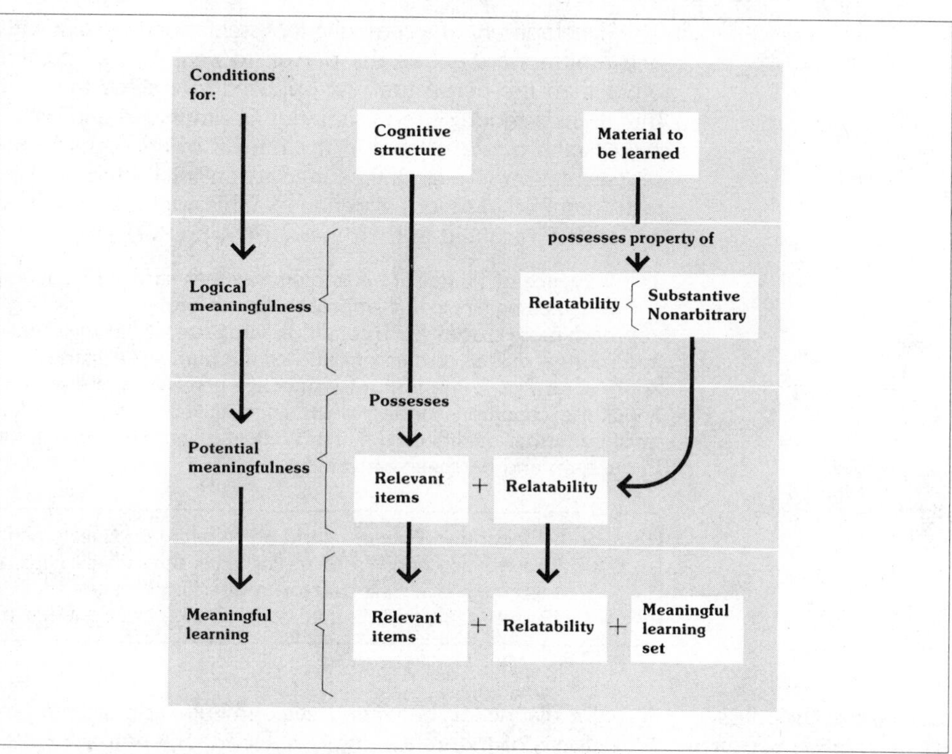

Source: Ausubel and Robinson (1969).

Substantiveness means that the information is capable of being paraphrased without changing the idea expressed. If the idea expressed in the information has a nonarbitrary relationship to another idea, then the information is said to possess "nonarbitrariness."

The statement "Whales are mammals" meets both criteria for logical meaning. It has substantiveness, that is, it could be restated "Whales are animals that nourish their young with the mother's milk" and not change in meaning. The relationship expressed between whales and mammals is certainly not arbitrary, rather it is asserted that whales are a subset of that set of animals that nourish their young with mother's milk. The typical paired-associate learning task, such as DOG–WEAK, lacks logical meaning. It is true that we could substitute synonyms for the terms, but still the relationship between the two is arbitrary.

Information with logical meaning is necessary for potential meaningfulness. Because of the qualities of substantiveness and nonarbitrariness this information is capable of being related to information existing in the cognitive structure of the learner. So we see that in order for the to-be-learned information to possess potential meaningfulness, two requirements must be satisfied: the information must have relatability (logical meaning), and the learner must have relevant information to which this information can be related. Next we consider the acquisition of potentially meaningful information in a meaningful manner.

Meaningful learning. When the learner approaches potentially meaningful material (that is, information with logical meaning that can be related to existing information in the learner's cognitive structure) with the intention of relating the new information to cognitive structure in a substantive and nonarbitrary manner, the result is meaningful learning. If this meaningful learning set is absent, then the result is the rote learning of meaningful material, in which case the material is said to "lack meaning" to the learner.

Meaningful learning has numerous advantages over rote learning to the learner. Rote learning occurs without comprehension and therefore the only performance supported by it is verbatim repetition. Furthermore, as we saw earlier in this chapter, information learned verbatim (not encoded) is forgotten quickly. Meaningful learning of information, on the other hand, facilitates the further learning of new related information and retention of learned information. So, economy in both learning and retention is promoted by meaningful learning.

Returning to the learner's cognitive structure, learning and retention of meaningful verbal material are influenced by two characteristics of cognitive structures: the availability of relevant anchoring ideas in conjunction with the stability and clarity of these anchoring ideas. The meaning of new information is a function of the degree of relatability of this information to ideas already in the individual's cognitive structure. As relevance of available anchoring information in cognitive structure decreases, we can expect less learning and retention to occur. The type of idea that is relevant to the learning of new information is determined by the relationship that exists between new information and the anchoring idea.

The possible types of relationships between new and existing ideas are shown in Figure 5–17, taken from Ausubel and Robinson (1969). A subordinate relationship exists when the new idea is subsumed under a more inclusive item. Our earlier example of "Whales are mammals" illustrates this relationship, because mammal as a class is

FIGURE 5–17
Possible relationships between new and existing ideas

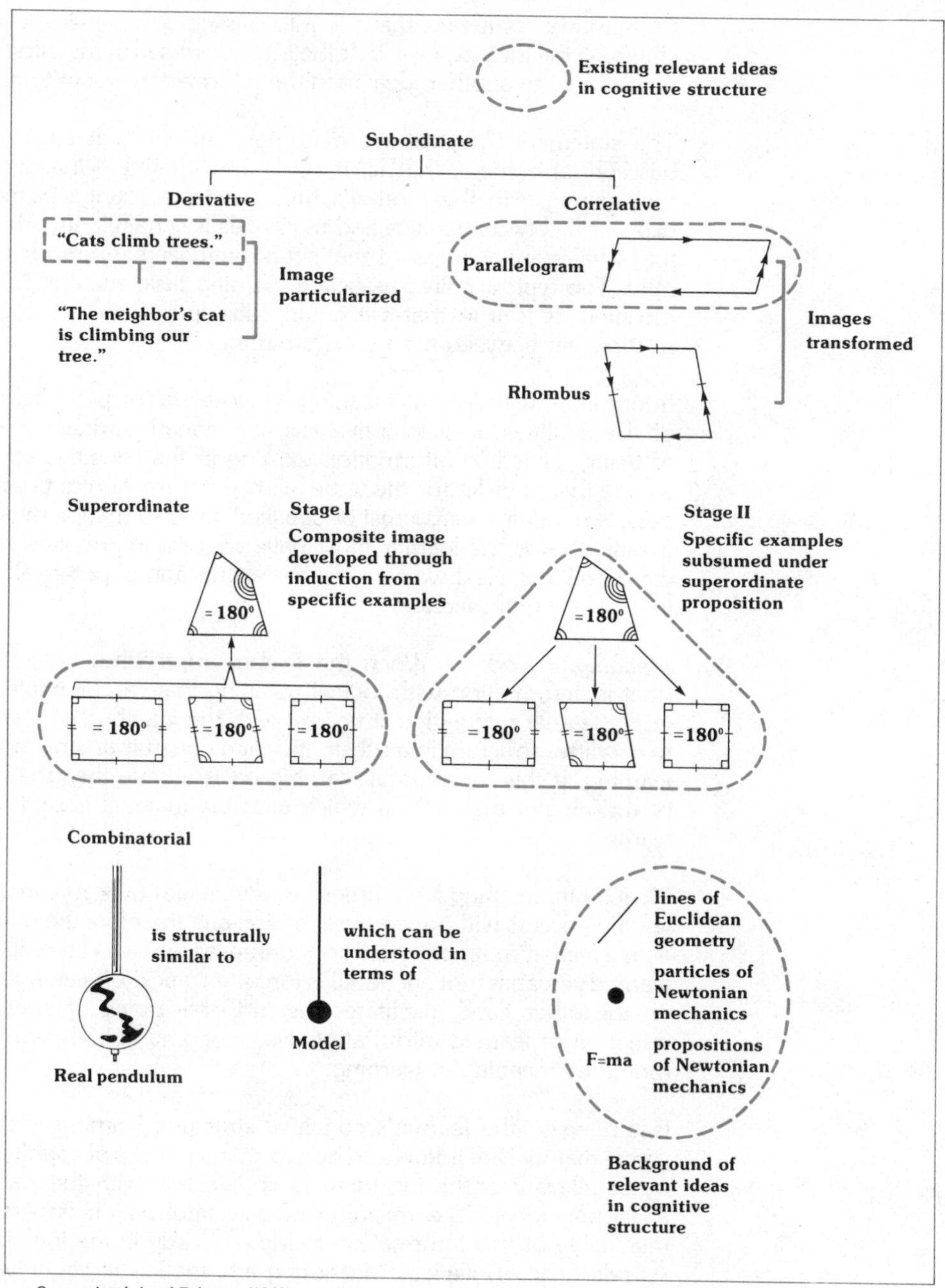

Source: Ausubel and Robinson (1969).

more inclusive than whale. Subordinate relationships can be derivative or correlative. In the example of derivative subordination from the figure, we see that the new information, "The neighbor's cat is climbing our tree" is a particular instance of a known idea "Cats climb trees." All the information necessary to derive the particular is contained within the general idea. However, in correlative subordination the new information elaborates on the subsuming idea by reducing its inclusiveness. Using the example from Figure 5–17, we see that the person has already learned the meaning of parallelogram (four-sided figure with opposite sides parallel) and now learns that a rhombus is a parallelogram with four equal sides.

A superordinate relationship occurs when the new information is more inclusive than the anchoring ideas. If a person has previously learned that the sum of the angles in each square, rectangle, and rhombus equals 360° and then acquires the idea that the sum of the angles for any quadrilateral totals 360°, we have a superordinate relationship between the new and anchoring information.

The third type of possible relationship called "combinatorial" by Ausubel and Robinson is neither superordinate nor subordinate, but rather is based on similarity between the new and known information. Since the new idea is analogous to a known idea, concepts and principles that apply to the known also apply to the new idea. As the example shows, a real pendulum is similar to a model; consequently principles demonstrated to explain the behavior of the model can be extrapolated to the behavior of the real object.

With an understanding of the types of relationships between new and known ideas, consideration of the availability of relevant anchoring ideas is simplified for subordinate relationships, the more inclusive term must be learned and available in the cognitive structure of the learner prior to reception of the new information. When dealing with superordinate relationships, a number of instances, not just one, must be incorporated into the existing cognitive structure before introduction of the general idea. In learning new information involved in a combinatorial relationship, the learner's cognitive structure must contain the relevant explanatory concepts and principles.

Another major characteristic of cognitive structures influencing the learning and retention of meaningful verbal learning is the stability and clarity of available anchoring ideas. Known relevant ideas that lack stability and clarity provide a weak anchor to which new information can be related. This weakness makes it difficult to relate the new information to cognitive structure and results in a more ambiguous meaning being established. Consequently, a new idea related to such a cognitive structure would be less discriminable from subsuming information, a major cause of forgetting according to Ausubel (1968).

This section has been a brief overview of Ausubel's theory of meaningful verbal learning. His theory is an important milestone in educational psychology because it was developed to directly account for learning in the complex environment of the classroom. As we have seen, most theories of learning require the educational psychologist to extrapolate from a relatively simple laboratory situation to the classroom. Several examples of the application of Ausubel's theory to instruction can be found in Chapter 11 of this book.

Robert M. Gagné: Domains of learning. Robert M. Gagné is one of the most influential contemporary educational psychologists. His work, while concerned with the structure of human knowledge, is not really a schema theory; however, his theory can be interpreted within that framework. Gagné's major contribution has been the development of a taxonomy of learning by which the vast field of learning research can be organized and applied appropriately to the design of instruction. According to this approach, regardless of the subject matter or the level of instruction, what can be taught can be classified into one of five domains of learning.

These domains are defined by (1) the performance capability established, and (2) the distinctive conditions of learning necessary to establish each domain. These conditions of learning are further subdivided into internal and external conditions.

The link between assimilation-to-schema theory and Gagné's theory is the concept of internal conditions of learning. Certain specific conditions must exist within the learner if an instance of learning in any domain is to be established. In Gagné's theory these necessary internal conditions are previously learned capabilities. According to Gagné (1977) two types of essential internal conditions can be identified: (1) capabilities that support new learning, and (2) capabilities that will be incorporated in the to-be-learned capability. These internal conditions are often referred to as *prerequisites.* Previously learned capabilities that support new learning are referred to as *general* prerequisites in this book and include, but are not limited to, reading, study skills, and memory strategies. Capabilities that are incorporated into new learning are referred to as *specific* prerequisites in this text. A student faced with learning long division must have first learned addition, subtraction, and multiplication. These latter arithmetic operations are specific prerequisites that are part of (become incorporated into) the performance of a long division problem.

Viewed within an assimilation-to-schema paradigm, the world knowledge needed to produce a specific instance of new learning will be a specific type of previously learned capability. Furthermore, the exact type of learned capability necessary will be determined by the domain involved in the new learning and whether the prerequisite will be incorporated into the new learning or merely support its acquisition and retention. Because of this specificity concerning prerequisites, among other reasons, Gagné's theory has had much application in the design of instruction. The procedure for deriving prerequisites and their use in instruction will be the focus of Chapter 8.

In addition to internal conditions, there is a unique set of external conditions associated with the establishment of new learning in each domain. These essential conditions for each learning domain and their deployment in the design of instruction are discussed in Chapters 10 and 11, so they will not be covered here. For now we will consider each domain in terms of the characteristic performance capability established by learning in that domain.

Domains of learning. Gagné (1965b) originally proposed eight types of learning outcomes which he had derived from research on learning. Later he modified and reorganized the eight types into five domains (Gagné, 1972). What value does the concept of learning domains hold for educational psychologists and teachers? According to Gagné (1972, p. 2), they serve three important functions:

1. To distinguish the parts of a content area that are subject to different instructional treatments.
2. To relate the instructional procedures of one subject to those of another.
3. To specify the different techniques of assessment required for each domain of learning.

A summary of the five domains of learning follows.

Verbal information. The learning of verbal information occurs when a student restates in verbal form previously acquired information. A young child reciting a nursery rhyme and a high school student writing a chronology of events leading up to the American Revolution are both demonstrating the learning of verbal information. The verbal information acquired in school ranges from names through facts to knowledge or organized bodies of related facts.

Intellectual skills. Earlier in this chapter we saw that children come to manipulate their environment by mental actions performed on internal representations rather than acting directly on the environment. These mental operations performed on symbols are termed *intellectual skills* by Gagné. He identified four major types of intellectual skills: discriminations, concepts, rules, and higher-order rules (Gagné, 1974a). Additionally, these skills are related in a hierarchical manner, such that the learning of one depends upon the prior learning of the simpler types as specific prerequisites. Thus learning a rule presupposes the previous learning of relevant concepts, which require as a prerequisite previous learning of appropriate discriminations.

Discrimination as a learned capability occurs when a person learns to "see differences in" or otherwise distinguish between two objects on the basis of a specific attribute or attributes. Concept learning occurs when the person comes to treat objects as equivalent on the basis of common attributes. The young child who calls both a collie and bassett hound "dog" is demonstrating concept learning, even though the relevant common attributes of dog as a concept cannot be verbalized by the child.

Gagné (1977, p. 134) defines a rule as "an inferred capability that enables the individual to respond to a class of stimulus situations with a class of performances." A person who has learned a rule can demonstrate application of that rule in a specific situation. Consider the rule, "To multiply exponentials, one adds exponents." A person who has learned this rule would be able to finish the equation, $A^6 \cdot A^3 = A^X$, or any other equation involving multiplication of exponentials. Higher-order rules are produced by combining simpler rules, and the learned capability would resemble that of a learned rule. The distinction is that the higher-order rule is more complex than any of its component rules and presumably more difficult to learn.

Cognitive strategies. This learning domain refers to the means or strategies people have learned to manage their own learning and remembering. Gagné (1974a, p. 64) views these strategies as "internally organized capabilities which the learner makes use of in guiding his own attending, learning, remembering, and thinking." The student who constructs questions to answer while reading a text, or the student who after finding a misunderstood word in the dictionary uses it in three different sentences, is demonstrating the use of cognitive strategies.

Attitude. The choices a person makes in a given situation are influenced by prior learning. Thus a child who chooses to read instead of some other activity does so on the basis of a preference established by previous learning. This internal state that influences a person's choice of action toward some class of things, persons, or events is called an "attitude" by Gagné.

Motor skills. Preschool children struggling to print their names legibly and the aspiring basketball star trying to master a lay-up while maneuvering around an opponent at a full run are all in the process of acquiring a motor skill. Both the above tasks require the coordinated execution of muscular movements.

A REORGANIZED TAXONOMY

Throughout this book we will be using a taxonomy of learning domains to aid in making various decisions about teaching. Knowledge of learning domains will be applied in determining the outcomes of instruction, designing instruction, evaluating instruction, and making other decisions concerning teaching in the classroom. Gagné's taxonomy represents an advance over other taxonomies in that it is derived from the literature on learning and so is firmly rooted in our scientific knowledge of the learning process. Because of this base his domains of learning have great value in organizing our knowledge of the learning process for its application to teaching. We have tried to maintain this value of Gagné's domains while reorganizing them into a form more familiar to teachers.

Teachers and other educators have traditionally classified educational goals into three domains: cognitive, affective, and psychomotor. We have maintained these distinctions with one exception. Like Gagné we have kept cognitive strategies as a separate domain, but to reduce the confusion with the cognitive domain we have renamed it the *mathemagenic* domain (the label is explained below). This type of skill is so important in the education of the student that we thought it desirable to maintain its distinctiveness by placing it in a separate domain. What follows is a description of the domains to be used in describing the learning outcomes of education in the remainder of this book.

Affective domain

Learning outcomes in this domain are referred to as *affective states.* They are internal states that predispose a person to act toward a class of objects or people in a certain way. The types of affective states established in schools are morals, values, opinions, and attitudes.

Affective states are manifested in the approach and avoidance behaviors of students. Approach behaviors bring the student in contact with the affective object, and avoidance behaviors move the student away from such objects. Many of the affective states learned in school are acquired incidentally through our experiences. But teachers do intentionally instill values, attitudes, and other affective states in students, so they do represent important outcomes in school.

Psychomotor domain

Outcomes in the psychomotor domain represent learned capabilities of motor skills as Gagné refers to them. Motor skills involve the performance of coordinated sequences of muscular actions. The most obvious examples are those athletic skills such as swimming, throwing a ball, or high jumping. Other examples are handwriting, speaking as in learning a new sound in a foreign language, or some aspects of sculpturing in clay. Learning outcomes involving motor skills occur most frequently at the lower grade levels or in courses such as physical education. However, even in higher grades tasks involving motor skills have to be mastered by the student.

Cognitive domain

Under the cognitive domain we have combined Gagné's verbal information domain and the learning of concepts and rules from his intellectual skills domain. These types of learned capabilities correspond most closely to Bloom et al.'s (1956) cognitive level of knowledge, comprehension, application, and evaluation.

Memorization. In this type of task the student has to recall or recognize information previously presented during the course of instruction. This information can range in complexity from a name to an entire body of knowledge. The student's performance can demonstrate either verbatim reproduction or comprehension as evidenced by substantial paraphrasing of the information.

Concept learning. This type of learning occurs, as we have seen, when the student classifies objects or events according to some superordinate category. A student identifying a painting as being of the Hudson Valley style or the biologist classifying a new organism as aerobic or anaerobic is demonstrating concept learning. Furthermore, the task of concept learning requires that the student be able to transfer this skill to new examples.

Rule learning. Rules are statements of cause-and-effect relationships between two or more concepts. A rule-learning task requires the student to demonstrate understanding of the rule by applying it in a particular situation. The learned capability established by rule learning is rule using. A student who understands the rule for forming the plural of words ending in *ch* can use that rule in novel situations.

Mathemagenic domain

We have taken the name of this domain from the phrase, *mathemagenic activities,* coined by Ernst Z. Rothkopf (1970). He describes mathemagenic activities as those in which students engage as they come in contact with instructional materials and which are critical in determining what the student will learn from the interaction. According to Rothkopf, mathemagenic activities are those that give birth to learning. The original focus on mathemagenic activities was involved with attentional processes, but we have borrowed the phrase to apply it to all strategies that the learner uses to facilitate learning (for a discussion of the range of these activities, see Chapter 16). Gagné has referred to these activities as *cognitive strategies.*

Mathemagenic skills or strategies are applied to bring about other learning outcomes, so tasks involving mathemagenic skills result in multiple outcomes. Tasks involving mathemagenic skills we have referred to as *problem-solving* situations. In a problem-solving situation the person must find a solution by applying past knowledge and mathemagenic skills. The solution usually represents a capability such as rule learning but can be any other type of learned capability such as an affective state or memorization. What is critical about problem solving is that it results in either the acquisition or practice of a mathemagenic skill in addition to the other learned capability acquired by the student.

9. What three factors are necessary for meaningful verbal learning according to Ausubel?
10. The potential meaningfulness of information depends upon:
    a. Logical meaningfulness.
    b. Cognitive structure.
    c. Meaningful learning set.
11. Learning to apply concepts and rules are examples of what Gagné calls:
    a. Verbal information.
    b. Cognitive strategies.
    c. Intellectual skills.
12. Learning that outlining a chapter as you read it helps you to remember better the information from that chapter illustrates what type of skill?
    a. Concept learning.
    b. Memorization.
    c. Rule learning.
    d. Mathemagenic.

SUMMARY

The human memory was described as being the common core of cognitivist interpretations of learning. This memory or information-processing system is composed of a sensory registor, a short-term or working memory, and a long-term store. Emphasis was given to the processes involved in the storage and retrieval of information from this long-term store. The storage process requires that the to-be-learned information be encoded in either verbal or imagery form. The retrieval process is aided by retrieval cues developed in the encoding process. The second half of the chapter examined how our world knowledge is represented and organized in the long-term store. This knowledge was said to be organized into schemata, and learning was described as a process of assimilation to schema. Two views of this assimilation-to-schema process were presented: developmental and learning. The developmental view stressed the qualitative changes in schemata occurring with growth, while the learning view focused on the conditions necessary to facilitate the assimilation-to-schema process.

SELF-TEST

1. A teacher saying "Listen carefully to the paragraph I am going to read, so you can answer the *what* question!" is trying to establish:
   a. An expectancy.
   b. Sensory orientation.
   c. Processing.
   d. Memory set.
2. The prevention of information loss from short-term memory is a function of what process?
   a. Pattern recognition.
   b. Attention.
   c. Chunking.
   d. Rehearsal.
3. Suppose a person was given the following sequence of letters to study for one minute and was told to say it in 30 seconds—AAAAEEEDDDDDDCCCC-CCC. This person repeats—A4 E3 D6 C7. This illustrates:
   a. Chunking.
   b. Cue-dependent retrieval.
   c. Information overload.
   d. Rehearsal.
4. In learning the Spanish word for *house,* which of the following encoding strategies should facilitate recall the least?
   a. Imagine a house with the word *casa* in neon on the side.
   b. Remember the saying, "A man's home is his casa."
   c. Repeat to yourself, "House equals casa."
   d. There should be no difference in the strategies.
5. Labeling a picture should facilitate its retention, according to the dual-encoding hypothesis. Why?
6. If some information you learned in Chapter 2 of the text for this course interfered with the recall of some information on this test, it would be:
   a. Proactive interference.
   b. Retroactive interference.
   c. Trace decay.
   d. Acoustical interference.
7. Which theory says forgetting in long-term memory is a function of time?
   a. Retrieval theory.
   b. Interference theory.
   c. Decay theory.
   d. Dual-encoding theory.
8. Distinguish between a *representation* and an *operation.*
9. One major distinction between Piaget and Bruner concerns the growth of modes of representation as opposed to stages. Explain this difference.
10. Information that can be related to another idea in a nonarbitrary and substantive manner has what quality according to Ausubel?
11. Gagné's equivalent of a schema is called:
    a. A prerequisite.
    b. An anchoring idea.
    c. A concept.
    d. A cognitive structure.
12. Mathemagenic skills are perhaps the most important class of skills acquired by people. Think of three mathemagenic skills you have mastered and list them.

ANSWER KEY TO BOXED QUESTIONS

1. *d*
2. *d*
3. *a*
4. *a*
5. *c*
6. *a*
7. False
8. *a* and *c*

9. Exposure to meaningful information, availability of relevant schema in cognitive structure, and activation of a meaningful learning set.
10. *b*
11. *c*
12. *d*

ANSWER KEY TO SELF-TEST

1. *a*
2. *d*
3. *a*
4. *c*
5. Because that would encode the information in both the verbal and imagery systems, and encoding in both systems leads to greater retention than does encoding in only one.
6. *a*
7. *c*
8. A *representation* is a mental substitute for an object or event, and an *operation* is a mental action performed on a representation.
9. Each new mode does not replace or eliminate the preceding, as do stages.
10. Logical meaning.
11. *a*
12. Any strategy you have acquired to aid your learning.

Chapter 6

The process of decision making: Systems perspective

UP TO THIS POINT we have tried to provide you with a broad perspective of the educational system, the learning process, and the field of educational psychology. We have also asked you to examine your beliefs relative to these issues. Now we begin to narrow the focus somewhat and explore how these factors interact with each other.

One critical point of interaction among the school system, students, and your beliefs is when you have to make decisions. The utility of the decisions to a great extent will be based on the quality of the decision-making process and the quality of information used to make those decisions. As the title of this text indicates, we believe the field of educational psychology can make a major contribution to improving those decisions affecting classroom instruction through research findings on the decision-making process and how information is gathered and used.

In this chapter we first explore the nature of educational problems and decision makers. Next, strategies for information gathering and decision making are discussed. Finally, we present our views on the utility of a rapidly developing approach to decision making and also your future role as a decision maker.

The main point to be made in this chapter is that in order to make sound decisions, you need a broad base of reasonably unbiased information and a sound, pragmatic decision-making strategy. By systematically using these two factors, your decisions should be workable and more productive, and relate to the total problem rather than merely portions of it in an unorganized and less productive manner. Using these two factors will also help you to avoid unintentionally creating problems that will have to be dealt with at some future time. In short, the content of this chapter should provide you with a pragmatic and integrated perspective for dealing with instructional problems.

After having read and studied the material in this chapter, you should be able to:

1. Outline several characteristics of educational problems.
2. Describe three limitations of humans as decision makers.
3. Describe three biases humans are subject to when making judgments.
4. Describe the process and three rules used in making small-group decisions.
5. Describe the process of making individual decisions.
6. List the main characteristics of five information-gathering strategies and the major usefulness of each technique.
7. Describe five phases of the instructional process in terms of *(a)* the main function, *(b)* the decisions to be made, and *(c)* the activities to be carried out in each phase.

NATURE OF EDUCATIONAL PROBLEMS

Basic problem

We have made the point that learning is a process that can be inferred only by a change in behavior occurring under fairly well-defined conditions. We have also pointed out that the process of teaching is primarily aimed at bringing about specific changes in behavior. The basic problem, then, is deciding how to bring about the changes we wish to see in the students' performance capability.

Compounding the problem is the fact that learning and teaching are both complex, interactive processes likely to create simultaneous change in both the learner and the teacher. As we progress through the interactive processes, nothing remains constant except possibly the furniture in the room, the paint on the walls, and often the material (you have so carefully designed) on the bulletin boards. Not even for a minute does the teacher, the student, or the topic remain constant.

The fact that learning/teaching is so complex and subject to change rules out the possibility that you can reach a point when you can decide that a problem is solved. Instead of being solved, problems merely evolve into new problems. As a teacher, you will usually be expected to take the initiative in directing this process of change, but to some extent your students will be expected to take some initiative, too. Even when students are given such opportunity, you are expected to maintain some control over the process. If you do not, you may find some students only too willing to take over the task. When this happens, you might have some really *big problems* to deal with, such as where to find another job or what other career to choose!

In addition to bringing about and coping with change, we usually need to deal with several factors simultaneously. These factors also tend to interact; that is, when one factor is changed it tends to change the characteristics of other factors. It would be impossible to outline all of the factors involved, but we believe there are a few broad ones that help to define the nature of the problems. These factors include the context in which we must make our decisions, and also the expectations and limitations imposed on us by society and the school system.

General context

One factor that tends to define the types of problems educators encounter is the general context within which the problems occur. In the broadest sense, this involves the type of educational system we have developed. Glaser and Nitko (1970) have identified three general models on which these systems seem to be based. The first is a system in which "educational goals and instructional methods are relatively fixed and inflexible. Similar goals are set for all students and individual differences are taken into account chiefly by dropping students along the way" (p. 15). One assumption of this model is that some students are more capable than others and the less capable will be "weeded out" at some point. This appears to have been the predominant model in the past and we will refer to it as the *traditional model* (Figure 6–1). As Jerome Kagan (1971, pp. 4–5) has noted:

> Since the system worked efficiently, our society was not concerned with early school failures. Early failure simply indicated how sensitive the procedure was in eliminating those who did not have the proper temperament or ability to take responsibility for their fellow man.

As Kagan further notes, there is a different orientation toward education today and more concern for the many early failures that were ignored in the past. In response to this concern, other models have been developed. Glaser and Nitko (1970, p. 15) describe one such model in which students, instead of all proceeding toward a common goal, are "channelled into different courses such as academic courses, vocational courses, or business courses." This type of system adapts to individual differences by first determining the prospective future role of the individual and then placing the student in a relatively fixed instructional program leading toward that goal. These programs are often referred to as *tracks,* so this model could be appropriately labeled the *tracking model.*

Glaser and Nitko describe the third model as having a variety of instructional treatments that can be implemented in several ways. One approach is to have all students proceed through a common instructional sequence; students are taken out of it only when

FIGURE 6–1
At times similar goals are set for all children

remedial work is necessary. When, and if, the remedial work is successfully completed, the student is put back into the general sequence of instruction. At the other extreme, a student's individual "learning habits and attitudes, achievements, skills, cognitive style, etc." are assessed. Based on this analysis, the student is "guided through a course of instruction specifically tailored to him" (1970, p. 16). Glaser and Nitko believe that a pattern falling somewhere between the two extremes of the third model will be adopted by many schools in the future. We have chosen to label this the *individualized model.*

Regardless of the exact model upon which any school is based, the broad orientation of the school defines the nature of the problem confronting the individuals involved. In some systems, the problems center on the weeding-out process, whereas others focus on the identification of individual differences and the specification of individual goals and programs. Within each model there will also be wide differences in the staff and the amount of flexibility allowed by the school administrators. The general context, then, is one factor that tends to shape our problems.

Specific context

In a narrower sense, educational problems arise and need to be dealt with during class discussions, at conferences with students and parents, during committee meetings, and at home alone. While it would be nice if these problems arose in a quiet, relaxed atmosphere, many times they do not. Because they do not, it is well to devote some time, when we are not so harried, to deciding on a decision-making strategy suitable for a context of change, complexity, and limited time. Having such a strategy may allow us to act in haste without needing to repent at leisure.

Goals

Adding to the unique character of educational problems are the goals that schools and teachers set and try to attain. As Glaser has pointed out, these can be limited to a few or expanded to a wide variety. Even between school systems where each has only a single set of goals for all students, we are likely to find wide differences.

Whether a few or many goals are involved, the exact types of goals chosen by our educational system define the problems facing us. For instance, to attempt to have all students attain a certain minimum level of reading achievement poses a different problem than to have all students attain an awareness of current social problems.

Learners

In the preceding chapters we identified some of the characteristics of the learning process that are believed to be universal to all humans. This does not mean, however, that all learners are the same and can be dealt with in a similar manner. Students are different and these individual differences need to be taken into account. Regardless of whether these differences are biological or environmental, we cannot ignore them and, therefore, they add another dimension to educational problems.

Resources

One aspect of educational problems which educators and the tax-paying public are well aware of is the matter of resources. As presently organized, schools use buildings, books, and fuel oil, and employ a large number of people. This involves raising and spending public monies. As you are aware, this also leads to much controversy. The fact that resources are limited imposes on us the need to take them into consideration as yet another facet of educational problems.

A less obvious effect that resources have on educational problems stems from the human resources involved. While most people tend to think of resources in terms of dollars, the most important resource of the schools is the staff that plans and carries out the functions of the school system. While it is not our intent to derogate the competence of these people, we feel it is well to keep in mind that there is a bias built into this staff. This bias is due to the fact that almost every person working in the American school system is a product of that system (Figure 6–2). In terms of seeing ourselves as we are, this needs to be recognized and considered in our decision making since it may severely limit the range of alternatives we will generate or consider.

Many studies have been aimed at trying to find those characteristics of teachers that make for an effective teacher (Dunkin & Biddle, 1974). We are still, however, very much in the dark on this issue. Wallen and Travers (1963) offer some suggestions about the origins of the general patterns of teacher behavior. They see these patterns as derived from:

1. Teaching traditions.
2. Social learnings.
3. Philosophical traditions.
4. The teacher's own needs.
5. Conditions existing in the school and community.
6. Scientific research on learning.

The teaching tradition origin is primarily a matter of teachers imitating the behavior of teachers they have observed in the past. The social learning origin refers to a teacher's beliefs about what is appropriate social behavior and values, as we have noted earlier. These beliefs will influence what the teacher will set as goals and tend to reward or punish in the activities of students. In a similar manner, as we have also noted, a teacher's philosophical beliefs will influence the teacher's goals and the general methods used to achieve them. The teacher's own needs are more closely related to what might be called the teacher's "personality." A warm, friendly teacher

FIGURE 6–2
Teachers training class of 1916 ready to reenter the educational system

Courtesy of New York State Historical Association, Cooperstown.

may adopt a very positive approach that calls for a great deal of student-teacher interaction, whereas a more reserved and antagonistic teacher might use an entirely different approach. The conditions existing within the school and/or community may suggest to a teacher that one approach is likely to be more accepted and productive than another. For instance, in some schools a more relaxed classroom atmosphere is compatible with the building principals' beliefs about appropriate classroom climate and also the previous experience of the students, while in other schools this may not be the case. The influence of research on learning is the final origin that Wallen and Travers (1963) mention. As Clifford (1973) notes, the amount of influence one can attribute to research is difficult to determine. In many cases the research is merely confirming the acceptability of a long-established educational practice. However, Clifford (p. 27) concluded that research contradictory to "personal or group opinion won neither notice nor acceptance". Clifford also pointed out that E. L. Thorndike, who we have mentioned as one of the early leaders in the field of educational psychology, expected a lag of 30–50 years between his experimental work and its implementation in the classroom. From some research evidence it appears that the lag is closer to 20 years. It may be that it takes that long for this single origin of teaching patterns to modify or overcome the other five origins.

In this text we are assuming that your present beliefs are largely a matter of your perception of the educational process you have been through and the role your teachers have played in that process. Our goal is to help you clarify, broaden, and modify your perceptions on the basis of current research data so as to increase the range of possibilities you can generate or consider as useful.

From the perspectives we have presented, a teacher can be viewed as a part of the process. But, to the extent that any human is a product of the past, this is also a constraint on the possibility of any rapid changes occurring within the system. While some may deplore this state of affairs, we view it with mixed feelings. We are anxious to bring about some improvements in the educational system where we see faults, but we are also satisfied that the system does not shift with every fad, fancy, and new theory. We would be quite happy, however, to see changes take place more rapidly when justifiable. We feel this can be accomplished through the use of a more systematic method of making decisions, which is capable of integrating new research information into our thinking to meet a changing educational environment.

1. How would the four characteristics of educational problems just discussed apply to a specific unit of instruction?

NATURE OF DECISION MAKERS

Your present decision-making skills

As you face the problems of classroom teaching, you will have to make decisions. Even now, if you had to teach, you would be able to arrive at some reasonable decisions, but because you have had relatively little training you would probably have many doubts about the wisdom of your decisions. The reason you would be able to make these decisions is that you have been through the educational system and have had a chance to observe what teachers and students do. Your experiences have been limited, however, to relatively few classrooms and teachers. And, your perception of those situations has been distorted by your general philosophy, value system, and role as a student. In this chapter we present a broad organizational framework that we believe will help you to integrate your experiences and make classroom decisions in a more systematic, less biased, and more productive manner. To aid you in that decision-making process, we now take a careful look at some factors that influence an individual's decisions.

The 7 ± 2 problem

One interesting research finding relative to our problem-solving ability is that people can retain only a limited amount of information at one time. For example, in human memory studies the average adult can remember only about seven bits of information at a time in short-term memory (Miller, 1956). Some individuals seem to be able to remember nine bits of information, while others can cope with only five bits at a time, thus the term 7 ± 2. This capacity apparently increases from age three, when only one bit of information can be retained, to age 16, when the adult level is reached (Case, 1972). Related to this finding, one of the authors of this text was recently surveying many psychological theories and models for an advanced course. In the analysis he discovered that every theory or model he reviewed was designed to deal with nine or fewer categories within any specific component of the theory. Likewise, none of the theories reviewed had more than nine major components. This is not offered as "proof" of the 7 ± 2 factor, but it is interesting to find that even with relatively sophisticated thinkers, the inability to keep in mind or the unwillingness to consider more than nine factors is apparent. We refer to this as the 7 ± 2 factor. While science is supposed to be parsimonious, this tendency to simplify and reorganize fantastically complex phenomena into only 7 ± 2 bits of information may, in fact, be a human limitation. Parsimony is supposed to simplify complex explanations but should not be used to distort the data and ignore the possibility of additional factors.

The satisficer strategy

An interesting point, possibly related to the 7 ± 2 factor, is that individuals like to operate with a minimum of information when trying to make a decision (Kogan & Wallach, 1967). The term used to describe this type of decision-making strategy is *satisficer,* indicating that the main strategy is to accept the first decision that appears to satisfy the requirements of an acceptable solution. The more traditional approaches to decision-making theory view people as attempting to maximize their gains and thereby seeking the best solution. To a considerable extent, people do try to maximize gains and minimize losses but, because of the cost of obtaining more information, it appears that people settle for less than optimal gains in many decisions. Expressed differently, because time and effort are involved in acquiring information, it may be more practical to use a satisficer strategy rather than a maximizer strategy in most situations in which we have to make decisions. With frequent use of this strategy it may become habitual and, rather than arriving at workable solutions that are responsive to the total problem, we are likely to arrive at a series of partial solutions that may not even be compatible.

An example of the satisficer strategy is when a teacher decides to use a certain set of materials simply because they are more colorful than others or "look as if" the students will enjoy them. Selecting on the basis of one factor and ignoring all other factors certainly makes it easier to come to a decision, but we may not obtain the maximum performance from our students. It is the old story: "Don't confuse me with facts."

This strategy is apparently not simply a matter of human laziness but rather the result of a limited capacity that further reduces the 7 ± 2 phenomenon. Cox (1978) presents evidence indicating that the 7 ± 2 phenomenon is a measure of short-term, static memory capacity. Distinct from this static memory capacity is processing capacity. His evidence indicates that this processing capacity is limited to actively manipulating approximately four bits of information. He also suggests that this capacity does not increase with age but can vary on a momentary basis and may be subject to improvement with specific training. While Cox does not make the suggestion, it seems reasonable to assume that the use of external aids, similar to written lists for increasing our static memory capacity, can be used to increase our processing capacity. People are frequently seen diagraming complex problems, which may be one strategy they have developed to cope with a limited internal capacity.

> 2. What are the three major ways in which your judgments are likely to be limited? What effect might these limitations have on your judgments?

Three other judgmental strategies

Our basic strategy of trying to maximize gains and minimize losses is affected by strategies other than the satisficer strategy. Tversky and Kahneman (1974) suggest three other strategies that tend to affect our decisions. These strategies distort our ability to predict an uncertain quality (values) or the likelihood of an event happening (probabilities), for example, how useful a particular instructional strategy may be with our students or how often particular student errors occur.

Representativeness. One strategy is that of representativeness. To illustrate this strategy, Tversky and Kahneman use as an example a situation in which a person is asked to judge, on the basis of a verbal description of an individual, whether that

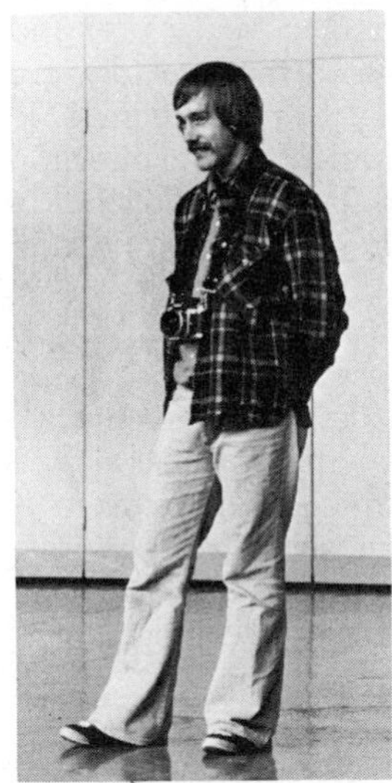

FIGURE 6–3
The representativeness of our stereotypes affects our judgment of a person's occupation

individual is a farmer, salesperson, airline pilot, librarian, or physician. To make the judgment we apparently assess the degree to which the description of the person is representative of, or similar to, our stereotype of the various occupations. In using this strategy we tend to ignore the actual frequencies with which the various occupations occur. In other words, we overlook the fact that there are many more farmers than there are librarians, and instead decide whether a person is a librarian on the basis of the description being representative of our stereotype of librarians (Figure 6–3).

In addition to ignoring the actual frequencies of events, reliance on the representativeness strategy results in our ignoring the number of observations with which we are dealing. If we take random samples from a population, the larger the sample the more likely it is to be representative of the population from which it was taken. We tend to overlook this fact and instead react to both large and small samples in the same way, namely, that regardless of size, any sample truly represents the population. In addition, we also expect a short-term run of events, such as one or two performances of a student, to be representative of the student's performance over a long time interval.

Another aspect of using the representativeness strategy is that it results in our being insensitive to the reliability of our data and the expected accuracy of our predictions. As an example, Tversky and Kahneman point out a study in which individuals were asked to read several paragraphs, each describing the performance of a student teacher during a practice lesson. Some subjects were asked to evaluate the quality of the lesson, while others were asked to predict the standing of each student five years into the future. The judgments were identical even though the reliability of predicting five years into the future on the basis of one practice lesson is probably quite low.

Using the representativeness strategy also tends to affect our feelings of confidence in our decisions. The more the description matches the stereotype of a librarian, the higher will be our confidence in the decision. This gives us the illusion of validity in our decision even though we may be aware of factors that should limit the accuracy of our predictions and also our confidence.

Because of our reliance on the use of the representativeness strategy, we also overlook the fact that extreme performances, either high or low, are usually not followed by similar extreme performances. This phenomenon is known as *regression toward the mean.* A common example is that an outstandingly high performance on an achievement test is not likely to be followed by one that is quite as high. In spite of much evidence to the contrary, we expect the high performance to be representative of all future performances.

As an example of the effects of the representativeness strategy, we may have a boy enroll in our fifth-grade class during the middle of the year who is well-groomed, handsome, friendly, and known to be the son of a college professor. On his first math test he gets a perfect score, while no other student in the class does as well. On the basis of his physical characteristics and family background we are likely to stereotype the boy as being of at least normal intelligence and probably above. On the basis of the one test result, it is likely that we will leap to the conclusion that the boy is actually brilliant, will do well on all tasks, and probably will go on to college.

Availability. Another strategy we commonly use in making a decision about the frequency of objects or the probability of events is based on the ease with which we can recall past instances or occurrences. This strategy is referred to by Tversky and Kahneman as *availability*. Because certain events are remembered more vividly, are recalled more often, or have occurred more recently, it is easier to recall them. Due to this increased availability, these events tend to distort our judgments in the direction of believing that they occur more frequently than they actually do. This sort of distortion may lead us to categorize a student as being disruptive simply because of one, and possibly only one, particularly disturbing situation.

The search process we use in trying to recall instances of a certain object or event has a bearing on the availability strategy. In cases where we have developed an effective search process to recall certain instances, those instances will be more available than those for which we have not developed an effective search strategy. For instance, if we have a more effective search strategy for remembering instances of aggressive behavior than for remembering cooperative behavior, we are much more likely to overestimate the amount of aggression that occurs and underestimate the amount of cooperative behavior that occurs.

The availability strategy is also affected by how easy it is to imagine certain instances that have not occurred but might occur. In our example of the disruptive boy, it might have been the usually quiet, polite, mild-mannered boy with whom he was fighting who actually instigated the conflict but, because it is difficult for us to imagine that this is the case, we place the blame on the wrong child.

An illusion that two factors are related also affects our reliance on the availability strategy. If we assume that two factors are closely related, we are likely to conclude that they have occurred together quite frequently. These relationships are more likely to be available and, therefore, have a stonger effect on our decisions than other relationships may have, even though the latter may be more accurate. Returning again to our misjudged, aggressive student, if he is in more than one fight with the same child we are quite likely to overestimate the proportion of fights they have had during the year.

Adjustment/anchoring. The third strategy is termed *adjustment/anchoring* and refers to the relationship between the effect of our initial decision and the effect of subsequent information related to that decision. Our initial decision tends to act as a base point, or anchor, for all subsequent decisions on the matter. For instance, if we initially decide that a particular student is very aggressive, the decision affects our future decisions. The initial decision anchors our subsequent perceptions, and additional information results in insufficient adjustments in our decisions. The net effect is that, in spite of receiving a great amount of data subsequent to our initial decision that our hypothetical child has a normal level of aggressive behavior, we still are likely to perceive the child as more aggressive than he actually is although not as aggressive as originally estimated.

The three strategies of representativeness, availability, and adjustment/anchoring may all affect our decisions about a single child. For example, it is possible that a certain child may have eyelids that droop to a slight degree and a pale complexion, both of which fit with our stereotype of a "dull" child as opposed to a "bright" child. This initial judgment will act as an anchor on subsequent judgments, and we are not likely to ever completely overcome the effect of this initial decision. As a result, we might react too little to the child's high achievements. Because of this, all signs of normality will be underestimated, giving us a large number of perceptions of the child's performance that are biased toward our original perception. This would leave us with few, if any, perceptions of high performance and many of low performance. Because some of the low performances are likely to be seen as even poorer than they were, they are also likely to appear to be outstandingly low. Here the strategy of availability adds to our perception of the child. Because the poor performances stood out at the time and because they appear to occur more frequently, we are more likely to recall them in the future. By using the availability strategy in future decisions about the child, these recollections will also tend to bias our decisions to treat the child as having low intelligence. Our original decision about the child, the fact that we will probably make insufficient revisions of that decision, and the fact that we will make future judgments on the basis of the memories that are easiest to recall may lead us to the conclusion that the child is retarded and does not belong in a regular classroom—all because this child has somewhat droopy eyelids and a pale complexion. Some teachers do it on the basis of dirty sneakers or socially unacceptable behaviors, but the results are the same!

3. What are the three biases in human judgments suggested by Tversky and Kahneman, and what will be their effect?

Individual decisions

Before we get into the more pragmatic presentation of decision-making strategies, we feel it will be useful for you to have a more concrete conceptualization of the decision-making process used by individuals. Leaving aside the complexities of the inner functions of the brain, there is a complex interaction between the information people receive and the decisions they make. We have already pointed out how we tend to distort this information. Here we discuss the source of information and how it relates to our decisions.

As we noted previously, our basic strategy is to maximize our gains and minimize our losses (Figure 6–4), but this is tempered by the satisficer strategy. You will recall

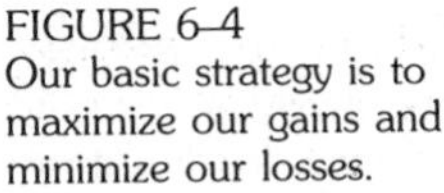

FIGURE 6–4
Our basic strategy is to maximize our gains and minimize our losses.

that the satisficer strategy is our tendency to use a minimum of information to make a decision. In making these decisions, we are also working from biased data due to the three strategies described by Tversky and Kahneman. Regardless of how well-informed or biased we may be, the individual decisions we make are based on our personal store of information. We also associate a certain level of confidence with those decisions. For example, suppose you are one of five second-grade teachers in a school and you are asked to make an *individual* decision as to the best reading series. After you have made your decision you may feel quite firmly that you have decided on the best series, or you may have a considerable amount of doubt about your decision. Your confidence level may have very little relationship to the quality of your decision.

If later you are informed of the differing decisions that the other teachers have made, without knowing the bases for their decisions, you are likely to interpret the data as subjective or merely the opinions of others. Depending on the level of confidence you hold in your initial decision, you may or may not revise it. If you attach a high level of confidence to your decision, you are not likely to change it, probably feeling that your decision is as good or better than anyone else's. If you have a low level of confidence in your decision, there is more likelihood that you will revise your decision and move toward the positions of the other persons. Affecting this situation will probably be the feelings you have about the competence of the other teachers.

Still later, if you are exposed to additional data you were not aware of, in the form of the reasons for the other teachers' decisions, there is a possibility that you will move somewhat toward the more informed teachers' position. It is more likely, however, that you will move toward some weighted average of the arguments. If each of the five teachers in our hypothetical group is exposed to this same information, it is likely that there will be greater consensus among the *individual* decisions. It may not result in complete agreement as to which is the best series to use, but there is likely to be more agreement than there was before the individuals were exposed to the other teachers' decisions and their reasons for making them.

Once the process of exchanging information has been accomplished and the information has had its effect on the various individuals, the teachers are likely to remain fairly fixed in their opinions until some new information is introduced into the situation. That is, if the exchange of information has not resulted in complete agreement or consensus, further discussion is not likely to revise anyone's personal opinion as to which is the best decision. One reason for this is the fact that, during the individual decision-making process, everyone develops a feeling of high confidence in their decision. Without new information being introduced, these opinions probably will not change even if the teachers are forced to compromise on a single reading series. While the group will be able, no doubt, to arrive at a compromise, one should not be deluded into thinking that the individual opinions in the group have changed. The process of individual decision making is represented in Figure 6–5.

Small-group decisions

Not only do we make decisions as individuals, but we also make group decisions in conjunction with other people. We may be a member of a committee, an ad hoc group, or a professional oganization faced with making a decision among several alternatives. In a small-group context a different problem is encountered. In order to arrive at a group decision, not only must each individual form an opinion but these individual opinions must be reduced down to a single decision. This may be

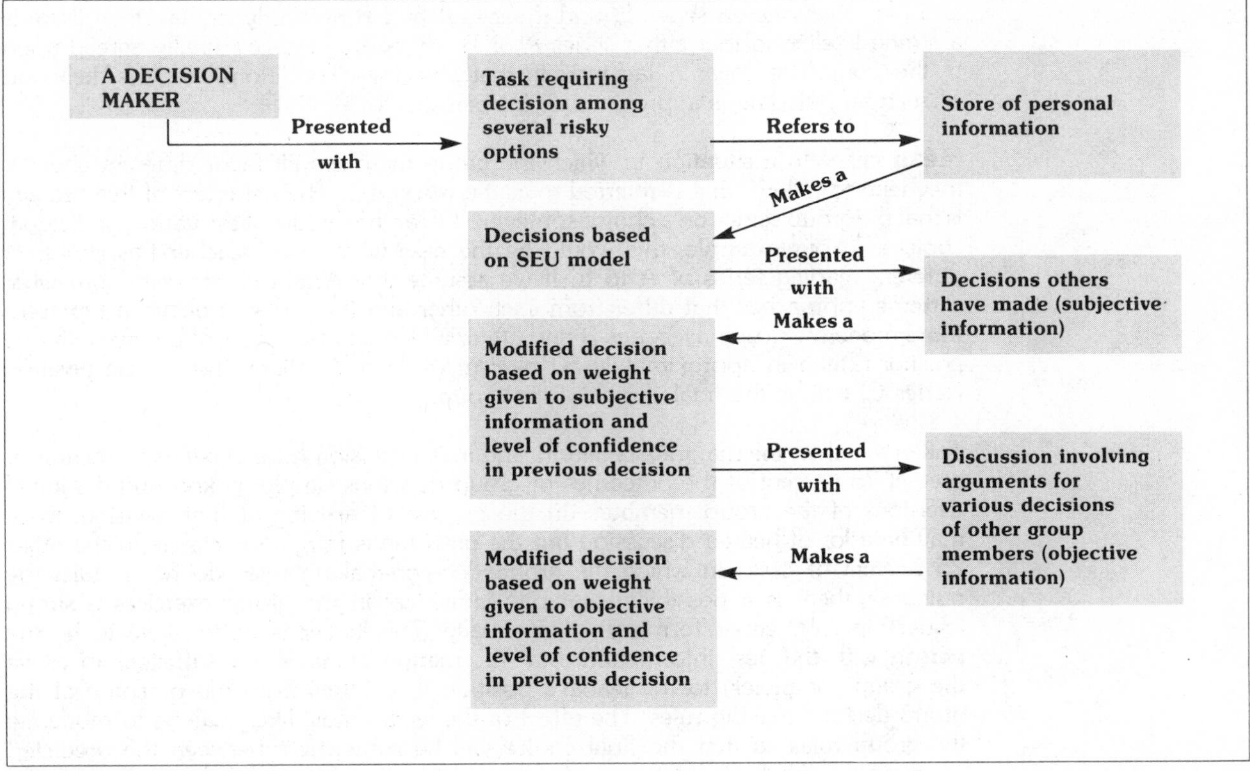

FIGURE 6–5
The individual decision-making process

achieved through the information-exchange process just described if the sharing of information leads to consensus, when all group members hold the same view as to which course of action is the best. More commonly, the sharing of information does not lead to consensus or complete unanimity of opinion. People may still disagree as to which course of action they believe to be the best. In these situations, a process leading to compromise is also necessary. In most small-group situations, the individual and the group decision-making processes probably occur somewhat simultaneously so that the group decision may be a combination of consensus and compromise.

Majority Rule. In order to arrive at a compromise, small groups adopt one of several strategies (Cartwright, 1971). If a majority favors one position, then the group is likely to adopt this choice as the group decision. This strategy is referred to as the *majority rule.* In our example of the five second-grade teachers, if three agree that reading series B is the best alternative, then approximately 70 percent of all groups in a similar situation are likely to follow the majority rule and adopt series B (Alverson, 1976; Cartwright, 1971).

Coalition Rule. If some members are close together in their choices but not similar, while others are fairly dissimilar, then the strategy referred to as the *coalition rule* will prevail. In this situation the group members who are fairly similar will form a coalition, decide on one of their choices, and then persuade the dissimilar members to also adopt their position. Referring again to the group of five second-grade teachers, if *two* teachers have decided on series A, *one* teacher on series B, *one* on series D, and the other *one* on series E, and if series A and B are fairly similar, then there is a strong likelihood that either series A or B will be the decision finally agreed upon by the group. The research data indicate that when these conditions exist, the likelihood of such an outcome is approximately 80 percent.

Mean rule. In a situation in which the group members all favor different choices, they tend to follow what is referred to as the *mean rule.* The net effect of this strategy is that the group settles on a choice somewhere near the middle of the various individual choices. In our example, this would be the case when each teacher has chosen a different reading series of A to E. If we assume that A and E represent somewhat extreme approaches that differ from each other and the series in between represent more moderate positions (series B and D), or a blending (series C) of the two extreme positions, then in approximately 50 percent of such situations the middle position (series C) will be the final choice of the group.

Taken together, the majority, coalition, and mean decision rules allow us to accurately predict 75 percent of the outcomes of group decisions simply by knowing the initial decisions of the group members. In the process of arriving at that decision, there may be a lot of heated discussion but the outcome is fairly predictable. In the other 25 percent of cases in which the group decision-making rules do not predict the outcome, there is a possibility that one individual in the group exercises a strong leadership role, either formally or informally. The leader is quite likely to be the person with the best information, but information alone is not sufficient to move the group completely to the leader's position if it differs from the outcome of the group decision-making rules. The effect of the leader most likely will be to moderate the group rules so that the final choice will be somewhere between the predicted outcome on the basis of the group decision-making rules and the leader's initial position.

As we noted earlier, after a group comes to some compromise on a decision, even though all members have agreed on the choice there is a high likelihood that the individuals within the group will still favor the same decison they did before the compromise. In other words, the compromise has done little to bring about consensus. The group members will probably have almost the same diversity of opinion, each believing their pre-compromise decision to be the best. In view of this, there is little reason to expect all of the group members to behave as though the choice were the best one. This may account for why, even after a group has seemingly agreed on a course of action, there is still a great deal of complaining and foot-dragging in the implementation.

The process of group decision making is depicted in Figure 6–6. It can be thought of as being added on at the end of the individual decision-making process shown in Figure 6–5.

By being able to distinguish between the results one may expect from the individual and the group decision-making processes, as a group member you may be able to see when the process of developing consensus in the group has terminated and the process of compromise must begin. If you view the situation in this manner and know the positions of the various group members, you may be able to decide which of the various group decision-making rules will prevail and suggest a compromise to the group. In this way you can become a facilitator of compromise and, as a side benefit, shorten the meeting time (which is bound to be popular).

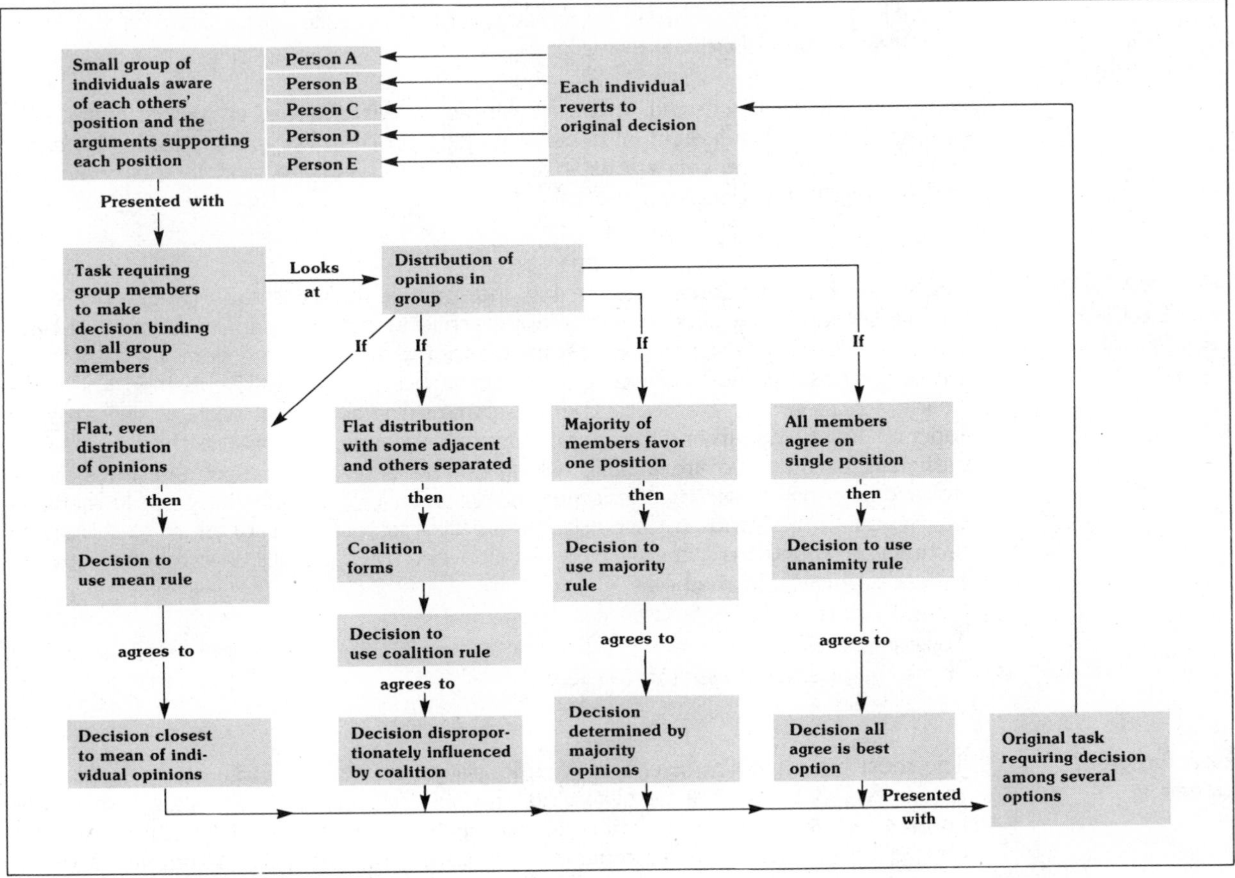

FIGURE 6–6
The small-group decision-making process

4. What factors affect the individual decision-making process and the small-group decision-making process? In relation to decisions and confidence levels, what are their effects?

In this section we have pointed out that with no further training, most individuals reading this text can make reasonably acceptable decisions about how to cope in the classroom teacher's role. However, these decisions are likely to be less than optimum. First of all, they would be made with a limited set of background experiences on which to base a decision. Second, the decision makers would be limited in the number of relevant factors and bits of information they would consider before arriving at a decision. Even the information they use would be likely to be biased due to the representativeness, availability, and adjustment/anchoring strategies used in obtaining and evaluating information. We also pointed out that the opinions of other people would more likely affect these decisions if the decision maker has little confidence in their own decision. More factual data would also have a weighted effect on the personal decisions regardless of the individual's confidence level. Finally, arriving at a compromise decision with several other individuals would probably be accomplished through the use of the majority, coalition, or mean rule, depending on the initial positions of the individuals in the group.

What we will be discussing in the remainder of this chapter, and most of the text, will involve only the individual decision-making process. We are primarily concerned with the instructional process as it relates to the classroom, and in this context by far the majority of decisions are made by individuals.

INFORMATION-GATHERING STRATEGIES

We have pointed out some biases in thinking and how this information affects decisions. In this section we will cover some approaches to gathering information that have been used to reduce the impact of our biases for distorting the data we gather in a random, nonsystematic fashion. These approaches are generally classified under the heading of *scientific methods.* There are many methods and each serves a useful function in our continuing development of knowledge. No one method by itself is sufficient, because we are usually asking several different types of questions as we investigate a new topic or phenomenon. We usually start with fairly crude methods but, as our understanding develops, we are able to make use of more sophisticated techniques. Along the way we may develop new perspectives that require a return to less sophisticated methods.

To acquaint you with some of these methods, we will briefly point out the characteristics of the major types of scientific studies.

Observational studies

The most basic type of scientific investigation is an observational study. In contrast to our everyday methods of observing, the observations are collected systematically and are usually aimed at isolating relevant factors or possible relationships that may have a bearing on the phenomenon being studied. One good example of this is when a teacher systematically looks for and records the frequency of a behavior. The teacher who claims that a child is always fighting, for example, is obviously not correct, since at least a part of the child's time is likely to be devoted to other activities. Through a systematic observation we can determine with whom the child fights, under what conditions, how frequently the fights occur, and other important data. We can also determine the conditions under which the child does not fight. With this information, the precise nature of the child's fighting behavior can be analyzed. This type of scientific methodology is probably by far the most useful for classroom teachers. It can be done simultaneously with other teaching activities and requires no knowledge of any statistical procedures beyond charting the results on a graph if one wants to display them visually. We will have more to say about systematic observations and where they should be applied in later chapters.

Correlational studies

A second level of scientific inquiry involves correlational studies. Here the search is centered on an estimation of the degree to which various factors show a relationship. A high relationship between two factors is expressed as a high correlation. The correlation can be a positive one, such that as one factor increases or decreases the other factor increases or decreases in the same direction. With a negative correlation, as one factor increases or decreases the other factor changes in the opposite direction. This type of study leads many to assume that a change in one factor is caused by a change in the related factor. This is not necessarily true. A third factor, which may not even be identified, may affect the relationship. It is also possible that the relationship may be entirely spurious.

For example, in the fall of the year people begin to wear more clothing. Soon afterward the trees in that area begin to lose their leaves. To assume that the trees lose their leaves because people wear more clothes is obviously false, even though there is a strong relationship between the amount of clothes people wear and the amount of foliage on the trees. One does not cause the other, nor apparently does the temperature cause both. The most basic relevant factor is the manner in which the earth revolves around the sun. This factor has an indirect relationship to both changes, a fact one would miss by focusing merely on the relationship between clothes and leaves.

In education, a perfect example is the relationship between left-handedness and mental retardation. The greater the degree of mental retardation, the more likely it is that the student will be left-handed. In fact, in an institutional setting consisting of a profoundly retarded population, one half of that population is likely to be left-handed or show no hand preference. Would you be willing to attribute the retardation to the students' handedness? If so, training students to be right-handed should cause them to be normal! This is why so many psychologists are suspicious of correlational studies in which any hint of causation is implied. You cannot assume causal relationships from correlation studies!

Experimental studies

A third type of scientific study used to further investigate the relationship between factors is an experimental study. In this case, the term *experimental* is used in a limited way rather than to simply refer to any systematic observation. An experimental study involves a research design in which one factor is varied systematically (the independent variable) in order to observe the effects on a second variable (the dependent variable). If changes are noted in the second variable, these changes are said to be dependent on the first variable (hence the term *dependent variable).* The first variable is termed the *independent variable* because it was varied independently of any results the study might have produced. If the study is well designed, all other factors that may have an effect on the experiment are held as nearly constant as possible. Depending on the ability to do the latter, we can then state with some degree of confidence that changes in the independent variable result in changes in the dependent variable.

An example would be a case in which we are trying to decide whether teaching method A using one set of materials is more effective than method B. We define effectiveness as producing a higher score on an identical final exam. In this example, the method used is the independent variable and the scores on the final exam are the dependent variable. It is possible to have more than two groups and more than one independent or dependent variable, but these add to the complexity and not to the clarity of our example. If we can hold constant such variables as the effects of prior student achievement, differences between teachers' effectiveness, and many others, then we may infer that any differences between scores on the final exam are related to the use of the materials.

$N = 1$ studies

One type of experimental study, called an $N = 1$ study, resembles the teaching role in some respects. This is often used in behavior modification studies. The initial phase

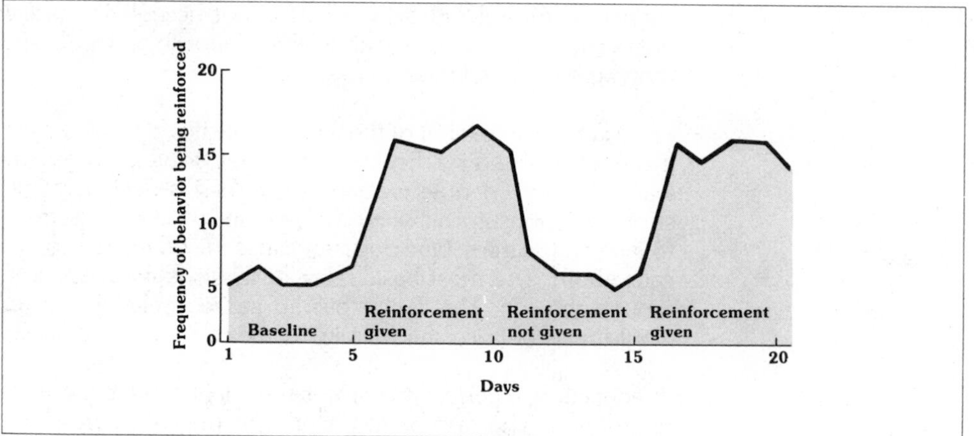

FIGURE 6–7
Generalized diagram of $N=$ 1 studies and typical operant conditioning results

of these studies is used to gather baseline data. Roughly stated, this is equivalent to determining the child's starting point in terms of the behavior being observed. The second phase involves some procedure designed to either increase or decrease the particular behavior being studied. In the third phase, the experimental procedure is removed to see whether the frequency of the behavior returns to its original level. Some, but not all, studies have a fourth phase, in which the experimental procedure is again instituted. The similarity between this type of study and the classroom is that there is more interest in bringing about specific changes in individual children; in other words, the comparisions are made in terms of an individual's change in behavior. The $N=1$ studies differ from the classroom situation in that the classroom teacher usually wants to see the new behavior continue and not return to its original level, as in the phase three portion of the $N=1$ study (Figure 6–7).

Post hoc studies

A fourth type of study is a variation of the experimental method. Here an attempt is made to take data that have been gathered already and then inspect the data to generate possible post hoc explanations of the data. Due to the post hoc nature of these studies, we are limited in the ability to state that one factor results in changes in the other. An example is when we compare two groups of students, one having a problem mastering reading and the other not having a problem, and then examine their birth records to see whether the students having the problem were also the babies from a difficult pregnancy or delivery. We may find that the children with reading problems are more likely to be the result of a difficult pregnancy or delivery. We cannot assume, however, that the pregnancy or delivery caused the problem, since there will be some poor readers who do not have this medical history and some good readers with this history. These discrepancies make it impossible to state that the medical history causes the poor reading in later life. It may be one of many contributing factors in some cases but under different educational conditions does not necessarily lead to poor reading.

5. What are the five main types of research strategies and the purpose each serves?

Limits on usefulness of research methodology for the classroom

The various research methods just outlined have been very useful for educational psychologists and have helped to produce a vast amount of information about the learning process. This has been accomplished because the research methods serve four important functions. One function is to reduce the amount of bias in our observations of phenomena. A second is to help isolate relevant factors and relationships. The third function is to reduce the amount of bias in the analysis and interpretation of data. Notice that the methods only reduce bias in our observations, analysis, and interpretation, and may not eliminate the bias. How much the methods actually reduce the bias is more a function of the researcher's expertise and care in designing and executing the research study. Because of this, the quality of research can vary considerably. The research process does over time also provide a fourth function, which corrects for errors in the research process. As additional data about a specific subject are collected with more refined techniques, some previous results and conclusions tend to be supported and others are not. Until these corrections are made, the faulty research data can mislead us.

Trying to apply these traditional research techniques to the classroom situation is difficult, even for those who are specialists in research methods. There are two major problems. First of all the classroom is a complex and dynamic environment, and second it is difficult to effectively control many of the factors that may influence the results of a study. The wisdom of a classroom teacher applying the typical research methods is questionable not only from the standpoint of training but also from the standpoint of basic orientation. Whereas researchers wish to hold constant the environment in order to *study* the changes associated with various factors and relationships, classroom teachers want to *use* the factors and relationships to bring about specific changes. Stated differently, the researcher typically studies the effect of A on B or the relationship between A and B. Teachers are usually faced with the task of bringing about B and wanting to know what A's will help to accomplish the task. A teacher can, however, often benefit in an indirect way from the use of these traditional techniques by reading what researchers have found out about the learning process and its application to the classroom. Reading reviews of research in a reputable journal is probably the most pragmatic method. At times it also may be of value to read original research articles that are relevant to the classroom problems and decisions to be made. In Chapter 22 we discuss in detail how this task may be approached. Now we will focus on a different approach to systematically looking at the problems and decisions relevant to a classroom.

DECISION-MAKING STRATEGIES FOR THE CLASSROOM

Due to the limited *direct* utility of traditional scientific techniques to the classroom context, some educational psychologists have become interested in developing alternate strategies. The interest is not primarily in the learning process of humans but rather in the formal instructional process that humans use to bring about learning. The area of interest is commonly referred to as *instructional psychology* or a *systems approach* to instruction. A systems approach does not imply any fixed method of instruction or even any single method of solving instructional problems but rather a general way of looking at them. As examples, it is common to hear people refer to a communication system or a transportation system. We also hear reference to the educational system. These systems can be large or small, but regardless of size they all exist within a larger system and may have smaller systems within them. We can refer to the American system of education that exists within the social system of the United States. On a smaller scale each state has an educational system divided into

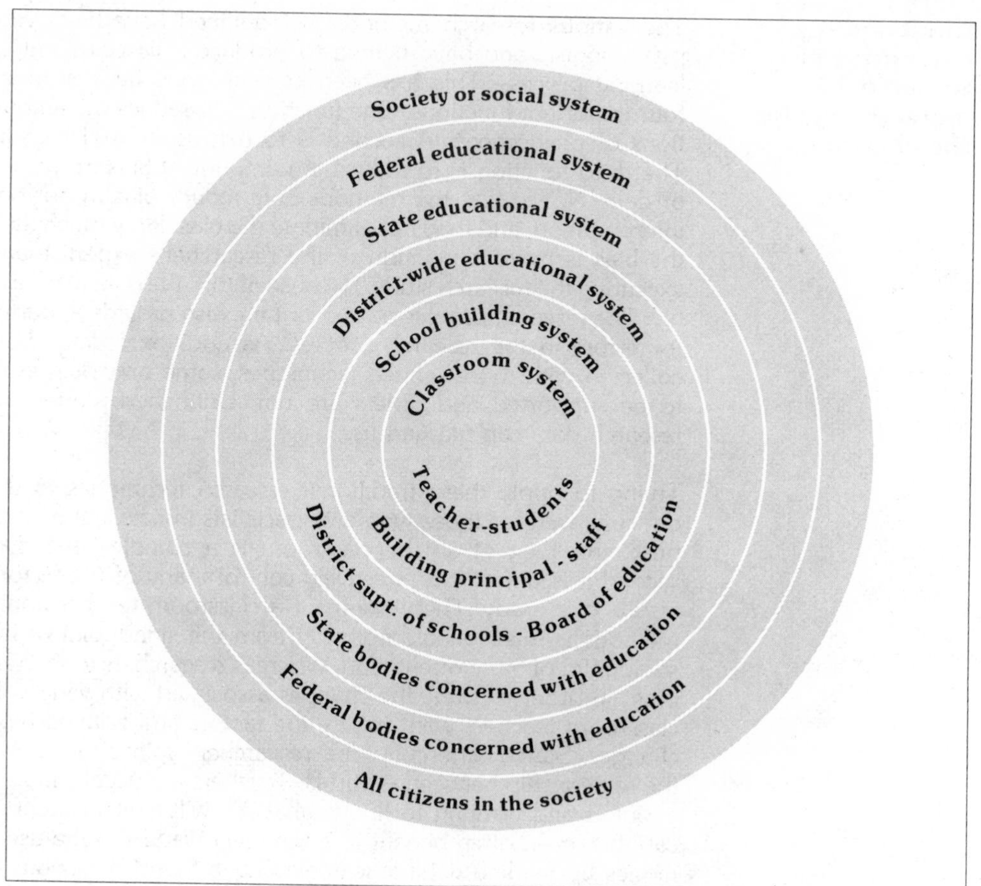

FIGURE 6–8
Levels of educational systems

smaller school districts or systems. Some districts are large and composed of several buildings, each of which is a somewhat separate system. At the heart of these systems is the smallest administrative unit or system, the classroom (Figure 6–8). This is the system that is in direct contact with students.

What defines each of these examples as a system is that each is a somewhat well-defined unit that has a purpose and performs certain functions to achieve that purpose. A system also operates in an organized manner both within itself and in relation to other systems with which it interacts. A classroom is certainly a well-defined unit that functions in an organized manner both internally and in relation to the other classes and school administration. On a hectic day some teachers may argue about this, but even on those days the classroom is far from utter chaos. The following decision-making strategies are based on this general view and attempt to sort out the various components of educational systems that are related to developing more effective instructional programs.

Glaser's model

An early attempt to illustrate the general characteristics of the instructional process from a systems perspective was made by Glaser (1962). He presented a general model of instructional development, which has been widely referred to and adopted for its utilitarian value. In a later description of his model, Glaser and Nitko (1970) refer to the model as having six components. Each component is described as a step in the process of planning or specifying an instructional system. Each step has a related set of decisions. Briefly, the six steps are:

1. Specifying outcomes of learning.
2. Diagnosing the starting level of a learner.
3. Designing instructional episodes adapted to the learner.
4. Monitoring student performance.
5. Adjusting Steps 1–4 based on the learner's performance.
6. Collecting information to improve the overall system.

The model makes the point that we need, first of all, to specify our goals in measurable terms. Next we need to determine the student's *pre-instructional* level of performance related to our goals. This determination of goals and starting point should be done prior to deciding on instructional procedures. We then need to provide instructional procedures that are adapted to the particular student, but these do not necessarily have to be provided on a one-to-one basis. The student's performance must be monitored on a fairly continuous basis and the information *used* to make adjustments in goals and instructional procedures as they are carried out. Finally we need to monitor the effectiveness of the various components of our system so that future revisions of it will be improvements. In essence, the model outlines the general flow of the instructional process in terms of both short and long-term planning.

Classroom-oriented model

Since Glaser's basic model was first presented, many versions have been developed to provide more detail about the process. One such version recently has been proposed by Hughes (1977) and currently is being applied in the development of large-scale instructional programs. Hughes's model has been modified to enhance its utility for classroom instruction (Alverson, 1978).

The model views instructional development as composed of five major phases. Each phase includes a distinct set of decisions and activities directed toward an intended purpose. The main distinction between phases lies in the intended purpose guiding the activities. Within each phase the decisions and activities are distinguishable from each other by the subpurpose they are intended to serve. The model, therefore, describes not only the process of instructional development but also a classification system for decisions and activities. By taking this dual perspective the model can serve as a checklist in developing instruction and also as a useful guide when evaluating instructional efforts.

The subdivisions and organization of the model enhance the ability to concentrate on certain activities during the development of a program without losing sight of the relationship of those activities to the total endeavor. This conceptual organization is the primary function served by the model in the development and implementation of classroom instruction. It helps to outline the many issues related to program development and at the same time integrate the different activities in a manner that facilitates the application of research data to small segments of instructional activities. The model does not limit the user to any particular set of instructional activities or theoretical orientation. It is more likely to point out shortcomings in less organized efforts and actually broaden the range of alternatives that may be used. In other words, the model offers a more systematic approach to how the problem is conceptualized and solved without limiting the range of solutions that may be generated.

In a broad sense the five phases of activities are sequential. They are also cyclical when applied to an instructional program that is used more than once and being improved. The phases are identified and their relationships are illustrated in Figure 6–9.

The purpose in the analysis phase is to define the dimensions of the instructional task or problem. The decisions and activities in this phase are related to finding out what the task is and the resources available to accomplish the task. The design phase has as its purpose the development of plans to accomplish the task. The decisions and activities focus on the specification of how various tasks will be carried out. In the preparatory phase the purpose is to have everything in a state of readiness for actual instruction. Activities in this phase follow the development of plans and involve getting ready for the planned instructional activities. The decisions are related to determining whether preparatory activities and products are adequate to accomplish the task. The implementation phase has the purpose of putting the planned instructional activities into operation. Activities in this phase are commonly associated with classroom instruction and management, which involve a teacher and students in an interaction. During this phase many decisions are made that adapt the plans to the immediate instructional context and student performance. In the evaluation phase of instruction the purpose is to judge how successful the activities and decisions have been in achieving the purpose of each phase and also the larger purpose of the total instructional process. The activities and decisions involve a review of what has been accomplished, how it has been accomplished, and how future efforts may be improved. In a sense the evaluation phase is a period of active reflection and anticipation—reflection about what has been done and anticipation about how it may be done better in the future.

While the model is depicted as a linear progression of activities, this is true only in a general sense. Typically there is considerable looping back to earlier phase activities, especially from the design to the analysis phase. For instance, if you were asked to

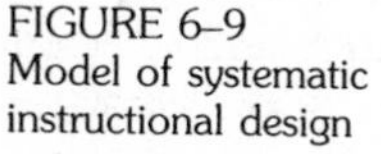

FIGURE 6–9
Model of systematic instructional design

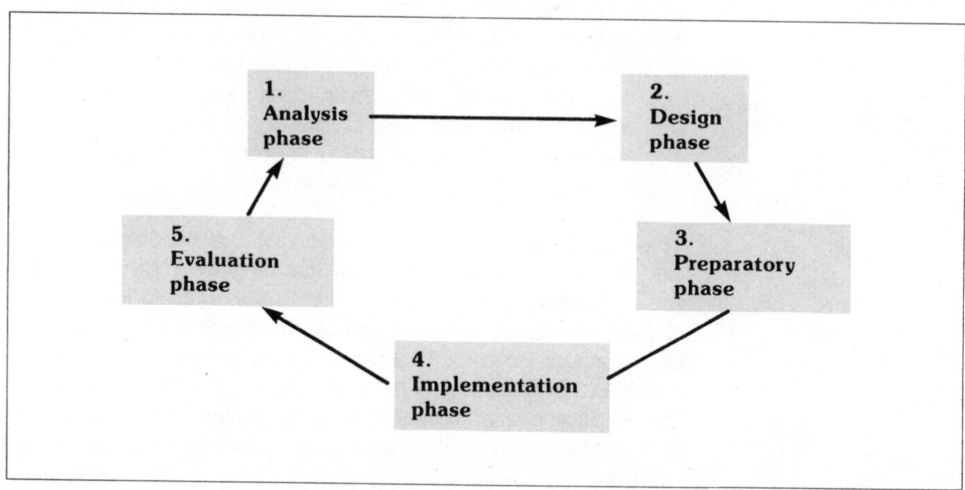

develop a program for an unknown group of learners and given no information about the task, the learners, or the resources available, there is obviously insufficient information to design an instructional program for the learners. If you were told that the learners are all 18 years of age, the information may not help you decide what to include in an instructional plan but it may lead you to exclude certain activities. Additional information that you are expected to teach these 18-year-olds the fundamentals of bartending would help to define the problem, so at least the general content of the instructional plan could begin to take shape. Before the plans could become more concrete and sophisticated, you would need more precise information about how much this group of 18-year-olds already knows about the topic and what resources you may or may not have at your disposal. The point we wish to emphasize with this example is that as our plans begin to take shape we typically find that more information is needed about the task, the learners, or the resources.

During the preparatory phase we may find that we do not have much time or sufficient materials to develop some instructional device. This will require a return to the design phase to form a decision about what can be substituted.

Some error made during the analysis, design, or preparatory phase may become evident during the implementation phase. Depending on the error it may have a trivial or disastrous effect on the implementation phase activities. When the effect is great enough to upset the effective flow of instruction, it results in the return to some previous phase's decisions or activities.

Even during the evaluation phase flaws or omissions in our evaluation may become evident and require a return to earlier phase decisions and activities in order to interpret data that have already been gathered.

With this brief overview of the model we will now look at the context within which the process normally operates and what it is expected to accomplish. Following this we will outline in more detail the decisions and activities of the five phases.

Social context of the model

Earlier we pointed out that a classroom is embedded within several larger systems. These all have some influence on how the classroom-sized system must operate. These influences can be described as expectations and constraints. The expectations define the general problem a classroom teacher has to solve, and the constraints impose certain limitations on how the problem can be solved. Within these general guidelines there is a wide range of choices left for the teacher's decision. Many teachers see themselves as more limited in their choices than is actually the case. Often they present a traditional program with few innovations, and then only if someone else has perfected the innovations. We believe it is probably wise to start from this position, but a competent teacher soon should be able to, with the aid of a systematic approach and a solid base of knowledge, add innovative improvements that enhance the effectiveness and efficiency of the process with little fear of any major failures.

It is difficult to pin down with any certainty the source of many expectations and constraints. We suspect that a future teacher has acquired much of this information as a student through observing a variety of teachers and hearing people make comments about schools. In the course of a teacher's professional training, the expectations and constraints are probably highlighted and clarified in course work and field experiences. The school administrators clarify the local ground rules with explanations of school policies and assignments. While the teacher is in service, the other staff members, students, parents of students, people in the community, and professional sources of information all tend to shape and refine a teacher's perception of the expectations and constraints. A teacher needs to recognize these sources and their impact. But, a teacher should also remain aware of the freedom granted and exercise this freedom to improve the instructional process.

Small, functional units in the classroom

The exercise of this freedom within the classroom is in relation to the many decisions about smaller, functional subsystems that a teacher needs to cope with and develop. For instance a high school chemistry teacher with a combination laboratory-lecture class has a variety of tasks to accomplish. Various topics must be taught, the laboratory area must be kept stocked with equipment and materials, the laboratory must be kept clean, an inventory of supplies must be maintained, and new materials must be ordered to replace those used or broken. Each of these tasks requires that certain activities be carried out, but there are a variety of ways to accomplish each task. Not all methods may require the teacher's direct effort in carrying out the task, but they will most likely require some planning on the teacher's part. To continue our example, the chemistry teacher may develop a system for teaching each of the units in the curriculum that utilizes a considerably different approach to instruction. One topic may be done primarily through a lecture-demonstration mode. Another may utilize reading materials and individualized techniques. Cleaning the lab may be organized around a student cleanup system, while the inventory, stocking, and ordering tasks may be delegated to the science club members and merely supervised by the chemistry teacher.

The point we wish to convey is that most teacher planning and efforts are in terms of these smaller systems. The planning of larger systems is left to committees, administrators, and boards of education. For the most part our discussion is not aimed at these larger instructional systems but is directed toward the classroom-teacher level of instructional development. Having completed our discussion of the context and purpose of the model, we now elaborate more fully on the activities and decisions within the five phases of the model.

Analysis phase of instruction

In a broad sense this phase involves those decisions and activities that are related to determining *what* needs to be accomplished. Generally the major portion of the instructional task is specified by the school system when a teacher is assigned to a certain group of students and portions of the curriculum. More specifically the learning tasks are defined by the textbooks and instructional materials the school system provides the teacher. Given this amount of direction on the macro-level goals to be accomplished, a teacher is still faced with many micro-level decisions. In making these decisions a teacher is likely to engage in the following five separate types of analyses:

1. Life space analysis.
2. Task analysis.
3. Learner analysis.
4. Instructional space analysis.
5. Staff analysis.

Life space analysis. Students come from a wide range of cultural and family backgrounds (Figure 6–10). Due to this diversity they come to school with different educa-

FIGURE 6–10
Students come from various backgrounds

tional needs and desires. Determining the student's general background and desires is a portion of a life space analysis. Another portion is a look at the general society the students will enter as adults and the requirements for successfully living in that society. This dual look at where the student is coming from and heading toward should take into account not only personal views but also the views of leading authorities in this area. Out of these activities decisions should be made as to what broad educational goals should be established. In a sense these goals should be idealistic and then adjusted to reality through the decisions made in the other four analyses.

Our coverage of information related to a life space analysis began with the previous discussion about the four philosophical positions and the various psychological perspectives related to the nature of humans. We hope the information will help you to analyze your students' life spaces in a broader, more objective framework. In Chapter 7 we focus more sharply on this issue and how the analysis can be translated into instructional goals.

Task analysis. A task analysis is to some extent a continuation of a life space analysis in that a task analysis is the process of dividing broad educational goals into smaller instructional objectives. The need for these activities is well recognized by teachers who frequently help students through a task by pointing out the substeps involved. The traditional approach to task analysis has been on the basis of a logical analysis within a subject area or topic. Limitations in the usefulness of the traditional task analysis approach, and the need for a different approach, became evident to psychologists attempting to develop a systematic approach to designing instruction (Glaser, 1962). Gagné's identification of different learning types is one such attempt to develop alternative types of task analysis that overcome the shortcomings of the traditional approach. These newer approaches provide a strategy for analyzing a task that not only helps to divide the task but is also grounded in the psychological research data. By doing this, the task analysis is associated with information indicating the conditions that must be provided if the student is to master the task.

The major activities associated with a task analysis are obtaining the sources of instructional goals, carefully inspecting them, and specifying the various tasks identified in terms of an instructional sequence. The questions to be asked during a task analysis are: (1) What subtasks are required to reach the goal? and (2) In what sequence can the subtasks most easily be mastered? Chapter 8 is devoted entirely to this topic and provides a continuation of the discussion about Gagné and his contribution to our knowledge of the structure of human learning and knowledge.

Learner analysis. The process of learner analysis is also to some extent a continuation of a life space analysis, but the unique characteristics of the learner are more closely analyzed in relation to the learning tasks rather than the student's past and future social context. The reason a learner analysis is needed is evident in the fact that we teach both preschool and college students neither the same topics nor in the same manner. We may cover the same general subject area at various times in a student's life but always on a more sophisticated level that assumes some prerequisite level of understanding to cope with the new learning task. Our judgments of "readiness" for the new task are based on our analysis of the learner. If we have done a good learner analysis we will match our instruction to the student's level of achievement. If our analysis is poorly done, we are likely to bore the student with repetitious tasks or confuse the student with information that requires too large a step in the learning process.

The activities in a learner analysis are those necessary to identify the student's starting capabilities in relation to the learning task. The major question is: What performance capabilities does the student now have? The answer to this question may have considerable impact on the actual goals we establish for any group of children and probably an even greater impact on the goals we establish for any single child.

The previous discussion of the learning process has been included to provide, in very broad terms, a framework for learner analysis, but this only helps to structure our general impression of the learner. Due to the importance of this class of teacher activities, we have devoted Chapters 9 and 15 to the topic. Chapter 9 narrows our discussion to types of learner analyses, and then in Chapter 15 we return to the topic in relation to the realities of the classroom.

Instructional space analysis. Obviously a teacher needs to look at, and make plans in relation to, the realities of the school building and available resources. The physical layout of the building and the available instructional areas must be known because they either open up possibilities or impose restrictions on what can be taught or how it can be taught. Included in an instructional space analysis is a look at what is, or is not, available in that space. Such things as room furnishings, instructional materials, equipment, resource personnel, and special programs can make the task in the classroom easier and should be looked at before making any definite plans about what, or how, to teach. The results of the analysis may have some impact on *what* we teach but will more likely have an effect on *how* we teach a topic.

Over time a teacher is likely to become aware of the instructional space through a variety of activities. A systematic approach to these activities may speed up the process of deciding what is available, or can be obtained, to enhance the teacher's effectiveness. There seems little justification for not using all the resources available that can lead to more effective and efficient instruction. By being more effective and efficient it may be possible to add considerably more "openness" to the curriculum and a wider variety of student choices about topics or learning styles.

The major question is: What resources do I have to work with? and therefore this type of analysis is highly related to the specific situation and requires a considerable amount of personal resourcefulness. In Chapter 13 we discuss some general factors you should consider about the school and classroom environment to help you carry out this type of analysis and incorporate it in your plans.

Staff analysis. Most would agree that the most important resource in the schools is the instructional staff. At the classroom level of organization, a staff analysis is primarily a self-analysis by the classroom teacher. Every teacher is an individual with certain strengths, weaknesses, and preferred ways of doing things. These should not be ignored, nor do they need to be apologized for, as some teachers seem to do. A frank appraisal of these personal characteristics can have two benefits. First of all, it may simply make a teacher feel more comfortable to design and implement strategies that are both effective and compatible with the teacher's personal characteristics. Second, an honest self-analysis may help a teacher to spot weaknesses and either overcome them or make adjustments for them so they do not have a detrimental effect on the outcomes of instruction.

One point we would like to stress about a self-analysis is that it should be done in a constructive frame of reference. To be constructive it needs to start with a self-accepting, positive view of oneself. It also needs to be carried out in an honest manner with the intention of maximizing the long-term personal gains. Part of this self-analysis should encompass a look at one's philosophy and beliefs about human nature before moving into more specific areas.

Even at the classroom level of analysis, a staff analysis often includes a look at other individuals because of the many specialists, aides, and parent volunteers that are commonly found in schools. When instructional programs are being developed, the expertise, preferences, and limitations of these individuals should also be analyzed.

All of this analysis of self and others leads to decisions about the capabilities, preferences, and limitations of the staff. This determination may have some impact on what goals we attempt to attain, but, like the physical resources, it is more likely to effect how we will try to reach the goals. These staff differences can, however, result in considerable variation between teachers in terms of the social behavior and work-study habits they try to instill in their students.

6. What is the main function of the analysis phase? For each of the five specific types of analyses included in the phase, what are the main decision and set of activities?

Design phase of instruction

Having analyzed the instructional problem from the five perspectives outlined above, the next step is to make some specific plans about how to achieve the goals. While it is possible to enter a classroom without any prior planning, this is apt to be a disaster, especially for a beginning teacher. An experienced teacher may be able to carry it off simply because the teacher has, over the years, developed an effective plan of action that needs only minor adjustments to make it suit a new situation.

Most often these plans are not in written form but can be described by a teacher if asked how a particular problem is handled.

The format of the plans is of much less concern than the content. At first the content is likely to be general and somewhat vague. As these plans are developed and made more specific, we may have to return to the analysis phase activities in order to gather more information so as to make a decision about a particular aspect of the plans. This recycling through the two phases results in an increasingly more sophisticated set of plans.

Most teachers recognize the need for lesson plans that outline their intended activities related to a small unit of instruction, but this is only one type of plan. There are at least four types of plans that can be helpful: (1) comprehensive plans, (2) component plans, (3) evaluation plans, and (4) preparatory plans.

Comprehensive plans. A comprehensive plan is broad and outlines the major tasks to be accomplished, the order in which they will be done, and the approximate time schedule to be followed. It may specify the major strategy to be used to accomplish a task, but it does not provide much detail. These plans often appear as some sort of time line, such as a calendar with notes jotted down for different dates (Figure 6–11).

The utility of a comprehensive plan is that it provides an outline for identifying and scheduling a great many activities well into the future so that they are more compatible with each other, the seasons of the year, the school calendar, the availability of materials, and the plans of other staff members.

The decisions about what to teach and the order in which to teach the various tasks are part of the analysis phase. The decisions in developing a comprehensive plan

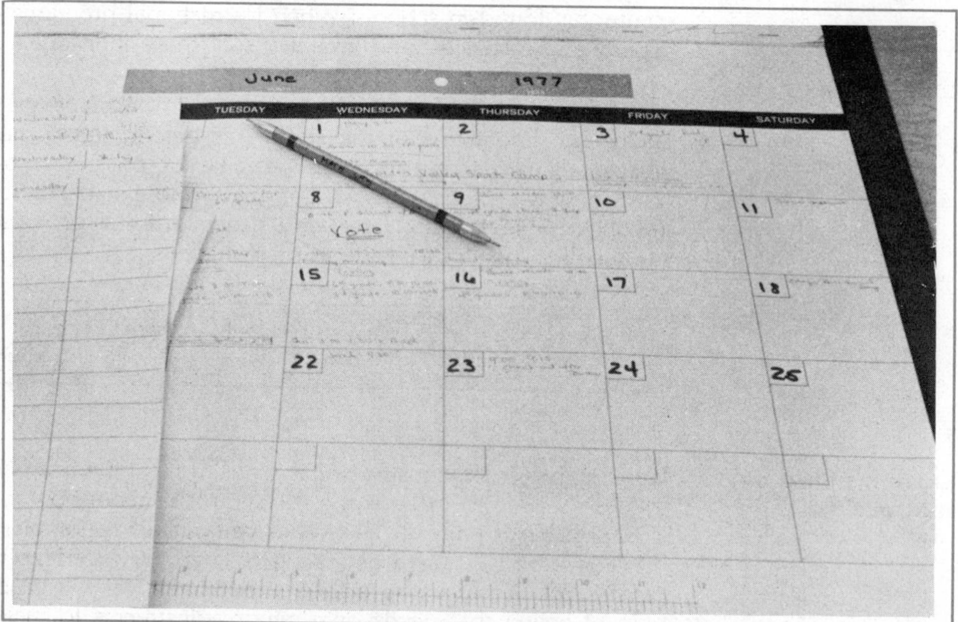

FIGURE 6–11
Comprehensive plans often have the form of notes on a calendar

involve how best to match the general pattern of instruction to the various realities just mentioned. The activities involved in making these decisions are those needed to determine the realities.

The development of these plans requires no skills beyond those necessary for an orderly approach to daily living and a sense of responsibility to other people with whom we work and interact. For this reason we do not deal with this set of activities in any specific section of the text.

Component plans. These are the common lesson plans that cover a small, specific unit of instruction. We refer to them as *component plans* to highlight the fact that they deal with only one component of a teacher's total set of activities. Our reference to them as lesson plans identifies the most common type of component plan; but it is also likely for a teacher to have component plans that are not lesson plans. For instance, how the chemistry teacher mentioned earlier would handle the problems of keeping the laboratory stocked and clean would require two component plans. There are a great many housekeeping and administrative activities that require some amount of planning. In many cases the problem is relatively simple and the solution equally simple and obvious. At other times the problem and solution may be more complex and the need for planning more obvious.

Many component plans covering instruction of a topic are derived from teachers' manuals provided with textbooks. These manuals can provide a good starting point, but most teachers modify the suggestions to suit their particular characteristics and situation. One of the major aims of this text is to help you develop the understanding necessary to select and modify plans to be effective.

Sometimes a teacher is dealing with a topic for which there are no sources, or at least no good sources, from which to start planning. In these situations a solid set of skills is more obviously needed to design an effective component plan. Without a good plan there are many pitfalls, and even with one there may be some hidden problems. The decisions involved are many, but in general they can be summed up as decisions about what instructional techniques and materials will be used. In the analysis phase the range of materials and staff resources is determined, and in the design phase selections are made from the possible choices. The activities engaged in may include a closer inspection of the available materials, the actual writing of plans, or at least some notes that outline the plan. It is also possible that the activities include the designing of some instructional aid that is needed but not available.

Chapters 4 and 5 are intended to set the broad perspective for your design of component plans. Chapters 10, 11, and 12 are included specifically to add some insight into issues that need to be considered in planning for instruction in each of the four domains of learning. Chapter 10 discusses general issues related to all domains, while Chapters 11 and 12 focus on specific instructional and measurement conditions that need to be provided for each domain.

Evaluation plans. One set of activities that is often ignored, even if a teacher is aware of them, is the design of an evaluation plan. If improvements are to be made in instruction, our efforts need to be looked at closely and systematically. To do this requires some prior planning, or else the data needed to make valid judgments may not be available. At no time are the three biases pointed out by Tversky and Kahneman more relevant to the classroom. In looking back over a unit or year of instruction in an unsystematic approach, we are likely to be seriously misled. Our feelings are apt to have a considerable impact and may be based on only sketchy and highly misleading data about one or two students. When this happens we may modify our future activities in a way that is detrimental to effective instruction. We may do this with a strong conviction that we are right as long as we are unaware of the true data.

In order to develop effective evaluation plans we need to decide which aspects of student performance we are most interested in and what data we need to make judgments. Since the focus of the evaluation plan is on both the results of current instruction and the improvement of future instruction, decisions also need to be made about which instructional techniques and materials have the most impact on the students and the rest of the instructional program.

The activity involved is a close look at our objectives and plans. We may write up our evaluation plans, but again the plans are likely to be a set of notes. At times we may also have to design specific materials to aid in the evaluation such as questionnaires or recording forms.

In Chapter 4 we discussed the need for observations of behavior in order to make valid inferences about learning. In Chapters 12 and 19 we continue this discussion on a more specific level. Chapter 12 covers the actual measuring of student performance levels, and Chapter 19 deals with the evaluation of the systems you develop based on how effectively and efficiently they help to bring about these performance levels.

FIGURE 6–12
Some people always seem well-prepared

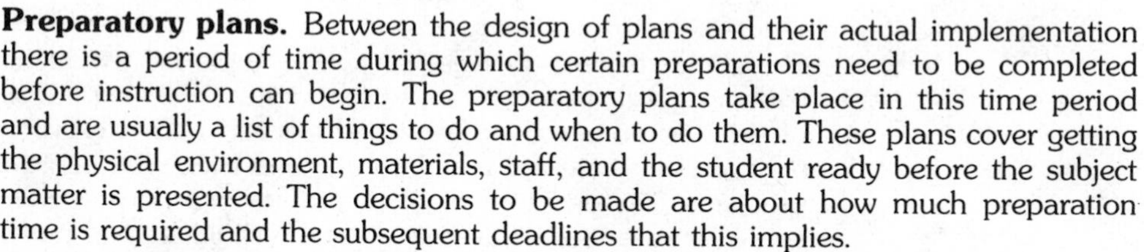
Preparatory plans. Between the design of plans and their actual implementation there is a period of time during which certain preparations need to be completed before instruction can begin. The preparatory plans take place in this time period and are usually a list of things to do and when to do them. These plans cover getting the physical environment, materials, staff, and the student ready before the subject matter is presented. The decisions to be made are about how much preparation time is required and the subsequent deadlines that this implies.

Developing these plans is highly dependent upon the component plans and the immediate situation and is as much a matter of attitude as of specific skills. Some people always seem to be well prepared ahead of time (Figure 6–12), while others are usually poorly prepared or at least terribly rushed to get prepared. We touch on this topic to some extent in Chapters 13 and 14, but we feel there is little that needs to be said to add to your capabilities.

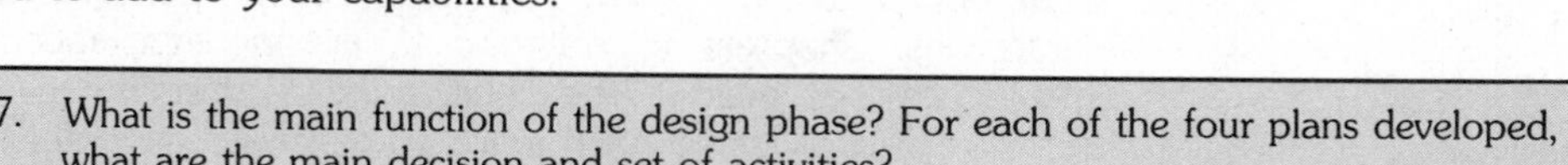
7. What is the main function of the design phase? For each of the four plans developed, what are the main decision and set of activities?

Preparatory phase of instruction

This phase is a plan following rather than a plan development phase. It covers the time period and activities that were specified in the preparatory plan. The plan should be used as a guide and not as an absolute course to be followed blindly. As the plan is being implemented, small adjustments (or even large ones in poorly constructed plans) may be needed to adapt it to the immediate situation. For example, a particular room, piece of equipment, person, or type of material may not be available as expected and substitutions may need to be made. Also changes may need to be made in the timing of events due to unforeseen conflicts with other people's schedules.

In this phase the emphasis between decisions and activities changes. In the analysis and design phases the major emphasis was on decisions, and the activities served to help make these decisions. In the preparatory phase the major emphasis is on doing the activities specified in the preparatory plan, and the decisions determine when the activities need modification or have been adequately completed.

As we mentioned in the description of the preparatory plan, there are four main areas within which preparatory activities can be classified: (1) physical setting, (2) materials, (3) staff, and (4) students.

Physical setting. Preparing the room so it creates a pleasant, convenient learning area is related to learning not only in the cognitive domain but also in the affective domain. The room itself, the room decorations, and the furniture all need to be readied. When these factors are prepared by others, they are often taken for granted. When they are not so well taken care of, they become very obvious and can create many problems in the implementation phase. Teachers often must do these preparatory activities themselves. At other times they may require the activities of a custodian, secretary, or some other person. In these cases the teacher should make sure the requirements are clear and some follow-up action is taken to decide whether what has been done is adequate.

Materials. The stimuli you present to your students must be available on a timely basis and have the characteristics necessary to fulfill their function. To prepare these materials, the activities involved are those needed to obtain or produce the materials specified in the component plans and have them in a readily available and usable form. The production of materials that were designed during the previous phase often requires layout, writing, drawing, typing, inspection of rough drafts, revision to improve, and reproduction of multiple copies before the component plans can actually be implemented. What was previously a mere specification of what is needed takes a concrete form during this phase. In Chapter 19 we point out some factors that need to be evaluated in relation to these activities, but the general skills needed in the development of these materials are not the subject of this text. We believe the materials should be well produced, but our primary interest is in the design of the materials.

Staff. Preparing staff members involves a training period requiring the same skills as any instructional setting and should be outlined in the preparatory plan. When you are the only staff member involved, your main activity may be reading or reviewing materials. At times it may also involve more formal and extensive training in the form of courses or workshops to develop new skills. It also can be a matter of reviewing priorities when several activities must be accomplished in a relatively short time.

When paid aides or volunteer staff are also involved, the activities should be carried out more systematically and early enough to make sure the training is adequate. Such techniques as walk-through demonstrations or practice periods may be helpful. Again you can develop most of these skills through years of interacting with people, but in this case you need to assume a leadership role.

We discuss these skills to some extent in Chapter 21, but many of the skills are those you would use in teaching a specific set of skills to any student. In many cases the skills are not new to the staff member, but it is more a matter of familiarizing the person with the context in which the skills need to be performed.

Students. Before actual instruction takes place, it is often necessary to introduce students to the topic or explain certain instructional procedures. These activities are not directly related to the content to be covered during instruction but serve to direct students' attention to either the instructional content or some activity they must perform in order to learn the content. If the student activities involve new and relatively complex procedures, actual instruction may also be involved to prepare the students. The actual activities a teacher performs are not distinguishable from other instructional activities when directing attention and explanations are needed. They are distinguishable, however, in the purpose they serve. Decisions regarding these activities should focus on the purpose and whether the purpose is being, or has been, accomplished.

In Chapter 10 we elaborate more fully on the purpose of these activities and how they can be used in the classroom.

8. What is the main function of the preparatory phase? For each of the four subareas of this phase, what are the main decision and set of activities?

Implementation phase of instruction

This can be considered the main event in the instructional process in terms of time but not necessarily in terms of importance. During this phase the activities specified in the various component plans are put into action according to the sequence and timing specified in the comprehensive plan. This phase is not, however, a simple implementation of these component plans, since the instructional process involves an interaction between the teacher and all of the individual students in the class. It also involves interactions between the students themselves. Since an interaction implies change, we have outlined the activities in the implementation phase on the basis of the changes that are likely to be required of a teacher. We have identified five sets of teacher activities involved in the interactive process: (1) follow component plans, (2) observe student performance, (3) analyze student performance, (4) adapt plans to student performance, and (5) collect evaluation data.

Follow component plans. Following a set of plans provides a set of cues for our activities and also gives them direction (Figure 6–13). If the plan is faulty, it can misdirect our activities to the point where learning is slowed down or inhibited. In any event the activities associated with this part of the implementation phase should be those specified in the component plan. As we point out below, we do not advocate a blind following of plans but rather the intelligent use of plans in this phase. In relation to plan-following activities, there are relatively few decisions to make unless the instructional context suggests that a revision of the plans would make them more appropriate. In this regard we are referring to the general instructional context where some recent world or classroom event could be incorporated into, or substituted for, the planned examples or general problem. The point we wish to emphasize is that the decisions are made on the basis of information other than student reaction to activities specified in the plan. We discuss that issue later.

Reference is sometimes made to teacher-proof plans, meaning plans that are not subject to any variation by the teacher. Seeing a well-planned activity destroyed by some disastrous variations made by the teacher makes some wish for teacher-proof

FIGURE 6–13
Following a plan provides a set of cues

plans. Also in research studies in which a particular set of activities is being investigated, teacher-proof plans seem to have a great deal of utility. In the regular classroom context, however, where the plans are generally the product of the teacher's planning, the issue seems less critical and there is more need for teacher tampering. Later when the teacher evaluates the results of the plan, this tampering should be taken into account. If there is no tampering it certainly simplifies the evaluation process, but the decision to modify the planned activities should be based first on the impact it will have on the learner and only second on administrative convenience.

The actual activities involved in following the plans will cover a wide range and each will probably have qualitative differences. For example two professors delivering the same lecture can do so in very different styles. Variations in inflection, volume, and body movements can mean the difference between an attentive or inattentive class. Generally we have not dealt with these qualitative issues in the text, but some distinctions we make in later chapters do have a bearing on these factors. We believe these skills are more appropriately developed and perfected in methods courses, classroom participation, micro-teaching labs, and student teaching.

Observe student performance. Change in student performance is the focal point of the entire instructional process. It is critical that we look at student performance carefully and with a well-trained set of skills to see the precise characteristics of the students' behavior in order to determine whether or not the expected changes are indeed occurring. In Chapter 4 we started the discussion of this issue, and in Chapter 5 we outlined the behavioral characteristics of learning in each of the four domains and several subtypes within the domains. In Chapters 10, 11, and 12 we continue to emphasize what to look for. In Chapter 12 and 17 we also point out how to observe student performance beyond the obvious looking and listening activities involved.

Analyze student performance. These activities may be some of the most important in terms of effective implementation of plans, but they take by far the least amount of time. Humans have the capability to react very quickly to stimuli, and in that short interval between a student's action and a teacher's reaction to it there is a quick analysis of the student's activity. For instance, a student may respond as expected and we say something complimentary in return and go on to the next activity in our plans. If the student's response is inconsistent with our expectations, we also react very quickly in a manner that we believe to be appropriate on the basis of our split-second analysis. We hope our analysis is more often correct than incorrect.

In our normal observation techniques there is often not much overt teacher behavior. In relation to our analysis of student behavior there is even less. In most cases there is no overt behavior involved. For the teacher this brief period is a time of decision in relation to the meaning of the student's performance. In Chapters 2 and 3 we introduced the broad philosophical and psychological issues that establish the context of our analysis. Chapters 4, 5, 10, and 11 narrow it down somewhat, but in Chapter 17 we deal specifically with the process of analyzing student performance.

Adapt plans to student performance. This set of activities is what we believe makes the difference between a good teacher and an excellent teacher. It is necessary to observe and analyze student performance, but if this analysis has no effect on our subsequent activities the process is often a waste of time, especially when errors in performance have been observed. Our changes may be only slight shifts in our original intentions, but at other times they may be large shifts. For the most part our component plans specify only the major characteristics of our activities simply because we cannot anticipate the momentary reactions of our students. For this reason the activities in this category are not changes in our plans but rather the filling out of those plans on a very specific and impromptu basis. How they are filled out is the major decision we face, and this is determined by our analysis of student performance and by the momentary conditions that prevail. We devote all of Chapter 18 to this issue, but at many points in the text we touch on the issues, especially in Chapters 10 and 11.

Collect evaluation data. For short-range use we need to observe specific behaviors of students in order to decide if we should adjust our plans and how to adjust them. We just discussed this in the last three topics above. On a long-term basis we need to decide these same issues on a broader basis. To accomplish this task we typically need to work from generalizations of several performances. These generalizations may be about a single student's performance over a period of time or a series of tasks. It can also be a generalization about the performance of several students at a single time or on a single task. The broadest type of generalization is when we summarize the performance of a class of students over a period of time and a series of tasks.

Most often we gather the generalized data to see if, and how, we need to change our activities in the distant future when implementing the plan with a new group of students. These same data may help us revise other component plans. To make these decisions in any valid manner we need unbiased data. To obtain data that are unbiased we need to collect them on a systematic basis as they occur. Some data, such as student work sheets or test results, are fairly permanent products. However, in order to cope with the clutter in a classroom, these products are often disposed of soon after they are looked at and are not available during the evaluation phase. Other performances, such as actual behaviors, are fleeting events and therefore not subject to storage for later use in evaluation. Some events, such as student attitudes, are not open to direct observation and therefore are difficult to collect unless planned for in advance. We do not wish to imply that these student-related data are any different than those you observe, analyze, and react to during the course of implementing your plans. Most of them are the same data. There may be some student performance data collected at the end of the instructional sequence that are in addition to the above data. Final exams are the most notable example. In addition to these normal performance data, measures of student work time may be called for in the evaluation plan as well as measures of teacher time and activity.

The activities in this category relate to collecting these various types of data so they are available for use in the evaluation phase. The decisions involved are related to the momentary conditions as to how best to collect, record, and store the data.

In Chapters 9, 12, 17, and 19 we discuss how to collect these data more extensively; in Chapter 12 we cover the measurement of specific skills; and in Chapters 9, 17, and 19 we discuss in more detail the collection of generalized types of information.

9. What is the main function of the implementation phase? For each of the five subareas of this phase, what are the main decision and set of activities?

Evaluation phase of instruction

The evaluation plan defines the general set of activities in this phase. Simply because it is impossible to anticipate all of the outcomes of instruction, this phase also includes those activities related to any unplanned evaluations that may be carried out. Some of these unexpected outcomes may be of major interest to us, and we may wish to evaluate our instructional process in relation to them so as to increase the future probability of the desired outcomes and eliminate any reoccurrence of the undesired outcomes.

The five major sets of activities that are performed in an evaluation of a program include: (1) organization of data, (2) analysis of data, (3) interpretation of data, (4) communication of results, and (5) revision of the program.

Organization of data. Getting a large quantity of varied data into some type of organization makes it easier to cope with them. One example of this activity is a teacher's class book used for recording test scores and other bits of data about students. There are other types of organization that can be used such as charts and graphs to display data. It is quite possible to have our organization of data distort our perception of them or hide some of the more subtle characteristics, and therefore the primary decision is about whether the organization will help or distort our analysis of the data. In Chapters 9 and 19 we point out some of the common techniques for organizing data for an evaluation.

Analysis of data. These activities are primarily the comparisons we make in our data or our attempts to find patterns in the data. The major decision concerns the correctness of our analysis in terms of any calculations of the data we use. The point is that the decisions are about the actual activity of the analysis and not the appropriateness of the analytic techniques used. The latter would be a decision more appropriate for the design phase when the evaluation plan is developed. In Chapters 9, 12, and 15 we again refer to some aspects of data analysis, but this is done more specifically in Chapter 19 and the Appendix.

Interpretation of data. Having looked at our data we may see a pattern in them but we still need to make sense of those data. For instance we may find that test scores start off at a low level at the beginning of the year, take a rapid climb upward, and then gradually drop down for the rest of the year. The question is: Why does this pattern occur? We need to interpret the data in reference to student, teacher, and environmental factors that may be related to the observed pattern. The pattern may not be directly related to our activities, but if we want to change the pattern we have to decide what factors are responsible for the pattern and what can be done to eliminate or modify the effects of the relevant factors. In other words, our interpretation should identify needed changes. The question most relevant to these activities is: Have I considered all of the relevant factors that may account for the data?

In a sense this entire text is devoted to helping you interpret the data you generate in the course of instruction. We do not attempt in any particular section or chapter to deal with the topic. We would like to caution you, however, against falling into the satisficer trap and accepting the first plausible explanation.

Communication of results. Not all of our evaluation efforts or conclusions need to be communicated to someone else. At times it may be useful to make our more favorable outcomes known or to make our interpretation of particularly disastrous, and obvious, results known to others (Figure 6–14). It is also quite possible that

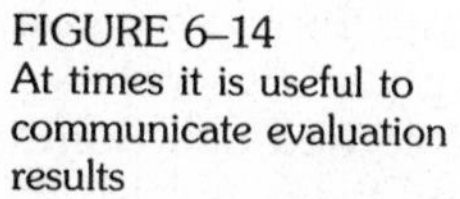

FIGURE 6–14
At times it is useful to communicate evaluation results

just letting an administrator know that we are seriously conducting a self-evaluation of our efforts may be to our advantage.

Another type of communication of results may be to the parents of the students or members of the general community. Letting them know of successes and a desire for improvement can conceivably help create better school-community relationships and interactions.

The activities can be as varied as the media used to communicate. The major questions can be narrowed down to whether or not to report the results, to whom, and in what form? The communication skills needed are developed over a long period of time and in many ways that are beyond the scope of this text. We do in Chapters 19 and 21 point out some factors that are specifically relevant for classroom-level communication of program results.

Revision of program. Any evaluation that simply ends with a conclusion is less than complete in relation to the long-term improvement of instruction. The conclusions, if they suggest change and where that change should take place, need to be put into practice. If we have written plans, we may rewrite them. With less formal plans we may simply make a note in our teacher's manual, a note in the margin of the text, or a mental note about how the change can be implemented. We may also decide how to make changes in our analysis, preparatory, or implementation phase activities. Given that humans often forget, it may be well to write the changes down. To make no changes in what we do is not likely to be a viable alternative because we are faced with a rapidly changing social environment that forces us to change. Planned change, if done well, is likely to create the fewest problems for us and our students. Complete lack of change is also professional stagnation, and today's school system usually attempts to prevent this from happening. The primary questions are: What changes will improve the instructional system, and how can they be implemented?

This chapter and also Chapters 19 and 22 are the ones in which we try to suggest ways for revising our plans on a rational basis.

10. What is the main function of the evaluation phase? For each of the five subareas of this phase, what are the main decision and set of activities?

UTILITY OF THE SYSTEMS APPROACH

The systems approach is mentioned more and more frequently in the literature, probably because of its adaptability and utility. It can be used with systems of varying size and complexity in a great many contexts. It can be used as the basis for written descriptions of systems or merely as a way of thinking about them. Because the systems approach allows us to describe the complexity of the systems we create, it allows us to monitor, assess, and revise what we are doing in a coordinated manner.

Planning instructional activities

When we are trying to start any new enterprise it is easy to overlook certain critical factors or to ignore the interactive effect between two factors that may lead to disaster. The 7 ± 2 phenomenon is probably an extremely important factor during the planning process, as is the satisficer strategy. It is thus important to make use of some strategy to help overcome these two limiting factors. The systems approach to planning calls our attention to details in a way that helps us maintain our overall perspective when making decisions. By organizing our planning in this way we can gradually make more and more refined decisions about the various matters. This is especially true when planning more complex programs. This advantage of allowing us to think through our plans more clearly prior to implementing them should not be overlooked.

We should also test our plans by having someone else review them. Our presentation is likely to be more organized and integrated when the plans have been systematically developed. If the person raises questions or makes comments, we should be able to interpret them at a more refined level than we would with a less organized view of the problem.

Monitoring instructional activities

In the same way that the systems approach helps us to see various aspects of our plans more clearly, it also helps us to monitor them more effectively. For one thing, we are alerted to watch for specific factors that may have a critical effect on our system. Are our goals reasonable and clear to the students? Is our analysis of the task correct? Have we correctly determined the starting level of our students? Is the handout on a particular unit accomplishing what we expected of it? What was the reaction to our examples? Did we measure what we wanted to measure? You should ask yourself these and many more specific questions as you implement your plans. We believe it is more productive to be able to ask yourself precise questions about specific factors when there is still time to modify them to improve results. Waiting until you have completed the lesson and then asking yourself simply whether it went well does nothing in the present context to improve your effectiveness. Asking the question may teach you how to do better next time, but this will be a slow and unproductive approach to improving your results. To bring about effective change more quickly, you need to monitor the effectiveness of each of your decisions while they are being implemented. The more detailed and analytic monitoring of your efforts afforded by the systems approach allows you to collect relatively refined and organized data about the operations of your system. If nothing else, it helps you to see that not everything you decided to do was incorrect but more likely only a few decisions were unwise. It may add a small amount of comfort to an otherwise very trying and discouraging time.

Assessing instructional activities

As we pointed out, the systems approach allows us to gather relatively detailed information regarding the operation of our system. The more detailed the data we are working with, the more detailed our assessment can be. We can look at each small segment of the system as well as the total system and ask ourselves how well it performed. Our questions, therefore, can be more refined and critical than with a less organized approach. For instance, we can deal with the effectiveness of a single sentence, paragraph, or section in a textbook rather than judging the entire text as a single unit. In this way we can decide where and how to supplement the text in specific ways. In Chapter 19 we cover this aspect of the systems approach more fully.

Revising instructional activities

An attitude one should develop is that regardless of how long or how effectively a system has been operating, it constantly needs to be revised. The need to revise may occur due to changes in society, federal regulations, or local school policies as well as our own perception of needed improvements in the system. Our own critical assessment of the internal performance of our system and the external factors influencing it should help us to make changes on a more timely basis. Often changes are made only after the effects of a factor are evident rather than estimating the effects and knowing how to adjust for them in advance. Since the systems approach allows us greater specificity in anticipating the performance of our system, it follows that these revisions can be made at a more sophisticated level of specificity. Also, if the situation requires major revisions in our system, the adjustments can be integrated more easily with the remaining segments of the system so that all portions of it are compatible with each other. What may happen in these cases is that the entire system will function more smoothly and at a higher level of sophistication and efficiency.

SHORT-RANGE USE OF THE MODEL

Our comments about the use of the systems approach have been in terms of your applying it as a classroom teacher. There is also a more immediate application to which it can be put. As you read the remaining chapters in the text, we suggest you use the model as an integrative tool to help place the issues in perspective with each other and the teaching role. It should also aid you in relating these issues to your current view of the instructional process and how you would cope with it. The model used in this integrative manner also can provide the basis for analyzing suggestions and demonstrations of specific practices you are exposed to in other courses and field experiences.

SUMMARY

In this chapter we made the point that educational problems are complex. We also indicated that, while we are all capable of making decisions about these problems, we are likely to be limited in dealing with the scope of the problem and use the minimum amount of data we believe necessary for a suitable solution. Even the data we use are likely to be distorted by our use of the representativeness, availability, and adjustment/anchoring strategies. A description of the process of both individual and group decisions was outlined along with what might be expected of each process in terms of consensus and compromise.

Several scientific approaches to information gathering were briefly presented, plus our views of the problems confronting a classroom teacher. A systems model approach to decision making was presented which has as its major phases: (1) analysis, (2) design, (3) preparation, (4) implementation, and (5) evaluation. The utility of the model as it relates to systems development, monitoring, assessment, and revision was also discussed.

SELF-TEST

1. The traditional model of education has been based on:
   a. Matching instruction to student capabilities.
   b. Matching instruction to student interests.
   c. Providing alternative tracks for students.
   d. A weeding-out process.
2. The average human adult can remember how many bits of information at a time in short-term memory?
   a. 7
   b. 5
   c. 9
   d. 12
3. When given a choice of how much information they may have to solve a problem, it appears that individuals prefer to:
   a. Gather all the relevant data before making a decision.
   b. Make decisions on the basis of no information.
   c. Operate with a minimum of information when making a decision.
   d. Gather some irrelevant information in addition to all of the relevant information before making a decision.
4. Assume teacher A has Tom in class this year, last

SELF-TEST *(continued)*

year had Dick in class, and the year before had Harry in class. Dick and Harry are older brothers of Tom. When making decisions about Tom, the teacher's judgment is likely to be biased by:
a. The fact that the teacher has had fewer observations of Tom.
b. A lack of confidence in making decisions about different members of the same family.
c. The average performance of Tom rather than his extreme performance.
d. The degree to which Tom looks like his two older brothers.

5. Once a person has made an initial decision, subsequent information is likely to have:
a. No effect.
b. Less effect than it should have.
c. An appropriate amount of effect.
d. More effect than it should have.

6. There are four types of scientific studies. Which study can be described as follows: the search is centered on an estimation of the degree to which various factors show a relationship.
a. Observational studies.
b. Correlational studies.
c. Experimental studies.
d. Ad hoc studies.

7. Mr. C teaches two tenth-grade geometry classes of equal academic abilities. Class I is given 30 minutes to do a test and class II is given 60 minutes to do the same test. Mr. C compares the results. Which of the following types of study was used?
a. Observational.
b. Ad hoc.
c. Correlational.
d. Experimental.

8. The general sequence of phases in program development is:
a. Analysis, design, preparation, implementation, and evaluation.
b. Design, analysis, evaluation, preparation, and implementation.
c. Evaluation, analysis, design, preparation, and implementation.
d. Preparation, design, evaluation, implementation, and analysis.
e. Design, analysis, preparation, implementation, and evaluation.

9. The primary activities associated with the design phase are:
a. Goal setting.
b. Determining learner capabilities.
c. Development of plans.
d. Checking plan effectiveness.

10. Which of the following is not a part of the analysis phase activities?
a. Task analysis.
b. Learner analysis.
c. Life space analysis.
d. Program analysis.

ANSWER KEY TO BOXED QUESTIONS

1. In any unit of instruction:
We intend to bring about specific changes in student performance.
As we teach, and the student learns, the problem will change.
The changes will result in the evolution of a problem into new problems.
We need to deal with several factors simultaneously.
The general context will shape the general nature of the problem.
The specific context will be hectic, requiring many quick decisions.
The learners will have individual differences that need to be taken into account.
Resources may be limited.
Our experiences are likely to limit our view of the problem and possible solutions.

2. Limited experiences will limit the total data base you have to draw upon.
Immediate memory capacity limited to 7 ± 2 bits of information will limit the amount of information you can use from the total pool of information.
Satisficer strategy is used due to limited processing capacity, so you are likely to draw on and use less information than is needed to arrive at an optimal solution.

3. Representativeness—Judgment of human characteristics and performance is likely to be biased by how well it matches our stereotyped beliefs.
Availability—Judgment of human characteristics and performance is likely to be biased by the ease with which we can recall previous experiences.
Adjustment/anchoring—Our initial judgment forms a base for later decisions and reduces the effect of additional information on future decisions.

4. Individual decision-making process:
Decisions of others may affect our initial decision if we have a low level of self-confidence in it but not if we have a high level of self-confidence in our initial decision.
Reasons for other people's decisions—The information provided by the more informed individuals may

cause us to move toward some weighted average of the arguments.

Further discussion is not likely to have any effect on opinions. Self-confidence in our final decision is likely to be high.

Small-group decisions:

Majority rule—In 70 percent of all groups having a majority favoring one position, the group will compromise on that position.

Coalition rule—When subgroups within the total group have close but differing opinions, they will decide on a single opinion and then, as a coalition, in 80 percent of these situations they will move the remainder of the group members to adopt this position.

Mean rule—Where all members favor different choices, in 50 percent of these cases they will compromise on a position close to the average of all positions.

Leadership—In 25 percent of all small-group decisions a leadership effect modifies the effects of the three group decision rules.

Compromise is not likely to bring about consensus.

5. Observational studies isolate relevant factors or possible relationships.

Correlational studies establish the degree to which various factors show a relationship. The finding of a relationship cannot be interpreted as a cause-and-effect relationship.

Experimental studies determine the effects of one factor on another. With well-designed studies cause-and-effect statements can be made.

N = 1 studies are a form of experiment used to study the effects of one factor on a single individual.

Post hoc studies are used to study previously gathered data to determine relationships between factors.

6. The main function is to determine the parameters of the instructional problem.

Environmental analysis—What goals should be set to prepare students for living in the general society and how should they be modified to meet their current and future lifestyles? Activities include an analysis of the current and expected state of our society and an analysis of the current lifestyles of individual students.

Task analysis—What subtasks are required in order to reach the instructional objectives, and in what order are they most effectively and efficiently learned? Subdividing the task and arranging the smaller units in an instructional sequence are the activities involved.

Learner analysis—What is the learner's current level of functioning in relation to the learning task? Collecting various measures of performance is the primary activity.

Instructional space analysis—What tangible resources are available or can be obtained for use during instruction? Seeking out and listing the various resources are two major activities.

Staff analysis—What are the instructional staff's strengths, weaknesses, and preferred ways of doing things? In most instances this is a self-analysis by the classroom teacher but may also require some observation and discussion with other staff members.

7. The main function is the development of plans to guide subsequent instruction.

Comprehensive plan—What should be the timing of the various instructional segments so they are most compatible with each other, the seasons of the year, the school calendar, the availability of materials, and the plans of other staff members? The activities are determining school realities and possibly making some notes about the timing of events.

Component plans—What instructional techniques and materials will best meet the conditions of learning or accomplish the goal of the program being developed? The main activities are covert, or thinking about the best alternatives. Also involved may be inspecting materials, specifying the characteristics of materials to be produced, and probably writing some notes about certain segments of the plan.

Evaluation plan—What should be evaluated and how will it be accomplished? A close inspection of objectives, possibly the design of evaluation materials, and sometimes written plans would cover the activities.

Preparatory plan—What needs to be done before the plans can be implemented, when should the preparations start, and when do they need to be completed? Writing a list of things to do and when to do them is an activity.

8. To prepare the physical setting, materials, staff, and students prior to the actual implementation of plans. The activities will vary with the plans and the task. The decisions are whether the preparations are proceeding on time, and whether they are adequate when completed.

9. The main function is to implement the component plans. In following the plans the activities will be those specified in the plan. When adapting plans to student performance, the activities of providing feedback and other follow-up activities are called for. The term *collecting evaluation data* describes the activities involved. The observation and analysis have no special activities. The decision that may be involved is whether to modify the plans to make use of some current event or situation. With observations there are no decisions specified. The analysis of student performance involves decisions about the meaning of a student's performance. When adopting plans the major decision is how to fill out the component plans to match the students' performance level and the immediate context.

Collection of evaluation data requires decisions about how to collect, record, and store the data to meet the current context.

10. The main function is to implement the evaluation plan and judge the effectiveness of the instructional activities and materials. The activities include the organization and inspection of the data so that regularities and relationships between the various factors involved in instruction can be determined. At times the information is communicated to others, but in all cases the process should result in using the information to improve future instruction. Several decisions are involved. One is relative to whether the evaluation procedures have been correctly completed. Decisions about whether or not to communicate the results, to whom, and in what form are also pertinent. The major decision should be how to use the results to improve future instruction.

ANSWER KEY TO SELF-TEST

1. *d*
2. *a*
3. *c*
4. *d*
5. *b*
6. *b*
7. *d*
8. *a*
9. *c*
10. *d*

SECTION II

PLANNING INSTRUCTION

Much of the teacher's work is accomplished before the teacher enters the classroom. This is the work of planning instruction, which is a major role of the teacher. In this role the teacher performs two related tasks: program adaption and development. In program adaption the teacher modifies a commercially prepared curriculum series to the particular purposes of the local classroom; and in program development the teacher constructs lessons to supplement the commercially prepared materials.

In making these decisions the teacher has a multitude of concerns, including the goals of instruction and the readiness of the students for instruction. Taking these into consideration the teacher plans instruction to achieve a desired set of outcomes with the available resources and time. An understanding of this planning process will allow the teacher to use available resources and time more wisely and efficiently.

In this section of the book we present the decisions faced by a teacher in planning instruction and the critical factors that should be considered in making these decisions. Chapter 7, "Educational and Instructional Objectives," describes the derivation of worthwhile objectives and their instructional uses. Chapter 8, "Sequencing Instruction," presents a rationale for making sequencing decisions in designing instruction. The process of identifying the student's level of readiness for instruction is discussed in Chapter 9, "The Learner: Analysis of Instructional Level." The design of specific events in instruction to achieve different learning outcomes is treated in Chapters 10 and 11. Finally, Chapter 12, "The Evaluation of Student Performance," details the important steps in planning evaluation of student learning outcomes.

Chapter 7

Educational and instructional objectives

IN PLANNING INSTRUCTION two basic decisions must be made: what to teach and how to teach it. The decision of what to teach concerns the goals and objectives of education. This chapter pertains to that process of deriving worthwhile objectives on which the design of instruction will be based. After reading this chapter you should be able to accomplish the following objectives:

1. Describe the role of performance objectives in planning instruction, as an adjunct aid, and in evaluating performance.
2. Identify missing components in statements of performance objectives.
3. Construct performance objectives for educational goals.

FUNCTIONAL STATEMENTS OF EDUCATIONAL GOALS

A teacher develops instruction to support the broad educational goals of the school. From these broad goals the teacher develops both long-range and short-range objectives for instruction. The long-range objectives refer to broad internal dispositions we expect the student to develop over the course of instruction. Such long-range objectives are "is competent in addition and subtraction of whole numbers," "reads with ease," and "appreciates music as a leisure-time activity." At the next level objectives represent specific learned capabilities that we expect the student to acquire in a relatively short time span. Finally, teachers develop test items to determine whether a student has attained a specific learned capability. The relationship between these levels of outcome is shown in Figure 7–1.

Level A statements are broad educational goals and they are the most inclusive, representing the ideal for which education should strive. As such, this level reflects the educational philosophy of a school. In Chapter 2 we identified the four major philosophies of perennialism, essentialism, progressivism, and reconstructionism from which these goals are derived.

With Level B statements or long-range objectives we have moved to individual subject disciplines. The most important and inclusive concepts and principles of the discipline are identified, and some dispositional state of knowledge or affect on the part of the student in regard to these principles and concepts is expressed. Level B statements serve two important functions according to Jenkins and Deno (1970). One of these functions is to serve as an economical framework for organizing and conceptualizing curriculum development. Additionally, Jenkins and Deno view Level B statements as a bridge from the most abstract level to the more specific and technical levels of C and D. In fulfilling this function, Level B statements allow us to obtain greater understanding and acceptance of specific goals among a wider and more diverse group of people.

Statements of outcome at Level C, or short-term objectives, describe the performance capability to be acquired by the student as a result of instruction. These statements are typically referred to as *performance objectives* or *behavioral objectives.* Performance objectives express learner outcomes that correspond to the performance capabilities comprising the various learning domains. Thus this level of objectives specifies classes of learned capabilities referred to in an earlier chapter as motor skills, affective states, and cognitive and mathemagenic skills.

Objectives stated at Level C are utilized by teachers in the design, implementation, and evaluation of instruction. As such, these objectives are the blueprint a teacher uses to develop the specific test items (or any other evaluation instruments or strategies)

FIGURE 7–1
Levels of educational outcomes

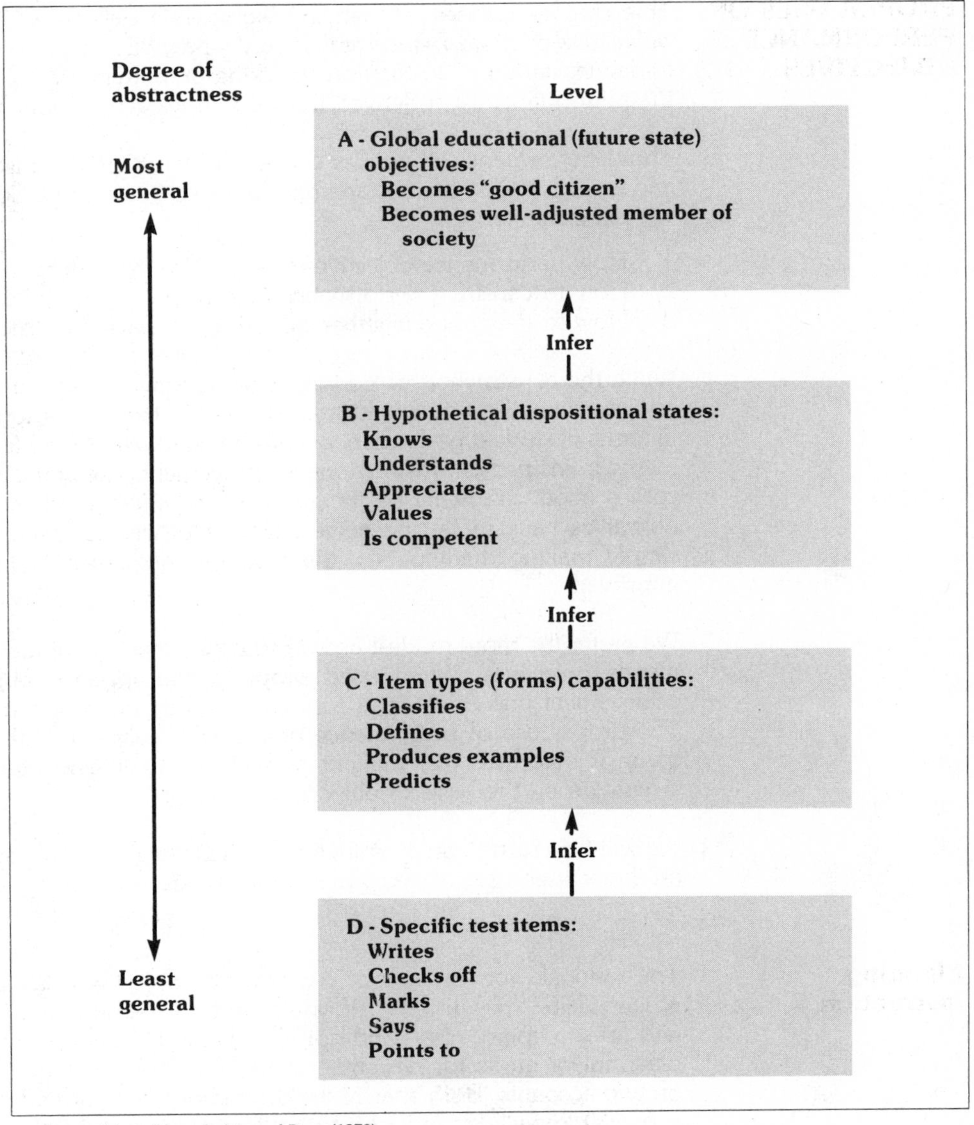

Source: Adapted from Jenkins and Deno (1970).

to measure student achievement resulting from instruction. Such test items are the Level D outcome statements. Information gathered at Level D provides the data on which the sequence of inferences depicted in Figure 7–1 operates. All of a teacher's decisions concerning instruction, ranging from deciding whether or not an individual student has achieved a specific goal to determining the success of an entire course, proceed on data from Level D. Notice that here we use a very inclusive definition of test item: any observation of a student's performance by a teacher in a formal testing situation or any informal classroom situation, or for that matter, *any* situation outside of the classroom. What is important is that the teacher observes some valid evidence of learning.

PROPER USES OF PERFORMANCE OBJECTIVES

This chapter focuses on deriving worthwhile objectives at Level C, referred to as *behavioral* or *performance objectives.* As previously mentioned, the planning and day-to-day execution of instruction are done predominantly on the basis of objectives at the performance level derived from the more general long-range objectives.

These performance objectives are at the heart of the instructional design process, and as such stating them is an important step in teaching. Consequently in this chapter we will examine:

1. How performance objectives are used in instruction.
2. How to construct performance objectives.
3. How to determine whether the ones you have constructed are worthwhile.

While the construction of performance objectives is an important step in the design of instruction, it is not an educational cure-all. The expression of educational outcomes in terms of student performance is not going to lead to tremendous overnight improvements in instruction. Instructional improvement, like any other worthwhile endeavor, comes about gradually as the result of *hard work!* Many advocates of behavioral objectives have made the naive claim or otherwise created the impression that by simply making them public, the expected outcomes of instruction will be greatly improved.

We prefer the more modest answer to why a teacher should construct and use performance objectives. When used properly, performance objectives increase student achievement and affect, and furthermore they increase the efficiency of instruction. The proper use of performance objectives involves: (1) planning instruction on the basis of objectives, (2) making objectives available to students, and (3) designing evaluation on the basis of objectives.

We will now turn to an examination of the logical rationale and the empirical research on these three uses of performance objectives.

Planning instruction

The rationale for this use of performance objectives has been succinctly stated by Mager (1962, p. vii): ". . . if you're not sure where you're going, you're liable to end up someplace else—and not even know it." Performance objectives provide the blueprint or guide for designing instruction. This analogy to blueprints is warranted on two accounts. Both specify the desired outcome or end product; and both require a special knowledge in order to implement procedures for the establishment of the desired outcomes. In other words, both a blueprint and a performance objective tell you in specific terms where you are going. Just as a blueprint requires special knowledge on the part of the carpenter or engineer to construct the house or building specified, so a teacher needs special knowledge to design a lesson to achieve a specified objective. As Gagné (1965a) points out, one advantage to the specification of objectives in performance terms is to identify the domain of learning involved in the task. With the domain of learning identified, the teacher may then incorporate into the lesson the distinctive instructional conditions that most facilitate attainment of the given domain.

McNeil (1967) reports the results of a series of studies relating to the value of planning instruction to achieve performance objectives. In the first two studies, the difference between the experimental and control groups was the criteria on which they were told their grades would be based. Student teachers in the experimental groups were told their grades would be determined by how successful they were in promoting the attainment of specified performance objectives by public school pupils. Student teachers in the control group were told their grades would be determined by their appearance, deportment in class, how well they executed their lesson plan, and other behavior. Results of the first study showed that student teachers in the experimental group were judged by their cooperating teacher to be more successful on three criteria than the control-group student teachers. The three criteria used to evaluate the student teachers were:

1. Success in teaching as evidenced by pupil achievement.
2. Poise and personality.
3. Application of the learning principles taught in the course.

Participating student teachers in both the experimental and control groups of the second study were compared on how well they improved the punctuation skills of their public school pupils. Public school pupils assigned to the experimental group student teachers scored significantly better on two measures of punctuation skills than did pupils in the control classes. These pupils showed greater improvement in the remediation of their deficiencies than did pupils taught by the control-group student teachers. Besides this improvement in deficient skills, the experimental pupils also showed a greater gain in other punctuation skills than the control group.

The final study reported by McNeil concerned data from a questionnaire given to all the student teachers who participated in the second study. Interestingly enough, there were no significant differences on the questionnaire between the two groups. Results of the study showed that 98 percent of student teachers from both groups preferred to have their teaching evaluated by the learning progress of their pupils. Both groups reported spending about half an hour per day on punctuation skills. Likewise, both groups perceived themselves as equally free in the selection of teaching procedures.

The research by McNeil suggests that instruction based on performance objectives leads to greater achievement by students. Furthermore, teachers seemed to prefer objectives as a basis for designing instruction. Perhaps with performance objectives both teacher and students perceive the purpose of instruction more clearly and remain on task better. As we shall see in the next section, making the intent of instruction known to the students can facilitate their learning.

The availability of objectives as an aid to student learning

Common sense suggests that providing students with descriptions of expected learning outcomes will aid them in determining what to study, and consequently should lead to greater achievement. Students themselves often report that after the initial test in any course, they do better on subsequent tests because they have learned what course content the teacher will emphasize and the type of test that will be given. The public disclosure of the intended outcome of instruction appears to be a simple technique by which the teacher may facilitate student achievement.

Objectives as directions to the learner. The means by which a student's knowledge of performance objectives affects learning has been the subject of much research. Performance objectives function primarily as orienting stimuli that focus the student's attention on the relevant information to be learned (Figure 7–2). In other words,

FIGURE 7–2
Objectives can direct student attention to relevant information in the learning task

performance objectives serve as goal directions to the student, which aid in locating the relevant information in instructional materials.

Evidence for the orienting function of performance objectives was obtained by Rothkopf and Kaplan (1972) in a study of learning from text. A test comprised of completion-type items was constructed from a reading passage, and test items were assigned to one of two subtests. One subtest was labeled *intentional learning* and it represented the test items from which the performance objectives were developed. The other subtest was labeled *incidental learning* and the test items on it measured learning of information from the reading passage for which there were no performance objectives. People in the experimental group were given the set of objectives with the reading passage and informed that they would be tested only on the stated objectives (i.e., the intentional subtest). Members of the control group were given the reading passage without the set of objectives and were simply told to learn everything in the text. However, after reading the text selection, both groups were given a posttest composed of both the intentional and incidental learning subtests.

The results of the study are presented in Figure 7–3. The group that had the objectives available did better on both subtests than did the group receiving general learning directions. However, most impressive is the difference between the two groups on the intentional learning subtest, with the objectives-available group's scores more than three times higher than those of the general learning directions group. Furthermore,

FIGURE 7–3
Retention of intentional and incidental information with performance objectives

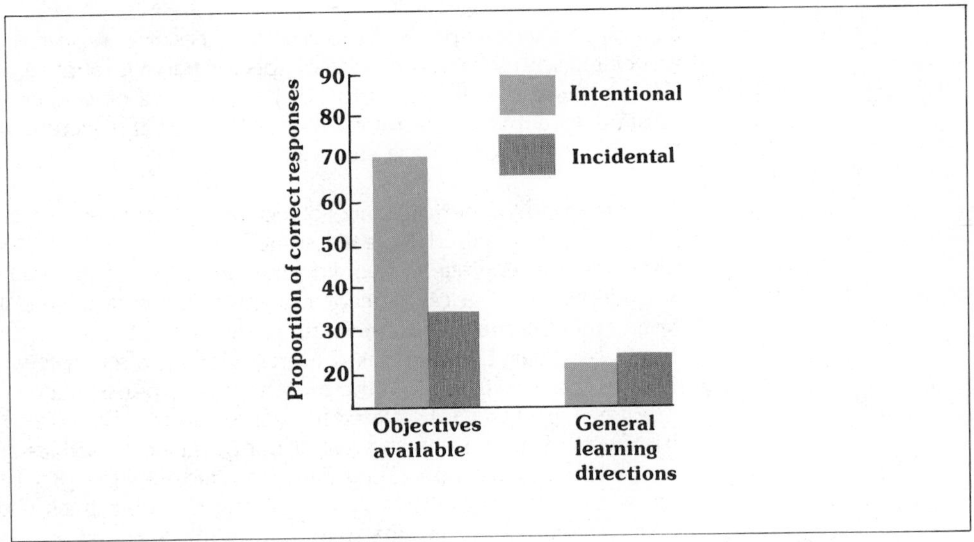

Source: Adapted from Rothkopf and Kaplan (1972).

the objectives-available group's scores on the intentional learning subtest were more than twice their scores on the incidental subtest, while for the general learning group there was not a significant difference between the intentional learning and incidental learning subtests. This whole pattern of results confirms the role of performance objectives as directions to the learner. Objectives facilitate learning by focusing the student's attention on relevant information. This in turn determines what the student studies and hence what is learned.

Other studies have supported the view of performance objectives as orienting stimuli. Duell (1974) showed that the difference in achievement for a group of students given objectives compared with a different group of students not receiving objectives could be attributed to performance on test items that measured information judged unimportant by a majority of students. She concluded that objectives direct students to information that they would have most probably overlooked in their independent studying.

Duchastel and Brown (1974) demonstrated that students perform better on test items measuring objectives provided to them (intentional learning) and performed less well on items covering information in the text that was not covered by an objective (incidental learning). These results were at odds with previous research, and Duchastel and Brown attributed this difference to the students' familiarity with objectives. The students participating in this study had prior experience with objectives and their use in learning and evaluation. According to Duchastel and Brown, these students focused their attention on the information in the text that was relevant to the supplied objectives while minimizing attention to information irrelevant to the objectives (hence the reduced incidental learning). Furthermore, students may need to learn to use objectives as orienting stimuli by practical experience with objectives as "true" descriptors of test type and content.

Other effects of performance objectives. We have seen that objectives increase learning by directing student attention to relevant information, but objectives can also have an effect upon student behaviors other than achievement. Tiemann (1968), in a study of a videotaped college economics course, reported a more favorable attitude associated with the presentation of specific behavioral objectives. More recently, Staley (1978) found that the inclusion of performance objectives with a videotaped lecture resulted in a more favorable attitude toward the lecture as an instructional mode among a group of college students.

The provision of performance objectives can influence the efficiency of instruction (i.e., the time required to learn something). Mager and McCann (1961), in a study with graduate engineers involving the provision of objectives and learner control of instruction, found a 65 percent reduction in training time with both methods used. Noting that the Mager and McCann study confounded learner control and the availability of objectives, Duchastel and Merrill (1973), after reviewing the available research, reached the conclusion that the presentation of performance objectives increased study time when groups were equated for learner control. Staley and Wolf (1979) investigated the effects of training on the use of performance objectives as a study aid for learning from written instruction. They demonstrated that the provision of objectives can decrease study time. Both groups receiving the objectives with or without training in their use learned more than did the reading-only group, although the differences were small. More important, the training group learned more in one-third less study time than the control group, as can be seen from an inspection of Figure 7–4. Staley and Wolf explain the difference between their results and Duchastel and Merrill's conclusion with the explanation that objectives influence study time as a function of the type of learning task. Of the five studies cited by Duchastel and Merrill to support their conclusion, one reported no significant difference in study time between objectives and no-objectives treatments, and three studies involved some form of computer-assisted instruction of short duration. Computer-assisted instruction typically provides for interactive instruction, which implies control of student attention, and hence has less need for an orienting stimulus like performance objectives. Yet it would seem that most texts are not tightly edited learning documents and they probably contain

FIGURE 7–4
Study time as a function of the availability of performance objectives and training in their use

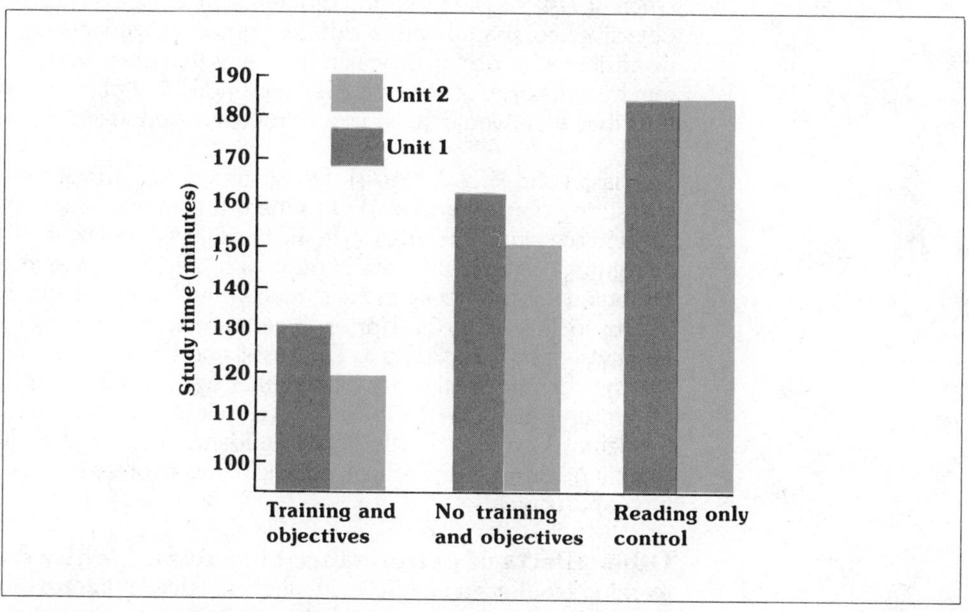

Source: Adapted from Staley and Wolf (1979).

much information that is not directly relevant to a set of performance objectives. Given such reading assignments, objectives allow the student to reduce study time by scanning and then passing over information judged irrelevant to the given set of objectives. Hartley and Davies (1976) offer a similar explanation in that they concluded objectives would be of little help to students with highly structured learning materials such as programmed instruction.

Conditions under which objectives facilitate learning. We have just seen that objectives have a greater influence upon student behavior as the structure of the instructional setting decreases. The more structure in an instructional setting, the more likely it is that instructional strategies are used to direct student attention to relevant information, and consequently the provision of objectives is redundant. Now we will examine other factors influencing the effectiveness of objectives as adjunct aids.

The provision of performance objectives increases student achievement when the expected learning outcomes are at the verbal information or memorization level. Several studies by Duell (1974, 1977) support this conclusion. She found that providing students with a list of objectives for a reading passage can increase performance on test items that require the learned capability of verbal information, but this did not increase performance on test items that required comprehension such as concept learning or rule learning. Apparently objectives, while serving as directions to students, do not necessarily induce the level of encoding required by comprehension questions.

Most studies of performance objectives as study aids have used the instructional medium of printed material, but several have utilized lecture as the instructional mode in investigating the effects of performance objectives on learning (Royer, 1977; Tiemann, 1968). Results of these investigations are in agreement with those studies using textual materials. Students supplied with a list of objectives learned more than did students not supplied with objectives. Furthermore, Staley (1978) demonstrated that the use of objectives facilitates the learning of memorization objectives but not the learning of concepts from lecture.

Earlier in this chapter we remarked that some advocates of performance objectives have made exaggerated claims about the benefits of using objectives on the achievement of students. In this section of the chapter we have tried to show that under certain conditions knowledge of performance objectives by students can facilitate learning. However, the degree to which performance will be facilitated is small in relation to some of the exaggerated claims made about objectives. Duchastel and Merrill (1973) offer the teacher some sage advice about objectives as adjunct aids in instruction, which they attribute to Rothkopf:

> To make instructional objectives available to students sometimes aids their learning and is almost never harmful. Therefore if to make objectives available does not consume much time or resources then one might as well provide them as not (p. 63).

The use of performance objectives in the evaluation of learning

Tests designed to measure the achievement of specific performance objectives are referred to as *criterion-referenced tests.* The type of information obtained from a criterion-referenced measure is more useful than information obtained from other types of measurement for instructional purposes (Glaser, 1963; Glaser & Klaus, 1962).

The use of performance objectives as the basis for test development can facilitate student learning in several ways (Figure 7–5). Foremost is that the student errors

FIGURE 7–5
Objectives facilitate evaluation of student learning and allow the teacher to offer more specific help to the student

on a criterion-referenced test provide the teacher with an excellent source of information on which to base corrective feedback to the student. Feedback derived from errors on a criterion-referenced test provides the student with detailed and thorough information with which to judge the learning effort, and the completeness of information in feedback has been shown to be an important variable in determining the effectiveness of the feedback (Bourne & Pendleton, 1958; Travers et al., 1964). Instructional feedback is examined thoroughly in Chapter 10 if you wish to pursue it further at this time.

Empirical revision of instruction is another important function that utilizes the data of student performance on measures of performance objectives. Instruction that has been tested and revised on the basis of student performance data is more effective in terms of student learning than is instruction designed to teach those same objectives but not subjected to empirical revision. The value of such revision has been demonstrated in a variety of instructional modes (Gropper, 1975). Quite possibly, empirical revision is the single most important step in the systematic design of instruction. This reflects the fact that, given our current state of knowledge, the design of instruction is more frequently empirically guided than theoretically guided.

1. For each use of performance objectives below, list a benefit associated with its use.
   a. Planning instruction.
   b. Adjunct aid in instruction.
   c. Evaluation.

WRITING PERFORMANCE OBJECTIVES

Statements of performance objectives focus our attention on what the student will be able to do as the result of instruction by describing either the behavior to be performed or the product to be produced by that performance. Such objectives are precise and unambiguous communications of the intended outcome of instruction because they state what the teacher will actually observe as evidence of the desired learning. Additionally, performance objectives facilitate the design of instruction and evaluation by conveying the type of learned capability (e.g., attitude, motor skill, rule learning) required by the student's performance. As we shall discuss in Chapter 11, after we classify the learned capability required by a performance objective into a domain, then we may apply our knowledge of the necessary conditions of learning for that domain to the design of instruction.

Performance objectives are derived from more general statements of educational outcomes or goals. Most typically, these statements represent long-range objectives and, while such statements serve other useful purposes, they are too general in meaning to function as an effective guide in designing specific units of instruction. For example consider the educational goal:

> The student will understand the importance of a proper diet to good health.

This goal says something about the content of instruction, especially to a health teacher. From reading the goal statement anyone could surmise that the students are to be *exposed* to information about the effects of nutrition on one's state of health; however, what the student will be able to do in demonstrating the acquired understanding is not answered. Now consider the following statements:

> Given a list of ten diseases, the student will check all the diseases that result from dietary deficiencies.
>
> The student will write a paragraph describing the importance of a balanced diet to good health, listing a minimum of three out of the five reasons given in the required health education text.
>
> The student will eat an overall balanced diet on a weekly basis within the caloric range appropriate for a person of the student's body type and activity level.

These performance objectives, as opposed to the educational goal statement, clearly specify the intended learner outcome in such a way that it would be relatively easy for two or more observers to agree on whether the objectives have been attained.

To obtain appropriate performance objectives, teachers start with an educational goal and ask the question: What student performance or performances are an acceptable indicator of successful attainment of this goal? In this light we may view the process of deriving performance objectives as one of translating long-range objectives into observable indicators.

Components of objectives

To be most effective as meaningful statements of intended instructional outcomes, performance objectives should contain three components: student behavior, conditions, and standards of performance. Let us examine several performance objectives for each of these components.

> The student will state orally the three primary colors, the three secondary colors, and the three achromatic colors.
>
> Behavior: State orally the three primary colors, the three secondary colors, and the three achromatic colors.
>
> Conditions: When asked to state the three primary, three secondary, and three achromatic colors (these conditions are implied by the nature of the objective).

Standards: One hundred percent, since each color class is composed of three colors.

Given ten different mushrooms from the northeastern geographic area, the student will be able to identify all the edible mushrooms.
Behavior: Identify the edible mushrooms.
Conditions: Given ten different mushrooms from the northeastern geographic area.
Standards: All, or 100 percent.

These two examples illustrate several important points about the construction of performance objectives. In a statement of a performance objective, the behavior component encompasses the verb and its object. Appropriate verb phrases denote an overt action on the part of the student and the results of this action, or simply an observable product resulting from some unspecified action by the learner. In our first example, the verb *talking* is an overt behavior to be performed by the student. Furthermore, words are not to be said randomly, but rather the student is to name the primary, secondary, and achromatic colors. Even when the verb in a behavior component specifies an overt action on the part of a student, the product of that action must be considered in determining the meaning of the performance.

The second performance objective has a behavior component of *identifies edible mushrooms.* In this example there is no overt behavior indicated by the verb; instead there is an observable product that could have resulted from a variety of overt actions. A person can identify edible mushrooms by engaging in a number of overt actions such as pointing to, picking up, or saying "that one." In objectives such as this (and many important learning tasks fall into this category), the actual overt behavior is not important; what is important is the product of the behavioral performance.

As the preceding examples show, a behavior component of a performance objective can specify either an overt action or a product produced by some action. In either case, there is some observable and measurable evidence from which the teacher can conclude that the desired learning has indeed taken place. What is significant about this is that a performance objective unambiguously states a *specific observable* outcome as evidence of learning, not whether it is an overt or covert action.

Just as the result of a behavior is important in interpreting the meaning of a behavior, so is the context in which the performance of a behavior occurs. However, very often the importance of the conditions component is overlooked or misunderstood. The following quote from an essay by Hyman (1972, p. 396) arguing against the use of specific objectives in behavioral form illustrates very well the importance of the often misunderstood conditions component:

> . . . Teachers are interested not only in what a student does, but *why* he does it. To state merely what a student should do (for example, answer test questions on his own) is thus inadequate. An objective stated in behavioral terms without further specification of reasons is not a useful tool for curriculum development or evaluation. Teachers desire that their students not cheat due to a commitment to honesty and respect of other people and prefer this to not cheating due to fear of the hickory stick. But, if all a teacher knows is that Jonathan did not cheat on his last exam, then he has insufficient data for evaluating both his own teaching efforts and Jonathan's progress in regard to cheating.

Another way of stating Hyman's argument is to say that in order for a teacher to obtain valid information about a student's learning progress, the teacher must observe not only performance of the desired behavior but also the conditions surrounding that performance. In the example of cheating, the teacher must determine that Jonathan refrains from looking at his neighbor's paper while taking a test; however, these data alone are inadequate, as Hyman points out. The teacher must also determine when Jonathan refrains from obtaining answers from his classmates. In this case the teacher wishes Jonathan to avoid cheating out of moral conviction. Now it can safely be assumed that a person with a moral value opposed to cheating would not cheat even when it is possible to safely do so. So our teacher needs to ascertain whether or not Jonathan would cheat in a situation when it is possible to do so with relative impunity.

The conditions components must also include any tools or constraints to be used by the student in the performance of the desired behavior. Consider this performance objective:

> The student will perform an imitation of any three animals of their choice using only bodily movements. Two of the imitations should be correctly recognized by a majority of the class members.

In this objective restrictions are placed on the imitative performance; it can consist of motor responses only, with no verbal responses allowed. Special conditions that restrict performance should be noted in the conditions component, but those that aid performance should be noted also, as in the following objective:

> Given a sample of 100 observations, the student will be able to compute the mean and standard deviation of the sample. Both calculations must be correct to the nearest hundredth and all arithmetic operations may be performed on an electronic calculator.

In this case, the student will be allowed to use a calculator to perform simple arithmetic operations, so this is a special condition that should aid student performance.

Now we turn to the third component of a performance objective: the standards component. If you recall from Chapter 4, as the sample of performance observations upon which an inference regarding learning is made increases, then the greater is the confidence we can place in the accuracy of that inference. I have more confidence in an inference that a student has learned a given capability if I have seen that student perform ten times than if I have observed only five performances of that behavior. So, quite simply, the standards component gives the minimal level of performance acceptable for indicating successful achievement of the intended learning outcome.

Two types of standards can be distinguished. Type 1 standards occur when one is dealing with discrete behaviors that (1) require little judgment to determine whether or not they have been successfully performed and (2) take a short time to perform. For these types of behaviors or products, it is convenient to have the student perform them a number of times. Consequently this type of standard specifies the proportion of correct responses set as the minimal level of acceptable performance. Below are several examples of Type 1 standards.

> Given a sample of 20 elements from the periodic table, the student will match them with their symbol from a list of 30 supplied symbols. The student must get 18 out of 20 correct for mastery of the objective.
>
> The student will name five of the seven continents.

Given a golf ball within a three-foot radius of the cup, the student will one-putt 85 percent of 20 such shots.

Type 2 standards occur when a judgment must be made about the qualitative aspects of some complex performance or product. With Type 2 standards, the purpose is to reduce personal bias or error in judging the complex performance or product by making explicit the important observable qualities to be judged. Below is an example of a Type 2 standard adapted from Coffman (1971, pp. 291–92).

The student will write an essay comparing the "policies of isolation" in American foreign policy during the period 1789–1826 and during the 1930s. Each of the following topics should be described in an acceptable answer:

a. Rationale of isolation, 1789–1826.
b. Specific isolationist practices, 1789–1826.
c. Rationale of isolation in 1930s.
d. Specific isolationist practices, 1930s.
e. Comparison of policies of isolation of both periods.
f. Appropriateness of "isolationism" as description of foreign policy of both periods.
g. Quality of english.

Each point will be scored on the following (note that rating system is given for only one point as illustrative of all).

Guide for Point B

Specific isolationist practices, 1789–1826

1. Neutrality proclamation, 1793.
2. Jay's Treaty, 1794 (to avoid League of Armed Neutrality).
3. Pinckney's Treaty, 1795 (to avoid Franco-Spanish U.S. alliance).
4. Washington's farewell address, 1796.
5. Jefferson's first inaugural address, 1800 ("entangling alliances").
6. "Neutrality" legislation—Embargo Act, 1807.
7. "Neutrality" legislation—Non-intercourse Acts, 1809–1810.
8. "Neutrality" legislation—Macon's Bill #2 1810.
9. The Monroe Doctrine.

Check appropriate blank.

_____*a.* Discusses four of the above, describes each accurately, and connects each with the "rationale" in A; or mentions six.

_____*b.* Discusses three of the above, describes each accurately, and connects each with the "rationale" in A; or mentions four.

_____*c.* Discusses two of the above, describes each accurately, and connects each with the "rationale" in A; or mentions three.

_____*d.* Discusses one of the above, describes it accurately, and connects it with "rationale" in A; or mentions two.

_____*e.* No credit.

Additionally, the standards would contain a system for assigning weights to the check marks for each point, and then the distribution of weight scores and the total score of a minimal acceptable answer would be described.

A Type 2 standard is a rating and scoring system for the judgment of a complex performance or product. As such it does not have to be stated as a formal part of a statement of a performance objective. An illustration of a Type 2 standard was included here to make the point that such rating systems should be constructed prior to the design of instruction to teach the skill. When the teacher attempts to determine beforehand the qualities that distinguish skilled performance from nonskilled performance, then the teacher develops a clearer conception of what is being taught and thus instruction should be approved. How to construct such rating and scoring systems will be covered in Chapter 12. For now it is sufficient to be cognizant of the fact that the standards for judging a complex performance require the development of a detailed outline of the qualities to be observed, which should be developed prior to the design of instruction.

Objectives for different learning domains

Since performance objectives indicate what the student is to learn from instruction, they reflect the domains of learned capabilities. Each domain, as we discovered in Chapter 5, is an internal state resulting in differing performance capabilities. The domain of learning involved in the intended outcome expressed by a given objective dictates that the behavior and conditions components of that objective meet certain specifications. The exact capabilities represented by each domain were presented in greater detail in Chapter 5. Our purpose here is to demonstrate how this information applies to the construction of performance objectives.

Affective domain. With objectives in this domain the teacher is attempting to specify valid observational data that will warrant the inference that the student has acquired a desired affective state. The behavior component must specify some action that brings the student into contact with the object in the case of positive affect and a behavior that avoids an object for a negative affect. Such behaviors are referred to as *approach* and *avoidance* behaviors, respectively. The conditions component should be one in which the student can choose to approach or avoid the object free from external influence. Under these conditions we can conclude that the behavior is a preferred activity on the part of the student. Below are two examples of affective objectives, one from high school biology and the other from elementary school social studies (Lee & Merrill, 1972, pp. 87–88).

Behavior: Coming to class early.
Conditions: Teacher does not ask students to come early, but has room open so that they may; does not reward those who come early, but has biology books available for students to browse through.
Standards: One third of the students will come early each day throughout the semester and 90 percent of the students will come early at least once.

Behavior: Asking parents questions about family lifestyle.
Conditions: During a unit on human development the teacher discusses family life styles but does not ask individual students about their life styles. Teacher distributes a worksheet "for the students' own information" which lists questions to ask parents to help identify lifestyles. Teacher informs students that she will not collect the worksheets. A week later the teacher contacts one third of the parents randomly.
Standards: At least one half of the parents will report that their children asked them about their family lifestyle.

Motor skills domain. Performance objectives in this domain are concerned with the student's ability to execute physical movements. Most typically motor skill objectives specify a complex performance of a sequence of muscular actions. The product of the performance is important, but the assumption is that the product automatically follows as a result of the correct movements.

The conditions components of motor skill objectives usually describe the tools and constraints involved in the student performance. Examples of performance objectives in the motor skills domain are:

Behavior: Hit a golf ball with the proper swing.
Conditions: Given a 2, 3, or 5 iron and a straight fairway.
Standards: The ball will travel a distance of at least 100 feet and remain within the bounds of the fairway on seven out of ten shots.

Behavior: Saw a corner joint.
Conditions: Given a hand saw, miter box, and quarter round molding.
Standards: The two pieces of molding will fit at the joint so that the largest separation of the two pieces is not greater than 1/16 of an inch. This level of performance will be demonstrated on 90 percent of a sample of ten joints.

Cognitive domain. In this domain learning outcomes are further divided into three subtypes: memorization, concept learning, and rule learning. Each of these is distinguished by the performance capability established as the result of learning. With memorization the performance of the student reproduces information to which the student has previously been exposed. In most objectives involving memorization, it does not matter whether the student reproduces the information orally or in writing, except for the teacher's convenience in evaluating the performance. Written prose leaves a permanent record which the teacher may return to at a more convenient time.

The conditions components of memorization objectives are frequently not stated in the formation of these objectives. This is so because memorization objectives require the recall of information from memory and the specific retrieval cue is usually the directions to recall the information: For an objective like:

The student will list in descending order the ten largest cities in the world.

The appropriate conditions component would be:

Given the question, "List the ten largest cities in the world in descending order."

So to have such a conditions component in the statement of this objective will be an unnecessary redundancy. However, some memorization objectives require that the information set to be learned be only sampled on a test; such objectives have an explicit conditions component. An example of this type of objective is:

Behavior: State the correct sum.
Conditions: Given a sample of 20 facts from the "addition facts" set of 1 to 5 (i.e., 2 + 1, 3 + 4, etc.).
Standards: Ninety five percent.

Performance objectives at the concept learning level require a performance indicating that the student can distinguish between instances and noninstances of the concept(s) under consideration. At this level the important element is not the actual behavior of the learner, but rather the product of the behavior (the identification of the instances of the concept).

Two features of the conditions component are critical for valid statements of concept learning objectives: (1) the student should be presented with both instances and noninstances of the concept, and (2) these instances and noninstances should be ones previously unencountered during instruction. Note the following examples (Boutwell & Tennyson, 1971, p. 8).

Behavior: Identify paintings by artist and period.
Conditions: Given four reproductions, not previously seen in class, from each of the ten major Western art periods (40 total).
Standards: Correctly identify the period and artist of at least three of the four paintings from each period.

Behavior: Classify rock fossils by geological age.
Conditions: Given ten previously unencountered rock fossils.
Standards: One hundred percent.

Rule learning as a learned capability implies that the student will be able to apply a general rule or principle in a specific situation; consequently, a rule-learning objective must state evidence open to such an interpretation. The behavior component will typically focus on a product that demonstrates the application of the desired rule.

The conditions component would consist of situations representing the range to which we expect the student to apply the rule. Furthermore, these instances should be ones not presented to the student during instruction on the rule. Examples of performance objectives involving rule learning are the following:

Behavior: Writes a topic sentence.
Conditions: Given ten previously unencountered paragraphs of four to seven sentences and with the topic sentence deleted.
Standards: Each topic sentence written by the student, in order to be counted correct, must express (1) a general proposition, (2) a question, or (3) offer the basis for a comparison or contrast. Eight out of ten topic sentences must be correct for mastery.

Behavior: Writes a paragraph predicting future trend in wages for a ten-year period according to Ricardo's Iron Law of Wages.
Conditions: Given a free-market economy and a chart projecting the population trend for the ten-year period immediately in the future.
Standards: Direction of the prediction must be appropriate.

Mathemagenic Domain. Problem solving objectives indicate that the student has to generate and verify a solution to the posed problem. A sample objective is:

Behavior: Constructs a persuasive essay on one of the following topics: (1) hazards of smoking, (2) the death penalty (pro or con), or (3) the abortion issue (pro or con).
Conditions: Given one week to prepare.
Standard: Essay will be scored on the following points:

I. Defensible assertions.
   a. Avoids absolutes.
   b. Open about uncertainties.
II. Evidence for position.
   a. Credible sources.
   b. Supports major assertions.
   c. Evidence applied correctly.
III. Addresses objections to view.
   a. Presents opposing views clearly.
   b. Presents logical (not emotional) arguments against objections.

In the objective the problem to be given the student is described and qualifications placed upon an acceptable solution are specified. The teacher makes the assumption that to achieve a correct solution the student must apply both cognitive and mathemagenic skills. Therefore such objectives usually focus on a product rather than an overt action by the student.

2. Determine which of the following statements *(a–d)* best applies to each objective below:

   a. Behavior component is inadequate.
   b. Conditions component is inadequate.
   c. Standards component is inadequate.
   d. All three components are present and adequate.

   1. Given a printed list of five good business principles, the student will know them.
   2. Given a description of ten different organisms and their position in the food chain, the student will correctly identify the trophic level of eight out of ten organisms.
   3. The student will not make more than two grammatical errors.
   4. Given an assortment of wood and metal screws, the student will sort them into appropriate categories.
   5. The student will demonstrate understanding of the importance of swimming pool safety rules.

THE SELECTION OF WORTHWHILE OBJECTIVES

The preceding section in this chapter analyzed the procedure used in formulating specific performance objectives for which instruction will be designed. The relevant question for this section is: How can teachers determine if the objectives they have formulated will be of value to their students? This question relates to the life space analysis described earlier in Chapter 6.

The Tyler rationale

To date the most viable framework for the generation and selection of worthwhile objectives is the model first proposed by Ralph W. Tyler (1950). An illustration of the model and how it relates to the levels of educational outcomes presented early

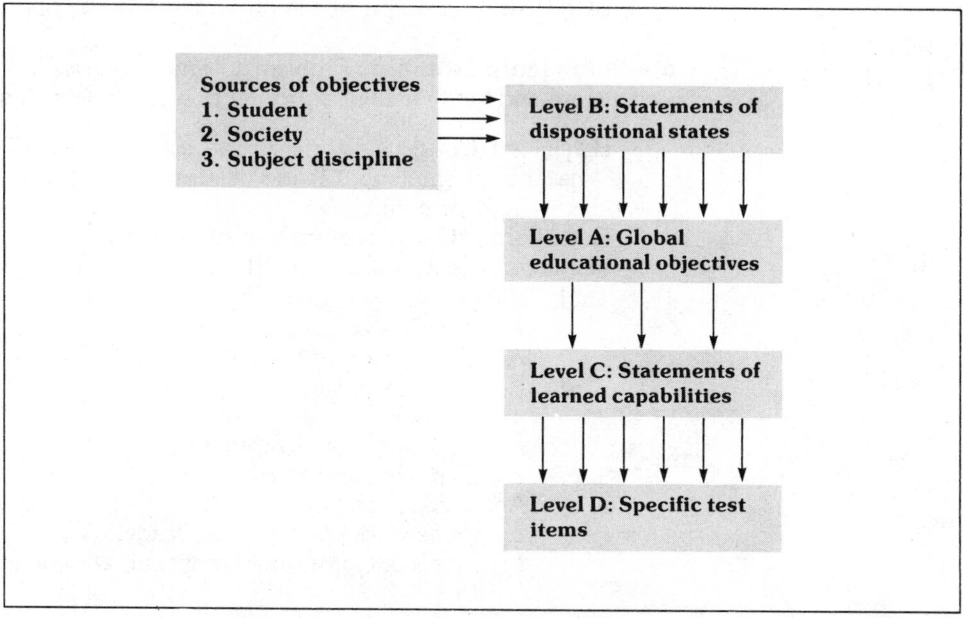

FIGURE 7–6
The Tyler rationale: Broad objectives are judged against the criteria of educational philosophy and the psychology of learning, then translated into specific performance objectives

in this chapter is shown in Figure 7–6. Objectives stem from a study of three sources: (1) the student's needs and interests, (2) society's needs, and (3) individual subject disciplines. Possible objectives identified through these studies are screened for agreement with the school's educational philosophy and for practicality by the criterion of the psychology of learning. After this screen, the remaining objectives are translated into specific performance objectives.

Student needs and interests. One of the most important sources of what to teach is the student. What students already know, their interests, and what we can reasonably ascertain they will need in order to function as contributing individuals in their society are all important considerations in the development of objectives. What the student already knows—entering behaviors—affects the statement of appropriate objectives in several ways. If a student already possesses the capability, then it need not be taught. More important, knowledge of student entering behaviors allows us to determine whether a student will profit from instruction on a given objective (for a full discussion of this, see Chapter 9).

Taking account of student interests and concerns in the formulation of instructional aims usually results in a higher level of student motivation (Figure 7–7). One way to insure representation of student interests among the objectives of instruction is to allow students to play a role in the determination of objectives. Such a role is typically accorded to older students; however, many educational critics argue that this responsibility is given most frequently too late and too rarely. Younger students are also capable of making such decisions, as many successful open classes have shown. In preparing students to be mentally and physically healthy adults, schools are responding to the needs of students as individuals. Student needs can be derived for a diversity

FIGURE 7–7

Student interests should be taken into consideration in determining the objectives of instruction

of areas, such as health, social relations, consumerism, occupational pursuits, and use of leisure time.

Society. Schools are social institutions and as such must serve the needs of society as well as the needs of the individual. A democratic and pluralistic society like that of the United States requires that its citizenry possess certain knowledge, skills, and values. A good citizen in a democracy respects the rights of others, takes an interest in government, and votes in an informed manner. As another example, society needs to maintain various occupational skills among the populace in order to function properly. The school has a responsibility to study the society's needs and respond to them by incorporating them into the school's objectives.

Subject matter disciplines. The third source of objectives is the subject matter specialist. This is by far the most common source of instructional objectives available to the teacher. National councils of various subject matter disciplines routinely make available curriculum guides and rationales about their discipline's contribution to the student's education. Tyler states that in the past these subject matter specialists have mistakenly developed objectives as if each student was to become a master of a particular subject. However, what has been needed is a set of objectives suitable for the layperson. In other words, the objectives should be developed in reply to the question: How can my discipline contribute to the education of the nonspecialist?

These three sources of objectives tend to overlap and so should not be considered mutually exclusive. For example, subject matter specialists would probably consider the demands of contemporary life in determining how their discipline could contribute to the general education of the layperson. A study of society's needs should identify areas of student needs, and vice versa. However, it is important to consider these three sources as focal points for study in determining the objectives of instruction. Valid objectives have their origins in one or all of these areas of inquiry.

Conscientious study of the preceding three sources would result in a very large collection of objectives. This set of objectives would contain much redundancy and incompatibility; additionally, it would be too lengthy to function as a guide in the design of instruction. What is needed is some screen or criteria against which the objectives could be judged and the most important objectives selected while discarding the others. Tyler suggested two screens: educational philosophy and the psychology of learning.

Philosophy of education. Chapter 2 presented in some detail how different educational philosophies stress different educational goals. Teachers tend to select objectives that are consonant with their educational and social philosophy and the school system within which they are employed. Tyler (1950, p. 24) states:

> For a statement of philosophy to serve most helpfully as a set of standards or a screen in selecting objectives it needs to be stated clearly and for the main points the implications for educational objectives may need to be spelled out. Such a clear and analytical statement can then be used by examining every proposed objective and noting whether the objective is in harmony with one or more main points in the philosophy, is in opposition or is unrelated to any of these points. Those in harmony with the philosophy will be identified as important objectives.

Tyler is advocating a systematic statement of one's philosophy and a thorough examination of one's objectives as they relate to this philosophy. Most teachers, and most schools for that matter, do not attempt a feat such as developing a complete and explicit statement of their educational philosophy, yet it is an important step in the derivation of valid objectives.

Psychology of learning. The psychology of learning allows us to screen the set of potential objectives for those that are attainable within the context of school. In addition we may use this screen to determine at what level of schooling to emphasize selected objectives. To illustrate the first point, we know enough to teach students to write clearly and grammatically, but we do not know enough to make the student a Henry James or a John Steinbeck. In reference to the second point, let us assume we wished to teach some of the abstract concepts of science. Our knowledge of the psychology of learning would tell us that this should be postponed until the student develops an understanding of the concept referents upon which the abstract concepts are built. Studies would indicate that the appropriate time for such objectives would be late junior high or high school grade levels.

Another very important use of the psychology of learning in the selection of objectives relates to determining whether a given objective is likely to be of future value to the student. For example, a given cognitive objective is most likely to be of value to a student if it can be applied to a situation outside of the school. This issue involves a consideration of the transfer of learning, and research tells us that the capabilities of concept learning, rule learning, and mathemagenic skills transfer to a much wider variety of situations than does memorization. So an objective that requires memorization on the part of the student has little transfer value, whereas one emphasizing rule learning would have the desired transfer effect.

The value of the Tyler rationale is that it relates specific objectives to more general educational goals. It provides a systematic procedure for the collection of data from a wide array of sources and for applying these data in the derivation of objectives. While it is not as explicit a set of procedures as we should like, it does provide direction and general criteria for the origination and selection of performance objectives. Objectives generated in this manner stand a much greater chance of being important in the life of the student and go a long way toward making school a meaningful experience for the student.

3. List four to five interests or needs of students in the age range you expect to teach which would be important in the selection of worthwhile objectives for these students.

CRITICISMS OF THE USE OF PERFORMANCE OBJECTIVES

The last decade has seen a resurgent interest in the use of behaviorally stated performance objectives. Concomitant with this interest has been a debate on the advantages and disadvantages of objectives. Earlier in this chapter we presented the positive aspects of the use of objectives; now we attempt to summarize for you the major objections to the use of performance objectives.

Arguments against the use of behaviorally stated performance objectives predominantly center around one of two major themes. One theme is expressed in the question: What are or should be the real goals of education? The second theme concerned what the critics of performance objectives believe to be undesirable side effects that result from the use of behavioral objectives.

True goals of education

Ebel (1970) states that to consider the student performance specified in a performance objective as the goal or objective of education is misleading and inaccurate. The true objectives of education are the knowledge and understanding, the attitudes and values that made possible the performances stated in the objectives. The student's behaviors are only the products or manifestation of these underlying knowledges and attitudes.

The fact that student performance is only an indicator of these underlying mental processes leads us to two further conclusions. For many of these understandings and attitudes we cannot specify in advance the behavior or behaviors that will be acceptable evidence. There are some situations or experiences we would like the student to have because the experience itself, independent of any performance outcome, is valuable. These kinds of educational encounter are referred to by Eisner (1969) as *expressive objectives.* Eisner makes the point that expressive objectives build upon performance objectives, but that most frequently the major goals of education are best described as expressive objectives. An educational experience as described by an expressive objective not only affects each student differently but can have a multitude of effects on a given student. Therefore it is premature and even foolish for us to think that the effects of an experience that we can specify and measure are the most important ones. We cannot even be sure that we are cognizant of the most important effects.

Undesirable side effects

In addition to the preceding objections, the use of performance objectives in curriculum design and instructional development has undesirable side effects according to the critics. A statement of expected student behaviors as the basis of curriculum development may hinder innovation and creativity. Atkin (1968) claims that early articulation of performance objectives by curriculum developers will cause them to design a program specifically to achieve these outcomes, and thereby blind them to other potentially important aspects of subject matter. Eisner (1967) has argued that specification of performance objectives as the first step in curriculum development can be supported on a logical basis, but it is not necessarily supported on a psychological basis. Eisner (p. 258) states:

> The means through which imaginative curriculums can be built is as open-ended as the means through which scientific and artistic inventions occur. Curriculum theory needs to allow for a variety of processes to be employed in the construction of curriculum.

Both Atkin and Eisner see performance objectives as narrowing the focus of curriculum development analogous to blinders narrowing the field of vision. Curriculum development instead should be an open-ended project allowing for a diversity of approaches. As Eisner expresses it, the use of performance objectives in curriculum development can be defended on a logical basis, but what are the best procedures for developing curricula is an empirical question.

Another undesirable side effect raised by critics of performance objectives involves the value of the objectives specified. The reasoning goes as follows. Objectives that are stated are those we are capable of measuring. Given the state of measurement theory at present, we are much better at measuring lower levels of cognitive abilities than higher levels, or cognitive as opposed to affective outcomes. Consequently performance objectives tend to concentrate on lower levels of cognitive abilities and hence to represent trivial educational outcomes. The goal of education should come from philosophy and needs; just because an objective is capable of being measured does not make it an important objective according to Atkin (1968). Ebel (1970, p. 172) states the point quite well, when he says: "Simply stating that something is an objective does not make it a desirable one."

The third side effect often cited by opponents of performance objectives concerns spontaneous, unplanned instructional outcomes. Teachers often find themselves in a situation in which an outcome can be accomplished that is more valuable than the one around which the instruction was based. We can refer to this outcome, other than the intended one, as *incidental* learning. On occasion a situation will present itself in which the potential incidental learning is of greater importance than the intentional learning. According to Atkin (1968) and Eisner (1967), a teacher who utilizes performance objectives is more likely to ignore or miss these opportunities for valuable incidental learning than are teachers who do not use behavioral objectives.

Criticisms in perspective

Popham (1968) replied to critics of behavioral objectives on a number of points, three of which concern us here. First, Popham argued that, contrary to emphasizing trivial outcomes, explicit objectives would result in more worthwhile objectives. Colleagues would examine explicit objectives and select the ones more worthwhile for instruction. The second point relates to spontaneity in the classroom. Explicit objectives do not tie the teacher to set instructional means. Teachers would be able to take advantage of unexpected opportunities if they could be justified as relating to significant objectives rather than mere entertainment.

The third point involves the difficulty of measuring objectives in such fields as the fine arts and humanities. Popham argues that it is difficult to identify and measure objectives in these areas but that is no reason not to attempt it. Teachers in this area must have criteria or they could not make judgments. By attempting to make explicit these criteria, they would be improved and instruction would benefit. Recent critics of objectives have realized that the issue is not an either/or decision and have tried to place performance objectives in their proper perspective in the design of instruction. Posner and Strike (1975) described two ideological interpretations of performance objectives and their place in the educational process. One interpretation, the behaviorist, views behavior as the goal of instruction. The empiricist interpretation, as the other view, perceives behavior as the evidence that the goal has been attained. The essential characteristics of the two interpretations are presented in Table 7–1.

TABLE 7–1
A comparison of two interpretations of behavioral objectives

	Behaviorism	*Empiricism*
Behavior	Behavior is the goal	Behavior is merely evidence that the goal has been achieved
Goals	Hostile to any goal which cannot be expressed as a finite list of behaviors	Hostile to a goal only if that goal is incapable of being tested empirically
	Hostile to all goals expressed in cognitive language	Requires that cognitively stated goals be capable of empirical verification
Concept of education	Education is solely the acquisition of a behavioral repertoire	Education is not only the acquisition of a behavioral repertoire but also other sorts of objectives

Source: Adapted from Posner and Strike (1975).

Posner and Strike contend that the majority of criticism is directed at the behaviorist interpretation of the role of performance objectives in education. The behaviorist model has two interrelated consequences that are undesirable for education. First, the view that behavior is the goal of education leads to an attempt to produce an exhaustive listing of specific objectives. The specificity is so great as to render each objective worthless when considered individually. The second point concerns the attempt to reduce a cognitive or affective state to a list of specific objectives and the nature of these cognitive and affective states. Posner and Strike (1975, p. 32) explain this objection in the following passage:

> It is reasonable to expect that goals (cognitive and affective states) which exhibit this property of having numerous and varied exemplifications will be substantially eroded by the demand for specific and exhaustive enumeration of objectives. The assumption here is that such goals are not equivalent to any finite list of their exemplification. It immediately follows that any attempt to replace such goals by a finite list of their exemplifications is unworkable and may be expected to effectively eliminate such goals together with the numerous and varied potential behavioral repertoire implied by them, substituting at best a much narrower and limited set of goals.

Posner and Strike's argument is that the whole (a cognitive or affective state) is greater than the sum of its indicators (specific behaviors). A cognitive state, such as comprehension, or an affective state, such as appreciation, has more meaning than simply a listing of specific behaviors. These behaviors, while acceptable as evidence of the cognitive or affective state, are not sufficient as a definition of the state. The acceptable use of performance objectives is then contained within the empiricist interpretation. Viewed in this perspective, performance objectives are a valuable tool in determining whether or not one has attained the desired goals.

MacDonald-Ross (1973) examined the issue of performance objectives as a central concept in the rational planning approach to education. He analyzed the claims for performance objectives and the evidence bearing on these claims, both pro and con. The major deficiencies of performance objectives according to MacDonald-Ross are the following.

1. There is no coherent set of rules for the derivation of worthwhile objectives.
2. There are no rules for determining the correct level of specificity for objectives.
3. Objectives do not prescribe clearly or fully the instructional conditions necessary to attain them.
4. Objectives do not describe completely valid measures.

However, MacDonald-Ross was not attempting to argue that the specification of performance objectives was worthless. He attempted to place them and the systems approach to instruction in perspective. All schemes (at least all we have concocted so far) have their faults and limitations. The attempt to discover these deficiencies and to propose new paradigms is the essence of progress. To quote MacDonald-Ross (1973, p. 47):

> This article has not argued that behavioral objectives are worthless, nor is it doubted that the systematic approach represents an advance on purely intuitive methods of curriculum design. The criticisms of traditional methods were entirely justified—no one wishes to put the clock back. But the application of behavioral objectives and the systematic approach needs to be tempered with an understanding of its inherent deficiencies.

Elsewhere in this chapter the statement was made that performance objectives are not an educational cure-all. We have shown that when performance objectives are derived from more general and significant educational goals, they serve useful purposes in the planning of instruction. First, they serve as indicators of whether or not the true goals of education, namely, broad cognitive and affective dispositions, are being achieved. Second, by exemplifying domains of learning they allow us to apply knowledge of learning conditions in a systematic manner to the design of instruction. Statements of objectives can play a role in the facilitation of student learning when they are provided to students as adjunct aids. Finally, objectives guide the construction of valid tests of learning outcomes expected from instruction. For all these reasons the construction of worthwhile performance objectives is an important step in the design of instruction.

> 4. Assuming the following statement is true, does it then negate the value of performance objectives in education? Explain your answer.
>
> Performance objectives are not the true goals of education.

SUMMARY

An important step in planning instruction is the identification of relevant performance objectives. Teachers can use objectives as a plan for instruction, as an adjunct aid for directing student attention, and as a blueprint for the construction of tests. The construction of performance objectives requires the teacher to identify acceptable evidence of the student's attainment of higher goals. Selection of worthwhile objectives occurs when the teacher considers objectives in the broader context of society's and the individual's needs.

It was shown that most criticisms of performance objectives are aimed at the view that holds that behaviors are the goals of education. However, it was shown that when performance objectives are viewed as indicators of broader goals, they serve a useful purpose in planning and evaluating instruction.

SELF-TEST

1. The presentation of objectives to students facilitates learning by what means?
2. What value does the psychology of learning have in identifying significant educational outcomes?
3. Which of the following statements is in agreement with the empiricist interpretation of performance objectives?
   a. Education is the acquisition of adaptive behaviors.
   b. Words like *comprehends* and *appreciates* must be avoided in goal statements.
   c. Behaviors are indicators of the true goals of education.
   d. Performance objectives blind teachers to unexpected but valuable outcomes.

Determine which of the following statements *(a–d)* best applies to each objective (4–8) below.

a. Behavior component is inadequate.
b. Conditions component is inadequate.
c. Standards component is inadequate.
d. All three components are present and adequate.

4. Given a number, the student will find its square root.
5. Shown a map of the United States with the states outlined, the student will write in the names of all 50 states.
6. States the value of π to three decimal places.
7. After visiting a local hospital, the student will appreciate the work of doctors and nurses.
8. The student will read two editorials supplied by the teacher and then identify one of the two as propaganda. The student must give reasons for the choice.

ANSWER KEY TO BOXED QUESTIONS

1. *a.* Planning instruction.
   1. Greater student achievement.
   2. More positive attitude by teachers.

   b. Adjunct aid.
   1. Greater student achievement.
   2. Direct attention to relevant information.

3. Greater positive attitude by student.
4. Less study time under some conditions.

c. Evaluation.
1. A more valid assessment of student achievement.
2. Better evidence for improving instruction.
3. Greater amount of information in feedback to student.

2. 1. *a, c*
   2. *d*
   3. *a, b*
   4. *c*
   5. *a, b, c*
3. We cannot give a prepared answer to this question; your answer should give attention to the following factors, among others: age, socioeconomic and cultural background, ability level, and social and occupational roles.
4. No; as Posner and Strike state, performance objectives are *indicators* that the real goals of education are being attained. Because of this they have value in the design of instruction and the evaluation of its outcome.

ANSWER KEY TO SELF-TEST

1. By directing student attention to relevant information.
2. The psychology of learning helps the teacher decide which objectives can realistically be taught and at what age they may be taught. Additionally, knowledge of transfer of learning will help determine if the instruction will facilitate performance outside of the school situation.
3. *c*
4. *c*
5. *d*
6. *d*
7. *a, c*
8. *c*

Chapter 8

Sequencing instruction

SCHOOLS OPERATE on a yearly basis; consequently, teachers are responsible for educating a class of students over a nine- to ten-month period. Because of this responsibility, as we have stated previously, teachers must engage in both long-term and short-term planning. A major decision in this planning relates to the sequence of instruction. Sequencing decisions faced by the teacher can range from ordering information within a lesson to arranging the content of an entire course.

On what basis do we make decisions about the sequence of instruction? As we shall see in this chapter, the specific considerations applying to our decisions will differ depending upon the level of sequencing under consideration; however, two general criteria should be considered in any sequencing decision. First, our sequence in instruction should support the attainment of our major goals; that is, the sequence of instruction should help transmit information to the student in a form that will facilitate its use in the intended situation outside of instruction. Second, we want a sequence of instruction in which the intended outcome of a given lesson is facilitated by the instruction preceding it.

Both of these general criteria relate to what educational psychologists refer to as *transfer*. Transfer of learning is one of the basic and most important concepts of both education and psychology. Simply stated, transfer of learning means that the learning of one task has an effect upon the learning of another. Note that the definition states an effect without specifying the direction of the effect on new learning and that this effect can be either facilitating or interfering. If the effects of prior learning are facilitating, then we refer to it as *positive* transfer. When prior learning has an interfering effect upon a new learning task, it is called *negative* transfer.

Of course, teachers are interested in promoting positive transfer within the school setting. In this chapter we shall explore what is known about the conditions that facilitate positive transfer.

After studying this chapter you should be able to:

1. Describe the factors that influence positive transfer between two learning tasks.
2. Derive a learning hierarchy for a simple learning task.
3. Specify the instructional uses of learning hierarchies.

ON THE TRANSFER OF LEARNING

The predominant learning theory at the foundation of education up until the early 20th century had at its core a concept of transfer called the "doctrine of formal discipline." Transfer as conceptualized in the doctrine of formal discipline was a highly generalized effect. The mind was viewed as being analogous to a muscle; consequently mental abilities could be improved and strengthened through exercises. So students were given a curriculum of Greek, Latin, geometry, and rhetoric, not because of content knowledge per se, but because these subjects were disciplines that provided rigorous exercise of the mental faculties. Students spent much time reciting passages in Greek or Latin, conjugating verbs, and memorizing geometric proofs, and the mental faculties improved through the study of these subjects would transfer to all types of situations experienced in life, or so the theory postulated.

It has been very difficult to dislodge the doctrine of formal discipline from the foundations of education. Still today one encounters in various guises the expectation of such a vague and generalized transfer effect as a benefit to be derived from various curricula and educational programs. Yet, research on the transfer of learning overwhelmingly illustrates that transfer is a more specific phenomenon occurring under a more limited set of conditions than that suggested by the doctrine of formal discipline. As early as the first decade of this century, E. L. Thorndike conducted experiments demonstrating that transfer effects among educational tasks are quite specific and depend upon the presence of similar elements in both tasks (Thorndike, 1923; Thorndike & Woodworth, 1901). The theory he postulated was called the "identical elements theory of transfer." The degree of transfer between two learning tasks, according to Thorndike's theory, is a function of the number of identical elements shared by the two tasks.

Before turning to an examination of the two types of transfer occurring in educational settings, we shall describe the basic method educational psychologists use to study transfer. Remember, an educational psychologist studying transfer basically asks the question: How does the prior learning of task 1 influence the learning of task 2? To answer this question requires an experiment that compares the performance of two groups on task 2, with the difference between the two groups being that one group has learned task 1 prior to learning task 2, whereas the other group has not learned task 1. This basic design is represented by the following chart:

Group	*Task 1*	*Task 2*
Experimental	Learns	Learns
Control	Rests	Learns

If there is a difference in the performance of the two groups on the learning of task 2, then it can be attributed to the difference in experience with task 1.

Types of transfer

Earlier in this chapter it was stated that teachers wish to sequence instruction according to two general criteria. These standards were the applicability of learning to new situations and the facilitation of new learning by prior learning. Respectively, they refer to what Gagné (1965b) has termed *lateral* and *vertical* transfer. In this section we shall further define each type and survey the conditions that advance each type of transfer.

Lateral transfer. When a learned capability is performed appropriately in a new and different situation of approximately the same level of complexity as that of original learning, the effect is said to be one of "lateral transfer." For example, students in a first-aid course practice techniques in simulated situations and later are able to perform these same procedures at the scene of a real accident. Students in an English class practice writing in grammatical, clear prose and later can transfer this capability to other situations outside the English class. This ability to transfer previous learning to new and different situations is at the heart of education. The purpose of education is often described as preparing the person for the future. In other words, knowledge acquired in school is expected to apply to life outside of school.

An important form of lateral transfer is learning to learn. L. B. Ward (1937) had people learn consecutively 16 different lists of paired associates. By the 16th and final list, the average person was learning the list to criterion in half the number of trials that had been required to reach criterion on the first list. Since the specific paired associates were different for each list, the improvement across lists could not be accounted for on the basis of learning shared elements among the lists. Therefore, the people in Ward's study must have acquired some general learning strategy or strategies that applied to the paired-associates learning tasks and allowed them to learn the lists more efficiently. Research by Duncan (1964) demonstrated that this general transfer occurs not only with simple learning tasks like the paired-associate task, but also with more complex learning tasks that place greater demands upon the learner. Duncan's study has even greater practical significance in that the learning to learn effect was of a higher magnitude for the complex task than for the simple task.

Lateral transfer involving general learning skills was demonstrated in a situation that more nearly approximates classroom conditions in a classic study by Woodrow (1927). This study illustrated that instruction on how to memorize resulted in greater amounts of verbal information being memorized than did an equivalent amount of undirected practice of memorizing. The control group received no training on how to memorize and no practice memorizing before memorizing the test material. The practice group practiced memorizing material for a total of 177 minutes over a four-week period before memorizing the test material. Members of a third group, called the "training group," were taught specific techniques of memorization such as active recitation, imagery and other mnemonic devices, and motivational devices. For the training group, 76 minutes were spent in learning the memorization strategies and 101 minutes were devoted to practicing memorization. Figure 8–1 presents the average gain scores (posttest minus pretest) for the three groups. As can be seen, the training group made gains in the ability to memorize over the course of the study, whereas the other two groups did not.

The preceding examples of lateral transfer involve learned capabilities referred to in Chapter 5 as mathemagenic skills or "strategies which give birth to learning." However,

FIGURE 8–1
Average gain scores in memorization for the control, practice, and training groups

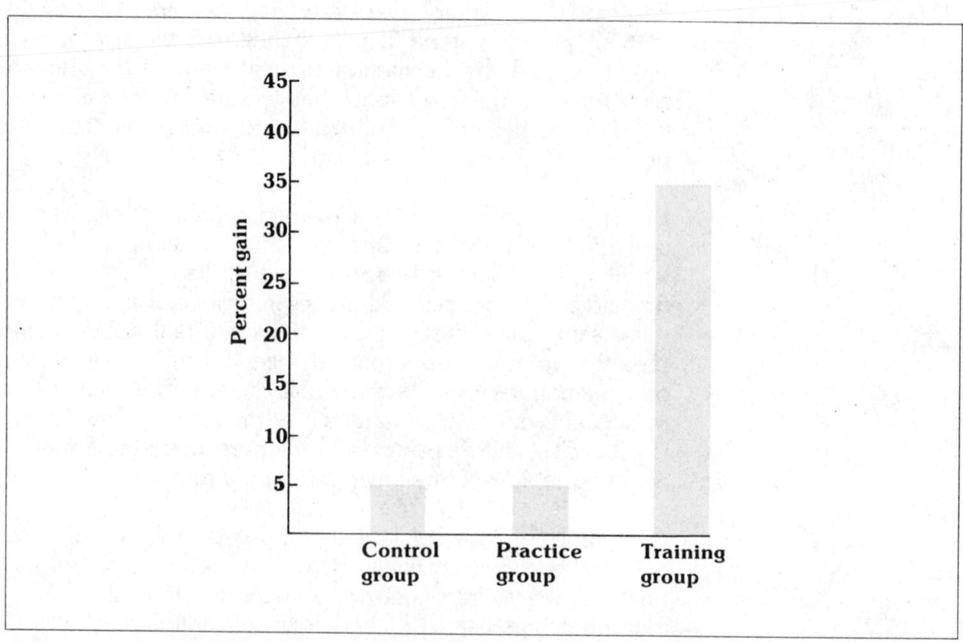

Source: Adapted from Woodrow (1927).

lateral transfer is also involved in more specific learned capabilities such as intellectual or motor skills and other general learning, for example, learning attitudes. Therefore, we expect that a young student who has learned the specific social rule "A person does not break in line" from experiences in the school cafeteria will transfer this learning to other settings involving lines such as the movies, McDonald's, and the playground.

The number and diversity of situations in which the learned capability is performed will determine the degree or breadth of lateral transfer. Consequently, the greater the generality of the to-be-learned capability, the more and diverse are the situations in which it must be practiced. The importance of practice in a number of situations was demonstrated in Ward's (1937) experiment in which trials to criterion decreased as each new list was learned. Wittrock and Twelker (1964) demonstrated that the variety of situations had an effect on transfer beyond that of practice alone. In their study the number of situations was held constant between two groups while the variety was varied and the resulting transfer measured. The groups receiving the diverse set of problems showed the greatest transfer to new situations.

Vertical transfer. When a learned capability at one level facilitates the learning of a capability at the next higher level, the influence is called "vertical transfer" (Figure 8–2). Much educational research is concerned with identifying lower-level tasks that will produce vertical transfer to important educational objectives. An example from the area of reading will illustrate this research. Samuels (1972) observed that a number of studies reported that those children most successful at learning to read in first grade had entered with letter-name knowledge, and he decided to test whether learning to name letters would transfer to learning to read words composed of those letters. He performed the experiment twice and both times failed to find vertical transfer between the two tasks. Jenkins, Bausell, and Jenkins (1972) compared training in letter naming and letter sounding as a transfer task to learning to read. They found that with beginning first-graders learning letter sounds facilitated learning to read, but learning letter names did not have this vertical transfer effect.

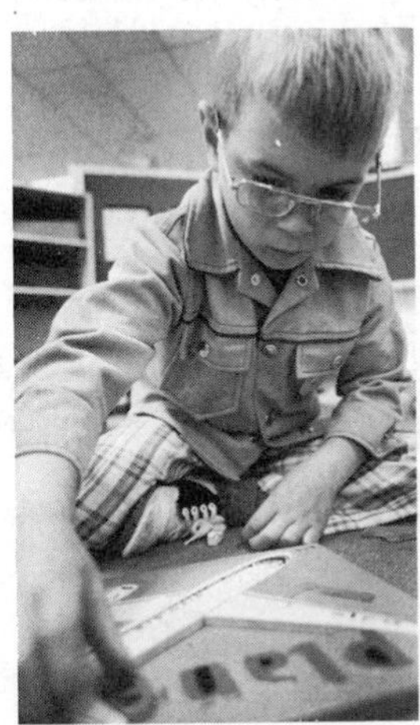

FIGURE 8–2
Learning on one task can facilitate learning on another task

Often, vertical transfer is thought of as involving transfer from an easy to a more difficult task. Holding (1962) found transfer to occur equally often from difficult to easy situations as from easy to difficult situations. So the degree of difficulty does not appear to be the critical attribute in accounting for vertical transfer. Research on transfer by stimulus predifferentiation by Gagné and his associates suggests that vertical transfer occurs when the lower-level skill is critically incorporated in performance of the higher-level skill. In this type of relationship, as we saw in Chapter 5, Gagné (1977) names the lower-level skill a specific *prerequisite* of the higher-level skill.

We examine a representative stimulus predifferentiation study in order to further clarify the relationship between the two tasks involved in vertical transfer. Gagné and Baker (1950) required people to learn to flip a switch when a particular light was activated. There were several lights in various positions on a panel and a person had to learn to associate a different switch with each light. Prior to learning this task, one group of people learned to associate different letters of the alphabet with each light. Another group that did not receive this pretraining made twice as many errors in the first 20 trials on associating lights and switches as the group that did receive the training. Goss and Greenfeld (1958), in an extension of this study, reported the same type of results.

To understand why positive transfer occurred in the situation above we first must analyze the task of associating the lights and switches. First, the lights must be made distinctive from each other (if you cannot tell the difference between two stimuli, how can you respond differently to them?), and then each switch must be associated with each light. The first component of the task, then, is learning to discriminate among the lights, and this skill was also learned in the training task. So people who received training learned a skill that was incorporated into the other learning task.

The importance of vertical transfer produced by stimulus predifferentiation training has been demonstrated by Samuels (1973) in a task more similar to classroom experiences. One group of students was given training on perceiving the distinctive features of letters before learning letter names. The control group learned the letter names without the perceptual training. The perceptual training group learned the letter names in appreciably less time than the other group. As this example illustrates, vertical transfer is an important consideration in sequencing instruction. Later in this chapter we shall see how it applies to more complex learning tasks.

1. Which of the following is an example of lateral transfer?
   a. Learns to identify proper subject-verb agreement, then learns to construct sentences with proper subject-verb agreement more quickly.
   b. Learns to saw with hand saw, then learns more quickly on a power saw.
2. Which sequence below would most probably lead to vertical transfer?
   a. Learns to distinguish between types of electrocardiogram (EKG) patterns, then learns to interpret EKG patterns for heart damage.
   b. Learns to interpret EKG patterns for heart damage, then learns to distinguish between types of EKG patterns.

LEVELS OF SEQUENCING DECISIONS

In Chapter 7 we stated that teachers describe the outcomes of education at varying levels of abstraction. The reasons for doing so are numerous, but primarily the different levels of objectives are used in different phases of planning for instruction. Before examining these levels of instruction and the corresponding sequencing decisions, we will review the levels of educational outcomes:

Level A—Statements describing the overall purposes of education (i.e., what does a person get from a high school education? a college education?).
Level B—Statements describing the knowledge, skills, and values obtained from a particular course supporting the broader goals of Level A.
Level C—Statements describing the specific learned capabilities by which the student will demonstrate the knowledge, skills, and values of Level B.
Level D—Specific situations in which the student will perform the learned capabilities of Level C.

Starting from the overall goals of education, the planning of instruction can be thought of as involving four levels. In each of these levels the teacher is concerned with learning outcomes of greater specificity and the sequence in which these outcomes should be taught. Consequently the teacher must make four related but separate decisions about sequencing instruction. The relationships between the levels in planning instruction, the different levels of educational outcomes, and the sequencing decisions are shown in Figure 8–3.

FIGURE 8–3
Sequence of planning instruction, levels of outcome, and sequencing decisions

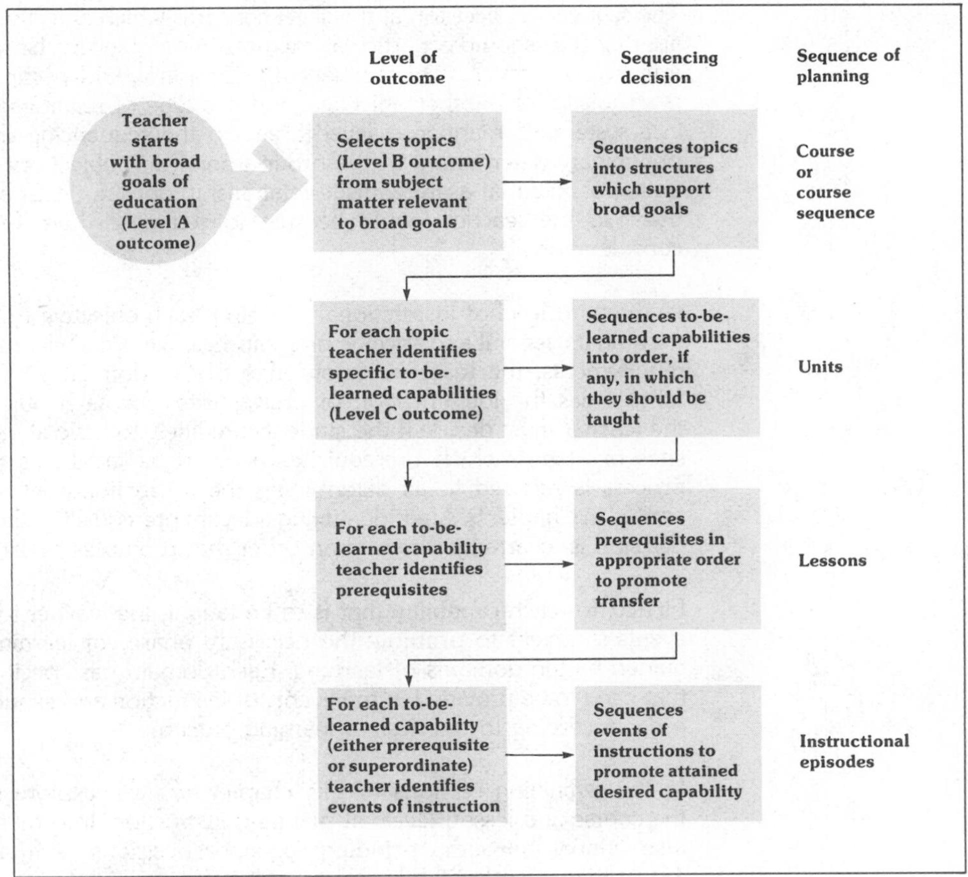

At level one, the course level of instructional planning, concern is given to what role the course has in the education of the student. The relevant question is: To what purpose will the knowledge, skills, and values regarding the subject matter be used by the student? Is the course a foundation for learning at a more advanced level? Will the student use it in the pursuit of leisure or is the course intended to have vocational applications? The purposes of the course will affect both the content selected and the organization of that content.

At the units level the teacher has identified the learned capabilities by which the student will demonstrate the knowledge, skills, and values around which the units were developed. This will result in a number of performance objectives reflecting the different learning domains, as the following example illustrates.

Topic: Energy balance (course is nutrition).

Objectives:
1. Defines the basic unit of measurement for the energy value of foods (memorization).
2. Calculates a factorial estimate of the patient's total daily energy needs (rule learning).
3. Identifies foods with high coefficient of digestibility (concept learning).

The sequencing decision at this level concerns which objective should be taught before another (i.e., should a particular memorization objective be taught before a particular affective objective?). This sequencing decision would occur when one objective is a prerequisite for another objective, and this type of relationship would be determined in a systematic manner at level three. So the sequencing decision in level two is a preliminary determinant of the order among unit objectives. On the other hand, it is quite possible that a prerequisite relationship does not exist among most of the objectives, so the teacher would be free to sequence them in accordance with other considerations.

At the third level of instructional planning, each objective from level two is examined for both its general and specific prerequisites. Since each learning domain has differing requirements, the teacher's knowledge of the domain within which each objective falls guides the identification of prerequisites for each objective. Also at this point the teacher must decide if the students are likely to have already learned the prerequisites or, if not, which prerequisites need to be taught as part of instruction. This process is referred to as determining the instructional level of the students and is treated in Chapter 9. After identifying relevant prerequisites, the appropriate sequencing decision is to arrange them in an order that promotes maximum vertical transfer.

Finally, for each capability that is to be taught, the teacher identifies the instructional events sufficient to promote the necessary phases of learning. Again, the teacher is guided by the domains of learning. Each domain has specific conditions of learning that need to be provided in the events of instruction and sequenced in the appropriate order according to the desired learning outcome.

In the remaining sections of this chapter, we will explore sequencing decisions at the course and lesson levels of planning instruction. Information relevant to planning instructional episodes, including sequence decisions, is found in Chapters 10 and 11. At the lesson level, this chapter will investigate analysis procedures for identifying and sequencing prerequisites for problem-solving and rule- and concept-learning objectives. Most instruction involves these skills, and systematic methods have been developed to analyze these tasks. Identifying and sequencing prerequisites for other domains require different criteria; information relevant to them will be found in Chapters 10 and 11.

SEQUENCING DECISIONS AT THE COURSE LEVEL: CONTENT ANALYSIS

In the previous section it was stated that the content of a course is partially determined by the role of the course in the education of the student. A common example is the difference in the high school mathematics curriculum for students choosing a vocationally oriented education and those choosing a college preparatory education. The fact that these two mathematics courses taught to students of the same age and the same grade differ in content is obvious, but we are interested here in the principles for sequencing content, not selecting it. Our question is: Are there different means of sequencing content that support different broad goals or outcomes? To answer this question, we must first determine the ways in which curricula can be sequenced.

Posner and Strike (1976) developed a categorization scheme for classifying curriculum structures based upon the sequence principle used to generate the structure. The scheme has five major classifications with more specific subdivisions within each. We present a brief summary of each division and an example of each type of structure.

World-related. The sequence among content elements reflects some aspect of their relationship in the empirical world, such as spatial, temporal, or physical attributes. A typical example of this sequencing scheme is the chronological order of events in history.

Concept-related. The sequence among content elements reflects some logical relationship among the elements. An obvious example of this scheme is teaching the characteristics of elements via the periodic table.

Inquiry-related. The sequence among content elements reflects the process or method by which the discipline generates knowledge. An example of this scheme would be a laboratory course in science where a series of experiments is performed by which the student induces the key concepts and principles of the discipline.

Learning-related. The sequence among content elements reflects some theory about how people learn. An example of this scheme was presented earlier in this chapter in the example in which letter-sound knowledge was taught before reading words because of a transfer of learning effect.

Utilization-related. The sequence among content elements reflects some personal, social, or vocational need of the student. An example of the scheme is a physical education course organized around life activity sports such as tennis, golf, and backpacking.

Posner and Strike (1976) state that no definitive answers on sequencing a curriculum can yet be given; however, teachers should be aware of the structures of curricula with which they work to insure that they meet their particular needs and purposes. This advice is particularly appropriate in light of research showing that content structure influences the cognitive structure acquired by the student (Rudnitsky & Posner, 1976; Shavelson, 1972, 1974).

The content elements of a unit on vascular plants in a college botany course were ordered by two different sequences in the Rudnitsky and Posner (1976) study. Students in two groups received content that was the same but sequenced differently according to either a world-related or concept-related sequence. Measures taken after the unit of instruction revealed that both groups learned the same amount of information, but that there were differences in the ways these students had the information organized in memory and the relationship they perceived among the elements.

Since the course structure influences how students organize information in memory from a course, the next question is: What types of course structure support different educational goals? A general answer to this question can be found in the work of Reigeluth, Merrill, and Bunderson (1978). They developed a set of five content structures that resemble those of Posner and Strike; however, more relevant to our present purposes, they conceive of three of these structures as representing three possible course orientations. They define the goal or orientation of a course as the overall emphasis of instruction with respect to how the student is expected to use it. These three orientations are conceptual, procedural, and theoretical.

The emphasis of instruction with a conceptual orientation is upon understanding the major concepts of the discipline and the interrelationships among them. A theoretical orientation is aimed at understanding the cause-and-effect relationships among the concepts comprising the subject matter. As the name implies, a *procedural* orientation would be concerned with applying a procedure in some life situation.

The structure of a conceptually oriented course would be some type of taxonomy going from superordinate to subordinate concept categories. A theoretically oriented structure would be represented by a model. For example, the content of a course in human memory could be organized around the model of human memory presented in Chapter 5. The structure with a procedural orientation would involve a general procedure under which other more specific procedures could be included. For example the structure for a course in automotive mechanics could be the general procedure of diagnosing an engine problem, then under this would be the procedure for fixing a carburetor, a water pump, and other features.

Reigeluth, Merrill, Wilson, Norton, and Spiller (1978) observe that the goals of a course can prescribe more than one orientation. Consequently, we could expect to find courses in which one section has a conceptual orientation and another section has a theoretical orientation. Additionally, courses can have suborientations, so it would be possible to have a procedural structure subsuming a theoretical substructure.

Procedures for developing course structures are in a preliminary stage. However, as has been demonstrated in this section, course structure does have an influence upon student achievement (Figure 8–4). The teacher should not ignore this aspect of planning

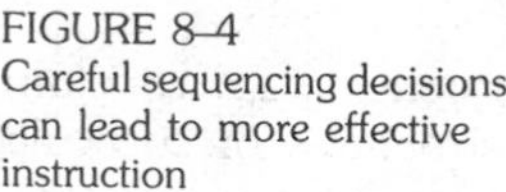

FIGURE 8–4
Careful sequencing decisions can lead to more effective instruction

instruction. Examination of the content structure of the course in light of the course's broad goals should be a serious part of the design of instruction. When instruction has long-term goals and the course content is related to these goals, it is less likely that any lesson will be "busy work" for the students.

SEQUENCING AT THE LESSON LEVEL: TASK ANALYSIS

Once the performance objectives for a given unit of instruction have been established, we examine each objective for its prerequisites. In doing so we are trying to determine what the student must already know or be able to do in order to acquire the new capability stated in the performance objective. If students do not enter instruction possessing these prerequisites, then they should be taught them as part of the instruction. A sequencing decision is involved when prerequisites are part of instruction because we wish to arrange the order in which they are taught to maximize vertical transfer.

To determine the prerequisites for a performance objective, we must take into account the domain of learning involved. Attainment of an objective in each domain requires activation of different prerequisites in the learner's memory. Each learning domain and its prerequisites are shown in Table 8–1.

The prerequisites for concept learning, rule learning, and problem solving form structures referred to as *learning hierarchies* by Gagné (1962). Prerequisites can be identified for affective and motor skill objectives and even memorization tasks, but they do not show this hierarchical structure as do the preceding tasks. The methods that have evolved for identifying these hierarchical structures are termed *task analyses* and it is to these task analysis methods that the remainder of this chapter will be devoted.

Two steps are involved in conducting a task analysis: logical analysis and empirical analysis. Logical analysis is the initial attempt at identifying the prerequisites of the desired performance objective and the order in which they should be taught. In this step the teacher is guided by knowledge of the prerequisite capabilities necessary for concept learning, rule learning, and problem solving. In empirical analysis the learning structure derived in the preceding step is tested in some manner to determine its validity. To refer to an earlier example, if the knowledge of letter sounds is a

TABLE 8–1
Learning domains and prerequisites

Domain	*Prerequisites*
Affective	Possession of concept of object toward which attitude or value is to be formed; possession of information relevant to attitude or value
Motor skills	Ability to perform component movements; knowledge of order of execution of component movements
Cognitive	
Memorization	Existence of previously learned information in memory to which new information can be related; ability to use an appropriate encoding strategy
Concept learning	Ability to distinguish between objects on the basis of important concept attributes
Rule learning	Identification of instances of component concepts
Mathemagenic skills	
Problem-solving	Existence of previously learned content knowledge and rules relevant to the task given the learner

prerequisite for learning to read, we would expect to find a transfer in instruction for a sequence of letter sounds to learning to read; or we would expect to find more people with knowledge of letter sounds than people without this knowledge among a group of readers.

Logical analysis

Within logical analysis a further distinction will be drawn between Gagné's learning hierarchies and Resnick's components analysis. These two approaches overlap to a large extent, since both are based on a principle of vertical transfer. There is an important distinction in the first level of skills in the learning structure derived by each approach. Consequently the two methods are presented separately for discussion and then compared to emphasize commonalities.

Gagné's learning hierarchies. The constituents of a learning hierarchy are learned capabilities, which Gagné refers to as *intellectual skills.* As we saw in Chapter 5 the varieties of intellectual skills are discriminations, concepts, rules, and problem solving. Furthermore these intellectual skills exhibit a hierarchical relationship among themselves such that the learning of a specific problem-solving capability requires the prior learning of rules, which require the prior learning of concepts, and so on. This hierarchical relationship can be exploited to derive learning hierarchies for any performance objective requiring the learning of an intellectual skill.

The pertinent question now is: How does one perform a task analysis? According to Gagné (1968b, p. 2) we start with an examination of a performance objective, which we will call the "superordinate skill," and attempt to answer the following question: "What would the individual already have to know how to do in order to learn this new capability simply by being given verbal instructions?"

This results in identification of the immediate prerequisites for this superordinate skill. Then each of these prerequisites or subordinate skills is addressed and the question, What would the learner already have to know in order to learn this capability simply by being told? is asked of the subordinate skill. In this manner the prerequisite(s) for each subordinate skill is identified; then this process could be repeated for each newly identified skill. This process of derivation could continue until we have exhausted the most elemental prerequisites involving discriminations. However, it is rarely necessary to carry the process of task analysis to the most elemental level of learning. A teacher will typically stop a task analysis when the level of subordinate skills has been reached that, in the opinion of the teacher, the greatest majority of students already can perform. This level of skills is referred to as the *instructional level* of the students, because the students begin instruction already possessing the capability to perform these skills. The ultimate test of whether or not a group of students has a particular set of entering skills is empirical (i.e., measurement of their performance on these skills); however, the teacher must utilize knowledge of both the subject matter and students to arrive at an initial estimate of the students' instructional level.

Learning hierarchies established through the process of task analysis are most often expressed in the form of a flowchart. Such a flowchart is presented in Figure 8–5 and represents a relatively simple learning hierarchy for the objective of solving physical work problems. The top box (IX) represents the superordinate skill, with boxes VI, VII, and VIII representing its immediate prerequisites. The prerequisites for box VI are boxes II and III, and so on. Let us examine this hierarchy in some depth as to

FIGURE 8–5
Solving physical work problems; a learning hierarchy pertaining to a science topic

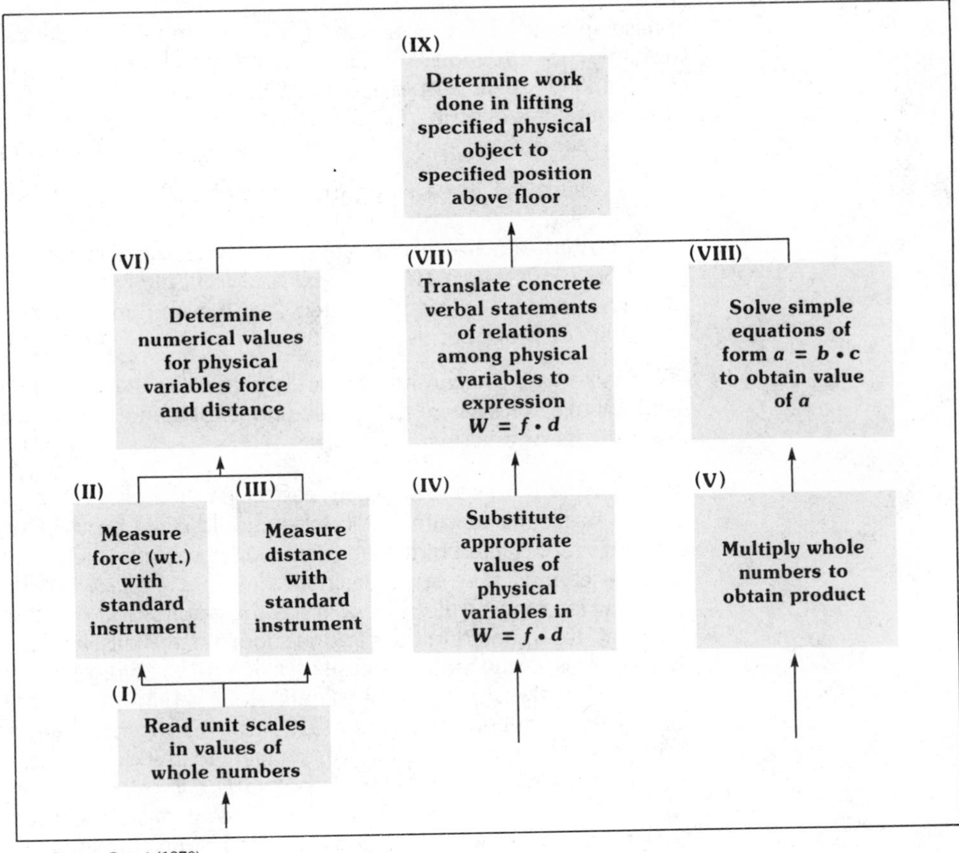

Source: Gagné (1970).

the nature of the learning tasks involved, since it illustrates some interesting points concerning learning hierarchies. First we will rewrite the superordinate skill as a more complete performance objective:

> Given the appropriate measuring instruments, the student will determine the work done in lifting various objects to given positions above the floor.

The capability required by this learning task is rule learning. Consider the following test of this objective. The teacher points to a 5-pound bowling ball, an object the student has not seen before this experience, and says, "Beth, how much work is done in lifting the ball to a height equal to this mark on the wall?" (The teacher points to a red mark 3 feet above the floor.) Now observe what Beth does in response to this query. First she puts the bowling ball on a scale, looks at the pointer, and writes down the number at which it points, in this case 5. Then she walks over to the wall, places a ruler against the wall, and looks to determine which mark on the ruler coincides with the red mark on the wall. Then she checks to see the numerical value of this mark and writes down 3 feet. Next she writes "5 • 3 = 15" on her paper. Then, turning to the teacher, Beth states, "15 foot-pounds of work was done."

Returning our attention to Figure 8–5 we see that Gagné has identified three subordinate skills or prerequisites for the superordinate skill of solving physical work problems.

These specific prerequisites are: (1) determine the numerical values for physical variables by measurement (VI), (2) translate verbal problems into mathematical statements (VII), and (3) solve simple equations of the form $a = b \cdot c$ (VIII). If a student possessed the capabilities described in the preceding three prerequisites, then this student should learn to solve physical work problems given *only* the following set of verbal directions:

1. Measure the force (weight) of the object to be moved and the distance it is to be lifted.
2. Substitute these specific values of force and distance into the equation, Work = Force • Distance $(W = f \cdot d)$, and multiply.
3. The product obtained in Step 2 is the amount of work done and is reported in units of foot-pounds.

This same type of examination could in turn be given to each of the three subordinate skills above. However, the preceding explanation should be sufficient to illustrate the process of analysis.

We move now to several points concerning learning hierarchies that the examination of this particular learning hierarchy should have brought to your attention. First, all the skills represented in the physical work problems hierarchy are of the type classified as rule learning. The superordinate skill is a *higher-order rule* in that the skill really involves learning a rule that governs the application of other rules. The other simple rules are represented in the various subordinate skills. So in the sense that this learning hierarchy is composed entirely of rules, it is atypical of most learning hierarchies. Quite often the various subordinate skills reflect the range of learning types, which brings us to our second point. This point concerns learning hierarchies in general, and it is that the derivation of a given learning hierarchy is dependent upon not only the teacher's knowledge of both the subject matter and learning principles but also the teacher's knowledge of the student population for whom the instruction is intended. This issue can be demonstrated quite simply with a quote by Gagné (1970, p. 264) in reference to the physical work problems hierarchy from Figure 8–5.

> Each of these [subordinate skills] in turn draws positive transfer from still other previously learned capabilities, which have been traced down to the point reasonable for, say, seventh-graders to have attained as starting skills. One could proceed further with the analysis if the topic were to be learned by fourth-graders. In such a case one might come to the level of defined concepts like *force, distance,* and *scale unit,* among others.

In other words, the level to which prerequisite analysis must be taken depends upon the level of students for which the instruction is intended. The younger the student population is, the more extensive will be the prerequisites identified.

Components analysis. Components analysis as a task analysis method is most often associated with the work of Lauren Resnick and her colleagues (Resnick, 1967; Resnick, Wang & Kaplan, 1973). While components analysis is not incompatible with Gagné's approach, it is sufficiently different as to merit separate consideration. Task analysis using Resnick's components analysis is a two-stage process: (1) identification of the components and (2) identification of the prerequisites for each component. According to Resnick et al. (1973, pp. 685–86), these two preceding stages of task analysis are accomplished in the following manner:

> The first step in performing an analysis is to describe in as much detail as possible the actual steps involved in skilled performance of the task.
>
> Once the components are identified, a second stage of analysis begins. Each component that has been specified is now considered separately, and the following question asked: "In order

FIGURE 8–6
Learning hierarchy illustrating components analysis

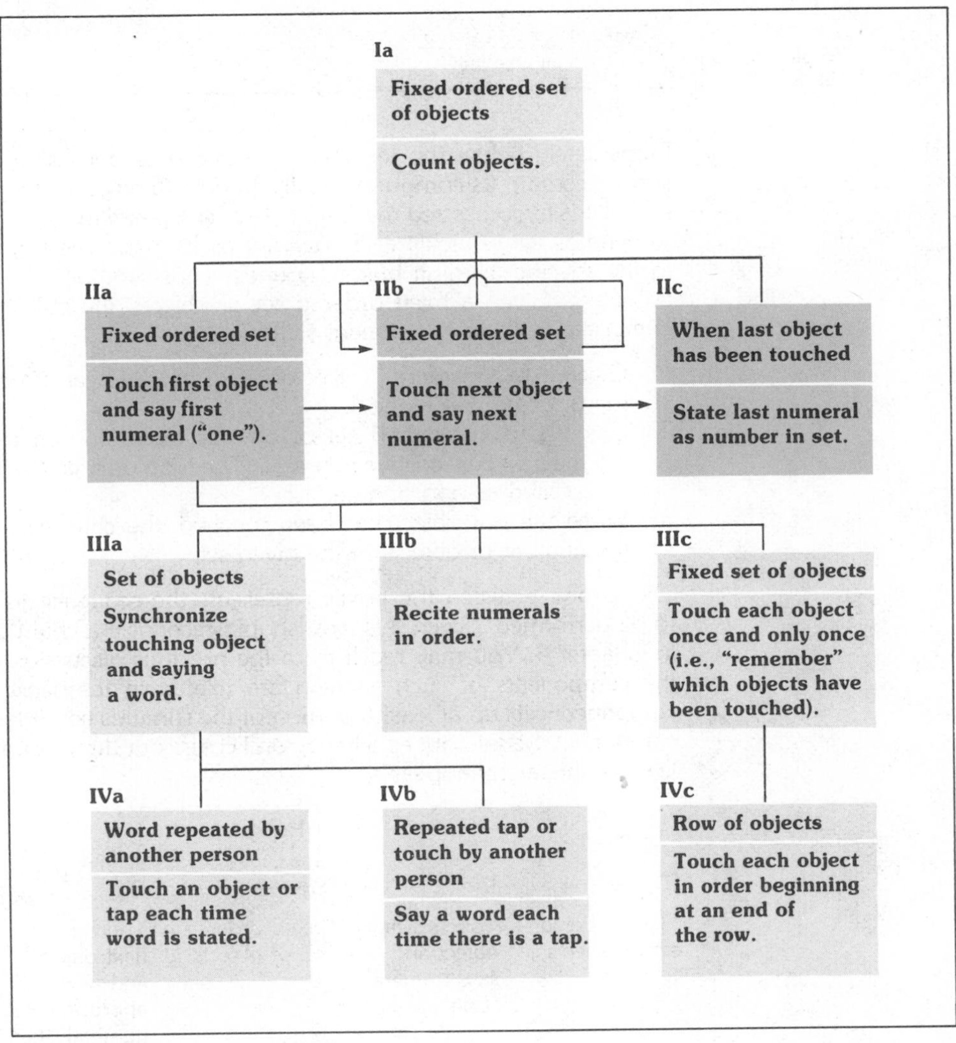

Source: Resnick, Wang, and Kaplan (1973).

to perform this behavior, which simple behavior(s) must a person be able to perform?" Here, the aim is to specify *prerequisites* for each of the behaviors.

Following Gagné, the product of a task analysis using components analysis is referred to as a *learning hierarchy*. A representative learning hierarchy is presented in Figure 8–6.

An examination of a learning hierarchy produced by the component analysis method will help clarify the nature of components and prerequisites. We will use the learning hierarchy presented in Figure 8–6 for the terminal objective: Given a fixed ordered set of objects, the child can count the objects. For ease of reading, notice that each box in the flowchart is divided by a horizontal line; above this line is the stimulus condition of the objective, and below the line is the learner's performance. Hence the performance objective above is represented in the box as:

Fixed ordered set of objects
Count objects.

Immediately below the terminal objective or superordinate skill, the boxes IIa, IIb, and IIc contain its component skills. In describing components Resnick et al. (p. 685) state, "it is hypothesized that the skilled person *actually performs* these steps (although sometimes very quickly and covertly) as he performs the terminal task." Returning to the specific learning hierarchy under consideration, we see that the performance objective—Given a fixed ordered set of objects, the child can count the objects—is *composed* of three component skills:

1. Given a fixed ordered set of objects, the child can touch the first object and say the first numeral ("one").
2. Given a fixed ordered set of objects, the child can touch the next object and say the next consecutive numeral. (The loop on this box indicates that the behavior is repeated as appropriate.)
3. When the last object has been touched, the child can state the last numeral as the number of objects in the given set.

The arrows between the boxes represents the sequence in which the behaviors are to be performed. Given this, you should recognize a chain of behaviors as illustrated in Chapter 4. You may recall from the previous discussion of behavioral chains that the components of such a chain are related in the sense that a given behavioral component sets up at least a portion of the stimulus conditions for the next behavioral component. So laid out as a behavioral chain, our three components for this particular learning hierarchy appear as:

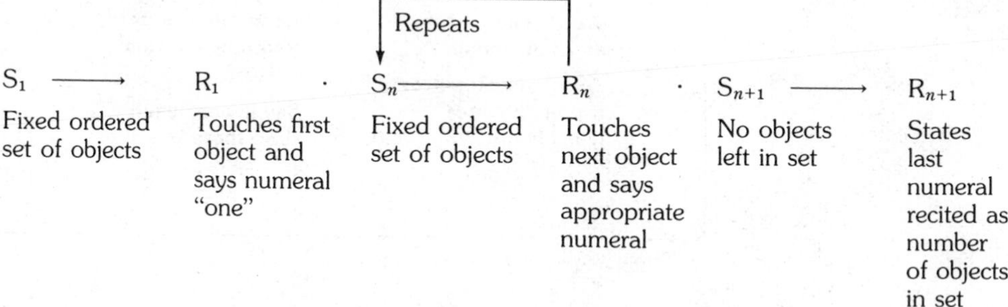

The second step in components analysis is to identify prerequisite(s) for each of the components from Step 1. Resnick et al. (1973, p. 686) offer the following description of prerequisites:

> Prerequisite behaviors, in contrast to component behaviors, are not actually performed in the course of the terminal performance. However, they are thought to *facilitate* learning of the higher level skill. More precisely, if A is prerequisite to B, then learning A first should result in positive transfer when B is learned, and anyone able to perform B should be able to perform A as well.

We will move to the learning hierarchy on size seriation illustrated in Figure 8–7 in order to examine prerequisites in a specific context. From this, we see that the learning task—Given three objects of different sizes, the child can select the largest object, IIIa—is a prerequisite for two components, IIa and IIc, of the superordinate skill. This prerequisite, IIIa, itself has a prerequisite IVa, of: Given two objects, the child

FIGURE 8–7
Learning hierarchy on size seriation

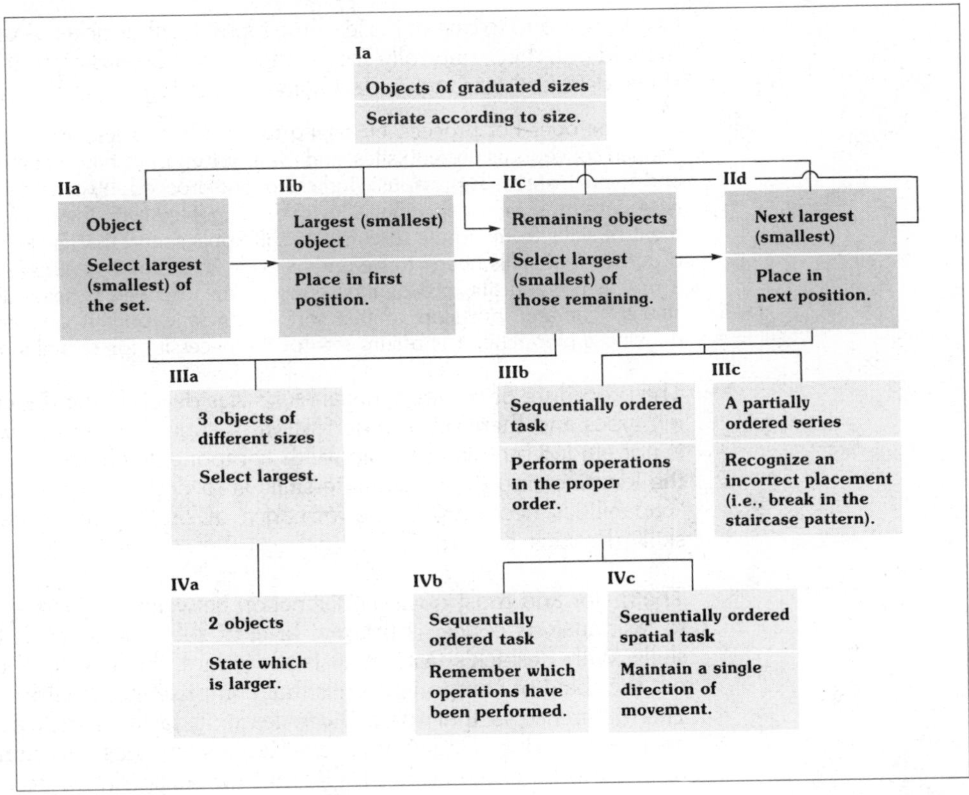

Source: Resnick, Wang, and Kaplan (1973).

can state which object is larger. These tasks, IVa, IIIa, IIa, and IIc, all require essentially the same behavior on the part of the student. They differ on the basis of the stimulus conditions under which the behavior is performed. However, while these stimulus conditions are different, they are also similar, so it appears that the difference is primarily one of complexity. As we go from the components IIa and IIc to the lowest prerequisite IVa, the number of objects with which the learner has to contend is fewer. Consequently we should get positive transfer from this sequence of tasks because, as we saw earlier in this chapter, positive transfer is maximized when tasks call for the same response under similar stimulus conditions.

A comparison of Gagné's and Resnick's methods of task analysis. As we have mentioned several times in this chapter, both Gagné and Resnick base their task analysis procedures on the concept of vertical transfer. Task analyses rest upon the assumption that for any given learning task there is a set of critical skills that can be identified, and the learning of these skills facilitates the learning of the superordinate skill. By identifying the subordinate skills and ordering them according to the relationships among themselves and to the superordinate skill, we have determined the blueprint for sequencing instruction to promote the attainment of this set of intellectual skills in the most efficient and effective manner possible.

Components analysis makes no assumption about learning types, whereas Gagné's approach to task analysis assumes that each successive level of subordinate skills will correspond to one of his learning types. Furthermore, as these levels of prerequisites are laid out, they "naturally" order themselves according to the hierarchy of intellectual skills identified by Gagné. As Gagné and Briggs (1974, p. 112) state:

> . . . One does not proceed by saying to oneself, this lesson is a rule, therefore it must have defined concepts as prerequisites, and these in turn must have concrete concepts as prerequisites, and so on. Instead, as previously indicated, one proceeds by considering what the critical subordinate skills must be for specific tasks of learning. However, the fundamental logic of the arrangement of skills from simple to complex still applies, and that is the basic reason why the nature of intellectual skills needs to be understood. An attempt to design a hierarchy which indicates a rule as prerequisite to a defined concept, or a defined concept as prerequisite to a concrete concept, or any inversion of this sort, is surely wrong. If one arrives at such inversions in deriving a hierarchy, it is a sure sign of the necessity for rethinking the entire structure.

The procedure of components analysis was developed independently of Gagné's learning types and therefore the derivation of subordinate skills with components analysis is not guided by this principle. With components analysis the major principle guiding the identification of subordinate skills is to derive *simpler* learning tasks that require "capabilities necessary to performance of or helpful in learning the superordinate skill" (Resnick & Ford, 1976).

The major and most obvious distinction between the Gagné and Resnick approaches to task analysis concerns the first level of subordinate skills below the superordinate skills. With Resnick's task analysis procedure, this first level of subordinate skills lays out the chain of component skills that comprise the superordinate skill under analysis. This difference is that for a given learning task Resnick adds one further level of analysis than does Gagné. Whereas Resnick analyzes a learning task into the sequence of steps to be executed by the learner for successful performance, Gagné prefers to deal with each learning task as an intact capability on the part of the learner. This distinction between the methods of Gagné and Resnick can be seen very clearly when each is used to generate a learning hierarchy for the same task. We have constructed a possible component analysis for solving physical work problems. This components analysis as depicted in Figure 8–8 (Gagné's learning hierarchy is in Figure 8–5) shows the two hierarchies to be essentially the same, with the difference being greater specificity at the first level of subordinate skills with components analysis. Gagné's original three subordinate skills, VI, VII, and VIII, are really the components and are even arranged in the sequence in which they would be performed (i.e., the product of performing skill VI provides an important aspect of the stimulus situation for performing skill VII) as a behavioral chain.

3. Describe the distinction between a *component* and a *prerequisite.*

Empirical analysis

One of the basic principles on which good teaching rests is that success in teaching is based on student outcome; or to put it another way, the proof of the pudding is in the tasting! Regardless of how theoretically correct or elegant a learning hierarchy is, it is of little or no instructional value unless it can be demonstrated that an instructional sequence based on this hierarchy is more effective or efficient in terms of student outcomes than a sequence teaching the same capability but not based on that learning hierarchy. Consequently to qualify as a valid structure on which to base decisions about instructional sequence, a learning hierarchy must be composed of a

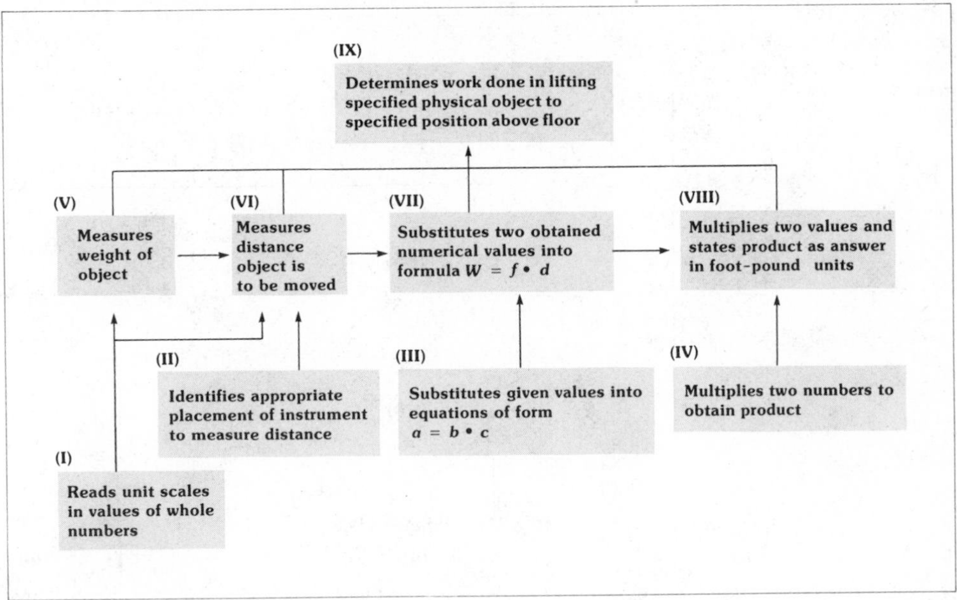

FIGURE 8–8
Learning hierarchy resulting from components analysis of the learning task; solving physical work problems

sequence of learning tasks in which learning the subordinate tasks facilitates learning the superordinate tasks through positive transfer.

The question of major concern now is: How does one determine whether a learning hierarchy represents a valid structure for sequencing instruction of a given objective? To answer this question adequately we must examine student performance on the tasks that comprise the hypothesized learning hierarchy; this is the second step in task analysis. Data pertaining to student performance can be analyzed by various statistical procedures, ranging from a simple "eyeball" test of percentage scores to sophisticated tests among ordered pairs of test items. Here we will describe only a sample of such procedures in brief detail, as a comprehensive explanation of these statistical procedures is beyond the scope and purpose of this book.

An empirical analysis is performed to determine whether the hypothesized vertical transfer among the hierarchy elements does indeed occur. The sequence of transfer is from subordinate to superordinate, or up the hierarchy, so if two tasks have a subordinate/superordinate relationship, we would expect that if a student could not perform one of the two skills, it would be the superordinate skill. For a given learning hierarchy, then, since we would not expect to find complete mastery of every skill by every person in a population, as we go up a hierarchy we would expect to find a decreasing percentage of mastery. A learning hierarchy that deviates from the preceding suggested pattern of mastery should be looked upon as suspect, and all that is required at this simple level of empirical analysis is to examine achievement of the skills comprising the hierarchy. Take as an example the hypothetical learning hierarchy in Figure 8–9. The numbers in parentheses represent the percentage of 100 students mastering each skill in the hierarchy after instruction.

When student achievement data are displayed in this visual format, it is easy to determine by visual inspection (the eyeball test) whether the data show the desired mastery

FIGURE 8–9
Hypothetical learning hierarchy with percentage of mastery for each skill

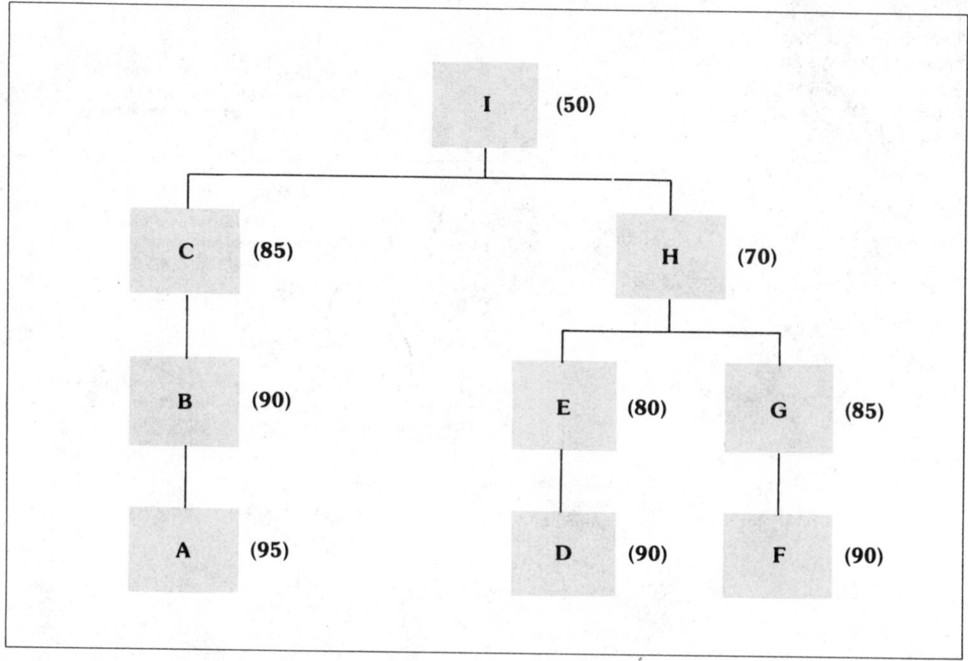

pattern; if so, we conclude that the subskills are ordered appropriately. However, in this particular case, the moderately low achievement of skill I suggests that either the instruction to teach skill I specifically should be improved or there is another prerequisite skill to I besides skills C and H.

Suppose for the prerequisites branch A to B to C, we got the following results:

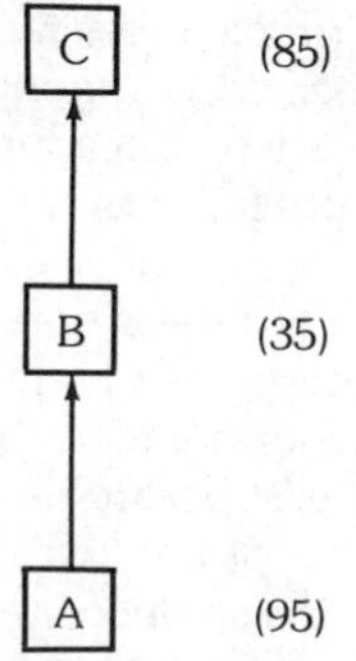

The obvious conclusion would be that skill B is not a valid prerequisite for skill C since more people learned C than did B. Consequently this branch of the hierarchy would have to be reanalyzed and a new sequence of prerequisites identified.

Gagné (1962) developed a simple set of statistics that allows assessment of the transfer relationships among the various skills comprising a learning hierarchy. Each superordinate/subordinate pair of skills represents a possible transfer sequence, so for our hypothetical learning hierarchy from Figure 8–9, we have the following transfer sequences.

Superordinate	←	*Subordinate*
I	←	C
I	←	H
C	←	B
B	←	A
H	←	E
E	←	D
H	←	G
G	←	F

There are four possible achievement patterns for a given superordinate/subordinate sequence. If both the superordinate and the subordinate skills are passed, Gagné represented this pattern with the symbol (1,1); therefore, the symbol (0,0) would mean that both the superordinate and subordinate skills were failed. If the superordinate skill were passed but the subordinate skill failed, it was symbolized (1,0) and the reverse of this was (0,1). The next step is to obtain a frequency count of the number of people showing each achievement pattern for all the superordinate/subordinate pairs comprising the learning hierarchies. The results of the frequency count can be placed in tabular form, such as in Table 8–2, to facilitate their interpretation and use in calculation of the statistic upon which we will base our evaluation of the hierarchy's validity.

The only achievement pattern that does not enter into the equation comprising the test of validity is the (0,1) pattern, superordinate failed/subordinate passed. Gagné did not utilize this particular achievement pattern in a test of the validity of a hierarchy, because it does not either confirm or disprove a transfer sequence and could be accounted for in terms of inadequate instruction. The dividend in our equation is composed of the sum of the frequencies for the two achievement patterns possible in a valid learning hierarchy; the divisor is the sum of the preceding two valid achievement patterns and the frequency of the invalid achievement pattern. Consequently our equation divides the number of achievement patterns indicating a valid hierarchy by the total number of observations providing information as to either the validity or invalidity of the hierarchy. Since the quotient from the equation tells us what percentage of the total observations are supportive of a valid hierarchy, the higher the value of the quotient the greater the validity of the hierarchy. There is no set minimum value that has been accepted as a standard for determination of a valid hierarchy, but 85–90 percent seems reasonable. If that were true then for our particular example, we would want to reexamine the H/G sequence to see if perhaps another prerequisite for H could be established. Other investigators reacting to what they consider to be inadequacies in Gagné's test for the validity of a learning hierarchy have devised tests of their own (Airasian, 1971; Capie & Jones, 1971).

TABLE 8–2
Frequency table of achievement patterns for 100 people on a hypothetical learning hierarchy

Superordinate/ subordinate pair	*Frequency of, achievement pattern* A (1,1)	B (0,0)	C (1,0)	D (0,1)	*Estimate of validity* $\frac{A+B}{A+B+C}$
I/C	80	15	5	0	0.95
I/H	70	20	5	5	0.95
C/B	85	5	10	0	0.90
B/A	63	20	7	10	0.92
H/E	90	10	0	0	1.00
E/D	70	20	5	5	0.95
H/G	60	15	15	10	0.83
G/F	79	15	3	3	0.97

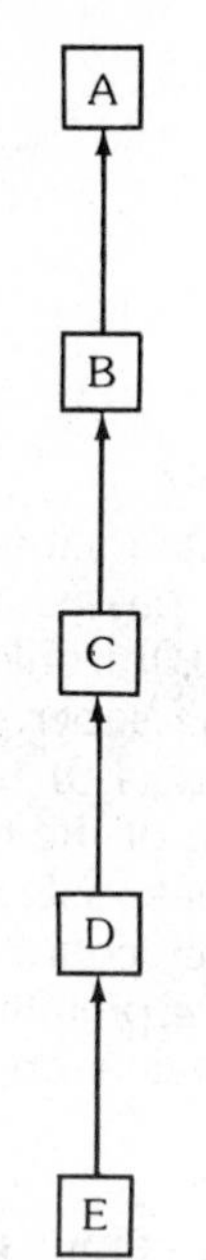

FIGURE 8–10
Sequence of skills in a hypothetical learning hierarchy

Much of the research done on the empirical analysis of learning hierarchies has used a statistical procedure called "scalogram analysis." A scale, as defined by Guttman, is a set of dichotomous items in which a person's score yields the number of items passed. This is so because the items constituting a scale are arranged from least to most difficult, so when a person fails a given item that person does not pass any further items, since they are more difficult than the failed item. Given a person's score on a Guttman-type scale, suppose a score of 12, we know this person passed the first 12 consecutive items on the test (scale).

In learning hierarchies an individual item on the scale represents a single subordinate skill from the hierarchy. Say we have a simple learning hierarchy represented in Figure 8–10. In a properly constructed learning hierarchy, no person passes a given superordinate skill without mastering its subordinate skill.

From this we see that the superordinate/subordinate pairs of a learning hierarchy form a Guttman-type scale. This fact can be seen more clearly from a graph demonstrating the possible patterns of achievement on our hypothetically perfect, learning hierarchy shown in Figure 8–11 (an X indicates mastery and no mark indicates nonmastery). Notice that the number assigned to each possible achievement pattern is the score on the corresponding Guttman-type scale.

Perfect learning hierarchies, as well as perfect Guttman-type scales, seldom occur in practice. Because learning hierarchies are composed of Guttman-type scales, we do have a statistic available that allows us to determine how close to a perfect hierarchy we have come. This statistic is called the "coefficient of reproducibility" and it is a measure of how well a person's response to a given pattern of items can be predicted from the score on a set of items. The higher the accuracy of the prediction, the closer that set of items approximates a perfect scale.

A number of investigators have used the coefficient of reproducibility as a measure in the empirical analysis of a proposed learning hierarchy with a good deal of success (Boozer & Lindvall, 1971; DiCostanzo, 1976; Resnick & Wang, 1969). We present the results of one such study to illustrate the value of empirical analysis in the development of valid learning hierarchies. DiCostanzo (1976) used a modification of Guttman's scalogram analysis to investigate a learning hierarchy from the Individualized Mathematics Curriculum developed by the University of Pittsburgh's Learning Research and Development Center. The purpose of DiCostanzo's study was to develop a procedure for the integration of logical and empirical analyses in the development of curricular structures. DiCostanzo used a version of scalogram analysis to investigate a logical analysis empirically. As the accompanying figures show, the results of this process can be both interesting and informative. Figure 8–12 presents the learning hierarchy proposed through the logical analysis. Figure 8–13 shows the learning structures de-

FIGURE 8–11
Possible achievement patterns in hypothetical learning hierarchy

Possible achievement patterns	*Skills*				
	E	*D*	*C*	*B*	*A*
5	X	X	X	X	X
4	X	X	X	X	
3	X	X	X		
2	X	X			
1	X				

FIGURE 8–12
Learning hierarchy derived from logical analysis

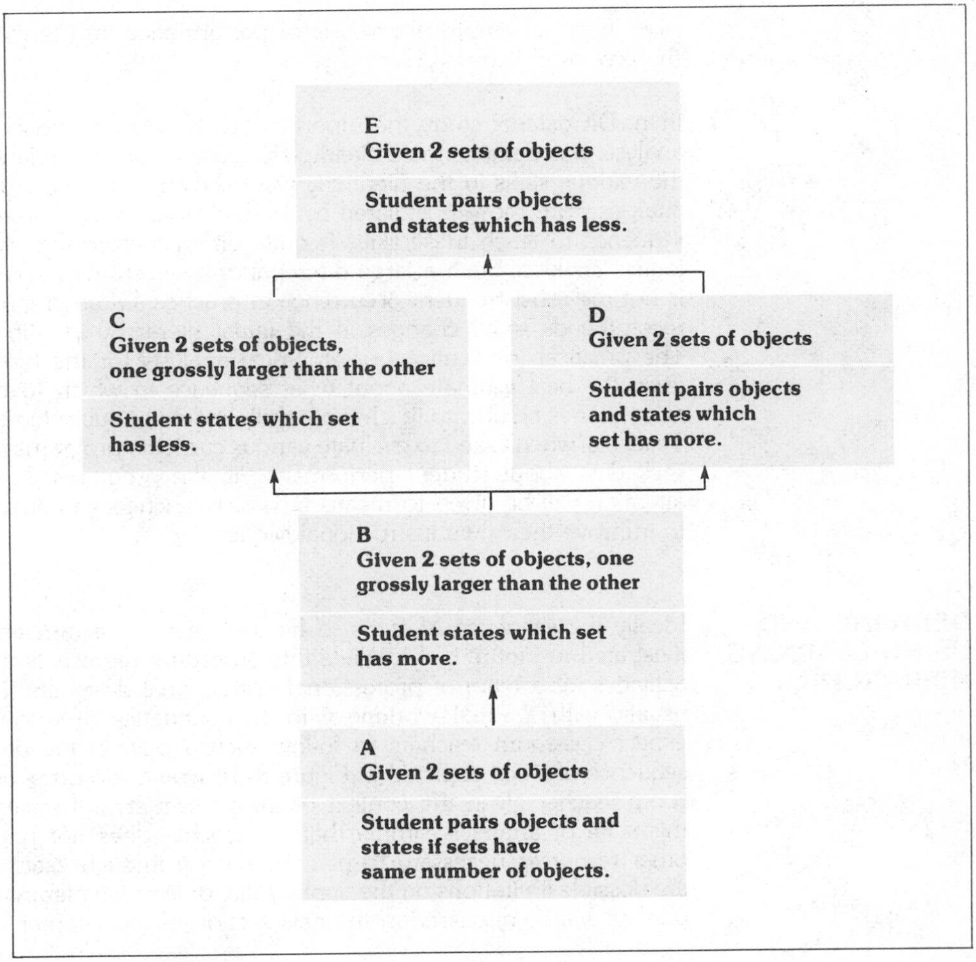

E
Given 2 sets of objects
Student pairs objects and states which has less.
C
Given 2 sets of objects, one grossly larger than the other
Student states which set has less.
D
Given 2 sets of objects
Student pairs objects and states which set has more.
B
Given 2 sets of objects, one grossly larger than the other
Student states which set has more.
A
Given 2 sets of objects
Student pairs objects and states if sets have same number of objects.

Source: DiCostanzo (1976).

FIGURE 8–13
Learning hierarchy derived from empirical analysis

E
Given 2 sets of objects
Student pairs objects and states which has less.
A
Given 2 sets of objects
Student pairs objects and states if sets have same number of objects.
B
Given 2 sets of objects, one grossly larger than the other
Student states which set has more.
D
Given 2 sets of objects
Student pairs objects and states which set has more.
C
Given 2 sets of objects, one grossly larger than the other
Student states which set has less.

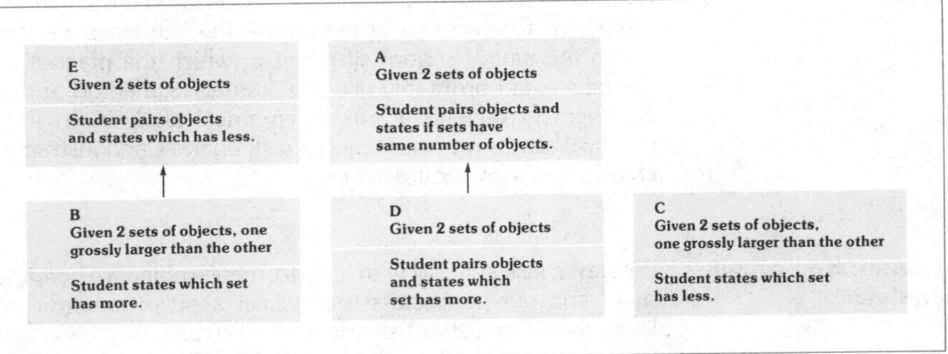

Source: DiCostanzo (1976).

rived from an empirical analysis of performance on the individual skills comprising the proposed learning hierarchy.

In the DiCostanzo study, the importance of the interdependency of logical and empirical analysis was demonstrated clearly. The positive transfer relationships existing between the various skills in the hierarchy were shown to be quite different by the empirical analysis from those postulated by the logical analysis. Consequently the instructional sequence to teach these skills is quite different from the sequence proposed by the logical analysis. Such a large discrepancy between the logical and empirical analyses is not the most frequent occurrence in practice. Often empirical analysis supports or recommends small changes in the initial hierarchy identified by a logical analysis. The practical implications of empirical analysis for the teacher are very important. Even the best estimate about what sequence in which to teach a set of skills and also theories on how to teach those skills should be subjected to proof in the classroom. Teachers, when asked to evaluate various curricula programs for classroom use, should seek data about student performance in the programs. In the next section further attention will be given to means by which teachers can collect and use student data to improve their own instructional sequencing.

DERIVING AND USING LEARNING HIERARCHIES

Ideally the sequence of steps to be performed in a task analysis procedure is that illustrated in Figure 8–14. While this procedure represents a reasonable sequence of activities for a team of professional instructional designers (highly trained personnel, usually with a PhD) working with an abundance of resources, it is unrealistic to expect classroom teachers to follow such a plan in the design of instruction. The sequence of steps depicted in Figure 8–14 would too often be impractical for a classroom teacher given the context of the present school system. The chief reason for this state of affairs is simply that the teacher does not have available the time or other resources necessary to plan instruction in such exacting detail. Further, there are possible limitations on the applicability of learning hierarchies to classroom instruction, as will be discussed in the next section of this chapter.

However, teachers do plan much of their own instruction and consequently they must make decisions about sequencing instruction. Therefore, the question is not whether a classroom teacher can use task analysis methods, but to what degree the classroom teacher can approximate the sequence of steps shown in Figure 8–14. Given the typical school situation in which the planning of instruction occurs, most teachers could profitably use a task analysis method and routinely—gathered student achievement data in a simple empirical analysis. In this section we present some practical advice on conducting a task analysis and instructional uses of learning hierarchies other than sequencing.

Conducting a task analysis

We start a task analysis with a performance objective hereafter called the "superordinate skill," and our purpose is to discover a set of subordinate tasks that are simpler to learn than our superordinate skill and that will contribute positive transfer to the learning of the superordinate skill. The first issue to settle is whether or not to use a components analysis method. As demonstrated earlier, Gagné's "intact skills" approach yields essentially the same structure as components analysis, so the choice is not critical. However, the nature of the chain formed by the component skills makes this method less likely, especially for the novice, to leave out a critical skill.

FIGURE 8–14
Sequence of steps in task analysis

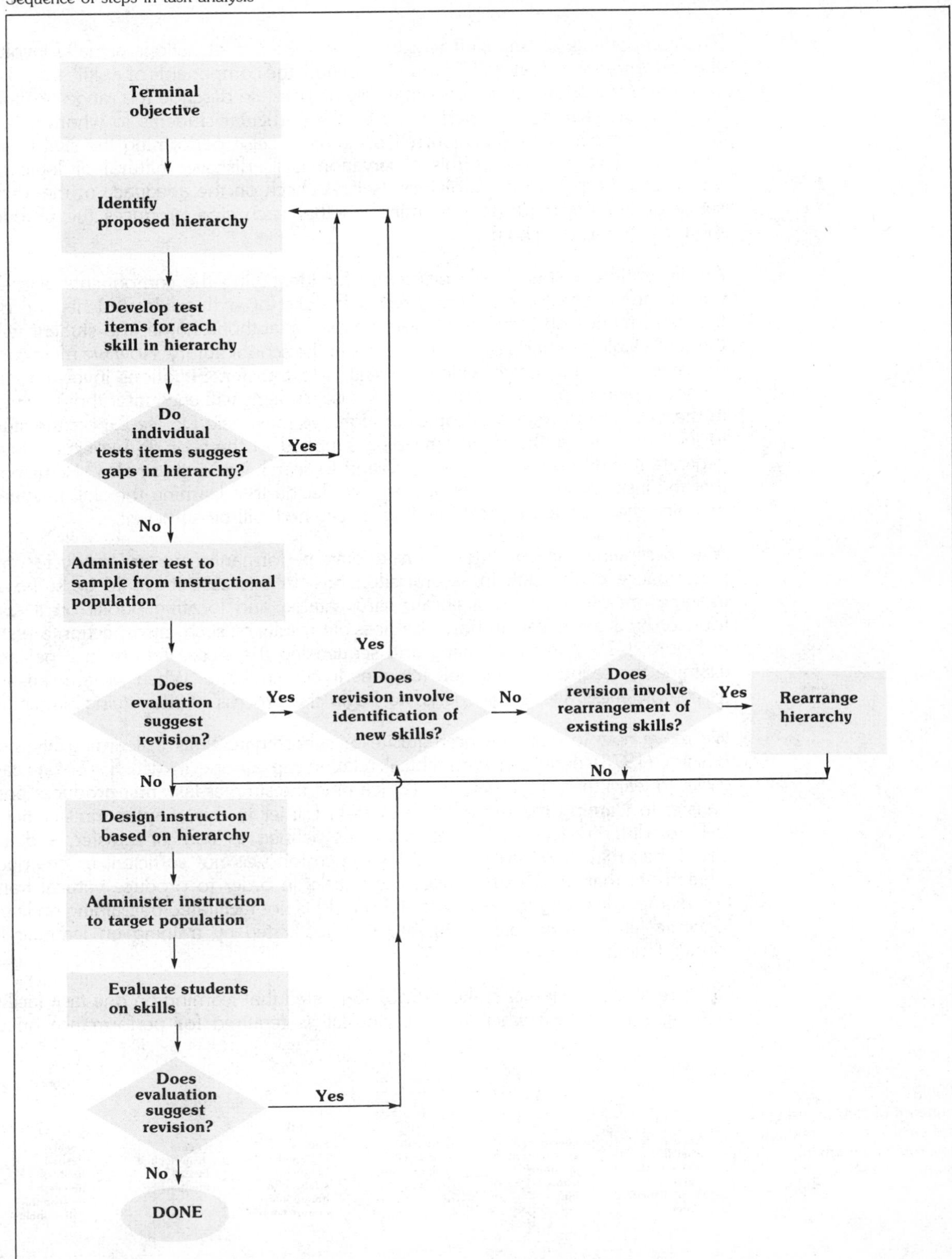

The components of any skill represent the sequence of actions actually involved in the performance of that skill. In order to identify the components of a skill, the following procedure is advised. First, as completely as possible describe the range of situations in which the skill is to be performed by the particular students to whom it is being taught. Next observe either yourself or someone else performing the skill in several situations. The purpose of this observation is to discover natural or logical steps into which the performance divides itself. A check on the adequacy of the identified series of steps is made to determine whether each step produces the product for the next step in the chain.

An illustration of this simple procedure for identifying the components of a skill is now in order. The topic is library research skills for sixth-grade students and one of the performance objectives is: Given a topic or author's name, the student will use the card catalog to find relevant resources in the school library. Now we must consider the range of situations to which the skill is to transfer. Situations involving authors do not appear to pose any problems because students will encounter those mentioned in their classes. In regard to topics though, we must ask: Do we expect the students to look only under the topical heading supplied to them or do we expect them to generate related topics and synonyms and to search under these also? Remembering that the instruction is for sixth-graders, we decide that learning the skill in situations in which the supplied topical heading is searched will be sufficient.

After describing the conditions surrounding performance, we are ready to observe performance of the skill in several situations. In this case it would be sufficient to imagine oneself going to a library card catalog and locating books on a specific topic or by a particular author. The possible results of such introspection are shown in Figure 8–15. After identifying and sequencing the steps, we are in a position to examine the sequence and look for gaps in the structure. When we are satisfied of its completeness, we are prepared to begin the process of identifying prerequisites.

We move now to examine prerequisite or subordinate skills in learning hierarchies. Resnick (1973) defines a hierarchical relationship as one in which: (1) one task is easier to learn than the other, and (2) learning the simpler task first produces positive transfer in learning the more complex task. Earlier in this chapter transfer between tasks of differing levels of complexity was defined as *vertical* transfer, and it was stated then that the simple-to-complex dimension was not sufficient to describe the relationship that must exist between two tasks in order to produce vertical transfer. For example, learning to read (a complex task) is not facilitated by training on learning to name letters (a simpler task), but it is facilitated by training on learning letter sounds (another simpler skill).

Other research (Gagné & Baker, 1950) suggested that learning on one task facilitates learning another task when a common skill is required for performance on both.

FIGURE 8–15
Sequence of steps in using card catalog to find relevant resources in the school library

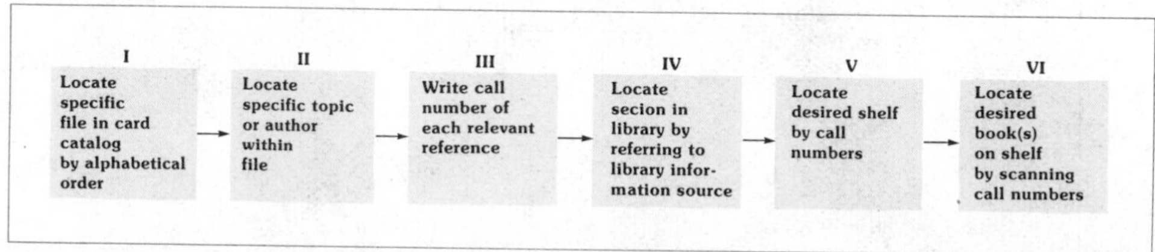

Thus learning to say letter sounds facilitates learning to read because reading involves saying and blending letter sounds; therefore, letter sounds are a subskill of learning to read. Saying letter names is not a subskill of learning to read and so there is no transfer between the two.

This leads to the conclusion that a prerequisite must be both a simpler task and one that provides practice on a subskill of the superordinate task. Our effort to identify essential subskills will be facilitated if we have knowledge of the possible classes of skills that can be required by any task. Glaser (1965) has categorized learning tasks into the two classes of demands they can make upon the learner: how to perform and when to perform. Return to our example of learning to read and imagine a young child learning to say "cat" when the word is encountered. In this specific instance the child has to blend the three sounds *k/a/t* into *kat,* which is learning *how,* and to say this sound only when the word *cat* is encountered in print, not when *cap, car,* or any other similar word is encountered. Furthermore, any *how* or *when* skill involved in a task can be broken into subskills. So for the above instance the subskill of saying the *k* sound of *c* is a prerequisite for learning the *how* skill of blending.

Seldom is it necessary to take an analysis to the level of specificity in our example above, except possibly with very young or special-education populations. Typically, a teacher can determine what critical subskill or subskills place the greatest demand upon the learner in a particular task and arrange to have it or them learned first in the context of a simpler task. For example, Figure 8–16 is part of the learning hierarchy for solving physical work problems presented earlier in the chapter. The subordinate skills II and III comprise the superordinate skill, and both have been identified as

FIGURE 8–16
Part of learning hierarchy for solving physical work problems

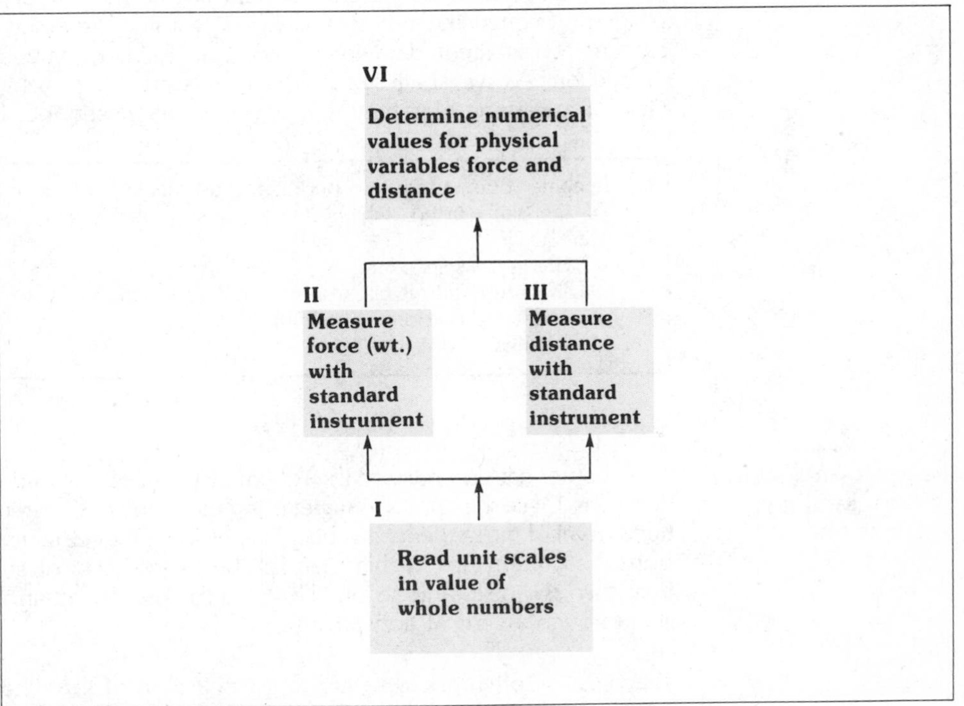

Source: Adapted from Gagné (1970).

prerequisites because they are independent subskills. However, notice that both have only one common prerequisite, that of reading unit scales, even though measuring both weight and distance requires other subskills besides reading scales. Probably from past experiences in teaching these skills, it was decided that the major learning demand was to read scales and once this was mastered the other subskills could be mastered readily.

In this section we have described in some detail how to conduct a task analysis. First, the teacher describes the task to be learned, paying close attention to the variety of situations in which the student is expected to learn. Next the task is broken into its components and arranged in order of performance. After the components are established, the prerequisites are developed. Here the intention is to identify the critical subskills of each component so that they may be taught first in a simpler context.

Emphasis was given to the important role of the teacher's knowledge of both subject matter and students in task analysis. This knowledge is critical in determining what and how many prerequisites should be identified. The relevancy of this knowledge also extends to the determination of the probable entering skills or instructional levels of the students.

Additionally, in the beginning of this section the need to check instructional sequencing decisions against student achievement was noted. It may be said that instructional sequences must be based on some rationale, so even though a teacher does not have the resources to permit an empirical analysis, a task analysis procedure is still a valuable sequencing tool. However, with or without task analysis, the ultimate test of any instructional program is student achievement and attitude resulting from the program. Sequencing on the basis of a learning hierarchy allows the teacher to use student achievement data in a more fine-grained analysis for the improvement of instruction. As we shall see in the next section, analyzing student achievement in view of a learning hierarchy is a powerful diagnostic tool for the classroom teacher.

4. Imagine yourself trying to perform a task analysis of the skill: arrives at class on time. Of the skills listed, which is the most probable component? The most probable prerequisite?
   a. States class schedule.
   b. Identifies various classroom buildings on campus.
   c. Locates classroom in building.
   d. Attends school.

Instructional value of task analysis procedures

This chapter has emphasized the role of task analysis procedures in making sequencing decisions. Once the appropriate learning hierarchy has been developed and the instructional level of the students has been established, the remaining prerequisites are taught from the bottom up. In this manner the lowest level of subordinate skills is taught first, then the next, and so on. The result is greater attainment of the superordinate skill through a vertical transfer effect.

Teachers are often asked to aid in the selection of the school instructional program. In this capacity a number of commercially prepared programs must be inspected and a choice among them based on an examination of the content and unsubstantiated claims by the publisher about the purposes of the materials. Task analysis offers the teacher a tool for analyzing and comparing the programs for intended outcomes and the adequacy of materials for attainment of the outcomes. In this manner the various programs could be related to the school's broad goals to determine which is most compatible.

Learning hierarchies represent a potentially powerful diagnostic tool for the classroom teacher. When a student encounters difficulty with a particular unit of instruction, rather than relying on the global and nebulous concept of readiness for learning, the teacher can pinpoint the specific prerequisite skill(s) that the student has not acquired in the learning hierarchy and that has produced the learning problem. By identifying the specific skills causing the learning problem, remedial instruction can be given that most effectively and efficiently uses both the student's and the teacher's time. Remedial instruction developed on this basis is more likely to be used, and hence the development of a realistic system of individualized instruction is promoted. For the description of such an individualized instructional system turn to Chapter 14 and read the section on *Individually Prescribed Instruction* developed by the Learning Research and Development Center of the University of Pittsburgh.

To examine this diagnostic function of learning hierarchies, we turn to Figure 8–17, the learning hierarchy for the skill of phonetic decoding in beginning reading. Suppose we have a student who has reached instruction on skill VIII—Pronounces regular "spelling patterns" involving same vowels in different phonemic values, and this student fails to acquire the desired capability from the instruction. By examining the learning hierarchy we see that the problem could arise from the student's failure to acquire any of the capabilities represented by skills I–VI in the hierarchy. Since it is most improbable that the student would have gotten to instruction on skill VIII without learning most of the skills subordinate to skill VIII, we need to assess the student's learning of them to pinpoint the specific deficiencies. Furthermore, due to the cumulative nature of learning hierarchies, deficiencies are most likely to be found in the immediate prerequisites of the problem skill. Therefore evaluation to determine the specific deficiencies works backwards through the learning hierarchy from the problem skill.

We close this section with one more illustration of the precision of the diagnostic information that can be obtained from learning hierarchies. Imagine two students who have failed to acquire the capability stated in skill VIII of Figure 8–17. Upon evaluation it was found that student 1 had failed to acquire skills VI, III, and II, while student 2 had not acquired skills VI and V. Typically these two students would be grouped together and given the same remedial instruction, consequently neither would probably receive the necessary remediation. The use of learning hierarchies in diagnosing learner problems allows us to avoid such unfortunate situations by determining with greater accuracy the skills needed by any given individual to succeed at the desired learning task.

5. Describe two instructional functions of learning hierarchies other than sequencing instruction.

LIMITATIONS OF TASK ANALYSIS PROCEDURES

Task analysis is not the only strategy for sequencing instruction, nor is it the most commonly used approach. What is unique about task analysis as a sequencing strategy is that it is an attempt to apply our knowledge of positive transfer to the design of

FIGURE 8–17
A learning hierarchy for a basic reading skill ("decoding")

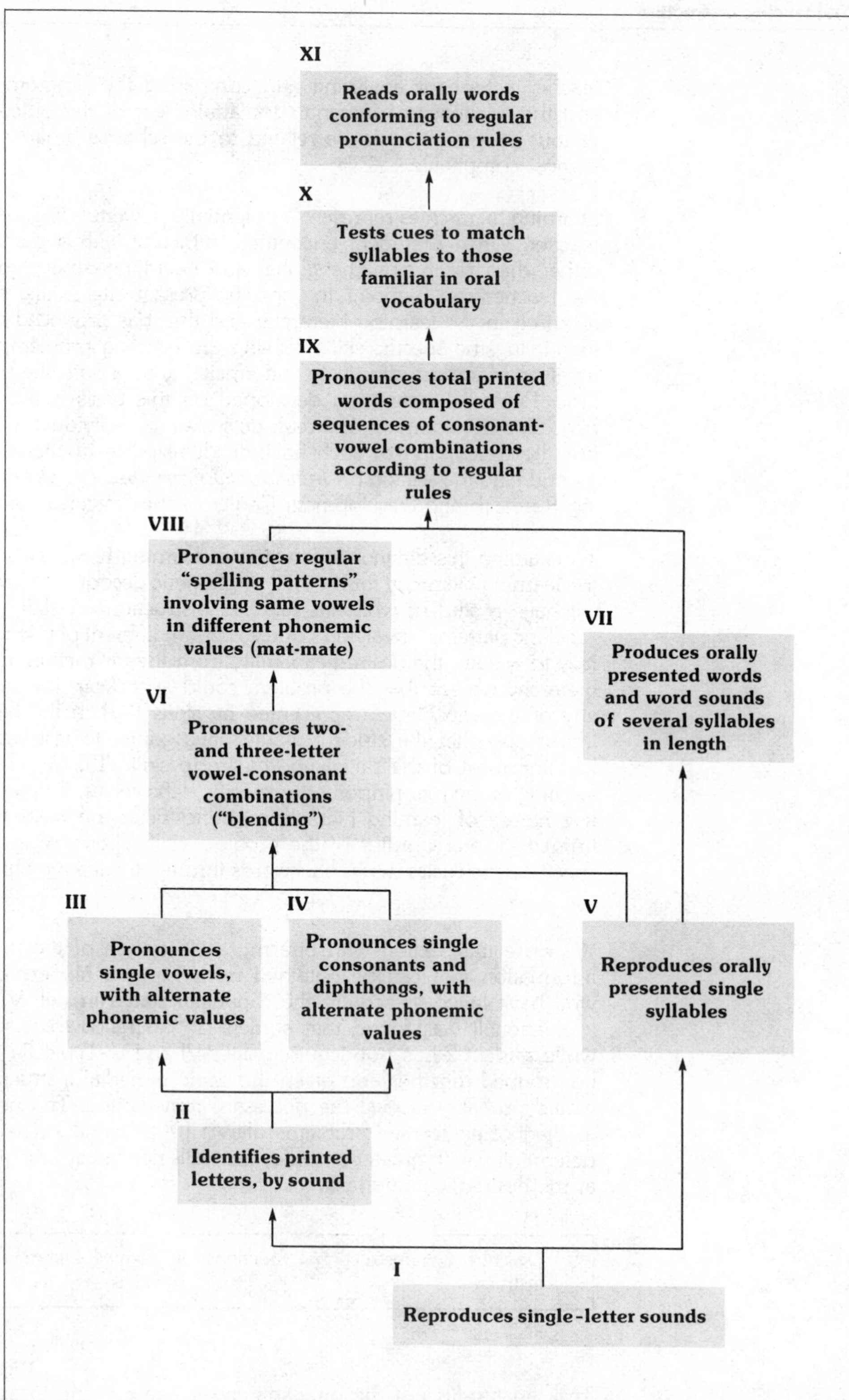

Source: Gagné (1970).

instructional sequences. However, task analysis as a tool in the design of instruction and teaching is not without its limitations. We now examine the major objections to task analysis.

R. T. White (1973) states that Gagné's approach to task analysis is of little practical value outside mathematics and the physical sciences. These subject matter areas are highly structured, and it is relatively simple to identify the rules and concepts involved in learning tasks in these areas. Actually it has been argued that these subjects are arranged according to a logical hierarchy of rules or principles. Students have long known that for subjects like math or physics you must keep up with your studying because to comprehend topic Y requires comprehension of the topics leading up to it; other courses such as history or psychology do not possess this interdependence of topics to the same extent. Hence in these areas you can let your studying "slide" and then you can cram the night before a test. Consequently Phillips and Kelly (1975) argue that Gagné's learning hierarchies are not psychological but rather logical in nature.

While it is true that it is easier to generate learning hierarchies in some subjects than in others, there are no a priori reasons to believe that learning hierarchies cannot be generated in the less structured subjects such as the arts and social sciences. Related to this point Merrill (1970) points out that it is commonly held that the subject matter dictates the level of learning (i.e., memorization, concept, rule using) to be attained through instruction. However, according to Merrill this is not the actual state of affairs, but rather the level of learning can be imposed upon the subject matter. For example, the idea of manifest destiny from American history could be the content of three instructional objectives reflecting three different types of learning.

The student will be able to define *manifest destiny* (verbal information).

Given various statements describing attitude toward American expansion on the North American continent, the student will identify those statements that reflect a belief in manifest destiny (concept learning).

Given a hypothetical incident concerning American citizens being barred from a western territory in the 1800s, the student will write a letter to the editor expressing a manifest destiny attitude toward the incident (rule learning).

White and Gagné (1974, pp. 23–24) said the following about the presences of learning hierarchies in various subject matter disciplines:

> Since hierarchies show promise of being useful instructional tools, it seems important to find out how widely they exist across subject areas. It is already apparent that the bulk of what is learned in mathematics and physical science is intellectual skills of the principles or rule-applying type, for which hierarchies can certainly be drawn up. But hierarchies should also be sought in other subject areas, even though this may be difficult and the chances of success may appear low. One probably fruitful area is language skills, both in the learner's mother tongue and in language foreign to him. In subjects which consist largely of verbal information, such as history, there are many intellectual skills of the concept type, but rules are less common, and so hierarchies may be rarer and less useful than in mathematics. There is the possibility, however, that such subjects do contain subtle and complex hierarchies leading to principles that at present are difficult to identify. Discovery of hierarchies of that type could lead to important changes in the teaching of these subjects.

Another limitation on task analysis as a sequencing strategy is that teachers typically work with prepared curricular materials so that the sequence of instruction is largely determined for them. Even if the task analysis does suggest a different instructional sequence than the one utilized by the commercially prepared materials, the teacher may not have the time necessary to develop instruction based on a new sequence. Although a teacher may not actually design instruction on the basis of a task analysis, the information derived from task analysis can be of value in examining the effectiveness of commercially prepared curricular and instructional materials.

Task analysis can facilitate the examination of instructional materials in a number of ways. One important way, according to Gagné (1974b), is the identification of intended learning outcomes. Gagné (p. 16) states:

> The analysis of existing content, using a task analysis method, may have a number of useful purposes. Chief among these may well be the clarification of what any given lesson is "all about." Many of us have had the experience of being able to inform a teacher that the type of learning outcome which seems to be intended by a text is very different from the learning outcome desired by the teacher. Thus, a task analysis of an existing text, film, or other instructional package may reveal some exceedingly important information for those concerned with selection of instructional materials.

Once the intended learning outcomes have been identified, a task analysis will specify the essential prerequisites for the intended objectives. With this information, the teacher can examine the prepared lesson to determine whether it covers all of these prerequisite skills. If any are lacking, the teacher can develop supplementary instruction to cover the missing prerequisite skills. Proceeding in this manner, the teacher can improve the effectiveness of the instructional program and simultaneously utilize scarce time resources wisely.

SUMMARY

This chapter described the sequencing decisions a teacher must make in planning instruction. Sequencing decisions and criteria were shown to change with the unit of instruction being planned by the teacher. Broad decisions involve sequencing content units on the basis of the course goals and purposes. Most specific decisions involving learned capabilities require the derivation of learning hierarchies. Learning hierarchies are composed of the components and prerequisites necessary to acquire a more complex skill. Prerequisites are identified on the basis of their ability to provide positive transfer to the higher skill. The need for subjecting proposed hierarchies to a tryout with students was discussed, and simple procedures for use by the teacher were presented. Finally, the difficulty of identifying hierarchies in such areas as the humanities and social sciences was detailed.

SELF-TEST

1. Under what condition will vertical transfer occur between two tasks?
2. Describe the relationship between logical and empirical analyses.
3. Try a logical analysis of some skill in a subject you expect to teach.
4. Which is *not* an instructional value of a learning hierarchy?
   a. Basis for individualizing instruction.
   b. Basis for pinpointing specific skills not acquired by student.
   c. Basis for sequencing subskills in instruction.
   d. Basis for matching instruction to the average skill level.
5. Learning hierarchies have not been obtained in such low-consensus fields as the social sciences by researchers. True or false?

ANSWER KEY TO BOXED QUESTIONS

1. *b*
2. *a*
3. A component is a subskill actually performed in carrying out the superordinate skill, while a prerequisite simply facilitates the learning of the superordinate skill.
4. Component is *c;* prerequisite is *b.*
5. Evaluating curriculum materials and as a diagnostic tool.

ANSWER KEY TO SELF-TEST

1. When one skill is an integral part of the other.
2. A logical analysis suggests a possible hierarchy and an empirical analysis verifies whether it actually exists.
3. You must evaluate your own hierarchy by referring to the criteria in the section on deriving learning hierarchies.
4. *d*
5. False.

Chapter 9

The learner: Analysis of instructional level

ONCE THE GOALS OF INSTRUCTION have been decided and the subordinate behaviors necessary to reach the terminal objective have been identified, the process of matching instruction to the learner's unique characteristics is in order. To do this it is first necessary to assess the present status of the learner's capabilities. This assessment should indicate an appropriate starting point for instruction and perhaps a revision upward or downward of the original goals. Not all learners are the same, and not all learning tasks require the same learning conditions. The assessment process, therefore, should start before making any micro-level decisions about methods or materials.

In this chapter we discuss five main topics. First, we explore some of the general issues related to assessing a student's capabilities at the outset of instruction. To give you a fuller understanding of the concepts and terminology related to measuring and describing human behavior, we briefly cover these two topics. The discussion then turns to a consideration of various approaches used in the analysis of learners. Our final topic is the use of the analytic data.

After reading this chapter, you should be able to:

1. Define entering behavior from a psychological perspective.
2. Distinguish between the function and process of assessing entering behavior.
3. Distinguish between measurement and evaluation.
4. Define reliability, and describe three ways in which it is determined.
5. Define four types of validity.
6. Describe several of the descriptive statistics that a teacher may encounter or use in descriptions of students' entering behavior.
7. Describe the six basic approaches to an analysis of a learner's initial characteristics.
8. Describe some uses and misuses of assessment data.

GENERAL CONSIDERATIONS

It is a long-standing axiom in education that we need to meet students at their current performance levels and let them move at their own pace. Most would agree that this is good advice if we are to treat each child fairly and as a unique individual. In spite of the many criticisms claiming that teachers do not match instruction to individual differences, almost every teacher attempts to do it in some way. This is not to say that teachers are entirely successful in their attempts. Their success is dependent upon the frame of reference one uses to judge their efforts. Often we believe there are serious errors in the way teachers (1) define students' capabilities, (2) assess these capabilities, and (3) use the assessment data. Also there is often very little consistency between the three processes. Teachers may define capabilities in one framework, assess them in another, and then plan instruction without regard for either framework. When these errors and inconsistencies exist, it is difficult for even the best-intentioned teacher to match instruction to the child's present level of performance.

Entering behavior defined

The term *entering behavior* is used to refer to a student's capabilities at the beginning of instruction. The term *readiness* has also been used but typically it has a more general meaning. The term *readiness* is often used by teachers and parents, but in psychological journals the term *entering behavior* is more common in serious discussions of learning.

In the preceding chapter about task analysis it was pointed out that tasks can be analyzed and described in terms of a superordinate response capability and the set of subordinate response capabilities necessary to learn the higher-level skill. These learning hierarchies are often expressed in terms of performance objectives, which describe specific behaviors that are used to infer that the performance capability has been acquired. The strictest definition of the term *entering behavior* refers to the actual set of behaviors an individual is able to perform at the beginning of instruction in relation to a specific learning hierarchy, and not to an internalized set of performance capabilities necessary to acquire some higher-level capability.

While a strict definition of the term *entering behavior* refers only to the overt behaviors of an individual, it is also used to refer to the performance capabilities. How the term is used depends to some extent on the context in which it is used. If the context involves the actual measurement of an individual's performance on some test item, or in Jenkins and Deno's framework (1970) at the D level, then the term is likely to refer to the individual's actual behavior. If the context is referring to the individual more generally, then the term is more likely to be used in relation to the performance capability, or at Jenkins and Deno's C level of specifying performance. Regardless of whether the term entering behavior is used to refer to an actual set of behaviors or to the capabilities inferred from behaviors, the reference is always to an individual's subset in relation to the total set embodied in a specific learning hierarchy. The definition is not used in reference to general performance, achievement, readiness, intelligence, or grade level in relation to some broad, undefined learning task.

This narrow definition is very useful in theoretical discussions but has, however, limited utility for the classroom. As a practical matter it is often necessary to make decisions about how to match instruction to broadly stated goals and objectives. To identify and measure all of the relevant behaviors that are theoretically needed to make decisions would require an exorbitant amount of time (Figure 9–1). For this reason the

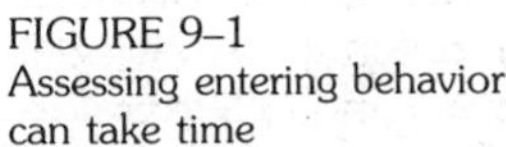

FIGURE 9–1
Assessing entering behavior can take time

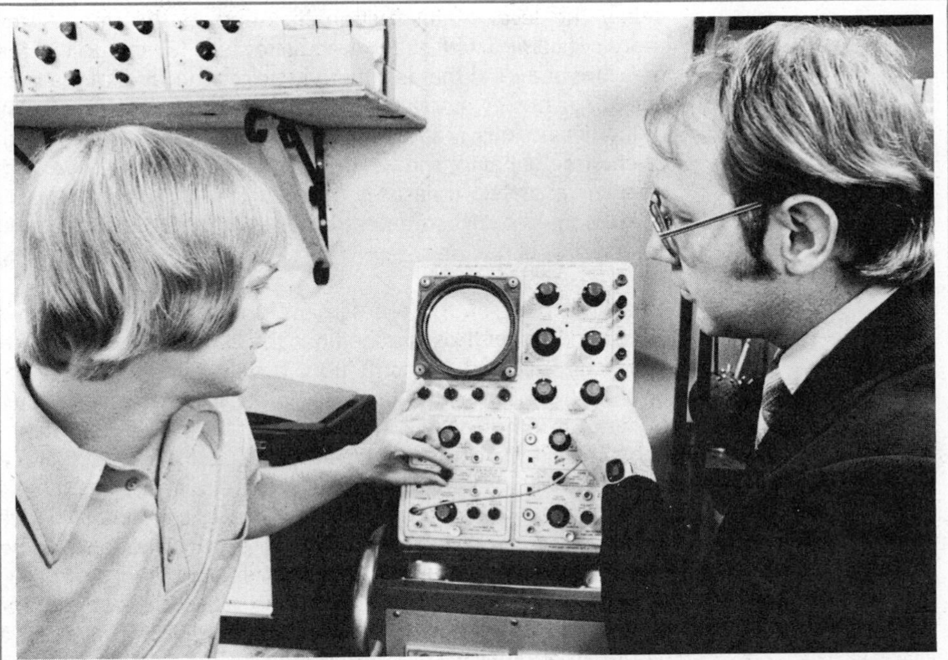

term *entering behavior* is often used more broadly by teachers and psychologists to refer to capabilities and levels of readiness for a task. Any actual behaviors referred to are used as indicators of these broad capabilities.

In this text we use the term *entering behavior* in this broader sense in recognition of the practical necessities of the classroom. We do wish to make clear, however, that in our usage of the term there is always implied a close relationship between the behaviors, or the capabilities, referred to and the learning hierarchy involved in the goal or objective the learner is to attain. Used this way, we believe, the basic concept has added utility without loss of meaning. We would also agree, however, with the argument that the more broadly the concept is applied, the less utility it has for making specific instructional decisions about individual students.

Function and process of assessing entering behavior

Fundamentally the assessment of entering behavior does not differ from other assessments of human capabilities. The basic function of any assessment is to measure, under a specific set of conditions, those behaviors that the individual is capable of performing. The unique function provided by an assessment of entering behavior is to determine the performance capabilities of the learner prior to the time instruction begins. As the definition of entering behavior was stated, the function of assessing entering behavior is also limited to only those behaviors believed to be prerequisite to learning the instructional task. It is not a general fishing expedition without any relationship to the instructional tasks.

A distinction needs to be made, however, between tests of entering behavior and pretests. Both are used to measure students' entering behaviors in relation to a unit of instruction, but there is a difference in the base point of the skills measured by the two types of tests. A pretest is used to measure performance that is to be developed in the instructional unit. The content of the test will, therefore, not measure performance below the level of instruction included in the unit. A test of entering behavior is more concerned with the prerequisite skills for the unit of instruction and will therefore measure at a level that is generally below the level of instruction. The entering behavior test may, however, overlap with the content measured by a pretest because these higher-level skills may also be entering behaviors. It is quite possible to have a test of entering behavior measure skills below, at, *and* above a particular unit of instruction, whereas a pretest measures only skills within the level of the instructional unit. This overlapping of measurement aims suggests that many pretests can be used as tests of entering behavior.

The final goal of the assessment process should be, in most cases, a micro-level determination of those capabilities the learner has acquired that are part of the learning hierarchy involved in instruction. It will not be possible to do this in all cases. First of all, the goals may not be stated precisely enough to allow for this level of specificity. Second, it is not always necessary to determine a student's precise level of entering behavior if instruction will begin at a fixed point and proceed to another fixed point because only certain instructional materials are available for the instructional task. In this case, if the student has the necessary entering behaviors but not all of the terminal behaviors to be developed, the instruction will be repetitious to the extent that it repeats previously learned tasks. It may be more pragmatic to forego a precise assessment of entering behaviors and allow the overlapping of instructional effort to occur. Trying to completely match the entering level of every student in the class would, in addition to the time it takes to conduct the assessment, create a tremendous scheduling problem unless the instructional materials were designed for individualized instruction.

Whereas the final goal of assessing entering behavior should be at the micro level, during the early stages a macro level may be more appropriate for two reasons. The first is that during the early planning stages more general estimates of the performance level may be all that are necessary for the macro-level decisions being made at that time. The second reason is that a macro-level assessment can also act as a screening process for determining those levels at which a micro-level assessment is most appropriate.

Between the early macro-level goals and the final micro-level goals, there may be several levels at which assessment takes place. This will depend on the instructional task and the particular circumstances.

Implied in the above statements is the suggestion that the assessment of entering behavior should start in the earliest planning stages. In fact, at the broadest macro level, assessment starts when you are told the age and grade level of the children. Since it is obvious that not all children at the same age or grade level are similar, the process needs to be pursued further. Assessing entering behavior will usually continue from the earliest planning phase on into the actual implementation phase. One reason is that during the earliest planning phase a teacher has not yet had any actual contact with the learners. Only macro-level information may be available at that time, and micro-level assessment will need to wait until the teacher has had a chance to interact with the students.

A second reason that assessment of entering behavior is likely to continue on into the implementation phase is because a teacher does not deal with one set of goals and plans but with a series of goals and plans throughout the year. While we may have the year's curriculum planned ahead, we usually cannot make too many micro-level decisions about our later plans until we have gotten some feedback on the results we obtained with our earlier plans. In other words, we will not be able to obtain accurate and up-to-date information about a student's entering behavior for a particular task until we have completed the instruction of some lower-level tasks.

One aspect of assessing entering behaviors is that the process occurs in a variety of contexts. During the planning phase the context may be rather quiet and relaxed, but during the implementation phase it may need to occur under fairly hectic conditions in the classroom. Without a clear focus on the function of the process and an efficient means of achieving it, the distracting context can result in much information being missed that could be used to improve the micro-level decisions still to be made.

1. How do the objective and process in an assessment of entering behavior distinguish this type of assessment from other assessments of human behavior?

MEASUREMENT AND EVALUATION

Before proceeding any further into the various approaches used to analyze entering behavior, we believe it will be useful for you to understand more fully some issues related to the measurement and evaluation of human behavior.

Distinction between measurement and evaluation

As with any assessment process, the evaluation of entering behavior involves the collection and evaluation of data. Psychologists working in the field of tests and measurement use the term *measurement* to refer to the collection portion of the process. According to Stevens (1951, p. 1), "in its broadest sense, measurement is the assignment of numerals to objects, or events, according to rules." We measure height and weight following certain rules and then assign some numerical value to the measurements. We do not assign numbers in all cases of measurement, especially when using criterion-referenced measuring instruments. Here the symbols assigned may be equivalent to + or −, since the measuring instrument sets a single standard and the individual either meets or fails to meet the absolute standard set by the objective.

When evaluating data we go beyond the concept of measurement and make a judgment about the measurements taken. The judgments can be in terms of either a norm-referenced standard or a criterion-referenced standard. Applied to the process of assessing entering behavior, the distinction between measurements of behavior and evaluating these measurements should be clearly made, since separate problems are associated with each.

Reliability

One of the basic rules of measurement is that we need a measuring instrument that is reliable (Figure 9–2); that is, we need an instrument that reduces the error in our measurements and gives us identical or consistent measures from one time to the next regardless of who may be using the instrument. For measuring height we usually use a ruler made of a relatively solid material. We do not use a rubber band. If we did, our measurements would be unreliable due to variations in how much the rubber band was stretched.

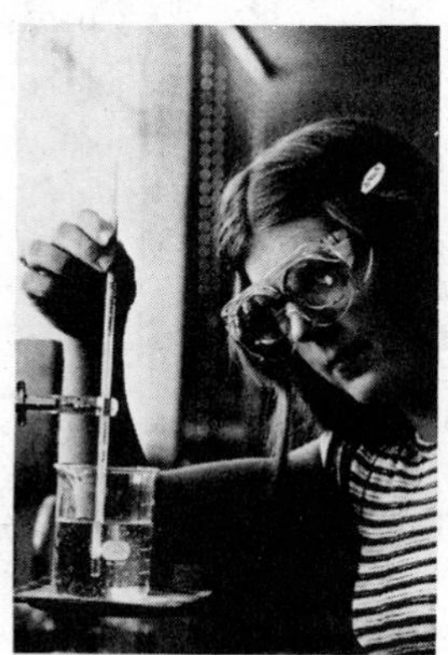

FIGURE 9–2
Measurement requires reliable instruments

When measuring human abilities we are faced with the same problem. The instrument we use must give us similar measurements time after time regardless of who is administering it. If the instrument is not reliable, it is useless. Several procedures are used to determine the reliability of a test instrument. All involve the taking of two or more measurements and determining the amount of agreement between them.

Test-retest reliability. One procedure used to obtain an estimate of reliability is to have the same individual take the same test on two different occasions. Generally, the longer the time interval between administrations of the test, the lower will be the reliability of any test. Some tests are not reliable for even very short periods and therefore are useless as measuring instruments.

Alternate-forms reliability. The reliability of a test is also determined by giving the same individual two separate forms of a test to determine the amount of agreement between the two. It is assumed that each test is a sample of items that could be used to measure the same characteristics.

Split-half reliability. Where alternate forms are not available, the internal consistency of a test will serve as an estimate of the reliability and is called the "split-half reliability." Here the individuals' performance on the odd-numbered items is compared with their performance on the even-numbered items.

These three measures of reliability are used with pencil-and-paper tests such as the commonly used achievement tests. We are not always dealing with pencil-and-paper tests, however; quite often psychologists and teachers are rating or classifying behavior.

Inter-rater reliability. An estimate of inter-rater reliability is used to express the amount of agreement between two or more people observing the same behavior. When an observational strategy results in a high degree of inter-rater reliability, it is much more likely to be a useful technique because of the agreement on what has been observed. If there is little or no inter-rater reliability when using a particular technique, then it is useless because we cannot be sure what it is we are observing. The more these observational techniques rely on the observation of actual behaviors that are objectively described, the more likely they are to achieve higher levels of inter-rater reliability. Techniques requiring observers to draw inferences or classify behaviors on the basis of loosely stated standards will result in lower inter-rater reliability.

Validity

It is possible to have highly reliable measurements that are useless. In order to be useful, a measurement must be reliable and also valid for its intended purposes. The weight of a desk, even though we may have almost perfect reliability of measurements, is an invalid measure for determining whether or not it will fit through the doorway of a room.

Applied to psychological and educational tests, validity does not have a single meaning but at least four meanings.

Face validity. Probably the most widely used and possibly the most deceptive measure of validity is how well a test appears to measure what it is intended to measure. One of the serious problems in evaluation is that many psychological tests have a high level of face validity but nothing else to justify their use.

Content validity. When referring to content validity, we are trying to determine whether or not a test measures the domain of learning or subject matter it is designed to measure. For example, if a test is to measure a student's knowledge of life in the early American colonies, then all of the test questions should be clearly related to that topic and presented in a manner the student is able to understand. To have a high level of content validity the test should not include unrelated topics, nor should it become a reading test for the poor readers in the class.

Predictive validity. Another type of validity is how well one measure of behavior is able to predict another measure of behavior. Different authorities have used different terms and subdivisions for this concept, but the basic notion is that of prediction. In an attempt to simplify the issues, we have chosen to ignore some of the traditional terminology.

How validly a test is able to predict some future measure of behavior is one aspect of predictive validity. The second measure of behavior is sometimes on a similar task but not always. Another aspect of predictive validity is when we use one measure of behavior as an estimate of a person's current capability on another task. The instrument used to predict may measure a small sample of a larger set of response capabilities or it may be a different but highly related set of behaviors. Regardless of the measures taken, if they are intended as a means of predicting the person's current capability in the larger or second set of behaviors, then the relevant question is how accurately the measure is able to do this.

When tests do claim to have predictive validity, the validity is likely to decrease as the time span increases. Also, as the differences in behavior between the two measures increase, the validity is likely to decrease. In view of the concept of transfer of training, this is quite logical since in both cases there is a greater demand on the transfer in terms of either time or task, and in most situations both.

Construct validity. Compared with other types of validity, construct validity is by far the most difficult to deal with. It is used in relation to how well a test measures some intangible property such as intelligence or creativity. We are not concerned primarily with this type of validity in this chapter and therefore will delay fuller explanation until Chapter 23, where we discuss in some depth the hypothetical construct of intelligence. We would like to point out, however, that many poor decisions can be made on the basis of test results due to a lack of understanding of construct validity. The same is also true of content and predictive validity, but in those cases errors may be more apparent. Labeling a test as measuring some hypothetical construct such as visual perception often leads people to judge the test on the basis of face validity alone. With hypothetical constructs this is likely to be a deceptive estimate of validity. Having deceived ourselves into believing that the test measures what it says it measures, we may then go on to make some totally erroneous decisions if the test does not have a fairly high degree of construct validity.

2. How does (do):
   a. The concept of reliability differ from the concept of validity?
   b. The four measures of reliability differ from each other?
   c. The four types of validity differ from each other?

DESCRIPTIVE STATISTICS

Closely associated with measurement and evaluation is the field of descriptive statistics. Some techniques such as graphs and averages are encountered in our everyday lives. Other techniques are less familiar. Because you are likely to encounter these statistical concepts at some time in your career, we have included a description of them here. These concepts are also necessary for a fuller understanding of psychological tests and the evaluation of human behavior.

At times you may have occasion to use these statistical procedures. For this reason we present the formulas and computational procedures involved in using the techniques. Since you may not need these skills at the present time, we offer this information in the Appendix at the end of the book.

Raw scores

The data used in descriptive statistics are the measurements we take. The measures derived from psychological and educational tests are referred to as *raw scores.* By themselves they have very little meaning. It is only when a raw score is considered in relation to other scores or some standard that it takes on meaning. For instance, to state that a child had a raw score of seven on the Boehm Test of Basic Concepts is probably meaningless. Only if we know the age or grade level of the child and how that score compares with those of other children of a similar age does it take on meaning. In this case even knowing which seven items were responded to correctly may be of little value because by sheer chance the child should have gotten more than seven correct. For that reason we should not assume that the score of seven means the child has mastered that many concepts. Without knowing how many items are on the test (there are 50), we would not even know how many the child apparently does not know.

Frequency counts and graphs

One use of descriptive statistics is to describe a set of raw scores. The most common descriptive statistic is a simple count of how frequently a certain raw score is observed. For instance, in a particular class of 30 children we may find the frequency count of the students' heights shown in the accompanying table.

Height	*Frequency*
68″	1
67″	2
66″	2
65″	3
64″	3
63″	4
62″	5
61″	4
60″	3
59″	2
58″	1
57″	0
Total	30

To illustrate the data we can present it in the form of a bar graph as in Figure 9–3. Frequency counts and graphs are used to present information in a manner that makes it easier to interpret or understand. They are essentially a means of imposing some organization on the data.

Normal distributions

In many populations of naturally occurring objects or events, the frequency distribution of measures shows a fairly consistent pattern. For instance, if we measured all children in all classrooms of the same grade level as our hypothetical class, we have a fairly good idea of what the scores would look like when plotted on a graph. Assuming that our hypothetical class is not unusually tall or short for most children in that grade level, the scores of the total population will tend to cluster around 63 inches. As the measurements get greater or less than 63 inches, we will encounter fewer

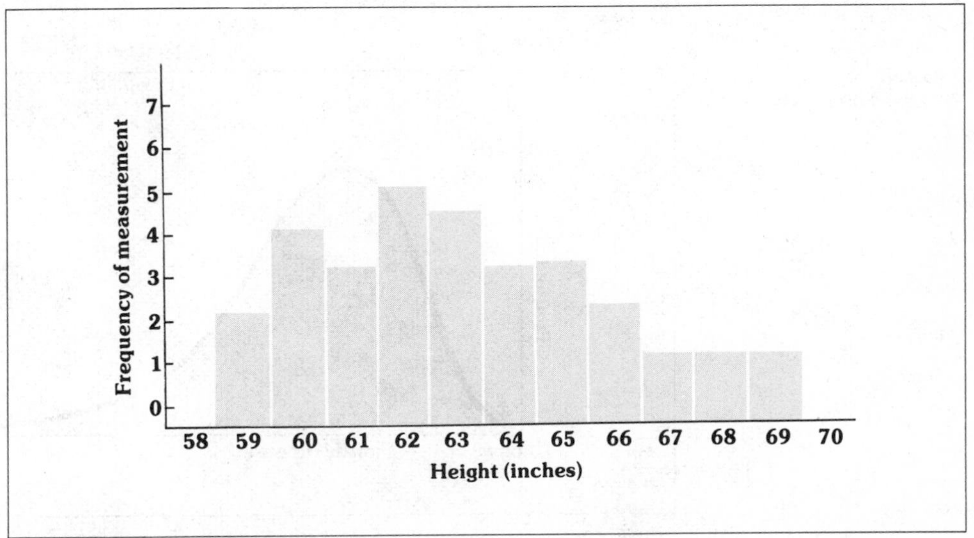

FIGURE 9–3
Heights of the children in the class

FIGURE 9–4
A normal distribution

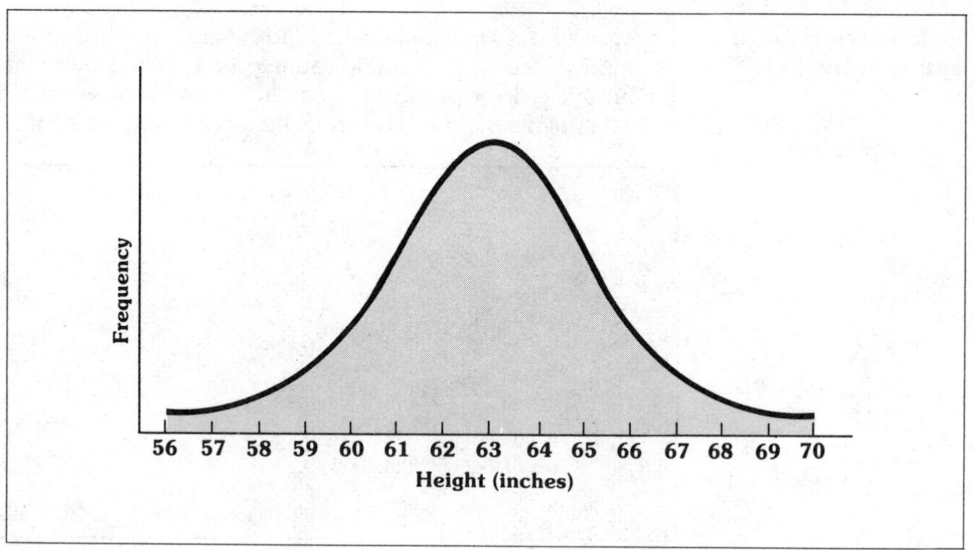

children having that height. In fact, beyond a certain point the frequency with which we encounter specific measurements will decrease rather rapidly and then gradually level off. If we plot the data in the form of a line graph, they will resemble a bell shape (see Figure 9–4). This is referred to as a *normal distribution.*

Skewed distributions

We do not always find data fitting the normal distribution. For example if we were to plot the family incomes of our large population of children, we would find the bell shape somewhat distorted. Because in the population a few families will have extremely high incomes, the bell will have a long sloping curve on the side toward the high incomes. A curve of this shape is referred to as a *skewed distribution;* an example is shown in Figure 9–5.

FIGURE 9–5
A skewed distribution

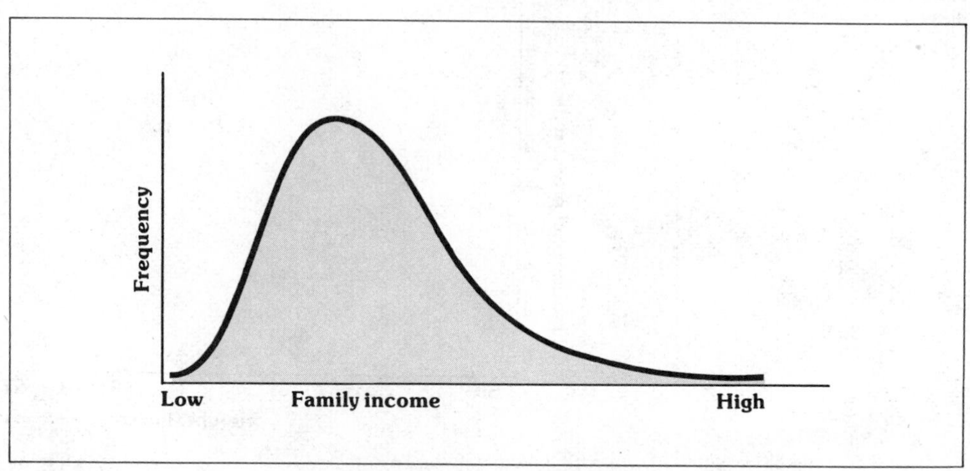

Distributions can be either positively skewed or negatively skewed depending on the direction of the few relatively large or small scores. In our example the distribution is *positively skewed.* A distribution with a few relatively small scores would be *negatively skewed.*

Mean, median, mode

At times we are presented not with data but with a description of what is called its "central tendency." Here the object is to reduce the data down to a single figure that best describes all the data. One way of doing this is to compute the average height, which in our example is 63 inches. More technically this is referred to as the *mean* height. This measure takes into account the frequency of the various measures and the absolute value of the various measures.

Another measure of central tendency is the *median.* This descriptive measure indicates the point at which half the scores are above and half below. In a normal distribution the mean and the median would be the same. In our example, 15 scores are above 62½ inches and 15 are below. This differs from the mean of our data because the mean is more sensitive to the few taller heights. The median as a measure ignores the absolute values of the measurements and describes the data only in terms of its frequency around a central point.

A third measure of central tendency, the *mode,* considers only the frequency of measures. The mode is the most frequently occurring score without regard to the value of the score. Often it is a single score somewhere near the middle of the set of scores, but it does not have to be either a single score or in the middle. In our case it happens to be because of the numbers we chose (it is 62 inches). With other data the mode could occur at any point along the continuum of measures. It is also possible that two measures will be tied for the highest frequency. In this case we refer to the data as being *bimodal* to indicate that there are two modal scores in the data.

Range

In addition to describing the central tendency of data, there are ways of describing how a set of measures spread out from the central point. One way is to state the range of scores. The range describes the distance between the highest and lowest scores in the distribution of measures. It does not, however, describe the way the measures distribute themselves between these two points.

> 3. What do the concepts of mean, median, and mode have in common? How do they differ from the concept of range?

Variance

To describe the amount of deviation of individual measures from the mean score, we use the statistical concept of variance. The variance refers to the dispersal of a set of scores around the mean of that set. This is an extremely useful statistic in formal analyses of data but by itself less useful for classroom teachers.

Standard deviation

In describing the variation found in test scores and other types of human performance, the standard deviation is frequently used. It is a statistical concept based on the square root of the variance for a set of measures. Regardless of the set of measures we are working with, the standard deviation provides a way of transforming data into a uniform measure of the spread of scores. One standard deviation is, in effect, the average of the deviations from the mean for the group. By knowing the mean for a group of scores, we usually view any particular score as being average, above average, or below average. By knowing the mean and the standard deviation for a set of scores, we can tell whether above- or below-average scores deviate from the mean more or less than the average for the group. For instance a score that is not only below average but also deviates below the mean by more than the average deviation, or standard deviation, is likely to be considered low on two measures of what is average for most of the population.

Standard deviations are always stated relative to the mean for the group (i.e., above or below the mean, or plus or minus). Approximately two thirds of all scores for a group will fall between one standard deviation below the mean (−1 standard deviation) and one standard deviation above (+1 standard deviation). Approximately one sixth of the scores will be above one standard deviation and a similar amount below one standard deviation. Only 2.5 percent of all scores are two standard deviations above the mean and a similar percentage are two standard deviations below the mean.

For instance in some states part of the legal definition of mental retardation is based on an intelligence score that is at least 1.5 standard deviations below the mean score for that test. Knowing this much information, we can reasonably assume that for every 1,000 children living within a school district, 6.7 percent or approximately 67 children could, on the basis of test scores alone, be classified as mentally retarded. This does not mean that this many children will be placed in special-education classes in the school district. Some may be so severely handicapped that they are institutionalized and never attend the regular school. Other children, whose scores would be low enough to allow the school to classify them as mentally retarded, do well enough in the regular classroom so that they are not placed in special classes. The standard deviation does allow us to estimate the number of individuals that may have special educational needs.

Standardized scores

There are a variety of other standardized scores, such as the z score and T score, but all are a transformation of the mean and standard deviation of a set of scores. For example, a score of 500 on the Scholastic Aptitude Test of the College Entrance Examination Board is not the student's raw score on the test but is a standardized score derived from all the raw scores of those who took the test. On this particular test the mean is always represented by a score of 500. Scores of 400 and 600 represent the standard deviation multiplied by 100. A raw score that is one standard deviation below the mean of all scores would, therefore, be reported as a score of 400. In the other direction a score two standard deviations above the mean would be reported as a score of 700. Since only 2.5 percent of all scores are likely to be two standard deviations above, a score of 700 or more would indicate a very high level of achievement. Most scores (68 percent) fall between 400 and 600, and only 13.5 percent fall below a score of 400.

This same type of transformation is used for T scores, except in this case the mean is 50 and the standard deviation is multiplied by 10. Some IQ tests have a mean of 100 and use a multiplier of 15 for the standard deviation.

Percentile ranks

Another way of giving meaning to raw scores is to convert them to percentile scores. A percentile score ranks a person's score in relation to the scores of others without reference to variations in distance between scores. A person with a percentile rank of 80 is one who has met or exceeded the performance of 80 percent of the individuals in the group. For any given set of scores, there are typically several individuals with the same raw score near the middle of the distribution. For this reason near the 50th percentile an increase of one point in raw score may move a person up several percentile points since it moves the person above several others. At the lower and upper extremes one score point may have no effect on a person's percentile rank because there are no other raw scores in between. Percentile ranks therefore indicate only the sheer number of individuals equaled or surpassed, without reference to the absolute difference in raw scores.

Stanine scores

Because percentile ranks spread scores out on a scale that has many discrete points, people are led to interpret small differences in percentile scores as indicating a real difference. Whether there is any practical difference between a percentile rank of 52 and 53 is questionable, but people are apt to interpret it as indicating a real difference. As a means of avoiding interpretation difficulties of this type, stanine scores were developed. Stanine scores are reported on a scale of nine (Figure 9–6). The scores in effect are categorized into nine groups, with one representing the lowest category of scores and nine the highest. Within each stanine there will be a range of actual raw scores. In this way the fine distinction between individuals is somewhat blurred.

FIGURE 9–6
Stanine scores are reported on a scale of nine

Pupil Information Box

If a separate answer sheet is being used, do not make any marks on this test booklet.

Name ______ (last) ______ (first) ______ (initial)

Boy ☐ Girl ☐ Grade ______ Teacher ______

School ______ Date of Testing ______ (Year) ______ (Month) ______ (Day)

City ______ Date of Birth ______ (Year) ______ (Month) ______ (Day)

State ______ Age ______ (Years) ______ (Months)

	Number Right	Scaled Score	Grade Equiv.	%ile Rank*	STANINE*
TEST 1: Vocabulary					1 2 3 4 5 6 7 8 9
TEST 2: Reading Comprehension					1 2 3 4 5 6 7 8 9
TEST 3: Math. Concepts					1 2 3 4 5 6 7 8 9
TEST 4: Math. Computation					1 2 3 4 5 6 7 8 9
TEST 5: Math. Applications					1 2 3 4 5 6 7 8 9
TEST 6: Spelling					1 2 3 4 5 6 7 8 9
TEST 7: Language					1 2 3 4 5 6 7 8 9
TEST 8: Social Science					1 2 3 4 5 6 7 8 9
TEST 9: Science					1 2 3 4 5 6 7 8 9
Total Battery (Test 1 through Test 9)					1 2 3 4 5 6 7 8 9
Total Reading (Test 1 + Test 2)					1 2 3 4 5 6 7 8 9
Total Mathematics (Test 3 + Test 4 + Test 5)					1 2 3 4 5 6 7 8 9

***Percentile Ranks and Stanines based on tables for Beginning ☐ End ☐ of Grade**

Source: Reproduced from the Stanford Achievement Test. Copyright © 1973 by Harcourt Brace Jovanovich, Inc. Reproduced by special permission of the publisher.

Describing errors of measurements

Standard error of measurement. Any time we take measurements we are likely to find variations because not all sources of error can be eliminated. If we take a large number of measurements and we know the variance and number of measurements we are dealing with, we can estimate the amount of variation, or error, we are likely to find in our measurements. This estimate is referred to as the *standard error of measurement.* Generally when we have a large number of measurements and the variance is small, the standard error of measurement is small. Conversely, when the variance is large and/or the number of measures is small, the standard error of measurement is likely to be large. In interpreting scores we should take this factor into account, especially if the standard error of measurement is large. Under these conditions, we are less certain whether any particular measure represents an individual's true performance level.

Confidence intervals. The standard error of measurement is often reported as confidence intervals. The confidence interval of a person's score is reported in terms of a range of scores and a certain level of confidence (for instance, 95 percent) that if tested again this person's score would still fall within that range.

4. In order to give meaning to a student's raw score, what four statistical techniques were presented? What were the two statistical methods of describing errors in our measurements?

DIFFERING APPROACHES TO THE ANALYSIS OF LEARNERS

There are many ways that teachers can, and do, look at their students. Most analytic views seem to fit in two dimensions: descriptive and comparative.

Descriptive and comparative dimensions of analysis

Descriptive dimension. There are many terms used to describe the characteristics of humans. Some are part of our everyday language and others are technical terms in the field of psychology. The terms can describe a person's general traits, abilities, motivation, cognitive processes, physical characteristics, socioeconomic status, and specific behaviors. As we have pointed out previously, our choice of descriptors is based on our observations of the person's behavior. In some cases the descriptors are references to the person's behavior; at other times the descriptors express our inferences about the person.

Descriptors also seem to be used to make generalizations about a person. For instance, when we say a person is kind, we are inferring that the intent behind his/her acts is primarily to benefit someone else. If we use the term to refer to the person's typical way of responding to people, then we are not only making an inference but also generalizing across situations and would probably be surprised to see the person commit an unkind act.

The degree to which a descriptive approach uses terms that describe behaviors, inferences, and generalizations needs to be considered. Our emphasis on behaviors may lead you to expect us to reject the use of inferences and generalizations, but these can be very useful at times. The decision as to when inferences and generalizations are more useful depends on many factors such as the amount of data available, the importance of the decision, and the kind of decision to be made. We do believe, however, that descriptors of behavior are less subject to misinterpretation.

Comparative dimension. Our descriptors, in addition to describing a person's characteristics, have some implied comparative basis. Probably most descriptors are based on a comparison between the individual and other individuals or groups. If we say a person is intelligent, the implied comparison is with other individuals of the same age and circumstances with whom we have had some contact or know about. The comparison group provides a norm against which we make our comparisons, hence it is norm-referenced.

We can also make criterion-referenced descriptions such as, "John can write his name and count to ten." There is no comparison implied between John and anyone else. There is only a comparison between John's performance and the requirements of the task; does John reach the standard or not? A nonbehavioral example would be to state that John is tall enough to reach the cookie jar. The comparison is between John's height and the normal position of the cookie jar.

To some extent our descriptions may be both criterion-referenced and norm-referenced. To say, "John can write his name and count to ten, and he is only four years old," we use only criterion-referenced statements, but the norm-referenced implication that John is also ahead of most children his age is achieved through the pairing of criterion-referenced statements. The inference, if it is made, has to be attributed to the receiver of the information but this is often clearly intended.

Whether to use an analysis based on a comparative or descriptive dimension depends to a large extent on the decision to be made and the conditions under which they need to be made. Generally, however, norm-referenced comparisons may be more appropriate when the decisions involve grouping of students, whereas the criterion-referenced approach may be more useful for selecting specific tasks to present to the student.

Maturational approach

The term *maturation* as it is used in the study of child development has a fairly precise meaning. It refers to a biologically controlled process whereby an individual from the moment of conception until death proceeds through a series of qualitative changes. The sequence never varies but may proceed at different rates for different individuals. An example of maturation is the attainment and loss of deciduous and permanent teeth. Each step in the process is dependent upon attainment of the earlier steps. Some proponents of the approach depend upon measurements of skeletal growth and dental records to derive an estimate of the individual's maturation level. For some children the rate of maturation is much faster than for others.

Adherents of this position point out that development is dependent upon the complementary and interacting processes of maturation and learning (Figure 9–7). Learning will not affect the rate of maturation but it is necessary to enhance the progress of maturation. Adherents also present evidence to demonstrate that given a large number of measures on a child, including achievement tests, the data will all tend to show a similar rate of progress. Even more interesting is data which indicate that efforts to speed up academic achievement have only short-term effects. As soon as the efforts to accelerate achievement cease, the rate of progress drops back to the general rate of development. Also, periods of deprivation are shown usually to have only short-term effects.

While these proponents of the maturational approach put forth considerable evidence to support their position, from the standpoint of evaluating entering behavior, the position presents a problem in circularity. Since maturation per se cannot be observed directly, we first need to gather various measures about the child. Having gathered these, we can compute a growth curve for the child and establish the child's current maturational level. This presumably should guide our presentation of tasks. The data we gathered to compute the guide could, however, have just as easily served as a guide.

A different approach to maturation is taken by Piaget and his followers. They share many of the same assumptions as the other maturational proponents; however, what they study is considerably different. Rather than attempting to demonstrate the effects of maturation, they accept it as an important variable in cognitive development and try to explain its relationship to learning.

FIGURE 9–7
Development is dependent upon maturation and learning

Piaget's stages of cognitive development indicate that certain tasks cannot be logically presented to children until they have reached a certain level of maturity. The maturity coupled with appropriate experience is the key to further development. For instance, according to Piaget, asking a kindergarten child to take on the role of another person is beyond the child's capabilities.

Some of Piaget's ideas have been seriously questioned by recent research and we do not know how well his theory will stand up. There is no doubt but what maturation places some limitations on what can be learned, especially during the preschool years. Beyond the motor skills domain, however, it is not certain what restrictions maturation places on our goals and instructional strategies.

The concept of maturation is often used by teachers and parents much more broadly than it is in the psychological literature. It is common to hear teachers refer to a child as being too immature for certain situations or experiences. What is meant when a teacher contends that a student is not mature enough for junior high school is far removed from Piaget's notion of maturity. It is often difficult to get from teachers a very firm definition of what they mean when they use the term *maturity.* Often it appears to be used in relation to self-control, social behaviors, or study habits. There is very little indication that maturation has anything to do with these behaviors, but on the basis of research findings, past learning experiences are heavily implicated.

In the analysis of learners, the maturation of the learner should be taken into consideration but not confused with the role of experience. No one seriously questions that maturation and experience need to be matched to maximize learning. The real questions are about what aspects of maturation are relevant for an adequate analysis of the learner.

There is little doubt that motor skills are dependent upon sufficient neurological, bone, and muscle development. Beyond the motor skills domain there is little evidence that maturational factors are involved to any great extent. Bruner has investigated to some degree the same issues as Piaget, and he contends that we can teach any topic at almost any age level in a logical way. To Bruner it is not so much a matter of the maturational level as it is the match between the cognitive processes and the organization of the task.

Demographic approach

A long-standing approach to analyzing learners, which may have been fostered by case studies in child growth and development, is to gather data about the individuals' social background including family and community data. There is considerable correlational data linking socioeconomic factors to achievement level. These data describe populations of individuals.

When making macro decisions about large groups of students, this approach may give us some indication about the goals and level of language development we may expect from the student, and amount of support we may expect from the family. It may also help establish rapport between ourselves and the students and thereby enhance our chances of acting as a model of desirable behavior.

When we are making micro-level decisions, some demographic data may help us to gain a better understanding of an individual's perspective as it interacts with the goals and techniques used in the classroom. The demographic data may be only suggestive, however, and lead to stereotyped thinking. As long as the data about the student's family and social context are used to supplement relevant behavioral data, they may be useful in achieving some objectives in the affective domain. Also, by being aware of the student's environmental context, examples can sometimes be slanted to make them more relevant.

Personality approach

Developing out of personality theories, a large number of traits have been described. These are Maddi's peripheral characteristics we mentioned earlier. They are learned ways of behaving that are fairly general across situations. A person who is relatively reserved in one situation is to some extent reserved in other situations. One problem with using personality traits in assessments of entering behavior is that some of the older measuring instruments tend to describe only what we observe. A second problem is that the predictive validity is often fairly low; sometimes a short observation period will yield the same information as a formal test. For these reasons the use of personality tests has probably decreased considerably over the last 25 years. Also adding to this decline is the advent of behavior therapies developing out of a learning theory approach. In these therapies there is little if any concern for the "unconscious" and the "inner person" and more focus on specific behaviors and environmental stimuli. There has been a great deal of research evidence supporting this approach and little if any support for the notion that the therapies treat only the surface manifestations of the problem but not the underlying causes.

More recently many traits such as impulsiveness versus reflectivity, hyperactivity, field dependent versus field independent, and self-directed versus environmentally controlled are being studied in relation to learning. The relationship between these traits and how well a student may learn in a specific situation is sometimes weak when attempting to use the data in relation to a single student. The research evidence indicating that some of these traits are preferred ways of responding, but that the alternate mode of responding can be used by the person, may account for some of the difficulty in using this approach.

Abilities and processes approach

Personality traits are learned characteristics that guide the direction and form of our behavior, whereas abilities refer to capacities within the individual to monitor, learn from, and respond to the environment. In using the term *abilities* in reference to a particular student, we are often implying that the student either has the ability or does not have it in sufficient quantity to cope with specific tasks.

Probably the most widely studied and used (as well as misused) concept of abilities is intelligence. Intelligence tests were developed as selection devices to predict future school achievement. For this purpose they are relatively effective. While intelligence tests may act as good predictors of future school achievement, the results of intelligence tests give us very little information about what to do with the student. They do indicate in a very broad way the person's general achievement level. Some tests use a single type of task while others use a variety of tasks. The latter are obviously more likely to represent the full range of a person's capabilities.

The main problem in using an abilities approach, whether it is associated with intelligence, or musical-artistic, or mathematical abilities, is that the measures are based on current achievement levels. Those who have achieved more are assumed to have more of the ability, and vice versa. This does not rule out the possibility that on any specific task the low-ability student can master it as well as, and as fast as, the high-ability student provided the prerequisite skills are first developed. Quite often this point is ignored by teachers when using the data from tests of abilities. Due to the face validity of the test, it is easy to make the error of overlooking its inferential nature and leap to the conclusion that we have an absolute measure of a capacity for future learning. What we actually have is a measure of how full the cup is presently, but not how full the cup can become!

Another common approach to assessing students is to analyze how well they handle certain conceptual processes. Two major themes in this approach are the visual and auditory perception processes. The basic notion is that these processes follow some developmental sequence. With continued experience the individual gradually becomes more proficient in the ability to process information.

Gibson and Gibson (1955) have shown that older children are able to make finer discriminations between visual stimuli than younger children. They also found that even though there are age differences in visual discrimination, a short training period for the younger children eliminates the age differences. This called attention to two important points. The first is that visual perception does develop sequentially, and the second is that for these tasks maturation is apparently not a controlling factor even at the preschool ages involved in the study.

Source: Reprinted from the Goldman-Fristoe Test of Articulation

FIGURE 9–8
The ability to produce sounds follows a developmental sequence

The ability to produce sounds also follows a developmental sequence (Figure 9–8) from cooing, babbling, baby talk, to adult speech. A similar effect is also found with perception of speech sounds. Goldman, Fristoe, and Woodcock (1967) have developed tests measuring the ability to discriminate between speech sounds. In children between the ages of four and six, a dramatic increase in auditory perception occurs. Some children are considerably poorer than other children at distinguishing between speech sounds, and the lower performance may persist beyond the six year age level. This low performance is often taken as an indication that the children have difficulty with oral instruction. The rationale is that because they are unable to discriminate between the spoken sounds they may think something else was said to them.

While the visual and auditory tests of the discrimination process show differences in processing that follow a developmental sequence, it is questionable how much low performance on the test indicates interference with perception during instruction. A review of the literature indicates that training does improve performance on the test but has very little, if any, effect on performance in other areas. It might be that there are enough cues in the environment to supplement the discrimination ability to a point at which the person can function effectively.

Achievement approach

A more task-oriented means of assessing entering behavior is through an achievement level approach. This is done in two ways, one more general than the other. Both use a sampling procedure but the bases for the sampling are considerably different. Achievement tests are one approach with which you are all familiar. These are the yearly tests given to children in schools under very controlled conditions. Another example is the college entrance exams. Tests in this category are designed to emphasize differences between students in their general achievement level. These tests do not sample the content of instruction very systematically because items from the test are selected on the basis of their difficulty and ability to discriminate between students who have a higher or lower level of overall achievement. The result of this selection process is a test that distributes student scores widely but also one that does not measure all areas. Those areas likely to be left out of the test are those that a great many students master. These areas are also likely to be ones to which a great deal of instructional time is devoted to insure that all students will master the tasks due to their perceived importance.

Diagnostic tests also sample a person's achievement level, but the sampling is much more systematic in relation to a specific topic area or set of skills. The intent is not to rank students but to pinpoint specific strengths and weaknesses.

Both the achievement and diagnostic test methods provide data that are easier to integrate into an assessment of entering behavior than the maturational, personality, and abilities approach data because they measure student characteristics more directly related to the content of instruction.

Teacher-made tests also fall within the achievement level approach. When we refer to teacher-made tests we include formal tests, quizzes, work sheets, and homework. If an assignment requires a student to demonstrate the attainment of some behavior, then we would consider it a test. The assignment does not have to be directly related to the assigning of grades but it may be used for this purpose. The formal tests that teachers give are likely to be used for assigning grades by sampling skills that allow the teacher to discriminate between different levels of achievement; therefore they are similar to the former type of achievement test mentioned. The less formal tests, such as work sheets, are likely to serve the same function as diagnostic tests. The focus may not be on overall performance but more on specifics within the total performance.

While the maturational, personality, and abilities approaches to analyzing learners may receive a good deal of attention, when a particular child is having an unusual amount of difficulty in the classroom, the day-to-day analysis of learning occurs most often and regularly through teacher-made tests of achievement. There is a wide variation in how well this analysis is handled by different teachers. Some do an excellent job, while others know comparatively little about their students. In later chapters we shall expand on how you might improve your skills in this area.

Transfer approach

In a very general way the faculty psychologists who advocated teaching certain subjects to exercise the "muscle of the mind" were considering the problem of transfer. They believed that learning Latin and mathematics would make the person a better problem solver in all subject areas. This particular belief has been shown to be false (Thorndike & Woodworth, 1901). In a modified form the belief in the transfer of training, however, is alive and thriving. Presently transfer of training is conceived of in a variety of ways but all of them are considering much smaller, and more specific, units in the relationship.

As Wittrock (1968) points out, for teachers the transfer of training involves two aspects. One is that learning leading to the achievement of a particular objective should transfer to problems of a similar nature. This he refers to as *applicational transfer.* A second aspect of transfer is that achievement of one objective should have some transfer to achievement of other objectives. This transfer reduces the time needed for learning to occur and is termed *savings transfer.* In Gagné's approach to learning hierarchies (described in Chapter 8), savings transfer is involved, but Gagné distinguishes between lateral and vertical transfer. The lateral transfer involves transfer between component skills, whereas vertical transfer is to tasks at a higher level or transfer between sequentially related tasks. Both, however, would fit Wittrock's conception of savings transfer.

Another point Wittrock makes is that research into the phenomenon of transfer has been carried on from three perspectives. One, the most recent, is the Gagnéan approach in which transfer between tasks is considered. A second, the oldest and most simplistic, is the stimulus-response conceptualization. We have discussed transfer from this aspect in an earlier chapter. We pointed out that stimulus and response similarity was the determining factor in whether positive or negative transfer would occur. The third approach to research is through the study of verbal labels and the effect they have on learning. The verbal labels act as mediators in the learning process, and hence are often referred to as *verbal mediators.* We have also discussed the fact that learning certain labels does have a savings effect on tasks for which the mediators are appropriate. Having these labels can also have the reverse effects with other tasks, or negative transfer.

The research evidence clearly indicates that transfer of training does exist between certain tasks. This suggests that an analysis of learners should consider whether the specific prerequisite knowledge is possessed by the learner in order to enhance learning of the new task or permit application of previous learning to a specific problem.

The problem in all of this for analyzing learners is that we know very little about what is needed to bring about transfer in most school situations. At this point research is limited to a few specific situations. Beyond this, a teacher is left to make educated guesses.

In making these educated guesses a teacher should, however, distinguish between the types of data related to achievement of specific content as opposed to the transfer effect that may have been learned along with the content. As Wittrock (1968, p. 157) states it, "Transfer is not 'glued on' after learning. It is a product of learning and of the conditions of learning." As such, transfer of training is clearly in the mathemagenic domain as we define it.

5. What is the main characteristic of each of the six basic approaches to an analysis of a learner's entering behavior?

USE OF ASSESSMENT PRODUCTS

The process of analyzing learners with reference to their entering behaviors wil in a product; the product will be data. On the basis of these data (and sometin without benefit of any data) you will need to make many decisions. Throughout the text we have referred to macro- and micro-level decisions. Here we discuss the use of assessment products in terms of the macro- and micro-level decisions you will need to make prior to, or early in, the implementation of your instructional plans. Since macro-level decisions usually precede micro-level decisions, we discuss the topics in that sequence.

Macro-level decisions

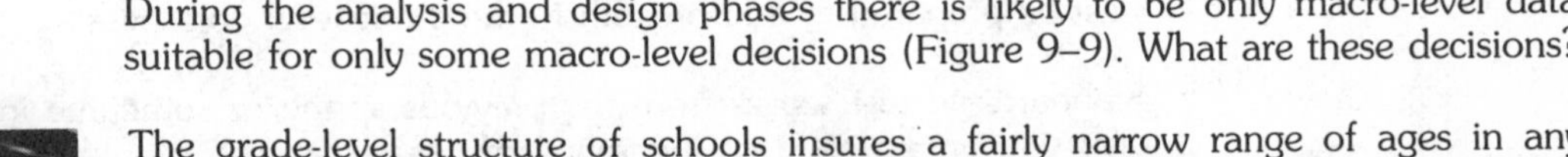

During the analysis and design phases there is likely to be only macro-level data suitable for only some macro-level decisions (Figure 9–9). What are these decisions?

FIGURE 9–9
During planning many decisions are made

The grade-level structure of schools insures a fairly narrow range of ages in any particular classroom. The maturational rates of the students are more likely to have a greater range than the chronological ages would indicate. Given the large number of students who successfully master the curriculum, it hardly seems as if there are any maturational factors that need to be adjusted for except in the motor skills domain. This view appears particularly sound when one considers that school achievement has a stronger relationship to the socioeconomic level of the students' families.

Although teachers may point to specific children whose physical maturation is slow and use this to explain why they are achieving at a low level, there are probably just as many children who could be used as examples of the reverse relationship. If this is true, then the maturational approach is adequately taken care of by the decisions that led to the present-day age/grade level organization of schools.

The fact that family socioeconomic level has a strong relationship to school achievement suggests that the demographic approach may have some utility for decisions. As we pointed out earlier, these data may suggest that for particular groups of students the *initial* level of our goals may need to be adjusted downward, but this does not mean that our terminal objectives need to be modified. Decisions about the starting point are likely to be made prior to instruction and involve the amount of review that will be included. Also, as we pointed out earlier, the demographic data may be used in decisions about the types of examples that will be worked into lesson plans to make them relevant.

For most children there is not likely to be much formal data on personalities, abilities, or cognitive processes. Informal data in the form of teachers' comments may be available. Given the variability of human behavior to match situational conditions, these data may be of very little value at the macrolevel of decisions.

Formal data about students' IQs are apt to be available in many schools. It should be remembered that an IQ is a fairly good predictor of academic achievement for most students although it may not be a valid predictor for any single individual. Even if one were to accept the notion of it being a valid predictor for an individual, it is usually the teacher's goal to upset the prediction for students with low IQs. On this basis IQ data, if used at all, may serve to alert a teacher to particular students as possibly having a higher or lower level of general achievement than the classroom-gathered data would indicate. One should be careful, however, that the teacher's view of the student is not distorted by this information. There is some evidence that teachers are seriously affected by early information of this type. Generally the bias is overcome with subsequent contact with the child, but there is no doubt some anchoring effect from the early information. An awareness of these factors should allow one to use the data without adverse side effects.

Achievement data may have more utility than other types of data in making macro-level decisions. One decision you should consider is the range of the curriculum that should be included in your instructional plans. The school assigns you that portion normally allotted to your grade and content areas. To assume that this is your total range of content is rather naive, as any experienced teacher well knows. For some students you also need to be prepared to instruct at lower levels. For other students, even if you do not intend to go above your grade-level objectives, you should at least be prepared to add breadth to the grade-level objectives.

Standardized test scores from the previous spring or sometime in the early fall can give you an estimate of the range of objectives you should be prepared to work with. You may find that particular students or small groups of children are probably far short of, or well beyond, the regular objectives. For these particular students, if their actual responses on the test are available, you may be able to detect specific problem areas. Decisions of this nature should be very tentative and more in the form of general strategies you may want to adopt to cope with the range of capabilities suggested by the test results. You may also decide to make an early search for material suitable for the upper and lower performance levels indicated by the achievement scores. A decision at this point to assign a particular student a particular task on the basis of these data would *not* be appropriate. Micro-level decisions of this type should be delayed until some contact has been made with the student. Once instruction has begun, the student's response should provide more precise data on which to base the micro-level decisions.

The achievement data should, in addition to helping you decide the range of goals you may need to cope with, help you decide the levels at which you should be prepared to begin micro-level assessment. These decisions can be in terms of either the entire group or particular students. For particular problems the students may have to solve, you may ask yourself which rules will be prerequisites and how you may test for them. For particular concepts you may want to decide whether the concept is learned at various levels of sophistication or as it relates to particular subject areas. You also may want to test for related concepts that may be fairly synonymous with the necessary concepts that may be missing. In this way you may be able to quickly establish a starting point for a micro-level assessment.

Past classroom work also may provide some useful data for decisions about starting level. If the products are fairly recent, they usually will be more helpful than those produced longer ago in time. An exception to this may be in the area of data pertaining to affective and mathemagenic behaviors, since these tend to be relatively persistent over time. Cognitive and motor skills are more likely to be affected by additional training and, with memorization, prolonged periods of disuse are likely to result in lowered levels of performance. If forgetting is apt to be a problem, the former performance should be an aid to relearning, thus affecting decisions about the time you may need to devote to reviewing the material.

Micro-level decisions

Once the process of assessing entering behavior has reached the micro level, the range of decisions narrows down to whether or not the student possesses the particular entering behavior and what should be our next procedure. If we assume the student does have the capability, we have three decisions confronting us. One is whether or not we should assess the next higher level of performance to see if this might not also be an already developed behavior. If it is, it makes little sense to spend instructional time since there would be no increase in performance level. There may even be detrimental consequences if the student finds the instruction boring or develops poor work habits in the nonlearning situation.

A second possibility may be that we decide the student has the necessary entering behavior at the level assessed but is not likely to have the next higher level. In this situation we may decide to assess for other entering behaviors that are also necessary for the instructional objective under consideration. If these have all been assessed and the learning hierarchy has several branches that may be followed, then we may need to decide which of several tasks should be the next for instruction.

The third possibility is that our assessment process has led us to the conclusion that the student does not have the necessary entering behaviors due to failure on the measurement item. From a pragmatic standpoint, this is the point at which micro-level assessments are most likely to begin in the classroom. It is not when a child succeeds that we are likely to focus on the micro levels of performance.

As long as the macro-level measures of behavior are acceptable, it is clear that we should move to higher levels or new topics. As we move up or begin new topics we are likely to observe failures, and these in turn should direct our attention to micro-level concerns (Figure 9–10). One concern should be: If failure occurs on any task, what are the lower-level tasks involved? Since the school curriculum is normally presented in terms of subject areas, this question may involve a different analytic approach to the task than is provided in the instructional materials. For example, if the materials provide for relevant practice on the task as a normal condition of learning and the practice still fails to bring about the performance, then we should begin a micro-level assessment on a lower level to see why the practice is not effective.

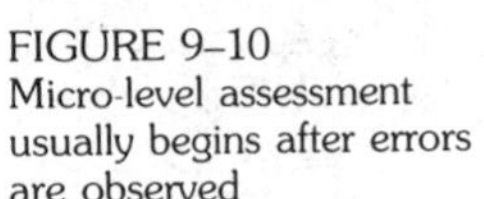
FIGURE 9–10
Micro-level assessment usually begins after errors are observed

With failure, then, our first decision should be whether relevant practice is likely to bring about learning. If this seems unlikely, then our second decision should be: What lower-level behaviors are necessary to achieve the task? This, in effect, is a decision to return to the use of our task analysis skills. It may not always be necessary to do this since it may already be clear to us which behaviors are necessary and also which may be lacking from the evidence contained in the student's performance that was judged a failure. In this case our decision may be either whether further assessment of entering behavior is necessary to pinpoint the student's actual entering behaviors, or whether review and/or instruction of the missing entering behavior should be the next step. Making the latter decision may serve both assessment and instructional functions if there are no lower levels of entering behaviors that are missing. If instruction proves to be unsuccessful, then the process needs to be moved down to more basic levels. This approach may or may not result in wasted time and effort depending on how well one judges whether or not to assume that certain prerequisite behaviors are present in the student's response repertoire.

Discriminatory assessment

In our discussion of macro-level uses of the results of assessing entering behavior, we have pointed out that you can make some grouping decisions. We have tried to make it clear that these are groups for which a common, specific instructional objective is to be attained by all members. We have also tried to make it clear that these groups are composed of children having a common minimal level of specific entering behaviors. In short, we have tried to stress focusing on an instructional perspective. We hope that we have made clear the logic for this approach, which is not always found in common educational practice.

It has been a common practice to use IQ scores or other measures of "abilities" to group children. One problem with grouping procedures on the basis of abilities is the phenomenon of the "self-fulfilling prophecy." The phenomenon is that once a person is classified or labeled, the person and others around him react as if he has all the general characteristics of the category. People with low intelligence are treated as if they *cannot* learn, rather than that they *have not* learned. The reaction to this problem has been a great deal of criticism and resistance to testing of all types. There is objection to what is currently being labeled *discriminatory assessment.* As pointed out earlier, all measurement is intended to make distinctions or discriminations. The term *discriminatory assessment* does not refer to this characteristic of assessment. Instead it refers to objectional ways in which data are *interpreted* and *applied.* If the data are interpreted as indicating some capability that affects the way a person perceives herself or others perceive her, it can be detrimental to that person. Setting the person apart from the normal population sometimes has the effect of discriminating against her so that she will not have the same opportunities in life as the rest of the population. For instance, if a person is classified or stereotyped as having a learning disability on the basis of some test scores, there is a strong possibility that he will act and think as if he is not capable of learning. He is likely to avoid learning situations, thereby shutting himself off from the possibility of learning. This is to his detriment and restricts his future opportunities. The reverse can also be true. Telling someone that she has a very high IQ can result in that person assuming that all learning tasks will be easily mastered and she will inevitably know more than her peers on all topics. This can seriously affect her social relationships and create unrealistic expectations on her part. In effect, discriminatory testing creates minority groups that may be treated in a way that is detrimental to their overall development. It is a real and serious issue that needs some careful answers and a great deal of awareness on the part of educators and others who interpret test data.

This discussion is particularly relevant at this point because we have suggested that certain types of data may be profitably used by teachers and administrators to group students *to their benefit.* It is also apparent that we can group students *to their detriment.* While we want you to utilize fully the former possibilities, we *do not* want you to make the latter mistake.

It is in response to the issue of discriminatory assessment that many individuals advocate an end to standardized testing, believing it serves no useful purpose. While we agree that standardized test data are often misused and these abuses should be stopped, we do not agree that the data serve no useful purpose. We believe norm-referenced test data serve at least a limited purpose in terms of macro-level decisions. We leave it up to you and others to make the value judgment as to whether the abuses outweigh the uses, or whether another alternative will serve the same purpose and avoid the abuses. Only by focusing attention on the problem, however, will the issue be resolved.

Instructional perspective

We may not be able to avoid the possibility of discriminatory assessment, but to some extent we can lessen the effect by changing the perspective of our data interpretation. The main reason our assessment is discriminatory is because of the comparative basis for reporting data. A person's performance is compared with that of some reference group of a specified chronological age or grade level. Since grade level is largely a matter of chronological age, all normative scores are basically a matter of comparison between the child's level and the level normally found at that age. Very little consideration is given to other factors, at least on the individual level. Because this is so, we are left with the conclusion that certain individuals are progressing at a much slower or faster rate than others. It seems to be a common error to then leap to the conclusion that the variations are due to differences in ability which are thought of as innate or developmentally based. Even people well versed in the techniques of tests and measurement, or well aware of the effects of environmental factors, will make statements about an individual that imply that the level of performance is due to factors within the child and therefore outside of the teacher's control. The statement thereby becomes potentially discriminatory in its effect.

We do not mean to imply that there are no innate differences between individuals; there are. We are just pointing out that psychological and educational tests do not measure innate differences directly. They give us an indirect measure of these differences, and because the measures are indirect we are on very shaky ground in making these inferences. Also, because making these inferences can have serious and negative consequences for an individual, we should not make them in a way that may be detrimental.

To avoid this trap the assessment data can be interpreted in terms of various aspects of the broad curriculum. The argument goes like this. If progress through the curriculum is perceived as a normal, cumulative progression through a series of learning tasks that are not, and do not have to be, universally achieved at any particular chronological age, then we have a basis for a different interpretation of the assessment data. It also needs to be understood that for each of the tasks under consideration, there was a point in each person's life at which it could not be done and a point at which

FIGURE 9–11
Mastery of a task requires time

it could, with an intervening period of time when the task was being acquired and mastered (Figure 9–11). Because each person is in these same three positions at some time or other, it is a way of reacting to the basic data in a nondiscriminatory manner. It is nondiscriminatory if we are willing to leave out our value judgments concerning the age at which these points are reached. Viewed in this way the child's achievement level is interpreted as an educational or instructional statement and not as a value statement about the person.

Since we can also use the data to group the children, our groups should *not* be formed on the basis of ability to learn but rather on what is not learned and has to be learned. In this way we are less likely to view the group members in a judgmental manner and more in terms of instructional tasks.

The matter of discriminatory assessment is not inherent in the tests themselves, we contend, but is rather inherent in the eye of the beholder (and interpreter of the data). The same data can be viewed and used from a discriminatory point of view and from an instructional point of view. We certainly hope you do not use the former.

6. How are the data gathered in an assessment of entering behavior used in making both macro- and micro-level decisions? How might this information be unintentionally misused?

SUMMARY

In this chapter we first made the point that entering behavior has many meanings but has its greatest utility when used to define a student's specific set of prerequisite capabilities related to a particular learning hierarchy. Measurement was distinguished from evaluation by describing the former as assigning some numerical quantity to a characteristic or at least noting the presence of a specific quantity, whereas the latter is making judgments based on our measurements. The importance of reliability and validity was highlighted and there was a discussion of how the two are measured and used. The statistical techniques of describing measures of student performance in terms of standard deviation and standardized, percentile, and stanine scores were briefly outlined as well as the techniques of describing errors in our measurements in terms of the standard error of measurement and confidence intervals. The maturational, demographic, personality, abilities/processes, achievement, and transfer approaches to the analysis of learner capabilities were described and related to the process of assessing entering behavior. As a final set of issues, entering behavior assessment data were described as being helpful at the macro level for making grouping decisions and at the micro level for making instructional decisions. The discriminatory abuses of assessment data were brought to your attention with the suggestion that an instructional perspective can help to avoid the abuses.

SELF-TEST

1. The term readiness:
   a. Is synonymous with *entering behavior.*
   b. Is used in more serious discussions of learning.
   c. Has a *narrower* meaning than *entering behavior.*
   d. Has a *broader* meaning than *entering behavior.*

2. Assessment of entering behavior:
   a. Involves the usual assessment skills.
   b. Involves different assessment skills.
   c. Implies the timing of the assessment process.
   d. Both *a* and *c.*

3. The concept of measurement refers to:
   a. Following certain rules to assign numbers or symbols to certain characteristics of objects and events.
   b. Making judgments about certain characteristics of objects and events.
   c. Both *a* and *b.*
4. If a test has a low level of reliability:
   a. It cannot have a high level of validity.
   b. It is relatively unimportant if its validity is high.
   c. It is possible that its validity will be high.
   d. It does not effect its usefulness.
5. Measuring instruments are useful if they are:
   a. Valid but not reliable.
   b. Reliable but not valid.
   c. Both reliable and valid.
   d. Neither reliable nor valid.
6. Hilda's teacher makes the following statement: "Hilda does not comprehend what is required of her in the math lesson. I need to pinpoint the specific skills she lacks or she will never master the new skills in this lesson." Which approach to learner analysis is implied in this statement?
   a. Maturational approach.
   b. Abilities and processes approach.
   c. Achievement approach.
   d. Transfer approach.
7. A macro-level assessment of entering behavior can help you decide all of the following *except:*
   a. The range of the curriculum you will actually need to be prepared to include in your plans.
   b. The level at which micro-level instruction should be started.
   c. A general level at which instruction can be started.
   d. How to assign a particular student a particular task.
8. We are most likely to focus on a micro-level assessment:
   a. Before we start instruction.
   b. When a student is mastering a task.
   c. After instruction is completed.
   d. When a student has made an error.
9. Discriminatory assessment refers to:
   a. Using a test that can discriminate between those students who know the year Christopher Columbus came to America and those who do not.
   b. Interpreting test data from an individual in a way that may cause others to view that person as an exceptional child.
   c. Using a test that is known to show differences in language usage between black and white students.
   d. Giving one achievement test to bright students and another test to the slow students.
10. An example of nondiscriminatory assessment is:
   a. Giving a test of a particular skill and then grouping together those who have the skill needed to learn the next task.
   b. Giving all students an IQ test and grouping them into fast and slow classes for instruction.
   c. Giving different ethnic groups different tests of abilities to group them into fast and slow classes for instruction.
   d. Not using formal tests but rather relying on observations of social and emotional behavior to group students into fast and slow classes for instruction.
   e. Not using formal tests but rather relying on observations of social and emotional behavior to group students to learn the next task.

ANSWER KEY TO BOXED QUESTIONS

1. The objectives differ in that the focus of assessing entering behavior is on the prerequisite skills needed to master the instructional task. The process does not differ from other assessments of human performance except in its timing.
2. *a.* The concept of reliability refers to the stability of our measurements, whereas validity refers to the appropriateness of our measures for making certain decisions.
   b. All four measures of reliability involve a comparison but differ as to the type of comparison. Test-retest reliability is derived from two measures on the same test given at different times. Alternate-forms reliability is derived from administering different forms of the test that supposedly measure the same capability. Split-half reliability is an internal measure of reliability on different portions of the test. Inter-rater reliability is the amount of agreement found between independent raters.
   c. Face validity is a judgment of how well a test appears to measure what it is intended to measure. Content validity is in reference to how well an instrument measures a specified content area. Predictive validity is an indicator of how accurately the measure will predict either future performance or performance on some other specified task. Construct validity refers to how well a test measures some intangible, hypothetical construct.
3. All three are a single descriptor for a set of data. The range describes the variation found within the set of measurements.
4. Standard deviation, standardized scores, percentile ranks,

and stanine scores can all give meaning to a student's raw score. Standard error of measurement and confidence intervals are used to describe measurement errors.

5. Maturational approach—Measures of physical growth and achievement are combined to determine developmental patterns.
   Demographic approach—Social and historical data are gathered to determine individual characteristics.
   Personality approach—Measures are taken to identify stable traits.
   Abilities and processes approach—Measures are taken of achievement level to determine the presence of assumed abilities or psychological processes related to learning.
   Achievement approach—Measures of achievement are taken to sample a broad level of achievement or specific skills.
   Transfer approach—Measures are taken of very specific behaviors believed to be prerequisite to learning a particular task.
6. Data about broad capabilities are most appropriately used to tentatively group students, or determine the range of the instructional tasks that may be needed to meet individual differences. More precise measures of specific capabilities are appropriate for making micro-level instructional decisions about the specific tasks to assign and the techniques to be used during instruction. The information may be used to inappropriately group and/or discriminate against an individual.

ANSWER KEY TO SELF-TEST

1. *d*
2. *d*
3. *a*
4. *a*
5. *c*
6. *d*
7. *d*
8. *d*
9. *b*
10. *a*

Chapter 10

General learning conditions

HAVING ESTABLISHED our performance objectives and the instructional level of our students, we are now in the position to plan the instruction to achieve these objectives. Traditionally, instructional planning has focused on what the teacher will do or say. This is an incomplete frame of reference and has very frequently led to the implicit assumption that learning is an automatic consequence of teaching; that is, teachers have often operated on the assumption that exposure equals learning. Under this approach if students have seen, read, or otherwise come into contact with the prescribed instructional material, then it is assumed they have learned it or have learned it as well as they are able.

What is needed is a new concept of instruction as an interactive process between teacher and student, not as a one-directional relationship of teacher to student. True, in planning instruction, teachers are making decisions about what they will do, say, or present, but these decisions always must be made by considering what function or purpose the given act is intended to serve. The ultimate purpose of instruction is to promote acquisition of the desired learned capabilities. Consequently, the teacher's actions in instruction should be directed toward accomplishing this goal and not just toward "covering all the material."

The objectives for this chapter are to:

1. Demonstrate effective techniques for directing student attention to relevant information in a learning task.
2. Describe the effects of various study activities on learning and retention.
3. Develop effective questions for a lesson.
4. Identify appropriate feedback procedures.

AN OVERVIEW OF THE TEACHING/LEARNING PROCESS

By viewing teaching as an interactive process, we arrive at a definition of instruction as a set of events usually, although not necessarily, initiated by a teacher to guide the learning process of the student toward a specified outcome. Furthermore, it is possible to specify individual events in instruction and to describe their purpose in terms of their effect on the learning processes of the student. Such an analysis has been performed by Gagné (1974a) and is depicted in Figure 10–1. In his analysis, Gagné has related the individual events of instruction to the phases of learning and the processes operating in each phase.

As Figure 10–1 illustrates, the first two events of instruction establish an appropriate expectancy in the learner. Since motivation is the energizer of behavior, the first task of the teacher in instruction is to activate relevant motivation. Teachers accomplish this task in a number of ways, such as appealing to students' interests, explaining the value of what is to be learned, arousing curiosity, and other school-related motives. (For a thorough discussion of school motivation, see Chapter 24 of this book.) Next, the teacher channels this motivation into the specific task at hand by informing the learner of the expected outcome of learning, thus establishing an expectancy in the learner.

The next event of instruction is to attract and direct the student's attention to the relevant information in the learning situation that will be involved in the acquisition of the to-be-learned capability. What is important here is to make the relevant information easily discernible from the irrelevant. Teachers utilize a number of tactics to achieve this task, such as underlining or coloring, pointing to important information,

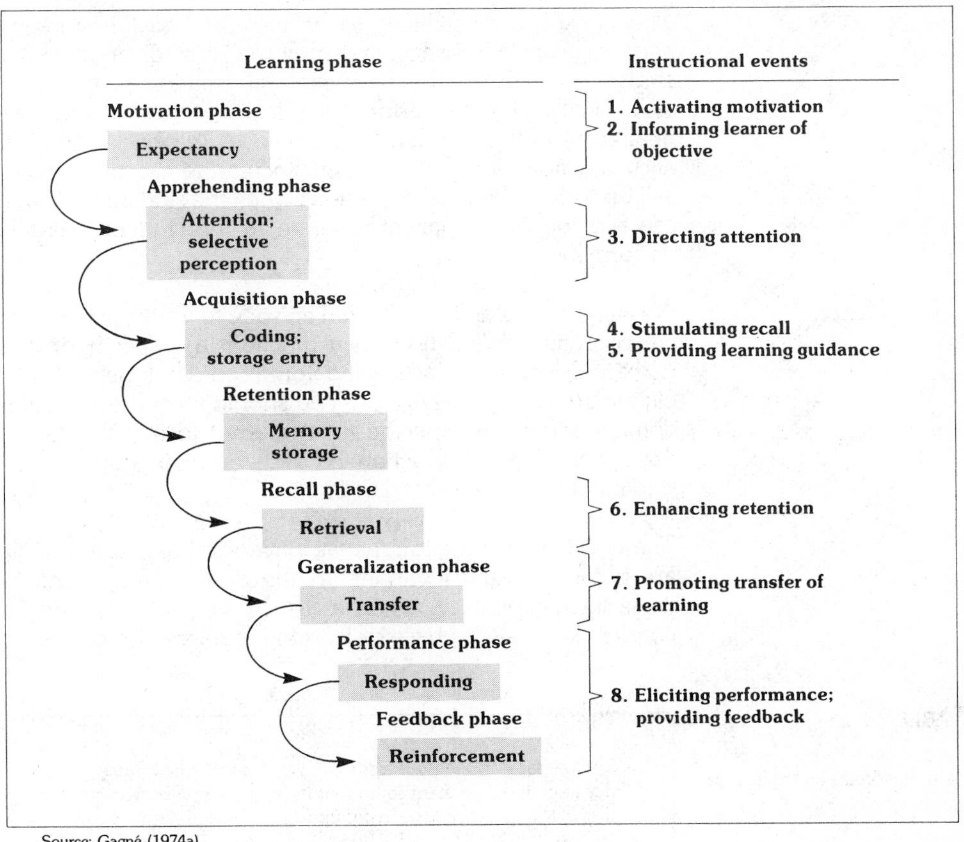

FIGURE 10–1
Relations between phases of learning and events of instruction; the latter events represent the functions performed by instruction which support internal learning processes

Source: Gagné (1974a).

and most typically giving verbal directions. We often direct attention with statements like, "Look at the example on the blackboard. Notice that the first *F*-ratio is less than one!"

According to Gagné, the fourth and fifth events of instruction support the transformation of information into the form in which it will be stored in long-term memory. This encoding requires two instructional events. First, recall of the appropriate prerequisites must be stimulated, and second, the teacher offers learning guidance by either providing or suggesting an appropriate elaborative encoding strategy. The recall of appropriate prerequisites usually can be done with the use of a verbal cue; however, the form of the learning guidance depends to a large extent upon the domain of learning to be acquired through the instruction.

Enhancing retention and facilitating the transfer of learning are executed by the presentation of additional situations that exemplify the information or skill to be learned. Especially important in facilitating the transfer of learning is the presentation of a variety of differing situations. Succeeding this presentation of examples is the instructional event of eliciting student performance. At this point in instruction the student should have acquired the intended capability; requiring its performance now serves several important purposes. First, it allows the teacher to determine whether the desired learning has indeed occurred and, if not, to apply corrective procedures immediately when they are most likely to be beneficial to the student. Second, instruction that encourages active responding of some form or another is more likely to induce the student to perform the necessary information processing required by the learning task. Finally, student performance supplies the basis for feedback to the student, the final event in the instructional sequence. Feedback that matches the student's expectancy functions as reinforcement, increasing the probability that future performance will be correct. On those occasions when the student performance is incorrect, feedback can provide additional information to the student that allows for correction of the performance.

We will examine an instructional episode to illustrate how Gagné's events of instruction are coordinated and how they function in a specific instance. The example chosen is that of a teacher instructing fourth-grade students on how to locate words in a dictionary using guide words. You should recognize this skill as being in the cognitive domain and of the specific type referred to as rule learning. A brief description of the lesson and the function of each event in guiding the learning process of the student is given in Table 10–1.

The events of instruction, as we have tried to illustrate with the preceding example, are not necessarily invariant. In the design of instruction, a teacher does not use these instructional events as a list. Rather, in designing instruction, a teacher must consider what each phase of learning requires of the student and what external events

TABLE 10–1

Lesson on locating words in a dictionary by the use of guide words

Event	*Function*
1. Teacher says, "When we want to spell a word or find its meaning, we don't want to look at every page in a section of the dictionary or read every word on a page. We may need to find the word in a hurry."	Activating motivation by describing an undesirable situation to be avoided
2. "There is a better way to find words in the dictionary. It is with the use of *guide words* provided in all dictionaries. And that's what we are going to learn now—how to use guide words to find other words."	Establishing expectancy by informing students of learning outcome to occur
3. Teacher reflects transparency of a dictionary page onto a screen at the front of the class. Points to guide words and says, "See the words in bold print at the top of the page. These are guide words. Notice there are two guides on each page, one at both the left and right columns of the page." Points to left and then right guide words.	Directing attention by both verbal directions and pointing
4. Referring again to transparency, teacher asks, "How are words arranged in dictionary?" (alphabetically) "Of the words on this page, where does the left guide word fall in the alphabetical order? The right guide word?"	Stimulating recall of previously acquired information and rules
5. Teacher states, "Notice the guide word in the left column starts a page and the right guide word ends the words on a page. As a reminder of this we can say, 'left begins, right ends.' "	Verbal guidance, including the introduction of a mnemonic, to facilitate encoding
6. Teacher asks students to get out their dictionaries and hands out sheets with five words. Students are told to find these words in the dictionary and write the guide words for each in the appropriate blanks on their sheets.	Additional examples for retention and transfer of learning, and elicitation of student performance
7. Teacher goes over the work sheet with class, calling on individual students for answers.	Providing feedback

(verbal directions, stimulus presentations) can be provided by the teacher to guide and promote the necessary learning processes. It is possible that one act or statement from a teacher can encompass several instructional events. So a teacher must not feel that eight discrete elements must be developed for each lesson to correspond to the eight instructional events of Gagné. These separate events should be looked upon as criteria for determining the adequacy of a lesson.

Many of the principles for designing instructional events can be used in teaching any learning outcome. These principles can be termed *general conditions of learning* and most often include activating motivation, directing attention, eliciting performance, and providing feedback. Other instructional principles are specific to learning outcomes in a particular learning domain and are labeled *specific conditions of learning.* These specific conditions include stimulating recall of prerequisites, providing guidance for encoding, and promoting retention and transfer of learning.

In the ensuing sections of this chapter we will examine the general conditions of learning as they are incorporated into instruction. Then we will move to an investigation of the specific conditions of learning for each of the four domains in Chapter 11. Our discussion of general learning conditions will exclude student motivation, as this topic is considered in a later chapter; therefore we will begin with the instructional event of directing attention.

DIRECTING ATTENTION

Attention can be further subdivided into phases of orientation and selective attention, or attracting and focusing the student's attention on the relevant information. Initially, the student's appropriate sensory receptor is oriented toward the source of stimulation; this capture of the student's attention is best accomplished through stimulus change. All of us have had the experience of being rousted from a state of somnolence by a monotone-voiced lecturer loudly clearing his throat. This sudden change of stimulation attracted our attention to say the least! Teachers can use stimulus change or other aspects of stimulus novelty to orient students to the appropriate source of stimulus.

Following this orientation to the stimulus source, the student must attend to those attributes of the nominal stimulus that are to be encoded into the working memory. Selective attention can be influenced in instruction by three types of events: (1) highlighting relevant information, (2) giving verbal directions and other teacher actions, and (3) providing prequestions and objectives.

Highlighting relevant information

Much laboratory work has demonstrated that the most distinctive or vivid items of information in a presentation are the most likely to be remembered by a person, as we saw in Chapter 4. This memory phenomenon is called the "von Restorff effect" after the investigator who first formally noted it. The inference is made that since a person remembered this information best, then it must have been attended to more than other information in the passage. Also, your personal experience suggests to you that the information you retain longest is that to which you attended most.

There are a number of ways teachers can make information more distinctive from its accompanying information. For printed material one can use italics, capitals, underlining, or differing colors. Pauses, differing intensity of speech, and repetition can be utilized with the spoken word. Pictorial presentations can use arrows, differing colors, or exaggerated proportions.

Klare, Mabry, and Gustafson (1955) underlined selected words in a technical training manual. Trainees who received the underlined version showed greater retention than did those who received a nonunderlined version of the same information. This result was obtained even though the trainees were given no rationale for the underlining. Cashen and Leicht (1970) highlighted by underlining in red three reading passages given to college freshmen. Students receiving the highlighted passages showed greater learning on test questions concerning the underlined statements than did the students receiving nonhighlighted passages. Students in the highlighted group also showed greater learning on test questions about statements adjacent to the underlined statements. Crouse and Idstein (1972) also found underlining to be an effective means for directing students' attention to important information in a passage.

Highlighting does not improve learning under all conditions. Hershberger (1964) examined the effects of complex typographical cues on learning from written instruction with fifth-grade students. No differences between the cued and the noncued conditions were discovered for either immediate or delayed retention. Another study by Hershberger and Terry (1965) investigated the effects of simple versus complex cues in an eighth-grade history lesson. As part of the study, three versions of a text were prepared: a version with no typographical cues as a control (1C); a version with essential content printed in red (2C); and a third version with different classes of essential content distinguished by underlining, variation in type size, and variation in ink color (5C). The results of the study are presented in Figure 10–2. Students who were given the text passages with simple cuing did not have higher overall achievement scores. However, the achievement proportion of essential content (highlighted) to enrichment content (not highlighted) was significantly higher for the simple cuing group than for either the control or complex cuing group. The simple cues seem more effective at directing attention to the cued information.

FIGURE 10–2
Mean gain scores for all subjects as a function of typographical format and type of lesson content tested

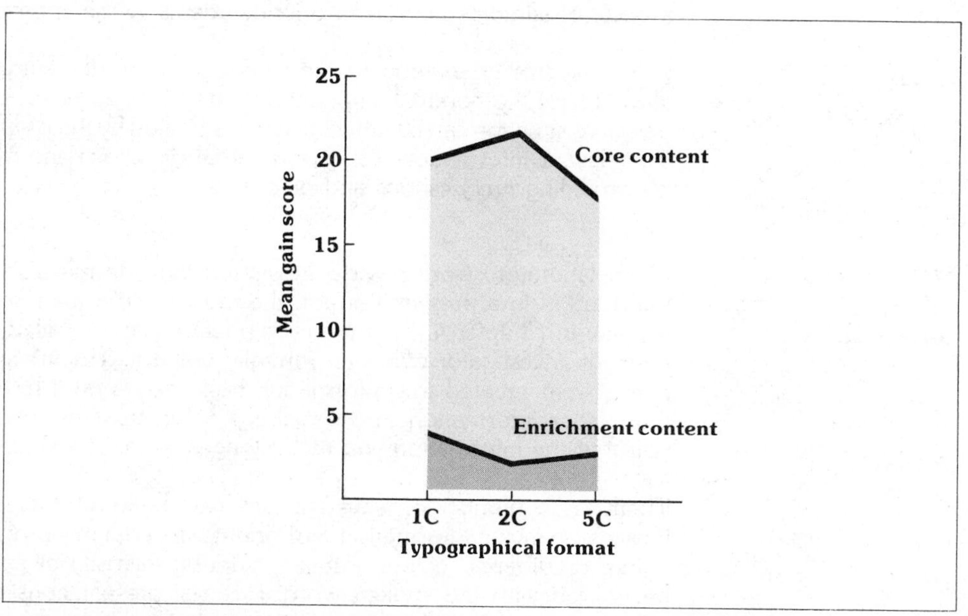

Source: Adapted from Hershberger and Terry (1965).

More recently, Bausell and Jenkins (1977), in a study involving high school and college students, found that with study time held constant underlining did not have an effect on overall retention. However, it did have an effect on what was learned, with students receiving highlighted material learning more highlighted and less non-highlighted information. This finding is in agreement with the role of highlighting in directing attention, and points to the need on the part of the teacher to insure that material highlighted in the text is indeed important information for the student.

Another potentially important application of highlighting involves elementary school children and some poor readers with comprehension problems. These people could not reliably identify informational units on the basis of their importance to the meaning of a passage (Brown & Smiley, 1977; Smiley, Oakley, Worthen, Campione & Brown, 1977). Highlighting of the most important information could direct these students' attention to this information and make it more likely to be encoded.

Most textbooks use typographical cues or some other form of highlighting material. In evaluating this feature, teachers should look for simple systems of cuing and insure that the most important information is highlighted. On occasion teachers may utilize highlighting as a means for directing student attention, especially for students who experience difficulty locating important information. Again, the teacher should use a simple highlighting technique, focusing on the most important information.

Verbal directions and other teacher actions

The predominant mode of directing attention in classroom instruction is verbal direction by the teacher. Frequent use is made of statements like "Notice the difference between . . . , Look closely at . . . , Watch carefully." Besides verbal directions, teachers often physically point in order to focus attention on relevant stimulus attributes, and obviously verbal directions and pointing are used in conjunction. Holen and Oaster (1976) obtained results showing that in a lecture a simple verbal cue such as, "this seems to be an especially significant point," led to greater retention of the information immediately following the statement. A study of note-taking habits of college students in 12 different courses discovered that students missed only 12 percent of the information noted on the board by the professor, but missed over 50 percent of the information not noted on the board (Locke, 1977). As these studies suggest, even very simple verbal statements can be effective cues for directing attention.

The effectiveness of verbal cues in directing attention varies considerably according to the age of the students. Pick, Christy, and Frankel (1972) concluded that older elementary school children have a more effective selective attention strategy than younger children. In their study, older children (sixth-graders) were better able to take advantage of knowledge given prior to stimulus presentation about what aspects of the presentation were relevant and irrelevant to the given learning task. Grote and Lippman (1972) found that providing contradictory verbal information about a task to preschool children interfered less with the performance of that task when they were given a demonstration of the desired performance, than did a contradictory demonstration when they were provided verbal direction. Smith, Ramey, and Brent (1973) taught third-grade, fifth-grade, high school senior, and college students a simple learning task with either visual or verbal cues. Verbal cues were less effective than visual cues for third-grade students, but for all other students there was no difference in the two classes of cues. Meacham and Nicolai (1975) investigated the relative efficacy of pointing, verbalizing, and looking by the teacher as cues for preschoolers. Conflicting cues for a performance task were presented to children ranging in age

FIGURE 10–3
Physical directions may work best with young students

from three to six years, then the cue the children followed was recorded. The children were more likely to follow the pointing cue when it conflicted with either verbalizing or looking. The verbal cue was preferred over the looking cue.

From the preceding studies, the conclusion can be drawn that the younger the student, the less likely it is that verbal directions from the teacher will effectively guide selective attention. With young children verbal directions should be accompanied by compatible concrete actions on the part of the teacher (Figure 10–3). For example, a preschool teacher who wishes to draw the students' attention to an object should simultaneously point and verbalize. For older students both verbal and physical directions appear to be effective in influencing selective attention.

Questions as orienting stimuli

In Chapter 7, we saw that a statement of performance objectives functions as an orienting stimulus in directing attention to relevant information. Questioning a student during learning can also serve this orienting function. Rothkopf (1963, 1966) was one of the first writers to discuss the effect of testlike events on study behaviors, or as he named them, *mathemagenic behaviors.* One very important mathemagenic behavior is selective attention. The student's attention to classes of information in an instructional presentation can be strongly influenced by questions asked during that presentation.

Rothkopf and Bisbicos (1967) developed test questions based on four categories of information contained in a 36-page reading passage. The categories of information were: (1) common phrases, defined as any common nontechnical English words; (2) technical terms; (3) measures including quantities of size, numerosity, distance, and dates; and (4) names, defined as any proper geographical or personal names or namelike words. Twenty-four completion-type test items were constructed for each category of information, and items were equally, but randomly, selected from each category to form several 48-item tests. One form of this test was used as the dependent measure and administered to all the experimental groups at the conclusion of the study.

Another form of the test was used as a pool from which to select questions to be interspersed throughout the reading passage. Some experimental groups got inserted questions before a three-page section of the passage that contained the information answering the questions; others got the questions inserted after the relevant three-page sections. More important for our current discussion, some of the experimental groups received inserted questions covering restricted information categories. For example, one group saw questions concerning only common phrases and technical phrases, while another group got questions involving only measures and names. However, after reading the 36-page passage, all groups received the posttest on all information categories.

Data analysis showed that people that had been presented restricted categories performed higher on new items from those same categories than other people. So the people that encountered measure and name questions during reading scored higher on new questions from those two categories of questions. This effect was even greater for information contained in the second half of the reading assignment.

The simplest explanation for this finding of the Rothkopf and Bisbicos study is that limiting the category of information quizzed by inserted questions focused the learner's attention on that category of information. This interpretation is further buttressed by including in the study a group designed to measure the direct informative effect of exposure to the experimental questions. This group learned the correct answers to all 48 inserted questions, then took the second test used as the dependent measure by the experimental groups. Practice on the first test did not transfer to the second test. Consequently, inserted questions in a reading passage have indirect effects on achievement by influencing selective attention and other mathemagenic behaviors.

In the next section on the student response in instruction we will review the conditions under which inserted questions improve student achievement from instruction. This brief introduction was to show how questions can direct student attention to those stimulus features to be encoded into working memory. For the teacher this research implies that the questions asked in class will lead the student to focus attention on that information and perhaps on similar information for which questions were not asked. This means that it is important for these questions to be related to the intended outcome of instruction or they could lead the student off-task. Furthermore, if all classes of intended outcome are not represented in the questions, then the student will learn a restricted set of objectives.

Attention: A caveat

Cues provided by a teacher to direct student attention can have a detrimental effect on learning, rather than the intended facilitating effect. This effect has been demonstrated in several studies by Anderson and Faust (1967). They investigated the effects of cues in learning from programmed instruction. For their studies they developed a simple self-instructional program to teach Russian vocabulary. Each frame (the information presented to a student at any one time) consisted of five simple sentences giving the Russian equivalent of an English word. Sentences were constructed such that the English word was always the subject of the sentence and the Russian word always the predicate noun. Five such sentences were arranged in paragraph form, and below each paragraph one sentence from the paragraph was repeated with the Russian word deleted and a blank in its place. The student's task was to read each frame, go to the sentence below it, and write the correct Russian word in the blank there, and then do the same for each succeeding frame.

Two versions of this program were developed; they were identical except in one version the Russian word to be placed in the blank was underlined in the paragraph. In the other version the word was not underlined. Anderson and Faust hypothesized that this typographical cue would affect how students inspected the information contained in the frame. The patterns of inspection for the same frame from the underlined and nonunderlined versions of the program are presented in Figure 10–4. After working through the program, students were given a cued recall test consisting of sentences with English nouns as subjects and their Russian predicate nouns replaced by a blank as in the program itself.

Since the learning task required the learner to associate English and Russian nouns, it was predicted that those learners who received the underlined version of the program would learn less than those with the nonunderlined program. The reason for this is that with the underlined version learners would not have to attend to the English noun to correctly fill in the blank with the Russian noun; consequently, association between the English noun and its Russian equivalent would not occur. However, as Figure 10–4 shows, learners given the nonunderlined program would have to attend to the English noun in order to correctly locate the Russian noun with which to fill in the blank. Results of the studies supported this hypothesis with the nonunderlined program learners scoring higher on the cued recall test than those learners who worked through the underlined version of the program.

FIGURE 10–4
Two versions of the copying frame (the lines trace the minimal eye movements that can be used to correctly fill in the response blank)

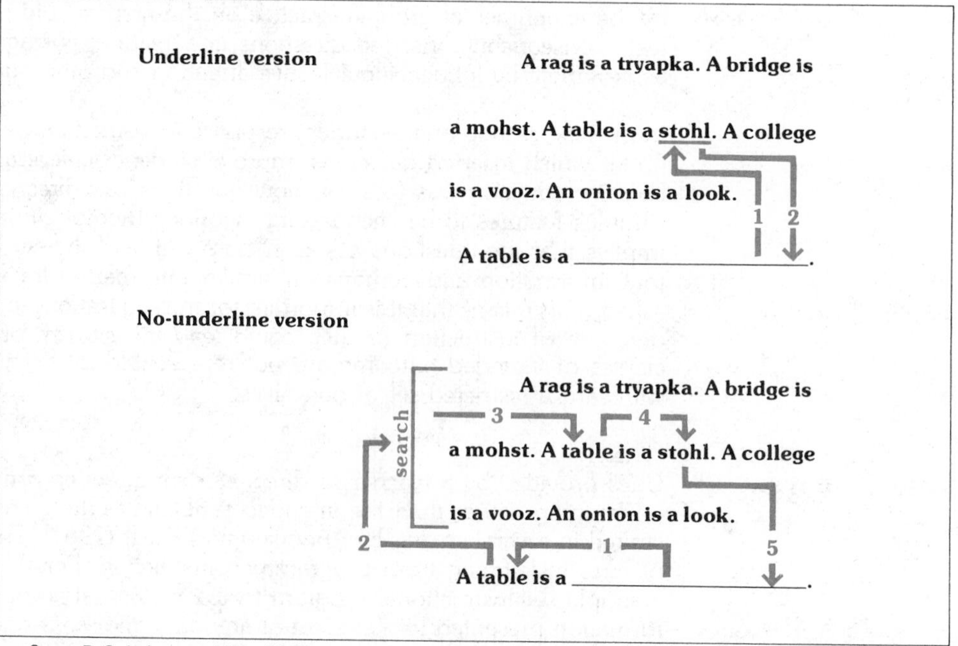

Source: R. C. Anderson and Faust (1967).

The implications of the Anderson and Faust studies for directing student attention in instruction are simple and worthy of note by teachers. Instructional cues can allow the student to bypass critical learning processes and still perform successfully at the task. But, when such cues are withdrawn there will be a resulting deterioration in student performance. To be effective in guiding the learning process in the apprehension phase, instructional cues should direct the learner's attention to all the crucial stimulus elements in the learning situation. Care should be exercised so that cues do not allow the learner to make the required performance without attending to all the critical stimulus features.

1. Italicized information tends to be remembered better than other information in a passage, because by italicizing it it is rendered more distinctive. The phenomenon on which this is based is called:
   a. The serial position effect.
   b. The von Restorff effect.
   c. Helmholz's law.
   d. Highlighting.
2. Which of the following directions would most probably be ineffective with first-graders?
   a. Teacher tells students to notice the addition sign.
   b. Teacher points to the addition sign.
   c. Teacher simultaneously points and says to notice the addition sign.
   d. Teacher draws red arrow pointing to the + sign.
3. A teacher developed a technique for teaching young children to read number names by placing the number name next to a corresponding set of stick figures as in the following examples:
   three ♀ ♀ ♀
   five ♀ ♀ ♀ ♀ ♀
   Unfortunately the children did not seem to learn with the technique even though they could count the figures correctly. Analyze this approach for a possible problem with student attention.

ELICITING STUDENT PERFORMANCE

A cardinal principle of education is that active student involvement in instruction results in greater gains for the student. Advocates, as diverse as educators extolling the virtues of drill to those in extreme free schools that allow complete freedom in student activities, have invoked this principle as a rationale for their respective approaches. Yet much difficulty has been encountered in defining explicitly the meaning of student involvement, and even more confusion is produced by adding *active* to the phrase.

Active involvement in instruction is usually understood to imply some form of student activity during instruction. Possible student activities during instruction range from listening or looking through reading to the production of a complex product. These activities vary on several important defining dimensions. They can be covert, internal processes or observable performances and products developed by the student. Also, they can be tasks of a general nature, such as listening carefully, or tasks of a specific nature, such as writing the answer to a math problem. Our major concern here is that the activity be an instructionally relevant one, that is, that the activity be functionally related to learning. By this we mean some demonstration is required that instruction that provides for, or induces, this student activity results in greater learning on the part of the student than does instruction not including this student activity.

Two classes of student activities that facilitate learning in instruction can be distinguished. One class, which we will call "study activities," includes reading, reviewing, underlining, and note taking. These activities tend to be initiated by the student in the context of general task requirements such as: "You will be responsible for the information in Chapters 1, 2, and 3," or "You will be held responsible for the information in my lectures not covered in your text." The second class of student activity is called "specific responses." With this class, the student is responding to a specific query or request to produce a specified product such as: "Name the authors of this text." As can be seen, in this type of task the expected outcome is well defined, whereas in situations in which study activities occur the expected outcome may not be specified so clearly to the learner. Both classes of student activity are performed frequently in instructional situations, but what do the two have in common? As previously stated, both classes are functionally related to learning. They are either mathemagenic strategies used by the student to facilitate learning, or else they provide direct practice of the to-be-learned capability or some component of it.

Student performance is a particularly important instructional event because of its influence on the information processing of the student. R. C. Anderson (1970) has observed that people follow a law of least effort in that they tend to engage in only the processing demanded by a given task. This principle is often humorously referred to as the "electric current theory of behavior." This theorem states that people follow the path of least resistance, analogous to an electric current. Instruction that requires a demonstration of performance competency places a greater processing demand on the student and increases the probability that the student will engage in the necessary processing to produce the desired learning.

Study activities

A variety of student activities fall within this class of events. We will focus on three activities that have been the objects of research within an instructional context: reviewing, underlining, and note taking. Reviewing is defined here as recall and rehearsal of information to which one has been exposed. Underlining as one means of identifying important information was analyzed in the preceding section. There the discussion centered on teacher-provided underlining, while here emphasis is on student-generated underlining as a study activity. Note taking is self-explanatory as a study activity; however, it should be recognized that its result is to transform information into a form more meaningful to the learner and to provide a permanent record for later study.

Review. Review has been defined as recall and rehearsal of information presented in instruction. We have restricted use of this term to free recall of the information and have included recall to specific questions in the specific response class of student activities. At one time, a form of review or recitation called "drill" was the predominant instructional activity of the school day. The practice of drill fell into disrepute because of its association with *rote memorization,* a term used to signify learning devoid of any comprehension.

Despite the decline of recitation as a formal instructional activity, research has demonstrated that under appropriate circumstances recitation in the form of review can lead to improved immediate and long-term retention. In Chapter 5, it was shown that rehearsal of information was the primary determinant of retention in working memory and that the longer information was in working memory, the more probable it was to be meaningfully encoded and transferred to long-term memory storage. This function of rehearsal has been demonstrated many times in laboratory work and we can reasonably expect it to operate in a similar fashion in an instructional setting.

An early study of recitation as a learning strategy was completed by Gates in 1917. He had children in grades four through eight memorize lists of either trigrams or short biographies composed of six or seven facts. He investigated retention immediately after study and four hours later as a function of the percentage of study time spent in recitation. Both immediate and delayed retention increased as the percentage of recitation in study time increased. This effect was more pronounced for the trigrams than for the biographies. Del Giorno, Jenkins, and Bausell (1974) compared a read-recite to a read-reread procedure as a study activity. Retention was measured with a cued recall test immediately after study and one week later. The read-recite group scored significantly higher on the immediate and delayed retention tests. The difference was most marked for delayed retention, with the recitation group scoring 23 percent higher than the reading only group.

Ross and Di Vesta (1976) studied oral summary as a review strategy. Students studied a nine-page passage for 14 minutes and then participated in one of three experimental conditions. In one condition students, referred to as *verbalizers,* presented an oral summary of the passage to another student and the experimenter. This other student, called an *observer,* while not presenting an oral summary, did hear such a summary and this constituted the observation condition. Members of the control group simply studied the passage for the allotted 14 minutes. Retention was measured one week after the study and review session with both multiple-choice and cued-recall tests. Participation in oral review as either verbalizer or observer had a positive effect on retention as measured by both recognition and cued recall. The effect of verbalization was greatest on recall, with the verbalizers scoring higher than either the observers or the controls. On recognition, the verbalizers and observers performed equally well and both retained more than the controls. Ross and Di Vesta take this pattern of results as evidence that both active and passive participation in oral review enhances storage of information in long-term memory, but active participation has more influence than passive participation on the retrievability of information from long-term storage.

Two further conditions can enhance the effectiveness of review as a study activity. The student should not recite information verbatim but rather should paraphrase it. By putting it into terms more meaningful to the individual, the student has encoded it in a form that can be retained better (Kurth & Moseley, 1978; Pio & Andre, 1977). Teachers can facilitate this process by encouraging students to phrase answers in their own words and not demanding textbook copies. The second condition concerns the timing of reviews. Gay (1973) found that spaced reviews result in greater retention than consecutive reviews. A group that reviewed one and seven days after the original learning retained more than did a group that reviewed for the first two days after original learning.

FIGURE 10–5
Student activities during instruction are critical in determining what is learned

Review as a study activity has been shown to be an effective strategy for promoting both immediate and long-term retention. Instructional programs that allow for and encourage review (or even exposure to a review) should result in greater learning on the part of the student. However, it may be more advantageous to allow students to engage in covert review (as in the Del Giorno et al. study) than to require overt and public review. Again, Ross and Di Vesta reported that students who were required to verbalize during oral review reported considerably more anxiety than the observers. While this increase in anxiety does not necessarily interfere with learning, it most definitely could lead to a negative attitude through the process of classical conditioning, as illustrated in Chapter 11. Meaningful encoding in review can be facilitated by encouraging students to paraphrase, rather than merely repeat, information and by providing spaced reviews (Figure 10–5).

Learner-generated underlining. In an earlier section of this chapter, we surveyed teacher-provided underlining as a cue for directing attention to relevant information to be encoded by the learner. Now, student-generated underlining will be inspected for its effectiveness as a study activity. The importance of underlining as a study activity was described by Fowler and Barker (1974). They reported that a random sample of used texts in a college bookstore showed that 92 percent of the books bore the results of various study activities of the former owners, and chief among them was underlining. Fowler and Barker conducted an investigation to compare the effects of active underlining of information in a text to reading a text with information already underlined. On a one-week retention test the active underlining group remembered more underlined information than the group that read underlined material.

Two recent studies have contributed much information about the conditions influencing the effectiveness of underlining as a study activity. Smart and Bruning (1973) investigated; (1) the relevancy of the underlined information to the posttest, and (2) the source of the underlining (whether the student or experimenter). Students who underlined relevant information or read the passage with this information underlined scored higher on a recognition test than did students who read a nonunderlined version. Irrelevant underlining provided by the experimenter did not impair performance compared with that of the other underlining groups, whereas the underlining of irrelevant information by the learner did severely impair performance on the achievement test.

Rickards and August (1975) conducted a study similar to the preceding one but with several important differences. Performance on an immediate recall test was compared for five experimental groups and a no-underlining–reading-only control group (C). The five experimental groups were: (1) student-generated underlining of any one sentence (SA), (2) student-generated underlining of sentences with high structural importance (SH), (3) student-generated underlining of sentences with low structural importance (SL), (4) experimenter-provided underlining of sentences with high structural importance (EH), and (5) experimenter-provided underlining of sentences with low structural importance (EL). Only one sentence in each paragraph of the reading passage was underlined for each of these conditions, whether by the student or by the experimenter. The structural importance of each sentence in the passage was defined as its importance to the meaning of the passage as determined by an empirical rating system independent of the present study.

Results for the recall of underlined and nonunderlined information separately and combined as total recall are presented in Figure 10–6. The SA and SH groups scored higher on underlined information than all other groups. This means they remembered more of the information they underlined than did other groups who underlined information or who were provided with underlined information. Additionally, the SA group remembered more nonunderlined information than any other group.

One very intriguing finding of the Rickards and August study concerns the sentences underlined by those students who were free to underline sentences of their own choosing, and those students directed to underline sentences with high structural importance. The sentences underlined by both groups did not differ from each other in rated structural importance, but neither group chose the most structurally important sentences to underline. Yet, students who were free to underline any sentence performed significantly higher on tests of the recall of nonunderlined information than did students directed to underline the sentences with high structural importance. Rickards and

FIGURE 10–6
Recall scores for six study groups

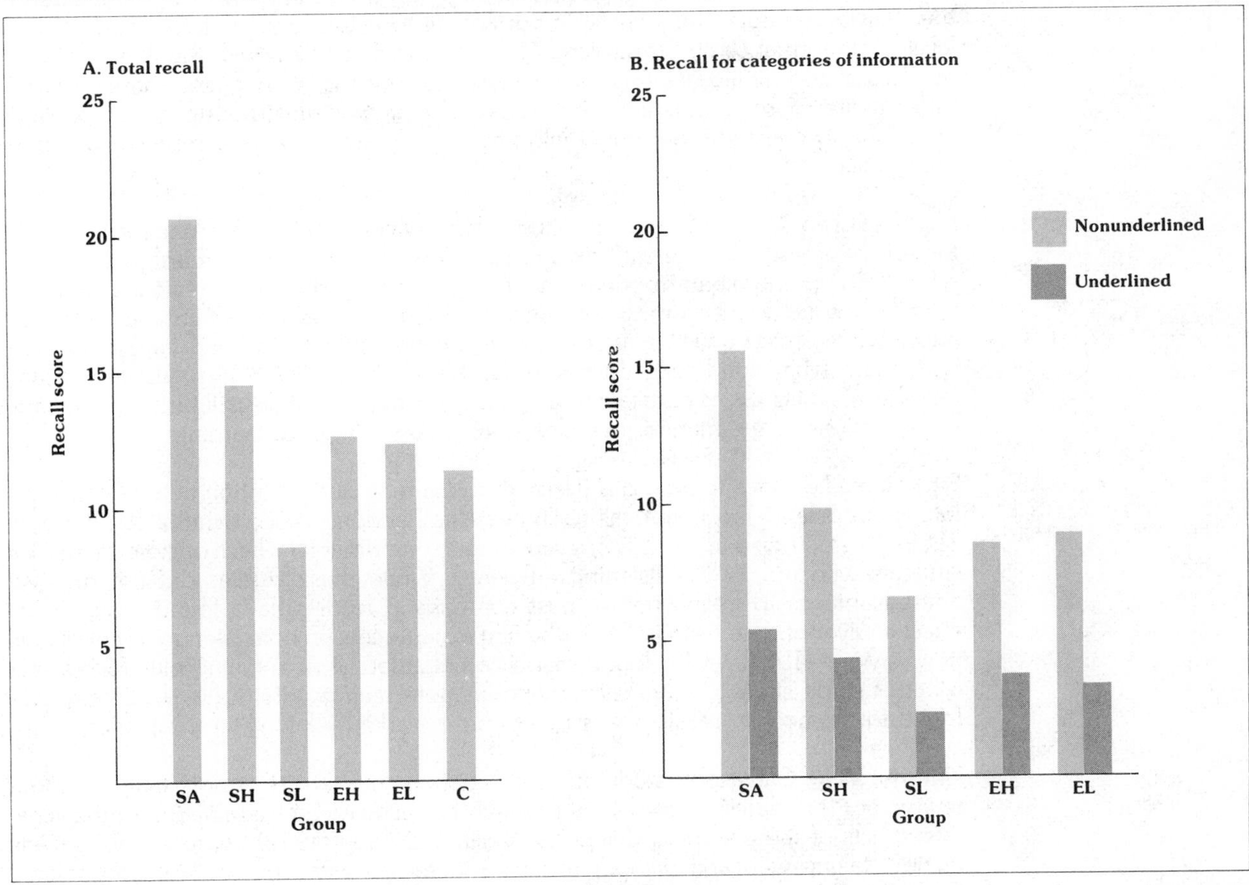

Source: Adapted from Rickards and August (1975).

August interpreted these results as evidence that students, free to choose, underline the sentences that best fit into their individual "cognitive structure" and are most conducive to the assimilation of subordinate information to them. In other words, these students choose the sentences most meaningful in terms of their prior knowledge. Hence these sentences are better retrieval cues for the recall of related information from their respective paragraph.

Several conclusions about underlining as a study activity can be drawn from the preceding studies. First, student-generated underlining can facilitate learning if the student underlines relevant and important information. If students are encouraged to underline the information most meaningful to them, then it appears advantageous to have them do the underlining themselves. Both the Smart and Bruning study and the Rickards and August study restricted the amount of information underlined by the students, while a study by Idstein and Jenkins (1972) did not. The two former studies found a difference for student-generated underlining over repetitive reading only, but the latter study did not obtain such a difference. These findings suggest that the advice to use underlining sparingly is sound advice for the student.

If students underline irrelevant information, then the activity of underlining can have a detrimental effect on learning. This was demonstrated in both studies. Apparently this activity disrupts attention to important information, thereby producing a lower level of performance by the student. This fact, in conjunction with the demonstration by Brown and Smiley (1977) that children below the sixth grade cannot reliably differentiate informational units on the basis of their structural importance to a passage, leads one to conclude that underlining as a study activity is best reserved for more mature learners.

Note taking. As one views the classroom activities in typical American schools, there is a large qualitative shift as the transition is made from primary to secondary school. The predominant mode of instruction becomes the lecture and the most frequent study activity becomes note taking. Given this state of affairs, an important and long-neglected question is: Does note taking facilitate learning, and if so, how and under what conditions does it have this positive effect? First we will inquire into the effectiveness of note taking as a study strategy. Then we will turn our attention to an analysis of the manner in which note taking influences learning.

Several studies have found no differences in learning and retention between students taking notes and those not taking notes (McClendon, 1958; Schultz & Di Vesta, 1972). A study by Peters (1972) even found a detrimental effect of note taking for students who are low in listening efficiency. While these studies did not discover any advantages to taking notes, most comparison studies have found a significant effect in favor of note taking. One of the first experiments on note taking was conducted by Crawford (1925b), who found that a combination of note taking plus review was a better study strategy than review without note taking. While this superiority was found for immediate recall, it was much more marked for long-term retention.

Unfortunately, Crawford's study did not determine the effects of note taking without review, but fortunately, more recent research has allowed an examination of the separate effects of these study activities. Di Vesta and Grey (1972) compared the effects of note taking with and without review, and review with and without note taking. Both note taking and review led to greater recall of ideas from the lecture. However, the effects of the two study activities were not additive; that is, a combination of the two was not greater than the effects of note taking or review alone. In a second study, Di Vesta and Grey (1973) examined the effects of note taking on both immediate and delayed retention. Taking notes resulted in the recall of more ideas than did not taking notes. On two recognition measures there was no difference for immediate retention, but long-term retention was higher for the note-taking condition.

Most studies on note taking have worked with instruction in a lecture-type situation; that is, the students received the information by listening. Kulhavy, Dyer, and Silver (1975) evaluated note taking as a study activity in learning from text. They had junior and senior high school students study a 845-word reading passage by reading and note taking, reading and underlining, or reading only. Immediate retention was tested with both cued-recall and multiple-choice items. The note-taking group studied significantly longer and learned more than either other group.

Other studies of note taking, rather than comparing it with other study activities, have focused on the relationship between the content of study notes and later performance. Most of these studies have obtained quite interesting and informative results. Crawford (1925a) correlated student notes with exam performance by using an outline of the lecture. He counted the number of ideas from the lecture in each student's notes and the number of ideas recalled on the tests. For seven classes participating in the study, the correlations ranged from .35 to .66, with a median of .50. Again, using the outline of the lecture, Crawford compared the notes and exams for ideas common to each. He found that of the ideas included in the lecture and missing from the notes, 86 percent were also absent from the examination papers. For the lecture ideas present in the notes, he found that 51 percent were also present on the tests. Crawford concluded from these data that taking note of an idea did not insure its recall on a test, but not taking note of it greatly decreased the probability of its recall. Crawford's conclusion was upheld in a more recent study by Howe (1970), in which students listened to a 160-word selection from a novel and took notes on the passage. A week later, they attempted recall of the passage. Comparisons were made of the content in both the notes and recall tests. An item appearing in a student's notes had a .34 probability of being recalled, but an item omitted from a student's notes had only a .047 probability of recall. Additionally, Howe developed a ratio measure of the efficiency of a student's notes:

$$\frac{\text{Number of items in notes}}{\text{Number of words in notes}}$$

This efficiency score was correlated with recall and found to have a coefficient of .53. This means that the fewer words it takes a student to place an information unit into notes, the better is the recall of that idea. Fisher and Harris (1974) found that the quality of notes, defined as the number of ideas from the lecture, correlated .52 with free-recall scores and .54 with multiple-choice scores.

Research has demonstrated that note taking is indeed an effective study strategy. Students who take notes during a lecture or while reading remember more of the information than students who do not take notes. Furthermore, the quality of notes directly relates to retention. Information contained in the notes has a much higher probability of being recalled than information omitted from the notes. Now we divert our attention to the issues of how and under what circumstances note taking affects learning and retention.

The encoding and external storage functions of notes. Note taking is thought to exert an influence on retention in two ways. First, note taking serves an encoding function; that is, in the process of taking notes the student transforms the information presented into a form that is more meaningful on an individual basis, thereby making the information more retrievable. The external storage function of notes means that notes provide a record of important information to which a student may return later for review. The encoding function implies that the value of notes is in *taking* them, while for the external storage function, the value of notes is in *having* them.

This testable difference concerning the value of notes has led to research aimed at determining whether one of these two functions of notes has a greater influence on retention than the other. Fisher and Harris (1973) manipulated note taking and review conditions to judge the effects of encoding only, external storage only, and the two in combination. A group that took notes (encoding) and then reviewed those notes (external storage) did the best, followed by a group that took no notes but reviewed a set of the lecturer's notes (external storage only). The worst performance was turned in by a group that took no notes and reviewed without notes. These results indicate that retention is best when both the encoding and external storage functions of notes are served by the student's own activities. However, when only one of these functions is operational, it appears that the external storage function is more important than the encoding function.

Carter and VanMatre (1975) investigated the comparative effects of note taking versus no notes in learning from a lecture. On both immediate and delayed recall, a group that took notes and reviewed them scored higher than both a group that listened without taking notes and then reviewed and a group that took notes and reviewed without them; these latter two groups do not differ from each other. Carter and VanMatre reasoned that if notes serve a strong encoding function then students who took notes, even though they did not review them, should recall more than students who listened to the lecture without taking notes. Since this was not the case, they concluded the encoding function of notes is only a weak effect. However, since having notes to review resulted in significantly more retention, it was concluded that the major value of notes is as external storage for later review and processing by the student.

Research by Rickards and Friedman (1978) supported both the encoding and external storage functions of notes. On a recall test, both students who took notes and students who had notes to review performed better than did a group who mentally reviewed the material without having taken notes. Having notes to review was shown to have a reconstruction effect; that is, notes enhanced recall by functioning as a retrieval cue for other information not recorded in the notes.

Further support for the encoding function of notes comes from studies by Shimmerlik and Nolan (1976) and Peper and Mayer (1977). Shimmerlik and Nolan showed that instructing junior high school students to reorganize information into specified categories as they took notes produced better recall than that of students who did not reorganize information in their notes. Peper and Mayer demonstrated that students who take notes during instruction perform better on novel problems involving application of information from the instruction than students not taking notes. They concluded that note taking activates a meaningful learning set rather than just increasing attentiveness to information in the instruction.

Note taking appears to serve both encoding and external storage functions, with perhaps the latter being most important. Quite possibly the encoding function plays a strong role when it occurs, but often students are not able to engage in encoding while taking notes under classroom conditions and also remain attentive to new information. If students are encouraged to encode as they take notes, this encoding is more likely to occur and influence retention. Even without encoding though, notes serve a valuable function for the student because they can be returned to later and used in review for further processing. Therefore conscientious students who go to the effort to obtain notes after their absence from class are rewarded for their effort by greater learning and retention!

We saw in the preceding section that note taking facilitates long-term retention, and now we will explore procedures by which the teacher can increase efficient and effective note taking strategies by students. Aiken, Thomas, and Shennum (1975) concluded that segmentation of a lecture, so that students are given pauses in the lecture to take notes, results in greater learning than concurrent note taking. Besides this finding, they showed that a fast speaking rate by the lecturer led to less learning, but repetition of information at this high rate aided learning. Earlier in this chapter it was stated that simple verbal cues ("This point is critical to understand," etc.), statement of objectives, and writing a point on the blackboard greatly increase attention to cued information and make it more likely that students will take notes on it.

These results suggest a simple procedure whereby a teacher may facilitate the effectiveness of student note taking. First, the rate of presentation must match the student's listening comprehension. Attempts to cover all the material are futile if they speed the rate of information presentation beyond the student's listening ability. Next, the lecture could be interspersed with pauses, especially after an important point, so that the student may make note of the information. Transparencies, verbal statements, and provision of objectives and outlines are some of the means that can be used by the teacher to cue important information to the student. In all probability, these strategies are typically used by teachers who are "good lecturers."

Note taking can actually interfere with learning from a lecture under certain conditions. The process of taking notes can distract the student's attention from important information as it is presented. This debilitating effect should be most marked for students with low abilities. Evidence for such an effect with low-ability students has been obtained in several studies. As reported earlier in this section on note taking, Peters found that students low in listening efficiency learned more from a lecture without taking notes. Berliner (1971) found that students high in memory ability were effective note takers, but this was not necessarily so for students low in memory ability. The requirement of specific responding (answering a specific question) was more beneficial for low-memory-ability students than was the general activity of note taking. With low-ability students it is even more important to follow the advice just given to speak slowly, pause frequently, and cue important information.

4. Review as a study activity would have its greatest effect on retention when a student is tested by:
   a. A multiple-choice test.
   b. An essay test.
   Explain your answer.

5. If you attended a lecture but did not take notes, which of the following would be the most effective study strategy?
   a. Obtain someone's notes to review.
   b. Review but do not bother to secure a set of notes.
   c. The two strategies described in *a* and *b* should be equally effective.
   d. Skip review because it would be ineffective since you did not take notes.

6. Student-generated underlining of information has the greatest effect on recall when:
   a. Students are reviewing previously learned information.
   b. Students underline limited information composed of information most meaningful to them.
   c. Students underline limited information composed of information most important to the overall meaning of the passage.
   d. Students have sufficient aptitude to comprehend the instruction.

Specific responses

The second major class of student activity in instruction we have labeled *specific responses.* This we define simply as a response on the part of the student to a specific question. This inquiry can be encountered while reading a text, listening to a lecture, or watching a film or other media presentations, or it can be asked by the teacher or another student during a discussion or tutorial situation. What is important is that the activity engaged in by the student must require the composition of an answer to a relatively well-defined question.

The distinction between specific responses and study activities involves several interrelated dimensions. With specific responses the teacher's influence on the actual performance is greater than with study activities. Consequently, attention is centered on the performance capability to be demonstrated as evidence of attainment of the intended learning outcome, or components of such performance. With study activities, the student has greater control over what behaviors are performed, so the performance desired by the teacher may or may not occur, or may or may not even be facilitated. Of course, the orienting stimuli and other information provided by the teacher can influence the student's study activities and thereby make it more likely that the desired performance capability will be acquired.

Clear evidence of the value of eliciting student responses was obtained in a study by Bruning (1968). He had students read a 1,500-word prose passage divided into six sections. Inserted at the end of each section was either a review statement or a test question. The test questions were constructed by deleting a key term from the equivalent review statements, thus they were essentially identical except for format. Students who received the review statements made twice as many errors on a posttest as did the questioned students. This effect held, although the magnitude of difference was not as large, even when the information presented in the review statements and corresponding questions was irrelevant to the posttest.

As we shall see in this section of the chapter, specific responses to instructional queries influence learning and retention in two ways (Figure 10–7): by direct practicing of the to-be-learned capability and by activating mathemagenic strategies that facilitate learning and retention.

Exactly what effects will be produced by requiring specific responding is a function of several characteristics related to the question that stimulated the response. Chief among these characteristics are: the placement of the question in relation to the information necessary to answer the question (i.e., before or after the information), the frequency of occurrence of the questions, the type of learned capability necessary to answer the question (i.e., memorization, concept learning), and the source of the question (i.e., teacher, student). Finally, individual differences in students' aptitudes influence the effects of specific responding on learning and retention.

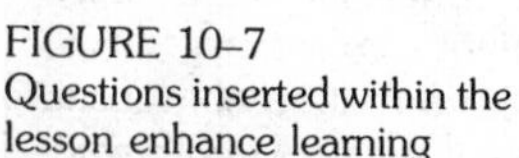
FIGURE 10–7
Questions inserted within the lesson enhance learning

Question placement. In a paper that gave impetus to the current interest in the use of adjunct questions to facilitate learning, Rothkopf (1966) studied the effects on learning of inserting questions at various points in a reading passage. While he included a number of groups in the study, we will examine only a few of them. One group had questions inserted after the information necessary to answer them, and another had these same questions placed before the section of the passage containing the necessary information. A third group served as a control and read the passage without the inserted questions. After reading the textual materials, all groups were given a test that covered both the questioned information and other information contained in the text passage but not tested by any of the inserted questions. Results showed that both questioned groups scored higher by about 40 percent than the reading-only group on the questioned information (the direct effect). Only the post-question group scored higher than the reading-only control group on a test of the nonquestioned information, with the difference being about 10 percent (the indirect effect).

Since Rothkopf's original study, much research has replicated and confirmed these trends. Anderson and Biddle (1975), analyzing the data for 35 such studies, concluded that questions after sections of text more frequently have a positive rather than a negative effect on new test items. Concerning the effects of pre-questions, Anderson and Biddle (p. 93) state, "Questions asked before the relevant passage more frequently inhibit than facilitate performance on new criterion test items. . . ." Figure 10–8 displays results from a study by Boker (1974) that typify these effects of pre- and post-questions on learning. Also, this study is important because it investigated delayed

FIGURE 10–8
The effects of adjunct question placement on immediate and delayed retention

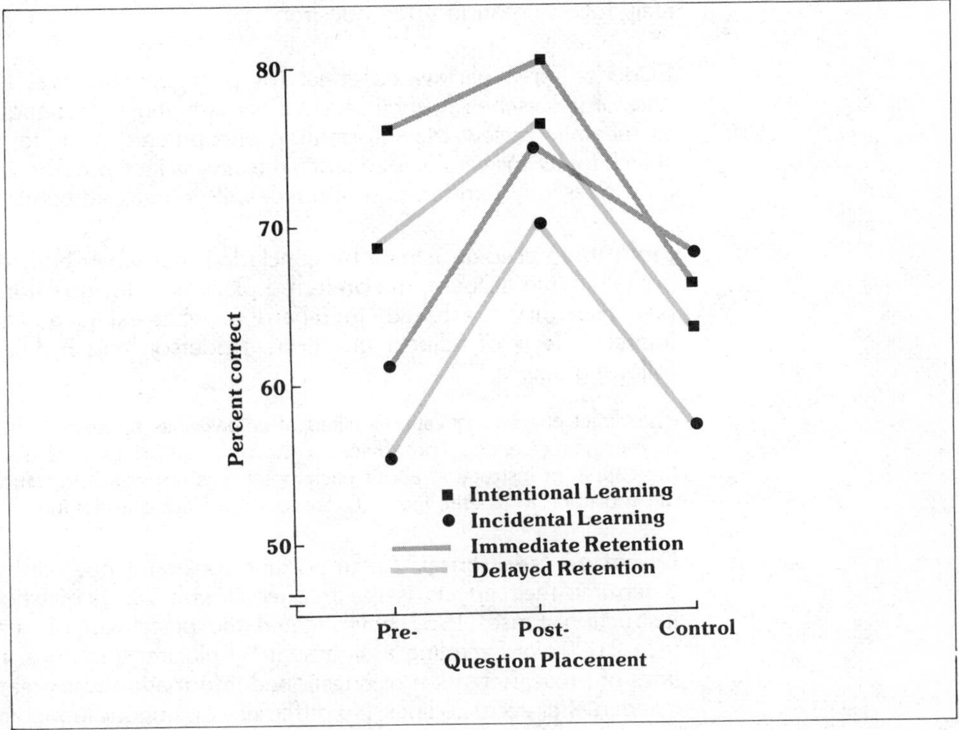

Source: Adapted from Boker (1974).

retention. As the figure illustrates, the superior performance of the post-question group on both questioned and nonquestioned information was maintained after a week.

Why does the placement of questions determine their influence on the student's learning effort? The answer to this question involves the strategies adopted by learners as they are faced with different types of learning tasks. Earlier in this chapter, pre-questions, like objectives, were said to serve as orienting stimuli. Pre-questions and objectives, when encountered by the student, establish an expectancy that leads to selective attention for a given class of information. Given this set, the student adopts a search strategy for answers to the specific pre-questions and rehearses and encodes this information to the exclusion of other information. This neglect of other information shows in the lower test scores for nonquestioned information. Pre-questions can even result in students having lower scores on nonquestioned information than a group given no adjunct questions (Frase, Patrick & Schumer, 1970).

The influences of post-questions on learning strategies are much more complex. Post-questions share with pre-questions a direct practice effect demonstrated by equal achievement for the two groups on questioned information. In addition to this direct practice effect, the indirect effect of post-questions may have as many as three separate components (McGaw & Grotelueschen 1972). They postulate a forward effect comprised of two components. One forward component works to shape appropriate inspection behaviors; that is, if the way a student inspected a text segment resulted in the correct answers on the post-questions, then the student is more likely to engage in that same inspection strategy for the following segment. Additionally, there is an increase in the general attentiveness or alertness of the student after encountering an inserted question. This is reflected by increased retention of the information immediately following an inserted question.

Evidence for a backwards effect for post-questions was also obtained by McGaw and Grotelueschen in their study. Encountering a post-question influences a student to mentally review the information encountered prior to the question in order to search for its answer. Consequently this review increases the likelihood that information, both questioned and nonquestioned, will be retained better.

From the preceding it may be concluded that when both direct and indirect effects are taken into account, the preferred placement for questions is after the information on which they are based. In regard to what extent a teacher should rely on the indirect effects of adjunct questions, Anderson and Biddle (1975, p. 92) offer the following advice:

> The direct effect of questions asked after passages appears to be about four times as great as the indirect effect. The advice to the practical educator is obvious: Ask questions during the course of instruction about each point it is important for students to master, rather than depend upon a general, indirect consequence from questioning.

Question frequency. An important constraint operating on adjunct questions to determine their effects is the frequency with which questions are presented during instruction. Frase (1967) investigated the placement of questions at various points in a 2,000-word reading assignment by placing questions after every 10, 20, or 40 lines of prose. Retention of questioned information was greatest for adjunct questions inserted after every 20 lines. No difference on nonquestioned information was observed among groups getting inserted questions at varying prose lengths.

FIGURE 10–9
Total retention as a function of question placement and frequency

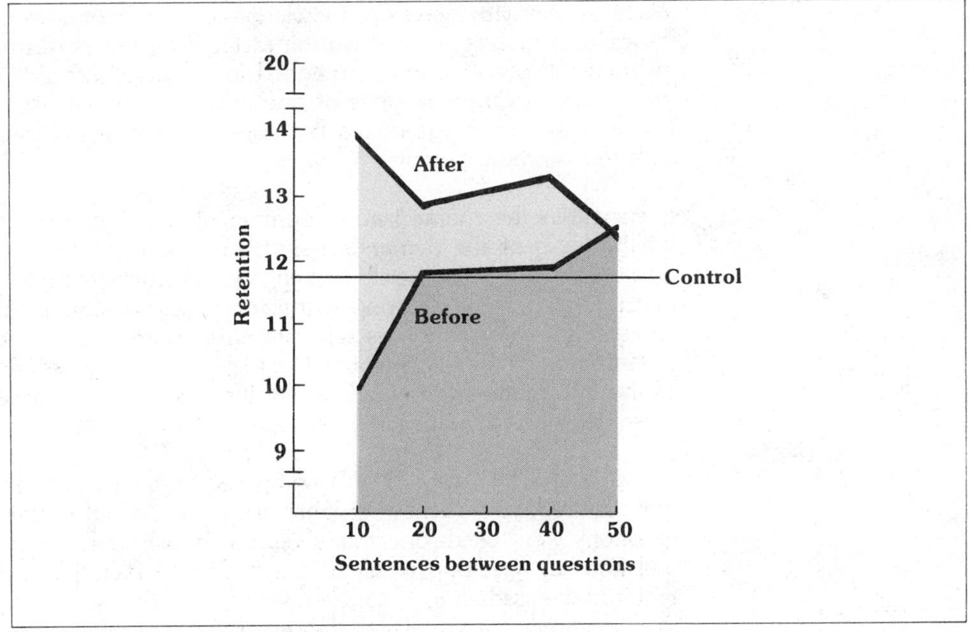

Source: Frase (1968).

Frase (1968) studied the frequency of questions in a second study with the same prose material. Questions were interspersed every 10, 20, 40, or 50 lines, so that all conditions received the same total of questions; the difference between groups was that two groups received one question either after or before every 10 lines, two other groups received two questions either after or before every 20 lines, and so on. As can be seen from Figure 10–9, the facilitative effects of post-questions increased with their frequency of occurrence. Conversely, an increase in the frequency of pre-questions amplified their negative influence on overall retention.

It is not clear how the frequency of adjunct questions interacts with their placement to influence the retention of questioned and nonquestioned information. In the study by Frase just cited, it was found that the frequency of pre-questions decreased retention of both questioned and nonquestioned information. Frase, Patrick, and Schumer (1970) demonstrated that frequent prequestions (one question per paragraph) reduced incidental learning compared to a reading-only control group. With reference to post-questions, Boyd (1973) determined that retention of questioned information was greater with one question after each paragraph than with five questions after every five paragraphs. There was no effect on nonquestioned information for either of these two conditions.

Type of question. Type of question is classified here by learning domain; that is, what learned capability must the student demonstrate in answering the question? A majority of the studies reported in the literature on adjunct questions involve verbatim or near-verbatim recall of information. Questions often are formed by taking an important sentence from the instructional presentation and deleting a key word from it, usually a technical term or proper name. Coincidentally, Gall (1970) reports that approximately 60 percent of questions asked by classroom teachers fall into this category.

We hope that with increased knowledge of the role of questions in specific responding, the type of questions used will be dictated by the performance objectives the given instructional presentation is designed to achieve. With this in mind, we will examine the effects of different types of questions on student achievement. Since we stated that a high percentage of teacher questions are at the memorization level, we start with that learning outcome.

Even within the memorization domain of learning, questions can be distinguished on the basis of the demands they place upon the student. As stated above, some questions require that the student engage in verbatim or near-verbatim recall of specific information presented during instruction. These questions require only that the student rehearse the information as separate units or entities; they do not force encoding by organization of the information. The focus of other questions is upon the organization of the information presented during instruction. In other words, in order to answer these questions the student must organize or otherwise elaborate on the information.

Rickards and Di Vesta (1974) compared verbatim post-questions to post-questions that required the student to organize the presented information. Two types of verbatim questions were used: one that required the verbatim recall of a superordinate idea and another requiring recall of a subordinate fact. The third type of post-question required the student to organize a set of subordinate facts around their superordinate idea. Post-questions involving the organization of information resulted in greater retention of both questioned and nonquestioned information than did either type of verbatim post-question. This finding held when the questions occurred after every two paragraphs, but not when they occurred after every four paragraphs. Rickards and Di Vesta suggested that the more frequent use of organizing questions was necessary because of the more thorough processing required to answer such questions.

In a separate study, Rickards (1976a) compared verbatim adjunct questions with abstraction questions. The latter type requires the student to relate a set of specific facts by producing a descriptive term for the set. On tests of total recall the abstraction pre-questions were more effective than abstraction post-questions, while the verbatim post-questions were better than verbatim pre-questions. For tests of delayed recall only the abstraction pre-questions group was superior to a control group. Additionally, strong evidence was obtained to demonstrate that abstraction pre-questions induced organization and consolidation of information in memory storage to a much greater extent than did the other question conditions.

The implications of these studies for classroom teachers are quite clear. Questions that facilitate the organization and relatedness of the information to be remembered are preferred to questions requiring only verbatim recall of information. By requiring organizational encoding, questions produce greater recall of both questioned and non-questioned information and more long-term retention of such information. To be used effectively such questions require frequent deployment during instruction.

Many performance objectives go beyond the memorization domain, so an important question is: Can specific responses to adjunct questions engender higher levels of comprehension? Based on the available research, the answer to this question seems to be yes. Adjunct questions involving the comprehension of concepts or rules result in a higher level of learning and a greater degree of learning than do verbatim recall questions. Experiments by Watts and Anderson (1971) support this conclusion about the effects of higher-level adjunct questions. They had high school students read a short prose passage describing and explaining five psychological concepts. The students were assigned to one of three groups distinguished by the type of inserted questions they received. Two types of verbatim questions were used: (1) questions that required the student to recognize the name of a psychologist associated with each concept; and (2) repeated example questions that required the student to identify examples repeated from the prose passage of each concept. The third question condition required the student to identify new examples of the five concepts.

All three groups were given a multiple-choice test that tested performance on names, repeated examples, and new examples. The new-example adjunct questions yielded greater total retention than either of the other two types. Furthermore, the new-example group scored higher on other previously unencountered examples than did either the names or repeated-examples group, while at the same time equaling these latter two groups on retention of names and repeated examples.

Felker and Dapra (1975) compared verbatim adjunct questions with questions requiring rule learning on the part of the student. In conjunction with a multiple-choice posttest measuring verbatim and rule learning, Felker and Dapra gave a comprehension test composed of five problem situations that required a written solution based on rules from the text. Students who received rule-learning questions scored significantly higher on the problem-solving criterion than did those given verbatim questions. Problem solving was further enhanced by placement of the rule-learning questions after the relevant passages as opposed to before these passages.

Studies in this section of the chapter have illustrated that questions are a practical means by which teachers can direct the students' learning processes toward attainment of learning outcomes at various levels of the cognitive domain. Of particular importance is the finding that questions can promote higher levels of comprehension by the student. Questions that require the student to organize information or apply a concept or rule produce performance gains greater than questions requiring only verbatim or near-verbatim recall. Care should be taken to insure that higher-level questions occur more frequently because they place greater processing demands upon the student that the student may not otherwise engage in.

Source of questions. Most of the work on specific responses to questions has involved written adjunct questions with textual materials. An important issue to be explored is the effect, if any, of questions presented in a medium other than print. Berliner (1971), as reported in an earlier section, demonstrated that oral questions inserted in a lecture had a facilitative effect on retention, especially for students with low memory ability.

Rothkopf and Bloom (1970) found that the interpersonal value of questions asked by a teacher had an effect on learning more positive than questions in print. High school students studying geology had the same questions either provided in print form or asked orally by a teacher. Questions, regardless of the presentation mode, resulted in greater learning than studying without questions. However, students receiving oral questions learned more than students getting printed questions.

Teachers do not necessarily have to ask questions and, on occasion, it is more desirable that students generate questions so that they may check on their own progress as they learn. Evidence has been obtained in two studies reported by Frase and Schwartz (1975) in support of the benefits of student-generated questions on learning. They had high school students construct questions as they studied a prose passage either individually or in a tutorial situation. Recall was greater in both question situations than in a study-only condition. Both the students who asked questions and those who answered them in the tutorial situation scored significantly higher than did their study-only comparisons.

In this segment of the chapter we discussed conditions under which specific responses are effective in promoting desired outcomes in instructional situations. It was seen that the type of question teachers should ask to promote learning and retention are comprehension questions going beyond verbatim recall. These questions should be asked frequently and after the presentation of relevant information in order to be maximally effective. Questions and students' responses to them are important to the teacher for another reason. The student performance is critical in making decisions about instructional actions. One of these decisions based on student performance is what feedback to give the student. This question will be addressed in the following section.

7. Which of the following statements concerning the level of inserted questions is correct?
   a. Questions requiring higher levels of comprehension should occur more frequently than lower-level questions.
   b. Higher-level questions should occur less frequently than lower-level questions because they place greater processing demands on the student.
   c. Higher-level questions should be used as pre-questions but not as post-questions.
   d. Lower-level questions should be used only in conjunction with instructional objectives.
8. In presenting a lecture, the teacher may ask a number of questions. Should this teacher pose the questions to the students before or after the lecture? Why?

INFORMATIONAL FEEDBACK

After responding in an instructional situation, some event either supplied by the teacher or inherent in the task usually informs the student about the adequacy of the response. This information can take a variety of forms: (1) the teacher stating whether the answer is right or wrong (2) providing the correct response (3) asking another question, or (4) explaining what the correct response should be. What all these events have in common is that they provide information to students that allows them to judge the correctness or incorrectness of their performance. We will refer to all these instructional events that provide students with a basis for evaluating their performance as *informational feedback*. For now, we will treat all feedback procedures, regardless of content, as the same. Later in this section we examine various feedback procedures to determine whether they have differential effects on learning and performance.

Postperformance information: Reinforcement or corrective feedback?

The predominant view of feedback has been one of reinforcement. From this frame of reference, the primary function of feedback is to increase the probability that a correct response will be repeated. Therefore the major influence of feedback would be exerted on the learner following appropriate performance.

However, reviews of research have consistently failed to find support for the reinforcement interpretation of feedback (Anderson, 1967; Kulhavy, 1977). Rather, a picture of feedback or postperformance information as corrective feedback has emerged from the research. Corrective feedback exerts its greatest influence on occasions of incorrect responding by the student. In this manner, feedback functions to increase the likelihood of the learner changing to the correct response following initially incorrect performance.

A study by Guthrie (1971) offers a direct comparison of the reinforcement and correction interpretations of feedback. He determined the reinforcement value of feedback by calculating the probability of repeating a right response from the learning phase of the study on the retention test. The corrective value of feedback was measured by determining the probability of changing a wrong response given during the learning phase to a correct response on the retention test. The probability of repeating a correct response was .43 with feedback and .44 without feedback. The corrective measure showed that the likelihood of correcting an incorrect response was .32 with feedback and .06 without feedback. Substantially the same results have been obtained by Surber and Anderson (1975). They demonstrated that feedback had a significant effect on changing an incorrect response but no effect on the repetition of an initially correct response.

Melching (1966) conducted a descriptive study of student feedback patterns in programmed instruction and found that feedback was requested by the students on only 31 percent of the frames. Of these frames, errors were made on 28 percent, while on nonrequested frames a 4 percent error rate was obtained. All of the experiments cited above lead to a preference for the corrective interpretation of informational feedback over the reinforcement version. The implication of this for the classroom teacher is clear. Since the major effect of feedback is corrective, care should be taken to provide feedback to students after incorrect performance. Feedback for correct responses obviously will do no harm and quite possibly could have motivational effects. However, correction of errors is likely to occur only if students are provided informational feedback, while correct responses tend to reoccur regardless of feedback.

The effective use of feedback

We expect feedback to exert its primary influence on the learner after an incorrect response, but are there other factors that determine the influence of feedback on learning? In this section we investigate factors in the instructional setting that affect feedback as a learning variable in instruction.

If students have access to informational feedback before they compose their answer to a question, then it is possible for them to bypass the necessary processing needed to respond correctly. The extent to which students bypass this processing determines the degree of learning from the instruction. No learning would occur from the extreme condition in which the student uses the available feedback to "copy" the answer.

Programmed instruction and independent work by a student are good examples of instruction in which feedback is readily available before responding. While working on a program, all a student has to do to obtain the answer to any frame (question) is to look ahead to the correct answer provided. In evaluating the effectiveness of such a program with high school students, R. C. Anderson (1969) asked students to state how frequently they had looked ahead to an answer for a difficult question before answering the question. More than 40 percent of the students said they sometimes did, and 20 percent said they usually did, so Anderson examined learning from the program as a function of copying answers. Figure 10–10 shows that as the frequency of copying increased, learning from the program decreased.

In two further studies, Anderson and his associates experimentally manipulated the availability of the correct response to programmed material (Anderson, Kulhavy & Andre, 1971, 1972). Students in both studies who had access to the correct answers

FIGURE 10–10
Achievement as a function of the reported frequency of copying correct responses to difficult frames.

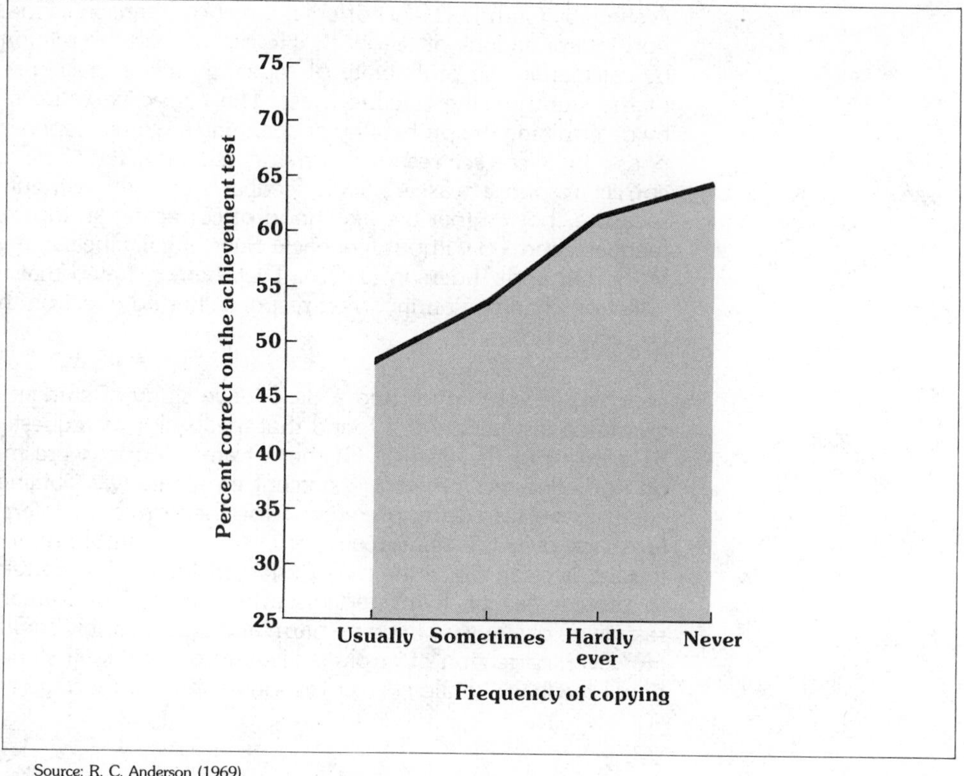

Source: R. C. Anderson (1969).

prior to responding worked through the instruction quickest and with the fewest errors but learned the least. The lesson from this for the teacher is to insure that the student's performance is based on relevant information in instruction and not on information that allows the learning process to be bypassed.

The research by Melching (1966), mentioned earlier in this section, showed that when students are provided feedback only upon request, they ask for it about one third of the time. It seems reasonable to further infer that students who are routinely provided with feedback attend to and use this information only part of the time. Furthermore, these occasions are most likely to have the greatest control over the student's learning effort.

So what distinguishes those occasions on which students attend to feedback from those on which they do not? An ingenious study by Kulhavy, Yekovich, and Dyer (1976) has provided much understanding of the conditions under which students effectively utilize feedback to promote desired learning outcomes. In this study, two groups of students read a program on the human eye and answered questions based on it, with one group receiving feedback and the other without feedback. The innovation in this study is that students in both groups were required to rate their confidence in the correctness of their response to each question immediately after answering it. The performance on a test of immediate retention for both the feedback and no-feedback groups at each confidence level is shown in Figure 10–11, as well as time spent studying feedback following error and correct responses. Students given feedback

FIGURE 10–11
Feedback study times and response probabilities, both plotted as a function of initial confidence ratings

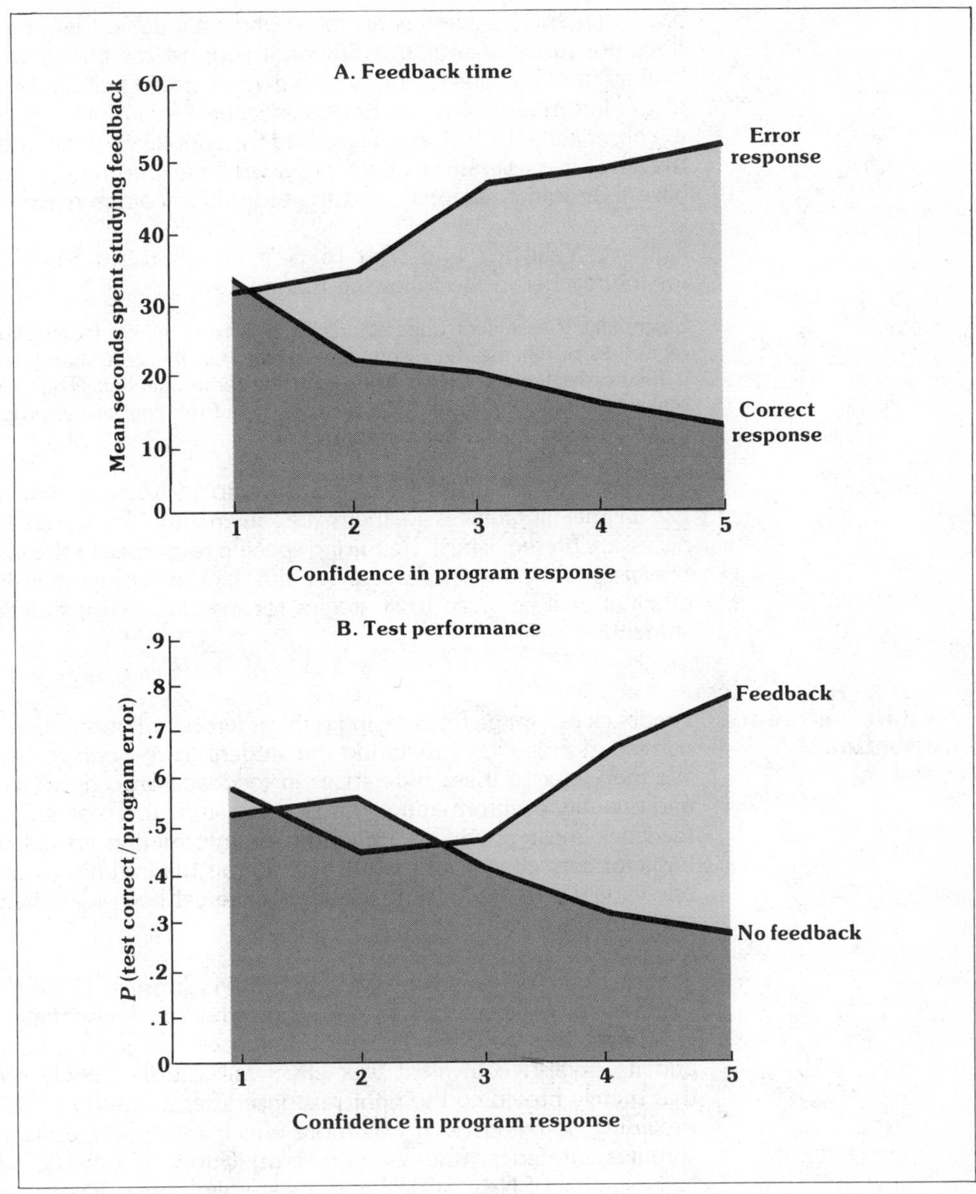

Source: Kulhavy (1977).

were very likely to correct high-confidence errors on tests of both immediate and delayed retention. Feedback was studied longest after high-confidence errors and least after high-confidence correct responses.

Overall, feedback had little effect on either errors or correct responses at low confidence levels, and Kulhavy, Yekovich, and Dyer explain this as a lack of understanding. When a student does not comprehend the information presented in instruction, the student has no basis for answering questions and simply guesses at the answer. Feedback after such a guess is no more understandable than the prior instruction and so does not further learning. Additional support for this view is found in research by Kulhavy and Parsons (1972), which demonstrated that errors due to low understanding of the information tend to be repeated on tests. More evidence for this comes from the observation by Kulhavy, Dyer, and Caterino (1975) that most research that obtained the error perseveration effect provided little information on which students could base their initial response, and therefore little comprehension was possible.

Kulhavy, Yekovich, and Dyer (p. 527) summarize the implications of their research for the teacher in the following manner:

> Essentially, if a student understands what is read, seeing feedback increases test performance regardless of whether he responds correctly. On the other hand, feedback is ineffective when it follows material which is only partially comprehended. The priority sequence is obvious. Make sure that the design and content of the material are appropriate for the student, then provide feedback after every response.

Students do not profit from exposure to instruction containing much information low in meaningfulness to them (i.e., instruction for which they do not possess the necessary prerequisites). Requiring specific responses to the information and providing feedback will not compensate for this lack of comprehension. In the next chapter attention will be given to strategies for insuring that instruction is meaningful to the student.

The information in informational feedback

Feedback can range from saying right or wrong following a response to more elaborate correction procedures requiring the student to respond to new remedial information. We may refer to these differences in feedback procedures as a matter of the quality and quantity of information provided the student. To be effective in correcting errors, feedback must provide a minimum of information so the student has a sufficient basis for correcting errors, while beyond this minimum level of information no systematic variables in feedback procedures have yet been identified and related to student performance.

Travers, Van Wagenen, Haygood, and McCormick (1964), in a study of learning German vocabulary by elementary school children, found that saying "No, that's wrong" was ineffective feedback. However, feedback that included the German word missed and its English equivalent was effective. Guthrie (1971) obtained results showing that merely providing the right response after a question was no more effective than providing no feedback. It was more effective to provide the correct response and its stimulus antecedent (the question stem). Suppose a teacher asks the question "What is the capital of New York?" and the student replies incorrectly, "Buffalo." According to Guthrie's finding, it would be ineffective to reply, "No, it's Albany." Rather the teacher should reply, "No, the capital of New York is Albany."

Sassenrath and Garverick (1965) compared four feedback procedures, differing in amount of information, following a midsemester examination in a college course. The feedback procedures were (1) no feedback—these students were told their total score and grade without review of the exam, (2) correct answers—the students' exams were returned with correct answers on the blackboard and they were given a period to review the exam, (3) correct answers and text reference—students were given correct answers with relevant pages in the text for an opportunity for review, and (4) discussion—instructor briefly discussed each exam question as students reviewed their exam.

FIGURE 10–12
Informative feedback facilitates learning

Performances for these four groups were compared on the final exam in the course for both items repeated from the midterm and new items. All three groups that received some form of feedback showed greater retention on repeated items than the no-feedback group. Only the discussion group did better on new items than the no-feedback group.

Research on more complicated feedback procedures, such as branching techniques that require the student to answer additional remedial questions, have not secured consistent effects due to the particular feedback procedure (Anderson, 1967). However, Anderson concluded that correction procedures, when used by a competent teacher, probably facilitate learning (Figure 10–12). In line with this conclusion is Kulhavy and associates' comprehension interpretation of error perseveration. Any instructional event, correction procedure or whatever, that promotes understanding will lead to a greater correction of erroneous performance by the student. A skilled and knowledgeable teacher interacting with an individual or small group of students should offer them an explanation that will further their understanding of the material, or else recognize that students do not possess the prerequisites to profit from the intended instruction and change plans accordingly.

Immediate or delayed feedback

Another cardinal principle of education has been that to be most effective, feedback should follow as immediately as possible the student's response. How has this principle held up under empirical analysis? Kulhavy and Anderson (1972) cite 11 studies comparing immediate and delayed feedback with meaningful materials. Eight out of 11 studies found a difference in retention in favor of delayed over immediate feedback.

Kulhavy and Anderson advanced the interference—perseveration hypothesis to explain the advantage of delayed feedback. They (p. 506) state:

> Our explanation is very simple: learners forget their incorrect responses over the delay interval, and thus there is less interference with learning the correct answers from the feedback. The subjects who receive immediate feedback, on the other hand, suffer from proactive interference because of the incorrect responses to which they have committed themselves.

In support of their interference-perseveration hypothesis, Kulhavy and Anderson offer several lines of experimental evidence from their study. First, a group receiving delayed feedback scored significantly higher than a group receiving immediate feedback. Next, the immediate feedback group was almost twice as likely to make an error on the same test items as were the delayed feedback students. Finally, the immediate feedback students could recall their choices on the first test better than the delayed feedback group. This research led Sassenrath (1975) to reanalyze data from his previous work on immediate and delayed feedback. He discovered that students who got delayed feedback were more likely to change an initially wrong response to a correct response on a second retention test.

In their experiment, Kulhavy and Anderson (1972) discovered that students in the immediate feedback condition studied the feedback less than those in the delayed feedback condition. This suggested that, in addition to less interference, part of the cause for the superior performance produced by delayed feedback is that after taking a test students attend less to informational feedback. This reduction in attention to feedback after a test could be due to fatigue, frustration, anxiety, or other factors associated with testing situations.

What does the reseach on delayed feedback mean for classroom practices? On a retention test covering a large unit of instruction, it would probably be best to delay feedback or discussion of the test until the next day. This should be especially relevant if attention is a factor in the delayed feedback effect, as Kulhavy and Anderson indicate. Immediately after the test, particularly a difficult one, students are not likely to attend very closely to the feedback and therefore do not profit from it. However, in the acquisition of new information the student is checking on comprehension, so providing immediate and frequent feedback should most facilitate the understanding process.

The most important function of feedback appears to be as corrective information after an incorrect response. Therefore, sufficient information beyond a simple right or wrong must be supplied to the student to provide a basis for correcting performance. Feedback cannot be used to augment poor instruction because students who do not comprehend the original instruction will not comprehend the feedback either. Care and planning must be used to insure that the initial instruction is understood by the student in order for feedback to be effective. In the next chapter further attention will be given to requirements for the design of such instruction.

9. Which of the following is true concerning the effective use of feedback?
   a. Access to feedback before responding reduces learning.
   b. Feedback after incorrect responding is more important than feedback after correct responding.
   c. Students do not profit much, if at all, from feedback when instruction is low in meaningfulness.
   d. All of the above.
10. In going over a test Ms. Carr supplies the correct answer but does not offer an explanation for any answer because it is too time-consuming. Evaluate this policy on the basis of feedback.

SUMMARY

Three general events occurring in all instruction were presented in this chapter: directing attention, eliciting student performance, and providing feedback. Teachers need to provide cues in instruction that direct the students' attention to relevant information; they can do so by a variety of means such as highlighting important information, giving verbal directions, and stating objectives or pre-questions. Requiring student performance was described as having two effects: direct and indirect. The direct is a practice effect and the indirect is the general effect of encouraging the student to engage in critical learning activities. Finally, providing feedback as an event of instruction was described. The conclusion was reached that feedback serves a corrective function to the student, so it should be rich in information.

SELF-TEST

1. Textbook A is advertised as being an effective learning tool. The most important information is printed in red, second most important in green, third in blue, and fourth in brown. Textbook B has only the most important information printed in red, while textbook C has no information differentially printed. Assuming these textbooks contain the same information, we would expect:
   a. Students to learn more from A than B or C.
   b. Students to learn more from B than A or C.
   c. Students to learn more from C than A or B.
   d. Students to learn equally well from A or B, which will both be greater than C.
2. Orienting stimuli, such as underlined words, pre-questions, and verbal directions, can reduce learning by:
   a. Promoting rote rehearsal.
   b. Diverting attention from relevant stimuli.
   c. Reducing expectancy.
   d. All of the above.
3. A student who asks the professor to repeat a statement and then writes it down word for word is demonstrating:
   a. Evidence against the external storage hypothesis.
   b. Processing too much information.
   c. Evidence against the encoding hypothesis.
   d. How to be a nuisance.
4. If inserted questions require concept learning or rule learning on the part of the student, it is important that the questions:
   a. Not occur too frequently.
   b. Be placed after the relevant information.
   c. Be placed before the relevant information.
   d. Require overt answers.
5. List two factors influencing the effectiveness of review as a study strategy.
6. In regard to note taking, research shows:
   a. Note taking does not facilitate learning when the information is low in meaningfulness to the learner.
   b. Note taking exerts a greater influence on retention when the lecture is highly structured.
   c. The greater the number of ideas per unit of words in a person's notes, the better is recall.
   d. Quality of notes correlates with a recall measure of retention but not with a recognition measure.
7. What appears to be the relationship between underlining and learning?
   a. It is a strategy most likely to be successful with mature learners at about the sixth-grade level and beyond.
   b. It is a strategy that can be successful with any student at any age if the student is able to read the material.
   c. Learning is positively related to the amount of material underlined—the greater the amount underlined, the greater the amount of learning.
   d. Being provided with information already underlined is better than self-generated underlining because the author is better able to pick out the important material to be remembered.
8. Mr. Neutron was very mad at his class because no one seemed to profit from his explanation of a question that everyone missed on the test. Actually this outcome could quite possibly be attributable to the original instruction. Explain this puzzling conclusion.
9. Which of the following would be evidence against a reinforcement interpretation of feedback?
   a. The interference-perseveration hypothesis.
   b. The tendency to repeat errors on a retest after feedback.
   c. The tendency to correct errors without feedback.
   d. No difference in correct responding on a retest for students receiving or not receiving feedback.
10. Research on the source of questions has demonstrated that:
    a. Student-generated questions are typically of lower levels than a teacher's and have little effect on learning.
    b. Oral questions facilitate learning from text better than printed questions.
    c. Oral questions inserted in a lecture do not facilitate retention for low-ability students.
    d. Printed questions provided as an adjunct to lectures facilitate retention better than oral questions.

ANSWER KEY TO BOXED QUESTIONS

1. *b*
2. *a*
3. The stick figures serve as a prompt for correct performance without attending to the number names.
4. *b;* review facilitates encoding and retrieval, so we would expect a student who has engaged in review to do much better on any essay than a student who has not.
5. *a*
6. *b*
7. *a*
8. After, because post-questions enhance both intentional and incidental learning, while pre-questions can actually reduce incidental learning.
9. *d*
10. Feedback serves a corrective function; the more information students have on which to base future performance, the better.

ANSWER KEY TO SELF-TEST

1. *b*
2. *d*
3. *c*
4. *b*
5. Factors influencing effectiveness of review: amount of time devoted to review, paraphrasing important information, spaced review, and constructing questions to answer.
6. *c*
7. *a*
8. The original instruction could have been beyond the comprehension of the students and therefore was low in meaningfulness to them. In this case, feedback would also be low in meaningfulness to the students.
9. *d*
10. *b*

Chapter 11

Domain-specific conditions of learning

IN CHAPTER 10, we looked at the requirements of effective instruction that are general to all learning domains. We saw that effective instruction requires that the teacher:

1. Activate and channel student motivation toward attainment of the desired outcome.
2. Direct student attention to the critical information in the instructional presention.
3. Promote direct practice of the desired performance capability or an appropriate class of study activities (note taking, underlining, mental review) that is instrumental in bringing about the desired behavior.
4. Provide feedback to students about the level of performance exhibited.

The significance of instructional events in facilitating phases of learning was discussed.

In this chapter, we will explore the instructional procedures that are most closely related to what Gagné (1974a, 1977) refers to as the instructional events of stimulating recall of prerequisites and providing learning guidance. Both these instructional events have an influence on various learning phases as well.

An instructional presentation designed to facilitate recall of prerequisites and provide learning guidance contains directions and stimuli specific to the particular learning domain required by the instructional objective. For example, teaching a task requiring concept learning necessitates different directions and stimuli for the learner than those necessary to teach a motor skill. The establishment of an affective state requires different directions and stimuli than does the establishment of a motor skill. We will refer to these directions and other instructional events particular to a learning domain as *specific* conditions of learning.

Again it should be noted that these instructional events, especially learning guidance, operate on many learning phases. Directions and stimuli provided to guide learning facilitate encoding, which affects retention and transfer directly. Of course, the presence or absence of prerequisites has a direct influence on the type of encoding that takes place, or even whether or not encoding takes place at all.

After reading this chapter, you should be able to specify the steps in teaching:

1. Affective objectives.
2. Motor skill objectives.
3. Memorization objectives.
4. Concept and rule learning objectives.
5. Mathemagenic objectives.

TEACHING AFFECTIVE OBJECTIVES

In Chapter 5 we saw that affective states are composed of three components: emotion, cognition, and behavior. If we view affective states as being directed toward classes of persons or objects, then the emotional component would be the subjective feelings directed toward that class. The cognitive component would be the information a person possesses and believes about that class of objects or people. The behavioral component would be the actual overt behaviors displayed by the person toward the object of the attitude. As we have seen earlier, such behaviors have the effect of moving the person either toward the object (approach behaviors) or away from the object (avoidance behaviors).

The learning of affective states such as attitudes, opinions, values, and morals represents important goals in the school curriculum. All schools want students to develop civic responsibility, tolerance of cultural differences, appreciation of the arts, love of learning, and other positive traits. Many affective states are taught intentionally, such as respect for the rights of other people, while others are acquired incidentally or secondarily during the pursuit of other goals. For example many of your experiences during art class help to mold your attitude toward the arts even though they may not have been intended to do so.

Another very important source of incidental learning of affective states is the teacher as a person. The values, beliefs, and other affective states reflected in the teacher's actions serve as a model of how the students should behave. Communities have long recognized this important function of teachers and demanded that teachers adhere to the moral code of the community. In this section of the chapter we will explore modeling and other means by which affective states may be acquired and modified.

Stimulating recall of prerequisites

One may not think so, but even the learning of attitudes requires prerequisites. Gagné (1977) describes two major classes of prerequisites for the acquisition of affective states: information and concepts. Both can be acquired during or before learning the affective state. However, for successful affective change, the information and concepts associated with the affective state must be available to the learner.

Affective states, as was stated previously, are directed toward classes of objects or people. These classes of objects or people are concepts and the person's understanding of them represents the cognitive component of affective states. Suppose a teacher wishes to change the attitude of students toward ethnic minorities. In order to do this the students must already know or acquire some conceptualization of ethnic group and prejudice.

Another prerequisite is information related to the affective state under consideration. According to Gagné (1977) information most likely to be important pertains to situations in which choices of action are to be made. In our example of prejudice against minorities, information about situations in which prejudice is most likely to occur would be presented to the student.

These two types of prerequisites are necessary in the modification of affective states. Often they are incorporated into the materials designed to influence the affective state. In this case they are learned as the affective state is acquired and changed. If they are not taught as part of the instruction, then the teacher must first determine that the students have the necessary information and concepts as entering behavior.

Providing learning guidance

Affective states can be acquired or changed by many different events. The change can be abrupt, as when we experience a very powerful or significant event, but more usually affective states evolve through many contacts with the class of events forming the object of the affect. At any rate, affective states appear to be acquired and modified through one of three means: (1) conditioning, (2) observational learning, and (3) exposure to persuasive communications.

Conditioning. In Chapter 4 classical conditioning was shown to be an effective means by which emotional responses are learned. Watson and Rayner (1920) conditioned a fear of white rats in little Albert through the classical conditioning paradigm. Staats, Staats, and Crawford (1962) demonstrated that words acquire emotional or affective meaning through classical conditioning. For example, a child may get a spanking from a parent. During the spanking the child is told several times that he is bad. *Bad* acquires negative affect from this pairing. Now *bad* is paired with *Chinese* when the child hears his parents say, "The Chinese are a bad risk, you cannot trust them." Again, through classical conditioning, *Chinese* acquires the negative affect associated with *bad*. In this way the emotional component of affective states can be learned without the person ever being exposed to the actual object. Zanna, Kiesler, and Pilkonis (1970) have found results similar to those of Staats et al. using a slightly different procedure.

Some affective states developed by the school are negative attitudes. The teacher desires that the student avoid certain habits, such as smoking or using drugs, for the student's own safety. In these instances, a teacher will often resort to "scare tactics." Does such an approach work? Classical conditioning suggests that if an unpleasant emotion is elicited, then it will become associated with any stimulus contiguous to it. Leventhal, Watts, and Pagano (1967) reported a greater desire to stop smoking from a group shown a vivid and gory movie of a lung operation performed on a lung cancer patient than from a group given statistics on the relationship of lung cancer to cigarette smoking. Presumably the visual concreteness of the film elicited a negative emotional response, while the abstract statistics did not.

A positive attitude toward an object can be developed if that object is associated with another object that already elicits such a response. Janis, Kaye, and Kirschner (1965) had two groups of people read a passage designed to change their attitude on an issue. One group was provided with cokes and snacks while reading the passage, and the other group was not provided with any snacks. The group given the snacks changed their attitude in a more positive direction than the other group. Galizio and Hendrick (1972) had college students read a persuasive passage with or without folk music as a background accompaniment. Students who received the music version developed a more favorable attitude toward the topic of the passage.

Studies like these support the common belief that school should be a pleasant experience for the student. Such architectural innovations as open space, carpeting, and cheerful colors can help students form a positive attitude toward schools. Teachers may aid the development of such an attitude by providing many interesting and varied displays and equipment in the class. For example, many elementary school classes have a reading corner, an area set aside exclusively for reading with perhaps a nice rug or large pillows. Something like this is not going to make children "love" school, but combined with other practices it should promote a more positive attitude toward school (Figure 11–1).

The preceding studies all suggest the relevance of classical conditioning to affective change; however, affective states can be modified through operant conditioning as well. In this situation the person performs some behavior for which reinforcement is received, and through this process the person's affective state toward the object of the performance is changed. Very often the behavior reinforced is expressing an attitude such as "I like school!" Hildum and Brown (1956) reinforced either positive or negative comments about Harvard's educational system. Students reinforced for positive comments subsequently made more similar comments than students reinforced for negative comments.

Lott and Lott (1960) studied the effects of reward on children's preference for playmates. By manipulating experiences in a game, they developed a preference for play-

FIGURE 11–1
A pleasant environment can be more conducive of positive affect.

mates among fourth and fifth-graders for partners associated with past experience. Insko (1965) found that attitudes conditioned by a simple reinforcement procedure are maintained over time. Students enrolled in a course were contacted by telephone and reinforced verbally with the comment "Good" for target verbal responses. One week later in class students were given an attitude survey, with the results that the attitudinal response conditioned over the phone was maintained.

Reinforcement in a learning task is given contingent upon appropriate performance, and school tasks are no exception. Consequently we would expect a child who experienced frequent success in school to develop a more positive affect toward school than a child whose experiences are predominantly failure. Furthermore, affective states have motivational properties in that the more we value an object, the more effort we will expend to attain that object. Hence the relationship between affect and achievement becomes cyclical because as a student experiences success in a subject, a positive attitude may develop. Then with a more positive affective state the student works harder and longer at the task and is therefore more likely to succeed. This new success in turn reinforces the affective state. For this reason and others reviewed earlier, reinforcement theorists have long advocated that instruction should be carefully designed and sequenced so that all students are successful with a very high frequency.

Observational learning. People often learn to perform a novel response by watching others. We have all noticed the person at a formal dinner who, not knowing the appropriate utensil for each course, looks about to see which utensils others are using to eat a course. In just such a way young children acquire the behavioral and other components of affective states by observing their parents and significant others in their lives. How we learn by observing others has been extensively studied by Albert Bandura and his associates, resulting in the social learning theory described in Chapter 4.

In a classic study of observational learning, Bandura, Ross, and Ross (1961) showed that young children can acquire aggressive behavior by observing an adult model. Perhaps due to such research, social learning theory has received wide application in the study of the effects of mass media on the affective states of young viewers. Much of this research has been concerned with the effect of viewing television violence on a person's future aggressive tendencies. After reviewing 33 studies of television violence and aggression, Stein and Friedrich (1975, p. 30) drew the following conclusions:

> The correlational and experimental studies indicate that viewing violence often instigates aggressive behavior. Such viewing is also associated with positive attitudes toward violence and with the belief that events on television reflect reality. These effects occur across a wide age range for both sexes and for children from varying social class backgrounds. The fact that the same findings result from differing methods and measures strengthens the conclusion drawn; although methodological weaknesses can be identified in any study, the strengths and weaknesses across studies fall in different areas. There is virtually no evidence that violence reduces aggressive behavior tendencies through catharsis.

More important for the classroom teacher than the effects of violence is the fact that research has demonstrated that people can acquire prosocial attitudes by observing a model. Bryan and Walbek (1970) demonstrated that children who observed a generous model were themselves more willing to share monetary rewards earned from playing a game. Stein and Bryan (1972) showed that third and fourth-grade students who observed a model displaying self-control in a game were more likely to engage in self-control during the same game than were children who had not seen such a model.

Children can learn prosocial attitudes and behaviors from watching television in natural settings such as the home and school. A successful and long-running children's program that focuses on social and emotional development is "Mister Roger's Neighborhood." Friedrich and Stein (1973) identified the following list of themes from a sample of shows: cooperation, sympathy, sharing, affection, friendship, understanding the feelings of others, verbalizing one's own feelings, delay of gratification, persistence and competence at tasks, learning to accept rules, control of aggression, adaptive coping with frustration, fear reduction, self-esteem, and valuing the unique qualities of each individual.

Stein and Friedrich (1975) reviewed nine studies concerning the effects on children of watching "Mister Rogers' Neighborhood." These studies include observations of performance on a contrived experimental task and children's play in natural settings. They concluded that children learned a variety of prosocial attitudes and behaviors from watching: respect for others, acceptance of individual differences, cooperation, independence, and self-control, to name a few. These attitudes generalized to a variety of settings. Short exposure to the program could produce these type of results, but the changes were more likely with more frequent exposure to the program.

Besides being models themselves, teachers often provide or direct students' attention to models of desirable characteristics. For example, students are frequently taken on field trips to observe various "work-world" models. Inspirational models of athletes, scientists, and other famous people who have persisted in the face of great adversity and accomplished significant feats are often held up to students as examples of conduct. The question naturally arises: What constitutes a model likely to be attended by the student?

As stated in Chapter 4, imitation of a model is most likely to occur when two conditions are met: (1) the model is reinforced for performance, and (2) the model is of high status to the student. So teachers want to choose a high-status model with which their students can identify. Just because a given model is successful in a particular field does not insure a high status for that model with a given student. An adolescent is more likely to attend to and therefore learn from the behavior of a popular singer or actor than from a Nobel laureate. For this reason it is important for a teacher to know about the personal interests of students in the class.

Persuasive communication. A teacher trying to develop a negative attitude toward smoking or a sense of civic responsibility in students will often present an argument in favor of the desired trait. For example, in making the argument in favor of civic responsibility the teacher may cite a list of historical events illustrating what does or does not become of an informed and concerned citizenry. Furthermore, the list of illustrative events is so sequenced as to lead to a logical conclusion, which may or may not be explicitly drawn for the student but which persuades the students to adopt the point of view expressed in the message.

We will define *persuasive communications* as verbal messages designed to convince people to change their opinion or belief about an issue on the basis of factual and rational information. Emphasis here is on the basis for this change because propaganda often carries the connotation of misleading and less than truthful information. We will assume the information is factual and the students are compelled to change their opinion because of the "sheer logical weight" of the argument. Notice that the content of the message is aimed at the cognitive component of affective states, not the emotional component.

The design of a persuasive message must consider three factors: (1) source of the message, (2) content of the message, and (3) student characteristics. The source of the message includes both the person who delivers the message and the authority who actually generated the information. Presentation of one or both sides of the argument, explicitly or implicitly drawn conclusions, and which side to present first are aspects of a message's content. Third, we need to consider the students and their initial attitude, frame of reference, and other characteristics likely to affect receptivity to the message.

Source of the message. A major determiner of whether or not a message will produce a shift in opinion is the source of that message. The effectiveness of an information source is influenced by two related factors: credibility and trustworthiness.

Hovland and Weiss (1951) were among the first researchers to examine the communicator's credibility as a variable in producing attitude change. In their study students who were led to believe that an argument came from a high-credibility source showed greater attitude change than students led to believe the same argument originated from a low-credibility source. Aronson and Golden (1962) performed essentially the same experiment with sixth-grade students. A man spoke to the students about the importance and usefulness of arithmetic. He was introduced to one group of students as a prize-winning engineer and to another as a dishwasher. As expected, there was a greater positive shift in the attitudes of the sixth-graders exposed to the high-credibility communicator.

One element of credibility in communication is expertise. We are more likely to accept the opinion of an expert than of a person without credentials in an area of endeavor, especially if we ourselves have little knowledge in this area. Another element determining the credence of an information source is trust. A trustworthy source is one in which we are willing to place reliance on the truthfulness of the information.

A particularly effective means for increasing trustworthiness in a persuasive communication is to have the message delivered by someone arguing against their own self-interest. For example, would you be more willing to believe an advertisement sponsored by a large oil company that argues for or against allowing big oil companies to expand into other energy fields? Or an advertisement by the American Bar Association for or against no-fault automobile insurance? Walster, Aronson, and Abrahams (1966) tested the relationship between self-interest and trustworthiness experimentally. One group of students read an article attributed to a convicted criminal that argued for more severe treatment of criminals, while another group read an article from the same source arguing for more lenient treatment. Students who read the argument for harsher treatment of criminals changed their opinion in that direction.

The preceding evidence indicates that the source of the information presented in a persuasive communication is critical to the effectiveness of that communication. The implications for teachers are simple: students' opinions are most likely to be changed by sources perceived by them as credible and trustworthy. Teachers should seek such sources when attempting to influence opinions.

Content of the communication. A persuasive communication as used here has been defined as a message designed to change a person's opinion or attitude on the basis of factual and logical information. Thus we have restricted the term to messages appealing to reason, although, in the case in which a group of smokers reported greater intent to stop smoking after viewing a lung cancer operation on film, an appeal to emotion is quite effective in inducing attitudinal change. If our message is to appeal to the person's rationality, then it should lead to our point of view. So concern should be given to the content of a message and its organization in order that they logically build to the appropriate conclusions.

One-sided or two-sided arguments. In presenting an argument we have the option of giving only those facts that support our conclusions or stating the arguments both pro and con. One line of reasoning states that presenting only the facts supporting an argument makes these facts appear stronger and more logically compelling. Another view hold that if people can think of counterarguments to a one-sided presentation, they are less likely to change their opinion. Therefore according to this view people should be exposed to both viewpoints so they do not generate counterarguments.

Hovland, Lumsdaine, and Sheffield (1949) found that two-sided arguments were more persuasive to people who started with an opposing opinion, and a one-sided argument was more effective in strengthening the opinion of those people who initially agreed with the opinion expressed in the communication. While there are conditions in which it is more advantageous to present a one-sided argument, overall the best strategy is to present both points of view. Lumsdaine and Janis (1953) demonstrated that people exposed to a two-sided argument are more resistant to a later counterargument about that same topic. Jones and Brehm (1970) showed that a one-sided argument is effective in changing opinion only if the person is unaware of logical counterarguments. Unless one is sure that counterarguments will not be generated, it is best to present both sides of the issue in a persuasive communication.

The order of presentation. If we present pro and con views in an argument, then we must decide whether to present our own point of view first or last. Of course, we wish to place our point of view in the position attracting the greatest attention by the students. Hovland (1957) lists five conditions that favor putting the desired viewpoint in the first position in an argument:

1. When the opposing view does not focus on weaknesses of the other side.
2. When the contradictory information is presented by the same communication.
3. When committing actions are taken after only one side of the issue has been presented.
4. When the issue is an unfamiliar one.
5. When the recipient has only a superficial interest in the issue (low cognitive need).

Stating a conclusion. Should the logical conclusion(s) of the facts presented in a persuasive communication be stated explicitly for the listeners or should listeners be required to infer these conclusions for themselves? Hovland and Mandell (1952) found that, regardless of the listener's intellectual level, attitude change was much greater for a group receiving the argument with explicitly stated conclusions than for one without. Consequently, rather than depending upon the students to draw the appropriate conclusions from the argument, it would appear that the teacher should summarize the argument by stating the desired conclusions for the students.

Student characteristics. A persuasive communication is not constructed without regard for the audience for which it is intended. Without due consideration of important student characteristics, our communication may lack effectiveness or, even worse, have an opposite effect of the one we intended. For example, our argument must be presented in terms comprehensible to the students. Additionally, we would expect that logical arguments in general would be more effective with older as opposed to younger students and also with more intelligent students.

The student's initial opinion or attitude on the issue we wish to influence is an important determinant of the position we should take in order for our message to have maximum impact. If our position is too divergent from that of the students, then we run the risk of our opinion being ignored or rejected by them.

Hovland, Harvey, and Sherif (1957) have conducted research demonstrating that the effectiveness of a given communication on attitude change depends upon the audience's initial opinion on the issue. They postulated that on a given issue people had both a latitude of acceptance, which represents the range of acceptable opinions different from their own, and a latitude of rejection comprising the range of unacceptable opinions different from their own. Furthermore, their research found that a person holding a strong opinion has a wide latitude of rejection and a narrow latitude of acceptance on that issue. This would suggest that for an issue on which strong feelings are exhibited, it is extremely important to consider the students' initial position in order to properly plan the message, since they will be more attuned to small variations from their position. Additionally, Hovland, et al. found that the greatest attitude change occurred when the opinion communicated was moderately discrepant from that held by the audience.

Communications that express opinions widely divergent from that of the audience can be effective in modifying opinion under certain conditions. Aronson, Turner, and Carlsmith (1963) found that with a high-credibility source, the greatest opinion change occurred when there was a large discrepancy between the audience's and the communicator's opinions. Moderate discrepancy between opinions produced the greatest attitude change when the credibility of the communicator was low or questionable. So, when the source of the communication is an acceptable expert or other highly credible figure to the students, the expression of a widely deviant opinion is most successful in changing opinion.

The degree of opinion change among a group of people is also influenced by the commitment made by those people to the stated opinion. People who make public their opinion on an issue are more resistant to counterarguments on that issue than people who, while possessing similar attitudes, do not make such a public commitment. Kiesler, Mathog, Pool, and Hovenstine (1971) reported that women who favored the dissemination of birth control information and signed a petition advocating it were much less affected by exposure to information arguing against the availability of birth control information than a similar group of women who did not sign a petition. Furthermore, the women who signed the petition were much more willing to do volunteer work concerning the dissemination of birth control information.

Using a technique somewhat analogous to the behaviorist's use of shaping, which they called the "foot in the door" technique, Freedman and Fraser (1966) demonstrated that people were more likely to make a significant public commitment if first they complied with a simpler act of commitment. This research suggests that over a period of time, through the use of careful planning, teachers could have a significant impact on students' affective states. By the use of gradually more difficult public actions students can be induced to strengthen a commitment toward a given point of view.

In this section on affective change we have seen that a teacher influences students' affective states in a number of ways. Often this influence is unintentional, as when the teacher's actions model behaviors that the students adopt. Instruction, while specifically designed to teach cognitive objectives, engenders attitudes toward school in general, the specific subject matter, and the individual teacher providing the instruction. Over time through this learning process students who experience success in school develop a positive attitude toward education and achievement, whereas students who consistently experience failure come to possess a negative attitude toward education and eventually may drop-out of the process.

Finally, teachers often intentionally attempt to change students' opinions on important issues. As we have seen, this is best done through a well-prepared and organized persuasive message. Such communications are most successful when the students' initial attitudes are taken into account in designing the message and the information is received from a source perceived as credible by the students.

1. Which of the following is a prerequisite for affective learning?
   a. Emotional empathy for the affect object.
   b. Specific approach responses.
   c. Information relevant to the affect.
   d. None of the above.

2. In presenting a lesson designed to change student opinion about an issue a teacher should:
   a. Present both sides of the issue.
   b. State the desired conclusions explicitly.
   c. Give the desired point of view first.
   d. All of the above.

TEACHING MOTOR SKILL OBJECTIVES

Skilled movement of the body and its various limbs is of great importance in human endeavors for a number of reasons. Skilled performance of a set of motor skills is quite often a critical component of the occupations by which we earn our living.

The skilled craft occupations often require a long apprenticeship while the apprentice acquires the capability to perform the appropriate skills. Not only our vocation, but frequently our avocation also, demand the mastery of motor skills. Many leisure activities are sports or other skilled performances like woodworking, sculpturing, modelmaking, and dancing. Furthermore, various motor skills are the media by which intellectual operations manifest themselves. The most noticeable, although not the only possible, media are speech and writing.

Much of our early life is spent gaining proficiency in basic motor skills and building these skills into more complex repertoires. For example, most children are encouraged by their parents at a very young age to scribble on paper. As these children enter kindergarten this scribbling is channeled into more skillful performances such as copying and drawing shapes. As the child enters school, progress is made in printing letters and finally in cursive writing. Even though most instruction on motor skills occurs while we are young children, we still encounter tasks demanding the acquisition of motor skills throughout our educational careers.

The nature of motor skills

Motor skills are typically complex performances involving the execution of a sequence of movements. This sequence of skill is often represented as a program that the person executes. Figure 11–2 shows the program involved in the task of opening a door.

From such analysis of motor skills we can see that mastering a motor skill has two aspects: (1) learning to execute the component movements comprising the skill and (2) learning the sequence in which the movements are performed. We will refer to this sequence of movements hereafter as the *program.* The student first learns the program cognitively, that is, as a rule, and after learning it in this manner it may be recalled to guide performance in learning to actually execute the program.

Phases in learning motor skills. These aspects of motor learning described above proceed in an orderly fashion through three phases of learning. Fitts and Posner (1967) have termed these phases: the early or cognitive phase, the intermediate or associative phase, and the final or autonomous phase. Fitts and Posner view these phases as overlapping, with no distinctively observable transition between them.

Cognitive phase. In this initial stage of skill learning, the students attempt to comprehend what the task requires of them. This means that the program of the skill is learned as a rule by which execution of the movements will be guided. Furthermore, the learner must attend to cues to guide movement that will later be ignored as performance becomes more expert. For example, the beginning student in golf must visually attend to the grip of the club while swinging is practiced. As he becomes more proficient in the skill, the golfer does not notice the grip but assumes it "naturally" without thought. Finally in this phase previously acquired movements are selected to serve as the component movements of the new motor skill.

Associative phase. Two important events in learning a motor skill occur in this phase. First, the previously acquired movements selected in the cognitive phase are modified to fit the requirement of the task. Second, coordination of the individual components in an integrated sequence in the execution of the skill is practiced. As a result of these two events, errors that are initially quite frequent begin to decrease.

FIGURE 11–2
Program involved in execution of a simple motor skill

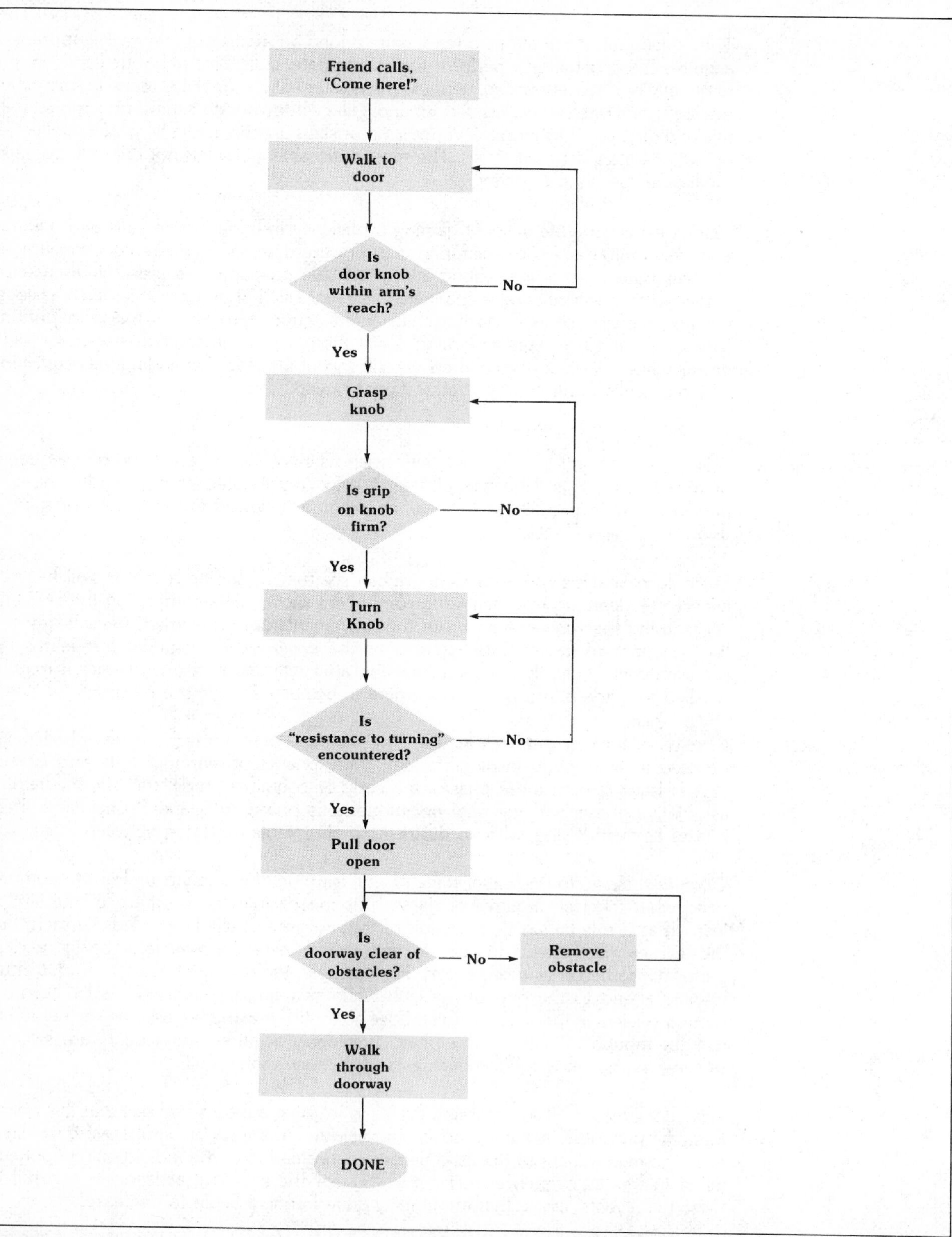

Autonomous phase. Here the skill becomes more or less automatic. By this is meant that the skill is less dependent upon cognitive control and less susceptible to distraction from other events. These two characteristics have important connotations in the performance of motor skills. Less cognitive control implies that the student has to place less conscious effort in the guidance of the skill. Verbal cues are less important or drop out and are replaced by appropriate internal cues. Since the skill is less susceptible to distraction, it can be performed in more diverse and complex contexts. Furthermore, it means the student can attend to and perform other tasks while executing the learned motor skill.

Performance is this phase is quite smooth. Fitts and Posner (1967) note a high degree of similarity between reflexes and highly practiced skills in this phase. Once the performance starts it tends to run off without hesitation. However, performance continues to improve with practice even in this phase.

We now move to a consideration of specific instructional events in the teaching of motor skills. As we shall see, these specific events must occur to guide the learner through the three phases outlined above. Therefore it is very important that teachers recognize the phase under consideration and the demands it places upon the student in designing motor skills instruction.

Stimulating recall of prerequisites

According to Gagné (1977) learning a motor skill requires two prerequisites on the part of the learner: recall of component movements and recall of the program comprising the skill. The component movements from which a new motor skill is built usually have been acquired earlier in a different context. If the motor skill to be learned by the student possesses a component movement unfamiliar to the student, then depending upon its difficulty it may be learned singularly or during practice of the total skill.

The availability of the skill program in the working memory of the student prior to instruction is unlikely. This is typically the initial emphasis of instruction. The reason for this is simple: the student must be able to recall the skill program in the associative phase of learning. Recall of the skill program, then, is a prerequisite to the associative phase of motor skill learning.

Providing learning guidance

Learning guidance in teaching motor skills usually consists of verbal instructions, demonstration of the skill, or some combination of the two. Demonstrations and verbal instructions are most important in the early or cognitive phase of motor skill learning. In this beginning phase, demonstrations and verbal instructions fulfill the following three important functions:

1. Inform the student of the skill program.
2. Cue specific component movements as the program is initially practiced.
3. Focus student attention on critical cues in skilled performance.

As the above functions suggest, learning guidance by the teacher affects the efficiency of motor skill learning. It allows students to more quickly perceive critical information in the learning situation. In many cases, left to their own devices students may never attend to this critical information. Davies (1945) compared two separate groups on the acquisition of archery skills. One group learned by trial and error, while the second group received verbal instruction on the correct form and how to practice it. Both groups received equal amounts of practice, but the verbal instruction group demonstrated far greater proficiency at the end of the course of study than the trial-and-error group. Davies observed that a major reason for the poor performance of the trial-and-error group was that they never adopted effective practice procedures but rather persevered with inadequate methods often acquired early in the course of study.

Verbal instruction or directions alone are usually insufficient to teach motor skills. Most typically either live or filmed demonstrations augmented by verbal instructions are used to teach motor skills. In this case the demonstration provides a model that the students can imitate in initial practice of the program. Later, with the performance of the model stored in memory possibly as an image, the students can compare their performance to the model's and determine its correctness. When used to augment a demonstration, verbal directions function as orienting stimuli. In this capacity they focus the students' attention on some external or internal stimuli that must come to control the execution of a particular component movement in the skill program. On other occasions they may be used by the teacher to cue performance of a component movement if for some reason student performance of the program falters at that movement. In either case, verbal instructions should be brief so they do not distract the students' attention from other relevant information.

Eliciting student performance

The importance of student performance to effective instruction was stressed in Chapter 10. Actual overt practice on the learning task is extremely important when our performance objective specifies the acquistion of a motor skill, unlike outcomes in the other domains where covert practice is sufficient to insure learning. Overt practice is so important in learning motor skills that little gain can be expected without it. But with continued practice the efficiency of motor skill performance can be facilitated even over very long periods of time. Crossman (1959) provided data to illustrate that performance improvements on a motor skill are evidenced even after four years of experience, as shown in Figure 11–3.

Apparently for motor skills the saying, "Anybody can do anything better than they are currently doing it," is a good principle by which to plan.

Practice of motor skills seems to be necessitated by the type of stimulus cues that come to control the skilled performance of muscular movements. Such skills are under the control of external environmental stimuli and internal stimuli arising from the muscular movements themselves. The only way, then, for the student to attend to these cues and to associate them with correct movement is to actually perform the desired skill. As Gagné (1977, p. 219) explains:

> Practice is necessary, then, because only by repeating the essential movements can the learner be provided with cues that regulate the motor performance. As practice proceeds (with suitable feedback), internal cues leading to error are progressively rejected, and internal cues associated with performance smoothness and precision become established and retained as regulators of skilled performance.

In designing the practice component of motor skill instruction, the teacher must make two decisions. First, should the student start with practicing the component movements and then practice the entire program after mastery of the components, or just practice

FIGURE 11–3
Performance of operators with varying amounts of experience in an industrial skill (cigar making)

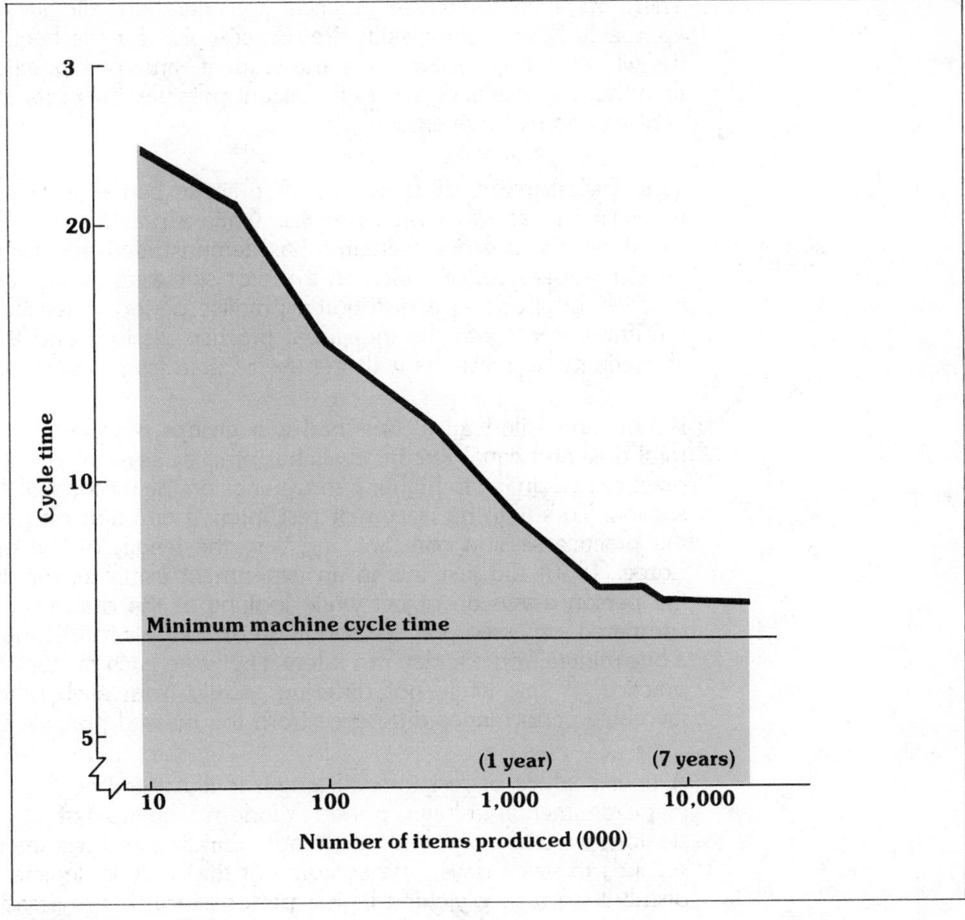

Source: Crossman (1959).

the entire program of movements? Second, should the practice period be interspersed with rest periods or not? To make these decisions the teacher must first determine the difficulty and novelty of the motor skill to be learned, and then decide upon the type of practice sessions, as we shall see in the succeeding paragraphs.

Part versus whole skill practice. On some occasions the teacher may prefer to have the student practice the individual component movements before practicing the entire skill program. On other occasions the teacher may omit the parts practice and have the student practice only the entire skill program. Research involving different types of tasks has been inconclusive on the superiority of either part or whole practice. Fitts and Posner (1967) offer the following advice in choosing whether to use part or whole practice. If the motor skill has component movements with a high degree of independence, then part practice would be more beneficial than whole practice. However, the major demand imposed on the student by most motor skill tasks is the integration of the component movements into a smooth sequence of responses. In this latter type of situation, practice of the whole skill program would be the obvious choice.

There are skills for which practical considerations dictate a part or whole practice approach. Some motor skills are too complex for the beginning student to practice the whole skill program. Here the student must first practice parts of the skill and then the whole skill. Again, to the extent possible, the parts should represent independent component movements.

The distribution of practice. A practice period interspersed with rest intervals is referred to as *distributed practice,* while a practice period without rest periods is called *massed practice.* Research has demonstrated that distributed practice leads to greater student performance on a motor skill than an equivalent amount of massed practice. In choosing a distributed practice period, a teacher needs to decide upon the duration of both the individual practice sessions and the rest intervals. We will examine these questions with the use of data from several studies.

Kimble and Bilodeau (1949) had two groups practice a motor skill with the same total time and equal rest intervals but practice sessions of different lengths. A shorter practice session led to higher performance on the motor skill than did the long practice session. To study the effects of rest interval duration on performance, we can hold the practice session constant and vary the length of the interspersed rest interval. Lorge (1930) did just this in an experiment using mirror drawing, a task in which the person draws an object while looking at the drawing effort in a mirror. Lorge compared a massed practice condition of 20 trials to distributed practice using either a one-minute or a one-day rest interval between each practice session. Both distributed practice groups, while not differing greatly from each other, showed a large and favorable performance difference from the massed practice condition.

A finer analysis of rest interval length is illustrated by the work of Kientzle (1946). Her experimental task was printing random sequences of letters upside down. Practice sessions were of a constant one-minute duration and rest intervals varied from several seconds to seven days. The outcome of the study is depicted in Figure 11–4. Again, distributed practice yielded higher performance than massed practice. There was no advantage to increasing the rest interval beyond 40 seconds.

From the preceding discussion, the optimal strategy for the distribution of practice in motor skill instruction is short practice sessions interspersed with short rest intervals. Of course, deciding the relative proportions of time to spend in practice and rest requires that other factors be taken into account. The nature of the task is one such factor; some tasks require a relatively long period of time to perform. Another important factor is the amount of available instruction time for practice and the amount necessary for most students to reach the specified criterion level.

When available instruction time is limited and rest intervals would subtract from the time necessary to achieve the specified criterion level, then rest intervals should be reduced or, if necessary, eliminated. Rest intervals may be safely eliminated because distributed practice affects performance, not learning, of motor skills (Irion, 1966; Whitely, 1970). After a rest period, performance of a skill practiced under a massed condition will recover to the level of performance that would result from an equal amount of distributed practice. Why then use distributed practice? As Gagné (1977) discusses, massed practice is more likely to lead to greater fatigue and less motivation on the part of the learner. Additionally, poorer student attitudes could result from such conditions as these combined with the lower level of performance with massed

FIGURE 11–4
The effect of time between trials on the performance of subjects learning how to print upside down

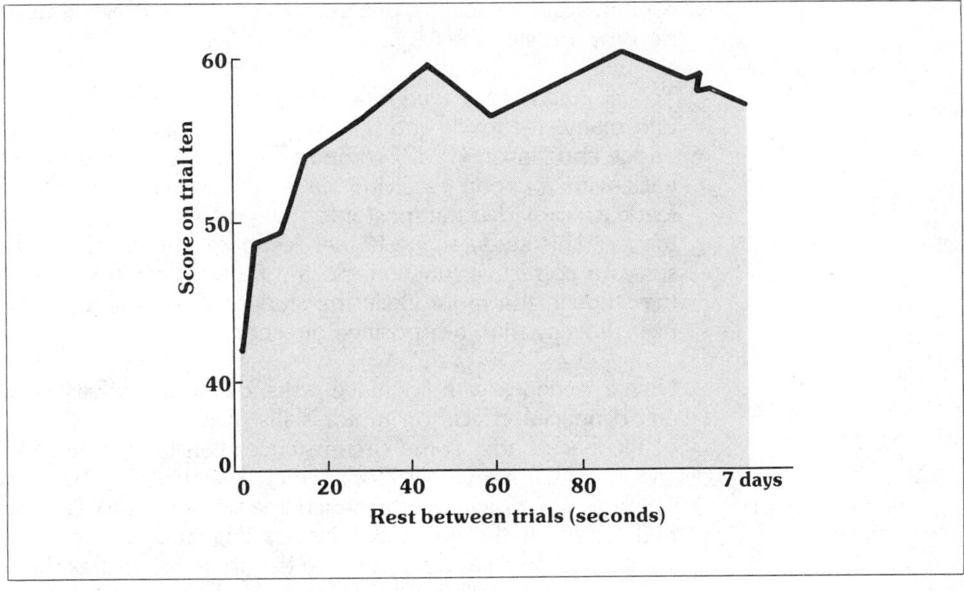

Source: Adapted from Kientzle (1946).

practice, consequently when possible distributed practice should be used in the design of motor skill instruction.

Providing feedback

Feedback and practice are critical events in instruction designed to promote motor skills. The nature and timing of feedback in the acquisition of motor skills are more critical than in instruction aimed at cognitive objectives. Two sources of feedback for motor skills can be identified: intrinsic and extrinsic.

Intrinsic feedback arises from execution of the skill. This information is often called a "natural consequence" of the action and can be either internal stimuli produced by muscular movements or external stimuli in the environment. For example in archery, intrinsic feedback can be either the "feeling" in the arm when the bowstring is pulled to the appropriate position or seeing the position of the arrow in the target. The latter is an external stimulus and the former is an internal stimulus, but both are intrinsic feedback because they are part or the result of performing the skill task.

Extrinsic feedback carries the connotation of "artificial" feedback because it is external stimuli added to the situation in which the skill is performed. Because of this characteristic, extrinsic feedback is alternately referred to as *augmented* feedback. Using our example of archery, suppose after a shot the student is told, "Your shot landed to the left of the bull's-eye because you pulled your bow arm after releasing the arrow." In this example the instructor is providing information to the student that is not a natural consequence of the action, so the intrinsic feedback is being augmented by the instructor.

In teaching a motor skill we want the student ultimately to depend upon intrinsic feedback to regulate performance. However, the acquisition of this motor skill is greatly enhanced by the appropriate use of augmented feedback. Especially in the cognitive and associative phases, augmented feedback is necessary for efficient progression toward skill mastery.

To use augmented feedback effectively, a teacher must observe two rules: (1) give informative feedback, and (2) give it as soon as possible following performance. Trowbridge and Cason (1932) compared groups receiving three types of augmented feedback with a group receiving no feedback. The most effective form of augmented feedback provided the most information to the students about the accuracy of performance. This study suggests that feedback with motor skills, as with cognitive tasks, serves a corrective function. So the more information augmented feedback supplies the student, the more likely the student will be able to change performance on the next practice trial in a positive direction.

Unlike feedback with cognitive tasks, delay of feedback has not been shown to have any beneficial effects on motor skills. Rather, research has demonstrated that delay of feedback under some circumstances can be harmful to skill performance. Greenspoon and Foreman (1956) studied delay of feedback with a simple motor skill. The task was drawing a three-inch line while blindfolded. Feedback consisted of being told "right" if the line was between 2¾ and 3¼ inches; for anything longer they were told "long"; and for any line less than 2¾ inches they were told "short." Experimental groups receiving differing feedback delays were compared with a control group receiving no feedback. The outcome of the study is illustrated in Figure 11–5.

In the Greenspoon and Foreman study, a short delay of ten seconds had little if any effect on performance. Other research has shown that longer delays of feedback can be tolerated with motor skills instruction (Bilodeau & Bilodeau, 1958). The situation in which a delay of feedback can be harmful involves intervening practice. Suppose

FIGURE 11–5
Mean number of "right" responses for control and experimental groups for successive blocks of five trials

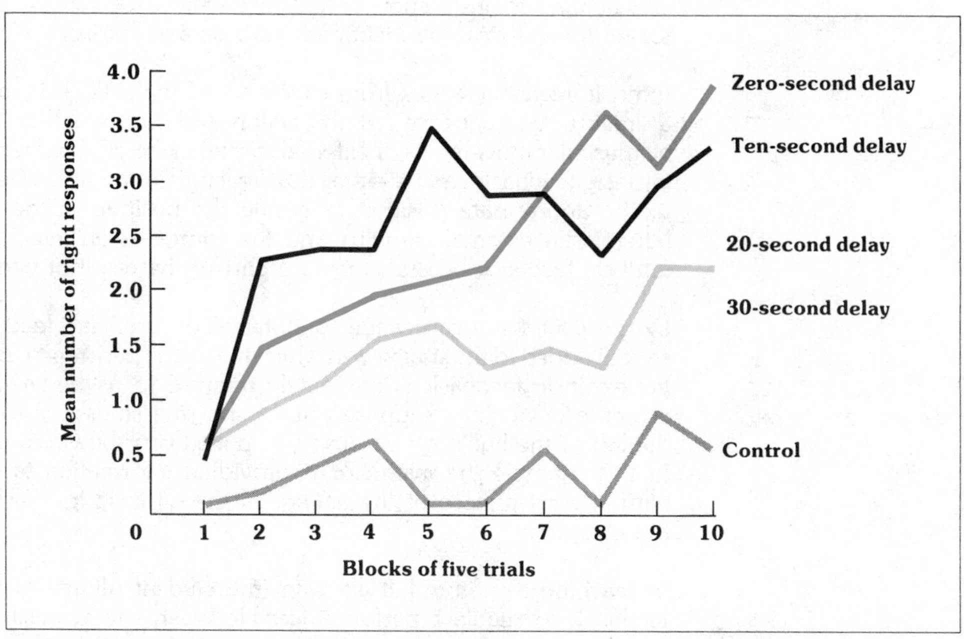

Source: Greenspoon and Foreman (1956).

a student commits an error while performing a movement and then practices the movement again before the teacher informs that student of the reason for the error. In a case like this the effectiveness of the feedback is diminished (Bilodeau, 1956; Lavery & Suddon, 1962). The solution to this problem is for the teacher to pace the practice trials, especially during the cognitive phase of learning, to avoid interfering activities by the student.

In this section of teaching model skills we have presented a teaching cycle of demonstration, practice, and feedback (Figure 11–6). Emphasis was on the importance of practice and feedback to successful instruction on motor skills. Appropriate practice and feedback, while important for learning in any domain, are essential components of motor skill instruction when the objective requires any degree of mastery. When motor skills are involved, practice does make "perfect" when used with sufficient and informative feedback to the student. Verbal directions and other cues are most important in the cognitive phase, where they focus the student's attention on critical features of the performance.

3. Which of the following represents the optimal strategy for the distribution of practice in motor skill instruction?
   a. Short practice sessions interspersed with short rest intervals.
   b. Short practice sessions interspersed with long rest intervals.
   c. Long practice sessions interspersed with short rest intervals.
   d. Long practice sessions interspersed with long rest intervals.
4. Describe the two critical features of effective feedback for motor skill learning.

FIGURE 11–6
Motor skills tasks can involve either total body movements or fine movements

TEACHING MEMORIZATION OBJECTIVES

Memorization occurs when the learner can recognize or reproduce information that was presented during instruction. Gagné (1977) refers to it as the *learning of verbal information* because we typically verbalize the information in sentence form. He further defines verbal information by distinguishing three categories based upon complexity: (1) names or labels, (2) facts, and (3) knowledge. Names are the verbal labels or words associated with objects or classes of objects (concepts). Facts are propositions referring to single and unique events ("Columbus discovered America in 1492") or to classes of events ("Geese fly south for the winter"). This last fact would also be a rule, whereas the former would not. Knowledge would be a collection of related facts about some subject or topic such as the history of the Pennsylvania Dutch or quantum mechanics in physics.

Learning in this domain spans performances ranging from the verbatim recall of a name to stating in one's own words a collection of facts. This latter capability Tiemann and Markle (1973, p. 155) call a "verbal repertoire," and they describe a person who possesses one with the following phrases.

> His behavior is characterized by restatement "in his own words," by summaries, by the comparing and contrasting of information from several sources, and other such activities that elevate his performance beyond the category of verbatim reproduction.

In providing learning guidance for the acquisition and retention of verbal information, the teacher's primary concern is to lead the student to encode the information in a meaningful and organized fashion. This is important because, as we have seen in Chapter 5, the type and degree of encoding determine whether information will be placed in long-term storage and also influence its retrievability from long-term memory.

This meaningful encoding is most likely to occur when information is presented in a meaningful context and is organized in a manner conducive to proper encoding. In a corollary to this principle, the student must be prepared for the instruction by possessing prior knowledge to which the new verbal information can be related and by having available an appropriate elaborative strategy for encoding the new information. This student preparedness for learning new verbal information is referred to as a *prerequisite* by Gagné (1977) and elsewhere in this book as *entering behavior.*

Stimulating recall of prerequisites

The instructional event of stimulating recall of prerequisites establishes the meaningful context in which the new verbal information is delivered. As we have just indicated, for the acquisition of verbal information the two prerequisites are (1) the existence of previously learned information to which the new information can be related, and (2) the availability of an elaborative strategy suitable for encoding the information. We will inquire first into the contribution of previously learned information to the learning and retention of new information.

The writings of Ausubel (1963, 1968) have been very influential in elucidating the role of prior learning in the acquisition of meaningful verbal information. As stated in Chapter 5, meaningful verbal learning occurs when the student relates the to-be-learned information to information already existing in the student's cognitive structure. If an individual does not have a relevant or adequately organized cognitive structure to which the new information can be related, then according to Ausubel, this anchoring information can be provided through an advance organizer. According to Ausubel, even if a student does possess relevant superordinate information in existing cognitive structure, an advance organizer presented by the teacher should still facilitate meaningful verbal learning.

Ausubel and his associates (Ausubel, 1960; Ausubel & Fitzgerald, 1961, 1962; Ausubel & Youssef, 1963) have carried out studies of the effects of advance organizers on the learning of verbal information with topics as diverse as metallurgy and religion. Ausubel and Youssef (1963) used a comparative organizer with consecutive reading passages on Buddhism and Zen Buddhism. These comparative organizers emphasized the similarities and differences between Buddhism and Christianity or between Buddhism and Zen Buddhism. Students in the control group read historical and biographical material related to the reading passages. There was a significant difference in learning between the two groups on the first reading passage but not on the second passage. This is understandable because both the experimental and control groups apparently had acquired knowledge of Buddhism from the first passage under which they could subsume or relate information from the second passage on Zen Buddhism.

In these studies, the effective organizers presented more general and inclusive information, while the ineffective ones presented information at the same level of specificity as the to-be-learned information. Ancillary to this, several studies have shown that advance organizers are a greater aid to students of low ability as opposed to students of higher abilities (Ausubel & Fitzgerald, 1962; Schulz, 1966). Presumably, the former students have less relevant cognitive structure for learning a given task or less skill at relating new information to existing knowledge. Under certain circumstances this can be reversed, and advance organizers can have a facilitating effect on the learning of high-ability students while not benefiting students of lower ability (Ausubel & Fitzgerald, 1962; Grotelueschen & Sjogren, 1968).

Many studies have failed to find any advantages of advance organizers in the learning of verbal information. Barnes and Clawson (1975) reviewed 32 studies and concluded that advance organizers do not facilitate learning. Lawton and Wanska (1977) disagree with this conclusion and point out that advance organizers are only potentially a variable in learning. Organizers play a role in determining learning only when the student does not have appropriate cognitive structure or when the student's existing cognitive structure needs reorganization or clarification. Therefore, according to Lawton and Wanska, negative results do not necessarily lead to the conclusion that advance organizers do not facilitate learning.

A study by Rickards (1976b) has done much to clarify the role of advanced organizers in the learning and retention of new verbal information. Most studies of advance organizers have examined merely the resulting quantity of learning while ignoring any possible qualitative differences in learning. However, Rickards postulated and obtained such qualitative differences in learning associated with the use of advance organizers. He demonstrated that advance organizers containing a statement of superordinate information produced greater recall of information than did organizers composed of coordinate information. More important, students given superordinate organizers showed greater organization in their recall than other students.

Several other lines of research evidence lend credence to the importance of a meaningful context established by prior knowledge in the acquisition and retention of verbal information. Wittrock (1974) has proposed a generative model of learning in which the student generates meaning for new information from past experiences. Comprehension and retention are greatest when the student is stimulated to form both abstract and distinctive concrete associations from long-term memory for the new information. One of the major variables determining the extent to which such generative processes occur is the specific context in which the information is encountered. Marks, Doctorow, and Wittrock (1974) replaced 15 percent of the words in an unfamiliar story given to elementary school children with high-frequency words. The frequency with which words occur is a common measure of their meaningfulness, which increases as the frequency increases. Comprehension and retention of both a story at the student's reading level and a story above reading level increased by an average of 25 percent for recipients of the high-frequency-word story versions.

In a second study, Wittrock, Marks, and Doctorow (1975) replicated and elaborated the study cited above. High- and low-frequency-word versions were developed for each of three stories used in the experiments. A sentence taken from one of the stories illustrates the difference between the two versions. Words in parentheses are low-frequency synonyms used to replace the high-frequency words they follow: "I saw that the flowers (blossoms) and leaves of the mirror were moving (stirring)." Students in the experimental condition read the high-frequency version of the story first, then the low-frequency version. Control-group students read the low-frequency version twice. Both groups were given a comprehension test after their first reading and then immediately after the second reading. Both groups were given a vocabulary test on the low-frequency words from the story. One week later, all students were given a retention test based upon the low-frequency version of the story. Dramatic results were obtained on the comprehension and retention tests from the group who first read the high-frequency version of the story; their performance was twice as good as that of the other group.

A meaningful context facilitates the acquisition and retention of verbal information because it allows the student to relate previously acquired knowledge or meaning to the new information. Several studies by Royer and Cable (1975, 1976) have shown that this transfer is a function of the type of information both previously learned and to be acquired. In their studies they demonstrated that previously acquired concrete information can facilitate the acquisition and retention of abstract information on a similar topic, but they did not discover a facilitative effect for the reverse relationship. The effect was very large, with the concrete-to-abstract groups recalling over 40 percent more of the abstract information than any other groups. Apparently students who learned the concrete information first had it available for encoding the abstract information, and consequently they remembered the abstract information better than students who had not learned the concrete information.

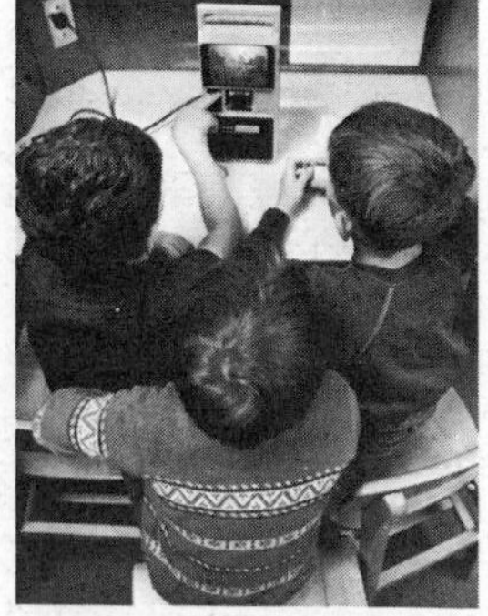

FIGURE 11–7
Presenting information in a meaningful context enhances retention

The preceding studies all support a simple but very important principle for the classroom teacher. As Ausubel (1968, p. vi) has written: "If I had to reduce all of educational psychology to just one principle, I would say this: The most important single factor influencing learning is what the learner already knows. Ascertain this and teach him accordingly." Students learn and remember verbal information best when they can give it meaning by relating it to their existing cognitive structure. The context in which new information is presented should promote the relating of this information to the existing knowledge structure (Figure 11–7). If the student does not possess the necessary cognitive structure to assimilate the new information, then such structure should be established prior to reception of the new material. Appropriate knowledge structure is most important when the new material is abstract and presumably least familiar to the student. Structure can be established by providing concrete and specific illustrations or other information that relates the new information to information already known by the students.

Facilitating student use of encoding strategies

In past chapters the role of encoding in the storage and retrieval of information from long-term memory has been emphasized. This section of the chapter will focus on how a teacher can promote student use of effective encoding strategies in the acquisition of new information. Additional emphasis will be given to important age differences in the use of encoding strategies as they relate to the design of instruction.

To review briefly, there are two types of elaborative encoding strategies: verbal and imagery. With verbal encoding strategies the student relates the new information in some manner to more meaningful verbal information that can be recalled more readily and hence serves as a retrieval cue for the new information. Such encoding schemes occur with frequency in classroom settings. For example, the student confronted with the task of learning the nine planets and their order from the sun learns the sentence: My very excellent mother just served us nine pies. When asked to name the planets in their order from the sun, the student recalls this sentence and decodes it into Mercury, Venus, Earth, Mars, Jupiter, Saturn, Uranus, Neptune, Pluto.

Imagery encoding strategies involve increasing the meaningfulness of information by association with concrete sensory experiences. Such encoding strategies usually entail visual imagery, but they do not have to do so. Consider the simple singsong way most children learn to recite the alphabet. If a child falters in saying the alphabet, then humming a few bars of this tune is usually sufficient to retrieve the appropriate sequence of letters. The tune is this case functions as an aural encoding image or cue.

Rohwer (1972) has classified the conditions necessary to induce elaborative encoding by a student. He refers to these triggering conditions as *prompts* and distinguishes four categories based on the degree of explicitness: maximal, substantial, moderate, and minimal. According to Rohwer, a maximal prompt is an actual demonstration, whereas a substantial prompt requires a description or representation using pictures, words, or both. With a moderate prompt, the teacher instructs the student to think of an event for use in encoding the information to be learned, while a minimal prompt directs the student to learn the information without even suggesting that the student use an elaborative strategy. In the remainder of this section we explore the instructional use of substantial and moderate prompts in teaching memorization objectives. The more inclusive term *teacher-provided encoding strategies* will be substituted for *substantial prompts,* and the term *student-generated encoding strategies* for *moderate prompts.*

Teacher-provided strategies. Many lessons contain within them the verbal mediator or imagery by which the student organizes and relates the information to existing cognitive structure. Very often this mnemonic is a picture or some type of graphic illustration. In this manner the mnemonic serves as an adjunct, not as the primary source of information. Quite often therefore the illustration is a redundancy of the information to be learned.

A frequently encountered instance of school tasks involving the learning of names or labels is vocabulary in either a first or second language. Richard C. Atkinson and his colleagues at Stanford University have developed a mnemonic technique, called the "keyword method," for learning foreign language vocabulary (R. C. Atkinson, 1975; Atkinson & Raugh, 1975; Raugh & Atkinson, 1975; Raugh, Schupbach & Atkinson, 1977). First tried out in the laboratory, the method has more recently been implemented over an eight- to ten-week period in a second-year Russian language course.

Vocabulary learning proceeds in two stages with the keyword method. The first stage establishes an acoustic link between the spoken foreign word and a similar sounding English word (the keyword). In the second stage an imagery link is formed between the keyword and the English translation of the foreign word. R. C. Atkinson (1975, pp. 821–22) gives the following examples of the keyword method for Spanish:

> In Spanish the word *caballo* (pronounced something like "cob-eye-yo") means horse. The pronunciation of the Spanish word contains a sound that resembles the English word *eye*. Employing the English word *eye* as the keyword, one might form a mental image of something like a cyclopean eye winking in the forehead of a horse, or a horse kicking a giant eye. As another example, the Spanish word for duck is *pato* (pronounced something like "pot-o"). Using the English word *pot* as the keyword, one could image a duck hiding under an overturned flower pot with its webbed feet and tufted tail sticking out below.

In one experiment, Atkinson and Raugh (1975) had students learn 120 Russian vocabulary words in three 40-word groups over three days with and without the keyword method. The probability of recalling a word on each day for both groups is presented in Figure 11–8. Furthermore a test over all 120 words was given the day after learning list three and then six weeks later. The keyword group recalled 72 percent of the words immediately and 43 percent on the delayed test, while the no-keyword group recalled 46 percent on the immediate test and 29 percent on the delayed test. Other research has shown that students are more likely to use a keyword for difficult vocabulary words or after making an error on a word (Raugh & Atkinson, 1975).

Other studies have supported the effectiveness of imagery strategies in learning names and labels. Ott, Butler, Blake, and Ball (1973) found that either providing students

FIGURE 11–8
Probability of a correct response on test trials on Day 1, Day 2, and Day 3

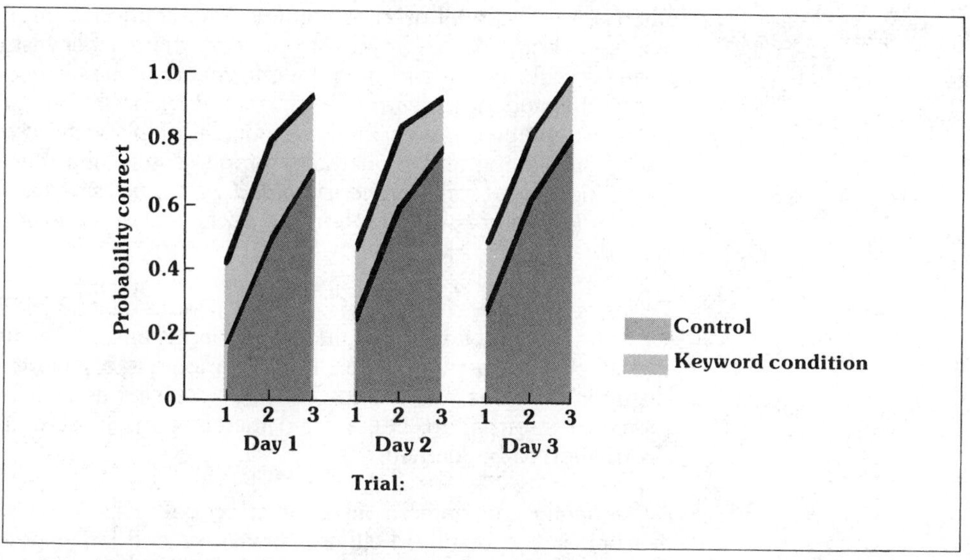

Source: Atkinson and Raugh (1975).

with pictures or having them generate imagery results in greater learning of German words. Lippman and Shanahan (1973) concluded that pictures facilitate vocabulary acquisition in third-grade students providing the to-be-learned word and its equivalent interact in the picture. Finally, Raugh and Atkinson (1975, p. 2) state that an effective keyword must meet three criteria:

1. The keyword sounds as much as possible like a part (not necessarily all) of the foreign word.
2. It is easy to form a memorable imagery link connecting the keyword and the English translation.
3. The keyword is unique (different from the other keywords used in the test vocabulary).

Illustrations as adjuncts. Teacher-provided encoding strategies can be used for learning not only names but also more complex verbal information such as facts and organized bodies of knowledge. One commonly used technique is to present pictures or other illustrations along with the oral (lecture) or printed (book) prose. Used in this way, the illustrations supplement the verbal information and are not the primary or only medium used to present the information. While research shows that memory is much better for visual information than for verbal information (see Ghatala & Levin, 1976; Levin, 1976, for further discussion), in this chapter we consider pictures in their adjunct role because this is their typical classroom role.

College students provided with graphic descriptions of chemistry concepts recalled more than a group given verbal descriptions of the same concepts (Rigney & Lutz, 1976). Other measures indicated that students, given the illustrations, reported more imagery while studying the concepts and also had a more positive attitude toward the instruction. Arnold and Dwyer (1975) showed that information from a reading passage on the physiology of the heart was retained better by high school students when it was accompanied by pictures. Peeck (1974) established that fourth-graders who read a simple story with illustrations performed higher on immediate and delayed recognition tests than a group who read the same story without the illustrations. When the two groups were compared on information presented only in the text or in the text and illustrations, it was found that the illustrations group performed higher on the text-plus-illustrations information but not on the text-only information. Furthermore, some of the information presented in the illustrations conflicted with test information. When given a multiple-choice test item that required choosing between the conflicting information, the illustrations group most often chose the information from the illustrations rather than from the text. This pattern of results suggests that pictures are an effective technique for directing students' attention to relevant information. Since students remember the information from illustrations better than information presented only by text, illustrations should be designed to depict the most important information.

Pictures can also be utilized to increase prereaders' comprehension of oral prose (Guttman, 1976; Lesgold, Levin, Shimron & Guttman, 1975). In one such study (Levin, Bender & Lesgold, 1976), one group of first-grade students heard several stories as they viewed a set of cutout pictures, and two other groups of students either repeated each sentence of the stories themselves or had the teacher repeat the sentences. After each story the students were asked five questions based on the story. Comparisons involving this measure showed that repetition, regardless of the source, facilitated learning and so did the inclusion of pictures. Interestingly, though, pictures produced greater learning than repetition. This leads to the conclusion that the effects of pictures on learning cannot be attributed to a simple repetition effect but rather to an encoding effect.

As we have seen, teacher-provided encoding strategies can have a very beneficial effect on the retention of verbal information. Depending upon the nature of the information, this encoding strategy can take the form of a verbal mediator or imagery. The most common type of imagery is the illustration, and the effects of illustrations are most noticeable when the information to be learned is abstract and difficult. In this case, the illustration helps to "concretize" the information and therefore relate it to past experiences in memory store. The most effective illustrations obviously are drawn from the most important information to be retained.

The use of pictures or other illustrations as adjunct aids does not always have a beneficial effect on learning. Samuels (1970) and Singer, Samuels, and Spiroff (1974) found that adjunct pictures interfere with the acquisition of sight words in reading taught by the commonly used flash card method. Samuels's (1970) explanation for this finding is that pictures divert the student's attention away from orthographic information (the printed letters). In this situation pictures are an inappropriate cue, analogous to underlining in the Anderson and Faust studies (see Chapter 10 of this book), which interfered with the appropriate learning.

Organization as a teacher-provided encoding strategy. Teachers can facilitate student encoding of information by presenting the information in a well-organized manner. Kulhavy, Schmid, and Walker (1977) suggest that recall differences in learning information from a text are closely related to how well students can match the structure of their recall to the structure of the textual passage.

A basic unit of organization in prose is the paragraph. The inclusion of a superordinate theme sentence in a paragraph can enhance recall of the other sentences comprising the paragraph. Gagné (1968a) demonstrated that retention of facts from a paragraph by fourth- and fifth-grade students was greater when the paragraph contained a superordinate theme sentence rather than an additional coordinate factual sentence. To illustrate this, consider the following four-sentence paragraph:

> The incidence of heart attacks is lower for high-IQ people than for the general population. On the average people with IQs over 100 live 4.7 years longer than people with IQs below 100. Statistics show that the probability of a stroke before the age of 50 is negatively related to intelligence. The occurrence of ulcers is most frequent in people with below average intelligence.

Information from this paragraph would be remembered better if it began with a sentence such as: "High-intelligence people are healthier than the general population," as opposed to starting with a sentence such as: "Arthritis occurs three times more frequently in the general population than among college graduates."

The organization of prose across paragraphs also can influence retention. A number of studies have established that college and high school students learn more from a logically organized presentation of information (Frase, 1969, 1973; Friedman & Greitzer, 1972; Kulhavy, Schmid & Walker, 1977; Myers, Pezdek & Coulson, 1973; Perlmutter & Royer, 1973; Schultz & Di Vesta, 1972; Yekovich & Kulhavy, 1976). Danner (1976) has extended this finding to children as young as eight years of age. He studied the effects of organizing prose by topic on the recall of second-, fourth-, and sixth-grade students. For all three grades, recall was greater and showed greater clustering (organization) for topically organized passages than for unorganized passages. Furthermore Danner obtained data that led him to conclude that the older children were more likely to notice the structure and to utilize it as a study strategy. These studies taken as a group give strong credence to the importance of a well-organized lecture or instructional presentation.

Learning is facilitated most when the organization of the information presented during instruction is congruent with the instructional objectives to be attained. Kulhavy, Schmid, and Walker (1977) presented the same information to groups of high school students organized around a semantic, temporal, or random theme. After studying their respective passage, all students were given a free-recall test, a semantically cued test (i.e., list all the livestock you read about), and a temporally cued test (i.e., write the events from the story in the order in which they occurred). Both organizational forms resulted in greater performance on the free-recall test. Each groups' performance on the two cued-recall tests is presented in Figure 11–9. As can be seen, recall performance was best when its organizational requirement matched the structure of the information presented in instruction.

Student-generated encoding strategies. Very often during the course of instruction, teachers make comments such as the following: "How does this relate to what we discussed last week?" "Try and imagine how it would have looked if . . . ," and

FIGURE 11–9
Recall performance as a function of prose organization across type of test cue

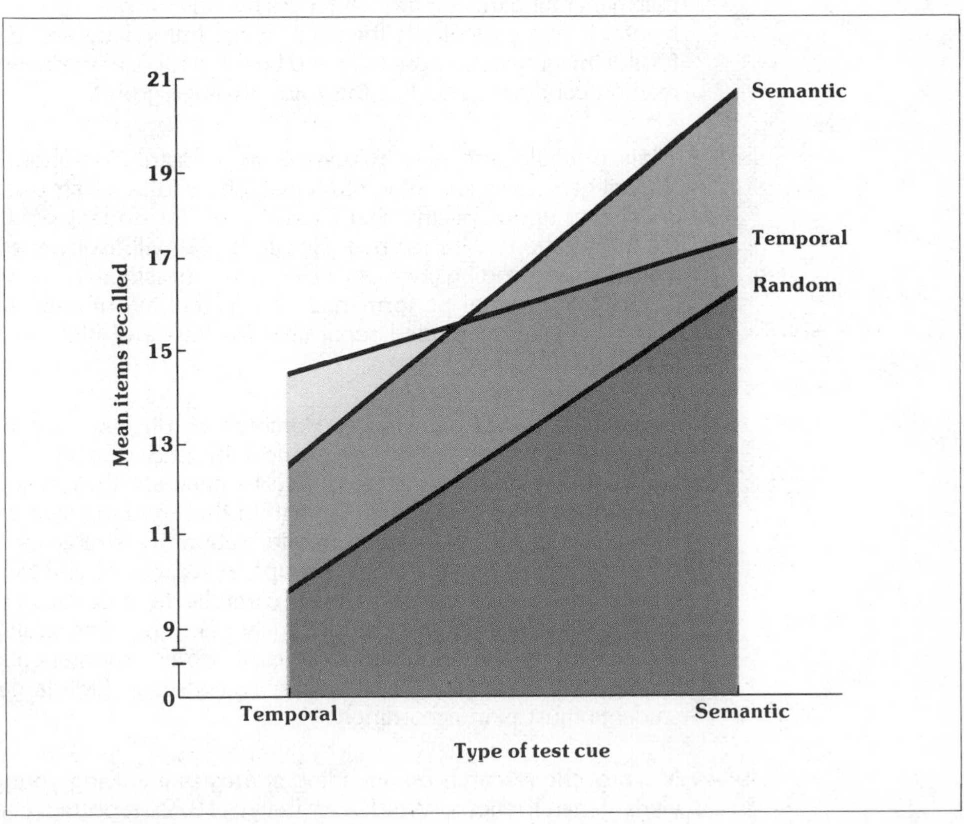

Source: Kulhavy, Schmid, and Walker (1977).

"What similarities do you recognize between this and . . . ?" Such statements are intended to induce the student to encode information in a meaningful form. In such instances the teacher is providing the students with directions that lead the students to generate their own encoding strategies.

Student-generated encoding strategies involving either verbal mediators or imagery have been demonstrated to be highly effective retention strategies (Anderson, 1971; Bower & Winzenz, 1970). The generation of mental imagery can exert a very powerful influence on learning even when there is no intent to learn. Anderson and Hidde (1971) asked one group of college students to rate 30 sentences for their imagery value and another group to rate them on their pronounceableness. The students were shown each sentence for seven seconds, and after one presentation of all 30 sentences, they were given a cued-recall test. The recall for students who rated imagery was more than three times that of students who rated pronounceableness.

Several reports have indicated that having students generate their own encoding strategy promotes learning and retention more than providing them with one. Bobrow and Bower (1969) found that college students who constructed a sentence associating two nouns remembered the association better than those who simply read a sentence relating the nouns. Bower and Winzenz (1970) had college students learn the associates for a list of 30 concrete noun pairs using one of four learning strategies. The four strategies were rehearsing by rote, studying meaningful sentences relating the noun pair, generating meaningful sentences relating the noun pairs, and generating interactive mental imagery involving the noun pairs. Immediate and delayed recall was greatest for the imagery condition, followed by the sentence production condition, the sentence reading condition, and last the rote rehearsal group.

While it would appear that preference in instruction should be given to the use of student-generated encoding strategies, the choice of an optimal encoding strategy is dependent upon specific characteristics of the student population and the nature of the information to be learned. Recall, if you will, Rohwer's classification of prompts that induce encoding. Rohwer (1972) has investigated the type of prompt necessary to facilitate optimal performance on a verbal information task as a function of age. This function is described separately for low- and high socioeconomic status (SES) students in Figure 11–10.

Two of the trends depicted in Rohwer's graph have important implications for the design of instruction. Both low- and high-SES students between the ages of seven and nine are developing the ability to generate their own encoding strategy when directed to do so. Consequently, within this age range we would expect to find large differences in the ability to generate elaborative strategies both within and between different socioeconomic status groups. A teacher of children in this age range, then, should assess entering skill levels carefully to determine whether instruction must include teacher-provided or student-generated encoding strategies. The next implication is that even by age 18, low-SES students do not spontaneously generate an encoding strategy with reliability. Teachers whose classes include large proportions of low-SES students must plan accordingly.

Much of the research on encoding strategies involving young children supports Rohwer's generalizations. Wolff and Levin (1972) reported evidence on an associative learning task that indicated that third-grade students benefited from instructions to

FIGURE 11–10
Summary of prompt types required to achieve optimal performance as a function of age; schematic patterns for high-SES (upper panel) and low-SES (lower panel) populations

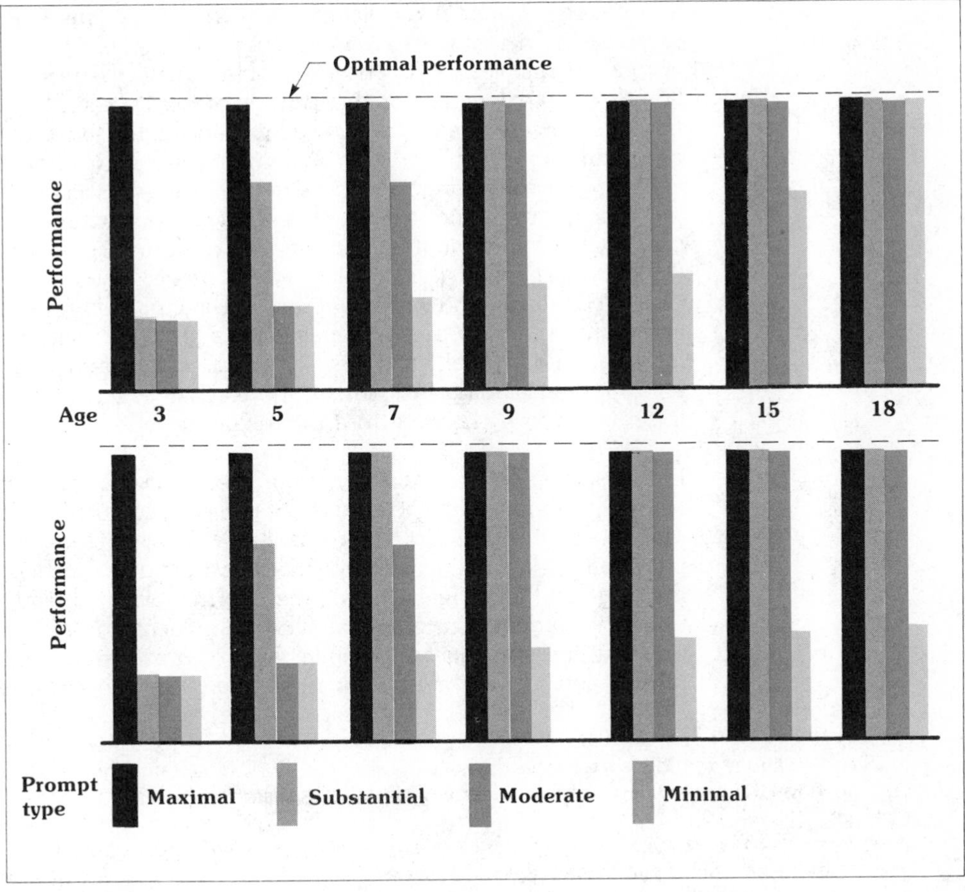

Source: Rohwer (1972).

form interactive imagery but kindergarten students showed no such effect. The difference in performance level was quite remarkable for the third-graders (77 percent correct with imagery instructions versus 32 percent correct without imagery instructions). However, children younger than seven years of age can benefit from teacher-provided elaborative strategies. Children as young as five years have been shown to recall more after listening to a story if they see or construct illustrations to accompany the story (Lesgold et al., 1975; McCabe, Levin & Wolff, 1974).

Kerst and Levin (1973) compared fourth- and fifth-grade students' use of teacher-provided and student-generated encoding strategies on an associative learning task. Both strategies were equally effective and both resulted in students performing better than a control group given no specific strategy. Closer examination of the data showed that the ability to utilize a teacher-provided strategy was more uniform among children of this age, whereas there was much greater variability in the use of student-generated strategies. As Levin (1976) has pointed out, this greater variability in the student-generated condition means two things: (1) not all students at this age profit from directions to generate their own encoding strategy, and (2) the performance of those who can encode exceeds that of students given an external encoding strategy.

In addition to student characteristics such as age, characteristics of the instructional presentation determine the effectiveness of teacher-provided and student-generated encoding strategies. Levin and Divine-Hawkins (1974) established that imagery directions had a greater effect on the learning of fourth- and fifth-graders when the information was delivered orally as opposed to in print. Presumably this effect occurs because processing textual information and mental imagery both involve the visual system and so were competing for processing capacity. However, listening involves the aural processing system and therefore does not compete with visual imagery for processing capacity. Support for this interpretation is found in a study by Rohwer and Matz (1975). They found that fourth-grade students learned better from instruction that presented information with oral prose and pictures than from material with oral prose and print. Teachers of children in this age range may want to present important information both orally and visually (pictures and print). For example, after or before an important reading assignment, the teacher could orally summarize the important information to be learned from the assignment.

In this section we have examined the specific events of instruction that are designed to teach memorization objectives. Teachers need to activate relevant information in the students' cognitive structure as a first step. If students do not possess relevant information, it should be supplied in instruction. Teachers then guide learning by insuring that the students encode the information in a meaningful fashion. Depending upon the students' current capabilities the teacher may supply the encoding strategy or allow the students to generate their own encoding strategy. When students are reliably able to generate their own strategy, learning will be maximized.

5. In which situations would we expect an advance organizer to have the greatest influence on learning and retention?
   a. When our objective calls for the learner to organize the information in some meaningful manner.
   b. When our advance organizer is on a level of specificity equal to the to-be-learned information.
   c. When the learners are of high-ability as opposed to low-ability level.
   d. When the advance organizer is composed of information superordinate to the to-be-acquired information.
6. For elementary school children (fourth and fifth grades) a student-generated imagery strategy would work best when:
   a. The students are low-socioeconomic-class students.
   b. The students are high in IQ.
   c. The students are required to practice the strategy overtly.
   d. The information is presented orally.
7. On what basis would we predict that providing the student with the outline of a lecture would facilitate retention of information from that lecture?

TEACHING CONCEPT AND RULE-LEARNING OBJECTIVES

Learning concepts and rules result in the capability to perform in novel situations in which students are asked to identify a specific instance of the concept or to apply the rule in a specific instance. Given this characteristic of concept and rule learning, it can be concluded that the major task of the teacher in providing instruction at this level is to insure that the transfer process is activated to a sufficient extent. This high degree of transferability is the hallmark of concept and rule learning as well as mathemagenic strategies. The distinction of these learning types from memorization is largely based on the transfer of learning.

In this section we cover the specific conditions of learning to be incorporated in instruction for both concept and rule learning. These two have been combined because, while the stimuli and performances involved in concept and rule learning differ, the underlying structure of the two are essentially the same. For example, even though concepts are typically divided into two classes and further distinguished from rules, both classes of concepts represent rules for classifying objects on the basis of common attributes. As defined in this book, rule learning occurs in transfer situations in which the performance to be demonstrated is one other than classification. Typically, the performance required of the student by a rule is to produce a new concept by the application of a specified change operation on another concept. An illustration of a simple rule would be to obtain the color green (a secondary color) by mixing blue and yellow (primary colors).

Since the capabilities acquired in learning a concept or rule are essentially the same, the specific conditions of learning needed to establish each are the same in terms of critical features. They are basically stimulating recall of appropriate prerequisites and providing learning guidance. Learning guidance for the acquisition of concepts and rules consists of three components: (1) a statement of the rule or definition of the concept, (2) a set of instances and noninstances, and (3) attribute prompts.

Stimulating recall of prerequisites

A child has learned the concept of red (a concrete concept) when that child can correctly identify any red object regardless of its shape, size, or function. Most frequently the child learns to identify red objects by responding with the verbal label "red." What is important is that because the child associates the response "red" with a sample of red but not other colors, we can infer that the student can perceive a difference between red and other colors. In other words, the student can discriminate red from other colors. Since learning a concrete concept involves learning to classify objects on the basis of a particular physical quality, the student must first be able to reliably distinguish this physical quality from other similar qualities.

Defined. Concepts and rules are defined by the relationship between two or more concepts. Therefore, the essential prerequisite for learning a defined concept or rule is the previous acquisition of those component concepts. In other words, the student should be able to identify previously unencountered instances of the component concepts comprising the new concept or rule. Suppose a high school English teacher is teaching the defined concept, *complement.* A complement is defined as an element in the predicate clause that identifies or describes the subject. In order to learn to correctly classify individual instances of complements, the student should already have learned the concepts of predicate clause, subject of a sentence, and identifying and describing prior to instruction on complements.

A teacher must insure that the necessary discriminations or component concepts are active in the student's working memory as instruction on the new concept or rule proceeds. Usually recall can be induced with a simple verbal cue such as "You remember earlier in the course we learned to identify predicate clauses?" On occasion the teacher may need to supply a stronger recall cue such as defining the concept and giving several instances of it.

Providing learning guidance

A teacher guides a student in learning a concept or rule with a series of expository steps. First, the teacher provides a definition of the concept or statement of the rule, which helps to focus the student's attention on the commonality among the various situations in which the learned capability is to be applied. Next, a set of specific instances is presented to illustrate the range of situations to which the student will be expected to apply the learned performance. While these specific instances are being displayed to the student, the teacher explains the application of the concept or rule in each situation, thereby focusing the student's attention on relevant information and facilitating its encoding.

Analysis of concepts and rules. The first step in designing this instruction is an analysis of the rule or concept for its relevant and irrelevant attributes. From this analysis the teacher derives the definition and a set of instances and noninstances to be presented in instruction.

A concept analysis results in a listing of the relevant attributes and the most common irrelevant attributes likely to be encountered by the student. Relevant attributes are those attributes that define class membership. All the relevant attributes for a concept must be present in an object for it to be included as a member of that concept class. In the case of a rule relevant attributes are those defining situations in which application of the rule is appropriate. Irrelevant attributes are other attributes present in a situation or object that are not critically related to class membership or application of the rule. These irrelevant attributes are important because their presence increases the difficulty of concept or rule learning. Basically a student has to learn to ignore irrelevant attributes and focus attention on relevant attributes in learning concepts and rules. The accompanying analysis of the concept *insect* is by Markle and Tiemann (1970).

Relevant attributes	**Irrelevant attributes**
1. Three-part body consisting of head, thorax, and abdomen.	1. Size.
2. External skeleton.	2. Color.
3. Three pairs of legs.	3. Style of locomotion.
4. All legs connected to thorax.	4. Ecological niche.
	5. Colonial or noncolonial.
	6. Presence or absence of wings.

As this analysis shows the student will be taught that any animal with the four relevant attributes is an insect regardless of the six irrelevant attributes. After the analysis is complete, the teacher is in a position to construct the concept definition or rule statement and the set of instances and noninstances to illustrate the concept or rule.

Statement of rule or concept definition. Providing the student with a definition of the concept helps direct the student's attention to the relevant attributes and thereby facilitates learning. Anderson and Kulhavy (1972) demonstrated that a one-sentence definition of a concept could greatly enhance performance on identifying previously unencountered instances of the concept. College students given the one-sentence definitions correctly identified 91 percent of novel instances presented, while students without the definitions answered only 28 percent of the questions correctly.

The conclusion should not be drawn from the Anderson and Kulhavy study that merely providing the student with a verbal statement of the concept or rule is sufficient instruction. As Klausmeier (1976) points out, the availability of a definition can eliminate the necessity of the student having to induce the relevant attributes from exposure to a number of instances and noninstances. However, a student who receives only a definition of a concept or rule may end up learning it as a verbal chain rather than being able to perform appropriately in novel situations. Research by Klausmeier and

Feldman (1975) demonstrated that a definition in combination with a set of instances and noninstances resulted in greater concept attainment than either alone. Furthermore, a definition with three sets of instances and noninstances was a better instructional procedure than a definition with one set; therefore a definition should be viewed as an adjunct that increases the transfer derived from a set of instances and noninstances.

The form of a definition helps to determine its effect on learning. To be maximally effective the definition of a concept or statement of a rule must be complete in terms of relevant attributes. Markle and Tiemann (1972) discovered that the capability to classify new instances or noninstances was greatly impaired following instruction containing an incomplete definition either with or without instances. The incomplete definition was obtained from a dictionary and lacked one relevant attribute.

The statement of the definition or rule must also be phrased in terms suitable to the instructional population. If the definition is stated in technical terms beyond the vocabulary of the students, then it will have little impact on student identification of relevant attributes. Feldman and Klausmeier (1974) compared the concept attainment of fourth- and eighth-grade students with two types of concept definitions. One was a technical definition specifying all relevant attributes, while the second was derived from a children's dictionary and lacked four of the six relevant attributes. Fourth-graders performed better with the dictionary definition and eighth-graders performed better with the technical definition. For the fourth-graders the technical definition apparently was not easily understood, resulting in more usable information being abstracted from the simpler and less complete dictionary definition.

Rational set. Perhaps the most important variable in determining how well the student will learn a rule or concept is the scope of the set of instances and noninstances presented in the instruction (Figure 11–11). The minimum set of such instances and noninstances necessary to teach a concept or rule is referred to as a *rational set* by Markle and Tiemann (1969). They define rational set as the number of instances necessary to vary each common irrelevant attribute once (each instance possesses all relevant attributes) and the number of noninstances necessary to delete each relevant attribute once. An important instructional decision determined by a concept or rule analysis is the composition of a rational set necessary to teach the concept or rule. Consider the analysis of insect as a concept; there were four relevant attributes and six irrelevant attributes. Therefore for this concept a rational set would consist of four noninstances and six instances.

The number of rational sets necessary to teach a concept is dependent upon several variables. The level of mastery to which the concept or rule is to be taught is a primary determinant of the number of sets needed in instruction. As the level of mastery increases, so does the number of rational sets necessary to teach the rule or concept. Another important determinant of the number of rational sets needed is the difficulty of the concept or rule. This difficulty is largely a function of the number and type of irrelevant attributes. Scandura and Voorhies (1974) showed that students took longer to learn a rule as the number of irrelevant attributes associated with instances increased. The greater the similarity between relevant and irrelevant attributes, the more likely is confusion between the two to occur, and the more rational sets will be required to teach the proper distinction.

Determining the difficulty level. After constructing a set of instances and noninstances the difficulty of each is identified by the teacher. This is done for two reasons;

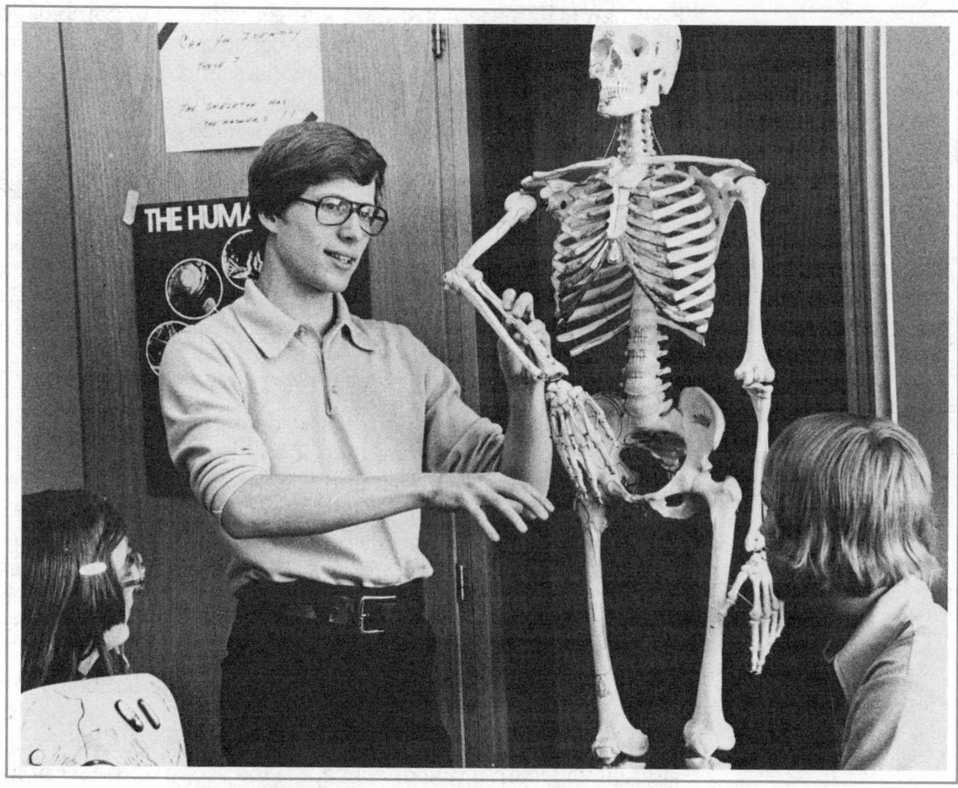

FIGURE 11–11
Provision of examples is very important in teaching concepts and rules

going from easy to difficult instances will facilitate acquisition of the concept or rule, and exposure to the total range of difficulty is necessary to insure mastery of the concept or rule. Tennyson and Boutwell (1974) have developed a systematic technique for determining difficulty level. Their approach is composed of two parts; a subjective rating of instances and noninstances by the teacher on the basis of the difficulty of attributes, and an empirical analysis resulting from a sample of students responding to the set of instances and noninstances.

Assuming the teacher has already generated a number of instances and noninstances, the first step in a subjective rating is to develop a matrix of the relevant attributes and common irrelevant attributes based on the rule or concept analysis. This matrix consists of the relevant and irrelevant attributes listed vertically and weights for the judged difficulty of each listed horizontally. A scale from one to five for rating the difficulty of each attribute can be used, with one the least difficult and five most difficult.

We will examine a sample of subjective ratings for a concept to illustrate the procedure. The concept is that of *performance objective* as defined in Chapter 7 of this book. Analysis of *performance objective* as a defined concept yielded the accompanying list of attributes.

Relevant attributes

1. Observable behavior or permanent product.
2. Conditions under which performance is to occur.
3. A quantitative criterion.

Irrelevant attributes

4. Subject matter.
5. Type of learning.
6. Syntax of sentence expressing objective.

An estimate of the difficulty level of an instance and noninstance of a performance objective follows:

Instance: Given 20 chemical elements randomly drawn from the periodic table, the student will write the atomic weights with 90 percent correct.

Noninstance: The students will correctly read a short story of their choosing.

	Weight of difficulty				
	Least				*Most*
Attributes	*1*	*2*	*3*	*4*	*5*
1. Observable behavior or permanent product	I*				N
2. Conditions of occurrence	I		N		
3. Criterion	I			N	
4. Subject matter	I N				
5. Type of learning	I N				
6. Syntax	I			N	

* I = instance, N = noninstance.

For the instance, the ratings were based on the following decisions:

1. The behavior of writing is very concrete and of high frequency in school.
2. The conditions are explicit in that they are preceded by the common word "given."
3. The criterion is a simple percentage, which from personal experience of the teacher is the type most often used by students learning to write objectives.
4. A highly structured subject matter is involved for which students encounter little trouble in writing objectives.
5. Learning type is memorization, and again the teacher's experience indicates that most objectives written by students are of this type.
6. Syntax follows the formula "Given X, the student does Y at Z level" by which objectives are typically expressed.

For the noninstance, the ratings were based on the following decisions:

1. *Reading* is a shorthand term for a set of complex performances and does not refer to a single observable act.
2. The conditions are: given a story of their own choosing, but due to the sentence structure this is obscured.
3. *Correctly* implies a standard but without mentioning a behavior or product this cannot be determined.
4. Subject matter presents no difficulty.
5. Type of learning presents no difficulty.
6. Even though syntax is an irrelevant attribute in this case the syntax used makes identification of components (relevant attributes) more difficult.

The total difficulty score for the instance was six, which would make it a very easy instance. For the noninstance the total score was 18 out of a possible 30, suggesting a middle range of difficulty. The range of scores for the available instances and noninstances would inform the teacher whether a sufficient spread had been constructed. For example, if this examination showed that more examples for a given difficulty range were needed, then the teacher could develop more.

Empirical analysis of difficulty level is a straightforward procedure. A sample of students is asked to identify the instances and noninstances developed by the teacher. The students are asked to perform this task prior to any instruction and are given only a definition of the concept or rule. The percentage of students correctly classifying the instance or noninstance under these circumstances determines its level of difficulty. For purposes of classroom instruction, individual items could be placed into one of three categories of difficulty: low, medium, and high.

The use of both subjective ratings and empirical analysis offers the most precision in instruction; however, many teachers lack the time and other resources for an empirical analysis given the realities of the classroom. When an empirical analysis is not possible, subject ratings can still provide a basis for systematically developing a range of instances and noninstances for instruction. Additionally, research by Tennyson (1973) showed that the difficulty level as determined by subjective rating sufficiently approximates that from an empirical analysis to justify its use. Use of the examples during instruction does provide a means of gathering data for an empirical analysis open to the teacher.

Presenting instances and noninstances. Once a number of rational sets of instances and noninstances have been constructed and rated for difficulty, decisions concerning the sequence of these instances and noninstances in instruction must be made. An instructional model for making such sequencing decisions has been developed by Robert D. Tennyson and his associates. Instances and noninstances are presented to the student in a display composed of two instances and two noninstances. Three variables must be considered in selecting the instances in a display and for sequencing a set of displays within this approach. A single display has the following physical format:

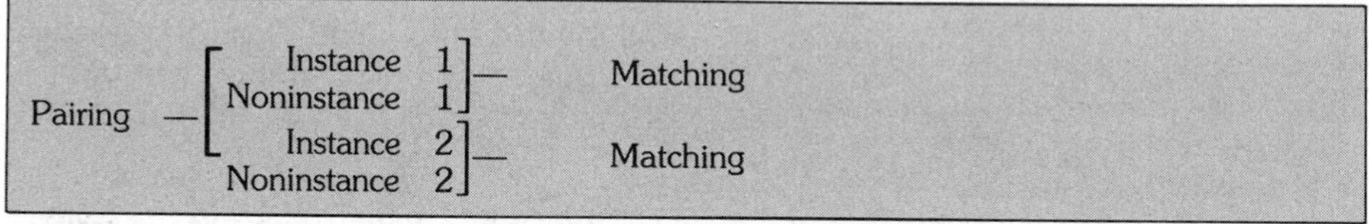

Matching as a variable refers to the relationship between the instances and noninstances in a display. They are matched if they share the same irrelevant attributes and differ only on the basis of relevant attributes. For example, with the concept of insect, the insect and other animal would be the same color, size, etc., but the other animal would have four sets of legs, not three sets. An instance and its corresponding noninstance are unmatched when they differ on both relevant and irrelevant attributes (e.g., different number of legs, size, color, etc.). Learning is facilitated when matched displays are presented because the presence or absence of a relevant attribute is more discriminable. Hence matching promotes the discrimination of noninstances from instances.

Pairing refers to the relationship between the two instances in an instructional display. Since all instances will contain all relevant attributes, pairing of instances is on the basis of irrelevant attributes. A divergent pair of instances would differ as much as possible in terms of irrelevant attributes, while a convergent pair would be equal on irrelevant attributes. According to Woolley and Tennyson (1972), divergently paired instances reduce the acceptance of irrelevant attributes as relevant to the concept or rule. Consequently, presenting divergent pairs of instances helps the student to correctly classify instances regardless of irrelevant attributes.

Mastery of a concept or rule requires that the student receive a range of difficulty in the instances and noninstances presented in instruction. Within a display all instances and noninstances should be of approximately the same level of difficulty; however, across a sequence of displays the difficulty level should increase from easy to difficult. For example, an early display would have large variations in size and color while later displays would exhibit greater similarities.

If students are not given instances and noninstances sampling all levels of difficulty, a restricted concept or rule will most likely be learned. The most typical error is to provide a student with only a few easy instances. This results in limited capability to apply the rule or concept which is largely restricted to simple situations similar to those encountered in instruction.

Research has supported the validity of the Tennyson et al. model of concept teaching. Tennyson, Woolley, and Merrill (1972) investigated the effects of probability level, matching, and pairing on the learning of a concept related to poetry. As predicted students who studied instructional displays with divergent instances, matched instances and noninstances, and the entire range of difficulty scored higher on a classification test than other groups. Tennyson (1973) reported the results of two experiments on concept acquisition. One was a direct replication of the study cited above with the concept of adverb; similar results were obtained. The second experiment was a replication of the first but without the inclusion of noninstances in instruction. Without the noninstances, students showed no learning on the concept classification test.

Markle and Tiemann (1972) reported the results of a study by two of their students on the separate effects of instances and noninstances in concept learning. Instances exerted their influence on the classification of new instances, and the presence or absence of noninstances affected correct classification of new noninstances.

An organized sequence of instances and noninstances results in better classification performance than a random sequence. Tennyson, Steve, and Boutwell (1975) organized the sets of instances and noninstances from easy to difficult or presented the sets randomly. Students who received the ordered set learned the concept in less time and made fewer errors on a posttest.

Attribute prompting. As we have seen earlier, prompts are cues that make it more probable that a student will perform correctly. In concept and rule learning prompts emphasize the relevant attributes on which student performance will depend. Their purpose is to focus the student's attention on the relevant attributes and aid in detecting the presence or absence of such attributes. Klausmeier, Ghatala, and Frayer (1974) report that when prompts are used in conjuction with a concept definition, they serve an encoding function by helping the student remember the definition and apply it in classifying instances and noninstances.

Prompts in concept and rule learning usually, although not necessarily, take the form of verbal statements clarifying the classification of a particular instance or noninstance. An illustration of this function of prompts is found in the instructional display to teach the concept of performance objective in Figure 11–12.

Tennyson, Steve, and Boutwell (1975) demonstrated that students learned more from an organized, matched, and divergent set of instances and noninstances that included attribute prompting. Furthermore, the students who received the prompts took less

FIGURE 11–12
An instructional display from a set used to teach the concept *performance objective* with attribute prompting

Presented with ten different mushrooms from this geographic location labeled by number only, the student will write the numbers of the edible mushrooms with 100 percent accuracy.

This example is an acceptable performance objective. The statement communicates the three essential components of an objective. "Write the number of edible mushrooms" is an observable behavior and leaves a permanent record, too. Conditions under which this behavior is to be performed are stated as "Presented with ten different mushrooms from this geographic location." Third, the standard for attaining this objective is explicit—"with 100 percent accuracy."

Presented with ten different mushrooms from this geographic location labeled by number only, the student will know the edible mushrooms with 100 percent accuracy.

This is not an example of an acceptable objective. While the conditions and standard are present (same as above), there is not an observable behavior. To "know" can be demonstrated by a very large number of behavioral performances.

The learner will state orally three of the four reasons for wearing safety glasses around the shop when asked to do so on a test.

This is an acceptable performance objective. All three essential components are present. "State orally" is an observable behavior. The learner will state it "when asked to do so on a test," so this is the condition of performance. How well he will perform is answered by "three of the four reasons."

The learner will state orally reasons for wearing safety glasses around the shop when asked to do so on a test.

This is not acceptable because there is no statement of how many reasons the learner will state; therefore, we have no standards for determining attainment of the objective.

time to study the material even though it was nearly twice as much information. Tennyson and Tennyson (1975) found that high school students learned to apply a rule to a greater degree when they were given explanations of how given instances represented application of the rule. Verbal explanations of specific examples supplied by the teacher are an effective technique for increasing the instructional value of a set of instances and noninstances. By offering such explanations in conjunction with a definition or statement of the rule, the teacher can reduce the number of instances and noninstances necessary to teach the concept or rule.

A note on rule learning. Until now most of our examples have involved concept learning. However, the information in the section is equally applicable to the teaching of rules. Nevertheless, we will examine a sample instructional display for teaching a rule to see how it embodies the principles discussed in this section. The display is shown in Figure 11–13 and it is actually teaching two rules simultaneously.

The examples within the display are matched and divergent with respect to each other as recommended by the teaching model. The first instance of the extraposition rule is matched on irrelevant attributes with the first instance of the "It" deletion rule. The relevant attribute on which they differ is the operation specified by each rule. The extraposition rule corrects the sentence by rearranging the phrases. With the "It" deletion rule the sentence is corrected simply by dropping the *it.* So the sentences have the same content (irrelevant attribute) but they are corrected differently (relevant attribute). If a single rule were being taught, then the noninstance would have shown a similar but different operation than that specified in the rule; in other

FIGURE 11–13
Instructional display to teach coordinate rules

Rule 1: *Extraposition* is an optional rule which may be applied whenever a sentence follows the pronoun "it" in a noun phrase. The sentence after "it" may be moved to the end of the larger sentence.

Rule 2: *"It" deletion.* Whenever the conditions for extraposition exist, but this transformation is not applied, then the pronoun "it" must be dropped.

Extraposition rule:
*It that she is sick worries me.
It worries me that she is sick.
That she is sick is the embedded sentence. The basic sentence is *It worries me.* The embedded sentence can be transferred, altogether, to follow the basic sentence.

"It" deletion rule:
*It that she is sick worries me.
That she is sick worries me.
If the embedded sentence is not moved, then the *it* that comes right in front of *that* must be dropped.

Extraposition rule:
*John wrote it that the car is new is exciting.
John wrote, "It is exciting that the car is new."
The choice in this sentence is to move *That the car is new* to follow *exciting.*

"It" deletion rule:
*John wrote it that the car is new is exciting.
John wrote, "That the car is new is exciting."
If the extraposition rule is not applied, the *it* pronoun which stands for *that the car is new* must be dropped.

Source: Adapted from Tennyson and Tennyson (1975).

words, an incorrectly worked instance. Furthermore the two extraposition rule instances and the two "It" deletion rule instances in the instructional display are divergent; that is, they differ in terms of their irrelevant attributes.

We close this section of the chapter with a note of caution on teaching concepts and rules. Klausmeier (1976) states that sets of instances and noninstances of many concepts and rules taught in the classroom cannot be specified with the precision recommended by the above approach. Many concepts could be called "fuzzy," that is, their boundaries are not clearly delineated. Take for example the concept of *car* or *automobile.* Almost everyone knows the concept but identifying its relevant attributes is difficult. Most people would list the relevant attributes as four-wheeled vehicle for transporting people. But what is the difference among a car, a truck, and a bus? Is a Volkswagen microbus a car or a bus? How about certain models of the Morgan (a three-wheeled sports car)? Would they be cars or motorcycles?

Even though many concepts fall into the fuzzy category, when teachers teach a concept, they define the limits of that concept or rule in a very real sense by the instances and noninstances they select. So teachers must use instances and noninstances in teaching concepts and rules, and the model presented in this chapter represents a guide to the development of instruction. A teacher may not be able to fulfill all the requirements of this model in any one lesson, but they stand as a goal toward which one should strive. The closer a given lesson approximates the requirements put forth in this section, the more effective we can expect it to be in fulfilling its intended purpose.

8. In concept learning a statement of the concept definition:
   a. Should not be given to the learners because it allows them to bypass necessary processing.
   b. Should contain all relevant attributes in order to maximize learning.
   c. Should be presented to the learner after correct responding on a set of instances and noninstances.
   d. None of the above.
9. Try a concept analysis of the concept *book*.
10. Discrimination of noninstances in concept learning is facilitated when an instructional presentation contains:
    a. Instances and noninstances matched on irrelevant attributes.
    b. Instances and noninstances not matched on irrelevant attributes.
    c. Instances convergent on the basis of irrelevant attributes.
    d. Instances divergent on the basis of irrelevant attributes.
11. A simple way to determine the difficulty of the instances and noninstances used to teach a concept is:
    a. To divide the number of relevant attributes by the number of irrelevant attributes present in a given instance or noninstance.
    b. To have a subject matter expert rate the instances and noninstances subjectively.
    c. To have students rate their confidence in their ability to identify the instances and noninstances correctly.
    d. None of the above.

TEACHING MATHEMAGENIC OBJECTIVES

One of the most important goals of education is to prepare students to solve the problems of tomorrow's society. This assignment is complicated by the fact that many of these problems are unknown today. Faced with this situation, schools have tried to give students a broad range of knowledge and a set of general problem-solving skills to meet the future. Furthermore, students are given practice in applying knowledge and skills to problems under the assumption that sufficient practice of this nature will transfer to those new problems encountered later in life.

In this section of the chapter we will examine the problem-solving process and how to design instruction to increase the learner's capability to solve problems. We will briefly review our definition of a problem from Chapter 5 and the capability established in the student who has learned to solve a given class of problems. Finally we will explore factors that influence the likelihood that the student will successfully solve a problem and their implications for the design of instruction.

The outcome of problem solving

A problem exists when a student is asked to produce a particular product under specified conditions but is not told how this goal is to be achieved. We describe the major task for students in such problem situations as one of discovering the solution. Problem-solving situations almost always involve multiple outcomes that are important to the student and teacher. Typically these outcomes are cognitive and mathemagenic in nature. Usually the cognitive outcome is the acquisition of a complex rule. Gagné (1977) has referred to this type of outcome in problem solving as a higher-order rule because it is a rule for applying a combination of previously acquired rules. The other outcome of a problem-solving situation is the acquisition of a mathemagenic skill or greater proficiency in its use.

Gagné (1977) stressed the cognitive outcome of problem solving and so classified it in his intellectual skill domain with rules, concepts, and discriminations. In this book we have placed problem solving in the mathemagenic domain because we wish to stress the mathemagenic aspect of problem solving. Perhaps the accompanying diagram will clarify the distinction between rule learning and problem solving.

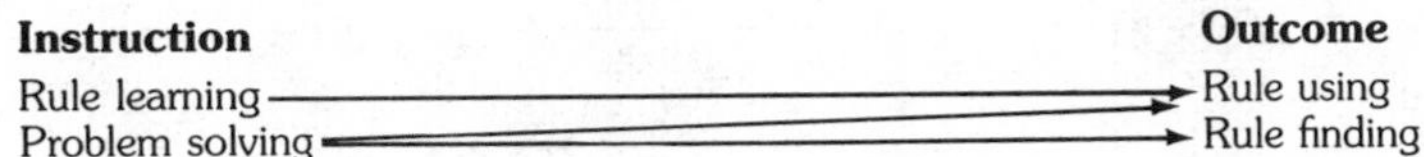

The outcome of rule learning is establishment of the capability to apply a specific subject matter rule without any appreciable increase in the ability to find new and similar rules. Instruction on problem solving results in both learned capabilities: application of a specific subject matter rule and increased ability to find new and similar rules.

In this chapter we will focus on problem-solving situations involving the cognitive outcome of rule using, but it should be remembered that mathemagenic strategies exist for facilitating all types of learning outcomes. For example, we have seen how the acquisition and retention of verbal information can be enhanced by various student-generated encoding strategies and other study skills. Similarly, a student who learns self-control strategies that influence motivation to work has acquired mathemagenic strategies that operate on affective states. These types of strategies are discussed in Chapter 16 along with a description of the means by which teachers can promote their acquisition and use.

Stimulating recall of prerequisites

For the purpose of determining prerequisites, problem-solving tasks can be separated into two major classes: problems involving the acquisition of mathemagenic skills and problems involving the practice of mathemagenic skills. The latter type necessitates the acquisition of relevant mathemagenic skills prior to instruction. It is very important for the teacher to determine the class of problem involved in instruction, because students often fail at a task due to lack of appropriate mathemagenic skills when the teacher had assumed these skills were acquired before instruction.

All problem-solving situations have prerequisites of a cognitive nature. If the student is to acquire a higher-order rule, then the component rules must have been previously mastered by the student. A study by Egan and Greeno (1973) demonstrates the importance of specific cognitive skills to learning in a problem-solving situation. They taught students to calculate the probability of a sequence of events (i.e., what are the odds of two heads, one tail, and two heads in that order on five flips of a coin?). One group, called the "rule-learning group" here, was given the formula, definitions of component terms, and practice in applying the formula. The other group, called the "problem-solving group," found the formula for themselves by working through a series of "nontechnical" problems.

Prior to learning to calculate the joint probabilities, the students were tested on a number of abilities, two of which concern us here. Egan and Greeno labeled one a test of *probabilistic concepts* and the other they called *generating permutations.* Both capabilities were postulated to be components of the to-be-acquired cognitive skill. After learning to find joint probabilities, the students were given a posttest designed to measure learning and transfer. Results as shown in Figure 11–14 indicated that students low in the two cognitive skills learned less from the discovery or problem-solving approach. As the graphs demonstrate, both instructional procedures produced greater learning outcomes when students possessed relevant prerequisites. However, the prerequisites were more essential in the problem-solving situation, as evidenced by the poorer performance of the students lacking the prerequisites in that situation as opposed to those in the rule-learning condition.

FIGURE 11–14
Problem-solving performance with and without prerequisites

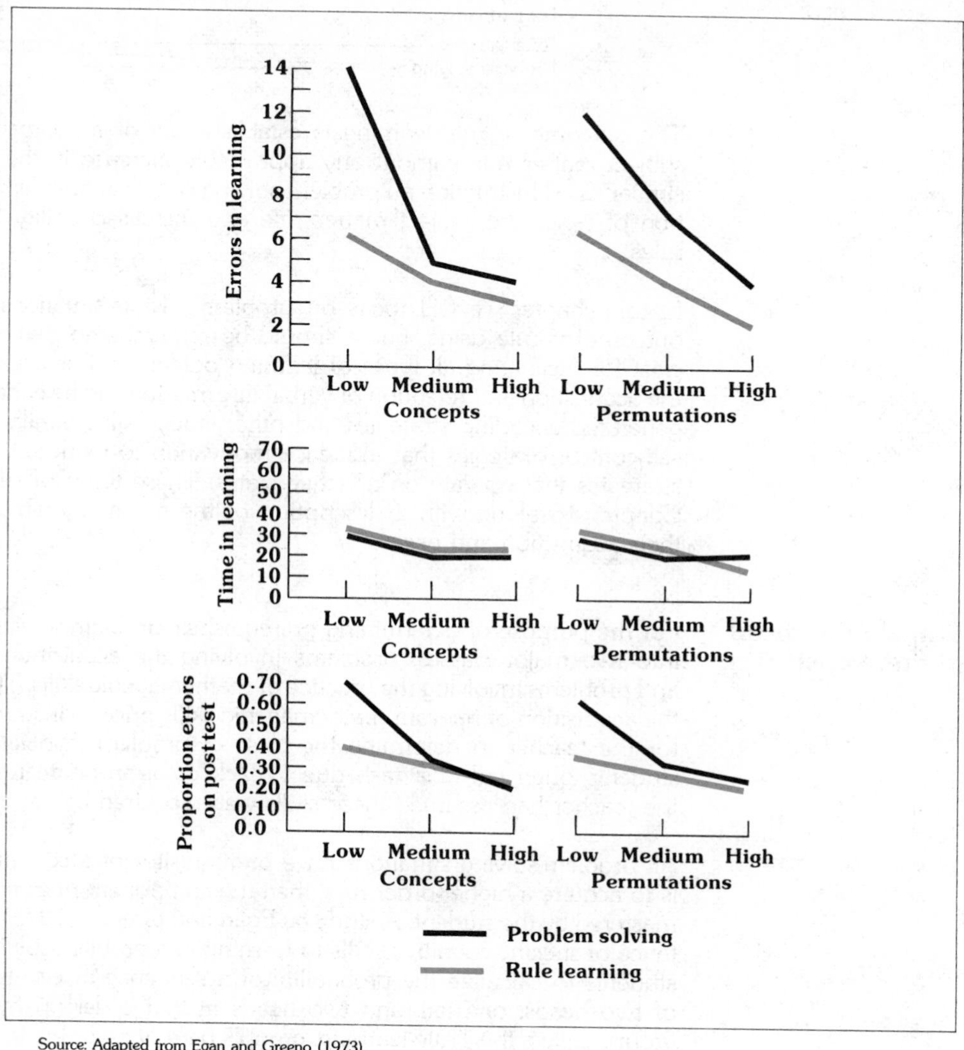

Source: Adapted from Egan and Greeno (1973).

Problem-solving instruction places strong demands on the learning ability of students, and because of this students should be well-prepared for the task. This means great emphasis must be placed upon the availability of prerequisites to the student. Without these prerequisites a student may come away from the instruction with no feelings of accomplishment and satisfaction but instead with feelings of failure and frustration

Providing learning guidance

A problem presents the student with a goal, and the student's task is to determine and apply an acceptable means to achieve that goal. For example, in a music class a student may be asked to write a short piece of original music meeting certain requirements. In solving this problem the student proceeds through four steps according to Dewey (1910). In the first step the student encounters the problem, while in the second step the student attempts to identify information in the situation and past experience relevant to the problem. Next the student formulates a possible solution to the problem, and in the fourth step verifies if indeed it is the correct solution.

Hayes (1978) captures the essence of these steps in two problem-solving processes: understanding and solving. In understanding the student applies past knowledge to construct a representation of the problem. This representation includes what is known relevant to the problem and what is possible given the known. The solving process involves selecting or constructing a solution from the possible in the representation and then verifying the solution.

In this section we will examine what the teacher can do to influence the steps or processes in solving a problem. Most frequently in instruction on problem solving, the teacher presents the initial problem or sequence of problems to the student and provides verbal directions suggesting a suitable representation of the problem or a form of an appropriate solution strategy. This type of instruction is called "guided discovery."

Guided discovery. Several studies have shown that performance on problems involving new rules is greater following a discovery procedure than following a rule-learning presentation (Guthrie, 1967; Worthen, 1968). Guthrie taught college students to decipher cryptograms, in this case scrambled words, by either a discovery or expository (rule-learning) approach. Students receiving rule-learning instruction showed greater ability to apply the learned rule to new examples and learned this capability in half the trials needed by the discovery students. However, the students receiving discovery instruction demonstrated greater skill in solving cryptograms involving new rules both similar and dissimilar to the rules practiced in instruction. As a matter of fact, students who received rule-learning instruction performed poorer on the cryptograms involving new and dissimilar rules than did a group of students given no instruction on solving cryptograms.

Worthen (1968) has obtained essentially the same results as Guthrie using mathematical rules with fifth- and sixth-grade students. He found that the students taught with rule learning had greater retention of the rules at both 5- and 11-week retest intervals than did the discovery group. When tested for their ability to discover a new mathematical rule, the students taught by the discovery method outperformed their counterparts in the rule-learning group.

These studies support the conclusion that instruction using a discovery presentation facilitates the student's ability to find and apply new subject matter rules. In doing so the student acquires or practices mathemagenic skills that further facilitate the student's ability to perform successfully in novel situations (Figure 11–15). Discovery instruction aids this transfer process because it gives the student an opportunity to practice problem solving in a situation which, as Olson (1976b) notes, is "more representative of actual problem solving" than is expository instruction.

Factors influencing the effectiveness of discovery learning. Since a teacher's primary purpose in teaching with a discovery procedure is to improve problem-solving skills, it is important that the student succeed in the instructional setting. If a student does not discover the solution to the problem during instruction, then it is not reasonable to assume that the student has acquired adaptive problem-solving skills. The importance of success during discovery instruction to later transfer of mathemagenic skills has been documented by Anthony (1973).

FIGURE 11–15
Discovery learning promotes the acquisition of mathemagenic skills

Anthony examined seven conflicting studies that investigated the effects of rule learning and discovery instructional presentations on the ability to find new rules. He found that in studies yielding no difference between the two approaches or a difference in favor of the rule-learning approach, there was a low rate of performance during learning for the discovery group. In studies in which there was a high rate of successful performance during instruction, the discovery group showed a greater capability for discovering new rules than the rule-learning group. Analysis revealed that this relationship between learning during discovery instruction and success in finding new rules was very high and significant.

This research suggests a very important consideration for the teacher planning a discovery lesson. If a high degree of student success cannot be insured, then students will most likely profit more from a rule-learning lesson. However, if the teacher's intention is to increase the student's problem-solving capability, then a well-constructed discovery lesson would be the preferred instructional means. Care must be exercised to insure that the students actually discover the desired rule from the instructional presentations, which we have seen is greatly dependent upon the availability of cognitive and/or mathemagenic prerequisites.

Student success in a discovery lesson is maximized by the skilled use of instructional guidance on the part of the teacher. Gagné and Brown (1961) compared two discovery presentations with differing degrees of learning guidance to a rule-learning presentation with a high school population. The learning task was deriving formulas for determining the sums of number series. In the rule-learning presentation a formula was given and then the students worked a series of examples. A discovery group was first asked to state the rule for determining the sum of a number series, then prompts were given until the student could state the rule. Under guided discovery another group of students were led to derive the rule by verbal directions that focused their attention on critical information in an example.

After this initial learning all three groups were given a test of their ability to discover new rules for previously unencountered number series. On this problem-solving task the guided discovery group performed best, followed by the discovery group, and last the rule-learning group. Gagné and Brown's explanation for these results is that during learning the guided discovery method requires the student to recall and apply previously learned concepts, while the rule-learning method does not require this recall. Furthermore, the discovery method requires this recall and application of concepts but in a more haphazard manner, and so the guided discovery method produces greater learning because the recall of concepts was more systematic.

Another factor that can have a facilitative effect on student performance in a discovery lesson is student verbalization. Gagné and Smith (1962) found that students required to verbally explain their actions while solving problems performed better than students not given these directions. Finally, Traub (1966) showed that sixth-grade students given a heterogeneous sample of problems evidenced greater transfer than another group provided with an equal number of homogeneous problems.

In this section we have seen that successful problem-solving instruction involves much more than simply presenting the student with a problem and allowing discovery to "run its course." Student performance in a discovery lesson is crucial to the attainment of desired results, perhaps more so than with any other instructional means. To secure successful performance with the discovery approach, the teacher must provide a minimum of two conditions: (1) stimulation of prerequisites and (2) guidance that leads the student to actually discover the rule. This guidance, while stimulating recall of the necessary concepts and directing the learner's attention to relevant information in the problem situation, does not give the student the solution but merely makes it more probable that the student will discover it. With this intermediate amount of guidance, problem-solving skills are better learned than either when the student is left to flounder in a discovery situation without guidance or when there is an expository lesson. Additionally, rule learning and mathemagenic skills will have greater transfer value if the student is given practice in a diversity of situations.

Alternate conceptions of problem solving and instructional implications

Discovery teaching is often viewed as being synonymous with problem-solving instruction, and most writers have identified induction as the essential aspect of discovery. In inductive sequencing the student is presented specific instances of the rule from which the general rule is induced. During the process of discovering the new rule, the student acquires and practices skills that transfer to new problem-solving situations. Yet many analyses of discovery and problem solving have questioned the importance of this inductive process to the learning of problem-solving skills (Ausubel, 1968; Wittrock, 1966). In this section of the chapter we will present three alternate views of problem solving and their educational implications.

A philosophical analysis. Strike (1975) described the shortcomings of the inductive conceptualization of discovery learning and argued that the process of verification is the real essence of discovery learning. By verification Strike means that the learner comes to know a proposition is true by a means that would be necessary if no one else knew the truth or falsity of the given proposition.

Strike goes on to analyze verification as requiring two types of skills: heuristic and epistemic. Heuristic skills are involved in formulating hypotheses and are operational as the learner conceptualizes the nature of the problem. Epistemic skills relate to the verification of the hypothesis. Through the application of these skills the learner gathers the appropriate evidence to prove or disprove the hypothesis. Strike concludes that appropriate heuristic and epistemic skills will vary among subject matter disciplines and even among levels of sophistication within disciplines.

Induction is only one set of all such possible heuristic and epistemic skills. Therefore the induction conceptualization of discovery is too narrow to accurately describe the range of student performances possible in problem-solving situations. According to Strike a more adequate model of discovery is that of verification. A student has discovered a proposition when in the course of solving a problem the student has hypothesized this proposition and has independently obtained the appropriate evidence to ascertain the truth of the proposition. As we have seen, this process may or may not involve induction on the part of the learner.

Epistemic skills as Strike has defined them are very important to the education of the student. After leaving school we expect students to be capable of verifying the truth of much information thrust at them rather than accept it on faith in authorities. Consequently, teachers should seek to identify the process used by their discipline to evaluate data and allow the student to practice this process, rather than teach only the content of their discipline. Furthermore, this view suggests that on occasions teachers should present "errors" for the student to detect and verify as false.

Extra scope transfer. Scandura and his associates have taken a different approach to the analysis of problem solving and the discovery method. They have gathered evidence from a number of studies examined below that indicates the degree of transfer observed in a problem-solving situation is more accurately determined by the scope (range of situations to which the rule applies) of the rule learned by the student than by the type of instructional presentation by which the rule was learned.

Scandura, Woodward, and Lee (1967) demonstrated that students who learned a general rule showed transfer of this rule to a wider array of problems than students who learned a more specific rule. However, the specific rule was easier to learn than the general rule. The problem situation used by Scandura et al. in this study was a number game played by two people. In this game a predetermined sum is selected along with a set of consecutive integers. Then the players take turns choosing an integer from the agreed set while keeping a running sum. The winning player is the person who selects the last integer to total to the predetermined sum.

Three different rules were taught to separate groups of students. The most specific rule taught was appropriate for winning games only where the set of integers was 1–6 and the predetermined sum was 31 (6, 31 games). An intermediate rule was taught appropriate for winning games in which the set of integers was 1–6 and the predetermined sum was any number, referred to as (6,*m*) games. The most general rule taught was appropriate for winning games involving any set of integers and any sum *(n,m)* games. Instruction was identical for the groups except for the statement of the rule, which of course differed in scope or applicability. After instruction all groups played a game from each of the forms described above: a (6, 31) game; a game of the form (6,*m*); and a game of the form *(n,m)*. Performance on these games was the measure of transfer and is summarized in Table 11–1.

Inspection of Table 11–1 shows that the most specific rule resulted in greater learning, as evidenced by the comparative performance on the (6, 31) problem. The breadth

TABLE 11–1
Percentage of students using appropriate game strategy for each rule condition

Group	*(6,31) problem*	*(6,m) problem*	*(n,m) problem*
Specific rule	76	0	6
Intermediate rule	29	24	0
General rule	29	29	24

Source: Adapted from Scandura, Woodward, and Lee (1967).

of transfer increases directly with the generality of the rule. Furthermore it may be concluded that while a general rule is most difficult to learn, once learned it provides a greater basis for transfer than a more specific rule.

Working with this knowledge, Roughead and Scandura (1968) postulated that since a discovery lesson promoted greater transfer than a corresponding rule learning approach with the same content, it was quite possible that students learned a more general rule with the discovery approach. They taught students either a general derivation rule for finding the sum of number series or three formulas for finding the sum of specific number series.

On a transfer test involving new number series both within and outside the scope of the general derivation rule, Roughead and Scandura found no performance differences between students taught the general rule by a rule learning method and students taught the specific formulas by a discovery approach. However, both groups performed more efficiently than did a group of students taught the specific formulas by a rule-learning presentation. From this Roughead and Scandura concluded that students in the discovery group had learned the more general derivation rule, while their counterparts in the rule learning/specific formulas group had not. Furthermore, what is learned in discovery can be identified and taught by an expository means as evidenced by the equal performance of those taught the general rule by the exposition method and those discovering the general rule.

Assimilation to schema. Richard E. Mayer has proposed a three-stage model of the information processing that takes place as a person learns to solve problems. The flowchart in Figure 11–16 illustrates the sequence of processing according to Mayer's model. As can be seen, the three factors involved in learning to solve problems are: (1) reception of information, (2) existence of prerequisite knowledge, and (3) activation of an appropriate assimilative set.

While all three factors are important in determining the learning outcome, we will focus on how the type of assimilative set activated during learning influences the quality of the learning outcome. In problem solving the quality of learning would be reflected in the types of problems the student could correctly perform. We expect students to be able to transfer their learning to problems different from those encountered during instruction as a result of problem-solving instruction.

According to Mayer (1975b) important variables influencing the student's assimilative set during learning are sequencing and emphasis in instruction. In several studies (Mayer, 1974; Mayer & Greeno, 1972) students were taught a formula for finding the probability of a series of events by two instructional methods with differing emphases. One instructional presentation focused on substituting specific values into the general formula and calculating the probability. The other presentation emphasized how the components of the formula relate to common experiences.

FIGURE 11–16
Three-stage model of problem solving

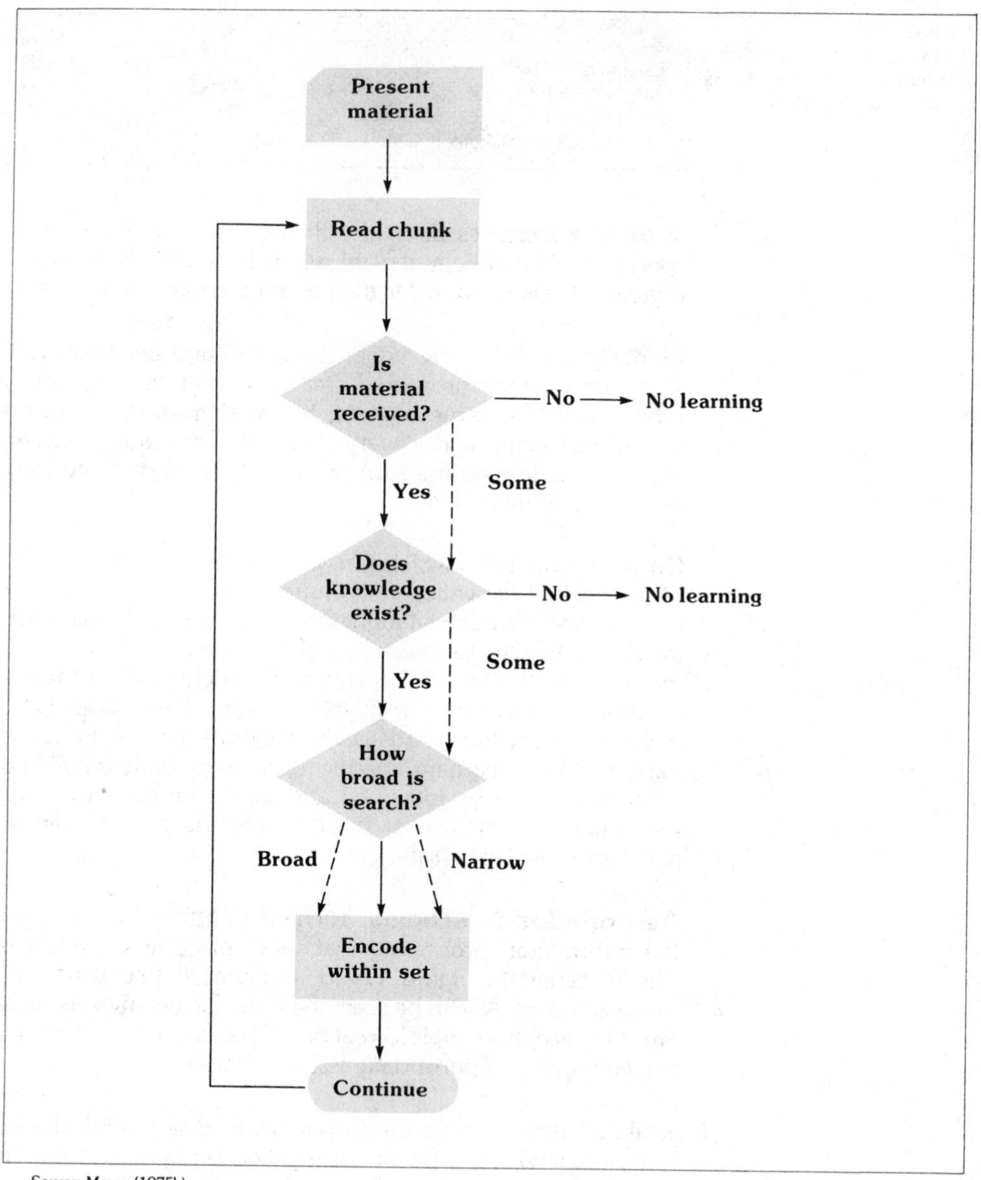

Source: Mayer (1975b).

Not surprisingly, the calculation instruction produced the highest performance on problems in which the students had to determine the probability of an event by substituting specific values into the formula. However, students given the instruction relating components of the formula to common experiences showed greater performance in novel situations involving story problems or unanswerable problems. Presumably, these latter types of problems demand greater transfer of learning on the part of the learner. Mayer (1975b) observed that this pattern of results was very similar to the results from the Egan and Greeno study of rule learning and discovery instruction discussed earlier in this chapter. He concluded that the common experience presentation and discovery instruction result in greater transfer because they both activate a broader assimilative set in learning.

Further research has focused on the sequencing of events in instruction and the activation of an assimilative set (Mayer, 1975a, 1976). In these two studies students were taught simple computer programming statements by one of two instructional presentations. These presentations were identical except for the sequence of components within the instruction. In both instructional presentations students read a text explaining seven basic programming statements, with the difference being exposure to a concrete model of computer operation before or after reading the text. Students who received text instruction followed by the model performed best on problems similar to those in the text. Performance on problems different from those in the text were solved best by those students who received instruction consisting of the concrete model preceding the text.

In another study, Mayer (1977a) taught college students to count in base three using the letters *w, d,* and *r* as digits. Students were given a letter-to-digit conversion list ($w=0$, $d=1$, $r=2$) either before or after learning to count in base three with the letters. On a transfer task involving addition in base three using the letters, students given the conversion list before learning performed at a higher level. To be more specific, the before group had 2.5 times more correct answers to the addition problems than did the after group.

The results of these studies suggest that the sequence of events in instruction influences when an assimilative set will be active and consequently determines what is learned from instruction. In summarizing the preceding sequencing studies, Mayer (1977b, p. 377) stated:

> These findings provide an independent complement to those involving induction-deduction comparisons, and suggest that assimilation to a meaningful set of past experiences (model) serves not to increase the amount of learning and retention per se but results in a broader, more integrated learning outcome than when the same information must be assimilated to narrower sets lacking the model. Apparently, sequencing of the model is crucial because a meaningful learning set must be available and active during the learning of incoming new information; once material is encoded, activation of a set may have little effect.

From the preceding three lines of investigation we can draw several important conclusions concerning instruction designed to teach problem-solving skills. Inductive sequencing is an effective instructional means to facilitate the acquisition of such skills; however, it is not the only means for teaching problem solving. Problem solving can be taught in a diversity of contexts, and the type of context to use depends to a large extent upon the particular subject matter being taught. Instruction should allow the student to verify the new rule by using skills characteristic of the subject matter.

Successful problem solving is promoted by instruction that requires the student to relate the new information to a broad set of experiences. Apparently, induction sequencing facilitates this broad encoding, but such encoding also can be achieved with other types of instruction. Furthermore, care should be taken to insure that the student acquires a rule of sufficient scope to result in the desired degree of transfer. Again, while the research suggests that inductive sequencing promotes acquisition of such wide-scope rules, such rules may also be taught with other instructional presentations.

On some occasions, such as those involving pressing time demands, an approach other than the discovery approach may be preferred; then the teacher must take care that the rule taught is sufficient in scope for the required problem-solving performance.

12. Which of the following is an advantage of the discovery as opposed to the rule-learning method?
    a. Greater ability to find and apply new subject matter rules.
    b. Greater ability to apply the specific rule taught.
    c. Greater efficiency in learning.
    d. All of the above.
13. A child wishes to take a new toy to school and show it to her playmates. Fearing she may forget it the next day, she places it on the breakfast table that night. In this way she will remember it in the morning when she sees it. Would you infer that in solving this problem the child has applied a mathemagenic skill? Why?

In this chapter the conditions of learning for each learning domain were presented in the context of designing instruction. Primarily, these conditions concern the design of two events of instruction: stimulating recall of prerequisites and providing learning guidance. In teaching affective objectives, teachers typically supply a model of the desired trait or present an argument designed to change student opinion. Additionally, many affective objectives are learned incidentally through students' experiences in school. Motor skills involve learning to execute a program of skills. Students first learn the program cognitively and then practice executing the actual skill. Furthermore feedback about performance should be given immediately. The learning of memorization objectives requires that the teacher lead the student to encode the material in some meaningful manner. This task was viewed as involving both prior knowledge to which the new information can be related and an appropriate encoding strategy. In teaching concepts and rules the teacher presents a definition, a variety of instances and noninstances, and verbal cues directing student attention to relevant attributes. Care must be taken to insure that the instances and noninstances reflect the range of the possible situations in which the student is to perform. Finally the teaching of mathemagenic skills was illustrated as a problem-solving process. The outcome of problem solving was said to involve both cognitive and mathemagenic skills. Guidance in the problem situation should direct the student's attention to information relevant to the solution but should not provide or "give away" the solution. Finally, alternate views of problem solving were presented and their implications for education discussed.

SELF-TEST

1. Which of the following is a determinant of credibility in communication?
    a. Communicator argues against self-interest.
    b. Physical attractiveness of communicator.
    c. Degree to which audience identifies with communicator.
    d. Age of communicator.
2. In what way would asking a student to state his/her opinion for the class facilitate the opinion-change process?
3. In which phase of motor skill learning are the component movements integrated into a "smoother whole"?
    a. Cognitive phase.
    b. Associative phase.
    c. Autonomous phase.
4. List three important functions of verbal instructions in motor skill learning.
5. If information presented in pictures and text conflict, then the student will probably:
    a. Remember the information in the picture.
    b. Remember the information in the text.
    c. Not learn either due to an interference effect.
    d. None of the above.
6. The comprehension and retention of prose can be facilitated by:

a. The use of concrete analogies for abstract information.
b. The use of high-frequency synonyms for difficult information.
c. Increasing the meaningfulness of the context in which the information is presented.
d. All of the above.

7. Describe the type of situation in which the teacher should provide an encoding strategy for the student, and a situation in which a student should generate his/her own encoding strategy.
8. The purpose of attribute prompting in learning concepts and rules is to direct the learner's attention to relevant attributes and facilitate learning to determine their presence or absence in a given situation. True or false?
9. If I wanted to teach the concept of circle and presented the following circle to the student:

   ○

   Which of the following nonexamples should I present simultaneously?

   a. □ *c.* □
   b. □ *d.* □

10. Given the circle from Question 9, which is the succeeding instance that should be presented?

    a. ○ *c.* ○
    b. ○ *d.* ○

11. Which is *not* a factor in problem solving according to Mayer?
    a. Reception of the to-be-learned information.
    b. General and specific problem-solving abilities.
    c. Existence of prerequisite knowledge.
    d. Activation of an appropriate assimilative set.
12. Describe specific actions a teacher can take to promote learning in a discovery situation.

ANSWER KEY TO BOXED QUESTIONS

1. *c*
2. *d*
3. *a*
4. Effective feedback should be immediate and augmented (provide information about the movement and its effects).
5. *a* and *d*
6. *d*
7. The basis would be organization as an encoding strategy.
8. *b*
9. According to the dictionary consulted by your author, a book is "a set of written, printed or blank sheets bound together in a volume". From this we derive two relevant attributes: *(a)* more than one sheet, and *(b)* bound. Irrelevant attributes are many. We list only a few: *(a)* size, *(b)* thickness, *(c)* hard or paper cover, *(d)* content, and *(e)* color of cover.
10. *a*
11. *b*
12. *a*
13. Our answer is yes. The child puts the toy where she would be sure to see it, thus having it serve as an external retrieval cue.

ANSWER KEY TO SELF-TEST

1. *a*
2. Public commitment toward an opinion influences change in that direction.
3. *b*
4. Inform student of skill program, cue specific components, and focus attention on critical cues.
5. *a*
6. *d*
7. Teacher should present the encoding strategy when students are low in ability or young or when the material is low in meaningfulness to the students. Students should generate the encoding strategy when they are able to do so.
8. True
9. *d*
10. *c*
11. *b*
12. Insure activation of cognitive prerequisites, provide verbal cues that direct the learner's attention to relevant information, and encourage students to think about reasons for actions performed in the situation.

Chapter 12

The evaluation of student performance

THE PURPOSE OF THIS CHAPTER is to discuss how a teacher can measure and evaluate cognitive and affective goals in the classroom through the use of various teacher-designed evaluation instruments. One of the main functions of teachers is to evaluate students. Regardless of the age of the student, the type of student, or the subject matter area, teachers have to make numerous instructional decisions about students and the effectiveness of instruction based on some type of classroom evaluation strategy. With younger children there is much less emphasis on formal testing and more emphasis on simple observation. For older students, particularly in the areas of cognitive subject matter, teachers tend to use more formal strategies for making evaluative decisions. This chapter is concerned with many of these strategies. In a later chapter we discuss how a teacher might observe a student in the classroom and then derive an instructional strategy based on the observation.

The first part of this chapter discusses the purposes of teacher-designed evaluation. The second section deals with how a systematic evaluation program might be developed for the cognitive objectives of a particular subject matter. In the third part we get down to the nuts and bolts of how to prepare, administer, score, and evaluate the effectiveness of teacher-made tests. Proper testing requires quite a lot of preparation and expertise. Following the nuts and bolts of testing is a section on assigning grades and reporting the results of evaluation. All too often teachers construct reasonable tests, only to invalidate the evaluation process by using poor grading practices. Concluding the chapter is a section on how to evaluate the affective domain.

At the conclusion of this chapter the reader should be able to:

1. Describe the purposes of systematic evaluation.
2. Develop a plan for sampling different levels of objectives for any sized unit of instruction.
3. Prepare different types of test items and state how to administer, score, and evaluate the effectiveness of teacher-made tests.
4. Generate a grading strategy for norm-referenced and criterion-referenced testing procedures.
5. Prepare different types of questions in the affective domain and state how these items might be used for making instructional decisions.

PURPOSES OF SYSTEMATIC EVALUATION

Evaluating student learning in the classrooom as the result of instruction is one of the major roles teachers have to perform. To do this task properly takes time and considerable expertise. Without a carefully developed evaluation program it is easy to make poor instructional decisions based on subjective impressions.

Gronlund (1976) defines evaluation as a systematic process of determining the extent to which instructional objectives are achieved. This definition implies that the evaluation process should be systematic and based on the instructional objectives of a course of study. To develop a good strategy for evaluation takes a lot of careful planning. It is not easy for teachers to perform the evaluation role fairly, objectively, reliably, validly, and efficiently. The task is made much easier, however, if the teacher has a clear evaluation purpose in mind and a well-developed plan for evaluating student performance in the context of the classroom.

Before we continue we would like to make a distinction between evaluating a student's performance in a naturalistic setting and evaluating it on a test. Educators would probably unanimously agree that the real purposes of any educational program are to help make students better independent learners and problem solvers in nonschool environments. In other words, the real purposes of education are concerned with transfer of training to the real world.

To insure that these goals are attained requires observing the student's independent performance in a nonschool environment. Given the number of students we have in our schools as well as other constraints, observing a student perform in a nonschool environment on a variety of tasks learned in school is not practical or efficient. Although there are always dangers associated with predicting a student's performance in a nonschool setting from the performance on some simulated task in school or on some paper-and-pencil test, this is usually the best we can do. Recognizing the inherent limitations of paper-and-pencil tests, we realize that economic constraints dictate some type of classroom evaluation rather than evaluation in a natural environmental setting. When we talk about systematic evaluation in this chapter, therefore, we are talking about classroom evaluation and, more specifically, we are usually talking about classroom tests designed by teachers. Within this limited framework, the first question to be discussed centers around the purposes of systematic classroom evalauation.

What are the purposes of systematic classroom evaluation? Tyler (1966) suggests that the purposes of evaluation fall into one of four categories:

1. The appraisal of academic achievement in individual students.
2. The diagnosis of learning difficulties in a student or a class.
3. The appraisal of a curriculum or some teacher innovation.
4. The appraisal of a large population.

Most often, classroom evaluation implies some type of formal test. Tests can have many purposes other than those identified by Tyler. Others include motivating students, providing relevant feedback for students, deciding the teaching approach to be used with different students, determining how the students may be best grouped for instruction, assigning grades, comparing different students or groups of students, determining the accountability of teachers, allocating resources, and predicting the future performance of a student based on current academic status.

All of these purposes suggest that the evaluation procedure used by a teacher ought to be purposive and systematic. To make well-founded instructional decisions requires careful and systematic planning based on a clear rationale of what should be evaluated. This point of view implies that a test should be developed neither haphazardly nor by choosing items in a random manner. Rather, each test item should be written to reflect some objective or domain of the course. Further, the item ought to be written in such a manner as to provide the teacher with useful instructional information.

Experts have tended to classify tests into one of three categories depending on whether the test is administered before instruction is to start (a pretest), during instruction (a formative test), or at the conclusion of a large component of instruction (a summative test).

A pretest can be administered to determine whether the student possesses the necessary prerequisites for a course (at the macro level) or for a unit of instruction (at the micro level). Information from such tests can be used to place students in appropriate groups, to assign appropriate tasks to students, to review some prerequisite lessons

FIGURE 12–1
Tests can be used to place students in advanced units of instruction

for students who do not possess the prerequisites, or to give a student a more advanced test if he/she passes the pretest satisfactorily (Figure 12–1).

Contrasted with the pretest, the formative test is designed to measure a student's performance while instruction is proceeding. The purpose of this strategy is to provide frequent, useful feedback to students concerning the quality of their performance, as well as to provide the teacher with information concerning the teacher's performance. Usually criterion-referenced, these short tests are most often administered at the conclusion of some small segment of instruction for diagnostic, prescriptive purposes. Depending on the general practices of the teacher, performance on these tests may or may not be graded.

The summative test, on the other hand, is given at the end of a fairly large segment of instruction to determine whether the student mastered the general content of the segment of instruction and to assign a grade. Either norm-referenced or criterion-referenced tests can make gross comparisons between students in different sections of the same course, between different programs, and between different methods. With a broader nature than formative tests, the summative test is used for macro decisions associated with such topics as grading, general class placement, and prediction of future performances.

Even though these general distinctions are made among pretests, formative tests, and summative tests, you should recognize that the types of information provided by these tests can be identical in some situations. For example, performance on specific items of a summative test can be used to recycle a student through a unit of instruction or can be used by a teacher to monitor the teacher's effectiveness in a segment of instruction. It is also possible that some of the items could be identical for each of these categories. The main differences among these categories concerns the time frame in which the tests are administered with reference to the instruction, and the types of general decisions usually arrived at after the tests have been administered.

In conclusion, based on clear purposes and a systematic plan for evaluating student learning, test construction can be challenging, productive, and interesting. Without a well-developed evaluation strategy, however, test construction can be a very unpleasant task for the teacher. The experience from a student's perspective can be equally unpleasant when the teacher uses unfair, unreliable, or invalid procedures in evaluation. Many of the complaints from students about faulty testing procedures can be minimized by developing a well-conceptualized, systematic testing program. It has been our experience that most complaints about testing stem *from poor test construction and poorly conceived evaluative strategies* in general rather than testing or grading per se. We cannot stress enough the importance of having a clear rationale upon which an evaluation strategy should be founded.

DEVELOPING AN EVALUATION PROGRAM FOR COGNITIVE OBJECTIVES

As seen from Gronlund's definition, evaluation is a total systematic process for determining how well students perform the stated instructional objectives for a course of study. To evaluate how well a student can achieve the cognitive objectives, the following steps should be taken:

Steps in the process

1. Determine the objectives for the course based on the goals and general domains of learning.
2. Determine the purpose for the evaluation.

3. Generate a table of specifications from the unit instructional objectives.
4. Based on the table of specifications, determine the *type(s)* of items that need to be written.
5. Write and/or choose valid and reliable items for learned capabilities specified by the objectives.
6. Assemble the test, including the answer sheet.
7. Determine how the test is to be scored.
8. Plan how the test is to be administered. Include:
   a. How the test will be announced.
   b. A policy on grading and makeups.
   c. A description of the testing policy—routines, seating arrangements, etc.
9. While developing the plan for evaluation, keep in mind how the plan might be efficient and objective. Also decide how the reliability and validity of the test for its stated purposes will be determined. Be sure the procedure is fair to the students.

Table of specifications

As we have stated previously, a wise procedure in planning and constructing a test is to write most of the test items at the time the unit is planned. We also stated that the test items should reflect the objectives of the unit. If our items do not measure performances that reflect our objectives, the test items are invalid measures of performance. Also items that surprise or trick students or measure some obscure part of the unit are neither appreciated nor necessary. In designing a test many teachers skim through the textual material and pick out any material that happens to stand out. Although this strategy may guarantee that the material is thoroughly covered on an exam, it is not recommended because it does not thoroughly sample the various levels of learning, it tends to create obscure items, the student is left guessing about the intentions of the teacher, and it does not guarantee that the important material is emphasized. A more consistent strategy for relating the content of the course to the objectives is to prepare a table of specifications.

A *table of specifications* is a two-dimensional chart having the contents or topics along one dimension and the levels of learning or some systematic taxonomy along the other. For example, Figure 12–2 shows a hypothetical unit of instruction in U.S. history at the high school level. The horizontal axis reflects the levels or types of learning and the vertical axis reflects the content or topics in the unit. The numbers in each box represent the number of test items in that topic at that level of complexity. This systematic strategy increases the likelihood that the various levels of learning will be sampled adequately, decreases the likelihood that obscure items will be written, and guarantees that the important material in the unit of instruction receive the proper weighting. Furthermore, since you should now possess the skills to do a task analysis on your units of instruction, it should be very easy to construct a test around a hierarchy of objectives prerequisite to the terminal instructional objectives for a unit of instruction. Thus, the test could be constructed to provide the teacher and the student with relevant feedback concerning those prerequisite skills still needed to perform the terminal objectives.

Writing a table of specifications for preparing a test is particularly useful when constructing formative tests at the unit level. You should also note in Figure 12–2 that mathemagenic responses are included along the horizontal axis. All too often courses tend to focus on the body of knowledge in a text with little or no concern for the broader goals of increasing the student's general competence as an independent learner. Since

FIGURE 12–2
Table of specifications in U.S. history based on a Gagnéan learning approach

	Memorization	*Concepts*	*Rule learning*	*Problem solving*	*Mathemagenics*
Conditions leading up to American Revolution	5	3	2	1	2
Leaders on the American side	5	4	0	0	0
Leaders on the British side	5	4	0	0	0
Chronology of the war	5	0	0	0	0
Outcomes of the war	5	4	2	1	2
American government philosophy at conclusion of the war	5	4	2	1	2

we have suggested that mathemagenic skills should be an integral part of the goals of a course, it makes sense to include those general skills on a test, if appropriate. We suggest that the table of specifications be presented to the students as an aid in advance of a test so that the student will have a very clear idea of the test's content.

Since many teachers have not been trained to use a Gagné-type approach, Bloom's taxonomy of educational objectives (Bloom, Englehart, Furst, Hill, & Krathwohl, 1956) is used by many teachers for one of the axes (Figure 12–3). You will recall that Bloom's taxonomy includes a variety of objectives in the areas of: knowledge, compre-

FIGURE 12–3
Table of specifications in U.S. history based on Bloom's taxonomy

	Knowledge	*Comprehension*	*Application*	*Analysis*	*Synthesis*	*Evaluation*
Conditions leading up to American Revolution	5	4	2	3	1	1
Leaders on the American side	5	4	2	3	1	1
Leaders on the British side	5	4	2	3	1	1
Chronology of the war	5	4	0	3	0	1
Outcomes of the war	5	4	2	3	1	1
American government philosophy at conclusion of the war	3	4	2	3	1	2

hension, application, analysis, synthesis, and evaluation. Whether a Gagné-type approach or Bloom's approach is used to construct a table of specifications, the key point to be made here is that some systematic approach needs to be followed to insure that the performance of the student is sampled in all areas of the subject matter proportionate to the importance of the material as well as the different levels of objectives in the course. Of particular importance is that this strategy insures the inclusion of many higher-level cognitive test items instead of the traditional verbal-association (rote memory) items found on many teacher-made tests.

One other point needs to be made about generating tables of specifications. We purposefully constructed two tables that in some ways are very broad (all about the American Revolution). On another level, however, the tables of specifications presented in this chapter are rather narrow. The real question an instructional developer or test designer must constantly ask is: *Why* is this unit or test item important?

From a theoretical standpoint the answer is clear. The unit or test item per se is *not* the critical outcome. The real purpose of instruction is not to teach the specific content of a course as an end in itself, but rather to teach the student how to generalize from the content of a course to previously unencountered instances beyond the content category of the course but within the general domain of the topic. For example, the American Revolution is just one instance of a revolution. The importance of studying the American Revolution is not just for understanding our revolution, although that is important; rather one of the purposes is to identify common elements in revolutions in general, to speculate how revolutions may be avoided, and to identify the possible outcomes of revolutions. With this perspective the emphasis shifts to generalizations, syntheses, comparisons, diverse relationships, and solving previously unencountered problems. Although beyond the scope of this book, the serious student might want to consult a fine paperback book on domain-referenced testing edited by Hively (1974). A serious concern for broad domains can significantly reduce the number of unimportant lessons and test items at the memory level which tend to permeate our schools and colleges.

CHOOSING THE ITEM FORMAT

The format of test items is generally classified according to the type of response required of the student. One type of test item requires students to generate long answers. Typically called "essay items," these take several forms. Another type of test item requires students to *supply* short answers to questions. A third type of item requires students to *select* an answer from two or more alternatives. Included in this category are the popular multiple-choice, true-false, and matching items. And of course there are other item types that combine several of these forms. In this part of the chapter we discuss the advantages and disadvantages of each type of test item, as well as identify those factors that should be considered when choosing the type of item.

The essay item (extended answer)

As described above, essay items require students to generate or supply answers. Depending on the purpose of the question, the answer may be restricted or extended (Gronlund, 1976). The extended-answer essay appears to be best suited to these situations in which the student is required to go beyond the information given by producing or organizing new ideas, integrating diverse material into a single answer, or evaluating the worthiness of some idea.

In general, the advantages of the essay item are:

1. If written properly, essay items require complex learning and thinking. Research indicates that students tend to study more thoroughly and are more likely to synthesize the course content when studying for an essay test.
2. Essay items have the potential to require an integration of diverse material, which is more difficult to achieve on selection-type questions.
3. Essay items require recall.
4. Certain type of essay questions require advanced communication skills.
5. Well-written questions designed to have students synthesize and originate solutions to complex problems require a literacy in the subject area that is difficult to measure with selection-type questions.
6. Essay items are less restrictive for the student.
7. Although many teachers would not want to measure attitudes and divergent problem-solving skills with an essay item, the extended essay testing format allows for this possibility.

From this list, it would appear that the essay item is the best format to use. Unfortunately, although it is very useful, it also has many disadvantages:

1. It is the most unreliable test item to score. Handwriting, the student's general verbal ability, the student's ability to organize, and the mood of the scorer all influence the scorer's interpretations of the answer.
2. It is very time-consuming to read, particularly if a teacher has a large number of students. From the teacher's perspective, evaluating essay tests can be tedious and boring. And it can even be more tedious if the test is used to provide students with relevant feedback concerning the quality of their answers.
3. Unless the test items on an essay test are constructed very cleverly to include a great deal of material from the unit(s) of instruction, the essay test limits the amount of material that can be assessed. In other words, the content validity of a pure essay test can be very low.
4. Good essay questions are deceivingly difficult to write. Poorly written questions are usually very vague, and a vague question encourages student bluffing.

The decision to use essay questions on a test obviously implies a trade-off between the inherent advantages and disadvantages of this format as well as several other factors. In general, the essay test can best be used in the following situations:

1. When the objectives are higher-order cognitive skills at the rule-learning and mathemagenic levels.
2. When the objectives require a great deal of synthesis.
3. When the number of students to be assessed is small.
4. When the skills to be assessed on the exam are related to organizational and/or written expression. Although sometimes secondary to the main cognitive content area of a course, these skills are too often downplayed or ignored.
5. When the time is too short to prepare an objective exam and the objectives of the course lend themselves to the essay format. Obviously in this situation the teacher will have to spend more time in evaluating the answers.

Notice how we constantly refer to the objectives of a course of study. Too often tests are planned with little or no consideration for the objectives of the course. The result of this unfortunate practice is that students do not receive a fair assessment of their ability to use their knowledge, skills, concepts, and principles in important problem-solving situations acquired during a course. A second result of this unfortunate practice is that unimportant, trite items at the memorization level tend to be assessed disproportionately on the tests.

The short-answer test (restricted answer)

The restricted-essay test item varies according to the response expected of the students. The test item can require a several-sentence answer or a one-word answer. Generally this type of question is reserved for those testing situations in which the teacher is interested in assessing the student's knowledge of the subject area at the memorization level, although ingeniously written questions may be written to sample a student's ability to use concepts, apply rules, and solve problems. By careful planning, such questions as discussing cause-and-effect situations, generating a list of relevant arguments on an issue, formulating a simple hypothesis, and describing the limitations of some experiment can be assessed using the restricted-answer format.

The advantages of a restricted-answer format are many:

1. Contrasted with the extended-answer essay format, the restricted-answer format allows the teacher to assess the student's knowledge on a wider range of material.
2. More precise than the extended-answer format, the restricted-answer format is more accurate for assessing specific objectives, particularly at the memorization and concept levels.
3. Since the student is required to supply the answer without cues, this format assesses recall rather than recognition.
4. Compared to multiple-choice or matching questions, the restricted-answer format is easy to write.
5. Compared to the extended-essay format, the restricted-answer format is much easier to score and is generally more reliably scored.

Although the restricted-answer format may appear to be very appealing, there are several major problems:

1. While the restricted-answer format is particularly useful for testing certain types of objectives, it is difficult to write questions designed to assess higher-order cognitive skills requiring analysis, synthesis, rule using, problem solving, or originality.
2. Some items are difficult to score, particularly if the question is not written explicitly.
3. Scoring the restricted-answer format is more tedious than the multiple-choice, true-false, or matching format.
4. Scoring the restricted-answer format is less objective than scoring a multiple-choice, true-false, or matching format test.
5. To insure that the intent of the question is very clear, the teacher must prepare well-written questions that can be quite time-consuming if done properly.

The restricted-answer format should be used when the skills on the exam require one-word or short answers. It is particularly useful to assess memorization-type information when the teacher does not want to provide any cues to the student. With this type of test, recall rather than recognition is assessed. Second, this format is useful in science or math, which often requires short answers to complex problems. It is particularly important in this regard to recognize that any test item must accurately reflect the course objectives. Assume a problem is given in math and the student is allowed to select the correct answer from among four or five choices. This testing procedure is poor from two perspectives. Providing the student with the correct answer embedded among a variety of choices is unrealistic; in the real world the answers are not in front of the problem solver. Second, by seeing the answer provided, the student might be able to work backwards to generate the solution, thus invalidating any decision a teacher might make concerning whether the student can solve the problem without the provision of the answer.

In conclusion, the teacher has to be very careful to write items that accurately reflect the objectives of a course and not to provide inadvertent cues or answers that may invalidate the conclusions to be derived from the test. Items of this type have low content validity—the item does not assess the performance the teacher wanted to assess.

Items requiring selection of an answer (multiple choice)

The two previous categories of test items require the student to supply or generate the answer. Contrasted to the supply type item are those that require the student to *select* the answer from among two or more alternatives. Depending on the complexity of the item, it can assess memorization learning or the higher levels of learning. As a generalization, the select-type item lends itself very well to various memorization tasks and is the preferred testing mode to assess this level of learning. It is also an excellent way of assessing many of the higher-level cognitive objectives. The most popular form of testing in this country, the multiple-choice item has the following advantages:

1. Although capable of being used for memorization items, the multiple-choice item can be adapted to measure higher-order cognitive tasks requiring a convergent answer.
2. For large-group instruction, the multiple-choice format reduces the load for evaluating the students. If care is taken to be sure the test does not get distributed to students outside of class, the test may be reused on future occasions.
3. The multiple-choice format is better than the true-false format because it reduces the likelihood of high scores by chance and it can discriminate better between actual high- and low-performing students.
4. When test scores are needed in a hurry after a test is administered an objective-type test should be given (Figure 12–4).
5. Scoring of a multiple-choice test is generally impartial, efficient, and fairer than scoring of the more subjective-type tests.
6. The results of a multiple-choice test tend to be more reliable than the extended essay tests.
7. Because more items can be included on a multiple-choice test than on essay tests, the material in a unit of instruction can be covered more comprehensively.
8. If written properly, the multiple-choice test can provide the teacher with much useful diagnostic information.

Even though this list of advantages is very impressive, all is not well with the multiple-choice format. Some of the disadvantages of this popular format include:

1. Writing multiple-choice items is time-consuming. To write a good multiple-choice item requires testing skills and some originality to generate plausible but incorrect answers for the distracters.
2. The multiple-choice format *is not applicable* for some types of higher-level cognitive objectives that require originality, novelty, or an extended answer. The content of the item as well as the item type should be based on the objectives of the course. To use the multiple-choice format just because it is easier to score and is generally more reliable is an inappropriate testing practice.
3. As mentioned in the previous section, the multiple-choice format is not applicable

FIGURE 12–4
Short multiple-choice tests can be scored quickly to provide immediate feedback

for some science and math problems in which the student is required to generate an answer to a formula-type problem.

4. Since the correct answers are provided with a multiple-choice item, some guessing is possible. Furthermore, sophisticated students can raise their scores on multiple-choice tests by paying close attention to inadvertent subtle cues in questions written by inexperienced teachers.
5. The multiple-choice format cannot measure organizational skills or expressive ability. In many courses, these skills are deemed important.
6. If the teacher is not careful, it is easy to write ambiguous items.
7. If the teacher has a small class, another mode of testing might be desired.
8. To a large extent the multiple-choice test measures recognition-type responses rather than responses requiring total recall.
9. Some critics of the multiple-choice tests have claimed that the tests measure only superficial material. Proponents of this form of test claim that almost any type of learning can be measured with this item more thoroughly, objectively, reliably, and validly for its stated purposes.
10. Finally, some statement needs to be made about the divergent, creative, and original students' performance on multiple-choice tests. Critics of the multiple-choice test claim that it measures convergent-type behaviors and does not provide creative students with either the challenge or the freedom to use their creative skills to their advantage.

Ironically, as it may seem, other forms of testing may put the creative student at an even worse disadvantage. For example, with the propensity to respond divergently on an essay test, the creative student might be penalized for originating a divergent answer. Given the research findings suggesting that the creative student performs about as well as highly intelligent but noncreative students, the multiple-choice format may not be as blameworthy as once thought. The key to this argument centers around the nature of the teacher's evaluation strategies, the extent to which multiple-choice tests are used in evaluation, and the extent to which divergent productive responses are valued. In sum, the argument of whether the multiple-choice test is good or bad for the divergent student is not really important when viewed from the broader context of a total system for evaluation, which takes into consideration divergent responding as one objective in the course. And the reader should keep in mind that divergent responding may not be appropriate in all contexts. *The objectives of the course determine whether divergent responding should be a desired outcome and to what extent divergent responding should be evaluated.* If divergent answers are desired, then the item ought to reflect that goal.

As stated previously, the multiple-choice test is very flexible from a teacher's perspective. The inherent weakness of this testing format is that it is difficult or impossible to measure organizational skills, originality, and writing skills. In addition, this format should not be used when the instructor wants the student to solve problems for which the provision of an answer gives the student a subtle cue concerning the solution.

The true-false item

Of somewhat limited value, the true-false item is not particularly well thought of as a type of evaluation item. Although the item is easy to write, easy to score, and useful for measuring the recall of certain types of factual information, there are many inherent problems. Some of the criticisms of the true-false tests are: (1) true-false items that do not measure trivia are difficult to write (2) the results from a true-false test are not very diagnostic (3) the test promotes guessing, and (4) there is a tendency for true-false items to measure trivia. Another major philosophical consideration is that truth is rarely absolute, thus the relative aspects of "truth" cannot be assessed very well with true-false items. As a generalization, true-false items should be used only in those situations in which there is a need to assess the student's knowledge of some discrete factual material and there is no other way to assess this knowledge.

The matching item

Another test item of somewhat limited value, the matching item is useful to assess *homogeneous* factual material. With some ingenuity, concepts and rules can be assessed on some occasions. Since matching items are initially difficult to write (the stems and choices must be equivalent) and the item is limited in what can be assessed, decisions to use this format should be based on whether the factual material is of an equivalent form. The matching item lends itself nicely to paired-associate-type material (names–dates, events–dates, diagrams–labels, etc.). As with the true-false test format, the matching format encourages the assessment of trivia and should be used sparingly as a testing strategy.

1. A teacher decides to give a midsemester test to determine the students' grades. What type of test is this characterized as?
   a. Formative.
   b. Summative.
   c. Pretest.

2. Describe a strategy to insure that a variety of objectives at different levels of complexity will be systematically evaluated on a midsemester test.
3. State three advantages of the extended essay test that other tests do not have.
4. As a generalization, why is the multiple-choice item better than most essay tests for sampling the content of the course? Implicit in this question is the recognition that the multiple-choice question cannot measure certain objectives.

WRITING DIFFERENT TYPES OF ITEMS

The essay test item

One of the unfortunate aspects of essay test questions is that teachers tend to assume writing the question is a very simple procedure. Writing a good essay question is not very difficult if several basic guidelines are followed. The difficulty occurs when these guidelines are not followed or when the item is written in a hurry with little consideration given to the objectives of the course or the outcomes expected on the test.

FIGURE 12–5
Great care needs to be taken to write good test items

To write a good essay question at the rule-learning or problem-solving level reflective of the course objectives takes some careful planning (Figure 12–5). Some general guidelines to use in writing essay questions include:

1. Write the question based on your objectives and the domains suggested by the course. Use a table of specifications to aid in generating the question.
2. Use the essay-item format for higher-level cognitive objectives at the rule-learning or problem-solving level. From Bloom's taxonomy, certain objectives at the application, analysis, synthesis, and evaluation levels of the taxonomy are appropriately assessed by essay-type questions. Do not use the essay-item format to assess factual material at the memorization level.
3. Generally write the question while planning the unit of instruction rather than near the conclusion of the unit. The advantage of this strategy is that it helps the teacher focus more clearly on the objectives of the course.
4. The most common error teachers make in writing essay questions is to make the question too vague and broad. To counter these common errors, the question should be fairly explicit and generally *limited* in scope.

The question should be explicit in scope to communicate the teacher's intent to the student so that the student understands what type of answer is expected on the test. Consider the difference between the following two questions:

Unclear: Discuss President Carter's foreign policy.

Clear: Discuss President Carter's foreign policy with reference to:

a. The emerging third-world countries.
b. Diplomatic relations with communist countries with whom the United States has no current official diplomatic relations.
c. The impact on the balance of payments problem.
d. The energy problem.
e. Military deployment of troops.

Indicate how these policies differ from those of the Nixon-Ford administrations, and predict the outcomes of these policies for the early 1980s. Equal weight is given to each of the five sections of the question.

Although more difficult to write, the clear question has at least five specific advantages:

1. The student knows what is expected on the test and how the answer will be evaluated.

2. By being explicit, the second question guarantees that the material in the unit will be covered in the answer if the student knows the material and is able to apply the material.
3. Unless the material about the early 1980s has been discussed in class, being able to predict future occurrences is a problem-solving task dealing with previously unencountered material. The broad question does not insure that the answer reflects problem-solving skills.
4. Since the question is already outlined, the student will not have to spend time outlining and organizing the question.
5. Although the second question is not limited in scope in comparison to a question dealing with just one of those issues, the outlining of specific aspects of Carter's foreign policy has the same effect as a limited question. The advantage of a limited question in contrast to a general question is that it allows for a wider assessment of the course objectives because more questions can be written, requiring less time to answer.

Again compare the two questions presented above. Confronted with the question "Discuss President Carter's foreign policy," the student might write an outstanding answer on only one aspect of Carter's foreign policy. Since the question is so general, the teacher could expect to get many varying answers, thus any means of comparing student responses or determining the extent of a student's knowledge on the course objectives is limited when general questions are asked. Also, general questions tend to encourage student bluffing, are more difficult to evaluate (the scoring tends to be more influenced by the student's writing abilities), and are less popular from a student's perspective (the students feel uneasy about general, vague questions). All these factors tend to make general questions less fair to students.

Of course, if the instructor is interested in organizational abilities and that is one of the course objectives, then a clearly outlined question may provide the ideal organization, thus negating the validity of the question to sample the student's organizational skills. As we have suggested, unless a student's organizational abilities are one of the cognitive objectives of the course, we prefer to provide the student with the organizational structure for the question. Our reason for this position is that it is quite possible for a student to present a highly novel, competent solution to a complex problem even though the essay question may be somewhat disorganized. Instructors opposing this viewpoint suggest that the ability to organize is a general goal of education and should be constantly assessed. The preference is clearly based on the values of the instructors.

As soon as the essay question is constructed, a general key, or a statement concerning the characteristics of good answers should be written. This increases the likelihood that any ambiguities or unrealistic questions might be eliminated before the student sees the test. Second, the key should be used in scoring the answer, thus increasing the reliability of scoring an essay test.

If the test requires a great deal of writing, it is a good practice to indicate to the students how much time should be spent on each question.

If grammar, spelling, writing ability, or organizational skills are assessed on an essay test, the student should be informed in advance. Hidden agendas are not appreciated by students, and these types of grading strategies can lead to unnecessary student resentment. Before a teacher decides to evaluate these skills on a test, a great deal of thinking should be done. As we have suggested, it is very possible that a student might be very competent with the specific cognitive content of a course and not very competent in expressive skills. To what extent a grade should reflect these expressive skills is a philosophical and pragmatic question requiring a great deal of thought.

In general, *don't* give students a choice on essay items unless there are different objectives for different students in the course. And even when there are different objectives for different students, the questions should be specified for each student. A choice of questions actually is very advantageous to the poorly prepared student.

In general, do not ask questions that only sample a student's opinion or attitude without having the student justify the answer in terms of the cognitive content of the course.

A useful suggestion for having the student integrate a lot of verbal information in a problem-solving question is to ask the student to generate a list of facts and then have him/her use that list to solve some problem. Note the following example:

List at least three factors that contributed to the Cold War between the United States and Russia at the conclusion of World War II (3 points). Limit the description of each factor to no more than *four* sentences.

Generate a *plausible* current solution to the Cold War that benefits both sides from a military, political, social, and economic standpoint. Your solution must take into account those factors which initially contributed to the cold war (8 points).

The advantage of this format is that it helps the student organize the answer, it is easier to evaluate than a regular extended answer, and it integrates the memorization and problem-solving objectives into one question.

The multiple-choice item

More difficult to write than essay items, the multiple-choice item presents four distinct problems to a test constructor. The first concerns how the item should reflect the level of the objective. Given that multiple-choice items can be written at many cognitive levels, care should be taken to insure that many of the items reflect higher-level cognitive objectives. The best strategy for insuring this is to provide the student with previously unencountered examples, problems, or conflicting evidence from which he/she must choose an appropriate answer.

A second problem is concerned with making the stem clear to the student. The stem of a multiple-choice item is the introductory part; it takes the form of an incomplete statement or a question. Great care should be taken to make it clear and explicit.

A third problem is concerned with generating plausible foils, the alternate answers to a multiple-choice question. Much of the time needed to write a multiple-choice question is spent in generating plausible foils. With experience, this gets easier.

Finally, attention needs to be given to the correct answer. The correct answer should be written in such a manner that experts would agree on it. In some fields this is difficult to achieve. Some guidelines for writing multiple-choice questions are:

1. Be sure that the item reflects or is related to one of the objectives of the course.
2. For higher-level objectives, be sure that the stem or the foils deal with a previously

unencountered example. Do not repeat scenarios or examples from the book or class notes. The objective is to determine whether the student is able to generalize to a new situation or example. Be sure the examples are novel.

3. Place all the items reflecting one objective in the same section of the test. It is easier to use the test as a diagnostic-prescriptive instrument if all such items are together.
4. When writing the stem, pose a question, problem, discrepancy, or situation for which the student must choose some plausible solution. Do not write a stem that does not specify what should be done. For example, compare the following questions:

   February:
   a. Is the shortest month.
   b. Has 31 days.
   c. Occurs in the summer.
   d. Has 30 days.

   Which month is the shortest?
   a. February.
   b. April.
   c. June.
   d. August.

   In the first question it is not explicit what is expected of the student. This is one of the most common mistakes of a novice test constructor. Also notice that when the question is explicit, the alternative answers are more homogeneous. There is some research evidence to indicate that homogeneous alternatives are more useful to measure a student's higher-order skills.
5. When writing the stem, keep to the point; do not put in extraneous information. Compare the following two questions:

   Which of the following types of behavior is B. F. Skinner, a leading radical behaviorist and father of modern behaviorism, concerned with?
   a. Classical conditioning.
   b. Operant conditioning.
   c. Observational learning.
   d. Cognitive learning.

   Which of the following types of behavior did B. F. Skinner study most frequently?
   a. Classical conditioning.
   b. Operant conditioning.
   c. Observational learning.
   d. Cognitive learning.

   Not only is the first example poorer because of the extraneous information, "a leading radical behaviorist and father of modern behaviorism," but also the fact that Skinner is identified as a behaviorist may help the student eliminate the alternative answer *d.*
6. When writing the stem or foil, the language ought to be clear and the choice of words commensurate with the student's vocabulary level. It is very unfair to penalize a student on questions due to unnecessarily difficult vocabulary words if the vocabulary words do not reflect the objective.
7. If the item reflects an opinion of some authority, the name of the authority should be cited (e.g., According to Jones . . .).
8. After all the items have been written for the test, they should be reread to

determine whether answers to specific questions are found in other questions. Interrelated items in which the answer to one question is found in another should be avoided.

9. When writing the foils, each should be a genuine alternative. Sometimes students can eliminate one or two faulty foils by identifying inadvertent cues.
10. Do not provide other inadvertent cues to students, such as varying the length of the foils in some systematic manner (e.g., having the correct answers longer or shorter) or placing the correct foil in a specific location (e.g., having the correct answer appear more frequently in the third or fourth location).
11. Multiple-choice items should have from three to five foils. The optimum number of foils is four or five. If necessary, the number of foils may vary from item to item as long as no inadvertent cues are present.
12. Avoid the use of words like "always," "never," "all," and "none" except in unusual circumstances.
13. Be sure that the foils are grammatically consistent. Inconsistent grammar in the foils is distracting and may provide subtle cues to the student.
14. The use of "none of the above" should be used very sparingly. The problem with this phrase is that if "none of the above" is correct you really do not know whether the student is able to identify the correct answer; you know only that the student is able to identify certain incorrect answers.
15. Do not repeat the same words over and over again in the foils. Rewrite the question to include those words in the stem if they are germane to the question.
16. The use of double negatives is a no-no. Double negatives are so confusing that the student may know the answer but become mixed up in attempting to understand the meaning of the question.
17. When writing the foils, there should be only one correct answer which experts would choose.
18. Do not make the test so long that reading speed becomes a main determinant of the student's score.
19. Make the options homogeneous. Heterogeneous options can be more difficult to read, and sometimes students can eliminate from consideration several foils because they do not fit with the stem.
20. If it is very difficult to generate a third and fourth foil, drop the question as a multiple-choice question and rewrite it using some other format.

The true-false item

Although true-false items are generally not the preferred format for most tests, the ease with which this type of item can be written and the amount of material that can be covered sometimes outweigh the inherent negative qualities. As with the other item formats, there are a series of guidelines to follow when writing a true-false item.

1. Make the item significant. Do not test for trivia. If you follow a table of specifications, the number of trivial items will be reduced significantly.
2. True-false items can be written at the higher levels of learning by presenting the student with previously unencountered problems to solve or previously unencountered situations to identify. For example, a graph could be presented to students with a series of true-false statements. The student's task would be to interpret the graph. Or a brief scenario could be presented followed by some interpretive true-false questions. Consider the following example:

   A teacher asked a question to the sixth-grade class. Dick practically jumped out of his seat waving his hand frantically and saying, "Ooo-ooo." The teacher called on quiet George for the answer. George had raised his hand and remained quiet. Are the following true or false?

a. By calling on *George,* the teacher was applying positive reinforcement principles with *Dick.*
b. By calling on *George,* the teacher was applying positive reinforcement principles with *George.*
c. By not calling on *Dick,* the teacher was applying extinction procedures to *Dick.*
d. By calling on *George,* the teacher was attempting to apply the principles of modeling to *Dick.*

3. Specific determiners like "never," "all," "sometimes," "always," and "frequently" should be used very infrequently. Generally absolute determiners are false and relative determiners are true.
4. Do not get into the pattern of writing longer true statements than false statements, or vice versa.
5. *Never* take a sentence verbatim from a text. Petty items are not appreciated.
6. When writing a true-false statement include only a single point. Having several ideas to contend with in a compound or complex sentence is confusing to a reader.
7. Be simple and to the point. Extraneous material is not needed in an item.
8. Do not use negatives in a true-false item.
9. Try not to use qualitative words like "few," "many," and "old." Be specific by substituting quantitative language if possible.
10. If a true-false item has a main clause and a subordinate clause, make the main clause true and the subordinate clause true or false.
11. Tuckman (1975) suggests that writing true-false items may be facilitated by making all the items initially true, and then changing about one half of the items to false. This strategy increases the likelihood that the items will be approximately the same length and decreases the likelihood that other extraneous cues will be present in the item.
12. To counter the tendency of students responding "true" when in doubt, several suggestions are recommended:
    a. Ebel (1974) recommends making more items false on the test. Of course, if the students catch on to this strategy, then an inadvertent clue would be present, thus negating the value of this technique.
    b. Instead of two choices, have three choices: "true," "partially correct," and "false."
    c. Write a corrected true-false item, in which the important point of the item is underlined. If the item is false, it is the student's task to change the underlined word to make the statement true. It should be noted here that students tend to feel uncomfortable with this practice.
    d. Although more difficult to correct and less reliable, another procedure is to have the student justify each answer. The disadvantage with this technique it that it reduces considerably the number of items that can be used on the test.

The matching item

You will recall from our previous discussion of matching items that on most occasions these items are appropriate for verbal-association-type relationships such as names–dates, people–events, authors–books, diagrams–labels of the diagrams, and cause–effect. With some ingenuity, a matching test can be written to measure certain limited higher-order skills at the rule-learning level such as principles → applications or problems → solutions. These items are not very difficult to write once the categories have been identified, but the following rules should be followed:

1. Be sure that there are very clear directions at the beginning of the item. Indicate that the items in the right-hand column may be used once, several times, or not at all.
2. Write from 5 to 10 items in the left-hand column and from 9 to about 14 items in the right-hand column. There should be three to four more items in the right-hand column than in the left-hand column.
3. Both columns should be as brief as possible. Put the longer column on the left so that the student will have to spend less time searching for the answer.
4. Be sure that the two columns contain only homogeneous items.
5. Be sure that all the items and the instructions are on one page. It is extremely difficult to have to answer a matching test with items divided over two pages.
6. Arrange the choices in the right-hand column in alphabetical or some logical order to minimize subtle cues.

5. Under what conditions, if any, would you want a student to answer a very general, relatively vague essay question? Justify your answer.
6. How can a test writer increase the likelihood that the multiple-choice questions on a test are at the concept or rule-learning level?

OTHER PLANNING CONSIDERATIONS FOR CLASSROOM TESTING

As we have repeatedly suggested, a test should reflect the objectives of a unit or course of study based on a table of specifications or some systematic outline. Assuming that the objectives of a course of study vary from memorization objectives to problem-solving objectives, it would seem likely that most tests would consist of several types of items.

Composing the test

We have also tried to point out, however, that the choice of item types has to be related to the amount of time the teacher has for preparing and/or evaluating the answers. Even though some units and course objectives might logically suggest using extended essay items, the reality of having to read 100–150 answers may limit the choice of items to the restricted-answer, multiple-choice format. In conclusion, the choice of item types to be included on a test should be based on the objectives of the unit and the time constraints of the teacher to prepare and evaluate the students' answers. Additional consideration should be given to the purposes of the test, the amount of material the test represents, and the advantages of each item type when choosing the type to be used in a test.

Assembling the test

Although there are not many rules for assembling a test, it is very important that the test be assembled to minimize student difficulties with the format and organization. The purpose of testing is to evaluate the student's competence with respect to course objectives. A poorly structured test interferes with this objective. Some suggestions include:

1. Put the same item types together. Mixing up types is very confusing to a student.
2. Have the items arranged in such a manner that the test can be readily used for student feedback. To accomplish this, place together all those items that deal

with a particular topic, identify each item as representative of specific course content or specific objectives, or identify the page or pages in the text in which the answer may be found. These procedures make relevant feedback easier. Even if the test is used as a summative device, we recommend this procedure. The information obtained from the students' performance on the test can be used to help the teacher redesign the unit or reteach certain material, if necessary.

3. Although there is no particular research to back up this third suggestion, most authorities suggest that the first several items should be fairly easy. The logical rationale for this suggestion is that several easy items placed at the beginning of the test should decrease initial text anxiety and increases motivation to do well on the text.
4. Clear instructions should be available to the students at the beginning of each section of the test.
5. There should be a space between each multiple-choice item as well as between each true-false item.
6. At the time of test construction the answer sheet should be prepared. Care should be taken to make the answer sheet easy to use by the students and to design it to minimize cheating by copying. Several excellent ways to minimize copying on exams include:
   a. Writing two forms of the test with the same items on the test, but in a different order.
   b. Preparing two different answer sheets so that it would be virtually impossible to copy. For multiple-choice tests, this strategy can be achieved very nicely by jumbling up the answers as follows:

Answer sheet A	*Answer sheet B*
1. C A B D E	1. E B C A D
2. B A C E D	2. B D A E C
3. D A C E B	3. C E A B D

Designing the answer sheet

Several strategies are recommended in designing the format for short-answer, multiple-choice, or true-false answer sheets. First, if the items are arranged according to the levels of learning, then the student can use the answer sheet when it is corrected to determine the level of understanding of the unit as well as to identify what needs to be done to improve test performance. Second, the answer sheet can provide the student with the page sources from which the item is derived. This procedure makes feedback more useful. If some of the items are taken from class discussion or class lectures, this can also be noted. This information could be particularly useful to the student when there is a discrepancy in scores between those items reflecting printed material and those reflecting classroom discussion or lectures. In our opinion, the main purpose of most forms of testing is to provide *useful* feedback to the student and to the teacher about what needs to be done to improve the student's and teacher's performances (Figure 12–6). Gross raw scores or letter grades do not provide this type of information, whereas a purposefully designed answer sheet can.

Scoring the test

Since the strategy for scoring the test should be communicated to the students in the test instructions, it is very important to plan how the test is to be scored at the time it is constructed. For multiple-choice and true-false tests the student needs to know whether guessing is encouraged or penalized. For extended essays, the student needs to know how much emphasis is placed on each part of the essay and how

FIGURE 12–6
A test should provide useful feedback to a student

much on other considerations such as organization, grammar, spelling, and paragraph construction.

On the multiple-choice and true-false tests we do not recommend excessively penalizing a student for answering an item incorrectly unless the test is very lengthy and the student's raw score could be raised significantly by blind guessing at the end of the test in order to finish it. Since we do not recommend this practice, rarely should a "correction for guessing" formula be necessary. If necessary, you can consult the Appendix of this book for the rationale and description of how to correct for guessing.

To increase the efficiency of scoring a short-answer, multiple-choice, or true-false test, appropriate scoring keys can be devised to minimize the time needed to score the test. Answer sheets designed to correspond with specially designed answer keys are much easier to use than referring back to the answers in the test booklet.

Because the essay test is more difficult to score and usually is scored less reliably than the more traditional short-answer or choice-type tests, the teacher should be aware of some special procedures to be followed when evaluating extended essay answers:

1. At the time the essay question is written, an outline of the ideal answer should also be written. When evaluating the students' responses, the outline can be used as a guide. Also, when the answers are evaluated the teacher ought to determine

if the ideal answer is a realistic guide. By quickly reading some of the answers in a random fashion, a rough estimate can be obtained about the wisdom of using the ideal answer as a key for evaluating the answer.

2. A decision also ought to be made about how to assign credit for a student who went beyond the required answer, and/or to what extent points will be taken off for extraneous material or incorrect answers.
3. If the essay test is to be used on a comparative basis, some authorities suggest that the papers be assigned to piles based on the quality of the answer. After all papers are distributed into various qualitative piles, differentiated credit can be assigned to each pile. Of course, this decision relates to the instructor's philosophy of grading (to be mentioned soon).
4. If the exam has several essay questions, all the responses to one essay question should be read at one sitting before any responses to other questions are read. This strategy decreases the "halo effect" (the tendency to judge a second answer as good or bad based on the student's response to the first question). This practice also increases the likelihood that the examiner will be more consistent in evaluating each test question because of mood changes or some extraneous factors that might intervene between two or more sittings.
5. A decision needs to be made prior to administering an essay test concerning how organization, writing skills, spelling, and similar factors are to be evaluated. These issues are obviously dependent on the course objectives and we would suggest that careful consideration be given to them. If a teacher values written communication skills, perhaps a separate score may be assigned to students in that area. In fact, a teacher has to be very careful not to allow poor writing skills or some similar factor bias the opinion of the student's cognitive response to the specific essay question.
6. To increase scoring objectivity further on essay tests, it is suggested that some system be developed to keep the test papers anonymous. Having students place their name on the back of the answer sheet and shuffling the test papers between questions helps increase scoring objectivity.
7. To increase the teacher's capability of providing pertinent feedback to students a shorthand notation system ought to be developed, such as *N.S.* = not a sentence, *V* = vague, *SP.* = spelling error, *I* = incorrect statement, *WW* = well-written, *E.P.* = excellent point, and others. When writing comments to students, try to write as many positive comments as negative comments. If the comment has to be negative, try to suggest some direction a student might take to improve the answer.
8. If an essay exam is to be used for an important decision (acceptance into some unique program or for some reward), several raters ought to read each answer using the same criteria. This increases the reliability of scoring the test. For a typical classroom essay test, however, this does not appear very realistic.

Generating a testing policy

To be as fair as possible to the students, the testing policy should be discussed with the students at the beginning of the year. To aid the students further, written statements about the policy should be distributed. Minimally, a publicized testing policy should include:

1. *A statement about when the exams will be given.* Included in this is some indication of how long the students will have to prepare for a test after it is announced.

2. *Some reference to the frequency of tests.* Distinctions should be made between unit quizzes, surprise quizzes, and larger summative exams.
3. *A description concerning the type of test to be expected.* Some examples of previous test items, a sample table of specifications, and the amount of material that is generally covered on a test are helpful information to students.
4. *The grading policy.* Students should know how test scores are related to the course or subject matter grade.
5. *A statement about makeups.* Included in this should be some reference to absenteeism on the day of the test as well as some reference to makeup exams for those students who did not perform to some specified level or to a personal level of satisfaction on the first exam. For most testing situations, makeup exams are a positive improvement in a testing program. The possibility of having two or more chances on an exam decreases test anxiety and increases the likelihood of bettering a student's overall performance in a subject.
6. *The teacher's intentions about the problem of cheating.* Students ought to know that the teacher is seriously opposed to cheating. A description of the testing routines and a statement about what the consequences of cheating will mean should be public. Under no circumstances should a teacher make some *idle threat* about cheating.

Administering the test

Factors to be planned prior to the administration of a test include the following.

1. *Seating arrangement.* If possible, have students spread out. It does not make sense to increase temptation if not necessary.
2. *Notebooks, books, etc.* Generally it is a good idea to have all extraneous material away from the examination area.
3. *Delivering instructions.* Preciseness and brevity are the keys to instructions for a test.
4. *Distributing the tests.* Depending on the size of the class the teacher may:
   a. Put the test and answer sheet on the desk before the students sit down.
   b. Distribute the test and answer sheet after the students are seated.
   c. Ask the students to pass out the test booklets.
5. *Proctoring the test.* Care should be taken that cheating does not occur. Ignoring the class once the testing starts is both naive and myopic. If the class is very large, several proctors may be warranted. In this case, one proctor at the rear of the room and one at the front greatly decrease the possibility of cheating. If the students are allowed to sit anywhere in the room, particular attention should be paid to those students in the back corners of the room or those who appear to sit behind someone in the center of the room in such a manner as to hide themselves from view. If the teacher has a sloppy testing procedure, students particularly will be prone to cheat when the teacher is preoccupied with a student question, or at the end of the class when tests are being returned. Be aware of these vulnerable times; preventive measures can be taken.
6. *Answering questions about the test.* Students should be asked to raise their hands to ask questions about the test. Discussing questions out loud with a student is improper and distracting, and inadvertent clues may be given to the class.
7. *Collecting the test.* Particular care should be taken to have a smooth operation for collecting the tests. To insure that all test booklets are returned, the booklets and answer sheets may be prenumbered, thus keeping the pilfering of tests to a minimum.

DETERMINING THE EFFECTIVENESS OF THE TEST

As we have indicated throughout this chapter, the main purpose of a test is to provide feedback to a student and to the teacher so that both parties may improve their performances. The decisions that can be made about performance can be only as good as the test in terms of reliability, purported validity, objectivity, fairness, and efficiency. This brief section of the book describes how a teacher can determine whether a test meets those five criteria.

Reliability

To make wise decisions about a student's score on a test, the teacher should be reasonably sure that the score is a consistent representation of the student's knowledge and skills. For example, if students were to take two alternate forms of a test and the scores varied considerably, then any decision about students' specific scores would be very tenuous. The teacher would be unable to determine which of the two scores more faithfully represents the students' "true" scores with reference to the knowledge and skills sampled on the two tests. Thus the teacher would be in a quandary concerning any instructional decisions that need to be made based on the test data.

This problem is somewhat compounded by whether the teacher decides to use a norm-referenced or criterion-referenced test as well as the state of the art in statistical measurement.

For norm-referenced testing approaches although there are some very clear statistical guidelines for computing reliability, there still is a fair amount of disagreement over how the statistical data should be used and interpreted.

For a norm-referenced approach the level at which a test is considered reliable enough depends on such factors as the homogeneity of the class (the more homogeneous, the more a lower-reliability score would be acceptable); the importance of the decision (the greater the importance, the more reliable the score must be in order to be acceptable); and the nature of the test (commercial test publishers are expected to produce tests that have much higher test reliabilities than teacher-made tests). The point to be made here is that there is some arbitrariness about the level of the statistical reliability of a test that is acceptable for instructional decision making.

As a generalization, there are several simple practices teachers can use to increase the reliability of a test. For one thing, the reliability of a test can be increased by simply increasing its length as long as the students have a reasonable time to finish the test. In addition, from a norm-referenced perspective there are a variety of statistical practices to determine the general reliability of a test as well as to determine the effectiveness of each item. For those interested students, these practices are discussed in the Appendix.

For a criterion-referenced test, the issue is a little different. Based carefully on the objectives of a unit or a course, a criterion-referenced test may be very long, very short, very easy, or very hard. The purpose of a criterion-referenced test is to determine the degree *to which the student has mastered the objectives,* not to determine how much better or worse the student performs in relation to other members of the class. Ideally, in a well-run school, if a criterion-referenced test were given to a class *before* instruction, the class should do extremely poorly, while at the conclusion of a unit of instruction the scores should be very high.

Traditional measures such as test-retest reliability and internal consistency measures are not applicable with criterion-referenced tests (Beggs and Lewis, 1975). According to Beggs and Lewis, if a criterion-referenced test possesses a good content validity (measures what it purports to measure), the reliability takes care of itself. Theoretically, a poor item on a criterion-referenced test would be one that the student answers correctly on one day and incorrectly on a future occasion. In a criterion-referenced testing system it is assumed that if a student answers an item correctly, he/she has mastered the item; an incorrect answer on a second occasion would be incongruous with that assumption. You should be aware here that we are not talking about the test-retest reliability procedure mentioned above. Since the data obtained from a criterion-referenced test should be used for determining what additional instruction needs to be implemented, any test-retest correlation should be low if instruction is successful.

Validity

For our purposes here, the most important type of validity for teacher-made tests is content validity. You will recall that *content validity* refers to whether the test is measuring the content and objectives that the teacher set out to accomplish.

There are several strategies a teacher might use to determine the degree to which the test actually samples what it is supposed to sample. Ideally, since tests are supposed to reflect accurately the objectives for a course of study, the teacher should carefully inspect the test items to determine whether the objectives are actually being measured. Several consistent errors in test construction contribute to invalid tests. Pressed for time, teachers might write insignificant items based on some trivial aspect of the course rather than use a table of specifications or some outline as a basis. Another common error is to write an item at the memorization level that is supposed to represent rule-learning or mathemagenic objectives. To write a test item at the rule-learning or mathemagenic level requires that the item represent a previously unencountered example or problem. Often the teacher has the student repeat a solution to a problem already encountered. In this case the item may be a memorization item rather than an item representative of rule-learning or mathemagenic skills. A third consistent error is to select and write test items in a haphazard way; thus the final test is not based on any weighted considerations of what is very important and what is not so important. Finally, the teacher may use the objective as a guideline in writing the item but may inadvertently write an item that does not clearly reflect the objective. Consider this silly but useful example. Assume that one of the objectives in an English course is that the students be able to spell correctly a list of words. What would be the conditions of testing? The teacher would have to dictate the words to the student in a different order than they were initially presented, and the student would have to write the words from memory. What would happen if the teacher decided to make the spelling test a multiple-choice format in which the student has to choose the correct word from a list of five different spellings? This testing situation violates the spelling objective. Given a recognition rather than a recall task, the student might be able to recognize misspelled words without being able to spell the words from memory.

Remember we talked about task analysis in Chapter 8? If some of the test items have been written to assess various levels of a learning hierarchy, then those items based on a task analysis could be inspected to determine whether the lower-level items are actually prerequisite to the higher-level items. In this situation, if a student is able to answer the higher-level items while missing some of the prerequisite items, then the task analysis was incorrect, or the test item itself was faulty. In any case, something needs to be examined more closely.

In conclusion, if a teacher-made test has high content validity, the test should be in close agreement with the objectives of the course and should reflect the degree of emphasis identified in the initial course objectives.

Objectivity

Careful consideration needs to be given to objectivity. Essentially, objectivity refers to the degree to which subject matter experts agree on the answer to an item. A test item in which the experts disagree on the answer is said to lack objectivity (Ebel, 1965). Particular attention should be paid to the objectivity of evaluating extended-answer essay items, because answers to essay questions are very difficult to evaluate in a manner so that "experts" would agree. Obviously, some multiple-choice questions may be criticized from the same perspective. Of course, the unfortunate consequence of a test that lacks objectivity is that a student might receive a grade that does not reflect his/her actual level of knowledge and skills. Receiving an undeserved grade is a by-product of testing that should be avoided as much as possible. Unnecessary arguments, dislike for the teacher, and a lack of motivation to perform well can result from such a practice.

The teacher can do many things to alleviate some of the above negative outcomes of subjective testing practices.

1. Reread all test questions several times to be sure they express the desired intent very clearly. Having a second party read the items for expression can help clear up poorly worded items.
2. Be sure the question refers to specific factual material. If the question deals with opinion questions, generate some plausible acceptable answers in advance.
3. On essay questions, the answer key should be written at the time the item is written.
4. Try not to look at the student's name on the answer sheet.
5. Be sure to follow the suggestions on grading essay questions found earlier in this chapter.
6. If a lot of the good students in a course miss an item, reread the item. It may be poorly written or deceptively tricky. Do not be afraid to drop items from the test if they are bad. Do not be afraid to admit that you have made a mistake, but don't confuse student arguments over the ambiguity of the item for a lack of ability to make the fine distinctions needed to answer the question. Students appreciate honesty and teachers who appear to have a concern for their well-being.

Fairness

Fairness is a relativistic term based on the students' perception of the general testing situation and the specific system of evaluation (Figure 12–7). From a student's perspective such practices as surprise quizzes, unannounced content covered on a test, picky or tricky questions, ambiguous questions, points taken off for misspelling or grammatical mistakes in a non-English course, long tests covering a lot of material with no chance for a makeup, a great deal of emphasis placed on one test score for the determination of the course grade, and the missing of a higher grade by a point or a fraction of a point are some of the more frequent complaints about testing.

Of course, some of the above practices *are perfectly justifiable* if the student is told about them in advance. Some of the other practices are seriously debatable, and those associated with poor item construction or poor choice of an item can result

FIGURE 12–7
Students should perceive the testing procedure as fair

in student disatisfaction. The main point here is to be aware of the practices students complain about, and if the course objectives can be met without engaging in those that might engender antagonism, then generate alternative testing practices. Avoid unnecessary negative attitudes toward a course because of questionable testing or evaluation practices that may be altered somewhat and still meet the same objectives.

Efficiency

One final quality of an evaluation program needs to be mentioned briefly. Consideration needs to be given to the efficiency of the evaluation and testing program. Time is invaluable; wasting the students' or the teacher's time because of inefficient testing practices is unproductive. Three specific questions need to be asked with reference to efficiency.

1. Can the time for preparation of the testing material be reduced and still achieve the course objectives?
2. Can the grading of test papers be streamlined?
3. What is the minimal amount of time needed to evaluate students in the classroom and achieve the same cognitive and affective objectives?

For example, it is often suggested that frequent unit-level quizzes are better than longer summative tests covering many chapters. Frequent testing requires distributed practice and provides a greater opportunity for frequent feedback. Frequent testing, however, often can be more time-consuming for both the students and the teacher. To what extent should one factor be weighed against the other? Of course, the real payoff from any testing program is the cognitive and affective outcomes. Another question concerns the type of question. Preparing essay tests takes very little time compared with writing a multiple-choice or short-answer test. Evaluating an essay test takes a long time and the scoring is generally less reliable. Given the objectives of the course and a limited amount of time available for evaluation, decisions about how the time might be best used are the paramount concern. The key consideration when deciding whether the testing program is efficient is to determine whether less time might be spent in preparing the tests, whether the time spent in testing might be reduced and still achieve the same objectives, and whether a less time-consuming strategy might be developed for evaluating the students. All these questions must be framed in terms of the course objectives.

7. Generate a workable and realistic strategy for preventing cheating.
8. How does the issue of testing frequency relate to the question of testing efficiency from the teacher's perspective?

GRADING AND MARKING

Assigning grades to students or making evaluative statements about their performances is part of a teacher's role—perhaps the most onerous and difficult task teachers face. While many critics of education have been extremely distressed by current grading practices, schools must serve an evaluative function. The question does not appear to be: Should we evaluate? but rather: How should evaluative statements be derived and communicated about students?

Most serious educators are very cognizant of the limitations and dangers of grading—problems such as the tremendous diversity in assigning grades, the unclear definition of what the grading system means, and the lack of objective data upon which grades are assigned. The purpose of this section is not to attempt to resolve the above issues; those issues have been around for years and are indeed complex! Instead, the purpose of this section is to help you arrive at a system of grading and reporting grades with which you will feel comfortable given the probable demands placed upon you as a teacher. Four questions are addressed:

1. What are the purposes of making evaluative statements about students and assigning grades?
2. What factors should be considered in arriving at an evaluative statement or grade for a student?
3. What are the characteristics of the major grading or evaluative systems?
4. How might evaluative statements or grades be communicated, and to whom should the statement and grades be communicated?

Purposes

Before we attempt to answer this question, notice that we make a distinction between evaluative statements and grades in this section of the book. By *evaluative statements* we mean some reference a teacher makes about the quality of a student's performance. More specifically, an evaluative statement makes some reference to the degree of desirability of the student's performance, and if the performance is less than desirable some suggestion is made concerning how it might be improved. These statements may vary from several words to lengthy suggestions for improvement. Compared with an evaluative statement, a *grade* is a qualitative, symbolic summary about the degree of worthiness of the performance. Usually in a letter form (A–E), *a grade does not suggest how the performance might be improved.*

The first objective of any evaluative or grading system should be that it benefits the student. More specifically, evaluative statements should provide feedback for students in order to maintain quality responses or to increase the quality of inadequate responses. Also, with reference to students, a good evaluative system can motivate students to work harder. An inadequate evaluative system can have deleterious outcomes with students. Of course, if the students do not care about receiving positive evaluative comments or high grades, then the system takes on a superfluous role with respect to motivation. It should be pointed out here that some students purposefully strive for negative comments or low grades to get back at their parents or to impress their peers. In these situations other contingencies would have to be available to the students to have any positive outcome on their performance. Finally, if students understand very clearly how the evaluative statements or grades are derived and they care about performing well, the students should get a clearer picture of their general capabilities with reference to either the subject matter or other members of the class. Having this type of information, the students should be in a better position to plan for the future with a little more assurance.

From a teacher's perspective, while the task of grading papers can be tedious, the information obtained from making a careful evaluation can be used in two major ways. With respect to a particular student or group of students, the information can be used in a diagnostic fashion to reteach the material. If a careful analysis of the students' errors is made, the teacher should be able to determine quickly with what level of learning the student is having difficulty (memorization, discriminations, concepts, rules, problem solving, or mathemagenic skills) and then rearrange the teaching environment accordingly. A cleverly written test can be designed to provide this type of information systematically. By providing for optimal learning conditions at the level at which the student is having difficulty (e.g., practice repeatedly, present examples and nonexamples, recall relevant prerequisite skills or concepts), successful reteaching of the task should be maximized. Second, the teacher ought to be able to use the information from a careful evaluation to reanalyze the effectiveness of the lesson. From a mastery point of view, failure by a large number of students indicates that something in the classroom environment needs to be changed. Having analyzed the students' responses on the test or project, *error patterns* can be detected that provide the teacher with some excellent cues about how the lesson ought to be restructured in the future.

Evaluative information about a student is also needed at the school level to determine his/her appropriate placement within a school system (retention, promotion, graduation, admission to a special program) as well as whether the student should receive certain honors.

Finally, other parties concerned about a student's progress include parents and possibly various outside agencies such as a potential employer or some other educational agency. In the latter respect, care should be taken to insure that the student's records are clear, accurate, and informative. Negative information that has no bearing on a student's employability or future academic success should be removed from a student's record.

In conclusion, the question is not whether evaluative statements are needed; the question is how an evaluative procedure should be established to benefit the student and to provide various concerned people and agencies with the necessary information to make enlightened and fair decisions about a student.

Deriving evaluative statements and grades

Making evaluative statements or grading is based on the value system of the teacher and the school system. It is very important that these value systems be made public and articulated clearly to students in order that the students understand the basis upon which they are graded and can plan accordingly. So far in this chapter we have discussed the rules for making a grading or evaluative system reliable, valid, objective, fair, and efficient. All evaluation and grading strategies should reflect these characteristics.

In this section of the chapter we are referring to the decisions a teacher has to make about the relative importance of different components of a subject matter and the strategies a teacher can use to combine different components into a strategy that is reliable, valid, objective, fair, and efficient. To do this the teacher has to decide on the objectives and those behaviors that are acceptable proof that the objectives have been performed satisfactorily. Further, the teacher has to decide on the relative importance of each of the objectives (weighting) and on how the different behaviors may be "averaged" together to derive an aggregate grade reflective of the course objectives. With a criterion-referenced system it is quite possible that each of the objectives will be reported separately on a checklist or similar arrangement.

As we have stated many times in this book, deciding upon course objectives and their relative importance is a value judgment. We have tended to value independent problem-solving and rule-learning objectives, and therefore we feel that much more emphasis should be placed on these higher-level tasks than on lower-order tasks when deriving a grade. The exact percentage figures for each objective or series of objectives reflects the teacher's subjective opinion about what is important and valued. These decisions should be made in advance of the course, unit, or lesson and should be communicated to the students.

If a grading system is to accurately reflect the teacher's intent, then care should be taken to see that procedural errors are not made in assigning weights to different objectives of the course or in combining different components of a course into an aggregate score. These errors invalidate the grading system and are terribly unfair to the student. Often, however, errors in weighting and combining different scores are made because the teacher is not aware of the correct procedures. At any rate, the grading system should be made available to the students at the beginning of the year for their scrutiny.

Weighting

In a norm-referenced testing situation in which a teacher has given a series of quizzes or tests and the standard deviations have tended to vary considerably from test to test, the results will contribute unequally to a student's conglomerate score in a manner directly related to the magnitude of the standard deviation. In other words, the greater the standard deviation on a test, the greater that score disproportionately influences the aggregate score. For example, if a teacher's intention is to give equal weight to five quizzes and the ranges and standard deviations vary considerably from quiz to quiz, a simple averaging of the five quizzes will not accurately reflect a student's aggregate score related to the rest of the class. Since one of the qualities of a desirable evaluation and grading program is fairness and another is validity, the teacher should do everything possible not to undermine these goals. If the teacher has decided upon a grading system that is based at least partially on a norm-referenced approach, then the teacher should insure that each test or quiz is truly comparable to each of the other quizzes or tests.

For the teacher who intends to use a norm-referenced approach, however, there is a fairly easy way of equating the quiz scores when the standard deviations vary considerably. A discussion of and the rationale for the approach are found in the Appendix.

In our opinion, to apply the normal distribution curve to a class of highly competent or incompetent students is grossly unfair. In our way of thinking, a criterion-referenced approach is much fairer and allows for much more explicitness. Needless to say, the statistical manipulation of the standard deviations has no place in a criterion-referenced approach to evaluation.

With criterion-referenced testing the problem is entirely different. First of all, the grade obtained from a criterion-referenced approach should have nothing to do with how other students in the class perform on the quizzes or tests. Second, with many criterion-referenced approaches the report card will not have an aggregate score; rather it will reflect the objectives of the course or some combination of objectives. Third, if an aggregate grade is required with a criterion-referenced approach, the grade will depend on the *number* of objectives performed successfully, or, in some instances, on the average of the quiz scores (if all the quizzes are measuring an equal number of objectives). Further, with a criterion-referenced approach to evaluation there is often an opportunity for students to improve their performance on a test by taking one or more makeup quizzes. In this case, the highest of the quiz scores is the one that counts.

Most teachers consider different types of tests, quizzes, projects, homework assignments, and class participation in arriving at a grade. As a rule of thumb, except at an advanced level, tests and quizzes should count more than projects and homework assignments. Tests are more objective, and the scores are less likely to reflect outside help or cheating. Put bluntly, there is very little a teacher can do to control for cheating or parental help on homework assignments or projects. Seen from this perspective, the purpose of homework is for relevant practice of the objectives. As such, the student's performance on homework should probably receive very little weight.

Careful consideration also ought to be given to assigning a lot of weight for classroom participation. Evaluating classroom participation is often very unreliable and to a significant extent is related to the student's ability to express an idea clearly as well as his/her willingness to participate. Further, we all know that some students tend to dominate classroom discussions. Theoretically for a class of 25 students meeting for 50 minutes, the time for each student to participate equally would be only two minutes, with no time for teacher comments. Quite frankly, with the exception of giving a grade to a student for an oral presentation on a topic, class participation should probably not receive much weight unless some overt activity is the product necessary to evaluate a specific performance objective.

Assume a teacher decides to grade a student by combining a major test with a major paper. Let us further assume that the teacher assigns double weight to the test. How should the scores be combined? From a norm-referenced approach, the teacher essentially needs to equate the standard deviations in each category. In this case, the teacher would have to use some system for converting the paper grade into a numerical score, and then equate the standard deviations of the two categories. If many quizzes are given during the semester, each quiz should be equated to a desired score as it is administered. Likewise if more than one paper were assigned, the same procedure would follow. An example of how to combine these scores is found in the Appendix.

Again, this statistical procedure is totally inappropriate for a criterion-referenced approach. Weighting in a criterion-referenced approach is achieved by simply multiplying the obtained score by the desired weight. In a criterion-referenced system, the performance of other members of the class is irrelevant. Obviously, if the report card refers to only performance on specific objectives, there is no problem of weighting.

Care should be given to insure that the grading practices used by the teacher actually reflect the teacher's intentions. Faulty grading practices can distort a teacher's intention and are unfair to students. Also, careful consideration should be given to the choice of the grading practice. Different practices will bring about entirely different grading distributions.

GRADING SYSTEM AND REPORTING SYSTEM RELATIONSHIPS

Essentially there are two types of grading systems: one based on predetermined standards and the other based on comparisons between students. All other systems are deviations or combinations of these two. We have discussed these systems at length, so there is no need to repeat. There is a need, however, to discuss how a teacher's evaluation of a student should be reported.

In report cards for the elementary grades there are typically several sections (a subject matter competence section and a work-study-attitude section) as well as several components within each section (Figure 12–8). More specifically, there are four ways to communicate in print a student's subject matter progress:

1. Grades
2. A list of objectives—each objective is checked off in terms of the degree of mastery.
3. A list of general characteristics—each germane characteristic is identified (e.g., tries hard, does what is expected).
4. Written comments.

Often report cards include three or all four of these forms of reporting. At the secondary level, a greater emphasis is placed on grades, with some room available for specific comments or a general rating system that is to be checked if appropriate. To some extent, the number of students assigned to a teacher dictates how much may be reported on each child.

Knowing what the reporting system is like, the teacher ought to gather information systematically to reflect what is needed on the report card. If aggregate grades are required, then plans should be made before school starts to determine how they will be derived. Above all else, keep in mind the objectives of the course and the welfare of the student; work toward those ends.

ASSESSING THE AFFECTIVE DOMAIN

Generally, the affective domain receives very little consideration in educational psychology texts. To some extent this text is no exception. This is not because the affective domain is not important; we just do not know as much about it as we do about the cognitive domain. In addition, there are some authorities who, while acknowledging the importance of the affective domain, feel the schools should not be tampering with this area except in a tangential manner related to the cognitive objectives of the course. There are other people who feel a student's personal belief system, attitudes, and values are private, therefore we have no right to measure or probe the student's private, "inner" self. Those people would argue that the only values education should

FIGURE 12–8
Examples of several types of report cards

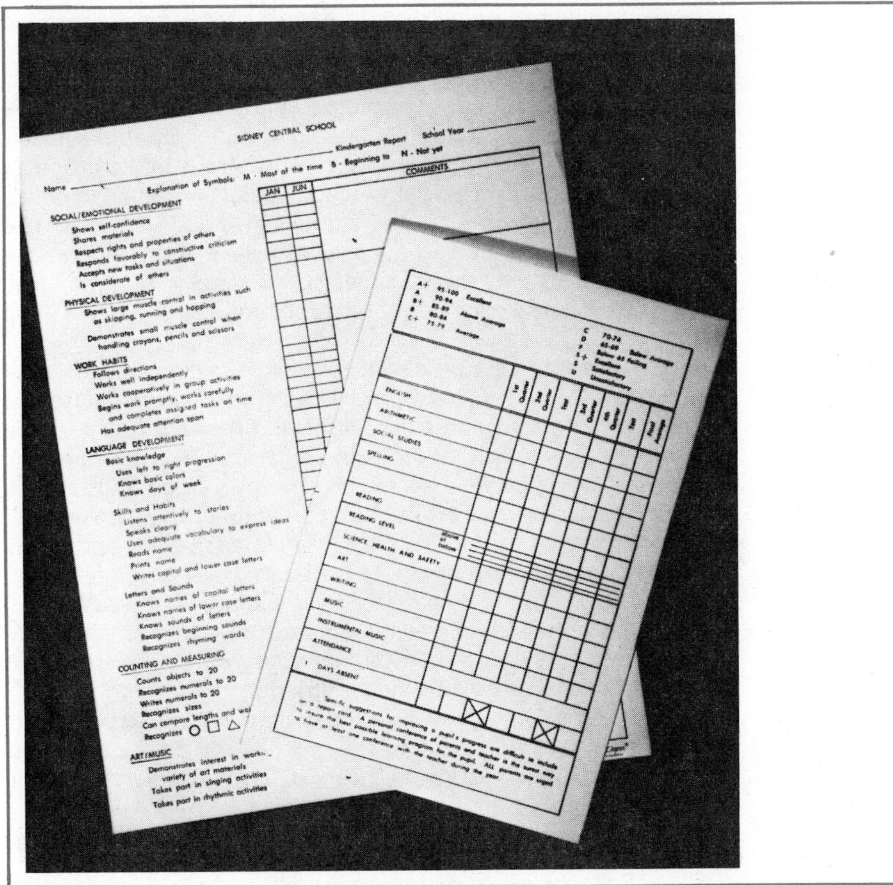

be concerned with are those attitudes expressed as overt behaviors that have an influence on classroom behavior or on society at large.

Contrary to the above viewpoints, the affective domain has taken on an increasingly significant importance in recent years. Discussions of such topics as one's political, religious, sexual, and social values are now commonplace in the schools. The purpose of this section is to discuss the possible positive outcomes of evaluating the affective domain and to describe some evaluation techniques.

Why assess the affective domain?

By using a thorough evaluation program in the affective domain, we can achieve at least five positive outcomes.

1. The student can get to understand his/her attitudes and feelings a little clearer if wise practices are used by the teacher.
2. From a careful analysis of the data obtained in the affective domain, a teacher could modify the general classroom program. For example, a question about minority groups might indicate that the students' attitudes are in conflict with a democratic form of government. These conflicting values might be discussed in class.
3. A good evaluative instrument in the affective domain might be used to determine

whether the objectives in the affective domain are being achieved, particularly if pretest and posttest measures are obtained.
4. To determine the student's opinion about a specific classroom event or practice, an anonymous questionnaire can be given to the class. This type of feedback can be invaluable in changing specific unpopular teacher practices!
5. At the elementary school level where a lot of group projects are used, a careful analysis of the social interactions in the class can be obtained. Particular concern should be given to the student in the class who is not chosen to be a member in a group (the isolate), especially if that student expresses a strong desire to affiliate with the members of the class. A great deal of careful planning and action can counteract this problem.

Attitudes can best be observed when a student has free choice and is not aware of being observed. An awareness of being observed can influence a person's behavior significantly. Since it is very difficult, time-consuming, and impractical to observe students in naturalistic settings in which they are unaware of being observed, we resort to paper-and-pencil tests to measure purported attitudes, beliefs, values, and feelings. You should be aware, however, that at times there is very little correspondence between an expressed attitude on paper-and-pencil tests and overt behavior. In one of the classic studies in this area, La Piere (1934) wrote letters to a number of restaurants asking whether they would serve a Chinese couple. Written receipts from the request indicated that a lot of restaurants would refuse to serve the Chinese couple; however, when a Chinese couple did attempt to get served in those restaurants they were refused service in only one. Although there were some methodological flaws with the research, the study does show that written, verbal statements do not always correspond to actual behavior. The reasons for such a discrepancy are very complex and well beyond the scope of this text. The importance of this finding, however, cannot be emphasized enough.

How should the affective domain be assessed?

Given the recognized limitation of paper-and-pencil tests, however, some useful information can be obtained if the items are written carefully. Generally, the strategies available to teachers fall into one of two categories. There are those observational strategies a teacher can use on occasions in the classroom or in some other environmental setting to measure a student's tendency to behave in a particular manner reflective of some desired attitude. An example might be some unobtrusive observations on a playground to determine whether a treatment program in the class is having any significant influence in making a student who is an isolate more socially acceptable. Another example would be a quick visit to the school librarian to determine whether a significant number of books have been taken out on a topic the class is studying even though no projects requiring library reading have been assigned. A third example would be recording on a prepared checklist a student's frequency of response in some attitudinal area. Essentially, in all three examples the teacher is trying to determine whether the student is willing to *approach* a given designated stimuli or situation.

The second strategy a teacher can use is some form of written questionnaire to measure attitudes. One of the most popular forms of evaluating written, expressed attitudes is through the use of a Likert-type instrument. Based on a five- or seven-point scale, the student is supposed to check off the point along the continuum that best reflects his/her attitude on a topic. The points on the continuum are distributed from extremely favorable to extremely unfavorable and are often written as: strongly agrees, agrees, neutral, disagrees, strongly disagrees. Care should be taken to use equivalent wording on both sides of the midpoint. With younger children, yes or no questions are used.

Another similar strategy is the semantic differential technique developed by Osgood, Suci, and Tannenbaum (1967). With this technique, the student checks his/her attitude toward some topic along a continuum in which two bipolar adjectives are at either end. Words such as "good–bad," "constructive–destructive," "useful–useless," and "happy–sad" are examples.

Other techniques include an adjective checklist in which a student checks off those words that appeal to him/her, a multiple-choice (forced-choice) technique in which the student is given several competing choices, a Q sort in which the student is given statements about an object and is asked to sort them into predetermined categories about the object, and open-ended questionnaires in which the student is asked to write an extended opinion on a topic. An excellent description of how to write affective questions is found in Tuckman's (1975) book, *Measuring Educational Outcomes: Fundamentals of Testing.*

The same general care and planning should go into developing a strategy for evaluating the affective domain as into one for evaluating the cognitive domain. To measure a student's attitude on a topic without a clear purpose is a waste of time. Often poorly conceptualized goals in the affective domain lead to poorly developed paper-and-pencil tests in this area as well.

SUMMARY

This chapter has been concerned with the strategies a teacher can use to evaluate a student's cognitive and affective responses to instruction with paper-and-pencil, teacher-made evaluation instruments given before, during, and after an instructional sequence. To evaluate reliably, validly, efficiently, objectively, and fairly with such evaluation instruments takes careful planning.

Divided into five main topics, the chapter discussed: the purposes of systematic evaluation strategies; how to develop a systematic strategy; how to prepare, score, and evaluate the effectiveness of teacher-made tests; how to develop a grading and reporting system; and how to evaluate the affective domain.

It was pointed out that all parts of an evaluation program ought to be integrated so that the total program meets the criteria of reliability, validity, efficiency, objectivity, and fairness. With careful planning, teachers can enhance their teaching effectiveness considerably. Without careful planning it is very easy to undo an otherwise effective plan of instruction.

SELF-TEST

1. From an instructional decision-making perspective, what are the two *main* purposes of systematic evaluation using teacher-made evaluation instruments?
2. State all the steps you should use when both *planning for evaluating* and *evaluating* an answer to an essay question.
3. What should a teacher do to insure high content validity on a teacher-made test?
4. What is the main reason for not assigning a lot of weight to homework assignments in determining a student's grade that reflects his/her knowledge and skills in the course?
5. State two general strategies a teacher could use to determine whether a student has a positive attitude toward music.

6. Generate a hypothetical table of specifications for a small topic in the area you intend to teach.

   For questions 7–10, construct a properly written test item for the category provided.
7. Extended essay—at the rule-learning or problem-solving level.
8. Short answer essay—at the rule-learning or problem-solving level.
9. Multiple-choice—at the concept, rule-learning or problem-solving level.
10. Matching.

ANSWER KEY TO BOXED QUESTIONS

1. *b*
2. Some type of strategy similar to a table of specifications is needed where the levels of objectives are along one axis and the content or topics along the other axis. The resulting boxes provide the tester with a framework to generate the test items.
3. The extended essay can measure:
   a. A student's ability to organize.
   b. A student's ability to write clearly and effectively.
   c. student's ability to originate divergent solutions to complex problems.
   d. A student's ability to synthesize a great deal of material in one question.
4. Since many more items can be answered in a short period of time, a greater amount of material can be sampled.
5. If you were interested in the student's ability to organize, write clearly, or generate an original synthesis to a variety of material, then a vague question might be appropriate. Generally, this type of question creates more problems than it is worth.
6. By being sure that the examples in the stem or foil were not previously encountered by the student. Examples from the text should *not* be provided.
7. Although there are many factors to consider in a strategy to prevent cheating, a few of the more obvious include:
   a. Having a good student-teacher relationship.
   b. Stating the objectives clearly.
   c. Attempting to have the students see the rationale for the objectives.
   d. Making sure the room is arranged so that cheating is difficult. This includes specially developed answer sheets; alternate forms of the test, if necessary; and precautions during the testing situation.
8. Enough testing should be conducted to insure that the students accomplish the objectives successfully. From a teacher's perspective, the question concerns the optimal amount of testing needed to reach the objectives. Obviously, the greater amount of time that is spent on any one instructional function, the less time there is for other functions. It is the teacher's task to determine what an optimal level of testing should be to reach the objectives of the course. Either too much or too little testing is inefficient.

ANSWER KEY TO SELF-TEST

1. Any two of the three answers are sufficient: to provide the student with relevant feedback, to determine how the student should be helped, and to modify the *teacher's* behavior by identifying areas in which the students performed poorly.
2. *a.* Identify an objective at the rule-using or problem-solving level.
   b. Generally, you should write the question just after you plan the lessons. The question should be explicit in what is expected.
   c. Generate an ideal answer or a statement concerning the characteristics of a good answer. Determine how writing skills, organization, and spelling are to be treated.
   d. When correcting the essays, insure anonymity of the student.
   e. Read a few of the answers before you start to evaluate them to determine if you want to use your answer key.
   f. Read all the answers to one essay question before reading the additional essays.
   g. Develop a notational system to provide feedback for students.
3. Be sure that the test measures the objectives of the course in a systematic way. The number and the type of test items should reflect the emphasis of the course. A table of specifications or some similar strategy should be used to guarantee a spread of questions.
4. Since homework assignments can be completed by getting a great deal of help from parents or peers, the grade on a homework assignment may not accurately reflect the student's capability.
5. *a.* Develop a questionnaire designed to determine the amount of time spent in music-associated activities.
   b. As unobtrusively as possible, observe the student participate in music-related activities.

6. Refer back to the relevant section to determine if the two general categories (levels of objectives and a list of topics) were included in your specification. Two other main points to consider in evaluating your answer are: Did you use a systematic approach for determining the topics? Did the number of questions in each box reflect your emphasis for each topic?

7–10. Refer back to the sections on the different item formats. Show your instructor how you wrote each item.

SECTION III

IMPLEMENTING INSTRUCTION

Section II of this book discussed how instruction should be designed to attain fairly specific performance objectives. In Section III, our concern turns to how the plans to achieve those objectives can be implemented best in the realistic context of the school and classroom. Much additional consideration is given to how these specific objectives might be integrated with the broader goals of schooling. In our opinion, an effective school should be able to attain both levels of outcomes. Each chapter in Section III addresses an aspect of the implementation process in teaching. Chapter 13 analyzes the types of considerations facing administrators and teachers when they create school and classroom environments supportive of the multilevel goals of schooling. In Chapter 14, the focus shifts to a discussion of various broad strategies teachers can use to implement those goals. To make effective decisions about instruction, the teacher also needs to evaluate the specific entering behaviors of the students with respect to the lessons. Chapter 15 addresses these considerations. Related to both Chapters 15 and 17, Chapter 16 describes the mathemagenic skills the student needs in order to be an effective learner in and beyond the classroom. Essentially, all instructional strategies should eventually lead the student to self-sufficiency.

The underlying theme in the latter part of Section III is that teaching is an interactive process and that the best of plans have to be modified at times. In Chapter 17, a very comprehensive strategy for analyzing student responses to tasks is presented. Chapter 18 discusses how a teacher might use the information obtained from analyzing a student's response in the context of the classroom, as well as strategies teachers might use to deal with disruptive classroom behavior. Section III culminates with a very concise and useful chapter on how to evaluate the effectiveness of the total instructional program.

Chapter 13

Creating the educational environment

THE LAST FEW CHAPTERS have been concerned with some of the micro instructional decisions based on the conditions of learning reflecting the different domains of learning. While all those decisions are very important for successful teaching, they can be undermined easily or made much less effective if the general school and classroom environment is at cross purposes with, or not supportive of, the specific objectives of a program. Achieving specific objectives at the expense of broad goals, or not achieving the narrow objectives because of a poorly arranged general classroom does not make good instructional sense. Specifically, care should be taken to insure (1) that the general curriculum is organized as effectively as possible, (2) that the physical arrangement of the school or classroom is appropriate, and (3) that the climate of the class is conducive to reaching the stated goals of the program. On the surface, these considerations appear to be three separate issues. It is our contention, however, that these three broad concerns are *the major components* of the general school and classroom environment that either contribute to or detract from the success of specific instructional events and, therefore, should be considered as a comprehensive plan.

Put another way, given that our hypothetical teacher has decided on the objectives for a course or a class, has identified all the prerequisites of the objectives, and has identified specific strategies that should be implemented to facilitate learning the objectives, the teacher now needs to think of how these strategies can be implemented in the context of the classroom environment. An inappropriate general classroom environment can be just as destructive of a teacher's goals as poorly planned and executed specific instructional strategies.

Most of us would agree that the general purposes of schools are to have students *maintain positive* feelings toward learning; *acquire* the necessary facts, concepts, and principles to solve important problems; become competent in *solving* important problems; and *feel reasonably good* about themselves. It follows, then, that the school's task is to arrange or to have the students arrange the school and general classroom environment to be supportive of these broad goals. David (1975) states it well: it is the responsibility of educators operating at various levels of our schools to purposefully design the school and general classroom environment necessary to bring about the combination of outcomes desired of students.

Oftentimes the process gets reversed. Finding ourselves in inappropriate environments, we tend to *react* to the environment as it is rather than *change* it to be consonant with our purposes. As in other chapters in this book, we are optimistic that much can be done to improve our classroom environments if great care is given to thinking about what we want to accomplish. To be a prisoner in our own environment is a fault too often perpetrated by the authorities who have the power to change things for the better.

Agreeing with David, Krasner's (1976) point of view sets the stage for this chapter.

> The classroom should be viewed as a total environment *planned* by the teacher with advice and suggestions from students, parents, researchers, school administrators, and guided by state curriculum mandate. Implicit in such a concept are: a theory of human nature, goals as to individuals and society, and a philosophy of education. . . .

Different from the past few chapters, this chapter attempts to bring together a variety of research findings as well as some practical suggestions on how to plan for a well-organized curriculum and classroom consonant with your goals. As such, this chapter will be more applied in its orientation.

For example, at the school level, it is important that school administrators, in consort with teachers, recognize that the general organization and operation of the school can have a major facilitative or deleterious influence on the success of the instructional program. Such broad school organizational difficulties as disorganized curriculums, inappropriate scheduling of activities, inappropriate matching of students to curriculums, poor procedural arrangements for carrying out the instructional program, poorly conceived school rules, ineffective grading systems, and inappropriate architectural designs of buildings are examples of problems at the school level that can interfere with the instructional program.

Getting more specific, at the classroom level there are many other faulty practices that can undermine an otherwise well-planned lesson based on the conditions of learning research. Included in this category are such practices as inappropriate rules, disorganized classrooms, improper seating arrangements, poorly presented sequences of activities, a general lack of consideration for individual learning differences, dreary classrooms, ineffective interpersonal interactions between teachers and students or between students and students, a general lack of smoothness in conducting the class, and poorly developed classroom routines.

To repeat—to have spent hours on planning specific lessons only to have those lessons undermined by other factors that educators should have controlled does not make sense. The purpose of this chapter is to have you consider how specific plans can be implemented in the context of the total school program as well as the general classroom environment.

At the conclusion of this chapter, you ought to be able to:

1. Identify factors that should be considered when planning for and implementing the goals of instruction in the context of the general classroom environment.
2. Identify some of the more important common errors made by the schools and classroom teachers that interfere with reaching the goals of instruction that could be easily changed.
3. State how the goals of instruction may be best implemented in the general school and classroom environment by creating an appropriate physical and psychological climate for learning.

SCHOOL EXPERIENCES AFFECTING YOUR MOTIVATION, ATTITUDES, AND LEARNING

Before we start discussing the factors in a general school or classroom environment that need to be considered in planning for instruction, we feel it would be very appropriate to point out the significance of this topic by having you analyze your own school experiences. Quite frankly, with the current knowledge level we have in education, we believe as a profession we have done many things that we need not have done, and we have not done some things we could have done to make our schools and colleges more successful. By analyzing your own experiences we felt we could make our points more vivid and realistic, therefore impressing upon you the necessity of systematic and careful planning for the general school and classroom environments. Basically, we are interested in whether you have observed or been involved in any of the school experiences mentioned in the accompanying questionnaire. Circle your choice.

QUESTIONNAIRE ABOUT YOUR SCHOOL EXPERIENCES

1. Have you ever taken a course that was basically unnecessary repetition of previous course material? Yes No
2. Have you ever been required to take a specific course in college in which the *content* varied tremendously from professor to professor even though the objectives of the course would not imply that variability? Yes No
3. One of the basic purposes of a college education is to insure that the graduate can synthesize material from a variety of disciplines in order to live a better life and to solve complex problems. Has your college significantly helped you in that synthesis? Yes No
4. Have you ever taken a course or courses in junior high school or high school for which you could see very little possible utility? Yes No
5. In your total public school experience, were you ever involved with some *project* of your choosing for an extended period of time (at least several months, perhaps a year or longer) in which a significant product was produced or some advanced skill was acquired? Yes No
6. Through some school-related experience, did you ever participate in an activity that contributed significantly to some aspect of your community's well-being? Yes No
7. At the high school level, were there ample opportunities for you to become involved in work-type experiences in government, business, or industry? Yes No
8. Throughout your school experiences, were there ample opportunities for students to receive recognition in areas other than the formal academic subjects, athletics, music, or theatrical events? Yes No
9. Do all children in your hometown start first grade and the same formal curriculum at a specified age? Yes No
10. Have you ever seen a student promoted who did not possess the appropriate skills for the next grade? Yes No
11. Have you ever taken a course that was beyond your ability because you did not have the prerequisites? Yes No
12. Have you ever taken a test that you feel did not adequately reflect the stated objectives of the course? Yes No
13. Have you taken a test that you feel did not adequately reflect what had been taught in the course or what you had been required to do before the test? Yes No
14. In any of your classes, were you ever allowed to make some of the significant decisions concerning how the course might be organized? Yes No
15. Did you ever dislike any of your teachers because you felt the teacher really did not care about teaching? Yes No
16. Did you ever attend a class in which a great number of off-task behaviors occurred, such as fooling around, goofing off, or excessive talking? Yes No

Now let's look at your answers. Questions 1–3 deal with aspects of how the general curriculum should reflect the goals of the program, Questions 4–8 address issues related to motivation, Questions 9–13 are concerned with learning, Questions 14 and 15 are about interpersonal relationships and the climate of the class, and Question 16 refers to the ability of the teacher to identify precisely what is happening in the class.

If you answered yes to Questions 1, 2, 4, 9–13, 15, or 16 or no to Questions 3, 5–8, or 14 you may have experienced an educational or instructional situation in which there was either a mismatch between the stated goals of the program and the actual implementation of the program or some inappropriate general instructional strategy was used in the class. In either case, with some conscious effort expended by those in power, the problem could most likely have been resolved.

STRUCTURING THE GENERAL SCHOOL AND CLASSROOM ENVIRONMENT

To decrease the likelihood of such mismatches or inappropriate general instructional strategies, we present five broad suggestions from which it would appear that a more appropriate organizational structure and general operating procedures could be derived in the classroom. See Figure 13–1 for a list of these guidelines.

FIGURE 13–1
List of principles upon which the general school environment should be planned

1. The objectives of each class or subject should reflect the goals of the curriculum. Further, each grade level or subject should be carefully integrated within the total school curriculum.
2. When you are planning for the general school and classroom environment, care should be given *to design an environment that tends to keep students on-task* or to prepare students to be able to pursue a task in a variety of settings. The general environment should be supportive of on-task behaviors.
3. When you are planning for the general school and classroom environment, care should be given *to design an environment that tends to facilitate learning the cognitive objectives* of the program. As such, various general learning principles should be used as guidelines in the development of the general classroom environment.
4. The teacher should always know what is going on in the class, be able to predict potential trouble in the classroom, and be able to implement plans smoothly.
5. The teacher should attempt to maintain positive interpersonal relations both between the teacher and students and between students.

Although these principles are general in nature, the key to good teaching is the ability to implement these general guidelines in the contexts of the total school program and the individual classroom. In the remainder of this chapter we consider how these broad guidelines might be translated into a workable plan of action for classroom teachers. On our journey we will point out how these guidelines, if not followed, can get teachers or even the educational establishment into serious trouble. We might add that although these five broad guidelines appear to be somewhat self-evident, it is very apparent that these principles *are violated frequently!* For whatever reasons, the principles are not always followed.

Organizing the school program based on differing levels of objectives

PRINCIPLE 1

The objectives of each grade level or subject should reflect the goals of the curriculum. Further, each grade level or subject should be carefully integrated within the total school curriculum.

Essentially this principle repeats the general theme of this book. Your objectives should be identified prior to giving a great deal of consideration to the structural arrangements of the environment. Given the desired outcomes of instruction, concern should be given to arranging the environment to implement the objectives. Examples of general problems in this area are when the course structure of the curriculum is determined *before* the objectives of the program are delineated, when a textbook is chosen *prior* to carefully identifying the objectives, or when a general organizational arrangement of the class is designed *earlier* than the objectives are specified.

In our opinion, the common error made in most of these situations is a "structure function discrepancy" in planning. For the purposes of this discussion, *structure* is defined as the physical and/or psychological arrangement (rules, routines, schedules, etc.) of the class or school. *Function* refers to the outcomes that are desired from the program. In an ideal systematic plan (see Chapter 6) the outcome should generally reflect the objectives, but in a poorly developed plan the functions or outcomes often vary considerably from the desired objectives. To obtain a match between the structure of the school and/or classroom and the desired outcomes, the structure (the general school and classroom environment) should be planned after the outcomes have been carefully identified. As a parallel, in architecture the basic principle used by most architects is "form follows function." Obviously, there are some fixed features in the structure of any environment, but quite frequently the apparent given features of an environment can be significantly changed if desired. Often the given features of the environment are dictated by past tradition and are not based on good instructional practices. Let us see what can happen when these processes get reversed.

The first structural-functional discrepancy to be discussed in this section deals with a common high school and college problem. This problem is a course structure that is not based on the outcomes desired of the students. Results of this structural-functional reversal include unnecessary repetition of material already learned, a great deal of variability in the content of a course when the objectives have been clearly delineated, and a general inappropriate organization of the curriculum in which the content of the courses is divided in such a way to make it difficult for the student to get a broad educational perspective of the material.

If you have ever taken a course in high school or college that was basically an unplanned repetition of another course, you have experienced a typical structural-functional problem. This problem occurs frequently because decisions about programs start with the titles of courses before the goals and objectives are clearly identified. For example, briefly consider the organizational arrangement of this fictional but typical college curriculum in a teacher training program. Assume you attend Fogbound University and you are an education major. The requirements for graduation include Foundations of Education, Methods I and II, Techniques of Reading, Strategies for Individualization, and several electives. You should be able to immediately see the problem. Unless the Education Department places very specific limitations on what can be taught in these courses, the student is liable to receive a tremendous amount of repetition.

These courses are not discrete organizational structures; therefore a tremendous amount of overlap is likely to occur. *Planned repetition* can serve as a useful review or can aid a student to integrate complex subject matter. Haphazard repetition is the result of poor planning and is wasteful as well as boring to the students. Nonplanned repetition occurs because very little consideration is given to developing *programs* based upon goals and functions. It takes a lot of hard work to generate a purposeful program stemming from a series of *integrated* goals. Without that planning, however, the student suffers.

Even the concept of a course, itself can be an inappropriate structural arrangement. Try to think how you might arrange a program without courses. If a *program* were designed in which the objectives are clearly specified, well-developed projects, modules, assignments, and other appropriate resource materials could be made available to students on an individual or group basis reflecting the instructional objectives. Instead of assigning students to broad courses, students would be assigned to specified goals, objectives, or questions (Figure 13–2). Instead of assigning teachers to courses, the teachers would be assigned to specific goals, objectives, and questions. While this type of program could be criticized for not presenting the students with an integrated

FIGURE 13–2
Grouping students is one way to minimize structure-function errors

course of study, that criticism easily could be avoided by choosing and then sequencing the objectives to reflect an integrated curriculum. We are not suggesting that this is the approach we should take in higher education. We are suggesting, however, that there are alternatives to our current course system that could be implemented and that are *not* based upon nebulous and overlapping course content.

Another difficulty in the structural organization of traditional subjects is the implicit assumption that the same set of objectives will be implemented in the same subject when taught by two different teachers and that the objectives will be equally mastered by the students. Unless a subject is highly specialized and sequential, the content and emphasis in a subject tend to reflect the teacher's idiosyncracies and personal preferences. Variability of approaches, as well as different emphases and points of view, may be very desirable, particularly if the student is asked to use variable approaches to solve a problem. *Variability does not serve a useful function at all, however, when huge gaps exist in a student's education because of it.*

For an example, let us look at a fictional high school English course, which we will call English I. Let us assume the content of English I is supposed to place an equal emphasis on writing short themes, vocabulary building, reading American writers, and personal letter writing. At the end of that course, the student receives a composite grade for the course and then moves on to English II. The problem should be immediately apparent. It is quite possible that a student could be extremely competent in several of the above areas, perform very poorly in several other areas, pass the course with a C, and move onward. In this case, the course structure has not insured that the student is competent in all the areas. To pursue our example a little further, two teachers assigned to teach English I might emphasize different components of the course. Unless there is an overall check on the performance of the students, severe gaps can be created by a teacher's personal preferences and interests. This situation typifies a serious structural-functional discrepancy in our educational system.

For our final mismatch in this area we decided to choose a current college problem to indicate how important it is to determine the nature of a curriculum based on goals and instructional objectives *before* the structure is determined. Our discussion now centers on the liberal arts distribution requirements found in most colleges throughout the country. *One* of the main purposes of the distribution requirements is to have students be knowledgeable in various broad areas so that they can synthesize knowledge from the various disciplines in order to better solve previously unencountered problems and make enlightened decisions. Paradoxically, the current course distribution structure can work against the broad goals upon which most liberal arts curriculums are based. If colleges are ever going to realize their broad goals of enabling students to solve broad, previously unencountered problems that require a synthesis of disciplines, the curriculum should require that students attempt to solve, or at least consider, interdisciplinary problems. Exposing students to a distribution of courses in a variety of disciplines, however, *insures neither that a student will integrate different bodies of knowledge nor that the student will solve complex problems using diverse bodies of knowledge.*

While it is true that many of the broad problems we are referring to in this section require a type of synthesis for which clear guidelines are not necessarily available, when the student is not required to make some original synthesis the main stated goal of a "liberally educated person" is not realized. Put another way, the typical solution of requiring a wider distribution of courses (a current trend) or a greater quantity of courses in a particular discipline does not address the goal of having the student become reasonably competent in handling interdisciplinary problems.

In order to solve complex problems using information from different disciplines, the student should be able to define the terminologies in each discipline, identify the similarities and differences between the concepts and principles of each discipline, and integrate the material into a workable model to solve complex problems. The principles of transfer of learning discussed in Chapter 8 apply very well here.

Some colleges have recognized these points and have organized their curriculums around team-teaching approaches and interdisciplinary programs. Unfortunately, the instructors on an interdisciplinary team quite often teach their own course content without much consideration for student outcomes; thus the existing course structure never is overcome by the students. According to Petrie (1976), "all too often grandly conceived interdisciplinary projects never get off the ground, and the level of scholarship seldom exceeds that of a glorified bull session."

We suggest that an appropriately designed environmental structure based upon a series of clearly defined objectives and requiring that students attempt to solve problems across disciplines should alleviate some of the problems cited in Petrie's observations. To summarize, if the first principle presented in this chapter were followed, these mismatches and reversals of function and structure would be much less likely to occur.

1. According to the authors of this text, too many structural-functional reversals take place in education. What is a structural-functional reversal?
2. In terms of curriculum organization, give two examples of a structure-function reversal.

Keeping students on-task

PRINCIPLE 2

When you are planning for the general school and classroom environment, care should be given to design an environment that tends to keep students on-task or to prepare students to be able to pursue a task in a variety of settings. The general environment should be supportive of on-task behaviors.

By embedding the lessons and learning activities in a positive framework that constantly makes use of motivational principles, you are increasing the likelihood that a student will desire to *approach* additional learning activities. Although all of these principles are discussed in depth in other chapters of the book, a synthesis of some of the main generalizations on motivational research is in order to provide a framework from which these broad theories might be applied in a classroom environment. In other sections of the book, we talk about motivational research with respect to specific students.

As stated in the general principle, care should be taken to arrange the classroom in such a way as to keep students on-task (Figure 13–3). This implies keeping unnecessary disruptions to a minimum, having supplies and books easily accessible to students, and having rules and routines supportive of on-task activities. Further, in classrooms in which many different activities occur at the same time, appropriate seating arrangements need to be considered. The noisier activities should be as far away as possible from the students who are completing individual assignments.

Personal space also must be planned. Depending on the student activities, provision needs to be made for some privacy or for group seating arrangements, where appropriate. For example, in one particular school in which the teachers designed the classrooms, they decided that hexagonally shaped classrooms provided an optimal architec-

FIGURE 13–3
The classroom should be designed to keep students on-task

tural use of space. The six corners of the room were to be used for privacy, while the center of the room was used for group projects and group lessons (Rice, 1970).

As another example, some elementary schools have experimented with small portable octagons in which students can work on their individual assignments, thus affording each student maximum privacy. We are not suggesting that either of these examples needs to be used in a classroom, but that a flexible imagination can go a long way toward altering traditional spatial allocations.

Although it is sometimes difficult to think of all these factors before classes start in the fall, a careful observation of those factors that appear to contribute to classroom disruptions can be made early in the school year, and then appropriate changes in the environment can be made. No two groups of students perform in the same manner. Depending on the characteristics of the group interactions in the class, the teacher should respond accordingly.

In conjunction with the first suggestion, the classroom should be organized so that there are numerous types of activities for students to do *after* the major seat work assignments are completed. These activities should vary in scope, novelty, and interest level.

Third, in many classes it would appear wise to involve students in long-term projects of their own choosing. Obviously, this strategy is appropriate only in those classrooms in which it would make sense to give the students a choice. Certainly, in some classes, a choice would not be appropriate due to the nature of the topic or curriculum. *Participation in goal setting by the learner is a particularly useful motivating principle. As a generalization goal-oriented learners tend to perform better than non-goal-oriented learners.* This principle suggests that in planning for the general organizational arrangement of the class, consideration should be given to having the students generate some of their own goals in concert with the teacher. Providing the student with the opportunity and the organizational skills to develop a plan to implement personal goals often makes a great deal of sense and should be considered an integral part of instruction. Research from both the cognitivist and behaviorist points of view strongly supports this position. As a value, we hope you recognize that education *is more than* just insuring that students acquire a certain set of cognitive objectives. Getting the students to commit themselves to long-term projects would appear to be a valuable goal in its own right, particularly if our long-term goals in education are concerned with producing efficient, independent learners and problem solvers who are intrinsically motivated to pursue excellence.

Principle 2 also implies that students will have to do some of their work at different times than other students as well as to pursue different topics of their choosing at different times during the school year. To implement this principle, the teacher has to be a very good organizer and keep a close watch on the different activities as well as insure that students do not interfere with other students while pursuing their goals. Achieving one objective at the expense of other objectives is not a good instructional outcome!

While some of the previous suggestions deal with a student's choice of activities, we have pointed out that it is not always appropriate to give the students a choice. Many times students will be asked to do things that are not of their own choosing. Although learning cannot always be perceived as "relevant," exciting, fun, and intrinsically interesting to students, the teacher should consider using the students' interests wherever possible in the lessons. Such strategies as using purposeful interest centers, presenting the lesson in a novel way, providing the students with concrete experiences outside of the classroom context, and attempting to use the students' experiences in the lesson make a lot of motivational sense. Not all students are going to be intrinsically interested in the topic for the day.

Furthermore, having a close relationship with the community and involving the community in some of the planning of the school program might help to make the school experiences of students more worthwhile and realistic. In fact, with meaningful involvement of the community, the school could take on a role more in line with the community center concept and somewhat more in line with the essentialist and reconstructionist philosophies identified in Chapter 2.

In one school system familiar to one of the authors of this text, the culminating experience for high school students studying German was a two-week visit to Germany at the end of the second year. Realizing that signing up for German meant a trip to Germany, the students had to work on many money-making projects to attain their goal. To alleviate much of the expense, while in Germany the students stayed in German homes. The following year, high school students from Germany came to this country on a reciprocal arrangement. Not only were the students more motivated to study German (English was not to be spoken in the German homes), but the students also learned a great deal about cooperation and working toward a long-term goal. It should be pointed out that this program occurred in a rural community where the income level of families was very low. With a desire to make learning more interesting, a little ingenuity can go a long way toward making lessons more appropriate.

Finally, within the budgetary constraints of the school, the classroom should be as attractive as possible. Such features as painting the room a pastel color, placing a rug in the corner of an elementary school classroom with several lamps placed about, and having several attractive plants and art objects add to the pleasantness of the room. Your students will spend considerable time in your room; make it as pleasant as possible for them. As pointed out by Getzels (1975), the environment we construct tells us who we are and what we must do. The individual character of a classroom and the organization of the classroom can set the stage for the year and should be arranged accordingly.

Where have our schools gone wrong in this area? In our opinion, three major factors have contributed to motivational difficulties in the classroom. One of the factors at the secondary level is concerned with the focus of the school curriculum, and the other two factors are related to the way classrooms have been traditionally organized.

At the secondary level, quite frankly, we have a serious problem. Not seeing any purpose in many of our traditional high school courses and not possessing the general academic skills required by the courses, a significant number of high-school-aged students are not interested in school. Failing to provide for these students by not having a much closer relationship to realistic work experiences, by not providing for a wider distribution of experiences designed for carry-over into leisure-time activities, and by not allowing the students to be involved in community activities where they are able to contribute to the betterment of society results in many students who feel that their high school experiences are not germane to their own development. To meet some of these criticisms head on would require some significant changes in typical high school curriculums. As stated previously, certainly a much closer relationship between the schools and life outside of the schools could contribute to a more meaningful experience for many high-school-aged youth.

The two other general factors that appear to contribute to motivational problems in students are based on inappropriate classroom management. One of the typical organizational problems facing teachers is not designing a classroom environment that flows smoothly in its operation, thus contributing to off-task behavior in the students. Common errors in this area include not providing the students with enough meaningful activities that are incompatible with disruptive classroom behavior, and not arranging the physical classroom in such a way as to minimize off-task behaviors (seating arrangements, traffic flow patterns). Having free time with nothing to do, students are likely to engage in disruptive behavior.

The second organizational error that greatly influences the motivational pattern of students is actually the faulty implementation of several related learning principles. This error, therefore, is discussed in the next section.

Implementing instructional principles in the classroom

PRINCIPLE 3

When you are planning for the general school and classroom environment, care should be given to design an environment that tends to facilitate learning the cognitive objectives of the program. As such, various general learning principles should be used as guidelines in the development of the general classroom environment.

***a.* Students possess different constellations of abilities, and therefore the school and classroom should be designed to reflect these differences where appropriate.**

Psychologists have known for a long time that there are wide variations in students' capabilities and general development. More recently, Cronbach and Snow (1977) have postulated that these differences are of such magnitude that different treatments and classroom organizational arrangements might be in order for different students (the aptitude-treatment interactions model). Implied in this principle is the recognition that some consideration should be given to individual differences in the schools and classrooms. The traditional "lock-step" approach generally tends to ignore individual differences. Any plan for individualization, however, has to take into account the broad goals and objectives of the school as well as how the school is organized. Given that students are very different, this principle suggests that a plan designed to reflect individual differences and also to implement the cognitive and affective objectives of the program would most likely be the ideal arrangement in planning for instruction. A discussion concerning how a teacher might design an environment to reflect individual differences while meeting the given objectives of the curriculum is found in the latter half of this chapter and in the next chapter.

***b.* The general environment should be designed to help make the learner efficient in the acquisition and performance of skills.**

Having mastery as a basic goal, teachers should arrange the classroom environment to reach that goal. Traditionally, many classrooms have been organized around the "exposure" model of teaching. In the exposure model, the total class is given a unit of instruction and is required to go through it at the same pace. Very little consideration is given to individual differences in the rates of acquisition of skills and the rates with which students are able to utilize their skills. Sufficient meaningful practice of material, which facilitates transfer to previously unencountered situations, is a prerequisite for the acquisition of generalizable skills. By meaningful practice of material we mean practice that encourages the student to relate the new material to previous learning as well as to situations that have been previously unencountered. As Rothkopf (1968) has so well pointed out, the "calculus of practice" (rote practice) by itself is one of the least effective modes of learning. It cannot be emphasized enough that sufficient *meaningful practice is important* to facilitate the achievement of many of the cognitive goals of the classroom (Figure 13–4). With this perspective in mind, the teacher must require mastery and have the students learn the material to the mastery level in a manner that is as enjoyable as possible. Teaching lesson after lesson to a whole class without providing for or requiring the necessary practice to achieve mastery violates this "sufficient meaningful practice" principle. Different structural arrangements than are now currently in vogue are needed to give students the necessary time to acquire the appropriate knowledge or skill to perform the terminal objectives.

FIGURE 13–4
Meaningful practice facilitates learning

According to Carroll (1963), time is one of the key independent variables that needs to be manipulated in order for learning to occur. Carroll points out that if a student is placed in a learning environment that is reasonably matched to his/her academic skills and motivational tendencies, there should be little reason for academic failure if enough *time* is provided for the student to learn the tasks. Carroll astutely suggests that the student's willingness to persevere at a task and ability to perform the task correctly should not be thwarted by *teacher-paced* approaches that ignore individual differences in academic ability and motivational tendencies.

Of course, it should be emphasized that it is not time alone that is critical; rather it is the qualitative use of time that makes the difference in learning (i.e., how the student chooses to spend the time).

Even though teachers must complete a curriculum in a predetermined amount of time, this principle suggests that the pace of instruction needs to be at least partially determined by the students' capabilities to achieve the objectives; therefore, time should be varied realistically.

c. The general classroom environment should be arranged in such a manner that the learner should be making many appropriate active responses and should receive appropriate knowledge of results.

Essentially derived from the research on learning discussed in depth in the preceding chapters, this point emphasizes the importance of these principles in the context of planning for the general classroom environment. As a generalization, learning requires active responding. While it is true that a person can observe someone perform an activity and then at a future time imitate the activity, generally cognitive covert or overt active responding such as reconceptualizing, reorganizing, using principles to solve problems, relating diverse information to a new framework, or making appropriate overt responses facilitates learning. Although the theoretical issues associated with this principle are very complex, a guiding principle of teaching should be to have students make active responses (either overtly or covertly) quite frequently during instruction.

As an example of the distinctions made here, consider the lecture method. In our opinion, one of the tragic misuses of the lecture method is that many teachers view it as a means of *providing information* rather than as a means of activating a student to *rethink* issues. McLeish (1976) makes some of the distinctions identified here. Our digression into methods is to point out that two teachers could use the same general instructional or organizational strategy and yet get completely different results due to the type of responses a teacher typically requires the student to make. Providing information is passive; rethinking issues and problem solving are active, even though they may be covert. The guiding principle here is to ensure that the student has to go beyond the information given to solve some previously unencountered problems.

To aid the student in these problem-solving tasks, the teacher should arrange the general environment in such a manner that the student receives some relevant feedback about the quality of his/her performance. Repetitively practicing some behavior or performing some behavior that is incorrect generally will not improve the performance of the problem-solving skill. Whether that knowledge of results should be immediate or delayed, or in the form of positive or negative information, is immaterial to this discussion. The main point in this chapter is that the teacher should plan different strategies to insure that knowledge of results is meaningful, frequent, and contingent upon the students' responses.

While these two principles have been discussed much more thoroughly in previous chapters in the context of facilitating performance on specific objectives, the general organization of a classroom should also incorporate these two principles.

Based on some of the points made in this chapter, a careful analysis of some of the characteristic ways our school systems and classrooms have been organized suggests that many violations of these basic instructional principles are constantly perpetrated. For one thing, all too often students are given assignments beyond their capability. This mismatch occurs for a variety of reasons, but essentially it is a function of:

1. The student does not have the general prerequisites, such as reading, writing, or spelling skills, to perform the assigned task.
2. The student does not have the specific cognitive prerequisites, such as the rules, concepts, discriminations, and skills, to perform the assigned task.
3. Frequently the student does not possess the general organizational or other mathemagenic skills to perform the tasks successfully.
4. The student possesses the general and specific prerequisites to perform the task, but not enough time is allotted.

When this *assigned task–lack of prerequisites mismatch* occurs, the result is often off-task, disruptive classroom behavior. Further, confronted with impossible tasks, the student's motivational level deteriorates.

These mismatches frequently originate in kindergarten and continue throughout succeeding grades. Exposing *all* six-year-olds to a formal reading program, for example, before they possess the prerequisite skills appears to be our first mistake. Given our current practices in the teaching of reading, we can predict with a high degree of accuracy that at least 20 percent of first-grade students will experience a great deal of difficulty in learning to read, and in some schools the percentage is much higher. The reading mismatch problem becomes particularly acute in the upper elementary grades when teachers have to teach social studies, science, history, health, and similar subjects that generally require that a student acquire much of the factual information through reading textbooks written for students at a specific grade level. Advanced writing skills are also necessary for these subjects, at least as they are currently taught. The unprepared student *cannot possibly* perform the assigned task as *expected* due to poor reading skills! And these discrepancies continue to widen throughout the grades.

To resolve this discrepancy there are educators and educational psychologists who argue very forcefully that the instructional solution to this mismatch is to present materials and assignments to students commensurate with their academic entering behaviors. This matching sounds like a great instructional strategy based on various accepted psychological principles and, on the surface, it does make good instructional sense. Consider for a moment, however, the typical classroom teacher's responsibility, particularly in the upper grades. The typical high school teaching load, for example, consists of teaching 80–150 students per day. In addition, the typical teacher has from two to four different preparations, sometimes in different subject areas. Couple this high student load with the fact that commercial textual material is written at a level designed to reach typical students in that grade level, and the problem becomes magnified considerably. The teacher finds out that a significant number of students do not have the basic reading and writing skills necessary to complete the assignments. It is difficult to find material covering a particular content at a particular grade level that is written at a much simpler level of understanding. Furthermore, the teacher is caught in several subtle crossfires that are almost impossible to resolve. One comes from the public and parents: "Why can't Johnny read?" and "Don't water down the curriculum" are real criticisms that influence teachers.

Another cross fire comes from the Catch-22 situation in which teachers find themselves with reference to the preparation of the student for the next grade. Students who do not possess the skills for the current grade put the teacher in the absurd situation of teaching content that is beyond the student's current abilities, just so the student will be ready for the next grade, which is also beyond the student's grasp. Although it is apparent that easier and alternative teaching material is needed to help these students, the teacher's load often mitigates against such an approach—at least in the short-run.

FIGURE 13–5
Overt responses are important for learning

Trapped in these pressures, the teacher quickly comes to feel that his/her classroom can be only partially individualized. Ideally, the school system should be reorganized to minimize these mismatches, but practically, this reorganization will not occur for a long time to come. In Chapter 14 strategies for partially resolving this problem are discussed. Later in this chapter, some general organizational arrangements for the classroom are discussed which could help reduce these mismatches. We might add that if the principles discussed in the first part of this chapter were closely followed, this discrepancy *could not occur.*

A second common error in typical classrooms is not to require enough overt responding so that corrective feedback can be used (Figure 13–5). When taught by the exposure model rather than the mastery model, a student is more likely to be confronted with inappropriate curricular material beyond his/her capability. To counter these two problems requires general classroom organizational patterns designed to match the student's ability level with curricular material at that level as well as to require diagnostic-prescriptive teaching on the part of the teacher.

3. Why is *time* considered to be one of the key independent variables which should be varied in teaching?
4. In terms of general learning principles, what appears to be the most frequent error made by the schools and teachers?

Keeping the class running smoothly

PRINCIPLE 4

The teacher should always know what is going on in the class, be able to predict potential trouble in the classroom, and be able to implement plans smoothly.

This chapter has discussed how the teacher can arrange or rearrange the general physical environment of the class to bring about the desired goals of instruction. Our concern now turns to the teacher. Even if a teacher presents "perfect" lessons based on the conditions of learning research and designs a physical environment derived from the suggestions presented in this chapter, the classroom can be a disaster without appropriate teacher-student interactions. The teacher is certainly a key factor that needs to be considered in the context of the general classroom environment.

Unfortunately, this section is relatively brief; not because this topic is unimportant, but because research in this area is extremely difficult to conduct and few concrete suggestions can be derived from the research. With between 200 and 300 different interpersonal relationships occurring every hour in a typical dynamic classroom setting (Ornstein, 1975), with the inability to get a clear handle on which aspects of an interaction should be studied (Berliner, 1975), and with the recognition that *different* interpersonal relationships and skills may be needed to teach younger children and students of different SES backgrounds (Brophy & Evertson, 1976; Soar, 1972), it is hard to make useful generalizations. Recognizing the serious difficulties associated with conducting research in this area, we do believe, however, that some generalizations are still in order.

In one of the most extensive reviews of the research on teaching effectiveness, Dunkin and Biddle (1974) found quite inconclusive results concerning what is currently thought of as good teaching. One of the most popular conceptions of a good teacher has stemmed from the work of Flanders (1969), who suggested that the degree to which a teacher is relatively indirective is the degree to which the teacher is good (i.e., the degree to which the student talks and initiates his/her own activity). From those variables studied (degree of indirectedness, amount of praise, willingness to accept student ideas, amount of criticism, amount of teacher talk, amount of teacher questions, amount of teacher lecturing, amount of teacher directions, amount of student talk, amount of pupil response to teacher initiation, amount of pupil initiation, and amount of silence or confusion), the only conclusion that Dunkin and Biddle could definitively arrive at is that *criticism should be used very sparingly.* All the other popular viewpoints about the characteristics of a good teacher were not supported from Dunkin and Biddle's extensive review.

In analyzing Kounin's (1970) creative work, however, Dunkin and Biddle were a little more positive. Kounin has done a great deal of work concerning classroom control and group management techniques. According to Kounin, good teachers acting within a social context possess the following abilities:

1. *Is with it*—The teacher knows what is going on at all times in the class.
2. *Is smooth*—The teacher is able to continue the flow of classroom activity, particularly at points of transition, so that the momentum continues.
3. *Is able to alert group*—The teacher keeps the students alert.
4. *Handles overlappingness*—The teacher is capable of handling several activities simultaneously.
5. *Fosters accountability*—The teacher holds the student responsible for the assignments.
6. *Arouses challenge*—The teacher is capable of maintaining enthusiasm, curiosity, and industriousness.
7. *Varies seat work*—The teacher varies the types of tasks assigned to students.

As a tentative generalization, we suggest that these capabilities or strategies would facilitate a well-functioning classroom. While the classroom may appear to be functioning very smoothly, the degree of learning and positive attitudes generated by these approaches still need further clarification.

Notice that Kounin's research suggests that *a good teacher easily can handle many activities simultaneously in a smooth and coordinated approach to teaching.* Essentially this means that a teacher ought to have good administrative skills. Later in this book we demonstrate how this principle might be used on a daily basis. For now, an example will suffice. Kounin's research findings indicate the student activities occurring in a classroom should not interfere with other student activities, and that when a teacher changes activities or topics in class the transition should not be abrupt. In other words, the activities, methods, assignments, and other events occurring in the classroom should blend together into a well-organized, integrated plan so that the student's attention is focused on the appropriate tasks. Sudden shifts and disruptions can detract from the goals of the class and should be avoided under most circumstances. As a specific example, assume two students are talking to each other while the class is having a teacher-student discussion. Rather than calling attention to the students who are talking out of turn, if the teacher were to walk slowly toward the two students while continuing with the class discussion, they would most likely stop talking and the class would continue the discussion unabated.

Having as a goal the continuation of the lesson, the teacher can use many general strategies such as this to help students achieve the objectives of the class. In summary, the general organization of the class should demonstrate a smooth organizational pattern reflecting the teacher's goals.

In another thorough review of classroom teaching procedures, Rosenshine (1976) indicated that a drill pattern consisting of questions that the student is generally capable of answering, followed by relevant feedback and additional questions, coupled with small steps of instruction at the student's achievement level appears to be a good strategy for teaching in the early grades. It should be pointed out that Rosenshine's research dealt with primary-grade pupils from lower socioeconomic backgrounds. The generalizability of these findings to different age levels and other types of socioeconomic status is undetermined. An earlier review by Rosenshine and Furst (1973) concluded that although a great many independent variables have been studied, few variables are consistently correlated with student achievement. Generally, clarity of presentation, variability of methods and assignments, teacher enthusiasm, and task orientation are positively related to teaching effectiveness.

The research on what type of teachers students prefer, however, is much clearer, and many of these findings are of the common-sense variety. For example, in a recent survey conducted with 1,200 junior high school students, Saunders and Wright (1974) found that the students wanted a teacher who is fair, explains work clearly, knows the subject matter well, and is friendly, dependable, and energetic. As Hamachek (1969) noted, a good teacher is first of all a good person. In the Veldman and Peck (1963) study, student teachers who were rated positively ran semidemocratic classrooms, had strict control, and were knowledgeable, friendly, and interesting. Whether any of these variables are strongly related to academic achievement or long-term motivation is still to be determined. It probably is safe to conclude that none of the characteristics identified in this paragraph would have a serious deleterious effect on learning or long-term motivation, and, therefore, as a "best bet" a teacher should strive to possess these characteristics.

It might be interesting for you to rate yourself on the checklist in Figure 13–6. According to Paul (1974), the characteristics in the left-hand column have frequently been found to be related to good teaching, while those in the right-hand column are usually associated with poor teaching skills. Although this questionnaire has not been validated, it may raise some important questions for you to consider about your general characteristics related to teaching. Paul's rating scale has also been reproduced for your benefit. In conclusion, if we were forced to speculate on what a good teacher should be like, our list would include the following characteristics:

1. Fair.
2. Good communication skills.
3. Firm.
4. Sure of self; reasonably systematic.
5. Well organized.
6. Enthusiastic and interesting.
7. Knowledgeable.
8. Friendly and warm.

PRINCIPLE 5

The teacher should attempt to maintain positive interpersonal relations both between the teacher and students and between students.

Before we leave this section, we need to discuss several topics related to the role of the teacher as he/she interacts in the physical environment. The point to be made here is that the classroom is not just a physical environment. It is a social environment, with many social interactions occurring between the teacher and students as well as among different students. Humans are social beings. Not only should humans learn to respond appropriately in social settings, but appropriate social interactions also tend to facilitate motivation and learning. For these reasons, the classroom environment should be based on positive interpersonal relationships.

Such factors as the degree of group cooperation versus individual competition; how status is determined in the class; the degree to which emotions are allowed or encouraged to be expressed; the degree of total democracy, shared student-teacher decision making, or teacher-centeredness; the degree of freedom to move about the room; the different social roles that the classroom encourages or discourages; and the formal

FIGURE 13–6
How do you rate?

	Positive traits	Negative traits
A	______ Analytical	______ Acrimonious
	______ Aware	______ Aloof
B	______ Broad (in thought)	______ Bitter
C	______ Careful	______ Capricious
	______ Cheerful	______ Captious
	______ Cooperative	______ Censorious
	______ Courteous	______ Cheating
	______ Curious	______ Childish
D	______ Decisive	______ Discouraging (to others)
	______ Disciplined	______ Dishonest
E	______ Encouraging	______ Exploitative
F	______ Faithful	______ Favoritism (overt or covert showing of)
	______ Firm	______ Fearful
G	______ Grammatical	______ Garrulous
	______ Growing (cognitively and affectively)	______ Grumbling
H	______ Hopeful	______ Hypercritical
	______ Humorous (at least appreciative of this quality in others)	______ Hypocritical
I	______ Integrity (exemplifying)	______ Impatient
	______ Intelligent	______ Inflexible
J	______ Just (in dealing with others)	______ Jealous
K	______ Kind	______ Kibitzing (e.g., meddling)
L	______ Loving	______ Lax
M	______ Mature	______ Messy
N	______ Natural (in manner)	______ Negative (to new ideas)
O	______ Open	______ Obtuse
	______ Orderly	______ Overbearing
P	______ Patient	______ Passive
	______ Persevering	______ Procrastinating
Q	______ Qualified	______ Querulous
R	______ Responsive	______ Ridiculing
	______ Retentive (in memory)	______ Rude
S	______ Sensitive	______ Selfish
T	______ Thoughtful	______ Temperamental
U	______ Understanding	______ Unclear
V	______ Vibrant	______ Vengeful
W	______ Warm (cordial)	______ Wasteful
	______ Willingness (exemplifying)	______ Weak-willed
X	______ X-factor (inner strength)	______ Xenophobic
Y	______ Youthful (in attitude and outlook)	______ Yes-person (inclined to be)
Z	______ Zestful	______ Zealotry (exemplifying)
	______ Positive points	______ Negative points

______ Net positive points (positive minus negative)

Rating scale

Net positive points	*Conclusion*
79–80	A paragon! Demand a continuing contract.
65–78	You serve as a real example to others.
50–64	See? You're human, too.
35–49	Still not too late to go back to the drawing board.
20–34	It's recycling time. (Is academe really for you?)
Below 20	You also serve as an example to others!

Source: Paul (1974).

versus informal social structure of the class all tend to contribute to the general classroom climate. *Climate* refers to the general feelings of students in the class toward themselves and toward others brought about by the *psychological structure of the class* (the various social relationships, rules of the classroom, and routines). Schmuck and Schmuck (1975) have attempted to define a positive classroom climate as meeting six basic conditions:

1. The students should expect excellence.
2. There is a great deal of teacher-student and student-student sharing of ideas and emotional support. Although the teacher is ultimately in charge of the outcomes of the class, this viewpoint stresses various democratic classroom arrangements for decision making.
3. Students like each other and the teacher.
4. The norms of the class support the pursuit of academic work and individual differences.
5. Open *dialogue* between teacher and student and among students is encouraged and maintained.
6. Group cohesiveness is emphasized.

According to Schmuck and Schmuck, such a classroom is very supportive of positive feeling toward oneself, resulting in a higher degree of motivation and effective learning. To a large extent, the view of the teacher as a facilitator of learning rather than an information provider is in line with this orientation. Trust and mutual respect within a nonthreatening environment in which excellence is expected and attained are the outcomes desired of this humanistic viewpoint. To achieve these ends, the six basic conditions of a positive classroom climate presented by Schmuck and Schmuck should be attained, if possible. The humanists suggest that the degree to which interpersonal processes such as those identified above are instituted in a class will be the degree to which these humanistic goals will be attained. At the heart of this viewpoint is striving for excellence within a supportive social environment. In line with Maslow's theory of self-actualization, in which the achievement of positive self-esteem is seen as a strong facilitator of achieving one's potential, emphasis should be placed on successful learning in a social context (Figure 13–7). To ignore this point, according to the humanists, is to deny the basic nature of humanity.

Our point of view on these suggestions is that the teacher should be willing to institute these guidelines to the degree possible while still attaining the cognitive objectives of the course. In instances where many students could care less about excellence and other students' social needs, however, direct teaching strategies might be more appropriate. To achieve an appropriate social atmosphere without achieving the cognitive gains, in our opinion, is faulty teaching. To achieve cognitive gains at the expense of positive social outcomes is also unnecessary. Except in unusual circumstances, a balance of both outcomes should be possible.

Several caveats to ponder

Many of the suggestions presented in this chapter derived from research findings have implied that there are some specific, but universal, characteristics of "good" teachers that appear to apply equally to different subjects, different age levels, different socioeconomic backgrounds, and different students. The purpose of this chapter was to identify those universals. In other words, we felt it was very important to identify some principles you could use to help you design your general classroom environment regardless of the above-mentioned differences. We suggest to you now that, although

FIGURE 13–7
A well-planned social atmosphere helps to develop positive attitudes

we feel fairly confident that the universals mentioned in this chapter are equally applicable for different subjects, age levels, socioeconomic backgrounds, and students, careful consideration must also be given to some of these differences.

Recently it has been suggested that the nature of the subject matter may necessitate different types of teacher-student interactions or climates, and that these climates influence students differently (G. J. Anderson, 1971; Hearn & Moos, 1978; Moos, 1978). This line of thinking implies that different classroom climates may be needed in different subject areas. As we have pointed out previously, it has also been suggested that different students in the same subject area might require different treatments if we are to maximize our effectiveness in teaching (Cronbach & Snow, 1977; Scandura, 1977a). Specifically, consideration needs to be given to the interrelationships between the subject matter, the cognitive processes required to complete the task, and individual differences. According to Scandura, since different subject matters appear to place different cognitive demands on students, and since some subject matters appear to have different inherent structures (e.g., botany—taxonomical relationships; mathematics—sequential, hierarchical, deductive relationships), different student strategies as well as different teaching strategies might be needed to maximize instructional and learning efficiency. What are the relationships between the patterns of teaching and different subject matters?

In an extensive review of 200 junior and senior high school classrooms, Moos (1978) found that teacher-student interactions could be classified into five general categories. See Figure 13–8 for a description of these categories.

Extending this work, Hearn and Moos (1978) studied the type of climates generally found in different subject areas [mechanical, vocationally oriented subjects; investigative subjects (science and math); art (art, band, language, theater); social (economics, history,

FIGURE 13–8
Patterns of teacher-student interactions in 200 junior and senior high school classes

Nature of the teacher-student interaction	*Number of classes observed having the trait*	*Description of the relationship*
Control-oriented	47	High emphasis on teacher control. In these classrooms, innovation, affiliation, task orientation, or competition was *not* emphasized. Classroom organization was generally poor.
Innovation-oriented	44	High emphasis on innovation—also high on involvement, affiliation, and teacher support but low on task orientation. Lack of classroom goals and unclear procedures a common complaint.
Affiliation-oriented	26	Emphasis on student-student interactions and group participation. Within this pattern are found two types of classroom organizational patterns. A structured classroom (20 classes) emphasized organization and clarity of rules and procedures. The unstructured classroom pattern (six classes) was low on the above characteristics.
Task-oriented	47	Emphasized specific academic objectives. The same two subpatterns were found as identified in the affiliation-oriented category. Only 8 of the classes could be characterized as structured; the remaining 39 were unstructured.
Competition-oriented	32	Emphasis on grades and recognition. Three subpatterns were found. Structured classes in this category numbered 14, 11 classes were characterized as supportive, and 7 classes were identified as instructional. The supportive classes emphasized competition, but in a friendly and cooperative context.
Total	196	(Of the 200 classes analyzed, 4 did not fit into any category.)

Source: Moos (1978).

social studies); and vocational, office work courses (bookkeeping, clerical, typing)]. The findings are presented in Figure 13–9.

In the Moos (1978) study, both students and teachers were more satisfied with an innovation-oriented pattern than with control-oriented patterns. A secondary finding was that a moderate amount of structure was preferred regardless of the orientation pattern. Paralleling the secondary finding, it was determined that students and teachers alike do not like classrooms that are out of control.

If we compare the Moos study with the Hearn and Moos study, it can be seen readily that certain subjects are characteristically taught in ways with which students report a strong dissatisfaction. Since it may be possible that different social climates are needed for different subjects (still to be researched), and since students characteristically tend to prefer certain types of social climates over others, where does this lead the teacher? Although this area certainly needs much additional research, the limited findings we now have pose some interesting challenges. What should a teacher do when the research suggests that climate A is better than climate B for optimal cognitive

FIGURE 13–9
Relationships between types of subject matter and classroom social climates

General subject matter area	*Characteristics of the social climate of the classroom*
Art (art, band, language, theater)	High on innovation and low on competition, rule clarity, and teacher control
Investigative (science and math)	High on task orientation and teacher control, low on involvement, affiliation, and innovation
Mechanical, vocational	High on competition, rule clarity, teacher control, involvement, affiliation, and innovation, while low on task orientation
Office, vocational	High on participation, affiliation, task orientation, competition, and rule clarity and low only on innovation
Social (economics, history, social studies)	Low on task orientation, rule clarity, teacher control, participation, and affiliation

Source: Hearn and Moos (1978).

results in a subject, while at the same time the research seems to indicate that the students clearly prefer climate B over climate A. While this problem may not pose too many difficulties for a specific teacher choosing to create a specific climate in the context of a classroom, it becomes very important, perhaps crucial, when we consider the collective results of these interactions over a long period of time.

So far in this discussion we have been talking about the relationships between the cognitive demands of different subjects and student preferences for particular climates. We have purposefully left out of this discussion any consideration of the relationships between a student's cognitive entering behavior and the climate of the class, or the student's motivational characteristics related to academic performance. For example, in an ATI study conducted in an Australian high school physics class, Gardner (1974a) found that high-achievement-oriented teachers had a very beneficial effect on achievement-oriented students but a very deleterious effect on low-achievement-oriented students. A traditional research study would have concluded most likely that there was no relationship between the teacher's characteristics of achievement orientation and the student's performance. Other evidence seems to indicate that students who perceive themselves to be in control of their lives may benefit more readily from a relatively unstructured class (Arlin, 1975; Daniels & Stevens, 1976), while students low in achievement may profit academically more from a structured class (Tobias, 1976). For a very comprehensive analysis of this topic, consult Cronbach and Snow's (1977) fine book on aptitude-treatment interactions. The point of this whole discussion is to remind you that a given instructional treatment *may* have different cognitive and affective results for different students. From a broad perspective, the teacher has two general choices in order to accommodate individual differences. The teacher can either have different goals for different students or different treatments for different students striving toward the same goal. Depending on the broad purposes of the program, both approaches could be appropriate. Discussion of these techniques is found in the next chapter.

5. Why is it usually important for the class to be conducted in a smooth manner?
6. What are the characteristics of a positive classroom climate?
7. What is meant by the term *attribute-treatment interaction* and what is its main implication for classroom instruction?

THREE SPECIFIC NON-TRADITIONAL ORGANIZATIONAL STRUCTURES

So far we have talked about five general principles that would appear to be beneficial guidelines in developing a general classroom environment supportive of the goals of instruction. We have also analyzed some of the current practices at different levels of the school and classroom that appear to run counter to these principles. Additionally, we discussed some current research on the relationship between the classroom climate and student preferences for climates. In this section of the book we discuss several broad educational and instructional strategies that incorporate many of these suggestions into a workable organizational structure for the schools. As examples of how these principles can be incorporated into a general school or classroom structure, the nongraded approach to school organization, the "open" classroom, and Hewett's (1968) engineered classroom are analyzed. Implicit in the discussion are some inferences about aptitude-treatment interaction findings related to the general school climate. In Chapter 14 we reintroduce these principles as they relate to the general broad question of teaching methods.

Before we start this section, we must point out that *there is nothing necessarily inherently bad with the graded, self-contained classroom IF individual differences are taken into consideration.* On the surface, though, nongraded and open education arrangements would appear to have some merit, because such structural arrangements make it easier to incorporate the principles related to individualizing instruction. The structural arrangements brought about by nongraded programs and open education, however, *will not guarantee* a closer fit between the student and the curriculum unless careful attention is paid to the student's performance during the school year, particularly with reference to the achievement of the instructional objectives. An open education approach requires greater awareness on the teacher's part to insure that a student does not engage in a lot of off-task behaviors. Behaviors must be carefully monitored if the open approach is ever to reach its *structural* potential.

The nongraded approach

The nongraded organizational structure is designed to do away with the traditional grades 1–12 or 1–6. In lieu of any grade placement the student is given appropriate curricular material at his/her academic and interest levels. The organizational pattern is based on the following premises (Goodlad & Anderson, 1963).

1. A year in a nongraded school may mean much more or much less than the traditional year of progress in graded schools.
2. A student's progress is irregular.
3. A student's progress is not unified across subjects.
4. Curricular content is seen as appropriate over a wide span of years. The content should not be artificially attached to a particular year in a child's development.
5. This system allows for slow or rapid vertical and/or horizontal progress.
6. This system allows flexible student movement at any time. There are no artificial chronological age barriers.

Of course, you should be aware that the nongraded organizational structure does not refer to any particular type of curricular program in the school. The nongraded arrangement is an *educational administrative strategy* to match the student more closely with material at his/her achievement and interest levels. The nongraded organizational structure can be used with any type of curricular approach.

The advantages resulting from this structural arrangement vary tremendously from school to school. The biggest advantage is the greater likelihood that students will be given work commensurate with their ability. The traditional placement of students in a specified grade based on chronological age increases the likelihood of a student-curriculum mismatch. Some undesirable effects of the nongraded approach, however, can occur if the teacher is not careful. If careful record keeping and organizational strategies are not adhered to, the student may not get the needed individual attention from a professional. In some ways, this nongraded structure requires additional planning and a tighter organizational pattern. Furthermore, transition by a student to a graded class structure can be difficult.

You should also be aware that there are many different organizational arrangements within the nongraded approach. Several contrasting arrangements give you some idea of the diversity within this approach.

1. The teacher can be assigned to a typical heterogeneous class of 25–30 children of the same chronological age and be charged with individualizing the classroom program in order to allow each child to develop at his/her own pace.
2. The teacher can be assigned a class of relatively homogeneous students for specific subjects based on ability grouping.
3. The students might be assigned a "homeroom" teacher and then regrouped during the day for specific subjects based on their achievement levels.
4. A team of teachers could be assigned a large number of students who vary in age. The team would be responsible for the total educational program of these students.
5. A teacher might be assigned specific modules within the school program. All students ready to study a particular module would be assigned to that teacher until the module is completed satisfactorily.

One final note: Since the teacher is expected to come in contact with small groups of students or individual students much more frequently, the teacher must be an efficient record keeper, possess good diagnostic-prescriptive skills, and be competent in instructional design and management procedures.

"Open" education approaches

We feel a little hesitant to discuss "open" education because educators have a tendency to use words that are faddish and lack agreement as to meaning. *Open education* is such a term. It would be remiss on our part, however, not to discuss this topic. Open-type arrangements will become more frequent in the years to come and you should be familiar with the general principles associated with this organizational arrangement. In this regard, you should be aware that all of the learning and motivation principles identified earlier in this chapter can be easily incorporated into an open approach.

Some educators equate open education with the free-school movement (another nebulous term). Others relate open education to the Montessori method (a structured learning environment for preschoolers). A third group of educators has been quick to note the similarities between open education and individualized instruction. In order to operationalize the definition, Bussis and Chittenden (1970) have developed a model that rates school environments along two continua: the degree to which the teacher contributes to the school environment, and the degree to which the child contributes to the program. According to Bussis and Chittenden, *high teacher contribution and high student contribution* are the ideal and should be defined as open education. The common element in open education approaches is to give the student some choice in the goals of the curriculum and some choice when these goals will be achieved.

FIGURE 13–10
The teacher acts as a guide in open education approaches

To further operationalize *open education,* Walberg and Thomas (1972) attempted to identify the critical characteristics of a school environment that would classify the school as "open." A revised list of the features presented by Walberg and Thomas follows:

1. Children can move freely about the environment and manipulate many materials.
2. Children are encouraged to make use of their own resources.
3. The teacher acts as a guide and uses test results to group children for instructional purposes (Figure 13–10).
4. The teacher plays the role of diagnostician and prescriber.
5. The teacher is warm and accepting.
6. The teacher is in control of the environment at all times.

Notice how these six characteristics use the five principles presented earlier in the chapter.

Although the teacher is supposed to be in control of the environment at all times and know what is happening, spontaneous and incidental learning is also valued strongly by those professing an open approach. According to advocates of this approach, learning should not be stamped into students in any systematic fashion because learning is not generally hierarchical (other psychologists would take exception to this conclusion, e.g., Gagné, 1977). While the student is expected to do some reading, writing, and arithmetic each day, the student is allowed considerable freedom concerning both the content and the time when the subjects are to be studied. Structured flexibility is one of the main principles upon which open education is based.

Since the physical arrangement is very important in open education, we would like to provide you with a clearer idea of how an open classroom might be arranged physically. A diagram of a typical open classroom is presented in Figure 13–11.

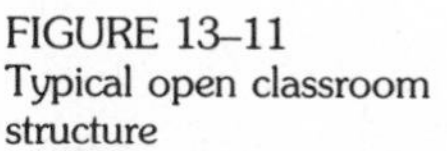

FIGURE 13–11
Typical open classroom structure

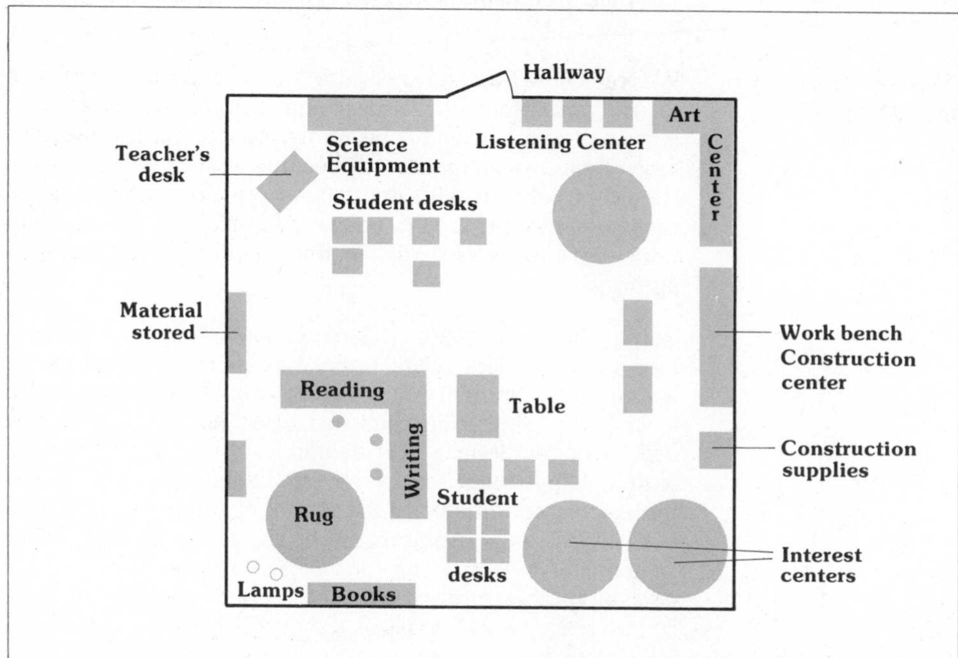

You should be aware that the physical arrangements, as well as the various objects in the room, serve specific purposes. While spontaneity and incidental learning are valued in the open education approach, the decisions concerning what resources and curricular materials are available to students are based on a set of goals and objectives. Within those specified limitations, spontaneity occurs. In other words, the open classroom is purposefully designed to bring about a series of objectives, some of which are not explicitly stated. Often this point is missed in a discussion of open education. It should not be equated with a "do your own thing" attitude! Proponents of this organizational structure are generally classified as progressivists and would tend to lean toward the cognitivist position in psychology, although there is nothing incompatible with behavior modification principles and openness—another misconception of considerable significance.

Teachers must constantly keep in mind that there are tremendous individual differences between students—in terms of both their willingness to approach appropriate tasks and persevere with them and their ability to learn what is expected of them. When a student appears to approach the appropriate curricular material willingly and effectively, there is no problem. The behaviorists would say that the appropriate contingencies are operating. With the reluctant student who is *not* willing to approach the curricular material, however, it would appear that some other contingencies need to be arranged, or that we should not require specific objectives. Since very few educators would be willing to dispense with specific objectives, the alternative solution is to design an environment in which the student approaches the curricular material based on some external contingencies. To assume that all students are very curious and have a strong desire to learn the specific objectives of a program is no more realistic than to assume that all adults would be equally willing to work at the same job! This is where behavioral modification principles fit nicely into the open education framework—to increase the likelihood that the reluctant learner will approach and persevere at some of the specific objectives of the program when other motivational techniques have failed. As we have pointed out in earlier chapters, at least in the loose sense of behavior modification, successful classrooms necessarily make use of these principles whether the teacher is a practicing behaviorist or not. Some behavioral principles are an inescapable part of human interpersonal relations (responding in a positive manner to someone when that person does something appropriate, and responding in a negative manner when someone does something inappropriate), so the question of whether behavior modification should be used in the classroom is an academic exercise. Of course, the degree to which human interactions should be calculated scientifically may be debated, but our point is that for the reluctant learner who would rather not be in school, the teacher will have to arrange the school environment to get the student to want to approach the school curriculum in a positive manner.

The advantages of an open approach are considerable. This approach makes it fairly easy to implement the general psychological principles of learning and motivation discussed earlier in the chapter. A maximum amount of socialization is possible with this approach. Learning can take place in a variety of settings. Finally, with this approach students are supposed to be more motivated toward school and respond more divergently. Research on these points, however, is equivocal.

Not all is well with this approach. Some authorities argue that it is too easy *not* to pay attention to the curriculum. It is a difficult procedure to implement; teaching under an open education approach is more work than conducting a traditional class and unless a teacher is careful, keeping track of the students' progress becomes a major problem. Fitt (1975) suggests that students respond differentially to open spaces—some students appear to thrive in an expansive environment, while others operate better in small spaces. Gump (1969) has found that a tremendous amount of time can be wasted between activities in a classroom—up to 40 percent of the day in some instances. With the emphasis on self-directed activities and a looser structure, an open education arrangement can be much more susceptible to off-task behaviors unless the teacher can monitor the students at all times.

Some authorities question whether this approach is appropriate for lower-SES students. At any rate, those advocating this approach should be warned against modeling the program after the British system, because British children have been brought up to respect authority to a greater degree than students in the United States and the British students appear to take their schooling more seriously than students in our country.

Finally an organizational continuity problem can occur when an elementary school decides to organize around the open approach and the secondary school is organized around a more traditional approach. Education is a system, and each component of the system should be coordinated. This point has been consistently raised throughout the book. This type of organizational discontinuity can create severe adjustment problems for students who suddenly experience a whole new set of expectancies brought about by different organizational arrangements.

To implement this organizational approach, the teacher should be well organized, keep careful records, and be able to construct a variety of appropriate learning environments. A teacher using this approach has a great deal of individual or small-group contact with students; therefore, the teacher ought to be able to deal equally effectively with students on a one-to-one basis, a small-group basis, and a large-group basis. In addition, the teacher should possess good diagnostic-prescriptive skills.

The interested reader ought to consult one or more of the following references for a more thorough description of open education: (Brown & Precious, 1969; Featherstone, 1971; Hassett & Weisberg, 1972; Hertzberg & Stone, 1971; Myers & Myers, 1973; Perrone, 1972; Sabaroff & Hanna, 1974; Silberman, 1973; Silberman, Allender & Yanoff, 1972; and Weber, 1971). Silberman (1973) is particularly useful in this regard.

Hewett's engineered classroom

Contrasted with the open education approach to education is Hewett's (1968) engineered classroom, which is based on many behavioral principles. See Figure 13–12 for a prototype diagram of a purposefully designed elementary classroom making use of Hewett's ideas. Recognizing that students have differing entering behaviors and that many different types of activities take place in a typical elementary school classroom, designers of this classroom structured it around clearly defined functions.

From the diagram you should note that the *order center* (where students who have difficulty working alone are given short tasks to accomplish) is in the lower right-hand corner of the diagram (close to the teacher's desk). It is important to note that all the desks in the order center face a wall so that there is less likelihood of distraction. For those students who need additional privacy, *special offices* are available near the order center. The *exploratory, social,* and *interest centers* are located at the

FIGURE 13–12
An example of a purposefully structured classroom

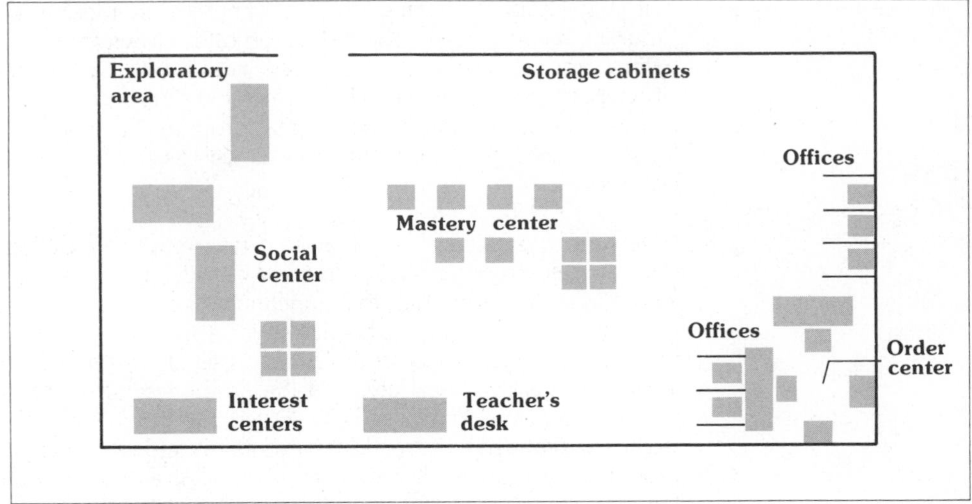

Source: Adapted from Hewett (1968).

other end of the room. Since more noise is generated in these centers, they are purposefully located as far away from the order center as possible. You should also note that the order center is not near the door, where a lot of activity and hall noises are likely to be heard. Ideally the whole room should be carpeted to further reduce the noise level. If this is not possible, at least the order center should be carpeted to cut down on desk, chair, and feet noises generated by restless students. *A few desks and chairs* might be bolted to the floor to further decrease the likelihood of noise. The *mastery center* is located in the center of the room. Students working in the mastery center should be capable of independent work and should not be distracted. The center of the room would be the worst possible location for a distractible student because of its proximity to the noisier activity centers and the door, and the nearness of other students. Figure 13–12 is presented so that you will more readily realize that, although it is unlikely that you will have to design such a complex environment, subtle environmental changes can bring about positive change in a student's behavior.

8. What is the essential difference between an open education approach and Hewett's engineered environment?
9. In what way are the open education approach and Hewett's engineered environment similar?
10. In what way does the nongraded approach to classroom organization make use of a major learning principle?

SUMMARY

This chapter was concerned with the general school and classroom environment. The general school and classroom environment was presented as consisting of the overall organization of the curriculum, the physical arrangement of the school and classroom, and the interpersonal relationships that take place in the classroom. When any of these factors gets out of balance, the program suffers.

In the beginning of this chapter, five general guidelines for constructing a general school and classroom environment were discussed. Time and again it was stressed that the school and classroom environment should be based on the goals of the program. It was pointed out that all too often structural decisions tend to be completed before proper consideration is given to the outcomes of instruction, thus creating a structure-function reversal. This unfortunate reversal of the decision-making process can lead to the establishment of inappropriate general environmental arrangements for the desired goals of instruction as well as for the more specific objectives of the classroom.

Given the five general guidelines, it was emphasized that the general school and classroom environment needs to be physically, psychologically, and socially consonant with those goals. Although the guidelines were synthesized from a variety of theoretical viewpoints, most of the principles suggest that some form of individualization ought to be a part of most classroom procedures at least some of the time. In this context, some consideration was given to the attribute-treatment interaction model proposed by Cronbach and Snow (1977). Given the guidelines presented in this chapter, it would appear that instructional events should be arranged so that the student is provided with *some* choice of tasks as well as some choice (within reason) about the time in which to complete the task. Implicit in such an arrangement is the point of view that students bring to any learning task different combinations of academic skills and interests which should be considered in planning instruction. The main generalization to be gleaned from this chapter is that the general school and classroom environment should be designed to achieve the goals of your program.

SELF-TEST

1. Define *structure-function reversal.*
2. Define *nongraded* approach.
3. Which of the following behaviors by a teacher would appear to violate a basic principle concerning how a classroom should be conducted?
   a. Giving homework based on the lesson.
   b. Having students sit in rows at their desks to take an exam.
   c. Giving some type of seat work to all members of the class.
   d. After starting a lesson, announcing to the class that the grades on the test the class took will be ready on Monday.
4. An example of a structure-function discrepancy is:
   a. Assigning a child to a specific curriculum based on the child's age.
   b. Using different teaching methods for different students.
   c. Requiring a *long-term* project in history class based on the objectives of the course.
   d. Making micro instructional decisions based on classroom criterion-referenced tests.
5. The advantage of a nongraded approach is that:
   a. When students do not receive grades, they do not get discouraged.
   b. A criterion-referenced approach to grading and testing can be used.
   c. General ability grouping will not occur.
   d. It is more likely that a student would be given work commensurate with the student's skill level.
6. The similarity between the open education approach and Hewett's purposefully structured classroom is that both approaches:
   a. Are based on behavior modification principles.
   b. Make use of space by assigning different activities to different locations within the room.
   c. Fall within a student-centered approach to instruction.
   d. Fall within a teacher-centered approach to instruction.
7. As a generalization gathered from the research on teaching effectiveness, it would appear that teachers should:
   a. Be more open and less demanding.
   b. Hold students accountable for their assignments.
   c. Be nondirective.
   d. Have students sit in small groups.
8. When Carroll talks about time as the key independent variable to be considered in teaching, Carroll is referring to:
   a. The lead-in time necessary to plan a lesson.
   b. The time needed to present an optimum lesson.
   c. The time the student needs to finish the task successfully.
   d. The amount of time it takes for the *average* student to complete the task.

9. According to the text, open education refers to a structural organization in which:
   a. The students and teachers both contribute a great deal to the course objectives.
   b. The students are essentially free to choose their own activities.
   c. The school has been architecturally designed to have no walls between classes.
   d. The student works independently on individualized tasks.
10. As opposed to *passive* responding, what is meant by *active* responding?

ANSWER KEY TO BOXED QUESTIONS

1. The decisions concerning the characteristics of the environment are made *before* the decisions about the outcomes of the program are finalized.
2. *a.* Unnecessary repetition.
   b. Variability of course content when objectives are the same.
   c. Wrong organizational arrangements of courses based on the objectives.
   d. Any other answer you originate that recognizes the principles of structure-function reversal.
3. Since students enter a program with differing scholastic abilities, having a flexible arrangement of time recognizes individual differences necessary to complete assignments successfully.
4. Inappropriate tasks are assigned to students for which the students lack some prerequisite.
5. Running a smooth classroom decreases the likelihood of unnecessary interruptions, thus making the best use of time. Disruptions create off-task behaviors. A lack of smoothness also tends to increase the amount of wasted time between activities.
6. The main factors include the expectancy and pursuit of excellence, an atmosphere of sharing between teacher and students, and a high degree of positive interpersonal relationships between teacher and students and among students.
7. As proposed by Cronbach and Snow (1977), this theory implies that in order to optimize instruction, different treatments will be needed for different students based on the students' entering behavior characteristics in the cognitive and affective domains of behavior. The obvious implication for the classroom teacher is individualization.
8. Open education is based on sharing between teacher and students—a humanistic viewpoint. Hewett's engineered environment is based on the teacher's control of the environment—more behavioristically oriented.
9. Both approaches emphasize the purposeful design of the classroom environments based on the objectives of the curriculum. The difference is in the degree of student sharing in the decisions.
10. The nongraded approach attempts to match the cognitive entering behavior level of the student with the curriculum. In traditional classrooms, students are placed in the class based on chronological age rather than specific academic skills.

ANSWER KEY TO SELF-TEST

1. A decision is made by determining the environmental arrangement of a school or classroom before the purpose or outcome is fully determined.
2. An administrative strategy for matching students with the curriculum based on the students' academic skills rather than chronological age.
3. *d*
4. *a*
5. *d*
6. *b*
7. *b*
8. *c*
9. *a*
10. Active responding is a response that requires a restructuring of information. Examples include rethinking an issue, solving a problem, and organizing material in some new order.

Chapter 14

Teaching methodology: The vehicle for blending instructional strategies

TO DEVELOP an overall strategy that is efficient in producing the desired cognitive, motor, and affective outcomes of instruction requires a lot of careful planning. In order to develop a good strategy the teacher needs to consider many interrelated factors. Obviously, these decisions should be based on the learning principles discussed in some of the previous chapters. Those factors, however, go far beyond the learning theories described in those chapters. For one thing, most lessons consist of *numerous* cognitive and affective goals which require *different* instructional strategies. Consideration needs to be given to how the material should be sequenced, integrated, and presented in the context of a general instructional strategy. Second, since it is very likely that students will have different levels of entering behavior with respect to the appropriate set of objectives, it makes sense in some instances to arrange for different lessons for different groups of students. Third, many additional outside factors need to be considered carefully when planning for the general instructional strategy, such as monetary constraints, the time needed to prepare lessons, the number of students assigned to a teacher, the teacher's talents and preferences for different general instructional strategies, and the fixed physical constraints of the classroom. In other words, an effective teacher has the task of incorporating many of the learning principles discussed previously in this book in the context of an environment that is often less than optimum for implementing these principles. The research we have discussed in this book needs to be applied in relation to these real-world issues.

Fourth, the overall structure of the subject matter itself should be considered when arriving at a general instructional strategy. A laboratory course in science, a mathematics course, a course on how to play tennis, or a course requiring divergent solutions to complex social issues each implies different general instructional strategies. Finally, even if several units of instruction consist of the same type of objectives, the general instructional strategy should vary from day to day. To approach each lesson in the same way is deadly. Novelty is needed in the stimulus presentation of the lesson as well as in the performance required to gain the students' attention and to maintain sufficient approach behaviors in the students necessary to perform the assignments.

When viewed from the previous perspectives, you ought to be quick to perceive that the general instructional strategy a teacher chooses is determined by many factors. Further, you should realize that the same objectives taught by two different teachers might very well be taught differently. There is no direct one-to-one relationship between a general instructional strategy and a specific objective; that is, it is very possible to effectively teach almost any objective by using a variety of teaching strategies. Additionally, within any given class period or instructional day, it is very possible that many different strategies and methods and combinations of strategies and methods might be used to implement the instructional objectives. Finally, when serious consideration is given to the affective goals of instruction in relation to the cognitive goals, the teacher should attempt to choose instructional strategies that integrate both goals simultaneously. To achieve cognitive goals at the expense of affective goals, or vice versa, is an unfortunate consequence of not being able to recognize that there are many purposes of instruction. Essentially, this chapter is divided into two major sections. The first addresses many practical questions that have not been specifically answered by the conditions of learning research and that need to be considered when planning for instruction. The second section of the chapter discusses how these questions and the conditions of learning research may be integrated into macro instructional strategies. General teaching methodologies are discussed. You should be aware, however, that the methods discussed in the second half of the chapter should not be viewed as independent strategies. Individual lessons may consist of three or four methods in a variety of combinations to achieve the instructional objectives of a unit. At the conclusion of this chapter you should be able to:

1. Identify those factors that need to be considered when choosing a general instructional strategy.
2. State the characteristics of each general teaching method presented in the second half of the chapter.
3. Identify the advantages, disadvantages, and the teacher's role implied by each of the general teaching methods presented in the second half of the chapter.
4. Based on the previous objectives, you should be able to generate appropriate general instructional strategies for aggregate sets of objectives.

CHOOSING INSTRUCTIONAL STRATEGIES: THE REALITIES

By now you should be aware that the decisions teachers have to make about instructional strategies and methods cannot and should not be made solely on the basis of what research has to say about the ideal instructional event for a specific cognitive objective. First of all, at times teachers have to choose an instructional strategy to reach goals that are obviously not the optimal methods for realizing a particular objective or series of objectives; given certain constraints (time to prepare, staff support, money, outside resources, number of students in the class) or other considerations, a realistic approximation is the best that can be accomplished. Teaching in the real world places many obstacles in the way of implementing the ideal lesson. Second, as we have pointed out, often teachers are faced with the problem of implementing a host of cognitive objectives, usually embedded in textual material. Since these objectives run the gamut from simple memorization objectives to complex problem-solving objectives, and since the conditions of learning for these objectives are quite varied, different instructional strategies would appear appropriate for different combinations of objectives. The implementation of a multifaceted approach to teaching is easier said than done, particularly since the instructional resources, including the textual materials, are not usually based on a systematic approach to learning. Third, if the decision to choose an instructional strategy were based solely on specific cognitive objectives, other considerations such as being flexible, using novelty and other techniques for maintaining motivation, bringing about broader cognitive competencies, and facilitating positive attitudes probably would be deemphasized. As stated before, this myopic strategy could lead to the unfortunate situation in which all the specific cognitive objectives in a class are implemented without insuring that any of the broader cognitive and affective goals are achieved. In fact, it could be possible to design a very efficient instructional strategy for implementing the specific course objectives while simultaneously undermining the broader cognitive, affective, and mathemagenic goals of the course or the schools. Unfortunately, the opposite can also occur; that is, the teacher can spend so much time attempting to facilitate motivation and positive attitudes that the cognitive objectives get lost in the lessons! Given that the decision to choose an instructional strategy is complex, what should the teacher do to plan a series of lessons?

FACTORS TO CONSIDER WHILE DERIVING INSTRUCTIONAL STRATEGIES

When deciding upon the nature of specific lessons, the teacher needs to consider the individual objectives of the unit in the context of the conditions of learning, how these objectives may be interrelated in specific lessons, how those lessons may be integrated into units of instruction, and how those units of instruction may be integrated into a semester, or yearly plan. At a general level, for example, Shavelson (1976) points out that it is the teacher's task to select a method or instructional strategy that takes into account the following five factors:

FIGURE 14–1
A teaching method can have many outcomes

1. *The set of goals.* The instructional strategy should help the students attain all the desired goals.
2. *The states of nature.* The instructional strategy should be consonant with the student's entering behavior.
3. *The predicted outcome.* The teacher needs to estimate the effect of the overall strategy on specific students (Figure 14–1).
4. *Constraints.* The availability of the instructional strategy and the teacher's knowledge of the strategy need to be considered.
5. *Utility.* The teacher's judgment (subjective interpretation) of the effect of the strategy should be made in terms of all the interrelated components that need to be considered in arriving at the decision.

Furthermore, these decisions are made at three different times: before the instructional act, during the instructional act, and after the act has been completed. Implicit in Shavelson's discussion is that a good teacher varies the strategy based on the above five considerations, and that the decisions are flexible enough to change if any of the above factors change. Decision making is an ongoing process. As Shavelson suggests, a teaching strategy is defined as "a sequence of teaching acts that arise from a *series* of decisions teachers have to make." The teacher's task is to select a strategy or a series of strategies that most likely would be effective for the various situations in which teachers find themselves.

In our opinion, consideration needs to be given to the nature of the specific subject matter as well as the conditions of learning research discussed in depth in Chapters 10 and 11. In addition, we will introduce some questions for which the conditions of learning research has failed to provide useful guidelines but which are important when planning for lessons. We start our discussion by addressing the issue of how to design a lesson when a set of interrelated goals is the desired outcome. Seven factors are discussed.

Set of interrelated goals

In essence, we have already alluded to this decision several times in our discussion. Care should be taken that the specific cognitive, affective, and motor objectives of the curriculum be implemented while at the same time insuring that the broader, long-term goals of the program are achieved. You will remember from our discussion about the general environment in Chapter 13 that it is very possible to develop a curricular program that does not insure that the long range goals of the program will be implemented. The same problem can occur with the incorrect choice of an instructional strategy. In choosing a method or instructional strategy, careful consideration should be given to the conditions of learning implied by the specific objective as well as to your estimation of the conditions under which the student has to perform the objective away from the instructional context.

Further, careful consideration should be given to the possible additive effect of the strategy on the student's general cognitive competency as well as the student's attitudinal state implied in the teacher's goals. Olson (1976b) has gone so far as to suggest that these broad considerations are critical to the choice of our teaching method. Often these considerations are ignored.

In essence, we are suggesting that the choice of a method should always take into account the specific goals of instruction as well as the broader general goals. Too often teachers fail to make their choices on the basis of an integration of these multilevel goals, thus falling short of reaching the desired outcomes of the program. We are suggesting here that a subtle combination of methods is needed to implement both the specific cognitive objective and the broader cognitive and affective goals of a curriculum. Too often a balance is not maintained.

To illustrate how a balance between cognitive and affective goals might be achieved, consider the following two objectives: one an educational objective and the other an instructional objective.

1. The student will work cooperatively with others (educational objective).
2. Given the necessary information concerning the natural resources for five geographic locations, the student will determine which location is most suitable for the development of a city (instructional objective).

It is obvious that our instructional objective in geography could be taught many ways. Students could be given individual reading assignments with accompanying work sheets, there could be a lecture-discussion format using discovery and inquiry techniques, or small-group projects designed to have students discover the principles of how people decide on the location of their cities could be assigned. From an efficiency standpoint, it would appear that the first instructional strategy might be best to implement the cognitive objective. That strategy would most likely insure that the task would be done rapidly, that the work would be the student's own work, and that the task would be completed in the least amount of time. From another perspective, however, the lecture-discussion format using discovery-type strategies might be a better approach because the student might acquire some cognitive discovery-type skills that would transfer to other types of problem-solving situations. And, of course, the small-group project may be the best approach because it would increase the amount of cooperation necessary to solve the problem in a group situation (Figure 14–2). Note

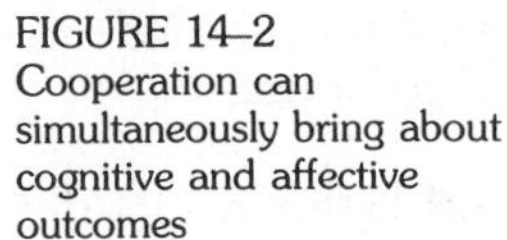
FIGURE 14–2
Cooperation can simultaneously bring about cognitive and affective outcomes

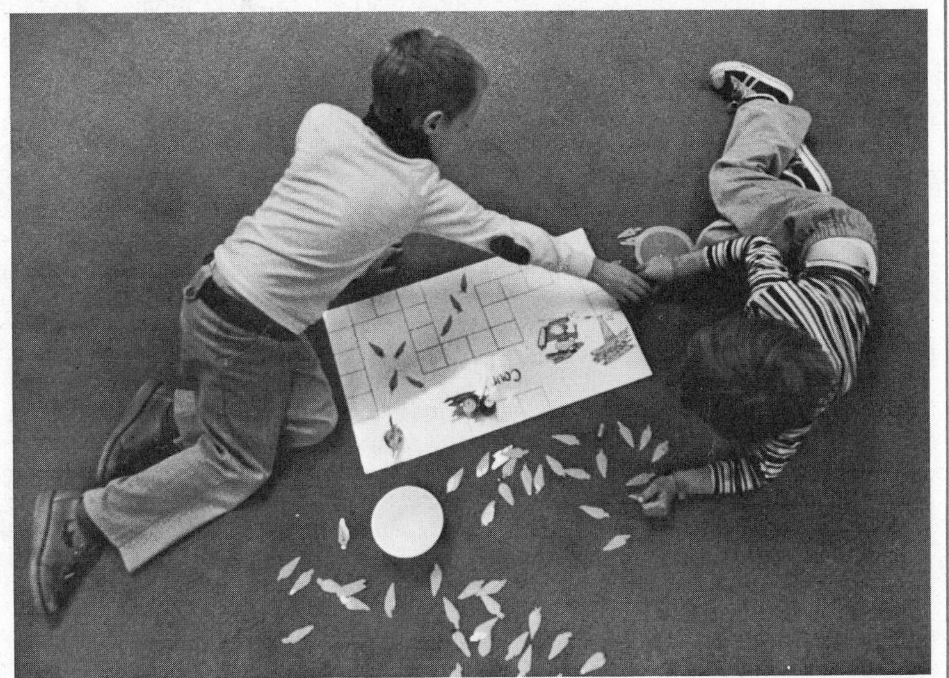

that under the reading assignment–work sheet strategy, sharing of information would be considered cheating, whereas under the group-project strategy sharing would be desirable; yet both of these methods are appropriate to reach the cognitive objectives. Stated another way, all three of the above strategies should implement the specific cognitive objective, but each of these methods, if used consistently, would appear to be best suited to achieve *different* cognitive and affective goals as well.

One other example suffices. Assume you are teaching a high school course in an area of your choosing, and you have spent a great deal of time planning. Let us further assume that you have identified ten terminal objectives that appear to require approximately the same conditions of learning. Would you then conclude that the method you would use to implement those objectives should never vary because each objective appears to require the same conditions of learning? We hope not. A very dull, uninspiring class might ensue. What we are suggesting in this chapter is that the teacher's decision to choose a method or series of methods is determined by many factors, in many cases the decision is a dynamic, ongoing process dependent on the students' responses in an instructional situation. In fact, as we pointed out before, in some situations three or four methods might be used simultaneously with different groups working the same objective!

The states of the learner

Such broad factors as the learners' general SES, age level, and interest level should provide you with a "ball park" estimate of some of the methods that may be appropriate or inappropriate for a class. For example, lecturing for any length of time to young children is not very appropriate. Giving a great deal of freedom to children who do not have the prerequisite motivational, attitudinal, or cognitive skills is not appropriate. Having a discussion in class with students who do not have the necessary experience, discussion skills, or knowledge for the discussion is a mistake frequently made by many teachers. Good teachers carefully monitor their effect on the class and are quick to make appropriate changes when the methodology is inappropriate.

As we have pointed out before, Cronbach and Snow (1977) and Gardner (1974a) suggest that there are optimal "fits" between the methods to be used and the characteristics of the student. Termed *aptitude-treatment interactions* (ATI), the implications for this viewpoint are far-reaching. Although premature to be used in the classroom with much precision, the ATI approach suggests that teachers ought to be very aware of the differential effects that different methods might have on various students. The optimal method for one student with a particular set of characteristics may be the worst method for another student in the same class. For now, all teachers can do is to keep a close record of their efficiency with different students under different treatments.

Not only should the teacher be asking questions about the student's *specific capabilities with respect to a specific objective,* but the teacher also should have a good idea of *what "phase" the student is in with reference to the appropriate objectives* of a lesson or course of study. According to Gagné (1977), the "phase" of learning and "phases" of instruction should parallel one another. You will recall that Gagné's phases of learning include:

1. *Motivation*—the student's willingness to approach a task.
2. *Apprehension*—the student's ability to attend to the appropriate stimuli.
3. *Acquisition*—the student's initial ability to "put" the stimuli into long-term memory. This process implies understanding, organizing, and coding the information.

4. *Retention*—the student's ability to "maintain" the stimuli in a state available for retrieval.
5. *Recall*—the student's ability to search memory and retrieve the appropriate information.
6. *Generalization*—the student's ability to use the retrieved information in previously unencountered situation, i.e., the student identifies the previously unencountered task as an instance in which a previously learned strategy is appropriate.
7. *Performance*—the student's ability to perform the task.
8. *Feedback*—the student's ability to monitor his/her performance and make the necessary adjustments in it (Figure 14–3).

Knowing which phase the student is in with respect to the objectives allows the teacher to plan with a little more precision as well as a little more compassion for the student's current level of competency or attitudes. For example, let us assume the student is assigned a chapter to read that has many different levels of objectives. Depending on an evaluation of which phase or phases the student is in, the teacher could attempt different instructional strategies or methods. A student who is not *motivated* to read the chapter perhaps needs a different initial teaching strategy than one who is ready to *perform* the final objective. A student who has not *acquired* the appropriate information or rules to perform the objective needs a different teaching strategy than the student who has performed the task and is now asked to assess the effectiveness of his/her performance.

To be more precise, for example, if the student has not acquired the prerequisites for a task, he/she needs *to be presented* with the prerequisite information in such a

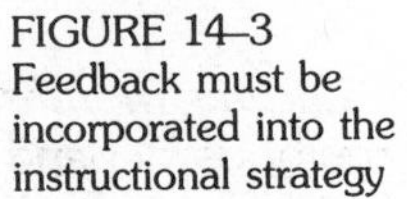
FIGURE 14–3
Feedback must be incorporated into the instructional strategy

manner that the student can understand the information and then use it to perform the task. If the student has been presented with the information and the teacher feels the student is capable of performing the task, practice is needed. Of course, the teacher may decide that the student should *discover* the prerequisites. That decision implies a different teaching strategy than simply developing within the learner the prerequisites to perform the task.

Institutional considerations

Within the context of the school, certain broad factors must be considered before the method is chosen.

The school structure. School policy, school organization, and subtle pressures from colleagues on whether to use certain methods can have a profound effect on teaching methodology. For example, certain value clarification procedures or types of self-paced programs in which the student is not necessarily expected to finish a specified amount of work during a year might not be allowed. A mandate from the principal that a particular method or program should be used has obvious implications for the teacher. Working in an institution implies that the method should be consonant with the school policy and organizational arrangements of the school.

The school resources. Certain methods require a great deal of physical or human support. Computer-assisted instruction requires a computer. Self-paced instruction usually requires a great deal of typing, which implies either a lot of secretarial help or excellent typing skills on the part of the teacher or unsuspecting spouse. Team-teaching implies a cooperative staff. Decisions cannot be made independent of the situation in which teachers find themselves.

Constraints. Some methods require a great deal of preparation *starting months in advance;* a modularized self-paced system is an example. Other methods depend on the spontaneity of a loosely structured class setting. Before choosing a method, the amount of effort needed to implement it should be carefully considered. For example, given other important considerations, *if a particular method takes a great deal of time to prepare, and the method appears to have the same general effects as another method that takes much less time to prepare, the choice should be made on the basis of the efficiency of the method* since a teacher has a limited amount of time. Another real concern for the teacher is the size of the group that needs to be instructed. As new organizational patterns are attempted (flexible scheduling, team-teaching, open architectural arrangements, nongraded schools) teachers more than likely will be confronted with varying group sizes to instruct. According to Berliner and Gage (1976) the size of the group to be instructed is related to the type of method that might be used with the group. Traditionally, when a teacher has wanted to deal with one student at a time, various types of individualized strategies, such as seat work, computer-assisted instruction, or some commercial system of modularizing instruction into small prepared units, have been used. With small groups of students (arbitrarily defined as 2–20 students) the discussion method or group problem-solving assignment has been used. For classes of 20–40 students, a combination lecture-discussion method has been used most frequently. This method has been variously called "classroom teaching" or the "recitation method." For older students in larger classes (40 or more), the lecture method has generally been the choice.

Of course, the decision to choose one method over another should not be based on the size of the class entirely; rather the choice of a particular method should be based on the set of interrelated goals for the class. For example, a large class does not necessarily imply the lecture method, nor does a small class necessarily preclude the lecture method. Certainly with an extremely large class, however, you would be limited in the types of performances you could expect from students unless you had considerable support to evaluate the students' responses. Although somewhat self-evident, giving weekly themes to a class of 150 would not be an appropriate assignment from the teacher's perspective.

The "state" of the teacher

Since what the teacher does in relation to the students is an important variable in instruction, there are several factors teachers need to consider about themselves.

The teacher's characteristics. Teachers vary in their effectiveness in using different methods. Some teachers are very dynamic, some less so; some teachers are very organized, others less so. Teachers also vary tremendously in their interpersonal skills. Some teachers are very friendly and nonthreatening; others are more cold and domineering. Some can thrive on and make the most of ambiguous situations; others do not enjoy ambiguity. Some teachers can communicate verbally very well; others do better in writing. Some teachers intuitively prefer certain methods over others for a host of reasons. Very little research has been done comparing these factors with teaching effectiveness. At any rate, given two methods that might be logically equivalent and require a different constellation of teaching characteristics, consideration of the teacher's characteristics and preferences should be a real concern. Disliking ambiguity, a teacher might be ineffective in leading a discussion in a topic with little consensus. Lacking a certain dynamic, enthusiastic quality, a teacher might not be very effective in conducting lectures. Being a good organizer, a teacher might be able to integrate many methods into a broad strategy, whereas the less organized teacher might make a mess at integrating numerous methods, or might even perform very poorly with a method that requires a high degree of organization.

The teacher's skill with the method and knowledge of the method's effectiveness. Some methods require a set of clearly specified skills that could not be implemented by a teacher who is not knowledgeable. To attempt to implement a method without the necessary skills is simply not a wise strategy. In addition, the teacher ought to have some idea of what the research has to say about the method's effectiveness.

The nature of the subject matter

It is interesting to note in recent years that psychologists are again beginning to consider the characteristics of the subject matter as well as the implicit structure within the subject matter as important considerations when choosing a method (Bruner, 1960; Scandura, 1977a,b). According to these "structural" psychologists, although there are general theories of learning that are applicable to all subjects, each subject has its own structure or unique combination of concepts that differentiates that subject from other subjects. For example, mathematics is generally hierarchical in its structure, whereas many other subjects do not require the same degree of hierarchical organization. In our opinion, it is no accident that proponents of the task analysis approach to instruction frequently use mathematical examples to demonstrate the utility of task analysis. While it is obvious that the subject matter does not necessarily dictate the method, it is also obvious that the characteristics of certain subjects are of such a nature as to imply the use or nonuse of certain broad methods. For example, any part of a mathematical curriculum that is hierarchical probably would not lend itself very well to the discussion method for any length of time unless the method were used in an advanced theoretical course. On the other hand, a course in which there is little agreement on the content because the field cannot agree on the solution to the issues might best be handled through a variety of discussion-type lessons.

Scandura (1977) suggests that the choice of method should take into account the structure of the subject matter as well as the performance objectives for the course. A general structural analysis of a course should suggest some underlying competencies a student might need, which a task analysis might not identify, thus giving the teacher further information about the appropriateness of a method.

Subjective trade-offs

Given the previous factors, the teacher is now in a position to assign values to each of the factors commensurate with the teacher's beliefs about education and people and arrive at a method. We think that there are two overriding concerns, however, that should suggest to a teacher the form the method should eventually take in the classroom. The first factor is to insure that the specific cognitive and affective objectives are achieved. The purpose of any method is to help achieve the objectives of the classroom. Often teachers lose sight of this basic point, and the method becomes the end rather than the means to reach the goals and objectives. In this case, a functional-structural reversal such as mentioned in the preceding chapter occurs. So far we probably have given you the impression that if a teacher departs from the objectives of the classroom, a "cardinal sin" is committed. You should remember from our earlier discussion that many of the methods are dynamic and require careful monitoring by the teacher. You should also remember that decisions about which method to use are made at three points along the instructional continuum: before, during, and after the instructional event. To continue with a teaching method in the implementation phase of instruction when an obvious tangential discussion would be in order, or to continue with the preplanned method when it is obvious that the students are not making adequate progress toward the objectives reflects poor decision-making skills on the teacher's part. The second factor to consider, therefore, is *planned flexibility* (Figure 14–4). The teacher should be ready at any time to depart from the plans that were made prior to the instructional event if he/she feels that a *useful outcome* is to be served by a change. The decision to depart from an original plan should be made on the basis of how the departure relates to the overall objectives as well as the possible positive additional outcomes to be derived from the departure. Being a prisoner to your original plans is foolish. Having no outcome in mind while instruction is occurring is also usually foolish. Good teaching requires that the underlying competencies related to the aggregate set of objectives for a classroom be acquired. And these competencies may be acquired at times independent of a specific course objective. When a teacher feels that some useful outcomes (either cognitive or affective) may be derived from a departure from the initial teaching plan, a departure is in order. Instead of ending up in meaningless bull sessions, these purposeful departures should serve useful functions.

In conclusion, know what factors to consider while deriving instructional strategies, choose your methods accordingly, and be willing to change your plans when appropriate. Methods are the tools to implement objectives. Artisans use their tools wisely, and teachers should do the same.

Structural questions

As we have pointed out repeatedly in this book, we appear to know a great deal about how to optimally arrange the environment to facilitate the learning of specific

FIGURE 14–4
Purposeful flexibility is an important aspect of instruction

objectives at different levels of learning. While this is a giant step forward in the design of instruction, much still needs to be done. Most lessons *do not consist of one objective;* many objectives are usually involved. We know much less about how lessons should be structured so that the various objectives can be optimally learned in an interrelated fashion. The real world of teaching, however, demands that these instructional decisions be made regardless of the state of research.

In essence, throughout the earlier chapters of the book we discussed how a teacher should analyze the component parts of instruction. In some sections we were very precise. It is now time to organize all the previous parts of the book into a workable general instructional strategy. Figure 14–5 presents a list of decisions a teacher should consider when planning specific lessons and combinations of lessons. Although most of these questions have been partially answered in the preceding chapters, it is at this point in the decision-making process that all the questions have to become integrated into the general instructional strategy. At best, all a teacher can do is to intuitively arrive at some of these decisions and then integrate them with what is now known about the conditions of learning.

By constantly focusing on the specific goals of instruction and the student's precise entering behavior level with respect to the instructional objectives, a teacher can answer each of these questions, although we have much more research evidence to back us up on the answers to some of the questions as compared to others.

With the exception of some aspects of the first set of questions, all the others have been addressed in previous chapters, therefore the implications of the first set of questions need to be mentioned. You will note that the first set includes questions about how objectives should be related. According to Reigeluth, Merrill, Wilson, Norton,

FIGURE 14–5
Some decisions to be made about the structure of lessons

Presentation decisions (acquisition and retention considerations):

1. How should the objectives be related?
   a. What types of *introductory presentations* can be developed to interrelate the objectives?
   b. How should the objectives be *sequenced* if they are at the same level and functionally equivalent?
   c. When should a cluster of objectives be *synthesized?*
   d. When should *summaries* be attempted? (Adapted from Reigeluth, Merrill, Wilson, Norton & Spiller, 1978.)
2. How should the material be presented?
   a. What *mode or modes* should be used in the presentation?
   b. To what extent should the presentation be *concrete or abstract?*
   c. What should be the *size* of the lesson? About *how many meaningful bits of information* should be presented to the students before the student is asked to perform an assignment?
3. While the information is being presented, *when* should the students respond to questions, *how often* should the students respond, and *who* should respond?

Performance decisions:

1. What should be the nature of the assignment?
   a. What should be the *sequence* in the assignment?
   b. How much *repetition* is initially needed in an assignment?
   c. What should be the *length* of the assignment?
   d. To what extent should students be given a *choice* of assignments and a choice of *when* to complete the assignment?
   e. What should be the *frequency* of assignments?
2. What type of responses should the students be asked to perform?
   a. Should the response be *oral* or *written,* or should the student *choose* a correct answer from among provided answers?
   b. To what degree should the response *match the real-life conditions* under which the student will be expected to ultimately perform?
   c. Should the student work *alone,* with a *tutor,* or with a *group?* Under what conditions would a *choral* response be appropriate?
3. How should the teacher plan to provide *feedback* and *reinforcement* in the context of the classroom?
4. When should a student be asked to *redo* an assignment?

and Spiller (1978), careful consideration ought to be given to the structural arrangements of a course because students often fail to see the interrelationships between course objectives.

Reigeluth et al. suggest that different courses will necessarily have one or more of the following organizational patterns:

1. *Lists*—The student is expected to reproduce an ordered list.
2. *Learning structure*—The student is expected to perform some hierarchical learning task.
3. *Taxonomic structure*—The student is expected to reproduce a taxonomy or is supposed to be able to categorize previously unencountered examples according to a taxonomic structure.
4. *Theoretical structure*—The student is expected to describe material events according to given theories, or to solve a class of problems based on the theory or combination of theories.

5. *Procedural structure*—The student is expected to perform a series of steps with a complex task based on either a procedural-prerequisite relationship or a procedural–decision-making relationship.

In any case, it is the task of the teacher to determine which superordinate structure the student needs to learn in order to interrelate the content of a course. Reigeluth et al. suggest that presenting the overall structure of the subject matter at the beginning of instruction will result in greater understanding, memory, organization, and student motivation. For conceptual knowledge, instruction should proceed from the general to the specific, whereas for theoretical and procedural knowledge instruction should proceed from the specific to the general. Further, each part of the whole should be gradually elaborated on in a systematic way to help the students see the relationships between the parts of the course and the structure of the total course. This implies that periodic synthesizers designed to relate specific objectives, and periodic summarizers designed to summarize logical components of a course need to be presented to the student for integrating the course content in a meaningful, structured, and well-organized manner. Although much of what Reigeluth et al. have presented needs to be validated, teachers cannot wait for the validation. Reigeluth et al. have presented a series of practical suggestions based on information-processing theories of the memory processes. Essentially, their instructional decision-making models have put some cement into the task analysis approach presented in Chapter 8.

1. Explain what is meant by the statement: Your choice of an instructional strategy should consider an aggregate set of interrelated goals.
2. Why is there not simply a one-to-one relationship between the identified objectives of a class and the choice of teaching methodology, i.e., once an objective is identified, a teaching method is automatically suggested?

IMPLEMENTING METHODS WITHIN VARYING CONTEXTS

We have already talked about many factors that need to be considered in order to choose an instructional strategy. This section of the chapter is devoted to a description of various teaching methods. Specifically, each method is discussed in terms of:

1. A description of the method.
2. The conditions under which the method might be appropriate.
3. The possible disadvantages of the method.
4. The general role of the teacher implied by the method.
5. The specific strategies a teacher might use or the specific skills a teacher might *need* to implement the method.

To make the chapter more understandable, we have chosen to categorize the methods along a continuum from highly structured to less structured methods. For the purpose of this part of the chapter three categories of methods are discussed.

1. *Commercially produced programs*—The content is standardized by an external agency and the teacher's role is clearly specified.
2. *Teacher-produced programs*—The content is predetermined by the teacher and remains relatively *static* during the lesson(s).
3. *Dynamic teaching methods*—Although there is a specified content for the lesson determined by the teacher, the lesson depends to a greater extent on the extemporaneous quality of the teacher's presentation and the student's discussion.

To decide on an appropriate general method, the teacher needs to simultaneously insure that the conditions of learning can be implemented and the broader instructional outcomes can be supported by the choice of the method. By broader instructional outcomes we are referring to strategies that facilitate independence, self-motivation, and efficient problem-solving skills in students as well as those skills necessary to work in a group context.

IMPLEMENTING METHODS WITHIN A COMMERCIALLY PRODUCED PROGRAM CONTEXT

With an increasing emphasis to design or implement classroom events based on instructional psychological principles, several trends have become apparent in teaching methodologies. One trend has been to use commercially produced, "packaged," sequential programs as an integrated method throughout the grades in a school system. Although not fully validated or used extensively in the schools, a description of these programs is in order so that you might better understand how such programs can be used in the classroom. Further, some of the ideas from these programs can be adapted to the traditional classroom in various ways. We have chosen to discuss PLAN and IPI, two commercially produced programs that are representative of these methods.

Programs for learning in accordance with needs (PLAN)

Project PLAN is a systematic computer-managed program in the areas of language arts, social studies, math, and science for students in grades 1–12. The program consists of the following five components (Flanagan, 1971).

1. Based upon approximately 1,500 objectives in four academic subjects, students are required to be competent with a core of the objectives in each subject area. Further, students are encouraged to select many additional objectives most directly related to their goals. The combined strategy of requiring competence with a core of the objectives while giving the student a great deal of choice is a positive feature of the program.

2. About five objectives constitute a module. A module consists of a series of readings, assignments, experiences, and similar activities centered around a unifying theme designed for about two weeks of work. Several forms of each module are available in order to more closely match a student's preference for learning through different approaches.

3. Assessment procedures consist of modular tests designed to measure the student's achievement in a module. In addition, long-term objectives that cover material over many modules are assessed periodically, thus providing the students with some synthesizing experiences.

4. Guidance and planning with students about their lessons on an individual basis are an integral part of PLAN. In the upper grades, the student is provided with much information about the world of work and leisure-time pursuits in cultural, recreational, civic, social, and similar activities. The student is also furnished with data concerning the development of his/her specific abilities, interests, and values. Third, each student is aided to develop long-term plans based on his/her abilities and interests. Finally, the student is encouraged to carry out the plan.

5. In order to be a teacher within this system, a short formal training program is required, which includes observing PLAN in operation, reading about the project,

attending a short workshop, and having considerable contact with a consultant during the early stages of implementation.

This program, or a program similar to this, is most applicable in a school system where the objectives have been clearly identified and the modules appear to reflect the objectives. Some advantages of this method are that students tend to work alone and at their own pace, the teachers claim to enjoy this approach, and the teachers are freer to work with individual students. As Bunderson and Faust (1976) note, "until the advent of the computer we were unable to manage the work associated with tracking the diversity of student paths through individualized systems, providing detailed practice with feedback, and collecting precise data for the revision and improvement of courseware." Computer-assisted instruction gives us these advantages (Figure 14–6). Another advantage of any type of computer program is that it is very easy to validate the effectiveness of the program. Disadvantages of this type of approach include the lack of group focus or discussion and the difficulty a teacher would have in planning modules when the information is not readily available in printed form or when an instructor's experiences should be shared with the students through a lively lecture-discussion format. In actuality, none of the disadvantages of PLAN is a disadvantage if the teacher incorporates these variations at other times during the day and does not use just PLAN as the only means of instruction. All methods appear to be valid in certain situations. The question is *not:* Should I ever use this method? Rather the question is: Under what circumstances is it appropriate to choose this method over another method?

Since the teacher's role in PLAN is very similar to that in IPI, the teacher's role for these commercial programs is discussed at the conclusion of our discussion of IPI.

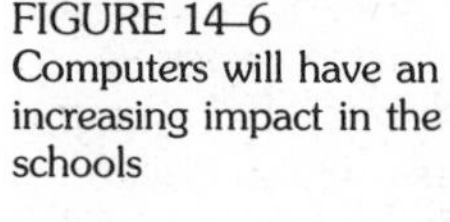

FIGURE 14–6
Computers will have an increasing impact in the schools

Individually Prescribed Instruction (IPI)

Initiated by the Learning Research and Development Center of the University of Pittsburgh, IPI is an individualized instructional system for grades K–6 in the subject areas of reading, mathematics, science, geography, handwriting, and spelling. The IPI system is based on a set of sequential behavioral objectives, related teaching materials, and integrated diagnostic tests. The objectives are arranged into units based on a specific content area and level of difficulty. Before a student may progress to another unit, the student must pass a criterion-referenced unit test at the 85 percent level of mastery. The students generally work independently on the units (Figure 14–7).

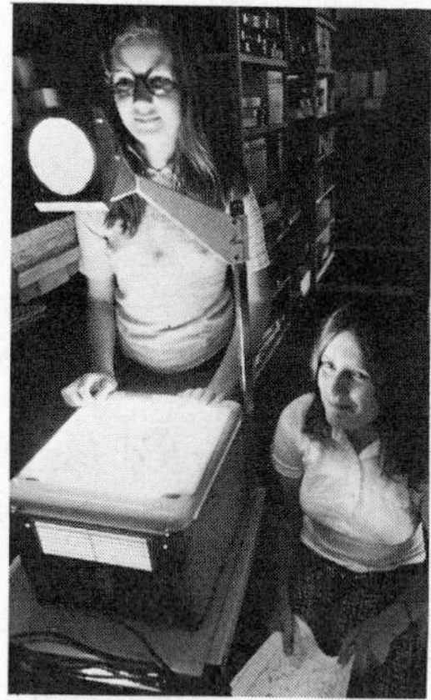

FIGURE 14–7
Students studying a module

The sequential steps in an IPI system include (Lindvall & Cox, 1969):

1. A placement test is administered by the teacher.
2. The teacher selects an appropriate unit for study.
3. The student takes the pretest on the unit.
4. If the student passes all *components* of the pretest, the student is given a new unit of study.
5. If the student fails one or more *components* of the pretest, the student is provided with appropriate instructional materials and lessons for that component.
6. The student studies the component and then takes a posttest. If the student passes the posttest, he/she moves on to a new unit. If the student fails the posttest, he/she restudies the missed component(s) of the unit.

The IPI method is based on constant monitoring of the student's achievement in the units. At the beginning of the school year the student is administered a series of placement tests in order to provide the teacher with specific information about which units the student should study. Each unit has a pretest to identify which objectives within the unit the student has mastered. The teacher evaluates the results of the pretest and generates a specific learning prescription. The student then proceeds to work on the specified objectives one at a time. Several times during the unit the student takes a "curriculum-embedded test" to assess the progress within the unit. When the student has performed at the 85 percent level on all the objectives in the unit, the student takes a posttest (an alternate form of the pretest) on the whole unit. If the student passes the posttest at the 85 percent level, he/she starts another unit. If the student's performance is below 85 percent, appropriate instruction and studying are repeated.

The advantages of IPI are basically the same as those of PLAN. The frequent teacher contact with students, the well-organized educational curriculum, the constant evaluation of a student's progress, and the fact that the necessary conditions of learning are usually met are among the assets of IPI. On the negative side, IPI is quite expensive, and a reorganization of the school is needed to implement IPI on a school-wide basis. Further, if not carefully monitored and supplemented with interesting material, an IPI approach can be boring and tedious. A great deal of research needs to be conducted on these individualized programs to determine the effects of individualization on such dependent variables as social skills, ability to solve problems in a group context, student attitude toward the subject matter, student ability to become an effective problem solver with material that is not prepackaged, student ability to plan time wisely when the contingencies are not as clearly identified and "artificially" engineered, and student ability to solve problems that require divergent solutions. Before deciding upon a commercial program as extensive as IPI or PLAN, a school must give careful consideration to the research findings.

General role of the teacher in IPI, PLAN, and similar prepackaged methods

The teacher's role in IPI and PLAN is to work with individuals or small groups of students based on student performance. Acting in a diagnostic-prescriptive role, the teacher constantly writes learning "prescriptions" for students based upon their achievement level, learning preference, and interests. To be an effective teacher in a system of instruction that has many different modules requires careful record keeping, well-developed diagnostic skills, and an ability to work with small groups of students. Being able to develop supplementary modules is also a very useful skill, as is the ability to develop criterion-referenced evaluation strategies. Some of the skills associated with developing modules are mentioned in the next section of the chapter.

3. Based on the conditions of learning research, identify what you consider to be the basic advantages to the commercially produced instructional strategies.
4. Given what we now know, or do not know, about these approaches, identify several problems that need to be researched.

IMPLEMENTING METHODS WITHIN A TEACHER PREPARED PROGRAM CONTEXT

Most schools do not use commercially produced, prepackaged programs such as IPI and PLAN, therefore if teachers want to match students with curricular material based on the students' skills and knowledge, teachers have to develop their own materials and instructional strategies. To be successful in this endeavor requires the use of *existing materials and resources* in a way that affords the students some latitude in progressing through various units of instruction based on their skills and interests. The strategies presented in this section include the Personalized System of Instruction (PSI), Bloom's mastery learning strategy, and the contract method. All three of these strategies impose a modularized structure on a course or subject matter in which the units of instruction are organized into sequential small steps.

Personalized System of Instruction (PSI)

Sometimes referred to as the Keller Plan or self-paced instruction, the PSI approach to instruction has generally been used at the college level, although it can be used at any grade level. According to Keller (1968), the originator of the approach, all PSI programs should consist of the following five instructional elements.

1. The student should be allowed to proceed through a course at his/her own pace.
2. The student must demonstrate a rather high level of mastery on frequent tests.
3. Detailed instructional guides with study questions and explicit behavioral objectives should be made available to the students for each unit of instruction.
4. The student is allowed to retake as many tests as necessary to reach mastery on a specified unit.
5. Immediate feedback on the student's performance should be provided. It is usually provided by student proctors, although the feedback may be given by the instructor.

In addition, many "enrichment" activities such as lectures, discussions, movies, demonstrations, and small projects should complement the approach. At the college level, most units are 20–40 pages long. At the end of the unit, a 10–15-item test consisting of multiple-choice, fill-in, and short-answer essay questions is administered to the student. Obviously, the units of instruction for younger children should be considerably shorter.

Depending on the length of the semester or school year and the length of the modules, 10–25 units are usually required during half a school year (one semester at the college level). A detailed study guide usually accompanies each unit. PSI courses have been offered in a wide variety of subjects at the college level, including psychology, economics, physics, engineering, chemistry, library science, mathematics, philosophy, and art history. In the lower grades, PSI-type organizational structures have been attempted for all the basic subjects. In other words, this technique is widely applicable.

Sherman (1974) suggests that PSI approaches should be used any time the instructor finds a great deal of repetition in the material, the same lectures are repeated to different sections of the same course, or the teacher cannot find enough time to get beyond the fundamental content of the course or subject. According to Sherman, *fundamentals* can better be taught by a PSI approach than by group instruction procedures.

From the students' perspective, the self-paced feature of PSI is very flexible, students receive immediate feedback on their performance, they may have more personal contact with the instructor compared with more traditional group methods, and they are graded solely on achievement, thus affording more objectivity. In addition, there is no permanent penalty for failing a test because students may retake the test as many times as necessary to complete a unit, and the students are very aware of what is expected on a unit. The objectives are usually clearly specified. Finally, more frequent and distributed repetitive practice is likely to occur with this approach because of the frequent testing practices.

Although there are many positive features of the PSI approach, there are also other factors that are not so positive and should be weighed carefully before designing a total course around a PSI approach. From a teacher's perspective, the course or subject can lose some flexibility because it is difficult to change in the middle of a semester. It is sometimes difficult to incorporate current material. If there is not an *adequate* text for the course or subject, the teacher may have to spend a great deal of time writing or preparing activity units. If it is a subject in a rapidly changing field, this approach would appear to be not very appropriate. If it is the type of course or subject that lends itself to a lot of discussion, the self-paced feature tends to get in the way of cohesive group participation, particularly if the students are progressing at significantly varying rates through the course. In the initial development of this approach, a great deal of preparation time is needed to write the modules, design the routine of the course, and write the unit tests. Significant secretarial help is a must. Finally, if the school system will not tolerate a large number of high grades, a teacher implementing this approach will be in trouble with the administration. The unlimited number of test attempts for each unit of instruction (within reason) guarantees a large number of higher grades. We should point out here that there is nothing incompatible with using many instructional approaches during the year. These decisions don't have to be either/or decisions. Rather the decisions should be concerned with when to use each method.

Since teachers are much more likely to use a PSI approach to teaching than some of the commercial programs now available, a brief analysis of the research findings in this area is appropriate. You should refer to Figure 14–8, which lists a selected number of studies designed to compare the effectiveness of a PSI course with the traditional college lecture course.

A quick glance at Figure 14–8 gives the impression that generally the PSI course is superior to the traditional lecture course when an objective final examination score is used as the dependent variable. A careful analysis of these data, however, suggests some other rather interesting conclusions. Consider the following interrelated points.

FIGURE 14–8
Studies comparing students' final exam performance in PSI versus traditional lecture approaches

Study	*Final exam results*	*Number of items*	*Additional comments*
Born & Davis (1974) (psychology)	Final exam score not reported "PSI students scored slightly higher on common course exams"		Particularly interesting since lecture students studied an average of 30.34 hours for the course, PSI studied 45.62 hours
Born, Gledhill & Davis (1972) (psychology of learning)	Lecture: 65.2 Modified PSI: 78.8 (allowed to choose size of study units, could take midterm test) PSI: 78.1 Combination PSI and lecture: 82.1	100-item test	
Cooper & Greiner (1971) (intro. psychology)	Lecture: 45.00 PSI: 53.17	78-item post-course quiz	On a follow-up "differences diminish on 5 month retake." PSI students studied twice as much as the lecture students
Corey & McMichael (1974) (intro. psychology)	Lecture: 65:1 PSI: 78.2	100-item test	
Jernstedt (1976) (learning)	Lecture: 58.04 PSI: 54.32	90-item test	
Lewis & Wolf (1974) (intro. chemistry)	Percent correct on final Fall 1971: Lecture: 39%, PSI: 50% Spring 1972: Lecture: 45%, PSI: 45% Fall 1972: Lecture: 65%, PSI: 61% Spring 1973: Lecture: 80%, PSI: 76%		Students in lecture class had a 0.33 lower GPA (had prior knowledge of which method was to be used)
McMichael & Corey (1969) (intro. psychology)	Lecture: 34 PSI: 40	50-point final	
Morris & Kimbrell (1971) (intro. psychology)	Median scores Lecture: 23.5 PSI: 28.5	40-point final	
Nazzaro, Todorov & Nazzaro (1972)	Lecture: 54.75 (range 38–66) PSI: 59.53 (range 53–66)	68-item test	
Sheppard & MacDermot (1970) (psychology of learning)	Lecture: 66.8 (S.D. 11.9) PSI: 73.1 (S.D. 12.1)	100-item test	

1. According to Keller and Sherman (1974), the originators of this plan, only about four fifths of the amount of material in a traditional lecture approach is usually covered in a PSI course.

2. It has been found that the study behavior pattern of those students in PSI differs significantly in two ways from that of students enrolled in a traditional lecture course. First, students in PSI courses tend to study 50–200 percent more than traditional lecture students. This finding appears to be consistent. Second, PSI students study much more frequently (they distribute their time), whereas traditional lecture students tend to cram for the exam (Born & Davis, 1974).

3. One final point: If you were to conduct a study comparing two methods in order to determine which is more successful in having students learn the greatest number of facts, concepts, and principles, and one method automatically provides the students with some additional material that the other cannot provide, how would you design your study? Assume a PSI course and a traditional lecture course are compared.

Let X represent the amount of knowledge, skills, concepts, principles, and problem-solving strategies the students are exposed to in their printed units. In addition, since the printed material is only a part of any lecture course, let Y represent the up to one-fifth additional added knowledge, skills, concepts, principles, and problem-solving strategies the student is exposed to in the lectures. Now, compare the two courses. What should be the dependent variable (i.e., what should be measured), X or $X + Y$? Should students be assessed at the conclusion of a course on material to which they have not been exposed?

Some would argue that it would be a methodological flaw to use the $X + Y$ dependent variable for the comparisons because it would bias the study against the PSI students. In one sense, those arguing against $X + Y$ as the dependent variable are right—it makes no logical sense to compare two groups on content that only one group has received. If the purpose of the study, however, is to compare the *absolute amount* of knowledge, skills, concepts, principles, and problem-solving strategies acquired through the two techniques in a fixed time (and almost all of the comparative studies were of this variety), then it would be a serious flaw not to include the Y content in the comparisons, particularly since the traditional lecture approach necessarily should provide an additional amount of material beyond the written content. In this sense, any study that does not assess the $X + Y$ dependent variable may ignore up to one fifth of the content of a course presented in lectures. To conclude that more is learned in a PSI course when perhaps the students have been exposed to only four fifths of the content of a lecture course is an example of a faulty conclusion.

Every study reviewed by DuBois (1976) used X as the dependent variable. Let us now relate the previous points. Given the fact that students exposed to a PSI format most likely study 50–200 percent more than students exposed to a traditional lecture approach, are usually responsible for only 75–90 percent of the content of a traditional lecture course (depending on the amount of additional content in the lecture), and are exposed to a method that is purposefully designed to maximize learning based on several generally well-accepted learning principles, are the differences in Figure 14–8 truly different, particularly when any additional amount of material acquired by the lecture approach was not even assessed? Any definitive statements about the relative effectiveness of either method would be necessarily premature, at best.

We took time out to provide you with this brief analysis of the research to show you what might happen if you were to read only a few research studies that appear to favor a particular approach without considering the total picture. Conclusions from research studies are only as good as the design and conceptual basis for them. Often poorly designed research studies are the rule rather than the exception. Be careful not to draw any firm conclusions after reading a few research studies on a topic.

In order to implement a program such as PSI, the teacher must be very well organized. A great deal of the planning and work involved in such an approach must take place before the first day of class. Appropriate material must be gathered, written, or chosen. Study guides must be prepared. Pre and posttests, the type of record-keeping system, and the procurement and training of proctors must be finalized. If the program is to be managed by computer, those details must be arranged. Since a substantial portion of the material is written by the instructor, enough lead time must be allowed for typing the study guides, tests, and adjunct handouts. The sytem of grading and strategies for dealing with student procrastinators must be worked out. The enrichment component of the program such as lectures, videotape presentations, movies, demonstrations, simulations, and similar activities should be conceived before the semester commences. In conclusion, if you tend to be somewhat disorganized, you had better acquire some organizational skills prior to instituting PSI. The degree of success with a PSI approach is dependent on the teacher's organizational skills.

The contract method

FIGURE 14–9
The contract method is an excellent strategy to focus a student's attention and increase motivation

The contract method is a form of learning guide in which the student, upon consultation with a teacher, agrees to perform a series of specified tasks. Contracts are initiated by either the student or teacher and afford much flexibility in the classroom (Figure 14–9). Although contracts are quite specific in design, they can be written in a manner to interest each student at an appropriate level of difficulty. Generally, contracts consist of a stated purpose, a series of clearly specified behavioral objectives, a method of evaluation so that the teacher and student understand how the evaluation is to occur, a list of resources and learning activities to be studied (including the sequential steps necessary to complete the project deadlines), and a method for relating the contract to the ongoing class activities.

In actuality, the contract method is usually not an independent method by itself; it is a method that supplements other teaching strategies. The decision to use the contract method for a unit or series of units of instruction generally would be the same as for the PSI method and, therefore, need not be discussed here.

The role of the teacher while using the contract method is the same as in other modularized approaches. The teacher should be able to generate appropriate contracts and determine the degree to which the student needs guided study, cooperative planning, a mini-lesson, or additional independent work (B. A. Ward, 1973).

Writing an appropriate contract consists of:

1. Specifying what the student should accomplish in performance terms at the conclusion of the contract.
2. Specifying the approximate time limit in which to complete the module.
3. Identifying the conditions under which the student will be evaluated.
4. Specifying or identifying the appropriate learning materials and activities.
5. Writing the appropriate tests, or specifying appropriate evaluation criteria.

Bloom's (1971) mastery learning strategy

Based on Carroll's (1963) model of learning, which suggests that time spent on a task is the most important factor contributing to school learning, Bloom's strategy is designed to be used in conjunction with *traditional group instructional procedures.* The steps in a "mastery approach" include:

1. Break the course down into one to two-week learning units.
2. Specify the learning outcomes.
3. Teach the unit *by typical group instructional* procedures.
4. Administer a test at the end of a unit.
5. Evaluate the results of the test.
6. Prescribe specific learning activities for those students who did not reach the mastery level.

7. At the end of the course, administer a comprehensive test to determine the student's grade.
8. Evaluate the system.

Bloom's system incorporates many of the features of individualized instruction while maintaining the traditional teaching strategy of group instruction. The student is allowed to spend as much time as necessary (within reason) on a unit after the first unit test has been administered in Step 4 to achieve the specified mastery level. Although somewhat arbitrary, Bloom suggests that an 85 percent level of proficiency on multiple-choice items and an 80 percent level of proficiency on short-essay items should be required of all students for each unit of instruction. For those students who do not achieve the level of mastery desired, alternative methods and materials should be available to learn the material.

Contrasted with the previous approaches, Bloom's mastery approach has many of the advantages of individualized instruction while allowing the teacher to use certain group approaches. Since the objectives are clearly specified for each unit, the student knows what to expect in a mastery approach. The semi-self-paced nature of this approach requires students to keep up with their work while allowing them extra time to restudy missed material. Further, the high level of mastery increases the likelihood that students will learn more material at the conclusion of the course. Finally, the small units of instruction force students to distribute studying time more evenly throughout the semester.

On the negative side, this method is generally more work for the teacher. And, as with the other modularized or self-paced approaches, some students complain about the frequent testing. No method will satisfy every student.

Since this teaching method incorporates modularized as well as group instructional strategies, the teaching role in this method is varied and includes all of the roles identified for both individualized and group instructional practices. Essentially, this method requires the teacher to be a "master of all the methods" (no pun intended).

Of particular importance is the teacher's skill in writing formative tests that are diagnostic-prescriptive in their emphasis and developing mini-lessons (handouts, tapes, student tutoring, practice assignments, etc.) to help those students who have not mastered the unit. This means that the questions on the test should systematically assess the different objectives of the course in some hierarchical manner (refer back to the table of specifications discussed in Chapter 12 or the task analysis discussion in Chapter 8), and that supplementary lessons or material designed to teach the missed facts, skills, discriminations, concepts, and principles necessary to perform the task be readily available to the students. As with the PSI and contract methods, the planning for this approach involves considerable time.

5. What are several basic, common underlying characteristics of PSI, the contract method, and Bloom's mastery strategy?
6. Which of the following methods is specifically designed to be used with any instructional approach?
   a. PSI.
   b. The contract method.
   c. Bloom's mastery approach.
   d. PLAN.

IMPLEMENTING METHODS WITHIN A DYNAMIC CLASSROOM PROGRAM

Contrasted with the types of programs mentioned earlier in this chapter are other programs characterized by group instructional procedures. Included in this category are the lecture-explanation, discussion, and classroom teaching methods.

The lecture-explanation method includes such diverse teaching strategies as a short explanation or statement about a topic lasting for perhaps a minute, a short presentation of a few minutes duration, and a formal 50-minute verbal presentation with very little opportunity for students to respond overtly. In these instructional situations, the common characteristic is the teacher taking on a verbal role with reference to the class, and the attention of the class focuses on the teacher.

Compared with programs using the lecture-explanation method to present the content are those instructional programs in which a group of students actively interacts with each other and with the instructor to either discuss some problem or achieve some concrete product through group cooperation or discussion of the program content. In any case, active overt responding by numerous students in a group is the common characteristic of this approach. This method includes discussions with the total class, small discussion groups, or group projects. The teacher's role is generally that of a facilitator and, depending on the role the teacher plays in the discussion, the attention of the class may focus on the teacher or on the other students.

When psychologists have gone into various classrooms to observe the teacher's behavior, however, it has been found that most classroom programs use a combination of the lecture and discussion methods (Bellack, Kliebard, Hyman & Smith, 1966; Dunkin & Biddle, 1974). Based on a synthesis of the lecture and discussion format, this approach may be described as an ongoing lecture-discussion strategy in which the teacher asks questions, poses problems, identifies issues, and presents information while the student is generally expected to respond to the teacher's queries and information. With this approach [often referred to as *classroom teaching* (Rosenshine, 1976)], the teacher takes on the simultaneous role of information provider and facilitator of discussions. This part of the chapter is concerned with those three methods.

The lecture-explanation method

For the purpose of this part of the chapter the lecture-explanation method is defined as any strategy a teacher uses to impart information concepts or principles to students through the spoken word in order to *enable the student to perform specific instructional objective(s).* We chose this definition to remind you that any method used by a teacher should constantly reflect what the students should be able to do after the method has been implemented. According to Gropper (1976), one of the biggest mistakes educators or teachers make is to forget that any instructional strategy should lead directly to the *objectives* and interrelated *goals* for a course of study. We might add that formal lectures as typically delivered in many instructional settings often do not meet Gropper's criterion for an appropriate instructional strategy because the teacher loses sight of the purpose of the presentation and rambles or repeats readily available, easily understood printed material.

Under attack since the advent of the printing press as an outdated instructional strategy, the lecture method has survived waves and waves of criticism at various times in educational history. Most recently, for example, proponents of the PSI approach have implied that since the lecture method appears to violate many principles of learning, it is generally an inappropriate instructional technique. If there has been so much criticism leveled against this method, why is it still used? McLeish (1976) argues

FIGURE 14–10
Although often misused, the lecture method can be very effective

strongly that the lecture method, just like any other method, is inappropriate as an all-purpose method, although it can serve many useful instructional functions (Figure 14–10). According to McLeish, the lecture-explanation approach, when used properly, can inspire enthusiasm and capture the students' imagination.

Other instructional situations for which the lecture method appears to be appropriate include:

1. When printed material is not available or is not easily accessible.
2. When the teacher is confronted with poor and/or inadequate readers who possess an adequate level of auditory verbal skills.
3. When the teacher is dissatisfied with a portion of the written material because:
   a. The student needs some prerequisite information in order to understand the reading.
   b. The student needs some organizing rules to interrelate diverse material.
   c. The reading material is inadequate in its coverage of the topic.
   d. There is too much to read (the student needs to discriminate between the important and the unimportant material).
4. When the instructor wants to provide a different point of view, place a book and/or reading assignment in perspective, or raise significant questions or problems not raised in a book.
5. To establish "relevancy" through the medium of a scholar.
6. To utilize the instructor's practical experiences.
7. To summarize a variety of diverse material.
8. To present newly dated material in a rapidly changing subject area.
9. When the instructor has some empirical evidence (past experience) that a section of the printed material is difficult to understand.

10. When the instructor has not had time to put the lecture material into a written format or there is not enough secretarial staff or monies available to print the lectures.
11. When the lecturer is an authority in a field, in which case the lecturer can serve as a provider of new information and a model to the audience.
12. When many students need to be handled at one time.
13. When an inexpensive method is needed.

In fact, with the exception of "classroom teaching," the lecture method is the most flexible method available from an instructor's perspective. When presenting a lengthy lecture, the instructor is limited only by his/her own lack of ingenuity and the clock.

Essentially, most of the above justifications for the lecture-explanation method are related to the instructor's opinion that the available printed material either is not satisfactory or is not available in printed form that is easily and realistically accessible to students. No book is perfect; no book is complete. The lecture-explanation method is *one way to supplement* readily available printed material. As an all-purpose method, the pure lecture, like any other method, is an inadequate strategy. Unless the lecturer is dynamic, thought-provoking, organized, and can communicate clearly, the lecture can be a very painful experience. Good lecturing is not easy. It requires a blend of skills. If the lecture is a repetition of readily available printed material that can be easily understood and remembered by the students, it is an inappropriate strategy. If the material is such that the student needs to make many overt responses, rehearse material, and be given feedback, the lecture is inappropriate except when the instructor has to provide the information for the students prior to rehearsal. Since the lecture is teacher-paced, the advanced students can be held back while the less capable students may not understand some of the content. As a method, the lecture approach is inappropriate for young students except in very short segments. Formal lectures of long duration appear to be appropriate for only upper-level high school students and college students.

Finally, the traditional approach to lecturing has been to place students in a relatively passive role rather than an *active,* learning role. Passively taking notes on material rather than reconceptualizing it can be an unfortunate but *avoidable* side effect of the lecture. Most of the negative features of the lecture, however, can be partially offset by planning carefully and by using several other complementary methods during a class period or during a longer time span, if necessary. However, the potential misuses of the lecture method are numerous.

The functions of a lecture-explanation method are to impart verbal information, concepts, or principles that are not found satisfactorily in printed form or to repeat material that needs to be highlighted or stated differently than in the printed form. The purpose of imparting the material is to enable the student to achieve the specified instructional objectives for the subject. Much of the criticism of this method has come about because instructors have traditionally viewed this method as a technique for imparting information without asking the student to do anything with the information. According to Nekrasova (1960), the task of the lecturer is to insure the active responding of students that is necessary to reconceptualize and rethink through the subject matter.

Seen in this framework, the lecture method takes on a new dimension. Requiring independent thinking by asking open-ended questions during the discourse, posing unfinished problems, having students relate diverse material, and having students originate well-thought-out questions and problems can effectively transform the lecture into a stimulating and productive problem-solving exercise. With this approach, the danger of having the student conclude that knowledge is a closed system is minimized. With this approach, there is a greater likelihood that the students will be covertly active while listening to the lecture. Finally, involving students in covert problem solving can provide students with the feedback that is so often missing in traditional information-providing lectures.

A well designed instructional program utilizing the lecture method as the primary means for presenting the course content can easily make use of the principles of learning mentioned earlier in this book. If desired, short tests can be administered on a frequent basis. For those students who perform poorly on tests, alternative lessons can be made available (refer back to Bloom's mastery approach). Having students actively apply the concepts and principles acquired during a lecture to solve relevant problems while the lecture is progressing is also a possibility. In this case, the student can receive immediate feedback about the efficacy of the solution. Just because the traditional lecture format has not been used in conjunction with these techniques, it does not mean that the lecture format cannot be restructured to incorporate these principles of instruction on a daily basis.

According to Musella and Rusch (1968), students claim that instructors who communicate clearly, organize their presentations, act knowledgeably, and present material in an enthusiastic manner facilitate thinking. Although not much has been done to analyze the structural qualities of a good lecture-explanation presentation, some tentative recommendations are presented.

1. The introduction of a lecture explanation should inform the listeners about its content (Ausubel, 1960; Klemm, 1976; McDougall, Gray & McNicol, 1972). A brief printed summary of the lecture can be helpful.
2. The introduction should gain the student's attention (Kounin, 1970). As such, a well-developed question or problem is in order to start a lecture. For example, an instructor may start a lecture by stating, "Today's discussion centers around the question of. . . . During the period we will consider. . . . By the end of the period you should be able to. . . ."
3. If the lecture is one of a series of lectures, a brief recapitulation of how the lecture to be presented relates to the previous lectures is in order. Research indicates that new information to be acquired is more likely to be remembered if it is related to information the student has already acquired.
4. Asking questions during a lecture and posing open-ended problems can have the effect of changing the lecture into an active information-processing medium. Through the medium of questions, students can answer the question either overtly or covertly and receive immediate feedback concerning the efficacy of their response.
5. Throughout the lecture, the lecturer should attempt to have the student relate the material in a meaningful manner. Some lecturers have attempted to insert mini-quizzes in the middle of a lecture to require the student to synthesize the material, respond overtly, and get immediate feedback.
6. The middle part of a lengthy lecture is most often forgotten (Thomas, 1972). Some strategy should be attempted to make the middle of the lecture more interesting and memorable. Varying the type of presentation and varying the student activities in the middle of a lengthy presentation are good strategies.
7. The end of a lecture should highlight the main points of the lecture. If the lecture

is one of an integrated series, an attempt to relate the lecture to future lectures in the series can help the student to integrate the material.

In conclusion, viewing the learner as an active information processor rather than as a passive recipient of knowledge can transform the lecture into a completely new medium. The purpose of a lecture explanation should be to facilitate the objectives of the course, not to present unusable information to passive listeners.

The discussion-group project method

This method includes any instructional situation in which the predominant activity is one where students interact with one another or with the teacher to exchange ideas verbally, solve complex problems through verbal interchange, or generate some concrete product through group cooperation to achieve the instructional objectives. The teacher may or may not be present during the discussion. Although discussion groups may be used for many different cognitive and affective outcomes, this chapter is only concerned with using the discussion method to implement cognitive objectives. A leader for discussion groups in the affective domain where the focus is on personal adjustment requires many skills beyond the scope of this book.

Although the discussion-group project method can be used with most types of objectives, it appears particularly well suited for those situations in which there are differences of opinion or fact, problems for which there are no known acceptable answers, and situations where group problem solving is desirable. In a pluralistic, democratic society, many decisions are arrived at through group consensus. Hill (1969) suggests, for example, that the discussion-group project method is particularly useful to:

1. Use knowledge gained from written material to solve complex problems in a group context.
2. Resolve issue-oriented problems.
3. Resolve problems that appear to be best solved through group processes.

Hill's suggestions are discussed in sequence. According to Hill, the discussion method may be used in conjunction with typical reading assignments. When the student is given a reading assignment, Hill suggests that the content of the assignment be discussed in the following order: defining and identifying the terms, concepts, and rules; identifying the author's message; stating the major themes of the article; integrating the material; applying the material; and evaluating the author's presentation. Notice that the order of the discussion proceeds from the restatement of factual material to the higher problem-solving objectives. Essentially Hill's suggestion parallels the task analysis viewpoint presented earlier in the book. According to Hill, "going beyond the information" in a problem-solving context is the usual terminal objective of this approach. Simply restating known facts without some application of the facts is a misuse of this method's potential.

Being involved in issue-oriented topics is another major use for the discussion method. An issue-oriented topic can provide the student with the opportunity to identify other student viewpoints, analyze divergent opinions critically, modify personal viewpoints, and change other viewpoints if necessary. One of the most important outcomes of this type of discussion is that it has the potential to help crystallize a student's belief or opinion about an issue-oriented problem. Note the similarity between this suggestion and the reconstructionist philosophical position discussed in Chapter 2.

Some problems that are complex and that resist simple resolution, would appear to be best discussed in a group context. Problems that require a great deal of knowledge in a variety of disciplines particularly require group solutions, with each person contributing his/her own expertise to the solution. Whether the problem is approached through a group discussion or a group project format, some concrete product should be required of the group. Knowing that a concrete product must result keeps students on-task.

Notice that the above three purposes of the discussion method emphasize problem-solving skills and a resulting product. Hill also points out that four other secondary effects of the discussion method include: it increases the likelihood that the students will improve their discussion skills; if used properly, the method can be a good motivational device; and it allows the teacher to assess a student's knowledge and thinking skills. In the affective domain, feelings of belonging to a group and the simple opportunity to express one's feelings, attitudes, or beliefs in a relatively spontaneous instructional situation can be positive assets of a discussion.

As with every other method, the discussion method has serious limitations and is not appropriate for every instructional situation. Because of the relatively spontaneous nature of the discussion method, unless the group is presented with a series of specific convergent questions, the method does not appear to be as useful for a subject where a well-defined body of knowledge needs to be replicated. Less systematic than other methods, there is a greater likelihood that some important material may not be discussed. It is not particularly useful in situations where divergent viewpoints need not be expressed, identified, shared, or debated. Using the discussion method to rediscuss easily understood material is inappropriate. In those situations where it is important for students to do independent work without the aid of peers, this method is generally inappropriate. Teachers also ought to consider their own skills with reference to the discussion method. Most discussions, unless rigorously controlled, create a certain amount of divergence, ambiguity, and disorder. Not all of us thrive on ambiguity. Further, there are a variety of subtle skills needed to conduct a good discussion. Conducting a discussion without these skills is like steering a ship without a rudder. Oftentimes the result is an unorganized bull session where very little is accomplished except for the sharing of ignorance. In fact, if the teacher is not very careful to insure that the students have the prerequisite cognitive and affective skills for the discussion a great deal of valuable time may be wasted. Finally, to use the discussion method for an extended period of time with young students would not be in order.

Teachers have to be careful when using the discussion method to be sure they understand their appropriate role with this method. The role of the teacher can vary significantly with the discussion group method depending on the objectives of the lesson and the entering behavior of the students. Some discussions may consist of well-organized lessons where a group has a number of clear, predetermined convergent-type questions to answer, contrasted with lessons where the goals are less clearly specified because it is expected that the outcomes should vary widely from group to group. In the first case, the teacher may take on a very active role in keeping students to the task (Figure 14–11). The second implies that the group should be allowed to consider many divergent avenues without much intervention from a teacher. The teacher has three broad roles with the discussion-group project method. These roles are concerned with *planning* and *initiating* the group lesson, *implementing* the discussion or project, and drawing some *summarizing conclusions* about the group's work.

FIGURE 14–11
The teacher can play a very important role in discussions by clarifying issues

In planning for a discussion, particular concern should be given to analyzing the purpose of the discussion. While discussion for the sake of a discussion is a nice luxury, it is not necessarily productive. The discussion method is unusually prone to wandering off the target. *Well-phrased questions or objectives stated in performance terms, clear instructions on how the discussion or project should be attempted, and a clearly specified time limit provide some necessary structure for the students.* Further, the teacher should be specifically concerned with the students' entering behavior. Giving students a discussion assignment or group project for which many members of the class may not have the prerequisites is a common teacher error. While at times this cannot be avoided, the teacher can do much to insure that the proper assignments have been read, prerequisite questions answered, or proper experiences have been undertaken prior to the assignment of the group activity. Participation in the group activity can be made contingent on having completed individual assignments.

The teacher can also do a great deal to structure the group for maximum efficiency. Gall and Gall (1976), after an extensive review of the research on the discussion method, make the following five recommendations.

1. The *ideal size* for a discussion group from which everyone should receive some benefit is about *five students.* A small number is better than a large number because of the opportunity to participate in the group. If the assignment is of such a nature that the members of a group will have to vote on issues, then the composition of the group should be an odd number, if five students cannot be assigned to the group. According to Gall and Gall, five is an optimal number because as the size of the group increases, a more complex social structure is needed to support it. Further, the greater the number in a group, the greater the likelihood of social diversity, thus increasing the likelihood of wasted time in the pursuit of the task.

2. Generally speaking, the group should be a *heterogeneous group* when the members are assigned controversial issues to discuss. Some consideration, however, should be given to group cohesiveness.
3. The group should be *moderately cohesive.* If the group is hopelessly fragmented, little progress will be made unless it is *required* to synthesize divergent viewpoints.
4. The seating arrangement of a group usually should be arranged to facilitate maximum interaction among the group members. The research seems to indicate that for simple convergent tasks, a centrally located leader facilitates the group processes (Collins, 1970). For more complex divergent tasks, decentralized structural arrangements appear to be more appropriate, such as a circle, square, or rectangle.
5. A democratically organized group appears to facilitate group discussion and promotes more positive attitudes by members of a group than does an authoritatively organized group.

In assigning specific students to a group, consideration should be given to the student's relationship to other members of the group, the student's academic entering behavior, the student's ability to discuss the issues or contribute to a group project, and other characteristics that may affect the performance of the group. Often students should be allowed to choose their own group based on their preferences. The decision to allow or not allow a student the choice to participate in a group of the student's choosing should be based on the course objectives.

How active should a teacher be in a group discussion? Although some psychologists might suggest that the teacher assume a very passive role with respect to the group on the grounds that the total group process is always a learning experience and ought not to be interfered with, we take a slightly different position. Our position is that the degree of teacher interference with a group should be based on the teacher's objectives for using the group discussion or project method. If the basic goal for the group is a process goal, such as to increase discussion skills, promote group cohesiveness, provide the students with the opportunity to listen to various viewpoints, or allow students to express opinions on controversial subjects, very little interference is necessary. If, on the other hand, the purpose of the group is a product goal, then some interference with the group might be necessary when it departs from the goal.

For example, assume you are listening to a group and you hear or observe one of the following: the student states an idea poorly so that the group does not understand the student; the student commits a logical fallacy that goes undetected by the group; the student states the facts incorrectly and the statement is accepted by the group as the truth; or as a result of a student's divergent suggestion, a lengthy digression or an unusually lengthy silence ensues. What do these examples have in common? The common element is that the group is "off-target" with respect to the terminal objective. The decision to intervene in one of these situations has to be based on the teacher's values and the teacher's best guess concerning what might happen if that situation is allowed to continue.

Having a clear *purpose in mind* concerning the outcome of the discussion or group project provides the teacher with reason to intervene or not to intervene. Whether a discussion deteriorates into a tangential bull session often depends on the teacher's ability to get the group back on-target and establish goal-directed behavior. Furthermore, providing the student with appropriate feedback concerning his/her inappropriate response based on the conditions of learning is certainly in order in some situations.

In fact, after the groups have finished their discussions, the teacher ought to insure that some conclusion is generated. Evaluating the groups' performances and synthesizing the results of the groups' deliberations are strongly recommended. Particular concern should be taken to determine whether the objectives have been met. Additionally, the teacher should attempt to relate the content of the discussions or the product of the group to the goals of the class. Without this final step, often discussions have the effect of being tangential to the objectives of the course, or appear to be fragmented in the student's perception.

If used properly, the discussion method is powerful. Less systematic than any of the other methods we have discussed, however, the discussion method is particularly prone to misuse. It is the teacher's task, based on a set of clear purposes and well-defined skills, to insure the proper implementation of this method.

The "classroom teaching" or "classroom instruction" method

Although we have indicated that the definitions of various teaching methods often are not very precise, we have attempted to present you with many of the common methods used by teachers. In doing so, we recognize the artificiality of our approach—*rarely do teachers use one method independent of other methods.* Even within given instructional time frames, teachers vary their methods considerably. For example, rarely is the lecture method presented in its pure form. Rarely do discussions occur without individual seat work. Most teaching consists of a synthesis of various methods into a purposeful, integrated instructional program. Recently various psychologists and educational researchers have attempted to summarize the vast amount of literature on teaching effectiveness based on what the teacher *really* does in the classroom. The typical teacher uses a combination of approaches and, therefore, according to these researchers, studies should be based on what the teacher really does in the classroom related to what the student does, rather than on some "pure" method that is rarely used by a teacher in a classroom situation. Some of these reviews include Bellack, Kliebard, Hyman, and Smith (1966); Brophy and Good (1974); Dunkin and Biddle (1974); and Rosenshine and Furst (1973).

Generally, at the core of most forms of classroom teaching is a lecture-discussion-recitation format or some derivative of that combination. Although not solely limited to this process, many teachers tend to structure their lessons around the following sequence:

1. The teacher *presents* some information or a framework within which a student-teacher interaction is to occur (i.e., the teacher sets the stage or the structure for the interaction).
2. The teacher *solicits* a response from one or more members of the class.
3. The student *answers* the solicitation (Figure 14–12).
4. The teacher *responds* to the student's response with an extended comment, praise, or additional question (Bellack, Kliebard, Hyman & Smith, 1966); the teacher provides relevant feedback.

Since all the specific strategies used in classroom teaching have already been discussed throughout this chapter, there is no need to discuss them or the role of the teacher in this approach. The role of the teacher is dependent on the specific strategy the teacher uses at any given time during the instructional event and, therefore, has already been mentioned.

In essence, the condition of learning research discussed in Chapters 10 and 11 points out how the environment ought to be structured specifically to facilitate different

FIGURE 14–12
The lecture-discussion-recitation format of classroom teaching insures many overt responses

types of learning given specific instructional objectives. As such, the principles mentioned in those chapters should be the framework upon which classroom teaching is based. In other words, the decision to present students with some information, the decision to solicit a student response, and the decision to react to a student's response, as well as the decision about how to react to a student or class, are based on the teacher's estimate of the student's capability to perform the objective consonant with the conditions of learning research.

SUMMARY

In this chapter we discussed the factors teachers should consider when choosing a general instructional strategy. We pointed out that instruction can have variable long-term outcomes beyond what is planned in the special objectives. To choose a method properly, consideration should be given to both short-term and long-term cognitive goals and objectives as well as the mathemagenic and affective goals of instruction. Without considering these multiple factors, the actual outcomes of instruction can differ significantly from what is desired. In addition, a plea was made for flexibility in being able to change the methodology during a lesson when it is apparently not successful. Factors to consider in choosing a general instructional strategy include the aggregate set of goals and objectives; the nature of the students; the nature of the institution in terms of its structure, resources, and other constraints; the nature of the teacher; the nature of the subject matter; the subjective trade-offs the teacher has to make in the final analysis; and the conditions of learning.

The second part of the chapter discussed three general categories of programs: commercially produced programs, teacher-produced programs in which the content is predetermined by the teacher, and the traditional group dynamic teaching methods characterized by spontaneity and teacher-student interactions. It was pointed out that all methods are appropriate under certain conditions because they serve different logical functions. In addition, with a little adaptability and flexibility on the teacher's part, all the methods in this chapter can be implemented to satisfy the required conditions of learning.

Further, you should realize that for any given instructional sequence, a variety of methods might be used within a class period to facilitate the acquisition of different types of objectives. The integration of methods into a coherent instructional program is up to the teacher. The main consideration for choosing method A over method B should rest on a careful analysis of the total educational context of which the teacher and students are a part.

SELF-TEST

1. According to the aptitude-treatment interaction model, what can be said about teaching methods?
   a. The student's genetic makeup will have a greater effect on achievement than will the student's learned aptitudes.
   b. Proper teaching methods can considerably increase a student's aptitude.
   c. The amount of variability in student differences on achievement tests cannot be related to teaching methods.
   d. This model suggests that different methods will work better with students according to what they bring to the task.
2. Which statement(s) is (are) true about the relationship between a cognitive objective and the method used to teach the objective?
   a. Since there are many methods that can be used to teach cognitive objectives, the consideration of the choice of methods should be much broader than just the cognitive domain.
   b. Since the identification of a cognitive objective clearly limits the teacher's choice to just several methods that meet all the conditions of learning, the choice of methods is fairly automatic once the objective is specified in instructional terms.
   c. Since a clearly specified instructional cognitive objective suggests a specific hierarchy based on the conditions of learning research, the use of novelty in the choice of methods would not be very appropriate to teach specific objectives, although novelty would be appropriate to teach general goals.
   d. It is very possible that a teacher, if basing his/her decision only on specific cognitive objectives, could choose instructional strategies that would efficiently get the students to perform all of the specific cognitive objectives without reaching any of the broader goals of the course.
   e. *b* and *c.*
   f. *a* and *d.*
3. As a generalization, commercially produced programs use the modular format. Most modules are designed to:
   a. Present one objective to a student to be completed in about one week.
   b. Supplement the regular curriculum, i.e., the commercially produced programs mentioned in the book are enrichment-type activities to be completed after the regular curricular work is performed.
   c. Present about five objectives to a student to be completed in two weeks.
   d. Insure mastery at at least the 65 percent level.
4. Probably there has been no method as misused as the lecture method. Which of the following characteristics of the lecture should and can be readily and realistically changed to make the lecture a more appropriate method?
   a. Turn the lecture into an active medium by posing different questions and problems related to the course objectives.
   b. Train lecturers to be more divergent in their approaches by including more tangential material in their lectures.
   c. Train a quiet person who is not very enthusiastic to be a dynamic, vital lecturer.
   d. Develop strategies to repeat the textual material in interesting ways.
5. The discussion method is misused often. One or more of the most frequent misuses of this method is/are:
   a. The method is used as a means without considering the end results.
   b. The students are given topics for which the prerequisites are lacking.
   c. Not requiring a clear problem-solving objective, the students get off-target very easily.
   d. *a* and *b.*
   e. *a* and *c.*
   f. *b* and *c.*
   g. All of the above.
6. As a generalization, although classroom teaching takes many forms, the most frequent is:

SELF-TEST *(continued)*

a. A group discussion followed by feedback.
b. The written module with related activities complementing the module.
c. A modified Bloom's format.
d. A lecture, discussion, and recitation sequence.

7. As a generalization, what percentage of mastery is expected before a student is allowed to progress in a mastery or commercial modular approach to teaching?
   a. 65.
   b. 75.
   c. 85.
   d. 95.
8. From the *teacher's* perspective, one of the advantages of PSI is:
   a. It should force closer contact with students if done properly.
   b. It allows the teachers to have control over the student's rate of progress through the course.
   c. It requires very little outside support from the secretarial staff.
   d. It is considerably easier to prepare for than other methods.
9. Which of the following methods is designed to be used with regular methods?
   a. PSI.
   b. IPI.
   c. PLAN.
   d. Bloom's mastery.
10. You are a teacher for 11th-grade history, and for a particular unit you chose the small-group discussion method. After two days with this method you note that the students appear to wander off the topic and, when they attempt to stay on the topic, their ignorance of the topic is terrible. State the two most probable factors associated with the students' poor performance and state how this problem should be resolved. You have already decided that the discussion method is appropriate for this unit.

ANSWER KEY TO BOXED QUESTIONS

1. Without considering the specific cognitive and affective objectives at the same time as the broader cognitive and affective goals, it is very possible to achieve all the outcomes in one or several of the categories at the expense of another category.
2. While it is true that broad instructional strategies or teaching methods should be based directly on the identified objectives of a program, many other factors such as the state of the learner, the nature of the institution, the nature of the teacher, and the characteristics of the subject matter must be considered when choosing a method. With slight modifications, almost all the teaching methods can reflect the appropriate conditions of learning.
3. Since these approaches are generally based on the conditions of learning research (relevant practice, immediate feedback, distributed practice, clear objectives, etc.), it follows that, given several other considerations, these programs should be successful.
4. Although based on the appropriate conditions of learning for cognitive objectives, these programs tend to deemphasize group interaction and problem solving as well as the student's general attitude toward the subject matter. There is nothing inherently incompatible, however, with incorporating the social and attitudinal aspects of instruction in these approaches.
5. All three approaches emphasize relatively small units of instruction, mastery of subject matter, and feedback.
6. *c*

ANSWER KEY TO SELF-TEST

1. *d*
2. *f*
3. *c*
4. *a*
5. *g*
6. *d*
7. *c*
8. *a*
9. *d*
10. The two most likely problems are: the objectives were not clear enough, and the students had not acquired the cognitive prerequisites. Most likely the students had not done their reading. To solve the first problem the teacher should be sure the purpose of the discussion is clear. A specific, well-defined instructional objective written in behavioral terms to be completed by a time deadline should solve the problem. The second problem can be solved by giving the students an assignment; then test the students on the assignment before they can participate in the discussion. If necessary, no student with scores below some cutoff should be allowed to participate in the discussion.

Chapter 15

Establishing the instructional level

IN THE CLASSROOM a means of matching instruction to the students' varied levels of achievement is needed. In this chapter we continue the discussion of analyzing the students' level of performance prior to instruction. The earlier discussion centered on the theoretical issues of assessing entering behavior. At this point we turn our attention to the problems of implementing an evaluation of entering behavior in the classroom context.

Our first point concerns the overall rationale for the assessment process. We then present three general principles to guide the process. Following this we outline a model that defines the content and procedures that may be used in an evaluation of entering behavior. We describe the process as a series of screening activities matched to the level of the instructional decisions that must be made.

The objectives in this chapter are for you to be able to:

1. Describe the theoretical and pragmatic issues that need to be considered in an evaluation of students' entering behaviors.
2. State three general principles that should guide the assessment process, and describe the implications these principles have for classroom instruction.
3. List the two main types of data and the five traditional types of data that may be needed in evaluating entering behavior.
4. List several places where the various types of data can be obtained.
5. Describe how various types of data may be obtained.
6. Describe the interpretation problems associated with the various types and sources of data.
7. List the sequence of events in implementing an evaluation of entering behavior.
8. Describe how a screening program can be refined.

INFORMATIONAL NEEDS

Idealistic instructional principles are constantly confronted with the realities of the classroom. The area of assessing entering behavior is one in which idealism is not likely to withstand the assault of reality as well as in some other areas. In an effort to present the entire curriculum and the required learning conditions, individual differences in students are likely to be overlooked or ignored. It may not be the teacher's desire to do so, but time and the necessary strategy may be lacking.

Theoretical considerations

You will recall that in Chapter 9 about analyzing students we identified six approaches:

1. Maturational approach.
2. Demographic approach.
3. Personality approach.
4. Abilities and processes approach.
5. Achievement approach.
6. Transfer approach.

From a theoretical standpoint all of these approaches can be justified as having some utility. The different approaches will add different perspectives to our view of the student, and each perspective has its own utility. However, the utilities of the various approaches may not be equal; the weighting used will be determined by the decisions to be made and the personal values of the teacher making the decision.

Theoretically there is no question but what the maturational approach and it's emphasis that biological development of the child needs to be sufficiently advanced so that he/she can profit from a particular experience.

Demographic data may have more relationship to decisions about the goals of the classroom than to decisions about the instructional procedures to be used to reach those goals. This is not to say that instructional procedures should not be adapted to match demographic differences. It is just that the data may define more closely differences in the lifestyles and goals of students but have little bearing on the basic conditions that need to be provided to reach the goals. This effect on goals could have far-reaching implications for outcomes in the affective and mathemagenic domains. These in turn could influence the outcomes in the cognitive domain, and vice versa.

There is little question that the development of personal traits, processing abilities, and understanding does not occur spontaneously but gradually expands. The expansion in a particular area may be rapid at times and slow or stopped at other times. Due to the incremental and related nature of cognitive development, information about the child's general level of functioning in terms of personal traits, processing ability, and achievement level is needed. Teachers have traditionally taken students through a series of instructional steps on the basis of these types of data. Apparently they have recognized the need for matching instruction to the student's level of achievement but have not always accomplished it too successfully.

The transfer approach points out the necessity for determining even more precise data in the form of certain mathemagenic behaviors. In a sense this is a continuation of the achievement approach but at a considerably refined level. The orientation also changes from a focus on the subject matter and the amount the learner has acquired to a focus on learner characteristics that make further learning possible.

Pragmatic considerations

Theoretically there is a need for many kinds of information about learners. At the achievement and transfer levels of analysis a considerable amount of very precise information is needed. To gather all of the information that is theoretically desirable would be an insurmountable task. Teachers have done a reasonably successful job in the past with most students without getting into any complicated assessment procedures. Part of the reason for this success story is that many teachers informally gather much of the information needed even at the transfer level. We suspect that success can also be attributed to the pace of the school curriculum, a great deal of backtracking, and the inclusion of many practice periods in the instructional procedures. What we are suggesting is that most teachers do a fair job of assessing entering behaviors. Any gaps between the assigned tasks and the student's entering behaviors are closed during the instructional process by shotgun techniques that by chance alone are apt to hit upon what is needed by the student.

This approach was perfectly acceptable when the schools served as a screening institution and a certain percentage of failures and dropouts was expected and accepted (Kagan, 1971). With today's concern for preventing dropouts and having all children reach a minimum level of competency, yesterday's failures become today's problems (Figure 15–1). If a particular child is not helped by the shotgun approach, there needs to be a clearer focus on the issue of entering behavior. Provided that other

FIGURE 15–1
Yesterday's dropouts can become today's problem

children mastered the task under the conditions presented, the child who has not mastered it is most likely lacking some of the prerequisite skills.

Quite often teachers will make the comment that a child has reached a plateau beyond which they cannot seem to move him/her. In the experience of one of the authors this appears to be a January phenomenon, since it is most often heard around that time of year. Incidentally, only the low-performance students seem to reach these plateaus. We suspect that the child has not reached a plateau but rather that the pace of the school curriculum is such that the assigned tasks have outdistanced the student's entering behavior. In many of these cases the mismatch between assigned tasks and entering behaviors is considerable, especially when the prerequisite behaviors have been included in the curriculum at a much lower grade level.

To avoid the problem of not being able to help students learn or progress beyond a particular plateau, we see a pragmatic need for the same information that is theoretically needed. Most of the information that is needed will be at the transfer level of specificity but some information from the other approaches can also be useful.

Once the need for information is recognized, the next pragmatic consideration involves how much information can be effectively used. Earlier we pointed out that people seem to be "satisficers" in that they like to deal with a minimum amount of information when making decisions. We also pointed out that people are apparently able to cope with only about 7 ± 2 bits of information at a time. This suggests that the pragmatic considerations include keeping the amount of information within these manageable limits. This can be done in three ways. One is to have a strategy for reducing the task into a smaller number of units. By doing this we can strip away many peripheral issues while we deal with the primary issue. A second way is to have a strategy that also relates the task requirements to the student information needed. The third way is to reduce the information about the student down to the most relevant data. Irrelevant information should also be discarded, but the strategy relating the task and the information should help do this. Less relevant information can be included depending on how much concern there is for maximizing the utility of the decision and how much information you feel you can cope with.

We believe that Gagné's model of learning provides a useful conceptualization for relating the task and information needs in the cognitive domain. We hope that we have in various ways made clear the relationship between the various domains. These four domains should provide an integrated view of the various tasks and the types of information one would need.

This leads us to the last pragmatic issue we will raise. The time of teachers and students is limited and needs to be used carefully. Many teachers, even if they were aware of the information needed, would argue that they do not have the time to gather it. Possibly if they would devote more time to analyzing their students' entering behavior, an equal or greater amount of time would be saved in other instructional activities with an increased likelihood of success. To decide how much time should be devoted to assessing entering behavior we need to consider both the time spent on unproductive activities and the techniques used to gather the data.

Unproductive activities may be teaching students material they have already mastered and teaching them at a level for which they are not prepared. The latter will be more evident than the former. If an assessment procedure takes less time than the unproductive activities, assessment should be the more desirable alternative. The procedures used may, however, place too great a demand on the teacher's time. If this cannot be overcome then the most practical solution may be to settle for a lower level of student productivity. By focusing on the issue of productive learning time and available teacher time, the teacher can achieve a more effective balance than is often the case in many classrooms. While we have no data to support our idea, it seems reasonable to assume that those teachers who initially do the poorest job of assessing entering behavior subject their students to larger amounts of unproductive learning time because of mismatches of entering behavior and assigned tasks. To keep up with the pace required by the school curriculum, the teacher is forced to move to new tasks and to fill the gap between the new tasks and the child's entering behavior with greater amounts of instructional time. This pressure is then likely to make the teacher devote even less time to assessing entering behaviors.

When due consideration is given to which information is useful, how much information can be managed, and how it can be gathered within the time constraints of the classroom, there are some serious restrictions on what might be done solely from an idealistic perspective. What seems needed is not a theoretically complete evaluation of entering behaviors, but rather a pragmatic screening process to determine the most relevant entering behaviors. The screening process, to be effective, should sample a student's response capabilities so that valid predictions can be made about the student's likelihood of achieving a broad set of tasks as well as specific tasks.

1. What are the three pragmatic considerations related to developing an assessment of entering behavior? What impact should they have on the process as it is applied to the classroom?

GENERAL PRINCIPLES GUIDING ASSESSMENT

In the process of assessing entering behavior, a clear focus on the function of the assessment is necessary if one is to avoid getting lost in the details of implementation. We believe three general principles should guide the assessment process if it is to remain consistent with a teacher's broader educational goals and still be useful in making specific instructional decisions.

Assess in a broad context

The assessment of entering behavior should be done in terms of all four domains of learning and how they interact with each other and fit into the individual's broad, life-span development. To assess too narrowly may cause us to lose sight of the fact that classroom instruction is not an end but merely a means to a broad education which is necessary if one is to cope with living in our modern society. This requires that a student have specific cognitive capabilities and a positive attitude toward using them if we expect transfer of these capabilities to nonschool situations. Also, if we expect a student to sharpen these skills later in life, the student must possess the appropriate mathemagenic behaviors to do so. Without a broad framework within which to view the function of assessing entering behavior, we are likely to overlook the significant aspects of what we should be assessing and instead focus entirely on behaviors useful in the classroom but having only limited utility beyond the demands of the classroom.

Assess systematically

Within the broad framework of the individual's unique life-span development we should systematically assess those aspects that the framework helps us to identify. Without a systematic orientation toward the process, we are likely to be unduly biased by certain data and overlook other data in reference to our decisions. This not only implies that we need to be aware of all the data that are needed for a comprehensive evaluation, but it also implies that the data need to be gathered systematically from all the available sources.

Assess efficiently

By being systematic, attention is called to getting all of the needed data from all the available sources. To gather and effectively make use of all the data we must use efficient techniques. The techniques must be not only efficient in terms of time and available resources but also compatible with the total instructional process and the learner's long-term development.

Efficiency in assessing entering behaviors is probably something that develops over time as one becomes more proficient with all of the interrelated tasks of teaching. Since a teacher sees students for a great many hours engaged in a wide variety of tasks, student information is readily available; and if a teacher knows what to look for, assessment of entering behavior can become to a large extent a matter of observation and awareness rather than a separate process. Done in this manner the assessment of entering behaviors requires very little time. Also, as teachers become more familiar with the learning tasks, they should be able to pinpoint key behaviors in order to reduce the amount of micro-level assessment that needs to be done to appropriately match the student with instruction.

2. What are the three general principles that should guide the assessment of entering behaviors? How would they apply to the instructional process?

SPECIFIC PROCESS QUESTIONS

To assess a learner's entering behavior we not only need a frame of reference and some general guidelines but also need to make specific decisions about the following four issues:

1. What data are needed?
2. Where can data be obtained?

3. How can data be obtained?
4. How should data be interpreted?

The four specific questions about assessing a student's entering behavior should be made in terms of all four broad domains of learning. The situation is diagramed in Figure 15–2.

What data are needed?

From the past discussion it will hardly come as a surprise when we state that the two main types of data needed are behaviors and products of behaviors. These types can be subdivided according to the four domains of learning and even further into subtypes within the domains. It is also possible to divide the two main types of data, behaviors and products of behavior, according to a more traditional framework. Behavioral data can be subdivided into observations and reports; and the products of behavior can be subdivided on the basis of standardized test results, classroom products of behavior, and miscellaneous products of behavior.

We will use both classification schemes. The first one is more relevant to the narrower definition of entering behavior and a micro-level assessment. The second scheme is more useful in a macro-level assessment approach and more related to present-day practices. We will first discuss the data needed in terms of the first classification scheme and then from the second classification scheme.

From the first general principle of keeping the assessment process broad in scope, and from the assessment outline in Figure 15–2, it is obvious that data from all four domains of learning will be needed. For the cognitive domain we need information about the three important types of learning outcomes: memorization, concept learning, and rule learning. You should recall that memorization requires recognition or recall of previously acquired information. The conditions under which it needs to be assessed have been given previously. Concept learning requires data indicating that the student can classify previously unencountered instances of the concept. For rule learning the student must *demonstrate* the general rule by applying it in specific situations that have not been encountered previously.

In the motor domain we need a performance that demonstrates the attainment of a particular capability or a specific unit of it that may be necessary for developing new motor skills. Again, the conditions of performance are also part of the data needed.

FIGURE 15–2
Outline of decision strategy for assessing entering behavior

	Learning domain issue			
Decision issue	*Cognitive skills*	*Motor skills*	*Affective state*	*Mathemagenic skills*
1. What data are needed?				
2. Where can data be obtained?				
3. How can data be obtained?				
4. How should data be interpreted?				

Data related to the affective domain are generally restricted to approach and avoidance tendencies of some type occurring under free-choice conditions. This may be difficult to obtain at times because of the requirement of free choice. There are many subtle contingencies operating that may affect approach and avoidance tendencies, and therefore these contingencies, or the possibility of them, also become some of the data needed since they are the conditions under which the behavior occurs.

Mathemagenic data are difficult to identify with any assurance since we know so little about them at this point. We will simply group them as any behaviors related to good work/study habits.

Data classified and labeled according to the four domains of learning are not likely to be found in schools today. This analytic approach is beginning to appear more often, but usually curricular materials are analyzed in a traditional framework according to topics. Usually these topics can easily be reclassified according to the various types of learning. The point is, however, that currently *you* will probably have to do the reclassification task in order to develop the data needed for a micro-level assessment.

Since much of the data normally found about students are in a more traditional form, we also need to consider data needs in the second framework mentioned earlier. These data will serve as a macro-level assessment data.

As we have pointed out, one type of data will be direct observations of behavior; by this we mean direct observations made personally by the teacher in the classroom or some other setting. We refer to observations made by others as reports of behaviors and we discuss these below. Some observations will be planned and more or less structured, while others will be unplanned due to the dynamic nature of the classroom. Regardless of the amount of planning or structure involved, they will be by far the largest amount of data you will have available and need to cope with.

Before going any further we wish to call your attention again to the distinction between observations and inferences and generalizations. It is relatively easy to transform observations into inferences and generalizations. Untrained observers often transform the observations into inferences with the result that the data they then work from are inferences and not observations. We believe this is a serious error. First of all, the data are one step removed from the learner and, second, they somehow distort the actual facts. How much of a distortion they may be is difficult to say, but Tversky and Kahneman (1971) have pointed out some of the typical distortions that are made, as we noted in Chapter 6. In short, the inferences transform the data from what the learner did into what the observer *thinks* the learner did or why it was done. The point we wish to make clear is that the data should be the observations and not the inferences one leaps to. The same is true of generalizations, except in this case the distortion is likely to be in the direction of an overgeneralization or magnification of a skill or skill deficit.

The second type of behavioral data commonly found in schools is reports of behavior. We have separated these from direct observations of behavior because they are second-hand behavioral data and often are more inferences and generalizations than actual reports of observations. The latter are seldom encountered, but with the Freedom-of-Information Law, which has made most records available to the parents or guardians of students, there may be more objective reports of observations and less inferential data available in the future. The reports of behavior may also be oral instead of written, and objective reporting may be mixed with a great deal of inferential information.

As we mentioned, products of behavior can be divided into standardized test results, classroom products, and miscellaneous products. We have used these divisions because each category comes from a different source and involves somewhat different interpretation problems. The second category, classroom products of behavior, is by far the most common and no doubt the most familiar to you. Included are classroom test papers, quizzes, work sheets, homework pages, projects, and other tangible products produced by the learner. We mention them here only briefly but this should not obscure their importance as data for assessing entering behavior. Next to direct observations they are the most valuable source for micro-level assessment.

Standardized test results are also a product of behavior that is common in schools. Presently, standardized tests come in a wide variety. They measure intelligence, reading achievement, language development, auditory perception, and personality characteristics, to name a few. The data are reported in many ways but probably all of those commonly found in schools report a numerical score or a series of subscores. Some of the tests measure very broad characteristics while others measure specific capabilities. They also differ as to whether they are criterion- or norm-referenced, the latter being more frequent. In a few cases a test is designed to be used as both a norm-referenced and a criterion-referenced test. We shall become more explicit about the actual data, or scores that are reported on the basis of the test results, when we consider the question of how to interpret data. For now it is probably sufficient to simply call your attention to this type of data.

The third type of products of behavior we have labeled *miscellaneous* to reflect the wide range of products a student may produce. Not only will the products vary widely, but so will the contexts in which they are produced. These may be craft articles produced at home or in some other setting. They may be stories or paintings. This category is limited only by the range of human abilities found in students. Although broad, the category may have limited utility in assessing entering behavior. Often these products are only tangentially related to the classroom effort or are an extension beyond what one tries to accomplish in the classroom. As such, these products seldom provide data specific enough for a micro-level assessment. These data may add, however, breadth to a macro-level assessment, especially in the affective domain. It is often useful to know of some particular interest a student may have and how proficient he/she may be in that area.

> 3. What are the two main types and five traditional categories of data? How do the two classification systems relate to each other?

Where can data be obtained?

Most of the data you will need for a micro-level assessment of entering behaviors can be obtained in the classroom. Because the domain and learning-level data are likely to be closely associated with the school curriculum and displayed by the student in the classroom, they may not be found outside of that context. Therefore, the observations of domain and learning-level data must be obtained in the classroom. We wish to qualify our use of the word *classroom,* however, to include any instructional setting in which the teacher is able to directly observe the learners. This would include not

FIGURE 15–3
The classroom sometimes extends beyond the regular class area

only the confines of the regular classroom area but also the recreation areas, auditoriums, cafeterias, and other school areas as well as any field trip environments (Figure 15–3). In this sense we use the term *classroom* in its broadest meaning.

As defined, classroom products of behavior are obtained in the classroom as a normal result of assigning tasks to students. The task may be a part of the current instructional objectives and as such may be used to measure progress toward that end. The data can also be viewed as indicating the presence or absence of entering behaviors for an instructional objective to be introduced later. These classroom products of behavior can be obtained by administering tasks specifically designed to assess entering behaviors before an instructional strategy is initiated. Most commonly this is done by administering a low-level review test designed to measure specific behaviors necessary for attainment of the new task.

Standardized test results, reports of behavior, and miscellaneous products of behavior may be obtained from a variety of sources. Most schools maintain several sets of records pertaining to each student. There are academic records, health records, psychological records, and possibly others, depending on the school's policies. Also depending on the policies of the particular school, these records may be stored in a single place or in a variety of places. In the past there have been very few restrictions to limit a teacher's access to this material unless it was considered by the school to be confidential material pertaining to the student or the student's family. It is more likely that classroom teachers imposed restrictions on themselves which resulted in not inspecting the available data. Teachers and college students often express the opinion that they do not believe it is appropriate to inspect a child's records until after they have had an opportunity to interact with the child for a considerable period of time. This attitude may be justified if the person inspecting the material cannot distinguish among observations, inferences, and generalizations. If an individual can make these distinctions then it should be possible to view the data with some objectivity and sort out the useful information from that which may lead us astray.

To contend that the information found in these sources is biased and that inspecting these data prematurely may bias one's view of a child in an unrealistic manner, one would have to assume that one's colleagues are incompetent to make accurate observations and form reasonable inferences. The individual is also expressing a lack of competence to accurately interpret data in an objective manner. With an understanding of some simple interpretation rules we contend that a teacher should inspect these data early in the planning phase. We would caution, however, that the data should be used as macro-level assessment data for making tentative decisions. From that point on a teacher should adopt an objective framework for observing the child that is based on the classroom objectives and is, as much as possible, criterion-referenced. In this way comparative judgments can be minimized. This is probably the basis for teachers' objections to inspecting the data earlier.

In addition to the formal records, many individuals in a school have been in contact with a child. Going to some of these sources may be useful in individual cases if one uses a directed approach. It is as much a matter of the strategy used to obtain the information as it is the source of the information that will determine the utility of the data obtained.

While we advocate a careful look at student information, a note of caution is in order. Recent legislation and court cases have more clearly defined how a teacher may use this information. Generally, sound educational use of the information to enhance a student's progress is not objected to, but other uses of the information may result in a lawsuit. Professional journals and school administrators should be consulted for up-to-date guidelines.

How can data be obtained?

Starting with the standardized test scores and reports of behavior, most data can be obtained by inspecting the student's records or by talking with others who have had contact with the student. With the written records it is simply a matter of locating and reading them. With oral reports there is some flexibility in the data that may be obtained depending on the techniques used. Having a clear idea of the data needed and the decisions to be made will guide you in probing for details. General questions are likely to elicit general responses, whereas specific questions are more likely to yield information about specific entering behaviors. It is not likely that you will need to solicit reports of behavior on all of your students in any great detail, but for an occasional child it may be a useful technique. Our suggestion is to pursue the assessment as close to a micro-level assessment as possible. At this level you will obtain more useful data and you may also avoid getting inferences and generalizations from the person giving the report.

Miscellaneous products of behavior are probably seldom, if ever, solicited but usually appear spontaneously from the student or others who know the student. One instance in which products are solicited is "show and tell" time. Here the teacher is making it possible for the student to display items without making it a requirement to do so.

Classroom products of behavior are normally collected through the routine assignments given to students, so not collecting these assignments after they are given would result in a loss of data. Even after the data are collected they need to be inspected if they are to be useful. If the product contains any errors the inspection should be at the micro-level of assessment. In Chapter 17 we will cover in greater detail a strategy for analyzing student responses; it can be used for assessing entering behavior as well as for making decisions about more immediate responses to students. Therefore, we will not pursue the topic any further at this time.

Direct observations of behavior are probably the main source of data and by far the most useful if done appropriately. Done inappropriately, they can be almost useless. The main factor determining the usefulness of the observational data is the orientation and extent to which they are done systematically. Since psychologists often use observations of behavior as a means of gathering data, workable procedures have been developed to provide objective data.

One aspect of observations is that the observer needs to have a clear definition of the behaviors to be observed. In the case of entering behaviors on the micro level, this means a clear definition of the behaviors within each of the domains of learning and the various subtypes as well as the conditions under which they need to be observed. Another aspect of normal observation is that data are often collected in terms of some time frame to determine the frequency of the behavior. Knowing how often a behavior occurs or the time patterns of a behavior can sometimes be helpful.

A common observational strategy used in behavior modification studies is to look for those stimuli in the environment that seem to precede certain behaviors and also for the consequences of the behaviors. This strategy is particularly useful when affective or mathemagenic behaviors are the target of attention. Since these have an impact on cognitive behaviors, this strategy can provide adjunct information to our observations of behavior in the cognitive domain.

The preceding stimuli, sometimes referred to as the *antecedent events,* immediately precede the behavior. Likewise, the *consequence* is the event immediately following the behavior. In this observational framework, Antecedent (A)–Behavior (B)–Consequence (C) form a sequence of interactions between the person being observed and the people and objects serving as functional stimuli. This A-B-C approach combines what appear to be principles of respondent conditioning and operant conditioning into one framework. In most situations the antecedent functions as a conditioned stimulus. The behavior itself then operates on the environment to bring about the consequence.

When particular behaviors are the focus of a teacher's goals, they are referred to as *target behaviors.* Usually the intention is to either increase or decrease the occurrence of the target behavior or have another behavior develop as a substitute response to the antecedent. This observational strategy provides the framework to analyze the ongoing interactions for any patterns that keep unwanted behaviors from occurring or may provide clues as to how an intervention may be used.

Another form of observation takes place during discussion periods or an interview. In this situation the teacher may be less interested in micro-level cognitive entering behaviors and more interested in the affective and mathemagenic domains. The interview may also provide a broad view of the student's goals against which to interpret some specific entering behavior information.

The key to any method of gathering information is to do it systematically and with a clear focus on the function of the assessment process (Figure 15–4). Odd bits of

FIGURE 15–4
The key to data collection is to have a clear focus on the purpose

information, while they may be interesting, are usually of little value unless they can be placed in some integrated pattern.

A strategy used in some published programs that have a series of integrated steps is to use a screening test to first establish the general capabilities and then to follow this with tests of the specific skills developed in the program. Too few programs have this type of macro-level assessment of entering behavior as an integral part. By using this strategy it is possible to determine in a few minutes a child's level of functioning in several skill areas and the follow-up micro-level assessment that will yield the most useful information for decisions.

A recent reading test, the Sipay Word Analysis Test (SWAT) (1971), does this for word analysis skills in reading, independent of any particular reading program. It is anticipated that more tests of this type will be produced in the future as researchers specify more clearly the learning skills necessary to accomplish various tasks. One interesting aspect of the SWAT is that it can be interpreted as assessing in both the cognitive and mathemagenic domains simultaneously. It assesses in the cognitive domain by identifying those reading skills acquired and necessary for moving to higher-level tasks. In the sense that reading is a behavior used for learning in many areas, it can be considered a powerful mathemagenic behavior and the SWAT results an indication of which mathemagenic skills are available for use in learning the content in other subject areas. For example, does the student have the reading skills needed to cope with materials that could possibly be assigned as part of the social studies instruction?

4. What is the main technique used to gather information for each of the five traditional classes of information?

How should data be interpreted?

The process of interpreting information is, beyond a doubt, one of the most critical areas in assessing entering behaviors. While we can make errors in observing behavior, it is more likely that we will make errors in interpreting our observations. Here we are concerned primarily with the interpretation process and therefore, for the most part, we will assume that the observations have been done appropriately.

The five main sources of information: (1) standardized test scores, (2) classroom products of behavior, (3) other products of behavior, (4) reports from others, and (5) personal observations of behavior, all have somewhat unique interpretation problems. Our presentation has been subdivided on the basis of the five main sources so as to point out the errors unique to each source and some control measures you should consider when interpreting information from that source.

Standardized test scores. While standardized test scores may not provide the most useful data, they are commonly encountered. Depending on the purpose for which they were designed, the scores are reported in a variety of ways. One general way describes the distribution of scores and another describes the accuracy of the measurements. Most of the better tests have been given to a relatively large sample of the population and individual scores are reported in relation to the results obtained from the sample. It is assumed, more or less accurately, that this sample is representative of the larger population. On this basis they are assumed to represent a norm for the population.

To gain a fuller understanding of the scores reported for students, it is advisable to obtain a copy of the technical manual pertaining to the test. At times it may also be advisable to consult a copy of Buros's *Mental Measurement Yearbook* which is periodically updated and read the comments that various reviewers have made in reference to the test. Whereas the technical manual is put out by those selling the test, Buros reviews the research concerning the reliability and validity of the test as well as a description of its general characteristics and therefore is more likely to point out weaknesses.

For the better tests the manual will describe the test, what it is intended to measure, and how it was constructed. The manual will also include estimates of the reliability and validity of the test and how these measures were obtained. It will also give tables of normative data that were collected and describe the sample of individuals from which this information was gathered. For this sample they also normally provide the mean, the standard deviation, and the standard error of measurement. Some tests provide the standard error of measurement as a confidence interval. If you do not have sufficient knowledge of statistics, some of this information may have little meaning. Interspersed in the manual will usually be enough verbal statements so you can at least gain some understanding of the intent and strengths of the test. As we mentioned, the manual may not point out weaknesses except in trying to explain them away.

In addition to the technical data the manual is also likely to provide some information about the interpretation and use of test results. Every reputable test also provides a set of instructions for administering the test. These directions are the standard conditions under which the test is to be given if one wishes to meaningfully use the normative data provided in the manual. The term *standardized test* refers to the standardized conditions under which the test is to be given. Deviation from these conditions may change the results you will get in ways that you may not notice or suspect. Comparing the normative data with results obtained from nonstandardized conditions may lead to some rather surprising (and erroneous) conclusions.

Depending on the particular test, the manual may have tables to convert raw scores into a standard score, z score, or T score. These are all based on the standard deviation and should be explained in the manual. Tables may also be provided to convert raw scores into percentiles or stanine scores.

Using a different reference point for comparison, scores are also reported as *grade-level ratings.* Instead of a comparison based solely on the reference group, grade-level ratings anchor the reference group to the normal school curriculum so that the individual's performance level can be compared with the average performance level at various grade levels (Figure 15–5). When a grade-level rating of 6.0 is reported for an individual, it indicates a performance level equivalent to that of the average performance level found for students at the beginning of sixth grade. The first number in the score indicates grade level and the decimal fraction indicates roughly the month during that grade level. Due to the procedures used in the construction of most achievement tests, tests usually do not sample the curriculum content evenly (Levine, 1976) and therefore are of limited value as a test of entering behavior. They do, however, provide a broad estimate of skills that may be useful during the planning stage or when a new child enters the classroom during the school year. Given the mobility of the American population, the latter is a common occurrence, probably more so in some school districts than in others and for some children than for others. One author of this text encountered an 11-year-old girl who had attended at least 16 different schools! In addition, at least one year was missing from her records, so the total may have been even more than 16. She had been in seven first-grade classes and during the year she had been in four different fifth grades. By September she had moved again!

The interpretation of the various tests should first of all determine whether the test is a valid measuring instrument for the type of decision to be made. As we pointed out earlier, if we are trying to decide whether a desk will fit through a doorway, weighing it is not a valid measurement. Next, we should ask if the measuring instrument is reliable. Placing our hands on either side of the desk and then walking over to

FIGURE 15–5
Grade ratings are sometimes reported

Name Mary Patrick Johnson Sex: M (F)
Date 6/6/x9 Birth Date 3/15/x0 Age 9-3
School Greenwood Elementary Grade 4
Referred by A. Smith Examiner P. Sanchez

Test Results:	Raw Score	Grade Rating	Standard Score	Percentile
Reading	54	3.8	94	34
Spelling	42	5.4	109	73
Arithmetic	30	3.9	99	47

Source: Wide Range Achievement Test (WRAT). Reprinted with permission of Jastak Assessment Systems.

the doorway is certainly not as reliable as using a standard ruler. With the ruler we are likely to get more agreement from one time to the next and from one person to another.

When evaluating the validity and reliability of a measuring instrument, one should remember that they are determined in various ways and may be misleading. If the test reports *predictive* validity, one should read carefully what the test is able to predict and how well it does that. Many times the predictive validity of the test is not given, but instead *face validity* is discussed. Here the issue is: Does the test indeed measure what it claims to measure? There is no objective means of determining face validity and therefore subjective judgments or logical arguments are given to support the face validity of the measuring instrument. If *content validity* is presented, it should be interpreted in terms of how well the test also samples the content of classroom instruction. If the test is related to a specific set of instructional materials that are being used, the content validity may be very high. On a standardized achievement test intended to be used on a nationwide basis, the content validity may be quite low for certain topics and high for others. When *construct validity* is reported in relation to some hypothetical entity such as intelligence or creativity, it is usually a measure of how well that test agrees with some other generally accepted test of the same hypothetical construct. Whether either test actually measures what it purportedly measures is often an open question.

A basic requirement for a test to be valid is that it be a reliable measuring instrument. If the alternate-forms or splithalf reliability estimates for the test are low, then we should probably not rely on the test results to provide any meaningful data. If these measures of reliability are high, then we should consider the test-retest reliability estimates. If these are high then the test is probably measuring characteristics that are fairly stable over extended periods of time. This indicates that these entering behaviors can more reliably be counted on to be available in future situations. When test-retest reliability is lower, this assumption cannot be made.

If the validity and reliability are satisfactory, we begin to determine what other meaning the reported scores may have in relation to the decisions we must make. Here, as we noted earlier, the standards used to derive the scores should be valid for the type of decision we need to make. Most norm-referenced tests should be interpreted with a clear understanding of who is represented in the reference group from which the norm was derived. Sometimes the reference group is considerably different than our classroom population, which would reduce the validity of any comparison between the two groups.

The results can also be interpreted in terms of comparisons between children within the classroom, but in this case the standard error of measurement and/or confidence intervals need to be considered. If the standard error of measurement is large, it may be that one can make very few distinctions between children or groups of children with any high degree of confidence. In these cases only the very high scores can be assumed to reflect any real difference from the very low scores. In between these extremes, interpretation becomes a large gray area in which the standard error of measurement is large or unknown.

If one attempts to use standardized test scores to detect differences in performance over time it is also very important to consider the standard error of measurement since, with any particular individual, any gains noted may be due to normal variation in our measurements.

Many standardized tests do not measure school-related achievement but rather general skills used to measure psychological constructs such as intelligence, creativity, personality, and perceptual skills, to name a few of the many. The predictive validity of these tests needs to be considered very carefully in relation to the decisions we need to make. For the very broadest decisions about class placement they may offer useful data. For some children this is the only precise data on which to make these decisions. Occasionally there is some legal requirement for using this type of data in making certain decisions, such as special class placement or participation in a remedial program. Data of this broad nature should be interpreted with a great deal of caution. In terms of micro-level decisions they are often too broad to be a useful means of providing any meaningful data about entering behaviors.

Another class of standardized tests is diagnostic tests. These are intended not so much to sample behaviors broadly as most achievement tests do, but rather as criterion-referenced tests. An example of a useful test in this category is the Stanford Diagnostic Arithmetic Test. This is actually a norm-referenced *and* a criterion-referenced test. Scores can be computed on several subtests and the total test, and compared with norms provided in the manual. The tables allow one to report the student's scores in terms of grade level or stanines. This gives an indication, therefore, of where in the general curriculum a child may be ready to enter. It also gives us an indication of how this child compares with other children at a particular grade level in terms of grouping.

One of the most useful instructional aids provided with the Stanford Diagnostic Arithmetic Test is an analysis of the skills measured by the test. The test appears to systematically assess these skills, and success on one task level would appear to be fairly good evidence that the learner has the necessary entering behaviors for the subsequent tasks in that skill area. It certainly is one of the more useful standardized tests known to the authors to get a quick, systematic estimate of a wide range of a child's arithmetic skills for use in making specific instructional decisions.

Additionally, some standardized, norm-referenced tests measure mathemagenic skills like reading and other self-management study/learning skills. Although we are still inept at identifying these skills exactly, they are roughly measured by some standardized norm-referenced tests. These mathemagenic skills are necessary for or at least facilitate learning in a number of subjects. Therefore, students who are proficient with these mathemagenic skills learn more, and quicker, than less proficient students and this will be reflected in higher test scores. Given the instructional procedures of the average school, these differences in mathemagenic skills may account for the wide differences in achievement scores following group instruction.

Classroom products of behavior. In addition to the results of standardized tests there are other products of behavior that are potentially useful. Some of these are classroom test results, seat work, special projects, and other tangible products of the student's effort.

The products produced in the classroom may give direct evidence of a student's entering behavior in a specific topic area or level of learning. The time lapse between when the product was produced and when the student starts the related task must be considered. It is quite possible that at the time the product was produced, the student was capable of performing the behavior but due to forgetting is not presently capable of doing so.

In addition to forgetting we also have to consider that additional instruction may have been given. In this case our data may be out of date and we would underestimate the student's level. Within certain limits, however, we would expect only a certain amount of increase (or decrease) within a known time span, so the old information would at least provide a rough guide.

Probably the most important means of assessing entering behavior in the classroom is a child's performance in class on tests and seat work. While a teacher has to make some judgments about levels of entering behavior during the planning phase of instruction, by far most judgments are made during the implementation phase. The judgments referred to are usually about whether or not a child is ready to move to the next task. At times these are made on the basis of the average of the performance levels of the students in a group. This may make sense in terms of group instruction, but in terms of individual differences it does not. If it is clear that some students have not mastered the task at all or have mastered it with a low level of facility, then it is a mistake to move them ahead. In other words, it is a mistake to overlook or ignore differences in levels of entering behavior when deciding to move a particular child ahead. It is also a mistake to overlook data about individual differences in the way students learn. For some students this information may be helpful for making decisions about a wide spectrum of tasks.

In deciding to move a child to the next task we may use either a topical or learning level approach to defining the tasks. Since most teachers will be following a somewhat structured program based on a topical type of task analysis, it makes more sense to use assessment categories consistent with the program. This is especially true when the students appear to be progressing satisfactorily. If one or more students are not progressing satisfactorily, we believe that shifting to a learning level approach in assessing their entering behavior has much merit. Using this type of assessment for decisions about how to respond to the student in terms of the topic or level of learning being taught at the time will be covered in a later chapter. Our main concern at this point is with decisions to move the child to another task.

Using a learning-level type of task analysis would allow you to view the task from a perspective of the relationship between the task and the student's level of entering behavior. Analyzed this way, the task could be divided into different, smaller learning units. Developing appropriate behavioral objectives for these smaller units would then allow you to assess the student's entering behavior on a micro level. By identifying the entering behavior in this way, you could then decide which behaviors are lacking and this would help you decide which learning task should be presented next. It may be possible that the assessment of entering behavior will indicate that you should move to a much lower level of learning than one would suspect on the basis of a topical analysis. The learning level approach to assessment may also point out the need to move to other topic areas that one might not suspect as causing the problem. In any event, the micro-level assessment would aid in making micro-level decisions about when, and which remedial instruction is needed and when the original topic should be returned to.

Miscellaneous products of behavior. Some of the products of behavior may not be directly related to the classroom but may give us an estimate of interest areas

FIGURE 15–6
Some products of behavior may give an indication of interest areas

or achievement levels in a nonacademic setting (Figure 15–6). These products may also provide a measure of motivational level in terms of nonacademic tasks. The child who performs poorly and only with much external motivation may, away from school, perform well at other tasks with little or no need for reminders or threats. This type of pattern should alert us to the fact that in terms of the affective domain the school has seriously failed. It may also give us a means of using the out-of-school positive attitudes to help develop some positive feelings toward school tasks and staff.

Reports from others. One general statement we can make about human behavior is that the best predictor of a person's future behavior is his/her past behavior. The best source of additional data in the schools is the student's past teacher(s). You may find these data either in their written comments in the child's official folder or through personal contact with the teachers. At times teachers will argue that they do not like to hear the opinions of past teachers but wish to form their own opinion of the child. They believe that the past teachers' personal biases may be transmitted to them by way of their comments and thereby bias their own observations of the child. There is no doubt that this is possible. On the other hand, by taking this position the teacher is ignoring a large amount of information about past patterns of behavior that cannot be acquired from any other source. While the data are apt to be biased, it is also true that given several observers, including the teacher who objects to using biased data, there usually will be an overwhelming amount of agreement among observations. This will be particularly true when the data you are dealing with are specific behaviors rather than inferences. Sorting out what is behavior or products of behavior, as opposed to inferences based on behavior, is the skill you need in order to use this data source effectively.

A behavior, as we have stated earlier, is a specific act. A description of behavior would let you imagine the exact action. An inference is a statement of an internal process, state, or propensity of the person. By distinguishing between behaviors and inferences, you can ferret out the unbiased data the teacher is able to supply in terms of actual behaviors and keep this separate from the inferences based on the teacher's experiences with a child (i.e., "volunteers frequently" versus "eager to participate"). If the teacher's inferences seem warranted on the basis of the data, then they move you ahead quickly to certain generalized aspects of the child. This approach will not eliminate all biases because you may interpret the data in the same biased way that the past teacher did. This approach, however, will help you to ask questions about behaviors rather than make inferences and also recognize which you are receiving. It will also help you spot some biases the past teacher may have had and thereby prevent you from being influenced by them. This information could be useful in future contacts with that teacher, since it will be easier for you to interpret that teacher's remarks more accurately.

Another reason for using data from previous teachers is that by tapping this source of information you gather data in all four of the main learning domains. In most instances this will be your only source of information prior to the instructional phase about the affective and mathemagenic domains. During the implementation phase of instruction you will have many chances to observe behaviors and gather more information in these two learning domains as well as the cognitive and motor skills domains.

Personal observations of behavior. Most personal observations will be made in the classroom. There are, in addition to products of behavior, actual behaviors occurring in class. In a great many instances we are interested only moderately in the actual behaviors such as writing, drawing, or some other performance that results in the production of a tangible product. In other instances we are not expecting a tangible product and must rely on the act itself to give us an indication of entering behavior.

One of the most useful observations of behavior is a student's attending behaviors over short periods of time. Often this is referred to as a student's *attention span.* Teachers usually interpret short periods of attention to a task as an indication of a short attention span. The inference is based on the belief that the attention span is a somewhat fixed attribute of the child. From this perspective a teacher tries to design tasks of a suitable length to match the supposed attention span. This approach overlooks the research data indicating that attending behaviors are more likely to be dependent on the match between the student's level of entering behavior and the stimulus situation. Even infants less than six months old will attend to a single stimulus (their hand) for periods of up to half an hour (Wolff, 1965). It is also known that the stimulus that will hold attention is constantly changing as cognitive development progresses (Fantz, 1958). Therefore, what may not hold attention for very long periods at one time may do so at another time.

One factor that helps to hold attention is the level of novelty associated with a specific stimulus. A stimulus that is too novel will be ignored or hold attention for only short periods of time. As a person gains some familiarity with a stimulus, the novelty is reduced and the length of attending behaviors tends to increase. However, beyond a certain point the attending behaviors begin to decrease. In this case what occurs can be thought of as analogous to boredom. For example, sections of this text may vary in holding your attention. The variation is to a large extent due to your level of entering behavior as you read the text. As we present novel ideas in a context that is meaningful and understandable to you, you are likely to maintain your attention to the text. When we present ideas you find difficult to understand, we are probably presenting the material too rapidly for you or in a context that is considerably different from what you are familiar with. At the other extreme if the material becomes too repetitious, it has too little novelty (Figure 15–7). Under either of these conditions you are more likely to begin looking at your watch, getting up for snacks, being distracted by sounds and motions around you, or worse yet, yawning and falling asleep.

This same phenomenon is apparent when we become bored and put aside some difficult reading but then get glued to the late movie and then the late-late movie and be wide awake the entire time and then feel drowsy soon after the television is turned off. The problem is that the heavy reading is too novel while the movies are neither too novel nor too familiar and therefore not boring. There is just sufficient novelty present to hold our attention.

In assessing entering behavior we can use this simple principle to make decisions about when to move a child ahead. If the learner's interest is being held by a topic, we can assume we have a good match between entering behaviors and the assigned task. If interest is short we need to ask ourselves if the task is too difficult or too easy. To determine this, an assessment more related to the cognitive domain is needed. The attention span is only an indicator of a match or mismatch between student and task.

FIGURE 15–7
If material is too novel or repetitious we lose interest

To pursue the assessment further we may proceed along topical lines, but if this does not indicate either a clear understanding or no understanding of the problem, we may wish to switch to a learning-level type of assessment. This will allow us to break the topical approach down into finer units of entering behaviors and make decisions about what the next learning task should be.

5. For each of the five main types of data, what is the major interpretation problem or set of problems?

IMPLEMENTING A SCREENING PROGRAM

As you start your teaching career you will be faced with a task of considerable proportions. All that you do may not be successful. Also some teacher errors are likely to have a greater impact than others. Unless you are a unique individual you will continue to make errors throughout your career. The errors should, however, become smaller and less frequent. Your primary concerns will be to maintain order in the classroom and achieve a reasonable degree of success in the cognitive and affective domains. These concerns set some priorities on what data may be needed first.

Identifying potential discipline problems

For a teacher to provide the conditions necessary for learning, a certain degree of order must be established in the classroom. Assessment of entering behavior related to establishing this order is best approached from an observational standpoint. Problems can arise either within the cognitive domain if the students do not understand your rules, or within the affective domain if they simply do not want to follow the rules. The first step is to decide which is the case. Students who verbally claim to have forgotten a rule or claim thay did not know the rule may have learned it but chose to ignore it.

Instances that disrupt classroom order should be observed to see which stimuli tend to trigger the disruption and what events immediately follow the disruption. This may help to isolate the response tendencies that exist and may need to be changed. In the analysis of response tendencies you should look for the response tendencies of other students to the disruptive students. Your analysis should not ignore your own responses. In a sense the response tendencies of the other students and yourself are all entering behaviors. The responses of the disruptive student are certainly relevant to the instructional task of changing them. The responses of particular students or yourself may also be relevant. The assumption here is that the student is reacting to a particular stimulus situation with a learned reaction and in some way the response is being reinforced. The task is to identify the stimulus eliciting the response or the reinforcer that results in the subsequent occurrences of the behavior. It may not be possible to remove the stimuli and it may then become necessary to modify the responses you or the other students make that are relevant to the disruptions.

Some problems of control may be anticipated from reports of other teachers. Humans tend to try previously learned behaviors in new situations. Students who have chronically been the most disruptive are likely to continue to perform the disruptive behaviors with a new teacher. They may initially practice a mild form of the behavior and only later practice a more extreme version of it. By looking at the reports of other teachers about the students you will have, you may see some disruptive behaviors described and what tends to elicit them. A conversation with the student's past teachers may be productive. In the conversation more specifics can be gained than are likely to be found in a written report or checklist of behaviors. The conversation should not deteriorate to a complaint session about students but should be maintained at a level at which the topic is disruptive behaviors that you may have to cope with, and the stimuli and consequences preceding and following them. There is a distinct difference between having a gossip session about students and preparing yourself to instruct students. As long as your purpose is the latter and that is evident to the other teacher, you should be able to obtain some reliable and valid data. The data can help you avoid eliciting certain behaviors at least until you are more confident you can cope with them. By knowing what behaviors are likely to occur, you are in a better position to recognize the milder forms of them and not inadvertently reinforce the behaviors. This may act as a deterrent to the more extreme forms. A mild punishment applied to a mild form of disruption may also eliminate the need for stronger punishments later on.

By being aware of certain disruptive behaviors that may occur, incompatible behaviors that are desirable alternatives can be identified and reinforced to circumvent the occurrence of unwanted behavior. This is probably the most productive approach, but often there is not enough early information about the student to plan ahead. It may have to develop as a reactive plan rather than as an anticipatory plan.

Identifying potential motivational problems

Assuming that control in the classroom is reasonably acceptable and any disruptions are mild or infrequent, the next major problem is having students approach and work on tasks at an acceptable level. This involves the affective domain. There may be sufficient intrinsic motivation or positive affect toward the tasks to satisfy most situations. For many students a certain amount of extrinsic motivation may be required. One of the most effective methods of extrinsically motivating students to approach tasks is through contingency management techniques. In this approach a task and a reward for correct task completion are paired together. The task and reward need to be commensurate in size and the reward given only after task completion. One of the tasks in establishing these contingencies is to determine what will act as a reinforcer. Usually any behavior a person likes to engage in will act as a reinforcer for engaging in less desired behaviors. Along with this principle there needs to be the satiation principle, since a person is likely to get tired of doing the same thing for very long no matter how enjoyable it may have been originally. We therefore need not a single behavior but a hierarchy of behaviors arranged in order from most desirable to least desirable. For the same-size task we should trade off more time engaging in the less desirable behaviors than in the more desirable behaviors. It will help to have some idea of which behaviors to offer as the contingency for completing a task successfully, and our conversations with past teachers may help to identify some of these. Another means is to observe what students do when given free time (Figure 15–8). A way that may speed up the process is to have students list in order of preference those things they would like to be able to do during the school day. By making the request in a laissez-faire context, the lists of preferred behaviors are likely to be acceptable and even highly desirable. Students usually take into consideration the social constraints and do not list unacceptable behaviors. Some of the behaviors they list can be undesirable if engaged in at an inappropriate time, but it usually is the timing of the behavior that is objectionable and not the behavior itself. The pairing of tasks and rewards should eliminate the objection to the behavior on the basis of timing.

An advantage of being obvious about gathering students' preferred behaviors is that you present yourself as a teacher concerned about the interests of your students and willing to satisfy their desires without shirking your responsibilities. The lists should also help to establish effective contingencies for productive behaviors early in the year. By doing this you establish a work-oriented environment that is balanced with an orientation toward pursuing socially acceptable interests. Creating this type of atmosphere early should have a positive effect on the further development of intrinsic

FIGURE 15–8
Observation of students during free time can identify preferred activities

motivation for some tasks that previously required extrinsic motivation to get students engaged in the task.

Identifying potential achievement problems

The third area of concern for teachers, but by no means the least of the three, is the matter of student achievement. Every teacher would like to have every student master all of the tasks normally presented in the curriculum. This probably never happens unless a teacher is working with a very limited number of children, has a limited number of objectives, or arbitrarily reduces the number of objectives to suit the student.

Because students are not likely to be very close in overall achievement level, as we mentioned earlier, past achievement scores can act as an initial means of screening the students. This at least gives a tentative starting point for instruction and the precise screening of entering behavior.

Review lessons are a common way of introducing many subjects. If the review sessions can be handled as assigned review tasks, the product may verify or refute the initial estimate of the student's entering behavior. Many teachers overlook this simple means of making adjustments in the initial grouping of children. Without using a tactic such as this the student is likely to be left in an initial, inappropriate group for several weeks before enough data are collected to convince the teacher to regroup. This review task tactic can be applied before the class is actually divided into groups but lists of tentative groups have been formed. For each of the groups a slightly different set of tasks may be administered or the groups may all be given the same tasks. On the basis of the products of behavior, the lists could be revised. This would avoid some of the problems associated with moving students to more advanced or lower-level groups in the middle of an instructional sequence of activities.

If the review tasks are well designed the grouping of students should be quite accurate in roughly matching them with a unit of instruction. A well-designed set of review tasks can also act as a diagnostic tool for making micro-level decisions about how to cope with the individual needs of students during instruction.

A student may have mastered one instructional unit, or at least enough components of the unit, to a level at which it does not seem advantageous to have the student repeat the unit. This does not mean that the student is completely ready for the next unit. The review tasks should systematically measure the component skills to more precisely establish the entering behavior level. Having identified various entering behavior deficits, the teacher may modify the review session to provide relevant practice to meet individual needs. For some the sessions will be not review but instruction in a new skill. After the necessary entering behaviors have been developed in the review sessions, group instruction can *then* begin with a greater certainty of success.

What we are advocating here does not involve extra time and may result in even less time spent overall. When entering behaviors are not sufficiently developed prior to group instruction, those students without the prerequisite behaviors are less likely to master the task without additional help. Without knowing specifically what help is needed, teachers are likely to give remedial efforts that are a modification of the original procedures used to teach the task. The modified procedures are also likely to fail when instruction at a lower level is actually needed. If the lower-level instruction is included in the modified procedures, or belatedly added, the procedures are more likely to be effective but more time-consuming than if the deficiency in entering behavior had been approached directly. While our suggestion may involve more preparatory time, it may save a lot more patch-up time.

Another advantage of the use of review techniques for assessing entering behavior is that you avoid placing the students in a failure situation. The review tasks are likely to be quick, and feedback on performance does not need to be given since in some cases there will be some advantage in withholding it. At this point feedback about failure does not have to be given, since the concern is not necessarily one of moving the students ahead but more of trying to find out the level at which they will most effectively move ahead. Once this is established initial instructional activities can have a greater likelihood of success. At this point only positive feedback may be given. This avoidance of giving negative feedback during the screening process and the greater likelihood of being able to provide positive feedback during instruction can help a teacher reach the goals in the affective domain while preparing to accomplish those in the cognitive domain.

6. What are the three major types of problems that may be identified and partially alleviated by the screening process?

REFINING A SCREENING PROGRAM

Once you have initiated the process of screening students for entering behavior and have collected some data about them, you are in a position to make your initial decisions. These decisions will be on a macro level such as which group to place the child in and what general set of activities and materials to start with. Having gotten this far, your next step is to determine more precisely the student's entering behavior. As an example you may have a child in a social studies group working on the economic productivity of some geographic area. The text may express production in terms of fractions, ratios, millions, and billions. Even though the child has been exposed to these concepts a year or two earlier, he or she may not have mastered them. It is also quite possible that many words in the reading materials or class discussion are referring to concepts the child has not mastered, has only partially mastered, or has learned incorrectly. In the context of the subject matter, the term may refer to a more sophisticated definition of the concept. This lack of concept clarity may result in the student not understanding the meaning of a sentence or section. It may also result in a distorted impression of what was being explained. To pick up these gaps in entering behavior requires a much more sophisticated type of assessment of entering behavior.

To refine the screening process for entering behaviors, the tactics do not need to change to any great extent but the focus does. First of all, the focus needs to shift from grouping decisions to micro-level instructional decisions (Figure 15–9), such as decisions about a particular child and the gaps that may exist between entering behaviors and instructional tasks. Second, the screening process will benefit, we believe, by a shift to a Gagnean type of analysis so that a much finer type of task breakdown is possible. These smaller units can then be more systematically pursued by either appropriate instruction or further assessment to pinpoint the student's level of entering behavior. It is one thing to meet students at their general level of functioning and quite another to meet them at a precise level. At times the former may be adequate, but not always. For those times when a general matching of instruction does not

FIGURE 15–9
Assessing entering behavior on the micro level for instructional decisions

meet the student's needs, you should have not only the desire to meet them on a precise level but also the capability.

For some students this shift in focus will occur when you observe errors in their performance. The shift will be toward identifying lower-level skills that are lacking. For other students signs of boredom or off-task behaviors may indicate that the focus should shift to higher-level skill assessment. In many cases the content of instruction is repetitious so that it does not hold the student's attention. Then assessment in an upward direction is appropriate. This can be difficult because a student may have learned a particular concept or rule but does not have the terminology to comprehend a question about it or express the knowledge in a satisfactory manner.

In many cases you will be faced with errors, off-task behaviors, and signs of boredom. For a student who is considerably below the average level of achievement in all areas, probably the shift in focus should be downward to identify gaps in knowledge or partial knowledge. This is particularly true for children who normally work hard on tasks but have difficulty mastering them. This off-task behavior may be the first sign that you are creating the illusion of the child reaching a plateau.

For other children who make errors, engage in off-task behaviors, and exhibit signs of boredom but show high levels of general achievement in several but not all areas, the task becomes more complicated. The complication arises because we have a discrepancy in performance capabilities and often a long history of low achievement motivation. For a student who fits this description, the shift in focus should probably go both upward and downward. It should go upward because the high achievement in some areas coupled with the low achievement motivation suggests the student is learning the information with a minimum of attention and effort. The lack of attention and effort may be a reaction to the curriculum constantly lagging below the student's entering behavior. The curriculum presents so little new information that only minimal attention and effort are needed to master the instructional tasks. This pattern may develop negative attitudes and poor mathemagenic behaviors. The effects of the negative attitudes and lack of adequate mathemagenic behaviors may combine to cause a learning problem in a specific area, especially when that area requires a great deal of student initiative in the learning process. Examples would be topics requiring a great deal of memorization and independent practice in the early part of mastering the topic. Because the necessary self-directed activities are not engaged in during the early part of instruction, the latter, more meaningful part of the instruction may be well beyond the student's ability to comprehend the material. This puts the student in a vicious cycle. At the beginning of this cycle the problem is usually recognized as motivational. Later on, as the missing skills begin to affect the learning of subsequent skills, the matter of causation becomes cloudy. Is it motivation or an inability to master the task? This is a difficult question to answer because both are involved. Before anyone really attempts to unravel the problem, the student may be so caught up in the cycle that downward assessment of entering behaviors is extremely difficult. A good example of this is found in students at the sixth grade and beyond who do not have a firm understanding of place value (i.e., ones, tens, hundreds, etc.) in our numbering system and the relationship between the various values expressed by the same numeral. These students may be able to work through the mechanics of simple addition and subtraction problems where simple counting will suffice to solve problems, but beyond this level they become overwhelmed.

7. In refining a screening program of entering behaviors, at what point would the focus shift upward and at what point would it shift downward?

SUMMARY

The theoretical needs for information on entering behavior were considered in relation to the limitations of the classroom context that necessitate decisions about what information will be most useful, how much information can be usefully managed, and how the data can be gathered within the limited amount of time available. It was suggested that we need a screening process that assesses broadly, systematically, and efficiently. The screening process should gather data in all four domains of learning.

The main issues involved in the screening process are: (1) what data are needed, (2) where can they be obtained, (3) how can they be obtained, and (4) how should data be interpreted? Following a discussion of these issues, the implementation of a screening program was described in terms of identifying potential discipline, motivation, and achievement problems. The refinement and shifting upward or downward of the screening process on the basis of specific indicators were the final topics covered in the chapter.

SELF-TEST

1. In screening for entering behaviors, which of the following approaches can be justified from a theoretical standpoint?
   a. Maturational approach.
   b. Demographic approach.
   c. Abilities and processes approach.
   d. Transfer approach.
   e. All of the above.
2. As a practical matter it is important in screening for entering behaviors:
   a. That all available information be gathered about the learner.
   b. That the task be ignored so it does not prejudice the teacher's view.
   c. That the information be kept within manageable limits.
   d. All of the above.
   e. None of the above.
3. Which of the following is *not* one of the three general principles outlined in the text?
   a. Assess only when students reach a plateau.
   b. Assess in a broad context.
   c. Assess systematically.
   d. Assess efficiently.
4. To assess a learner's entering behavior:
   a. Only behavioral data should be considered.
   b. Only products of behavior should be considered.
   c. Reports from others and classroom products of behavior should not be used.
   d. All of the above.
   e. None of the above.
5. Most of the data needed for a micro-level assessment of a learner's entering behavior:
   a. Will be unavailable.
   b. Can be obtained in the classroom.
   c. Can be obtained from the child's permanent records.
   d. Can be obtained from norm-referenced test scores.
6. In obtaining information about a child's entering behavior, talking to others who have had contact with the child should be:
   a. Avoided.
   b. Done by using broad questions.
   c. Done for all children in the classroom.
   d. Done by using specific questions.
7. Standardized test scores:
   a. Are of limited value in the assessment of entering behavior.
   b. Are the best means of measuring entering behavior.
   c. Provide a broad estimate of skills.
   d. Both *a* and *c.*
8. As a means of assessing a student's entering behavior, classroom products of behavior:
   a. Are potentially useful.
   b. Are too unreliable for this purpose.
   c. Seldom if ever are valid measures.
   d. Are too closely related to the task to be useful.
9. When implementing a screening program it was suggested in the text that the order of priorities in the classroom should be:
   a. (1) Motivation, (2) achievement, (3) maintaining order.
   b. (1) Achievement, (2) maintaining order, (3) motivation.
   c. (1) Maintaining order, (2) motivation, (3) achievement.
   d. (1) Achievement, (2) motivation, (3) maintaining order.
10. In refining a screening program:
   a. The tactics do not need to change nor does the focus.
   b. The tactics do not need to change but the focus does.
   c. The tactics need to change but the focus does not.
   d. The tactics need to change and so does the focus.

ANSWER KEY TO BOXED QUESTIONS

1. The three pragmatic considerations are:
   a. Information is needed but the assessment skills may be lacking.
   b. Only a limited amount can be used.
   c. There is a limited amount of time that can be devoted to gathering the information.

   Their impacts, in the order listed above, are:
   a. Time will be used to gather the information but the process may be defective and the results not too useful.
   b. Unless a strategy for integrating various bits of information is developed, much information that is available cannot be meaningfully used.
   c. The assessment process needs to become an integral part of the instructional process.
2. The three general principles are assess in a broad context, assess systematically, and assess efficiently. The first implies assessment in all four domains of learning on the basis of a wide variety of information and in relation to the student's life-span development. The second principle implies that haphazard assessment may lead to biases in our decisions. The last principle is in

recognition of the time constraints that exist in the classroom.

3. The two classification systems and their relationship to the five traditional categories may be diagramed as follows:

Behaviors	*Products of behavior*
Personal observations	Classroom products of behavior
Reports of others	Standardized test results
	Miscellaneous products of behavior

4. Personal observations—skilled observation of performance.
   Reports of others—reading reports or asking probing questions with a clear understanding of the distinction among observations, generalizations, and inferences in the comments.
   Classroom products of behavior—assignment, collection, and inspection of the product.
   Standardized test results—inspection of past results found in school records, administration of the test, and inspection of the results.
   Miscellaneous products of behavior—usually not solicited, but presented on an irregular basis.
5. Standardized test scores—reliability of the test and its validity for the decisions to be made; also the amount of error that can be expected in the scores.
   Classroom products of behavior—reliability of the performance capability and the validity of the measure for inferring the presence of a particular capability or that the capability will be available in the learning situation.
   Miscellaneous products of behavior—of limited utility due to the unsystematic pattern of the data, but may have some utility in assessing the affective domain if the products are generated in a free-choice situation.
   Reports from others—distinguishing among reports of observations, generalizations, and inferences.
   Personal observations of behavior—interpretation of the behavior in relation to the task characteristics rather than merely on the basis of some assumed internal state of the learner.
6. Identifying possible discipline problems, identifying possible motivational problems, and identifying possible achievement problems.
7. The process would shift downward when
   a. Errors are detected.
   b. Off-task behavior or signs of boredom are associated with a low level of achievement in all areas.
   c. Off-task behavior or signs of boredom are associated with low achievement in specific areas and errors in classroom performance are observed in these areas. Only for the low areas of general achievement would the focus shift downward.

   The process would shift upward when
   a. Off-task behavior or signs of boredom are associated with a high level of achievement in all areas.
   b. Off-task behavior or signs of boredom are associated with some high and some low levels of achievement. Only for the high areas of general achievement would the focus shift upward.

ANSWER KEY TO SELF-TEST

1. e
2. c
3. *a*
4. *e*
5. *b*
6. *d*
7. *d*
8. *a*
9. *c*
10. *b*

Chapter 16

Effective learner strategies: In and beyond the classroom

THE PAST FEW CHAPTERS in this book have focused on numerous general and specific strategies teachers can use to create the appropriate conditions of learning in instructional events. In this chapter the focus shifts to a description of the mathemagenic strategies a person needs to be a self-sufficient learner and problem solver in any context. We changed the focus in this chapter for three interrelated reasons. First regardless of what cognitive or motor objectives teachers may have for students, an equally important goal of education is to produce capable students who can work without the teacher's aid. To be able to implement these broad goals, teachers should use instructional techniques that facilitate these goals while simultaneously teaching the primary objectives of the curriculum. Second without knowing what a self-sufficient learner can do to increase competency, you can easily choose an instructional strategy that will not be commensurate with these broad goals. Further, although many of these abilities appear to come about through practice in a variety of situations over long periods of time, the initial acquisition of most of these strategies can be taught in the same manner as higher-order rules. Thus, once the skills of self-sufficiency have been identified, it should be possible to identify the prerequisites for the skills and then arrange instructional strategies to facilitate these skills. Third not only should a teacher plan to develop these skills, but a teacher also needs to be able to determine whether a student's inability to achieve the regular cognitive or motor objectives of a course of study is due to the student's inability to be self-sufficient. In Chapter 17 we discuss how a teacher may assess student errors, and in Chapter 18 we discuss strategies for correcting the errors. Without knowledge about the possible types of self-sufficiency skills students need to perform various assignments (e.g., study skills, planning time wisely, and general problem-solving strategies), any analysis of a student's error is incomplete, thus resulting in an incomplete plan to help correct the error.

Specifically, four questions are raised.

1. How can a student develop personal strategies to approach and attend to the relevant attributes of a task until it is completed?
2. How can a student use strategies to increase the amount learned from written and verbal material?
3. How can a student increase his/her effectiveness as an independent problem solver?
4. How can a student increase his/her motor proficiency?

In essence, we are concerned with the competencies students need in order to study effectively and solve varieties of problems. Consider the following situations which may have happened to you. How many times have you known all the facts, concepts, and principles of a problem and yet were unable to solve it? How many times have you been given a task to complete for which you did not meet the deadline or you barely met the deadline, simply because you did not organize your time wisely? How many times have you had a great deal of difficulty trying to remember a lot of facts for a test? How many times have you read a chapter in a book, only to discover you were not really attending to the chapter and therefore you were unable to recall the content? Each of these questions represents a situation in which students consciously can do a great deal by themselves to improve their own learning or performance independent of a teacher's support.

To be able to use these self-management strategies requires that the student be aware of these strategies as well as the conditions under which some conscious strategies can facilitate learning and performance.

Often tasks are failed not because students do not know or are not able to learn the specific skills, facts, concepts, or rules to perform a task, but simply because they are not capable of modifying their behavior to make the appropriate response to the task. From the student's perspective, we are talking about such strategies as organizing the task in an effective way to complete it, organizing time effectively, using specific memory techniques to learn the material, utilizing conscious strategies to maintain attention to a task, applying specific but generalizable problem-solving strategies to solve a class of complex problems, and using other effective study skills.

At the conclusion of this chapter you should be able to:

1. Identify various strategies a student can use to initiate an activity, and then be able to use those strategies in your own daily life.
2. Identify various strategies a student can use to acquire information, and then use those strategies in your own daily life.
3. Identify various strategies a student can use to solve convergent and divergent problems, and apply them to daily activities.
4. Identify various strategies a student can use to monitor and execute complex motor acts, and then use those strategies in your own daily life.

HOW TO READ THIS CHAPTER

Although this chapter attempts to identify many strategies students might use to increase their learning or performance proficiency, and therefore does not actually refer to what a teacher can do to bring about the acquisition of these strategies, we recommend that you take on the dual role of a prospective teacher and a student while reading this chapter. Refer back to Chapters 10 and 11 for relevant advice to teachers on some of these topics.

As a prospective teacher, you should recognize that any assignment given to students assumes a certain amount of self-sufficiency, whether the self-sufficiency takes the form of answering questions from a workbook, studying for a test, or writing a research paper. These self-sufficiency skills have to be taught just like any other skill. Unfortunately, rarely do the schools or teachers spend time on these skills, with the result that too many students remain generally incompetent when confronted with various types of assignments.

Reading this chapter from a student's perspective, you should use some of these strategies when you are given assignments to do in college or when you are confronted with a test.

One further note: Most of the suggestions in this chapter have originated from research conducted on high school and college students. If you intend to teach elementary school children you certainly cannot wait around until a set of verifiable studies has been generated and empirically validated. Our suggestion would be to attempt to teach those strategies you feel might work, and then *empirically validate* the results. To quote Brown and Smiley (1977), "The more we learn about the efficient learner, the more able we become to teach the inefficient how to learn."

A PROTOTYPE MODEL OF SELF-SUFFICIENCY

In this chapter we are concerned with those general skills and attitudes that contribute to self-sufficiency. Figure 16–1 portrays a prototype model of the general attitudinal and cognitive prerequisites necessary to perform any type of task. This model may

FIGURE 16–1
General stages in learning or performing tasks at a self-sufficiency level

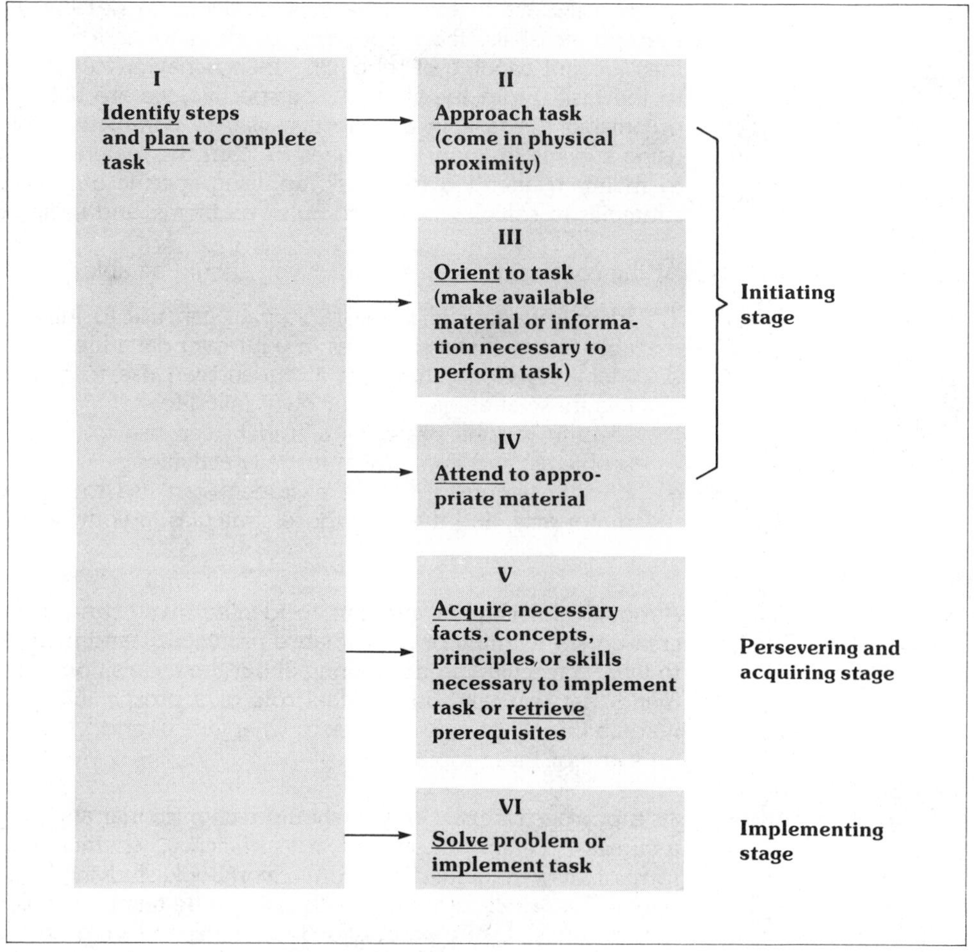

be seen as analogous to a general information-processing, task analysis model. Further, the model can be viewed from the perspective of either a student who is learning a new skill for the first time or a student who is asked to apply previously acquired skills to a previously unencountered task. Throughout the chapter these distinctions will become clearer.

According to Figure 16–1, to be self-sufficient at a task requires that a student initiate the task, acquire or retrieve the skills necessary to perform the task, and then perform the task. In addition, implicit in this model is the point that a plan to perform the task is also necessary for effective completion of a task. In simple tasks the plan sometimes is so automatic that the planner simply executes it without ever being aware of the plan. For more complex tasks, developing the plan may take considerable time before the student even attempts to approach or initiate the actual task. Since any plan a student might generate depends on the type of task as well as the sophistication of the student, the actual planning of how to execute a task often takes place before and during any of the steps identified in Figure 16–1. Because planning often takes place at each step during the process, we have chosen to discuss the superordinate strategy of planning at each step rather than to discuss planning as a separate category. Our discussion starts with the initiating stage.

INITIATING THE TASK

Strategies for approaching the task

At the most general level, the first response a student has to make to a task is to *approach* it. Regardless of whether a student's behavior is externally or internally determined, problems cannot be solved or tasks successfully executed or learned unless a student is willing to approach a task and then spend the sufficient amount of *time* to complete it successfully. Rosenshine (1971) refers to this behavior in a school context as "academic engaged time."

It should be pointed out here that a student's willingness to approach a task and spend the necessary amount of time to complete it is a function of the degree of success the student has had with similar tasks in the past, the probable current consequences of completing the task successfully or unsuccessfully, the degree of interest or lack of interest engendered by the specific task, the degree of achievement motivation or fear of failure operating within the student, and the degree to which other internal or external variables compete for the student's time (including peer pressures).

Even though willingness to spend time on a task is influenced by external factors, there is a great deal a person can do to control specific motivational tendencies. Several suggestions are identified in the following paragraphs. According to the classical conditioning principles presented in Chapter 4, a pleasant environment should increase the learner's approach tendencies. As an example, many artists and writers make use of this technique by creating special environments before they work in order to bring about a creative mood.

FIGURE 16–2
Self-motivational strategies are important to an effective student

Operant conditioning procedures can also be used to increase one's approach tendencies. Arranging schedules so that leisure-time pursuits generally follow the required work can act as a reinforcer for doing the required work [Premack's (1965) contingency management principle]. In other words, the student can design the workload in such a manner that the student will not engage in leisure pursuits until a specified amount of work is accomplished. Obviously, in those subject matter areas in which the student is intrinsically interested, he/she could schedule studying time during the time scheduled for leisure activities (Figure 16–2).

Sometimes tasks are not particularly attractive. People cannot like everything they have to do. With a little imagination on a student's part, however, an undesirable task can be related to some broad goal the student has, thus making the task more relevant. There is a great deal of evidence to indicate that students tend to do better when they have clear goals guiding their behavior. Perceiving tasks as related to long-term goals is helpful in this regard (Raynor, 1970). In addition, with a little effort the student can purposefully make some tasks novel or incongruent, thus utilizing Berlyne's (1960) theory that incongruent or novel situations create disequilibrium that needs to be resolved. Instead of being faced with an unpleasant task, many of the previous strategies have the effect of transforming the task into a desirable activity, thus increasing the likelihood of approaching the task and persevering until it is completed.

Oftentimes people fail to complete tasks because their goals or the chosen tasks are unrealistic. There are several strategies a person can use to pursue realistic tasks and goals. According to J. W. Atkinson (1964), a person should choose activities of moderate difficulty if given a choice. A task that is too simple, except in cases of individuals who have experienced a great deal of failure, has a tendency to become boring, whereas a very difficult task can lead to frustration and a fear of failure, resulting in withdrawal from the task. A moderately challenging task is attractive and can maintain interest over a long period of time.

Realistically, however, people are not always given choices over the types of tasks they have to complete. And sometimes the tasks may be quite difficult and somewhat inappropriate. When confronted with very difficult tasks, Atkinson's theory still applies. In this case, difficult tasks need to be reduced into manageable and more easily attained subtasks. This strategy increases the likelihood that the subordinate task will be more realistic, while at the same time increases the likelihood of successful completion of the total task. Sometimes large tasks have an overwhelming effect of incapacitating people who would have the competency to do the task if it were organized into smaller units.

As an example of how this strategy might be used, consider Toby, a fifth-grade boy of above-average mathematics ability. Given 20 math problems to do, Toby literally did not know where to begin. Rarely would Toby finish more than a few of the problems, although those he finished were correct. The teacher redesigned the task for Toby—assigning four groups of five problems in succession. To complete the task, Toby was instructed to cover all the problems on the page with a piece of paper except for the group he was currently solving. This conscious strategy to break down the task into smaller manageable units had an amazing effect on his performance. Regardless of whether Toby's problem was emotional, motivational, or perceptual, he quickly learned to break down his math homework in this fashion and successfully completed the assignments on time.

Not only is it helpful to break down long-term, difficult tasks into subtasks, but it is also helpful to perform the activity on a regularly distributed basis. Setting personal goals with clearly specified deadlines is an excellent strategy for getting started on a task. Let us assume a college student is taking five courses, and there is a great deal of work in several of the courses requiring long-term work on projects or term papers. Rather than procrastinate on the tasks, a wise strategy is to create a fairly rigorous schedule with built-in deadlines designed to distribute the workload over a semester. With judicious planning, the student's distributed workload can be organized around his/her daily schedule. Purposefully scheduling almost all the hours during the day for study and project work, the student is likely to realize that there is *more time* available during the prime time in the evenings to do activities of his/her choosing. A list of the steps to take in scheduling time is found in Figure 16–3.

The steps have two major points in common. First, each is a plan by the student to have more control of how time is spent. Put another way, using conscious strategies

FIGURE 16–3
Steps for scheduling time wisely

1. Identify the subcomponents of the task that need to be accomplished.
2. Place the subcomponents in a proper sequence.
3. Generate an estimated timetable for completion of each subcomponent as well as for the completion of the long-term task.
4. Make a personal contract so that upon completion of each of the concrete subcomponents, a reward of some sort will be forthcoming.
5. Keep a detailed record of progress and stick to the timetable. Monitor your progress.

to approach tasks in a systematic, semidisciplined fashion, the student should come to perceive that personal control is possible rather than responding to events in a haphazard, undisciplined, pawnlike fashion. According to De Charms (1968), the more people feel they are in control of their own lives and can plan for events, the more likely they will do so. Weiner and Kukla (1970) and Weiner and Potepan (1970) indicate that achievement-oriented individuals see themselves as the cause of their own behavior as well as the cause of the success that results from the behavior. Furthermore, as a by-product of successful planning, the person is more likely to have positive feelings about his/her own generalized competency as a student and problem solver. Seen in this light, a greater emphasis is placed upon the individual as an *originator* of his/her own *motivation.* Rather than waiting for motivation to come from external sources, the learner can do a great deal to control and monitor his/her own motivational state (Maehr, 1976). When viewed from this perspective, there can be fewer excuses for a lack of performance if the person possesses the skills to perform the task.

The second common element in these strategies is that each strategy is teachable, and therefore much could be done in the context of the school to teach these motivational strategies. More is said about some of these theories in Chapter 24.

Conscious strategies for processing information

Once a student becomes committed to perform some previously unencountered task, an effective student must orient to the task, attend to the relevant attributes of the task, use the appropriate memory strategies to aid encoding and retrieval, and develop a general study strategy. This section of the chapter describes each of these interrelated processes in considerable detail.

Orienting strategies. You should remember from our previous discussions that orienting strategies are general preparatory responses necessary to direct our attention towards any type of stimulus situation. A great deal of research has been conducted on how selective attention may be brought about by providing a student with some advanced knowledge about information found in textual material (Ausubel, 1963; Frase, 1975; Rickards, 1976a; Rothkopf, 1972). The generalization from this research is that students ought to have a general idea of what to expect before being exposed to a lesson. By purposefully reading the introduction and summaries to written material or by converting titles and subtitles into broad questions, the student can bring about the same general orienting effect as an adjunct question or advanced organizer. More will be said about these strategies as they are used in the framework of general study techniques.

Attending strategies. Earlier in the book we spoke about attention as a process that is brought about through a variety of external stimulus conditions presented by the teacher. In this part of the book, attention is spoken of as an internal process mediated by the student's conscious efforts to control the attentional processes.

Stemming from the original work by the famous Russian psychologist Luria (1961), who suggested that children can control their own behavior through internal verbalizations, many recent studies have been conducted confirming that attention can be controlled consciously through internal verbal commands. Of particular relevance to this section of the book are studies by Palkes, Stewart, and Freedman (1971) and Meichenbaum and Goodman (1971), which required second- and third-grade, highly distractible children to use "stop, listen, look, and think" strategies and "talkout" strate-

FIGURE 16–4
Conscious "stop, look, and think" strategies can increase attention

gies while performing tasks that they could not have performed without paying careful attention. Essentially, these self-induced strategies were successful in increasing the children's attention to the tasks (Figure 16–4). The importance of these studies cannot be overlooked. In the past, psychologists might have claimed that talking to yourself signified abnormal behavior; today we are suggesting that talking to yourself might significantly increase your attention processes!

Another example of an attention problem is a young student who loses the place on a printed page. To alleviate this problem, the student can use a finger to focus on the appropriate line, take a small card and place it under the appropriate line, or take a card with a "window" in it and move it across the page accordingly. Each of these strategies increases the likelihood that the student will attend to the appropriate stimuli. When the student begins to develop the attending skills necessary to read without these aids, they can be withdrawn.

The common elements in these two examples are that students should be seen as capable of modifying their own environment to bring about optimal learning conditions, and that conscious strategies such as these can be effectively taught to students.

1. Distinguish between an orienting response and attention.
2. How can a student make use of Premack's principle when given a required task for homework?
3. State two orienting-response strategies a student may employ before reading a chapter in an assigned text.

ACQUIRING TASK-RELEVANT INFORMATION

Memory strategies

In order to put information into long-term memory, conscious encoding strategies such as reorganizing large amounts of information into logical relationships and manageable chunks of information, relating the information in a meaningful way to previously learned material, utilizing a variety of mnemonic strategies, using effective rehearsal strategies, and employing general elaborative strategies can be used.

Typically, most school-related tasks require students to learn a significant amount of information in one lesson. Faced with these types of tasks, the student should be able to reorganize the material in the lesson(s) into manageable and logical clusters to facilitate long-term memory. For example, for tasks that require memory of a group of words, research has shown that adults efficient at remembering tend to rearrange the words according to categories. These categories include such semantic relationships as conceptual categories (animals, fruits, objects); sense impressions (the perceptual quality of the object—round, rough, sweet, etc.); and, less frequently, the *stereotypic* masculine or feminine connotation of words (e.g., football—male, cooking—female) (Wickens, 1973). The important point to be made here is that it has been found that upper-elementary-school-aged children can make conscious use of categorization strategies to increase their memory proficiency, although the degree to which students at this age level use these strategies independently is somewhat limited. As Hagen, Jongeward, and Kail (1975) suggest, developmental differences in memory appear to be the result of an expanding repertoire of acquired memory strategies rather than a major shift in general cognitive efficiency.

In addition to breaking down the information into clusters, students should be able to arrange information in a superordinate hierarchical order if there is any inherent structural relationship in what has to be learned. The more active the learner is in restructuring the material in a meaningful manner, the more likely the material will be retrieved at a future time.

Since the human short-term memory system seems to be able to remember only about 7 ± 2 bits of information at one setting, it would make additional sense for the student to structure memory tasks to require only about seven bits of information to be remembered *in one isolated instructional event* (G. A. Miller, 1956). With younger children, this span should be reduced to three to five bits of information. For example, in a very clever study with adolescent, mentally retarded students, Butterfield, Wambold, and Belmont (1973) found that these students were incapable of properly sequencing rehearsal techniques and they could not coordinate their techniques. In this study, the students were given a sequence of six letters to remember. The adolescents who were taught a chunking, rehearsal, and sequencing strategy statistically outperformed the group who did not receive this training.

Not only should students be able to reorganize material in lessons, but they also should be able to consciously use a variety of cognitive processes to increase their learning efficiency. In a recent paper, Weinstein (1977) points out that the degree to which students can use *elaborative* memory strategies will be the degree to which they will effectively learn the content of the assignments. According to Weinstein, in order for the student to retain important information, the information must be *restructured* within the student's own cognitive structure (Figure 16–5). Strategies based on mnenomics, generating images (Paivio's (1971) dual coding system), relating new material to previously learned material, and incorporating a list of words to be memorized into a meaningful sentence are some examples. By teaching these strategies

FIGURE 16–5
Each student has to develop an elaborative memory style

to a group of ninth-graders, Weinstein was able to increase the students' learning efficiency considerably. As another example, Yuille and Catchpole (1973) ingeniously taught first- and third-grade students to create images of a pair of items by having the items interact with each other in the image. The students easily were able to learn this strategy. Although you should be forewarned that many of the studies reported in this section have been conducted in laboratory settings, the evidence is rapidly accumulating that students can become much more effective learners by using a variety of interrelated cognitive strategies to process the information.

One more example of a memory strategy should suffice. Let us assume you have to study for a test in psychology that requires you to restate the four stages of Piaget's theory (sensorimotor–preoperational–concrete operational–formal operational). The first letters of each stage are SPCF. Since SPCF is an unpronounceable nonsense word, note that the first three letters (SPC) are the same letters in the acronym S.P.C.A. Now that the nonsense word SPCF is related to the familiar acronym S.P.C.A., you should have no difficulty in remembering SPCF and, in fact, you could make up a nonsense society—Society for the Prevention of Cruelty to Furry Animals, and then generate an image of a fox. In this case, you would be combining several of the previously mentioned strategies to facilitate your retrieval processes.

From this discussion it should be evident to you that a student can do a great deal to increase memory efficiency. The trick is to rehearse the information needed to be remembered by creating easily remembered cues that can be reused when retrieving the information at a future date. By remembering the cue at a future date, it is easier to retrieve information associated with the cue than it is to remember information that may not have a very recallable cue (low associative value). To summarize, using active memory strategies rather than rote memory strategies increases learning efficiency.

4. State in your own words the significance of the statement: The more active the learner is in restructuring the material to be learned, the greater the likelihood the material will be learned.
5. If you were given an assignment to learn a list of 50 chemical elements which had to be learned for a quiz in two weeks, what principles should you follow to learn the list?

Study skills

Our discussion starts with the popular SQ4R study method (scan, query, read, reflect, recite, review) developed by Thomas and Robinson (1972). Although this technique is designed mainly for studying printed material, aspects of it can be used for any type of study situation. According to Thomas and Robinson, there are six stages to this process.

1. *Scan the material.* The student should briefly scan the written material including the introduction and summary. Scanning familiarizes the reader with the overall organization of the material by providing the "intellectual scaffolding" from which the material might be related and providing the student with knowledge about the general characteristics of the material. From this initial reading, the reader should know what to expect. In one sense, this strategy allows the reader to develop a personalized advance organizer (Ausubel, 1963). Put another way, these techniques should orient the student toward the material.

2. *Make up questions.* This strategy consists of translating the expository material into a series of questions that need to be answered while the material is being read.

One of the best techniques for generating questions is to turn the major headings of the chapters into *who, what, where, why,* and *how* questions. In terms of studying for a test, the question should be of the same type expected on the exam.

3. *Read the material.* The student reads the material in order to answer the questions posed in Step 2.

4. *Reflect upon the material.* Upon reading the material, the student should attempt to:

a. Relate the material to what the student already knows.
b. Relate the subtopics in the text to superordinate concepts or principles.
c. Resolve disparate information, if appropriate.
d. Attempt to use the information to solve simulated problems covering the material.

5. *Recite it.* This phase of the strategy consists of rehearsing the material by reanswering the questions. If possible, the rehearsal should take the format of the final test. This strategy should enhance the retrievability of the information on the test because it makes use of the horizontal transfer principles discussed in Chapter 8.

6. *Review it.* Just before the test, the student should actively review the material, generally repeating any step necessary to understand the material and make the material more accessible in long-term memory.

FIGURE 16–6
Systematic study skills are an important component of self-sufficiency

Essentially, Thomas and Robinson are suggesting that the learner needs to use a systematic, disciplined, and purposive approach to studying (Figure 16–6). As Dansereau, Collins, McDonald, Diekhoff, Garland, and Holley (1978) so well point out, effective studying consists of a conscious, sequential series of interrelated steps and processes. Based on an information-processing approach and the SQ4R approach to studying, Dansereau et al. have developed a very interesting and systematic learning strategy curriculum to help college students learn how to study. The program consists of two major components entitled *comprehension/retention* strategies and *retrieval/utilization* strategies. In the comprehension/retention component, the student is systematically taught how to *understand* difficult material, develop *recall* strategies, use strategies to *digest* the material, and use strategies to *expand* the material. In the retrieval/utilization component, the student is taught how to *analyze* a task to determine what is required, develop strategies to *recall the main ideas* as well as *retrieve specific information,* effectively *organize* the body of information, and *create appropriate terminal* and *evaluation responses.* In addition, the student is given training in the support strategies of goal setting and scheduling, as well as strategies to maintain attention. Each of the broad processes consists of many component processes that are also taught as part of the program.

Although the total program is well beyond the scope of this text, one promising component process deserves mention. Based on Quillan's (1969) network model of memory, this strategy consists of identifying key ideas or principles of subject matter and the interrelationships between those ideas and principles. In the Dansereau et al. program 13 possible specific interrelationships have been identified. The next task for the learner is to label the key ideas as well as the nature of the interrelationships. Aside from the obvious advantages that this study program is systematic and requires a lot of cognitive *elaboration,* the program encourages the student to study the same material in a variety of ways, thus increasing the probability of retrievability. Although much more research needs to be conducted on this approach, much of what Dansereau et al. have done makes a lot of cognitive sense.

Although not as systematic as the Dansereau program, other researchers (Briggs, Tosig & Norley, 1971; Greiner & Karoly, 1976; Van Zoost & Jackson, 1974) have also reported success in teaching generalized study strategies. All of these approaches have included internal motivational techniques such as contingency management, self-monitoring techniques, and general methods of planning as well as some specific memory components. The common element in all of these study skill programs is the dual emphasis on motivation and cognitive variables.

With the increasing emphasis on aptitude-treatment interaction models, some consideration should also be given to ATIs when teaching study skills. Biggs (1976) found, for example, that liberal arts college students can be successful either by applying a general reproductive study strategy (giving back prescribed material intact) or by applying a transformational study strategy (injecting a great deal of personal meaning into the material). Success in science, on the other hand, does not appear to be related to either strategy. Considering another dimension of study style, Svensson (1977) has found that an atomistic strategy (attempts to remember specific details by rote) can be used for factual and relatively unimportant material, while a holistic strategy (attempts to identify and remember the main message) is needed for deeper understanding. Although some aspects of these findings are not particularly surprising, they do suggest that different study strategies might be used by different students with equal results, and that different strategies should perhaps be attempted with different types of subject matter as well as different levels of subject matter. All three of these points need to be researched further.

GENERATING AND VERIFYING PROBLEM SOLUTIONS OF A TASK

Problem solving refers to strategies a person engages in to generate or originate a solution to a previously unencountered question where the solution is unknown to the person before he/she attempts to solve the problem. In rule-using situations, the student has to retrieve the appropriate rules necessary to solve a problem, whereas in rule generating a student actually has to generate new rules to solve a problem.

A general problem-solving model

Any type of problem solving, whether it be painting a portrait, creating a new invention, solving a math problem, or writing a theme, appears to require these general stepwise stages. To a large extent, *all* problems require the same set of broad decisions prior to the final solution. The model presented in Figure 16–7 represents an extension of Wallas's (1926) depiction of the general stages a person uses in order to arrive at a solution to a complex problem. An awareness of the various decisions that have to be made in complex problem solving should help a person understand systematic problem solving a little more thoroughly. Of course, the ultimate understanding of complex problem solving can come about only through practice.

Figure 16–7 indicates there are six general decisions a problem solver must make in order to prepare for the solution to a problem in Stage I (preparation). The problem solver must (1) recognize that there is a need to solve the problem; (2) identify the pertinent characteristics of the problem (Is it like any other problem I've encountered?); (3) formulate the appropriate question and hypothesis concerning the problem; (4) choose or generate a plan to solve the problem; (5) identify the appropriate sources of data; and (6) gather the appropriate data. In Stage II (incubation) the problem solver must analyze, evaluate, and interpret the data in terms of the initial query. Obviously, a reformulation of the query or a decision to gather additional data may be made at this time. Based on the general questions, hypotheses, strategies, and data gathered in Stage II, the student generates or originates a tentative solution to

FIGURE 16–7
A schematic description of general problem solving

Stages in problem solving	*Conditions to bring about the solution*
I. Prepares	1. *Needs* to solve the problem because either the: *a.* Student observes the situation—becomes dissatisfied with current situation. *b.* Student is assigned a problem—someone else decides that the problem is worthy of solution.
	2. *Identifies* the pertinent characteristics of the problem.
	3. *Formulates* the appropriate questions and hypotheses concerning the problem.
	4. *Chooses* or *generates* the strategy needed to solve the problem (generates a plan).
	5. *Locates* the sources of useful data.
	6. *Gathers* the appropriate data.
II. Incubates	7. *Organizes* the data so that they can be analyzed, evaluated, and interpreted; during this stage, the person may work on other matters before returning to task.
III. Illuminates	8. *Generates* and/or *originates* a tentative solution based on the questions/hypotheses and the gathered data.
IV. Executes	9. *Elaborates* the solution overtly—produces an overt product.
V. Evaluates	10. *Assesses* the fit of the solution—how well does the solution answer the questions and solve the problem? If the solution is not satisfactory, the problem solver must reanalyze each stage to determine where the solution must be improved.

the problem in Stage III. At this time, the student is ready to execute the solution (Stage IV). Basically, Stage IV consists of elaborating upon the solution. The final stage (V) in this schematized model is when the problem solver determines the fit of the solutions, i.e., determines whether the solution fits the situation.

We should warn you now that we are a little reluctant to present such a highly schematized figure. Our concern is that you might misinterpret the figure to mean that all problems are solved in the same sequential fashion. Although all problems appear to require the processes identified in Figure 16–7, the order and magnitude of the processes vary considerably for both the person and the nature of the task. Instead of viewing this schematized figure as the exact stages and sequence in which solutions to problems are derived, the figure should be viewed as a portrayal of the decisions that a person must resolve before solving a complex problem. Certain problems appear to require a very logical step-by-step process; others appear to require a trial-and-error approach or at least a "lateral" strategy (DeBono, 1967) for solution. Still other problems appear to require intuitive-type solutions. For most complex problems, there is no set, predetermined order in which the decisions are made, although a relatively systematic order generally prevails. In other words, we are not suggesting that problem solving is a unidirectional process occurring in a predetermined time sequence; rather we are suggesting that decisions made later in a problem-solving sequence may influence earlier decisions, in which case the latter decisions serve as feedback for reconceptualizing earlier decisions.

For example, let us assume a student has systematically progressed through Steps 1–5 in Stage I and is now gathering appropriate data for solving the problem. It is very possible that the student may find out that the initial question needs to be reformulated, hence Steps 1–5 have to be repeated *before* Step 6 is reattempted.

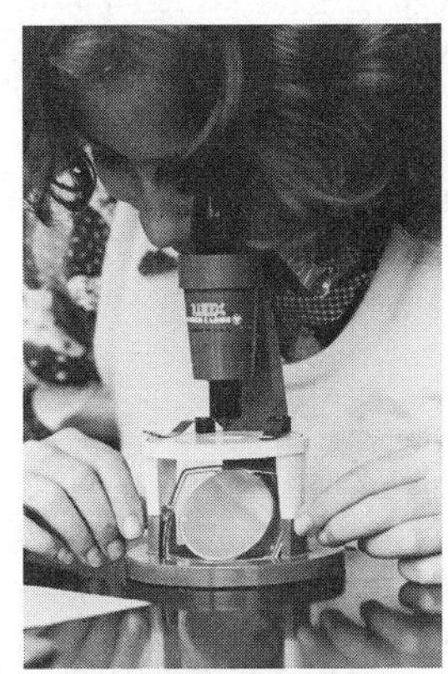

FIGURE 16–8
Problem solving consists of a series of interrelated stages

Keeping in mind the complexity and interrelationships involved in problem-solving, there is some evidence to indicate that certain systematic decision-making strategies can be applied to problem-solving situations which increase the probability of solving the problem. To make this point even clearer, Hayes (1978) indicates there are two general stages to problem solving (Figure 16–8). Initially the student must *understand* the problem; it is only *after* the problem is understood that the appropriate solution can be retrieved or generated and then used in the solution to the problem. In order to understand a problem, people have to use selective strategies while processing the data, as well as use their specific syntactic knowledge, semantic knowledge, and knowledge about the specific class of problem represented. Depending on the familiarity of the problem, its solution requires either that the student recognize the similarity between the problem in question and a previously learned class of problems or that the student originate a novel solution. Although beyond the scope of this part of the text, Hayes has written a very nice description of the variety of search strategies people use to find answers to problems. For anyone interested in this topic, we strongly recommend Hayes's highly readable but scholarly description of the problem-solving process.

Systematic problem-solving strategies

There have been many general programs developed recently to increase problem-solving efficiency (DeBono, 1967; Feldhusen, 1978; Olton & Crutchfield, 1971; Parnes, 1971; Wickelgren, 1974). Parnes's program is of particular importance because of the recognition that the initial problem-solving process is so important to the solution. In Parnes's program, there are three general processes, each of which involves two subprocesses:

1. Fact finding
   a. Problem definition—picks out and points up the problem.
   b. Preparation—gathers and analyzes the pertinent data.
2. Idea finding
   c. Idea production—generates tentative ideas as possible leads.
   d. Idea development—selects from the resulting ideas, recombines and modifies.
3. Solution finding
   e. Evaluation—verifies the tentative solution.
   f. Adaption—implements the final solution.

In a modification of Parnes's program, Feldhusen (1978) also proposes a six-stage model of creative problem solving. Feldhusen's model consists of problem generation, problem clarification, problem identification, idea finding, synthesizing a solution, and implementing the solution. Feldhusen's model is worthy of note for the ingenious way in which Guilford's structure of intellect model (discussed in Chapter 23) and the Parnes program have been incorporated into the model as well as for the emphasis on several strategies that come before the problem definition or identification stage. Regardless of which model is chosen, the important point to remember is that any type of problem solving consists of a series of quasi-systematic and sequential processes that can be taught. Of course, the degree to which an efficient general problem solver can be trained in the use of the discrete stages is a very important question for research.

Conscious strategies to eliminate unproductive "sets" to complex problems

It should come as no surprise to you that psychologists have noted that a person's "set" (an established tendency to respond in a certain manner) can greatly impede problem-solving efficiency, particularly if the problem requires a divergent solution (DeBono, 1967; Duncker, 1945; Gardner & Runquist, 1958; Luchins & Luchins, 1959). It would appear, therefore, that a problem solver should attempt to be particularly flexible in the initial stages of solving problems which may require a divergent solution in order to decrease the likelihood of premature closure.

Often a solution to a divergent-type problem may never be generated because the problem is not formulated correctly in the initial preparatory stage. Posing incorrect questions to problems, failing to identify the relationship between a current problem and a similar previously encountered problem, and generalizing inappropriately from a previously encountered problem are just three of the common errors people make in starting to solve a problem. Many scholars of the creative problem-solving process, therefore, have noted that the questions and perceptions the problem solver generates in the initial stage of solving a problem greatly influence the ultimate form the solution takes in solving the problem. As Socrates noted centuries ago: "A question is a midwife which brings ideas to birth." Incorrect questions can give birth to incorrect ideas, and then prevent the birth of needed ideas. Six strategies designed to help a person reformulate a problem in a productive manner are presented in this section.

Individual brainstorming. According to Osborn (1957), individual brainstorming consists of consciously generating as many ideas and questions as possible on a particular problem. The zanier the idea, the better. The greater the number of ideas, the better. The purpose of this strategy is to generate a quantity of ideas and questions from which a possible solution to the problem might be generated. This strategy is said to decrease the likelihood that a divergent question or solution to a problem will be discarded in the early phases of decision making.

Systematic brainstorming. As a modification of Osborn's technique, W. J. Gordon (1961) suggests that brainstorming on a very general topic germane to a specific problem before brainstorming on the specific topic increases idea production. For example, let us assume a politician is concerned with ways in which the welfare problem in this country ought to be resolved. Instead of brainstorming on welfare per se, the initial brainstorming should occur at a broader level, perhaps on the general economic situation of our country. Based on the ideas generated in the broad brainstorming session, the problem solver is then able to brainstorm at a more specific level related to the welfare problem on each of the topics raised in the general session. This strategy has the advantage that the problem solver may see the specific problem in a broader context, thus exposing him/her to ideas that most likely would not have been generated if the problem solver had initially focused on the specific problem.

Systematic questioning. Another useful strategy for systematically analyzing the nature of a problem is to attempt to ask a series of specific predetermined questions about the problem or task before attempting to solve the problem [Davis, Roweton, Train, Warren, and Houtman (1969)]. Although Davis's strategy has been used mainly to improve inventions or products, with a little ingenuity a list of questions germane to any field can be easily generated. Davis's list includes:

1. Adding and/or subtracting parts.
2. Changing colors.
3. Varying materials.
4. Rearranging parts.
5. Varying shapes.
6. Changing size.
7. Modifying the design or style.

Synectics. This strategy is designed to have problem solvers join together different and apparently irrelevant elements in order to identify possible relationships that would not ordinarily be identified by more typical thought processes. To facilitate problem solving by using synectics, the problem solver is asked to generate certain analogies or fantasies, including:

1. *Personal analogy*—The person tries to become the object of investigation. How would you feel and work if you were the object?
2. *Direct analogy*—The person attempts to note the similarity between the assigned problem and similar problems in other fields of investigation.
3. *Symbolic analogy*—The person attempts to use a metaphor or a short phrase that describes the problem abstractly.
4. *Fantasy*—The person uses his/her wildest imagination to solve the problem.

W. J. Gordon (1961) reports that many highly creative solutions to problems have been generated by people using these techniques.

Attribute listing. Attribute listing is a strategy in which a person lists the perceptual characteristics of an object or situation, and then uses the perceptual attributes to generate new ideas or associations. For example, Torrance (1962) has developed a test for creativity in which the student has to think of as many ways as possible to improve an object such as a toy. Identifying the perceptual attributes of the toy (smooth, small, round, rough in spots, yellow, wooden), the student focuses on the attributes of the object rather than on the object itself. This strategy helps the problem solver to perceive the object systematically in ways not ordinarily perceived.

Circumrelation. Developed by Laverty (1974), this technique is designed to have a problem solver relate as many dimensions in a problem-solving task to as many other dimensions in the task as possible. We have modified Laverty's strategy to make it easier to implement.

1. Define the issues or problem in general terms.
2. Identify three or more major divisions of the problem.
3. Relate each subfactor in one division of the problem to every other subfactor in each of the other divisions. This strategy results in a complex matrix so that every subfactor is systematically juxtaposed with every other subfactor.
4. Reflect on the obtained interrelationships and evaluate the results. Use the obtained interrelationships as a springboard for new ideas.

This technique forces a person to engage in "combinatorial analysis." Recognizing that creative problem solving is often the result of relating diverse elements, the problem solver must systematically relate all the identifiable components in a task to every other component of the task. Manipulating and playing with ideas aid in finding original solutions to complex problems. Einstein recognized the importance of this type of activity when he wrote to Jacques Hadamard that "combinatory play seems to be the essential feature in productive thought—before there is any connection with logical construction in words or other kind of signs which can be communicated to others" (Ghiselin, 1952).

For a review of other programs designed to facilitate creative problem-solving strategies, consult Treffinger and Gowan (1971), F. E. Williams (1973), Davis and Scott (1971), as well as more recent articles in the *Journal of Creative Behavior* on other specific strategies.

6. Explain what Einstein meant by the statement: Combinatory play seems to be the essential feature in productive thought.
7. What is the common underlying similarity between brainstorming, attribute listing, and circumrelation?

STRATEGIES TO IMPROVE MOTOR PERFORMANCE

Oftentimes motor skills as a category of behaviors become relegated to the lower levels of taxonomies. There are many types of motor responses, however, that should be viewed in relationship to complex problem solving. For example, while any complex motor task can be logically analyzed in terms of a series of finer and finer responses (refer back to the section on motor responses in Chapter 11) and therefore can be viewed as a *chained response,* the *decision of when* to emit that chained response or *how* that chained response might be improved or modified under certain conditions could be classified as problem-solving behavior. In these cases we are referring to problem-solving strategies as related to the execution of motor skills.

As Marteniuk (1976) states in a fine little book on *Information Processing in Motor Skills:*

> There is at least a similarity between the processes underlying this ability (perceptual-motor skills) and an ability like the logical thinking required to solve intellectual problems. Just as an individual can mentally solve a problem without overtly expressing it, so too can an individual plan a movement in advance and imagine its outcome without actually physically moving.

As we mentioned earlier in this book, when a teacher attempts to teach a motor task, the teacher is generally concerned about the execution of the response in a correct sequence under the proper conditions. One excellent instructional strategy for increasing motor proficiency and/or the proper execution of the response under varied conditions (in a game situation, for example) is *to have the student verbally state the appropriate rule* under which the response should be emitted. These verbally stated rules can serve the function of guiding a complex motor response, changing a poorly executed motor response, or helping a person to decide upon which appropriate motor chain should be performed in a complex situation.

In order to make these suggestions clearer, concrete examples are provided for each of these complex situations.

Language guiding motor performance

Throughout your life you have been taught a variety of motor tasks in which the task has been demonstrated while the teacher provided you with verbal instructions or a verbal chain to correspond to the execution of the task. Generally, the execution of the square knot is taught in this fashion. The student is told to pick up a piece of rope in two hands, to take the ends of rope and place the end of the rope in the right hand over the end of the rope in the left hand, and then bring the right-hand rope under and around the left-hand rope. Then the process is reversed. To simplify, the student is told to remember the verbal chain: "Right, over and under; Left, over and under." The verbal chain comes to be associated with the execution of the chain. In one sense, we could say that the verbal chain comes to control and guide the motor response.

Language used to change a motor response

Let us assume a person is in a situation in which he/she is executing a motor response incorrectly. Although the goal of teaching any motor response is perfect execution, there are many factors that interfere. Serving a tennis ball is a good example. The perfect execution of a serve is a very difficult accomplishment. It requires a series of carefully integrated motor movements. If any one of the movements becomes altered in any fashion, the execution of the serve quickly becomes faulty. For example, if the server throws the ball too far out in front of the body, the ball will tend to be hit into the net. Conversely, if the ball is not thrown out far enough, the ball will tend to be hit too long. Now, consider a game in which you are serving and your ball constantly hits the net on the first serve. What should you do to alleviate this problem? Recalling the previous verbal rule, you should adjust your toss by throwing the ball up closer to your body. In this case, knowledge of the rule concerning the toss of the ball should help you modify your execution (Figure 16–9). That rule will only help you, however, if it is recalled under the proper conditions and you are able to change your motor execution accordingly. When a player is able to correct improper motor executions such as this, it is said that the player's behavior is rule-governed and planned.

Language used to choose a motor act

In many situations involving motor performance, there may be different types of chained responses that are appropriate under certain conditions and inappropriate under other conditions. For example, a baseball player has to decide *where* to throw the baseball when there are runners on base; the basketball player has to decide *whether* to drive for the basket, shoot a jump shot, or pass; the quarterback on the

FIGURE 16–9
Strategies are also needed to monitor and improve motor performance

football team has to decide *whether* to throw the ball or run on the pass option; the soccer player has to decide *whether* to cut inside or outside on a rapidly developing play. While many of these decisions require almost instantaneous action, many can be made in advance of the play. For example, an outfielder in baseball ought to know where to throw the ball *before* it is hit; the basketball player may have noted that the defensive player plays too far away to be effective in defending against a jump shot, while a driving layup would be inappropriate offensive strategy; the quarterback may have observed that one of the defensive backs is slow in deciding how to defend against the pass option play. By verbally stating to oneself a plan of execution, fewer mistakes are made. In this case, *stating the complex rules comes to control future* executed motor chains. Generally, these rules are stated in an "if, then" format—if this situation develops, I'll do this; if another situation develops, I'll do that. Obviously, in the previous examples, complex discrimination skills are needed to facilitate the decision-making process.

SUMMARY

This chapter has been concerned with strategies a student can use to increase his/her learning proficiency and performances in a variety of tasks. Specifically, strategies dealing with ways in which a student might come to approach, orient, attend, persevere, learn, solve problems, and improve motor performance are considered. Traditionally, most of these competencies have been left to chance by our educational institutions, which have tended to view them as the incidental goals of education. Perhaps there should be a much greater effort to insure that these generalizable skills are taught to students at various levels in the students' progress through the schools. Rather than leaving these skills to chance and serendipity, we would suggest that teaching self-sufficiency strategies should become an *integral* part of the curriculum.

Critics of the public school system from both sides of the political spectrum have indicated that our schools have produced many passive, alienated students who are not very capable of independent learning. In refocusing our efforts for the future, it would appear to make a great deal of sense to emphasize those skills a student needs to become a competent *problem solver* and an *efficient learner.* There are many specific skills that a student can acquire to increase his/her effectiveness in these areas. Producing effective learners and problem solvers should also have the effect of developing attitudes of self-confidence and self-determination. According to De Charm's (1968) the type of skills emphasized in this chapter should have the effect of producing a person who is in control of his/her behavior rather than one who is a pawn in the game of life.

SELF-TEST

1. When applying Premack's principle, the independent learner should be sure to:
   a. Make the place where one works pleasant, thus making use of classical conditioning.
   b. Make the task relevant, thus making use of a motivational principle
   c. Do something of one's choosing before doing the assigned task, thus insuring that a good mood will prevail while doing the task.
   d. Do something of one's choosing after doing the assigned task, thus making use of reinforcement principles.
2. The strategy to make the place where one studies a pleasant location is derived from:
   a. Cognitive theory.
   b. Classical conditioning principles.
   c. The schedules of reinforcement research.
   d. Premack's principle.
3. Generally, almost all current *motivational* approaches in education have as their basic emphasis:
   a. The manipulation of internal factors within a learner which attempt to make the learner an originator of motivation.
   b. The manipulation of external factors that need

SELF-TEST *(continued)*

to be changed before the learner will seriously approach a task.
c. Establishing a positive home background of the learner.
d. Reinforcement theory as the explanation for motivation.

4. The relationship between orienting responses and attending responses is:
   a. Orienting occurs before attending.
   b. Attending occurs before orienting.
   c. Attending to a task naturally orients the learner to the relevant features of the task.
   d. Attending to a task is a broader response than orienting to a task.
5. An accurate summary statement concerning the suggestions for increasing memory efficiency is:
   a. Active overt rehearsal is important.
   b. Reinforcement theory should be applied while memorizing material.
   c. Elementary-school-aged children cannot use memory strategies very well.
   d. An idiosyncratic restructuring of the material to be learned is in order.
6. Both synectics and circumrelation strategies help a problem solver to:
   a. Combine diverse material in a novel way.
   b. Obtain feedback about the quality of one's novel response.
   c. Synthesize the plan to solve a novel problem.
   d. Execute the solution to a problem after the idea has been generated.
7. One of the greatest problems people have in generating novel solutions to problems is their inability to generate a "set" to be flexible. Which of the following techniques is designed to minimize this problem?
   a. Synectics.
   b. Systematic questioning.
   c. Circumrelation.
   d. All of the above.
8. State three ways in which language can be used in relation to one's motor performance.
9. Which of the following categories does *not* belong in the initiating phase of learning or performing a task?
   a. Motivation.
   b. Orienting.
   c. Memorizing.
   d. Attending.
10. State how you would teach any of the strategies listed in this chapter based on the conditions of learning research.

ANSWER KEY TO BOXED QUESTIONS

1. The main difference between an orienting response and attention is that the orienting response refers to the general preparatory response a person makes to a stimulus situation in order to perceive the relevant stimuli, while attention refers to the processes involved in actually discriminating the relevant stimuli from the stimulus situation once that preparatory response is made.
2. By planning to do something the learner wants to do *after* completing a required task, the learner makes use of Premack's principle.
3. *a.* By scanning the whole chapter prior to reading it, the learner should get a better perspective about the content and organization of the chapter.
   b. An excellent way to study a chapter is to turn the titles of sections into questions, thus increasing the likelihood that the important material in a section will be identified. Of course, the danger in this strategy is that other important material may be overlooked in the process.
4. It is important to remember that humans tend to categorize and restructure stimuli in idiosyncratic ways that have *personal meaning* to themselves. Thus, the learner who restructures and recategorizes stimuli in a way that has a personal meaning is more likely to remember the material than material that has been categorized according to someone else's notion of what makes sense. Of course, on numerous occasions there would be a match between what one person conceives of as a logical category and what another person conceives.
5. *a.* The list should be broken down into manageable units (5–10 elements at a time).
   b. Attempt to restructure the list in a way that has some personal meaning (logical categories).
   c. Use imagery and mnemonics strategies where appropriate. The creation of meaningful sentences in which the first letter of each word represents the words to be memorized may be helpful. In general, any strategy that restructures the list to make it more retrievable is useful.
6. Combinatorial play allows a person to relate diverse elements or ideas in ways that never would be found based on logic or semantic relationships. A characteristic of creative thought is that diverse ideas and elements become associated in novel ways. For example, Pasteur's conceptualization for pasteurization was based on the apparent "illogical" connection "safe-attack."

7. These are semi-systematic strategies for generating uncommon ideas about a problem. A creative solution to a problem requires reconceptualizing the problem in a manner never before considered.

ANSWER KEY TO SELF-TEST

1. *d*
2. *b*
3. *a*
4. *a*
5. *d*
6. *a*
7. *d*
8. Language can be used to *guide, monitor,* or *plan* a response.
9. *c*
10. Any type of answer is acceptable for this question if you included the recognition that the conditions of learning associated with rule learning should be used in the lessons, and that relevant practice of those rules in a variety of diverse tasks should be required.

Chapter 17

Analysis of student responses

UP TO THIS POINT we have focused primarily on learning principles and strategies that should be considered when making instructional decisions. The decisions are intended to bring about a specific response, or perhaps a general class of responses, from the student. We now focus on the student's response to the instructional activities and how you might analyze that response in terms of your expectations. We leave for Chapter 18 decisions about which follow-up activities might be appropriate for the response.

One premise of this chapter is that no matter how carefully plans are made, students will not always attain the desired goals. You will be confronted with, and therefore need to analyze, less-than-perfect student performance. To help you prepare for this analysis we present some general issues involved and then two specific approaches representing the behaviorist and cognitivist perspectives. Synthesizing these two approaches, we offer an error analysis process composed of six phases. We then go on to show how the process can be applied to the four domains of learning.

After studying this chapter you should be able to:

1. Define the attitudes and role of a teacher analyzing student responses.
2. List the three types of data needed to analyze student responses.
3. Outline the steps in one behavioral approach to analyzing responses.
4. Outline the cognitive functions in one cognitive approach to analyzing errors.
5. Describe the six phases and five questions in the analysis model, which synthesizes the behavioral and cognitive strategies.

GENERAL ISSUES

In several of the preceding chapters we have dealt with the measurement and evaluation of human performance. In Chapter 4 we indicated the relationship between the definition of learning and the need for observations of behavior. In Chapters 9 and 15 we discussed more fully the assessment of entering behaviors and the evaluation process that should take place prior to instruction. Chapter 12 focused on the assessment of learning that should take place after instruction is completed. The latter is, as we noted, *summative* evaluation. In this chapter we deal with assessment of learning during the time instruction is occurring. This is generally referred to as *formative* evaluation to denote the fact that it occurs while the new capability is being developed or formed.

Before we delve into more specific matters, there are three general issues we will consider in order to clarify the context of the assessment process. The first issue concerns your instructional attitude, the second, your classroom role, and the third, the data you will need to collect and the conditions under which they must be gathered.

Instructional attitude

Several times we have made the point that any plans you develop should be considered tentative—a set of working hypotheses rather than a hard and fast course to follow. If we consider our decisions from this perspective, then the instructional episode is a means of testing and revising our working hypotheses. This testing and revising process is, in effect, a learning process in which the *teacher* is the learner, as well as the students. If the working hypotheses are reasonably accurate, *the students will learn* the objectives and *the teacher will learn* that the strategy was effective. If the plans or hypotheses are inaccurate, there may be only one learner in the classroom: the teacher may learn that the strategy used was ineffective and the student's behavior may remain unchanged (except for an increase in saying "Huh?").

Our plans or working hypotheses are usually in the form "If I do *X*, then I will expect the student to be able to do *Y*." Most of the time, if we have planned well, we will find student behaviors within the range we expect. When this occurs our working hypotheses are accurate enough to allow us to predict the outcome in terms of student performance. When we do not find student behaviors within the range of our expectations, we must be prepared to modify our plans or working hypotheses, since they are apparently inadequate to bring about the desired results. Note the emphasis we have placed on the failure of our hypotheses and not on the student's failure, even though it is student performance that does not meet our standards. This places the responsibility for failure on the teacher rather than on the student; in some way we have failed to help the student attain the goal. This position was emphasized prior to the early 1800s but, with the emergence of the age-grading system in schools, it gave way to the notion that some children have a learning disability because they do not progress at some established rate (Levine, 1976). While the concept of learning-disabled children has become firmly entrenched, it is too often applied in situations where the disability is more accurately an instructional disability.

We do not mean to imply that all student errors are the fault of inadequate instruction. Some errors may be due to inappropriate student initiative or other variables, as we pointed out in the preceding chapter. The point we wish to make is that when a student error does occur it should not be noted simply to determine test scores or grades. Rather, errors should be analyzed to see why they have occurred and what might be modified in the instructional plans in order to decrease the probability of the error being made again in the future.

Classroom role of teacher

Another point we wish to emphasize is that you, as a classroom teacher, will be functioning in two roles. One will be the traditional one of the classroom teacher. You will be implementing a series of instructional strategies. Not only will you be implementing the strategy by providing the conditions necessary for learning to occur, but you will also be a part of these conditions. Some of these strategies will have been largely developed for you in the form of materials and instructors manuals which you may use, more or less closely, as a guide. Other strategies will be entirely your product. Especially when dealing with strategies developed entirely by yourself, you are likely to be both the developer and the implementer of the strategy.

While performing this typical teacher's role of implementer, you should not lose sight of the fact that someone else could have been selected and trained to implement the strategy. With those programs that you have designed this usually does not happen but if it did you would want to observe the implementation process and see how it was carried out. In this capacity as observer you would be serving more clearly in an administrative role. Therefore, as the teacher in the classroom, you should be wearing two hats: one as the primary implementer of the plan and one as the administrator observing the implementer. It is useful to keep this distinction in mind because, when a student is responding, you should be objectively observing in both capacities.

Response data and collection context

In order to analyze student responses the data you will need are: (1) observations of behavior, (2) products of behavior, and (3) observations of response conditions. Any errors a student may make will be found when making observations of behavior or examining the products of behavior.

Usually the general characteristics of the behavior or product are sufficient to indicate that an inappropriate performance has occurred. In addition to these general characteristics, more subtle, specific ones may be needed in order to determine the type of error made and what factors may have helped bring about the erroneous performance. To determine the latter, one must also identify and analyze the conditions of learning, practice, and performance. This interest in the subtleties of performance and the conditions leading up to the performance will necessitate a sharpening of observational skills to detect the relevant aspects of the student's behavior and the stimuli which brought about the behavior.

Ideally, the process of formative evaluation implies that the data will be gathered, evaluated, and used to modify the instructional plan during the implementation phase of instruction. Of necessity, this also implies a limitation on the amount of time available to evaluate the data and revise the instructional plan. Another implication is that the functions of data collection, evaluation, and revision of plans need to be carried on almost simultaneously in the short time available. This may make the process somewhat hectic and open to teacher errors in judgment. These errors may occur because certain data are lacking or have been ignored. The teacher's errors may also occur due to faulty interpretation of the data or as an inadequate decision-making strategy.

Since the collection conditions are embedded in the implementation phase of instruction (Figure 17–1), you are likely to be distracted not only by your ongoing actions but also by the actions of the students. For these reasons, even the most experienced and careful observer may miss much of what goes on in a classroom. To some extent, this can be offset by an awareness of certain aspects of behavior that tend to influence our inferences. By developing an awareness of these aspects before entering

FIGURE 17–1
Collection of response data is embedded in the implementation phase

the classroom, you are less likely to miss the data needed to test or revise your working hypotheses. Without data that are relatively precise and relevant to the learning tasks, it will be virtually impossible to make productive decisions.

Having sound data is not enough. We must also be aware of the inferences that can reasonably be made on the basis of the data. This awareness will allow us not only to make more accurate inferences but also to arrive at them more rapidly. This awareness should also provide us with a greater feeling of confidence in our decisions.

> 1. What should be your attitude and role in the analysis of student responses? What data will be needed to conduct the analysis?

TWO PERSPECTIVES FOR ANALYZING ERRORS

Throughout this text we have pointed out the divergent viewpoints of the behaviorists and the cognitivists. At no point is the dichotomy more apparent than in their description of how to analyze student errors. They do, however, have a common starting point, which is the student's behavior. From that point they diverge not only in the types of tasks they discuss but also in the types of inferences they make. Before we present the divergence of the two viewpoints, we present the commonality.

Common starting point

In the early days of psychological research, a great deal of the research focused on introspection or personal reports of one's internal experiences. Due to the unreliability of this type of data, American psychologists abandoned it in favor of observations of overt behaviors. These are much easier to quantify and more open to verification based on agreement between various observers. This approach is shared by behaviorists and cognitivists alike. Psychologists of both persuasions collect observations of overt behavior, or observable products of behavior, as data in their experimental studies.

From an analysis of experimental studies, Gilbert (1962) suggests that the behaviors referred to in the studies are usually described along seven dimensions. Five of the seven describe temporal measurements and the other two describe spatial measurements. The dimensions are used to describe the characteristics of behavior that are used to determine whether a behavior will be considered an instance of correct or inadequate performance. While some behaviors may require the use of all seven dimensions to describe them, most can be described in reference to one or two dimensions. Beyond their use in research studies, these seven dimensions can provide an objective, multidimensional model for observing behavior in the classroom.

The temporal dimensions are:

1. Latency—the time between the first opportunity for a behavior and its initial occurrence.
2. Tempo—the rate of the continuously ongoing behavior.
3. Perseveration—the proportion of time in which the behaviors are actually occurring.
4. Duration—the total time from the start of the behavior to the end of the behavior.
5. Output—the total number of behaviors or products of behavior the individual engages in.

The spatial dimensions are:

6. Intension—the amount of movement of any one body part.
7. Extension—the amount of the total body involved in the movement.

To help clarify the meaning of these dimensions let us assume that we have handed out a work sheet with ten angles on it and the student has been instructed to circle all of the right angles. After we hand out the work sheet we make the following observation. For one minute the student alternately looks at his paper and his neighbor's paper. His neighbor is doing the same. Then the student, in three seconds, circles the first three angles. He then looks at his watch and proceeds to wind it. He looks up at the teacher and then quickly back down at the work sheet. He remains looking at his work sheet and yawns several times until the teacher says, "Hand in your work sheets." He then quickly circles three more examples. It has been five minutes since the work sheet was handed out. The completed work sheet looks like this:

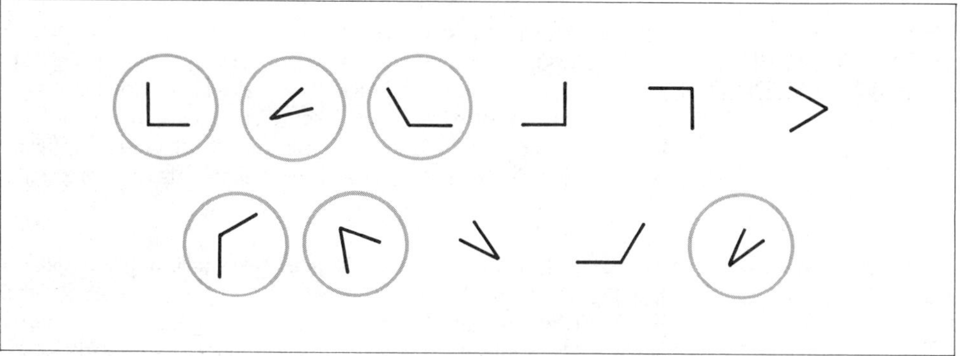

An analysis of the behavior and product of the behavior (the circled angles on the work sheet) will probably effect our thinking in several ways. First of all, we were expecting a circling of all 90-degree angles but no circling of the other angles. Using the taxonomy of cognitive skills, we would classify the expected behavior as concept-using behavior because we expected the student to classify the angles according to the concept of "right angles." On the basis of our observation of the student's behaviors, we might suspect that the student has not learned the concept. A look at the product of his behavior (the work sheet) would confirm our suspicions.

What arouses our suspicion and confirms it? First of all, the slow start on the task might arouse our suspicions. Since it took one full minute to make the first response, we have a long latency period. A student who has learned the concept would not need a long study period but would start (or at least could start) to circle the right angles within a few seconds of being told to do so.

The tempo, or rate, of the student's response was high when he was actually circling the angles. Until we actually inspect the completed work sheet, this may lead us to feel that the student knows how to complete the task successfully (but because the student looked at the other student's paper he may be able to only copy the correct responses).

Our student's perseveration at the task is relatively low since there is a great deal of nontask behavior occurring during the time period. This may not affect our judgment of how well the student may be able to perform the task, but it may lead us to infer that the student is disinterested in the task, has a short attention span, or does not understand the concept of right angle.

Duration as a dimension is not, on the surface, relevant to our evaluation of the student's competence, since we are not especially interested in a measure of endurance or how long the student will continue to work on the task. In this case, however, the fact that the two periods of on-task behavior are of relatively short duration is also likely to lead us to assume that the student is disinterested, has a short attention span, or does not understand the task.

In our example the student's output of circling behaviors should arouse our suspicions about his competence. Since there are only three correct answers to be circled, an output of six circles indicates the student has made at least three errors and possibly six.

The dimension of intension, or amount of movement of the student's hand while circling, will probably not give any indication of the student's competence. If the student circles the various items with an obvious flourish, we may assume that the student is responding with a great deal of confidence. The amount of wrinkling of the forehead, raising of the eyebrows, or squinting while studying the various angles may also affect our estimate of the student's level of confidence and involvement in the task.

The example we have used is not primarily a motor task, and only the hand is expected to be involved in performing the task. If, as we noted above, the forehead, eyebrows, and other facial parts are also moved, this would represent an increase in terms of the extension dimension and would be likely to influence our judgments. Students are intuitively aware of this and often engage in a great deal of body movement to convince others that they are actively trying to produce the desired response. Sometimes, when we privately thump our own foreheads, we may actually even be trying to convince ourselves that we are more capable than our inadequacies at the moment would imply.

From this example it can be seen that even though our explicit criterion for success on the task may involve only how many and which angles are circled, our observations of the student along the seven dimensions may also affect our judgments in determining proficiency (Figure 17–2).

A behavioristic approach

From the behaviorist position, Gropper (1974, 1975) offers what appears to be a fairly comprehensive strategy for analyzing student errors. Since the behaviorists describe the learners' responses in terms of environmental stimuli, the environment is seen as the key to explaining the errors. In keeping with this position, Gropper's main emphasis is on analyzing errors in terms of flaws in the response capability related to flaws in the stimulus situation. This is an extremely useful approach to the analysis of errors since it also identifies the environmental factors that may need to be modified.

Basically, the model has five main points. The first is an emphasis on 11 factors that tend to influence our judgments of response adequacy. This portion of the model appears to be a modification and extension of Gilbert's seven dimensions of behavior.

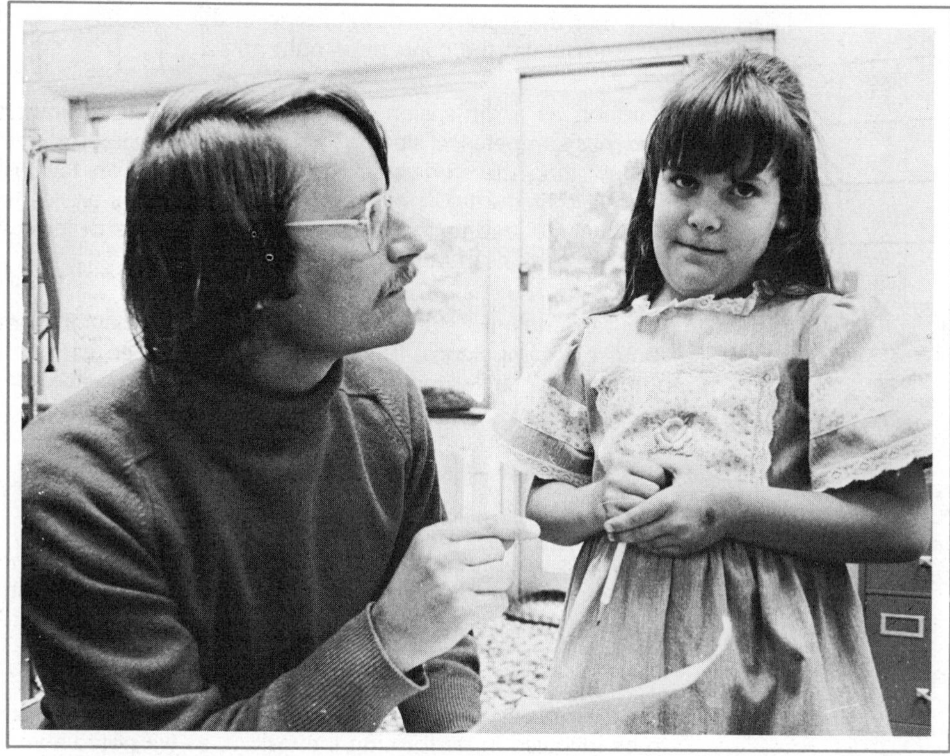

FIGURE 17–2
Various dimensions of student behavior may influence important teacher decisions.

While Gropper does not make the point, it appears to us that his 11 factors can be categorized as either performance characteristics or task characteristics.

The performance characteristics are:

1. Latency—similar to Gilbert's definition.
2. Completion time—time needed to complete task.
3. Duration—similar to Gilbert's definition.
4. Output—similar to Gilbert's definition of tempo or rate at which behaviors occur or products are produced.
5. Some/all—either a partial or complete performance of some of the steps or discrete units of a complete behavior.

The task characteristics are:

6. Recall versus transfer—remembering previously given information versus using knowledge in a new situation.
7. Immediate versus delayed—performance soon after training versus long after training.
8. Recognition versus production—recognizing correct or incorrect information versus recalling correct information.
9. One versus two-directional performance—performing in the sequence taught versus being able to vary the sequence of behaviors.
10. Content difficulty—beginning level skills versus more advanced skills.
11. Aids versus no aids—use of notes, tables, tools, etc. versus no prompts or devices.

The task characteristics have the effect of making it either easier or more difficult for the student to successfully complete the task. Because of this, changes in any of these characteristics will most likely lead to changes in our judgment of performance adequacy.

The second point in Gropper's model is that, based on our judgments of response adequacy, student performance is classified in one of four ways:

1. At criterion level—All performance characteristics meet or exceed criterion level.
2. At substandard level—Some but not all performance characteristics are at acceptable levels.
3. Unacceptable level—None or very few performance characteristics are at acceptable levels.
4. Competing behavior—An incorrectly learned behavior is substituted for the correct behavior.

Gropper's third point is based on the fact that he considers behaviors that can be classified according to the domains and types of learning, as we have discussed them, are actually complete behaviors. He believes the complete behaviors are developed on the basis of four subskills. When the performance of any complete behavior, such as rule using, does not meet criterion level, it is due to a failure in the use of one of the four subskills. The four subskills are discrimination, generalization, association, and chaining, all of which were discussed in Chapter 4 when we covered the behaviorist learning position. By focusing on these four subskills, Gropper's analytic framework becomes a form of task analysis on a much finer level than we presented in Chapter 8. The skills are not subskills of each other and, therefore, can be thought of as micro-level component skills.

The fourth point in Gropper's model is that we need to distinguish among failures that occur during the acquisition, retention, and transfer stages of learning. Gropper (1974) makes a clear distinction between learning-related factors and performance-related factors. He is less specific about retention-related factors, at least in diagnosing errors. This is due, no doubt, to the behavioristic orientation, which focuses on stimuli and responses rather than internal, unobservable processes. From this perspective, retention problems are viewed as a failure to provide sufficient relevant practice in instruction so that learning will persist at least until we assess performance. In effect, retention conditions are included under the broader heading of learning conditions. The cognitivists take a substantially different view of this; we elaborate on this point shortly.

Consistent with the behaviorist concern with the environment and functional stimuli, Gropper's final point is that several stimulus properties in the learning and performance situations are responsible for difficulties in learning the four subskills of discriminations, generalizations, associations, and chains. In order to correct the errors, we need to identify the related environmental factor and modify it appropriately.

Discriminations are made more difficult if the stimuli or responses to be discriminated are highly similar. Also, as the number of stimulus attributes or classes increases, it is more difficult to acquire discriminations. For example, it is usually easier to learn to distinguish between large classes of fish than to distinguish between subspecies. It is also easier to deal with 15 rather than 50 different classes of fish because more features are likely to be needed to make the larger number of discriminations.

On the other hand, generalizations are acquired more easily as the similarity increases and the dissimilarity decreases. They are more difficult to acquire, however, as the number of properties, or number of members in the class, increases. In other words, it is easier to learn how two bananas are alike than to learn how a banana and a strawberry are alike, and even harder to see how a banana, eggplant, strawberry, and coconut are alike.

New associations are more difficult to learn if a stimulus is already associated with a response that is different from the new one with which it is to be associated. For instance if a friend gets a new phone number we may find ourselves starting to dial the old number for a while. New associations are facilitated, however, when a well-learned behavior can be used to aid in learning. This is an endorsement of the notion that there are mathemagenic behaviors and these do indeed enhance the formation of associations. An example of this would be the use of rhyming or acronyms as a mnemonic device by a person well practiced in the use of rhyming and the formation of acronyms.

Learning chains is made more difficult as the length of the chain increases. For instance, it is easier to learn a short poem or tune than a much longer one.

In summary, Gropper's position is that on the basis of certain performance and/or task characteristics, we tend to classify student behaviors in one of four ways. If the behavior does not meet criterion level, it is due to a failure in one of four basic subskills. During the acquisition, retention, and transfer stages of learning, the four subskills are affected by several learning or performance conditions that can be identified and modified to improve student performance in the future. Gropper's approach would lead one to deal with errors by revising the stimulus situation or requiring a different response mode that is more compatible with the child's capabilities (Figure 17–3). This implies that learning is almost entirely controlled by the environment, since all that needs to be done to correct the performance error is to modify the stimulus situation or the response characteristics. This is not, however, the only view of how to analyze and react to the student errors.

2. What are the five main points in Gropper's strategy for analysis of student responses?

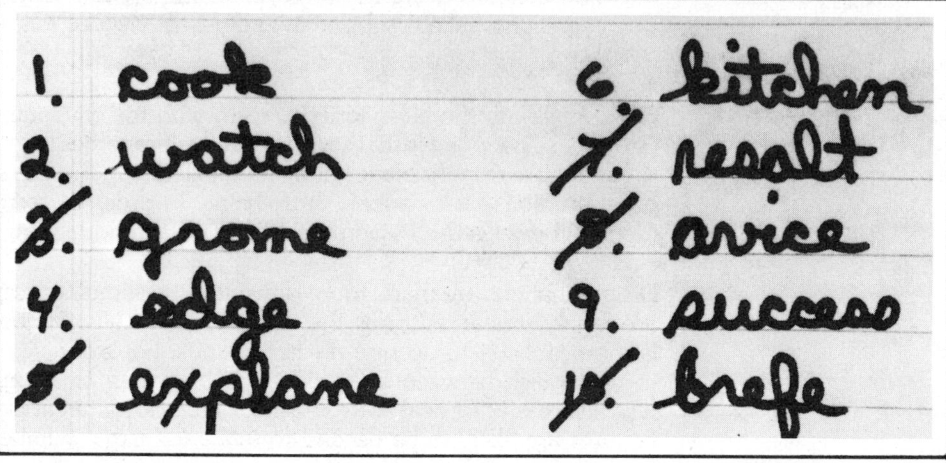

FIGURE 17–3
Careful attention should be given to student errors in planning for future instruction

A cognitivistic approach

Clinchy and Rosenthal (1971) offer another view on the analysis of errors. These two authors do so from an information-processing perspective. They are careful to point out that they make a distinction between errors in the process and products of learning. Errors in products of learning are incorrect responses. Process errors are those that lead up to a product error. They divide process errors into three broad categories: intake, organizational, and executive. It should be noted that these process errors can be inferred only from observations of behavior or examination of the products of behavior. This emphasis on processing errors is not necessarily in conflict with Gropper's position but merely considers the question of errors in terms of the influence of inferred internal processes rather than in terms of external, observable factors.

Intake errors. The two major types of intake errors are *errors in task perception* and *errors in data perception.* The learner can make an *error in task perception* either because of an *ambiguous goal* or because the learner is pursuing a *conflicting goal.* With *ambiguous goals* the learner's errors would be a failure to perceive what is expected due to the teacher's failure to specify the goals well enough. Depending on how the teacher has specified the goal, all students may make the same type of error, each student may make a different error, or only a small number of students may interpret the goal statement incorrectly and make an error. In many situations teachers do not explicitly state the expected goals, and therefore the learner is left to discover the goals implicit in the learning context. As Clinchy and Rosenthal point out, learners from different cultural backgrounds may perceive the goals in a situation differently, and for some the perception may be erroneous in terms of the teacher's expectations.

Instead of misperceiving the goal, the student's error may be one of following a *conflicting goal.* Here the learner may have a correct perception of the goal expected but simply pursues a different short- or long-term goal. The teacher may want a composition, "My Summer," and the student's goal may be to hand in whatever involves the least amount of time but is likely to be accepted.

The second type of intake error, errors in *data perception,* are made because the learner (1) *omits,* (2) *distorts,* or (3) *imports* data. *Omission of data* occurs when the learner is subjected to an overload of information, is distracted, or engages in insufficient scanning of the data. Clinchy and Rosenthal point out that all three of these factors are related to a need for redundancy or, expressed differently, the meaningfulness of the material. The point they make is that the more familiar or meaningful the data are to us, the more data we are able to successfully take in at one time. Also, if we are dealing with material that is familiar to us, we can successfully absorb it even with some distractions. It is only when the material is less familiar to us that small distractions cause us to omit data. Apparently the familiarity or meaningfulness allows us to fill in the gaps in the data that were omitted during the intake process. An example of this is your ability to follow most television stories without paying total attention to what is said and shown. Our scanning of the television program, in terms of watching and listening, needs to be only minimal because the total situation is so familiar to us that we need only a limited number of cues to follow the story. Differing from this situation is when we are reading new and novel information in a textbook. Here we are likely to be faced with an informational overload. Repeated readings or scanning of the material is likely to result in additional information being gained each time we go through the material. The rereading process is a systematic method of adequately scanning and subdividing the material into manageable units.

With other types of tasks the scanning process also needs to be systematic enough to insure that information is not omitted during the intake process. The most likely material to be omitted in the scanning process is that which is too novel or unfamiliar to have any meaning for us. It is only as we become aware of various attributes of stimuli that we develop the ability to focus our attention on them. As Clinchy and Rosenthal point out, redundancy of information has a fundamental effect on how much data a person is likely to omit. With wide variations in achievement levels of students in a class, we can expect those students at the lower levels of achievement to make errors of omission during the intake process and also to require more time to take in all of the information.

Distortion of data occurs when the learner has *inappropriate expectations,* uses *loose criteria,* or uses *brute simplification.* If we have inappropriate expectations about the data we will be presented with, then our perceptual set is likely to cause us to distort the data. Kahneman and Tversky's observations about biases in judgments, which we presented earlier, are relevant to this issue. In distortions caused by using *loose criteria,* we tend to match incoming data inappropriately with information we already possess. Apparently, certain relevant aspects of the information are so loosely defined by the learner that the new information appears to be similar to previous information. Clinchy and Rosenthal state that this type of distortion is particularly true with younger children rather than with adults. *Brute simplification* leads to distortion errors during the encoding of information. Clinchy and Rosenthal point out that brute simplification is both an intake and an organizational error. Normally encoding facilitates the intake process by simplifying data. If, however, the encoding process uses brute simplification, then the data are simplified to a point where they are distorted during the encoding process. Again, certain relevant distinctions in the data are ignored during the intake process and they are grouped or organized inappropriately.

Importation of data occurs when the learner adds to the data presented from his/her personal store of experiences. When these additions are appropriate, there is no apparent error but rather some enrichment of the data. However, when the additions are inappropriate, the student has a data base that is different from the one needed to deal with the learning task and, therefore, is likely to make a performance error.

In our discussion of intake errors we have listed ten different types. Since this exceeds the normal 7 ± 2 capacity to deal with information, it occurred to us that you may be experiencing a concrete example of information overload and subsequently make errors. To help you cope with this overload and also as a means of illustrating our next topic of organizational errors, the ten types we have just described can be outlined as follows:

I. Intake errors.
   A. Errors in task perception.
      1. Ambiguous goal.
      2. Conflicting goal.
   B. Errors in data perception.
      1. Omission of data.
      2. Distortion of data.
         a. Inappropriate expectations.
         b. Loose criteria.
         c. Brute simplification.
      3. Importation of data.

If you perceived the ten types of errors as being organized differently, you would see different relationships in the information we presented. If the informational overload was great enough so that you could not organize it and thereby "chunk" it, you would probably do poorly on a test of this specific information.

Organizational errors. According to Clinchy and Rosenthal (1971, p. 116), organizational errors are those made in "isolating certain elements of the data (analysis), combining these elements in new ways (synthesis), and ordering a series of such operations inappropriately (sequencing)."

As pointed out, analysis errors are due to a failure to isolate relevant aspects of the data. They appear to be close to what Gropper refers to as discrimination and association errors, where the learner fails to respond to a particular aspect of the stimulus situation that requires a different response to different specific stimuli.

The learner makes synthesis errors by not synthesizing two or more relevant bits of information into the appropriate combination. In some respects these errors are similar to Gropper's generalization errors in that Clinchy and Rosenthal cite instances of synthesis errors where the learner failed to generalize appropriately.

As Clinchy and Rosenthal outline them, sequencing errors involve conceptual strategies, or hypotheses, used in seeking a solution to a problem. In this respect these errors involve mathemagenic behaviors, as we have described them, and differ from Gropper's notion of chaining errors. In relation to mathemagenic behaviors, the strategies are a means of organizing a task or ordering data in some sort of sequence or arrangement of categories. It is essentially the conceptual outline we use in working on a task. Clinchy and Rosenthal (p. 119) express this as "the use of a systematic plan for arranging information in a coherent sequence." In the sense that Gropper uses the term *chaining,* we are dealing with the sequential ordering of the content of a problem or the sequence of actions in a response rather than the total strategy we use to acquire the content.

Executive errors. Errors of this type do not involve a failure to understand the problem but rather an error in executing a particular strategy that is presumably learned. The error occurs primarily in the form of what are often referred to as "careless" or "stupid" errors or are sometimes classed as "sloppy" work habits (Figure 17–4). These also occur with lengthy sequences of operations. It appears that this may be due to cumbersome or poorly organized methods used during the execution of a problem-solving task. To some extent it involves errors in which learners lose sight of the response strategy needed and get bogged down in the maze of details involved in the task.

Now that we have presented error analysis from the behaviorist and cognitivist perspectives, we would like to call your attention to the fact that both positions relate the errors to environmental factors. Whereas Gropper relates product errors, Clinchy and Rosenthal relate process errors. Since the product errors are more concrete and the process errors more speculative, a focus on product errors appears to be a more secure approach to the analysis of errors. The behaviorists would certainly agree with this argument. The problem is that the same product error can be the result of different process errors. As long as we start from the sure ground of product errors and move with caution to the softer ground of speculating about process errors that may be involved, we see no harm. In fact it seems like a pragmatic strategy for the

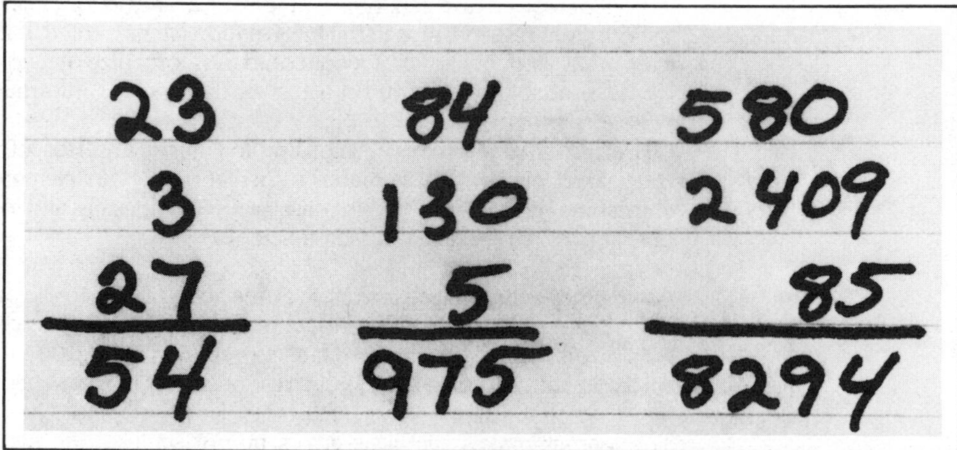

FIGURE 17–4
Some executive errors occur in the form of sloppy work habits

teacher that may help us more quickly decide which factors require some modification. In the remainder of the chapter we offer our synthesis of these positions to call attention to the fact that both environment- and student-controlled factors may lead to errors. While the behaviorists and cognitivists would both modify the environment to overcome the error, in some cases they would modify very different things.

> 3. What are the three main types of errors that Clinchy and Rosenthal focus on? In what basic way is their focus different from Gropper's?

THE PROCESS OF ERROR ANALYSIS

As we pointed out earlier, responding to student errors is an integral part of the instructional episode because the classroom provides an ongoing flow of stimuli, some of which will *elicit* student responses. The teacher *expects* certain responses to these stimuli. As the student is responding, the teacher *observes* the student's behavior and afterward the product of the behavior. The teacher then *evaluates* the student's performance or product and if the performance or product does not meet the teacher's expectations, the teacher *hypothesizes* about the possible reasons for the erroneous performance. After the teacher has finished hypothesizing, the final step in the process is to *follow up* with some remedial activity designed to insure that the error does not occur in the future.

During the process of reacting to student responses, five basic questions can arise. The first two questions arise during the evaluating phase.

1. Were the performance conditions appropriate for the type of learning being evaluated?
2. Does the student's response and/or product of behavior meet my criteria?

Assuming we judge the performance conditions to be appropriate but judge the student's response or product of behavior as not meeting our criteria, we would be faced with a further set of questions.

1. At what stage in the learning process did the error develop?
2. What student-controlled factors may have contributed to the error?
3. What environmental factors may have contributed to the error?

For the purpose of describing the process of error analysis we have divided it into the following six phases:

1. Eliciting phase.
2. Expectancy phase.
3. Observation phase.
4. Evaluation phase.
5. Hypothesizing phase.
6. Follow-up phase.

The six phases of the error analysis process are presented graphically in Figure 17–5. Each of the five questions is shown in relation to the various factors associated with each phase in the process. Lines and arrows indicate the normal flow of activities in the error analysis process. To indicate the continuous nature of instruction, the lines form a continuous loop.

The relevant environment (eliciting phase)

As shown at top left in the diagram, the process begins with an eliciting phase. This phase is actually not part of the error analysis process; more accurately it is a prelude to the process. We have included it here to point out the major ways that student responses are elicited. For instance a teacher can change the physical stimuli in the environment and thereby bring about a student response. At other times, when no changes occur, the monotony of the physical environment will induce a response. The most common means of eliciting student responses is for the teacher to ask questions, make statements, assign tasks, or otherwise interact with the student. Another common way that student responses are evoked is through interactions with peers or other individuals in the environment. Activity can also be self-induced by a person's thoughts, which may or may not be directly related to stimuli in the environment. Those that are unrelated, or only tangentially related, are sometimes of major concern to the student. Due to the wide variety of eliciting stimuli and because a teacher is interested in all four domains of learning, errors in a wide range of student performance may be noted. Thinking of errors in terms of merely the cognitive domain is the typical approach and appears to be a result of focusing too narrowly on the instructional goals of teachers, thereby losing sight of the broader educational goals of schools.

The relevant characteristics of the eliciting phase are outlined in Figure 17–9, which is presented after the description of all six phases.

Teacher expectancies (expectancy phase)

Returning to Figure 17–5, at the second level the ongoing stream of stimuli in the classroom also elicits at least three expectancies within the teacher. A teacher expects the student's response to occur under a certain set of conditions. The teacher also expects the student's response to those conditions to have behavioral characteristics of a specific type or to be within a certain range. If the student's behavior results in a product the teacher also has certain expectations about what it will look like.

Performance conditions. We have pointed out in earlier chapters the general performance conditions that should exist in order to assess whether a particular bit of learning has occurred, such as a concept or rule. These conditions may not exist in all situations. Sometimes we are aware of inappropriate performance conditions but at other times we are not so aware. Stated differently, we may expect certain conditions to exist that are appropriate for assessing a particular bit of learning and

FIGURE 17–5
The context and phases of the error analysis process with associated instructional questions

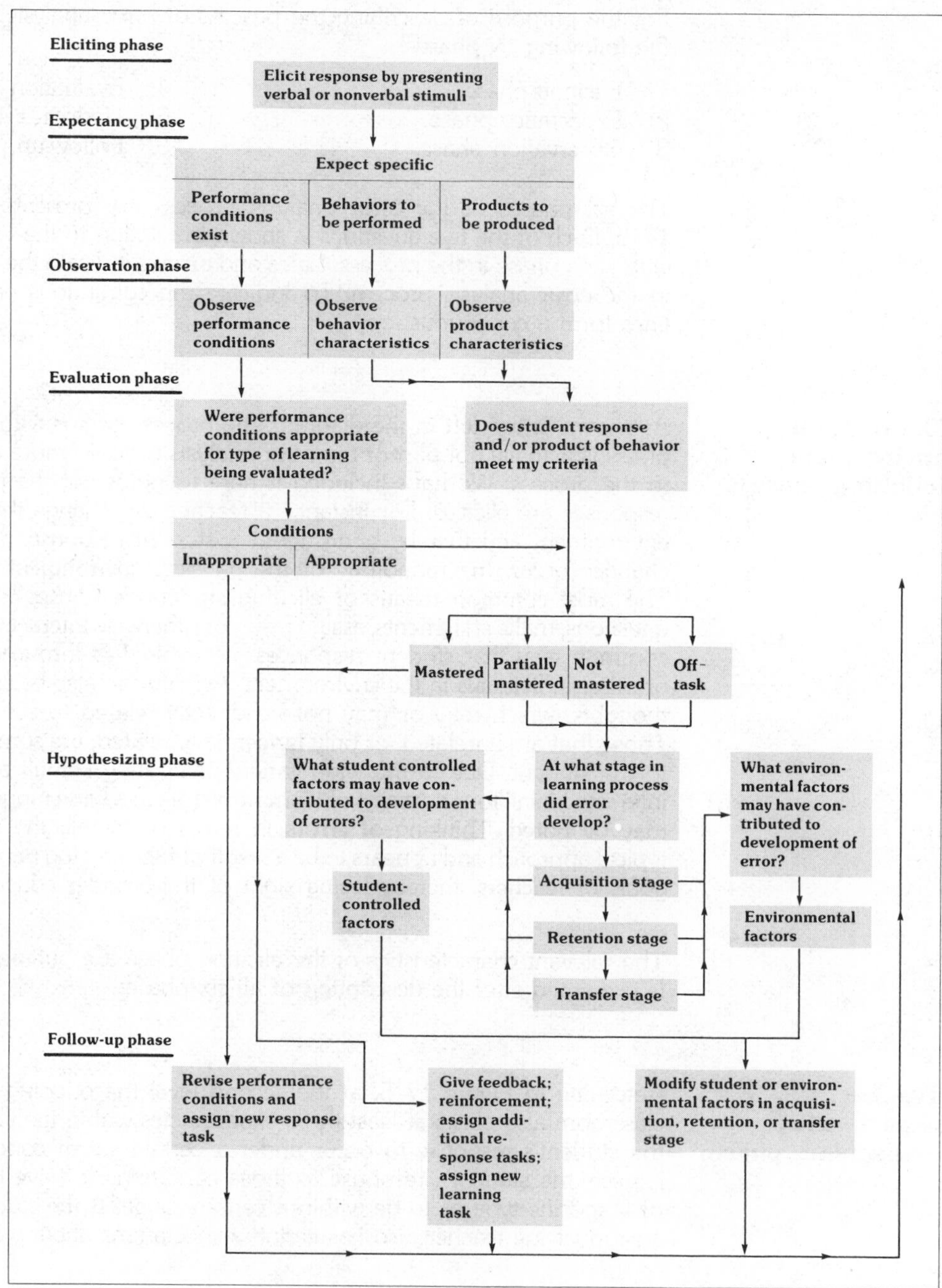

these expectations will influence our judgments. If our expectations in terms of performance conditions do not match reality, then our judgments are likely to be faulty.

Within the broad performance conditions more specific task characteristics must also exist for assessing the various types of learning. Gropper has specified what appears to be a fairly comprehensive list of specific task characteristics. With a small modification we have incorporated Gropper's list into our model of analyzing errors as follows:

1. Encountered versus unencountered task.
2. Immediate versus delayed performance.
3. Recognition versus recall task.
4. One-directional versus two-directional performance.
5. Simple versus complex content.
6. Aided versus unaided performance.

Only some of the characteristics will be appropriate for any particular type of learning and the task to which the student will be responding.

Behavioral characteristics. In addition to our expectations about the performance conditions, we have certain expectations about the behaviors various stimuli will elicit. For instance, a question about the causes of the Civil War is not likely to elicit a headstand from the student, but we may not be as surprised by a groan or an incorrect answer from the student. In terms of the various domains and types of learning, we have, in other chapters, described the general behavioral characteristics that are expected. Briefly, the expectation is that the student will name, classify, or approach in response to various stimuli. On a more specific level, the behavioral characteristics described by Gilbert (1962) and Gropper (1974, 1975) sharpen our expectations. Gilbert and Gropper differ only slightly in the characteristics they outline. Our adaptation of their characteristics is as follows:

1. Latency—the time (i.e., short–long) between the first opportunity for a behavior and its initial occurrence.
2. Intension—the amount (i.e., small–large) of movement of any one body part.
3. Extension—the amount (i.e., small–large) of the total body involved in the behavior.
4. Tempo—the rate (i.e., slow–fast) of the continuously ongoing behavior.
5. Perseverance—the proportion (i.e., small–large) of time in which the behaviors are actually occurring.
6. Completion time—time needed (i.e., short–long) to complete the task.
7. Duration—the total time (i.e., short–long) from the start of the behavior to the end of the behavior regardless of whether or not the task is completed.
8. Output—the total number (i.e., few–many) of behaviors or products of behavior the individual engages in.
9. Completeness—the number (i.e., some–all) of steps in a complete behavior that are performed or the parts of a complete product that are produced.

Our reasons for including in our list the dimensions of latency, completion time, output, and completeness should be fairly obvious since they are criteria commonly used by teachers. The dimensions of intension and extension also appear necessary for defining behavior in the motor domain. Since body movements tend to influence our judgments in the affective and mathemagenic domains, this is an additional reason for including them in our list of behavioral characteristics. While tempo and perseverance tend to determine completion time, they were incorporated into the list because in particular situations they may give a more precise meaning to our expectations and observations. Duration differs from perseverance and completion time in that duration is stated as an absolute value in terms of the length of time a behavior persists; perseverance is stated as a proportion of a time period during which the behavior occurs; completion time is stated as an absolute value but in relation to the task to be performed. At times it may be more meaningful to describe a behavior, such as reading, in terms of the length of time one instance of the behavior is carried on regardless of whether the entire reading task was completed. At another time it may make more sense to describe the behavior as a proportion of the time it is engaged in. In still other situations we may wish to describe how long it takes to read a specified unit of material.

To the above nine dimensions we add another set from behavior modification techniques.

10. Timing—when a behavior occurs in terms of time of day, or spacing between occurrences of behavior.
11. Frequency—the number of times a behavior has occurred, usually with respect to a specified time period.
12. Location—where a behavior occurs in terms of general location or proximity to specific stimuli such as physical objects or specific individuals (Figure 17–6).

These have been added for those instances in which a task has not been assigned, but we wish to describe a behavior that occurs only occasionally. These dimensions are more likely to be used in conjunction with the affective domain, although they can at times be used with the other domains.

Product characteristics. The third set of expectations is about the characteristics of the products we may elicit. Many student products of behavior are assigned tasks and therefore the product characteristics are likely to be defined by the criteria of our instructional objectives. These criteria form a set of ideal expectations toward which we expect students to progress. Elsewhere we have described the product characteristics one should expect as evidence of learning in the various domains. These products are also defined by commonly accepted criteria within the various academic subject areas.

FIGURE 17–6
Sometimes we are interested in the location of specific activities

Quite often the social standards of the community help define acceptable product characteristics. For instance in a language class a student may have to write a short composition. We would expect, in most cases, to see the usual conventions of grammar and spelling followed. Based on the values of the community we would not expect certain topics, assumptions, or words to appear in these compositions, whereas in another community we might expect these to appear.

The mode of responding also affects the product characteristics. If we require a student to describe a typical day's activities we may want a written, pictorial, pantomime, or oral presentation. The latter two would be transitory products but could be tangible if taped or filmed. Depending on the response mode we might focus on punctuation, smoothness of line, expressiveness of motion, or inflection.

To summarize, during the expectancy phase the ongoing stream of stimulus events affects our prior expectations or psychological set, which will bias our observations of a student's behavior, the products of student behavior, and the performance conditions. Due to this bias we are likely to "see" what we expect, even when it does not actually exist. In other words, teachers are as susceptible as anyone else to intake errors such as omission, importation, and distortion. In order to reduce the amount that our expectations distort our observations, we believe it is well to look carefully and objectively at our expectations as teachers.

The relevant characteristics of this phase are summarized in Figure 17–9, which is presented after the discussion of all six phases.

Observation of responses (observation phase)

The observational phase, depicted at the third level in Figure 17–5, includes that portion of time when we are actively observing the student's actual behavior, the conditions under which it is occurring, and the product of the behavior. Since student behaviors and the conditions under which they occur can be very brief, our observation time is often limited. With products of behavior we sometimes have the advantage of being able to examine them at our convenience and also take more time to complete our observations. These products are, however, sometimes produced at home or in situations where we cannot be sure of the actual conditions under which they were produced.

The factors we focus on in the observation phase are, therefore, the same as those described in the expectancy phase. As we pointed out in our discussion of that phase, our expectations guide our observations but care must be taken that they do not distort our observations. This is most easily avoided by having a clear understanding of what it is we need to observe and what may distort our observations.

In Figure 17–9, which is presented later, the relevant characteristics of the observation phase are found. The content of the column headed Observation is similar to the expectancy phase column. Even though the contents of the two phases look similar in the model, it should be remembered that the content of our expectations may not match what we actually observe even though we use the same dimensions to describe both expectations and observations.

Evaluation of responses (evaluation phase)

During the evaluation phase the basic function performed is to match the observed performance or product characteristics with our expectations. If we have a well-stated objective that clearly indicates the characteristics of the performance or product in some quantifiable means, then the evaluation task is well defined. More often we enter the evaluation phase with only vague evaluative standards. This is true even for teachers who take the time to explicitly state many of their objectives in performance terms, because teachers are compelled to cope with an extremely wide range of behaviors that are not easily quantifiable. For example, it may be easy to state the exact answer to 2 + 2, or what proportion of addition examples we will accept as a minimum standard of acceptable behavior. It is much more difficult to quantify how cooperative or courteous a student should be. The latter may be a part of a teacher's goals just as the learning of addition may be, yet the teacher may not have any explicit criteria against which to judge cooperation or courtesy. While the criteria may not be explicit, as we pointed out in preceding chapters, they nonetheless exist. It is against this more or less implicit set of standards or expectations that we tend to evaluate students' responses.

Gropper has identified four useful categories for evaluating performance. Three of his categories have the advantage of agreeing with categories used in many educational materials you may encounter. It is common to find evaluation checklists with three levels of mastery such as mastered, partially mastered, and not mastered. In our model we use the mastery headings for the evaluation categories because of the more general usage of this terminology. The term *mastery* implies that a student's performance or product meets all of our criteria under appropriate conditions. *Partial mastery* refers to a performance that meets our general criteria but does not meet all of our specific criteria. *Not mastered* refers to performances in which our general criteria have not been met but the performance is a reasonable approximation of the behavior or a commonly occurring error.

Based on the student's performance we may also observe a behavior that does not appear to have any relationship to our expectations and associated standards of performance. We will depart from Gropper's lead and refer to this as *off-task behavior*. Gropper uses his term to refer to behaviors related to the task that block the desired behavior from occurring. We will broaden his definition to include any and all behaviors that do not allow us to make any inference about the degree of learning that has occurred. Included in this category would be unusual errors and non-task-related behaviors. More generally the responses would appear to be related to a different stimulus than the one we presented or the one we assume elicited the response.

In addition to evaluating the student performance or product, we need to evaluate the adequacy of the assessment conditions in terms of the type of learning we have evaluated. The simplest approach to this is to classify the conditions as either appropriate or inappropriate on the basis of whether or not all of the necessary conditions existed. It is quite possible that some but not all conditions have been met. In this situation it is probably not valid to assume that learning has occurred at a particular level. For this reason a two-category system of evaluation appears to be sufficient for a general strategy. If all conditions are appropriate then we can go on and evaluate the student's performance or product. If all conditions are not met then we need to observe the behavior under appropriate conditions.

An outline of the main characteristics of the evaluation phase is given in Figure 17–9.

Hypotheses about contributing factors (hypothesis phase)

Following our evaluation of a student's performance, one of three things usually follows. If the performance conditions are not appropriate, we may elicit another response under appropriate conditions. If the performance conditions are appropriate and we judge the performance or product to be at the mastery level, we usually react to it in a positive manner. If the performance is judged to be below mastery level, we ask ourselves why the error has occurred and eventually what can be done to prevent it from occurring in the future. In asking ourselves these questions we usually have no data beyond our observations. We cannot physically enter the student's thought processes and observe what may have gone wrong. We do, in a sense, attempt to do this by making inferences about what may have gone astray. Based on an integration of Gropper's and the Clinchy and Rosenthal's approach to error analysis, it appears that three major hypotheses can be made. One is about the learning stage at which the error has developed, a second is about which student-controlled factors may be involved, and the third is about which conditions in the environment may be inappropriate. For convenience we are presenting these three hypotheses as if they develop in the sequence just mentioned. It is possible for them to develop in any sequence and for one or two hypotheses to be made without the others. Too often in classrooms none of the inferences is made and this we believe to be a mistake. From an instructional perspective errors indicate that further activity is needed, but the question is: What activity? Only by trying to decide what may have gone wrong will we be able to most effectively and efficiently help the student. Repeating the previous activities may not be the solution.

Hypothesis 1: Learning stage. As Gropper notes errors can occur during the acquisition, retention, and transfer stages of learning. For instance a student may not have acquired the necessary information for some reason (Figure 17–7). It is also possible that the student may have acquired the necessary information but failed to retain it. The third possibility is that the transfer situation is such that the student

FIGURE 17–7
Errors can occur during the acquisition of learning

is unable to perform properly. In this case the student may be able to respond appropriately to other transfer tasks.

To clarify our use of the three terms, the acquisition stage is used to refer to situations in which the student is presented with new information or an expansion or modification of previous information. On the student's part it involves the perception and storage of information. The retention stage of learning includes the retrieval of information from long-term storage and its rehearsal on a covert level. It also includes *unobserved,* overt rehearsal of information or a response. By distinguishing between observed and unobserved overt responses we make a distinction between the responses we do and do not analyze for errors. The unobserved, and unanalyzed, overt and covert behaviors are beyond our control but may be partially responsible for the characteristics of the behavior or product we do observe and can react to. Within the transfer stage we include any and all observed, overt behaviors that make use of previously learned information to respond to a new situation. The transfer can be across a relatively narrow or wide gap between training and response conditions.

Hypothesis 2: Student-controlled factors. Speculating even further as to why a student performs at a less than criterion level, you may infer that a particular cognitive process is at fault during one or more of the three learning stages. We have adapted Clinchy and Rosenthal's approach as the primary organization for this portion of our error analysis model. We have integrated into this the four subskills Gropper views as being a partial basis for errors.

As we have defined the *acquisition stage* of learning, a student could make intake and organization errors but not executive errors because we have excluded from this stage any form of response. In the *retention stage* intake, organization, and executive errors could all occur. The intake errors would occur when the information to be rehearsed is incorrectly retrieved from long-term memory storage. Organization errors could occur as a result of a new organization being imposed upon the information at this stage. Executive errors could occur in the covert rehearsal of information or subsequent returning of information to long-term memory storage. During the *transfer stage* of learning intake errors from memory or of the transfer task could occur because we use information from both sources. Organization errors could also occur relative to the information from memory, but more likely they will be in relation to the transfer task since this will be new information requiring some organization. Executive errors are especially relevant in the transfer stage of learning because it is during this stage that we are dealing with observed, overt responses. The relationship of learning stages to cognitive processes is depicted in Figure 17–8.

The *intake, organization,* and *executive* processes involve distinct types of errors. Errors in the *intake process* include omission, addition, and distortion of data. In our view, these are different forms of discrimination error. With omission or addition errors some aspect of the data is either missed or added. With distortion errors Clinchy and Rosenthal's use of the concepts of brute simplification and loose criteria lead

FIGURE 17–8
Relationship of learning stages to cognitive processes

Learning stage	*Cognitive processes*
Acquisition	Intake (from environment), organization
Retention	Intake (from memory), organization, executive
Transfer	Intake (from environment and/or memory), organization, executive

us to conclude that these are generalization errors resulting from previously learned discriminations. If the discriminations we have learned are not accurate or precise, we are likely to overlook subtle but relevant aspects in the data we receive. Having overlooked these characteristics in the data, we are likely to misclassify the data and deal with them as a more general or different class of stimuli. Because of this relationship between discriminations and generalizations we believe it is reasonable and simpler to consider various forms of intake errors as discrimination errors due to omission, addition, or distortion and treat generalization errors as occurring in the organization process. In short we consider intake errors to be discrimination errors.

The *organization process* we have retained intact from Clinchy and Rosenthal in terms of *analysis, synthesis,* and *sequencing* errors. *Analysis errors* we view as discrimination errors. *Synthesis errors* we treat as encompassing both association and generalization errors since both of these imply some joining together. With associations it is the joining of discrete units, whereas generalization involves a set of criteria to relate various stimuli. *Sequencing errors,* as Clinchy and Rosenthal explain them, are analogous to an overall strategy for solving a problem. Chaining errors as used by Gropper are more related to the sequencing of a response developed as a result of the organization process. The distinction between the two terms lies in the different perspectives of the behaviorists and the cognitivists. The behaviorist meaning of *chaining* is more closely associated with environmental data or responses intended to reflect the environmental data in terms of ordering. The cognitivist use of the term *sequencing* is more closely associated with the cognitive strategy or particular mathemagenic behavior used to cope with a problem, and as such is independent of the environmental data and observable response reflecting the environmental data. Due to the differences in the two concepts, we have retained both terms but use the term *chaining* in relation to executive errors since this appears more appropriate.

The *executive process* we have portrayed as occurring in the retention and transfer stages of learning. In both of these stages there is likely to be a response from the learner. In the rehearsal stage the response is unobserved, and in the transfer stage it is observed. As we described them earlier, executive errors may be due to *poorly organized* or *cumbersome response strategies* that have been developed. These errors would occur during the performance of a response or as a product is being produced. Some executive errors would be *chaining errors* in that the ordering of the response chain or product is not appropriate. It is also possible to have a response run off in an acceptable sequence but not have it done smoothly. We are also likely to observe self-correcting changes in a response chain. We apparently monitor our performances as they are being run off, and when an error is detected it is corrected by the individual (Welford, 1976). Instances in which an individual becomes bogged down in task-related details and cannot perform a reasonable approximation of the required response we would view as organizational errors and not as executive errors. The distinction between organizational and executive errors would be difficult to maintain with any rigor. We suggest that a reasonable approximation of an acceptable response be treated as an executive error. At this level of performance, if the individual has more practice in responding, the errors are likely to disappear even though the executive strategy used is more cumbersome than some others that could be used. The increased practice is likely to organize any poorly organized strategies that led to the previous executive errors. With more drastic errors, more than practice of the executive function is required.

Hypothesis 3: Environmental factors. When making inferences about environmental factors we are on firmer territory because we can refer to the conditions of learning and performance derived from research studies. The acquisition stage of learning should call our attention to the conditions of learning. The retention stage should call our attention to certain of these conditions. Errors in the transfer stage of learning should focus our attention on performance conditions including both the general transfer conditions and the more specific transfer conditions we have listed earlier under the heading of performance characteristics.

Discussion of these three types of inferences expands our model considerably. This expansion is illustrated in Figure 17–9, which follows the next section.

Follow-up (follow-up phase)

This phase of the process is really epilogue in that it occurs after the error analysis process is complete. We included it in Figure 17–5 for the sake of making clear the continuity of activities in instruction. We will cover in detail various follow-up activities in the next chapter. For now we will simply point out that mastery level performances are usually followed by moving on to new tasks. The desired performance should be followed with reinforcement more often than generally occurs in many classrooms. Incorrect performances need to be followed with additional instruction in the form of corrective feedback or other instructional activities.

The behaviorists and cognitivists differ somewhat in the recommendations they make about follow-up activities. The behaviorists would, because of their focus on environmental conditions, recommend manipulating environmental factors to eliminate the errors. The cognitivists are not as convinced that we should completely structure and simplify the learning environment to make sure a specific bit of learning will occur. Some contend that overstructuring the learning environment does not develop the mathemagenic behaviors necessary to cope with complex problems.

See Figure 17–9 for the relevant characteristics of all six phases.

> 4. What are the six phases described in the model for the analysis of responses? What are the five main decisions that are required?

ANALYSIS OF COGNITIVE DOMAIN RESPONSES

In Figure 17–9 we outlined our response analysis model. In the remainder of the chapter we show how it can be applied. The presentation assumes that you have observed the student's behavior or product of behavior and have made an evaluation of the behavior. The discussion therefore focuses on the hypothesis phase and tries to point out some of the complexities involved. We discuss each of the four domains separately on the basis of the four evaluation categories since each will tend to generate different hypotheses.

Performance at mastery level

If all the behavioral characteristics and product characteristics meet criterion levels, then an inference that the student has learned the skill seems logical. However, there is always a possibility that this inference is incorrect. To test our inference, it is useful to require one or more responses from the student. This, in effect, would be a means of measuring the reliability with which the student can respond appropriately. Another strategy that should be used to test the inference is to examine the conditions under which the performance was made. It is possible that there are unintended cues in the situation that reduce the amount of transfer required, or we may have used a transfer task that inadvertently requires less transfer than intended.

FIGURE 17–9
Model for error analysis indicating phases and relevant characteristics of phases

Eliciting	*Expectancy*	*Observation*	*Evaluation*	*Hypothesis*	*Follow-up*
1. Teacher-initiated 2. Physical environment-initiated 3. Peer-initiated 4. Other person-initiated	**Performance conditions** 1. Encountered vs. unencountered task 2. Immediate vs. delayed performance 3. Recognition vs. recall task 4. One-directional vs. two-directional performance 5. Simple vs. complex content 6. Aided vs. unaided performance **Behavioral characteristics** *General characteristics* Cognitive domain 1. Rule—demonstrate 2. Concept—classify 3. Memorization—reproduce Motor domain 1. Skilled performance 2. Muscle movement Affective domain 1. Approach 2. Avoidance 3. Escape Mathemagenic domain 1. Problem solving 2. Mathemagenic behaviors *Specific characteristics* 1. Latency 2. Intension 3. Extension 4. Tempo 5. Perseveration 6. Completion time 7. Duration 8. Output 9. Some/all 10. Timing 11. Location **Product characteristics** Defined by: 1. Subject matter criteria 2. Social norm criteria	**Performance conditions** 1. Encountered vs. unencountered task 2. Immediate vs. delayed performance 3. Recognition vs. recall task 4. One-directional vs. two-directional performance 5. Simple vs. complex content 6. Aided vs. unaided performance **Behavioral characteristics** *General characteristics* Cognitive domain 1. Rule—demonstrate 2. Concept—classify 3. Memorization—reproduce Motor domain 1. Skilled performance 2. Muscle movement Affective domain 1. Approach 2. Avoidance 3. Escape Mathemagenic domain 1. Problem solving 2. Mathemagenic behaviors *Specific characteristics* 1. Latency 2. Intension 3. Extension 4. Tempo 5. Perseveration 6. Completion time 7. Duration 8. Output 9. Some/all 10. Timing 11. Location **Product characteristics** Defined by: 1. Subject matter criteria 2. Social norm criteria	**Performance conditions** *Inappropriate* → *Appropriate* **Performance characteristics** Mastery → Partial mastery Nonmastery Off-task	**Learning stage** Acquisition Retention Transfer **Student-controlled factors** *Intake process* Omission errors, discrimination skill Addition errors, discrimination skill Distortion errors, discrimination skill *Organization process* Analysis errors, discrimination skill Synthesis errors, association skill, generalization skill *Executive process* Poorly organized response strategy, cumbersome strategy, chaining skill **Environmental factors** *General factors* Presentation strategy Task requirements *Specific factors* Conditions of learning Task requirements	Initiate new response under appropriate conditions Check performance conditions. Give feedback. Reinforce. Assign additional practice tasks. Assign new learning tasks Modify student-controlled and/or environmental factors in acquisition, retention, or transfer stage

Rule learning. Rule learning is fairly resistant to forgetting (Gagné, 1970). Therefore, one response may be sufficient to infer that learning has occurred, but you should check to make sure the task was previously unencountered and you may want to check on the reliability of the performance by requiring other responses. Also, as a check on the predictive validity of transfer to other situations, you should ask yourself how big a gap in difficulty level there is between the present task and the transfer situation in terms of complexity. In a more complex situation the student may not be able to make the discriminations and generalization necessary to see that the rule applies.

Concept learning. The ability to retain and use learned concepts is also relatively stable. Again, the task should present previously unencountered examples and nonexamples for the student to classify. A check on reliability can be made by presenting more examples for classification. By varying the difficulty of the stimuli presented for classification, you can also vary the level of predictive validity to new situations in which new stimuli will be encountered.

Memorization. With this type of learning, retention is relatively short-lived and any inference that learning has occurred should be tempered in terms of the length of time you expect the learning to be retained. You may have been able to name every child in your first-grade class when you were in it, but unless you have had subsequent contact with these individuals or periodically rehearsed their names, you probably will not be able to recall all their names now. In school much of the factual material taught is not expected to be retained during a person's lifetime but is required to be retained for short periods of time in order to point out similarities, differences, categories, and relationships. The use of this verbal information is in many respects merely a vehicle to aid learning of concepts and rules.

The measurement situation must present the student with a question designed to elicit the desired information, but some determination should be made that no unwanted cues are present. Also, if recall rather than recognition is the level on which a student is expected to transfer the learning, then performance on recognition tasks would not provide the predictive validity to infer learning at the recall level. The recognition task would provide more cues than would be available in the transfer situation. For many real-life transfer situations the recognition level of performance is all that is required, and therefore using recognition tasks is appropriate for an inference that learning has occurred.

Performance at partial mastery level

At the partial mastery level a student's performance or product of performance is not completely acceptable. We need to look more closely at the exact characteristics of that performance or product in relation to the transfer task in order to most effectively decide what needs to be done next.

Rule learning. When rule learning is only partially mastered, the error can be due to (1) nonmastery of one of the concepts involved in the rule, (2) a misunderstanding of the relationship between the concepts, or (3) a misunderstanding of the transfer task. The first possibility is a case of not having the prerequisite skills to learn the rule and would therefore occur during the acquisition stage of learning. A misunderstanding of the relationship between concepts would most likely occur during the acquisition stage but also could occur during the retention stages. A misunderstanding of the transfer task is clearly related to the transfer stage. These are the possibilities, but the problem facing the teacher is to decide which alternative is involved in any particular partial mastery performance. To ferret out the correct alternative we have to consider a series of alternatives, which we can diagram as follows:

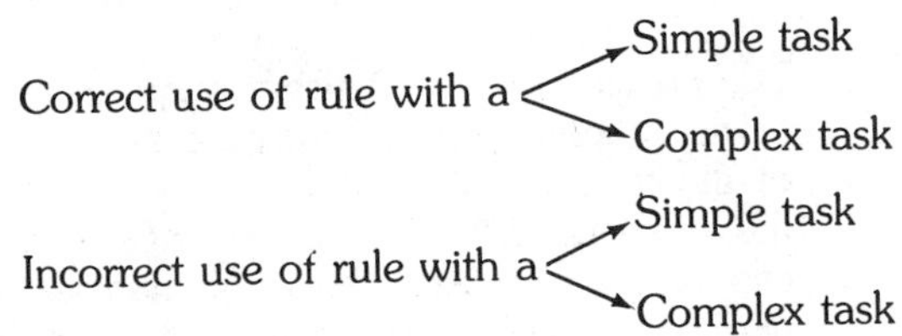

Taking the first alternative, a student can correctly apply a rule to a simple task, but because of a long latency period (slow to respond) we may judge the performance level as partial mastery. Since the response was correct we can rule out any errors in the acquisition or retention stages of learning. The hesitation can be due to the fact that we are requiring transfer over a long period of time and the executive function of recalling the rule is deficient. Even if the transfer time is fairly short, it seems more logical to consider the problem as occurring in the transfer stage since time is the only variable that has been changed.

For the second alternative the acquisition and retention stages can be ruled out for the same reasons as given above; namely, the student has, after a delay, demonstrated correct usage of the rule. In this case the complexity of the task may have resulted in our observing a long latency, a long completion time, a slow tempo, or if several tasks are involved, a small output in the specific characteristics of the student's performance. Since the student has successfully applied the rule, the information given in the task was successfully taken in and the rule was accurately recalled. This would narrow the problem down to the process of organization or execution. An organizational problem is most reasonably assumed when the complexity of the task mainly involves large amounts of relevant or distracting information (Figure 17–10). An execution error is more reasonable when the complexity of the task is related to the type of response that is required.

FIGURE 17–10
Organizational errors may be due to large amounts of stimuli

Moving to the third alternative in which the student has incorrectly responded to a relatively simple task, the acquisition and retention stages of learning are likely to be involved. The student may have failed to learn the correct rule or distorted the rule during the retention stage. The general characteristics of the student's performance or product may make it obvious which rule the student did apply in the situation. The characteristics of the task should be inspected to see whether an intake error could have occurred due to some ambiguity in the task statement.

The final alternative when an incorrect response was obtained to a complex task opens up a whole host of hypotheses. Failure may have occurred in any of the stages of learning. We will not attempt to outline all of the possibilities but simply suggest that some of the specific characteristics of behavior can provide useful leads. Also with incorrect responses to complex tasks, the use of probing questions in relation to specific student behaviors is extremely useful. For example when a long latency period is observed, the student may be questioned as to whether the latency was related to recall of the rule, organization of the task, or execution of the response. Questions of this nature can probably be answered by the student. The more general question: Why were you incorrect? may not be answered as easily because the student cannot sort out the various intake, organization, and execution processes required by the task. If students could independently and successfully diagnose their own errors, we would have less need for teachers. If teachers could more successfully use probing questions, we would probably have more successful students.

The precise probes a teacher might use will depend on the topic and the particulars of the situation. The probing process should try to determine the student's interpretation of the task and the student's use of prerequisite knowledge. If the probes narrow the problem down to the student's interpretation of the task, more precise probes can then be formulated to further narrow the problem. When the problem is sufficiently narrow, the process of overcoming the problem can begin and should be more effective because of the specificity that can be achieved. This outcome, however, hinges on a teacher's ability to observe the relevant characteristics involved in the situation and formulate precise hypotheses that are reasonable alternatives. The need for careful observations is often expressed, but we believe a greater awareness of the hypothesizing process is also needed if these observations are going to be translated into effective teacher activities.

Concept learning. Concept learning is essentially the learning and using of definitions of categories into which we classify objects and events. The definitions are statements of the relevant attributes needed to be a member of the concept class. When dealing with a single concept, the task of analyzing errors is narrower than it is with rule-learning errors. An incorrect performance must be due to learning either an incorrect definition of the class or an error in applying the definition to a particular stimulus. The former would obviously occur in the acquisition or retention stage of learning, while the latter would occur in the transfer stage.

Failure to acquire or retain an acceptable definition can be an intake or organization error involving a discrimination. If certain discriminations have not been made, the resulting effect will be omission, distortion, or importation of relevant attributes.

Errors in using an acceptable definition can be intake, organization, or executive errors. Intake errors are failures to make adequate discriminations in terms of the stimulus attributes. Again omissions, distortions, or importations of relevant attributes could occur, resulting in a misclassification of the stimuli. Depending on the stimulus and how it was classified, we would judge the performance as an overgeneralization or an undergeneralization in relation to the concept definition. The generalization error would presumably occur in the organization process when the information that has been taken in about the stimulus is compared with the learned definition.

In the sense that Clinchy and Rosenthal seem to use the idea of loose criteria, it is possible that a more basic type of generalization error may have occurred. For example, if part of the defining attributes of a class of objects were an insect with long legs and thick black wings, our criteria for defining insects are also involved when we classify specific objects according to the total definition. If our definition of insects is very loose, we would be likely to make an overgeneralization on the basis of any of these attributes. In terms of the stimulus to be classified this could certainly be considered an intake error. In terms of the definition that was learned it could be considered an intake or organizational error. If the criteria for these subparts of the definition are clearly specified when the definition is presented to the student, then it would be an intake error due to omission, importation, or distortion. If the subpart criteria are not specified, because it is assumed that the student has adequate criteria for the subparts of the definition, then an intake error involving loose criteria should be considered. What you would probe for would be not only the concept definition the student has learned but also the criteria the student use for the subconcept attributes.

Memorization. With this level of learning the analysis of errors is still narrower. The student must rely on making discrete associations or a series of them as a chain. Since we are considering the issue of partial mastery, the student has apparently done one of three things. The student may have given all of the information but done so slowly. Another possibility is that the student requires additional cues in order to produce the information. The other possibility is that the student has been able to produce only part of the information required.

When a student produces the information after a long latency period or produces a list of required terms in short groups with pauses between, it is obvious that the acquisition stage is not involved. The retention stage may be involved if the performance reflects the use of an ineffective mnemonic device or reflects the pattern of responding used during rehearsal of the material. The most relevant issues are likely to be related to the transfer phase. Whether the task requires immediate versus delayed performance or recall versus recognition of the information will have a large impact on a student's performance level. If later use of the information will be under delayed recall conditions, then the student needs to learn to perform under these conditions.

The second possibility when a student can produce the information only after cues are given is probably not an acquisition error but a retention stage error if the mnemonics required for recall are considered to be a part of the retention process. Again if it is a delayed recall task, it can also be considered a transfer stage error.

The third possibility when a student can accurately recall or recognize some but not all of the required information may be due to an error in any of the three stages of learning. The student may have made an intake error of omission during the learning stage and therefore cannot reproduce it. The student in the same stage may have made a distortion error and therefore reproduces the incorrect distortion. The distortion could also have occurred during the retention stage. As mentioned before, lack of a mnemonic or the poor use of one could also involve the retention phase. Task characteristics such as length of delay and recall would implicate the transfer stage.

Probes may be used in the form of questions or the amounts of cues that are needed to stimulate recall of the information. If cues about a mnemonic that has been provided or could be used elicit a response, the information and the mnemonic are available but are not being used. If the cues do not work and a mnemonic must be given, the student reaction to the mnemonic should be noted. If the student reacts to the mnemonic as if it were forgotten information, then it has been learned but not available. On the other hand, if there is no recognition of the mnemonic, it was not acquired or developed by the student during the acquisition or retention stages. Providing the mnemonic may result in the student giving the information. In this case, acquisition of the information has taken place but retention or transfer needs to be improved. If the mnemonic does not elicit the correct response, we are probably going to classify the student's performance at the nonmastery level, which we discuss next.

Performance at nonmastery level

At the nonmastery level of performance we can assume that the general characteristics of the student's performance or product do not meet any of our criteria. Since we are considering analysis of errors in the context of implementing our plans rather than assessing entering behavior, we can also assume that the performance or product does not meet our criteria after instruction has been given, we obviously need to look closely at the acquisition and retention stages of learning. We should also look at the transfer stage because it is possible that the student has acquired the knowledge but our measurement techniques are inappropriate for what we need to measure.

It will probably be easiest to consider the transfer stage of learning first by looking more closely at the transfer task. Ambiguous tasks or errors in precisely stating the required response are common even with well-trained and experienced individuals. If some flaw in the transfer task is found, it can be corrected and a new measure taken.

When the transfer stage of learning has been ruled out as a possible problem for the student, the retention stage is the next to consider. Often this can be done by probing. In the case of rule and concept learning, retention of the rule or defining attributes can be determined by having the student recognize them when presented. If they are not recognized then it is probably well to consider the error as having originated during the acquisition stage of learning. If cues are effective for memorization then it can be considered a retention error. If the cues do not elicit a correct response then the acquisition stage is suspect.

The most likely alternatives for nonmastery after instruction, especially when it involves only a small number of students in the classroom, are that the student lacked certain prerequisite skills when the instruction was being given and/or the student was not attending to the instructional events. Probing may easily determine which is the case by asking the student whether the information was missed or misunderstood. In the case of rule and concept learning a question asking why students responded as they did may also reveal the rule or defining attributes that were used.

If inattention on the part of the student is involved it should be easily corrected by repeating the instruction. When a student lacks certain prerequisite skills, the teacher should not repeat the instruction until after the skills have been developed. This will first require a micro-level evaluation of the student's entering behaviors.

Performance of off-task behaviors

Most off-task behaviors are a matter of the student's attitude and we will consider them in the discussion of the affective domain later in this chapter. Gropper's category of competing behaviors that inhibit correct performance would be viewed as errors caused by inappropriate mathemagenic behaviors. By viewing off-task behaviors as a reflection of the student's performance in these two domains, we can analyze them in terms of our goals in those domains. This puts them in a more precise, goal-directed framework where our view of them may be more meaningful and possibly more positive.

> 5. In what ways are the four classes of performance different from each other in the cognitive domain? For each class what should be the main data for the analysis?

ANALYSIS OF MOTOR SKILLS DOMAIN RESPONSES

Within the motor skills domain of learning we are more directly concerned with performance of a behavior and somewhat less so with the product of the behavior. For instance, if we are teaching a student to drive a golf ball, then we would probably focus on the student's stance, position of hands on the club, and movements in the action of hitting the ball as well as the follow-through movements. We would probably consider the product of the behavior (the direction and distance the ball traveled) as merely an indicator of how well the total performance is executed.

As we have pointed out, in this domain we generally deal with two types of performance. One is meaningful units of performance such as hitting a golf ball and the second is the smaller stimulus-response subunits making up the larger unit. In almost all instances we teach meaningful units of motor skills and also measure student performance in terms of the total performance. If we do not observe an acceptable level of performance, then our focus shifts to the chain of stimulus-response units comprising the total behavior.

Performance at mastery level

With motor skills we are in the fortunate position of not needing to make an inference that a person has learned a particular capability. If the person performs a skilled motor response in a smoothly flowing, appropriate sequence and all of the behavioral characteristics meet our standards, then we do not need to infer that learning has taken place, since an occurrence of the capability has been observed (Figure 17–11). The predictive validity of our inferences in terms of other transfer situations may be questionable if we do not check for stimuli or aids that may have helped the student with performance that would not be in the transfer situation. In most cases these are usually very limited or at least easily detectable. An example would be a student preparing a slide for viewing under a microscope who is still dependent on the written directions penciled on the lab table. In this case the performance would probably not run off smoothly and either the tempo, duration, or output would be below acceptable levels. In addition, other behaviors such as glancing down at the table during pauses in the ongoing behavior may alert us to a less than acceptable performance.

Performance at partial mastery level

If a student's performance has the general characteristics of the performance we desire, we are likely to infer that some learning has occurred. The errors we are likely to observe in the motor chain are omitted or extra stimulus-response units, an improperly sequenced series of units, or some of the specific behavioral characteristics indicating a less than smoothly flowing, perfected level of performance.

FIGURE 17–11
Errors in motor skills are sometimes obvious

If units are omitted, added, or performed out of sequence, the most useful inference is that there has been an error made in either the acquisition or retention stage. Units may be omitted because the student has made a discrimination or a sequencing error. If the student spontaneously recalls the missing stimulus-response unit and recognizes that it has been omitted, then there is likely to be a failure in retention of the chain. If the stimulus-response unit is not spontaneously recalled, then it could be a failure to either make or retain the necessary discrimination. If prompting results in the student recalling the stimulus-response unit, then the error could be dealt with as a retention error. If prompting does not help, then the student can be considered as having made an omission in intake during the acquisition stage.

When the performance is essentially intact but not performed smoothly or to the level of perfection required, then it seems logical to assume that the error is confined to the transfer situation. Errors in the acquisition and retention stage are obviously ruled out since the performance has occurred. A further inference could be that the error is one of integrating the stimulus-response units into smoothly flowing chains. The poorly executed performance may be due to errors in discrimination of fine, kinesthetic cues which must be learned if the performance is to run off smoothly at the desired level. These fine discriminations can be learned only as the performance is being perfected.

Inferences about environmental factors may lead us to conclude that we have not provided certain cues or adequate models to have the student learn the various discriminations and chains involved. It may be that practice periods have also been spaced too far apart for retention or perfection.

Performance at non-mastery level

When a student performs a crude approximation of the expected behavior at a level no better than the entering behavior, then an inference of no learning is in order. It should be established however that the student is not just unable to start the motor skill but once started can perform at least parts of the chain. If this possibility is ruled out the error is apparently due to some factor in the acquisition stage of learning. The errors may be related to the cognitive domain in that the student does not understand the directions. It is also possible, especially with very young children, that the student does not have all of the entering behaviors needed to accomplish the task.

Performance of off-task behavior

If a student performs a different behavior than the one expected, leaving aside motivational issues, the problem could lie in the acquisition, retention, or transfer stage, but either the first or the last is most likely. In the acquisition stage the student may have failed to make the appropriate discriminations or associations. The discrimination error is likely to be a failure to distinguish between two stimuli or a failure to distinguish between two responses. The first case is more likely when the stimuli are highly similar and the latter when the two responses are highly similar. In either case the focus should turn to environmental factors that failed to make the differences distinctive enough to the learner.

It is also possible that a student is well aware of the necessary discriminations but in the transfer situation fails to make an adequate generalization of the relevant stimuli and therefore fails to respond appropriately. In this case the error would be an organizational error. Another possibility is that the student failed to detect the relevant stimuli in the transfer situation due to an overload of stimuli being presented and thus made an omission error.

> 6. In what ways are the four classes of performance different from each other in the motor skills domain? For each class what should be the main data for the analysis?

ANALYSIS OF AFFECTIVE DOMAIN RESPONSES

When observing responses in the affective domain we have in some ways a more complex problem and in other ways a simpler problem. The complexity comes about because affective behavior occurs in varying degrees and is usually in a context where the affective states of the individual are influenced by the choices of activities in which the individual might otherwise be engaged. For instance, a student may enjoy reading a particular book during a free reading time but may not prefer it to working on a science project or participating in a class party (Figure 17–12).

While the problem is complicated by the need to cope with degrees of affect and interrelated levels of affect, basically we are dealing with positive or negative values of affect. As Mager (1968) points out, to try and measure the degree of affect is rather difficult, but measuring whether the affect is positive or negative is considerably simpler. As we have mentioned, the indicators of positive affect are approach behaviors, whereas avoidance and escape behaviors indicate negative affective learning. If we confine our measures of affective learning to these three characteristics of a student's behavior, it simplifies our task. If we are also able to quantify various degrees of affective learning in terms of some criterion measure, then we are much more sophisticated.

FIGURE 17–12
A student may enjoy reading a book in preference to other tasks

Performance at mastery level

If we judge that a student has learned a particular attitude, feeling, or interest, it should be on the basis of some approach behavior performed under free-choice conditions. If the conditions do not allow the student to make a free choice, then our inference may not be justified. This restriction makes it very difficult to determine the amount of affective learning that has taken place in many situations. Even in the most "open" classrooms, the choices are not entirely free but are to some extent controlled by subtle contingencies. The very choice to attend school or not attend school is first of all not an option but is determined by state law for certain ages. Beyond this the teacher's suggestions about, or reactions to, certain behaviors may indicate to the student that these behaviors are likely to lead to rewards while others are not. Many choices, therefore, are made in terms of the extrinsic rewards to be gained rather than solely on the basis of intrinsic desire. For this reason any inferences we make about affective behavior must be checked against whether or not there is a subtle contingency operating that may influence the student's behavior. In an ongoing classroom situation these are often difficult to pinpoint unless we present alternatives that students see as being equally rewarded by teacher or peer group.

Many times if we are to make valid inferences, we need to observe students in free activity times or make our inferences in terms of pairs of behaviors. A student may choose to do a science activity rather than multiplication problems. This does not necessarily indicate a positive attitude toward science. The child may not like either task and choose only the science project as the lesser of two evils. Observation of long latency and short duration may help to detect approach behaviors that are really not so much approach behaviors as they are avoidance behaviors. For instance, while a student may approach a task it may only occur after a long delay and/or then only be engaged in for a short period of time.

Performance at partial mastery level

All of the difficulties associated with inferences that learning is at criterion level apply to this level as well, but in addition this level implies some ability to detect degrees of affective behavior. This is difficult but unavoidable since teachers do try and develop positive levels of affective state and need a means of measuring shifts in attitude. This will probably require a close look at the specific characteristics of a student's behavior. For instance we may observe during the school year that a student has shorter latency periods, has a faster tempo, perseveres at a task, produces more products, or involves more parts of the body in more extensive movements. These will all act as indicators of increased positive affect toward the task. Only if we try to quantify these behavioral signs and take periodic measures of them can we detect changes in attitude with any validity.

Performance at nonmastery level

Of all the judgments in regard to affective learning it is easiest to arrive at valid inferences that a student has not learned a particular feeling, attitude, or interest. If the student avoids or needs constant extrinsic motivation to approach or persist in a task, it is fairly evident that it is not done of any inner desire. Also any of the behavioral characteristics may be indicators of negative affect.

In making inferences about the affective domain we are dealing not with cognitive processes directly but rather with a somewhat separate learning system. For this reason we cannot make the same types of inferences about input, organization, and executive functions that we can with the cognitive and motor domains. We can, however, make inferences about whether the lack of positive learning is due to the acquisition or transfer stages. In both stages of learning the conditions surrounding the task to which the affect is to be attached must be pleasant for the learner, or at least as pleasant as possible. For this reason we can make inferences about how pleasant the conditions were for the student in either the learning or transfer situation. In the learning situation manageable-size learning units need to be presented in an interesting, novel, or otherwise pleasantly stimulating mode or at least attached to a reinforcing contingency. In the transfer situation reinforcement and fairly high levels of success with low levels of frustration and punishment need to be provided.

Performance of off-task behaviors

When the student has learned the correct approach behavior and it is clear that it is appropriate to approach, and if we observe competing off-task behaviors, we can make an inference that the student has a more positive attitude toward performing the competing behavior than the desired one. In social psychology they discuss approach-approach conflict situations in which an individual can engage in one or the other of two, but not both, behaviors. With competing behavior inferences it is therefore not valid to assume that no positive affect has been learned. It could be the momentary pairing of choices that accounts for the competing behavior. A series of observations over time should clarify the student's hierarchy of preferences.

7. In what ways are the four classes of performance different from each other in the affective domain? For each class what should be the main data for the analysis?

ANALYSIS OF MATHEMAGENIC DOMAIN RESPONSES

We have described the mathemagenic domain as composed of two subtypes of behavior. Problem-solving behaviors are one type and they help to develop new mathemagenic behaviors. Mathemagenic behaviors themselves are the other type and they are the cognitive strategies used in learning. To a large extent when we are making inferences about the cognitive processes that may have led to a student making an error, we are making inferences about the student's mathemagenic behaviors since they are the processes that lead to further learning.

Performance at mastery level

As with any type of cognitive learning we are dependent on behavioral signs to make inferences. When we find a student successfully solving new problems or learning cognitive and motor tasks quickly, it is fairly safe to infer that the student has acquired and is using the necessary mathemagenic behaviors (Figure 17–13). This is especially true if the learning occurs with a minimum of direction from the teacher.

Problem solving. To assume that a student has mastered the new mathemagenic skill necessary to solve a problem requires that the student actually engages in the task and produces a solution. If the solution is acceptable, there are a few pitfalls that may reduce the validity of our inference of mastery. One is when a student has focused on producing the solution rather than developing the problem-solving strategy. Without developing the problem-solving strategy, the student will be blocked from arriving at a solution and may become frustrated to the point where the teacher supplies small bits of help. This help, while well intentioned, may inadvertently circumvent the development of the skill and allow the student to produce an acceptable solution with the use of previously acquired mathemagenic skills or pseudo-mathemagenic behaviors. One such pseudo-mathemagenic behavior in these situations is to ask the teacher for help at the first sign of frustration. Since problem solving is likely

FIGURE 17–13
The use of mathemagenic behaviors is often inferred from specific behavioral signs

to involve some degree of frustration, the development of frustration tolerance is a related affective domain capability.

Another situation in which our inferences may be questionable is in group problem solving. Here, only one student of the group may have developed the skill. It is also possible that each of the students has acquired a portion of the strategy but none possesses the entire strategy. On the surface the cooperative product is perfectly acceptable, but the real intent of instruction has not been met. While the cooperative action has the blessings of the teacher, it has the same effect as letting the students cheat. We do not mean to imply that these group activities are undesirable. As an instructional technique in the early development of the mathemagenic skills they may be useful and avoid some unnecessary frustration that might be encountered by some students. The point we wish to make is that group problem solving should be followed by individual problem-solving tasks as a means of arriving at more valid inferences.

Mathemagenic behaviors. The student who rapidly acquires cognitive and motor skills must be using effective mathemagenic skills unless he/she is cheating. Only in a relatively few cases will the latter be a problem. The mathemagenic strategies used might not be the same for all students and some may be more effective than others.

Problem solving. Our inference that a new mathemagenic skill is partially mastered as a product of problem solving is probably the result of observing a partial or inefficient solution. Solutions that are ineffective or incorrect would lead to an inference of partial mastery only when they show a correct sequence of steps but a poor organization of information or a poor execution of some steps. In other words the solution indicates that the appropriate strategy has been developed but is being poorly applied. For instance a student may have to solve a long division problem given in the form of a word problem. The steps in the actual division may have been carried out in the proper sequence even though the numbers for the divisor and the dividend have been reversed and some of the addition is incorrect.

Mathemagenic behaviors. During the acquisition, retention, and transfer stages of learning, various mathemagenic behaviors will be needed. If they are all mastered and used appropriately, learning should proceed quickly and smoothly. If they are not mastered, learning will not take place. Judgments of partial mastery are reserved for those instances in which learning in the cognitive and motor skills domains is successful but occurs slowly and does not require the development of new mathemagenic behaviors. Our judgment is therefore based primarily on the specific behavioral characteristics of latency, tempo, duration, and output. If any of these do not meet our level of expectation for the cognitive or motor skill task, we need to consider the behavioral characteristic in relation to the part of the task the student is working on. With some tasks we may be able to see from simple observation the part of the task involved. At other times probes in the form of questions to the student are in order. Unless we suspect that the student is using an ineffective, alternative mathemagenic behavior, we would probably have little interest in determining which mathemagenic behavior is only partially mastered. The reason is that regardless of which mathemagenic behavior is involved, we probably would have the student practice more on the task and in this way develop the cognitive or motor capability and also practice the mathemagenic behavior. We may, however, also try to help the student develop a different mathemagenic behavior if we see the student having difficulty on several similar tasks and it appears that the student does not have the appropriate mathemagenic behavior to cope with them.

Performance at nonmastery level

In the cases of both problem solving and mathemagenic behaviors, classification of nonmastery is likely to be on the basis of general performance or product characteristics. Looking more closely at the characteristics of the performance or product may not help with problem solving but should be done when we are considering mathemagenic behaviors. From the observed characteristics we may be able to determine which mathemagenic behavior is not mastered. Instruction could then be directed toward its development before the main learning task is again attempted by the student. The instruction would most likely combine the two tasks by using the learning of the cognitive or motor skill as the problem-solving task to develop the new mathemagenic behavior. This way the student would still work on the major task but also would be shown a means of developing the mathemagenic behavior. As with nonmastery of any problem-solving task, we may also want to simplify the problem in order to develop the rudiments of the new mathemagenic behavior. More complex problems could be given later to enlarge on the strategy or give the student practice in its use to a level at which it is useful as an independent learning skill.

A student not having the necessary mathemagenic behaviors may be difficult to differentiate from one with a lack of the positive affective learning necessary to approach and persist in the learning task. It is quite possible that lack of one will lead to a lack of the other. When these two deficiencies exist and combine, a student is also likely to have high rates of failure in specific cognitive or motor tasks. It is difficult to imagine a successful student who both is unwilling to approach a learning task and does not have the cognitive strategies to cope with it successfully. This starts a vicious cycle: the lack of success results in even lower positive levels of affective behavior; the lack of approach tendencies reduces the likelihood of the mathemagenic behaviors being developed. This cycle makes future learning even more difficult for the student and more frustrating for the teacher.

Performance of off-task behaviors

We view off-task behaviors as a block to learning and as such related to the mathemagenic domain in that they are counterproductive. As Shavelson, Berliner, Loeding, Porteus, and Stanton (1974) point out, if mathemagenic behaviors are those that give birth to learning then we might label these counterproductive behaviors as mathemathanic behaviors or those that kill learning.

Some of these counterproductive strategies will be honest attempts by the student to master the learning task. A long, drawn-out, all-night cram session covering many subjects is one example of a student using a counterproductive strategy. It may improve the student's test score over not studying, but it is not the most effective means of mastering the material on a meaningful level. The cram session is likely to focus on the memorization of factual material rather than concept or rule learning. Some children are quite capable, it appears, of memorizing enough material to meet the standards in classrooms but still lack many mathemagenic skills that may prove useful in later life. Others cannot even cope with the classroom tasks but, as we have already pointed out, these students are apt to fall into a cycle of failure and negative attitudes.

Another type of competing behavior is general off-task behaviors. Here the student never actually attempts to master the material but instead engages in a competing behavior that precludes the occurrence of the appropriate behaviors. Analysis of these behaviors is probably more appropriately related to the affective domain, since they can be considered to be indicators that negative feelings have been associated with the specific task, the teacher, school, or learning in general. The frequency and timing of the off-task behaviors will give some indication of how generalized the negative affect has become.

8. In what ways are the four classes of performance different from each other in the mathemagenic domain? For each class what should be the main data for the analysis?

SUMMARY

Careful planning will result in a great many successful student performances. Errors in performance will also occur and should be analyzed to modify or refine our plans. To do this the instructional process should be viewed from the perspectives of an instructional designer as well as the implementer of the program. In the process you will need to gather data about student behaviors, products of behavior, and the conditions under which these occurred or were produced. Gathering these data may be hectic but a sound error analysis strategy will help organize the process.

Whether we view student errors from the behaviorist or the cognitivist perspective, we need to start from observable events or products. From this starting point the behaviorists would focus on environmental conditions that may have resulted in the less than acceptable behavior. The cognitivists would focus on internal processes that are under the control of the learner and could have resulted in the error.

One behavioral and one cognitive strategy for error analysis were presented. As a synthesis of the two positions, a third strategy was offered that describes the error analysis process as a series of six phases. The series starts with eliciting a student response in a specific situation in which the teacher holds some prior expectations about the performance conditions and what the student will do. With these expectations the teacher observes the situation, the student performance, and the product. On the basis of these observations the student's performance or product is judged according to the criterion associated with the task and categorized as indicating mastery, partial mastery, nonmastery, or off-task behavior. For those responses categorized as indicators of partial mastery, nonmastery, or off-task behavior, hypotheses are formulated as to why the behavior does not meet criterion level. One set of hypotheses is about whether the error is due to a problem in the acquisition, retention, or transfer stage of learning. A second set of hypotheses is about which learner-controlled factors may be involved, and the third set of hypotheses is about the environmental factors that may have contributed to the error. Depending on the outcome of the analysis process, some form of follow-up activity is usually indicated.

To illustrate the use of the model it was discussed in relation to the four domains of learning and the four response categories outlined in the model.

SELF-TEST

1. Instructional plans should be treated as:
   a. Tentative.
   b. Working hypotheses.
   c. A set of hypotheses to be tested.
   d. All of the above.
   e. None of the above.
2. The most appropriate list of data necessary to analyze student responses is:
   a. Observations of behavior, products of behavior, and observations of response conditions.
   b. Observations of behavior and products of behavior.
   c. Observations of behavior and response conditions.
   d. Products of behavior and observations of response conditions.
3. Which of Gilbert's five temporal dimensions of behavior is represented by a child who answers a question only after a long pause?
   a. Output.
   b. Perseveration.
   c. Latency.
   d. Tempo.
   e. Duration.
4. Gropper's approach to the analysis of errors:
   a. Avoids the need to classify student responses.
   b. Deal with only the transfer of learning.
   c. Emphasizes the need to revise the stimulus situation to overcome student errors.
   d. Emphasizes the role of both the stimulus situation and student-controlled factors in overcoming student errors.
5. From the cognitivist perspective, intake errors:
   a. Cannot be overcome by the teacher.
   b. Are errors in task or data perception.
   c. May be due to the teacher's method of task presentation.
   d. *a* and *b.*
   e. *b* and *c.*
6. Fewer intake errors are likely to occur with:
   a. Very novel information.
   b. Very familiar information.
   c. Rapidly presented information.
   d. Large amounts of information.
7. Organizational errors, according to Clinchy and Rosenthal, are due to:
   a. Analysis, synthesis, or sequencing errors.
   b. Loose criteria, brute simplification, or inappropriate expectations.
   c. Task perception, analysis, and executive errors.
   d. All of the above.
   e. None of the above.
8. According to the suggested strategy for error analysis, a teacher:
   a. Should not observe student performance with prior expectations.
   b. Observes behaviors, products of behavior, and response conditions with prior expectations.
   c. Should not engage in hypothesizing about internal events.
   d. Should ignore the environment and concentrate on the learner.
9. The evaluation phase of the suggested strategy for error analysis:
   a. Is the final phase in the analysis of errors.
   b. Is related only to behaviors and products of behavior.
   c. Involves a matching of observations against expectations.
   d. Is best accomplished without making judgments.
10. The hypothesis phase may involve hypotheses about:
   a. The learning stage at which the error has occurred.
   b. Which student-controlled factors may be involved.
   c. Which environmental conditions may be inappropriate.
   d. All of the above.
   e. *a* and *b.*

ANSWER KEY TO BOXED QUESTIONS

1. Your attitude should be that plans are a tentative set of working hypotheses. Your role is that of both program implementer and observer of the implementation process. The data needed are observations of behavior, products of behavior, and observations of response conditions.
2. *a.* Eleven factors influence judgments of response adequacy.
   b. Student performance is classified in one of four categories.
   c. Behaviors at the domain and learning level of description are developed on the basis of four subskills.
   d. Errors need to be categorized as occurring in one of three stages of learning.
   e. Environmental stimuli are responsible for errors.
3. The intake, organization, and executive errors Clinchy and Rosenthal focus on are processing errors and are not product errors which is Gropper's focal point for analysis.
4. The six phases are eliciting, expectancy, observation, evaluation, hypothesizing, and follow-up. The five main decisions are: (1) Were the performance conditions appropriate? (2) Does the student's performance meet my criteria? (3) At what stage in the learning process did the error occur? (4) What student-controlled factors may have contributed to error? and (5) What environmental factors may have contributed to error?
5. *Mastery level*—A correct response or product of behavior for the appropriate level of learning. Rule and concept learning should involve previously unencountered situations or stimuli. Memorization can be either recall or recognition depending on the level of final transfer required.
   Partial mastery level—A flawed set of general behaviors, a flawed product of behavior, or a less than smooth and rapid set of specific behaviors. Data are task complexity, specific behavioral characteristics, and general behavioral characteristics.
   Nonmastery level—General characteristics of behavior and/or product do not meet performance criteria. Data are specific factors in acquisition and retention stages of learning.
   Off-task behaviors—More appropriately interpreted in the affective and mathemagenic domains.
6. *Mastery level*—A skilled motor performance; data are unintended cues or other aids in performance situation.
   Partial mastery level—General characteristics of motor chain are evident but some errors or roughness in performance is noted; Data are observations of stimulus-response units involved.
   Nonmastery—Crude approximation, at best, of motor chain; data are factors in acquisition and retention stages of learning.
   Off-task behavior—A different behavior is performed; data are factors in learning and acquisition stage.
7. *Mastery level*—Approach behavior under free-choice conditions; data are contingencies involved.
   Partial mastery level—Somewhat slow or halting approach behavior under free-choice conditions; data are contingencies involved and specific characteristics of behavior.
   Nonmastery level—Avoids or needs extrinsic motivation to approach task; data may be avoidance or escape behaviors or specific behavioral characteristics during extrinsic motivational context.
   Off-task behaviors—Approach behavior has been learned but is not being used in a situation where it is clearly appropriate.
8. *Mastery level*—Successfully solving problems or mastering cognitive domain tasks; data are requests for help and level of aid provided.
   Partial mastery level—Partial solutions, inefficient solutions, or slow, uneven acquisition of cognitive domain skills.
   Nonmastery level—Incorrect solutions or nonmastery of cognitive domain skills; data are characteristics of general behaviors, specific behaviors, or products of behavior.
   Off-task behaviors—Counterproductive behaviors that inhibit learning; data are general or specific behavioral characteristics.

ANSWER KEY TO SELF-TEST

1. *d*
2. *a*
3. *c*
4. *c*
5. *e*
6. *b*
7. *a*
8. *b*
9. *c*
10. *d*

Chapter 18

Adjusting plans to classroom dynamics

THE PREVIOUS CHAPTERS have discussed how a teacher should plan for the classroom. Ideally, if a teacher's plan works smoothly, the teacher should simply arrange the environment accordingly to insure that the objectives are met, and then proceed to the next lesson.

Far from the ideal, the real world of teaching is not that simple. Teaching is a very complex act, and planning systematically for all the possible deviations from the plan that might occur in the classroom is an impossible task. Second, to believe that you have been so successful with all the students in the class that no further consideration needs to be given to those who did not perform very well is neither a wise nor a fair instructional decision, particularly if the subject matter is hierarchically organized. As we have stated throughout the book, a mastery approach to teaching for at least part of the course material makes a great deal of philosophical and psychological sense. Given the possibility that even the best of instructional plans does not always work, a teacher should be prepared to modify the lessons and assignments, often on the spur of the moment. To be able to change plans successfully requires good diagnostic skills on the part of a teacher as well as a *repertoire of alternative teaching strategies* that can be used in such instances.

More specifically, we pointed out in the last chapter that teachers should develop a systematic strategy for assessing errors and then use that strategy for determining what should be done about the errors. We also suggested that the teacher should be able to assess errors *rapidly* in order that the lessons proceed at a smooth pace.

Essentially, our point of view in this chapter is that a good teacher ought to know the skills necessary to maximize the conditions of learning in the context of an ongoing class. Good teaching, regardless of the philosophical orientations or general teaching arrangements of the class, consists of finely timed implementation practices, including highly sophisticated diagnostic skills, knowledge of how appropriate feedback should be given to students, and well-developed group management strategies. The preceding chapters have tended to discuss these topics separately. This chapter is concerned with the integration of these skills, particularly as they are related to student errors or off-task disruptive classroom behavior. The two topics are not totally separable. *Often a student engages in off-task disruptive behavior as a result of not being able to do the assigned tasks.*

The first part of this chapter addresses the decisions that need to be made when a student commits an error. Based on an analysis of how important the error is as well as whether the error is the result of an acquisition, retention, or performance problem, the teacher needs to decide whether to reteach aspects of the lesson or to move to the next lesson. The strategy the teacher uses to reteach the lesson or parts of the lesson can be more effective if the teacher is capable of identifying the learning stage in which the error occurred as well as those environmental and student factors that most likely contribute to the error. As stated previously, often the teacher has to make these decisions in relationship to the total class—a skill that necessitates good group organizational and management skills.

In the second part of the chapter our attention turns to a consideration of how teachers may interact with a student or group of students who are engaging in off-task disruptive classroom behavior. Being able to deal effectively with disruptive behavior is clearly a prerequisite for good teaching. At the end of this chapter, you should be able to:

1. Identify proper instructional strategies to use with students who have performed inappropriately on an assigned task. Consideration has to be given equally to classroom environmental changes and to techniques a teacher should use to reteach the prerequisite skills for the task.
2. Given simulated classroom situations in which off-task behaviors are occurring, generate appropriate strategies to resolve the problem.

RESPONDING TO VARIOUS CLASSES OF ERRORS IN LEARNING AND PERFORMANCE

Unimportant, infrequent, and unusual errors

Errors are not equally undesirable. To decide whether student errors need to be corrected, the value of the objectives in relationship to the broader educational goals needs to be established. Several questions must be asked: How important is complete mastery of the objective? Is it crucial to the understanding of a subject or topic? Is it crucial to the performance of a broader objective? Is mastery of a particular objective or objectives *necessary* for performance in a later unit of instruction? Finally, might it not be important for students to discover their own errors and derive self-corrective measures to alleviate the errors? These questions cannot be considered in isolation. We believe that if these questions would be taken seriously by the teaching profession, significantly fewer learning problems would be experienced by students.

To allow students to commit errors over and over again without having significant errors corrected is a faulty teaching practice which is too often perpetrated on students. In effect, if a teacher can answer yes to any of the above questions, then the teacher should provide the opportunity for the student to relearn that objective, particularly those skills needed for future units of instruction.

If the answer is no to the above questions, then perhaps all the teacher should do is present the student with relevant feedback and, depending on the circumstances of the error, give the student an opportunity to correct the error. This strategy may be particularly useful if the errors occur on unit quizzes. Obviously, in many cases the error may be ignored.

We should add here that if a teacher is capable of predicting in advance that many students will have trouble with a unit of instruction, the teacher probably ought to consider alternative ways of teaching the unit as well as to prepare additional backup materials for the troublesome units.

Student acquisitional errors

As pointed out in Chapter 17 the teacher needs to make three interrelated decisions concerning student errors:

1. Is the error a problem in acquisition, a problem in retention, or a problem in performance?
2. Is the error the result of a faulty student strategy?
3. Is the error the result of some environmental factor in the classroom or home environment that can be realistically changed?

Of course, any error may be the result of a breakdown in several stages of learning brought about by faulty student strategies or faulty environmental factors. To be effective in correcting a student error, essentially the teacher has to identify the underlying student or environmental factors that have contributed to the error. After identifying the precise factors that produced the error, the teacher's strategy should be fairly self-evident. The remainder of this chapter discusses how a teacher can help students

FIGURE 18–1
Student acquisition errors

1. Lack of general cognitive prerequisites (e.g., poor reading ability or inadequate vocabulary resulting in a lack of understanding of the spoken word).
2. Lack of specific prerequisites necessary to understand or acquire the specific skills to perform the task (student did not learn an important prerequisite for the task).
3. Lack of mathemagenic skills (inability to plan, inability to take notes, poor underlining skills, poor scanning strategies).
4. Affective factors interfering with incentive (trait and state).

who have made some significant errors in their work or are engaging in off-task behaviors.

When a teacher analyzes a student error or combination of errors, the first task is to determine whether the student ever acquired, or was capable of acquiring, the necessary information, skills, or understandings to perform what is expected. Four factors may interfere with the student's ability to acquire the prerequisites for a unit of instruction (Figure 18–1).

One of the first factors a teacher needs to consider with reference to student errors is whether the student possesses the general cognitive prerequisite skills necessary to acquire the prerequisites for a task.

As pointed out in Chapter 13, our current organizational arrrangements in the school often create mismatches between what the student is expected to do and the student's general achievement level of entering behavior. Although this faulty practice is the result of an inappropriate school structure as well as many subtle pressures from various sources, the teacher must be aware of this problem and attempt to arrange the classroom tasks accordingly.

As we mentioned in Chapters 9, 13, and 17, it is important to match the curriculum to the student's entering behavior level. To do less than that creates many problems, one of which is off-target disruptive classroom behavior. This is perhaps one of the biggest mistakes we make in teaching. Teachers should be aware of the general entering behavior levels of their students and arrange their instructional practices accordingly (Figure 18–2). For those students with poor reading skills, a variety of simple handouts as well as auditory lessons might be in order. For those students who cannot take appropriate notes because of poor writing skills, other presentational modes are in order. For those students lacking specialized mathemagenic skills, help on these skills should be forthcoming. Needless to say, at a broader level, the educational institutions must attempt to increase reading, writing, study, and organizational skills for a goodly proportion of our youth.

FIGURE 18–2
A student should be assigned tasks only if he/she is capable of acquiring the skills to perform the tasks

Very careful consideration needs to be given to the second acquisitional factor. Frequently, inappropriate classroom behavior (partial mastery of a task, lack of mastery of a task, or off-task behavior) is a result of not having acquired the necessary specific motor skills, facts, concepts, or rules necessary to acquire the prerequisite and/or to perform the task. Not possessing the necessary prerequisites, the student attempts the task and makes a lot of errors, withdraws from the task, or disrupts the class. *Lacking the prerequisites to do a task is one of the most frequent contributing factors to disruptive classroom behavior.*

To alleviate this problem, the teacher should attempt to ascertain which specific prerequisites are lacking. The preceding chapter addressed many of these points. Having identified which prerequisite is lacking, the teacher should apply the appropriate conditions of learning suggestive of that prerequisite as well as appropriate corrective feedback strategies.

Another major concern for teachers is those errors students make that are the direct result of mathemagenic skills such as poor organizational skills, poor acquisitional study skills, poor information-processing skills (including attention), or similar internal variables. Too often tasks are assigned to students for which the student does not possess the skills to work independent of a teacher's guidance, with the result that the student's faulty performance remains uncorrected. In order to help a student in this area, the teacher needs to assess the skills necessary to perform a task independent of a teacher. Chapter 16 discusses many such skills. Second, the teacher needs to teach those skills to the student in the same manner as other cognitive skills are taught, except that care should be taken that those skills will transfer to new situations. Requiring students to use those skills in a new situation aids in the transfer process.

Because many teachers are pressured, however, to teach the cognitive objectives of a subject and cannot realistically spend the needed time on these important tasks, the best we can suggest is to try to teach these skills concurrently with the subject matter content. A second suggestion is that these skills need to be taught in a more systematic fashion. To neglect teaching those skills necessary for the student to be an effective independent learner is an undesirable side effect of poor planning.

Finally, consideration needs to be given to the motivational variables that might interfere with the acquisition of skills. Essentially, it is the teacher's task to attempt to motivate students to perform the assigned tasks. Ideally, the goal of education is to produce intrinsically motivated students. Practically, many students will respond only to extrinsic rewards, and therefore it would appear likely that these students have to be dealt with at that level. These points are discussed at other locations in the book. For now we would like to reemphasize that tasks of moderate difficulty should be given for which the students *have a reasonable chance of success.* Constantly exposing students to failure should be avoided whenever possible!

Environment-induced errors in acquisition

A list of environment-induced errors in acquisition is found in Figure 18–3. Essentially, environment-induced errors occur as the result of inappropriate goals, a poorly structured environment, or inappropriate tasks.

FIGURE 18–3
Environment-induced errors in acquisition

1. Faulty purposes.
   a. Inappropriate goals and objectives.
   b. Goals and/or objectives not clear.
   c. Important goals and/or objectives not identified.
2. Poorly structured environment.
   a. Poorly designed general environment (rules, procedures, organization, etc.).
   b. Poor climate (inappropriate teacher-student and student-student interactions).
   c. Failure to teach general and/or specific skills (appropriate conditions of learning not established including entering behavior–learning situation mismatches).
   d. Did not establish incentive in student.
   e. Too much information presented to student.
   f. Inappropriate discovery task given to student.

When a teacher has chosen inappropriate objectives or has ignored some important objectives, the student outcomes can be disastrous. If students determine that the goals or objectives are not important, incentive problems are likely to surface quickly, resulting in an unwillingness to put forth maximum effort. The same situation can occur when students are not sure of the purposes of a unit of instruction. The research presented in Chapter 7 on the relationship between making instructional objectives available to students and student performance should be apparent to you by now. One of the clues that problems in this area are contributing to student errors is the amount of time students are willing to spend on the tasks with respect to latency, perseverance, duration, and output (Gilbert, 1962; see Chapter 17 for a discussion of these dimensions). To rectify these problems, the teacher should be able to justify the objectives as significant and communicate that significance to the students. Further, the students should be able to see how the objectives fit into the big picture of the unit or the course.

Students may also not acquire the desired objectives because of poorly designed environmental factors. Faulty practices in this area include a poorly designed general environment or social climate, poorly executed lessons, failure to establish student incentives, and poorly designed discovery tasks. Since the dynamics of each classroom are unique, the best strategy a teacher can use is to carefully observe the students who do not perform well when given tasks or attending to a group lesson. Often simple environmental changes (a seat change, a change in the type of lesson, or a change in a couple of classroom procedures) are all that is needed.

Poor performance may also be the result of specific faulty teaching practices (the student has not acquired some specific skill or some generalizable skill necessary to understand the lesson) (Figure 18–4). In one sense, it does not matter whether the student's poor performance is self-inflicted or the result of poor teaching practices; the role of the teacher is to reteach the material. In another sense, however, it is very important to determine the nature of the student's poor performance in order to give the student appropriate feedback. As mentioned, if many students in the class perform poorly, then it is incumbent on the teacher to analyze why the teaching strategy failed to get better results in order that better lessons might be prepared for the future. A very detailed analysis of each error should give the teacher the necessary cues in order to correct the deficiencies and identify which part of the lesson was faulty. Further, particular care should be taken to be sure when discovery lessons are presented that the students have the performance capabilities to derive the necessary concepts and rules to perform the terminal task.

Once the errors have been correctly identified, it should be evident to the teacher whether the student's error is the result of not having acquired a specific prerequisite or having a faulty mathemagenic skill. In some cases, it may be that the teacher did not provide the student with enough time to acquire the skills. In other cases, enough varied examples may not have been given or the discriminative stimuli were not made evident. In still other cases, direct instruction in an acquisitional strategy would be helpful, such as training in the use of imagery or mnemonics.

Another problem can occur when the teacher presents the lesson and fails to get the student's attention. Finally, perhaps not enough relevant practice was provided for the student, or the teacher failed to provide corrective feedback while the student was acquiring the initial skills.

FIGURE 18–4
The teacher needs to determine if an acquisition error is the result of faulty teaching practices

Student retention errors

Assuming that a student is capable of acquiring the content of a lesson, there may be three factors that would interfere with retention (Figure 18–5).

Since learning takes time, it could very well be that our hypothetical student did not invest enough time in rehearsing the material. Time by itself, however, is not often the problem; it is the *qualitative use of time* that is important. Put simply, many students do not know how to use their time effectively in order to learn what is expected in a unit of instruction. Since general study skill strategies and organizational strategies as well as more specific encoding strategies such as mnemonics, use of imagery, and chunking are needed to remember material effectively, the student needs to be taught these skills and then *needs to practice them in the context of a lesson.* As stated previously, it has been our experience as college instructors and public school teachers that students are rarely taught these skills in any systematic manner.

FIGURE 18–5
Student retention errors

1. Insufficient time on task.
2. Use of poor encoding techniques.
    a. Organization.
    b. Imagery.
    c. Mnemonics.
    d. Study skills, etc.
3. Inability to retrieve acquired information.

Another factor related to memory is the student's ability to retrieve information from long-term storage. Quite frequently students store information in long-term memory only to find out that they are unable to retrieve it at a future time. As we mentioned earlier in the book, problems in this area usually occur because the student did not associate the original material with a cue that can be readily retrieved (Figure 18–6). For young children (ages 7–9), teacher-provided encoding strategies are often necessary. Further, as pointed out in Chapter 11, even older students from lower socioeconomic levels have difficulty generating their own encoding strategies (Rohwer, 1972). Providing students with direct instruction on how to increase their encoding strategies makes a great deal of sense.

Environment-induced errors in retention

As can be seen in Figure 18–7, errors in retention produced by faulty environments include poor instructional presentation strategies, inadequate practice or rehearsal conditions, and ineffective retention strategies.

FIGURE 18–6
Students need to learn effective memory skills

A reanalysis of how the material was presented coupled with an analysis of the specific characteristics of the errors (were the same errors committed by a large number of students?) ought to provide the teacher with enough information to reteach the material. For example, assume a task was given to the class in which most of the class missed one component while performing well on another component. Assuming that the two sections of the task were of comparable difficulty, we can most likely assume that the presentation of the material was at fault. Contrast this situation with one in which most of the class performed poorly on the overall task, and no specific error pattern was apparent. It could very well be in this case that not enough time was allowed for the students to retain the material or incentives were not established. Further, the overall organization of the lesson may have been at fault, making it difficult for the students to retain the information in a meaningful sequence. By attempting to analyze the environmental factors that might have contributed to the error, the teacher will be able to reteach important material better as well as make fewer mistakes the next time the material is presented.

A good example of a common faulty teaching practice in this area is the assignment of a large number of math problems to students who have not learned the basic number concepts. This practice requires that the student spend an inordinate amount of time solving the problems, and can easily result in a very strong negative attitude toward arithmetic.

Simply put, if a teacher assigns tasks that have a strong memory component, it is incumbent on the teacher to arrange the instructional time to increase the student's chances of retaining the prerequisites *prior to the assignment* of the terminal performance objective. And, of course, as we have stated previously, the teacher may have

FIGURE 18–7
Environment-induced retention errors

1. Presentation was insufficient or deficient.
   a. Adequate prompts were not provided in initial presentation.
   b. Material was not organized properly in presentation.
   c. Some material was not presented.
2. Study conditions were inadequate; there was too much information to be learned for amount of time; motivation was not established, resulting in an unwillingness to spend time on study; or environmental stimuli interfered with rehearsal.
3. There was a failure to teach study skills necessary to be an independent learner.

failed to teach good retentional strategies, thus the student fails to become an efficient learner.

Student performance errors

As identified in Figure 18–8, a student may not perform a task correctly because he/she failed to initially acquire the prerequisites, failed to retain or retrieve the prerequisites, did not spend enough time on the task in order to perform the task effectively, or failed to note the similarities between the assigned task and previous tasks and then transfer the solution accordingly. Since we have already discussed in this chapter all of the above factors except the point about the student's inability to generalize, our attention now turns to that factor.

FIGURE 18–8
Student performance errors

1. Initial failure to acquire the general or specific prerequisites of the task.
2. Failure to retain or retrieve the prerequisites.
3. Failure to spend enough time on the task in order to effectively perform the task.
4. Failure to recognize the similarity between the assigned task and previous tasks or generalizable problem-solving skills.
5. Failure to organize the task appropriately.

In order for a student to generalize from a problem to a class of similar problems, the student needs to identify the similarity between the original problem and the class of problems, recall the solution to the original problem, and transfer that solution to the new class of problems. Essentially, this means that the student has to identify the similar, relevant stimuli in the problem and then solve the problem by using previously acquired rules. To determine whether the performance error is the result of a classification error or a rule-using error is simple. If the student cannot classify the problems, then he/she needs practice in applying the definition of the problem (discrimination and generalization skills). On the other hand, if the student has classified the problem correctly, then the error lies in the execution of a rule or procedure.

In a sense, the student needs knowledge of and practice in a generalizable superordinate rule or series of rules that permit the student to solve a class of problems (Figure 18–9). With reference to this point, Scandura (1977) suggests that the role of teachers is to present the superordinate structure of a field to students in order that a student can more readily organize the content of a subject and note the similarities between classes of problems. More specifically, students need practice in systematically applying superordinate rules to the solution of problems. Although premature as a conclusive instructional strategy, work by Bassler, Beers, and Richardson (1975), Ehrenpreis and Scandura (1977), Kantowski (1977), and Post and Brennan (1976) in the area of mathematical problem solving suggests that teaching generalizable problem-solving strategies, heuristics, or algorithms appears to be a promising approach. With respect to a student's inability to apply a rule correctly, if a specific error is evident, the aspect of the rule that was not applied needs reteaching. On the other hand, if the error is not evident, then asking the student to state each step of the problem should uncover the error. In either case, the teacher should consciously attempt to teach generalizable problem-solving strategies while working with the student. Refer to Chapter 16 for a fuller coverage of this topic.

Environment-induced errors in performance

An environment-induced error in performance can be produced by any of the factors previously discussed in the acquisition and retention sections of this chapter. The difference between an environment-induced acquisition or retention error and an envi-

FIGURE 18–9
Students need to learn superordinate rules in order to solve a class of problems

ronment-induced performance error is simply whether the factor interferes with the acquisition or retention process or with only the terminal performance (Figure 18–10). For example, if the teacher has developed a poor rationale for the goals of a unit of instruction, that factor can interfere with the acquisition of skills (the student fails to pay attention), the retention of skills (the student refuses to exert effort to learn the material), or the actual performance of the task (the student fails to put in enough effort to perform the terminal task). To make a distinction between the first two categories and the latter category, the teacher needs to determine whether the student possesses the appropriate skills to perform the task.

In addition, if many students have made the same error in performance the teacher needs to determine whether the necessary prerequisites were adequately taught as well as whether the task is appropriate. Many times poor performance on a task is a result of an inappropriate task.

Such factors as ambiguous tasks, nonrepresentative tasks, and poor task conditions (a lack of time to do the task, an inappropriate length of the task for the amount

FIGURE 18–10
Environment-induced errors in performance

1. Faulty purposes—poor goal identification and development.
2. Poorly structured general or specific instructional environment—inadequate organization, inappropriate instructional strategy, incentive not established.
3. Inappropriate performance conditions—ambiguous task, nonrepresentational task, task conditions inappropriate (poor constraints, lack of tools, not enough time).
4. Acquisitional and/or retention conditions not successful.

of instructional payoff, poor constraints, and a lack of tools necessary to perform the task) can contribute to poor performance.

1. Under what conditions should errors be ignored?
2. Under what conditions should errors be corrected *after a unit of instruction has been completed?*
3. What can a teacher do for students in the upper grades who do not possess the general prerequisite skills to perform the assignments?
4. How can a teacher determine whether a specific student error is the product of a faulty environment or the product of a specific deficiency within the student?

RESPONDING TO DISRUPTIVE CLASSROOM BEHAVIOR

General principles of classroom management

Given that a teacher has attempted to implement an effective lesson and one or more students start to misbehave, how should the teacher respond? As a generalization, there are several broad principles you might want to follow in dealing with a disruptive student. Since the purpose of any instructional program is to have students pursue appropriate activities, most interactions between the teacher and student should have the appropriate objective as the desired outcome. To accomplish this in the context of the classroom, the degree to which there are as few inappropriate disruptions as possible during the instructional event is the degree to which the students ought to remain on-target (Kounin, 1970). For example, assume a class discussion of some type is in progress and two students start talking to each other. At that moment, what is your goal? Your goal should be conceptualized as twofold: *to continue the discussion without disruption,* if possible, and *to get the two students to attend to the discussion.* Strategies for achieving those objectives include continuing the discussion while subtly walking toward the two offenders; raising your voice slightly while continuing the discussion; and achieving eye contact with the two offenders. If a teacher works with very young children, the teacher can arrange the group discussion so that the chronic offenders are within arm's reach of the teacher. If a student starts to act inappropriately, a hand placed on the student's head while continuing the class discussion is often effective in achieving both goals simultaneously. Notice that these strategies have the effect of keeping the class running smoothly, the focus is on the task, and the teacher's attention is *not* inordinately focused on the inappropriate behavior. If, on the other hand, many students started talking while a discussion was in progress, the inappropriate behavior of the group should be seen as a sign that something is wrong with the teaching strategy and that some major shift in strategy would be appropriate.

While the previous strategy works in some situations, more direct means might have to be taken to insure that a student stays on-task. If a teacher has to intervene with a student, the teacher must keep the desired outcomes in mind during the intervention. As simplistic as this notion is, teachers tend to lose sight of this fact, with the unfortunate consequence that when an inappropriate behavior occurs teachers tend to emphasize how to *stop* the inappropriate behavior rather than how to *maintain* the appropriate behavior or channel the student to the appropriate task. Notice the difference between "Johnny, you stop that right now. You are disrupting the whole class," and "Johnny, do you need any help on your work? I see you are not finishing the assignment. See if you can finish it in the next ten minutes." In the first example, the teacher has not told the student what to do. In the second, the teacher has told the student what to do and has helped establish a *goal* to complete the assignment in ten minutes. Of course, there are other ways of getting the student back on-task. The teacher could have asked Johnny how long he thought it would take him to finish the task. If this were a chronic problem, other steps might have been more appropriate. A second major reason for focusing on appropriate behaviors to a greater extent than inappropriate behaviors is that the teacher should reward good behavior on occasions. Could you imagine your grade school teacher saying, "Class, we have done our work so well today that we are going to take a 20-minute break by going outside"? We do not mean this to be critical of teachers. For whatever reason, most people tend to be more critical than complimentary. Emphasizing the positive, there should be an increase in appropriate behaviors.

If a confrontation with a student is necessary, regardless of the strategy the teacher intends to use, the following guidelines should be followed if possible:

1. During the confrontation be as pleasant as possible. If you are angry, express the anger in a manner helpful to the student.
2. Be as firm as necessary to get results. If a classroom situation has deteriorated to a point where confrontation is necessary, being less than forceful is a sign of weakness.
3. Unless the teacher wants to make an object lesson of some student who has committed an inappropriate response, the teacher-student confrontation should not have the whole class as a witness. It is disruptive to the class, and if either the teacher or student is "put down" during the confrontation, a loss of face is possible. One good technique for having a discussion with a student during class time is to remove the student to the hall and talk quietly. A particularly good strategy for the teacher is to stand in the doorway and place the student out of view of the class. In this manner, the students in the class cannot see what the disruptive student is doing and the teacher can keep watch over the class, if necessary. This strategy also removes the student from any vicarious reinforcement he/she might receive from classmates while the confrontation is in progress.
4. Under no circumstances should the teacher generate an idle threat. One of the authors of this book had invited some friends over for dinner. About half an hour before dinner, one of the friend's children started to misbehave. In frustration, the parent announced that if he did that again they were going home. Such a threat done in haste is idle and the child knew it. Another example of this practice is the harried parent in the supermarket who attempts to reprimand a child from picking up unwanted packages by announcing loudly to the child, "If you pick up another package, I will call the police." Ludicrous, yes. A little sad, too.

As a generalization, all of the previous strategies have certain characteristics in common. First, although there are subtly different explanations for behavior, the basis for these strategies is that most behavior is *learned* through interactions in the environment. Second, behavior patterns are *maintained* through environmental factors. Third, those factors that contribute to the maintenance of a behavior pattern are *current*. The past has an influence on behavior only insofar as it is represented in the present. As an example, it is not the trauma of a past event that influences current behavior; rather it is the current reconstructed memory of the past event that influences behavior. Finally, since behavior is learned and maintained by current environmental factors, a restructuring of the current environment or the student's perception of the environment is in order. This restructuring can take place through external manipulation of those stimuli that apparently have an influence on the student (behavior modification and social learning approaches); through providing the student with conscious, internalized strategies for becoming actively constructive; or through a combination of both approaches.

Establishing internalized goals for students

Since self-initiated, goal-directed behavior should be the overriding aim of most school programs, we thought it would be logical to discuss techniques teachers might use to establish this type of behavior. We will then discuss specific teacher-control techniques for modifying specific behavioral patterns through external manipulation of the environment. Rather than discuss a specific technique, our discussion centers on an integration of strategies based on the life space interview technique (Redl, 1959), Glasser's (1969) reality therapy, T. Gordon's (1974) teacher effectiveness training and Carl Rogers's (1951) techniques in accepting student responses.

Assume a situation has developed in a classroom in which a student is engaging in a lot of off-task behavior and the teacher has determined that the student has the general and specific capabilities to perform the task. In this case the teacher wants the student to resolve the problem by setting up some internal goals to perform the tasks appropriately (Figure 18–11). The purpose of a confrontation with a student in this instance is to clarify the student's perceptions of the situation, communicate to the student the teacher's displeasure with that behavior, help the student to derive a workable plan for resolving this difficulty, and maintain a positive relationship with the student. Confrontations using these techniques work best with reasonably verbal

FIGURE 18–11
Helping students establish internalized goals should be an important outcome of schooling

students who appear to like the teacher and are reasonably willing to change their ways. With nonverbal students or students who are openly antagonistic toward the teacher and/or the school, a more direct means would be appropriate. Obviously, some simplified techniques would have to be adapted for young students. Given that a teacher has decided to help a student develop some internal goals, how might the teacher proceed? Based on an integration of some suggestions by Glasser, Gordon, Redl, and Rogers, the following steps are delineated.

1. Confront the student with the inappropriate behavior. Indicate to the student *what* is inappropriate and *why* it is inappropriate. *Calmly* indicate to the student that the behavior cannot continue.
2. Indicate to the student or ask the student *what* it is in the environment that is precipitating the problem.
3. Ask the student *how* the problem might be resolved.
4. Get the student to derive a plausible solution to the problem. If the student has no solution, suggest several solutions, if possible.
5. Get a *commitment* from the student that the inappropriate behavior will not continue. More important, get from the student a *concrete plan* to behave appropriately which the student is capable of completing.
6. Be accepting of the student's ideas. Do not be punitive or mad. The relationship should be friendly but to the point. If the student suggests some ideas that are impractical, try to indicate something positive about the suggestion, but then point out the unacceptable part.
7. Do not get off the topic. The purpose of the meeting with the student is to resolve the problem, not to talk about tangential points.
8. A decision should be made about the consequences of successful or unsuccessful completion of the task. The student should be made to see that successful completion of a task should result in a positive outcome, while the continuance of inappropriate behaviors may have to result in a negative outcome. It is best that the student understands very clearly what the consequences of the appropriate behavior will be.
9. The discussion should *not* be witnessed by other students. It is a private matter between the teacher and student.
10. At the conclusion of the meeting, the results of the meeting should be summarized. In addition, the student should have the opportunity to ask any questions. Some teachers find it useful to write out a contract of the agreement reached in the discussion as an additional reminder to the student.
11. The meeting should always end on a positive note.

Several of the above points need additional comment. If the confrontation with the student is based on some inappropriate behavior the student committed and you know the student committed the behavior, do not be cute by asking, "Did you do so and so?" You know the student did it, so inform him/her of that fact. By asking the student if he/she behaved inappropriately, you tempt the student to lie, thus compounding the problem.

Asking the student *what* it is in the environment that precipitated the response rather than *why* the response occurred is a good idea. *What* questions elicit concrete answers. *Why* questions tend to elicit more abstract answers such as "I hate her" or "This is silly."

Having the student agree to the consequences of behavior is also an excellent idea. If in the future the teacher is forced to administer some punishment (a last-resort technique), the student is less likely to be mad since the student had agreed to the consequences.

If you feel the student is terribly upset about having committed some inappropriate behavior, attempt to minimize the perceived severity of the act by saying something similar to: "Everyone gets into trouble at times. It's okay. What is important is how we might try not to do this again." In other words, the focus should be on the plan for resolving the problem, not on the inappropriate response.

Finally, an interview can be used to interpret to a student *what* is happening in the environment that is precipitating the inappropriate behavior. Recall your school days. Do you remember students in many of your classes who were basically well behaved but tended to get "sucked into" inappropriate situations by other more aggressive students? Helping the student perceive those situations is one function of this type of interview. One of the authors of this text recalls an incident with one of his fifth-grade students in which the student came to the teacher and complained that a lot of students were wrestling with him during lunch hour on the playground and he was tired of it. Not knowing what was precipitating the wrestling, the author agreed to observe the student on the playground. Within five minutes it was evident what was happening. The boy was creating those wrestling situations by provoking other students with such tantalizing strategies as intercepting a ball, pushing students from behind and running, and taking a student's hat. His behaviors were designed to elicit wrestling behaviors from the total school population and beyond! To solve this problem, the author told the boy of his observations. To make the student more aware of what was precipitating the wrestling, the boy was asked to stay near the teacher on the playground the next day. Whenever the boy started to provoke a situation, the teacher had agreed to blow his whistle, and point out to the boy just *what* was happening. Within several days the problem was resolved. As unrealistic as it may seem, often people are unaware of the effect the environment has on their behavior. An external, objective observer can sometimes quickly identify the precipitating factor(s).

5. Given a verbal confrontation with a student who has committed some inappropriate disruptive classroom behavior, what should be the main goal of the confrontation?

Using behavioral techniques in the classroom

From a behaviorist perspective, behavior is a function of the learned relationship between stimuli in an environment and a person's response repertoire. To the behaviorist, the solution to bringing about effective change in a student's response is to manipulate various appropriate stimuli in the environment in a systematic manner, thus effecting the desired behavioral change. This section deals with a potpourri of techniques a teacher can use to change the environment in a systematic way in order to bring about desired behavioral changes in students.

In one sense, everyone uses behavioral techniques. It is an inescapable function of being human. When another person responds in a positive manner, we respond through praise, smiles, verbal agreement, or some other accepting response. When another person responds in a manner that we deem inappropriate or incorrect we respond with criticism, frowns, verbal disagreement, or some other unaccepting response. This selective responding often has the effect of either maintaining or decreasing the other person's behavior accordingly. The difference between the spontaneity in human interactions and behavior modification techniques is simply the degree to which the stimuli are consciously and systematically manipulated to bring about the desired behavior.

There can be no disagreement that the environment has a strong influence on behavior. The question is to what extent the teacher can purposefully arrange the environment in a classroom to bring about the desired end results, and how the teacher might do this.

Human behavior is extremely complex, particularly when it occurs in a group context such as a classroom. In a laboratory setting a psychologist has a great deal of control over the independent variables and can easily control for the influence of extraneous variables that might influence behavior. In a school setting, it is very difficult to control all the important external variables. Sometimes we are not even aware of what an effective independent variable might be, nor are we aware of the degree to which a student desires to behave in such a manner just for the sheer joy of behaving that way! Given the complexity of a classroom, how might a teacher use some of these laboratory-derived techniques to bring about the desired change in a student?

We saved this section for last, not because we did think behavior modification techniques are unimportant, but because we felt there were other things a teacher could do that were much simpler and more realistic. Quite frankly, a classroom run on *strict* behavioral modification procedures is neither needed nor very practical. In fact, there is some evidence that systematic behavior modification procedures in which a lot of concrete rewards are administered to students who appear to be *intrinsically* interested in their work may have undesirable consequences. De Charms (1968) points out that external rewards may have the effect of giving a person a feeling of being a pawn to the rewards. Deci (1971) found that paying college students for solving puzzles decreased the amount of time a student was willing to work on a puzzle independent of external observation. Confirming these results, Lepper, Greene, and Nisbett (1973) conducted a study in which one group of nursery school children received a reward for drawing pictures and the control group did not receive a reward. Lepper et al. found that on a subsequent occasion the group who received a reward spent significantly *less* time drawing when given the opportunity than did the control group. Although this area of research is far from resolved, a second look at the influence of rewards on behavior is certainly in order. For a fine coverage of this topic, consult Deci (1975).

Since in many classrooms the students are already performing most of the desired activities, even from a behavioral point of view the contingencies must be working successfully. To run a systematic behavior modification program using specified schedules of reinforcement principles through token economies or highly complicated contingency management procedures is not very practical in a large class without a lot of additional adult aid. Record keeping and dispensing the rewards require so much time that the teacher would have difficulty providing instruction.

Finally, since the goal of most educators is to have students perform independently of external control, reliance on a program that purposefully uses external control techniques could have an adverse outcome on producing independent learners unless a great deal of care were taken to develop the willingness and ability to perform independently of external controls. For example, in one study, Taffel, O'Leary, and Armel (1974) found that simple reasoning with second-grade children was as effective or more effective than praising the children for performing arithmetic tasks. Knowing what is expected, *most* students will perform the tasks.

In our opinion behavior modification procedures are quite appropriate in those situations in which a student, group of students, or the class is off-task and the student is capable of performing the task. At times a teacher ought to recognize good work by praising a student or giving a student a well-deserved reward. To overpraise or overreward, however, should be avoided. We would say that if students come to expect the reward and do not perform without the reward, then an overrewarding situation has been created.

In this section of the chapter we discuss how a teacher might use behavior modification procedures in a typical classroom. Technically, behavior modification programs require careful observation, the systematic application of reinforcers and punishers, and a detailed record-keeping system. Based on the premise that people generally behave fairly consistently due to the consequences that their behavior brings about, it is clear that the teacher should emphasize systematic positive control techniques wherever possible in order to get students to *remain on-task* rather than aversive control techniques to get students *back on-task*.

As stated, except in unusual circumstances in which the teacher is especially trained in these procedures and the environment is purposefully designed to implement such a program, it is unrealistic that a typical classroom teacher can use a fully designed behavior modification program. It is highly likely, however, that a teacher could use many of the behavior modification principles in a typical classroom. Included in this brief discussion are the techniques of positive reinforcement, shaping, modeling, contingency contracting, token economies, negative reinforcement, stimulus change, counterconditioning, satiation, extinction, time-out, and punishment.

Positive reinforcement. In essence, positive reinforcement is a reward contingent upon some behavior (Figure 18–12). For a typical classroom, the teacher needs to realize that what is reinforcing for one student may not be reinforcing for another student. Oftentimes teachers make the mistake of assuming a stimulus event is reinforcing, when in fact the event may be aversive to the student. Great care should be taken to insure that the stimulus event is, in fact, a reinforcer.

Approaches that recognize these important points should be more successful than ones that attempt to treat all students the same. Examples of reinforcers include: primary reinforcers (those that satisfy basic physiological needs), social reinforcers (recognition by adult or peer group), symbolic reinforcers (those reinforcers that are substituted for other reinforcers—including tokens, money, and grades), and preferred activity reinforcers (under free-choice conditions the student is allowed to choose a desirable activity). The choice of which reinforcer to use, the amount of reinforcement, and the frequency of the reinforcer, will have to be based on the classroom situation and the system designed by the teacher to dispense the rewards.

Shaping. For the reluctant student who is *incapable of performing an assigned task,* perhaps the task could be broken down into small, manageable units. Termed *shaping,* this strategy is designed to start with the smallest manageable task the student is capable of performing, and then gradually increase the complexity of the task. This strategy has been particularly successful in establishing some verbalization skills in nonverbal autistic-like children (Lovaas, Berberich, Perloff & Schaeffer, 1966), but it

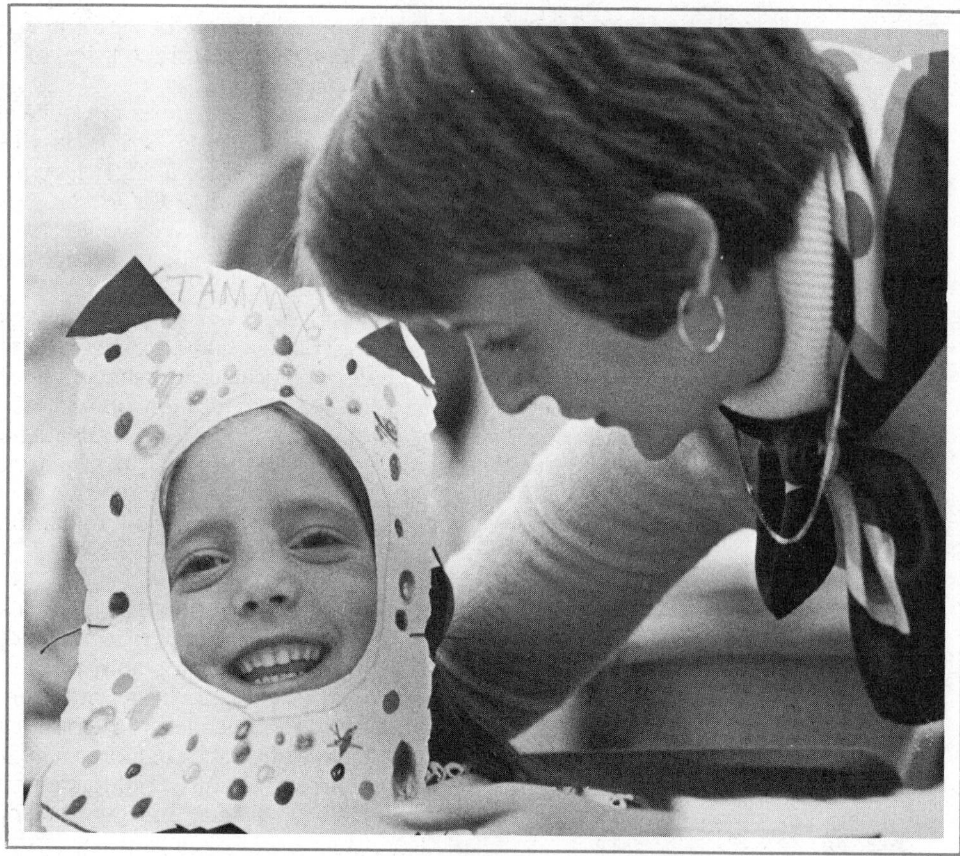

FIGURE 18–12
Positive reinforcement should be an integral part of teaching

can be appropriately used in numerous classroom situations. For example, Skinner and Krakower (1968) have developed a handwriting program based on this principle in which students are taught the basic skills of handwriting in a sequential, step-by-step approach. At each step the student receives reinforcement for successful accomplishment of the task. As a generalization, if a teacher has a reluctant student, the rewards should be frequent, of small value, and follow immediately after the desired performance is emitted. Gradually the number of the rewards may be lessened.

Schedules of reinforcement. Theoretically, as we pointed out in an earlier chapter, positive reinforcement may be continuous or intermittent. For continuous reinforcement, every proper response should be reinforced. For intermittent reinforcement, the correct response may be reinforced only after *a specified number of correct responses* (a ratio schedule of reinforcement) or only after *a specified period of time has elapsed* (an interval schedule of reinforcement). Many other schedules of reinforcement may be derived from the two basic types (Ferster & Skinner, 1957). For a teacher in a typical classroom, a continuous-ratio schedule of reinforcement may be instituted by giving a student some type of reward for every assignment turned in that meets the standards of the course. Since a continuous ratio schedule of reinforcement has the effect of establishing fairly rapid, consistent responding, it can be used very nicely with the reluctant student. Realistically, most forms of behavior in a classroom are reinforced intermittently by a teacher (e.g., raising hands, seat work, cooperative behaviors). Intermittent reinforcement has the effect of maintaining responses and is fairly resistant to extinction. For these reasons, paying attention to appropriate behaviors by reinforcing them on an intermittent basis is a good idea. Because positive reinforcement does have such a strong effect on behavior, it is also very important for teachers to analyze the classroom environment very carefully to determine what might be precipitating certain inappropriate behaviors. A simple change in the environment by either removing a reinforcer or changing some strategy may be all that is needed to stop some inappropriate behavior.

Contingency contracting (Premack's principle). There are several systematic programs that make use of behavior modification procedures and can be adapted for the classroom. One of the most successful of these approaches is contingency contracting, a procedure based on a principle put forth by Premack (1959). According to Premack (Premack's principle), any behavior that has a high probability of occurring at a specified time can be used to reinforce any behavior that has a lower probability of occurring. As described by Homme, Csanyi, Gonzales, and Rechs (1970), the steps in a contingency contracting program consist of:

1. Identifying the task for the student to do.
2. Identifying the reinforcer (something the student would rather do). This can be done by observing the student or, better yet, by asking the student what the student prefers to do with free time. A list of reinforcers is developed from which the student chooses the preferred activity. The preferred activity must be approved by the teacher and cannot be disrupting to the class.
3. Writing the contract. The contract is written in the form: If you do the specified task (developed by the teacher), then you may do or get the reinforcer identified in Step 2. It is very important that the contract specify the amount of work to be completed as well as the criteria of acceptability of the work, the exact nature of the reinforcer, and when the reinforcer is to be dispensed.
4. Oftentimes a section of the room is set aside where the students can go to get the benefits of the reinforcer after the assigned task has been completed.

You should remember, however, that the purpose of such a program, or any similar program, is to get the student to work independently of the teacher. In a *student-controlled* contingency management system, the student performs all the steps initially performed by the teacher. Essentially, in such a program, the student comes to control his/her own extrinsic motivational patterns through contingency management procedures. Ideally, the final step in the program would be to have the student perform the appropriate tasks just for the sake of performing them (intrinsic motivation).

Token economy. Another systematic procedure using positive behavior modification principles is the use of a token economy. In a token economy the student receives tokens for performing a task correctly (or for *not* performing an inappropriate behavior). Upon the receipt of a designated number of tokens, the student is allowed to cash them in for a reinforcer of the student's choosing that has been approved by the teacher. This system has been used successfully in a variety of settings with many different age groups. See Ayllon and Azrin (1968) for a more complete description of this approach. We would not recommend either a contingency management program or a token economy, however, unless the teacher were faced with a lot of students who consistently tend to be off-task or one who is a particularly difficult problem to motivate otherwise. In such instances, additional adult help would be in order to implement the program.

Negative reinforcement. You will recall from Chapter 4 that negative reinforcement also increases the probability that a response will occur. In negative reinforcement situations the person is faced with an aversive or negative situation in which getting away from or removing the negative situation is reinforcing. A variety of avoidance behaviors, including procrastination, would be classified as examples of negative reinforcement. Another example would be a threat announced to the class, such as "If your seat work is *not* finished by 2:45, you will have to remain after school to finish it." Working hard to finish the seat work, in this instance, is an example of negative reinforcement because the completion of the assignment removes the possibility of staying after school (an aversive stimulus event). If the teacher is not successful with positive approaches, a combination of positive and negative approaches should be attempted, such as rewarding the successful completion of a task while applying an aversive consequence if the task is not completed successfully. Of course, in the latter example, the *administration* of the aversive stimulus is categorized as a *punishment.* Because of the side effects often associated with punishment, this procedure should be used only as a last resort. For this reason we do not recommend this procedure unless many other strategies have been attempted. Often a combination of techniques employed in an instructional event is effective.

For example, frantic hand writing and shouting "oo-oo" is a typical response that many teachers find distracting to a class discussion, and yet many teachers inadvertently reinforce that precise behavior by calling on that student so that the hand waving and shouting will stop. This behavior can be easily changed by applying a combination of behavioral techniques. First, the teacher should announce to the class the exact behaviors expected of the students. Second, the teacher should choose only those students who put up their hands appropriately. Depending on the nature of the frantic hand-waving behavior, the teacher should purposefully not respond or perhaps give some sort of mildly disapproving look to the student. When choosing the student who is putting up his/her hand appropriately, the teacher could announce to the class why that student was chosen, particularly if he/she is a popular member of the class. From social learning theory you will recall that people tend to model their behavior after other people they respect if they see that person receiving reinforcement. The strategy of rewarding appropriate behavior in front of other students is particularly successful with young students.

So far we have been talking about strategies to increase or maintain desired behaviors. In this section, we turn briefly to some behavioral modification techniques designed to *stop* inappropriate behaviors. We saved this section for last because, as we have repeated many times, the teacher's emphasis should be on *insuring that appropriate behaviors occur.* Being successful in establishing appropriate behaviors, a teacher will not need to use aversive control techniques. If needed, however, the following are some of the common techniques that can be used to stop inappropriate behaviors from occurring.

Stimulus change. In essence, this strategy requires the teacher to analyze the stimulus situation in which the appropriate behavior is occurring, and then to change whatever it is in the environment that appears to be provoking the inappropriate behavior. Such simple strategies as a change in the seating arrangement, a change in teaching methods, or a modification of certain rules might be all that is needed for this strategy to be successful.

Counterconditioning. A counterconditioning strategy requires that a teacher identify very specifically what behaviors are appropriate and what behaviors are inappropriate in the classroom context. More specifically, the teacher's task in this instance is to reinforce the desired appropriate behaviors that are incompatible with performing inappropriate behaviors. Several examples should suffice. Let us assume that a student gets out of her seat quite frequently and wanders about the classroom during seat work time. In this case, the on-task appropriate behavior is completing the seat work successfully and the off-task inappropriate behavior is wandering around the room. Realistically, if a teacher were faced with this situation and had tried a variety of positive approaches unsuccessfully, the teacher should assign the student some short tasks commensurate with her ability, and then plan to reinforce the student upon successful completion of each of those tasks. Success in this instance is defined as completing the task successfully without getting out of the seat. This approach could be used very nicely with a contingency contracting technique. Ayllon and Roberts (1974) indicate that it is possible to eliminate inappropriate behaviors with this technique by simply reinforcing appropriate academic behaviors that are incompatible with performing inappropriately.

One other example should suffice. Assume a teacher has a great deal of difficulty having students line up to go to lunch, gym, or some other preferred activity. In this example, the question of whether students should line up has been resolved in the affirmative. The appropriate behavior in this instance would be some sort of reasonably quiet and orderly line; inappropriate behavior would be defined as excessive noise, running, and shoving. In this example, what is incompatible with excessive noise, running, and shoving? A quiet and orderly line is incompatible, therefore that type of behavior should be reinforced. The number of techniques to reinforce that behavior is limited only by the teacher's imagination. The "best" row could go first, or the class could go to gym by making a game out of going in the most quiet manner (tiptoeing, marching, walking like a ghost).

Satiation. Satiation is the strategy of practicing an inappropriate behavior over and over again to the point at which it loses its effect and ceases to be reinforcing. An example comes to mind of the infamous "spitball club." To achieve membership in this esteemed body, the student has to be caught throwing spitballs in class. Being caught at throwing spitballs automatically makes the student a member of the club. The club meets at 3:00 in the afternoon and practices the following ritual. Each student has to make 500–1,000 spitballs. The next part of the ritual consists of throwing spitballs all around the room. If the spitballs are not thrown all around the room, the student has to pick up the spitballs and start over again. Of course, at the completion of the ritual the student has to pick up all the spitballs. For some strange reason, the announcement of tryouts for the varsity spitball team tends to bring out fewer and fewer students from year to year. Obviously this example also makes use of punishment. Often a stimulus event consists of three or four different behavioral strategies intertwined into an integrated strategy. It is unusual to find a "pure" example of a behavioral principle in a classroom setting.

Extinction. Extinction is defined as the absence of reinforcement by purposefully ignoring an inappropriate response. We put this strategy near the bottom of the list of techniques a teacher can use because it is not always practical. In a group context, if a student starts to *disrupt the class with inappropriate behaviors* the teacher cannot afford to ignore the behavior. Furthermore, disruptive behavior is usually maintained by the effect the behavior has on other members of the class. For a teacher to ignore such behavior is foolhardy; in many situations the student is attempting to get his/her peers' attention instead of the teacher's attention. Recognizing that peer influence is a very strong determinant of behavior, some teachers have incorporated group extinction procedures.

In one experiment the whole class purposefully ignored inappropriate behavior by turning their heads away from the student every time the student disrupted the class. This procedure works particularly well in situations in which the teacher reinforces the total class for appropriate behaviors. In the latter case, the disruptive student soon receives a lot of social pressure to conform to the rules of the class.

FIGURE 18–13
Sending a student to get a drink of water can help get a student out of a difficult classroom situation

Time-out. In a time-out, the student is removed from the reinforcing event and is not allowed to return to the classroom until the teacher determines the student may return. Care needs to be taken in using this technique so that time-out does not become a positively reinforcing stimulus event for the student. As a generalization, this technique ought to be used infrequently. Whelen and Haring (1966) reported that they were quite successful in stopping "emotionally disturbed" students from engaging in a lot of inappropriate classroom behaviors with such a technique. When using these "negative" techniques it is important to keep in mind that the various "positive" techniques described earlier should be used as well. As an offshoot of time-out, another strategy is to have a student momentarily leave the room when the student has lost control of a situation (uncontrollable giggles or crying). A drink of water or a quick visit to the library can work wonders in such a situation (Figure 18–13). In this case, the student saves face and the class is not unnecessarily disrupted.

Punishment. Punishment should be used as a last resort, and then only in consort with other more positive approaches. If punishment is necessary, it should occur as close in time as possible to when inappropriate behavior occurred. Be sure to tell the student why the punishment is necessary and, more important, what the student should do to receive positive reinforcement and avoid punishment. Punishment should be as private as possible. Generally, the purpose of punishment is not to ridicule but to change the student's behavioral pattern. In a well-organized classroom, particularly a classroom in which the teacher carefully monitors those points mentioned at the beginning of this section of the chapter, students should not need to be punished very often.

Effective punishment will *stop* an inappropriate response, but punishment does not guarantee that the appropriate response will be emitted. Further, if a teacher has to give out punishment the student might resent the teacher as well as the assigned work. Finally, often punishment will work for only a short time. As a generalization, the positive approaches mentioned earlier should be tried first.

SUMMARY

This chapter has generally been concerned with what a teacher should do when a student or group of students has only partially mastered a task, has not mastered any of the task, or engages in off-task disruptive behavior. The first section of the chapter pointed out that a teacher must first determine the relative importance of correcting a student error. All errors are not equally important and need not necessarily be corrected.

A distinction was then made between student-induced errors and environment-induced errors. Further, distinctions were made among acquisition errors (errors made when the student initially comes in contact with the material), retention errors (errors made by a student when he/she fails to retain the material appropriately over a period of time), and performance errors (errors made by a student when executing the final task). Instructional strategies were discussed that could alleviate each type of error.

The remainder of the chapter discussed at length strategies teachers could use to minimize as well as deal with disruptive classroom behavior. In order of priority, those strategies designed to help a student become an independent worker were discussed first. Second, positive behavior-control techniques were analyzed. Last, "negative" control techniques were identified. It was pointed out that the techniques a teacher uses in the classroom should generally follow the above sequence. Doing everything possible to keep a student on-task by using strategies that give the appearance of spontaneity as well as have the effect of being smooth by not disrupting on-task behaviors of the class appears to make good instructional sense.

SELF-TEST

1. If one desires to conduct a classroom in which inappropriate, disruptive responses are at a minimum, one should focus on (choose the *best* answer):
   a. Clearly defining what is meant by an "inappropriate" response to the students.
   b. Clearly defining the consequences of the inappropriate, disruptive response to the students.
   c. Generating appropriate lessons, assignments, and presentations.
   d. Maintaining positive peer associations.
2. A student commits an inappropriate behavior, and the teacher responds by applying an aversive stimulus (from the teacher's perspective). The teacher notes that the student's inappropriate behavior increases in frequency. In this situation, the teacher has actually presented a:
   a. Counterconditioning technique.
   b. Negative reinforcement.
   c. Punishment.
   d. Positive reinforcer.
3. Gail constantly has been in trouble in class. She has an excellent arm and is very accurate in spitball throwing. In fact, she is so accurate in spitball throwing that she just made the teacher's spitball-throwing-for-accuracy team. This team practices after school by making 1,000 spitballs, throwing the spitballs around the room, and then cleaning up the room. Upon this initial tryout for the team, Gail decides she is not interested in playing with the varsity spitballers, so she doesn't throw spitballs in class any more. The most precise label for the teacher's strategy in this case is:
   a. Positive reinforcement.
   b. Negative reinforcement.
   c. Punishment.
   d. Satiation.
4. A very comptetent sixth-grade boy constantly gets into trouble because he finishes his work quickly and accurately and then has nothing to do. What *general* principle, if followed by a teacher, should alleviate this situation?
   a. Time-out.
   b. Counterconditioning.
   c. Respondent conditioning.
   d. Extinction.
5. One of the students in your fifth-grade class rarely gets assignments in on time, and when the assignments are finished on time, there are many mistakes. In addition, you are sure the student possesses the skills to do the assignments correctly. What would be an appropriate and realistic strategy to deal with this situation?
   a. Contingency management.
   b. Extinction.
   c. Time-out from schoolwork.
   d. Punishment.
6. One of the poorer academic students in your eighth-grade class, who usually gets between 50 and 70 percent correct on classroom assignments, fools around a great deal during class. Which strategy would be most appropriate?
   a. A life space interview.
   b. Give the student different assignments.
   c. Group extinction procedures.
   d. Change of seat to the corner of the room between your desk and the door.
7. Why might an extinction procedure work in a one-to-one situation but not in a situation where a *teacher* attempts to extinguish a student's response by purposefully ignoring the response? *Limit your answer to one sentence.*
8. What can be a negative effect of positive reinforcement?
9. Why is it generally not necessary to conduct a classroom on strict behavioral principles?
10. Consider the following situation from the teacher's perspective. A student in the class starts waving his

SELF-TEST *(continued)*

hand frantically and makes a lot of unnecessary noise. To stop the noise, the teacher calls on the student. Which behavioral principle explains why the *teacher* called on the student due to the environmental contingencies of the situation?

11. Many students in Mr. Erzenbop's second-grade class performed poorly on a simple workbook quiz covering the addition facts. In which category should this error most likely be classified? Explain your choice.
    a. Environment-induced performance error.
    b. Student performance error.
    c. Student retention error.
    d. Environment-induced retention error.
12. What would be the best instructional strategy to eliminate those addition errors mentioned in Question 11?
    a. Give the students additional work sheets.
    b. Design some lessons to help students rehearse the material.
    c. Provide more time for the students to complete their work sheets.
    d. Provide instruction for the students on how to develop internal motivation strategies.
13. A student in Ms. Verbly's high school English class failed to turn in several homework assignments related to linguistics. The student's score on a unit quiz covering that material was 95. All the other students in the class turned in their work. In which category should this error most likely be classified? Explain your choice.
    a. Environment-induced acquisition error.
    b. Student acquisition error.
    c. Environment-induced performance error.
    d. Student performance error.
14. Seven students in your junior high school social studies class generally perform very poorly on the unit exercises accompanying each chapter. On a standardized test it was determined that these students read at approximately the fourth-grade level. In which category should this error best be classified? Explain your choice.
    a. Environment-induced retention error.
    b. Environment-induced acquisition error.
    c. Environment-induced performance error.
    d. Student retention error.
15. What type of error is classified as failure to provide the students enough time to complete an assignment?
    a. Environment-induced performance error.
    b. Environment-induced retention error.
    c. Environment-induced acquisition error.
    d. Student performance error.

ANSWERS KEY TO BOXED QUESTIONS

1. Errors can be ignored when the skills represented by those errors are not necessary for the general understanding of the curricular content or for other units of instruction. The instructor has to determine the relative worth of each objective within the framework of the overall objectives of the curriculum.
2. If poor performance on a specific objective is likely to interfere with future performance in the subject matter, and that material cannot be incorporated into a new unit of instruction, then provisions should be made for the student to relearn the material.
3. Realistically speaking, the teacher should devise other means to present the content to the students (handouts designed to summarize the content, tape recordings, etc.) as well as additional methods for evaluating the students.
4. If a significant number of students in the class made the same error, then the teacher can assume that either some aspect of the presentation was faulty or the teacher did not provide enough time and relevant feedback necessary for the student to acquire and retain the prerequisites.
5. The main goal should be to have the student *behave appropriately*. You should not receive credit if you mentioned something about stopping the inappropriate response. Given that you get a student to respond correctly, the inappropriate responses won't occur. Establishing positive goals rather than stopping inappropriate behaviors should be the first principle in good teaching.

ANSWER KEY TO SELF-TEST

1. *c*
2. *d*
3. *d*
4. *b*
5. *a*
6. *b*
7. In a group situation the student is most likely to be reinforced by other students, therefore the teacher's ignoring the response would have no effect.
8. If the student appears to be intrinsically motivated toward a task, there is some evidence that positive reinforcement may decrease the intrinsic motivation.

9. In most classes, most of the students will behave appropriately most of the time.
10. Negative reinforcement explains the teacher's behavior because the teacher is *attempting to get away* from the aversive stimulus of the student's inappropriate hand waving.
11. *d;* since many students in the class performed poorly, this error would be categorized as an environment-induced error. Essentially the students had not been provided enough time to rehearse the number facts, therefore it is a retention error.
12. *b*
13. *d;* since the student performed well on the unit quiz it could be assumed the student had acquired and retained the unit objectives. Since all the other students in the class turned in their homework, the teacher would most likely assume it is a student error, and therefore some type of specific incentive needs to be established for that student or the task needs to be changed.
14. *b;* this type of error is always categorized as an environment-induced acquisition error because the students are given tasks that are inappropriate for their level of entering behavior. The teacher (and the system) has made a faulty instructional decision.
15. *a*

Chapter 19

Evaluating the instructional program

IN THE CLASSROOM you are both evaluator and the subject of evaluation. You will evaluate student performance, your own activities, instructional materials, suggestions others make, and the activities of your colleagues. You will also be evaluated by your colleagues, administrators, parents, and pupils in terms of your professional role and personal characteristics. With the tightening of the job market in education, accountability is now, more than ever, a fact of life.

Student performance is the primary concern of these evaluations but classroom discipline, cooperation with other staff members, promptness, responsibility for assigned tasks, smooth transitions from one task to another, effective and efficient handling of routine housekeeping duties, and the social model you provide for your students are all aspects of performance that enter into an evaluation of a teacher. To help insure that these evaluation results are positive, we believe a teacher should carry on a continuous process of self-evaluation. This chapter is designed to acquaint you with some of the issues and techniques for evaluating your activities.

The objectives for this chapter are for you to be able to:

1. Describe the focus of program evaluation in terms of evaluation context, purpose, judgment criteria, and data.
2. Describe the process of program evaluation in terms of the evaluator's task, the appropriate persons to perform the task, and the thoroughness with which an evaluation should be conducted.
3. Outline the steps that may be taken by a classroom teacher in developing an evaluation program.

FOCUS OF PROGRAM EVALUATION

Unit being evaluated

In the psychological literature evaluation is discussed in terms of two distinct units. One unit is the learner and the other is the program of instruction presented to learners. Until now we have been discussing evaluation in terms of making judgments about whether or not a particular student has mastered a specific skill or attitude. This type of evaluation can include taking similar measurements on a large group of individuals at the same time or a series of different measurements at various times. As we have pointed out, the evaluation can be for the purpose of identifying entering behaviors, discovering errors in learning, or assigning grades. In these evaluations the relevant issue is whether or not the student has acquired and can demonstrate various capabilities. This type of evaluation is critical in making decisions about our current instructional activities with individual students. It is, however, too narrow for evaluating and improving our overall performance.

In program evaluation the unit being evaluated is not the learner per se but the instructional program presented to a learner, or usually a group of learners. *Programs,* as we use the term, can involve units of various sizes. In the sense that a program is an organized means of accomplishing a specific purpose, our use of the term *program* is synonymous with the term *system.*

We may have federally funded programs such as Head Start which involve many children nationwide and include a variety of instructional goals and techniques. We can also have statewide and school-district-wide programs. At the classroom level of organization we can think of the teacher's total set of activities as a program made up of many smaller units or programs. Some of these may be entirely teacher-designed or commercially produced. Usually they are a combination, such as a teacher who uses a commercially produced program that supplies a text, workbook, instructional aids, and a teacher's manual but does not follow the suggestions in the manual. The program actually used is a unique blend of the publisher's program and the teacher's ideas of how to make it more suitable for local conditions and the teacher's preference. For the academic curriculum this is probably the most common type of program used in the classroom.

In addition to academic programs a teacher usually has some plan of action or a system for handling the many housekeeping and administrative duties that are involved in managing a classroom. These programs may not have a direct relationship to any particular unit of instruction, but they can have an indirect effect on a teacher's efforts to achieve the academic goals in the curriculum. In this chapter we are primarily interested in these smaller instructional and management programs that have a fairly limited and precise purpose.

It should be recognized that although the unit to be evaluated has changed, the issues of reliability and validity of measurements still apply. We still need to take measures of human behavior as part of the process, but with program evaluation there is an additional set of issues to which we apply the concepts of reliability and validity.

Context of program evaluation

Regardless of the size or type of program evaluation, it is conducted within some context. Stufflebeam (1973) suggests there are four main contexts, which vary as to the amount of change involved and the amount of information available to guide this change.

Maintenance context. In this context a program is in operation and there is a desire to maintain the status quo in the program or system. These are usually the day-to-day management systems in the school and classroom (Figure 19–1). Examples of this situation would be the ongoing maintenance of routines such as scheduling bus routes, developing procedures for fire drills, taking attendance, collecting lunch money, and signing up for extracurricular activites. These programs remain relatively fixed and undergo very little change. The program may undergo some revision to adjust for changing environmental conditions, but the outcome of the program is usually expected to remain constant. Because these programs remain relatively fixed and are used for long periods of time, there is a great deal of information available about them.

Developmental context. A second context is one in which an existing program is being developed. Most academic programs are examples of this category. No matter how long schools or teachers (with a few exceptions) may use a particular program, they are constantly revising it to improve its content, organization, or implementation. In this context the intent is to retain an existing program but change it to improve the outcomes or functions. There may be a great deal or only a small amount of change within the program to bring about the improved results. However, as Stufflebeam describes this context, there is a greater amount of change intended than there is in a maintenance context. There is also less information on which to base these changes. This reflects the limited amount of empirical data available or used by those making the changes. There may be some empirical data available, but the changes being made involve a great deal of intuition to apply the limited information and arrive at decisions.

FIGURE 19–1
A maintenance context involves routine management programs

Innovative context. In a third context innovations are being made. This differs from the developmental context in that large, relatively novel changes are being made in existing programs or a new program is being tried. For a school this may be a change from a closed classroom to an open architecture-type of building organization, or from a highly structured to an open curriculum approach for determining instructional goals. Even more innovative would be a situation in which the building characteristics and the goal-setting strategy are both changed at the same time. At the classroom level, changing the general instructional strategy used with a particular unit from group instruction to some form of individualized approach would be an example. Changing the basic instructional materials such as the text or workbooks and changing the type of work assignments are other examples.

The program may not be new to other teachers and schools, but for those trying it out for the first time, information to guide the innovative process is likely to be limited in the sense that there are no guiding principles available. What information there is will be related to how the program worked in a particular situation, which may be different from the one in which the program is now being tried. This makes the outcomes of the program highly speculative.

Utopian context. The fourth context is found infrequently in education according to Stufflebeam. It is a utopian context in which complete changes are being proposed in terms of some organizing theory. An example of this would be decisions concerning large changes in a curriculum developed from some theory such as Piaget's.

The difference between the innovative and utopian contexts is the amount of guiding information. In the innovative context relatively small amounts of information are available to guide decisions, whereas in the utopian context the theory provides the general principles needed to make decisions. While the theory may provide the principles used to make decisions, it may be difficult to apply the principles to the realities of the classroom. How well developed the theory is and how well it is supported by empirical evidence will determine how much speculation is involved in predicting the outcomes of the program. This assumes, of course, that the idealism of the theoretical principles can be maintained in the face of classroom realities.

Purpose of evaluation

Determine program utility. Generally stated, the purpose of evaluation is to judge the social worth or utility of something (Glass, 1967). As Glass notes, research is often confused with evaluation because both are concerned with the systematic gathering of accurate data. Whereas research is aimed at developing new knowledge, evaluation is limited to making judgments about the application of knowledge to specific problems.

Within the general purpose of evaluation there can be a variety of specific purposes. Webster and Stufflebeam (1978) have identified six different types of evaluation, each with a distinctly different purpose. Without getting into the specifics of the various program types, the purpose can be to judge the value of an (1) institution, (2) policy, or (3) particular decision. The purpose of an evaluation can also be to judge the merits of a program from the perspective of (4) those it is intended to serve, (5) those involved in the operation and development of the program, or (6) some independent authority.

Webster and Stufflebeam also point out that there are quasi-types and pseudo-types of evaluation. The quasi-type evaluations generally have the purpose of developing knowledge about a program and therefore are somewhat synonymous with Glass's definition of research studies. The pseudo-evaluation studies have a distinctly different purpose. They are intended to serve a political or public relations function. Their purpose is not to make an unbiased judgment but rather to gather data to support an already established position or positive image. Unfortunately many studies fall within this type and are likely to mislead rather than help in the process of improving education.

Make program choices versus improvements. In relation to the purpose of program evaluation, Scriven (1967) has made a distinction between formative and summative evaluation. We have been using these terms in the text somewhat differently than they originally were proposed by Scriven. In the sense that Scriven used the terms, formative evaluation occurs during planning and tryout. The purpose for this type of evaluation is to provide information used to modify or form the program, hence the term *formative* evaluation. Summative evaluation is the evaluation of a program after it has been fully implemented. The purpose is to evaluate the effectiveness of the total program, not its component parts. This summing across program components and development efforts gives rise to the term *summative* evaluation. Scriven made these distinctions in reply to comments that the primary purpose of program evaluation should be to improve programs. Scriven's point was that, while formative evaluation is useful, in the final analysis we still need to consider the payoff value of programs and conduct summative evaluations to compare programs with other alternatives. From his point of view the purpose of evaluation should be to make judgments about programs as they are being developed, and also to judge the worth of a program after it has been developed.

Evaluate broad versus specific factors. Hammond (1973) presents a model that suggests the purpose of an evaluation should be focused on specific factors.

FIGURE 19–2
Evaluation can be directed toward making choices between programs or improving programs

He lists many specific factors but groups them into three main categories. One set is behaviors. Under this he lists the domains of learning somewhat as we have described them. A second set of factors relates to instruction. Here the organization, content, method, facilities, and cost are the relevant variables to be judged. The third set of variables he labels *institutional*. Under this heading he lists students, teachers, administrators, educational specialists, family, and community.

From the above it is evident that there can be more than one purpose for program evaluation. The primary purpose is to determine the utility of some entity and not just to gather information about it or give an unjustified rationalization for its existence. This does not negate the need to develop new information in order to have a more basic understanding of the instructional process, nor does it negate the occasional need to provide information about a program in order to describe or justify it. It is simply a matter of having different purposes at different times, which sometimes overlap and get confused.

The judgments of utility can be directed toward making choices between programs or improving programs (Figure 19–2). Following Hammond's suggestion, these evaluations should be based on specific factors within a program. This is especially true for a formative evaluation, but presumably would also apply to summative evaluation since it would give us a more detailed basis for making our judgments. This attention to specifics would also allow for the summative evaluation of portions of programs so that choices could be made about which parts of programs to retain, replace, or improve.

The exact purpose of an evaluation would be determined to some extent by the four evaluation contexts described by Stufflebeam. Summative evaluations seem to have the most relevance in a maintenance context since the general intent is to maintain some status quo. Formative evaluation would have less relevance since there is little emphasis on change in a maintenance context, but some summative evaluation might be appropriate.

Formative evaluation seems more clearly needed as an aid to guiding the greater amounts of change in the developmental, innovative, and utopian contexts. Since the developmental and innovative contexts have little prior information on which to plan the programs and predict program outcomes, the need for formative evaluation seems especially clear. The information from a formative evaluation, or a series of formative evaluations, could provide the information needed to insure more positive final outcomes for the programs. A formative evaluation would also be useful in a utopian context as a check on whether the theoretical principles were being implemented in an appropriate manner. As a check on the final outcome in all three contexts, summative evaluation also seems necessary to make decisions about whether the large changes in the innovative and utopian contexts have sufficient utility to retain the program and also to decide whether the program may need further development. In the developmental context the summative evaluation serves as a check on whether past changes have had a desirable effect and should be retained or rejected. It also provides a means of deciding whether the program being developed needs further changes. If the summative evaluation is based on a number of specific factors, it also provides some direction for future formative and summative evaluations.

The final point we wish to make about the context and purpose of program evaluation is in conjunction with Webster and Stufflebeam's identification of true, quasi-, and pseudo-types of program evaluation. It is well to identify when we are actually making judgments, trying to simply gather or describe information about our programs, or trying to justify our programs rather than honestly judge them. It is also useful to be able to recognize when others are engaged in one of the three strategies so as not to be misled about the value of other people's programs.

Judgment criteria for evaluation

The specific basis on which major judgments should be made, assuming suitable data are available, can be summed up as three judgmental dichotomies: (1) desired versus planned, (2) planned versus observed, and (3) one program versus another.

Desired versus planned. The first dichotomy calls attention to the fact that often programs are intended to achieve a desired goal, but as they are being developed they may not have the characteristics necessary to achieve the desired goals. In short, our desires may not be met because our plans include activities that do not lead us to the desired goal.

Planned versus observed. The second dichotomy refers to judgments about how well our plans are reflected in what actually occurred. It is quite possible to plan for one set of activities or outcomes and have a different set occur.

One program versus another. The third dichotomy is between programs. Here the worth of one program is compared with that of another. The comparison might be between a new, fully developed program being considered to replace another older one. The comparison could also be between two programs currently used, with the intention of eliminating one or selecting one for further developmental efforts.

The first two dichotomies can be used in a summative evaluation but are more closely related to formative evaluation. The third dichotomy more clearly implies a summative evaluation. In the sense that comparisons between programs can be used to determine which of two parallel programs to abandon in favor of continuing development of the other, program comparisons can be considered to be tangentially related to formative evaluation.

Classroom teachers should, in our opinion, carefully consider the dichotomies between desired versus planned versus observed when evaluating programs they are developing. It is quite possible to make errors and overlook them unless we take a careful and critical look at how well our plans match our intentions and our actions match our plans. Between our intentions and actions there may be a large gap.

In addition to selecting programs for their own classrooms, teachers are asked to comment upon and make recommendations about the adoption of new programs by a school. For these reasons teachers also need to know how to make summative evaluations on the basis of the third dichotomy.

Other comparisons. In addition to the three major comparisons, other important considerations are the completeness, effectiveness, and efficiency of our efforts. Obviously our efforts should be effective. There are some practical limits to how complete our efforts should be. If they are too incomplete, they will not accomplish as much as we expect. If they are too complete, the returns on our efforts begin to drop and take time away from other activities we should pursue. Most of all, our efforts should be efficient in that we reach our goals with a minimum of time, effort, and resources.

Included in the question of efficiency is the amount of time and energy required of the learners. This should be kept to a minimum so there will be time for other activities.

Data base needed for evaluation

In order to make judgments we need to have data that are reliable and valid for the judgments to be made. This requires that data are gathered by systematically using sound measurement principles.

Output data. Since the purpose of any program is to bring about or maintain some state, data about the products of the program are obviously needed. With academic programs the product is going to be our measures of student performance in the four domains of learning. To this extent student evaluation and program evaluation overlap. Since programs are usually presented to groups of students, the product being evaluated is not any single student's capability but rather a generalization drawn from the performance of all students receiving that instructional program. In other words, in program evaluation we are not particularly interested in how Mary did but rather in the general effect of using reading series A on the total group. In situations where we realize that we have different groups of students, such as high and low achievers, we may wish to ask the same question in relation to the subgroups, since the program may be effective with one group and not the other.

For classroom management programs the purpose may be too broad to be related to any specific student performance. For instance, our strategy for recording student performance on tests has little to do with learning but is a normal part of the teacher's activities. Here the product would be the test scores or other indicators of performance as we have recorded them. Another example is when a teacher tries to enlist the aid of parents to act as volunteer tutors. Here the product would be the number of hours of parent tutoring time that was actually volunteered. In this last example the hours of volunteer time would be valid for judging our enlistment efforts, but if we also wish to evaluate the overall effectiveness of the program we would need additional data about the effect the volunteer help had on student performance.

Process data. Data related to process variables may be measures of student or teacher time on certain tasks, the number of students selecting a particular study option, the number of examples needed before all students acquire a particular concept, or the number of times parent volunteers could not come as scheduled (Figure 19–3). The examples we have given are only a few that may be used in a formative evaluation. For any particular program there may be a great many process variables about which we would need to collect data, or there may be only one variable. The model of the instructional design process presented in Chapter 6 that outlined various sets of activities and decisions related to the analysis, design, preparation, implementation, and evaluation phases provides one means for identifying these process variables. There are certainly many other descriptions of the instructional process that can be used. Which description is selected as an aid in evaluation should be based on how well it describes the process in a meaningful manner and how well it subdivides that process into measurable units. Without these two qualities we are left with very little help in planning an evaluation and using the results to improve our future efforts.

1. In a development context, *(a)* what is likely to be the purpose, or purposes, of the evaluation, *(b)* what judgment criteria might be used; *(c)* when would the judgment criteria be used; and *(d)* what data are apt to be needed?

FIGURE 19–3
Program evaluation may need data about student selection rates among options

PROCESS OF PROGRAM EVALUATION

The process of program evaluation will vary with the size and complexity of the program being evaluated. The process should not start, however, after a program has been implemented. As we pointed out in Chapter 6, during the design phase of instruction we should be developing our evaluation plans along with our instructional and management plans.

Role of evaluator

Over the years, the definition of evaluation and the role of evaluators in education have gradually expanded. Earlier evaluation was limited to evaluating student performance, but since the 1930s evaluation has gradually expanded to encompass evaluating programs. As discussed in the literature, some see the role of professional program evaluators as limited to gathering data on which sound judgments can be made. Others believe the evaluator should present the data and also make recommendations to decision makers as to what their course of action should be. Advocates of the latter position therefore argue that judgments should be made about the performance of a program and also about whether a program should be retained, improved, or replaced. Which of the two positions a person may adopt probably depends on how much responsibility the person wants to assume or has been delegated.

In the narrowly conceived role of evaluator, the judgments would be restricted to decisions about which data are needed, how the data can be gathered, and how they can be most meaningfully interpreted. The judgments to retain, improve, or replace the program would be left to others. For professional evaluators this may be a common role when some administrator or committee is responsible for the final decision about what to do with a program.

For most classroom teachers the broader role of evaluator is more relevant, because most evaluations they conduct have the purpose of improving classroom programs. There is no administrative request for these evaluations, but teachers are expected to recognize major flaws in their programs and take whatever initiative is needed to correct the problems. Most teachers recognize this and like to spot and correct flaws before they become evident to administrators and colleagues around them.

Occasionally a teacher is asked to judge a commercially produced program, and here the role may be limited to making recommendations about the adoption of a particular program or textbook series. In these situations the teacher is usually functioning as a knowledgeable professional on a committee, and each individual's opinions are only part of the total information input leading to the final evaluation. In a democratic atmosphere this would not limit the person's evaluative role, since a full range of opinions could be expressed.

Who should be the evaluator?

External evaluation. Typically the role of program evaluator is discussed in the literature from the perspective of someone outside the program making judgments that are supposedly objective and unbiased about relatively large programs involving more than one teacher. They are generally not discussing the issue from the perspective of a classroom teacher, who may be evaluating a year's effort or some other segment of what has been planned and occurred in the classroom. These outside evaluators, as contrasted with teachers, are usually trying to generalize their judgments to other teachers, schools, and groups of children. For any particular teacher, the amount of generalization is usually limited to show that the results of this year's efforts may apply to other groups of children within the classroom, either this year or next.

From the professional evaluator's perspective the task is highly complex and requires many technical skills (Figure 19–4). They are quite right and it comes as no surprise when they suggest that well-trained professional evaluators should make many of the judgments. They particularly frown on salespersons as being inadequate evaluators for programs they are trying to sell. It is not that they question the salesperson's honesty, but many of the commercially produced programs do not offer any summative evaluation or even any objective data on which to base an adequate evaluation. Usually any data presented are in the form of subjective opinions and impressions based on unsystematic examination or use of the program.

Evaluators treat subject matter experts somewhat more kindly than salespersons, but only in the context of certain goals, content, and methods do they see the skills of the subject matter expert as being relevant to evaluation. In other areas, such as data collection, data analysis, and interpretation of the data, they are viewed as lacking the necessary skills. Into this category could be grouped most classroom teachers who are subject matter experts in delivering programs and the characteristics of children but usually do not have the skills to adequately analyze or design programs. For instance, teachers may be unaware of certain effects of a program because their interest in having students like them personally may cause them to weigh too heavily the matter of having students enjoy themselves. Student attitudes should certainly be a part of any evaluation, but they should not be the entire focus of the evaluation.

FIGURE 19–4
Program evaluation can involve many technical skills

Administrators or other decision makers are sometimes suggested in the literature as the appropriate individuals to make the final evaluation. In regard to large programs they are the only ones who can because they are the ones with the broadest decision-making authority. Even though a professional evaluator can recommend specific courses of action, the decision maker has to evaluate the evaluators recommendations and decide on some course of action. The distinction between the power to decide and the power to recommend is often ignored by many individuals because recommendations are often accepted and appear to have the same power as decisions.

Another suggestion in the literature is that groups of individuals should be used as evaluators. This is not suggested as a means of diffusing responsibility but rather as a means of providing a variety of expertise in arriving at a judgment. This suggestion is most often raised when either the programs are large, the programs will affect many individuals, or the consequences of the judgment will have a large social or economic impact.

When teachers are mentioned in connection with evaluation it is in reference to judging the worth of programs beyond the narrow confines of their own classroom. In this sense professional evaluators do not believe teachers have the expertise to be the primary evaluator but can play a very useful informative role. Due to the complexity of large-scale evaluation these comments on a limited teacher role in evaluation are probably well taken.

Internal evaluation. Our position is that teachers, because of their role in the educational process, do a great deal of evaluation. Unfortunately much of it is haphazard, is based on very little data, and ignores many factors that should be considered. As we noted earlier the usual evaluation responsibilities are related to the teacher's own programs. In regard to this level of evaluation we believe the teacher is in the best position to do the most comprehensive and productive type of evaluation. For one thing the teacher is usually presenting a unique program that is not defined completely until it is implemented. The teacher generally knows what the goals are and the general strategy to be implemented, but these are not in written form or available to anyone else. Since the teacher is the only one who has access to the plans, the teacher is the only one who can develop an appropriate evaluation strategy unless we require teachers to specify in advance the details of their plans. This is not realistic. Even if teachers did specify their plans in advance, they would have to follow the plans in a very rigid manner and not make adjustments for fear of invalidating our evaluation. This type of rigidity is even more unrealistic and educationally unsound. Having a general outline of content to be covered on specific days seems sufficient should a substitute teacher be needed.

The second point is that the classroom teacher is in the best position to collect the necessary data. It is easiest for the teacher to work this function in with the other activities of teaching because most of the data needed are readily obtained during the course of instruction.

Our last point is that the classroom teacher is the one with the most immediate need for the evaluation results. In order to do a better job of instruction, formative evaluation results need to be quickly fed back into the instructional process. Having the program planning, implementation, and evaluation functions all performed by the teacher reduces the communication delays to a minimum.

External check on internal evaluation. Even the best-intentioned person may not be an objective evaluator of his/her own performance. This is well recognized, and administrators are usually delegated the difficult and thankless job of providing some outside evaluation of a teacher's performance. From our perspective the evaluations are often made on a very limited number of observations and based on superficial criteria that have very little to do with actual student learning. In view of the confusing results of research on teaching methods, the administrators hardly can be criticized for their evaluations. As flawed as these evaluations may be, they do provide a teacher with some external standard against which to compare their own standards.

Those with probably the most valid right to evaluate instructional programs are parents and taxpayers. These people are probably also the ones least qualified to make judgments. What judgments they do make are likely to be on the basis of one or two visits to school or incidents learned through reports from others and quite likely taken out of context. We are firmly in favor of the schools being accountable to the public, but this accountability should be on the basis of reliable and valid data related to the achievement of educational goals.

Thoroughness of evaluation

Regardless of who does an evaluation, the issue of how thoroughly any particular program needs to be evaluated should be addressed. Some suggestions appear in the literature.

Importance and thoroughness. Stufflebeam (1973) suggests that the rigor of evaluation should depend on the importance of the decisions to be made. With programs affecting many students, or any program likely to have a large impact on students, a rigorous evaluation is needed. Less extensive or relatively inconsequential programs can be evaluated with considerably less rigor since the program will have only a small impact in relation to other forces in the student's life.

Stages of development and thoroughness. On a related issue Cronbach (1963) makes the point that in the early stages of program development, when flaws are likely to be large and obvious, less systematically gathered data may be adequate. In the later stages more systematic data-gathering procedures are needed to detect smaller or more subtle flaws. As Cronbach uses the term *stages,* he is referring to cycles of development through the five phases of program development outlined in Chapter 6, and each cycle would represent a more sophisticated level of program development.

Classroom factors and thoroughness. When one considers the fact that students are exposed to a great many teachers and their unique programs, it is doubtful that any single program in a classroom can be considered to have a large impact on the student's education. A teacher can certainly have a decided effect on short-range instructional outcomes but has only a partial effect on long-range educational outcomes. Also each teacher has only a relatively few students when the total school population is considered. From the professional evaluator's perspective they would consider the specific programs a teacher uses in the classroom as relatively unimportant and affecting relatively few students and therefore not in need of any rigorous evaluation. It appears that this is the current attitude guiding evaluations of classroom-level programs.

Considering the problem from the perspective of a particular teacher, the matter of evaluation is very different. The classroom and group of students are for all practical purposes the entire educational system upon which teachers will have any significant impact. For them the programs being used are important and they probably feel a need to evaluate them more thoroughly than do administrators and the lay public. We share the attitude and belief that at this level evaluation is most likely to bring about effective, smooth, and relatively rapid change within schools.

Assuming that a thorough evaluation of all programs is not possible, some determination needs to be made about which programs to evaluate, and for those selected how thorough an evaluation to conduct. Decisions about which programs to evaluate will rest almost entirely on personal judgments. The matter of how precise the data must be, according to Cronbach (1963), depends on the stage or level of sophistication of program development. The more times the program is used the more sophisticated it becomes and the more precise will be our data needs. This precision in data, we believe, should also be related to the five phases of program development by evaluating our program development activities in each of the phases. As we first start the process of program development, we would therefore consider each of the sets of activities at a very general level. In subsequent cycles through the five phases of program development we would consider these same sets of activities on a more precise level, because as major flaws are eliminated less obvious flaws can be detected. This directs our attention to other evaluation needs in subsequent cycles of program development.

All of this suggests that our innovative programs are likely to be good candidates for a relatively unrefined evaluation based on relatively general data. Our more utopian programs are especially in need of this type of evaluation. Once past the innovative stage, our evaluations need to be more refined and based on more sophisticated bits of information. Our maintenance programs should require the least amount of evaluation, because once established their operation is very familiar and we need to merely check to see that the program is maintaining the desired state.

> 2. For an innovative science program to be used in kindergarten as an enrichment program, *(a)* who would be an appropriate evaluator; *(b)* what role would be appropriate for the evaluator; and *(c)* how thorough an evaluation should be conducted?

SUGGESTED STRATEGY FOR PROGRAM EVALUATION

Consistent with our earlier emphasis on systematically approaching the development of instructional programs, we also believe that evaluation is likely to be more effective and useful if developed in a systematic manner. The major problems involved are the complexities of the programs and the expertise needed to develop and implement a productive evaluation. To help sort out the complexities of the problem we believe there are a few basic steps that can be helpful. Since developing an evaluation program is basically like developing any other instructional program, we will describe the process in terms of the five phases of instructional design.

Analyzing the evaluation problem

Environmental analysis. The first step in the development of an evaluation program is to consider the problem from a broad perspective so that instructional efforts are evaluated in a realistic context.

One fact you should consider in an evaluation is that you are a person with many aspects to your life, as depicted in Figure 19–5. Depending on your age, sex, marital status, and personal values you will have a particular lifestyle, which exerts certain pressures on you as an individual outside of the school environment. In addition to your professional life you have a family, social, and possibly a religious life. You have a recreational life in the form of sports, hobbies, or other leisure-time activities. There is also that part of your personal life of thoughts, memories, and feelings, which is not expressed in outward activities.

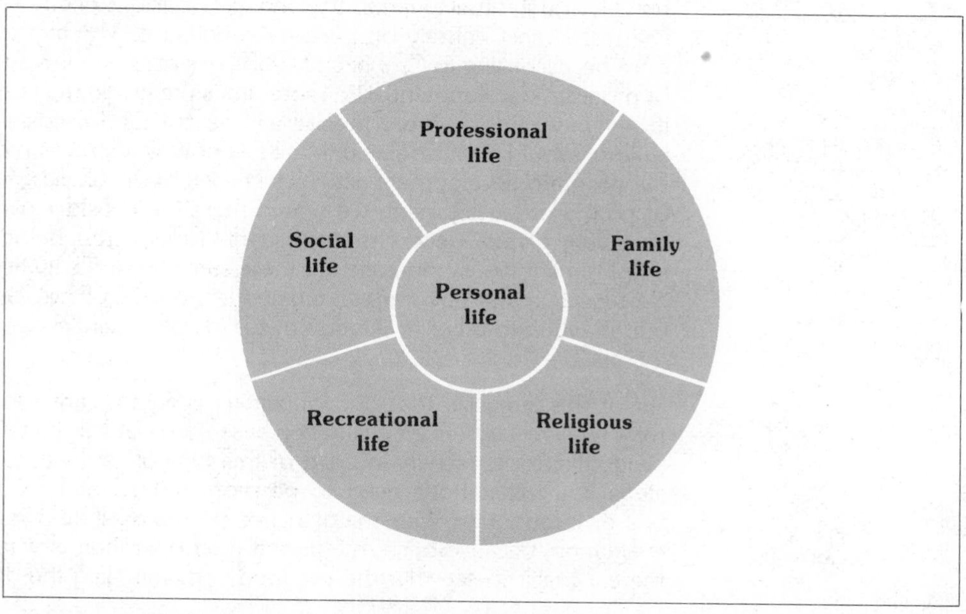

FIGURE 19–5
The multiple aspects of life can influence the teacher's role

Whereas we have depicted the various segments as being of equal size, they are more likely to be of unequal importance with respect to your commitment of time and energy. Each teacher needs to determine his/her personal values and commitments and reach a compromise between the amount of time and effort devoted to professional and other activities. The resulting hierarchy of personal commitments may very well be one factor seriously influencing effectiveness on the job and self-judgments of effectiveness.

Besides personal and nonprofessional considerations a teacher is influenced by the professional context. There are the expectations and limitations imposed by administrators, colleagues, parents, students, and other social forces. These forces usually make demands on time, effort, and methods that oppose the nonprofessional demands on time and energy. As such these professional forces provide a form of external evaluation of our professional commitment of time, energy, and competence. The two opposing forces of professional and nonprofessional demands, interacting with personal competence, will determine the level of professional effectiveness. These forces are not simple one-way relationships, because the personal level of competence also influences the demands made upon us. In addition the level of professional competence we display tends to influence the future level of our personal competence. For example a competent professional will probably be asked to participate in many activities and through this participation is likely to develop higher levels of competence. These relationships are depicted in Figure 19–6.

Task analysis. From the previous discussion of issues it is no doubt obvious that there are many considerations involved when attempting an evaluation. The other activities going on in the classroom make the problem even more complicated, so some means are needed to reduce the complexity down into manageable units. One way is to ignore many of the intricacies and deal with general characteristics. It is quite possible, and common, for teachers to simply judge a year's efforts on how they feel about them, the number of major problems they had, the average level of student achievement on some test, or some other single criterion. The same may be true in making judgments about a single lesson. This approach has some advantages and disadvantages. The advantage is that it is quick and easy. For some decisions about your subsequent actions it may be sufficient. The approach is summative in

FIGURE 19–6
Forces determining professional effectiveness

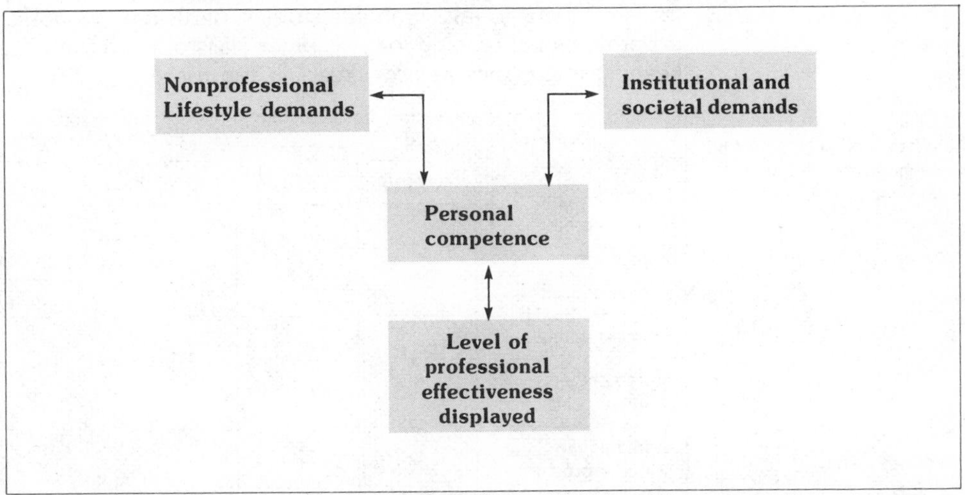

nature and therefore limited to decisions about whether to retain, modify, or abandon the previous set of activities. It may not give much indication of what modifications need to be made or which set of activities to substitute for the old ones. The disadvantage then is the lack of detail which leaves us with little direction for the future.

Focusing on specific details of our activities for evaluation will help us to make micro-level decisions about the future. It is neither possible nor necessary to look at each and every one of our actions. To do so would be too time-consuming and would overwhelm us with a mass of unrelated details. What is needed is a strategy that helps to sort out the complexities by gradually subdividing the problem to identify its various components. The process of subdivision should, however, also retain the relationship between the parts of the problem.

The second step in the development of evaluation programs is to try and identify the various programs that might require evaluation. One common way is to subdivide our efforts in the classroom on the basis of their purpose. For instance, teachers typically see their efforts directed toward helping students achieve certain academic goals and develop more productive social skills. They also see their efforts directed toward coping with the administrative duties of a teacher, interactions with parents, and their own professional development outside of the classroom. If these various types of efforts are viewed as programs that are more or less formally planned, then we can consider each one in terms of the five phases of development.

The above suggests a two-dimensional model for organizing our evaluation efforts based on the type of program along one dimension and the five phase of program development along the other dimension. We have, for descriptive purposes, identified five types of programs into which a teacher could classify activities, but other categories could be just as easily used. The model is illustrated in Figure 19–7 and provides a means of sorting out the evaluation problem for a teacher. It is obvious that in each of the five types of activities there can be subdivisions. Academic activities can be divided by subject area or domain of learning; socialization activities can be divided by dimensions of social behavior such as cooperation, independence, empathy, and eating habits, to name a few. Community activities could include efforts to enlist volunteer help for the classroom, enlist parental help at home, or inform parents of the activities at school or of their child's progress. Self-improvement can include a teacher's plans to take graduate studies, participate in workshops, attend conferences, do professional reading, or visit other classrooms. Housekeeping efforts may include keeping attendance records, keeping the room in order, or doing other activities of

FIGURE 19–7
Categorization scheme for identifying programs that could be evaluated

Program type	*Program development phase*				
	Analysis	*Design*	*Preparation*	*Implementation*	*Evaluation*
Academic					
Social development					
Housekeeping					
Community interactions					
Professional development					

this nature. This level of specificity can be included in the analytic framework by adding subheadings under the five major types of activities listed along the left margin of the model to suit the particular needs of your classroom. The utility of this type of subdivision is that it will call your attention to some areas that may otherwise be overlooked.

The five phases of instructional development listed across the top of the model can also be subdivided. These subdivisions are provided in the outline of the model of systematic instructional design presented in Chapter 6. For example, the analysis phase included five specific analyses that can be conducted. These help to further focus attention on what specific activities might be considered for evaluation. Ignoring these subdivisions may be a serious error because the problems we encounter in the classroom may not be due to our activities in the classroom but may be more directly related to our actions prior to the time we implement our plans.

Using this sort of strategy would provide a means of systematically looking at the entire range of activities a teacher is engaged in, but not all types of activities are of equal importance. Certainly those directed toward some academic or socialization purposes are of primary importance. The areas of housekeeping, community interaction, and professional development are secondary and derive their importance because they also serve some function in achieving our academic or socialization goals. They are apt to be too general, however to associate directly with any particular academic or socialization goal but may have an effect on many of our primary goals. Due to this inequality in importance, as a third step in developing evaluation programs, a teacher should set some priorities about what are the most pressing evaluation needs.

To set priorities it seems as if the degree of innovativeness should be considered. With innovative programs, as contrasted with well-established programs, we have had the least experience, and therefore we are more likely to need information. Somewhere in between the innovative and established programs are those we are still developing but no longer consider innovative because we have already implemented them and have some experience and knowledge about their utility. For these we would have a lower need for information but any information needed is likely to be relatively specific.

Another way of establishing priorities is to consider the importance of the program, or a component within a program, in relation to its possible effect on students since this is the ultimate purpose for all of the programs we are considering.

These two methods can be combined as illustrated in Figure 19–8. To use the model it is suggested that the various programs identified first be classified on the basis of how important they are in relation to students' learning. These programs should then

FIGURE 19–8
Categorization model for prioritizing evaluation needs

Priority level	*Innovativeness*		
	Innovative	*Developing*	*Established*
High			
Medium			
Low			

be classified on the basis of how innovative they are for the particular classroom. After the programs have been classified in these two ways, they should be examined more closely in terms of specific activities in each of the five phases of program development. Even in a very important and highly innovative program some activities are likely to be less important to the overall operation and outcome. Also, many of the specific activities in an innovative program are not new but well-established procedures currently being used in the classroom. Classifying the specific activities involved would result in a much more precise set of priorities. This type of specificity does not preclude, however, the classification of total programs that need an overall evaluation of results. For those programs that are very important or have a great many innovative activities, it would be appropriate just to list the entire program for an overall evaluation of major outcomes. Based on Cronbach's suggestion, the determination of how precisely program activities should be identified is probably dependent upon how well developed the program is.

The process of prioritizing our evaluation needs should proceed to those less innovative but still important programs. From there the analysis should move to the less important programs. These less important programs should not be ignored, especially if changes are being made in them. What we may want to do in these cases is follow Stufflebeam's suggestion and conduct a fairly simple and unsophisticated evaluation of the program's overall effectiveness or the major activities involved.

The final result of this process should be a rough hierarchy of evaluation tasks indicating the order in which they may be approached. To refine priorities between groups, the technique of comparing each program on a one-to-one basis with all other programs seems appropriate. For example suppose we have five programs labeled A through E. If we start with program B we would compare it on an individual basis with programs A, C, D, and E in any order. If we judge programs A and D as more important and C and E as less important, then program B would be the third most important. To decide first and second places we could then compare programs A and D to decide first and second place. We would do the same with B and E to decide fourth and fifth places.

Learner analysis. In the case of program evaluation the person conducting the evaluation, is in one sense trying to learn more about the program. From this perspective we can view the evaluator as a learner. As with any learner we should determine what the learner knows and does not know. Since we are discussing evaluation from a teacher's perspective the teacher doing the evaluation is both the evaluator and the learner. Therefore, the fourth step is to determine how much the teacher already knows about certain programs. To answer this question we conduct the equivalent of an analysis of the teacher's entering behavior in relation to the program (i.e., how much detail could the teacher provide about outcomes and process variables responsible for those outcomes). For those outcomes and effects of process variables that a teacher can accurately describe, there is no need for an evaluation. For those the teacher cannot describe there *may* be a need for evaluation. To finally decide on priorities we would then return to our task analysis data, in which the various program components were ranked as to their importance. By eliminating those tasks about which the teacher already has sufficient information, the remaining tasks could be used as a prioritized list of evaluation needs.

The process of task and learner analysis does not have to take place all at one time. It can occur as an ongoing process in which various types of programs are analyzed as time is available. As new programs are developed they can be inserted into the existing priority list. To the extent that we are able to accomplish the evaluation tasks on the priority list, items would be taken off the list and possibly more refined tasks added back to the list. This will require a periodic review of programs and evaluation priorities throughout a teacher's professional career.

Instructional space and staff analysis. In the analysis phase the physical and human resources available to accomplish the task are also a consideration. In most cases the physical resources required to conduct an evaluation are minimal and readily available. For a great many evaluation tasks a sound understanding of the program, the purpose of the program, and basic measurement principles are sufficient staff expertise variables. For some special problems your expertise may be deficient. To identify and correct for the deficiencies it may be a good strategy to locate some individual that has the needed expertise. This person may be able to help during the development of your evaluation plans and at the same time teach you the skills you will need in the future. Consulting a good measurement and evaluation text written on an understandable level is another method that may be used.

3. For a junior high teacher who teaches a single academic subject to students at two different grade levels and one accelerated class, what is the suggested sequence of steps this teacher should follow to identify which evaluation tasks to accomplish first?

Designing an evaluation

Comprehensive plan and component plans. Once we have analyzed out total evaluation task and our area of interest has been narrowed down to a relatively small set of activities, we need to develop evaluation plans. In developing these plans we need to deal with a second set of issues pertaining to: (1) the specific factors we will look at, (2) the questions we will ask in relation to those factors, and (3) the comparisons we will make.

Hammond (1973) has called attention to the need for focusing on *specific factors* in an evaluation and has listed many examples. The simplest division of these factors is on the basis of outcome and process variables. A summative evaluation should focus on at least the outcome variables, while a formative evaluation would have to focus on the process variables and their relationship to outcomes.

FIGURE 19–9
At times we need to evaluate the characteristics of texts and workbooks

Outcome factors may be student performance in any of the domains and subtypes of learning. The interest may be in the average test scores on a final exam or the percentage of students who have met a certain criterion on a particular task. Other outcomes may be related to the affective domain. As we mentioned earlier the number of volunteer tutors we recruit can be an outcome, or the number of students who sign up for and stay in an extracurricular activity may be an outcome factor.

Process factors can be the characteristics of instructional materials, such as a particular set of questions in a workbook, the equipment in a room, or the readability of a ditto sheet. The activities of the individuals involved are also a major part of the process factors. At times the poor quality of ditto can be related to the teacher's or a secretary's activities, and whenever this is possible it should be done not to place blame but to modify the human behavior to prevent future problems. Other instructional materials are relatively fixed such as texts, filmstrips, room characteristics, and published workbooks (Figure 19–9). Knowing who designed, produced, or selected them is not going to be a particularly useful factor to focus on, since the person will not be expected to modify the materials.

To identify specific human factors, a look at the activities involved in the five phases of the instructional design process will provide a useful outline. For example in the analysis phase of developing a math program we may conclude that a large number of students have an interest in baseball. In the design phase we may outline the characteristics of two or three problems we plan to hand out on a ditto sheet that involves batting averages. In the preparatory phase we would type up and run off our dittos for the students. During the implementation phase we would hand them out and the students would react to the examples. At any point our activities could have an effect on the outcomes of instruction. In the analysis phase we may have overestimated the interest in baseball. In the design phase, instead of designing original problems, available ones may have been better. We can evaluate not only the characteristics of the problems designed, but also the decision to design rather than select problems. It is also possible to evaluate the way in which the problems were used during the implementation phase. This evaluation would take into account the specific characteristics of how the problems were presented or the way they were used in relation to some outcome factor such as student achievement, failure, or student complaints.

The three major *questions* we ask about the various factors are their effectiveness, efficiency, and completeness. The main question is about the effectiveness of a factor in bringing about a particular outcome. The factor can be very effective, partially effective, totally ineffective, or even counterproductive by developing competing behaviors. Several factors may be effective in bringing about a particular outcome, but one may do it more efficiently in that the result is achieved more quickly with less cost or with beneficial side effects such as more positive student attitudes. The third question we may ask is how completely the factor brings about these outcomes, since it may be effective with some students but not with others.

To answer our questions about the various factors we have included in our instructional efforts we need to make some sort of comparison. *Comparisons* need to be made between the results we achieved and some standard we have selected. There are at least three major types of comparisons. They are between observed outcome and (1) intended outcome, (2) planned outcome, and (3) another program.

Which of the three comparisons are made will depend on the purpose of the evaluation. In many cases all three might be useful. This is especially evident when one considers the fact that we can make plans that are inconsistent with what we intended to do but were not evident at the time the plans were made. As we observe the outcome of our efforts the flaw may be very obvious. By the same token what we are doing may be turning out well, but a look at someone else's efforts may make it obvious that there are even better ways of organizing our efforts.

Preparatory plan. Once we have developed our evaluation plan there is sometimes the need to also develop a preparatory plan. This plan will outline the tasks that need to be accomplished prior to actually implementing the evaluation. This plan may specify the time schedule for the development of recording forms, evaluation instruments, or the acquisition of some published materials. The plan, like other preparatory plans, should specify what needs to be done and when.

Evaluation plan. One final point is that we should also consider how we will evaluate our evaluation efforts. This may simply be a plan to go over our evaluation data and conclusions with a colleague as a check on our personal biases. At times this outside evaluation can be performed by an administrator interested in your professional development and with whom you can communicate openly.

> 4. Having decided on the most important parts of our program to look at, what are the next three issues we need to consider in a component plan? How would we apply them to our program of handing out assignments to students in a fifth-grade, open-area classroom with the use of written instructions "mailed" to the students each day and picked up by them at their mailbox located near the teacher's desk?

Preparing for and implementing an evaluation

In most cases preparatory activities are minimal, but if they are needed and not done it can create real problems in data collection. Since a teacher's main interest is in the preparation and implementation of the instructional programs, preparations for evaluating those plans get left out or hastily done. For this reason it is well to leave plenty of lead time for accomplishing the task so it can be worked in with other activities.

The implementation of an evaluation plan starts during the implementation of the component plan. These two implementations have overlapping activities but also separate activities. The overlap in activities involves the gathering of student performance data. In spite of the overlap in activities it is useful to treat them as parallel sets of activities due to the difference in purpose. The purpose of gathering student information data during the implementation of the main instructional program is to make micro-level decisions about how to adapt the current student needs. This same student data, collected and stored in some form, also becomes the basis for the evaluation of the program and decisions about how it can be improved in the future. Since the data are being generated in the implementation of the main instructional program, that is when they need to be gathered. Analysis and interpretation of the data can be done when there is less competition for your time and more attention can be given to forming your judgments (Figure 19–10). The analysis and interpretation should not be delayed any longer than necessary because some of the details of what actually occurred during the instructional period may be forgotten and make it difficult to interpret our data and pinpoint specific ways in which the information may be used.

Evaluating evaluation efforts

A somewhat confusing point is that in addition to evaluating our other programs, we need to evaluate our evaluation program. In this case we need to determine how well we have analyzed and prioritized our evaluation needs. Most important, we need to evaluate how effective and efficient our evaluation plans were and how efficiently they were developed. In the same manner we need to evaluate how completely and efficiently they were prepared for and implemented. To answer these questions the friendly colleague or administrator mentioned earlier should be contacted and asked how the evaluation may be deficient and could have been improved.

> 5. Once an evaluation is completed and we have made our judgments as to the effectiveness, efficiency, and completeness of various factors, which two tasks remain to be accomplished?

FIGURE 19–10
Analysis and interpretation can be done when there is less competition for a teacher's time

USING THE EVALUATION STRATEGY

The utility in using a maximum number of categories in an evaluation is that greater precision is achieved in isolating factors for improvement. A disadvantage of having many categories is that it is difficult to cope with all of them at once. The models we have presented are, we believe, comprehensive in nature and fairly detailed in content. It is not expected that they will be memorized but rather will provide a conceptual framework and checklist for planning and implementing an evaluation.

The first model outlining the program types and developmental stages should help to outline the full range of evaluation tasks. Classifying the tasks according to context and importance should help narrow down the specific factors, questions, and comparisons that need to be considered. Using the factors, questions, and comparisons model as a checklist to draw up an evaluation plan should result in a vast improvement over what is normally produced, if any plan is produced at all. The process may seem overwhelming, but if taken one step at a time during free moments it can be done quite quickly. Once past the first step, it may be rather reassuring to find that during the process of prioritizing programs and activities you already know a great deal about your programs and activities. Even if the process does not go any further, you will be in a better position to react to any outside evaluations that may be made about your competence. We strongly suggest, however, that the process be carried on using as many precise factors as possible.

SUMMARY

In this chapter distinctions were drawn between program evaluation and student evaluation, research, and pseudo-evaluations. The contexts of maintenance, developmental, innovative, and utopian programs were described and related to the purpose of evaluation, as were the judgment criteria and data base needed for program evaluation. The process of evaluation was described in terms of the role of external and internal program evaluators. It was suggested that the classroom teacher is the logical choice to evaluate classroom-level programs, but some external evaluation should take place as a check on the validity of the self-evaluation efforts. The thoroughness of program evaluation was related to the importance and maturity of the program development efforts. The final part of the chapter was devoted to describing a program evaluation strategy for outlining the array of possible evaluation tasks, prioritizing the various tasks, and then identifying the factors, questions, and comparisons to be included in the evaluation.

SELF-TEST

1. Which of the following is true with regard to program evaluation?
   a. Validity is not an important consideration.
   b. Reliability is not an important consideration.
   c. Neither validity nor reliability is an important consideration.
   d. Both validity and reliability are important considerations.
2. In relation to learner evaluation, program evaluation has:
   a. An additional set of issues to consider.
   b. Fewer issues to consider.
   c. The same set of issues to consider.
   d. An entirely different set of issues to consider.
3. The objective of program evaluation is:
   a. To develop new knowledge.
   b. To judge the worth of a program in relation to another program.
   c. To modify a program as it is being planned and tried out.
   d. Both *b* and *c.*
   e. *a, b,* and *c.*
4. According to Stufflebeam, the context with the greatest amount of change and the least amount of information is the:
   a. Utopian context.
   b. Innovative context.
   c. Developmental context.
   d. Maintenance context.
5. The basis for making judgments could be:
   a. Desired versus planned.
   b. Planned versus observed.
   c. One program versus another.
   d. Both *a* and *b.*
   e. All of the above.
6. Program evaluation judgments can also be made on the basis of:
   a. Effectiveness and efficiency only.
   b. Effectiveness, efficiency, and completeness.
   c. Effectiveness but not efficiency.
   d. None of the above.
7. For purposes of program evaluation:
   a. Only systematically gathered data have any usefulness.
   b. Less systematically gathered data may be useful in the *early* stages of program development.
   c. Less systematically gathered data may be useful in the *later* stages of development.
   d. Less systematically gathered data are always preferable to systematically gathered data since they reduce the possibility of evaluation bias.
8. How rigorously a program is evaluated should depend on:
   a. The qualifications of the evaluator.
   b. The preference of the evaluator.
   c. The importance of the decisions to be made.
   d. All of the above.
9. Professional evaluators generally believe that teachers:
   a. Do not have the expertise to be the primary evaluator of a program but can fill a useful informative role.
   b. Should not be involved in program evaluation since they are more likely to provide misinformation than useful information.
   c. Have the expertise to be program evaluators but do not use their skills.
   d. Have the expertise to be program evaluators but are too close to the programs to be objective.
10. The evaluation strategy suggested in the text is intended as a means of:
    a. Outlining the complexity of program evaluation.
    b. Organizing the process of program evaluation.
    c. Eliminating certain instructional activities from the evaluation process.
    d. All of the above.
    e. None of the above.

ANSWER KEY TO BOXED QUESTIONS

1. Purposes—utility of program outcomes and process variables.
   Judgment criteria—desired versus planned versus observed or one program against another.
   When are criteria appropriate—Comparisons among desired, planned, and observed would be more useful in formative evaluations where the object is to improve the program, while comparisons between programs would involve summative evaluation to make choices between programs or decisions to terminate a program.
2. Evaluator—classroom teacher or outside evaluator.
   Role—Classroom teacher would assume broad role on the assumption that the purpose of the program will

be formative. Outside evaluator could assume a broad or narrow role depending on the status of the evaluator and the authority granted.

Thoroughness—The teacher's evaluation would be less thorough for this program than for a pre-reading or number concepts program due to lower priority in curriculum concerns. Outside evaluator would base thoroughness on the size of the overall project beyond the immediate classroom. If it will affect many children and involve a lot of money or changes, the evaluation should be very rigorous.

3. *Step 1.* Determine balance in various personal roles and check this against professional expectations for a competent and relatively well-motivated professional.
   Step 2. Identify array of programs that may require evaluation and activities involved in five phases of program development.
   Step 3. Set priorities on the basis of importance and innovativeness of programs and specific program development activities.
   Step 4. Determine current knowledge base of the evaluator with regard to prioritized evaluation tasks.
   Step 5. Inventory evaluation resources.
4. *Factors*—Output factors of "mail" being delivered on time and consistently; also student attitude. Process factors such as time consumed, individual time patterns, peers picking up mail for others, etc.
   Questions—Is it effective in getting assignments out? Is it efficient in terms of time and energy needed to get the "mail" ready, delivered, and picked up?
   Comparisons—Is it as good as intended, as planned, or as the former method?
5. Using the results of the evaluation to modify, terminate, or replace the program and evaluate our evaluation efforts possibly with the aid of an outside evaluator.

ANSWER KEY TO SELF-TEST

1. *d*
2. *a*
3. *d*
4. *b*
5. *e*
6. *b*
7. *b*
8. *c*
9. *a*
10. *d*

SECTION IV

FACILITATING SOCIAL SKILLS AND COMMUNITY INVOLVEMENT

Schools were created by society to serve a purpose. Some argue that their primary purpose is to exert a socialization influence on children. There is little doubt that this is done but mainly through the "hidden curriculum." While trying to achieve the explicit and implicit purposes for which the schools were intended, the schools are also charged with the responsibility to keep the public informed of their needs and progress. These two functions have a large impact on the teacher's role in and out of the classroom, and for this reason we have devoted a chapter to each topic.

Each of the two chapters in this section has a secondary function beyond the subject matter. In Section I, the presentation was intended to give you a broad perspective of the educational process. In Section II, the coverage was related to specific principles that should underlie the instructional process. Section III was intended to show how these principles can be applied in a classroom. The chapters in this section are organized not only to cover the particular topic but also to demonstrate how the instructional design process can be applied to developing programs in a particular content area.

In Chapter 20 the focus is on the socialization process from a broad perspective which cuts across the normal boundaries of the social studies curriculum, occupational training, and social interaction skills. Normally only the latter are covered in a text of this type but we wish to show the interrelated nature of the three areas and how they may be integrated. We do not present any new learning principles but instead build on those presented earlier. In Chapter 21 we follow the same general approach, but the topic is the communication process among the home, school and community. We point out the important role that teachers play in that process and indicate that the role may expand and become more critical in the future.

Chapter 20

Facilitating the development of social skills

IT HAS BEEN OUR EXPERIENCE that many students preparing to be teachers consider the development of social skills to be a major portion of their educational goals, if not their instructional goals. For this reason we have included it as a topic in the text.

The content of socialization skills overlaps to a considerable degree with the content of other subject areas. The learning principles involved are the same as those associated with the four learning domains. The most distinctive feature of social skills is their use. Socialization is a far-ranging area with many components and is discussed from a great many divergent points of view. Not only learning theorists but also others from the fields of personality, child development, social psychology, sociology, and biology are interested in the socialization process. This array of approaches has resulted in the study of many behaviors related to social interaction and a correspondingly large number of concepts and explanatory principles.

We have tried to organize the subject in a manner that is understandable in view of the material already presented and easily translated into classroom socialization programs. The chapter roughly follows the points to be considered in the analysis and design phases of instruction. Issues related to the preparation, implementation, and evaluation phases have been omitted because they have been discussed elsewhere.

After reading this chapter you should be able to:

1. Define society's expectations of the outcomes and methods of the socialization process.
2. Outline the major components of the socialization task and how each relates to the domains of learning.
3. Describe the macro- and micro-level assessments of entering behavior in relation to social skills.
4. Define the three general instructional techniques used to develop social skills.
5. Describe specific instructional techniques related to the four components of social skills.

EXPECTATIONS IN OUR SOCIETY—ENVIRONMENTAL ANALYSIS

In the analysis phase of program development one task is to analyze the environment. In this chapter we have done this at a general level by identifying some of the goals, historical trends, socialization agents, and constraints associated with the development of social skills.

Socialization goals

Elkin and Handel (1972) define socialization as "the process by which someone learns the ways of a given society or social group so that he can function within it." Taken at the level of the individual person, the process develops those behaviors we engage in when interacting with other individuals. The process is lifelong; it begins at birth and ends with death. Elkin and Handel identify four outcomes, or ranges of outcomes, that society expects of the socialization process. Paraphrased at the educational goals level, they are that a person:

1. Functions as a law-abiding citizen.
2. Displays a sense of loyalty to the society.
3. Adheres to social norms of society.
4. Performs as a competent citizen.

Within our society various subgroups may hold somewhat different interpretations of what behaviors exemplify each of the goals but, according to a recent Gallup (1976) poll designed to measure public opinion on the education issues, the following are the most important qualities in the development of a child along with the percentage of respondents choosing that quality (p. 194):

Learning to think for oneself	26%
Ability to get along with others	23
Willingness to accept responsibility	21
High moral standards	13
Eagerness to learn	11
Desire to excel	4

This suggests that the general goals of the socialization process are to develop a person who is law-abiding, self-sufficient, self-directed, friendly, agreeable, and responsive to the needs of others. In addition these characteristics are expected to gradually change and conform to social norms for various ages. In other words, what is considered responsible behavior for a 6 year-old child is not the same as for a 16-, 30-, or 90-year-old person. Society, therefore, does not have a simple set of socialization goals but a complex, age-related set of goals.

Historical note

With our current awareness of youth it is a surprise to many how recently the concept of childhood has emerged. Based on his analysis of French history Ariès (1962) suggests that the distinction between children and adults did not appear until the 16th century. He perceived the parents as being indifferent to infants and having no clearly defined approach to raising children. D. Hunt (1970) believes that Ariès may have overstated the amount of indifference with which parents treated their children, but there is apparently little doubt that after the first couple of years of life the children mingled freely with adults in all aspects of life. Being nursed by their mothers, usually until 18 months of age, they then ended the period of greatest dependency. From then on they were dressed and treated as miniature adults, sharing in the labors and the merrymaking. Until about age seven the child was primarily under the care and supervision of women. After that time the boys associated with the men and other boys while the girls continued to stay with the women and older girls.

Hunt sees the 16th century as characterized by a great deal of sociability and mixing between social classes and age levels. At the time the concept of family was that of a family line rather than the nuclear family of a mother, father, and children as we know it today. Property rights belonged primarily to the family line rather than to the current members of the family. By custom, marriages were often a matter of simple consent, but attempts were made to outlaw the practice. Planned marriages that were more compatible with the inheritance laws and useful in merging business interests were preferred by adults. In these mergers the two to be married were treated almost as if they were pieces of property to be traded off for some economic or political gain.

The practice of having children mingle freely with adults and share in the same activities continued well beyond the 16th century. Sudia (undated) describes the American colonies where everyone's labor was needed if they literally were to stay alive. At age four children were expected to work. As late as 1900, 95 percent of the population was classified as rural and working mostly on family farms. These, as a matter of

FIGURE 20–1
Agriculture required large amounts of manual labor until after World War II

Courtesy of New York State Historical Association, Cooperstown.

necessity, required the early involvement of children in the family labor supply. Not until after World War II, when the farms became much more mechanized with the coming of electricity and the expanding use of tractors instead of horses, did the need for large amounts of manual labor diminish (Figure 20–1). Boys grew up in the company of their fathers and other men, and girls with their mothers and other women. Idleness was treated as evil, partly out of religious conviction but also out of the realities of raising crops and caring for livestock and buildings. The sons stayed on the farm and eventually took over from their fathers or moved on to other farms. Life did not change too much between childhood and adulthood. Sometimes not even the location changed unless the lack of available land forced the sons to move westward. Before the move was made, however, enough resources had to be accumulated in order to start the new enterprise.

Even in the urban areas, Reynolds (undated, p. 289) reports that children as young as four years of age were employed in the yarn factories, and "one measure of the value of the machinery produced for use in the mills in the early 19th century was the degree to which it could be managed by 5–10-year-old children." Fathers and their children hired out to work in the factories on a single contract. The children's wages helped to support the family. Reynolds notes that as much as 95 percent of a girl's pay and 85 percent of a boy's pay went into the family budget. The boys were encouraged to move into better jobs, but the girls stayed at home until they married.

In a society such as this, which did not change to any great extent until the 1930s, the process of socialization was much different than it is today. Adult roles were readily apparent to children and taken on at an early age. Schooling was the unique work of children but it was sporadic and for most children lasted only a few years.

The advent of child labor laws, labor unions, more efficient modes of production, and a sophisticated technology has contributed to a dramatic and swift change in our society. Shorter working hours, higher pay, greater mobility, exclusion of children from the labor force, and the large variety of household appliances have left children with little to do but play and go to school. What household duties are required are usually accomplished in a few minutes. Most of their time is spent with other children of a similar age, and the only adult role many children come in contact with are those of parents, teachers, tradespeople, and some professionals. The vast majority of the labor force and the occupational role they perform are not visible to children. Children now grow up in a world of children which is shielded from, and oblivious to, many of the realities and contingencies of adult life. Few demands are placed on their time and large amounts of resources are devoted to their care, education, and amusement.

A central theme in all accounts of the relationship of parents and children prior to the mid-19th century is the belief that children were to be controlled. Control was necessary to thwart the basically evil nature of humans, which would manifest itself in the children's behavior if they were not punished. A more recent trend (Greven, 1973) is that children are viewed as pure and therefore need to be controlled to shield them from corruption. The earlier position is much harsher and probably motivated as much by economic matters as religious persuasion. Both positions are presently reflected in parental attitudes, but the amount of parental control, as well as that of all adults, is being eroded. Child development texts point out the strong influence the child's peer groups play in the socialization process especially during adolescence, which incidentally is an even more recently invented stage of growth. Indeed, Ariès (1962, p. 30) was prompted to describe the adolescent as "the hero of our twentieth century, the century of adolescence."

As Coleman (Panel on Youth, 1974, p. 29) points out, young people in our society "are simultaneously the most indulged and oppressed part of the population." As adults view it, the restrictions on activities "stem not from tyranny but from affection and consideration." The intent is to protect them from themselves and from unscrupulous persons who may take advantage of them.

In this recent unheaval and rapidly changing process of socialization, where different social classes have little contact with each other and children are raised apart from the adult world, the schools are increasingly involved. Most actively involved of all are classroom teachers, whether they wish to be or not. Compounding the problem for the teacher is the inability of many parents to maintain control over the activities of their children.

Socializing forces

Various individuals, groups, and institutions currently play a role in the socialization of young people. These agents of change have various amounts of influence at differing times in the child's life. Starting with the influence of parents and siblings, this is gradually extended to peers, teachers, and the school as an institution. There are many others, such as relatives, neighbors, and community workers, who also have an influence.

Parents and siblings. A child's parents, brothers, sisters, and other family members are expected to foster the development of social attachment to themselves and a basic trust in humans. The parents are also given the primary responsibility for establishing adult authority and appropriate rules of social interaction with which the child is expected to comply. Along with this responsibility, parents are held accountable for the nonsocial actions of their young children.

Even during the school years the parents maintain the major responsibility for control over the social actions of their children. To some extent the task is shared with the schools and other institutions, but the child remains primarily the ward of the parents and not the school. Only in instances in which parents are judged legally incompetent will the court consent to make the child its ward.

Peers. A child is expected to interact socially with a peer group of a similar age, and as long as the child reciprocates in a similar manner the peers are not expected to shun the child. Due to the frequent, varied, and more or less continuous peer associations, a great many of a child's interaction skills must be learned and modified in the peer setting. This interaction acts to broaden the child's awareness of differences in family structures, practices, and standards. This awareness modifies to some extent the socialization process started by the parents and sometimes conflicts with parental values, but not always.

Sheer closeness and probability of contact determine to a great extent who a child's peers will be. This means they are likely to live close by, have parents in a somewhat similar socioeconomic level, and have parents who share a great many values which they pass on to their children. The peer group is, therefore, likely to share many values and exert only a minimum amount of broadening influence (Figure 20–2).

Schools. The schools are expected to broaden a student's awareness of the cultural structure and institutions. Part of this is accomplished through the social studies curriculum. The purpose is apparently to teach what the social structure is supposed to be and to a lesser extent to teach how we deviate from the ideal.

Teachers are also expected to assist in the continuing development of the student's role and age-appropriate behaviors by modeling appropriate school and adult behaviors and maintaining a certain level of control over student interactions.

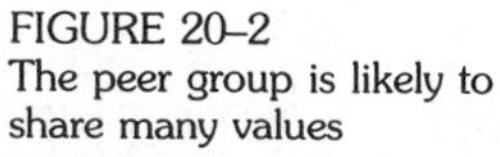

FIGURE 20–2
The peer group is likely to share many values

Others. All members of society by the example they set have a certain potential for influencing the student. This influence is largely unplanned, but some individuals are pointed out as good and bad examples of what the child should emulate. This is done in explicit ways at times but more often in subtle ways.

The mass media of television, movies, radio, books, magazines, and newspapers have a considerable effect on the socialization process because the media describe and portray a wide range of social roles and interactions which affect the child's perception of the social world. It is estimated that most children by age 16 have watched 10,000–15,000 hours of television and, as mentioned in Chapter 11, this helps to shape children's prosocial and aggressive behaviors.

Constraints on socialization practices

In the same subtle way that society sets expectations, society also imposes some constraints. These constraints are mainly limits on goals and methods.

Constraints on goals. The law generally defines the outer limits of social behavior that will be tolerated in our society. Most people's definition of acceptable social behavior is probably even more limited, and what may not be punishable according to law may be frowned on and socially punished. Teaching children these unacceptable behaviors is certainly not accepted by most adults. Because teachers come primarily from a middle-class social background (Charters, 1963), they may pursue an even more restricted set of socialization goals than the population at large would accept. Milburn (1975) found that teachers rated social skills related to order, rules, obedience, and responsibility in the classroom as more important than taking initiative and being outgoing and assertive in interpersonal relationships. Teachers apparently change during their first few years and move away from a concern for pupil freedom to place more emphasis on social controls (Hoy, 1967, 1968; Rabinowitz & Rosenbaum, 1960). This shift may not be related to the social backgrounds of the teachers as much as it is that "teachers are at once the executive (supervisory, directive, critical) and the counselor (supportive, advisory, knowledge-oriented)" (Edgerton, 1977, p. 120). Where at first they lean more toward the counselor side of the continuum, later they take on more of an executive stance. Regardless of why the shift takes place, it further limits the range of social behaviors that will be taught and tolerated in class. This shift in attitude seems compatible with the finding by Gallup (1977) that 26 percent of those individuals polled believed that lack of discipline is the biggest problem facing public schools. The public concern and teacher shift in attitude may not reflect a desire to inhibit certain socially accepted behaviors, but rather a wish to prevent the development of unacceptable behaviors.

Constraints on methods. In some countries the methods used to indoctrinate the students into the culture, and particularly the political culture, are much more extreme than would be tolerated in the United States. To bring about compliance with the social structure, we rule out harsh methods of punishment. While parents are allowed to use corporal punishment, they are not allowed to "batter" their child. Teachers are usually restricted to verbal coercion, verbal reprimands, and withdrawal of privileges as punishment.

1. What are the general goals of the socialization process as given in the text? What forces exert some influence on a child? What are the two constraints on the socialization process?

COMPONENTS OF SOCIALIZATION GOALS—TASK ANALYSIS

The broad educational goals of the socialization process listed by Elkin and Handel (1972) cover a wide range of activities. Stated at that level of generality they can include almost any educational objective, since they cover citizenship, personal interactions, and occupational functioning. Some components of these educational goals are clearly related to social interactions, whereas others are more environmentally functional. We have organized the social components differently than they are normally discussed in most educational psychology texts. We have deviated from tradition to point out the interrelatedness of the explicit social studies to the career development curriculum, and, the implicit curriculum to the development of interpersonal skills and self control. To place the development of social skills in a long-term perspective and to relate them more easily to the four domains of learning, we will discuss them under the following five categories:

1. Social roles.
2. Role relationships.
3. Social contexts.
4. Rules of interaction.
5. Personal role.

This division is based on the assumption that the socialization process is intended to help individuals learn the ways of our society and how to function within that social structure. The components of social roles, social structure, and social contexts generally define the social units, the relationships between social units, and the normal situations found in our society. The rules of interaction define the accepted means by which individuals interact in their various social roles. The personal role component is a means of describing a particular individual and the specific set of social roles that individual assumes at various times.

Relationship of domains and components

Learning to categorize social contexts, roles, and personal roles is at the concept level of learning. Learning the relationships between roles requires rule learning. The rules of interaction are obviously also at the rule-learning level.

One point that is stressed in the literature about social development is that a simple learning of the rules is not sufficient. The goal is to have the student *internalize* the rules. Once internalized these rules become a set of values and guiding principles that determine the manner in which the person interacts with others. The internalization implies that the rules are, therefore, a form of intrinsic motivation. Without internalization of the rules, external methods are needed to have the person follow the rule. An example would be the custom of saying, "Thank you." At one point parents may have to instruct a child by saying: "Say thank you to Grandpa." Later it may be "What do you say to Grandpa for the present?" Still later, without prompting, the child may say "Thank you" whenever someone treats her kindly. At this point the thank you rule is internalized. The person does not view it as a rule that *must* be followed but he/she does it voluntarily. Whereas learning the rule is a cognitive domain skill, the internalization portion of the socialization process is clearly related to the affective domain since it involves the development of values and attitudes.

We can also view the development of some social behaviors as being related to the mathemagenic domain in that they are likely to bring us into new social situations, thereby fostering further development of more sophisticated social skills.

The motor skills domain is also involved since some social behaviors involve games, recreational activities, and competencies in certain tasks. We have not dealt with this domain to any great extent in this chapter because it is related tangentially rather than directly. For the same reason we have slighted the mathemagenic domain. For any one individual in the process of developing social skills, either domain may have considerable impact, but at this point we are more concerned with an impersonal analysis of social skills and the type of learning involved so as to more easily relate the process to the instructional conditions that should be provided. In this way we hope to overcome some of the current lack of any obvious learning hierarchy in the social science and social development areas.

Social roles

The learning of social roles covers the normal activities, rights, responsibilities, and privileges associated with various roles. These roles can be those of students of different ages, men, women, parents, civil servants, people with various occupations, or those of a specific religious persuasion.

Role relationships

As we use the term *role relationships,* it includes the social organization within the immediate family, the extended family, the neighborhood, the school, small social groups, work groups, various levels of government, the economic world, and almost any other form of social organization involving humans (Figure 20–3). Some role relationships are defined by laws, but most are determined by social convention.

FIGURE 20–3
Within the family there are role relationships.

Courtesy of New York State Historical Association, Cooperstown.

These role relationships define a social pecking order. The relationships are based on the power and status related to the various roles and tend to define authority and the relationships between individuals. As we define it, power is derived from the ability to control certain resources and dispense or withhold them on a selective basis. Status is conferred because of certain personal characteristics or personal achievements. For instance, beauty, intelligence, height, singing ability, or home runs batted in may result in a high status being conferred on a person. A person's power, age, and occupational role also determine status.

Rules of interaction

As we pointed out earlier, learning the rules is one goal, but internalizing the rules is the final goal. There are many rules guiding our social interactions. Some apply to specific situations such as sports events, libraries, churches, and work. Others pertain to the interactions between parent-child, teacher-student, employer-employee, and lovers. Still others such as the thank-you rule apply more generally. As we pointed out earlier these rules first must be learned, but in addition the socialization process assumes they will be internalized as attitudes.

As individuals change in age and from one situation to another during the day they change roles. This necessitates a changing of the social interaction rules to match the roles. A person must also learn to be sensitive to changes in the content of the interaction as well as the situations and roles of other people. At times a student has the right to refuse to obey a teacher's order, and at other times because of the content of the order the student is expected to comply. The content may also determine the vigor with which a child refuses to obey an order.

Harré (1974) sees these rules of interaction as stemming from two main classes of problems. The first class includes "the problems created by the sudden appearance of other and strange human beings, and the need to quickly run up some sort of viable relationships with them." The second class are those "problems created by threats and challenges to an existing fragment of order" (p. 248). The first class of problems requires "socially constructive solutions"; the second class requires "socially maintaining solutions."

Examples of the former are when two strangers arrive at a doorway at the same time, pass in a hallway, or come into physical contact in a crowded area. The social rules generally define who goes through the doorway first, whether the two people will greet or ignore each other in the hallway, and whether one person will be offended if the other makes any type of physical contact.

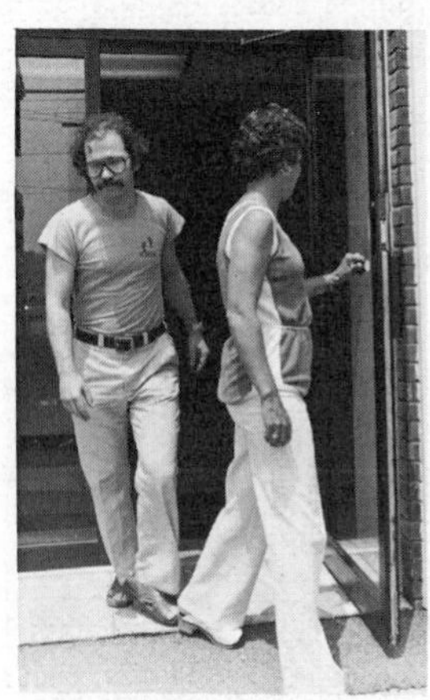

FIGURE 20–4
The ceremonial portion of a social encounter

In these interactions Harré contends that there are three components. The first is some form of greeting that recognizes the "autonomy" and "cognitive status" of the other individual. The second component is a ceremonial activity to resolve the situation. The third is "a competitive metagame to present the most acceptable self" (p. 251). Each individual in the situation attempts to use the ceremonial activity that will make himself look best. The awareness of the other is not just an awareness of physical presence but also of his/her role in the situation and thoughts and feelings at the time. These are detected through a variety of subtle facial expressions and social gestures the person makes. Depending on the situation a person may decide to ignore these signs but risks the disapproval of the other person.

The ceremonial portion of the action may be reaching back to partially hold open the door for someone following (Figure 20–4) or holding open the door and stepping back to allow the other to pass first. A person is most likely to display the ceremonial action that presents him/her in the most socially acceptable way. In essence the encounter should fulfill the requirements of an acceptable greeting and the appropriate ceremonial act that leaves a favorable impression on the other person. Not in all situations does the greeting have to be an obvious greeting. For instance in some situations the appropriate greeting may be to avoid eye contact and give no verbal greeting. At other times it may involve a glance at the bundle of papers in the other person's arms to indicate to them that you recognize their burdened state and right to pass first.

Problems associated with maintaining social order can arise when one person threatens the other's social territory or the image another person is trying to present. The social territory can involve physical territory or the perceived social rights and privileges to which a person feels he/she has a claim on the basis of social role. Harré treats both types of threats in a similar manner.

Threats to social order are dealt with in one of two ways. One is to acknowledge the threat and exchange apologies and acceptances of apology. The second way is to redefine the situation. Here the situations and actions are recognized, but one or the other of the two people may redefine the situation or the intent of the action so it is perceived as nonthreatening. In these interactions both individuals are likely to cooperate in the solution. Harré calls attention to standard and nonstandard solutions. The standard solutions are those laid down by convention. The nonstandard solutions occur when one individual has not learned the standard solution to the problem and therefore improvises. This would probably be a common occurrence with young children or peers moving into new areas of social behavior or new social situations.

Social contexts

Very young children are often seen talking to inanimate objects as if the object had all the qualities of a human. An adult doing the same thing may be referred to a mental health clinic or at least considered to be a bit eccentric. In both cases neither the child nor the adult is making the most basic distinction of a social context, the presence of other humans. On a more sophisticated level another human does not have to be physically present but may be present only in a larger context. For instance, a person picking wildflowers in the woods to give to another person, while it may be illegal if the flowers are an endangered species, is engaging in a social act.

How we interpret the social acts of others depends on the social context we use to interpret them. The flower picking can be interpreted within the context of the relationship between the flower picker and the intended recipient of the flowers. In this context the flower picking is a noble act of thoughtfulness and love. Placed in the context of everyone's right to enjoy endangered species, the flower picking takes on a different meaning. It is this subtle construing of the same situation in different social contexts that adds sophistication to social behaviors. Without this capacity a person may not view a particular situation as requiring a specific social response or offering a choice of social responses.

Personal role

A major part of the socialization process is to have the child assume a socially acceptable role. At early ages the child has very little choice of roles. Parents, older siblings, and teachers have a great deal of control over the child's life and, to a considerable extent, determine the child's role or at least the alternatives. By high school age the child's role is still primarily that of a student but the range of subroles is extensive.

Regardless of the roles students are given or choose, children will also develop a personal view of themselves. This is the self-concept—how one defines and classifies oneself. Related to this are estimates people make about their own worth or value. These estimates are referred to as self-confidence or self-esteem. The latter term is used more often in the psychological literature. Self-esteem is usually subdivided into general and task-specific self-esteem. The first is an estimate of overall value, whereas the latter is much narrower and associated with a limited set of skills.

> 2. What are the five components of the general socialization task? How do they relate to the four domains of learning?

LOOKING AT THE LEARNER—LEARNER ANALYSIS

During the analysis phase of instruction the learner's entering behavior must be measured or estimated. Obtaining measures or estimates of social behavior in any systematic manner is difficult to do in the classroom. One problem is that in order to measure the behaviors we first need to have the social situation occur. We cannot always do this. A second problem is that, since socialization implies an internalization of the rules, this internalization needs to be measured without imposing some external pressure to comply with the social rules. This is the typical problem encountered in measuring in the affective domain. For instance a child may allow another, smaller child to take the first turn in an activity when an adult is around but may not do so when the adult is absent.

Even though it may be difficult to measure a student's social behavior, we can usually get a rough estimate of the behavior or some characteristics of the environment that will affect it. This you will recognize as a macro-level approach to the assessment of entering behavior. Before we tackle this problem a brief review of the development and present-day characteristics of children's social interactions will help to put the task in context.

Early social development

The earliest social interaction is between an infant and the mother or primary caretaker. Gradually the infant begins to recognize this person through the many interactions that occur. The effect of these interactions are not one-way; both participants affect each other. Since there is research data indicating that even in the very first weeks of life an infant can learn to bring about changes in the environment, it seems reasonable to assume that the infant also learns to bring about specific responses in the mother. Certainly crying has the effect of bringing someone. Smiling, waving of arms, cooing, and babbling can also have the effect of prolonging that contact. Depending on the quality of these contacts a child may develop very strong or weak attachments to human adults.

In our culture contact with other infants is very limited, but in Russia and Israel children are raised together starting soon after birth. Groups of children are kept in large playpens or yards. Under these conditions the children are taught to interact in a positive manner. They do this in their play; the context of peer social interactions. Play develops through the stages of solitary play, onlooker, parallel play, associative play, and finally cooperative play.

FIGURE 20–5
Members of cliques are likely to share similar socioeconomic backgrounds, values, and interests

Beyond early childhood children develop friendships in a fairly consistent pattern. First two-person friendships are developed with another person of the same sex. Next small, single-sex cliques form with considerable attachment among members. There can be school, recreational, or institutional cliques. These three types of cliques develop out of the class groupings, play area boundaries, and social organizations, such as scouting or church groups which the child joins. The cliques that form are likely to be composed of members from families at the same socioeconomic level and thus members have similar values and interests (Figure 20–5). From these cliques larger groups, referred to as *crowds,* are formed that are similar but larger. The crowds are likely to be heterosexual as are the later-formed cliques and friendships. These various peer groups have a strong influence on the members and it is not until the late teen years that the crowds begin to break up when some go to college, begin an occupation, or get married.

Present-day characteristics of youth

Coleman (Panel on Youth, 1974), in describing the "youth culture," points out that it is indeed a recent phenomenon. It was not until this century (Hall, 1904) that adolescence was considered a separate phenomenon in development, and not until the 1930s and 1940s did teenagers begin to develop a culture of their own. Prior to this time the age group was oriented toward adult values and lifestyle. In the 1960s and 1970s an expansion of the age group to include college-age students resulted in the phenomenon of a youth culture. There are a variety of subcultures, but Coleman sees five basic characteristics of individuals in the youth culture:

1. Inward-lookingness to one another for preferences in clothes, music, and activities of interest.
2. Psychic attachment and intimacy with others of their own age.
3. Press toward autonomy from adults and self-control over their activities.
4. Concern for the underdog in relation to the political and corporate establishment.

5. Interest in change in the social structure whereby status is gained slowly through achievement.

The pervasive nature of these characteristics gives us some guideposts to social interactions of youth in general. It also points up the strong influence that the peer group is likely to have and the relatively low influence adults may have with adolescents and college-age individuals. While Coleman does not deal with preadolescent individuals, some of these same characteristics have probably permeated down into the younger ages. As Coleman points out, the youth culture has certainly permeated upward into older age groups. While some of these attitudes are not new, especially the press toward autonomy, they do seem to suggest a lack of movement toward adult roles and also a lack of orientation toward traditional methods of socialization.

Macro-level assessment

The points about adult attachments, play characteristics, peer groups, and youth culture characteristics give us some idea about the social behaviors of children in general but not the social behaviors of a particular child. This general information does, however, provide a norm against which any particular child can be compared. It also provides a starting point from which general assumptions can be made about how to handle a whole class of students of a particular age. From this point adjustments can be made to suit the particular group, subgroups, and individuals within the class.

A slightly more refined estimate of a student's level of socialization can be gained from the peer relationships a child develops. For children at the younger ages these are likely to be rather flexible and subject to the influence of immediate events. With increasing age the relationships become more stable and enduring.

First, the members of a friendship or school clique are likely to share a common attitude toward many topics including school work and adult authority. We hasten to stress, however, that this provides only a very broad estimate of what any particular student's attitudes and social skills may be. It does indicate, however, that the child is not totally lacking in social skills or the individual would not be accepted by the other group members. Occasionally you will encounter a child who attempts to interact with peers but is so inept that he/she is totally rejected by every student in the class. You may also find children who avoid social contact to the point where they are isolates in the class. The other children may not dislike them but they simply have no social contact with the individuals. It is difficult to tell whether the withdrawal is due to a past history of negative contacts or a lack of effective approach skills.

A second aspect of peer grouping is the stability of the membership. To maintain stability the members must have either a strong overriding interest holding them together or enough social skills to interact in a way that maintains the relationship. As Harré points out, nonstandard solutions may be used for lack of knowledge of a standard solution. It seems reasonable to assume that those children who are constantly in and out of group membership may lack the necessary social skills to resolve social problems and maintain the relationship.

A third aspect of group membership is the range of groups in which an individual has a membership. Some students have a single friend and no other social relationships, while others who interact with a great many children maintain a close friendship with several peers. It seems reasonable to assume that the latter children are better prepared to cope with the adult social world. This can be misleading, however. The apparently popular child may have only the skills to make friends easily but not the skills to maintain a long relationship. Conversely the student who maintains only a single friendship may be socially far advanced but not interested in associating with the less socially advanced peers. For this child, a stable friendship with a single peer may be sufficient to indicate that peer relationships can be established and maintained. As the peer group reaches adulthood and becomes more socially mature, individuals may be inclined to widen their range of friendships and they have the skills to do so.

One technique used to gather data about peer groups is to ask the students in a class to indicate preferences such as the person they would most like to sit next to, work on a task with, invite home for a visit, or play with. One or a series of questions can be asked. The responses can be plotted on a diagram with a series of concentric rings (Figure 20–6). These are called "sociograms." Each ring indicates the number of times a person was named by peers. The student or students most often named by other students have their names listed in the center circle. The children not named by anyone are placed in the outer circle.

FIGURE 20–6
Sociometric techniques can aid in determining classroom social dynamics

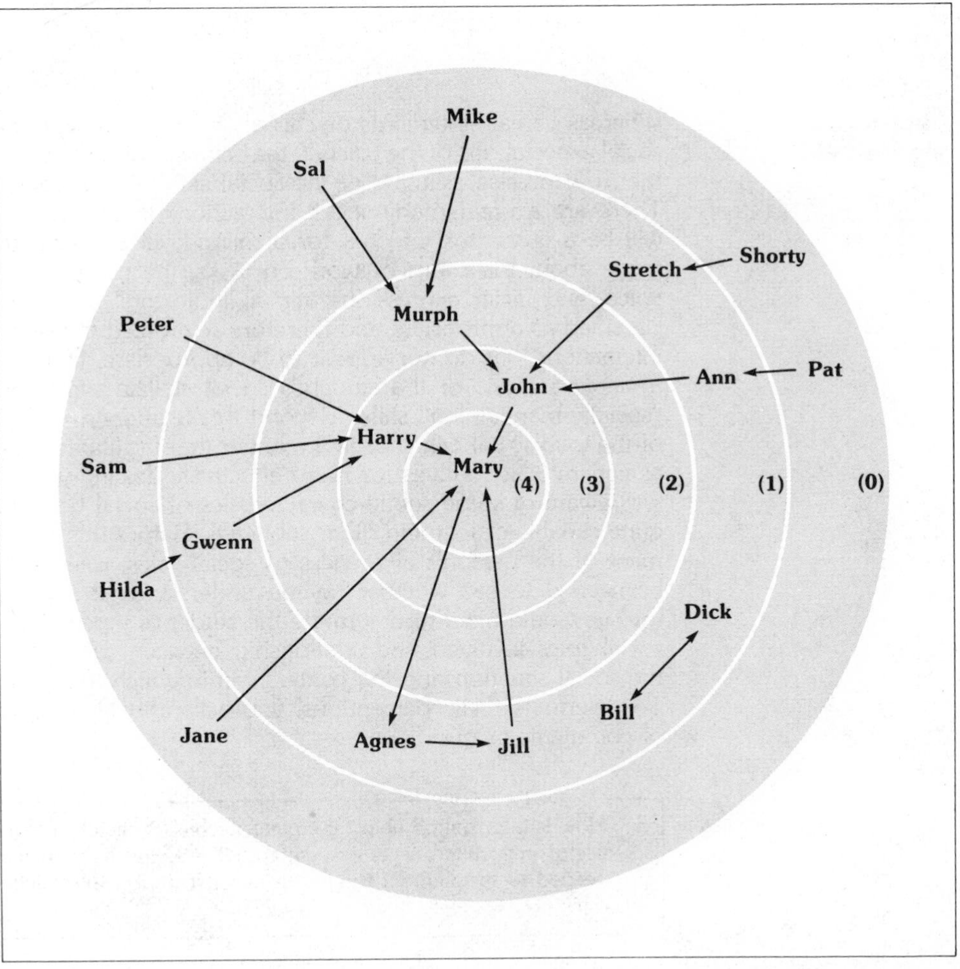

Arrows are used to reflect who named whom. An arrow between A and B pointing toward B indicates that A named B. Double-headed arrows are used to indicate a mutual naming. The data derived from these sociograms may be helpful in arranging groups that will facilitate the development of social skills. For example, a child who has few or no friends may express a preference for a child who is socially adept. The more socially adept child can serve as a good model for the less adept child if they are grouped together.

At the beginning of the year, or for examining areas of interpersonal relationships not easily observed, the sociogram technique can be useful.

It can also be used to measure students' estimates of their peers' ability to handle certain social situations or social skills by asking, "Who is the person most likely to settle an argument? Start an argument?" This may help to pinpoint social skills that children possess or need to develop.

In this process of looking at groups to determine the characteristics of any particular child in the group, there is a large measure of generalization involved. The process should, therefore, be treated as a rough estimate of entering behavior and a guide to a micro-level assessment.

Micro-level assessment

Whereas verbal statements or choices in response to questions may conform to the social expectations of the teacher, the behavior of the individual may not and, therefore, the most precise estimate of the social skill level is derived from direct observation. There are a great many social interactions taking place in the classroom so there will be a great deal of data for a micro-level assessment. For instance, as children move about the room or work on tasks, the physical actions, statements, tones of voice, and facial expressions are all indicators. Most of these interactions can be classified as appropriate and therefore reinforced (or more likely ignored). For those interactions that do not appear to be appropriate, Harrè's framework seems to offer a viable analysis of the student's social skill in terms of "socially constructive" or "socially maintaining" skills. Beyond this it offers a means of analyzing the subunits of the total social behavior in a manner that facilitates what you can offer the student as concrete alternatives for more effectively dealing with the situations. Students are well aware of some subtle characteristics of social behavior and therefore should be quite capable of learning other subtleties. Before this can be accomplished an assessment of the person's awareness of social roles, role relationships, and context may be needed to see whether he/she understands the overall social structure. To do this we would need to determine the student's perception of personal role, the other social roles involved, the relationship between roles, the relevant characteristics of the social situation and the context within which the student interprets the situation. To determine these perceptions, you will probably need to use probes in the form of comments or questions.

3. How is information about the general characteristics of children and friendship patterns useful in a macro-level assessment of entering behavior? What are the primary data needed to supplement the information so that a micro-level assessment can be carried out?

GENERAL INSTRUCTIONAL PRINCIPLES—DESIGNING COMPONENT PLANS

Teaching social behaviors does not differ in any substantial way from teaching other skills. There may be some basic human propensities that are genetically determined such as curiosity and activity level and that may have some effect on social behaviors, but the behaviors used to express these propensities are learned. In any event the learning capacity of humans is great enough so that any innate socialization characteristics are difficult to discern with any certainty. Due to this uncertainty and limited impact it is probably more productive to ignore innate social tendencies when planning how to develop social skills than to fall into the trap of using them to explain current behaviors. Assuming that certain social behaviors are innate implies that there are more constraints on what can be accomplished than may be true.

Asher, Gottman, and Oden (1977) identify modeling, coaching, and shaping as the general techniques in teaching social behaviors. It is necessary, however, to keep in mind the distinction that Bandura and Walters (1963) make between the acquisition of a behavior and the performance of a behavior, since social learning involves not only the learning of behaviors to be performed but also learning when the behavior is appropriate and when it should be inhibited. We point this out because the techniques of modeling, coaching, and shaping are not equally related to learning and performance.

Modeling

Bandura and Walters (1963) have made a distinct contribution to the perspective placed on social learning. We mentioned their theory of learning earlier, and you will recall the basic premise is that much of human behavior does not develop in small increments but as a complete act and in the correct context.

The role of modeling is generally recognized and people often make the comment "Let me show you how" or "Watch! Do it this way." Recognized, but less readily admitted, is that in addition to modeling desirable behaviors we model less desirable behaviors. As Bandura and Walters pointed out, it is not so much what we tell our children to do but what we do ourselves that influences what they will learn. The old adage of "Don't do as I do, do as I say" seems especially appropriate with social behaviors.

Modeling, in addition to helping in the process of learning a personal role, no doubt aids in the learning of social roles and social structure. Observing the leadership, compliance, authority, and submissiveness displayed by other models who are interacting also points out the status and power relationships between the roles.

Modeling of parental behaviors accounts for a great deal of the social behaviors one sees in school children, and many student behaviors are a reflection of parental behaviors. When children come from homes in which the parental behaviors are compatible with the social behaviors preferred by schools, there is less need for providing an appropriate model in school. For many children the provision of appropriate peer and adult models may play a considerable role in the socialization process.

Verbal coaching

The term *coaching* refers to direct instruction through verbal means in order to develop new behaviors (Figure 20–7). The coaching can be a verbal description of social roles, relationships between roles, and social interaction rules. It can also be a suggestion to try a particular behavior in a certain situation. Coaching can be effective when a student is dissatisfied with the quality or quantity of social interactions and has a

FIGURE 20–7
Verbal coaching can be a useful technique

desire to become socially more effective, but it may have little effect on a student who is not motivated to change.

Coaching differs from admonishment. Quite often admonishments are about what not to do in the future or a bit of hindsight about what should not have been done in the past. Many parents and teachers who use admonishment continually harp on the child's unacceptable behaviors without ever offering a suggestion as to the appropriate behavior. By contrast, coaching emphasizes appropriate behaviors and an indication of when and where in the future they are appropriate. The coaching should try to identify specific social cues to be attended to and the class of behaviors to be used in response to the cue. In some instances coaching may point out which cues to ignore, such as when other children are teasing. Another use may be to provide suggestions about self-control techniques such as telling the student to lightly clench the teeth so as to avoid making a retort to teasing.

An important part of coaching involves follow-up activities. Even though we may suggest that a student try a particular behavior, the response from the peers or other individuals may not always be reinforcing. In fact it may take quite a while for a new social skill to overcome the feelings created by previous nonsocial behaviors. This lack of reinforcers from the natural environment following the performance of the new social skill will make it necessary to provide an alternate form of reinforcement. This can be provided in the follow-up coaching session in the form of verbal praise and encouragement.

Shaping

Another way of developing social behaviors is through the process of shaping. Many adult social behaviors are modified versions of childhood social behaviors. Over the years a shaping process transforms childhood social behavior into new behavior or a more sophisticated version. Where a baby might bang a cup on the table to indicate that more is wanted to drink, an adult may hold the cup up or point to it as a means of asking for more coffee.

It is quite likely that most social behaviors are a product of a combination of modeling, coaching, and shaping. Modeling and coaching can bring about rapid learning of new behaviors that are modified and perfected by shaping to meet specific situational requirements. As originally performed the behavior may have been rather crude and somewhat inappropriate for the situation. Only through continued use and selective reinforcement does the behavior become perfected. This implies that practice of the behavior is needed if it is to be performed in a sophisticated manner.

4. What are the three general instructional techniques described? How do they apply to the socialization process?

SPECIFIC INSTRUCTIONAL PRINCIPLES

Interest in socialization, as we have broadly defined it, is shared by many fields, including education, psychology, sociology, medicine, and biology. The specific topics and terminology vary to a considerable degree. Presenting a comprehensive view of specific principles in developing social behaviors could cover several volumes. What we have presented here are a few of the major topics and research findings under the four components we identified as part of the socialization process.

Social roles

Learning about social roles is essentially learning the concepts we use to classify different categories of social functions and responsibilities. Generally it is accomplished through verbal definitions of the role, models in real life, and portrayals of the role in the mass media.

One way to measure a child's awareness of social roles is to place him/her in the position of another person's role or perspective through hypothetical examples. Piaget's studies led him to conclude that young children are unable to shed their own perspective and assume another's until adolescence. This inability to assume another's role he called "egocentrism," indicating that children view the world almost as if there were only one view—their own. While Piaget roughly identifies what he believed to be the lower age limits of the ability to take another's role, this does not mean that a person will necessarily develop the skill. Egocentric behaviors are often found in adult performance.

Since Piaget's work, the research findings have been extended and they suggest that role playing can begin at much earlier ages. Piaget's pioneering work was with *spatial role taking.* While standing in one position viewing a scene, a child is asked to describe what another person would be seeing from another position that the child had previously occupied. Typically, children younger than six years of age do not correctly describe the view from the other's position. Using simpler tasks children as young as one year old act in a manner indicating an awareness that the other person's position requires a different perspective.

When it comes to *inferring the emotions of others,* preschoolers can accurately identify the emotion conveyed by faces and situations (Figure 20–8). When the people used are dissimilar to themselves and in unfamiliar situations, it is not until the ages of 9–12 that children are consistently able to recognize the emotions.

FIGURE 20–8
At an early age we learn tc identify emotions conveyed by facial signs

The ability to *infer what another knows or thinks* is another aspect of role taking. Present research demonstrates that five-year-olds take into account the intentions of others when they are performing some acts. Even four-year-olds use simpler language when talking to younger children than they do when talking to adults, and two-year-olds show signs of starting to take turns when speaking to each other.

West (1974) presents data that lead him to believe that a certain amount of social interaction is needed in order to develop role-taking skills. Once a child has developed the skill, more training has little effect.

Still another facet of role-taking ability has been investigated by having students fake "good" and "bad" responses to personality tests. When asked to play the role, college students could do so but not consistently across all tests.

From the studies we cite it appears that children become aware of various roles in our social structure and can put themselves in the position of others at an early age but that the skill is perfected over time. West's results suggest that the skill per se, once it is developed, may not need further development. Only the content of roles may need further elaboration. This is speculation on our part but it appears to fit with the research results.

Empathy is another social behavior related to the developing awareness of social roles. It also forms a link between awareness of other social roles and some of the behavior exhibited in a personal role. Hoffman (1977) points out that empathy has two components. One is an awareness of the feelings of others, which we have just discussed. The second component is the arousal of a similar feeling in the observer. The first puts empathy partially in the cognitive domain and the second puts it in the affective domain.

Hoffman believes that empathy develops in four stages. The first two stages are rudimentary and occur during the first year or two of life and, therefore, we do not cover them here. In the third stage children become aware of the inner states of other individuals as being independent and possibly different from their own feelings. The fourth stage develops much later. "By middle or late childhood (research is unclear) awareness of others as having personal identities and life experiences that extend beyond the immediate situation" (Hoffman, 1977, p. 299) has developed. These are the *cognitive stages* in the development of empathy.

During the first two stages of development the affective state of the other person does not elicit a similar feeling in the child. In the third stage, when a child is cognitively aware of others' feelings, an affective state can develop in the child similar to the one experienced by the observed person. This transfer of affect is limited to the immediate situation. In the fourth stage this mirroring of affect can go beyond the immediate situation due to an awareness of the observed person's broader life experiences.

To integrate Hoffman's position in the framework we have presented in the earlier portions of the text, it appears as if training of empathy should proceed in two steps. The first step would involve concept learning in that the relevant attributes of the social situation and the roles of the individuals are made clear. In highly complex examples those characteristics of the situation that are likely to bring about specific affective states might be further emphasized. This clarification of the roles and social context may overcome some of the inconsistencies observed in children's ability to role play. If this results in the development of empathy, then making explicit the affect felt by the person in the situation may not be necessary but could be done by teaching the rule or relationships between the context and its effect on the person in the situation.

One interesting line of research indicates that there are universal facial expressions of emotion that are recognized across cultures. The feelings are happiness, anger, sadness, disgust, surprise, and fear (Ekman, 1973). This suggests that there are innate responses to specific affective states. While the responses to the affective state may be innately determined, the stimuli that elicit the affective states are learned and vary from one culture to another. In other words, stimuli that bring about a feeling of disgust in one culture may not do so in other cultures. Another interesting point about facial expressions that has been reported in the research is that persons who are unaware that they have been led to frown or smile report the associated feelings of anger and happiness. Also the greater a person's amount of cognitive involvement in a particular situation, the greater the depth of the feelings (Wexler, 1974; Laird, 1974).

These findings suggest that little, if anything, needs to be done to develop the actual feelings of the observer; they seem to be innate characteristics. However, to elicit the feelings in a child, the teacher needs to develop in the child an awareness of the situation and the role. In addition acting out of the facial expressions by the teacher and students may help to elicit the affective state as the situation is discussed.

Since any social role implies an interaction either directly or indirectly with at least one other individual, the discussion would need to include the relationship with other roles in the social structure.

Role relationships

Learning the relationships between various social roles adds structure to the array of roles. These relationships also provide further meaning to the roles. The relative power of one role over another is one such relationship. Related to this are the issues of dominance and submissiveness as well as leadership.

FIGURE 20–9
Some roles involve leadership

That some roles have more power and direct the activities of others is probably well learned by children of school age through the occurrence of natural contingencies, verbal statements, and modeling of behavior (Figure 20–9). Awareness of the social structure is probably also enhanced by various topics included in the regular curriculum that convey the relationship between certain roles. In this way the relative closeness, power, and status of the roles may be pointed out as an incidental part of the lesson. For instance incidental learning has probably contributed much to the generally lower status attributed to women than to men. In the past if women were depicted in a role it was generally a lower-status role than those assigned to men in the instructional material. This is now a matter of considerable concern in writing and editing instructional materials.

The status of various roles in our society remains fairly stable but does change. Again using the status of women as an example, one research study has found that as women move into an occupational role previously dominated by men, the status of that role drops (Touhey, 1974). This points out not only a problem for the women's movement for equality but also the changing nature of the social structure.

Judging from the lack of social upheaval that occurs at any particular age group, the techniques used to teach the social structure and have it internalized must be fairly successful. This is not to say that youth have always accepted the social structure without some dissent, but almost all do seem to function within it sooner or later. Coleman's observations that the youth culture is a relatively recent phenomenon characterized by an inward turning to its own interests and standards raises a question about when and how the individuals involved will make the transition from that culture to the larger culture. Within the youth culture there is, no doubt, a structure of roles, but the status of the roles seems to be based on somewhat different standards than those encountered in the larger society. To make the transition from the youth culture to the larger economic culture may be very difficult for many individuals.

Since schools impose the most demands on a student's time in a setting somewhat similar to a modern-day work setting, they provide a means for helping students bridge the gap between a life of play and a life of work and also to develop a set of values compatible with the demands children will face as adults. This will involve more attention to the affective domain and the development of positive feelings toward sustained effort to accomplish a task without constant supervision.

Social context

The learning of social contexts is primarily the learning of various perspectives and the way they affect a person's perception of a situation. As such, the topics covered in the discussion of social roles applies here as well and we will not belabor the point any further.

Interaction rules

It is not our intent to present the vast array of interaction rules that make up the content of social learning. Instead we will focus on the internalization of the rules.

As Hoffman (1977, p. 300) points out,

> most people do not go through life viewing society's norms as external, coercively imposed pressures to which they must submit . . . , they eventually become part of their motive system and guide their behavior even in the absence of external authority.

The process of internalization takes time and is apparently dependent upon a number of principles. First of all, the child needs to become aware of a rule. This can come about through modeling, shaping, or coaching. Modeling has been shown to aid in the development of many social behaviors such as moral judgments, altruistic behavior, resisting and yielding to temptation, aggressive behavior, self-reward, social interactions, facial expressions, teachers' preferences, perceptual judgments, and vocal and linguistic responses (Heatherington & McIntyre, 1975). Used by itself modeling of the desired behaviors can, therefore, be very effective in promoting the process of internalization.

In addition to behavior modeling, coaching or verbally stating a rule can have an effect. When a model merely espouses a particular social rule but does not follow it, the likelihood is much lower that the rule will be internalized. Having a warm and prolonged relationship with a child may make coaching more effective. A warm relationship is usually described as one in which the parent or teacher takes a positive view of the child by stressing the desirable behaviors of the child rather than the undesirable behaviors. It does not mean that the parents are necessarily more permissive. Children of these more positively oriented parents have been shown to display greater generosity and a greater concern for others (Olejnik & McKinney, 1973). Since the effectiveness of coaching is closely associated with modeling and shaping techniques, it is difficult to say how much of this is due to coaching and how much can be attributed to the other two approaches. There is ample evidence, however, that presenting rules verbally can be an effective strategy for having the student learn them, as long as the prerequisite concept learning has taken place.

Hoffman (1977) suggests that over time the ideas conveyed by parents may be retained by children, but the fact that the idea originated with the parent may be forgotten. Because of this Hoffman further suggests that the child, having forgotten where the idea originated, may attribute the origin to himself. Consistent with Hoffman's reasoning, memory studies also demonstrate that details are usually forgotten much sooner than the more general aspects of a situation. All of this suggests that using particular situations to teach social rules can help in the socialization process. The details of the situation should be used to recall and expand on the concepts involved and to make clear the relationship expressed in the rule. In this way the concrete aspects of the situation are not the main focus but are utilized as examples. By emphasizing the general attributes involved, as well as the concrete aspects, the instance should serve to make the rule both clear and applicable.

Shaping procedures make use of external rewards. The process of internalization suggests that the goal is the elimination of any need for external control. You will recall, however, that the process starts with external controls. From a reinforcement perspective the transition from external control to internalization becomes one of thinning the reinforcement schedule and also shifting from tangible to social reinforcers. The former increases the likelihood of long-term retention and the latter puts the reinforcement into a more naturally occurring form. Research evidence does indicate that tangible reinforcers presented after intrinsic motivation has developed may have the effect of reducing the intrinsic motivation. This suggests that the internalization process can be reversed. To avoid this, any externally applied reinforcers should be in the form of social rewards and should reward the intrinsic motivation, or internalization of the rule, that has developed. In other words, give praise to students for having developed a particular social trait and not merely for having performed a specific social act.

Personal role

In developing a personal role a person is actually developing several roles. A single woman can be an engineer, mother, daughter, sister, wife, aunt, niece, girl scout leader, bowling team leader, housekeeper, and lover. Most roles are imposed on children. As the individual grows older more roles are developed, but to some extent they are imposed by factors such as age, sex, physical characteristics, intelligence, and socioeconomic level (Figure 20–10). These roles are developed through a long series of the person's interactions with the environment and the people in it. The factors of modeling, coaching, and shaping all play a part. The opportunity to learn certain roles and to practice them is important, but probably equally important is the amount of success and reinforcement a person encounters while performing behaviors associated with these roles. Those behaviors that are more successful and more heavily reinforced are more likely to be performed in the future. Roles associated with these behaviors are more likely to be developed. As the person begins to see herself in a certain role and accept it, she is then likely to learn other behaviors associated with the role. What we are suggesting is that role development in the early stages is probably a matter of certain behaviors converging to suggest a role, and, once accepted, some divergence of skills takes place to fill out the role requirements.

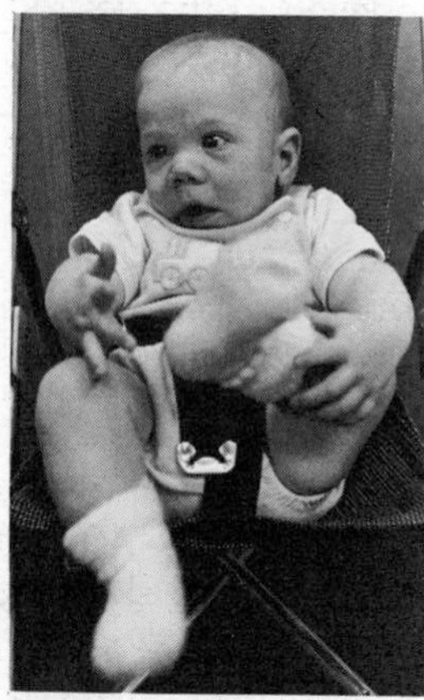

FIGURE 20–10
Roles are acquired slowly and depend to some extent on age, sex, and socioeconomic level

Another aspect of a personal role is the individual's perception of how well various roles are performed. This is often referred to as a person's *self-esteem*. In the research literature a distinction is made between general self-esteem and task-specific self-esteem. As is probably obvious, the former is in reference to a person's perception of overall ability to function adequately, whereas the latter is a judgment about adequacy on certain narrowly defined tasks. For instance a student may have a low level of general self-esteem but a high level of self-esteem with regard to running the 100-yard dash.

At least four important factors seem to determine a person's self-esteem:

1. The tasks assigned or attempted.
2. The performance level attained.
3. The accuracy of the person's perception of the performance level attained.
4. The standard against which the perceived performance level is judged.

A child who continually attempts tasks through personal initiative or assignment that are too far above the child's performance capability is going to meet with a great deal of failure. On the other hand, a child who generally attempts tasks that he/she can achieve with a reasonable amount of effort will most often meet with success. The first child is more likely to have a low level of general self-esteem than is the latter. In certain areas the former child may be more appropriately matched with tasks and therefore develop a higher level of task-specific self-esteem in relation to these tasks. Even the child who is usually successful and has a high level of general self-esteem is likely to perceive differences in terms of capability to handle different tasks.

In the development of self-esteem the actual performance is usually obvious to the person and often comparable to the performance of other people. This obscures the effect that task level has on the person's performance and emphasizes the person's ability as the main determinant of performance level. Since some performances may have little or no degree of success while others are highly successful, the degree of success on many tasks over a lifetime of experiences (regardless of the person's age) has a very strong effect on the person's level of self-esteem. Obviously the higher the degree of success, the higher the self-esteem.

Humans are not always (if ever) objective in their observations of performance, especially with regard to personal performance. It is quite possible that an individual will overlook certain characteristics of a performance, such as speed or smoothness, and therefore rate a performance as successful while another person may not. This ignoring of subtle characteristics of performance could lead to an overestimation of success and a higher level of general or task-specific self-esteem than is justified.

Possibly the most important factor of all is the standard against which a performance is judged. These standards may be set by others or self-selected. In a sense the tasks assigned set a standard, since the person is expected to master the task. Also people's comments about a performance in comparison with some norm or criterion set a standard that affects the self-esteem of an individual. If the norm or criterion they select to compare the performance against is continually higher than the performance level achieved, then the self-esteem of the individual will likely suffer. A common example of this is when parents or teachers point out another more capable child's performance on the same task. Given the fact that development and practice usually lead to a gradual improvement in performance, parents and teachers who compare a child's performance against an earlier performance are more likely to be pointing out improvement and more likely to have a positive effect on the self-esteem of the child. It is quite possible for parents, and at times teachers, to use such low comparative standards that they have a positive effect on self-esteem, but in a broader context the self-esteem is unrealistic and incompatible with other's judgments of the child's capability. A person can in the same manner select comparative standards that are continually well above, well below, or close to the performance level. Depending on the amount of discrepancy, the self-esteem may be lowered, raised, or unrealistically lowered or raised.

There is not much question that a student's self-concept has an effect on what and how much a student will learn. Every effort should be made to help a student develop a positive level of general self-esteem, but it seems unrealistic to expect a student to develop high levels of task-specific self-esteem in all areas. Assigning tasks that are appropriate for a child's capability, pointing out the positive performance characteristics, not reinforcing a child's inappropriate estimates of performance, and using appropriate comparative standards can do much to help the child develop a positive level of self-esteem. Probably the most direct technique is to use a realistic *but appropriate* set of standards against which we judge and comment on the child's performance.

Attempts to artificially raise a child's level of self-esteem as a means of making instruction more effective may be well intentioned but may not have any long-term effect unless the subsequent instruction is effective enough to actually bring the competence level up to the self-esteem level. Without this progress the vast numbers of subsequent performances in which the performance level does not match up to the external standards are likely to result in a lowering of self-esteem. Probably the most effective long-range technique is to provide effective instruction in a positive context followed by sufficient constructive feedback and reinforcement.

> 5. What are the specific principles of instruction discussed in relation to social roles, role relationships, social contexts, personal role, and interaction rules?

TEACHER'S IMPACT ON SOCIAL BEHAVIOR

As we have indicated, the process of socialization is lifelong and influenced by many individuals. As a teacher you will be picking up on the process in a student long after it has been started. Many of the student's entering behaviors will be well practiced and firmly entrenched. When these are appropriate it will make your task easy. When they are inappropriate you will be hard pressed to extinguish them and develop new ones. While you work to establish a new pattern of behavior, other individuals may continue to reinforce the old established patterns. Inadvertently you may even reinforce a more subtle version of the old behaviors. Dependency and aggressive behaviors are good examples of this. There are many ways of playing helpless and many ways of hurting people; because we have extinguished the more obvious forms of dependency and aggression in students, we may not recognize the modified versions for what they are until after we have reinforced them. What is more, we may not recognize them at all!

We are suggesting that rather than expecting dramatic effects on overall behavior you should at most hope to bring about modest effects and subtle changes. You may also strengthen present desirable behaviors, but there may not be any behavioral indicators of this change. There may be an increase in the frequency, vigor, or signs of enthusiasm related to the behavior that can be noted, but these are apt to be subtle and impossible to measure in the classroom.

Occasionally you will encounter a child who recognizes an inability to socialize with other children and genuinely wishes to develop the necessary skills. In these cases you can bring about dramatic change. It will require a great deal of empathy on your part to see the student's position and goals clearly enough to help. Your position and values may hinder you in the process, but a combination of modeling, coaching, and shaping can usually achieve significant results.

One thing you should recognize is that teachers occupy a unique position in terms of their own socialization because they have had close contact with adult models in their occupational role for many years. In this respect the teaching profession has preserved for its future members a way of life that was common prior to the 20th century. The continuity from childhood to adulthood has thus been made clearer, if not easier, for teachers. You should recognize that only a small portion of your students will be teachers, and you must adjust to the different circumstances they face and the values they may need to develop.

SUMMARY

Socialization was discussed in reference to developing programs for the classroom and defined as a process whereby children learn the ways of our society and how to function within it. Some general opinions about the goals of the socialization process were identified. The gradual segregation of children, teenagers, and youths was described from a historical perspective. Socializing forces and their current function were described as well as some constraints that society places on the goals that may be pursued and the methods that may be used to attain them. Having outlined the major dimensions of the problem in terms of expectation and constraints, we described the task as consisting of five components. The task of learner analysis was described by first outlining the process of early social development and then the present-day characteristics of youths. Techniques for macro- and micro-level assessments were described along with three general instructional techniques. The final topics discussed were specific instructional techniques related to each of the components of the socialization task and the teacher impact that may be expected.

SELF-TEST

1. As used in the text, socialization is the process whereby an individual learns:
   a. To develop a personal role in society.
   b. To interact with peers and develop friendships.
   c. About a particular society and how to function in it.
   d. To adhere to the social norms of society.
   e. All of the above.
2. In a recent Gallup (1976) poll at least 25 percent of the respondents expressed the opinion that two important qualities in the development of a child are:
   a. Ability to think for oneself and get along with others.
   b. Eagerness to learn and a desire to excel.
   c. High moral standards and a desire to excel.
3. The concept of childhood is:
   a. As old as recorded history.
   b. More than 1,000 years old at least.
   c. About 400 years old.
   d. About 80 years old.
4. In our society the family and schools are the only effective socialization agents. True or false?
5. The learning of social roles is primarily a form of:
   a. Affective learning.
   b. Rule learning.
   c. Concept learning.
   d. Memorization learning.
6. The learning of role relationships involves the learning of:
   a. Discrete bits of factual information.
   b. Concepts.
   c. Mathemagenic behaviors.
   d. Rules.
   e. None of the above.
7. Harré (1974) sees rules of interaction as stemming from two main classes of problems. Which of the following is an example of a socially maintaining solution? Two strangers meet at a wedding and one:
   a. Asks if he can get the other a drink.
   b. Who is an usher, asks the other if she is a relative of the bride.
   c. Greets the other by saying "I don't believe we've met but I wanted to come over and say how much I admired your dress."
   d. Spills champagne on the floor while trying to shake hands but the other person appears not to notice.
   e. All of the above.
8. Cliques are more likely to be composed of:
   a. Two individuals of similar background.
   b. Several individuals of similar background.
   c. Individuals who are attracted to each other because of wide differences in background.
   d. Both sexes at the younger age level.
9. The "youth culture," as described by Coleman (1974):
   a. Looks to peers for preferences.
   b. Develops strong attachments with others the same age.
   c. Strives for independence from adults.
   d. Wants the social structure to change so they can quickly gain status.
   e. All of the above.
10. Micro-level assessment of entering behaviors, in reference to social skills, can:
    a. Not be done in the classroom.
    b. Start with a search of the school records to determine the socioeconomic background of each student.
    c. Be based almost entirely on students' verbal description.
    d. Be more accurate if based on observations of the actual behaviors in preference to verbal statements.

ANSWER KEY TO BOXED QUESTIONS

1. The goals are summarized as developing a person who is law-abiding, self-sufficient, self-directed, friendly, agreeable, and responsive to the needs of others. The forces are the family, siblings, peers, school, and other individuals. The two constraints are on unacceptable goals and harsh training methods.
2. The five components are social roles, role relationships, social contexts, rules of interaction, and personal roles. Social roles, social contexts, and personal roles all involve concept learning, whereas role relationships and interaction rules involve rule learning.
3. The general characteristics of children and friendship patterns give us a starting point for micro-level assessment, but to carry out the micro-level assessment we need observations of actual behavior.
4. Modeling, verbal coaching, and shaping. Modeling is a potent means of developing social behaviors and verbal coaching can also be effective, especially if the student is motivated to change. Shaping is a more gradual process of modifying current behaviors into a new form.
5. *Social roles*—taught with verbal definitions, real-life models, or mass media portrayals of the role. To develop role-taking skills, a certain level of social interaction is a necessary condition of learning. Empathy should involve a two-step process in which the first is concept development and a clarification of the role relationships involved. The second step, if needed, would be to point out its effect on the individuals involved. Acting out facial expressions may help to elicit the affective state in the learner.

   Role relationships—Natural contingencies, verbal statements, and modeling can all enhance learning. Much of this may occur as incidental learning.

   Social contexts—similar to social roles.

   Personal role—Assigning tasks at an appropriate level, insuring a high level of success, and developing an objective perception of performance and a realistic criterion-referenced standard of judgments are the major principles.

   Interaction rules—The principles associated with rule learning are first needed to develop an awareness of the rule, and then affective domain principles are needed for the rule to become internalized as a value or attitude. When using examples the general attributes should be stressed and the concrete aspects used only to clarify the details of the situation.

ANSWER KEY TO SELF-TEST

1. *e*
2. *a*
3. *c*
4. True
5. *c*
6. *d*
7. *b*
8. *b*
9. *e*
10. *d*

Chapter 21

Communicating with parents and community

AS A PROFESSIONAL in the school system your primary interactions will be with students and the school staff. You will also serve as the contact between the school and members of the community in the school district. The manner in which you perform this interactive role can have direct and indirect effects on what happens in your classroom and the school system as a whole.

In this chapter we present some of the contacts you may have and the problems that may arise as a result. We outline the general position of the community and the schools as a starting point for understanding the interactive role. From there we proceed to a description of the components in the communication process. Having presented this analysis of the various factors that determine the goals of the communication process we provide an outline of the factors you will need to consider in designing effective programs for interacting and communicating with parents and others in the community.

After studying this chapter you should be able to:

1. Describe public attitudes about the quality of schools, the major problems of schools, control of schools, school curriculum, and methods for solving school problems.
2. Outline the major points of conflict between schools and the public.
3. Describe the school's attitude about the purpose of contacts, the areas of involvement, and restrictions in the process of home-school-community communication.
4. Define the five major components in the communication process.
5. Outline some of the major factors to be considered in the design of community programs.

HOME-SCHOOL-COMMUNITY RELATIONS

Schools are such an established part of our society that we often forget they were developed by the members of a community as a means of educating their children. The citizens in the community, especially those with children of school age, have a need and a desire to keep informed about the operation of the schools. The schools respond to these needs by providing various types of information. This communication function is carried on to a large extent by teachers, but they are certainly not the only line of communication between schools and community.

School boards and school administrators periodically disseminate information about school policies, programs, and finances. These interactions are typically accomplished through the news media, general announcements sent home to parents, or formal meetings. They also organize various citizens' committees to obtain input and recommendations from the community. At this level the communication process involves broad issues related to the school or the student body as a whole.

At a much more personalized and detailed level, teachers play a large part in the communication process. It is through these interactions that parents of children gain some insight into the current problems and methods of schools. In many cases these problems and methods have changed since the parents were students. These contacts also give the parents a means of judging the quality of the educational process their children are going through. Usually this access is limited to a couple of short parent-teacher conferences a year (Gallup, 1977) but involves between 55 and 80 percent of the parents in any one year, and therefore it would seem advisable to maximize the utility of these contacts and avoid creating unwarranted, unfavorable impressions.

The Florida Learning Resource System (1975) lists several ways in which you can come in contact with parents or involve them in the educational and instructional process. When you come in contact with them they may be in the role of an audience, a decision maker, a home teacher, volunteer, or paid employee. At times the parents may be in more than one of these roles at the same time. For instance, during a conference between yourself and the parents of one of your students, the parents would be an audience for your presentation of data and conclusions about their child's progress. If options are open concerning instructional alternatives, parents may then become involved as decision makers. The decision may then involve one or both of them in the role of home teacher or volunteer worker in the classroom. It may even lead to one of them serving as a paid employee of the school.

PARENT AND COMMUNITY ATTITUDES

To interact with members and groups within the community you should understand their position. Depending on the area of the country in which you will be teaching, the position will vary somewhat. We have presented some issues and opinions that are likely to affect your interactions with parents and others in any community. What we have presented on the topic is by no means exhaustive but should help you to identify some of today's issues.

Historical perspective

Reference is often made that the citizens of today feel thay have lost control of their government, including the regulations and taxes imposed. Proposition 13 in California and the frequent defeat of school budgets are often interpreted as a form of revolt against this feeling of helplessness. School budgets are especially vulnerable because they are usually directly voted upon by the citizens and are not decided by elected representatives who are open to the influence of small but politically powerful groups. This citizen protest is relatively ineffective in bringing about change since about 95 percent of a school budget consists of fixed costs such as negotiated salaries, heat, light, and maintenance of buildings. It does highlight the fact that the communication process is ineffective, the schools are unresponsive to citizen desires, or the schools are unable to respond and cannot effectively communicate this to the community.

In a provocative article, Zeigler, Tucker, and Wilson (1976) outline the progression of events that have gradually shifted control of schools from the local citizens to the national government. They see the progression as consisting of four phases.

During Phase I, from 1835 to 1900, local school boards were in charge of American education. The schools were small and the school boards attended to the day-to-day operations (Figure 21–1). Due to the fact thay many school districts had a common boundary with the political wards, the school boards were often influenced by partisan politics and open to corruption. Schools did, however, reflect the values of the local communities. Just prior to the turn of the century reformers reacted to the political influence on the schools. As Ziegler et al. note, the movement was largely an elitist response to lay control. In effect "the upper-class response was to provide power to *their* people . . . the experts" (p. 91). This movement drastically changed the composition of school boards so that they were composed largely of persons who were wealthy or well educated but not necessarily representative of the majority. This shift in school board composition set the stage for Phase II.

Phase II is characterized by the influence the school boards had on professional school superintendents. The superintendents were looked upon by the boards as experts

FIGURE 21–1
The school, teacher, and student body in 1907

Courtesy of New York State Historical Association, Cooperstown.

in their profession. As Zeigler et al. state, "School boards typically enact policies suggested by their professional staff in about 85% of the recorded votes" (p. 91). In this way the school administrators took on the major role for directing American education even though the school boards were still technically the governing body and the administration was under the board's direction. It was also during this period that the number of school districts in the United States was drastically reduced by consolidation to the present number of approximately 15,000.

The advent of Phase III was brought about by demands from the federal government and minority groups. The federal government sought to have the schools serve as institutions to eliminate inequalities in educational and economic opportunities. At the same time minority groups were demanding community control. The federal government made funds available for improving the education of the economically and educationally deprived, with the provision that certain guidelines be followed. The funds were welcomed by school districts because they provided for programs that could not be funded on a local basis. Less welcome were the guidelines and paper work involved. The movement toward increased federal control of the schools removed control even further from local citizens, but it did have the effect of making education responsive to a wider segment of the population. This does not mean that it is more compatible with local values; in many cases it makes it more incompatible.

Zeigler et al. point out that some evidence is accumulating that schools as they are presently organized cannot bring about the social changes necessary to equalize economic opportunity. If the present indicators are found to be accurate, then they see education moving into Phase IV. The characteristics of this phase cannot be predicted, but some alternatives are a return to Phase I or II, or a system of vouchers in which every parent contracts with the school of his/her choice.

Present position

Starting in 1969 Gallup has conducted polls of the public's attitudes toward the public schools. We have summarized here the results from the 1976 and 1977 polls (Gallup, 1976, 1977). As we view it, the five main issues covered in the poll concern the (1) quality of education, (2) major problems facing schools, (3) control of schools, (4) school curriculum, and (5) methods for solving school problems.

Quality of education. In recent years there has been a yearly decline in test scores on standardized achievement tests. When asked if this drop in test scores means that the quality of education is declining, those polled indicated it does by a two-to-one margin. This margin was common for all segments of the population.

When asked to assign a letter grade to public schools the results based on all responses ranked the performance of public schools somewhere between a C and a C+. It may be encouraging to know that the highest ratings come from the parents with children in school. Of this group, in 1976, 50 percent gave a rating of A (16 percent) or B (34 percent) and in 1977, 54 percent gave a rating of A (18 percent) or B (36 percent). The lowest ratings come from those who send their children to private or parochial schools, which is not too surprising when you consider that they are willing to pay extra to have their children attend these schools. As Gallup notes, the real test of public support is how willing citizens are to have taxes increased. In this case the parents are in effect imposing an added tax on themselves. Sharing the low opinion (but not necessarily the willingness to spend more on education) is the 18- to 29-year age group.

When citizens were asked what they felt was particularly good about the local public schools, the most frequent responses were "the curriculum" and "the teachers." This positive opinion is not the same for schools in small communities as compared with those in big cities. By a margin of six to one, people indicated they believe that students in small communities get a better education than students in big-city schools.

From these results it seems reasonable for a teacher to expect the parents of children in the school to have a fairly positive attitude toward the teachers and the curriculum, especially outside the big cities. Other taxpayers with whom they come in contact may not be as favorably disposed.

Problems. When asked, "What do you think are the biggest problems with which the public schools in this community must deal?" in both years, the top three concerns in order of mention were: (1) lack of discipline, (2) integration/segregation/busing, and (3) lack of financial support. In the latest poll Gallup (1977, p. 34) points out that:

> Discipline continues to top the list of major problems facing the public schools of the nation, as it has during eight of the last nine years. In fact, the percentage who cite discipline as the major problem is the highest found during the period in which these annual surveys have been conducted.
>
> Parents of children now attending public school, perhaps the group best suited to judge the schools, cite discipline as the number one problem and by the highest percentage yet recorded.

The three problems next most often cited in the past two years are: (4) difficulty of getting "good" teachers, (5) poor curriculum, and (6) use of drugs.

In 1977 the three were mentioned in the above order of frequency. This was a change from 1976 when "difficulty getting 'good' teachers" was in sixth place and the other two were one place higher on the list. The percentages of people responding to those problems in places two through six ranged from 7 to 15 percent, whereas lack of discipline was cited by 22 percent of those responding in 1976 and 26 percent in 1977, putting discipline well ahead of the others. Since teachers are the ones most responsible for maintaining student discipline, this reflects on their role but it does not necessarily mean that the public holds teachers entirely responsible for the lack of discipline.

The fact that poor curriculum was cited as a problem by 10–14 percent of those polled indicates that there is some dissatisfaction, possibly stemming from a concern about decreasing achievement scores and the fact that some students leave school as illiterates.

Considering the number of school budgets that get voted down, finances are certainly one of the major problems citizens have in relation to schools, even though only 12–14 percent see their school as having a problem of proper financial support. This suggests that most people believe the schools have sufficient monies to operate and may indeed feel they are asking for more than they need. Among the public there is considerable agreement to cut administration staffs (72 percent) and to reduce the number of counselors on the staff (52 percent). When the issue of declining enrollments in school is raised, the public agrees that school expenditures should be reduced accordingly (55 percent) to reflect the drop in student numbers. For those agreeing, the greatest number suggested reducing the number of teachers. The next most common suggestion was to close schools and combine classes.

Control of schools. A full two thirds of those polled favored giving the local school boards greater responsibility in running the schools. Only 10 percent wanted them to have less control. They also favored by a two-to-one margin giving local school boards more authority in deciding how federal money will be spent at the local level. The federal controls have apparently put the school boards and local citizens in a similar position of opposing greater federal control.

When asked if teacher bargaining power should be extended to include the right to negotiate about class size, the curriculum, and teaching methods, the public apparently agrees. Whether school boards are as ready to accept it is not answered by the poll. Those most in favor of the proposal were the people in the 18- to 29-year-old group (73 percent). This seems to be a substantial vote of confidence in teacher competency and a willingness to have them assume more control of the educational process. Coupled with the finding that the public overwhelmingly is in favor of cutting school costs by reducing the number of administrative personnel but not in favor of reducing the number of teachers by increasing class sizes (70 percent opposed) or cutting teacher salaries by a fixed percentage (74 percent opposed), the impression is given that there is more dissatisfaction with the administrative staff than with the instructional staff.

Not only is the public willing to give teachers a greater voice in the control of schools but citizens themselves express a strong willingness to take an active part in the process. When given a list of 20 problems for which a school board might form a citizens advisory committee, 90 percent of the individuals indicated at least one committee they would like to serve on. The most popular was a committee to deal with discipline and related problems (51 percent). Other popular committees were those dealing with student/teacher relations (31 percent), career education (29 percent), student dropouts (29 percent), teacher evaluation (28 percent), and handicapped children (26 percent) (Figure 21–2). Ranking below these were committees for educational costs/finances (22 percent) and the curriculum (21 percent). Low on the list were committees for extracurricular activities (11 percent), educational innovations (12 percent), public relations (13 percent), and school facilities (14 percent).

The public is not in favor of giving these committees the final authority to make decisions, because three quarters of those polled wanted school boards to retain decision-making authority over the curriculum, staff selection, and budget.

With regard to teachers unions and whether they have helped, hurt, or made no difference in the *quality* of public school education, the public has a mixed reaction. Only 22 percent felt they helped, whereas 38 percent felt they hurt. Another 27 percent felt they made no difference. Judging from this, union control is certainly not too popular but neither is it objected to very strongly.

All of this suggests that generally teachers as well as local boards of education are highly regarded as the ones best suited to control the schools. This is tempered with

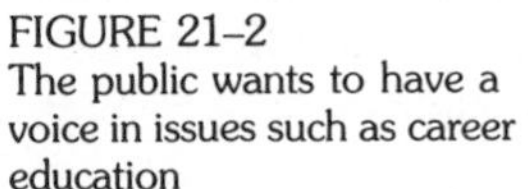

FIGURE 21–2
The public wants to have a voice in issues such as career education

a desire for more meaningful input from the lay public as advisors to the school board, which would retain its present decision-making authority.

School curriculum. The back-to-basics movement in education is probably very familiar to most educators, but in the 1977 poll only 41 percent of the general public in the poll had heard or read about the movement. Of those who were familiar with the movement, it was usually associated with reading, writing, and arithmetic, but some equated it with the educational process itself. Of those familiar with the term, 83 percent were in favor of the back-to-basics movement and only 11 percent were opposed.

Several suggestions offered as possible ways to reduce the budget involved the curriculum. Unfavorable reactions to reducing the number of subjects (53 percent opposed), reducing after-school activities (63 percent opposed), and reducing special remedial services (85 percent opposed) indicate that these parts of the curriculum, as it now stands, are fairly well supported by the public. This is especially noteworthy because these possibilities were raised directly in connection with school finances and how to reduce them. This gives some indication of which parts of the curriculum are supported but still leaves open the question of what the public wants added or dropped. Some questions in the poll indirectly relate to this issue.

One such question in the 1976 survey dealt with what the public believes is the most important quality of a child. The six qualities suggested (p. 194) and the percentages of those selecting each alternative as the *most important* quality are as follows:

Learning to think for oneself	26%
Ability to get along with others	23
Willingness to accept responsibility	21
High moral standards	13
Eagerness to learn	11
Desire to excel	4

In answer to which one is *most neglected by parents,* the responses were:

High moral standards	32%
Willingness to accept responsibility	30
Learning to think for oneself	14
Ability to get along with others	8
Eagerness to learn	5
Desire to excel	4

When the question was changed to which one is *most neglected by schools,* the results were:

High moral standards	26%
Learning to think for oneself	15
Eagerness to learn	13
Willingness to accept responsibility	12
Desire to excel	9
Ability to get along with others	8

In reference to high moral standards, Gallup (1976, p. 197) states, "The American people have reached the conclusion that many parents either won't or can't control the behavior of their children. They are ready therefore, to turn over part of the responsibility to the schools." A total of 67 percent agreed that schools should take on a share of the responsibility, while only 30 percent disagreed. All of this suggests that the current social development curriculum is felt to be inadequate for today's conditions and should be modified or supplemented.

Another area of public concern is with careers and career preparation. More emphasis at the high school level was favored by 80 percent of the individuals polled, with only 5 percent favoring less emphasis. Even at the elementary school level 52 percent felt that the curriculum should include information about jobs and careers; opposed were 39 percent. This is another indication that schools could be more involved in this aspect of the socialization process as well as with moral behavior.

When asked if courses offered as a regular part of the school system designed to help parents help their children in school were a good idea or a poor idea, 77 percent thought they were a good idea. Those who indicated it was a good idea were asked if they would be willing to pay additional taxes to support such a program. A total of 51 percent said they would. This, however, amounts to only 39 percent of the total number interviewed. It is, however, a substantial amount of support. If such a program could be demonstrated as a viable means of cutting costs in other programs, it might be even more popular.

In the 1977 survey (p. 42) a question was asked about which courses, from a list of 16, would be of the most interest to citizens.

Listed below in order of mention are the 16 suggested topics for parents whose eldest child is 13 to 20 years of age.

1. What to do about drugs, smoking, use of alcohol.
2. How to help the child choose a career.
3. How to help the child set high achievement goals.
4. How to develop good work habits.
5. How to encourage reading.
6. How to increase interest in school and school subjects.
7. How to help the child organize his/her homework.
8. How to improve parent/child relationships.
9. How to improve the child's thinking and observation abilities.
10. How to deal with the child's emotional problems.
11. How to use family activities to help the child do better in school.
12. How to improve the child's school behavior.
13. How to reduce television viewing.
14. How to help the child get along with other children.
15. How to improve health habits.
16. How to deal with dating problems.

Ranked below in order of mention are the 16 suggested topics for parents whose eldest child is 12 years or younger.

1. What to do about drugs, smoking, use of alcohol.
2. How to help the child set high achievement goals.
3. How to develop good work habits.
4. How to improve the child's school behavior.
5. How to improve the child's thinking and observation abilities.
6. How to deal with the child's emotional problems.
7. How to increase interest in school and school subjects.
8. How to help the child organize his/her homework.
9. How to improve parent/child relationships.
10. How to help the child choose a career.
11. How to use family activities to help the child do better in school.

12. How to encourage reading.
13. How to help the child get along with other children.
14. How to reduce television viewing.
15. How to deal with dating problems.
16. How to improve health habits.

Suggestions to change the curriculum by lowering the starting age met with only a 5 percent approval, but 46 percent favored establishing child-care centers as part of the public school system. This may be due to the large number of families in which both parents work.

A suggestion to allow students to take one year of college-credit courses during high school was generally favored by a two-to-one margin but was not as well supported in small communities where the school would presumably have difficulty making the necessary arrangements.

FIGURE 21–3
The public and teachers see a need to meet the individual needs of students

Methods. In a variety of ways the poll tapped public opinion about how education could be improved. One question asked the respondents to choose from a list those alternatives they thought would do most to improve the quality of education (Figure 21–3). The top choices regarding methods and the percent choosing them were (Gallup, 1976, pp. 189–90):

More attention to teaching basic skills	51%
Enforce stricter discipline	50
Meet individual needs of students	42
Improve parent/school relations	41
Provide opportunities for teachers to keep up to date regarding new methods	29
Raise academic standards	27
Raise teachers' salaries	14
Increase amount of homework	14
Build new buildings	9

Two ways of changing the present methods of education are to lower the age when children start school and to shorten the process. As we mentioned earlier only 5 percent were in favor of a lower compulsory age for attendance, but 46 percent favored establishing child-care centers as part of the public school system. Nonwhites favored this more extensively (76 percent). At the other end of the age continuum, suggestions to eliminate the 12th grade by covering in three years what is now covered in four years met with unfavorable opinions from 58 percent of those polled. Suggestions to permit students who can pass a basic competency test to take jobs or go to college at age 14 were disapproved by 66 percent and approved by only 30 percent of those responding. In the 1977 survey the question was asked whether those meeting academic requirements after three years instead of four should be permitted to graduate early. This was supported by a margin of three to one.

A suggestion to change the present school hours to a 9:00-to-5:00 schedule was not popular, nor was a suggestion to close the schools for a period of time in the winter to save energy and then make up the time in June and August.

While not directly related to methods, one question about desirable teacher qualities does imply some methods. With regard to the personal qualities a teacher should bring to the classroom, the eight most often named, in order of mention, were (Gallup, 1976, p. 195):

1. The ability to communicate, to understand, to relate.
2. The ability to discipline, be firm and fair.
3. The ability to inspire, motivate the child.
4. High moral character.
5. Love of children, concern for them.
6. Dedication to teaching profession, enthusiasm.
7. Friendly, good personality.
8. Good personal appearance, cleanliness.

As Gallup (1976, p. 195) points out, the public view of the ideal teacher "is one who becomes a model of behavior for the young. It is not startling to discover this; a survey 100 years ago would probably have revealed the same thing."

One final point in regard to methods is the results of the public's views about a national test students must pass before graduating. Gallup (p. 190) used the following question in 1958 and 1976: "Should all high school students in the United States be required to pass a standard nation-wide examination in order to get a high school diploma?" From 1958 to 1976 the percent favoring the proposal has risen from 50 percent to 65 percent. In 1976 those with less education were more in favor of it (76 percent) than were those with more education (53 percent). These was less support from younger people (56 percent) than from those in the older age group (71 percent).

In summary it appears that the public has a great deal of confidence in teachers but is not completely satisfied with schools. Citizens also have a considerable interest in having more control over the schools. The involvement they seek is not superficial but meaningful involvement in substantial problems. The matters of discipline and moral development are primary concerns at the time, but the basic curriculum and a minimum set of competencies are also important concerns. As new responsibilities, parents would like to have schools provide courses that would enable the parents to help their children in school. Parents are also apparently willing to have schools take over a larger share of the socialization process particularly in regard to moral development and career education. To accomplish these ends the public apparently does not see any need to make major revisions in the present school structure but does endorse a more individualized approach that includes more parent involvement in the process.

1. What are the major public attitudes about the:
   a. Quality of schools.
   b. Major problems schools face.
   c. Control of schools.
   d. School curriculum.
   e. Methods suitable for solving school problems.

Points of conflict

As we have pointed out, the educational system was created by society for a specific purpose. Society also has certain expectations regarding the system's effectiveness and places certain constraints upon the system. Bowles and Fruth (1976) see three basic points of conflict that require resolution. The conflicts stem from allocation of resources, choice of values, and distribution of power.

Resources. The resources for schools in the form of public monies come from three main sources: the federal government, state government, and direct from the taxpayer in the school district. Because all of these monies are eventually derived from the taxpaying public, it is not a question of who supports the schools but who has the power to specify how the monies will be spent. The answer to this seems to be everyone involved in the school process except the individuals who are supplying the monies. The federal and state governments set certain rules and regulations that schools must abide by and, as we pointed out earlier, sometimes earmark certain monies for specific programs.

As Gallup (1976) notes, approximately 80 percent of a school's budget is used to pay teachers' salaries, which are often negotiated between a teachers' bargaining group and the board of education. This places control of this money in the hands of these groups and it then becomes a fixed cost in the school budget.

Another 15 percent of the school budget is devoted to costs that are fixed in one way or another so that the taxpayers, at best, can control only a mere 5 percent of the school finances. Usually they do not even control this 5 percent unless the budget is divided and the specific budget items are voted on separately.

From the results of the Gallup Poll it appears that the public does not object to all school costs and might be willing to pay even more taxes if it would directly improve the education of children. Since a full 90 percent of the public wants to have a more substantial role in deciding the actual programs for which monies are being spent, the point of conflict may more accurately be over having some knowledge about, and some voice in, how the monies will be spent rather than the actual amount being spent. Public involvement may help to clarify the educational goals for which financial support will be given (Figure 21–4).

FIGURE 21–4
Objections to school budgets often reflect differing views of educational goals

Values. The results of the poll indicating that citizens have a great interest in serving on committees are a clear indication that the public wants to express its values. Apparently they do not believe that the values expressed by schools are similar to their own. It also appears that the public does not believe that parents in our society are capable of instilling acceptable values in their children, judging from their opinions about discipline, moral development, career education, the ability to think for oneself, and the development of responsibility. They want the schools to take more responsibility in these areas, and the public wants a clear voice in how it is to be done.

Power. The issue of having lay committees to advise school boards is most closely associated with the conflict over power. There is no strong indication that the public wants to do away with the present administrative structure of schools and is willing to act in an advisory capacity to school boards at this time. If they do not get this advisory power, or if they get the power and their advice is ignored, then the situation may change.

At the classroom level, parents are usually quite willing to take the advice of teachers and other school personnel about the education of their children. It is generally conceded, however, that parents have the power to make some decisions about how their children will be handled. Also, recently enacted legislation and Supreme Court decisions have helped to define who has the authority to make certain decisions. For the most part these are based on the principle of protecting the child's rights and welfare. A few issues are decided by law, but many others are established by school policy and it is advisable for teachers to become familiar with these. Many are not specified in writing but have become a matter of custom, such as retention policies and the manner in which students are assigned to classes. On both matters the school takes the initiative but is often responsive to parental pressure to change the decision. More often than not teachers are apt to raise the possibility of retaining a child at midyear partly as a means of trying to avoid the necessity for retention and partly as a means of determining the parents' attitudes about such a decision before it is made. In this way many confrontations are avoided before both sides have expressed a firm decision and one or the other has to relinguish its power to decide the issue. One tactic that is sometimes used is to phrase a school decision about a child in the form of a recommendation to the child's parents. If the parents do not decide to follow the suggestion, the parents are requested to give the school a note in writing to that effect. This is done as a means of avoiding conflict and also clarifying the situation in case there is any future question about the course of action that was followed. If the choice is unwise the child will suffer, but the responsibility for the error is neither in doubt nor a matter for grievance.

Recent U.S. Supreme Court rulings and federal regulations have made it necessary for schools to establish committees with some parents as members to consider on an individual basis the class placement and educational progress of every handicapped child in the district. It is now clearer that it is the school's responsibility to provide for the education of all children in the district, and they cannot exclude and ignore certain children because of some handicap. The decision from the Supreme Court is that each child will be educated in "the least restrictive environment" and for most children this means the regular classroom. These child advocacy laws give parents the power they need to secure a better education for their handicapped children than they were able to do just a few years ago. The law also places the school in an advocacy position if the school believes the parents are not acting in the child's best interests. Procedures for resolving conflicts are now in effect so that either parents or the school may bring the matter to an independent hearing officer for a decision.

A pattern of requiring the formation of parent committees was made a part of the federally funded Head Start programs. This is probably a result of resolving the Phase III shift in power toward the federal government and also the demand by minority groups for more of a voice in the educational process. It may also be an indication of what Phase IV of school control is going to be like. The present structure will be retained, but through federal mandates more and more lay people will be brought into the decision-making process. At present many of these people are not too vocal in the presence of the professional staff, but it is quite possible that as they become more comfortable in their role they will express their opinions more forcefully and even demand a larger representation on the committees. These are matters whose solutions lie in the future and about which we can only speculate. This would in effect bring about a Phase IV, which is a composite of Phases I, II, and III.

2. On what issues and in what ways do schools and the public seem to be in conflict?

SCHOOL SYSTEM ATTITUDES ABOUT COMMUNITY INTERACTIONS

Purpose of contacts

As Lake (1976) notes, school-community relations have recently expanded to home-school-community relations. In the former context the emphasis was on a public relations concept of interaction (Figure 21–5). How much these interactions were motivated by a feeling of responsibility and how much out of necessity is open to speculation. Based on the Zeigler et al. description of Phase II, it seems reasonable to assume that the attitude was to contact the parents only to report accomplishments or when conditions outside of school adversely affected the efforts of the school. Beyond this the attitude was probably to leave the process of instruction to the "experts." Lake believes the public relations approach is less credible now.

FIGURE 21–5
A public relations approach to public involvement has been the dominant theme in the past

Courtesy of New York State Historical Association, Cooperstown.

More recently, Lake contends, schools have taken a more political attitude. In addition to the public relations efforts they are inclined to more actively try to inform the public about the instructional process and involve them in not only the process but also the establishment of goals. Again, how much of this is internally motivated and how much is due to external pressure from the federal government and citizens' groups is an open question. Depending on the philosophy of the school administration, there is likely to be a considerable amount of variation between schools.

Involvement areas

Lake (1976) lists eight areas of involvement:

1. Citizen control.
2. Delegated power.
3. Partnership.
4. Placation.
5. Consultation.
6. Informing.
7. Therapy.
8. Manipulation.

Although Lake is referring to the system as a whole, all but the first two areas pertain to the individual teacher as well. The authority to relinquish control or delegate power will probably be done only at the administrative or broad levels of decision making. Certain instructional functions may, however, be performed by volunteer members of the community if the policy of the school permits this type of interaction. Murray (1974) lists several activities, such as classroom helper, tutor, and chaperone for field trips, as specific areas in which the public may be involved in the school. These are almost always done under the supervision of a professional educator and therefore the authority and responsibility are not relinquished to any great extent. The lay person has the responsibility for performing certain functions, but the professional still has the responsibility to see that the functions are carried out appropriately.

Restrictions on interaction

As a matter of protection for the rights and safety of students, many laws have been passed to guide the activities of educators, which, to some extent, extend and limit the interactions among schools, parents, and the community. Insurance regulations and laws sometimes restrict the use of nonemployees in transporting or supervising children during the school day. The Freedom-of-Information Act opens up the interaction by guaranteeing parents the right to see the school records kept on their children and also restricts some interactions because schools and teachers are required to keep data about the student confidential. This legislation has made the schools more aware of the records they keep and the responsibility the school has to protect a child's constitutional rights. It has also made teachers more cautious about what they put into records and what they say about a child. The data kept and the statements made are likely to be more objective than they have been in the past.

Court rulings have also made schools less capable of arbitrarily placing students into restrictive programs. As we mentioned, committees composed of parents and school personnel are now required to make these decisions. In the past it was often the decision of a single administrator acting on the advice of a single teacher. The abuses inherent in this system are apparent and the new procedures are a much-needed child advocacy reform.

> 3. What are the past and present reasons that schools communicate with the public? What areas are involved in these communications? What restrictions are there on a more open interaction between schools and the public?

COMPONENTS OF THE INTERACTION PROCESS

Having outlined the need for home-school-community interactions and the positions of the public and schools, we now turn the discussion toward the communication process and how it can be used to improve the educational process. This section draws almost exclusively on the description by Andersen (1972) of the communication process and related factors. We shall deal with only a few select topics, and anyone wishing a more complete treatment of the subject is referred to Andersen's text. First we present Andersen's definition of communication and his model of the communication process. Following this we present a discussion of the components as they relate to the role of a teacher who communicates with parents and others in the community.

Definition of communication

Several definitions of communication can be found. Some are very broad and others very technical. Andersen presents a definition that is fairly concise, limited to human communication, and expressed in terms compatible with the terminology used in this text. The definition is (p. 5): "a dynamic process in which man consciously or unconsciously affects the cognitions of another through materials or agencies and in symbolic ways."

The term *dynamic* is used to indicate the interactive nature of the process between the individuals involved. The terms *consciously* and *unconsciously* we would replace with the terms *intentional* and *unintentional*. The definition also points out that the process has an effect on the beliefs, attitudes, values, or actions of some person. The *symbolic ways* refer not only to oral and written language symbols but also to body movements, facial expressions, posture, dress, and other nonverbal forms of conveying information. As Andersen points out, even the presence or absence of a person has a symbolic meaning.

Model of communication process

Andersen also presents a simple model of the communication process that outlines several components of the process and identifies the context within which they must function (Figure 21–6).

The source and receiver are obvious references to the person who sends the message and the person who receives the message. The message is what is actually conveyed

FIGURE 21–6
A general communication model

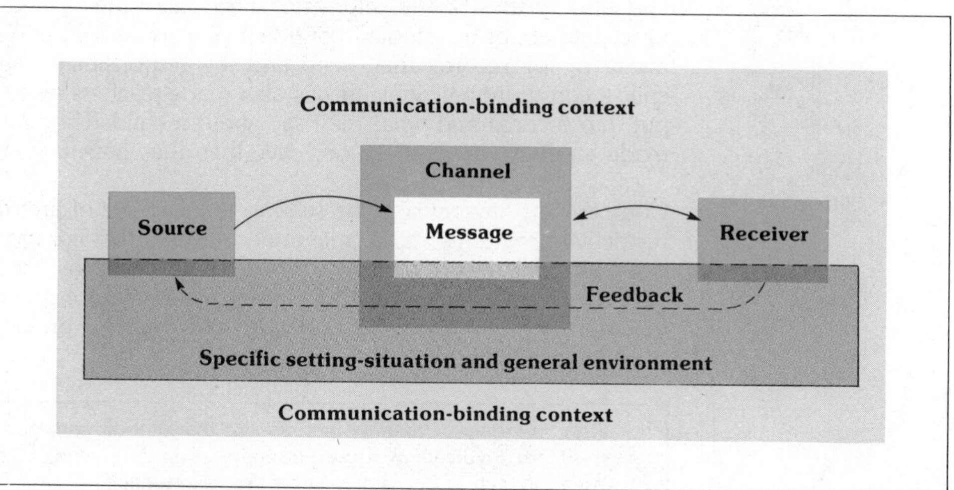

Source: Andersen (1972).

and is distinct from the source and the receiver. In other words, the message may not be the message the source intended to send, and it may not necessarily coincide with the message the receiver perceives. The channel is the means used to convey the message. Feedback from the receiver to the source is also included since the receiver's actions during the communication process have an impact on the source and any subsequent communication. Andersen also emphasizes the impact that the specific situation and the more general context have on the communication process. We return to each of these elements and discuss them more fully in later sections.

Purpose of communicatior

There are several purposes for communication but three general ones appear to cover the most common needs teachers may have for communication. They are exposition, persuasion, and facilitation. Exposition is primarily the presentation of information to enhance the understanding of the receiver. This is of primary benefit to receivers but may also benefit the source. Persuasion is used to bring about a change in a person's beliefs, attitude, values, or actions. The intent is not only to have an impact on a person's knowledge, as is the case with exposition, but also to bring about changes in the person's criteria, decisions, or actions. Facilitation involves communications that serve a secondary role in communication. Examples of facilitation are acting as a chairperson for a committee or as a master of ceremonies at a meeting. The communications involved in these roles are important only to the extent that they impose some order or organization that makes the primary communication process proceed more easily or smoothly.

Receivers

The term *receivers* can refer to one person in a one-to-one situation, a small group, or a large audience. The most salient feature of receivers is that they are not passive even when there are no outward signs of activity. In Piaget's terminology they are either assimilating or accommodating. These processes are likely to result in some distortion of the message but it may not be enough to have any noticeable difference.

In one-to-one and small-group settings receivers are more readily influenced. Andersen notes that in laboratory experiments experts have considerable influence on receivers but in real-life situations peer groups exert more influence. This may indicate that the advice of a teacher may have less influence than the advice of a neighbor or friend.

Another feature of receivers is that they selectively attend to communications. This means not only attention during a communication but also physical presence at a meeting or conference. Attendance and attention are closely related to the receiver's perception of the communication. If the message is relevant to the receiver he will attend to the message; if it is not he will focus attention on other stimuli. Attention to the message quickly changes if the message looses relevance or other stimuli gain relevance. This may result in only parts of the message being received.

Certain characteristics of recievers will influence how successful we will be in having an effect on any particular receiver. Around the ages of eight or nine people are most susceptible to suggestions and this gradually decreases with age. People with demanding parents, low self-esteem, and a feeling of being externally controlled tend to be more suggestible. Less suggestible are individuals with permissive parents, high self-esteem, and a feeling of being internally controlled. People with low self-esteem are not always easily persuaded because at times they simply do not respond to communications and are therefore not influenced. In contrast individuals with high self-esteem are apt to engage in communications that attempt to influence them, and eventually they are persuaded, so there are situations in which the general rule with regard to self-esteem and susceptibility to influence needs to be considered more carefully.

Sex and level of intelligence are two factors that do not correlate to any great extent with susceptibility to influence. On certain topics women are more easily persuaded than men but on other topics that is not true. While level of intelligence does not have much relationship to persuadability, people with high intelligence are more likely to ask for supporting data and fuller explanations than are receivers with lower intelligence.

Source

There are several characteristics of a source that affect the communication process. These characteristics do not need to actually exist in the source, but may exist only in the receiver's perception of the source. When a source is unknown to a receiver it is judged on two dimensions. One is an evaluation of the source in relation to general competence. The second dimension Andersen labels *dynamism,* which includes judgments of power, activity, and energy. Presumably a source judged more positively on these two dimensions has a higher chance of influencing a receiver than a source judged less positively. These judgments all take place before any message is received and therefore may affect the reception a message will get from the receiver, regardless of the content of the message.

During the course of communication we judge the source on three factors according to Andersen. The first is our trust in the source to convey accurate information. The second and third are again general competence and dynamism. At this point the message itself is heavily involved in our judgments, but some decisions are based on personal characteristics of the source. Physical appearance, ease of delivery, groups we associate with the source, and the reactions of others around us all influence our judgments of the source.

Message

You have all had a considerable amount of instruction in the importance of clear, concise, and well-organized messages. We will not elaborate on these issues here. We do wish to stress the importance of presenting data to support your claims, or at least having them available if requested. As we noted in an earlier chapter people are more apt to settle for a minimum of information rather than maximum amounts of it. In view of the 7 ± 2 phenomenon, it is probably difficult for receivers to cope with very much data unless they can be summarized into a few chunks. For this reason when data are presented they should be clearly related to the receiver's understanding of a situation or a decision that has been, or needs to be, made. It is easy to confuse and overwhelm the receiver when he/she is not as familiar with the types of data, or has not had as much time to analyze the data, as you have had. A practice of occasionally summarizing data in a way that reduces the amount that needs to be considered in making a final decision seems appropriate.

Channel

You are all familiar with many means by which we can transmit messages. Notes, telephone calls, conferences, newsletters, and informal conversations are all channels used by teachers. In each of these channels we should not overlook certain pitfalls.

In oral communications inflections, mispronunciations, and fluency may pose problems. Another means of communicating is through "body language," as it is popularly called. Facial expressions, posture, dress, and body movements all tend to convey a message that is part of the general message perceived by the receiver. Care should be taken that all channels carry the same message or at least consistent components of the message. With written communications spelling, punctuation, grammar, and legibility all have an impact, especially when parents or members of the community consider you as a model for teaching these skills.

We also wish to point out that not all receivers respond equally well to the same channel; therefore channel selection will need to recognize differences in receivers' preferences or abilities to communicate by way of a particular channel. When it is important that the message is communicated accurately, a variety of channels may have to be used.

Setting and context

We have pointed out the importance of pleasant surroundings in regard to the affective domain. These same factors apply in any communication (Figure 21–7). This is especially important when you consider that most communications with parents are aimed as much toward the affective domain as toward the cognitive domain. We may wish to inform parents about certain matters, but quite often we also intend to influence their attitudes, interests, values, and decisions.

Since teachers have approached higher levels of education and work in educational settings, it seems safe to predict that they have a relatively high regard for education. They may find fault with parts of the educational system but in general they believe in the value of education. This favorable attitude is not shared by all citizens. Many feel an education is a waste of time, their school years were miserable, and teachers are out to "get" their children. In communicating with these individuals, the general

FIGURE 21–7
A pleasant setting can have an impact on both the communication process and the affective domain

context of educational messages may make the process difficult if not impossible. Any teacher can readily cite examples of parents who ignore all communication attempts. Given the negative feelings associated with school buildings and teachers, school conferences with teachers loom as a particularly obnoxious prospect for some individuals. To start the communication process it may be necessary to begin in a setting where the school stimuli and the teaching role are not as evident. Gradually easing into a more school-oriented context may require a great deal of time and effort and may not be successful in all cases.

Another reason some individuals may avoid the communication context is a lack of oral and written communication skills. This lack of skill may have led to the initial alienation from schools and still may be present and very obvious. To avoid the embarrassment or to cover up the lack of skill, the individual may just avoid any and all contacts or keep them to a minimum.

4. What are the five major components of the communication process and the distinguishing attributes of each component?

DEVELOPING COMMUNITY INTERACTION PROGRAMS

Only a small portion of a teacher's time is devoted to interactions with parents and other members of the community. These contacts may have long-lasting effects, but because they occur with relative infrequency they may be difficult to modify. They should, therefore, be carefully planned.

There are many suggestions offered in the literature about various components of communication. The suggestions usually focus on certain aspects of the problem but exclude others. To integrate the many suggestions we discuss the problem in the context of designing interactive programs between a teacher and the community, and we have organized the discussion around the five phases of instructional design.

Analysis of communication problem

In the analysis phase the five areas of environment, task, learner, instructional space, and staff analysis are relevant with slight adaptations.

Environmental analysis. We have pointed out in a general way the attitude of the public. This provides only a starting point for the environmental analysis. The attitudes on certain issues may be different in your community or at least with certain parents. Also, other issues will be raised about which you will need to communicate. To pursue the environmental analysis further, other teachers can be questioned about community reactions to the issues. To avoid biases due to age differences or other factors, it is well to consult with a wide variety of people. These issues will be a part of the communication-binding context in Andersen's model. Your social and educational status in the community will also be involved in the communication context. This may vary considerably between communities but even more widely in comparison with specific families within the community. With some families your role may be readily accepted, whereas with other families it may create an antagonistic setting and form a block to communication. It may be wise to look at the occupations and educational levels of the parents with whom you will be communicating and ask others about the outcome of their attempts to communicate. Admittedly, use of this stereotype data can lead to errors in specific cases if adjustments are not made, but it does provide a starting point.

Also included in an environmental analysis is the more concrete and immediate environment. As we pointed out, the communication environment should be pleasant. It should also provide some degree of privacy and a minimum of distractions. At times the environment will be in the school building but it may also span the distance between the school and the home. For instance, sometimes you will have a parent come to school for a conference while at other times you will communicate by phone or written messages. In an environmental analysis, all the possibilities should be analyzed in terms of the factors of pleasantness and privacy. Involved in the pleasantness, besides the physical setting, is the convenience of those involved. Some environments will require less effort and disruption of schedules than others. An analysis of possible environments should focus on these issues. You should keep in mind that in the analysis phase the object is to determine the state of the general context, the choices of particular settings, and the characteristics of the specific settings. In the analysis phase a choice is not made. That is left for the design phase. Here the main task is to determine the goals we should establish.

Task analysis. From our point of view the task analysis starts with the final effect you wish to bring about. This may be an awareness and understanding of certain information, a willingness to engage in certain activities, or the making of a decision. From this point we can identify those concepts, principles, and terms that are needed in order to solve the problem. The analysis should include the perspective of the receiver since this is the person we wish to affect (Figure 21–8). In order to understand, be motivated, or make an intelligent decision, what does the receiver need to know? This analysis outlines the content of the message that needs to be delivered. It will not dictate the exact form of the message or the channel to be used. See Chapter 11 for principles of organization in persuasive communications.

FIGURE 21–8
Effective communication requires an understanding of the other person's perspective

Learner analysis This is equivalent to an analysis of the receiver's current knowledge or attitudinal state. You will probably have much less access to, and control over, receivers than you have with learners in the classroom. This necessitates an emphasis on the attitudes, values, and lifestyles of the receiver as well as the knowledge the receiver possesses. For instance the task analysis might identify certain principles you need to use. The learner analysis may point out that these principles are apt to be rejected by the receiver due to a difference in values. This may help to identify the type and amount of data needed in the message. A receiver who is aware of the concepts and principles embodied in the message and has a similar set of values will require a minimum of information. Providing the receiver with this information may make the message redundant and boring. A simple outline of the problem may be more appropriate for this individual. For others a more thorough message may be needed that is more persuasive than informative. The distinction between when a persuasive or an informative message is needed is not always inherent in the task but is inherent in the individual receiver.

The lifestyle of the receivers is particularly relevant because your message may have the effect of asking a family to change its lifestyle when you see it as merely asking them to perform one small task such as making sure their child comes to school each day. The lifestyle also needs to be carefully considered because it may set some limits on the channels of communication that are appropriate. In many families both parents are employed and unable to attend conferences during the day without a great deal of inconvenience. Lack of transportation is another consideration. A common situation is a one-parent family. Often there is another adult in the home who fills the role of spouse and parent. Regardless of whether they are legally married, both adults are likely to be receivers of messages from you so the characteristics of both need to be considered. Another frequent situation is when the parents of a child are having difficulties with their marriage and these difficulties may affect them as receivers. It may affect the time they can devote to the education of their children, the direction they want that education to take, and the methods they want used. While it may appear evident to you that one parent is more consistent with your beliefs, attitudes, and values than the other, it is wise to avoid having the communication process add to the family discord since it may eventually be detrimental to the child's welfare. If this is a distinct possibility, it may be better to minimize communication. Difficult problems of this nature are better left to family counselors.

Instructional space analysis. In relation to developing communication plans, this is an analysis of the channels available and the resources required in the various channels. You are no doubt aware of the many channels used in schools and we will not elaborate on them here.

Staff analysis. In addition to the physical and psychological factors, you should analyze yourself as a source of messages. You will have certain biases, preferences, and capabilities that will affect your ability to communicate well. In the analysis phase strengths and weaknesses should be identified. Where weaknesses are evident remedial action may be appropriate or substitute resources may have to be located. If you do not have personal resources such as information relevant to the message or certain communication skills, your ability to design an effective and efficient community program will be seriously hampered.

5. What are the main considerations in the analysis phase of developing community programs?

Design of communication plans

Comprehensive plan. To give community plans more meaning and continuity, a year-long, comprehensive, program adds an overall perspective. This plan should include the major goals we hope to accomplish, an outline of the component plans necessary, and a general timetable for implementing the component plans. Probably the advantage in having such a plan is that it puts a teacher in a proactive position and avoids some of the problems involved in functioning from a reactive position. By being proactive you are taking the initiative in opening up and guiding the direction of the communication process. Being reactive leaves the initiative to someone else to start and guide the process. In addition, when you are in a reactive role there is often very little time before you have to react, and this lack of time may mean the message is poorly organized and lacks sufficient data to support it. We may also be very defensive in our reaction and appear less open to suggestion than we are in a proactive situation.

Component plans. In this chapter we have presented some general principles of communication that should be included in the design of component plans. In Chapter 11 we presented many precise principles that should be taken into consideration when attempting to change the information and attitudes of another person. Principles germane to the fields of speech and composition are also important in the design of communication plans but we will not attempt to cover the issues from these fields except to emphasize that the message needs to be clear and concise. The problem, however, is that what may be clear and concise for one receiver may not be clear and concise for another. This suggests the need for a variety of component plans to match the characteristics of individual receivers. For those individuals with whom a particular plan is not effective, an alternate plan may be substituted. For instance, a request for a conference in school may be ignored. The parent may be disinterested in communication or more likely, judging from the results of the Gallup poll about participating on committees, unable to respond for some reason. The request may not have reached them, was inconvenient, or was impossible. Occasionally the parent cannot read or understand English and the request may not have been comprehended. Here the facilitative type of communication plan that was used did not successfully bring about the primary communication process. Under these circumstances a request written in the language of the home, a telephone call, a letter delivered through the postal service, or even a visit to the home may be needed if the process of communication is to be completed. How vital it is to communicate will determine the number of component plans that will be used and the intensity of the efforts expended.

Due to the individual differences between receivers, you may not want to send the same messages to all receivers. You may be trying to enlist the aid of one or two parents to help in the classroom. Your job will be easier if you communicate with those who already may be interested in helping and have the time. Your interest may be in specific receivers because they have the expertise you wish to tap or wish to develop. As an example, a teacher may ask a particular parent to come in and talk about an area of the world she grew up in or visited, or ask her to work in the classroom so she is better able to help her own child at home. The strategy of having the parent work in the classroom may also serve as a means of changing attitudes and values about other aspects of the educational process.

FIGURE 21–9
At times we need to gather data if communication is to be effective

Evaluation plan. The only point we wish to emphasize here is that without some evaluation plan you may continue to design and use very ineffective communication techniques (Figure 21–9). Your evaluation plans are apt to be very sketchy because it will be very difficult if not impossible for you to measure many of the effects you wish to bring about. Receivers are very adept at giving the impression of understanding or agreeing when in fact they do not. Also many of the actions you wish to bring about are going to occur when you cannot observe them. You are left therefore to draw inferences from indirect measures such as a change in their child's behavior.

Preparation plan. In the case of community programs our implementation plans to some extent involve a facilitative type of communication. These are the plans necessary to bring about the success of our comprehensive and component plans. They include such activities as calling or writing to parents to set up a more lengthy conference. It may also include introducing people in a group meeting or even suggesting some material to read or a television program to watch. The methods used should be effective in bringing about the main communication process.

At times other activities need to be planned such as gathering data, presenting data, and arranging the physical setting prior to conferences or meetings. These activities may not be needed in all situations, but if needed and neglected, they could have a detrimental effect on the outcome of our component plans.

6. What are the main considerations in the design phase of developing community programs?

Preparing for the communication process

In this phase the activities of authoring, tryout, and assembly are likely to be done by the teacher, but in some situations involving large audiences several people may perform the tasks. The most likely items to be produced are announcements of meetings or activities, agendas, short reports of specific activities, and displays of data. The latter may be displays of student work for open school meetings, formal meetings, workshops, or presented during individual conferences with parents. It is obvious these should be relevant, attractive, and well finished if they are going to generate interest and communicate a general competence on the part of the source. Poorly designed materials and displays have a message of their own and may have a greater impact than the main message. For instance, parents may be well aware of their child's capabilities in an area. A display of it may have little effect on their knowledge about the child, but how it is displayed may have a considerable effect on their perception of the teacher.

Communicating

In carrying out communication plans it is common to make errors or at least deviate from our plans. There appears to be three basic reasons for this: poor preparation, anxiety, and feedback from the receiver. Poor preparation is to some extent inexcusable but also understandable. A teacher with a classroom filled with active children may be interrupted often enough so that certain tasks are not completed or are forgotten. This is understandable and apt to happen to anyone. It does not happen with the same frequency for all teachers, indicating that good planning can help to avoid some bottlenecks in implementing plans.

Probably a common characteristic of all people is a certain amount of anxiety in meeting new situations. During communication several indications of anxiety are noticed. The voice changes due to tension on the vocal cords, perspiration begins to appear, fingers are clenched and unclenched, and there are a great many pauses and errors in the speech patterns. With written communication there is less anxiety because we are not in a face-to-face situation and we can modify our message and perfect it to our satisfaction. When we are not able to revise our written message or are not sure of the reaction it will evoke, there may also be a great deal of anxiety generated.

Andersen offers the assurance that we can vary a great deal from normal delivery patterns and the receivers still will accept it quite readily and may not even be aware of the variation. We ourselves are more likely to notice our errors and signs of anxiety, thereby raising the anxiety level and subsequent number of errors. As a remedy Andersen offers the suggestion that careful planning and gradual exposure to audiences over time will help alleviate the anxiety. It should also be remembered that our audiences are probably going to be quite understanding and cooperative in helping us gain our composure.

One thing that helps us (or may hinder us) in gaining our composure is the feedback we get from the receiver. Not only does this feedback help in overcoming our anxiety but it also causes us to modify our message. The verbal comments, facial expressions, and body movements of the receiver all provide feedback. The fact that much of this feedback is unavailable during telephone conversations may explain why many people do not like to use the telephone.

To the extent that we receive this feedback and interpret it correctly, the feedback may make the communication process more successful. One aspect frequently discussed about utilizing feedback is a person's ability to listen. This is certainly an important skill. Another aspect of this is the fact that words have a connotative as well as a denotative meaning. Not in all instances is the meaning of a word the same for all individuals, especially the connotative meaning. Techniques for clarifying the receiver's feedback are therefore necessary to the communication process. We mention these techniques only to alert you to their importance but will not attempt to elaborate on them here.

Evaluation of communication efforts

We have discussed the importance and techniques of evaluating programs at some length in previous chapters. At this point we only wish to reiterate that the evaluation phase should be a careful evaluation of the process and products of the first four phases as well as of our evaluation efforts. Our communication efforts are not simply a matter of constructing and sending a message. The evaluation process should focus on the entire range of activities in order to improve on future activities and results.

7. What are the main considerations in the preparation, implementation, and evaluation phases of developing community programs?

SUMMARY

In this chapter we have pointed out the purpose of home-school-community relations and how they have changed over time. Based on recent opinion surveys, the major attitudes of the public were discussed in relation to (1) the quality of schools, (2) the major problems facing schools, (3) who should control the schools, (4) the school curriculum, and (5) the methods that should be used to solve the problems. Points of conflict between the schools and the public concerning resources, values, and power were outlined, as was the school's position in the communication process. The communication process itself was described in terms of the six components of receivers, source, message, channel, setting, and context. The chapter concluded by discussing a variety of factors that need to be considered in the five phases of designing community programs.

SELF-TEST

1. When teachers are involved in the communication process among home-school-community, they are usually involved with:
   a. One-to-one interactions.
   b. Broad issues.
   c. Announcements through the media.
   d. Only a small proportion of the parents of children in class.
2. Over the years control of the schools has shifted from local control to professional control and now toward federal control. This shift has been prompted by:
   a. Research results indicating that lay people lacked sufficient expertise.
   b. Efforts to make all schools more consistent.
   c. Dissatisfaction with political influence and later elitist influence.
   d. Professional educators trying to gain a wider base of control.
3. With reference to dissatisfaction with schools, the public is:
   a. Overwhelmingly dissatisfied.
   b. Moderately dissatisfied.
   c. Moderately satisfied.
   d. Overwhelmingly satisfied.
4. Of the following, which is seen as the major problem facing public schools today?
   a. Use of drugs.
   b. Student discipline.
   c. Poor curriculum.
   d. Poor teachers.
5. If the question of school control over curriculum, staff selection, and budget was brought to a vote on the following four choices, which most likely would be chosen?
   a. Have citizens committees make final decisions.
   b. Have teachers make final decisions.
   c. Have school boards make final decisions.
   d. Have federal agencies make final decisions.
6. Generally the public wants the following curricular changes:
   a. Reduce after-school activities and remedial services.
   b. Reduce high school to three years for all students.
   c. Concentrate on academic subjects and leave student control to parents.
   d. All of the above.
   e. None of the above.
7. To improve the quality of education, most people are in favor of:
   a. Improving the buildings and facilities.
   b. Increasing the amount of homework and raising the academic standards.
   c. Lowering the mandatory starting age and adding a fifth year to high school.
   d. Increasing attention to teaching basic skills and enforcing stricter discipline.
   e. Lengthening the school day and closing schools during the coldest months to save energy and money.
8. The message is defined as:
   a. What the source intends to convey.
   b. What is actually conveyed.
   c. What the receiver perceives the message to be.
   d. All of the above.
   e. None of the above.
9. George Nudnick and Dick Klutz are both experts in their field but are talking to an audience who does not know either of them. George comes slowly on stage and quietly asks where to sit, followed by Dick who quickly walks on stage, shakes hands with the master of ceremonies and George before moving his chair closer to center stage, and then sits down. If the two differ on a particular point, who is more likely to convince the audience?
   a. George.
   b. Dick.
   c. Both will be equally convincing.
   d. Neither will be particularly convincing.
10. Receivers with demanding parents and low self-esteem as compared to receivers with permissive parents and high self-esteem:
   a. Are always easier to persuade.
   b. May not as consistently respond to all communication.
   c. Will more consistently respond to all messages.
   d. Are usually more difficult to persuade.

ANSWER KEY TO BOXED QUESTIONS

1. *Quality of schools*—Generally satisfied with teachers and curriculum, especially outside of big cities.
   Problems—Lack of discipline is main concern; costs are another concern.
   Control of schools—Want school boards to make final decisions but greater input from public through committees.
   Curriculum—Strongly in favor of back-to-basics in reading, writing, and arithmetic. Remainder of curriculum to remain unchanged except to add some

college-level courses and courses for parents of school children.

Methods—More attention to basic skills and discipline is the main suggestion, with meeting individual needs and improving parent/school relations as a second-level pair of concerns. The present age structure, school calendar, and time schedules should be maintained.

2. *Resources*—Public wants more input about distribution of funds.

   Values—Public wants its values expressed and wants schools to foster more acceptable values in students.

   Power—Schools are slow to share power and the federal government is seen as a foe to laypeople, school boards, and administration alike.

3. Past reasons were motivated by public relations. Present-day reasons are more political and are directed toward encouraging public participation in the process of education. The areas of involvement generally include different facets of authority to make decisions and the decision-making process itself. Restrictions are legal in regard to protection of the school district itself and the rights of students.

4. *Source*—the sender of a message.

   Message—the actual content conveyed, may differ from content intended or interpreted by receiver.

   Receiver—recipient of message.

   Channel—means of transmitting message.

   Setting—situation-specific characteristics within which communication takes place.

5. *Environmental analysis*—community attitudes.

   Task analysis—identification of discrete information, concepts, rules, or attitudes needed in order for message to have its intended effect.

   Learner analysis—estimate of receiver's current level of knowledge and affective states.

   Instructional space analysis—inventory of available channels, materials needed to prepare message, and communication settings.

   Staff analysis—inventory of source's communication skills, preferences, and weaknesses.

6. *Comprehensive plan*—outline of overall communication task with general time schedule for implementing various components of task.

   Component plans—a variety of alternate plans to meet differing receiver characteristics that meet principles of effective communication.

   Preparation plan—outline preparatory activities or facilitative messages.

   Evaluation plan—may be sketchy but needs to focus on measuring effects of communication process.

7. *Preparation phase*—make sure facilitative type communication functions are carried out and needed data are gathered and/or prepared for the main communication process.

   Implementation phase—avoid lack of preparation and anxiety, focus on feedback provided by receiver but interpret it carefully.

   Evaluation phase—interpret results in terms of intent of message and process used to communicate message.

ANSWER KEY TO SELF-TEST

1. *a*
2. *c*
3. *c*
4. *b*
5. *c*
6. *e*
7. *d*
8. *b*
9. *b*
10. *b*

SECTION V

FULFILLING PROFESSIONAL RESPONSIBILITIES

The purpose of Section V is to increase your general professional growth and make you aware of some significant changes taking place in educational psychology with several broad and timely topics.

In Chapter 22, suggestions are made concerning how to effectively use the library and read research articles. Being current is necessary for a competent professional. Chapters 23 and 24 focus on the broad topics of intelligence and motivation. No topic in our discipline has created as much controversy as intelligence. Chapter 23 thoroughly analyzes intelligence from an instructional psychology point of view. In Chapter 24, many current topics and theories of motivation are considered that have broad educational and instructional implications. Taken together, these topics should add a considerable amount to your professional growth. Much of what is said in Chapter 24 should have a direct bearing on planning and implementing the goals and objectives of our schools.

Chapter 22

Professional literature as a source of growth

NOT ALL OF A TEACHER'S TIME is spent preparing and implementing lessons in the classroom. One of the important tasks facing professional educators is to keep abreast with our discipline. This is accomplished by making periodic trips to a library, reading journal articles and similar periodicals, and attending conferences and workshops. The purpose of this chapter is to identify those library skills necessary to acquire professional sources in education and educational psychology quickly, thoroughly, and efficiently. After the source is located, additional skills are necessary to read any type of journal article without having a great deal of advanced knowledge in research design and complex statistics. At the conclusion of this chapter you should be able to accomplish the following three objectives:

1. Given a topic in education or educational psychology, you should be able to identify the most likely source for finding the information in the library and then locate the topic.
2. Given various types of professional articles to read (statistical studies, reviews of research, and opinion articles), you should be able to identify the rules needed to arrive at a reasoned conclusion about the article.
3. Given a journal article, you should be able to identify the most important information found in each section of the article.

All too often, professional teachers are severely limited in their professional roles because they have not acquired the above three skills. It is our contention that the worthiness of any professional decision is enhanced when a professional has considered as many as possible of the available sources before arriving at a final decision on an issue. Unfortunately, professional library skills and skills about how to read journal articles are frequently left to chance, with the result that the student is deprived of two valuable professional skills upon which reasoned decisions should be made. Being unaware of or unable to locate sources in the library, the student stays away from the library. Being unable to understand even the basics of research articles, the student does not read them. Although advanced skills in research design and statistics are needed from a research perspective to evaluate critically the methodological treatment and statistical manipulation found in research articles, a lot can be gained from reading research articles at a less intensive level. This is the purpose of the second part of this chapter.

USE OF THE LIBRARY BY THE PROFESSIONAL EDUCATOR

At various times during your professional career you will have the occasion to use a library in connection with your teaching role. The simple research skills to use a library effectively and quickly are invaluable and should be acquired in your undergraduate preparation. For the purposes of this chapter we assume you already have a working knowledge of the card catalog and its organization, as well as some of the secondary skills such as locating the proper stacks and the reference section of the library. Our purpose is to help you with using the specific materials available to our profession.

Locating information in periodicals

Assume you are interested in locating information on a specific topic in the library that you feel will help you in teaching, and you are particularly interested in up-to-date sources on the topic. You have looked through the card catalog, and now you are ready to find some appropriate journal or periodical sources on the topic. To find up-to-date journal sources, you should consult special indexes. In high school you were more than likely exposed to the *Reader's Guide to Periodic Literature,* a guide that lists sources in popular magazines. The professional indexes are similar in format to the *Reader's Guide.*

There are a variety of professional indexes available to help a reader quickly locate up-to-date journal sources as well as other current printed information. These indexes are located in the periodical section or the reference section of your library. To locate current material quickly and efficiently, you should be familiar with the *Current Index to Journals in Education (CIJE),* the *Educational Index,* and *Resources in Education (RIE).*

In addition, there are many other specialized indexes within our field as well as several other broad related indexes, which should be consulted depending on your topic. Each index is briefly described.

CIJE. Known as the *Current Index to Journals in Education,* this comprehensive index is put out by the CMM Information Corporation in cooperation with the various Educational Resources Information Centers (ERIC). ERIC is a federally funded project designed to identify pertinent articles of interest to professional educators. More than 700 journals and 15,000 articles are identified yearly. In the back of each *CIJE,* you will find an author index, journal content, and subject index. An example of a subject index entry is presented in Figure 22–1 to show you how to use *CIJE.*

FIGURE 22–1
A sample subject index entry in *CIJE*

Attention and learning disordered children: A review of theory and remediation, Journal of Learning Disabilities, V9n2, pp. 100–10, Feb 76. EJ 136 138

A summary of the EJ 136 138 subject index entry would be found by looking up that source under the entry EJ 136 138 in the front part of the index. An example of the EJ 136 138 entry is found in Figure 22–2.

FIGURE 22–2
A sample of a summary entry in *CIJE*

EJ 136 138

Attention and Learning Disordered Children: A Review of Theory and Remediation. Harris, Larry P. *Journal of Learning Disabilities,* v9 n2, pp 100–10, Feb 76

*Learning Disabilities, *Educable Mentally Handicapped, *Emotionally Disturbed, *Attention Span, *Academic Achievement Exceptional Child Research, Definitions, Drug Therapy, Stimulation, Operant Conditioning

Reviewed is research on the role of attentional deficits in the inferior school-related performances of mild-to-moderate learning disabled, emotionally disturbed, or mentally retarded children. (Author/DB)

Because of *CIJE*'s breadth, it is by far the most comprehensive journal source in our field. Since it was conceived in 1969, earlier journal sources have to be located in the *Educational Index.*

RIE (Resources in Education, a monthly publication of ERIC started in 1966). As a companion to *CIJE, RIE*'s purpose is to identify various articles, reports, pamphlets, and similar current materials that are not located in journals. Extensive government reports are indexed in *RIE.* If your library subscribes to the *RIE* publication and the accompanying microfiche service, all of the articles identified in *RIE* will be at your fingertips. If your library subscribes to only the *RIE* index, then it is necessary to purchase a microfiche copy or paper copy of the report identified in the *RIE* index. The microfiche is very inexpensive and can be ordered easily. If you need to have a particular area searched, information on how to use ERIC's search services is found in *RIE.* To thoroughly review a topic, a teacher ought to use this source. Since the structure of *RIE* is very similar to that of *CIJE,* there is no need to present specific examples of *RIE*'s entries.

Educational index. Published by the H. W. Wilson Company since 1929, this index identifies important educational articles from over 200 periodicals in addition to various other current publications and government reports. The reader can look for either a specific topic or a specific author; both are alphabetically arranged. Examples of a subject entry and author entry are presented in Figures 22–3 and 22–4.

FIGURE 22–3
Sample of subject entry in *Educational Index*

Reading

elementary school

Are individualized reading programs helpful?
D. C. Poll & M. J. Allegra.
Educ Tech 15:30–3 N '75

FIGURE 22–4
Sample of author entry in *Educational Index*

TAYLOR, Ronald L.

Psychosocial development among black children and youth: A reexamination bibl. Am J. Ortho psych 46:4–19 Ja '76.

Other general or specialized indexes useful to education. Depending on your topic, some additional general indexes include the *Social Sciences and Humanities Index,* the *New York Times Index, Sociological Abstracts, Dissertation Abstracts International,* and the *Psychological Abstracts.* Put out by the American Psychological Association, *Psychological Abstracts* is particularly helpful for identifying experimental studies in education, and has special sections devoted to educational psychology and developmental psychology.

In addition, there are some specific indexes that are very useful for some aspects of education. These include the *Child Development Abstracts and Bibliography,* the *Exceptional Children Education Abstracts* (which is cross-referenced with ERIC), and the *Mental Retardation Abstracts.* Most large libraries will have all these indexes.

Using specialized reference books

In addition to the many available indexes, there are a variety of specialized books that gather together a great deal of information concerning specific topics in education (Figure 22–5). Some of those germane to education include descriptions and reviews of tests in print or not in print, sources of grant monies, guides to reference books in general, the identification and review of good books in education, an analysis of acronyms in education, and a list of useful journals in our field (including editorial policies for publishing articles). Each of these topics is discussed briefly.

Testing. There are several useful sources of published tests. By far the largest source in this area is Buros's classic:

Buros, O. K. (Ed.). *Tests in print (II): An index to tests, test reviews, and the literature on specific tests.* Highland, Park, N.J.: Gryphon Press, 1974.

FIGURE 22–5
Making many professional decisions requires good library skills

This book identifies published tests in the fields of achievement testing, English, fine arts, foreign languages, intelligence testing, mathematics, multi-aptitude testing, personality, reading, science, sensorimotor, social studies, speech and hearing, and the vocational testing field. Buros has also written specific books on reading (1968) and personality (1970).

If you are interested in reading excellent, lengthy reviews on specific tests in print, the classic source to consult is:

Buros, O. K. *The 7th Mental Measurement Yearbook.* Highland Park, N.J.: Gryphon Press, 1972.

Published irregularly, on the average every six years, this book gives a good insight into the reliability and validity studies on each test as well as some book reviews about testing. Before deciding to choose a standardized test for a school district, you should carefully consider what the critics have to say about the test. Many of the misuses associated with current standardized testing could be avoided if more time were spent in choosing an appropriate test for the stated purposes of the school district.

If you are interested in an analysis of preschool and kindergarten tests, a source to consult is:

Hoepfner, R., Stern, C., & Nummedal, S. G. *CSE-ECRC preschool/K test evaluations.* Los Angeles: UCLA Graduate School of Education, 1971.

Included in this book are statements about the test's validity for its stated purposes, the appropriateness of the test, the administrative usability of the test, and the procedures used for establishing the norms and reliability of the test.

At the elementary school level, a companion to Hoepfner's preschool book is:

Hoepfner, R., et al. *CSE elementary school test evaluations.* Los Angeles: UCLA Graduate School of Education, 1970.

For those teachers interested in conducting classroom research and in need of some ideas about unpublished tests, there are several excellent books:

Goldman, B. A., & Saunders, J. L. *Directory of unpublished experimental measurements* (Vol. I). New York: Behavioral Publishing, 1974.

Johnson, O. G., & Bommarito, J. W. *Tests and measurements in child development: A handbook.* San Francisco: Jossey Bass, Inc., 1971.

These books describe the unpublished tests and indicate where the test may be obtained. Many useful ideas may be obtained by browsing through these books. More current reviews of recent tests would obviously have to be found in current journal articles.

Guides to good books and journals. If you ever need to identify good books or references about some aspect of education, several sources include:

Sheehy, E. P., Keckeissen, R. G., & McIlvaine, E. (Eds.). *Guide to reference books.* Chicago: American Library Association, 1976.

White, C. M., et al. *Sources of information in the social sciences.* Chicago: American Library Association, 1973.

These two books are general source guides that include the topic of education as one small component. Of a more specific nature, if a list of professional periodicals for some project is needed, two good books to consult are:

Arnold, D. B., & Doyle, K. O. *Education/psychology journals: A scholar's guide.* Metuchen, N.J.: Scarecrow Press, 1975.

Camp, W. L., & Schwark, B. L. *Guide to periodicals in education and to academic disciplines.* Metuchen, N.J.: Scarecrow Press, 1975.

Both of these books are excellent sources for the young professional who aspires to write and needs knowledge concerning the types of available journals as well as the standards for publishing articles. In this regard, the Camp and Schwark book is much more extensive, reviewing over 600 educational periodicals. The Arnold and Doyle book reviews 122 journals. Similar to these books is another published by Scarecrow Press which focuses on educational research topics such as government publications, knowledge of grants, reference materials, and similar information. If interested, consult:

Berry, D. M. *A bibliographic guide to educational research.* Metuchen, N.J.: Scarecrow Press, 1975.

Acronyms. With the burgeoning use of acronyms (an abbreviation of a multiple-word phrase generally formed by extracting the first letter of at least the most important major words), a need developed to identify these acronyms. A thorough source for the identification of acronyms of organizations, associations, and popular acronyms (e.g., IQ, IPI) is:

Kawakami, T. S. *Acronyms in education and the behavioral sciences.* Chicago: American Library Association, 1971.

Using general educational reference books

The purpose of general reference books is to provide the reader with an overview of a field or a topic and, as such, should not be viewed as a final source on a topic. In some cases, the overview or review might be quite thorough, but because of the nature of these books, the information can be dated in some instances. Some of the more popular, useful general reference books include:

Encyclopedia of Education, edited by L. C. Deighton, though dated, is an informative source on many topics in education.

Educational Yearbook, edited by R. Farmighetti, P. B. Randall, and J. Paradise, has many relatively current articles on such topics as accountability, behavior modification, students' rights, CBTE, early schooling, schools of the future, as well as some up-to-date statistical reviews.

Encyclopedia of Educational Research, edited by R. Ebel, has topics including developmental psychology, psychology of learning, human behavior, social foundations, curriculum, instruction, special education, measurement, research, and many others; extensive bibliography (published about every ten years).

Review of Research in Education, edited by F. N. Kerlinger, includes topics on learning and instruction, comparative education, teaching effectiveness, and methodology. The reviews are quite extensive and scholarly.

Second Handbook of Research on Teaching, edited by R. M. W. Travers, is a review of models and theories, methods and techniques of research and development, special problems in teaching, and research on teaching various subject matter content; thorough and scholarly.

Handbook of Contemporary Education, edited by S. E. Goodman, includes sections on change and planning (22 articles), administration and management of education (16 articles), teacher-faculty issues (7 articles), education and training of teachers and administrators (6 articles), students and parents (9 articles), special interest groups (7 articles), teaching and learning strategies (38 articles), and some alternatives and options in education (13 articles). Articles vary in breadth and scholarship. Some articles are excellent introductory sources to topics.

1. If your library subscribes to *CIJE,* the *Educational Index,* and *RIE,* state exactly where those indexes are located.
2. Using *CIJE,* the *Educational Index,* and *RIE* in your library, locate a topic of your choice or one chosen by your instructor.
3. Assume you have been assigned to a committee charged with the responsibility of choosing a published, standardized achievement test for your school. Which general review book would you consult?

READING GENERAL PROFESSIONAL ARTICLES: SOME SUGGESTIONS

Throughout this book, we have been critical of educational practices at various times. Our purpose for being critical is not to chastise the educational researcher or practitioners; rather we hope that you *become a careful consumer* of professional literature in your own right. As a critical consumer of literature, do not accept anything in print as the absolute truth never to be modified or reinterpreted in the future. Question; probe; play Hegel's thesis-antithesis role. Assume initially that the material you are reading might be incorrect in some manner. Pose counterhypotheses. Because our profession has not established a series of immutable instructional principles that have been totally validated under all conditions, you will note at times that our field tends to perform in a cyclical fashion. Assume that what you are reading is a new cycle, possibly to be modified in the future. Take the viewpoint that what you are reading may be very useful to you but may need some modification to be functional in your specific classroom. *Never assume that a study or a review of studies necessarily proves anything beyond all reasonable doubt.* What appears to be good today may be much improved tomorrow.

On the positive side, if after you carefully scrutinize the material it seems appropriate, adapt it to your specific class. Be aware that what is in print form might have to be adapted somewhat for your class. Make use of the many innovative ideas that find their way into print. We ask only that you not become so doctrinaire in your ways that you accept what is in print without carefully evaluating the results in your class. The purpose of education is to help students learn, not to espouse some viewpoint which upon careful analysis works to the detriment of your goals. Well meaning but ineffective teachers who do not verify what they do to their students are not likely to be an asset to our profession.

To become a critical consumer of professional articles requires that you use a few basic principles when reading articles of this type. If the article is found in a yearbook, encyclopedia, book, or similar source, the article should be viewed as an overview or generalization that should be pursued by the reader in more depth. Further, the reader should ask some very penetrating questions about the article or book. The purpose of expository writing is to identify the specifics. General articles or books are particularly susceptible to two dangers. There is the likelihood, first of all, that the author might be biased, and the bias most likely will find its way into print. Second, there is a strong likelihood that the article may be outdated, since significant progress may have been made in the field since the time of the writing. For these two reasons, scholars prefer to read original and current sources if they are available.

To read up-to-date journal articles requires some additional skills. If the articles are of the opinion format, the same precautions should be taken as mentioned above. If jargon is used, be suspicious. The writer should be required to define terms clearly. Terms such as *individualized instruction, self-concept,* and *underachievement* really do very little to clarify an article. Unless the author has used clear terminology that others have no trouble understanding, the article has failed.

Determine if there is instructional *payoff* to the article. Ask yourself how this article will help you in the classroom. There are many correlational studies in education that have very little relevance to instruction. Be selective. A study on the relationship between socioeconomic status and the student's performance on an intelligence test, for example, might be very interesting, but questions about how lessons should be presented at 9:00 in the morning will not be found in articles of this nature. Correlation does not mean causation. To draw any instructional conclusions, you should generally read studies that are experimental in design.

Two types of articles can provide the teacher with a maximum payoff: well-written unbiased scholarly review articles and experimental articles in which the experimenter has manipulated one or more dependent variables. Unbiased scholarly reviews can be an excellent source for a quick synthesis of an aspect of research. If you do not have enough time or the inclination to read original research articles, reviews are an acceptable substitute. You should be aware, however, that it sometimes takes from three to five years before studies are reviewed; therefore, the time lag between when a research study is reported in the literature and when it is reviewed by a scholar may be considerable.

Reading experimental studies unfortunately requires many additional skills beyond those required to read review or opinion-type articles. To read research articles at the level at which they can be critiqued from an experimental design or statistical perspective requires several advanced courses at the graduate level. Such competence is well beyond the scope of this book. This does not mean, however, that the undergraduate student or practicing teacher should be so handicapped that any understanding of experimental or correlational studies cannot be attempted by the neophyte. Much can be gained from reading these types of studies even though the complex statistical procedures and rationale for the research design are not understood. Ideally all teachers should possess the competence to read articles of this nature. Practically, this goal will not be realized for a long time to come. The purpose of this part of the chapter is to provide any reader not trained in statistical analysis or experimental design with enough skills to read a research article and identify its main highlights. Without those basic skills it would be highly unlikely that a teacher not possessing research competence would consult research articles. The unfortunate outcome of this is that a great source of rich information that a teacher might be able to use would not be read. To be deprived of the findings of research studies due to the lack of a few skills is an oversight of considerable magnitude in many teacher-training programs.

READING RESEARCH ARTICLES: SOME SUGGESTIONS

By definition, research articles require mathematical analysis of data. Mathematical analysis allows us to be more exact and definite and provides us with ways to draw conclusions, summarize our results, make predictions, and analyze complex relationships (Guilford, 1965). As a generalization researchers are interested either in how variables relate to one another (simple correlational procedures, factor analytic procedures, or multiple regression techniques) or in the degree to which two or more treatments differ from one another on the dependent measures (*t* tests, chi square, analysis of variance, and analysis of covariance). Within those two general categories other similar questions are raised. To be competent in statistical analysis and research design procedures, a reader must have enough advanced skills to be able to understand the underlying rationale of the statistics, to generate well-conceptualized clear hypotheses, to design appropriate studies including the use of the correct statistical procedures, and to generate correct inferences from the study. As mentioned previously, training in this area is rigorous, and it takes at least two to three advanced courses for a student to be competent in most of these skills. We bring this point up to remind you of the purpose of this part of the chapter. Obviously you will not learn the above skills here. What you *will* learn is how a research article is organized and how to read enough of the statistical notations so that most articles you might come in contact with in your professional career will make more sense to you than if you do not have these skills. In essence, you will learn how to interpret the statistical notations that are *common* to almost all research articles. As such, your professional literacy skills should increase significantly. We hope this surface introduction to the topic of research articles will whet your appetite for further study in this important tool subject.

Research articles almost always have the same structure. A 100–200-word abstract precedes the article, followed by an introductory section, a section on the procedure, a statistical section reporting the results, and a general discussion section of the results as related to the hypotheses and other research studies. Each of these sections is briefly reviewed. Figure 22–6 *portrays a prototypic organizational* design of a study.

The abstract

The abstract is designed to highlight the main points of the article in five to eight sentences. Usually the abstract begins with a one-sentence introduction about the purpose of the study, followed by a one- or two-sentence description of the experimental treatment. Third, several sentences cover the results of the study, while the implications of the study may be mentioned at the end of the abstract. Although abstracts vary in their structure, the above points almost always are included.

FIGURE 22–6
Organization of a prototypic study

Section of study	*Purpose*
Abstract	To summarize the study in five to eight sentences
Introduction	To discuss the general nature of the topic, review relevant research, identify the status of the research, and justify the current study
Method	To discuss how subjects were chosen for the study, the nature of the independent and dependent variables, how the data were gathered, and a rationale for the type of statistical treatment used in the study
Results	To report the statistical findings of the study
Discussion	To highlight findings, relate and compare to other research, specify implications, identify limitations of the current study, and suggest future research possibilities

Introduction

Introductions to research studies usually follow the same organizational pattern. The first paragraph discusses the general nature of the topic. The next several paragraphs review the research in a very concise manner. Following the review of the research, a statement is made about the status of that research (i.e., where it has erred, what is needed, how it is incomplete), thus justifying the current study. Finally, a precise one- or two-paragraph justification of the current study is presented. Included in these paragraphs, if appropriate, is a statement about the uniqueness of the current study in terms of its research design or statistical treatment of the data.

Method

The purpose of the method section of a research study is to state how the study was conducted in enough detail so that a sophisticated reader can identify its major strengths and weaknesses. As a rule of thumb, *enough detail should be written in this section so that a reader, if the reader desired, could replicate the study in its entirety.* Unfortunately, this basic principle is often violated. Statements about the number of subjects in the study, how the subjects were chosen, the rationale for the selection procedure, and how the subjects were assigned to treatment groups, if the study is of an experimental nature, are found in this section of the article. The reader should be aware that inappropriate selection or assignment of subjects to treatment groups can invalidate an otherwise fine study.

The second part of the method section of a research article should describe *in detail* the independent variable (what the experimenter provides or does to the subject) including a description of any apparatus used in the study. In addition, this section includes a description of the dependent variable (how the subject is evaluated) including a careful description of the dependent measure. Other points included in this section are a description of how the data were gathered or recorded, a discussion of the rationale underlying the statistical analysis used in the study, and a discussion concerning the experimental design of the study. Oftentimes these points are not adequately discussed, or have not been carefully considered in the implementation of a study; therefore studies should be read from a critical perspective. For excellent discussions on how to analyze the design of studies, consult Campbell and Stanley (1963), Barber (1973), and Kerlinger (1973a).

Results

The results section of a research article reports the statistical findings of the study. Looking through journal articles, an unsophisticated reader might think that an infinite number of statistical procedures are used in research studies, thus making the task of understanding these results hopelessly complex. Behind all these complex statistical notations, however, are a few basic concepts that can greatly simplify the nature of the results section of research articles.

As a generalization, there are five types of general statistical treatments a teacher would most likely identify while reading educational research articles. The five general treatments are discussed in Figure 22–7. In this figure the general purpose of each of the treatments as well as the statistical symbols representing the most frequently used statistics in each category are presented.

In the first category, statistics dealing with central tendencies, i.e., those that refer to the mean, median, or mode, are included. In research studies, by far the most frequent reported statistic is *M* (the mean or average score). Material on this was presented in the chapter on testing. The second category refers to variability (the amount of dispersion of scores within a group). You will find that almost any study that reports *M* also reports the degree of dispersal of scores *(S.D.)*. Since most other complex statistics dealing with group differences based on the difference between the means also use the *S.D.* in the computation, the *S.D.* is reported in the study. The computation of this statistic is found in the Appendix at the end of the book.

If the researcher is interested in the relationship between two or more variables, then some type of correlational statistic is reported. Theoretically it is possible to have correlational scores from +1.00 to −1.00. A correlation of +1.00 means that a perfect positive or direct relationship exists between the measured variables (as the value of one variable goes up, the value of the other variable goes up in the same manner). Conversely, a correlation of −1.00 means that as the value of one variable goes up, the value of the other variable goes down in the same precise manner. A third theoretical possibility would be a .00 correlation. In this situation the two variables would vary in a random fashion. Since perfect relationships are never obtained in studies, the correlations found are between +1.00 and −1.00. Depending on the type of study and the variables correlated, correlations are typically in the +.40 to −.40 range.

FIGURE 22–7
Most frequent statistics found in educational research studies

General category of statistical treatment	*Purpose of statistical treatment*	*Symbols of statistics frequently used by researchers*
Central tendency	To identify the average or most typical scores of a group	Mean *(M)*, median *(Mdn)*, mode *(Mo)*
Variability	To determine the degree of distribution of scores in a group	Standard deviation *(S.D.)*, variance
Relationship	To determine the degree of relationship between two or more variables; complex correlations are used to determine the interrelationships between several independent variables	Correlation *(r)*, multiple correlation *(R)*
Differences	To determine if there is a statistically significant difference between two or more groups	Between means—*t* or *F*, between variances—*F*, between correlations—*z*, between frequencies or proportions—χ^2
Factors	To determine the number of traits or abilities that underlie several variables	No symbol; discussed in terms of number of factors with eigenvalues over 1

Although many different types of correlational formulas are used, the most frequent is the Pearson product moment correlation. Other popular correlations include the point biserial *(r_{pb})* (used when dichotomous variables are studied, e.g., males and females) and multiple correlation *(R)*. In the latter case numerous variables are correlated to predict a single variable. Finally, when there is statistical need to control for a relationship between two variables and a possible contributing third variable, a first-order partial correlation technique is used. For example, let us assume an experimenter conducts a study in which two variables correlate significantly. As stated previously, correlation does not mean causation. It is possible that the relationship between the two variables is partially due to some other outside factor or factors that the experimenter had not considered. First-order partial correlation techniques allow the experimenter to identify complex statistical interactions of this sort.

One of the most popular statistical treatments of data in educational research is to determine whether differences exist between two or more means. In typical studies you will find differences computed between means *(t* or *F)*, between variances *(F)*, between correlations *(z)*, and between frequencies or proportions (χ^2). The most frequent statistical test of the difference between means is the *F* test, *usually* computed in connection with an analysis of variance (a statistic to determine whether the obtained means vary more than predicted from the population mean).

Finally, in your readings, you might find some studies that use factor analytic procedures. Generally factor analysis studies are conducted to determine whether certain clusters of traits or abilities can be identified on existing tests. For example, the WISC-R intelligence test has ten subtests. The researcher might want to conduct a study to determine the underlying nature of the ten subtests. Many psychologists have claimed that the subtest patterns can be used in clinical diagnosis. If those subtest scores do not represent "pure factors," then a clinical diagnosis could be faulty. A factor analytic study could be conducted with the WISC-R to determine the actual number of intellectual traits measured by the WISC-R. Generally the factor structure of the WISC-R has not been validated. As a statistical procedure, factor analysis is an extremely complex process which is studied by advanced graduate students in measurement.

Now that you have a vague idea of the general type of statistics you will most likely find in a journal, what does this all mean? Generally there are two statistical questions researchers are really concerned with: the degree of relationship between variables and the degree of differences between average group scores. Within this context, the broad concern of a researcher focuses on the nature of the relationship or difference obtained in the study. Since a research finding never proves any hypothesis conclusively, the researcher is interested to know the *probability* that the degree of the relationship between two variables or the obtained differences between group scores in the study is due to the treatment or the obtained relationship and is not due to chance.

To compute the probability that the degree of the relationship or the degree of difference between scores is due to chance requires special statistical tables. For example, assume a study is conducted comparing the relationship between performance on a readiness test (RT) and academic achievement in reading (R) and arithmetic (A) at the end of the first grade. For the RT-R relationship, the correlation is .42, and for the RT-A relationship the correlation is .27. Until such time as probability tables are consulted to determine the *statistical* significance of those relationships, nothing can be said about the probability *(p)* that the relationships could have been obtained by chance. When reading journal articles, you will note that the probability statement is written as $p < .05$, $p < .01$, and so on. The statement that the RT-R correlation is significant beyond or at the .01 level ($p < .01$) means that the odds are 1 in 100 of obtaining a correlation this large or larger, and the odds are 99 in 100 of obtaining a correlation this large or smaller. Since the experimenter has no way of determining whether the current study is one of the 99 in which the relationship was not due to chance or random error, the experimenter has to make a probability statement. If a relationship were reported significant at the .05 level ($p < .05$), the odds of that obtained relationship would be 95 out of 100. At the .001 level ($p < .001$), the odds of that obtained relationship would be 999 out of 1,000. Traditionally psychologists have used the .05, .01, and .001 levels. Depending on the purposes of the study as well as several other considerations, other significance levels may be used in studies.

Another way of looking at the *p* level is as a statistical statement of how much risk you are willing to take in believing that the obtained results are, in fact, worth believing. A .001 *p* level tells you that odds are less likely due to chance than if the *p* level were .01 or .05.

Although correlational studies are fairly popular with educational researchers, most researchers prefer experimental studies. In an experimental study, researchers are generally interested in the differences between two or more treatment and control groups. Oftentimes you will find in your reading a statistical treatment called an "analysis of variance" or "analysis of covariance." As a generalization, the findings from an analysis of variance or covariance will be reported in a form such as: "The main effect of grade was significant, $F(2,66) = 14.86$, $p < .01$. Essentially those numbers mean that an *F* score is computed based on an analysis of variance or analysis of covariance, and then the *F* score is referred to in an *F* probability table to determine to what extent the differences between whatever groups were studied could have been obtained by chance.

An interpretation of the above statistics is that the grade level contributed to a statistical difference in the means. Furthermore, the odds of obtaining such a difference are 99 out of 100. Just as in the correlational studies discussed, there is no way the experimenter can determine whether the difference was actually due to chance or due to real differences in treatments.

One final point needs to be discussed about statistical significance. It is very important for you to keep in mind that a statistically significant finding does not necessarily imply an "instructionally" significant finding. For example, assume an experimenter compared two groups of students on a 100-item multiple-choice test and these two groups had received two different treatments. Group A obtained a 74.1 average and Group B achieved a 70.2 average. A statistical comparison of the differences is computed and found to be statistically significant at the .01 level ($p < .01$). A glance at the average figures suggests that the real magnitude of difference between the two groups is not very large and probably does not represent any real *significant instructional difference* between the two treatments. In this case, common sense prevails over a statistical finding.

Discussion

The discussion section of a research article draws attention to the key findings of the study. Typically such statements as: "The results of the present research study suggest. . . . Compared to Jones's study, the current study. . . . These results can be explained by. . . . The results of the present study have implications. . . . Suggestions for future studies include. . . ." are found in this section of the article. The discussion sections of research articles focus on comparisons between the study in question and other studies; discuss implications based on theories, hypotheses, or models; point out the methodological limitations of the study; and identify future research possibilities.

SUMMARY

The purpose of this chapter was to identify the main professional library resources available to educators. Second, an introduction to the format and structure of research articles was presented to help you interpret statistical studies with a little more sophistication. Realistically, many educators are never exposed to statistics or research design, and are thus deprived of reading a great deal of professional literature. As stated previously, to be truly competent in this area you would need advanced training.

We urge you to read research articles. The good ideas in education are usually derived from research studies, but oftentimes it takes many years before the research ideas get translated for the classroom teacher. Complex decision making requires competence and contact with up-to-date information. To be deprived of a large body of current knowledge in our field because of a lack of skills in reading articles of this nature is unfortunate. A basic course in statistics or research design should help you become a better consumer of our literature.

SELF-TEST

1. What type of books are *CIJE* and *RIE?*
2. Which book would you consult if you were given an assignment to review the reliability and validity studies of a standardized published test?
3. In which section of a journal article would you most likely find a justification for the study?
   a. Abstract.
   b. Introduction.
   c. Method.
   d. Results.
   e. Discussion.
4. In which section of a journal article would you most likely find the justification for the choice of the statistical treatment of the study?
   a. Abstract.
   b. Introduction.
   c. Method.
   d. Results.
   e. Discussion.
5. In which two sections of a journal article would you most likely find an analysis of where other research on the topic has been in error or has been incomplete?
   a. Introduction, method.
   b. Introduction, results.
   c. Introduction, discussion.
   d. Method, results.
   e. Method, discussion.
   f. Results, discussion.
6. In which section of a journal article should a precise definition of the independent variable be found?
   a. Introduction.
   b. Method.
   c. Results.
   d. Discussion.
7. If you read a study in which a correlation of −.81 was obtained between variable A and variable B, what could be said about the nature of the relationship?
   a. As the value of one variable went up, the value of the other variable went up accordingly.
   b. Not enough information is given to draw any conclusion about the relationship of the two variables.
   c. As the value of one variable went up, the value of the other variable went down accordingly.
   d. Very little relationship exists between the two variables.
8. In study A the probability of the differences between a control and experimental group was found to be $p < .05$, in study B the probability of the differences was found to be $p < .01$, in study C the probability was $p < .001$, and in study D the probability was $p < .025$. Of the four studies, in which study could you be surest of the results?

a. A
b. B
c. C
d. D

9. State two reasons why journal articles are usually the preferred sources over review articles in a given research area.
10. Given a research article you have read, state the strategies you should use to apply the information to your class.

ANSWER KEY TO BOXED QUESTIONS

1–2. Answers to these questions obviously depend on your library and the topic you choose to research.

3. Buros's *7th Mental Measurement Yearbook.*

ANSWER KEY TO SELF-TEST

1. Comprehensive indexes to professional educational literature.
2. Buros's *7th Mental Measurement Yearbook.*
3. *b*
4. *c*
5. *c*
6. *b*
7. *c*
8. *c*
9. They are more current and less likely to be biased.
10. *a.* Determine whether the article has any instructional payoff for your class.
    b. Adapt the idea in the article to the class you are teaching.
    c. Verify the results in your class.

Chapter 23

Intelligence: A critical issue in schooling

AN EDUCATIONAL PSYCHOLOGY BOOK would be incomplete without a chapter on the nature of intelligence and its relation to educational and instructional decision making. At a broad level, such diverse topics as how preschool and elementary school programs should be run, issues associated with exceptional children (gifted, mentally retarded, and learning disabled), and issues associated with child-rearing practices have been profoundly influenced by many of the theoretical viewpoints reviewed in this chapter. Some examples of specific educational programs or administrative strategies that have been at least partially based on various theories of intelligence include numerous Head Start programs, cognitive training programs in special education, school busing issues, early environmental enrichment experiences for lower-socioeconomic children in the children's place of residence, and television programs for the preschooler.

Not only have the theories had a significant impact on broad educational decisions, but also teachers are constantly confronted with questions related to intelligence. Most schools administer group intelligence tests, employ psychologists who administer individual IQ tests, have parent-teacher conferences in which IQ test results are discussed, and make educational decisions about students based on their performance on intelligence tests. In addition, the topic of intelligence has taken on an increasing importance in educational circles due to the issues associated with the degree to which intelligence is related to one's genetic or environmental background.

Of particular interest is the Jensen controversy, a hotly contested topic concerned with the degree to which performance on intelligence tests by different groups of people in our population (blacks versus whites) is related to the genetic or environmental background of the group. For you to be aware of these issues and make enlightened decisions about these topics are the purposes of this chapter, if for no other reason than to enable you to answer questions from nonprofessionals in the community who are curious about this topic. Essentially, this chapter discusses the problems associated with defining this construct, traces how the conceptualizations of intelligence have evolved over the years, identifies six major current theoretical viewpoints concerning the nature of intelligence, presents some of the unresolved issues about intelligence, describes the nature of group and individual IQ tests, and thoroughly reviews the types of decisions that can be based legitimately on intelligence test data. The chapter concludes by discussing the topic of intelligence from an instructional point of view while identifying the trends that most likely will occur in the immediate future.

At the conclusion of this chapter, you should be able to:

1. Compare and contrast the various historical and current theoretical viewpoints concerning the nature of intelligence and how it is studied.
2. Identify the major issues and controversies in this field and explain the differing viewpoints on the issues.
3. Describe the characteristics of group and individual intelligence tests.
4. Identify the types of legitimate educational and instructional decisions that can be made based on IQ test data.
5. State what is likely to occur in the future concerning the study and measure of intelligence.

INTELLIGENCE DEFINED: A CRITICAL ISSUE

To start our discussion of intelligence, it would make sense to identify some of the more popular definitions of this construct. Compare your beliefs about the nature of intelligence to some of these definitions.

1. Intelligence is the ability to deal with abstractions.
2. Intelligence is the ability to deal with problems.
3. Intelligence is the ability to learn.
4. Intelligence includes the ability to withstand stress and distraction.
5. Intelligence is the general ability a person has to respond effectively to the environment.
6. Intelligence is the cumulative set of competencies an individual has acquired through interaction with an environment over a period of time.
7. Intelligence is whatever one chooses to measure on an intelligence test.

A careful analysis of these definitions should kindle some questions in your mind. Each definition emphasizes *a different aspect* of human behavior! Assume you are a psychologist and you need to develop a theory or a test to measure intelligence. What types of behaviors would you emphasize in your theory? What would be the content of your test items? What type of test items would you include? The behaviors you might emphasize in your theory based on the first definition of intelligence naturally would be quite different from the behaviors representative of the third definition. Obviously, the test items also would be different in each case.

Some psychologists would argue that a person's general ability to respond effectively to the environment best represents the nature of intelligence; hence, whatever one chooses to measure on an intelligence test is a valid measure of intelligence (Butcher, 1968; Eysenck, 1971). Aside from the circularity of this position, even if it possesses certain wisdom, the psychologist is still confronted with the same problem of choosing items to measure this construct. Stated succinctly, the psychology profession has been unable to agree upon those sets of behaviors that are thought to be representative of intelligence, and yet many people still think of intelligence as a specific existing entity that *causes* human behavior. That is, Johnny does poorly in school *because* he is lacking "intelligence."

We cannot provide you with a neat definition of *intelligence,* and you should be aware that the inability of our profession to originate some workable definitions of this construct has been a thorn in our side. To have developed tests, programs, and theories of intelligence without a satisfactory definition of the term is unsettling. At any rate, let us continue our discussion by taking a brief excursion back in time to the late 1800s.

HISTORICAL VIEWPOINTS OF INTELLIGENCE

Late 1800s: Galton, physical skills

In the late 1800s psychologists conceptualized intelligence as consisting of various tasks such as the ability to discriminate the weight of objects, the ability to make auditory discriminations, the speed of the subject's response, and similar tasks. This orientation was based on the belief that since the human body processed information about the environment through the senses, the ability to make sensory discriminations should be directly related to the intellectual capacity of the individual. Galton (1883) was one of the leaders of this orientation. Galton's approach, however, was soon discredited because performance on Galton-type tasks did not correlate with other tasks thought to represent intelligence.

Early 1900s: Binet, general ability

Aware of the inability of the Galton scales to predict academic achievement, Binet greatly influenced the mental measurement movement in the early 1900s by postulating that intelligence consists of a general intellectual ability ("g") to respond effectively toward the environment. Binet's interest in intelligence stemmed from his position with the Paris school system, where he was asked to help the schools identify potentially unsuccessful students.

Collaborating with Simon, Binet constructed a new type of intelligence test consisting of 30 "mental" items arranged in ascending order of difficulty. The items chosen for the test purportedly measured a student's general ability and were designed to predict academic successes and failures. Included on the early Binet test were items measuring comprehension, attention, memory, and logical abilities. The only rationale for including a task on the test was if the task discriminated the student's ability to perform successully or unsuccessfully on school tasks. The current Stanford-Binet Intelligence Test (a popular individual IQ test) is an offshoot of this approach. A description of the Stanford-Binet test is found later in the chapter.

Late 1930s: Thurstone, specific abilities

Within a few years after the Binet scales were developed some psychologists began to question Binet's conceptualizations concerning "g." These psychologists were quick to note that "g" did not address the issues related to uneven mental development. Psychologists of this persuasion observed that people are not uniformly competent; some are outstanding on some mental tasks but quite poor on others. Theories were thought to be needed to bridge the gap between the general ability ("g") notion of Binet and the observation that people possess unique constellations of abilities.

The early works of Thurstone (1938) typify this viewpoint. Thurstone eventually identified nine such abilities: space, perceptual speed, numerical facility, verbal comprehension, rote memory, induction, word fluency, deduction, and general reasoning.

CURRENT VIEWS OF INTELLIGENCE

Currently psychologists view the construct of intelligence or cognitive development from a variety of perspectives. There is no clear trend. Six different orientations are discussed in this section of the chapter.

In order to present you with an overview of some representative *current* approaches to the study of intelligence, Figure 23–1 summarizes each position. You may want to refer to the figure now in order to identify the underlying premise of each approach, or you may want to wait until the end of this section of the chapter and use the figure as an encapsulated summary of each position. For the purposes of this part of the chapter, psychologists and psychological approaches have been chosen that typify the six most frequently used approaches to study complex intelligent and cognitive behaviors in humans.

Guilford: Structure of intellect model

Some psychologists, as represented by Guilford (1967), have attempted to identify the nature of specific intellectual abilities by generating models of intelligence that postulate numerous intellectual skills. According to Guilford, most of the current theories of intelligence lack a systematic way of viewing the nature of intelligence. Since the nature of intelligence is not clearly specified, the current measures of intelligence suffer from the same difficulty. This point should become obvious when you study the characteristics of IQ tests. Guilford suggests that since people obviously possess uneven constellations of mental abilities, the theories, models, and measures of intelligence ought to reflect these differences in a systematic fashion.

FIGURE 23–1
The basic underlying principles for representative theoretical positions

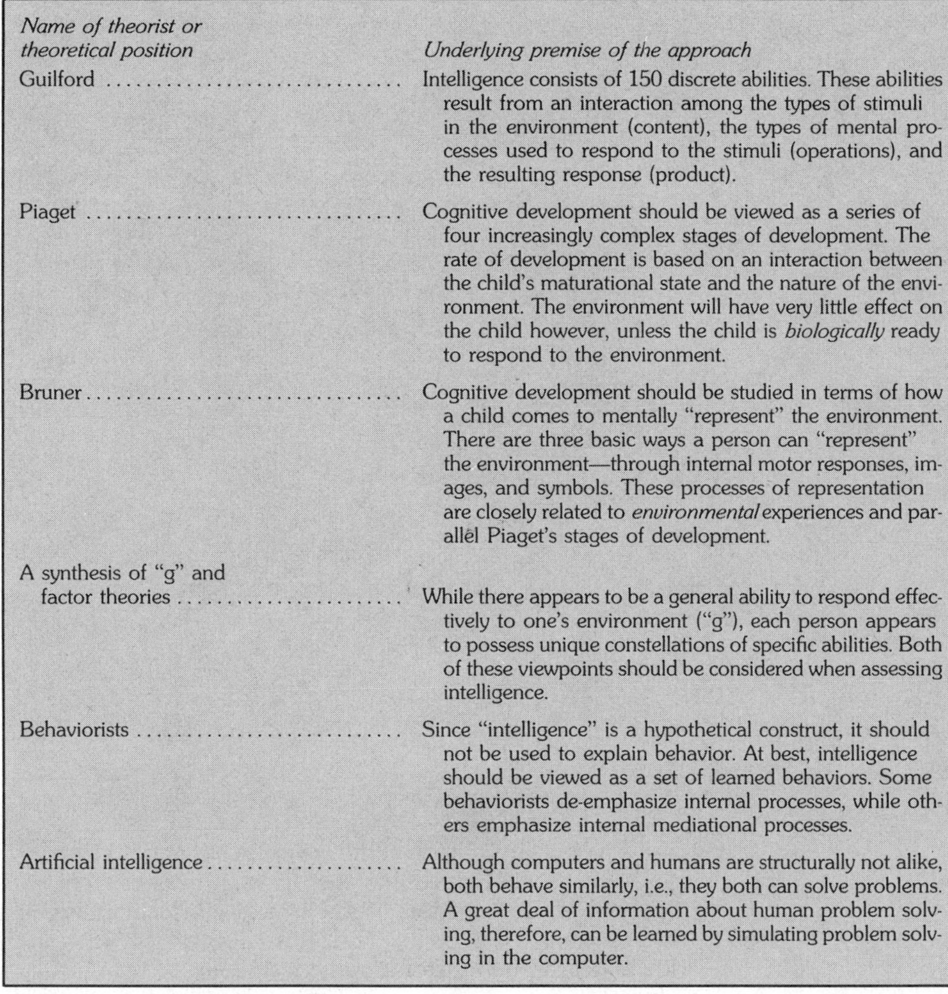

Name of theorist or theoretical position	*Underlying premise of the approach*
Guilford	Intelligence consists of 150 discrete abilities. These abilities result from an interaction among the types of stimuli in the environment (content), the types of mental processes used to respond to the stimuli (operations), and the resulting response (product).
Piaget	Cognitive development should be viewed as a series of four increasingly complex stages of development. The rate of development is based on an interaction between the child's maturational state and the nature of the environment. The environment will have very little effect on the child however, unless the child is *biologically* ready to respond to the environment.
Bruner	Cognitive development should be studied in terms of how a child comes to mentally "represent" the environment. There are three basic ways a person can "represent" the environment—through internal motor responses, images, and symbols. These processes of representation are closely related to *environmental* experiences and parallel Piaget's stages of development.
A synthesis of "g" and factor theories	While there appears to be a general ability to respond effectively to one's environment ("g"), each person appears to possess unique constellations of specific abilities. Both of these viewpoints should be considered when assessing intelligence.
Behaviorists	Since "intelligence" is a hypothetical construct, it should not be used to explain behavior. At best, intelligence should be viewed as a set of learned behaviors. Some behaviorists de-emphasize internal processes, while others emphasize internal mediational processes.
Artificial intelligence	Although computers and humans are structurally not alike, both behave similarly, i.e., they both can solve problems. A great deal of information about human problem solving, therefore, can be learned by simulating problem solving in the computer.

Guilford's approach makes use of a technique designed to identify and measure the nature of clusters of human intellectual abilities. Known as *factor analysis,* this technique determines which specific intellectual abilities appear to be correlated with each other, and which abilities appear to be independent of each other.

As currently conceived, Guilford's structure of intellect model postulates 150 specific components of intelligence based on *three* broad categories:

1. *Operations*—What one does to the environment, basic psychological processes.
2. *Contents*—The nature of the information in the environment, the kind of material or content to which the person responds.
3. *Products*—The result of an operation upon the content, which produces the final overt response.

As can be seen in Figure 23–2, within each broad category, there are subcategories that consist of five types of mental operations, five types of content (information from the environment), and six products. The products are the result of an interaction

FIGURE 23–2
Guilford's structure of intellect model

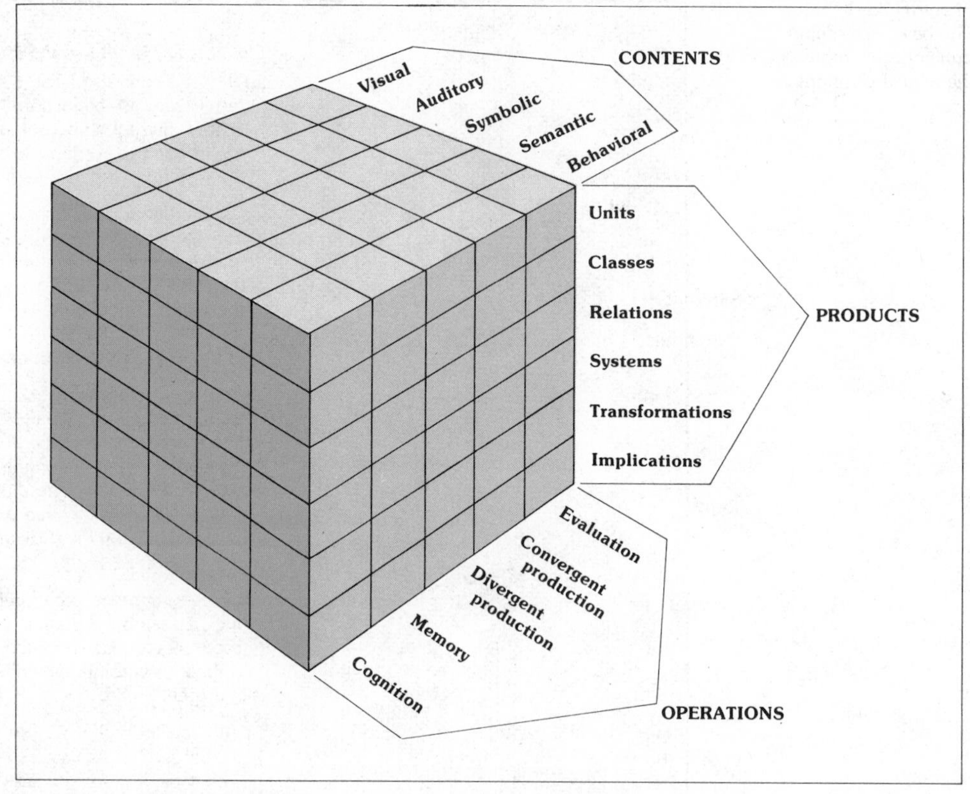

Source: Adapted from Guilford (1977).

between the information in the environment and a mental operation upon the information. Figure 23–3 identifies the 16 major components of the model and provides you with some examples of the type of intellectual tasks that each major component represents. At this point, more than 100 of the 150 postulated abilities have been identified through factor analytic techniques.

Guilford's structure of intellect model has served several useful functions for educators. Some school districts have used Guilford's model to develop aspects of their curriculum, and some commercial companies have used the model as a guide in the construction of curricular materials (Peabody Language Development Kit). Psychologists have also been quick to note that our most popular current intelligence tests [Stanford-Binet (S-B) and the Wechsler Intelligence Scale for Children–Revised (WISC-R)] *have almost totally ignored many of the abilities tapped by the upper levels of the operations and products categories* of the model. In other words, our current intelligence tests do not tap many of the abilities represented by the cubes of divergent production, evaluation, systems, transformations, and implications. Generally, convergent production rather than creative production has been measured on intelligence tests. Of course, the theoretical issue centers on whether the purpose of the IQ test is to assess the construct of intelligence or to predict academic performance. Since the manuals of both the Stanford-Binet and WISC-R intelligence tests (the two most popular individual IQ tests) make it abundantly clear that the purpose of the test is to assess an individual's potential for purposive and useful behavior (Wechsler, 1974a) or to provide a test that "differentiates between degrees of intellectual ability" (Terman & Merrill,

FIGURE 23–3
Guilford: 16 categories of intelligence

Category	*Nature of the category*	*Examples of possible test items*
Content		
1. Visual	Information in visual form	Color, shape, texture, size, continuity, dimensionality
2. Auditory	Information in auditory form	Music tones, phonemes, discrimination of spoken words, musical intervals, pitch, melodies
3. Symbolic	Information in the form of signs: the elements have no significance by themselves	Letters, numbers, codes, musical notations
4. Semantic	Information in the form of meanings	Words commonly attached to verbal thinking and communication
5. Behavioral	Nonverbal information involved in human interactions—awareness of other people and self	Interpret moods, states, and traits of oneself and others
Operations		
6. Cognition	Awareness, immediate discovery, recognition of information in various forms, comprehension	Recognition of stimuli that are incomplete (e.g., mutilated words or pictures), vocabulary words
7. Memory	Recognition and/or recall of previous stimuli in various forms and relations	Free recall, memory span, test for numbers
8. Divergent production	Generation of information from given information—emphasis on variety and quantity	Generate ideas, brainstorm, flexibility, and fluency
9. Convergent production	Generation of information from given information—emphasis on *one* solution	Relate diverse objects where a specific answer is required (in what way are a cat and dog alike?)
10. Evaluation	A process of comparing a product of information with known information	Must answer a "which," "is," or "does" question
Products		
11. Units	Things, segregated wholes, figures on grounds, or "chunks"	The student produces a product, such as filling in mutilated words, filling in incomplete words, defining vocabulary words, or identifying a characteristic of a person
12. Classes	Set of objects with one or more common properties	Student identifies the common attribute between two or more stimuli
13. Relations	Some kind of connection between two things	Student identifies the relational nature of two or more stimuli, e.g., "married to," "greater than"—analogies, serial order, etc.
14. Systems	Patterns or organizations of interdependent or interacting parts	Student identifies the rule to find the solution to problem, e.g., Which letter comes next? A, C, E, ______—What is the rule?
15. Transformations	Changes, revisions, modifications from one state to another	How would something look if it were changed? What would something be like if ______? How can the purpose of an object be changed to get a new result?
16. Implications	Something expected, anticipated, or predicted from given information	The ability to plan ahead, or predict what will *most* likely come next

1960), one wonders why these higher-order tasks are not included. For an excellent overview of Guilford's model, consult Guilford (1966 or 1967).

Piaget: A biological approach

Other psychologists such as Bruner (1964), J. Hunt (1961), and Piaget (1963) are not as concerned about studying the static structure of intelligence at a point in time as they are about studying the systematic, *dynamic* evolution of intelligence or cognitive development over a period of time. According to these developmental theorists, if we are to understand the nature of intelligence or cognitive abilities, it is very important to identify those processes that contribute to a change in development. What cognitive skills does an infant possess at birth, and how does the environment interact with the infant to produce qualitative and quantitive changes in development over a long period of time?

Piaget conceives of intelligence as the ability to adapt mentally to new situations. Viewed from a developmental perspective, the child is seen to evolve through four increasingly complex stages (Figure 23–4). Within each of the major stages are sub-stages. Based on a hierarchical sequential model of cognitive development, Piaget asserts that it is impossible for a person to solve the type of complex problems found in the formal operations stage of development unless that person has evolved through a series of prerequisite stages of development (Piaget, 1963).

According to Piaget, adult intelligence has as its basis sensorimotor activity that has undergone a qualitative series of changes. In the sensorimotor stage (0–2 years), much of the basic practical knowledge needed for the foundation of complex thought is formed. During the preoperational stage (2–7 years) the beginnings of language and the *reconstruction* of the sensorimotor experiences takes place. Images also develop during this stage. It is during the concrete operational stage of development (7–11 years) that the child begins to solve concrete problems, dealing with objects by using concrete mental operations. In this stage the child develops the ability to

FIGURE 23–4
Piaget's stages of intellectual development

*Stage**	*Characteristics*
Sensorimotor (0–2 years)	Basic perceptual-motor development; infant begins motoric interaction with the environment, begins to manipulate the environment
Preoperational (2–7 years)	Begins to use language in an egocentric manner, very self-centered intellectually; in latter part of this stage child can reach intellectual conclusions, but the conclusions are based on fleeting perceptual judgments; not based on a conceptual system of thought
Concrete operations (7–11 years)	Uses language system in a reliable, although concrete, fashion; understands concrete concepts such as $A > B > C \therefore A > C$ or $A + B = B + A$; begins to approach problems systematically, acquires conservational skills (knowledge that the *amount* of something does not change just because the outside appearance, shape, or length changes)
Formal operations (11+ years)	Can think abstractly, uses hypothetical-deductive reasoning, generalizes, can solve problems systematically, understands implications of past and future

* The ages associated with the stages of development should not be viewed as fixed. Children evolve through these stages at different rates of development.

FIGURE 23–5
Students in the formal operations stage of development should be able to solve problems systematically and logically

solve most of the famous conservation tasks (the principle that the number, volume, amount, weight, and mass of objects are not changed regardless of the shape or appearance of an object). For example, the child realizes that the amount of liquid in a beaker is the same even though it is poured into a different-shaped container, or the amount of pennies in a row remains the same even though the pennies are spread out. Piaget maintains that these tasks require complex mental operations characterized by flexibility in thought. The preoperational child, according to Piaget, does not have the flexibility in thought necessary to solve these tasks. The child in the concrete stage of development, however, cannot solve abstract problems requiring hypothetical-deductive mental operations. The child is also not very systematic in solving problems. As the child evolves into the fourth stage of development (formal operations—about 11 years of age in a typical child), the child begins to use hypothetical-deductive reasoning in a systematic fashion, loses the egocentric perspective of viewing the world, and comes to understand fully the implications of the past and the future (Figure 23–5).

According to Piaget, four factors determine the rate at which a child evolves through these predetermined stages of development:

1. *The biological maturation of the child*—Environmental experiences can have an effect on a child only when the child is biologically "ready" for the experience.
2. *The activity of the child*—A change in cognitive development can occur when the child actively interacts with the environment in some meaningful manner commensurate with the child's biological maturity.
3. *The influence of the environment on the child*—A change in cognitive development can occur when the environment provides the child with cognitive information

through teaching and/or social interaction if the child is biologically "ready" for the experience.

4. *Equilibration*—Ultimately, significant changes in cognitive growth are said to occur when a child is confronted with situations in which the environment is at variance with what the child believes to be correct. In order to reduce the uncertainty, the child changes his/her response accordingly.

In Piagetian terminology, the equilibration model is based on the processes of assimilation and accommodation. For assimilation, the child is said to acquire information from the environment, while in accommodation the child modifies the concepts (schemata or structures) the child has of the environment to more closely represent a better solution or another solution to a problematic situation.

As an example of this process, assimilation occurs when a person *responds* in the same way to a stimulus event that resembles a previous stimulus event. To provide a precise example, if a person wants to get into a room in which the door is shut, the person *responds* to the door in the same manner as she has done in the past. Accommodation, on the other hand, occurs when a person responds to a stimulus event differently than the manner in which he had responded in the past. To use the door example, the person may decide to fasten to the door knob an apparatus for doing arm and leg exercises, thereby using the door in a novel manner. Within the Piagetian framework cognitive growth is said to occur when a child learns to make new responses to old stimuli, particularly when the old responses are perceived as discrepant with the new responses. For example, the child learns to say "cow" when the child sees a cow instead of saying "horse."

Notice that Piaget emphasizes the interactions between biological and environmental variables. In Piagetian theory, the biological tendency to develop at a predetermined rate is the critical variable in the developmental interactive process. This *does not* mean that the environment is not necessary for cognitive development! It means that the experiences a child has with the environment will have little or no influence on cognitive development unless the child is *biologically* "ready" for the experience. From a Piagetian perspective, heredity and environment cannot be separated. The environment obviously plays an *extremely* important role in cognitive development, but only if the child possesses the maturational readiness for the experience. This point is often misunderstood. Put another way, the maturational readiness of a child at any given point in time is a product of the past interactions between numerous biological and environmental factors. Justice cannot really be done to Piaget's theory with this brief presentation. His prodigious output has been unequaled in 20th-century psychology.

To summarize his viewpoints, seven educational implications from his work are presented. Notice how many of these viewpoints coincide with the learning principles mentioned throughout this book.

1. Children should be active. They learn best when actively exploring their environment.
2. Children should not be pushed or accelerated into learning material beyond their level of development. The child will be incapable of accommodating to the experience.
3. Activities selected by the children aid in their cognitive growth.
4. Teachers should purposefully arrange classroom environments to facilitate cognitive development and to encourage active exploring.

5. When interacting with a child, the teacher should attempt to understand the child's cognitive level of development by applying the "clinical interview" technique to determine what the child believes is true.
6. Piaget's general theory would suggest that the open education or free-school format might be especially fruitful (Weber, 1971).
7. Some psychologists have attempted to construct tests to reflect Piaget's stages of cognitive development (Uzgiris & Hunt, 1975). Other educators have attempted to apply aspects of his theory to the teaching of reading (Elkind, 1967).

For the interested reader there are many well-written summaries of Piaget's work. Before you decide to read original Piagetian works, however, we suggest you read several overviews of his ideas. Piaget is a difficult writer to understand. Summaries include: Athey and Rubadeau (1970), Boyle (1969), Flavell (1963), Furth (1970), Ginsburg and Opper (1969), Phillips (1969), and Wadsworth (1971).

Bruner: An environmental approach

Although greatly influenced by Piaget, Bruner's views about the development of cognitive skills are not a restatement of Piaget's. Bruner has emphasized the role of culture and specific environmental influences in the development of cognitive abilities to a much greater extent than Piaget. According to Bruner, humans actively seek to reconstruct and recategorize the environment based on their learned conceptions of the environment. Evolving through three stages of development (enactive, iconic, and symbolic representation), humans come to *learn* those strategies for "representing" reality. Much of Bruner's research has focused on the "teachability" of cognitive abilities, particularly those cognitive abilities that Piaget claims cannot be taught unless the child is biologically ready for the experience.

Within the Brunerian viewpoint, enactive representation is the ability to represent reality through motor responses, iconic representation is the ability to represent images based upon the environment, and symbolic representation is the ability to represent reality through the use of symbols (either language or pictorial symbols). Only after a child can represent reality adequately through these modes does the child learn to manipulate the representations to solve complex cognitive problems.

Bruner postulates that any intellectual experience can be honestly understood by a child at almost any time in a child's development if the experience is commensurate with the child's representational level of development. This basic challenge to the Piagetian view has created considerable controversy in educational circles. Contrasted with Piaget, the task for educators operating within a Brunerian frame of reference is to convert what is known into a form that can be mastered by a child at any level of development.

Bruner's ideas have had a particularly strong impact on discovery learning strategies, theories of instruction, the modern math curriculum, and the role of language in cognitive development.

Since the Brunerian-Piagetian controversy is one of the most important controversies in developmental cognitive psychology, and since both of these theorists have had a significant impact on educational practices, we urge you to read additional sources on the subject. Some particularly pertinent articles and books include: Anglin (1973); Bruner (1971); and Bruner, Olver, and Greenfield (1966).

A synthesis of "g" and factor models

Some psychologists view intelligence as a very explicit concept (Butcher & Lomax, 1972; McNemar, 1964) and disagree with both the factor or specific abilities approach of Guilford and the developmental approaches of Piaget and Bruner. Other psychologists suggest that a synthesis must be reached between the "g" proponents and the factor theorists (Cattell, 1963; Eysenck, 1967; Vernon, 1961). While these psychologists feel that "g" is a somewhat useful construct, they think the nature of the structural relationship between "g" and specific abilities should be more clearly delineated. According to this viewpoint, people do possess unique constellations of abilities, and these factors ought to be studied. Figure 23–6 is a schematic diagram of the hierarchical relationships between "g" and specific factors. You should notice in this model that the specific factors in the verbal-educational and spatial-mechanical categories have an influence on the broader categories. Models such as Vernon's make an attempt to specify the relationships between specific factors and broad abilities.

Several behavioral positions

Some behaviorists argue strongly that since intelligence is nothing more than a hypothetical construct, any approach that attempts to specify the structure of this construct is doomed to failure and is folly at best (Skinner, 1953). Skinner points out that it is circular reasoning to use a *descriptive* label (e.g., "intelligence") as an *explanation* of behavior.

Other more moderate behaviorists maintain that intellectual development consists of combinations of gradual changes in specific performances resulting from environmental interactions. These behaviors can be studied by identifying the current environmental circumstances as well as the results of previous learning that have contributed to this behavior (Rohwer, Ammon & Cramer, 1974). Gagné's (1977) model, which postulates eight levels of learning from basic classical conditioning through problem-solving skills, is particularly germane to this point (see Chapters 5 and 8). According

FIGURE 23–6
A hierarchical structure of mental abilities

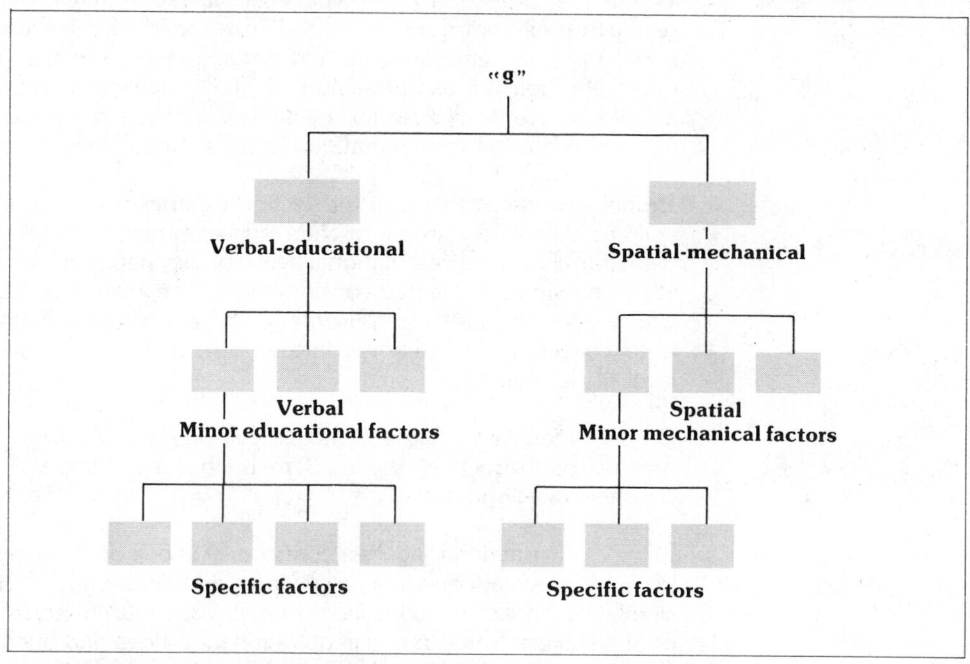

Source: Adapted from Vernon (1950).

to Gagné, all problem-solving skills or intelligence can be analyzed in terms of the prerequisite performance necessary to solve a specified problem; hence, once a problem has been analyzed in terms of its component parts, it is possible to teach the prerequisites necessary to solve the problem. Obviously the task analysis implications of Gagné have had a strong impact on the instructional design movement in recent years and, to some extent, contrast sharply with the Piagetian viewpoint.

Artificial intelligence

Artificial intelligence is a very specialized area concerned with simulating intelligent behavior by computer. This approach is based on the proposition that if a sophisticated person sitting in one room cannot distinguish between a computer's response and a person's typewritten response in another room, then intelligence has been created in the computer. Those psychologists who are studying this approach feel a great deal can be learned by analyzing how the computer responds to problems. Opponents of this approach indicate that a computer is not constructed like a human and does not solve problems in a manner similar to a human, therefore any data obtained by this approach cannot be extrapolated to humans. Since the computer is designed by humans and may not reflect the same structure and functions as humans, extrapolating information from a computer is tenuous at best.

For example, Neisser (1976) argues that computers differ from humans in three major ways. First, human thinking evolves over a long period of time in an environmental setting and requires a great deal of interaction. Second, human thinking is closely related to values, beliefs, attitudes, and feelings. Finally, humans have many different motives that interact simultaneously with the intellect. A particular behavior may be a function of many variables, all interacting with each other at the same time. What is important today may be far less so tomorrow, and vice versa.

Viewed from a different perspective, Simon (1976) suggests that we need a valid process theory that describes the performance underlying complex tasks, i.e., a model that describes the processes involved in performing a task as well as the interrelationships of the processes. When conceptualized from this framework, the noun *intelligence* is changed to the adjectival form *intelligent* to modify performance. Intelligent performance is any performance in which the task is performed correctly with little waste of motion. Since computers can simulate intelligent performance, perhaps a great deal can be learned from the computer and the process of programming used to simulate intelligence. More specific than a general theory of intelligence, this approach focuses on the performance of specific tasks. Recognizing that a computer and the human mind certainly are not analogous, we can still learn a great deal from a computer in terms of identifying the prerequisites necessary to solve complex problems. The relationship to task analysis is apparent.

Programs have been written so that the computer can *learn* the game of checkers, *solve* verbal algebra problems, *play* chess, *write* basic symphonic music, *recognize* verbal material in any book by stating the words (decode printed material), and *answer* complex questions within a specifically defined subject matter area. Although researchers are still a long way from totally simulating intelligent behavior in any general sense, a great deal of progress has been made in this area in recent years. When one considers the fact that computers have been in existence for only a very brief period of time, the progress has been phenomenal. Of particular interest for the serious student is Newell and Simon's (1972) book on simulated general problem solving and Klahr's (1976) thought-provoking chapter on an attempt to simulate on a computer the performance of the Piagetian conservation tasks mentioned earlier in this chapter.

Summary of current trends

As can be seen from the earlier part of this chapter, psychologists have studied the construct of intelligence and cognitive processes from many different perspectives. Some psychologists, such as Guilford, Vernon, and Thurstone, have tended to focus their efforts on the specific components of intelligence. Other psychologists have been more concerned with how people come to know and become competent problem solvers through interactions with their environment over time (Piaget and Bruner). Still others have argued strongly against studying the construct of intelligence per se. These psychologists suggest that the focus or unit of study should be the relationship between clearly identified stimuli, the responses that follow, and the results of the response. Representative of this viewpoint are the behaviorist positions of Skinner and Gagné's hierarchical learning model. Another strategy has been to simulate human intelligence through the use of computers. Based on the principle that computers are capable of simulating human intelligence, psychologists of this persuasion have been able to demonstrate the characteristics of many rudimentary forms of intelligent behavior with the computer.

We have certainly not exhausted all the viewpoints concerning human intelligence. Other psychologists have suggested that there are basically two types of intelligence with clearly delineated heredity and environment components. Although these theories have taken many different forms and emphases, the recent works of Cattell (1971), Hebb (1941), and Kagan and Klein (1973), as well as the controversial Jensen (1973) studies on hereditability and IQ discuss aspects of this viewpoint. Still other psychologists, as represented by Wechsler (1974b), have been concerned with the problems of measuring this construct. Many psychologists of this orientation have not been particularly concerned with the theoretical issues raised in this chapter. Other psychologists have been concerned with the very real pragmatic question concerning how a child's intelligence might be increased through a variety of early intervention programs (Deutsch, 1964; Scarr & Weinberg, 1976).

In the near future it appears that a major paradigm shift is going to take place in educational circles concerning the study of intelligence (Glaser, 1976b; Resnick, 1976). Given our inability to get a handle on this topic as currently conceptualized, we predict that instructional psychologists will start to study the general and specific prerequisites of academic tasks in such a way that diagnostic-prescriptive information can be obtained from tests designed to provide instructionally useful information to instructors as opposed to tests designed to give us broad predictive data of a comparative nature. Because of the interest in instructionally useful information, the heredity-environment dispute most likely will be replaced with questions concerning *how the environment* may be arranged best to help a student perform specific academic tasks. Further, we predict that the information-processing point of view as presented in Chapter 5 and the task analysis point of view expressed in Chapter 8 will be the bases from which new approaches to the study of intelligence will develop. Instead of focusing on intelligence, the new orientation will have as its basis the study of *intelligent behavior* and the concomitant underlying *mental processes* associated with intelligent behavior.

The point we wish to raise is that there is very little agreement concerning how this construct should be defined, *how* this construct should be studied, *what* should be studied, or what we can conclude about the nature of intelligence. One sound conclusion would be to proceed with extreme caution before making any pronouncements about a student's "intelligence."

To make this point even more emphatic, we have identified in a simplified, concise form some of the current major unresolved issues in this field. As you consider each of these issues, try to relate it to the inherent definitional problems identified at the beginning of the chapter. Four major issues are delineated.

1. *The heredity versus environment issue:*
   Since intelligence is basically learned, it is environmentally determined (Bereiter & Engelmann, 1966; J. Hunt, 1961).
   Approximately 80 percent of the variance of intelligence is genetically determined; the remaining 20 percent reflects the influence of environment on intelligence (Burt, 1966; Jensen, 1969).
2. *The heredity versus environment (racial differences) issue:*
   Depending on the study, a 10–15-point differential in IQ is found between whites and blacks on existing IQ tests. This difference is basically due to environmental differences experienced by the two groups (Dreger & Miller, 1968; Klineberg, 1963).
   Depending on the study, a 10–15-point differential is found between whites and blacks on existing IQ tests. This difference is due basically to hereditary differences between the groups (Jensen, 1969; Shuey, 1966).
3. *The heredity versus environment (importance of early intervention) issue:*
   "Intelligence" becomes a relatively fixed entity after the child is about eight years of age. Proper early intervention is important to insure that a child reaches his/her innate ability (Bloom, 1964; Deutsch, 1964).
   Generally speaking, the early intervention programs such as Head Start have not been overly successful in permanently increasing a child's "intelligence," although some programs have proven to be more successful than others (Cicirelli et al., 1969).
4. *The structural nature of intelligence issue:*
   Intelligence consists of 150 specific abilities (Guilford, 1977).
   Intelligence consists of eight or nine major abilities (Thurstone, 1938).
   Intelligence consists of two levels of abilities (Cattell, 1941; Hebb, 1941; Jensen, 1969).
   Intelligence consists of a general ability to respond effectively to the environment (Burt, 1955).
   Intelligence consists of a hierarchical order of abilities with a general ability at the apex (Humphreys, 1962; Vernon, 1950).

We could present many additional unresolved problems: statements about such issues as the *types* of early experiences necessary for intelligence to flourish, the *relationship between language* and intelligence, the *characteristics* of intelligence tests that purport to measure this hypothetical construct, the *relationship between personality styles and motivational tendencies* and intelligence, the *power* of existing IQ tests to predict academic achievement, the *general purposes* of IQ tests, the *neurophysiological basis* of intelligent behavior, and on and on.

As an interesting, although frightening, sidelight, all too often it appears that the conclusions arrived at by psychologists who study intelligence are more closely related to their politics [conservatives tend to be hereditarians and liberals tend to be environmentalists (Pastore, 1949; Sherwood & Nataupsky, 1968)] than to the inconclusive data, which suggest a suspension of judgment is in order. Read carefully the conclusion arrived at by Loehlin, Lindzey, and Spuhler (1975) after they did an extensive study of racial differences in intelligence.

> We have been concerned privately by the number of instances in which the political and social preferences of the investigation apparently have grossly biased their interpretation of data. Such distortions appear to be as prevalent at *environmentalist* as at *hereditarian* extremes [emphasis ours] . . . consequently, any evidence deriving from a single unreplicated study must be viewed with more than the normal caution stemming from statistical considerations.

Although we have been cautioning you to reserve judgment about many of these issues, from a practical perspective that is impossible. Practitioners cannot wait until all the theoretical and empirical data are validated. "Best bet" decisions have to be made daily. While ivory-tower theorizing continues, educators need answers now.

1. State two criticisms of the "g" theory of intelligence.
2. In what basic way are Piaget's and Bruner's theories similar and how do the theories differ?
3. Based on Guilford's structure of intellect model, how might current intelligence tests be deficient?
4. Although Piaget's theory may be characterized as emphasizing a biological point of view, the theory actually is strongly interactionist in its emphasis. Explain how Piaget's biological point of view relates to interaction with the environment.

BROAD DECISION MAKING AND INTELLIGENCE

As stated previously, many of the theoretical viewpoints expressed in this chapter have been used as the basis for the development of preschool programs, elementary school programs, and programs for various exceptional children (mentally retarded, gifted, and learning disabled). In addition, some of these theories have had profound implications for child-rearing practices. Again, to refresh your recall some of the *broad* educational decisions that have been made based on theories of intelligence include Head Start programs, cognitive training programs in special education, school busing issues, and early environmental enrichment experiences in the home. You might want to refer back to specific theoretical positions presented earlier in this chapter to identify additional instructional decisions influenced by the theories. Our purpose is to present you with a brief discussion of several of those broad decisions. Obviously, much work has been done on each of those decisions and a full chapter easily could be written for each.

Head Start

One of the rationales for Head Start programs (preschool intervention programs for the economically disadvantaged) is that experiences in the preschool age are *critical* for the development of intelligence, and therefore children ought to be exposed to an optimal environment at this age in order to stimulate intellectual growth (Bloom, 1964; Deutsch, 1964; J. Hunt, 1961). According to this viewpoint, if children are not exposed to an *optimal* preschool environment, permanent, subtle intellectual impairment may result. This issue is highly complex and has not been resolved easily. Such questions as the length of training necessary to effect a change, the type of environmental experiences necessary for optimal intellectual growth, the age of the child when these experiences may have an effect, and the degree of parental involvement in the programs simply have not been adequately addressed at this time. This type of program, however, probably will be with us for a long time to come. There is some indication that earlier intervention, more parental involvement, and a more extensive and integrated approach to preschool education are the trends of the future in this area of decision making.

Special education

Another example comes from the field of special education. Many programs for the young mentally retarded or learning-disabled child have as an integral part various sensorimotor and perceptual training activities. Based on the point of view that higher-order mental processes stem from sensorimotor and perceptual experiences, these programs attempt to teach lower-order skills in order to facilitate higher-order mental processes (Delacato, 1963; Frostig & Maslow, 1973; Kephart, 1971). Although based on different theoretical rationales, each of these programs assumes that a general vertical transfer takes place between the lower-order sensorimotor and perceptual skills and higher-order cognitive processes. Many research studies, however, have not substantiated the efficacy of this orientation. For an excellent review of the research on this topic, see Hammill, Goodman, and Wiederholt (1974). At this point, there is a de-emphasis on these approaches. In the immediate future a trend toward a task analysis approach is apparent.

Busing: Change of the social structure

As a final example, the works of Coleman (1966) and Jencks (1972) deserve mention. Coleman's famous report entitled *Equality of Educational Opportunity* makes the point that, regardless of the school a student attends, the greatest influence on the student's achievement is the general social class of the student body. Coleman suggests, therefore, that economically deprived students should increase their achievement level if placed in a school with many economically advantaged students. Jencks (1972) makes even a stronger proposal. According to Jencks, the only way to reduce the current inequality among the economically advantaged and disadvantaged is to change the whole social structure of the United States. Both of these viewpoints stem from an environmental position, which suggests that the intellectual endowment of students is basically environmentally determined. Change the environment and you will change a student's intelligence. Note the underlying optimism common to all these viewpoints.

We have presented you with a variety of examples in order that you sense the importance of these issues. Each of these issues is a broad question that must be faced ultimately by our society. Each one of these issues has had a significant influence on our current school programs and general educational practices. And, each has been subjected to considerable criticism. The works of Eysenck (1971), Herrnstein (1973), and Jensen (1969), for example, suggest that environmental intervention does not have a significant impact on intellectual functioning because intelligence is mostly genetically determined. In fact, Herrnstein posits that increasing the effectiveness of the environment *might* actually create a worse situation than now exists because the main intellectual differences between people functioning in an ideal environment would be almost totally due to genetic differences. Obviously, that viewpoint has produced numerous counterarguments. And so, the merry-go-round continues.

IQ TESTS

The difference between intelligence and IQ

So far we have dealt with the broad theoretical questions and concomitant broad educational decisions stemming from these viewpoints. We would like to turn our attention now to those tests that purport to measure the construct of "intelligence." Before we progress very far, however, we would like you to keep in mind the difference between intelligence and IQ. Intelligence is a theoretical construct—a label used as a description of behavior; IQ, on the other hand, is a derived statistic based upon a child's performance on an IQ test. To assume that an IQ score accurately reflects a child's intelligence is a very faulty conclusion that is made too often. First of all, authorities do not agree on the nature of intelligence! Second, none of the existing group or individual IQ tests is based on theories of intelligence such as those presented in the preceding section of the chapter. Instead, the current IQ tests are based on a relatively unsystematic collection of items. Finally, the IQ score is designed to represent a child's relative position on the IQ test with reference to a representative sample of the population; the score is not designed to measure a child's absolute quality and quantity of intelligence. These tests are not measuring an entity! They are measuring an aggregate set of behaviors thought to be representative of "g." The IQ score is a *relative* score, not an *absolute* score.

The norm-referenced model

Current IQ tests are almost always based on the norm-referenced statistical model. Stemming from Galton's (1869) statistical work on the measurement of a person's ability on sensory-type tasks, the application of the norm-referenced approach to intelligence testing has become firmly entrenched in psychology. This approach is designed to determine an individual's relative standing on a series of tasks compared with a standardized group. (Refer back to Chapter 9 for a more complete discussion of this concept.) Although some psychologists have questioned the use of the norm-referenced approach as a statistical model for IQ testing, the norm-referenced model is still very much an integral part of the mental measurement movement. It is appropriate, therefore, that you understand a few of the basic underlying principles of the model as applied to intelligence testing.

Assume that Johnny and Jimmy, two fourth-graders in Ms. Psyche's class, are referred to the school psychologist because of poor scholastic performance. After having a short discussion with Johnny and Jimmy, the psychologist administers the Wechsler Intelligence Scale for Children–Revised Edition (WISC-R). Upon completion of the testing session, the psychologist computes Johnny's and Jimmy's IQs. Johnny obtains an IQ of 130, while Jimmy's is only 85. What do these numbers tell the psychologist? Back in Chapter 9 you learned that the normal curve is a statistical model that purportedly portrays a hypothetical distribution of scores around a central location. In a perfect curve, the midpoint is both the median score (the 50th percentile) and the mean (the average score). Keep in mind that the normal curve is only a statistical model, but since many kinds of human performance scores tend to distribute themselves in a near-perfect symmetrical distribution, this model is generally thought appropriate to use when studying intelligence test performances.

Most current intelligence tests are purposefully designed both structurally and statistically to provide the examiner with this norm-referenced data. Each item of an IQ test is chosen based on its ability *to discriminate between high-performing and low-performing students.* To translate a child's raw score on an IQ test (the number of correct items) to a score that can be compared with other students' scores, the score must be converted in such a manner that a comparison is possible. For example, a raw score of 48 out of a 60-item test tells us nothing about a student's score in relation to other students who took the test. You have no way of knowing if the raw score is above average, below average, or average. In order to give meaning to the score and to make judgements about a student's relative performance, the score is usually transformed into a derived score or interpreted with reference to the group's mean and standard deviation. Some of the derived scores frequently used in test interpretation include grade scores, mental ages, percentile ranks, and deviation IQs. The purpose of derived scores is to provide psychologists with data concerning a student's standing with reference to a norm. To better understand some of these concepts, refer to Figure 23–7.

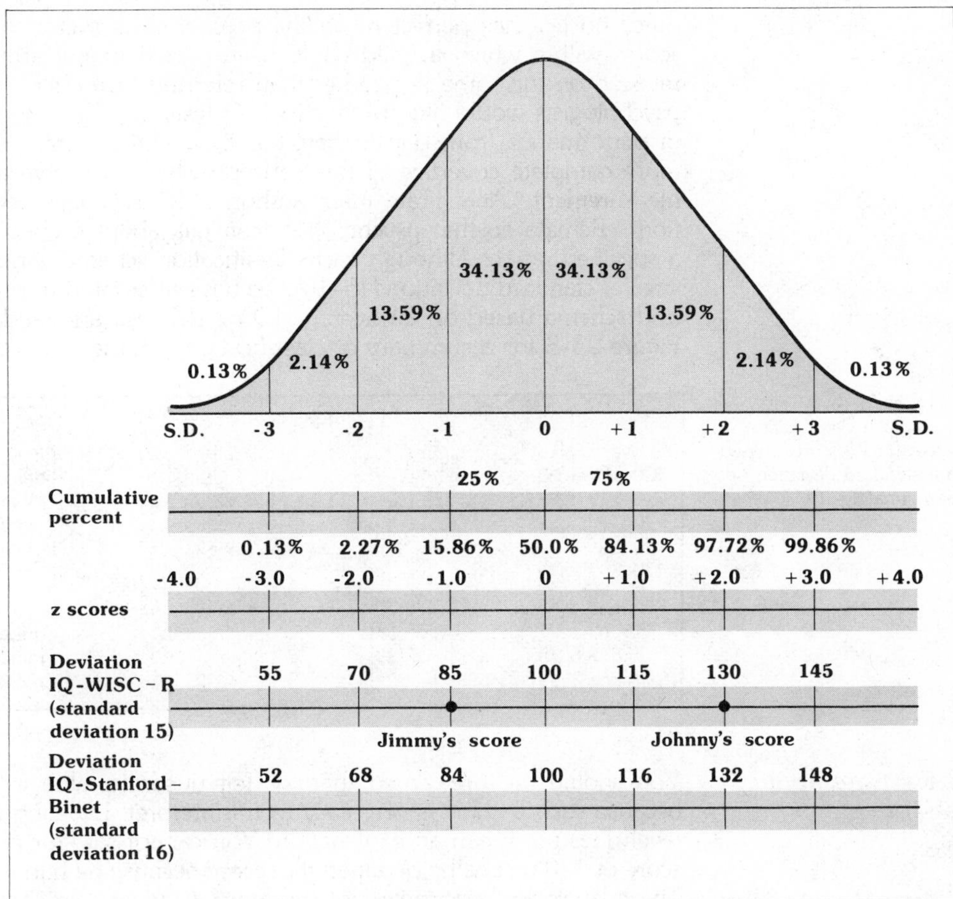

FIGURE 23–7
Application of the normal curve to intelligence test performance

Note how all the numbers in Figure 23–7 are interrelated. An IQ score of 100 on the WISC-R, for example, tells us that the score does not deviate from the average (0 standard deviation) and that the score is better than that obtained by 50 percent of the sample that took the test and also poorer than 50 percent of the sample. An IQ score of 100 represents 0 standard deviation from the mean and the 50th percentile. Refer to the Appendix for computational information about the standard deviation.

The meaning of an IQ score

You should now be ready to discuss Johnny's IQ of 130 and Jimmy's IQ of 85. Johnny's score of 130 places him +2 standard deviations from the mean, while Jimmy's score of 85 is −1 standard deviation from the mean. In other words, Johnny did better than 97.22 percent of the sample who took the WISC-R, while Jimmy did better than only 15.86 percent of the sample. Before we proceed, it is also important to note that the WISC-R and the Stanford-Binet (S-B) have standard deviations of 15 and 16, respectively; therefore the IQ scores on these two tests are not precisely equivalent. We mention this because some IQ tests have standard deviations that vary widely from 15 to 16, so IQ scores on different tests are not at all equivalent! To make any comparative sense out of an IQ score, *you must know the standard score and the standard deviation of the test.* To talk about a child's IQ score without identifying the test from which the score is derived is a very faulty educational practice.

Since no test has perfect reliability, psychologists prefer to talk about the range of scores within which a child could be expected to perform if the child were to be retested on the same test rather than referring to a child's specific IQ score. Ideally psychologists would like to construct IQ tests in which there would be no variability in performance from day to day, but that is impossible. Refer to Chapter 9 for a more complete coverage of this concept, which is known as "the standard error of measurement." At any rate, many authors of IQ tests have developed general classification schemata so that psychologists can talk about a child's IQ score falling within a specified range. Although each classification schema varies, particularly those with smaller standard deviations (5–10), we have attempted to present you with a generalized schema based on an average IQ of 100 and an standard deviation of 15. See Figure 23–8 for a summary of classification schemas.

FIGURE 23–8
Generalized classification system for IQ scores (based on a standard deviation of approximately 15)

Score	*Range*
Above 129/139	Intellectually gifted
120–129/139	Intellectually superior
110–119	Above average—bright
90–109	Average
80–89	Below average—dull—slow learner
70–79	Borderline—slow learner
Retarded (below 70 or 75)	
55–70/75	Educable
25/30–50/55	Trainable
Below 25	Custodial

A warning about labels

You should be forewarned that we felt uncomfortable in presenting Figure 23–8 because such a chart is very easy to misinterpret. Labeling is dangerous business. A label does not mean an explanation. You cannot say, for example, that Johnny's IQ score of 130 means he obtained that score because he had superior or gifted intellect. These labels are descriptive not causative! Account also should be taken that a score of 130 places Johnny in the intellectually gifted category in one classification system and in the superior range in another system. Categories of different authorities are not necessarily comparable. For example, in those school districts that have special programs for the intellectually gifted (a fuzzy term), different IQ cutoff scores are used on specified tests. In some districts, a 130 IQ is the minimum, in other schools a 140 IQ is the minimum, while in other school districts a child's achievement in a subject area is considered rather than an IQ score. Schools using the third strategy really are denying that the gifted category exists; the student is accepted into a program based solely on his/her academic competence, not on some hypothetical potential to perform. When you use a statistical categorical approach, what do you say about a child who misses an IQ category by a few points? Are you willing to say that an IQ of 89 should be characterized as a slow learner (dull) while an IQ of 91 is average? One final point needs to be raised. Would you be willing to say that because a child obtains an IQ score of 122 none of the child's behavior could be classified as academically very superior? Many children possess bumps, they are not well rounded; that is, many children may be characterized as possessing uneven academic abilities. Einstein is a case in point—highly proficient in some areas, not as proficient in other academic areas. Global IQ scores ignore these bumps. In conclusion, the categories in Figure 23–8 should not be construed to have any *instructional* purposes. Instead, they should be viewed as convenient labels from which one can make some potentially very dangerous generalizations.

In our opinion, the dangers associated with these labels far outweigh their minimal educational utility. However, since federal monies are made available to school districts based upon the categorical label of a child, these terms will continue to be used as an administrative device for funding and class placement.

5. What is the difference between intelligence and IQ? State why these terms should not be equated.
6. Identify three unfortunate outcomes that have been associated with the study of intelligence.

Types of tests: Group and individual

You should remember that psychologists do not agree on the definition of intelligence or on the nature of those factors that contribute to intellectual growth. Even though there is a great deal of disagreement concerning the nature of intelligence, intelligence tests have been used extensively in the schools to make important educational decisions about students. These tests will continue to be used, and therefore it would be remiss not to include a description of some of the most frequently used group and individual IQ tests upon which decisions are often made.

Traditionally, intelligence tests have been categorized into group tests and individual tests. As implied in the title, group intelligence tests are administered to groups of children at one or more sittings in a paper-and-pencil format. Individual tests, on the other hand, are administered to one student at a time, usually by a trained professional.

Group IQ tests. While not as reliable or valid for their stated purposes as individual intelligence tests, group intelligence and general ability tests are often used in the schools as preliminary screening devices to *predict academic performance* (Figure 23–9). Many of the group tests perform reasonably well at this function. Most group intelligence test manuals report correlations from .45 to .75/.80 between performance

FIGURE 23–9
Group intelligence tests are used for screening purposes

on the test and performance on standardized achievement tests. When a discrepancy exists between a student's group IQ test score and the student's academic performance, an individual intelligence test is frequently administered by a trained psychologist.

Depending on the nature of the group test, these tests take anywhere from 10 to 12 minutes (Wonderlic) to a series of testing sessions in which a test battery is involved (Differential Aptitude Test). Although group intelligence tests vary widely, some of their more common attractive features include:

1. Extensive representative sampling procedures are usually used when standardizing the tests.
2. The multiple-choice format of most group tests allows for easy scoring procedures.
3. Easy administration procedures are built into the testing format.
4. A large number of students can be administered the test at the same time.
5. Compared with individual tests, group tests are relatively inexpensive to administer.

Before attempting to describe group intelligence tests, caution must be raised about two problems associated with group testing in general. First of all, a group testing arrangement requires that the examiner administer the test to a large number of students at one time, therefore the examiner is rarely in a position to observe a specific student's performance on the test. Since good performance on an IQ test depends on steady work, reasonable rapport with the testing situation, and other similar factors, one should be very careful in making any definitive statements about a student's *poor* test performance on a group test. There are simply too many factors that might interfere with adequate test performance on the group test and have very little to do with the student's intellectual abilities. In an individual testing situation, a well-trained psychologist can easily identify through careful observation many of these factors that might interfere with optimal test performance. The fact that there is less control in a group testing situation is enough to contribute to a lower reliability and, therefore, validity of the group test for its stated purposes.

Second, since the format of many group tests consists of multiple-choice rather than open-ended questions, group tests tend to emphasize convergent responses of the *recognition* variety as opposed to recall-type questions. In other words, on a multiple-choice test the answer is provided to the student; in an open-ended question the student must recall the answer. Group tests and individual tests oftentimes require different types of responses. The tests should not be viewed as necessarily comparable.

If you were to take a group intelligence test, what would it be like? Although group intelligence tests do not have quite the same variety as individual intelligence tests, the variety of test items is still extensive. Some of the types of items might include vocabulary, verbal classifications, verbal analogies, arithmetic reasoning, verbal conceptualizations, sentence completion, general information, ability to follow directions, matrices of various types, figure classification, figure analogies, and number series.

Depending on the purpose of the group test, group intelligence tests may measure only one of two intellectual abilities or numerous abilities. In the early elementary grades, group tests often do not require reading. By the time a student is in junior high school, however, reading is usually required for at least a substantial part of the test. At the high school level not only do the tests usually require reading, but it is often very difficult to discriminate between an intelligence test and an achievement test. Obviously a poor reader is at a disadvantage on these tests. Again, you must keep in mind the purposes of most of these tests. Surely poor performance on a group intelligence test at the high school level should not be construed to indicate that a student necessarily possesses poor *inherent* ability. If the score were reliable, however, you could say with reasonable confidence that the student *probably* would not perform very well in the academic subjects. Figure 23–10 provides you with a sample of typical items on group intelligence tests. None of these examples is an actual item. Figure 23–11 lists many of the more frequently used group tests.

FIGURE 23–10
Twelve simulated group intelligence test items*

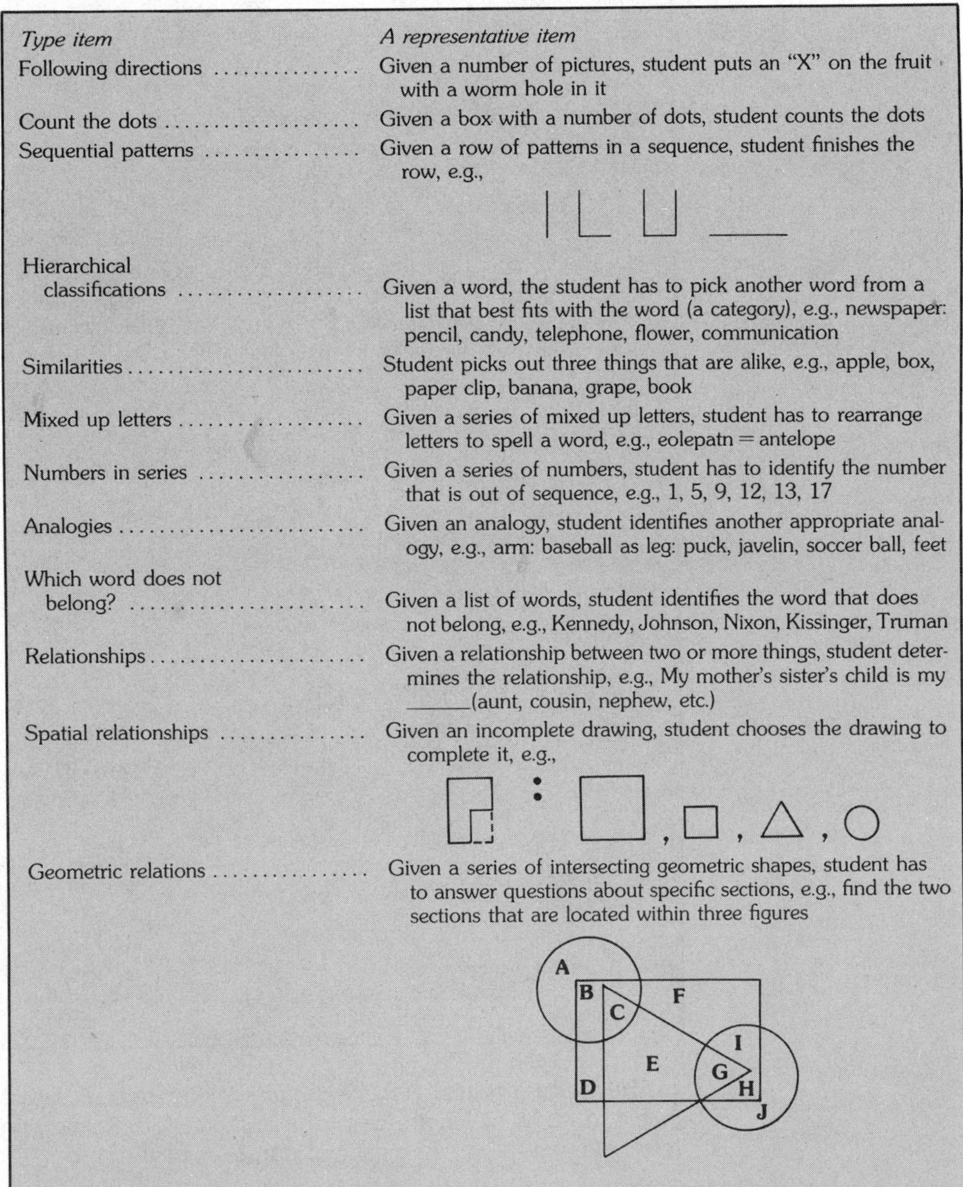

Type item	*A representative item*
Following directions	Given a number of pictures, student puts an "X" on the fruit with a worm hole in it
Count the dots	Given a box with a number of dots, student counts the dots
Sequential patterns	Given a row of patterns in a sequence, student finishes the row, e.g.,
Hierarchical classifications	Given a word, the student has to pick another word from a list that best fits with the word (a category), e.g., newspaper: pencil, candy, telephone, flower, communication
Similarities	Student picks out three things that are alike, e.g., apple, box, paper clip, banana, grape, book
Mixed up letters	Given a series of mixed up letters, student has to rearrange letters to spell a word, e.g., eolepatn = antelope
Numbers in series	Given a series of numbers, student has to identify the number that is out of sequence, e.g., 1, 5, 9, 12, 13, 17
Analogies	Given an analogy, student identifies another appropriate analogy, e.g., arm: baseball as leg: puck, javelin, soccer ball, feet
Which word does not belong?	Given a list of words, student identifies the word that does not belong, e.g., Kennedy, Johnson, Nixon, Kissinger, Truman
Relationships	Given a relationship between two or more things, student determines the relationship, e.g., My mother's sister's child is my ______(aunt, cousin, nephew, etc.)
Spatial relationships	Given an incomplete drawing, student chooses the drawing to complete it, e.g.,
Geometric relations	Given a series of intersecting geometric shapes, student has to answer questions about specific sections, e.g., find the two sections that are located within three figures

* The examples are not actual items from group intelligence tests but are designed to stimulate the type of items representative of group tests.

FIGURE 23–11
Some popular group intelligence tests

Name of test	*Outstanding characteristics or features*
Analysis of Learning Potential (ALP) (Harcourt, Brace, Jovanovich) Grades: 1, 2–3, 4–6, 7–9, 10–12	Purpose: to predict specific criteria of scholastic success. Subtests: subtests generally follow the categories of verbal classification, number series, numerical reasoning
Boehm Test of Basic Concepts (Psychological Corporation) Grades: K–2	Purpose: "to assess students' basic concepts widely but sometimes mistakenly assumed to be familiar to children at their time of entry in K or 1st grade." Subtests: space (location, direction, orientation, dimensions), time and quantity (number), plus several other types of items
California Test of Mental Maturity (CTMM) (McGraw-Hill) Grades: K–1, 1.5–3, 4–6, 7–9, 9–12, 12–16	Purpose: "to measure functional capacities deemed basic to learning, problem solving, and responding to new situations. Subtests: logical reasoning, spatial relationships, numerical reasoning, verbal concepts, memory, language total, and total score
Cooperative School and College Ability Tests (SCAT) (Cooperative Tests and Service) Grades: 4–6, 7–9, 10–12, 12–14	Purpose: to provide measures of basic verbal and mathematical abilities. Scores: verbal, mathematical, total
Henmon-Nelson Tests of Mental Ability (Houghton Mifflin) Grades: K–2, 3–6, 6–9, 9–12, 13–17	Purpose: to measure scholastic aptitude, especially at lower levels. Subtests: quantitative, verbal, total
Kuhlmann-Anderson Intelligence Tests	Purpose: to assess overall mental age. Subtests: verbal, quantitative, total—consists of 39 individual subtests
Lorge-Thorndike Intelligence Tests (LTIT) (Houghton Mifflin) Grades: 3, 4, 5, 6, 7, 8–9, 10–11, 12–13 (overlapping levels)	Purpose: to select curriculum materials and learning tasks for students, identify students who may need special help, vocational guidance, and other broad purposes. Scores: verbal, nonverbal, composite
Otis-Lennon Mental Ability Test (OLMAT) (Harcourt, Brace, Jovanovich) Grades: K, 1.0–1.5, 1.6–3.9, 4–6, 7–9, 10–12	Purpose: based on Vernon's structure of mental abilities—to assess the "verbal-educational" component of Vernon's model. Scores: classification, verbal conceptualization, quantitative reasoning, general information, ability to follow directions
Progressive Matrices (Psychological Corporation) Ages: 6 and over	Purpose: to measure "g." Scores: 1 score—series of matrices
Wonderlic (E. F. Wonderlic and Associates) Adults—candidates for business and industry	Purpose: to screen applicants for business and industry. Scores: one score consisting of verbal, numerical, and spatial items—12-minute test

Individual IQ tests. As with group intelligence tests, individual IQ tests vary considerably in terms of length, ease of administration, format, the age level for which the test can be used, and the general purposes of the test.

An individual intelligence test is a standardized test administered to one child at a time by a trained professional (most often a psychologist). Generally, when a child is referred for individualized testing it is because the child is experiencing either learning or adjustment difficulties in school. Depending on the reason for referral and the professional's initial assessment of the child, a specific battery of tests is usually administered. If the child is experiencing difficulty in learning, or if special education services or special class placement for the mentally retarded, gifted, or learning-disabled child is considered a possibility, an individual IQ test is used.

The testing session for individual IQ tests can last from 15 to 20 minutes [Slosson Intelligence Test (SIT) and the Peabody Picture Vocabulary Test (PPVT)] to one hour or longer [Stanford-Binet (S-B) and the Wechsler Intelligence Scale for Children–Revised (WISC-R)]. If a quick assessment of a child is needed, the PPVT or SIT can be used.

Peabody Picture Vocabulary Test (PPVT), American Guidance Service. The PPVT is a vocabulary test consisting of 150 pages of drawings, four drawings to a page. The child is asked a vocabulary-type question about each page and responds by pointing to the correct picture. The pictures are line drawings representing objects, animals, birds, human actions, nature scenes, plants, flowers, inanimate objects, and adverbs. Since this test does not require any spoken language from the child, the PPVT is frequently used with children who have difficulty speaking, who cannot speak, or who are very resistant to speaking (cerebral palsied, autistic, aphasic). Generally, vocabulary tests are very good predictors of academic achievement, and since the PPVT has a high correlation with the Stanford-Binet and with academic achievement, the test can be used for a quick assessment of the child's receptive verbal ability and for a tentative predictive score of academic achievement. The test can be used with children from 2 1/2 to 18 years of age and takes about 15 minutes to administer.

Slosson Intelligence Test (SIT), Slosson Educational Publications. The SIT is a short intelligence test used as a screening device to assess an individual's mental ability at any age level from infancy through adulthood. Since many of the items have been purposefully adapted from the Stanford-Binet (S-B), this test is reported to correlate very highly with it. Many of the preschool items below the one-year level consist of observing the infant in a natural environment to determine whether the child is developing typically (e.g., eyes follow a moving object, holds head erect, holds object in hand). Items for the school-age child almost always consist of verbal questions such as information, vocabulary, similarities, arithmetic, and rote memory. Many verbal arithmetic items are included beyond the ten-year level. Depending on the student, the test takes from 15 to 25 minutes to administer.

Stanford-Binet Intelligence Scale (S-B), Houghton-Mifflin. Unquestionably, the Stanford-Binet Intelligence Test is one of the most popular individualized tests. The origins of this test go back to the turn of the century. Charged with the task of identifying children in the Paris school system who would not be expected to perform well in school, you will recall, Binet constructed the original test to consist of 30 items of ascending difficulty that were considered representative of different aspects of general intelligence. The latest revision of the Stanford-Binet maintains the same format but has many more items. Starting at the two-year-old level, six subtests are administered to a child through adulthood. There are six subtests for each year of development. A child is administered the subtests at his/her appropriate age level until *all* six subtests in any given year are missed. In order to give you an idea of the types of items found on the S-B, Figure 23–12 depicts the nature of the subtests at Years VI, X, and XIII. Not based on any systematic theory or model about the nature of intelligence, the Stanford-Binet samples a variety of tasks in a rather unsystematic fashion to

FIGURE 23–12
Nature of Stanford-Binet subtests at Years VI, X, and XIII*

Name of subtest	*What it measures*
VI-year level	
Vocabulary	Define a list of words
Differences	What is the difference between . . . ?
Mutilated pictures	Pictures portrayed in which part of the picture is missing
Number concepts	Child is given three to ten blocks and is required to count blocks
Opposite analogies	Child is given four sentences such as: A car goes on roads; an airplane goes ______
Maze tracing	Simple mazes are presented to child and child has to trace shortest route to an end goal
X-year level	
Vocabulary	Define a list of words
Block counting	Child is shown a card with pictures of cubes arranged in rows and has to count number of blocks in the picture
Abstract words	Child has to define abstract words, such as *sorrow, justice*
Finding reasons	Child is asked to give reasons for common social practices: Why do we have schools?
Word meaning	Child names as many words as possible in one minute
Repeating six digits	Child is given six random numbers at a uniform rate of one per second and child has to repeat this list in the presented order
XIII-year level	
Plan of search	Child is asked to draw a path in a field to indicate how the child would proceed to find a lost object
Abstract words	Same as X-year level but more difficult
Memory for sentences	Examiner reads two 15-word sentences to student and student has to repeat the sentence with no errors
Problems of fact	Examiner reads a short paragraph to the student and the student has to predict a plausible conclusion
Dissected sentences	Student is given a card on which disarranged words are printed and student has to rearrange words to construct an appropriate sentence
Copying a bead chain from memory	Examiner makes a bead chain out of different-shaped beads in a predetermined order. The student watches the examiner make the chain, and after five seconds the student has to make the chain from memory

* Simulated examples are presented.

assess general intelligence. We shall discuss this issue more fully in the final section of the chapter.

The Wechsler Scales (WPPSI, WISC-R, WAIS), The Psychological Corporation. The other leading individual IQ tests are those developed by David Wechsler. These tests have been prepared for different age levels and, with the exception of the WAIS, are used extensively in the schools by trained psychologists. The Wechsler Preschool and Primary Scale of Intelligence (WPPSI) is designed for the four- to six-year-old child to assess the child's "overall or global intellectual capacity" (Wechsler, 1967). The school-aged child (6–16) is given the Wechsler Intelligence Scale for Children–Revised (WISC-R), while adults are given the Wechsler Adult Intelligence Scale (WAIS). All three tests have the same basic structure. Divided into a verbal section and a performance section, each test provides the examiner with a verbal IQ score, a performance IQ score, and a total IQ score. To help you understand the nature of the Wechsler tests, the WISC-R is described in Figure 23–13.

FIGURE 23–13
The organization of the Wechsler Intelligence Scale for Children–Revised (WISC-R)*

Name of test	*What it measures*
Verbal section	
Information	Information-type questions are asked, such as: "Who wrote *War and Peace?* "What does a cat say?"
Similarities	In what way are a ______and a ______alike?
Arithmetic	Verbal arithmetic problems—from counting to 12 to written verbal problems requiring sequential calculations with fractions to solve the problem (timed)
Vocabulary	Define a list of words—from very easy to highly technical words
Comprehension	A series of questions that deal with logical solutions, such as: "Why do we have a system of checks and balances in our government?" "What would you do if you saw someone unconscious on the side of the road?"
Performance Section	
Picture completion	Student is shown pictures with a part of the picture missing; the harder items become quite subtle (timed)
Picture arrangement	Student is shown cartoon-like pictures in a mixed-up order; student has to arrange the pictures in an appropriate order to make a logical story (timed)
Block design	Student is presented a series of cards with block designs; given some blocks, the student has to copy the designs (timed)
Object assembly	Student has to put together some puzzles; no color cues are available (timed)
Coding	Student is given a paper with a series of numbers out of sequence; the numbers are from 1 to 9. Under each number is a specific code representing that number. Given a series of numbers, without codes, the student has to mark each number with the appropriate code (timed)

* Simulated examples.

Unlike the S-B, each subtest of the WISC-R is administered to the student until the student misses a predetermined number of items; then the next subtest is administered in the same manner. To make the test more interesting, verbal and performance subtests are alternated.

Individual IQ testing decisions. Throughout this book we have been making the distinction between educational decisions and instructional decisions. The distinction applies here very nicely. At a general level, intelligence tests, when used properly, can predict a student's academic performance with a fair degree of accuracy. This is one of the purposes of the test. If your school has a special education program, these tests are used as one measure to place a student in a special class or, if appropriate, to keep a student out of a special class. To some extent, these tests can be used to protect a student from misplacement in an incorrect program. Obviously, the converse is also true, and this has been one of the arguments against the IQ tests.

You should be aware that often outside funding is based on data obtained with an individually administered IQ test. And, of course, group intelligence tests, when used as a screening device, identify some children for individual evaluations who might not be identified in a regular school program.

At a more specific level, individual intelligence tests can serve two functions. If a student is administered an individual intelligence test and the student's pattern of

FIGURE 23–14
Individual IQ tests allow professionals to make more precise decisions than group IQ tests

Source: Reprinted from the Peabody Picture Vocabulary Test.

response is atypical when compared to the norm, that atypical response pattern *may* reflect a serious difficulty (e.g., a neurological dysfunction or similar disturbance) which might warrant additional professional attention (Figure 23–14). There have been cases in which a school psychologist has referred a child to a neurologist for additional tests, only to find out that the child had an operable tumor. A trained psychologist is always on the alert for this type of problem. It should be noted here that the psychologist has no right to make a diagnosis of neurological dysfunction. The testing instruments have not been validated for that purpose. The unusual test performance of a child, however, can alert a psychologist that additional professional services may be needed and a referral is in order. Second, a good school psychologist is sometimes capable of identifying specific patterns of responses from a student on an individual intelligence test that suggest a particular instructional strategy that might be applied in the classroom. Remember though, these tests are designed to make predictions about a student's general *relative* ability, not the student's ability with reference to a specified curriculum or academic task. Designed to provide generalizations, the tests do not focus on specific instructional information. It is the school psychologist's competence rather than the design of the test that provides much of the instructional information gleaned from these tests.

AN INSTRUCTIONAL PSYCHOLOGY PERSPECTIVE

Since you intend to be a teacher we thought it would prove useful for you to consider from an *instructional* perspective some of the difficulties and problems associated with the study of intelligence. Quite frankly, considering the amount of effort some educational psychologists have exerted studying intelligence, the *instructional* payoff has not been very productive. Why should this be the case? At the conclusion of the chapter some possible instructional solutions to these issues are presented for your consideration.

In this part of the chapter some of the conceptual inconsistencies and sloppy thinking associated with this topic are analyzed. We include this section because our analysis leads us to believe that some of the criticisms leveled against many of the conclusions (or nonconclusions) concerning the instructional implications of intelligence are directly applicable to other educational psychology topics as well. After you read this section of the book, we hope you will not fall into some of the same faulty conclusions that have been made by many of the "experts."

IQ test results lack instructional utility

Since almost all the popular intelligence tests are designed to measure a person's general intellectual level, the tests consist of a series of items or subtests that supposedly sample aspects of general intelligence. For example, you will remember that the Wechsler Intelligence Scale for Children–Revised (WISC-R) consists of ten subtests (information, comprehension, arithmetic, similarities, vocabulary, picture completion, picture arrangement, object assembly, block design, and coding). No particular theoretical rationale is used in the choices of the subtests. These subtests are chosen for the WISC-R because they purportedly reflect aspects of general intelligence. This strategy leaves us still wondering what truly constitutes "g," particularly since the definitional issues are far from resolved. For example, many other types of subtests and items could have been substituted just as easily to assess other aspects of general intelligence. The same applies equally to the Stanford-Binet. In other words, the subtests and resultant items have no distinct, consistent instructional purpose other than to assess an individual's relative standing on a cluster of items designed to measure "g." Because the information obtained from a student's performance on an intelligence test provides the examiner with information about "g," very little can be said about *specific* diagnostic or prescriptive information necessary for instructional decisions. In fact, as now constructed, the intelligence tests are not supposed to be useful for instructional questions! And yet the most ardent hereditarian would admit that the environment has considerable impact on the development of intelligence.

This situation has created several major instructional difficulties. For the purposes of this discussion, let us assume we agree there is a useful construct called "intelligence" (to be debated shortly) and we also agree on a satisfactory definition of it. We should now be able to construct a test to sample the construct. Regardless of how we feel ultimately about the heredity-environment controversy, and regardless of how we feel about what subtests and items should represent intellectual functioning, we want to design a test in such a manner that it assesses in a systematic fashion those subskills thought to represent intelligence. The information gained from such a test should be theoretically, diagnostically, and instructionally useful from an environmental perspective. Even if one's intelligence is mainly a function of one's genetic makeup, the environment still has enough influence so that a psychologist would want information concerning how the child's environment should be changed to increase a student's intellectual functioning! Solely designed to measure "g," the current intelligence tests do not reflect these very important environmental questions. Instead of asking environmental-type questions, these tests focus on broad labels.

Incredible as it may seem, *none* of the items or subtests of popular standardized IQ tests is based on *systematic models* or *theoretical conceptualizations* of intelligence. For example, none of the current IQ tests is constructed to measure developmental hierarchies such as those postulated by Piaget. Some tests along these lines, however, are in the experimental stages of construction. No tests are based on the structural nature of intelligence reflecting primary, secondary, or tertiary hierarchies as proposed by Hakstian and Cattell (1974) and representative of Vernon's hierarchy. No tests are designed to sample discrete mental abilities such as those identified by Guilford (1966). In other words, the current tests lack a systematic theoretical basis, such as that provided by Guilford, Piaget, or Bruner. For the theoretician as well as the practitioner, this procedure is most unsatisfactory.

The emphasis on assessing "g" rather than assessing useful environmental information has created a number of related problems in the field of instruction.

1. Macro labels—making faulty conclusions and expectations. Macro labels can lead to faulty conclusions and expectations about human behavior. Knowledge that Jimmy or Johnny is very intelligent or very stupid does not tell the teacher where to begin with the student. Furthermore, there is always the danger of false expectancies. Although the research on false expectancies leading to self-fulfilling prophecies has not been fully resolved (Rosenthal & Jacobson, 1968), a safe conclusion would be to use no *broad* labels about students unless the label serves a useful instructional function.

2. Macro labels—ignoring uneven distribution of abilities. Unfortunately, IQ tests are not designed to measure the specific abilities necessary to perform specific academic tasks. Since abilities are distributed very unevenly, it makes little sense to talk about the expected performance of a child in a specific subject area (whether it be reading, arithmetic, or art) based on a general IQ score that purportedly measures "g." Einstein is a case in point. Although his IQ was reported to be exceptionally high, he was somewhat deficient in language-related activities in school. Is the claim that Einstein was underachieving in the language area, i.e., performing below his estimated potential, therefore a valid one? Current intelligence tests are not designed to take into consideration unique constellations of abilities. Is it not logical to suggest that the discrepancy between a child's score on an IQ test and the child's performance in school is a result of overprediction?

Let us assume that a child performs better in school than the IQ test would predict. How do educators explain this? The explanation most frequently put forth is that the student overachieved and thus overcompensated for his/her lack of ability. Give that explanation some serious consideration. How is it possible for a child to perform beyond one's potential? (Answer: It is not possible.) Is it not equally plausible in this case that an underprediction has occurred? Stated simply, in this case the IQ test did not measure the constellation of factors necessary to predict the specific achievement task with accuracy. By the way, one should not claim that the student may have overcompensated. This term lacks complete meaning in this context; it is simply *impossible* to overcompensate for something one does not purportedly have the ability to do. The fact that the student achieves the task indicates the student possesses the ability to perform the task! Educational jargon can be soothingly deceptive.

3. Studying behaviors that do not matter. Studying "g" rather than studying those specific skills prerequisite to academic functioning in the basic curriculum areas (reading, arithmetic, etc.) seems to be off-target behavior. As educators, our ultimate concern should be to design environments commensurate with students' skills in order to have the students reach a variety of goals. Current IQ tests do not measure those specific *skills* prerequisite for academic success. Stated another way, the information obtained from intelligence tests lacks the specificity necessary for designing environmental strategies. The tests have been designed independent of any curriculum decisions that must be made about students.

4. Using labels as explanations. Consider this analogy from a car mechanic's perspective. Admittedly the analogy is a spoof, but we feel it makes the point about a basic error that is made constantly in psychological and instructional circles. Assume an owner of a car seeks to have the car repaired. Based upon the owner's description of the car's malfunctioning, or based upon the mechanic's initial observation of the car's condition, the mechanic attempts to identify the precise malfunction of the car. To determine the accuracy of his hypothesis, the mechanic checks out each part of the car thought to contribute to the malfunction. The data obtained from the tests are designed to provide the mechanic with the information needed to fix the car. This is the method most mechanics use to fix a car.

Now let us assume the mechanic in this analogy is not interested in fixing cars. Let us assume, instead, that the mechanic is interested in comparing the performances of different cars. Our mechanic gets an ingenious idea. Having read several books on psychology, our mechanic decides to create a descriptive label to describe the car's condition to each customer. He decides further to call this label the "lemon quotient" (LQ). To assess accurately the LQ of his customer's car, everytime a car is brought in to be fixed the mechanic diligently checks the condition of the spark plugs, the pickup of the car in a specified time, the horn, the windshield wipers, whether the car starts as soon as the key is turned on, and the gas mileage to obtain a general score of the car's overall condition. Our mechanic decides to assign a score of 100 to cars of average condition, and then he recomputes all the other scores of cars referred to his station based on the average. Some mechanics would argue that the pickup of a car should be weighted higher than the gas mileage, but since we have agreed to accept our mechanic's definition of the lemon quotient, we will have to ignore this methodological difficulty.

Our mechanic is now ready to talk business with his customers. He can tell the owner of the car how far the car deviates from the average based on its current condition. No other gas station can provide this service. A low LQ signifies that the car is not in very good shape compared with other cars, and a high LQ means that the car is better than most cars. Try to picture the face of a customer who comes into the garage to have a flat fixed, and at the end of 1½ hours the mechanic explains with enthusiasm that the car possesses a high LQ and therefore should perform quite well for the customer. In fact, try to imagine mechanics spending time on this exercise! It simply lacks utility because it is circular reasoning at its best (or worst). While it is true that a low LQ would indicate to the mechanic that several things are wrong with the car, nothing of *functional* significance can be obtained by examining the LQ. Only by systematically examining the results of specific tests designed to assess specific mechanical difficulties can a mechanic fix a car. Mechanics are not interested in predicting self-evident phenomena; they are interested in fixing cars based on a precise diagnosis of a car's condition. Specific mechanical tests have a diagnostic-prescriptive purpose. Broad labels such as an LQ provide us with very little functional information. And oftentimes, the labels are off-target.

As mentioned, the subtests of IQ tests have not been designed to provide diagnostic-prescriptive information; they are designed to assess "g." In other words, the subtests of an IQ test, when averaged together, *do not explain behavior;* these subtests *describe* a person's relative performance on a series of items compared with a norm. The end result is a descriptive label placed upon a child which describes a child's *relative* standing on an IQ test. All too often this relative *descriptive label* becomes a pseudo-explanatory label, particularly if the intelligence test is viewed as measuring a specific entity defined in terms of the innate potential to achieve. The inherent dangers of engaging in circular reasoning should be obvious to you by now. Perhaps we could conclude that the construct of intelligence possesses a low LQ for instructional purposes! We might add here that this type of reasoning is all too prevalent in educational circles. Consider this statement: "I don't know what to do with Johnny in school. His low self-concept is interfering with his work." He could have substituted the phrase "self-concept" in our mechanic's analogy with the same results. The moral of our little analogy is: Be careful in using labels. If you have to use macro labels, don't use them as explanations.

Lack of consensus and premature conclusions

In case you still are not convinced, we thought we would conclude this part of the chapter by returning to the issue raised at the beginning of the chapter. What is "intelligence"? Wechsler (1974b) has defined intelligence as "the overall capacity of an individual to understand and cope with the world around him." According to Wechsler, intelligence should be viewed as a multidetermined and multifaceted concept. One should not attempt to single out any ability as necessarily important to the overall concept of intelligence, nor should one equate general intelligence with intellectual abilities (which are defined as specific skills). Rather, intelligence is viewed as the way in which intellectual abilities are combined in unique combinations with other internal variables such as drive and incentive to influence the total behavior of the individual. Intelligence is something that is *implied* from the way intellectual abilities are manifested under different conditions and circumstances.

In agreement with Wechsler, Butcher (1970) views intelligence as a "quintessentially high level skill at the summit of a hierarchy of intellectual skills." According to Butcher, intelligence serves the function of integrating specific skills into a workable whole; it should be seen as an open-ended concept because *the number of activities attributed as characteristic of intelligence has never been identified.* While such a viewpoint is indeed necessary at this time, where does this place the educational practitioner? Educational psychologists are concerned with understanding, controlling, and predicting educational phenomena. With such poorly defined models of intelligence, again you should be cautioned to proceed with extra care in making any pronouncements about a specific student's intellectual capacity. Making premature generalizations about this topic can have unfortunate repercussions.

For example, numerous psychologists on both sides of the heredity-environment issue have proceeded on the assumption that we do in fact understand intelligence and we are able to control human intelligence. Some preschool educational programs, for example, have been based on the belief that the nature of intelligence is understood well enough to warrant early intervention with students in order to increase their intelligence (Bloom, 1964; Deutsch, 1964). Contrary to this viewpoint, other psychologists have attempted to point out that approximately 80 percent of the variance in IQ scores is due to heredity (Eysenck, 1971; Jensen, 1969). You can imagine the difficulties experienced by educators when they started to find out that many, but not all, of the Head Start programs failed to reach some of their objectives, particularly when Jensen (1969) suggested that the programs should experience difficulty because not enough attention had been placed on the genetic aspects of behavior! It is indeed unfortunate this controversy exists. As Horn (1976) aptly points out, the evidence is equivocal and far from adequate to provide a convincing case for either a mainly genetic or a mainly environmental interpretation of human intelligence. To argue otherwise is premature and speculative at best. For a particularly good review of this controversy, consult Cancro's (1971) book entitled *Intelligence: Genetic and Environmental Influences.*

A suggestion

We have spent a great deal of time on this topic because we believe that many of the arguments about the nature of intelligence have not been well formulated or conceptualized from an instructional perspective. As we view this topic from an instructional framework, two main issues seem to surface. The first issue concerns itself with the nature of environmental experiences that might have a long-term effect on a child's development. The second issue deals with the basic purposes of IQ tests and, more specifically, the types of tests needed to provide examiners with useful *instructional* data about a child.

The research strategies that have been used to study the nature of intelligence have not been designed to provide answers to either of the issues we raised. From our perspective, studying group differences between identifed subpopulations (sex differences, SES differences, race differences) is nonproductive from an *instructional perspective* unless it can be demonstrated that every member of the one group is different from every member of the other group on the variable being studied. Since this is not the case, and since teachers have to be concerned with the characteristics of individual students, research studies that emphasize group differences can be very misleading. Given that Johnny acts one way and Jimmy acts differently, what should be the best treatment strategy for each of the boys? Studies on group differences rarely address this issue.

As a case in point, let us look at one of the topics on intelligence studied by psychologists to indicate how the topic itself is nonproductive from an *instructional* point of view. The topic is the popular heredity versus environment issue. From our point of view, the questions raised by this issue have been unproductive because the wrong questions have been asked. To determine that a certain percentage of the variance in IQ scores is attributable to heredity provides the theoretician or practitioner with no clues about how to improve the environmental component. That question is not asked with this type of study. As educators, we are concerned with those factors that can be changed in an environment in order to bring about a particular goal with a particular child. Many of our current research strategies only let us make broad educational generalizations; they lack the specificity necessary to provide information about the environment. We need information about how to proceed with *environmental* decisions for *individual* children. Even if ultimately it could be determined that 100 percent of the variance in IQ scores is attributable to heredity (an absurdity), we still would need to make environmental decisions!

How might this problem be reformulated from an instructional perspective? Instead of studying intelligence as an entity, perhaps educational psychologists should turn their attention to *individual* students. The instructional question we need answered as educators is: Given a student with a propensity to respond in a particular manner, how might we provide the best environment in which the student can develop optimally?

If an educator needs general predictive information about a student's likelihood to do well in a particular curriculum, would it not make more sense to assess carefully those knowledges, skills, and competencies thought necessary for the student to perform successfully in the particular curriculum rather than to gather data about the student's postulated general intelligence level? You should note the similarity between this suggestion and the general suggestions proposed in the chapter on task analysis (Chapter 8).

In lieu of the hodgepodge of items that are now found on intelligence tests, this new approach would provide educators with specific instructional data about where to proceed with the student as well as the *identical broad predictive data* that are now obtained from IQ tests. In other words, the tests would be prescriptive, not descriptive. This orientation totally bypasses the current intelligence test controversy. The approach we are suggesting says nothing about potential to perform, therefore the issue of whether an item is fair for children coming from different socioeconomic groups is not an issue. If the item predicts success or lack of success in a specified curriculum or provides the educator with useful *prescriptive* information about where to proceed with a child, it should be included on the test. These new tests would not be labeled *intelligence* tests; they would be entitled *academic predictor* tests or *academic placement* tests. No inferences would be made about a student's innate potential to perform a task, for these proposed tests would not be concerned with innate potential. In fact, using the label *intelligence* lacks instructional usefulness in this framework.

Why should we have spent so much of your time criticizing various issues related to intelligence? Quite frankly, we believe some members of our profession have not been as careful as they should be. When you become a teacher, we want you to be cautious in your statements about a student's "intelligence." In fact, we hope you begin to view intelligence tests from a different perspective. Act *intelligently*.

SUMMARY

This chapter discussed many of the major theoretical viewpoints concerning the nature of intelligence. The chapter started by analyzing how the concept of intelligence has changed over the years. Using different paradigms and asking different questions, current theoretical viewpoints run the gamut from biological and environmental positions to the new field of artifical intelligence.

Many issues were also discussed, particularly as they relate to educational and instructional decision making. Of specific concern in this chapter was the inability of psychologists to generate workable definitions of *intelligence*. Another major concern was how broad terms tend to become misused. Finally, the payoff of this topic in terms of instruction was addressed. The instructional decisions that can be derived from current intelligence tests are very minimal because the tests are not designed to provide diagnostic instructional information. The chapter concluded by providing an analysis of what future psychologists will likely study about human capabilities.

SELF-TEST

1. If one were to use *Guilford's* theory of intelligence to analyze current intelligence tests, what would be found?
   a. The current tests do not measure developmental processes.
   b. The construct of "g" is a fairly reliable measure.

c. Not enough consideration is given to normative data.
d. The upper levels of thinking are not measured.

2. Identify two conceptual problems in the statement: The reason Johnny is doing poorly in school is because he is an underachiever.
3. You are studying the phenomenon of intelligence in the late *1800s.* What would you most likely study in your work?
   a. "g."
   b. The senses.
   c. The relationship between "g" and specific abilities.
   d. The impact of the environment on development.
4. Which statement best represents the relationship between a group intelligence test and an individual intelligence test?
   a. A group test is more reliable than an individual test because of the larger norms used in standardizing the tests.
   b. A group test usually measures a wider variety of abilities than an individual test.
   c. Performance on an individual test is more variable due to the differences in examiners.
   d. An individual test is generally better able to predict future academic performance than a group test.
5. Which of the following theorists or theoretical viewpoints has *systematically* studied different types of stimuli in relation to internal responses?
   a. Piaget.
   b. Vernon.
   c. Guilford.
   d. The artificial intelligence group.
6. With an IQ of 120 on an IQ test on which the standard deviation is *10,* what is the percentile?
   a. 97th.
   b. 3d.
   c. 50th.
   d. 84th.
7. Through careful analysis a scientist discovers a new use for the sun's rays. This discovery is an example of:
   a. Accommodation.
   b. Assimilation.
   c. Conservation.
   d. Concrete operational thought.
8. The belief that anything can be taught to a child in some form if the child has the basic thought processes is best represented by:
   a. Bruner.
   b. Guilford.
   c. Piaget.
   d. Vernon.
9. Which theoretical viewpoint would recommend discovery learning as a means of learning new material?
   a. Gagné.
   b. The artificial intelligence group.
   c. Skinner.
   d. Piaget.
10. Assume you are a test designer, and you want to design a test that will be very useful to classroom teachers for their instructional decision making. Which characteristic(s) of the test would most likely give teachers useful information?
   a. A test based on "g."
   b. A norm-referenced approach to test construction.
   c. A criterion-referenced approach to test construction.
   d. A test based on a Gagné-type analysis of the curriculum.
   e. *a* and *b.*
   f. *c* and *d.*

ANSWER KEY TO BOXED QUESTIONS

1. The "g" theory of intelligence does not take into consideration specific abilities or uneven development patterns.
   From an instructional perspective, it does not provide educators with useful prescriptive information about what to do with a student who is not competent on a task or class of tasks.
   From a developmental perspective, the "g" theory does not address the quantitative and qualitative changes that take place during the formative years of development.
2. Piaget's and Bruner's theories are developmental in their orientation. The differences center around the degree to which biological development (Piaget) or environmental influences (Bruner) are emphasized.
3. Two major criticisms can be made against current intelligence testing using Guilford's theory:
   a. The tests tend to ignore the major factors at the upper levels of the model, such as divergent production, evaluation, as well as transformations and implications.
   b. The tests are not constructed in any systematic way to evaluate response patterns based on different stimuli and processes. Rather, the tests sample a hodgepodge of abilities thought to measure "g."
4. According to Piaget, in order to respond meaningfully

to the environment in a cognitive sense, the person must be biologically ready (mature) for the experience. Given a biological readiness, the environment plays a major role in development in terms of what the person does to the environment as well as the effect the environment has on cognitive development.

5. Intelligence is a label or hypothetical construct. IQ is a statistic derived from a person's performance on an intelligence test. Since intelligence is ill-defined, to assume that a particular test actually measures an entity entitled *intelligence* is premature. It is much safer to say that the IQ score represents performance on a constellation of tasks and is designed to predict academic achievement, or whatever else it is designed to predict.

   To equate IQ and intelligence lends credence to the proposition that intelligence is an actual entity. Further, it lends credence to the viewpoint that the nature of intelligence is known. Given that our state of knowledge in this area is limited, any attempt to equate IQ and intelligence is fallacious reasoning at best.

6. Some unfortunate outcomes have included:
   a. The problem of labeling human behavior and then using the label as an explanation of behavior.
   b. An unnecessary hereditarian-environmentalist debate that has resulted in premature pronouncements about the differences between racial groups.
   c. Premature closure on theorizing resulting in a dogmatism rather than a scientific questioning attitude toward the subject.
   d. The perpetration of a great deal of testing that provides very little instructional payoff for the time spent.

ANSWER KEY TO SELF-TEST

1. *d*
2. *a.* Underachievement is a description of a relationship between an expected performance and an actual performance. It is not an explanation.
   b. The label *underachievement* is derived from a global measure, thus ignoring the uneven distribution of abilities in people.
   c. Since, in actuality, we do not truly understand the nature of intellectual potential, to make a statement about underachievement is pretentious. Rather, it would be appropriate to say that the student performed at a lower level than predicted.
3. *b*
4. *d*
5. *c*
6. *a*
7. *a*
8. *a*
9. *d*
10. *f*

Chapter 24

Motivational theories: Implications for the classroom

ONE OF THE FIRST CONSIDERATIONS a teacher needs to make when planning a unit of instruction is how to insure that the students will spend enough time with their lessons to successfully complete the assigned tasks. Without the student's cooperation to learn the objectives, the unit comes to a standstill from the teacher's point of view.

To make this chapter both useful and provocative, we have chosen to discuss only those topics or theories that appear to have some bearing on motivational questions in a school context over which the schools or teachers have a direct or indirect influence. For example, since the schools really have no control over sex differences in motivation, SES differences, or child-rearing patterns, these topics are not considered. These topics are important considerations for a broad understanding of motivation, but the generalities that can be gleaned from research in these areas have little functional utility from an instructional perspective. At best, all we can suggest to you is do not treat students differently because of their membership in a group. Base your expectancies on the entering behavior of the student, and then act accordingly.

You should also be forewarned that the classical, operant, and social learning theories related to school motivation are not discussed because these theories have been addressed in other chapters. For the purposes of this chapter we are interested in those factors external to a student as well as those internal factors that appear to be responsible for *arousing, directing,* and *sustaining* desirable behaviors of students in a school-related context (Ball, 1977).

Our discussion starts with a summary of a selected group of broad theories that tend to view motivation as a general pervasive force responsible for giving direction to human behavior. Both developmental theories and broad process theories are considered. Our attention then turns to a selected group of persistent traits or motives students are said to possess that are related to instructionally relevant tasks. In this section we talk about such factors as motivational styles, achievement motivation, locus of control, interests, and school-related anxiety. Finally, we discuss motivation as a partial function of the state of the person at a given time in relation to specific environmental situations.

Throughout the chapter, four questions are addressed, where appropriate.

1. What external and internal factors tend to *energize* a student?
2. What external and internal factors influence a student's *choice* of activity?
3. What external and internal factors influence how long a student is willing to *persist* at an activity?
4. What appear to be the implications for educational and instructional decision making?

At the conclusion of this chapter, you should be able to:

1. Explain how different motivational theories have attempted to describe what energizes a person to make a choice and persist with the choice.
2. Identify the variables that appear to contribute to such *instructionally* relevant traits and characteristics as: intrinsic motivation, achievement motivation, internal locus of control, interests, and anxiety. Explain the underlying generalizations of the homeostasis model as it relates to instruction.
3. Identify how our schools might be structured and how classes might be conducted to bring about goal-directed behavior and intrinsic motivational patterns in students.

BROAD THEORIES OF MOTIVATION

At a broad level, motivation may be considered to be whatever appears to energize and direct a person's behavior. Some theorists have tended to focus on environmental variables in their search for explanations and descriptions of motivation. Taking the Lockean viewpoint that the human mind is essentially a blank slate at birth, the diverse viewpoints presented earlier in the book represent different aspects of the classical, operant, and social learning theories. As a generalization, these viewpoints emphasize that environmental factors are a main determiner of behavior. Contrasted sharply with the Lockean viewpoint, Leibnitz suggested that humans actively seek out and rearrange conceptualizations of the environment as a result of their inherent nature to do so.

Rather than viewing behavior as a function of the environment per se, the Leibnitzian viewpoint stresses that behavior results from internal processes and choices to behave in a patterned manner toward stimuli in the environment. A more current view of behavior incorporates aspects of both extremes and posits reciprocal relationships between those two positions. In this chapter we shall be discussing the latter two viewpoints.

Historically, most psychologists of the Leibnitzian persuasion described motivational variables by postulating various relationships among internal needs, drives, and motivation. Needs are said to come about as a result of basic physiological states (a primary need) or as the result of some acquired need to respond successfully to different aspects of the environment (a secondary need). Having a need creates an imbalance between a current state and a more desirable potential state. This imbalance sets up a drive that must be reduced in order to be satisfied. Of a general nature, drives are said to energize a person toward action. The direction the action takes is the result of motivation or a combination of motives. Based on a specific goal, motivated behavior is said to be purposive and is derived from experience.

Recently, however, this viewpoint has come under attack as being simplistic and incomplete. We start our discussion of motivation, therefore, with some modern theories that have rejected both the environmental explanations and the outdated drive-reduction version of motivated behavior.

Maslow's theory: Self-actualization

Maslow (1968) has developed a rather broad, general motivational and personality model that depicts the relationships among needs, drives, and motives. Maslow's theory posits that humans have an inborn tendency to become self-actualized (a general *positive* motivational force that is responsible for people reaching their potential and performing good works). According to Maslow, psychologically healthy people progress through the lower stages of physical needs, safety needs, needs for belongingness, and a need to respect themselves in order to reach the stage of self-actualization (Figure 24–1).

This theory was developed as a reaction against the stimulus-response (S-R) behavioristic viewpoints as well as against the early homeostasis models, which suggest that behavior is generally a function of attempting to reduce an imbalanced drive state. Maslow arrived at this position after rejecting the S-R or R-S theories for not emphasizing that humans are capable of executing internally conscious goal-directed decisions. Maslow also rejected the drive-reduction models for not considering what positive forces interact within a person to promote excellence and good works. Since the drive-reduction or homeostasis models emphasize that the primary goal of a person

FIGURE 24–1
Maslow's hierarchy of needs

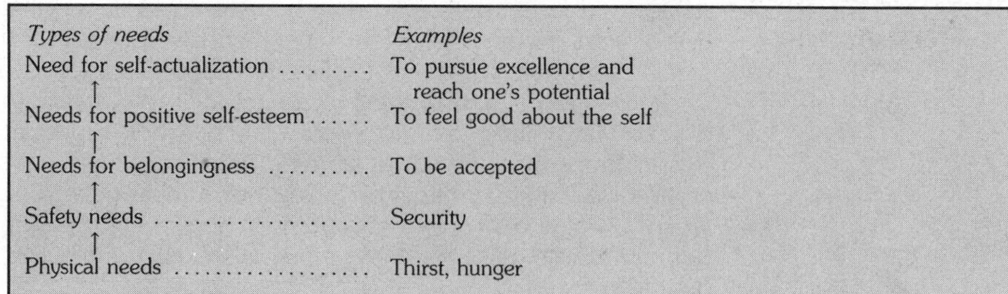

Types of needs	*Examples*
Need for self-actualization	To pursue excellence and reach one's potential
↑	
Needs for positive self-esteem	To feel good about the self
↑	
Needs for belongingness	To be accepted
↑	
Safety needs	Security
↑	
Physical needs	Thirst, hunger

is to reduce tension or disequilibrium, Maslow wondered why anyone would ever desire to produce anything that requires hard work. From the drive-reduction perspective, an attempt to produce a major work should result in a state of disequilibrium, and since a state of disequilibrium is postulated as unpleasant, people would attempt to reduce the disequilibrium by moving away from the unpleasant state. By moving away from an unpleasant state, homeostasis or psychological balance can be achieved but excellence cannot.

To account for differences in motivational patterns of behavior, Maslow postulated two types of motivational traits. Deficiency motivational traits are related to a reduction of states of deprivation or imbalance, while growth motivational traits are responsible for moving a person toward self-actualization. As one moves up the hierarchy from physical needs through the need for self-esteem, the growth motivational traits take on increasing importance. This model suggests that the degree to which a person has satisfactorily evolved through these stages of development is the degree to which growth motivational traits should be present. For example, according to Maslow, a person who has not satisfied the basic physical or safety needs of survival will hardly be in a state to move toward self-actualization. People in those stages will still be attempting to resolve various deficiency motivational states. In addition, people who do not feel very good about themselves are less likely to pursue excellence. Maslow suggests that when people are confronted with a choice, those who do not feel very positive about themselves will more than likely choose a "regression choice" (i.e., the person will move away from growth), much akin to Fromm's (1941) point about escape from freedom. Freedom is a threatening state for many people—in a free state there is no one to blame for failure except oneself. Another way of stating this is to say that when people are given free choices, those who do not feel very good about themselves tend to make *safe* rather than *risky* choices. In essence, people define themselves by the choices they make.

Erikson's theory: Critical choices in development

Similar in scope to Maslow's stage theory, Erikson's (1963) broad personality-motivation theory postulates that there are eight stages of development. See Figure 24–2 for a description of his model. As can be seen from the figure, at each stage of development the person has to resolve different external and internal forces, which tend to push and pull a person toward different actions. Often termed a *personality theory,* Erikson's theory was included in this chapter because of its similarities to Maslow's theory. Further, some very important motivational implications can be derived from Erikson's general theory.

You will note that each one of the eight stages implies a continuum from very positive characteristics (e.g., trust, autonomy, industry) to very negative characteristics (e.g.,

FIGURE 24–2
Erikson's eight stages of development

Stage	*Age*	*Positive characteristics*
Ego integrity versus despair	Late life	Puts life in perspective
Generativity versus stagnation	Adulthood	Interest in producing worthwhile products
Intimacy versus isolation	18 years–early adulthood	Able to share in a mature relationship
Identity versus role diffusion	12–18 years	Determines role, gets direction
Industry versus inferiority	6–11 years	Learns to become involved for the sake of the activity, active pursuit
Initiative versus guilt	3–5 years	Learns to interact aggressively with the environment
Autonomy versus shame and doubt	1–2 years	Learns some independence
Trust versus mistrust	0–1 year	Learns to depend on people, trust develops

mistrust, shame, inferiority). According to Erikson, the environment has a great effect on which side of the continuum the person tends to operate.

Contrasted with the broad developmental views of Maslow and Erikson, several broad internal motivational variables will now be considered. After these models are presented, we shall incorporate the four models in a discussion of intrinsic motivation.

White's (1959) competence theory

According to R. W. White, the events that occur between homeostatic imbalances in the environment are the periods of time that need to be explained by some motivational theory. Why does a person behave in a predictable manner? When a person is not moved to reduce some imbalance brought about by some tissue need (hunger, thirst), why would anyone want to seek out a challenging task? White suggests that the need to be competent in one's environment is a basic biological need that has survival utility. The more competent the person, the greater the chance of survival. According to White, people seek out stimulation between homeostatic states of imbalance because the stimulation is inherently a challenge. In other words, the person desires to be competent in a variety of stimulus situations to fulfill the basic biological need of competence. By seeking out stimulation when there is no significant stimulation, the person creates a challenge, particularly if there is an incongruity in the new situation. The reduction of the incongruity is said to bring about a feeling of competence. This viewpoint implies that intrinsically motivated behavior is the result of a general need to feel competent in interactions with the environment.

In young children, this motivation for competence is said to be undifferentiated, but as a child begins to develop the competence, motivation begins to evolve into specific motives such as achievement or the need for affiliation with others. As a parallel to the "g" explanation of intelligence, the general ability of a growing child becomes more and more differentiated and specialized due to environmental interactions.

Berlyne's arousal theory

Attempting to synthesize the drive-reduction models of motivation with the reinforcement theory approach, Berlyne (1966) noted that *both* the decrease and the increase of a drive state can be rewarding. To account for both of these conditions, Berlyne postulated that there must be an optimum level of arousal that is responsible for these two types of behavior.

Berlyne developed his theory by reasoning that humans are information processors who need to cope efficiently with their environment. This coping requires strategies to categorize and process information by comparing and contrasting stimuli and stimulus situations. If there is not enough stimulation in the environment, the person will actively seek out stimulation. Conversely, if there is too much stimulation, the person will attempt to reduce the stimulation or escape from the situation. Essentially, Berlyne was attempting to address the question of *why* people engage in problem-solving behavior. According to Berlyne, being in a stimulus situation characterized by a lot of novelty, change, surprise, incongruity, or complexity has the potential to bring about states of conceptual conflict. Six types of conceptual conflict are postulated (Figure 24–3). In turn, Berlyne suggests that people need strategies for reducing the conceptual conflict brought about by a discrepancy between the information provided by the environment and the cognitive state of the learner. The internal strategies identified by Berlyne include strengthening a response while weakening another response, introducing a new response that "swamps" the original, developing a superordinate strategy so as to make the incompatible information compatible, or ignoring the incompatibilities. In any case, the strategy the person uses serves the function of reducing the conceptual conflict initially brought about by an internal level of arousal. We return to this point later in the chapter when the specific state of the learner is addressed.

FIGURE 24–3
Major types of conceptual conflict

Doubt—to believe and not to believe
Perplexity—to believe A or B
Contradiction—to believe A and B when A and B appear to be contradictions
Incongruity—to believe that A and B cannot occur together
Confusion—not sure about A or B
Irrelevant—to solve for A and to be confronted by B which is not germane to the solution of A

Source: Berlyne (1960).

Intrinsic motivation

In reacting against the pure behavioristic theories, many psychologists feel that theories are needed to deal with the issue of choice—why does a person choose one activity over another and then persevere at a task? From a pure reinforcement perspective such issues as goals, plans, and choice are unimportant. A person does something simply because the person must do it; the behavior is determined by past reinforcements and contingencies. Inner processes are excess baggage from some behavioral viewpoints. Other behavioral theorists (Hull, 1943) have been concerned with internal processes, but only in terms of the internal drive states said to occur between stimuli and responses.

Those theorists outside of the behavioristic orientation who are concerned with inner processes generally posit that a person has a choice; people *voluntarily, purposefully,* and *consistently* interact with their environment and seek out the environment. Rather than attempt to explain behavior by focusing on the stimuli in the environment as the primary factor in producing a behavior, these theorists postulating internal processes have viewed behavior as under a person's control. For example, psychologists of an information-processing or cognitive persuasion suggest that many overt behavioral patterns in humans are under the influence of conscious goals and plans.

Not only do people tend to respond to their environment based on conscious choices, goals, and plans, but they do so because the activities often are apparently rewarding for their own sake. Koch (1956), for example, was one of the originators of the

FIGURE 24–4
Intrinsic motivation is one of the major goals of education

notion that intrinsic motivation must be considered when studying motivated behavior, and that any motivational theory must deal with the fact that intrinsically motivated behavior is under the partial control of conscious plans. Further, any theory of motivation has to deal with the observation that not only do people interact with their environment to reduce discrepancies (a drive-reduction explanation), but they also interact with their environment to *produce* significant discrepancies. Discrepancies are a challenge. When viewed from this perspective, the similarity between Maslow's, Erikson's, White's, and Berlyne's theories should be apparent. All four approaches suggest that *humans consciously choose to interact with their environments to bring about certain goals* that are perceived as challenging and reasonably attainable. One more point needs brief discussion.

Recently concern has been expressed over the relationship between extrinsic reinforcers and intrinsic reinforcers, (Figure 24–4). A host of studies on both animals and humans have found that the application of extrinsic reinforcers to an intrinsically motivated organism may have some deleterious influences on intrinsic motivation (Davis, Settlage & Harlow, 1950; Deci, 1971, 1972; Lepper, Greene & Nisbett, 1973). What are the implications of these findings?

Although much more research needs to be conducted on the origins of intrinsic motivation, as well as on the relationships between intrinsic motivation and extrinsic motivation, a summary of the research and theories suggests the following possibilities.

1. Born with a generalized drive to be efficient or competent, an organism seeks out challenging stimuli.

2. If there is no strong preference for one activity over another, the initial application of extrinsic motivation might increase the likelihood of a preference for an activity, particularly if that activity is moderately challenging and the organism experiences success. In this instance, extrinsic motivation can change to intrinsic motivation. At this point, all we can say is that much more work needs to be done to clarify these complex interrelationships.

3. Having achieved success in an activity that is perceived as interesting and challenging for its own sake, however, makes an extrinsic reinforcer less important. In fact, De Charms (1968) suggests that extrinsic reinforcers can destroy a person's sense of personal causation and contribute to a person's feeling of being a "pawn" rather than an "origin" of behavior.

4. From an instructional decision-making point of view, if a student is performing as expected, very little extrinsic motivation is necessary. On the other hand, if a student does not perform as desired and the reason for the nonperformance is diagnosed as a lack of motivation, some degree of extrinsic reinforcement might be necessary. To take advantage of a student's intrinsic motivation, the teacher should make the tasks of moderate difficulty and should attempt to choose interesting topics where possible. Providing the students with a choice of activities also makes sense if the choice is commensurate with the teacher's cognitive goals. For an excellent in-depth discussion of these issues, consult Deci (1975).

From the theories we have discussed so far, several other general instructional implications seem warranted. Maslow's general theory suggests that people have a need to be accepted and feel good about themselves. According to Maslow, if people do not achieve these needs they will have a great deal of difficulty reaching their potential.

Relate these points to Erikson's fourth and fifth stages of development. You will recall Erikson proposes that the elementary-school-aged child has to resolve the conflict of industry versus inferiority, and the adolescent has to resolve the conflict of identity versus role diffusion. Essentially, both of these macro-theories imply that students should become involved in long-term projects of their own choosing. To reach one's potential takes a lot of effort and long-term involvement. Certainly the senses of industry and purpose (an identity) are important factors in the development of competence and creativity. We remind you, however, that long-term projects cannot be completed without *acquiring the prerequisites* for the projects.

Contrast the implications of these general theories with the obtained results of Becker and Englemann's (1977) direct teaching model based on reinforcement theory and used with disadvantaged K–3 students. Using the principle of insuring success through progressing in small sequential steps, requiring overt responses, and applying immediate feedback to the students, Becker and Englemann's program has resulted in great success in increasing students' reading levels. More important, with respect to personality and motivational variables, it was found that students taught with this direct method, compared with students taught by more humanistic methods emphasizing the "whole" child or the child's own interests, were more motivated and had a better self-concept.

How might these apparent discrepancies be resolved? In our opinion there is no conflict between these approaches. It seems that in the initial stages of teaching young children great care should be used to insure *skill development, success,* and *positive attitudes* toward school. Instead of viewing positive attitudes and motivation as coming before teaching a lesson, it could well be that positive attitudes and motivation can be developed *as the result of being successful* at a task! Insuring that the prerequisites have been acquired for long-term projects, the teacher is then in a position to successfully involve students with those projects. A careful plan can incorporate both of these viewpoints.

So far we have talked about intrinsic motivation in relation to classroom tasks. If you would press us, however, we would claim that an equally important objective—in fact, maybe the critical outcome of education—is to facilitate continuing motivation in students beyond the context of the classroom. It seems to us that our ultimate goal in education is to produce students who are so turned on to some of the academic concerns of life that they will want to return to topics related to the school curriculum after they leave school. Certainly very little is known about this important area. With almost no research having been conducted on continuing motivation, all we can do is to take some broad guesses about how to produce these results. After an extensive review of related research, Maehr (1976) proposes that the most likely antecedent conditions of continuing motivation are to get students to see themselves as the cause of their own behavior, perceive themselves as capable of performing successfully, and join others who possess achievement values. Our goals and programs should aim toward these outcomes.

1. Why do most modern psychologists reject the drive-reduction model of motivation?
2. From a psychological point of view, in what way are Maslow's, Erikson's, White's, and Berlyne's theories alike?
3. From an instructional decision-making point of view, use components of *each* of the four broad theories to indicate how motivation might be increased in the context of the classroom as well as in the context of schools. What common element seems to underline all four of the theories for instructional decision making?

MOTIVATIONAL VARIABLES AND SCHOOL ACHIEVEMENT RELATIONSHIPS

The common element of the theoretical assumptions underlying the motivational theories discussed in this chapter is that there are general pervasive factors that tend to provide for a person both energy and a general direction for approaching various tasks. In this section we narrow our focus somewhat to consider some *specific* internal factors, variables, and motives said to provide the energy and the choices students make toward school-related tasks. Some of the specific motivational factors related to a student's school behavior include the student's motivation style, the student's desire to achieve (achievement motivation), the student's perception of whether behavior is internally or externally controlled (locus of control), the student's specific interests, and the amount and duration of anxiety related to various school tasks.

Motivational style

Earlier in the book we discussed the proposition that people have distinct identifiable styles or propensities to process, reinterpret, learn, and perform tasks in a consistent manner. Many such learning or cognitive styles have been postulated (Cronbach & Snow, 1977). More recently, the concept of style has been discussed with reference to motivational patterns of behavior (Ball, 1977). Based on Chui's (1967) factor analytic doctoral dissertation, which found that students report five distinct reasons for approaching school-related tasks, Ball suggests that it might be profitable to view motivated behavior in the same light as learning styles.

In other words, not only do students appear to prefer various distinctive characteristic modes to learn or process information, but students also have different distinctive preferences for what energizes and maintains their approach behaviors or nonapproach behaviors in a school-related context. According to Ball, those independent factors that emerged from Chui's study included the following general predispositions:

1. A general *positive feeling toward school-related tasks.*
2. A need to *avoid failure* on school-related tasks.
3. A predisposition to respond to the environment in a manner *to resolve an intense "curiosity."*
4. The need for *social acceptance* from teacher or peers.
5. The need to *conform* to teacher or peer pressure.

Although relatively new as an approach to the study of school-related behavior, this avenue of research has the potential of integrating the general motivational theories discussed earlier in the book with some of the specific motivational theories concerned with discrete motives. This integration would appear to be needed to derive a workable decision-making model for the classroom teacher. Put another way, knowledge about a student's motivational characteristics might help a teacher to make wiser instructional decisions for specific students based on the student's specific approach tendencies, particularly with reference to assigning long-term projects or tasks that are perceived by the student as too easy or too difficult.

Ball is careful to warn readers, however, that the issues involved with motivation are highly complex. According to Ball, any theory that ignores other school-related behaviors, such as the student's general and specific cognitive aptitudes toward specific subject matter as well as the student's preferences to learn and process information, will be less than successful as an instructional decision-making model. For example, does it make any sense to motivate a student who does not have the general or specific prerequisites to perform the assigned tasks?

Achievement motivation

Achievement motivation is defined as the relatively specific and stable characteristics of some people to thrive on pursuing and achieving excellence in activities for the sake of the activity. McClelland, Atkinson, Clark, and Lowell (1953) wondered why there are such tremendous individual differences in people's tendencies to pursue success and postulated that people differ in their need for achievement. Recently this topic has received much interest from our profession.

To get a perspective on this topic, let us assume you have been hired to follow a particular student around all day in school and observe all that the student does. You are asked to record every behavior you observe. Your first finding would be that the student engages in some type of activity at all times during the day. Your next conclusion most likely would be that your student would tend to engage in some behaviors much more frequently than in other types of behaviors. This is what achievement motivation is all about. The real questions concerned with achievement motivation deal with the *internal* inclinations of a person to pursue a variety of activities just for the sake of excellence instead of choosing activities that tend to lead to mediocre performance.

According to Atkinson and Birch (1974), whether a student will engage in a task to pursue excellence at any given time during a day is related to the student's consummatory needs (hunger, thirst, etc.), the student's hierarchical structure of internal motives to achieve success in various activities, and the student's tendencies to avoid failure in various activities. From a motivational point of view, in order to be able to predict what our student most likely would do with a difficult task we would have to be able to identify:

1. The student's general motive to achieve success (MS) as well as the student's tendency to avoid failure (MaF).
2. The effect of the immediate environment with respect to the student's perception of the difficulty of the task.
3. The relative attractiveness of a particular activity for that student as compared with other types of activities (work versus talking, English versus math).
4. The student's physiological needs, which result in consummatory behavior.

J. W. Atkinson (1974) has diagrammed the tendency to achieve success in any given situation as $TS = MS \times PS \times IS$, where TS = tendency to achieve success, MS = motive to achieve success, PS = the person's perception that engaging in a task will be followed by success, and IS = the relative attractiveness of a particular task. Given any task situation, all three variables should be optimum or at least in the right direction in order for a student to strive for success. Unfortunately, in the context of school, every student is not motivated to achieve success (MS); rather, many students are influenced by a motive to avoid failure (MaF). In addition, all tasks are not perceived as attractive to students.

How do these factors interact to produce persistent behavior? As a generalization, when a student's MS is greater than his/her MaF ($MS > MaF$), the student will tend to stick to tasks that are perceived as moderately difficult (Figure 24–5). If, on the other hand, the relationship between MS and MaF is: $MaF > MS$, the student will more likely pursue tasks that are perceived as either easy or difficult. It should be readily apparent why MaF students choose easy tasks; it is a little more complicated why MaF students would choose difficult tasks that would likely terminate in failure. The most plausible explanation for the choice of difficult tasks by MaF students is

FIGURE 24–5
Achievement-motivated students choose tasks of moderate difficulty

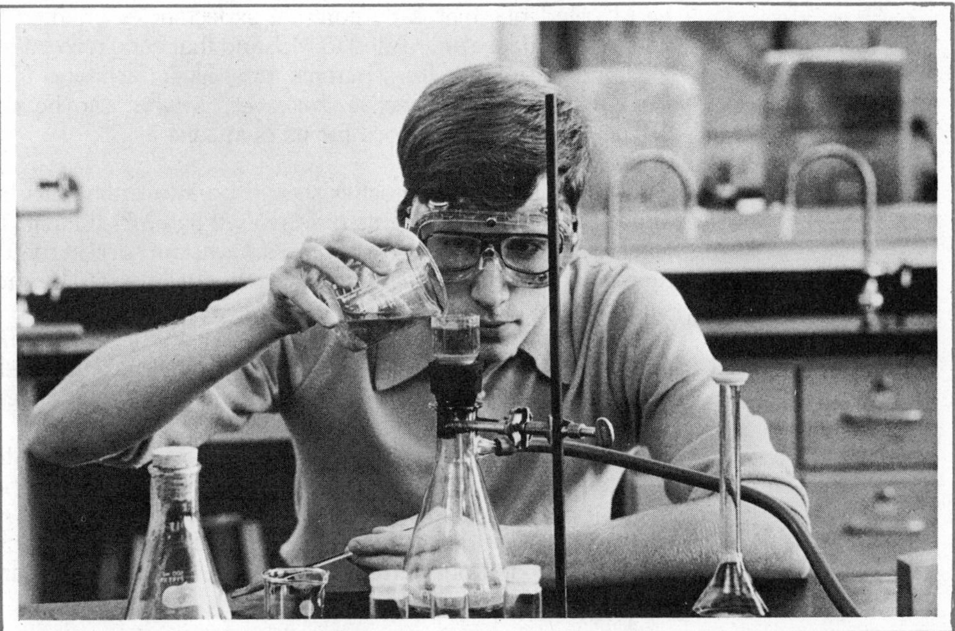

that the students, in actuality, create a situation for which they exempt themselves from the blame of failure; the task is simply too difficult. How can a student be expected to be successful when confronted with a difficult task? In this situation, by choosing a difficult task, the student has the task to blame when failure occurs rather than the student's personal inadequacies. Isaacson (1964), for example, found that MS students at the college level tend to enroll in moderately challenging courses, whereas MaF students tend to enroll in easy or difficult courses. Obviously, if the student has very little or no interest in a task, these findings are not as pervasive. It would be interesting in this respect to identify the underlying motivations of students choosing the pass-fail option in grading for some of their college work.

To get a clearer picture concerning the characteristics of MS and MaF students, Vidler (1977) has summarized a variety of studies conducted on these students. Vidler has found that students for whom MS > MaF:

1. Are interested in excellence for its own sake as opposed to extrinsic rewards.
2. Will not be greatly affected by external rewards.
3. May, in fact, respond negatively toward tasks if too much success is associated with completing the task.
4. Tend to pick experts rather than friends when assigned group projects and given a choice of partners.
5. Prefer task situations in which the person responsible for getting the work done is apparent.
6. Prefer to rely on their independent judgments rather than the judgments of others.
7. Tend to have clearer goals than typical students, particularly with reference to intermediate and long-term goals.

A great deal of work has been done to identify the early environmental and organismic factors thought conducive to producing MS > MaF students. It should come as no shock to you that students coming from higher SES levels are more than likely to be MS students, that early parental expectancies oriented toward achievement tasks and independence are related to MS, and that early recognition of achievement through love and acceptance from parents most likely facilitates MS. The important question from a teacher's perspective, however, is what can be done to increase students' desires to pursue excellence for its own sake.

At a general level, the teacher should be aware that success and failure experiences appear to influence students differently. High-MS students are said to thrive on challenging and moderately difficult tasks. Constant success may *decrease* the MS student's motivation to achieve; therefore, a teacher will have to be careful not to always present simple material. Conversely, the MaF student oftentimes responds very poorly to failure. This line of research suggests that the level of difficulty of a task should be matched to a student's MS or MaF style; a MS student should receive moderately difficult material, whereas a MaF student initially should receive relatively easy material.

There is, however, possibly a greater implication for education. Since most psychologists tend to view MS as a learned characteristic to respond positively toward tasks, might it not be possible to teach students to develop MS > MaF tendencies, thereby developing in students the desire to pursue excellence for the sake of excellence? Although beyond our current capabilities, this line of research warrants much further investigation.

While there have been numerous studies reported in the literature that have attempted to increase achievement motivation and hence a student's grades (Kolb, 1965; McClelland, 1965; McClelland & Alschuler, 1971; McClelland & Winter, 1969; Ryals, 1969; Smith & Troth, 1975; Tang, 1970), the findings have not been overwhelmingly positive. Some of the studies have reported increases in certain desirable outcomes, however, such as a lesser tendency to drop out of school (McClelland & Winter, 1969). Another study has reported increases in grades in some courses in which the teachers who taught the course were also involved in the achievement training program (Ryals, 1969). Finally, Kolb (1965) found that increases in the grades of students who participated in the training program were influenced by achievement motivation training. In each case, however, the numbers in the study were very small, and any generalizations to the school population at large are somewhat tenuous. Further, in many of the studies a large number of students dropped out of the treatment conditions before the study was completed, thus compounding the results.

At this time, the following conclusions appear warranted with reference to achievement motivation training:

1. It is possible to increase a student's motivation to achieve through training programs *as measured by selected achievement motivation instruments* if the student has a desire to be trained.
2. The change in achievement motivation generally does not correspond to a change in the student's grades, although in individual cases there may be *marked* changes.
3. Oftentimes, as summarized by Alschuler (1973), concomitant changes have been reported outside of school where students are more in charge of their lives.
4. Comparable studies conducted with businesspeople have been found to be more successful (Arnoff & Litwin, 1971; McClelland, 1965) than training programs in a school context.
5. Regardless of the specific components of an achievement training program, it is generally agreed that the training should consist of at least:

a. A training session carried out over *a long period of time* (perhaps a semester or longer).
b. An emphasis on *doing tasks well*—an attitude of excellence.
c. An emphasis on *generating realistic and attainable goals.*
d. Training *on how to plan* tasks appropriately.
e. An emphasis on *living fully* in the here and now while at the same time *developing capabilities to be future-oriented.*

To attempt to analyze the reasons for the rather weak relationships found between achievement motivation training and performance in school is well beyond the scope of this text, although several brief possible explanations are in order. First of all, there may be different reasons for motives to achieve; therefore different treatment programs would be needed for different types of achievement motivation. For example, Wolk and DuCette (1973) postulate two types of achievement motivation: an internally motivated person who accepts responsibility for actions and an externally motivated person who attributes outcomes of actions to environmental sources, in which case the task itself becomes somewhat immaterial. More recently Veroff (1975) has suggested six varieties of achievement motivation. Veroff has found that some people desire to do tasks because the tasks provide the opportunity for the person to become *autonomous, responsible,* or *competent.* In these instances, Veroff suggests that the main motivational variable contributing to the person's behavioral pattern is the desire to pursue the task for its own sake. Veroff has found other people who tend to do tasks because the tasks provide the person with the opportunity to have influence over others by developing a sense of *power, competing* with others, or having some other *social impact.*

Second, a high GPA implies that the student has acquired the prerequisites of the curriculum and is able to apply them to the curriculum. *No amount of achievement motivation training* is likely to change a student's GPA if the student does not have the necessary prerequisite skills or abilities to perform at a higher level. Third, it would be only logical to assume that a person high in achievement motivation would respond differently to different aspects of the environment based on specific interest patterns. Adults high on achievement motivation in one area of their lives certainly do not have that same high level in all areas. A successful person *must* be selective in how time is spent. Why should it be any different with children? There is no reason to assume that a high achievement motivation level should have the same outcome on all aspects of a student's school life. A person's skill level and specific interests must be considered in relation to any achievement motivation variable we choose to study. Most of the achievement motivation studies have not taken these considerations into account even though Atkinson specified this as a factor in determining the tendency to achieve success. Finally, the types of criticisms leveled against the research on intelligence and academic performance pointed out in Chapter 23 are also applicable here.

To help make students independent problem solvers desirous of pursuing excellence is clearly one of the major goals of education! With the growing emphasis in psychology to view people as capable of consciously controlling their own destiny, it is apparent that this line of research bears close watching.

Locus of control

The student's perception of his/her locus of control is postulated by Rotter (1954) as the degree to which individuals believe they have control over their own environment.

Educational psychologists have recently become interested in the relationship between a student's locus of control over the environment and the student's academic achievement. As with the need for achievement research, it has been posited that an increase in a student's internal locus of control should have a positive outcome on the student's level of achievement. Rotter's theory suggests that people are distributed along an "internal-external" continuum. People along the internal end of the continuum feel that their abilities, skills, personal effort, competence, and similar variables control their destiny. In other words, *internal* people feel that the outcome of events is generally under the control of the person. Contrasted with the *internals* are those people who characteristically feel that whatever happens to them is "in the cards"—controlled by chance, other people, and luck. Termed *externals* by Rotter, these people tend to feel that events in the environment are beyond the control of the individual.

The implications for education should be apparent. In an extensive review of the research comparing the relationship between locus of control and academic achievement, Bar-Tal and Bar-Zohar (1977) found that in 31 of 36 studies in this area there was a significant relationship between internal locus of control and high academic achievement (Figure 24–6). In the famous Coleman Report (1966), internal locus of control was found to be the *best* single predictor of successful academic achievement with disadvantaged students!

As with any correlational studies, care needs to be taken not to conclude a cause-and-effect relationship between the variables. With that caution in mind, however, there do appear to be some consistent patterns exhibited by internal people which need to be considered. Internals tend to have less anxiety than externals. They are more goal-oriented, thus behaving much more aggressively in seeking information germane to their goals and using the information appropriately. They persist at tasks

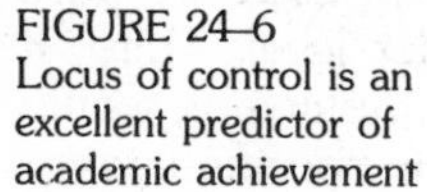

FIGURE 24–6
Locus of control is an excellent predictor of academic achievement

more readily and show much more initiative in challenging situations. Being aggressive and seeking out information germane to their goals, they are quick to study tasks in a systematic way to arrive at an effective solution. As a generalization, externals behave at the opposite end of the continuum on each of these characteristics. From a teacher's perspective, the ideal student is one at the internal end of the continuum who is oriented toward success and who is reasonably interested in the subject matter. Obviously, not all internals respond the same way toward school. In addition to locus of control, the student's specific abilities, specific expectations and interests, and similar characteristics are closely related to the student's behavior in school.

Given that students with internal locus of control tend to perform better in school, the question must be raised whether changing a reasonably capable student from an external locus of control orientation to an internal orientation will have any concomitant effect on the student's school achievement. Although much additional research needs to be carried out in this area, most studies that have attempted to increase a student's internal locus of control have been successful (Bar-Tal, Bar-Tal & Leinhardt, 1975; Chandler, 1975; De Charms, 1972, 1976a; Shore, Milgram & Malasky, 1971; Wang & Stiles, 1975). Further, each of these studies reports that changing students from externals to internals had a facilitating effect on academic achievement.

As you can see from the previous studies the common element in each program was to give the student responsibility and hence some choice over his/her own destiny. In the Bar-Tal et al. (1975) study, students who had been exposed to an individualized self-paced program in which progress depended upon the student's initiative were reported to be higher in their perception of internal locus of control. Wang and Stiles (1975) report the same finding for second graders in an inner-city setting. Chandler (1975) determined that using underachieving junior-high-school-aged students as tutors for second- and third-grade children had a very positive outcome on the junior high school students' internal locus of control. Apparently the role of a tutor requires responsibility as well as the cognitive realization that in order to teach material to younger students, the material has to be reorganized, thus putting the junior high student in an active relationship with a lesson rather than a passive, powerless role. Other studies have also reported success in increasing a student's performance by placing a student in a tutorial role with other students.

According to De Charms (1972, 1976a) the key to any program designed to facilitate an internal locus of control must move a learner from a "pawn" relationship with the material to an "origin" relationship. De Charms (1976) suggests that programs should give students small *but real* choices followed by an expectancy of commitment and responsibility to get the tasks completed. As an example, De Charms describes how a slight alteration of the old-fashioned spelling bee might be used to help a student achieve commitment and responsibility. Instead of having each student compete against the class, De Charms suggests that two teams be formed. The spelling test is given on Monday, and a list of words each student missed is recorded. The words are then categorized as easy, moderate, or difficult. In the spelling bee, each student is asked to choose an easy, moderate, or difficult word to spell. Based on the student's performance, the student receives points for the team. With a little ingenuity many classroom activities can be designed to promote an emphasis on internal locus of control. Bolvin (1968), for example, suggests that the whole classroom structure should be based on having students pursue tasks at their own rate (with needed encouragement if necessary) and then having the students evaluate and record their own rate of progress.

While all of these suggestions appear to be worthwhile, two major cautions are in order. First of all, such programs could be a disaster if the teacher is not careful to monitor the types of assignments. Providing students with assignments and tasks well beyond the students' general or specific skill levels could have an extremely negative outcome on a student's perception of internal locus of control. Further, if a student has no initial desire or interest to do well on the assignments, a closely monitored contingency management program would be in order. As Friend and Neale (1972) so aptly state, if the student has no pride in the successful completion of work that requires some effort, then the desire to put effort into an assignment will be lacking. Lacking an initial desire to do the work, an internal locus of control would have little influence on the student—the task would be perceived as useless. For an up-to-date review of this line of research, consult De Charms (1976a) or Fanelli (1977).

Interests of a student

While it has been suggested that broad motivational variables (need for self-actualization or need to be competent) as well as narrower motivational variables (the specific need for achievement and an internal locus of evaluation) influence a person's behavior, consideration also needs to be given to a person's specific interests. Obviously, the specific interests of a student are a strong motivating factor that influences a student's willingness to both pursue a task for an extended time and repeat a task at a future time. It could very well be that an intense dislike or lack of interest in some task plays a more significant role in whether the student chooses to approach a task than the student's general competence motivation or internal locus of control or achievement motivation. Faced with students who lack interest in an area or who are not likely to have an interest in a specific topic, the teacher should try to generate interest. Within reason, teachers should attempt to make lessons interesting by relating the potentially dull lesson to something that the teacher is sure the students will enjoy (Figure 24–7). Lacking a realistic possibility in this area, a variety of reinforcement procedures would be in order. For additional suggestions, consult Rust (1977).

Anxiety-achievement interactions

Although the research on the relationship between anxiety and academic achievement is extensive, very few generalizations can be derived. Generally viewed as a vague state or trait within a person that causes the person to feel uneasy, fearful, and self-deprecating, anxiety has a very complex relationship to academic performance.

FIGURE 24–7
High-interest material should be used in the classroom whenever possible

Stemming from the work of Spence and Spence (1966), who postulated a curvilinear relationship between learning and anxiety, many researchers have attempted to determine whether instructional strategies differing in levels of complexity have differential effects on students' performances. Spence and Spence's formulations led investigators to predict that the amount of anxiety related to learning would be optimum at some *intermediate state of anxiety;* that is, low levels of anxiety as well as high levels of anxiety should be equally debilitating on learning. As Cronbach and Snow (1977) have so well stated, however, to determine the interrelationships between anxiety and learning researchers have to go far beyond Spence and Spence's initial theory. At best, to get a handle on these interrelationships, consideration must be given to the ability of the learner and the nature of the treatment (including the perceived complexity of the task) as those factors interact with the nature of anxiety (Cronbach & Snow, 1977). And even if we could definitively measure these variables, we would still be a long way from predicting a particular student's response toward a task. People respond to states of anxiety differently. Some people withdraw, others act impulsively, and others attempt to compulsively control their behavior. In addition, other motivational variables such as achievement motivation and locus of control certainly would appear to have an influence on any anxiety-achievement relationship. Although it would be premature from an instructional perspective to make many definitive statements about anxiety-academic achievement relationships, some generalizations are in order.

1. All too often there is too much anxiety engendered by our public schools (Hansen, 1977).
2. To minimize unnecessary anxiety, steps should be taken to minimize failure and not place students in potentially embarrassing situations. Giving opportunities for retaking tests, emphasizing cooperation rather than competition, allowing students a realistic amount of choice, and designing an environment in which students progress at their own pace are some of the more obvious suggestions put forth by Hansen (1977) to reduce anxiety.
3. Students differ in their reaction to anxiety provoking situations. What works for one student will not necessarily be as successful with another student. Careful monitoring of students' responses and then treating students accordingly appear to make instructional sense. While the general suggestions made in this section of the chapter emphasize individualization as a means of adjusting to both student motivational and cognitive differences, *great care needs to be taken to insure that the standards of excellence are expected and maintained!* Fuzzy, ill-defined goals tend to bring on mediocrity—letting students "do their own thing" is *not* what is meant by individualization. Allowing students some choice in the curriculum need not detract from the goals of the curriculum.

4. Considering only motivational factors, how would MS > MaF and MaF > MS students differ in the context of the schools?
5. Combining the research on achievement motivation and locus of control, what generalizations can be made about the types of attitudes and skills a student needs in order to become competent in school? Consider only motivational factors and skills, not cognitive skills in the subject matter field.
6. Even though a teacher may be able to produce a student who we would say has high achievement motivation or an internal locus of control (two highly desirable qualities), this does not mean that the student's performance in school will necessarily improve. Explain why this might be the case.

RELATIONSHIP OF THE STATE OF THE STUDENT TO ENVIRONMENTAL DISCREPANCIES

So far we have discussed the interrelationships between some very broad motivational traits and some narrower traits that are thought to interact in various ways to produce motivated behavior. In this section, we focus on a few theories that analyze a person at a given time with respect to specific environmental events. Specific attention is given to the implications for instruction.

Theoretically, any of the *trait* patterns mentioned earlier in this chapter can interact with people in a variety of ways to produce specific *states* of imbalance. These specific states of imbalance are what move a person toward either increasing or decreasing such states as uncertainty, novelty, dissonance, incongruity, doubt, perplexity, and contradiction (Berlyne, 1960). Note that we said these traits can have the outcome of either *increasing* or *decreasing* imbalance. From this viewpoint, being in an imbalanced state produces an internal desire to reduce the imbalance. Being able to reduce the imbalance implies a competency over the environment. In other words, when a person who has some type of need to feel reasonably competent over the environment or some environmental situation is confronted with a discrepant cognitive state with reference to a specific environmental event (e.g., the student believes one thing and the environment appears to be telling the student something different), the student will attempt a strategy to reduce the discrepancy. According to Berlyne (1971) the reduction of the discrepancy brings about an internal consequence that is satisfying (Figure 24–8).

Paradoxically, being in a state of balance can also be unsatisfying to a person because there is no challenge or discrepancy to be resolved. In this *unsatisfactory state of balance,* a person driven by the general need to be competent will tend to seek out an imbalanced state (i.e., a person will engage in a challenging activity). This sounds like the story of the person who kept banging his head against the wall because it felt good when he stopped. Hence, upon completing a crossword puzzle in the newspaper, the person seeks out another puzzle. Upon writing one book, the author produces another. Upon conducting a scientific experiment, the scientist designs another experiment. It should be noted, however, that people most likely will attempt to resolve discrepancies only in those situations that *interest* them, those that are perceived as a *challenge,* and those in which people perceive themselves as *having the capability* of resolving the discrepancy. Resolving a discrepancy just for its own sake will *not* occur unless the person cares about resolving the discrepancy, i.e., unless the discrepancy has some type of personal meaning to the person.

Although this is well beyond the scope of this text, you should be aware that there are numerous subtle variations of this general homeostasis model. Historically, McClelland, Atkinson, Clark, and Lowell's (1953) discrepancy from the adaptation level model; Hebb's (1955) optimal arousal theory; Dember and Earl's (1957) optimal

FIGURE 24–8
A state of disequilibrium can bring about desired approach responses

incongruity formulations; and Berlyne's (1971) optimal level of arousal model all are derivations of the above viewpoint.

Regardless of the specific explanation for why people tend to reduce as well as seek out discrepant situations, each of the theories postulates that there is some optimum level of stimulation toward which a person strives—a moderate level of activation. Being in a situation in which too much discrepancy is present produces fear or anxiety; too little discrepancy produces boredom. If either of these situations occurs in a classroom, a large number of misbehaviors are likely to occur.

Evans's (1969) finding that students appear to be most interested in textbook material that is slightly beyond their usual level of comprehension seems to substantiate these theories. Also, educators espousing the discovery approach to teaching suggest that, aside from the fact that the student learns certain cognitive strategies, being able to discover a solution to a complex problem is itself a rewarding outcome confirming the student's competence.

As a generalization, the theoretical implications of this line of work suggest that teachers ought to place students in moderately discrepant situations. We would suggest that these discrepant situations generally be introduced *after* the students have acquired the necessary skills to resolve the discrepancy. When a teacher purposefully creates moderate amounts of incongruity, doubt, perplexity, uncertainty, dissonance, or contradictions, the student most likely will orient and attend to the lesson to reduce the state of imbalance. Placing students in discrepant situations, however, for which the students have no desire to resolve the discrepancy will have little or no effect on behavior.

SUMMARY

This chapter was concerned with those internal factors thought to be related to school motivation that tend to *arouse, direct,* and *sustain* a behavior. In the first part of the chapter, an emphasis was placed on broad motivational factors or theories. Such factors as a general need to reach one's potential (Maslow), a need to be industrious (Erikson), a need to be competent (White), a need to attain an optimal level of arousal (Berlyne), and variables related to intrinsic motivation (Deci) and continuing motivation (Maehr) were discussed. Common elements underlying these theories or topics are that people need to see themselves as the cause of their own behavior and that they are capable and desirous of performing tasks of moderate difficulty.

The next section of the chapter discussed the nature of specific internal motivational factors said to influence school behavior. Included in this section was a review of such factors as motivation style, achievement motivation, internal locus of control, interests, and school-related anxiety. This chapter consistently made the point that an understanding of school motivation requires that these factors be considered from an interactive perspective. Studying each of these factors in isolation can lead to only a superficial understanding of motivation. As a generalization, the main implications to be derived from this section are the following.

1. Behavior is highly complex. Simple theorizing will not provide us with the necessary answers in this area.
2. Even though it is abundantly clear that students respond very differently to their environment using this knowledge in instructional decision making is very difficult.
3. The pursuit of excellence should be a goal of the schools. School programs should motivate students to become independent and autonomous students who are

capable of pursuing tasks for the sake of the tasks. Furthermore, producing students who are capable of cooperation should be a major goal of the schools.

The last section of the chapter analyzed a series of common theories that view motivated behavior as being a partial function of the relationship between the state of a person and the nature of the environment. According to these theories, each person possesses an optimum level of arousal, and if the environmental situation is not consonant with the given level, the person will act to increase or decrease the arousal level accordingly.

As a generalization, school programs should demand excellence, promote a sense of industry, and individualize to the extent that the student has *some* choice over the content and pace of the material. These general suggestions appear to be some of the desirable qualities of school programs that the research on school motivation seems to support.

SELF-TEST

1. All the theories discussed in this chapter clearly represent either the Lockean or Leibitzian viewpoint of human behavior. Which viewpoint is supported by the theories presented in this chapter? Support your choice with a one-sentence justification.
2. What are the similarities in the Maslow, Erikson, White, and Berlyne theories of motivation?
   a. All four theories stress the importance of a positive early upbringing.
   b. All four theories stress different aspects of the competence motive as an explanation of behavior.
   c. All four theories emphasize the relationship between cognitive and motivational development.
   d. All of the theories are closely aligned with the S-R viewpoint on motivation.
3. According to Erikson, setting a goal to help make a student industrious should initially take place within which chronological era?
   a. Preschool.
   b. Early elementary school (K–2).
   c. Elementary school (K–6).
   d. Junior high school.
   e. Senior high school.
   f. College.
4. Which statement best characterizes the relationship between extrinsic motivation and intrinsic motivation?
   a. Extrinsic motivation comes about through intrinsic motivation.
   b. Extrinsic reinforcers may interfere with intrinsic motivation.
   c. In order to bring about intrinsic motivation in any situation, the S_1's and S_2's of the stimulus situation must be optimal.
   d. Intrinsic motivation interferes with extrinsic motivation.
5. Whose theoretical viewpoint stresses the mental health of the student?
   a. Maslow.
   b. White.
   c. Berlyne.
   d. Deci.
6. According to Berlyne, the instructional strategy of purposefully producing conceptual conflict on various occasions should:
   a. Create MaF > MS students.
   b. Increase internal locus of control.
   c. Increase approach responses toward the task.
   d. Increase intrinsic motivation.
7. Which type of behavior would you predict of a MaF > MS student?
   a. Choose a pass-fail grading option in an easy course.
   b. Choose to take a challenging, though not exceedingly difficult, course.
   c. Ask many divergent questions in class.
   d. Generate realistic goals based on careful decision making.
8. Which of the following could be validly offered as an explanation of why strong positive relationships have not been uniformly obtained between achievement motivation training and school grades?
   a. The independent variables have not been clearly specified.
   b. Incorrect statistical procedures have been uniformly misapplied in the studies.
   c. The control and experimental groups have not been carefully selected.
   d. Other internal variables operating within a student may negate the outcomes of achievement motivation training.
9. Assume a high school student you are teaching has a strong desire to become a doctor and that goal is realistic for that student. Which motivational characteristic would the student most likely possess?

a. MS > MaF pattern.
b. MaF > MS pattern.
c. High on external locus of control.
d. A student operating above an optimal level of arousal according to Berlyne's theory.

10. Internal locus of control is to extrinsic reinforcement as external locus of control is to:
a. MaF > MS.
b. Origin.
c. Pawn.
d. Anxiety.

ANSWER KEY TO BOXED QUESTIONS

1. Drive-reduction theories fail to explain why a person would purposefully interact with the environment to *increase* a state of disequilibrium. Further, modern motivational theorists suggest that the desire to achieve excellence or competence negates the state of disequilibrium one would obviously have to be in on various occasions in order to achieve excellence.
2. All four theories suggest that people purposefully interact with their environment to achieve feelings of competence in their pursuit of excellence. To produce something of significance is in itself satisfying. Each of these theoretical viewpoints is closely related to the topic of intrinsic motivation.
3. *Maslow*—Students should be accepted for their own worth, therefore students should be allowed to pursue some topics of their own interest consonant with the goals of the curriculum or program.
Erikson—The main motivational goal of the school should be to establish a sense of industry. This aspect of Erikson's theory suggests that long-term projects that require a sense of involvement are important instructional goals.
White—Having a classroom environment in which standards of excellence are expected, coupled with moderately difficult and challenging assignments within the student's ability range, are the general implications of White's theory.
Berlyne—Since each person is said to operate within an "optimum level of arousal," it is the teacher's task to make use of this postulated level by purposefully creating various types of cognitive imbalance (doubt, perplexity, contradiction, etc.) which the student is expected to resolve. The resolution of the imbalance is said to be self-satisfying.
4. MS > MaF students tend to make more realistic choices and desire tasks of moderate difficulty. MaF > MS students, on the other hand, make more unrealistic choices and tend to prefer very simple or very complex tasks. The ability to do simple tasks is no threat to the MaF > MS student, while the inability to perform complex tasks is also nonthreatening. Since the task is very difficult, the student could not be expected to perform well anyway, and therefore the student relieves him/herself of any blame for the failure.
5. Characteristics of high-achieving students with reference to achievement motivation and locus of control include:
a. A positive value toward achievement.
b. The desire to avoid failure.
c. Development of realistic goals, clearly defined.
d. Knowledge of how to plan a task competently.
e. A future orientation.
f. Low level of anxiety, but capable of being moderately anxious.
g. Persistence.
h. Systematic study strategies.
i. Seeing oneself responsible for one's own behavior (an "originator" instead of a "pawn").
6. Reasons for a discrepancy between a student characterized as high on MS > MaF with an internal locus of control and poor scholastic achievement scores include:
a. Student may not have the general or specific prerequisites for the subject(s).
b. Student may not be specifically interested in the subject(s).
c. These characteristics may come about because of high achievement in a subject, not because the characteristics produce high achievement.
d. There may be different types of achievement motivation (Veroff, 1975) or styles (Ball, 1977), thus compounding any simple interaction between these variables and achievement.

ANSWER KEY TO SELF-TEST

1. The Leibnitzian viewpoint is represented by these theories. Essentially all suggest that humans have internal motivational mechanisms that actively interact with a person to impart arousal, direction, and sustained behavioral patterns.
2. *b*
3. *c*
4. *b*
5. *a*
6. *c*
7. *a*
8. *d*
9. *a*
10. *b*

APPENDIX

Statistical procedures useful for making instructional decisions concerning evaluations on a norm-referenced test

Computing the variance and standard deviation
Standard error of the mean
Determining the reliability of a norm-referenced test
Index of item difficulty
Index of item discrimination
Assigning equal weights on tests with differing standard deviations
Procedure for correction for guessing

COMPUTING THE VARIANCE AND STANDARD DEVIATION

From a teacher's perspective these statistical procedures can be used for three interrelated reasons. Commercial tests almost always discuss the degree of dispersal of scores around a central value or mean. On a *standardized* test, one of the most frequent questions asked about a student's performance is its relationship to the performance of the group who took the test. Measures of variance and standard deviation allow us to answer this question. A student's percentile rank can be estimated if we know a student's raw score, the average score of the group, and the standard deviation of the scores on the test. If a classroom teacher wants to determine the degree of spread of scores on a test, or wants to compute how likely it is that a student's score is actually a reflection of the student's true score if the student were to retake the test, these statistical procedures are useful. Finally, variance and standard deviation are the bases from which more complex statistical procedures are used in sophisticated research studies.

With the exception of the research function, most frequently the standard deviation is used with the norm-referenced approach to testing. Although the criterion-referenced orientation to testing is more appropriate for most types of instructional decision making, any grading procedure that is at least partially based on comparisons should utilize these statistical procedures. To compute a standard deviation, the following steps should be followed.

Consider the scores in this example to be scores on a unit quiz in a high school history class. To simplify the example, we have only ten scores ranging from 4 to 9.

Quiz scores	*Scores squared*
4	16
8	64
9	81
8	64
9	81
5	25
8	64
8	64
9	81
7	49
75	589

1. Add the scores, 75.
2. Square the scores and total, 589.
3. Square the result obtained in Step 1, and divide by the number of scores. $(75)^2/10 = 5{,}625/10 = 562.5$.
4. Subtract the result obtained in Step 3 from the result obtained in Step 2, $589 - 562.5 = 26.5$.
5. Divide the result obtained in Step 4 by $(N - 1)$. Since there are ten scores in this example, $(N - 1) = 9$, $26.5/9 = 2.94$. This figure is the variance of the sample.
6. To compute the standard deviation, take the square root of the result obtained in Step 5, $\sqrt{2.94} = 1.714$.

This procedure is the common method to determine a precise standard deviation. When the teacher is interested in a gross estimate of the standard deviation, one of the following two procedures might be used.

1. $\dfrac{\text{Sum of the highest sixth} - \text{Sum of the lowest sixth}}{\text{Half the number of students}}$

   or $(18 - 9)/5 = 9/5 = 1.8$.
2. Obtain the range of the sample, $(9 - 4 = 5)$, and divide by k. To find k, consult the accompanying table developed by Hills (1976). The size of k depends on the approximate number of students in the class. In our example, since the class size is 10, k falls between 3 and 4, and by inspection it is apparent that the value is practically 3.0. For this example we will use 3.0 as k. Since 5 is the range, we divide: $5/3.0 = 1.67$.

Divisions for estimating standard deviation from the range

Number	k
4	2
9	3
27	4
98	5
444	6

* Source: Hills (1976).

Oftentimes one of these two procedures is acceptable to determine a gross estimate of the standard deviation. If a teacher were conducting a study, even a pilot study, we recommend using the precise statistical formula.

STANDARD ERROR OF THE MEAN

For a classroom test, once a standard deviation is computed, it is very easy to determine the standard error of the mean (S.E.M.). Essentially, the standard error of the mean can be obtained by dividing the standard deviation by the square root of the number of cases in the class. For the last example,

$$\text{S.E.M.} = \frac{\text{S.D.}}{\sqrt{N}}, \qquad \text{so } \frac{1.71}{\sqrt{10}} = \frac{1.71}{3.16} = 0.54$$

The standard error of the mean tells us how likely it is that a particular score would fall within a particular range if the test were administered again, or how far the test performance of the class in general would be likely to vary if the test were administered again. In any event, the S.E.M. gives us some idea of the reliability of the test.

The derived statistic can be applied by using the normal distribution curve. To interpret the 0.54 in the above example, we can say that the mean of the test, which is 7.5 in this case, would not be likely to vary 68 percent of the time by more than ±0.54 from 7.5, would not be likely to vary 96 percent of the time by more than ± 1.08 from 7.5, and would not be likely to vary 99 percent of the time by more than ±1.62 from the mean. In other words, the S.E.M. can be interpreted by applying the percentage of cases found in the distribution curve. We can also apply the S.E.M. to an individual score. Assume a student had a score of 6 on the test. With a S.E.M. of 0.54, we could predict that the student's score would not be likely to vary 68 percent of the time by more than ±0.54 from 6, would not be likely to vary 96 percent of the time by more than ±1.08 from 6, and would not be likely to vary 99 percent of the time by more than ±1.62 from 6. As can be seen from these examples, the S.E.M. gives us some indication about our willingness to accept the class distribution or the student's test score as representative of the "true" score. The greater the S.E.M., the less likely we would be willing to accept a given score as a reliable measure.

DETERMINING THE RELIABILITY OF A NORM-REFERENCED TEST

You have just seen how the reliability of a test can be estimated by computing its S.E.M. There are other ways to compute the reliability of a test. Given an objective, norm-referenced test in which all the items are of equal weight, it is easy to compute a reliability (rel) score. Diederich (1964) suggests the following formula:

$$\text{rel} = 1 - \frac{M(n - M)}{n(\text{S.D.})^2}$$

where: M = mean, n = number of items on the test, and $(\text{S.D.})^2$ = standard deviation squared.

Assume the following 60-item test was given to a class of 50 students. All items receive equal weight:

50 = 1	50	40 = 1	40	30 = 1	30
49 = 3	147	39 = 3	117	29 = 1	29
48 = 2	96	38 = 2	76	28 = 0	0
47 = 4	188	37 = 2	74	27 = 0	0
46 = 3	138	36 = 1	36	26 = 1	26
45 = 5	225	35 = 1	35		2,079
44 = 6	264	34 = 0	0		
43 = 4	172	33 = 2	66		
42 = 2	84	32 = 1	32		
41 = 3	123	31 = 1	31		

$$n = 60$$
$$M = 41.58$$
$$\text{S.D.} = 5.52$$
$$(\text{S.D.})^2 = 30.47$$

$$\text{S.D.} = \frac{\text{Sum of high sixth} - \text{Sum of low sixth}}{\text{Half number of students}} = \frac{387 - 249}{25} = \frac{138}{25} = 5.52$$

$$\text{rel} = 1 - \frac{M(n - m)}{n\,(\text{S.D.})^2}$$
$$= 1 - \frac{41.58\,(60 - 41.58)}{60\,(30.47)}$$
$$= 1 - \frac{41.58\,(18.42)}{60\,(30.47)}$$
$$= 1 - \frac{765.90}{1{,}828.2}$$
$$= 1 - 0.418$$
$$\boxed{\text{rel} = 0.58}$$

As we stated in the chapter on evaluation, the level of reliability that is accepted as satisfactory is somewhat arbitrary, but as a general rule standardized tests should be in the 0.90's while acceptable teacher-made tests are usually in the 0.60's, 0.70's, or 0.80's. A quick glance at the distribution scores in this sample should tell you why the reliability is a little low on this test; even though the test has 60 items and the highest score is only 50, many scores are clustered in the higher range. In other words, the reliability of a norm-referenced test increases in proportion to the degree that the scores are spread out. The larger the number of items on a test, the greater the possibility of a spread of scores. Given a reliability of 0.58, the teacher should inspect the items to determine whether each item is discriminating between high-scoring students and low-scoring students as well as whether the item is of moderate difficulty. With a norm-referenced testing strategy, it is desirable to construct items that are moderately difficult and discriminate between good students and poorer students.

INDEX OF ITEM DIFFICULTY

To determine whether an item is of the desired level of difficulty, a simple procedure is to arrange the test scores in descending order. The next step is to take the proportion of students in the highest 25–30 percent who answered the item correctly, and the proportion of students in the lowest 25–30 percent who answered the item correctly, add the two scores together, and divide by 2.

The formula looks like this:

$$\text{Difficulty index} = \frac{\begin{matrix}\text{Proportion of} \\ \text{students in} \\ \text{highest group} \\ \text{who answered} \\ \text{item correctly}\end{matrix} + \begin{matrix}\text{Proportion of} \\ \text{students in} \\ \text{lowest group} \\ \text{who answered} \\ \text{item correctly}\end{matrix}}{2}$$

The ideal difficulty index for each item is 0.50, with a spread of 0.25 to 0.75 as acceptable. With a difficulty index of less than 0.25, the item is too difficult, while an item with a difficulty index greater than 0.75 is too easy. Keep in mind we are talking about norm-referenced tests only. For criterion-referenced tests this procedure is inappropriate; many items on a criterion-referenced test should be very easy or very difficult depending on the objective. As a guideline on a norm-referenced test, an ideal item should be answered correctly by 60–70 percent of the class.

INDEX OF ITEM DISCRIMINATION

It is also desirable to write items that discriminate between those students who are truly competent with the subject matter and those who are less competent. To determine the index of discrimination, subtract the proportion of lowest scorers who got the item correct from the proportion of highest scorers who were successful on the item.

$$\text{Discrimination index} = \begin{matrix}\text{Proportion of} \\ \text{students in} \\ \text{highest group} \\ \text{who answered} \\ \text{item correctly}\end{matrix} - \begin{matrix}\text{Proportion of} \\ \text{students in} \\ \text{lowest group} \\ \text{who answered} \\ \text{item correctly}\end{matrix}$$

Theoretically, an ideal item discrimination would be 1.00, in which case all the students in the highest group answered the item correctly and none of the students in the lowest group did so. Realistically, items over 0.40 on item discrimination are acceptable, items in the 0.30–0.39 range might need some revision, items in the 0.20–0.29 range need revision, and items below 0.19 should be totally rewritten or discarded (Ebel, 1965).

Some teachers who use many of the same items from year to year keep a filing system of 3 by 5 cards to record the items. Included on the card are the difficulty and discrimination indexes of previous years. Needless to say, teachers reusing items from year to year ought to be very cautious not to let the students be aware of this practice. Particular care needs to be taken to have the tests returned at the end of the testing session.

ASSIGNING EQUAL WEIGHTS ON TESTS WITH DIFFERING STANDARD DEVIATIONS

The purpose of this procedure is to manipulate the scores statistically in order that the standard deviations of each quiz are equal. Without equating the standard deviations on a norm-referenced test, the greater the standard deviation on a particular test, the greater that score is weighted in assigning a grade. Since a teacher wants to be sure that all the test scores are equivalent in their weights, a statistical procedure is needed to equate the different distributions. To equate widely divergent quiz distributions, an ideal range and average score should be determined. Since scores in the 70–80 range traditionally have been considered average, perhaps an average of 75 with a range of 50 is in order. Let us do the following example for a class of 20 students. We are interested in equating these scores to a distribution in which 75 is average with a range of 50.

Student quiz scores
98 = 1
95 = 2
93 = 1
91 = 1
86 = 1
83 = 2
81 = 1
80 = 2
77 = 2
74 = 1
73 = 1
70 = 1
68 = 1
65 = 1
60 = 1
58 = 1

$$M = \frac{1{,}587}{20} = 79.35$$

Now we are ready to compute the estimated standard deviation. We will use Hills's (1976) procedure for estimating the standard deviation. Since the range on this quiz is 40 and the k is approximately 3.75, simply divide 40 by 3.75, which equals 10.66. For this example you will remember our goal is to convert the current distribution to a distribution in which the average score is 75 with a range of 50. On this particular quiz, the average score is 79.35 with a range of 40—not bad if you attempted to design a test in which the average is 75 with a range of 50. Still, if you are using the norm-referenced approach to grading, each quiz score should be made comparable to all the quizzes in terms of having an equal average score and identical range.

To make each quiz score equivalent in a norm-referenced sense to all other quiz scores, Hills (1976) suggests the following formula:

$$\text{Converted score} = \frac{\text{New standard deviation}}{\text{Old standard deviation}}\left(\begin{array}{c}\text{Difference between}\\ \text{obtained score and}\\ \text{old mean}\end{array}\right) + \begin{array}{c}\text{Desired}\\ \text{new mean}\end{array}$$

Applying this formula to our hypothetical example of 20 students, the new standard deviation is 50 (the desired range) ÷ 3.75 (*k* for a class of 20—this score is obtained from Hill's table and is interpolated roughly for 20 students). The resulting new desired standard deviation is 13.3. The old standard deviation is 40 ÷ 3.75, or 10.66. Let us assume you want to convert Mary's and Susie's quiz scores. Mary obtained an 81 and Susie's score was 68. For Mary, the formula is (13.33/10.66) (81 − 79.4) + 75 = 1.25(1.6) + 75 = 77. For Susie, the formula is (13.33/10.66) (68 − 79.4) + 75 = 1.25 (−11.4) + 75 = −14.25 + 75 = 60.75. This procedure can be computed for each quiz, and then the mean of the converted quiz scores can be tabulated.

Since each quiz score has been converted to make the scores equivalent in a norm-referenced comparative sense, the obtained mean for each student is a more accurate representation of that student's performance with reference to the class. How you eventually use the data is up to you. This procedure is designed to spread the scores and make the scores equivalent from test to test. We might add several warnings here. Implicit in this procedure is the assumption that the students in the class are randomly assigned and, therefore, the distribution is normal. Most of the time this requirement is not met. If a corrective formula is used such as Hills suggests, some consideration should be given to the characteristics of the class, and the grading procedures should be modified accordingly.

PROCEDURE FOR CORRECTION FOR GUESSING

The assumption for applying "correction for guessing" formulas is based on the proposition that students guess blindly when they do not understand the question and, therefore, the raw scores are inordinately high. Except in the case cited above, this assumption is generally not valid. Students make educated guesses at answers by eliminating known incorrect answers and then use some educated hunch to choose the final answer. If necessary, however, the following formula may be used to correct for guessing on multiple-choice or true-false tests:

$$\text{Corrected score} = \text{No. right} - \frac{\text{No. wrong}}{\text{Number of choices on the item} - 1}$$

To see how this assumption operates and this formula is computed, we shall compute and discuss the results of a typical test. Assume you have given a 50-item multiple-choice test with each item having four choices. Further assume a student missed 15 items. In this case, the student's corrected score for guessing would be 30. See the example illustrated below.

$$\text{Correct score} = 35 - \frac{15}{4-1} = 35 - 5 = 30$$

In this example, 35 represents the number of correct items, 15 represents the number of incorrect items, and 4 represents the number of possible choices on each item. Given that the student missed 15 items, it is assumed that the student may have guessed wildly at at least five other questions and got the correct answer by chance, therefore the corrected raw score is 30. As we stated previously, the assumption that a student just guesses wildly on questions is tenuous. At best, this correction procedure should be used only on a speed test which very few students may be able to finish. And even in this situation guessing may be reduced considerably by telling the students that wrong answers will be penalized more than items not answered.

REFERENCES

Adams, J. A. *Learning and memory: An introduction.* Homewood, Ill.: Dorsey Press, 1976.

Adler, M. In defense of the philosophy of education. In N. B. Henry (Ed.), *The 41st Yearbook of the National Society for the Study of Education. Part I, Philosophies of Education.* Bloomington, Ill.: Public School Publishing Co., 1942.

Aiken, E. G., Thomas, G. S., & Shennum, W. A. Memory for a lecture: Effects of notes, lecture rate, and informational density. *Journal of Educational Psychology,* 1975, *67,* 439–444.

Airasian, P. W. A method for validating sequential instructional hierarchies. *Educational Technology,* 1971, *11,* 54–56.

Alschuler, A. S. *Developing achievement motivation in adolescents.* Englewood Cliffs, N.J.: Educational Technology Publications, 1973.

Alverson, G. F. An investigation of the cognitive-social process underlying group induced shifts. *Dissertation Abstracts International,* 1976, *37,* 2729A.

Alverson, G. F. IEP's: Meaningful educational plans or meaningless collection of trivia? Paper presented at the annual meeting of the National Association of School Psychologists, 1978.

Andersen, K. E. *Introduction to communication theory and practice.* Menlo Park, Calif.: Cummings, 1972.

Anderson, G. J. Effects of course content and teacher sex on the social climate of learning. *American Educational Research Journal,* 1971, *8,* 649–663.

Anderson, R. C. Educational psychology. *Annual Review of Psychology,* 1967, *18,* 129–164.

Anderson, R. C. The comparative field experiment: An illustration from high school biology. In *Proceedings of the 1968 Invitational Conference on Testing Problems.* Princeton, N.J.: Educational Testing Service, 1969.

Anderson, R. C. Control of student mediating processes during verbal learning and instruction. *Review of Educational Research,* 1970, *40,* 349–369.

Anderson, R. C. Encoding processes in the storage and retrieval of sentences. *Journal of Experimental Psychology,* 1971, *91,* 338–340.

Anderson, R. C., & Biddle, W. B. On asking people questions about what they are reading. In G. H. Bower (Ed.), *The psychology of learning and motivation: Advances in research and theory* (Vol. 9). New York: Academic Press, 1975.

Anderson, R. C., & Faust, G. W. The effects of strong formal prompts in programed instruction. *American Educational Research Journal,* 1967, *4,* 345–352. Copyright 1967, American Educational Research Association, Washington, D.C.

Anderson, R. C., & Hidde, J. T. Imagery and sentence learning. *Journal of Educational Psychology,* 1971, *62,* 526–530.

Anderson, R. C., & Kulhavy, R. W. Learning concepts from definitions. *American Educational Research Journal,* 1972, *9,* 385–390.

Anderson, R. C., Kulhavy, R. W., & Andre, T. Feedback procedures in programmed instruction. *Journal of Educational Psychology,* 1971, *62,* 148–156.

Anderson, R. C., Kulhavy, R. W., & Andre, T. Conditions under which feedback facilitates learning from a programmed lesson. *Journal of Educational Psychology,* 1972, *63,* 186–188.

Anderson, R. C., Reynolds, R. E., Schallert, D. L., & Goetz, E. T. Frameworks for comprehending discourse. *American Educational Research Journal,* 1977, *14,* 367–381. Copyright 1977, American Educational Research Association, Washington, D.C. Material reprinted by permission.

Anglin, J. M. *Jerome Bruner: Beyond the information given: Studies in the psychology of knowing.* New York: Norton, 1973.

Anthony, W. S. Learning to discover rules by discovery. *Journal of Educational Psychology,* 1973, *64,* 325–328.

Ariès, P. *Centuries of childhood: A social history of family life.* New York: Knopf, 1962.

Arlin, M. The interaction of locus of control, classroom structure and pupil satisfaction. *Psychology in the Schools,* 1972, *12,* 279–286.

Arnoff, J., & Litwin, C. H. Achievement motivation training and executive advancement. *Journal of Applied Behavioral Science,* 1971, *7,* 215–228.

Arnold, T. C., & Dwyer, F. M. Realism in visualized instruction. *Perceptual and Motor Skills,* 1975, *40,* 369–370.

Aronson, E., & Golden, B. The effect of relevant and irrelevant aspects of communicator credibility on opinion change. *Journal of Personality,* 1962, *30,* 135–146.

Aronson, E., Turner, J., & Carlsmith, J. M. Communicator credibility and communicator discrepancy as determinants of opinion change. *Journal of Abnormal and Social Psychology,* 1963, *67,* 31–36.

Asher, S. R., Gottman, J. M., & Oden, S. L. Children's friendships in school settings. In E. M. Hetherington & R. D. Parke (Eds.), *Contemporary readings in child psychology.* New York: McGraw-Hill, 1977.

Athey, I. J., & Rubadeau, D. O. (Eds.). *Educational implications of Piaget's theory.* Waltham, Mass.: Ginn-Blaisdell, 1970.

Atkin, J. M. Behavioral objectives in curriculum design: A cautionary note. *The Science Teacher,* 1968, *35,* 27–30.

Atkinson, J. W. *An introduction to motivation.* Princeton, N.J.: VanNostrand, 1964.

Atkinson, J. W. Strength of motivation and efficiency of performance. In J. W. Atkinson & J. O. Raynor (Eds.), *Motivation and achievement.* New York: Wiley, 1974.

Atkinson, J. W., & Birch, D. The dynamics of achievement-oriented activity. In J. W. Atkinson & J. O. Raynor (Eds.), *Motivation and achievement.* New York: Wiley, 1974.

Atkinson, R. C. Mnemotechnics in second-language learning. *American Psychologist,* 1975, *30,* 821–828.

Atkinson, R. C., & Raugh, M. R. An application of the mnemonic keyword method to the acquisition of a Russian vocabulary. *Journal of Experimental Psychology: Human Learning and Memory,* 1975, *104,* 126–133. © 1975 by the American Psychological Association. Material reprinted by permission.

Atkinson, R. C., & Shiffrin, R. M. Human memory: A proposed system and its control processes. In K. W. Spence & J. T. Spence (Eds.), *The psychology of learning and motivation* (Vol. 2). New York: Academic Press, 1968.

Ausubel, D. P. The use of advance organizers in the learning and retention of meaningful verbal material. *Journal of Educational Psychology,* 1960, *51,* 267–272.

Ausubel, D. P. *The psychology of meaningful verbal learning.* New York: Grune and Stratton, 1963.

Ausubel, D. P. *Educational psychology: A cognitive view.* New York: Holt, Rinehart and Winston, 1968.

Ausubel, D. P., & Fitzgerald, D. The role of discriminability in meaningful verbal learning and retention. *Journal of Educational Psychology,* 1961, *52,* 266–274.

Ausubel, D. P., & Fitzgerald, D. Organizer, general background, and antecedent learning variables in sequential verbal learning. *Journal of Educational Psychology,* 1962, *53,* 243–249.

Ausubel, D. P., & Robinson, F. G. *School learning: An introduction to educational psychology.* New York: Holt, Rinehart and Winston, 1969. Copyright © 1969 by Holt, Rinehart and Winston, Inc. Material reprinted by permission.

Ausubel, D. P., & Youssef, M. The role of discriminability in meaningful verbal learning. *Journal of Educational Psychology,* 1963, *54,* 331–336.

Ayllon, T., & Azrin, N. *The token economy.* New York: Appleton-Century-Crofts, 1968.

Ayllon, T., & Roberts, M. Eliminating discipline problems by strengthening academic performance. *Journal of Applied Behavioral Analysis,* 1974, *7,* 71–76.

Azrin, N. H., & Holz, W. C. Punishment. In W. K. Honig (Ed.), *Operant behavior: Areas of research and application.* New York: Appleton-Century-Crofts, 1966.

Ball, S. Motivation in education. In S. Ball (Ed.), *Introduction.* New York: Academic Press, 1977.

Bandura, A. Influence of model's reinforcement contingencies on the acquisition of imitative responses. *Journal of Personality and Social Psychology,* 1965, *1,* 589–595.

Bandura, A. *Social learning theory.* Morristown, N.J.: General Learning Press, 1971.

Bandura, A. *Aggression: A social learning analysis.* Englewood Cliffs, N.J.: Prentice-Hall, 1973.

Bandura, A. *Social learning theory.* Englewood Cliffs, N.J.: Prentice-Hall, 1977.

Bandura, A., Grusec, J. E., & Menlove, F. L. Observational learning as a function of symbolization and incentive set. *Child Development,* 1966, *37,* 499–506.

Bandura, A., Ross, D., & Ross, S. Transmission of aggression through imitation of aggressive models. *Journal of Abnormal and Social Psychology,* 1961, *63,* 575–582.

Bandura, A. H., & Walters, R. H. *Social learning and personality development.* New York: Holt, Rinehart and Winston, 1963.

Barber, T. X. Pitfalls in research: Nine investigator and experiment effects. In R. M. Travers (Ed.), *Second handbook of research on teaching.* Chicago: Rand McNally, 1973.

Barnes, B. R., & Clawson, E. V. Do advance organizers facilitate learning? Recommendations for further research based on an analysis of 32 studies. *Review of Educational Research,* 1975, *45,* 637–659.

Bar-Tal, D., Bar-Tal, Y., & Leinhardt, G. *The environment, locus of control and feelings of satisfaction.* Pittsburgh: University of Pittsburgh, Learning and Research Development Center, 1975. (LRDC Publication 1975/27)

Bar-Tal, D., & Bar-Zohar, Y. The relationship between perception of locus of control and academic achievement: Review and some educational implications. *Contemporary Educational Psychology,* 1977, *2,* 181–199.

Bartlett, F. C. *Remembering: A study in experimental and social psychology.* London: Cambridge University Press, 1932.

Bassler, O. C., Beers, M. I., & Richardson, L. I. Comparison of two instructional strategies for teaching the solution of verbal problems. *Journal for Research in Mathematics Education,* 1975, *6,* 170–178.

Bausell, R. B., & Jenkins, J. R. Effects on prose learning of frequency of adjunct cues and the difficulty of the material cued. *Journal of Reading Behavior,* 1977, *9,* 227–232.

Becker, W. C., & Engelmann, S. *The Oregon direct-instructional model.* Eugene: University of Oregon Follow-Through Project, 1977.

Becker, W. C., Engelmann, S., & Thomas, D. R. *Teaching 1: Classroom management.* Chicago: Science Research Associates, 1975.

Beggs, D. L., & Lewis, E. L. *Measurement and evaluation in the schools.* Hopewell, N.J.: Houghton Mifflin, 1975.

Bellack, A. A., Kliebard, H. M., Hyman, R. T., & Smith, F. L. *The language of the classroom.* New York: Teacher's College Press, 1966.

Bereiter, C., & Engelmann, S. *Teaching disadvantaged children in the preschool.* Englewood Cliffs, N.J.: Prentice-Hall, 1966.

Berliner, D. C. Aptitude-treatment interactions in two studies of learning from lecture instruction. Paper presented at meeting of the American Educational Research Association, New York, 1971. (ERIC Document ED 046 249)

Berliner, D. C. A status report on the study of teacher effectiveness. ERIC Information Analysis Center for Science, Mathematics, and Environmental Education, Columbus, Ohio. 1975 (ERIC Document ED 114261).

Berliner, D. C., & Gage, N. L. The psychology of teaching methods. In N. L. Gage (Ed.), *The psychology of teaching methods: The 75th yearbook of the National Society for the Study of Education.* Chicago: University of Chicago Press, 1976.

Berlyne, D. E. *Conflict, arousal and curiosity.* New York: McGraw-Hill, 1960.

Berlyne, D. E. Exploration and curiosity. *Science,* 1966, *153,* 25–33.

Berlyne, D. E. What next? Concluding summary. In H. I. Day, D. E. Berlyne, & D. E. Hunt (Eds.), *Intrinsic motivation: A new direction in education.* Toronto: Holt, Rinehart and Winston of Canada, 1971.

Biggs, J. B. Dimensions of study behavior: Another look at ATI. *British Journal of Educational Psychology,* 1976, *46,* 68–80.

Bilodeau, E. A., & Bilodeau, I. McD. Variation of temporal intervals among critical events in five studies of knowledge of results. *Journal of Experimental Psychology,* 1958, *55,* 603–612.

Bilodeau, I. McD. Accuracy of a simple positioning response with variation in the number of trials by which knowledge of results is delayed. *American Journal of Psychology,* 1956, *69,* 434–437.

Bloom, B. S. *Stability and change in human characteristics.* New York: Wiley, 1964.

Bloom, B. S. Mastery learning. In J. H. Block (Ed.), *Mastery learning: theory and practice.* New York: Holt, Rinehart and Winston, 1971.

Bloom, B. S., Englehart, M. D., Furst, E. J., Hill, W. H., & Krathwohl, D. R. (Eds.). *Taxonomy of educational objectives: The classification of educational goals. Handbook 1: Cognitive domain.* New York: David McKay, 1956.

Bobrow, S., & Bower, G. H. Comprehension and recall of sentences. *Journal of Experimental Psychology,* 1969, *80,* 455–461.

Boker, J. R. Immediate and delayed retention effects of interspersing questions in written instructional passages. *Journal of Educational Psychology,* 1974, *66,* 96–98. © 1974 by the American Psychological Association. Material adapted with permission.

Bolvin, J. O. Implications of the individualization of instruction for curriculum and instructional design. *Audiovisual Instruction,* 1968, *13,* 238–242.

Boozer, R. F., & Lindvall, C. M. *An investigation of selected procedures for the development and evaluation of hierarchical curriculum structures.* Pittsburgh: Learning Research and Development Center, University of Pittsburgh, 1971. (Publication No. 1971/23)

Boring, E. G. *A history of experimental psychology* (2nd ed.). New York: Appleton-Century-Crofts, 1950.

Born, D. G., & Davis, M. L. Amount and distribution of study in a personalized instructional course and in a lecture course. *Journal of Applied Behavioral Analysis,* 1974, *7,* 365–375.

Born, D. G., Gledhill, S. M., & Davis, M. L. Examination performance in lecture discussion and personalized instruction courses. *Journal of Applied Behavioral Analysis,* 1972, *5,* 33–43.

Bourne, L. E., Jr., & Pendleton, R. B. Concept identification as a function of completeness and probability of information feedback. *Journal of Experimental Psychology,* 1958, *56,* 413–420.

Bousfield, W. A. The occurrence of clustering in the recall of randomly arranged associates. *Journal of General Psychology,* 1953, *49,* 229–240.

Boutwell, R. C., & Tennyson, R. D. Instructional objectives—different by design. *NSPI Journal,* 1971, *10,* 7–10.

Bower, G. H. Mental imagery in association learning. In L. W. Gregg (Ed.), *Cognition in learning and memory.* New York: Wiley, 1972.

Bower, G. H., Clark, M. C., Lesgold, A. M., & Winzenz, D. Hierarchical retrieval schemes in recall of categorized word lists. *Journal of Verbal Learning and Verbal Behavior,* 1969, *8,* 323–343.

Bower, G. H., & Winzenz, D. Comparison of associative learning strategies. *Psychonomic Science,* 1970, *20,* 119–120.

Bowles, B. D., & Fruth, M. J. Improving home-school-community relations. In J. M. Lipham & M. J. Fruth (Eds.), *The principalship and individually guided education.* Reading, Mass.: Addison-Wesley, 1976.

Boyd, W. M. Repeating questions in prose learning. *Journal of Educational Psychology,* 1973, *64,* 31–38.

Boyle, D. G. *Student's guide to Piaget.* New York: Pergamon Press, 1969.

Brameld, T. *Patterns of educational philosophy.* New York: Holt, Rinehart and Winston, 1971.

Briggs, R. D., Tosig, D. J., & Norley, R. M. Study habit modification and its effect on academic performance: A behavioral approach. *Journal of Educational Research,* 1971, *64,* 347–350.

Brigham, T. A., Finfrock, S. R., Breunig, M. K., & Bushell, D. The use of programmed materials in the analysis of academic contingencies. *Journal of Applied Behavior Analysis,* 1972, *5,* 177–182. Copyright © 1972 by the Society for the Experimental Analysis of Behavior, Inc. Material reprinted by permission.

Brophy, J. E., & Evertson, C. M. *Learning from teaching: A developmental perspective.* Boston: Allyn and Bacon, 1976.

Brophy, J. E., & Good, T. L. *Teacher-student relationships: Causes and consequences.* New York: Holt, Rinehart and Winston, 1974.

Brown, A. L., & Smiley, S. S. Rating the importance of structural units of prose passages: A problem of metacognitive development. *Child Development,* 1977, *48,* 1–8.

Brown, M., & Precious, N. *The integrated day in the primary school.* New York: Ballantine Books, 1969.

Bruner, J. S. *Process of education.* New York: Vintage, 1960.

Bruner, J. S. The course of cognitive growth. *American Psychologist,* 1964, *19,* 1–15. © 1964 by the American Psychological Association. Material reprinted by permission.

Bruner, J. S. The growth of mind. *American Psychologist,* 1965, *20,* 1007–1017.

Bruner, J. S. *Toward a theory of instruction.* Cambridge, Mass.: Harvard University Press, 1966.

Bruner, J. S. *The relevance of education.* New York: Norton, 1971.

Bruner, J. S. The growth of representational processes in childhood. In J. M. Anglin (Ed.), *Beyond the information given.* New York: Norton, 1973.

Bruner, J. S., & Kenney, H. Multiple ordering. In J. S. Bruner, R. R. Oliver, & P. M. Greenfield (Eds.), *Studies in cognitive growth.* New York: Wiley, 1966.

Bruner, J. S., Olver, R. R., & Greenfield, P. M. *Studies in cognitive growth.* New York: Wiley, 1966.

Bruner, J. S., & Postman, L. On the perception of incongruity: A paradigm. *Journal of Personality,* 1949, *18,* 206–223.

Bruning, R. H. Effects of review and testlike events within the learning of prose material. *Journal of Educational Psychology,* 1968, *59,* 16–19.

Bryan, J. H., & Walbek, N. H. Preaching and practicing generosity: Some determinants of sharing in children. *Child Development,* 1970, *41,* 329–354.

Bunderson, C. V., & Faust, G. W. Programmed and computer-assisted instruction. In N. L. Gage (Ed.), *The psychology of teaching methods: The 75th Yearbook of the National Society for the Study of Education.* Chicago: University of Chicago Press, 1976.

Buros, O. K. *Reading-tests and reviews.* Highland Park, N.J.: Gryphon Press, 1968.

Buros, O. K. *Personality-tests and reviews.* Highland Park, N.J.: Gryphon Press, 1970.

Burt, C. The evidence for the concept of intelligence. *British Journal of Educational Psychology,* 1955, *25,* 158–177.

Burt, C. The genetic determination of differences in intelligence: A study of monozygotic twins reared together and apart. *British Journal of Psychology,* 1966, *57,* 137–157.

Bussis, A. M., & Chittenden, E. A. *Analysis of an approach to open education.* Interim report of the Educational Testing Service, Princeton, N.J., 1970.

Butcher, H. J. *Human intelligence: Its nature and assessment.* London: Methuen, 1968.

Butcher, H. J. *Human intelligence: Its nature and assessment* (2nd ed.). London: Methuen, 1970.

Butcher, H. J., & Lomax, D. E. (Eds.). *Readings in human intelligence.* London: Methuen, 1972.

Butterfield, E. C., Wambold, C., & Belmont, J. M. On the theory and practice of improving short-term memory. *American Journal of Mental Deficiency,* 1973, *77,* 654–669.

Campbell, D. T., & Stanley, J. *Experimental and quasi-experimental designs for research.* Chicago: Rand McNally, 1963.

Cancro, R. (Ed.). *Intelligence: Genetic and environmental differences.* New York: Grune and Stratton, 1971.

Capie, W., & Jones, H. An assessment of hierarchy validation techniques. *Journal of Research in Science Teaching,* 1971, *8,* 137–147.

Carroll, J. B. A model of school learning. *Teacher's College Record,* 1963, *64,* 723–733.

Carter, J. F., & VanMatre, N. H. Note taking versus note having. *Journal of Educational Psychology,* 1975, *67,* 900–904.

Cartwright, D. Risk taking by individuals and group: An assessment of research employing choice dilemmas. *Journal of Personality and Social Psychology,* 1971, *20,* 361–378.

Case, R. Validation of a neo-Piagetian mental capacity construct. *Journal of Experimental Child Psychology,* 1972, *14,* 287–302.

Cashen, V. M., & Leicht, K. L. Role of the isolation effect in a formal educational setting. *Journal of Educational Psychology,* 1970, *61,* 484–486.

Cattell, R. B. Some theoretical issues in adult intelligence testing. *Psychological Bulletin,* 1941, *38,* 592. (Abstract)

Cattell, R. B. Theory of fluid and crystallized intelligence: A critical experiment. *Journal of Educational Psychology,* 1963, *16,* 191–210.

Cattell, R. B. *Abilities: Their structure, growth, and action.* Boston: Houghton Mifflin, 1971.

Chandler, T. A. Locus of control: A proposal for change. *Psychology in the Schools,* 1975, *12,* 334–339.

Chapman, D. W. Relative effects of determinate and indeterminate Aufgaben. *American Journal of Psychology,* 1932, *44,* 163–174.

Charters, W. W. The social background of teaching. In N. L. Gage (Ed.), *Handbook of research on teaching.* Chicago: Rand McNally, 1963.

Chui, L. H. *A factorial study of academic motivation.* Unpublished doctoral dissertation, Teacher's College, Columbia University, 1967.

Cicirelli, V., et al. *The impact of Head Start: An evaluation of the effects of Head Start on children's cognitive and affective development.* Washington, D.C.: Westinghouse Learning Corporation and Ohio University, 1969. (DED contract B 89–4536). Cited in J. Hellmuth (Ed.), *Disadvantaged child* (Vol. 3). New York: Brunner/Mazel, 1970.

Clifford, G. V. A history of the impact of research on teaching. In R. M. W. Travers (Ed.), *Second handbook of research on teaching.* Chicago: Rand McNally, 1973.

Clinchy, B., & Rosenthal, K. Analysis of children's errors. In G. S. Lesser (Ed.), *Psychology and educational practice.* Glenview, Ill.: Scott, Foresman, 1971.

Coffman, W. E. Essay examinations. In R. L. Thorndike (Ed.), *Educational measurement* (2nd ed.). Washington, D.C.: American Council on Education, 1971.

Coleman, J. S. *Equality of educational opportunity.* Washington, D.C.: U.S. Department of Health, Education and Welfare, 1966.

Coleman, J. S. The children have outgrown the schools. *Psychology Today,* 1972, *5,* 72–75, 82.

Collins, B. E. *Social psychology: Social influence, attitude change, group processes, and prejudice.* Reading, Mass.: Addison Wesley, 1970.

Conrad, R. Acoustic confusions in immediate memory. *British Journal of Psychology,* 1964, *55,* 75–84.

Cooke, T. P., & Apolloni, T. Developing positive social-emotional behaviors: A study of training and generalization effects. *Journal of Applied Behavior Analysis,* 1976, *9,* 65–78.

Cooper, J. L., & Greiner, J. M. Contingency management in an introductory psychology class produces better retention. *Psychological Record,* 1971, *21,* 391–400.

Corey, J. R., & McMichael, J. S. Retention in a PSI introductory psychology course. In J. G. Sherman (Ed.), *Personalized system of instruction: 41 germinal papers.* Menlo Park, Calif.: Benjamin, 1974.

Cox, W. F., Jr. Mental capacity-limitation on solving chaining problems. Paper presented at the annual convention of the American Educational Research Association, Toronto, Canada, 1978.

Craik, R. I. M., & Lockhart, R. S. Levels of processing: A framework for memory research. *Journal of Verbal Learning and Verbal Behavior,* 1972, *11,* 671–684.

Craik, R. I. M., & Watkins, M. J. The role of rehearsal in short-term memory. *Journal of Verbal Learning and Verbal Behavior,* 1973, *12,* 598–607.

Crawford, C. C. The correlation between lecture notes and quiz papers. *Journal of Educational Research,* 1925, *12,* 282–291. (a)

Crawford, C. C. Some experimental studies on the results of college note-taking. *Journal of Educational Research,* 1925, *12,* 379–386. (b)

Cronbach, L. J. Course improvement through evaluation. *Teachers College Record,* 1963, *64,* 672–683.

Cronbach, L. J., & Snow, R. E. *Aptitudes and instructional methods: A handbook for research on interactions.* New York: Halsted Press, 1977.

Crossman, E. R. F. W. A theory of the acquisition of speed-skill. *Ergonomics,* 1959, *2,* 153–166.

Crouse, J. H., & Idstein, P. Effects of encoding cues on prose learning. *Journal of Educational Psychology,* 1972, *63,* 309–313.

Daniels, R., & Stevens, J. The interaction between the internal-external locus of control and two methods of college instruction. *American Educational Research Journal,* 1976, *13,* 103–113.

Danner, F. W. Children's understanding of intersentence organization in the recall of short descriptive passages. *Journal of Educational Psychology,* 1976, *68,* 174–183.

Dansereau, F., Collins, K. W., McDonald, B. A., Diekhoff, G., Garland, J., & Holley, C. S. Development and assessment of a cognitively based learning strategy curriculum. Paper presented at the annual meeting of the American Educational Research Association, Toronto, Canada, 1978.

David, T. G. Introduction. In T. G. David & B. D. Wright (Eds.), *Learning environments.* Chicago: University of Chicago Press, 1975.

Davies, D. R. The effect of tuition upon the process of learning a complex motor skill. *Journal of Educational Psychology,* 1945, *36,* 352–365.

Davis, G. A., Roweton, W. E., Train, A. J., Warren, T. F., & Houtman, S. E. *Laboratory studies of creative thinking techniques: The checklist and morphological synthesis methods.* Madison: Wisconsin Research and Developmental Center for Cognitive Learning. (Technical Report #94, 1969).

Davis, G. A., & Scott, J. A. (Eds.). *Training creative thinking.* New York: Holt, Rinehart and Winston, 1971.

Davis, R. T., Settlage, P. H., & Harlow, H. F.. Performance of normal and brain-operated monkeys on mechanical puzzles with and without food incentive. *Journal of Genetic Psychology,* 1950, *77,* 305–311.

DeBono, E. *New think: The use of lateral thinking in the generation of new ideas.* New York: Basic Books, 1967.

De Charms, R. *Personal causation: The internal affective determinants of behavior.* New York: Academic Press, 1968.

De Charms, R. Personal causation training in the school. *Journal of Applied Social Psychology,* 1972, *2,* 95–113.

De Charms, R. *Enhancing motivation: Change in the classroom.* New York: Irving Publishers, 1976. (a)

De Charms, R. Pawn or origin? Enhancing motivation in disaffected youth. *Educational Leadership,* 1976, *34,* 444–448. (b)

Deci, E. L. Effects of externally mediated rewards on intrinsic motivation. *Journal of Personality and Social Psychology,* 1971, *18,* 105–115.

Deci, E. L. Intrinsic motivation, extrinsic reinforcement and inequity. *Journal of Personality and Social Psychology,* 1972, *22,* 113–120.

Deci, E. L. *Intrinsic motivation.* New York: Plenum Press, 1975.

Deese, J., & Hulse, S. H. *The psychology of learning.* New York: McGraw-Hill, 1967.

Deighton, L. C. (Ed.). *Encyclopedia of education.* New York: Macmillan Company and The Free Press, 1971.

Delacato, C. H. *The diagnosis and treatment of speech and reading problems.* Springfield, Ill.: Thomas, 1963.

Del Giorno, W., Jenkins, J. R., & Bausell, R. B. Effects of recitation on the acquisition of prose. *Journal of Educational Research,* 1974, *67,* 293–294.

Dember, W. N., & Earl, R. W. Analysis of exploratory, manipulatory and curiosity behaviors. *Psychological Review,* 1957, *64,* 91–96.

Deutsch, M. Facilitating development in the preschool child: Sociological and psychological perspectives. *Merrill-Palmer Quarterly,* 1964, *10,* 240–263.

Dewey, J. *How we think.* Boston: Heath, 1910.

DiCostanzo, J. L. The integration of logical and empirical procedures for hierarchically structuring an individualized curriculum. Paper presented at meeting of the American Educational Research Association, San Francisco, 1976.

Diederich, P. B. *Short-cut statistics for teacher-made tests* (2nd ed. series #5). Princeton, N.J.: Educational Testing Service, 1964.

Di Vesta, F. J., & Gray, S. G. Listening and note-taking. *Journal of Educational Psychology,* 1972, *63,* 8–14.

Di Vesta, F. J., & Gray, S. G. Listening and note-taking: II: Immediate and delayed recall as functions of variations in thematic continuity, note-taking and length of listening—review intervals. *Journal of Educational Psychology,* 1973, *64,* 278–287.

Dooling, D. J., & Lachman, R. Effects of comprehension on retention of prose. *Journal of Experimental Psychology,* 1971, *88,* 216–222.

Dooling, D. J., & Mullet, R. L. Locus of thematic effects in retention of prose. *Journal of Experimental Psychology,* 1973, *97,* 404–406.

Dreger, R. M., & Miller, K. S. Comparative psychological studies of Negroes and whites in the United States: 1939–1965. *Psychological Bulletin Monograph Supplement,* 1968, *70*(3), Part 2, 1–58.

DuBois, N. F. PSI: The inconclusiveness of conclusive data. Paper presented at Northeastern Educational Research Association, Ellenville, N.Y., 1976.

Duchastel, P. C., & Brown, B. R. Incidental and relevant learning with instructional objectives. *Journal of Educational Psychology,* 1974, *66,* 481–485.

Duchastel, P. C., & Merrill, P. F. The effects of behavioral objectives of learning: A review of empirical studies. *Review of Educational Research,* 1973, *43,* 53–69.

Duell, O. K. Effect of type of objective, level of test questions, and the judged importance of tested materials upon posttest performance. *Journal of Educational Psychology,* 1974, *66,* 225–232.

Duell, O. K. Overt and covert use of objectives at different levels. Paper presented at the meeting of the American Educational Research Association, New York, 1977.

Duncan, C. P. Learning to learn in response-discovery and in paired-associate lists. *American Journal of Psychology,* 1964, *77,* 367–379.

Duncker, K. On problem solving. *Psychological Monographs,* 1945 (#270), 58, 1–113.

Dunkin, M. J., & Biddle, B. J. *The study of teaching.* New York: Holt, Rinehart and Winston, 1974.

Dunn, L. M. *Peabody Picture Vocabulary Test.* Circle Pines, Minn.: American Guidance Service. Reprinted by permission of the publisher.

Ebel, R. L. *Measuring educational achievement.* Englewood Cliffs, N.J.: Prentice-Hall, 1965.

Ebel, R. (Ed.). *Encyclopedia of educational research.* New York: Macmillan, 1969.

Ebel, R. L. Behavioral objectives: A close look. *Phi Delta Kappan,* 1970, *52,* 171–173.

Ebel, R. L. How to write true-false test items. In T. W. Covin (Ed.), *Classroom test construction: A sourcebook for teachers.* New York: MSS Information Corporation, 1974.

Edgerton, S. K. Teachers in role conflict: The hidden dilemma. *Phi Delta Kappan,* 1977, *59,* 120–122.

Egan, D. E., & Greeno, J. G. Acquiring cognitive structure by discovery and rule learning. *Journal of Educational Psychology,* 1973, *64,* 85–97. © 1973 by the American Psychological Association. Material reprinted by permission.

Ehrenpreis, W., & Scandura, J. M. Algorithmic approach to curriculum construction: A field test in mathematics. In J. M. Scandura (Ed.), *Problem solving: A structural/process approach with instructional implications.* New York: Academic Press, 1977.

Eisner, E. W. Educational objectives: Help or hindrance? *School Review,* 1967, *75,* 250–260.

Eisner, E. W. Instructional and expressive objectives: Their formulation and use in curriculum. In J. Popham (Ed.), *Instructional objectives: An analysis of emerging issues.* Chicago: Rand McNally, 1969.

Ekman, P. (Ed.). *Darwin and facial expression: A century of research in review.* New York: Academic Press, 1973.

Eliot, T. S. *Selected essays.* New York: Harcourt, Brace, 1950.

Elkin, F., & Handel, G. *The child and society* (2nd ed.). New York: Random House, 1972.

Elkind, D. Piaget's theory of intellectual development: Its application to reading and special education. *Journal of Special Education,* 1967, *4,* 357–361.

Englander, M. F. Educational psychology and teacher education. *Phi Delta Kappan,* 1976, *57,* 440–442.

Erikson, E. *Childhood and society.* New York: Norton, 1963.

Evans, D. R. *Conceptual complexity, arousal and epistemic behavior.* Unpublished doctoral dissertation, University of Toronto, 1969.

Eysenck, H. J. Intelligence assessment: A theoretical and experimental approach. *British Journal of Educational Psychology,* 1967, *37,* 81–98.

Eysenck, H. J. *The IQ argument, race intelligence and education.* New York: The Library Press, 1971.

Fanelli, G. C. Locus of control. In S. Ball (Ed.), *Motivation in education.* New York: Academic Press, 1977.

Fantz, R. L. Pattern vision in young infants. *Psychological Record,* 1958, *8,* 43–49.

Farmighetti, R., Randall, P. B., & Paradise, J. (Eds.). *Education yearbook.* New York: Macmillan Educational Corporation, 1974.

Featherstone, J. *Schools where children learn.* New York: Liveright, 1971.

Feldhusen, J. An alternative creative problem solving approach. Paper presented at the Creative Problem Solving Institute, Buffalo, N.Y., 1978.

Feldman, K. V., & Klausmeier, H. J. Effects of two kinds of definition on the concept attainment of fourth and eighth graders. *Journal of Educational Research,* 1974, *67,* 219–223.

Felker, D. B., & Dapra, R. A. Effects of question type and question placement on problem solving ability from prose material. *Journal of Educational Psychology,* 1975, *67,* 380–384.

Ferster, C. B., & Skinner, B. F. *Schedules of reinforcement.* New York: Appleton-Century-Crofts, 1957.

Fisher, J. L., & Harris, M. B. Note taking and recall. *Journal of Educational Research,* 1974, *67,* 291–292.

Fisher, J. L., & Harris, M. B. Effect of note taking and review on recall. *Journal of Educational Psychology,* 1973, *65,* 321–325.

Fitt, S. The individual and his environment. In T. G. David & B. D. Wright (Eds.), *Learning environments.* Chicago: University of Chicago Press, 1975.

Fitts, P. M., & Posner, M. I. *Human performance.* Monterey, Calif.: Brooks-Cole, 1967.

Flanagan, J. C. Project PLAN: Basic assumptions, implementation and significance. *Journal of Secondary Education,* 1971, *46,* 173–178.

Flanders, N. A. Teacher effectiveness. In R. L. Ebel (Ed.), *Encyclopedia of educational research.* New York: Macmillan, 1969.

Flavell, J. H. *The developmental psychology of Jean Piaget.* Princeton, N.J.: Van Nostrand, 1963.

Florida Learning Resource System/CROWN. *Working with parents.* Jacksonville: Florida Learning Resource System/CROWN, 1975.

Fowler, R. L., & Barker, A. S. Effectiveness of highlighting for retention of text material. *Journal of Applied Psychology,* 1974, *59,* 358–364.

Frank, F. Perception and language in conservation. In J. S. Bruner, R. R. Olver, & P. M. Greenfield (Eds.), *Studies in cognitive growth.* New York: Wiley, 1966.

Frase, L. T. Learning from prose material: Length of passage, knowledge of results, and position of questions. *Journal of Educational Psychology,* 1967, *58,* 266–272.

Frase, L. T. Effect of question location, pacing and mode upon retention of prose material. *Journal of Educational Psychology,* 1968, *59,* 244–249. © 1968 by the American Psychological Association. Material reprinted by permission.

Frase, L. T. Paragraph organization of written materials: The influence of conceptual clustering upon the level or organization of recall. *Journal of Educational Psychology,* 1969, *60,* 394–401.

Frase, L. T. Integration of written text. *Journal of Educational Psychology,* 1973, *65,* 252–261.

Frase, L. T. Prose processing. In G. H. Bower (Ed.), *The psychology of learning and motivation* (Vol. 9). New York: Academic Press, 1975.

Frase, L. T., Patrick, E., & Schumer, H. Effect of question position and frequency upon learning from text under different levels of incentive. *Journal of Educational Psychology,* 1970, *61,* 52–56.

Frase, L. T., & Schwartz, B. J. Effect of question production and answering on prose recall. *Journal of Educational Psychology,* 1975, *67,* 628–635.

Freedman, J. L., & Fraser, S. Compliance without pressure: The foot-in-the-door technique. *Journal of Personality and Social Psychology,* 1966, *4,* 195–202.

Friedman, M. P., & Greitzer, F. L. Organization and study time in learning from reading. *Journal of Educational Psychology,* 1972, *63,* 609–616.

Friedrich, L. K., & Stein, A. H. Aggressive and prosocial television programs and the natural behavior of preschool children. *Monographs of the Society for Research in Child Development,* 1973, *38,* Serial No. 151.

Friend, R., & Neale, J. Children's perceptions of success and failure: An attributional analysis of the effects on race and social class. *Developmental Psychology,* 1972, *7,* 124–128.

Fromm, E. *Escape from freedom.* New York: Farrar and Rinehart, 1941.

Frostig, M., & Maslow, P. *Learning problems in the classroom: Prevention and remediation.* New York: Grune and Stratton, 1973.

Furth, H. G. *Piaget for teachers.* Englewood Cliffs, N.J.: Prentice-Hall, 1970.

Gage, N. L. The theories on teaching. In N. L. Gage (Ed.), *Handbook of research on teaching.* Chicago: Rand McNally, 1964.

Gagné, R. M. The acquisition of knowledge. *Psychological Review,* 1962, *69,* 355–365.

Gagné, R. M. The analysis of instructional objectives for the design of instruction. In R. Glaser (Ed.), *Teaching machines and programed learning. II: Data and directions.* Washington, D.C.: National Education Association, 1965. (a)

Gagné, R. M. *The conditions of learning.* New York: Holt, Rinehart and Winston, 1965. (b) Copyright © 1965 by Holt, Rinehart and Winston, Inc. Material reprinted by permission.

Gagné, R. M. Context, isolation and interference effects on the retention of facts. *Journal of Educational Psychology,* 1968, *60,* 408–414. (a)

Gagné, R. M. Learning hierarchies. *Educational Psychologist,* 1968, *6,* 1–6. (b)

Gagné, R. *Conditions of learning* (2d ed.). New York: Holt, Rinehart and Winston, 1970. Copyright © 1970 by Holt, Rinehart and Winston, Inc. Material reprinted by permission.

Gagné, R. M. Domains of learning. *Interchange,* 1972, *3,* 1–8.

Gagné, R. M. *Essentials of learning for instruction.* New York: Holt, Rinehart and Winston, 1974. (a) Copyright © 1974 by The Dryden Press, a division of Holt, Rinehart and Winston, Inc. Material reprinted by permission.

Gagné, R. M. Task analysis: Its relation to content analysis. *Educational Psychologist,* 1974, *11,* 11–18. (b)

Gagné, R. M. *The conditions of learning* (3d ed.). New York: Holt, Rinehart and Winston, 1977. Copyright © 1977 by Holt, Rinehart and Winston, Inc. Material reprinted by permission.

Gagné, R. M., & Baker, R. E. Stimulus pre-differentiation as a factor in transfer of training. *Journal of Experimental Psychology,* 1950, *40,* 439–451.

Gagné, R. M., & Briggs, L. J. *Principles of instructional design.* New York: Holt, Rinehart and Winston, 1974.

Gagné, R. M., & Brown, L. T. Some factors in the programming of conceptual learning. *Journal of Experimental Psychology,* 1961, *62,* 313–321.

Gagné, R. M., & Smith, E. C. A study of the effects of verbalization on problem solving. *Journal of Experimental Psychology,* 1962, *63,* 12–16.

Galizio, M., & Hendrick, C. Effect of musical accompaniment on attitude: The guitar as a prop for persuasion. *Journal of Applied Social Psychology,* 1972, *2,* 350–359.

Gall, M. D. The use of questions in teaching. *Review of Educational Research,* 1970, *40,* 707–721.

Gall, M. D., & Gall, J. P. The discussion method. In N. L. Gage (Ed.), *The psychology of teaching methods: The 75th yearbook of the National Society for the Study of Education.* Chicago: University of Chicago Press, 1976.

Gallup, G. H. Eighth annual Gallup poll of the public's attitudes toward the public schools. *Phi Delta Kappan,* 1976, *58,* 187–200.

Gallup, G. H. Ninth annual Gallup poll of the public's attitudes toward the public schools. *Phi Delta Kappan,* 1977, *59,* 33–48.

Galton, F. *Hereditary genius: An inquiry into its laws and consequences.* New York: Macmillan, 1869.

Galton, F. *Inquiries into human faculty and its development.* London: Macmillan, 1883.

Gardner, P. L. Pupil personality, teacher behavior, and attitudes to a physics course. *British Journal of Educational Psychology,* 1974, *44,* 123–130. (a)

Gardner, P. L. Research on teacher effects: Critique of a traditional paradigm. *British Journal of Educational Psychology,* 1974, *44,* 123–130. (b)

Gardner, R. A., & Runquist, W. N. Acquisition and extinction of problem solving set. *Journal of Experimental Psychology,* 1958, *55,* 274–277.

Gates, A. I. Recitation as a factor in memorizing. *Archives of Psychology,* 1917, *26* (Whole No. 40).

Gay, L. R. Temporal position of reviews and its effect on the retention of mathematical rules. *Journal of Educational Psychology,* 1973, *64,* 171–182.

Gerst, M. S. Symbolic coding processes in observational learning. *Journal of Personality and Social Psychology,* 1971, *19,* 7–17.

Getzels, J. W. Images of the classroom and visions of the learner. In T. G. David & B. D. Wright (Eds.), *Learning environments.* Chicago: University of Chicago Press, 1975.

Ghatala, E. S., & Levin, J. R. Children's recognition memory processes. In J. R. Levin & V. L. Allen (Eds.), *Cognitive learning in children: Theories and strategies.* New York: Academic Press, 1976.

Ghiselen, B. (Ed.), *The creative process.* New York: Times Mirror, 1952.

Gibson, J. J., & Gibson, E. J. Perceptual learning: Differentiation or enrichment? *Psychological Review,* 1955, *62,* 32–41.

Gilbert, T. F. Mathetics: The technology of education. *Journal of Mathetics,* 1962, *1,* 7–73. Reprinted in M. D. Merrill (Ed.), *Instructional design: Readings.* Englewood Cliffs, N.J.: Prentice-Hall, 1971.

Ginsburg, H., & Opper, S. *Piaget's Theory of intellectual development.* Englewood Cliffs, N.J.: Prentice-Hall, 1969.

Glaser, R. (Ed.). *Training research and education.* Pittsburgh: University of Pittsburgh Press, 1962.

Glaser, R. Instructional technology and the measurement of learning outcomes: Some questions. *American Psychologist,* 1963, *18,* 519–521.

Glaser, R. Toward a behavioral science base for instructional design. In R. Glaser (Ed.), *Teaching machines and programed learning, II: Data and directions.* Washington, D.C.: National Education Association, 1965.

Glaser, R. Cognitive psychology and instructional design. In D. Klahr (Ed.), *Cognition and instruction.* New York: Wiley, 1976. (a)

Glaser, R. The processes of intelligence and education. In L. B. Resnick (Ed.), *The nature of intelligence.* New York: Wiley, 1976. (b)

Glaser, R., & Klaus, D. J. Proficiency measurement: Assessing human performance. In R. M. Gagné (Ed.), *Psychological principles in system development.* New York: Holt, Rinehart and Winston, 1962.

Glaser, R., & Nitko, A. J. *Measurement in learning and instruction.* Pittsburgh: University of Pittsburgh, Learning Research and Development Center, 1970. (ERIC Document ED 038 873)

Glass, G. V. Reflections on Bloom's "Toward a theory of testing which includes measurement-evaluation-assessment." Research paper No. 8. Boulder: Laboratory of Educational Research, University of Colorado, 1967.

Glasser, W. *Schools without failure.* New York: Harper & Row, 1969.

Glaze, J. A. The association value of non-sense syllables. *Journal of Genetic Psychology,* 1928, *35,* 255–269.

Goldman, R., & Fristoe, M. *Goldman-Fristoe Test of Articulation.* Circle Pines, Minn.: American Guidance Service. Reprinted by permission of the publisher.

Goldman, R., Fristoe, M., & Woodcock, R. W. *Goldman-Fristoe-Woodcock test of auditory discrimination.* Circle Pines, Minn.: American Guidance Service, 1967.

Goodlad, J. I., & Anderson, R. H. *The nongraded elementary school.* New York: Harcourt, Brace and World, 1963.

Goodman, S. E. (Ed.). *Handbook of contemporary education.* New York: Bowker, 1976.

Gordon, T. *T.E.T. Teacher effectiveness training.* New York: Peter H. Wyden, 1974.

Gordon, W. J. *Synectics: The development of creative capacity.* New York: Harper & Row, 1961.

Goss, A. E., & Greenfeld, N. Transfer to a motor task as influenced by conditions and degree of prior discrimination training. *Journal of Experimental Psychology,* 1958, *55,* 258–269.

Greene, R. R., & Hoats, D. C. Reinforcing capabilities of television distortion. *Journal of Applied Behavior Analysis,* 1969, *2,* 139–141. Copyright 1969 by Society for the Experimental Analysis of Behavior, Inc. Material reprinted by permission.

Greenfield, P. M., & Bruner, J. S. Culture and cognitive growth. In D. A. Goslin (Ed.), *Handbook of socialization theory and research.* Chicago: Rand McNally, 1969.

Greenspoon, J., & Foreman, S. Effect of delay of knowledge or results on learning a motor task. *Journal of Experimental Psychology,* 1956, *51,* 226–228. © 1956 by the American Psychological Association. Material reprinted by permission.

Greiner, J. M., & Karoly, P. Effects of self-control training on study activity and academic performance: An analysis of self-monitoring, self-reward, and systematic planning components. *Journal of Counseling Psychology,* 1976, *23,* 495–501.

Greven, P. J. *Child-rearing concepts, 1628–1861: Historical sources.* Itasca, Ill.: Peacock, 1973.

Gronlund, N. E. *Measurement and evaluation in teaching* (3rd ed.). New York: Macmillan, 1976.

Gropper, G. L. *Instructional strategies.* Englewood Cliffs, N.J.: Educational Technology Publications, 1974.

Gropper, G. L. *Diagnosis and revision in the development of instructional materials.* Englewood Cliffs, N.J.: Educational Technology Publications, 1975.

Gropper, G. L. What should a theory of instruction concern itself with? *Educational Technology,* 1976, *16,* 7–12.

Grote, B., & Lippman, M. Z. The influence of conflicting verbal and visual information on the performance of preschool and primary children. Paper presented at the meeting of the Western Psychological Association, Portland, Oregon, 1972.

Grotelueschen, A. D., & Sjogren, D. O. Effects of differentially structured introduction materials and learning tasks on learning and transfer. *American Educational Research Journal,* 1968, *5,* 191–202.

Guilford, J. P. *Fundamental statistics in psychology and education.* New York: McGraw-Hill, 1965.

Guilford, J. P. Intelligence: 1965 model. *American Psychologist,* 1966, *21,* 20–26.

Guilford, J. P. *The nature of human intelligence.* New York: McGraw-Hill, 1967.

Guilford, J. P. *Way beyond the I.Q.* Buffalo, N.Y.: Creative Education Foundation in cooperation with Creative Synergetic Associates, Ltd., 1977.

Gump, P. Intra-setting analysis: The third grade classroom as a special but instructive case. In E. Willems & H. Raush (Eds.), *Naturalistic viewpoints in psychological research.* New York: Holt, Rinehart and Winston, 1969.

Guthrie, J. T. Expository instruction versus a discovery method. *Journal of Educational Psychology,* 1967, *58,* 45–49.

Guthrie, J. T. Feedback and sentence learning. *Journal of Verbal Learning and Verbal Behavior,* 1971, *10,* 23–28.

Guttman, J. The effects of pictures and partial pictures on children's oral prose learning. Paper presented at meeting of the American Educational Research Association, San Francisco, 1976. (ERIC Document ED 120 695)

Guttman, L. A basis for scaling quantitative data. *American Sociological Review,* 1944, *9,* 139–150.

Hagen, J. W., Jongeward, R. H., & Kail, R. V. Cognitive perspectives on the development of memory. In H. W. Reese (Ed.), *Advances in child development and behavior.* New York: Academic Press, 1975.

Hakstian, A. R., & Cattell, R. B. The checking of primary ability structure on a broader basis of performance. *British Journal of Educational Psychology,* 1974, *44,* 140–154.

Hall, S. G. *Adolescence: Its psychology and its relation to physiology, anthropology, sociology, sex, crime, religion, and education.* New York: Appleton, 1904.

Hamachek, D. B. Characteristics of good teachers and implications for teacher education. *Phi Delta Kappan,* 1969, *50,* 341–344.

Hammill, D. D., Goodman, L., & Wiederholt, J. L. Visual-motor processes—can we train them? *Reading Teacher,* 1974, *27,* 469–480.

Hammond, R. L. Evaluation at the local level. In B. R. Worthen & J. R. Sanders (Ed.), *Educational evaluation: Theory and practice.* Worthington, Ohio: Charles A. Jones, 1973.

Hansen, R. A. *Anxiety.* In S. Ball (Ed.), *Motivation in education.* New York: Academic Press, 1977.

Harré, R. The conditions for a social psychology of childhood. In M. P. M. Richards (Ed.), *The integration of a child into a social world.* New York: Cambridge University Press, 1974.

Harris, F. R., Johnston, M. K., Kelley, C. S., & Wolf, M. M. Effects of positive social reinforcement on regressed crawling of a nursery school child. *Journal of Educational Psychology,* 1964, *55,* 35–41.

Hart, B., & Risley, T. R. Using preschool materials to modify the language of disadvantaged children. *Journal of Applied Behavior Analysis,* 1974, *7,* 243–256.

Hartley, J., & Davies, I. K. Preinstructional strategies: The role of pretests, behavioral objectives, overviews and advance organizers. *Review of Educational Research,* 1976, *46,* 239–266.

Harvard University. Harvard weighs plan to reform college curriculum: Harvard's report on the "core curriculum." *The Chronicle of Higher Education,* 1978, *16,* 1, 15–19.

Hassett, J. D., & Weisberg, A. *Open education: Alternatives within our tradition.* Englewood Cliffs, N.J.: Prentice-Hall, 1972.

Hayes, J. R. *Cognitive psychology: Thinking and creating.* Homewood, Ill.: Dorsey Press, 1978.

Hearn, J. C., & Moos, R. H. Subject matter and classroom climate: A test of Holland's environmental propositions. *American Educational Research Journal,* 1978, *15,* 111–124.

Heatherington, E. M., & McIntyre, C. W. Developmental psychology. *Annual Review of Psychology,* 1975, *26,* 97–136.

Hebb, D. O. Clinical evidence concerning the nature of normal adult test performance. *Psychological Bulletin,* 1941, *38,* 593.

Hebb, D. O. Drives and the conceptual nervous system (c.n.s.). *Psychological Review,* 1955, *62,* 243–254.

Herrnstein, R. J. *I.Q. in the meritocracy.* Boston: Little, Brown, 1973.

Hershberger, W. A. Self-evaluation responding and typographical cueing: Techniques for programing self-instructional reading materials. *Journal of Educational Psychology,* 1964, *55,* 288–296.

Hershberger, W. A., & Terry, D. F. Typographical cueing in conventional and programed texts. *Journal of Applied Psychology,* 1965, *49,* 55–60. © 1965 by the American Psychological Association. Material reprinted by permission.

Hertzberg, A., & Stone, E. *Schools are for children: An American approach to the open classroom.* New York: Shocken Books, 1971.

Hewett, F. M. *The emotionally disturbed child in the classroom: A developmental strategy for educating children with maladaptive behavior.* Boston: Allyn and Bacon, 1968.

Hildum, D. C. & Brown, R. W. Verbal reinforcement and interviewer bias. *Journal of Abnormal and Social Psychology,* 1956, *53,* 108–111.

Hilgard, E. R. *Introduction to psychology* (3rd ed.). New York: Harcourt, Brace and World, 1962.

Hilgard, E. R., & Bower, G. H. *Theories of learning* (4th ed.). Englewood Cliffs, N.J.: Prentice-Hall, 1975.

Hill, W. F. *Learning through discussion.* Beverly Hills: Sage Publications, 1969.

Hills, J. R. *Measurement and evaluation in the classroom.* Columbus, Ohio: Charles B. Merrill, 1976.

Hitt, W. D. Two models of man. *American Psychologist,* 1969, *24,* 651–658.

Hively, W. (Ed.). *Domain referenced testing.* Englewood Cliffs, N.J.: Educational Technology Publications, 1974.

Hoffman, M. L. Personality and social development. *Annual Review of Psychology,* 1977, *28,* 295–321.

Holding, D. H. Transfer between difficult and easy tasks. *British Journal of Psychology,* 1962, *53,* 397–407.

Holen, M. C., & Oaster, T. R. Serial position and isolation effects in a classroom lecture simulation. *Journal of Educational Psychology,* 1976, *68,* 293– 296.

Homme, L., Csanyi, A. P., Gonzales, M. A., & Rechs, J. R. *How to use contigency contracting in the classroom.* Champaign, Ill.: Research Press, 1970.

Horn, J. L. Human ability: A review of research and theory in the early 1970's. *Annual Review of Psychology,* 1976, *27,* 437–485.

Hovland, C. I. (Ed.). *The order of presentation in persuasion.* New Haven, Conn.: Yale University Press, 1957.

Hovland, C. I., Harvey, O., & Sherif, M. Assimilation and contrast effects in communication and attitude change. *Journal of Abnormal and Social Psychology,* 1957, *55,* 242–252.

Hovland, C. I., Lumsdaine, A., & Sheffield, F. *Experiments on mass communication.* Princeton, N.J.: Princeton University Press, 1949.

Hovland, C. I., & Mandell, W. An experimental comparison of conclusion-drawing by the communicator and the audience. *Journal of Abnormal and Social Psychology,* 1952, *47,* 581–588.

Hovland, C., & Weiss, W. The influence of source credibility on communication effectiveness. *Public Opinion Quarterly,* 1951, *15,* 635–650.

Howe, M. J. A. Using students' notes to examine the role of the individual learner in acquiring meaningful subject matter. *Journal of Educational Research,* 1970, *64,* 61–63.

Hoy, W. K. Organizational socialization: The student teacher and pupil control ideology. *Journal of Educational Research,* 1967, *61,* 153–155.

Hoy, W. K. The influence of experience on the beginning teacher. *The School Review,* 1968, *76,* 312–321.

Hughes, J. A. Team organization in large scale instructional development projects. Paper presented at the annual convention of the American Educational Research Association, New York City, April 1977.

Hull, C. L. *Principles of behavior.* New York: Appleton-Century-Crofts, 1943.

Humphreys, L. G. The organization of human abilities. *American Psychologist,* 1962, *17,* 475–483.

Hunt, D. *Parents and children in history: The psychology of family life in early modern France.* New York: Basic Books, 1970.

Hunt, D. E., & Sullivan, F. V. *Between psychology and education.* Hinsdale, Ill. Dryden Press, 1974.

Hunt, J. McV. *Intelligence and experience.* New York: Ronald Press, 1961.

Hutchins, R. M. The great anti-school campaign. In R. M. Hutchins & M. J. Adler (Eds.), *The great ideas today.* Chicago: Encyclopedia Britannica, 1972.

Hyman, R. T. Means-ends reasoning and curriculum. *Teachers College Record,* 1972, *73,* 393–402.

Idstein, P., & Jenkins, J. R. Underlining versus repetitive reading. *Journal of Educational Research,* 1972, *65,* 321–323.

Inhelder, B., & Piaget, J. *The growth of logical thinking from childhood to adolescence.* New York: Basic Books, 1958.

Insko, C. A. Verbal reinforcement of attitude. *Journal of Personality and Social Psychology,* 1965, *2,* 621–623.

Irion, A. L. A brief history of research on the acquisition of skill. In E. A. Bilodeau (Ed.), *Acquisition of skill.* New York: Academic Press, 1966.

Isaacson, R. L. Relation between achievement, test anxiety, and curricular choices. *Journal of Abnormal and Social Psychology,* 1964, *68,* 447–452.

Janis, I. L., Kaye, D., & Kirschner, P. Facilitating effects of "eating-while-reading" on responsiveness to persuasive communications. *Journal of Personality and Social Psychology,* 1965, *1,* 181–186.

Jeffrey, R. W. The influence of symbolic and motor rehearsal on observational learning. *Journal of Research in Personality,* 1976, *10,* 116–127.

Jencks, C., Smith, M., Acland, H., Bane, M. J., Cohen, D., Gintis, H., Heyns, B., & Michelson, S. *Inequality: A reassessment of family and schooling in America.* New York: Basic Books, 1972

Jenkins, J. G., & Dallenbach, K. M. Oblivescence during sleep and waking. *American Journal of Psychology,* 1924, *35,* 605–612. © 1924 by the University of Illinois Press. Reprinted by permission.

Jenkins, J. R., Bausell, R. B., & Jenkins, L. M. Comparisons of letter name and letter sound training as transfer variables. *American Educational Research Journal,* 1972, *9,* 75–86.

Jenkins, J. R., & Deno, S. L. A model for instructional objectives: Responsibilities and advantages. *Educational Technology,* 1970, *10,* 11–16.

Jensen, A. R. How much can we boost IQ and scholastic achievement? *Harvard Educational Review,* 1969, *39,* 1–123.

Jensen, A. R., *Educability and group differences.* London: Methuen, 1973.

Jernstedt, G. C. The relative effectiveness of individualized and traditional instructional methods. *Journal of Educational Research,* 1976, *69,* 211–218.

Jones, M. C. A laboratory study of fear: The case of Peter. *Pedagogical Seminar,* 1924, *31,* 308–315.

Jones, R. A., & Brehm, J. W. Persuasiveness of one and two-sided communications as a function of awareness there are two sides. *Journal of Experimental Social Psychology,* 1970, *6,* 47–56.

Kagan, J. *Understanding children: Behavior, motives, and thought.* New York: Harcourt, Brace, Jovanovich, 1971.

Kagan, J., & Klein, R. E. Cross-cultural perspectives on early development. *American Psychologist,* 1973, *28,* 947–961.

Kantowski, M. G. Process involved in mathematical problem solving. *Journal for Research in Mathematics Education,* 1977, *8,* 163–180.

Keller, F. S. "Good bye, teacher . . ." *Journal of Applied Behavioral Analysis,* 1968, *1,* 78–89.

Keller, F. S., & Sherman, J. G. *The Keller Plan handbook.* Menlo Park, Calif. Benjamin, 1974.

Kephart, N. C. *The slow learner in the classroom.* Columbus, Ohio: Merrill, 1971.

Kerlinger, F. N. *Foundations of behavioral research.* New York: Holt, Rinehart and Winston, 1973. (a)

Kerlinger, F. N. (Ed.). *Review of research in education.* Itasca, Ill.: Peacock, 1973. (b)

Kerst, S., & Levin, J. R. A comparison of experimenter-provided and subject-generated strategies in children's paired-associate learning. *Journal of Educational Psychology,* 1973, *65,* 300–303.

Kientzle, M. J. Properties of learning curves under varied distribution of practice. *Journal of Experimental Psychology,* 1946, *36,* 187–211. © 1946 by the American Psychological Association. Material reprinted by permission.

Kiesler, C. A., Mathog, R., Pool, P., & Hovenstine, R. Commitment and the boomerang effect: A field study. In C Kiesler (Ed.), *The psychology of commitment: Experiments linking behavior to belief.* New York: Academic Press, 1971.

Kimble, G. A., & Bilodeau, E. A. Work and rest as variables in cyclical motor learning. *Journal of Experimental Psychology,* 1949, *39,* 150–157. © 1949 by the American Psychological Association. Material reprinted by permission.

Klahr, D. Steps toward the simulation of intellectual development. In L. B. Resnick (Ed.), *The nature of intelligence.* New York: Wiley, 1976.

Klare, G. R., Mabry, J. E., & Gustafson, L. M. The relationship of patterning (underlining) to immediate retention and to acceptability of technical material. *Journal of Applied Psychology,* 1955, *39,* 40–42.

Klausmeier, H. J. Instructional design and the teaching of concepts. In J. R. Levin & V. L. Allen (Eds.), *Cognitive learning in children: Theories and strategies.* New York: Academic Press, 1976.

Klausmeier, H. J., & Feldman, K. V. Effects of a definition and a varying number of examples and non-examples on concept attainment. *Journal of Educational Psychology,* 1975, *67,* 174–178.

Klausmeier, H. J., Ghatala, E. S., & Frayer, D. A. *Conceptual learning and development: A cognitive view.* New York: Academic Press, 1974.

Klemm, W. R. Efficiency of handout skeleton notes in student learning. *Improving College and University Teaching,* 1976, *24,* 10–12.

Klineberg, O. Negro-white differences in intelligence test performance: A new look at an old problem. *American Psychologist, 1963, 18,* 198–203.

Knight, M. F., & McKenzie, H. S. Elimination of bedtime thumbsucking in home settings through contingent reading. *Journal of Applied Behavior Analysis,* 1974, *7,* 33–38.

Koch, S. Behavior as "intrinsically" regulated: Work notes toward a pre-theory of phenomena called "motivational." In M. R. Jones (Ed.), *Nebraska Symposium on Motivation.* Lincoln: University of Nebraska Press, 1956.

Kogan, N., & Wallach, M. A. Risk taking as a function of the situation, the person, and the group. In *New directions in psychology* (Vol. 3). New York: Holt, Rinehart and Winston, 1967.

Kolb, D. Achievement motivation training for underachieving high school boys. *Journal of Personality and Social Psychology,* 1965, *2,* 783–792.

Kounin, J. S. *Discipline and group management in classrooms.* New York: Holt, Rinehart and Winston, 1970.

Krasner, L. The classroom as a planned environment. *Educational Researcher,* 1976, *5,* 9–14.

Kulhavy, R. W. Feedback in written instruction. *Review of Educational Research,* 1977, *47,* 211–232. Copyright 1977, American Educational Research Association, Washington, D.C.

Kulhavy, R. W., & Anderson, R. C. Delay-retention effect with multiple-choice tests. *Journal of Educational Psychology,* 1972, *63,* 505–512.

Kulhavy, R. W., Dyer, J. W., & Caterino, L. C. On connecting connected discourse: A comment on methodology. *Bulletin of the Psychonomic Society,* 1975, *5,* 146–148.

Kulhavy, R. W., Dyer, J. W., & Silver, L. The effects of note taking and test expectancy on the learning of text material. *Journal of Educational Research,* 1975, *68,* 363–365.

Kulhavy, R. W., & Parsons, J. A. Learning-criterion error perseveration in text materials. *Journal of Educational Psychology,* 1972, *63,* 81–86.

Kulhavy, R. W., Schmid, R. F., & Walker, C. H. Temporal organization in prose. *American Educational Research Journal,* 1977, *14,* 115–123.

Kulhavy, R. W., Yekovich, F. R., & Dyer, J. W. Feedback and response confidence. *Journal of Educational Psychology,* 1976, *68,* 522–528.

Kurth, R. J., & Moseley, P. A. The effects of copying or paraphrasing structurally-cued topic sentences on passage comprehension. Paper presented at meeting of American Educational Research Association, Toronto, Canada, 1978.

Lahey, B. B., & Drabman, R. S. Facilitation of the acquisition and retention of sight-word vocabulary through token reinforcement. *Journal of Applied Behavior Analysis,* 1974, *7,* 307–312. Copyright 1974 by the Society for the Experimental Analysis of Behaviors, Inc. Material adapted by permission.

Laird, J. D. Self attribution of emotion: The effects of expressive behavior on the quality of emotional experience. *Journal of Personality and Social Psychology,* 1974, *29,* 475–486.

Lake, R. V. An analysis of a home-school-community relations program in an IGE school. Madison: Wisconsin Research and Development Center for Cognitive Learning, University of Wisconsin, 1976. (Technical Report No. 395)

La Piere, R. T. Attitudes vs. action. *Social Forces,* 1934, *13,* 230–237.

Laverty, F. Creative ideas through circumrelation. *Journal of Creative Behavior,* 1974, *8,* 40–46.

Lavery, J. J., & Suddon, F. H. Retention of simple motor skills as a function of the number of trials by which KR is delayed. *Perceptual Motor Skills,* 1962, *15,* 231–237.

Lawton, J. T., & Wanska, S. K. Advance organizers as a teaching strategy: A reply to Barnes and Clawson. *Review of Educational Research,* 1977, *47,* 233–244.

Lee, B. N., & Merrill, M. D. *Writing complete affective objectives: A short course.* Belmont, Calif.: Wadsworth, 1972. © 1972 by Wadsworth Publishing Company, Inc., Belmont, California. Material reprinted by permission of the publisher.

Lepper, M. R., Greene, D., & Nisbett, R. E. Undermining children's intrinsic interest with extrinsic rewards: A test of the "overjustification" hypothesis. *Journal of Personality and Social Psychology,* 1973, *28,* 129–137.

Lesgold, A. M., Levin, J. R., Shimron, J., & Guttman, J. Pictures and young children's learning from oral prose. *Journal of Educational Psychology,* 1975, *67,* 636–642.

Leventhal, H., Watts, J. C., & Pagano, F. Effects of fear and instructions on how to cope with danger. *Journal of Personality and Social Psychology,* 1967, *6,* 313–321.

Levin, J. R. What have we learned about maximizing what children learn? In J. R. Levin & V. L. Allen (Eds.), *Cognitive learning in children: Theories and strategies.* New York: Academic Press, 1976.

Levin, J. R., Bender, B. G., & Lesgold, A. M. Pictures, repetition, and young children's oral prose learning. *AV Communication Review,* 1976, *24,* 367–380.

Levin, J. R., & Divine-Hawkins, P. Visual imagery as a prose-learning process. *Journal of Reading Behavior,* 1974, *6,* 23–30.

Levine, M. The academic achievement test: Its historical context and social functions. *American Psychologist,* 1976, *31,* 228–238.

Lewis, D. K., & Wolf, W. A. Keller plan introductory chemistry student's performance during and after the Keller experience. *Journal of Chemical Education,* 1974, *51,* 665–667.

Liebert, R. M. Television and social learning: Some relationships between viewing violence and behaving aggressively. In J. P. Murray, E. A. Rubenstein, & G. A. Comstock (Eds.), *Television and social behavior, Vol. II: Television and social learning.* Washington, D.C.: U.S. Government Printing Office, 1972.

Light, L., & Carter-Sobell, L. Effects of changed semantic context on recognition memory. *Journal of Verbal Learning and Verbal Behavior,* 1970, *9,* 1–11.

Lindvall, C. M., & Cox, R. C. The role of evaluation in programs for individualized instruction. In R. W. Tyler (Ed.), *Educational evaluation: New roles, new means, Part II. 68th yearbook of the National Society for the Study of Education.* Chicago: University of Chicago Press, 1969.

Lippman, M. Z., & Shanahan, M. W. Pictorial facilitation of paired-associate learning: Implications for vocabulary training. *Journal of Educational Psychology,* 1973, *64,* 216–222.

Locke, E. A. An empirical study of lecture note taking among college students. *Journal of Educational Research,* 1977, *71,* 93–99.

Loehlin, J. C., Lindzey, G., & Spuhler, J. N. *Race differences in intelligence.* San Francisco: Freeman, 1975.

Lorge, I. Influence of regularly interpolated time intervals upon subsequent learning. *Teachers College Contributions to Education, 1930, No. 438,* 57.

Lott, B. E., & Lott, A. J. The formation of positive attitudes toward group members. *Journal of Abnormal and Social Psychology,* 1960, *61,* 297–300.

Lovaas, O. I., Berberich, J. P., Perloff, B. F., & Schaeffer, B. Acquisition of imitative speech by schizophrenic children. *Science,* 1966, *151,* 705–707.

Luchins, A. S., & Luchins, E. H. *Rigidity of behavior: A variational approach to the effect of Einstellung.* Eugene: University of Oregon Press, 1959.

Lumsdaine, A., & Janis, I. Resistance to "counter-propaganda" produced by one-sided and two-sided "propaganda" presentations. *Public Opinion Quarterly,* 1953, *17,* 311–318.

Luria, A. R. *The role of speech in the regulation of normal and abnormal behavior.* New York: Liveright, 1961.

McCabe, A. E., Levin, J. R., & Wolff, P. The role of overt activity in children's sentence production. *Journal of Experimental Child Psychology,* 1974, *17,* 107–114.

McClelland, D. C. Toward a theory of motive acquisition. *American Psychologist,* 1965, *20,* 321–333.

McClelland, D. C., & Alschuler, A. S. The achievement motivation development project. Final report to USOE project No. 7-1231, Bureau of Research, 1971.

McClelland, D. C., Atkinson, J. W., Clark, R. W., & Lowell, E. L. *The achievement motive.* New York: Appleton-Century-Crofts, 1953.

McClelland, D. C., & Liberman, A. M. The effect of need for achievement on recognition of need-related words. *Journal of Personality,* 1949, *18,* 236–251.

McClelland, D. C., & Winter, D. G. *Motivating economic achievement.* New York: Free Press, 1969.

McClendon, P. T. An experimental study of the relationship between the note-taking practices and listening comprehension of college freshmen during expository lectures. *Speech Monographs,* 1958, *25,* 222–228.

McDougall, I. R., Gray, H. W., & McNicol, G. P. The effect of timing of distribution of handouts on improvement of student performance. *British Journal of Medical Education,* 1972, *6,* 155–157.

McGaw, B., & Grotelueschen, A. Direction of the effect of questions in prose material. *Journal of Educational Psychology,* 1972, *63,* 580–588.

McLeish, J. The lecture method. In N. L. Gage (Ed.), *The psychology of teaching methods. The 75th yearbook of the National Society for the Study of Education.* Chicago: University of Chicago Press, 1976.

McMichael, J. S., & Corey, J. R. Contingency management in an introductory psychology course produces better learning. *Journal of Applied Behavioral Analysis,* 1969, *2,* 79–83.

McNeil, J. D. Concomitants of using behavioral objectives in the assessment of teacher effectiveness. *Journal of Experimental Education,* 1967, *36,* 69–74.

McNemar, Q. Lost: Our intelligence? Why? *American Psychologist, 1964, 19,* 871–882.

MacDonald-Ross, M. Behavioral objectives—A critical review. *Instructional Science,* 1973, *2,* 1–51.

Maddi, S. R. *Personality theories: A comparative analysis* (3rd ed.). Homewood, Ill.: Dorsey Press, 1976.

Maehr, M. L. Continuing motivation: An analysis of a seldom considered educational outcome. *Review of Educational Research,* 1976, *46,* 443–462.

Mager, R. F. *Preparing instructional objectives.* Belmont, Calif.: Fearon, 1962.

Mager, R. F. *Developing attitude toward learning.* Belmont, Calif.: Fearon, 1968.

Mager, R. F., & McCann, J. Learner-controlled instruction (1961). Cited in R. F. Mager & C. Clark (Eds.), Explorations in student-controlled instruction. *Psychological Reports,* 1963, *13,* 71–76.

Mancuso, J. C. (Ed.). *Readings for a cognitive theory of personality.* New York: Holt, Rinehart and Winston, 1970.

Markle, S. M., & Tiemann, P. W. *Really understanding concepts: Or in frumious pursuit of the jabberwock.* Champaign, Ill.: Stipes, 1969.

Markle, S. M., & Tiemann, P. W. Behavioral analysis of cognitive content. *Educational Technology,* 1970, *10,* 41–45.

Markle, S. M., & Tiemann, P. W. Some principles of instructional design at higher cognitive levels, 1972. In R. Ulrich, T. Stachnik, & J. Mabry (Eds.), *Control of human behavior, Vol. 3: Behavior modification in education.* Glenview, Ill.: Scott, Foresman, 1974.

Marks, C. B., Doctorow, M. J., & Wittrock, M. C. Word frequency and reading comprehension. *Journal of Educational Research,* 1974, *67,* 259–262.

Marteniuk, R. G. *Information processing in motor skills.* New York: Holt, Rinehart and Winston, 1976.

Maslow, A. *Toward a psychology of being.* Princeton, N.J · Van Nostrand, 1968.

Mayer, R. E. Acquisition processes and resilience under varying testing conditions for structurally different problem solving procedures. *Journal of Educational Psychology,* 1974, *66,* 644–656.

Mayer, R. E. Different problem-solving competencies established in learning computer programming with and without meaningful models. *Journal of Educational Psychology,* 1975, *67,* 725–734.(a)

Mayer, R. E. Information processing variables in learning to solve problems. *Review of Educational Research,* 1975, *45,* 525–541.(b) Copyright 1975, American Educational Research Association, Washington, D.C.

Mayer, R. E. Some conditions of meaningful learning of computer programming: Advance organizers and subject control of frame sequencing. *Journal of Educational Psychology,* 1976, *68,* 143–150.

Mayer, R. E. Different rule systems for counting behavior acquired in meaningful and rote contexts of learning. *Journal of Educational Psychology,* 1977, *69,* 537–546.(a)

Mayer, R. E. The sequence of instruction and the concept of assimilation-to-schema. *Instructional Science,* 1977, *6,* 369–388.(b)

Mayer, R. E., & Greeno, J. G. Structurally different learning outcomes produced by different instructional methods. *Journal of Educational Psychology,* 1972, *63,* 165–173.

Meacham, J. A., & Nicolai, P. Pointing, verbalizing, and looking as cues for preschoolers. Paper presented at the meeting of the American Psychological Association, Chicago, 1975. (ERIC Document ED 119 860)

Mechner, F. Behavioral analysis and instructional sequencing. In P. C. Lange (Ed.), *Programed instruction: The sixty-sixth yearbook of the National Society for the Study of Education, Part II.* Chicago: University of Chicago Press, 1967.

Meichenbaum, D. H., & Goodman, J. Training impulsive children to talk to themselves: A means of developing self-control. *Journal of Abnormal Psychology,* 1971, *77,* 115–126.

Melching. W. H. Programmed instruction under a feedback schedule. *National Society for Programmed Instruction Journal,* 1966, *5,* 14–15.

Merrill, M. D. Necessary psychological conditions for defining instructional outcomes. *Educational Technology,* 1971, *11,* 34–39.

Milburn, J. Special education and regular class teacher attitudes regarding social behaviors of children: Steps toward the development of a social skills curriculum. *Dissertation Abstracts International,* 1974, *8,* 5174A–5175A.

Miller, G. A. The magical number seven, plus or minus two: Some limits on our capacity to process information. *Psychological Review,* 1956, *63,* 81–97.

Montague, W. E., Adams, J. A., & Kiess, H. O. Forgetting and natural language mediation. *Journal of Experimental Psychology,* 1966, *72,* 829–833.

Moos, R. H. A typology of junior high and high school classrooms. *American Educational Research Journal,* 1978, *15,* 53–66.

Morris, C. J., & Kimbrell, G. McA. Performance and attitudinal effects of the Keller method in an introductory psychology course. *Psychological Record,* 1971, *22,* 523–530.

Morris, V. C. *Philosophy and the American school.* Boston: Houghton Mifflin, 1962.

Murray, A. *Parent power in the schools.* Chelmsford, Mass.: Merrimack Education Center, 1974.

Musella, D., & Rusch, R. Student opinion on college teaching. *Improving College and University Teaching,* 1968, *16,* 137–140.

Myers, J. L., Pezdek, K., & Coulson, D. Effects of prose organization upon free recall. *Journal of Educational Psychology,* 1973, *65,* 313–320.

Myers, P. A., & Myers, L. (Eds.). *Open education re-examined.* Lexington, Mass.: Heath, 1973.

Nazzaro, J. R., Todorov, J. C., & Nazzaro, J. N. Student ability and individualized instruction. *Journal of College Science Teaching,* 1972, *2,* 29–30.

Neill, A. S. *Summerhill: A radical approach to child rearing.* New York: Hart, 1960.

Neisser, U. General, academic and artificial intelligence. In L. B. Resnick (Ed.), *The nature of intelligence.* New York: Wiley, 1976.

Nekrasova, K. A. On the activation of thinking in students in the process of teaching by lecture. *Voprosy Psikhologii,* 1960, *6,* 166–171 (in Russian). In J. McLeish, The lecture method. In N. L. Gage (Ed.), *The psychology of teaching methods: The 75th yearbook of the National Society for the study of Education.* Chicago: University of Chicago Press, 1976.

Newell, A., & Simon, H. A. *Human problem solving.* Englewood Cliffs, N.J.: Prentice-Hall, 1972.

O'Brien, F., Azrin, N. H., & Bugle, C. Training profoundly retarded children to stop crawling. *Journal of Applied Behavior Analysis,* 1972, *2,* 131–137.

Olejnik, A. B., & McKinney, J. P. Parental value orientation and generosity in children. *Developmental Psychology,* 1973, *8,* 311.

Olson, D. R. Notes on a cognitive theory of instruction. In D. Klahr (Ed.), *Cognition and instruction.* New York: Wiley, 1976.(a)

Olson, D. R. Towards a theory of instructional means. *Educational Psychologist,* 1976, *12,* 14–35.(b)

Olton, R. M., & Crutchfield, R. S. Developing the skills of productive thinking. In G. A. Davis & J. A. Scott (Eds.), *Training creative thinking.* New York: Holt, Rinehart and Winston, 1971.

Ornstein, A. C. Can we define a good teacher? *Peabody Journal of Education,* 1975, *53,* 201–207.

Osborn, A. F. *Applied imagination.* New York: Scribner, 1957.

Osgood, C., Suci, G., & Tannenbaum, P. *The measurement of meaning.* Urbana: University of Illinois Press, 1967.

Ott, C. E., Butler, D. C., Blake, R. S., & Ball, J. P. The effect of interactive-image elaboration on the acquisition of foreign language vocabulary. *Language Learning,* 1973, *23,* 197–206.

Paivio, A. *Imagery and verbal processes.* New York: Holt, Rinehart and Winston, 1971.

Paivio, A., Smythe, P. C., & Yuille, J. C. Imagery *versus* meaningfulness of nouns in paired-associate learning. *Canadian Journal of Psychology,* 1968, *22,* 427–441.

Palkes, H., Stewart, M., & Freedman, J. Improvement in maze performance of hyperactive boys as a function of verbal training procedures. *Journal of Special Education,* 1971, *5,* 337–342.

Panel on Youth of the President's Science Advisory Committee. *Youth transition to adulthood: Report of the Panel on Youth of the President's Science Advisory Committee.* Chicago: University of Chicago Press, 1974.

Parnes, S. J. Can creativity be increased? In G. A. Davis & J. A. Scott (Eds.), *Training creative thinking.* New York: Holt, Rinehart and Winston, 1971.

Paul, W. I. How do you rate? *Phi Delta Kappan,* 1974, *56,* 33.

Pastore, N. *The nature-nuture controversy.* New York: Kings Crown Press, Columbia University, 1949.

Peeck, J. Retention of pictorial and verbal content of a text with illustrations. *Journal of Educational Psychology,* 1974, *66,* 880–888.

Peper, R. J., & Mayer, R. E. Note taking as a mathemagenic activity. Paper presented at meeting of American Psychological Association, San Francisco, 1977.

Perlmutter, J., & Royer, J. M. Organization of prose materials: Stimulus, storage and retrieval. *Canadian Journal of Psychology,* 1973, *27,* 200–209.

Perrone, V. *Open education: Promise and problems.* Bloomington, Ind.: Phi Delta Kappa, 1972.

Peters, D. L. Effects of note taking and rate of presentation on short-term objective test performance. *Journal of Educational Psychology,* 1972, *63,* 276–280.

Peterson, L. R., & Peterson, M. J. Short-term retention of individual verbal items. *Journal of Experimental Psychology,* 1959, *58,* 193–198.

Petrie, H. G. Do you see what I see? The epistemology of interdisciplinary inquiry. *Educational Researcher,* 1976, *5,* 9–15.

Phillips, D. C., & Kelly, M. E. Hierarchical theories of development in education and psychology. *Harvard Educational Review,* 1975, *45,* 351–375.

Phillips, J. L. *The origins of intellect: Piaget's theory.* San Francisco: Freeman, 1969.

Piaget, J. *The construction of reality in the child.* New York: Basic Books, 1954.

Piaget, J. *The origins of intelligence in children.* New York: Norton, 1963.

Piaget, J. Piaget's theory. In P. H. Mussen (Ed.), *Carmichael's manual of child psychology.* New York: Wiley, 1970.

Piaget, J., & Inhelder, B. *The child's conception of space.* London: Routledge and Kegan Paul, 1956.

Pick, A. D., Christy, M. D., & Frankel, G. W. Developmental study of visual selective attention. *Journal of Experimental Child Psychology,* 1972, *14,* 165–175.

Pio, C., & Andre, T. Paraphrasing highlighted statements and learning from prose. Paper presented at meeting of the American Educational Research Association, New York, 1977.

Popham, W. J. Probing the validity of arguments against behavioral goals. Paper presented at meeting of American Educational Research Association, Chicago, 1968. Reprinted in W. J. Popham, E. W. Eisner, H. J. Sullivan, & L. L. Tyler. *Instructional Objectives. AERA Monographs on curriculum evaluation, No. 3.* Chicago: Rand McNally, 1969.

Posner, G. J., & Strike, K. A. Ideology versus technology: The bias of behavioral objectives. *Educational Technology,* 1975, *15,* 28–34.

Posner, G. J., & Strike, K. A. A categorization scheme for principles of sequencing content. *Review of Educational Research,* 1976, *46,* 665–690.

Post, T. R., & Brennan, M. L. An experimental study of the effectiveness of a formal vs. an informal presentation of a general heuristic process on problem solving in 10th grade geometry. *Journal for Research in Mathematics Education,* 1976, *7,* 59–64.

Premack, D. Toward empirical behavioral laws: Positive reinforcement. *Psychological Review,* 1959, *66,* 219–233.

Premack, D. Reinforcement theory. In D. Levine (Ed.), *Nebraska symposium on motivation* (Vol. 13). Lincoln: University of Nebraska Press, 1965.

Prytulak, L. S. Natural language mediation. *Cognitive Psychology,* 1971, *2,* 1–56.

Quillan, M. R. The teachable language comprehender. *Communications of the Association for Computing Machinery,* 1969, *12,* 459–476.

Rabinowitz, W., & Rosenbaum, I. Teaching experience and teaching attitudes. *Elementary School Journal,* 1960, *60,* 313–319.

Raugh, M. R., & Atkinson, R. C. A mnemonic method for learning a second-language vocabulary. *Journal of Educational Psychology,* 1975, *67,* 1–16.

Raugh, M. R., Schupbach, R. D., & Atkinson, R. C. Teaching a large Russian vocabulary by the mnemonic keyword method. *Instructional Science,* 1977, *6,* 199–222.

Raynor, J. O. Relationships between achievement related motives, future orientation, and academic performance. *Journal of Personality and Social Psychology,* 1970, *15,* 28–33.

Redl, F. Strategy and techniques of the life space interview. *American Journal of Orthopsychiatry,* 1959, *29,* 1–18.

Reese, E. P. *The analysis of human operant behavior.* Dubuque, Iowa: Brown, 1966.

Reigeluth, C. M., Merrill, M. D., & Bunderson, C. V. The structure of subject matter content and its instructional design implications. *Instructional Science,* 1978, *7,* 107–126.

Reigeluth, C. M., Merrill, M. D., Wilson, B. G., Norton, R. F., & Spiller, R. T. The structural strategy diagnostic profile project: A progress report. Paper read at the annual meeting of the American Educational Research Association, March 1978.

Resnick, L. B. *Design of an early learning curriculum* (Working Paper 16). Pittsburgh: Learning Research and Development Center, University of Pittsburgh, 1967.

Resnick, L. B. (Ed.). Hierarchies in children's learning: A symposium. *Instructional Science,* 1973, *2,* 311–362.

Resnick, L. B. Introduction: Changing conceptions of intelligence. In L. B. Resnick (Ed.), *The nature of intelligence.* New York: Wiley, 1976.

Resnick, L. B., & Ford, W. W. *The analysis of tasks for instruction: An information-processing approach.* Pittsburgh: Learning Research and Development Center, University of Pittsburgh, 1976. (Publication No. 1976/4). Also in A. C. Catania & T. M. Brigham (Eds.). *Handbook of applied behavior analysis: Social and instructional processes.* New York: Irvington Publishers, 1978.

Resnick, L. B., & Wang, M. C. Approaches to the validation of learning hierarchies. *Proceedings of the eighteenth annual western regional conference on testing problems.* Princeton, N. J.: Educational Testing Service, 1969.

Resnick, L. B., Wang, M. C., & Kaplan, J. Task analysis in curriculum design. A hierarchically sequenced introductory mathematics curriculum. *Journal of Applied Behavior Analysis,* 1973, *6,* 679–710.

Reynolds, J. Two hundred years of children's recreation. In E. H. Grotberg (Ed.), *200 years of children.* Washington, D.C.: U.S. Department of Health, Education and Welfare, Office of Human Development, Office of Child Development, undated.

Rice, A. H. Should you let your teachers design their own schools? *Nation's Schools,* 1970, *85,* 18–19.

Rickards, J. P. Interaction of position and conceptual level of adjunct questions on immediate and delayed retention of text. *Journal of Educational Psychology,* 1976, *68,* 210–217. (a)

Rickards, J. P. Processing effects of advance organizers interspersed in text. *Reading Research Quarterly,* 1976, *11,* 599–622. (b)

Rickards, J. P., & August, G. J. Generative underlining strategies in prose recall. *Journal of Educational Psychology,* 1975, *67,* 860–865. © 1975 by the American Psychological Association. Material adapted with permission.

Rickards, J. P., & Di Vesta, F. J. Type and frequency of questions in processing textual material. *Journal of Educational Psychology,* 1974, *66,* 354–362.

Rickards, J. P., & Friedman, F. The encoding versus the external storage hypothesis in note taking. *Contemporary Educational Psychology,* 1978, *3,* 136–143.

Rigney, J. W., & Lutz, K. A. Effect of graphic analogies of concepts in chemistry on learning and attitude. *Journal of Educational Psychology,* 1976, *68,* 305–311.

Rogers, C. R. *Client-centered therapy: Its current practice, implications and theory.* Boston: Houghton Mifflin, 1951.

Rogers, C. R. The interpersonal relationship in the facilitation of learning. In R. R. Leeper (Ed.), *Humanizing education: The person in the process.* Washington, D.C.: Association for Supervision and Curriculum Development, 1967.

Rohwer, W. D., Jr. Decisive research: A means for answering fundamental questions about instruction. *Educational Researcher,* 1972, *1,* 5–11. Copyright 1972, American Educational Research Association, Washington, D.C. Material reprinted by permission.

Rohwer, W. D., Jr. Ammon, P. R., & Cramer, P. *Understanding intellectual development: Three approaches to theory and practice.* Hinsdale, Ill.: Dryden Press, 1974.

Rohwer, W. D., Jr., & Matz, R. D. Improving aural comprehension in white and black children: Picture versus print. *Journal of Experimental Child Psychology,* 1975, *19,* 23–26.

Rosenshine, B. *Teaching behaviors and student achievement.* Slough, England: National Foundation for Educational Research in England and Wales, 1971.

Rosenshine, B. Classroom instruction. In N. L. Gage (Ed.), *The psychology of teaching methods: The 75th yearbook of the National Society for the Study of Education, Part I.* Chicago: University of Chicago Press, 1976.

Rosenshine, B., & Furst, N. The use of direct observation to study teaching. In R. M. W. Travers (Ed.), *Second handbook of research on teaching.* Chicago: Rand McNally, 1973.

Rosenthal, R., & Jacobson, L. *Pygmalion in the classroom.* New York: Holt, Rinehart and Winston, 1968.

Ross, S. M., & Di Vesta, F. J. Oral summary as a review strategy for enhancing recall of textual material. *Journal of Educational Psychology,* 1976, *68,* 689–695.

Rothkopf, E. Z. Some conjectures about inspection behavior in learning from written sentences and the response mode problem in programmed self-instruction. *Journal of Programmed Instruction,* 1963, *2,* 31–46.

Rothkopf, E. Z. Learning from written materials: An exploration of the control of inspection behavior by test-like events. *American Educational Research Journal,* 1966, *3,* 241–249.

Rothkopf, E. Z. Two scientific approaches to the management of instruction. In R. M. Gagne & W. J. Gephart (Eds.), *Learning research and school subjects.* Itasca, Ill.: Peacock, 1968.

Rothkopf, E. Z. The concept of mathemagenic activities. *Review of Educational Research,* 1970, *40,* 325–336.

Rothkopf, E. Z., & Bisbicos, E. Selective facilitative effects of interspersed questions on learning from written material. *Journal of Educational Psychology,* 1967, *58,* 56–61.

Rothkopf, E. Z., & Bloom, R. D. Effects of interpersonal interaction on the instructional value of adjunct questions in learning from written material. *Journal of Educational Psychology,* 1970, *61,* 417–422.

Rothkopf, E. Z., & Kaplan, R. Exploration of the effect of density and specificity of instructional objectives on learning from text. *Journal of Educational Psychology,* 1972, *63,* 295–302. © 1972 by the American Psychological Association. Material adapted with permission.

Rotter, J. B. *Social learning and clinical psychology.* Englewood Cliffs, N.J.: Prentice-Hall, 1954.

Roughead, W. G., & Scandura, J. M. What is learned in mathematical discovery. *Journal of Educational Psychology,* 1968, *59,* 283–289.

Royer, J. M., & Cable, G. W. Facilitated learning in connected discourse. *Journal of Educational Psychology,* 1975, *67,* 116–123.

Royer, J. M., & Cable, G. W. Illustrations, analogies, and facilitative transfer in prose learning. *Journal of Educational Psychology,* 1976, *68,* 205–209.

Royer, P. N. Effects of specificity and position of written instructional objectives on learning from lecture. *Journal of Educational Psychology,* 1977, *69,* 40–45.

Rudnitsky, A. N., & Posner, G. J. The effects of content structure on student learning. Paper presented at meeting of the American Educational Research Association, San Francisco, 1976.

Rundus, D., & Atkinson, R. C. Rehearsal processes in free-recall: A procedure for direct observation. *Journal of Verbal Learning and Verbal Behavior,* 1970, *9,* 99–105.

Rust, L. W. Interests. In S. Ball (Ed.), *Motivation in education.* New York: Academic Press, 1977.

Ryals, K. *An experimental study of achievement motivation training as a function of moral maturity of trainees.* Unpublished doctoral dissertation, Washington University, 1969.

Sabaroff, R., & Hanna, M. A. *The open classroom: A practical guide for the teacher of the elementary grades.* Metuchen, N.J.: Scarecrow Press, 1974.

Samuels, S. J. Effects of pictures on learning to read, comprehension, and attitudes. *Review of Educational Research,* 1970, *40,* 397–407.

Samuels, S. J. The effect of letter-name knowledge on learning to read. *American Educational Research Journal,* 1972, *9,* 65–74.

Samuels, S. J. Effect of distinctive feature training on paired-associate learning. *Journal of Educational Psychology,* 1973, *64,* 164–170.

Sassenrath, J. M. Theory and results on feedback and retention. *Journal of Educational Psychology,* 1975, *67,* 894–899.

Sassenrath, J. M., & Garverick, C. M. Effects of differential feedback from examinations on retention and transfer. *Journal of Educational Psychology,* 1965, *56,* 259–263.

Saunders, J. O. L., & Wright, R. E. Good teachers: Loud and clear. *National Association of Secondary School Principals Bulletin,* 1974, *58,* 38–43.

Scandura, J. M. *Problem solving: A structural process approach with instructional implications.* New York: Academic Press, 1977. (a)

Scandura, J. M. Structural approach to instructional problems. *American Psychologist,* 1977, *32,* 33–53. (b)

Scandura, J. M., & Voorhies, D. J. Effect of irrelevant attributes and irrelevant operations on rule learning. *Journal of Educational Psychology,* 1974, *62,* 352–356.

Scandura, J. M., Woodward, E., & Lee, F. Rule generality and consistency in mathematics learning. *American Educational Research Journal,* 1967, *4,* 303–319. Copyright 1967, American Educational Research Association, Washington, D.C.

Scarr, S., & Weinberg, R. A. IQ test performance of black children adopted by white families. *American Psychologist,* 1976, *31,* 726–739.

Schmuck, R. A., & Schmuck, P. A. *Group processes in the classroom* (2nd ed.). Dubuque, Iowa: William C. Brown, 1975.

Schultz, C. B., & Di Vesta, F. J. Effects of passage organization and note taking on the selection of clustering strategies and on recall of textual materials. *Journal of Educational Psychology,* 1972, *63,* 244–252.

Schulz, R. W. The role of cognitive organizers in the facilitation of concept learning elementary school science. Unpublished doctoral dissertation, Purdue University, 1966. Cited in D. P. Ausubel & F. G. Robinson, *School learning: An introduction to educational psychology.* New York: Holt, Rinehart and Winston, 1969.

Scriven, M. The methodology of evaluation. In R. W. Tyler, R. M. Gagne, & M. Scriven (Eds.), *Perspectives of curriculum evaluation.* Chicago: Rand McNally, 1967.

Shavelson, R. J. Some aspects of the correspondence between content structure and cognitive structure in physics instruction. *Journal of Educational Psychology,* 1972, *63,* 225–234.

Shavelson, R. J. Some methods for examining content structure and cognitive structure in instruction. *Educational Psychologist,* 1974, *11,* 110–122.

Shavelson, R. J. Teachers' decision making. In N. L. Gage (Ed.), *The psychology of teaching methods. The seventy-fifth yearbook of the National Society for the Study of Education, Part 1.* Chicago: University of Chicago Press, 1976.

Shavelson, R. J., Berliner, D. C., Loeding, D., Porteus, A. W., & Stanton, G. C. Adjunct questions, mathemagenics and mathemathanics. Paper presented at the meetings of the American Psychological Association, New Orleans, 1974.

Sheppard, W. C., & MacDermot, H. G. Design and evaluation of a programmed course in introductory psychology. *Journal of Applied Behavioral Analysis,* 1970, *3,* 5–11.

Sherman, J. G. *Personalized system of instruction.* Reading, Mass.: Benjamin, 1974.

Sherwood, J. J., & Nataupsky, M. Predicting the conclusions of Negro-white intelligence research from biographical characteristics of the investigator. *Journal of Personality and Social Psychology,* 1968, *8,* 53–58.

Shimmerlik, S. M., & Nolan, J. D. Reorganization and the recall of prose. *Journal of Educational Psychology,* 1976, *68,* 779–786.

Shore, M. F., Milgram, N. A., & Malasky, C. The effectiveness of an enrichment program for disadvantaged young children. *American Journal of Orthopsychiatry,* 1971, *41,* 442–449.

Shuey, A. *The testing of Negro intelligence* (2nd ed.). New York: Social Science Press, 1966.

Sigel, I. E., & Cocking, R. R. *Cognitive development from childhood to adolescence: A constructivist perspective.* New York: Holt, Rinehart and Winston, 1977.

Silberman, C. E. *The open classroom reader.* New York: Vintage Books, 1973.

Silberman, M. L., Allender, J. S., & Yanoff, J. M. *The psychology of an open teaching and learning: An inquiry approach.* Boston: Little, Brown, 1972.

Simon, H. A. Identifying basic abilities underlying intelligent performance of complex tasks. In L. B. Resnick (Ed.), *The nature of intelligence.* New York: Wiley, 1976.

Singer, H., Samuels, S. J., & Spiroff, J. The effects of pictures and contextual conditions on learning responses. *Reading Research Quarterly,* 1973–74, *9,* 555–567.

Sipay, E. *Sipay word analysis tests.* Cambridge, Mass.: Educators Publishing Service, 1971.

Skinner, B. F. *Science and human behavior.* New York: Macmillan, 1953.

Skinner, B. F. *The technology of teaching.* New York: Appleton-Century-Crofts, 1968.

Skinner, B. F., & Krakower, S. A. *Handwriting with write and see.* Chicago: Lyons and Carnahan, 1968.

Smart, K. L., & Bruning, J. L. An examination of the practical import of the Von Restorff effect. Paper presented at meeting of the American Psychological Association, Montreal, 1973. (ERIC Document ED 102 502)

Smiley, S. S., Oakley, D. D., Worthen, D., Campione, J. C., & Brown, A. L. Recall of thematically relevant material by adolescent good and poor readers as a function of written versus oral presentation. *Journal of Educational Psychology,* 1977, *69,* 381–387.

Smith, J. C., Ramey, C. T., & Brent, S. B. The developmental effects of visual and/or verbal cues on learning and memory. *Proceedings of the 81st Annual Convention of the American Psychological Association,* Montreal, Canada, 1973, *8,* 89–90.

Smith, R. L., & Troth, W. A. Achievement motivation: A rational approach to psychological education. *Journal of Counseling Psychology,* 1975, *22,* 500–504.

Snelbecker, G. E. *Learning theory, instructional theory and psychoeducational design.* New York: McGraw-Hill, 1974.

Snyder, B. R. *The hidden curriculum.* New York: Knopf, 1971.

Soar, R. Teacher behavior related to pupil growth. *International Review of Education,* 1972, *18,* 508–526.

Spearman, C. E. *Psychology down the ages* (Vol. 1). New York: Macmillan, 1937.

Spence, J. A., & Spence, K. W. The motivational components of manifest anxiety: Drive and drive stimuli. In C. D. Spielberger (Ed.), *Anxiety and behavior.* New York: Academic Press, 1966.

Sperling, G. The information available in brief visual presentations. *Psychological Monographs,* 1960, *74,* 1–29.

Staats, A. W. *Learning, language and cognition.* New York: Holt, Rinehart and Winston, 1968.

Staats, A. W., Staats, C. K., & Crawford, H. L. First-order conditioning of meaning and the parallel conditioning of a GSR. *Journal of General Psychology,* 1962, *67,* 159–167.

Staley, R. K. Presentation of instructional objectives by set or subsets in learning from lecture. Paper presented at the meeting of the American Educational Research Association, Toronto, Canada, 1978. (ERIC Document ED 151 358)

Staley, R. K., & Wolf, R. I. Learning, study time, and note-taking with instructional objectives and training in their use. Paper presented at meeting of the American Educational Research Association, San Francisco, 1979.

Stappler, M. Letter to editor. *Today's Education,* 1976, *65,* 6–8.

Stein, A. H., & Friedrich, L. K. *Impact of television on children and youth.* Chicago: University of Chicago Press, 1975.

Stein, G. M., & Bryan, J. H. The effect of a television model upon rule adoption behavior of children. *Child Development,* 1972, *43,* 268–273.

Stevens, S. Mathematics, measurement, and psychophysics. In S. Stevens (Ed.), *Handbook of experimental psychology.* New York: Wiley, 1951.

Strike, K. A. The logic of learning by discovery. *Review of Educational Research,* 1975, *45,* 461–483.

Stufflebeam, D. L. An introduction to the PDK book educational evaluation and decision making. In B. R. Worthen & J. R. Sanders (Eds.), *Educational evaluation: Theory and practice.* Worthington, Ohio: Charles A. Jones, 1973.

Sudia, C. E. Historical trends in American family behavior: An essay. In E. H. Grotberg (Ed.), *200 years of children.* Washington, D.C.: U.S. Department of Health, Education and Welfare, Office of Human Development, Office of Child Development, undated.

Sullivan, E. V. An investigation into the use of different degrees of filmed verbal explanations on the activation, generalization, and extinction of the conservation of substance problems in children. *Dissertation Abstracts International,* 1967, *28,* 1177B–1178B.

Sulzer-Azaroff, B., & Mayer, G. R. *Applying behavior-analysis procedures with children and youth.* New York: Holt, Rinehart and Winston, 1977.

Surber, J. R., & Anderson, R. C. Delay-retention effect in natural classroom settings. *Journal of Educational Psychology,* 1975, *67,* 170–173.

Svensson, L. Symposium: Learning processes and strategies—III. On qualitative differences in learning: III—Study skill and learning. *British Journal of Educational Psychology,* 1977, *47,* 233–243.

Taffel, S. J., O'Leary, K. D., & Armel, S. Reasoning and praise: Their effects on academic behavior. *Journal of Educational Psychology,* 1974, *60,* 291–295.

Tang, K. *Inducing achievement behavior through a planned group counseling program.* Unpublished doctoral dissertation, University of Hawaii, 1970.

Tennyson, R. D. Effect of negative instances in concept acquisition using a verbal learning task. *Journal of Educational Psychology,* 1973, *64,* 247–260.

Tennyson, R. D., & Boutwell, R. C. Methodology for defining instance difficulty in concept teaching. *Educational Technology,* 1974, *12,* 19–24.

Tennyson, R. D., Steve, M. W., & Boutwell, R. C. Instance sequence and analysis of instance attribute representation in concept acquisition. *Journal of Educational Psychology,* 1975, *67,* 821–827.

Tennyson, R. D., & Tennyson, C. L. Rule acquisition design strategy variables: Degree of instance divergence, sequence, and instance analysis. *Journal of Educational Psychology,* 1975, *67,* 852–859. © 1975 by the American Psychological Association. Material adapted by permission.

Tennyson, R. D., Woolley, F. R., & Merrill, M. D. Exemplar and nonexemplar variables which produce correct concept classification behavior and specified classification errors. *Journal of Educational Psychology,* 1972, *63,* 144–152.

Terman, L. M., & Merrill, M. A. *Stanford-Binet intelligence scale.* Boston: Houghton Mifflin, 1960.

Thomas, E. J. The variation of memory with time for information appearing during a lecture. *Studies in Adult Education,* 1972, *4,* 57–62.

Thomas, E. L., & Robinson, H. A. *Improving reading in every class: A source book for teachers.* Boston: Allyn and Bacon, 1972.

Thorndike, E. L. *The psychology of learning.* New York: Teachers College Press, 1913.

Thorndike, E. L. The influence of first-year Latin upon the ability to read English. *School and Society,* 1923, *17,* 165–168.

Thorndike, E. L., & Woodworth, R. S. The influence of improvement in one mental function upon the efficiency of other functions. *Psychological Review,* 1901, *8,* 247–267, 384–395, 553–564.

Thurstone, L. L. *Primary mental abilities.* Chicago: University of Chicago Press, 1938.

Tiemann, P. W. Student use of behaviorally-stated objectives to augment conventional and programmed revisions of televised college economics lectures. Paper presented at the meeting of the American Educational Research Association, Chicago, 1968.

Tiemann, P. W., & Markle, S. M. Remodeling a model: An elaborated hierarchy of types of learning. *Educational Psychologist,* 1973, *10,* 147–158.

Tobias, S. Achievement-treatment interactions. *Review of Educational Research,* 1976, *46,* 61–74.

Torrance, E. P. *Guiding creative talent.* Englewood Cliffs, N.J.: Prentice-Hall, 1962.

Touhey, J. C. Effects of additional women professionals on ratings of occupational prestige and desirability. *Journal of Personality and Social Psychology,* 1974, *29,* 86–89.

Traub, R. E. Importance of problem heterogeneity to programed instruction. *Journal of Educational Psychology,* 1966, *57,* 54–60.

Travers, R. M. W. (Ed.). *Second handbook of research on teaching.* Chicago: Rand McNally, 1973.

Travers, R. M. W., Van Wagenen, R. K., Haygood, D. H., & McCormick, M. Learning as a consequence of the learner's task involvement under different conditions of feedback. *Journal of Educational Psychology,* 1964, *55,* 167–173.

Treffinger, D. J., & Gowan, J. C. An updated representative list of methods and educational programs for stimulating creativity. *Journal of Creative Behavior,* 1971, *5,* 127–139.

Trowbridge, M. H., & Cason, H. An experimental study of Thorndike's theory of learning. *Journal of General Psychology,* 1932, *7,* 245–258.

Tuckman, B. W. *Measuring educational outcomes: Fundamentals of testing.* New York: Harcourt, Brace, Jovanovich, 1975.

Tulving, E. Episodic and semantic memory. In E. Tulving & W. Donaldson (Eds.), *Organization of memory.* New York: Academic Press, 1972.

Tulving, E. Cue-dependent forgetting. *American Scientist,* 1974, *62,* 74–82. Material reprinted by permission, *American Scientist,* Journal of Sigma Xi, The Scientific Research Society of North America.

Tulving, E., & Psotka, J. Retroactive inhibition in free recall: Inaccessibility of information available in the memory store. *Journal of Experimental Psychology,* 1971, *87,* 1–8.

Tversky, A., & Kahneman, D. Judgement under uncertainty: Heuristics and biases. *Science,* 1974, *185,* 1124–1131.

Tyler, R. W. *Basic principles of curriculum and instruction.* Chicago: University of Chicago Press, 1950.

Tyler, R. W. The objectives and plans for a material assessment of educational progress. *Journal of Educational Measurement,* 1966, *3,* 1–4.

Underwood, B. J. Interference and forgetting. *Psychological Review,* 1957, *64,* 49–60.

Underwood, B. J. Ten years of massed practice on distributed practice. *Psychological Review,* 1961, *68,* 229–247.

Underwood, B. J., & Schulz, R. W. *Meaningfulness and verbal learning.* New York: Lippincott, 1960.

Uzgiris, I. C., & Hunt, J. McV. *Assessment in infancy: Ordinal scales of psychological development.* Urbana: University of Illinois Press, 1975.

Van Zoost, F. L., & Jackson, B. T. Effects of self-monitoring and self-administrated reinforcement on study behaviors. *Journal of Educational Research,* 1974, *67,* 216–218.

Veldman, D. J., & Peck, R. F. Student teacher characteristics from pupils' viewpoint. *Journal of Educational Psychology,* 1963, *54,* 346–355.

Vellutino, F. R., Steger, B. M., Moyer, S. C., Harding, C. J., & Niles, J. A. Has the perceptual deficit hypothesis led us astray? *Journal of Learning Disabilities,* 1977, *10,* 375–385.

Vernon, P. E. *The structure of human abilities.* New York: Wiley, 1950.

Vernon, P. E. *The structure of human abilities* (2nd ed.). London: Methuen, 1961.

Veroff, J. Varieties of achievement motivation. Paper presented at American Educational Research Association, Washington, D.C., 1975. (ERIC Document ED 106 737)

Vidler, D. C. Curiosity. In S. Ball (Ed.), *Motivation in education.* New York: Academic Press, 1977.

Wadsworth, B. J. *Piaget's theory of cognitive development: An introduction for students of psychology and education.* New York: McKay, 1971.

Walberg, H. J., & Thomas, S. C. Open education: A class validation in Great Britain and the U.S.A. *American Educational Research Journal,* 1972, *9,* 197–208.

Wallas, G. *The art of thought.* New York: Harcourt, Brace and World, 1926.

Wallen, N. E., & Travers, R. M. W. Analysis and investigation of teaching methods. In N. L. Gage (Ed.), *Handbook of research on teaching.* Chicago: Rand McNally, 1963.

Walster, E., Aronson, E., & Abrahams, D. On increasing the persuasiveness of a low prestige communicator. *Journal of Experimental Social Psychology,* 1966, *2,* 325–342.

Wang, M. C., & Stiles, B. *An investigation of children's concept of self responsibility for their school learning.* Pittsburgh: University of Pittsburgh, Learning Research and Development Center, 1975. (LRDC Publication 1975/11)

Ward, B. A. *Minicourse 15: Organizing independent learning, intermediate level: Teacher's handbook.* New York: Macmillan, 1973.

Ward, L. B. Reminiscence and rote learning. *Psychological Monographs,* 1937, *49* (Whole No. 220).

Watson, J. B., & Rayner, R. Conditioned emotional reactions. *Journal of Experimental Psychology,* 1920, *3,* 1–14.

Watts, G. H., & Anderson, R. C. Effects of three types of inserted questions on learning from prose. *Journal of Educational Psychology,* 1971, *62,* 387–394.

Weber, L. *The English infant school and informal education.* Englewood Cliffs, N.J.: Prentice-Hall, 1971.

Webster, W. L., & Stufflebeam, D. L. Educational evaluation: Ten years later. A paper presented at the annual convention of the American Educational Research Association, Toronto, 1978.

Wechsler, D. Manual for the Wechsler Preschool and Primary Scale of Intelligence. New York: Psychological Corporation, 1967.

Wechsler, D. *Manual for the Wechsler intelligence scale for children—revised.* New York: Psychological Corporation, 1974. (a)

Wechsler, D. *Selected papers of David Wechsler.* New York: Academic Press, 1974. (b)

Weiner, B., & Kukla, A. An attribution analysis of achievement motivation. *Journal of Personality and Social Psychology,* 1970, *15,* 1–20.

Weiner, B., & Potepan, P. A. Personality characteristics and affective reactions toward exams of superior and failing college students. *Journal of Educational Psychology,* 1970, *61,* 144–151.

Weinstein, C. E. Cognitive elaboration learning strategies. Paper presented at the annual meeting of the American Educational Research Association, New York, 1977.

Weisberg, P., & Waldrop. P. B. Fixed interval work habits of Congress. *Journal of Applied Behavior Analysis,* 1972, *5,* 93–97. Copyright © 1972 by the Society for the Experimental Analysis of Behavior, Inc. Material reprinted by permission.

Welford, A. T. *Skilled performance: Perceptual and motor skills.* Glenview, Ill.: Scott, Foresman, 1976.

West, H. Early peer-group interaction and role-taking skills: An investigation of Israeli children. *Child Development,* 1974, *45,* 1118–1121.

Wexler, D. A. Depth of experiencing of emotion and the elaboration of meaning. Paper presented at the Western Psychological Association, San Francisco, 1974.

Whelan, R. F., & Haring, N. G. Modification and maintenance of behavior through systematic application of consequences. *Exceptional Children,* 1966, *32,* 281–289.

White, R. T. A limit to the application of learning hierarchies. *Australian Journal of Education,* 1973, *17,* 153–156.

White, R. T., & Gagné, R. M. Past and future research on learning hierarchies. *Educational Psychologist,* 1974, *11,* 19–28.

White, R. W. Motivation reconsidered: The concept of competence. *Psychological Review,* 1959, *66,* 297–333.

Whitely, J. D. Effects of practice distribution on learning a fine motor task. *Research Quarterly,* 1970, *48,* 576–583.

Wickelgren, W. A. *How to solve problems: Elements of a theory of problems and problem solving.* San Francisco: Freeman, 1974.

Wickens, D. D. Some characteristics of word encoding. *Memory and Cognition,* 1973, *1,* 485–490.

Williams, C. D. The elimination of tantrum behavior by extinction procedures. *Journal of Abnormal and Social Psychology,* 1959, *59,* 269. Copyright © 1959 by the American Psychological Association. Material reprinted by permission.

Williams, F. E. *Total creativity program.* Englewood Cliffs, N.J.: Educational Technology Publications, 1973.

Wispé, L. G., & Drambarean, N. C. Physiological need, word frequency and visual duration thresholds. *Journal of Experimental Psychology,* 1953, *46,* 25–31.

Wittrock, M. C. The learning by discovery hypothesis. In L. S. Shulman & E. R. Keislar (Eds.), *Learning by discovery: A critical appraisal.* Chicago: Rand McNally, 1966.

Wittrock, M. C. Three conceptual approaches to research on transfer of training. In R. M. Gagné & W. J. Gephart (Eds.), *Learning research and school subjects.* Itasca, Ill.: Peacock, 1968.

Wittrock, M. C. Learning as a generative process. *Educational Psychologist,* 1974, *11,* 87–95.

Wittrock, M. C., Marks, C., & Doctorow, M. Reading as a generative process. *Journal of Educational Psychology,* 1975, *67,* 484–489.

Wittrock, M. C., & Twelker, P. A. Verbal cues and variety of classes of problems in transfer of training. *Psychological Reports,* 1964, *14,* 827–830.

Wolff, P. H. The development of attention in young infants. *Annals of the New York Academy of Sciences,* 1965, *118,* 815–830.

Wolff, P., & Levin, J. R. The role of overt activity in children's imagery production. *Child Development,* 1972, *43,* 537–547.

Wolk, S., & Du Cette, J. The moderating effect of locus of control in relation to achievement motivation variables. *Journal of Personality,* 1973, *41,* 59–70.

Woodrow, H. The effect of type of training upon transference. *Journal of Educational Psychology,* 1927, *18,* 159–172. © 1927 by the American Psychological Association. Material reprinted by permission.

Woodward, A. E., Bjork, R. A., & Jongeward, R. H. Recall and recognition as a function of primary rehearsal. *Journal of Verbal Learning and Verbal Behavior,* 1973, *12,* 608–617.

Woolley, R. R., & Tennyson, R. D. Conceptual model of classification behavior. *Educational Technology,* 1972, *12,* 37–39.

Worthen, B. R. Discovery and expository task presentation in elementary mathematics. *Journal of Educational Psychology: Monograph Supplement,* 1968, *59,* No. 1, Part 2.

Yekovich, F. R., & Kulhavy, R. W. Structural and contextual effects in the organization of prose. *Journal of Educational Psychology,* 1976, *68,* 626–635.

Yuille, J. C., & Catchpole, M. J. Associative learning and imagery training in children. *Journal of Experimental Child Psychology,* 1973, *16,* 403–412.

Zanna, M., Kiesler, C. A., & Pilkonis, P. Positive and negative attitudinal effect established by classical conditioning. *Journal of Personality and Social Psychology,* 1970, *14,* 321–328.

Zeigler, H. L., Tucker, H. J., & Wilson, L. A. II. School boards and community power: The irony of professionalism. *Intellect,* 1976, *105,* 90–92.

Author index

Y–Z

Subject index

K–L

T

This book has been set VideoComp, in 10 and 9 point Souvenir Light, leaded 1 point. Section numbers and titles are 36 point Souvenir Bold. Chapter numbers are 30 point Souvenir Bold and chapter titles are 18 point Souvenir Bold. The size of the text area is 30 picas by 50 picas.